WINNICOTT'S THEORY OF THE MATURATIONAL PROCESSES

WINNICOTT'S THEORY OF THE MATURATIONAL PROCESSES

Elsa Oliveira Dias

KARNAC

First published in 2016 by
Karnac Books Ltd
118 Finchley Road
London NW3 5HT

Copyright © 2016 by Elsa Oliveira Dias

The right of Elsa Oliveira Dias to be identified as the author of this work has been asserted in accordance with §§ 77 and 78 of the Copyright Design and Patents Act 1988.

All rights reserved. No part of this publication may be reproduced, stored in a retrieval system, or transmitted, in any form or by any means, electronic, mechanical, photocopying, recording, or otherwise, without the prior written permission of the publisher.

British Library Cataloguing in Publication Data

A C.I.P. for this book is available from the British Library

ISBN-13: 978-1-78220-364-3

Typeset by V Publishing Solutions Pvt Ltd., Chennai, India

Printed in Great Britain by TJ International Ltd, Padstow, Cornwall

www.karnacbooks.com

In memory of my mother

To my dearest children Sandra, Claudia, and Paulo Manoel, who made me a mother each in their own way

"[…] We do need to try to get at a theory of normal growth so as to be able to understand illness and the various immaturities, since we are now no longer contented unless we can cure and prevent. We do not accept childhood schizophrenia any more than we accept poliomyelitis or the condition of the spastic child. We try to prevent, and we hope to be able to lead the way to cure wherever there is abnormality, which means suffering for someone".

—*Winnicott*, 1965b, p. 67

"Leave man undisturbed from the cradle on! Do not drive him out of the tightly closed bud of his being, out of the small hut of his childhood! Do not do too little, and thereby he shall not dispense with you and thus distinguish you from himself; do not do too much, and thereby he shall not feel your or his power and thus distinguish you from himself; in short, do not let man know until late that there are men, that there is anything else outside of him, for only thus shall he become a man. But man is a god as soon as he is a man. And when he is a god, he is beautiful".

—*Hölderlin*, Hyperion, p. 106

CONTENTS

ACKNOWLEDGEMENTS	xi
ABOUT THE AUTHOR	xiii
PREFACE TO THE ENGLISH EDITION	xv
PREFACE TO THE SECOND EDITION	xix
PREFACE TO THE THIRD EDITION	xxi
INTRODUCTION	xxiii
CHAPTER ONE Winnicott and the debate with related areas	1
CHAPTER TWO Basic concepts of the theory of maturational processes	27
CHAPTER THREE The primitive stages: absolute dependence	69
CHAPTER FOUR The stages of relative dependence and independence	115

FINAL CONSIDERATIONS	173
REFERENCES	177
INDEX	189

ACKNOWLEDGEMENTS

This book would not have been the same without the contribution of the colleagues and friends who read the first draft of this study, accompanied its development and helped it with valuable suggestions.

I would like to thank the Marsh Agency Ltd., incorporating Paterson Marsh and Campbell Thomson & McLaughlin for their permission to quote many excerpts (around 500 words) from Winnicott, D. W. (1988) *Human Nature*.

Many thanks also to my translators, Regina de Barros Carvalho and Jonathan Morris, for the dedication, skill, and rigour with which they undertook the translation of my book into English, each of them with their respective talents, sensitivity, and linguistic skills which they brought to the task of translation.

I would like to thank Meire Gomes, who revised the references in the text and their links to the final references, for her indispensable assistance.

Many thanks to Loris Notturni, Suze Piza, and Teresa Mendonça, for their diligent assistance in tracking down quotations in English.

Once again, my thanks to Zeljko Loparic, my life and working companion, for his characteristic boldness of thought and partnership in the task of teaching and research which expanded enormously, as well as for the enthusiasm with which he has incorporated Winnicott into his acute philosophical reflection.

Lastly, I would like to express my special thanks to and affection for my children, Sandra, Claudia and Paulo Manoel, for the joy which they, together with my grandchildren, André, João and Francisco, have brought to my life, for confirming my faith in human nature and for giving me a profound sense of continuity. I am particularly grateful to Claudia for being an alert and inquisitive reader of my work and a valuable conversation partner regarding Winnicott's theoretical and clinical work.

ABOUT THE AUTHOR

Elsa Oliveira Dias, PhD, is a clinical psychologist, psychoanalyst, and co-founder of the Brazilian Society of Winnicottian Psychoanalysis. She is also Deputy-Chairperson of the International Winnicottian Psychoanalysis (IWA), and the author of a number of books, including *A teoria do amadurecimento de D. W. Winnicott*, *Sobre a confiabilidade e outros estudos*, and *Interpretação e manejo na clínica winnicottiana*, as well as many articles on Winnicott.

PREFACE TO THE ENGLISH EDITION

The possibility of publishing a book in Winnicott's own language and with the publisher who traditionally edited a large part of his work, while he was alive and posthumously, has been a great joy to me. I have thus been delighted to devote myself to the task of preparing the English edition of *A teoria do amadurecimento de D. W. Winnicott*, published by Karnac Books.

The book is the corrected and expanded version of the first part of my doctoral thesis, submitted in 1998, to the Pontifical Catholic University of São Paulo (PUC-SP). Its objective was to present Winnicott's theory of psychoses in a coordinated and extensive way, highlighting the originality of his contributions to psychoanalytic thought, including the fundamentally temporal and relational nature of human beings, his new criterion for classifying psychic disorders, primarily maturational and only secondarily symptomatological, the fact that in his theory, creativity is a diagnostic criterion for distinguishing between sickness and health and the fact that he highlighted the existence of environmental deficiency disorders, as is the case for psychoses, related to the importance of the environment in constituting the individual and the idea of dependence. At the same time, and contrary to many of his commentators, I have attempted to show the extraordinary theoretical unity of thought and its clinical consequences, fully aligned with his new approach, in particular, his introduction of the concept of care-cure and management.

Considering the close connection established by Winnicott between the nature of psychic disturbances and their point of origin (aetiology) in the line of maturation, I found myself obliged, above all, to explain the stages of the maturation process, emphasising and describing the tasks and achievements which characterise each stage, so as to open the field in which the various types of emotional disturbances may be configured, in particular, psychoses. In dealing with these latter disturbances, like Winnicott, I have given priority to the early stages, since it is during these that the foundations of an integrated personality and psychic health are established, and for this very reason, it is here that the risk of this type of disorder lies.

Winnicott formulated this theory which, in his own view, forms the backbone of his work and thought, but not in the systematic manner which I present here after collecting its constituent conceptual elements which are scattered across his work; in these, however, the theory is absolutely clear and internally consistent, as I intend to demonstrate in my book, with this indeed being one of the reasons why I have included so many direct citations of the author. This is a theory of health or perhaps, more precisely, of fundamental human needs, from the start of life and throughout the entire process as well as of the way in which the environment, in a specifically Winnicottian sense, favours or fails to favour the processes by which a baby, who is initially immature and heavily dependent, becomes a viable person, capable of establishing relations with external reality, of identifying with it without an excessive loss of spontaneity, of finding some sense in the fact of being alive and being reasonably able to take care of herself. All in all, this is the subject matter of this book.

Published in 2003, by the Brazilian publisher Imago, *A teoria do amadurecimento de D. W. Winnicott* was favourably received by the Brazilian public, having become work of reference in Winnicottian studies, among both psychoanalytic and academic institutions. It represented one of the first systematic studies in Brazil of the central theoretical component of the Winnicottian paradigm, his theory of maturational processes. The first edition, which was reprinted several times, was followed by a second edition in 2012 and a third edition in 2014, both published by DWW Editorial, the publishing company of the *Sociedade Brasileira de Psicanálise Winnicottiana* (Brazilian Society of Winnicottian Psychoanalysis) (SBPW). Also in 2012, the book was translated into Spanish with the title *La teoria de la maduración de D. W. Winnicott* and made available in electronic form. A translation into French by Loris Notturni is in preparation and should be completed by mid-2017; another translation into Chinese is also in progress, under the coordination of Dr. Zhao Chengzhi, with the participation of Dr. Ling Sunang, by way of evidence for the growing international reception of the book and research programme which it follows.

The text which I am presenting here to an English-speaking public is based on the third Brazilian edition. The changes made reflect the inherent difference between the two languages and their forms of expression, as well as corrections to the text and references, with the inclusion of various footnotes.

I have not made any amendments or additions for the purpose of updating results, in particular, I have left unchanged the sections "The relevance of the study of the theory of maturational processes", and "Brief discussion of divergent readings", of the Introduction, in which I compare my own interpretation of Winnicott with those of his commentators, whose works were published in those years. The most recent studies of Winnicott's work have certainly made new and significant contributions. I nevertheless consider that this book remains timely, since it presents Winnicott's central contribution to psychoanalytic theory and clinical practice in a unified and comprehensive form, notably his theory of maturational processes, organised around the ideas of a tendency towards integration, the realisation of this tendency by virtue of environmental facilitation, at the same time as it reveals the possibilities of failure or even breakdown of this integration process.

The reader who reflects on these themes will be able to understand more readily what Winnicott had in mind when, already at the end of his life, he expressed the following wish: "I am asking for a kind of revolution in our work. Let us examine what we do" (Abram, 2013, p. 312). The reader will also understand that the revolution for which Winnicott was arguing had already been initiated and partially achieved by him. He will also note that works which attempt to clarify the nature of this revolution began to be realised several years before his request was made public in 2013, by a number of institutional groups of clinicians and researchers in various countries, who, going against the dominant minimising interpretations, independently noted the momentous advances which psychoanalysis owes to Winnicott.

What I desire, above all, with this publication in English is that an increased dissemination of this study will help to provide debate on the crucial questions which Winnicott introduced to psychoanalysis and the study of human nature.

PREFACE TO THE SECOND EDITION

It has been with great satisfaction that I have prepared the second edition of this book, which was first published in 2003 by Imago. The fact that the first edition, which went through several reprints, is once again out of print shows that it has achieved one of its objectives: the broad dissemination of Winnicott's psychoanalysis among the Brazilian public.

Developing a unified reading of Winnicott's work, which clarified the unity of his thought, was the goal of my doctoral thesis; its partially rewritten first section constitutes this book. Already at that point, it seemed to me that a coordinated presentation of Winnicott's thought around one of its main axes, the theory of maturational processes, would facilitate understanding and consequently, the acceptance of his highly complex and innovative theoretical perspective, resulting in far-reaching and highly effective clinical practice. In addition to this dissemination, I also had another objective: that of drawing the attention of specialised public to the fact that Winnicott, in addition to being an uncommon clinician, had developed a consistent unified theoretical framework, which represents a decisive step in the progress of psychoanalysis and which could be seen as a new paradigm within that discipline. Despite giving the impression of looseness or of a certain dispersion, Winnicott's work has an unrivalled internal organisation and consistency, which allows a radically renewed psychoanalytic vision of health, illness, and the clinic to be extracted from it without great effort, together with teachings of capital importance, applicable to areas which are not strictly clinical. After 2003, I developed some of these viewpoints in a series of articles, basically written to be read at conferences. Some of them are now gathered in my book *Sobre a confiabilidade e outros estudos* (On reliability and other studies) (DWW editorial, 2011).

The favourable reception of *A teoria do amadurecimento de D. W. Winnicott* (D. W. Winnicott's theory of maturation) made the book a work of reference in the disciplines of the Winnicottian School of Psychoanalysis, taught by the Winnicott Centres of the Brazilian Society of

Winnicottian Psychoanalysis (SBPW). I was also delighted to observe that the book began to be used in a number of other courses on Winnicott and became the object of study by various research groups. Dissertations and theses for Postgraduate Programmes at various universities refer to the book. Several of the articles in the review *Natureza humana* (Human Nature) and of *Winnicott e-Prints* take up and develop the viewpoints which I articulated. The results achieved by some of these authors may be found in the collection *Winnicott na Escola de São Paulo* (Winnicott in the School of São Paulo) (DWW editorial, 2011). The book was also the object of specialist reviews, including those of Edna Vilete and Ricardo Rodulfo. The emergence of interest in the book outside Brazil provided an impetus for translations, which are currently in preparation, in order to meet the demand which we have received from our foreign colleagues.

The book took an important step in the direction of providing theoretical support and promoting, as far as possible and in different contexts, the application of Winnicott's psychoanalysis both to the treatment of difficult clinical cases, especially those which, according to traditional psychoanalysis, fall outside their areas of expertise, and in different not strictly clinical fields, such as those relating to prevention policies in mental health, to adolescents in conflict with the law and to manifestations of anti-social tendencies, in broader fashion.

For this second edition, undertaken by DWW editorial, the publisher of SBPW, which is primarily devoted to publishing works on Winnicott and related topics, corrections and modifications were made to spelling, in accordance with the recent reform, and to bibliographic references, as well as alterations aiming at improving the clarity of the phrase, with a number of theoretical additions to the text which were suggested to me and/or which I understood to be necessary. Some footnotes were omitted and other new ones added. As a result, the pagination of the book was slightly modified relative to the first edition. As a consequence, the references listed in the index were amended.

Once again, I would like to thank Zeljko Loparic for his partnership in the project which has grown enormously in scope, and for the enthusiasm with which he articulates Winnicott with his acute philosophical reflection. I would like to express my gratitude to all of my friends and colleagues who took the trouble to read the first steps in this study, long ago, as well as its development, which they aided with valuable suggestions. In this second edition, I would like to thank Meire Gomes for her meticulous revision and Simone Novo for patiently scanning for errors in the references and citations. I also want to thank Claudia Dias Rosa for her readiness to help, Daniela Guizzo and Roseana Moraes Garcia for organising the index. I would also like to record my thanks to all of my colleagues who have shared the joy with me of discovering and using Winnicott's precious legacy and who have not only made valuable use of my study but have also advanced it in numerous directions. I would especially like to thank my beloved children Sandra, Claudia, and Paulo Manoel, whose existence in my life fills me with joy as I work, study, and write, and for giving me a deep sense of continuity. I am particularly grateful to Claudia, for being an attentive and inquisitive reader of my writings and a valued partner on Winnicottian paths; and Sandra, for using her talent for creating the book cover so well and affectionately.

Elsa Oliveira Dias

PREFACE TO THE THIRD EDITION

With the second edition of this book having sold out in only two years, I am extremely satisfied to be preparing this third edition, again with DWW editorial. The publisher and I decided that rather than simply reprinting, a new edition would be necessary, as it was necessary to correct errors of spelling and standardisation detected in the second edition and to introduce changes aiming to improve the clarity of one or other phrase or to refine the formulation of others.

Until recently, the idea of maturation was not regarded as central to Winnicott's work, even by scholars studying the author, both within Brazil and abroad, let alone as the horizon from which his thought is unified and from which it is possible to develop a theory of health and another of psychic disorders, with both phenomena endowed with a sense of maturation.

Already today, at least in Brazil, on the basis of the work of research, teaching, and dissemination that has been undertaken, this idea is being discovered and used, apparently to great advantage, in theoretical work, as a guide to clinical practice, in the guidelines and supervision of different institutional fields and for preventive policies in mental health. In study and research, rather than the habit of simply highlighting isolated concepts, more care has been taken in contextualising it in the whole of Winnicott's work or in locating the described phenomenon, within the line of maturation.

Scholars from other countries are also expressing interest in deepening the proposed reading and by virtue of this demand, this book has been translated into Spanish, with this edition now available as an e-book. Other translations are being undertaken into French and English, which are expected to be finalised soon.

I would like to express here how happy I am to enjoy the good fortune of being able to coexist with and rely on colleagues and contacts with whom I share the pleasure of studying, reflecting, and discovering the richness of Winnicott's thought, in ever greater detail, as well as of placing this richness and its clinical acuity at the service of therapeutic work of all kinds.

In this third edition, I would again like to thank Meire Gomes for her meticulous revision, Loris Notturni, my French translator for his thorough collecting of minor errors and inaccuracies, as well as Gabriela Galván who, on the basis of her translation into Spanish, has been indefatigable in detecting imprecise phrases or terms.

Elsa Oliveira Dias

INTRODUCTION

The theory of maturational processes in Winnicott's work[1]

Winnicott formulated a theory of *personal development*, which he subsequently termed the "Theory of Maturational Processes", based on the ideas that every human being has an innate tendency towards maturation and that no aspect of human existence, whether healthy or unhealthy, can be understood independently of the moment of the process to which it belongs or from which it originates. He regarded this theory as the backbone of his theoretical and clinical work.[2] The emphasis of this theory is on the initial stages, since it is during this period that the basis of personality and of psychic health is formed. By shedding light on what goes on in the special relationship between a mother and her child, Winnicott describes the fundamental human needs, which persist throughout life, from the most primitive stages until the death of the individual, and the environmental conditions which facilitate the gradual constitution of the unitary identity that every baby should achieve, with the ability to relate to the world and to external objects as well as to establish interpersonal relationships.

Winnicott's theory of maturational processes conceptualises and describes the different tasks, achievements, and difficulties inherent to the developmental process at each stage of life. It thus serves as a practical guide for understanding the phenomena of health and for early detection of emotional difficulties. His theory is useful not only for psychoanalysts and psychotherapists but also for parents seeking to assist the personal development of their children, for professionals whose work affects the emotional development of babies, children, adolescents, and adults in some way as well as for anyone made aware of the need for a reflection on preventive activities and policies in the field of psychic health.

Important in itself, the theory of maturational processes also provides the theoretical framework from which different aspects of the study of human nature can be developed, such as those related to cultural achievements and the entire field of creativity. It also forms the theoretical basis, both in Winnicott's own work and in the research project including this book, which allows a clarification of concepts of general psychic disorders, due to their intimate connection with the stages of development.

In order to understand the perspective from which Winnicott develops his theory of maturational processes and psychic disorders, we should underline that he was a paediatrician who became a psychoanalyst due to his conviction, confirmed by his clinical practice, that most of the problems which brought mothers and their babies to his office resulted from extremely primitive emotional difficulties. As his thinking evolved, he defined these as difficulties in establishing the relationship between mother and baby in the earliest stage of life. Once he had become a psychoanalyst, Winnicott devoted himself to the treatment and study of psychotic pathologies, albeit without ever abandoning paediatrics. In the parallel exercise of both clinical practices and in simultaneously observing psychotics and babies with their mothers, he came to realise that emotional development during the very early stages of life related to exactly the same phenomena as those which emerged from the study of the various forms of adult schizophrenia. In this way, the in-depth investigation of an individual of any age with a disorder of a schizophrenic type "becomes an intimate study of that individual's very early development" (1953a, p. 222). In essence, the difficulties shared by infants and psychotics concern the constitution of the self as a unitary identity and the contact with reality. In babies, these difficulties are due to extreme immaturity; in psychotics, to the fact that at some point they have strayed from the path leading to maturity.

The theory of maturational processes is thus the central point of Winnicott's analytical thought. The need for such a theory and the essential connection which exists between this theory and that of psychic disorders were made explicit by the author in 1962, a decisive year for the development of his new concepts, when he stated that:

> [...] we do need to try to get a theory of normal growth so as to be able to understand illness and the various immaturities, since we are now no longer contented unless we can cure and prevent. We do not accept childhood schizophrenia any more than we accept poliomyelitis or the condition of the spastic child. We try to prevent, and we hope to be able to lead the way to cure wherever there is abnormality, which means suffering for someone. (1965e, p. 67)[3]

As the theoretical *background* for the understanding of psychic disorder, the theory of maturational processes is an intrinsic part of therapeutic action:

> The only companion that I have in exploring the unknown territory of the new case is the theory that I carry around with me and that has become part of me and that I do not even have to think about in a deliberate way. (1971c, p. 6)

This book proposes to study and to present the concepts of Winnicott's theory of maturational processes in a unified way, clarifying its premises and providing an organised description of the various stages, their respective tasks and achievements. This study shall concentrate on the early stages, just as Winnicott did, since in the author's view, it is psychoses and not neuroses that form the paradigm of human illness. Referring to the fundamental tasks of the beginning of life, psychotic disorders derive from an environmental failure in facilitating the accomplishment of these tasks and in transforming them into achievements of maturation. In addition, Winnicott's thought demonstrates that it is from the observation and treatment of psychosis that a perspective emerges, which allows us to glimpse essential aspects of human existence that would otherwise be inaccessible when studying a healthy or even a neurotic individual.

The development and application of the theory of personal development for the characterisation of Winnicott's theory of psychic disorders shall be presented in a forthcoming study (in preparation), which refers specifically to psychoses. This more general project, of which this book is the first step, will consist of a unified presentation of Winnicott's theory of schizophrenic psychosis in the light of the theory of maturational processes, with an emphasis on the initial stages of life.

Although Winnicott insisted on the central role of the theory of maturational processes throughout his entire work, he did not go as far as presenting it in a systematic or organised fashion. The only book that offers a more explicit global presentation of the process of personal development was *Human Nature* (1988), which remained unfinished. With the exception of this book, which was conceived as a complete work, Winnicott's books are collections of independent articles, originally written as lectures for different audiences. Since Winnicott took account of the specific character of his public, these articles repeat the same principal theses, albeit from different perspectives, in the light of which one or other specific aspect of human existence is analysed. All of this makes it difficult to grasp the unity of his thought. The objective of this book is to present the various conceptual elements which constitute his theory of maturational processes in a unitary and organised manner. In order to achieve this, we have found it necessary to group and compare the most diverse texts, since the author refers to different stages in different parts of his work, without ever presenting them as a whole.

This study is based on a close reading of the whole of Winnicott's work directed towards the proposed theme. As in any other reading, the one made here has its own premises. The principal ones shall be explained in this Introduction; others will become clearer in the course of the exposition. Essentially, I shall use the classical principle of hermeneutics, according to which, each part of a work must be understood in the light of the whole of this work while, on the other hand, its structure must be reconstructed, taking into account each of its components.[4] In this case, I do not intend to offer an exhaustive reading of Winnicott's work as a whole, but to reconstruct its most central section: the theory of maturational processes. Applying the methodological principle of hermeneutics to this particular task, I shall proceed in such a way as to understand Winnicott's statements about the issue in question, in the light of the totality of his thought. This, as a consequence, will be illuminated as a whole, on the basis of his theory of maturation. I shall subsequently do the same for the theory of psychoses.

Some principles made explicit by Winnicott himself shall also be used, one of which, for example, recommends that an understanding of psychoanalysis in general and of one's own should be achieved by considering the historical route taken in seeking solutions for the problems raised. This is the reason why, for psychoanalytical topics,

[…] the reader must form a personal opinion in these matters, after learning what is taught as far as possible in the historical manner, which is the only way that the theory of anyone moment becomes intelligible and interesting. (1988, p. 42)

Unifying the general hermeneutic principle and this advice from Winnicott, the work will have, from a methodological viewpoint, the character of *internal and historical analysis* of the text. According to this procedure, I shall not attempt to justify Winnicott's theses, any more than he did himself. Nor shall I make a comparative study except in order to highlight the specificity of some of his points of view. This shall be done, above all, in relation to Winnicott's main interlocutor, traditional psychoanalysis, *but always starting from his own position*.[5] I shall not aim at exhaustiveness in these comparisons, but shall limit myself to questions regarding the theory of maturational processes.

Such a task, even within the indicated limits, has its difficulties. One of these is always considering the historical evolution of his thought. In general, leaving aside the texts from the 1930s, during which he wrote as a paediatrician, we may distinguish three phases of his work: the one from 1940 until the publication, in 1951, of his seminal article on transitional objects; the 1950s, during which the decision to develop his own theoretical perspective becomes more explicit; and finally, the phase starting from the 1960s, above all with the publication of the 1962 article "Ego integration in child development" (1965n), in which he introduces the central concepts of the innate tendency to maturation and of the subjective object.[6] The evolution of his thought shall be considered, albeit not in a systematic way, since such task would require another study, despite remaining limited to the presentation of the central theme.

The relevance of the study of the theory of maturational processes

In addition to the fact that the theory of maturational processes constitutes Winnicott's central contribution to psychoanalysis, its study is justified by the fact that, until now, the secondary literature has approached the theme without fully exploring its theoretical and clinical consequences. Furthermore, despite the fact that the author has stated, above all from the 1960s onwards, that this theory is the necessary theoretical horizon for understanding the concepts relating to psychic disorders and their classification, this point has not been emphasised by his commentators.[7]

The same is true of the various general introductions to Winnicott's works.[8] In most of these, we find careful and dense interpretations of aspects of his work but not the internal articulation of his thought as a whole, in a way that clarifies the conceptual key that gives it unity and coherence. There is no emphasis on the importance of the theory of psychoses (with no highlighting of the originality of his approach to the theme and of the fact that the fundamentals of human existence are revealed through the study of psychoses), or any mention of the intrinsic connection between this theory and the theory of maturational processes (i.e., the fact that the latter is the basis of Winnicott's conception of the nature and aetiology of psychoses). Since these are presentations which, while succinct, are intended to provide a general overview of the author, the fact that the core of his thought is not mentioned becomes incomprehensible.

We should consider a few examples.⁹ In *Boundary and Space: An Introduction to the Work of D. W. Winnicott* (1981), one of the first general presentations of Winnicott's work, the authors Madeleine Davis and David Wallbridge expose the central concepts of Winnicott's thought, but these are not articulated in terms of the maturational processes, as a function of its basic temporality.¹⁰ There is no reference to the fact that the theory of maturation is the theoretical foundation required for understanding and classifying psychic disorders. I found only one reference to the aetiology, which, moreover, is the only one made explicit by Winnicott when, while describing the false self, the authors say: The aetiology of the false self is to be found particularly in the failure in object presenting at the stage of absolute dependence (Davis & Wallbridge, 1981, p. 65). However, there is one passage in this work, in the item "Adapting to Shared Reality", in which the authors present a sequence that may suggest the various stages of development to the attentive reader.

A critical appreciation in the same vein would apply to the book *The Work & Play of Winnicott* (1990) by Simon Grolnick, which despite emphasising the developmental character of Winnicott's work, does not specify the singularity of what Winnicott understands by development, nor does it contemplate the essential internal articulations with the theory of psychic disorders.

In the preface to *Le Paradoxe de Winnicott* (Winnicott Paradox, 1987), Anne Clancier and Jeannine Kalmanovitch¹¹ assert that the work, made possible by the collaboration of "a profoundly Winnicottian team, *but a very objective one* [sic], takes up the highly original notions of this creative psychoanalyst […]" (p. xiv, preface). The 250-page book dedicates a chapter of only eight pages to an aspect undoubtedly central to the theory of psychoses: the fear of breakdown. In this chapter, there is allusion to psychoses *en passant*. There is no mention to the central character of the theory of maturational processes and its connection to a theory of psychic disorders. That is not surprising since the entire interpretation of Winnicott's thought is based on Freudian psychoanalytic theory, especially Kleinian theory.

In 1981, Claude Geets published her study *Winnicott*. The author describes Winnicott's concepts most properly, above all those which characterised his originality, for example, questions relating to primary creativity, to playing and to transitional phenomena. Since, however, the author does not consider the global theory of maturation she presents the concepts in an isolated manner, as if they were timeless, that is, without expanding the different meanings that they acquire according to the moment in the personal development process. As, in Winnicott's view, the language that is appropriate for describing one stage becomes *wrong* when used for another stage, since the tasks involved are of different natures, the indiscriminate use of terms promotes the impression that his theory is incomprehensible or inconsistent. In addition to the lack of distinction between the different stages, there is also some backsliding into the traditional theory. The following example demonstrates both problems. Geets begins an item called "From object relation to object usage" (De la relation d'object à l'utilization de l'object) with the following sentence:

> *The adaptation of the child to reality* may thus be described as this long path from subjectivity to objectivity. The *opposition* between me and not-me is supported by the *fantasy* (fantasme) of an *internal* reality, located in the body […]. The child has an "inside" in which he may accumulate

things and his growth is based on the form of an exchange between him (the internal reality) and the world (the external reality) [...] the progressive achievement of objectivity is *favoured by the inevitable frustrations*. (Geets, 1981, p. 100; my italics)

However, for Winnicott, in the first place, the child does not initially *adapt* to reality; if he does so, and it would not be to reality but to the environment, this could be the start of the formation of a pathological false self. In normality, *it is the environment that adapts to the baby*, and as the baby grows, in the presence of the facilitating environment, he *creates* not only one, but many senses of reality. Secondly, bearing in mind that the author announces that she is referring to the passage from the subjective to the objective, which as she herself concedes, is a "long path", it is necessary to discriminate the different stages of this long path. However, in dealing with the beginning of the process, the author not only goes straight to the end (speaking immediately of the "opposition" between me and not-me) but also interprets and uses terms that are alien to Winnicott (for the author, this is a question of *separation* between the me and not-me and not of opposition). The author also discusses the inside and the outside of the infant, when Winnicott clearly affirms that at the start of the process, the senses of internal and external realities have not yet been established and the baby lives in a subjective world, which is neither inside nor outside. Furthermore, the me/not-me separation is not supported by any fantasy (fantasme), nor is it favoured by frustrations, but is initiated by the experience of *no anger* destructiveness, which creates the externality of the world at the stage of object usage.

Adam Phillips, with his book *Winnicott* (1988), is largely an exception in this panorama. Emphasising the originality of Winnicott's theory of personal development, as well as the difference that separates it both from the Freudian theory of the development of sexual functions and the Kleinian "positions", he asserts that Winnicott not only introduced significant innovations into psychoanalytical theory and practice, but that his theory leads to "radical departures from Freud". The main point of this rupture consists of the fact that Winnicott "would derive everything in his work, including a theory of the origins of scientific objectivity and a revision of psychoanalysis, from this paradigm of the developing mother–infant relationship" (Phillips, 1988, p. 5). Phillips uses the term paradigm in the sense of "model" and not in the technical sense used by Thomas Kuhn, who, as we shall see below, uses this term to designate the exemplary problem and solution brought together by a scientific discipline.

In any case, what Phillips indicates is that Winnicott has constructed a theory that is not limited to enriching psychoanalysis with new contributions to an old model, but starts from another point crucial for the study of human nature, namely the initial vulnerability of the dependent infant and the importance of the environment. According to the commentator, these new propositions lead Winnicott to issues that had never been formulated by traditional theory, such as: "what do we depend on to make us feel alive, or real?" (cf. Phillips, 1988, p. 5). However, even this commentator, whose work appears to me to be one of the most significant expositions of Winnicott's thought to date, states that the theory of maturational processes seems to be vague and lacking in solid foundations. In a passage which highlights that, in Winnicott's view, "a too militantly knowing psychoanalysis had usurped, or simply lacked confidence in, what he called 'essentially natural process'" (ibid., p. 98), Phillips asks:

But were such "natural process" simple or complicated? What do we need to know about them in order to adjust to them when, in Winnicott's view, "if the parents have succeeded as parents they are unaware of the things in themselves that have made for success"? (Phillips, 1988, p. 99)

On the other hand, Phillips continues, Winnicott

comes to increasingly complex and often obscure formulations about the earliest "natural" stages of infant's development that involve him in a radical revision of the kinds of instinct-theory that psychoanalysis had been traditionally based on. (Phillips, 1988, p. 99)

The fact is that having glimpsed Winnicott's theoretical strength and originality, neither the meaning of maturation, nor the meaning of what Winnicott understands by natural processes or even the status of the theory of maturational processes are clear to an acute interpreter like Phillips. Perhaps it is for this reason that he did not refer in this work to the articulation of the stages of personal development to the theory of psychic disorders.

We have another example in Michael Jacobs, in his book *D. W. Winnicott* (1995). The author states the central character of the concept of development in Winnicott's work, highlighting it as the mark of the decisive influence of Darwin on him, but, nevertheless fails to indicate their profound differences; the fact that, in Winnicott, maturation is not reducible to the biological evolutionism, and the essentially personal character with which Winnicott endows his concept of development. There are two chapters in this book "Major Contributions to Theory" and "Criticisms and Rebuttals", in which we might expect a mention of the link between the theory of maturational processes and the study of psychic disorders, but there is none. In the last chapter, Jacobs declares that in Winnicott, "there is also little even in the way of a more theoretical position […] that can be debated as readily as, for example, Freud can be on instinct theory, the unconscious, the centrality of sexuality" but concedes, in parentheses "(…) except perhaps his theory of the development of the self" (Jacobs, 1995, p. 99). What would be an introduction to the theory of maturational processes is contained in an item named "From dependence towards independence" (p. 37). In it, not considering the specific character of development, Jacobs declares: "just as Winnicott moves away from a strict Freudian tripartite division of personality, so too he has little to say about the Freudian threefold development scheme of oral, anal and phallic or genital stages of sexuality"; also with the proviso that "like that of Freud, Winnicott's scheme contains three categories [*sic*] (rather than stages, although they are similarly progressive): absolute dependence, relative dependence and the phase 'towards independence'" (ibid., p. 37). That is, juxtaposing Winnicott and Freud, Jacobs does not conclude that there are differences in the theories, but that the former has a debt to the latter.

Although it is a dictionary and not an introduction to Winnicott's work, it is appropriate here to mention Jan Abram's book *The Language of Winnicott: A Dictionary of Winnicott's Use of Words* (1996). Abram selected twenty-two items that she regarded as the main themes of Winnicott's thought. In addition to making explicit, for each one of the chosen items, the main orientation of Winnicott's thought, she enumerates a list of contents in which she points out related themes, weaves her own comments and, as is appropriate to a dictionary of this kind, presents extensive citations of the original texts. The quality of the conceptual analysis of themes is uneven: in some of them the author keeps to what is essential in the theme, maintaining Winnicott's theoretical position accurately. In others, the analysis is vague, losing itself in secondary ideas. Despite being quite successful in the task of establishing links between the concepts, with this making her dictionary a kind of general introduction to Winnicott's work, the book suffers from a lack of a unitary interpretation of his thought. This becomes clear above all since the author has not considered the theory of the maturational process in a consistent fashion, making only isolated references to the connection between the stages of maturation and psychic disorders. This lack of a unitary interpretation also appears in the absence of certain fundamental concepts from the main list, for example, the theory of personal development itself, the subjective object, imaginative elaboration, unthinkable agonies, psychoses, family, Oedipus complex, and the establishment of morality. Psychoses, for example, do not appear in the central themes, being considered within the theme "environment", with the author highlighting the articulation of such disorders with the failure of the environment to provide the baby, during the initial stages, with the satisfactory conditions which permit the continuity of personal growth. Another reference to the aetiology of psychosis is found under the item "antisocial tendency".[12]

I shall now refer to Julio de Mello Filho, with his book *O ser e o viver* (Being and living), of 1989. This book, which marks the beginning of Winnicottian studies in Brazil, is also a rewarding surprise regarding the principal point: the reading of Winnicott's thought presented in it is made with a fearless appreciation of the originality of Winnicott's theory, even if the author does not always extract all of its implications, and demonstrates a vast knowledge of the subject. In the first chapter, "The man, the life and the work", Mello Filho provides what he describes as a bird's eye view, that is, a general and concise introduction, albeit very well elaborated, of a number of points which he regards as basic. In this chapter, what seems important to me and revealing of this scholar's understanding of Winnicott is his initiative of extending and I would say, correcting the list of Winnicott's contributions to psychoanalysis made by André Green, in a 1977 article. Green had distinguished seven theories in Winnicott's thought, including a "theory of pulsions", which was evidently an error. Green also mentions "the theory of development" as one of the theories and not as the theoretical horizon of all the others, in addition to mentioning it last. Correcting the French commentator, Mello Filho begins the list of Winnicott's contributions with the theory of development, leading us to believe that he has prioritised it. At the same time, neither the central position of this theory nor the interrelationship between the stages of maturation and psychic disorders are explicitly emphasised in the work. He also adds several other theories to the list which indeed deserved to be mentioned: for example, a theory of the self, a theory of psycho-somatics[13] and a theory of regression, in addition to re-describing those already mentioned by Green in a way which seems to me to be more faithful to Winnicott than Green himself had previously done. Lastly, he rightly modifies Green's note regarding the nature of a theory of pulsions in Winnicott, proposing a Winnicottian theory of impulses (the term used by Winnicott is *drives*).

Despite the fact that Mello Filho highlights important aspects of the theory of maturational processes here and there, it is mentioned only as a theoretical position to be described, without taking maturation itself into consideration. For example, in the second chapter, "Human development and the analytical situation", the author mentions "the three main processes which accompany the development of the infant: integration, personalisation and adaptation to reality", without distinguishing the stage when they begin. Shortly afterwards, without discussing the entire process and the various challenges which, from this point onwards, must be overcome in order to ensure integration into a unity, he states: "According to Winnicott, through the *conjunction* of the three described processes, [the baby] begins to distinguish a 'me' from a 'not-me', separated by the skin, operating as a limiting membrane" (Mello Filho, 1989, p. 37; my italics).

Brief discussion on the divergent readings

As a result of its subject and methodology, the present characterisation of Winnicott's theory of maturational processes offers a general view of his work that, while not completely new, differs considerably from some other existing readings. As there are several different ways in which Winnicott's work is read and evaluated regarding the extension of his contribution to psychoanalysis, the question here is of knowing exactly of what this contribution consists?

Some challenge the notion that Winnicott is an original thinker. Proponents of this reading deny the existence of a typically Winnicottian "theory" on any significant subject and, as a rule, include his contributions within the theoretical framework of traditional psychoanalysis (Freud & Klein). There is no shortage of this type of assimilation. Already in the title of Chapter Two, "L'enfant et ses fantasmes" (The child and his fantasies) (in Winnicott Paradox, by A. Clancier and Kalmanovitch, cited above) a concept of fantasy (*fantasme*) is used, which belongs to Klein's theory and which is totally alien to Winnicott. In this same chapter, which describes the baby-mother unity, the authors reproduce Winnicott's graphic illustrations of the baby as an isolated being, of the baby discovering the environment, etc.[14] Following this, by way of a caption they say:

> The emergence of id impulses makes it easier for the child to face the outside world. If the good breast realizes this experience of itself, all will go well. When the two do not meet, there will be a split. (Clancier & Kalmanovitch, 1987, p. 26)

In other words, everything here is Kleinian. The only Winnicottian element in this phrase is the movement towards an encounter but even in this case, the direction of the movement is wrong.[15]

Another good example in the same line is Luiz Meyer's 1994 article. Commissioned by the review *Percurso* to encourage reflection on the motives of a possible failure in psychoanalytical training, the article analyses the famous letter from Winnicott to Melanie Klein of November 1952. From any perspective, this letter is an alert regarding the uneasiness and the paralysing atmosphere for the evolution of psychoanalytical thought, resulting from the intransigence, sectarianism and abuse of power by the Kleinian group of the time, through the imposing of clichés and other types of constraint on thought. Meyer is prepared (se dispõe) to consider "the specifically Winnicottian concepts" in the letter, but only to analyse the precise nature of the criticism directed by Winnicott against Klein and particularly against the Kleinians. From this point onwards, Meyer skilfully and subtly undermines Winnicott's thought, shifting away from Winnicott's own concepts to a point outside the scope of the questioning which gave rise to them. This denaturing or even disfiguring reaches a crescendo until, in the final part of the text nothing of Winnicott is left, merely an anonymous and mimetic figure delivering Kleinian ideas.

Most commentators nevertheless do not hesitate in granting Winnicott a notable originality. An example of such an appreciation is provided by Geets (1981): "Winnicott's position in the field of contemporary psychoanalysis is original [...] his work has progressively imposed itself through the novelty of its language and the wealth of its perspectives [...]" (p. 15). In the article "Le concept de limite" (The borderline concept), Green himself states that Winnicott is specifically the analyst of borderline cases, pointing out that the apparent simplicity of the concepts of the British author frequently fails to note the subtle complexity of his discoveries (cf. Green, 1976).

Some interpreters, while acknowledging Winnicott's originality, deny that he is a theoretical thinker, insisting that his richness lies precisely in the fact that he is not "theoretical" or "systematic". Among those who seem to prefer this reading is Pontalis. In an interview with Clancier, the French psychoanalyst claimed that:

> [...] One can trace back Freud's thought, one can expound Melanie Klein's theory, one can systematize Lacan's theories even more. If you try to do that with Winnicott, you lose what is best in him. What I have been and remain sensitive to is the Winnicott effect.[16]

Rogério Luz, emphasising the fact that Winnicott's manner of theorising may result in this kind of approach, acknowledges that it leads to a narrowing down of his contribution. In a 1989 article, Luz points out the way in which Winnicott's text:

> [...] in approaching everyday language and since it refuses a scholarly systematisation, at times is seen merely as an expression of brilliant intuitions, linked to clinical practice, but incapable of responding to the demands of a theory of the subject and his relation to culture. (Luz, 1989, p. 26)

In the same sense, it also postulates the importance of not immobilising a thought that is rich and in continuous flux. For example, Claude Geets, draws attention to the risk of "paralysing a thought in incessant motion, of fixing within a rigid conceptualisation what, in principle, lends itself to being seen and heard as a clinical experience" (Geets, 1981, p. 17) a risk that would be particularly formidable in Winnicott's case. Part of this danger would be the possibility that Winnicott's thought could be transformed into a dogma if it were formulated into a theory. According to Geets, nothing would be more extraneous to the author's mentality than "the dogmatism of a system applied to living reality; detached from the experience that witnessed its birth, theory loses its sense and sheds its skin to become doctrine" (Geets, 1981, p. 17). A number of questions arise regarding this legitimate fear: why would conceptual clarity, unity, and rigour of theory become dogma specifically in Winnicott? If any work, once made public, is necessarily at the mercy of the reading that it receives, which is the equivalent of saying that the subjective world always interferes in the perception of objective reality, why enthrone this structural truth and recommend this subjective reading specifically in Winnicott's case? How can we establish a genuine dialogue with the author if what we do is use his name and language to dress up our old theories? Or also: which is the greater risk? Trying to understand exactly what Winnicott wanted to formulate (which ultimately is what we try to do with our patients) and so many times defended, using the enshrined method of reading and comparing his texts, or decreeing that his thought should be left to the discretion of every and any type of interpretation?[17]

I believe that it is the same kind of anxiety as that expressed by Geets that leads José Ottoni Outeiral, one of the most active disseminators of Winnicott in Brazil, to declare in his "Introduction to the Brazilian edition" of Winnicott's *Psychoanalytic Explorations* that in order to read Winnicott's work,

> it is necessary to do as he suggests in the *Squiggle Game*, with reader and author jointly creating a 'personal reading', a transitional space in which the reader 'will discover' as a personal finding what D. W. Winnicott wrote. (Outeiral, 1994, p. viii)

It is hard to agree with this reading method suggested by Outeiral. Firstly, in view of the same considerations as those made above with regard to Geets and secondly because the construction of a theory or the formulation of a concept is not a spontaneous gesture (which does not deprive them of creativity) as is required in the squiggle game. This game is a therapeutic method, a procedure for interpersonal communication that is entirely different from the procedure for constructing theories, which consists, as we shall demonstrate, of the elaboration and testing of hypothesis, which characterise the scientific activity of problem-solving. Furthermore, it does not seem to be legitimate for a reader to appropriate the ideas of an author without acknowledging his due merits; it is not fair to make a "personal finding" of what Winnicott wrote before trying to know what he actually wrote, forgetting that he was the one who wrote it. This would mean establishing a relationship with Winnicott's work, which had become a subjective object, which, according to the author, represented a "dead-end communication", a monologue instead of a dialogue; it would be to deny the fact that Winnicott and his work belong to external reality, with which each of us must deal if we hope to reach maturity. As was already mentioned, Winnicott actually recommends that "the reader must form a personal opinion in these matters", but only "after learning what is taught as far as possible […]" (1988, p. 42).

Curiously, this is not always Outeiral's position. Considering the subject of the father in Winnicott's thought, he concedes that "an extensive and unsystematic work […] complicates an in-depth study of certain issues" (Outeiral, 1997, p. 91). In another text, declaring that he was inspired by Hartmann, who once told Masud Khan that everybody referred to his work, but that nobody actually read it (cf. Khan, 1958, p. xxxi), Outeiral explains to the reader that the excessive number of citations of Winnicott in his article has the function of "preserving the true meaning of his ideas and not [favouring] a personal interpretation of them" (Outeiral, 1991, p. 133, note 1).

To the same group of interpreters, belong all those who acknowledging Winnicott as a great clinician, insist on the merely suggestive character of his work highlighting his preference for expressing himself in everyday and even poetic language as a proof of the non-existence of a theoretical interest.

The tendency to consider Winnicott uniquely from the perspective of a brilliant clinician or a "free" or "poetic" thinker is sometimes due to circumstantial reasons. According to Daniel Widlöcher, Winnicott counterbalanced in France, "a slightly intellectualist formalism" derived from Lacan's work, with those works which, on the contrary, gave priority to the therapeutic relationship and the feelings.[18] Having represented an alternative to Lacan's hyper-systematisation in France, in England, Winnicott served as an antidote against the dogmatism and sectarianism of the Kleinian group, not only in the theoretical plane, but also in the political-institutional and scientific one.

There are also those who, without necessarily denying the theoretical originality of Winnicott's texts, note their unscientific character and theoretical weakness. For example, Greenberg and Mitchell remarked that Winnicott's central themes "are generally presented in the form of evocative paradoxes that entice the reader playfully. The arguments are more discursive than tightly reasoned" (Greenberg & Mitchell, 1983, p. 189).

For his part, Jacobs, certainly supported by the absence of an unitary interpretation of Winnicott's thought, observes that although the name of Winnicott may be proverbial in the field of counselling,

> [...] his ideas attract little actual debate [...] within that related profession. [...]; if behaviourism [...] continues to have running battles with psychoanalysis, Winnicott does not attract any specific fire [...]. There may be reasons why there is little major criticism of his whole work. It is possible, for example, that the nature of his writing is such that debate is necessarily quite limited. He may have written prolifically, but he published little that was presented as a comprehensive theory [...]. There is no clear scheme in Winnicott, with the possible exception of *Human Nature*. (Jacobs, 1995, p. 98)

Rycroft, who is a prominent figure in the *Middle Group* laments the absence of a consistent theorisation in Winnicott's works. He concedes that the idea of a transitional reality "is perhaps the most important contribution made to psychoanalytic theory in the last thirty years" (Rycroft, 1985, p. 145). He nevertheless also states that "in spite of the occasional use of abstract nouns", Winnicott's theses are always:

> [...] a personal statement, too idiosyncratic to be readily assimilated into the general body of any scientific theory. He often sounds like a voice crying in a wilderness that is in fact inhabited, or like a visionary who is disguising himself as a thinker. (ibid., p. 144)

Finally, there are some who defend the existence of a profound originality in Winnicott with regard to his theory. In an even more radical way than Phillips, who, as we have seen, acknowledges the character of a break in Winnicott's thought with regard to traditional theory, Zeljko Loparic (2001b, 2006/2011) states that Winnicott's work introduces a new paradigm in the framework of psychoanalytical theory. In order to do so he starts from the idea that if psychoanalysis wishes to be scientific, then approximately in the same way as a mature factual science, it constitutes the framework within which *an activity of problem solving* develops that is similar to puzzles. The internal structure of this framework is characterised by a way of seeing the world and of talking about it that is shared by an institutionalised group and that is structured as a paradigm or a disciplinary matrix. (Loparic, 2006/2011, p. 29)

The notion of paradigm implied in it is that of Kuhn in his book *The Structure of Scientific Revolutions* (1970). Kuhn holds that a scientific discipline is defined by its "paradigms" and he already defines them in his first work on the issue as "universally recognized scientific achievements that for a time provide model problems and solutions to a community of practitioners" (Kuhn, 1970, p. viii). "A paradigm" consists of two kinds of paradigm. Paradigm I, composed of exemplary or paradigmatic problems, "concerning facts accessible in some form of experience (observation, experimentation, clinical practice) followed by their solutions" (Loparic, 2006/2011, p. 29). Paradigm II, also known as "disciplinary matrix" or "theoretical commitments", consists of the different theories which were formulated to solve exemplary problems. These theories are a) guideline generalisations, used as guides to the research in question; b) the ontological model of the studied domain; c) the methodological model and d) the values involved, including the epistemological ones: internal consistency, plausibility, etc. (cf. Loparic, 2006/2011, pp. 29–30). Paradigm II thus contains the group of hypotheses which serves as a theoretical basis for normal research, that is, for the resolution of problems in progress. Scientific research devotes itself to detecting and solving new problems and usually, the procedure consists of formulating the new problems on the lines of the exemplary or paradigmatic problems, solving them in the light of paradigmatic solutions. While it is capable of encompassing and solving the majority of the emerging problems, the paradigm (I and II) is maintained; however, as a large number of problems emerge which resist solution by an established paradigm, the so-called anomalous problems, a crisis begins which, in general, is slowly engendered. Little by little, research ceases to be "normal" and becomes "revolutionary", in the sense that now its effort is to find or to test a new paradigm capable of solving both the old problems and the new and anomalous ones.

According to Loparic, it is this situation of a change in paradigm that characterises Winnicott's work within psychoanalysis. To traditional psychoanalysis the exemplary problem is the Oedipus complex and the guiding theory is the theory of sexuality. The paradigmatic solution to the exemplary problem consists of the identification of the boy with the father, which means the resolution of the fear of castration and the abandonment of his intention of occupying the father's place as husband of the mother. "The new example proposed by Winnicott", the philosopher says,

> is the baby in the mother's lap, who needs to grow, that is, constitute a basis for continuing to exist and integrating itself into a unity. The most important guiding generalisation is the theory of maturational processes, of which the theory of sexuality is only a part. (Loparic, 2005, p. 314)

This is the new problem, which is anomalous for traditional psychoanalytical theory and refers not to issues of a pulsional order related to incestuous desire, but to the constitution of a sense of reality of the self and of the world. However, Loparic continues, besides altering the exemplary problem,

> Winnicott altered the disciplinary matrix as well. He rejected or significantly modified the use of fundamental concepts such as subject, object, object relation, pulsion (will, impulse), mental representation, mental mechanism, pulsional force. In their place and that of the theory of sexual development, he placed the theory of human development, as well as a series of new basic concepts to be used from that point onwards, in studying new and old problems. (Loparic, 2005, p. 314)

The attribution of the status of paradigmatic revolution to the psychoanalytical work of Winnicott is a polemical thesis of Loparic, surrounded by debate. For example, Roberto Graña, in the introduction to the 1997 Brazilian edition of *Thinking about Children* (1996a), disagrees with the philosopher, saying that this is a "statement which is difficult to maintain" (Graña, 1997, p. xi). Firstly, he says, because of the "inappropriateness of applying the Kuhnian method to the *Geisteswissenschaften*" and secondly, since Winnicott declared in many occasions that he was a Freudian psychoanalyst. Graña's first argument is incorrect, for the very reason that Freud himself declared that psychoanalysis is not a science of the spirit but a natural science.[19] Furthermore, although the main field to which Kuhn applies the notion of paradigm is that of natural sciences (physics, chemistry, biology, etc.) he maintains that *it can be equally applied to the social and human sciences*, with a difference: in these latter fields, the situation must be said to be pre-paradigmatic, since a paradigm I has not yet been established in an unambiguous way and research is seeking to do precisely this. In the field of the human sciences, however, if there is a science for which the paradigm has remained clear, it is psychoanalysis. Even if we were to consider psychoanalysis to be in a pre-paradigmatic situation, it is nevertheless important to read Kuhn when he says:

> [...] the members of all of the scientific communities, including schools of the "pre-paradigmatic" period, share the types of elements which I have collectively labelled as "a paradigm". What changes with the transition to maturity is not the presence of a paradigm but rather its nature. (Kuhn, 1970, p. 179)

In any case, the issue regarding the nature of Winnicott's contribution to psychoanalysis is a fertile discussion, which is still in progress. Graña's second argument concerning Winnicott's explicit affiliation to Freudian psychoanalysis is not convincing, since in addition to failing to resist an analysis of Winnicott's theoretical positions, as we will see in the current study, it refers to a declaration that was more political than theoretical. As Winnicott's thought evolved and he felt more free to express it, what we find is a highly critical analysis of Freud and Melanie Klein's positions, above all when it comes to the claimed breadth of the body of theory of these authors for understanding psychic disorders in general. This does not mean that Winnicott ceases to be a psychoanalyst but, believing psychoanalysis to be an evolving field of knowledge, he carries on with his task as researcher and modifies the theory in the light of new discoveries and from this perspective, he is indeed a follower of Freud.

Rogério Luz is another commentator on Winnicott who, without completely postulating a new paradigm, indicates the radical change that his work represents: "Winnicott introduces into psychoanalysis not only a new object, phenomenon or activity, but provokes a rearrangement of its field of problems and consequently, of its concepts" (Luz, 1989, p. 32).

Clarification of the overall vision of Winnicott's work

My starting point is the conviction that Winnicott's original contribution to psychoanalytical thought lies in the fact that he proposed a theory of the maturational processes of human beings and a theory of psychic disorders, especially psychoses, which are articulated internally and which are interconnected with each other. I also share the position of those who acknowledge that a series of Winnicott's concepts are radically new and extrapolate the available metapsychologies and even the philosophical tradition to which they belong, possibly announcing the emergence of a new paradigm for psychoanalysis as a whole. It is not my purpose to adduce the reasons why I accept this viewpoint. I shall limit myself to highlighting some aspects of Winnicott's procedure, not always noted, which prepare the way for the type of reading elaborated in this study. These observations concern forms of theorising practiced by him, in particular, (1) his conception of psychoanalysis and scientific work; (2) the dialogue which he maintains with the various areas of science; (3) his relationship with language; (4) the use that he makes of poetry and art in general; and finally, (5) the way in which he relates to non-scientific areas of knowledge, such as philosophy and theology (and religion, in general).

We shall initially look at aspects of his theoretical elaboration and in particular of his conception of scientific work. Winnicott always insisted on the fact that what he wrote derived from his own work and on how incapable he was of drawing up an inventory of an inheritance, of working from another person's conception. "My mind does not work that way", he affirmed (1945d, p. 145). In a letter of 1957 to Augusta Bonnard, he mentioned that it was of no importance to him whether or not he was the first to say a certain thing or whether it had already been said (cf. 1987b, p. 116) and also, "I'm not concerned either with being original or with quoting from other writers and thinkers (or even Freud)" (1968c, 193). The need to use his own language to elaborate his theories or as he put it, to formulate "my latest brain-child" in the most personal way is also well-known and has been stated on many occasions. This is undoubtedly due to the unusual freedom of thought that he practiced and of which he was an implacable defendant. His contemporaries are unanimous in affirming his extraordinary capacity to be himself, his aversion to dogmas or to any constraint on thinking.[20]

At the same time, he is the author who, by making explicit the fundamental paradox on which any access to reality is based, that the baby creates what he encounters, makes creativity pay tribute to tradition: "[…] in any cultural field it is *not possible to be original except on a basis of tradition*" (1967b, p. 134). When we are healthy, he says, we only create what we discover, that is, what is already there to be found. Even in the arts, "we cannot be creative into the blue unless we are having a solo experience in a mental hospital or in the asylum of our own autism" (1986h, p. 53). Creativity does not consist of an autistic invention, but "I mean seeing everything afresh all the time" (ibid., p. 41). Winnicott's originality does not come out of the blue and the same is true of scientific creativity; his ideas were forged from observation and within the debate with related areas: paediatrics, child psychiatry, and psycho-somatic medicine.[21] At the same time, his main interlocutor was traditional psychoanalysis. Winnicott always considered himself a psychoanalyst and acknowledged his debt to Freud and Klein on several occasions. Such acknowledgement is in full agreement with his conception of creativity. He states: "I am a product of the Freudian or psychoanalytic school. This does not mean that I take for granted everything Freud said or wrote" (1965i, p. 21).[22]

One of the aspects which Winnicott prised most highly in Freud's intellectual inheritance was the fact that the latter started a scientific approach to the problem of human development and created a method which allows for analysts to check the observations of others and contribute with their own (cf. 1965i, p. 21). A few years later, he would state that Freud gave us a method which we can use and which certainly leads us to something: "it's an objective way of looking at things and it's for people who can go to something without preconceived notions, which, in a sense, is science" (1989f, p. 574).

Winnicott leaves no doubts as to his choice of a scientific approach to the study of human development. Psychology, he stated as early as 1945, makes "no claim to priority in regard to the understanding of human nature, except in one respect: that is to say, in the making of this study a science" (1945b, p. 4). In the first part of *Human Nature*, we also find the formulation that the main objective of the book was to point out the ways in which emotional development was considered to be complex, albeit susceptible to investigation by scientific method (cf. Winnicott, 1988, p. 12).

As a student of human nature, however, with this conceived as essentially temporal, and in seeking to describe the stages of the maturational process, which refers to what is strictly personal in the human being, Winnicott nevertheless cannot accept any type of science and certainly does not accept the natural science to which Freud affiliated his psychoanalysis. What Winnicott rejects in the human sciences are the attempts to build closed systems or to reduce human life to physical entities or to quantifiable categories. He knows that such a science "boggles at the problem of human nature, and tends to lose sight of the whole human being" (1965f, p. 173). He also rejects the claim of a definitive solution for scientific problems. He manifests a singular indignation at Joan Rivière's declaration, in her Introduction to Melanie Klein's book, that the latter had produced an integrated theory which, while still in draft form, "nevertheless takes account of all psychical manifestations, normal and abnormal, from birth to death, and leaves no unbridgeable gulfs and no phenomena outstanding without intelligible relation to the rest" (1989b, p. 460). Winnicott remarks that this was: "A sentence which Melanie would have disallowed had she been truly a scientist" (idem).[23]

For him, there is the danger of science itself, when it is built on foundations which lead to the objectification of the human being and there is the danger of false science, or more precisely, of scientific praxis which is false, since instead of devoting itself to the ever greater clarification of its field of studies, it places itself in the service of "loyalties" and the preservation of power groups. All of this specifically legitimates the need *not to abandon* the task of

> [...] making the study of human nature a science, a process characterized by observation of facts, by the building of theory and the testing of it, and by modification of theory according to the discovery of new facts. (1945b, p. 5)

In this sentence, Winnicott seems to indicate the need to construct a new manner of doing science, adapted to the study of human nature, albeit while maintaining the essential character of the scientific spirit. His work gives us a sample of how to do it and, in this sense, constitutes a legacy and a responsibility.[24] Maintaining what seems to him to be fundamental in Freud's creation, the fact that any transformation in a person occurs within a human relationship, Winnicott formulates new exemplary problems and places the procedures of observation and description at the service of the phenomena which emerge in this new environment of interrogation. Since the rigour of a science consists precisely of the fact that its methodologies and procedures are adapted to its object of study, it is to be expected that a science dedicated to the study of human nature will be governed by another criterion of objectivity and rigour. Objectivity in human questions cannot in any way follow the standard of research in the physical or natural sciences; we cannot conceive of the human being on the basis of categories formulated for the study of natural and measurable entities. The research material for a science of human nature "is essentially the human being ... being, feeling, acting, relating and contemplating" (1965f, p. 175). Furthermore, objectivity, in this field, says Winnicott, "is a relative term because what is objectively perceived is by definition to some extent subjectively conceived of" (1971g, p. 88).[25]

The main thing to be preserved consists of the fact that in scientific research, the gap in knowledge is accepted as a challenge and does not lead the scientist to indulge in supernatural explanations. Ignorance is assumed, and around this, a research programme is devised. What matters to the scientist is to formulate questions; the answers which arise merely lead to new questions. Compared to the certainty of religion, it will be seen that science is completely different. "Religion replaces doubt with certainty. Science holds an infinity of doubt, and implies a faith. Faith in what? Perhaps in nothing; just a capacity to have faith" (1986c, p. 14).

In another text, he again emphasises that "the scientific approach to the phenomena of human nature enables us to be ignorant without being frightened, and without, therefore, having to invent all sorts of weird theories to explain away the gaps in knowledge" (1945b, p. 6). Psychoanalysis, he continues,

> [...] turns out to be a fine new instrument by which human beings may study themselves and their interpersonal relationships; but it does remain an instrument of scientific research or a therapy, and it never makes a direct philosophical or a religious contribution. (1945b, p. 11)

In a text of 1948, on mentioning, from an historical perspective, some of the theoretical developments which followed the pioneer work of Freud, he states that now

> [...] a highly complex theory of the emotional development of the human being has been worked out, so that with all our terrible and at the same time exciting ignorance, we now have useful working hypotheses, hypotheses, that is to say, that really work. There is now sufficient material available for attempts to be made to formulate things about infants which concern equally the psychiatrist and the children's physician, and I want to be one of those trying to say these things. (1948, p. 157)

The method which Winnicott recomends is essentially that of observing and recording phenomena in detail, testing new hypothesis within the perspective of the theory of personal development. We must not forget the example, as he states, of great masters of clinical medicine who loved to observe and to record, living in our minds and affections due to their belief in the value of carefully noting and collating small details (cf. 1969f, p. 255). In this regard, we should note, for example, that his much praised ability to observe and record what happened in his consultations with babies and their mothers, as well as in the clinical relationship with adults, was fed by two other capacities: that of being in actual personal contact with the individual whom he was treating and that of seeing phenomena which only became visible in the light of the theory of maturational processes. On account of the very nature of the phenomena which he studied, Winnicott was convinced that personal contact, far from going against the demands of rigour and objectivity of observation, was precisely what made them possible. These were the peculiarities which enabled him to describe aspects of human nature that had never been "seen" before. Perhaps without understanding the specific quality of Winnicott's clinical observation, but perceiving its result, the editors of his last book *Thinking about Children* (1996a) declared in the preface that

> [...] a striking feature of Winnicott's work was his great power of observation and description so that what he writes has an air of extraordinary familiarity—*one feels that one already has known what he reports all along*. (Shepherd, Johns, & Robinson, 1996a, p. xv; my italics)[26]

Another point which is convergent with what we have just outlined refers to the *sui generis* relation that Winnicott developed with language. In order to make explicit the phenomena that he intended to describe, Winnicott resorted to a language based on common language. In the introduction to the book *Through Paediatrics to Psychoanalysis* (1958a), Masud Khan asserts, not without a certain irony, that Winnicott

> [...] wrote as he spoke: simply and to relate. Not to incite conviction or indoctrinate. He made his idiom so much that of the ordinary cultured and common usage that everyone was illusioned into the make-believe that they have always known what he was saying. (Khan, 1975, p. xii)

In so proceeding, Winnicott often introduced concepts which were central to his theory, without showing a concern with defining, justifying, or providing a foundation for them through a conceptual abstraction. This is the case with "continuity of being", "feeling of real", "essential aloneness", "mutuality", "falling forever", etc. This does not imply that these concepts are lacking in analysable meaning, but rather that their sense must derive from the concrete situation, from the context in which they emerge. This, for example, is the case of "*good-enough mother*", where the "enough" cannot be explained in terms of rules of conduct and even less so is it quantifiable. On this point, Winnicott is incisive: the mother's knowledge derives from her ability to identify with the baby on the basis of her own experience of having been cared for; such knowledge cannot be learned from books or in lectures; regulating it is the same as destroying it, that is, depriving it of its main attribute, its relation to the personal nature and spontaneity of the mother. Defining his concepts by *use*, Winnicott's language is much more indicative than propositional. He allows the word itself to touch us; if this does not happen, it is no use explaining. It is more a question of a communication experience than the production of a verbal meaning intended for a purely intellectual understanding. He says, for example, that: "We can use words as we like, especially artificial words like counter-transference. A word like 'self' naturally knows more than we do; it uses us, and can command us" (1960a, p. 158).

The fact that the analyst, like the good enough mother, is affected by the patient is so intrinsic to the relationship that creating a concept to describe it appears to him to be totally artificial. Furthermore, on some occasions, in order not to misrepresent the phenomenon to be described or to violate it or cover it with a false and precipitated clarity, a certain degree of obscurity must be maintained. In a passage in his work in which a concept was particularly difficult to explain, Winnicott reflected that "just here one must allow obscurity to have a value that is superior to false clarification" (1989k, p. 240).

I would thus like to suggest that the singularity of Winnicott's language is not due solely to his freedom or need to be personal in everything that he did, but knowingly or not, to a well-established theoretical and methodological need, arising from his new perspective. The simplicity of Winnicott's language, at times poetic, is not literary charm, nor does his creativity reside in it; it is a need imposed by the phenomenon which he was able to see. When theorising about the achievements peculiar to the initial stages of development, Winnicott acknowledged that the language available in the context of psychoanalysis, and even in the human sciences, as well as within the framework of the philosophies that govern them, is not capable of addressing the specific nature of the phenomena which he intended to describe, without distorting them. In 1957, he had already stated that

> [...] a writer on human nature needs to be constantly drawn towards simple english and away from the jargon of the psychologist, valuable as this jargon may be in contributions to scientific journals. (1957a, p. 127)

Dealing with issues relating to human experience and not to a psychic apparatus, describing relations between persons and not between psychic agencies (*Instanzen*), indicating details of the mother/baby relation, in the "magic of intimacy" that governs it, Winnicott had to create another language. This is not merely a question of his idiosyncrasy, nor of neglecting descriptive rigour. It is a matter of extreme importance to know whether the language of metapsychology is adequate for describing the nature of human experience. His discussion with Freud and with metapsychology is not political, but methodological. With regard to Freudian psychoanalysis, we may perceive that Winnicott distinguishes two theories in Freud: an empirical one based on experience and another speculative one. These correspond to two types of language: the descriptive type, when Freud speaks of orality, anality, interests, rivalry of the boy with his father, etc.; and the language of metapsychology, which consists of abstract conceptual conventions, which he used to investigate clinical phenomena and to organise the results of those investigations: life and death pulsions, protophantasies, libido, cathexis, etc. Winnicott seems to accept Freud's descriptive theory very readily, while his profound suspicion regarding metapsychology is explicit. In a letter to Anna Freud, mentioning his tendency to say things in his own language instead of using the terms of metapsychology, he wrote:

> I am trying to find out why it is that I am so deeply suspicious of these terms. Is it because they can give the appearance of a common understanding when such understanding does not exist? Or is it because of something in myself? It can, of course, be both. (1987b, p. 58)

A philosophical benchmark for understanding and assessing Winnicott's difficulties with Freudian metapsychology can be found in Loparic's texts on the philosophy of psychoanalysis. Starting from his semantic interpretation of Kant's transcendental philosophy (Loparic, 2000c) and from the reconstruction of Kant's speculative method (Loparic, 1983) Loparic defends the thesis that: (1) Freud, as well as other members of the neo-Kantian School of Helmholtz, fall within the Kantian program of the critique of pure theoretical reason, (2) the basic concepts of Freudian metapsychology have the character of fictions introduced for heuristic reasons, (3) Freud's metapsychological propositions which employ these concepts are undecidable, (4) Freud's speculative method is a version of Kant's speculative method (Loparic, 1985). The philosopher writes:

> We find in Freud different series of observations that may serve to justify the *thesis of the impossibility of deciding about propositions that aim at determining the true nature of the unconscious.* They are all Kantian in inspiration. Firstly, Freud explicitly accepts the non-identity, established by Kant, between *the phenomenal world* given in unempirical experience and the *noumenal world* introduced by understanding, in order to satisfy the internal needs of its operation, in which Freud locates his unconscious [...] Furthermore, he accepts the Kantian thesis of the unknowability of the noumenal world, that is, the impossibility of deciding all of the propositions regarding the properties of noumenal objects [...]. In this way, Freud could only conclude that the problem of knowing what is the true nature of the unconscious is an insoluble one. (Loparic, 1985, p. 34)[27]

Loparic is not alone in adopting this position. In 1966, in a lecture to the British Psycho-Analytical Society, H. J. Home demarcated the theme of the article that he was going to present, saying that it was a philosophical text, which aimed to reflect on the following questions: what exactly does the psychoanalytical theory address and which types of theories can validly be constructed on the basis of it? Anticipating the conclusion, namely that psychoanalytical theory presents "serious logical difficulties, that many of its concepts are ill-defined and many terms in regular use for clinical description ambiguously employed" (Home, 1966, p. 42). Home affirms that the motivation for this study came to him from several scientific meetings with psychoanalysts and from his perplexity regarding the incomprehensibility of clinical articles, written in what was frequently called "technical language", and at what seemed to him to be "the philosophical naiveté of the theoretical papers" (ibid., p. 42). In order to illustrate this point, Home used a passage from Sandler's book "On the concept of superego", which states: "The two techniques of restoring a feeling of being loved (of increasing the level of libidinal cathexis of the self) [...]". Home comments: "The first part of this sentence seems to me completely comprehensible, the second part is, I believe, meaningless" (ibid., p. 42). One of the conclusions to be drawn from Home's article is the incapacity of metapsychological language, which is clearly metaphysical, to cope with the object of its study, the meaning of human experience.[28]

Continuing, Home writes that when, in 1954, Winnicott wanted to present his clinical experiences of regression to dependence, which could certainly be described by common use of language, as they indeed were, he realised that they did not fit either of the two already enshrined categories. "This meant", states Home, "that, strictly speaking, it could not exist as regression so far as psychoanalytic theory was concerned" (ibid., p. 46). That is, *there are human phenomena that cannot be encompassed by psychoanalytical theory, once it circumscribes its knowledge within the limits of the metapsychology language.* In this way, by insisting on using his own language to describe phenomena that had not yet been configured by the traditional theory and in stating, as it was mentioned before, that "a writer on human nature needs to be constantly drawn towards simple English", Winnicott was, even without knowing it, responding to a requirement imposed on thinking by the object of study itself.[29]

We should now highlight the importance ascribed by Winnicott to artistic modes of experience and to the poet who exists in all human beings, in performing the task of understanding human nature and its problems. Always preserving the value of scientific procedures in the building of knowledge, Winnicott never dismissed the fact that there are phenomena that can only be apprehended by the poetic gaze and voice. This refers in particular to his acknowledgement of a poetical truth about the human being, a truth that naturally is included in his theory of the individual personal maturation. Referring to the intimacy and the peculiar communication that develops within the unity baby–mother—central to the clinical work—he maintains that "it would be a pity to give examples lest this should seem to indicate that anyone but a poet could put into words that which has infinite variability" (1970a, p. 85).[30]

Manifesting a concern with the incessant eradication of poetic truth in current civilisation, Winnicott is aware of the danger that the power of technology represents for humankind, the objectifying power of which sweeps away all human sense from things, from the world, and from men and women themselves, with the aim of manipulating and controlling. In his text from 1969, "The Pill and the Moon", he recounts that one night while observing the moon, he raged at the recollection that there is an American flag stuck on it. The idea of a scientific exploration of the moon obscures "the waxing and waning of it and the majesty of it and the mystery" (1986i, p. 207). He continues: "if we can get back to the poetry and recover from the American landing on the moon, before it starts up on Venus, we might feel that there's some hope for civilization" (ibid).

At the same time, when he writes, Winnicott does not make poetry: at the most he places poetic truth at the service of knowledge. Moreover: at different points in his work, Winnicott imposed clear restrictions on a psychoanalytical work built exclusively on poetic truth, which can undoubtedly offer profound satisfaction and, he says, when an old truth encounters a new expression, there is an opportunity for a creative experience in terms of beauty. He nevertheless warns: it is very difficult to use poetic truth directly, since it is about feelings and not everybody feels the same with regard to a certain problem. In one of his most famous and important texts, "Fear of breakdown", he begins by stating that if there is any truth in what he is going to say in that article, the poets of the world would certainly have already addressed it. He nevertheless continues "[…] the flashes of *insight* that come in poetry *cannot absolve us from our painful task of getting step by step away from ignorance towards our goal*" (1974, p. 87; my italics).

For a student of human nature, the procedure is clear: it is about "moving step by step" as is proper to science, "the construction of a better, more accurate, and more serviceable theory of the emotional development of the individual human being" (1984f, p. 64). The scientific procedure "is not a matter of proving this or that by statistics", but instead "it is a matter of being free from knowing in advance. (Knowing in advance belongs to poetry)" (1996b, p. 236). Ivone Accioly Lins makes this point very well when she highlights that despite the evident affinity between Winnicott's ideas and the thought of the Romantic poets, "it would be a mistake to attribute the novelty of his conceptions only to this affinity" (Lins, 1997, p. 22). Unlike the poets, Winnicott was convinced of how necessary and painful the scientific task is and, Accioly continues, "although his research was animated by a poetic spirit, the type and the means of investigation were clinical and scientific" (Lins, 1997, p. 22).

Also with regard to intuition, generally so highly praised in him, Winnicott indicated the restrictions, especially in his classes for students in the field of health: "True intuition can reach to a whole truth in a flash (just as faulty intuition can reach to error) whereas in a science the whole truth is never reached" (1945b, p. 5). In this way, although we value this glimmer of truth that intuition can provide, we must always remember that "our feelings and our imaginings may get out of hand and may take us anywhere" (ibid., p. 5). There is also an ethical issue, in terms of professional responsibility, since intuitive understanding of human nature may prove unreliable as a guide in the field of social living.

> It might enable a doctor to be brilliantly understanding of a patient who was a thief, but unless the psychology of delinquency is studied as a science, intuitive understanding will not prevent doctors as well as other people from doing and saying all sorts of useless things when decisions have to be taken in a practical way, as, for instance, in a juvenile court. (ibid., p. 5)

Winnicott leaves no doubt about his position: in a lecture to paediatricians on child neurosis, he enumerates a few methods for treatment and says that he can "only stress that *intuition is not good enough in psychological practice*". Shortly afterwards, he asserts that "There *must* be those who dislike psychoanalysis, because of the fact that it studies human nature objectively; it invades the realms where previously belief, intuition, and empathy held sway" (1958k, p. 321). As a result of all of this, he concludes that

> […] what is important in science is a construction of a satisfactory road towards the truth. That is why a scientific training is so important for everybody; it enables you and me to test our own little bits of the world satisfactorily. (1945b, p. 5)

In 1946, in reply to a letter from Ella Sharp, Winnicott once again addressed the relation between psychoanalysis and art, stating that he was not sure whether he agreed with Sharpe's thesis that psychoanalysis is an art and that he preferred what he understood as the true psychoanalytical work, since in psychoanalysis, art occupies less space than technique based on scientific considerations (cf. 1987b, p. 10). Some years later, he would declare that the idea of psychoanalysis as art must gradually give way to a study of environment adaptation regarding to the regressions of patients, albeit while pointing out that "while the scientific study of environmental adaptation is undeveloped, then I suppose analysts must continue to be artists in their work" (1955b, p. 291). However, even if the psychoanalyst may be a good artist, "what patient wants to be someone else's poem or picture?" (ibid).

The therapeutic ability of the psychoanalyst, whose paradigm is the good enough mother clearly does not rest on purely intellectual knowledge, but above all on his personal sensitivity and ability to identify with the patient and understand his or her needs. However, apart from the fact that the analyst, unlike the mother, does not have twenty-four hours a day to be with the baby and to get to know him, he cannot count on the natural advantage of primary maternal concern. He may do better than the patient's own mother, but some humility is required in order to know that "[…] the clumsiness of the psycho-therapist as compared with the mother makes it inconceivable that regression to dependence even in a carefully controlled treatment is pleasurable" (1988, p. 159).

On the contrary, a period of regression to dependency requires that for a long period of time, analysts keep themselves within the strict limits dictated by the patient and, during this period, "the strain can be terrific" (1987b, p. 182). It is necessary, for example, to be prepared for the event which occurs when the patient, regressing to dependence, "goes mad" increasingly, while in search of the cure. In these cases, "if the analyst understands what is going on he or she is able to tolerate the very considerable tension that belongs to this kind of work" (1989q, p. 129). In this way although it is the patient who constantly teaches the analyst—who is capable of learning—about her own needs, as Winnicott points out, the analyst:

> […] should be able to know, theoretically, about the matters that concern the deepest or most central features of personality, else he may fail to recognise and to meet new demands on his understanding and technique. (1989o, p. 169)

On account of all of this, in his specialised work and above all in cases of patients with difficulties of a schizophrenic type, the analyst "must have a working theory of the emotional growth of the personality" (1968c, p. 194), learning to see, listen and understand through it. "That theory", says Winnicott, "is always there in the background" (1954c, p. 114), serving to shed light on the phenomenon and guide imagination, sensitivity and intuition. Starting from the observation of facts, we need to continue developing the theory "to arrive at an accurate and valuable theoretical statement, without which we are stuck" (1996c, p. 212).

The theory of maturational processes should not be understood as a merely intellectual tool to be applied to each case. On the contrary, highlighting the way in which it participates in clinical practice, Winnicott points out, as has already been mentioned, that his only company when facing the unknown territory of a new clinical case, is the theory which he carries with him, which, in this way, became such a part of himself that he does not even need to think about it in conscious fashion. He simply sees through it. Shortly afterwards in the same text, Winnicott compares himself to a cello player, who first works on the *technique* and then actually begins to play the *music*, most certainly using the technique (cf. 1971c, p. 6).

In an article from 1950, Winnicott expresses the hope that babies who have been offered a satisfactory presentation of external reality by their mothers, in small doses and in a comprehensible way, will grow up and develop "to be capable of making a scientific approach to phenomena", even being able to "carry a scientific method into the study of human affairs" (1965i, p. 28). This task is necessary since if what is good and natural in human nature and in the management of human beings in development is to be protected from being squashed out by science, it can only come about "by an extension of scientific inquiry into the whole field of human nature" (1965i, p. 28).

Another point to be considered refers to the fact that in order to clarify points with which he is dealing, Winnicott repeatedly refers his readers to philosophical and theological theses and even to religious and mystical practices. Some of these concepts effectively require an approximation to philosophy and many of them constitute fundamental philosophical themes.[31] Sometimes this occurs amid descriptions which seem to be restricted to the simplest everyday life. At a certain point, for example, Winnicott describes how the support of the maternal ego facilitates the organisation of the baby's ego. "Eventually", he says, "the baby becomes able to assert his or her own individuality and even to feel a sense of identity." And later: "There is the beginning of everything, and it gives meaning to very simple words like *being*" (1987e, p. 11). This is the text highlighted by Loparic (1995b) in his article "Winnicott and post-metaphysical thought". His philosophical reading leads him to perceive that,

> [...] suddenly, in a context which appeared only to concern mothering, the problem of identity emerges, which is one of the most difficult in philosophy. Moreover, the idea also arises that in the two-in-one of baby and mother, semantic questions are decided. Not the semantics of nipples and milk, nor even of the good and bad breast, but a semantics that metapsychology ignores, the semantics of the simple words, such as the word "being". Everything occurs as if, even for a philosopher thinking seriously, that is, not academically, about what the word "being" means, its original meaning would only be determined by a return to the original simplicity of the human being, initially experienced in the intimacy of the relationship between mother and baby. (Loparic, 1995b, p. 47)

As we have seen in Home's article, the description of what happens in the intimacy of the peculiar baby–mother relation cannot be made in an abstract language, built for dealing with systems. Winnicott accomplishes the not at all easy task of formulating his theme conceptually, without "insulting the delicacy of what is preverbal, unverbalised and unverbalisable, except perhaps in poetry" (1967a, p. 151).

All of the highlighted points deserve detailed analysis, although this is not what we intend to offer here; they were only enlisted in order to open the way and to outline the framework of interpretation. In the light of what has been set forth, we can only regard Winnicott as a scientific thinker. If this were not the case, it would lead us to an explicit contradiction with his text. On the other hand, we must acknowledge that his conception of scientific theorisation does not fit without further ado into the commonly held conceptions of what scientific work might be. This should not be understood, as the divergent interpretations mentioned here do, as a sign of lack of interest in scientific theorisation, of theoretical weakness, of inclination towards the poetic, etc. It instead means that in addition to his other scientific contributions, Winnicott introduced innovative proposals for the very way in which psychoanalytical knowledge is constituted.

It is perhaps also for this reason that some authors maintain, as we have seen, that his work constitutes a paradigm shift in the field established by Freud, including the form of theorisation. The paradigm shift frequently implies a change both in the scientific criteria which define a scientific discipline as a body of knowledge, and in the philosophical framework into which this body of knowledge is inserted. It is this direction that Rodman seems to tread, in the introduction to the book that assembles Winnicott's correspondence, when he writes that:

> Freud the great system builder probably meant less to Winnicott than Freud the originator of a method to plumb the human soul. One has the sense that Winnicott did not set his sights on Truth with a capital T, but on truths that would not stay still, the truth that is contained in the continuous interplay of people. He did not seem to require what Nietzsche has called "metaphysical solace", of the sort one may get, for example, from a convincing philosophical system. Yet this feature of his thought constituted a kind of philosophy in itself. (Rodman, 1987, p. xxvii)

On this point Rodman appears to align with Loparic when the latter states that Winnicott's theory of personal development constitutes a deliberate attempt to break with the metaphysics embedded in the language of Freudian metapsychology and for that reason, in the central body of traditional psychoanalysis.

In summary, if Winnicott certainly was not a "systematic thinker", he did not avoid the effort of articulating his thought internally. What characterises his thought, apart from its *total rejection of the objectification of the human being*, is absolutely not the rejection of any theorisation, but of *theories that are closed, definitive and unquestionable, susceptible to transformation into dogmas*. It is from this aversion that his much vaunted anti-dogmatism derived. Winnicott did not permit schools to develop around himself, since he understood that they tend towards proselytising and political games, to the detriment of a reflection based on experience. He even feared that some of the terms he created would become empty "Winnicottian" *slogans*, or impersonal applications of his conceptual findings, without the participation of the psychoanalyst's creativity. We can also observe in him a deep mistrust of abstract conceptualisations, unrelated to experience, which retreat from a commitment to life's intimate truth. We should not forget that his rejection of closed, abstract systems did not prevent him from seeking original theoretical paths, independent of those of Freud and Melanie Klein, rejecting traditional concepts that seemed unacceptable to him, from outlining his theoretical field with well-defined conceptual frontiers and from defending it effectively.

Notes

1. Until early 1960s, the expression most frequently used by Winnicott to refer to his central theme and theory was "emotional development". He took great care to clarify that the development which he was interested in did not concern just the growth of body and mental functions, but in the first place their integration in one individual person. In a paper published in 1960, Phyllis

Greenacre used the expression "maturational processes" in her considerations regarding the parent–infant relationship. She was not the first or the only one to use the expression, but the fact that she emphasised the role of maternal contact and care in these processes appealed very much to Winnicott. The point that interested him was not exactly that of Greenacre's. He nevertheless realised that this was the expression which he needed to make more accurate what he understood by "development": that it consists of several integrated maturational processes, and that the integration requires a facilitating environment in order to take place. Maturational processes thus imply dependence. Not only do we find Winnicott referring to his theory of "maturational processes" more and more frequently from 1960 onwards, but he also included the expression in the title of his very important book *"The Maturational Processes and the Facilitating Environment"*, published in 1965. In attempting to preserve the specific meaning of the language of Winnicott, I have chosen to name my study "Winnicott's Theory of Maturational Processes". However, I shall follow Winnicott and use the expressions "emotional or personal development" and "maturation" or "maturational processes" as synonymous.

2. Besides affirming on many occasions and throughout his work, that the theory of maturational processes is a central feature of his thought, Winnicott uses the decisive expression "backbone" in 1984e, p. 184.

3. Please note that all the quotations without an author's name are from Winnicott.

4. The procedure of text reading outlined here is that of the classical hermeneutical method, introduced by Schleiermacher in his reading of the Scriptures and restated by Dilthey for the study of Human Sciences in general. In Heidegger's early works and in Gadamer, Hermeneutics is raised to the condition of descriptive procedure par excellence. On all issues related to the method, cf. Hans Georg Gadamer (1976), especially the second section of Part Two.

5. I shall call traditional psychoanalysis the one represented by Freud and Melanie Klein, whose work may be considered as the matrix for that discipline. The naming is owed to Winnicott himself, who particularly dwelled on the discussion with these authors, referring to both their work with the expression "traditional", "classical" or "orthodox". Cf. Winnicott, 1969d, 1970b.

6. In a text from 1967, discussing his theoretical trajectory, Winnicott mentions that his view, constituted along the 1920s and 1930s while he worked as a paediatrician and started his psychoanalytical training, was reformulated in the 1940s when, he affirms in another text: "[…] I began to have my own way of stating the essential stages of the intertwined physical and emotional development of the human infant" (1968a, p. 218). Today, however, the historical perspective of the entirety of his work allows us to affirm that it was only from 1960 onwards, the year of Melanie Klein's death, that Winnicott felt himself freer to expose the new orientation of his thought clearly and incisively. Surely, the texts written in the 1940s already introduce a conceptualisation of his own, related to aspects of human nature that had not been considered by traditional psychoanalysis. However, because his ideas were not well established or for political reasons, or both, he expressed them timidly or, as Jan Abram puts it (1996, p. 1) "obliquely", sometimes even denying the originality that characterised them.

7. The only clear mention from others in this respect is found in the introduction to the first part of *Deprivation and Delinquency*, written by the organisers of the work: Clare Winnicott, Ray Shepherd and Madeleine Davis. (cf. Winnicott, C., Shepherd, & Davis, 1984).

8. I shall only mention the works which aim to introduce Winnicott's thought as a whole, leaving aside books or articles that linger over one or another aspect of his work.

9. The examples are restricted to the works in existence at the time of the first edition of this book, in 2003. There would be other references to be made today certainly.

10. This historical perspective does not appear even with reference to the development of Winnicott's work. In Chapter One, the section "The evolution of the theory", the authors, having already in hand most of the material that would only appear in public at a later date, refer only to the evolution from Winnicott's admiration of Darwin, while the former was still a student, to his discovery of psychoanalysis; from his fascination with Freud and then with Melanie Klein to his criticism of the Kleinian theory of jealousy. No reference is made to the gradual formulation of the theory of personal development, to the slow elaboration of the concepts of subjective object, of self and false self, to the new way of formulating the concepts of subjective object and object objectively perceived as respectively being and doing, to the last findings about destructiveness in terms of object usage, etc.
11. J. Kalmanovitch was the French translator of Winnicott's work *Maturational Processes and the Facilitating Environment*.
12. A more detailed analysis of Jan Abram's book may be found in the reviews by Dias, 2001 and by Bogomoletz, 2001.
13. In his text on psycho-somatic disorders (1966) and throughout the work, Winnicott uses the term "psycho-somatic" with a hyphen, to indicate that this compound expression is necessary to distinguish two domains of the whole person, the psyche and the soma, which cannot be reduced to each another, but through the specific tendency which characterises human nature, tend towards integration. This integration is not automatic and only takes place if there is environmental facilitation. It is an achievement of maturity. The hyphen, says the author, both unites and separates the two aspects of human nature; it is not a good sign when it merely separates them.
14. Cf. Winnicott, 1953a, p. 223.
15. According to Winnicott, when the care is good enough it is not the breast which makes the movement, imposing contact, but rather the baby, who by making the spontaneous gesture, encounters the breast, creating it. There are many examples of this kind of assimilation, which are equated in the same language and obscures the originality of Winnicott's proposals. In the same work, the authors, who are completely indifferent to Winnicott's insistence on the fact that reality is subjective and not internal at the beginning of life, named the next item of Chapter Two "From internal reality to external reality". A current way of assimilating Winnicott into the traditional theory without facing the questions that arise from his new conceptions, as if they belonged to the same theoretical horizon or, as Loparic puts it, to the same paradigm, is to say that Winnicott complements one single analytical theory, of which Freud would have described the more advanced cases, Melanie Klein, the more primitive disorders and Winnicott, those even more primitive. I shall attempt to show that this thesis is indefensible.
16. Cf. Pontalis' interview with Anne Clancier, in Clancier & Kalmanovitch, 1987, p. 143.
17. Some of Winnicott's commentators, defending the "free" interpretation of his thought, that is, without paying greater attention to what he actually wrote or defended, claim to be supported by a statement of Masud Khan in the preface to *Collected Papers: Through Paediatrics to Psychoanalysis*. Mentioning that he had never met someone "so inevitably himself" as Winnicott, Khan affirms that this is what allowed him to be multiple, and for everyone "to have his *own* Winnicott." If this was true, however, besides being inevitable with regard to Winnicott as a person, it is certainly not with regard to his theory, which he consistently defended whenever it was an object of distortion. Cf. among other examples, 1963a, p. 255/256, 1987b, letters 60, 74, 82, 89, and 125.
18. Cf. D. Widlöcher's interview to Anne Clancier, in Clancier & Kalmanovitch, 1987, p. 148.
19. Cf. Freud, 1933a (lectures 34 and 35) and 1940b.
20. Cf., in particular, the letter dated November 1952 to Melanie Klein (1987b, p. 33).

INTRODUCTION

21. As a psychoanalyst and paediatrician, Winnicott had long debates with medical psychiatry, paediatrics, and academic psychology, spread throughout his works, on various themes, such as human nature, the relation between mind and body, human growth and the issue of health and illness. Several moments of this debate are the subject of a detailed analysis in Chapter One.
22. To say that Winnicott was influenced or that he started from one idea or another, is not the same as to state, for example, like Adam Phillips does, that "his work, in fact, cannot be understood without reference to Klein" (Phillips, 1988, p. 9) or, as Luiz Meyer affirms: "In fact, we need to think about Winnicott starting from Melanie Klein" (Meyer, 1994, p. 83).
23. Cf. Winnicott, 1989b. In this same text, Winnicott refers to the fact that scientific discussion and the advancement of knowledge are often prevented not only by our "fear of doubts", but also by the play of "loyalties", frequent in groups inclined towards sectarianism, which, being more concerned with power than with the true discussion of ideas, stagnate thought and inhibit free expression. In this respect, cf. also Winnicott's letter to Melanie Klein, November 1952, in 1987b, p. 33.
24. Often in his work, Winnicott urges psychoanalysts to go on researching and increasing their understanding of phenomena which can be seen in the light of the theory of the maturational processes. "The analyst", he affirms in 1967, "has a great responsibility for the teaching of theory and for the development of theory according to what the patients are all the time trying to teach us [...]" (1996b, p. 252). The theory, Winnicott says, is too complex and "there are great gaps in our understanding" (1989q, p. 119); hence, any study which clarifies the nature of the infant at the time of birth and the first feed is welcome. (cf., 1988, p. 150).
25. It is interesting to note that the need both of a new science and the rigour that must characterise it finds a parallel in Heidegger. In the *Zollikon Seminars* (1987), addressing a group of doctors and psychiatrists interested in finding another way (not the scientific-natural one) of thinking about human issues related to the practice of their profession, Heidegger affirms that the rigour of a science resides in the fact that it corresponds to its object both in its project and in its method. However, he says, "Yet not every rigorous science is necessarily an exact science. Precision is merely a specific form of the science's rigour, for precision exists only where the object is posited as something that can be calculated before hand. But if there are matters that resist calculability due to their nature, then any attempt to measure them according to the method of an exact science is inappropriate" (Heidegger, 1987/2001, p. 132). Some time afterwards, bearing in mind the project of edifying a science of care for the man who falls ill, in the light of existential analytics, Heidegger would say: "Science means the systematic ordering of interpreted experience. Each science is rigorously bound to its subject domain, but everything rigorous does not involve exactitude *[Exaktheit]* in a [natural science's] calculative sense. The unifying pole in psychotherapeutical science is the existing human being" (Heidegger, 1987/2001, p. 207).
26. By emphasising Winnicott's profile as a scientist, the editors of the book *Thinking about Children*, neglected the fact that the science valued by him must not be understood in the terms of positivist or naturalistic science, but must be adapted to the study of human nature (cf. Shepherd, Johns, & Robinson, 1997).
27. Loparic also pointed out that Freud was familiar with the work of Ernst Mach, whose empiricism continued many aspects of Kant's criticism (cf. Loparic, 1984 & 1985). Details of the relationship between Freud and Mach were explained by Loparic in "Freud: contemporary of Brentano and Mach," a lecture delivered at the colloquium "Vienna in the beginning of the Century: a paradigm of modernity" (CLE, Unicamp, November 1985).

28. In a passage from *Zollikon's Seminars*, Heidegger says: "the whole starting point within the psychic and the point of departure from a consciousness is an *abstraction* and a *nondemonstrable construct [eine nicht ausweisbare Konstruktion]*. The relationships of a thing to the surrounding world *[Umwelt]* do not require explanation; they must simply be seen [in a phenomenological sense]" (cf. Heidegger, 2001, p. 162).
29. Although Winnicott did not clarify exactly what he understood by that, he knows that the metapsychology is metaphysical. He says: "Freud was able to develop the theory on which psychoanalysis is based very far indeed in his own lifetime, and this theory is usually called metapsychology (on the analogy with metaphysics)" (1986c, p. 15).
30. Ivone Accioly Lins points to the influence that English poets such as Wordsworth and Keats exercised on Winnicott's thought. In a passage from her article, she wrote: "Through the notion of 'negative capacity', Keats highlights the capacity to remain in uncertainty, in mystery, in doubt, without the 'irritating search for the facts or the rationale, that is, without the irritable flight to explanatory or scientific systems. Winnicott asks for the paradox to be tolerated and respected, instead of being resolved by intellectual processes" (Lins, 1997, p. 21).
31. As in the case of science, it is not any philosophy that addresses the questions raised by Winnicott's thought. The thinker who, in my view, favours the understanding of Winnicott's work the most, and who offers a philosophical foundation for some of his fundamental concepts, is Martin Heidegger, especially in his first phase, of *Being and Time* (1974). It is not the purpose of this study to explain the possible approximations between Winnicott's thought and that of Heidegger, and still less to apply Heidegger to Winnicott. It is nevertheless difficult, when studying Winnicott, not to observe Heideggerian resonances. Heidegger's ontology of finitude will be hence a background for the examination of certain aspects of Winnicott's thought which could not otherwise be understood by the traditional theory of psychoanalysis or philosophy. I shall mention it occasionally, when it appears opportune to me, in order to facilitate the understanding of the concept. Such approximation is entirely my responsibility, and is corroborated by the philosopher Zeljko Loparic, who has since developed a series of works around this fertile affinity (cf. Loparic, 1995a, 1995b, 1998, 1999b, 1999c, 2001). After having conceived this link, I found it in the book *De l'enfant à l'adulte* (1979), by the French psychiatrist Georges Amado. His interpretation of Winnicott and Heidegger, as well as the approximation that he made between them nevertheless diverge from my own to such an extent that I ultimately have not used his work in the context of this book. There is no evidence that Winnicott ever read Heidegger. The only possible proximity, highly indirect, is that Winnicott was R. Laing's supervisor before the latter went down the route of anti-psychiatry that was clearly influenced by Sartre. Adam Phillips, biographer of Winnicott and commentator on his work, states that the *Middle Group* was "obliquely influenced by existentialism" (Phillips, 1988, p. 11), without providing any further information. It would appear that this existentialism refers to the current created by Sartre in France. Nor there is any sign of Sartre in Winnicott's work; indeed, Sartre was not a follower of Heidegger, even if he wished to have us believe so. Moreover, Heidegger always rejected the epithet of existentialism for his philosophy.

CHAPTER ONE

Winnicott and the debate with related areas

Historical aspects of Winnicott's intellectual background

In examining Winnicott's conception of psychic health and illness in general, and of psychoses in particular, it is important to highlight some aspects of his professional and intellectual life that strongly influenced his theoretical positions. It will be equally useful to review the implicit or explicit debate within his work with the related areas of psychiatry, academic psychology, and traditional psychoanalysis. We may perceive the trend in the evolution of his thought through which certain concepts emerged and were consolidated as responses to the conceptions of his time which he judged to be inadequate and even unacceptable, starting with the general outlines of this debate.

At several points, Winnicott refers to the importance for his thought of his medical training. On the one hand, he had the obvious advantage of medical knowledge, which allowed him to identify clinical states with an active physical factor, which generated secondary psychological symptoms, or which allowed him to determine that a sick child was not suffering from a physical disorder, which indicated a psychological disturbance or a depression in the mother which manifested itself as an excessive concern for the child. Probably, however, his greatest debt to his medical training and practice lay in his clarity about what *not* to think or do in treating someone's health. Having lived among paediatricians and psychiatrists, Winnicott experienced the inadequacy of thinking about health and illness in purely organicist terms at first hand. He seems to have realised at a very early stage that health, and even more importantly, the feeling of being alive, could not be reduced to the effective functioning of the body and its organs and that the separation of the physical from the psychic was intellectually possible, but highly artificial.

In 1920, during his medical training, Winnicott was already firmly convinced of the impossibility of diagnosing disorders of relevance to paediatrics without considering their psychological aspects. While he was still a student, he encountered a work on Freud by the Swiss pastor Oskar Pfister and was delighted with the possibility offered by psychoanalysis of approaching psychic illness and somatic disorders from a predominantly psychological viewpoint. In a letter of 1919 to his sister Violet, he enthusiastically describes his discoveries regarding the Freudian theory of the psyche (cf. 1987b, p. 1). In 1923, he became an assistant doctor at the Paddington Green Children's Hospital, a position he held for forty years.[1] Having decided to include psychoanalysis in his training, he began analysis with James Strachey in the same year, which would last for a decade. The clinical care at the hospital gradually evolved from paediatrics to child psychiatry with an analytical orientation.

In the paediatric practice, carried out in terms of child psychiatry, Winnicott succeeded in verifying that most of the problems which brought mothers with their babies and children to a clinic were due to primitive emotional disorders. Furthermore, he observed that not only children but also physically healthy babies could already be emotionally ill during the first weeks of life. He was impressed by the precocity of the disorders and by the importance of psychic factors in their emergence; at the same time, the nature of these factors was not yet clear to him and in approaching psychoanalysis, he sought the field *par excellence* for investigating them. He indeed located them, albeit with the proviso that he would very soon realise that he did not agree with what the established traditional theory understood as psychic.

The discovery of the existence of these precocious emotional disorders decisively influenced the evolution of his analytical thinking. As a result of this finding, Winnicott could never be persuaded of the centrality of the Oedipus complex proposed by Freudian psychoanalysis. In 1967, during a lecture in which he presented a sort of intellectual autobiography to his analyst colleagues, he noted:

> When I came to try and learn what there was to be learned about psycho-analysis, I found that in those days we were being taught about everything in terms of the 2-, 3-, and 4-year-old Oedipus complex and regression from it. It was very distressing to me as someone who had been looking at babies—at mothers and babies—for a long time (already ten to fifteen years) to find that this was so, because I knew that I'd watched a lot of babies start off ill and a lot of them become ill early. (1989f, p. 574)

Marked by this evidence, Winnicott's theoretical efforts moved in the direction of clarifying what happens to babies at the very outset of life and the specific nature of the difficulty faced by or afflicting them.[2] In 1935, at Strachey's suggestion, he contacted Melanie Klein, who was already known for her interest in the more primitive anxieties of childhood. Regarding the study by Klein as being extremely important, Winnicott followed the path initiated by her, becoming her supervisee between 1935 and 1940 or 1941.[3] He soon realised that Klein knew a great deal and much more than he did about the topic and even during subsequent phases, when he decisively distanced himself from Klein's theoretical line, he always affirmed that he had learned much from her. There had nevertheless been theoretical differences between them from the start, which gradually deepened and became clearer as the basic conceptual elements of his theory became more precise, ultimately revealing a fundamental incompatibility between their respective theories. We shall examine some of these conceptual differences in greater detail below.

It was nevertheless during this period, at the end of the 1930s, that another professional experience decisively influenced the theoretical direction of his thought. During the Second World War, Winnicott was appointed psychiatrist-consultant to the Government Evacuation Scheme of one reception area in the UK and, according to Clare Winnicott, who was a member of his team as a social worker, this position had a profound effect on him, since he found himself facing a large scale and concentrated disruption of households and a massive disintegration of family life, allowing him to observe the effects of separation and loss on children and adolescents. In addition to the global situation, there was also the fact that the children for whom Winnicott became responsible were exactly those who, having already presented difficulties at home before the war, required special arrangements and could not be introduced into ordinary households which would "adopt" them, in accordance with the evacuation plans. Winnicott further observed that for such children, war was not only secondary but beneficial, as they found themselves removed from an intolerable situation in their own homes, for which they had not found an exit and were placed in a new situation, in which they could possibly obtain help. This was the experience that provided Winnicott with material for formulating his theory on delinquency and character disorders, clinical manifestations included in what he termed the *antisocial tendency*. From this point onwards, certain specific theoretical aspects of an as yet incipient theory of maturational processes were gradually outlined with greater clarity, with these relating to the importance of the environment in the aetiology of psychic disorders.

Until this point, character disorders such as delinquency and juvenile violence were seen by psychoanalytic theory as manifestations of the anxiety or guilt resulting from the inevitable unconscious ambivalence between love and hate, from the conflict which arises when the desire to destroy is specifically directed at the loved person. If the guilt cannot be repaired or sublimated, the individual is compelled to act out so as to give it a concrete outline. The aetiology of delinquency basically consisted of an intrapsychic conflict. For Winnicott, data from experience again led towards another hypothesis, namely, that the environmental factor was aetiologically decisive in these issues, with this undoubtedly already a tendency of his thought. This becomes clear, for example, in Winnicott's early texts from the 1930s, in which he describes several paediatric cases treated during the 1920s, for the elucidation of which he was already starting to use psychoanalytical theory. Although these articles point out unconscious conflicts that could form the origin of particular physical disorders, he did not fail to demonstrate the importance of environmental factors in the aetiology of the problem.[4] In 1967, when presenting a retrospective of his intellectual trajectory to his colleagues at the British Psycho-Analytical Society, Winnicott referred to the characteristic position of traditional psychoanalysis of emphasising internal factors and neglecting environmental aspects; he noted that for ten or fifteen years, psychoanalysts were the only ones who accepted the existence of anything other than the environment and that although everybody claimed that the delinquency of a particular boy was a consequence of his father's alcoholism, etc., psychoanalysts continued to attribute the problems to the constitution of the boy and to research into his internal conflicts (cf. 1989f, p. 577).[5] On several occasions, Winnicott tried to talk to Melanie Klein and to some Kleinians about the environmental factor, met with complete disinterest, if not suspicion. Soon afterwards, he stated that anyone interested in the care of children ran the risk of being considered "traitors to the cause of the internal processes" (1965h, p. 126).

In 1945, four years after leaving Klein's supervision, Winnicott wrote the article "Primitive emotional development", in which he made a number of statements indicating that he had decided to follow his own path. While he had always been interested in the child patient, he stated that he had decided to study psychosis and that he now had much to add to the current theories and "perhaps this paper may be taken as a beginning" (1945d, p. 145), that is, the beginning of the development of his own theory. In order to present his contribution, he nevertheless had to prepare the ground and would hence try "to describe *different types of psychoanalysis*" (ibid., my italics). At this point, Winnicott already seemed to be aware that both the Freudian version and the Kleinian revision of traditional psychoanalysis, which sought to cover psychoses, were incapable of dealing with the type of problem present in these serious disorders, especially those of a schizophrenic nature, which required an adjustment to the theory.

The debate with paediatrics

During the 1930s, as his psychoanalitical training progressed, Winnicott undertook to persuade paediatricians to abandon certain procedures resulting from a merely organicist background and to learn about psychological aspects in evaluating disorders in children. Although traditional psychoanalysis was his main point of reference over the whole of his intellectual life, Winnicott never ceased to address paediatricians, obstetricians, nurses, and nursery specialists in order to alert them to certain discoveries, which seemed to be essential to him, regarding child care and the implementation of health. During this period, he wrote several articles, as a paediatrician to paediatricians, in which he presented the emotional disorders which could form the basis of certain clinical situations typical of childhood and urged specialists to ensure that they were prepared to investigate the psychological motivations of such disorders.[6]

Winnicott was familiar with his potential readers and the traditional conceptions of illness and health which had dominated medical theories and practices since the start of the modern era. It was not only true that paediatrics and child psychiatry concerned themselves unquestioningly with their respective and traditionally separate fields, the body and the mind, but both areas also represented recent specialisations in medicine and general psychiatry which were still in the process of consolidating their specific characters. In addition, physical medicine had always tended towards a study of the classification of diseases, regardless of the age at which these occurred. Paediatrics became a necessity and was established as a specialist discipline in the mid-nineteenth century, when it became clear that there are morbid states specific to each age group and diseases typical of childhood. Even when syndromes are common to both childhood and adulthood, age imposes a peculiar characteristic from the perspective both of the etiological circumstances and of the clinical aspect.

At the same time, paediatrics limited itself to the physical and physiological aspects of growth. The paediatrician was a somatist whose specialisation was above all in terms of physiology. It was very hard, Winnicott observed in 1958, to find a paediatrician who did not restrict himself to the physical aspect. His background obliged him, for example, to be aware of the mental illnesses deriving from the rubella contracted by the mother during the second month of pregnancy, of orthopaedic malformations, of blood incompatibility between the mother and the baby, or of the damage caused to the meninges as a result of a delayed birth, etc. In the 1950s, many things had already changed in paediatrics theory and practice. These modifications, which included an incipient interest in the psychological aspects of development, were due in part to progress in research, to public sanitation, and to a general improvement in living conditions, which released doctors from a complete dedication to the study and treatment of primary diseases. Indeed, Winnicott conceded, until that point much specialised work had been necessary. In the mid-nineteenth century, he reported, the situation was even worse and the urgent task for the whole pioneer generation of paediatricians in the United Kingdom was to ensure an appropriate classification of the various physical illnesses peculiar to childhood and to try to eradicate them:

> In those days there was not much time or place for the consideration of health as such, nor for the study of the difficulties that beset the physically healthy child through the fact of growing up in a society that is composed of human beings. (1988, p. 9)

This quotation includes one of the main elements of Winnicott's conception of health and illness, a topic of his discussion with the entire medical field, from which important theoretical positions derived: the idea that health is a complex state which carries its own demands and must be conceived in its own right. Both in paediatrics and in psychiatry, health is generally conceived as the absence of illness, with Winnicott finding this negative definition grossly inadequate. On the other hand, illness was regarded as an evil to be eradicated. In the article "A note on normality and anxiety", Winnicott held that although from a purely physical viewpoint any deviation from health could be regarded as abnormal, "[…] it does not follow that physical lowering of health due to emotional strain and stress is necessarily abnormal" (1931b, p. 3). Reporting the case of a boy aged two and a half who had a strong adverse reaction to the birth of a brother, Winnicott stated that if the baby had not been born, the child would have been spared but would nevertheless have missed out on a real experience at an appropriate age. Such an occurrence, he continues, "justifies the statement that it can be more normal for a child to be ill than to be well" (ibid., p. 4).

The quotation highlighted above not only indicates the need to consider health as a state with its own profile but also contains the statement which permeates the whole of Winnicott's thought and has more extensive implications than may be apparent at first sight, namely, that, from the outset, *life itself is difficult* and the task of living, of continuing to be alive, and of maturing is a permanent struggle. It is thus necessary to study the difficulties that beset the physically healthy child through the fact of growing up in a society that is composed of human beings (1988, p. 9).

Furthermore, although paediatrics and child psychiatry began to take account of the psychological aspect of these phenomena and their specific character according to the stage of development, all of this refers to childhood from when children can already speak and not to babies. Neither specialisation viewed the baby as a human being capable of emotional states and of being affected by the environment. At birth, it was seen merely as an organism. Despite having observed babies becoming ill precociously, Winnicott himself admitted to having taken a long time to see them as human beings. He became capable of this through his own analysis, stating that this was indeed the principal result of his first five years of analysis with Strachey. In 1957, the author stated that he had observed an evolution in the attitude of health specialists towards babies and small children. Perhaps, he said, parents had considered the baby as a person for longer than specialists had done, sometimes seeing in him much more than was actually there, a potential little man or woman. This had initially been neglected and even rejected by science and, for a long time, children were considered as beings that were hardly human until they started to speak, but that recently, "it has been found that infants are indeed human, though appropriately infantile" (1957d, p. 107).

The contribution of psychoanalysis to this evolution had been decisive. Around the end of the Second World War, many research studies were being conducted on the normal emotional development of babies and children of different ages. This entire advance, Winnicott noted, was attributable to Freud, who proved, with the theory and treatment of neurotic disorders, that the analyst reaches the child in the adult. Winnicott stated that he had never abandoned paediatrics, since he understood that child psychiatry with a psychoanalytical orientation was an intrinsic part of it (cf. 1988, p. 1). His frequent assimilation of child psychiatry and psychoanalysis was due to the fact that the former has found its main stimulus during the second half of the twentieth century, in such research studies with a psychoanalytical orientation.

Convinced that psychic health is established in the early days of childhood and that as soon as the baby is born, he is already a human being, thrown like all of us to the task of living, Winnicott was concerned with advancing the work of those in contact with the infant and who could in some way facilitate or hinder the process of maturation. Since they occupied a privileged place in medicine, paediatricians are the only ones who, while specialising in one or other field, could monitor the process of maturation from the outset, when the baby's possibilities were still merely potential. In performing their duties, paediatricians were capable of detecting, if observant and alert, not only an incipient child neurosis which has already taken root, but also a latent tendency towards neurosis, which could become manifest at some point in adult life. And if this was true for neurosis, it was even more so for psychoses. The prevention of the illness which leads to the psychiatric hospital, says Winnicott, "(…) is in the hands of the paediatrician. It is safe to assert, however, that the paediatrician does not know it, and his life is thereby made sweeter" (1958k, p. 317).

By and large, paediatricians failed to use this privilege because they lacked training in psychology and would tend to provide guidance to parents without having the necessary knowledge of the difficulties relevant to emotional development.[7] It was nevertheless unlikely that a paediatrician already established in her carrier and relatively satisfied with the tools of an organicist approach would follow the path of an analytical training. One of the main obstacles to this is the fact that when someone studies psychology, even of a baby, this study brings the specialist back to herself as a person. Winnicott nevertheless stated that there were no shortcuts and there never would be any. The time would come when no further expansion of somatic paediatrics would be necessary and young paediatricians would be pushed towards child psychiatry. "I long for this day, and have longed for it throughout three decades" (1988, p. 10). The danger is nevertheless of avoiding the painful side of the new development and attempting to find a way round; theories will be reformulated, implying that the psychiatric disorder is a product not of emotional conflict but of heredity, constitution, endocrine imbalance, and crude mismanagement.

> But the fact is that life itself is difficult, and psychology concerns itself with the inherent problems of individual development and of the socialisation process; moreover in childhood psychology we must meet the struggles that we ourselves have been through, though for the most part we have forgotten these struggles or have never been conscious of them. (ibid., p. 10)

Winnicott not only disagreed with organicist theories (hormonal imbalances) and academic psychology (brutal environments) but also repudiated theories that conceived of psychic disorders in terms of constitution and heredity. In the latter case, he addressed not only psychiatry but traditional psychoanalysis as well.

Limits of academic psychology

During the 1950s, the new generation of medical students in England claimed a knowledge of psychology in order to deal with the task of which they were becoming increasingly aware, namely the close connection of the emotional factor with disorders of children. What they were offered, however, was knowledge of academic psychology, which did not have the answers to what was required and presented a real danger that the superficial aspects of child psychology would be overvalued. One of these refers to elements intended for the understanding of mental manifestations which, while psychological, were actually related to physical growth. When, for example, the academic psychologist studies the age at which the child is able to walk, he does not take into account the fact that a child may be led to walk earlier than the average or be delayed in this achievement due to emotional factors. The same occurs with research into skills, for which, using intelligence tests and measurement of intellectual capacity based on the quality of the brain as a functional organ, the academic psychologist isolates every single emotional factor that may interfere with the "pure" results. In other words, in the exercise of his functions, *the psychologist isolates the psyche in order to study the mind and the brain*; for Winnicott, however, dealing with and knowing the intellectual field was not the same as knowing the "psyche" of psycho-somatic existence.[8]

The major problem was nevertheless that in attempting to make explicit the role played by the environment in structuring the child's personality, academic psychology distorted the whole phenomenon, tending to concentrate on describing situations of brutality, effective abandonment and cruelty, constituting traumas which would, par excellence, be the causes of mental disorders, without considering the counterpart, the effective and necessary participation of the environment *in the establishment of health*. Psychoanalysis nevertheless specifically opposed this type of simplistic reductive conception, which saw human beings as products of the environment, and in this sense, Winnicott thought, it was not surprising that psychoanalysts were reluctant to consider the environmental factor, since

> [...] those who wished to ignore or deny the significance of the intrapsychic tensions chiefly stressed the bad external factor as a cause of illness in child psychiatric. However, psychoanalysis is now well established, and we can afford to examine the external factor both bad and good. (1963 a, p. 251)

This quotation is from a text of 1963 and it becomes clear that when referring to psychoanalysis in general, Winnicott was actually mentioning his own contribution, knowing that it was far from being accepted. In a letter to an editor of *New Society* whose name was not revealed, he wrote:

> I shudder lest my work should be taken as a weighting on the environmental side on the scales of argument, although I do hold the view that psychoanalysis can afford now to give full importance to external factors, both good and bad, and especially to the part played by the mother at the very beginning when the infant has not yet separated out the not-me from the me. (1987b, p. 141)

In Winnicott's work, the concept of environment, or of an external factor, is extremely complex and in the same way that it constitutes one of the main keys to the understanding of his thought, it is also one of the major sources of mistakes, if misunderstood. When referring to the initial stages and taking into account what the baby's viewpoint would be, the author speaks of the external environment, which is only external from the observer's perspective. At the beginning of life, the environment is subjective and, in this sense, is neither external nor internal. Insofar as it is subjective, the environment participates intrinsically in the constitution of the self and is not merely an *external influence*. It is only during the maturational process that the child will be able to achieve a sense of externality. Only then can the environment be seen as external and even then, not entirely or always.

The debate with psychiatry and with child psychiatry

Winnicott's dialogue with psychiatry revolves around the conceptions of health and illness, of the body/mind dichotomy and its consequences for theory and clinical work, and the conception of the aetiology of disorder from which the nature of the proceedings and the care provided to the patient derive. To these points we add one relating to child psychiatry: its need to protect its own specific field of research and to avoid being driven by the parameters of adult psychiatry.

The mind/body opposition may well be the oldest and most controversial of the distinctions to which the health specialist is subjected and has also been one of the most persistent in philosophy. It is sufficient to recall here the endless series of discussions both scientific and philosophical rekindled in the West by Cartesian dualism and the physicalist medicine based on it. For classical psychiatry, above all of the pre-psychoanalytic kind, psychiatric disorders are interpreted as symptoms of pathological processes of the organism, relating to an acquired organic dysfunction or to hereditary transmission. Psychiatry, which understands itself as a science of the somatogenesis of the psyche, views the psychic disorder as a "symptom".

This psychiatry is a specialised discipline of scientific clinical pathology, based on the body considered as an aetiological field.[9] Even when classical psychiatry adheres to certain psychogenic hypotheses, in reality, this psychogenesis continues to be somatogenesis, since what is termed psychic refers to the brain and to brain tissue. In medical psychiatry, the concept of mind, opposed to that of body, was assimilated with the concept of psyche, with the entity mind/psyche being located in the brain. When a patient, as a result of problems in the maturational process, develops a defensive hyper-mentalisation, which tortures him or her and points to a schizophrenic picture, the psychiatric diagnosis assumes that there is something wrong with his brain, since, in scientific medical thought, the brain has been equaled with the mind. The type of patient mentioned feels the mind to be an enemy, something that persecutes him inside the cranium. With this,

> [...] the surgeon who does a leucotomy would *at first* be doing what the patient asks for, that is, to be relieving the patient of mind activity, the mind having become the enemy of the psyche-soma. (1954 a, p. 253)

In Winnicott's conception, mental activity whether compulsive or not, has nothing to do with the brain. In this way, says Winnicott, one cannot claim that the patient is helped by a lobotomy through the visible relief of his suffering, since

> [...] there is no such thing as relief of suffering *in vacuo*; some person who suffers can be relieved; but it does not seem possible (to one holding my view on this point) to take responsibility for changing the person from one who suffers into quite something else, a part-human that does not suffer but which is not the original person who was brought for treatment. (1988, p. 53)

From the mid-1940s onwards, Winnicott engaged in a genuine campaign against shock therapies and, above all, against the practice of lobotomy, sending letters to the health authorities and writing articles in specialist magazines. In 1967, still involved in this struggle, he wrote that he would simply ignore those specialists who intended to provide physical treatment for psychic disorders, since

> [...] there will still be the patients there, persons like ourselves, with a history in each case of the onset of the disorder, and with a load of personal striving and suffering, and with an environment that is simply bad or good or else confusing to a degree that can be bewildering even to relate. (1968c, p. 194)

Another of Winnicott's objections to psychiatry concerns the fact that, just like the medical area in general, it only sees the illness and not the individual. This is a long tradition and even when, under Kraepelin's influence, in the late nineteenth and early twentieth century, classical psychiatry admits the heterogeneity of madness and starts to distinguish and divide the different categories of mental illnesses into groups, it does so with regard to the illnesses and not to individuals in their relations and in their history.[10] It is thus not surprising that health is not an interesting state to study and has a purely negative definition. In this way, all that matters is symptomatology and it is around it that the nosographic entities are built.

It is probable that from Kraepelin onwards, the new task of observing, describing, and recording the acts and symptoms of patients in order to match them to the label or diagnosis provided by his classification aroused a desire on the part of the specialist to know the hows and whys of those acts and symptoms, with this leading him to explore the patient's biography. The fact is that at a certain point, this became a mandatory part of the psychiatric file. Since a well-organised biography leads to the beginning of the patients' life, in the early twentieth century, psychiatry for the first time began to take an interest in childhood. This was nevertheless a biographical, retrospective interest, which failed to establish a direct relationship between childhood events and the sick individual who appeared and whose history was never examined from the perspective of the nature and meaning of his primitive experiences. It was Freud who revolutionised this situation. Around 1890, when the majority of Kraepelin's work was published, the incipient Freudian psychoanalysis began to introduce a dynamic conception in opposition to the static or nosographic psychiatry of the previous era. Recovering the meaning of the symptoms, psychoanalysis opened the field to studying the psychiatric disorders *of individuals* according to their history and unlike the psychiatrist, who catalogued symptoms, the psychoanalyst became a specialist in obtaining the life history of the patient.[11] In Winnicott's view, this was one of the great contributions of psychoanalysis to psychiatry: the suppression of the old idea of nosological entities. Mental illnesses cannot be considered illnesses in the same sense as rheumatic fever or scurvy; it is false to label psychic disorders in a manner characteristic of the classification in physical medicine.[12]

Another point relates not only to the debate but also to Winnicott's struggle to preserve the specific character of child psychiatry. This only emerged as a branch of specialised study in the early twentieth century; until then, with a few rare exceptions, psychiatry saw the child, who could already speak, as an adult in miniature and applied to him or her the clinical and psychopathological criteria of general psychiatry. There was no place, for example, for the conception of child psychosis and even less for disorders of that nature in babies. At this point, adult psychosis was defined as the degeneration of mental processes, with this definition not applicable to children.[13]

The fact is that all of nineteenth century psychiatry, under the influence of the dismemberment of Pinel's notion of idiotism, in the idiocy-dementia distinction established by Esquirrol and also with the advent of psychometrics and its premature generalisation to grave intellectual deficiencies, viewed child mental pathologies, especially those disorders understood today as child psychosis, as a form of mental deficiency or disorders of character. Even during the second half of the nineteenth century, as Misès noted, any reference to child psychosis was still inconceivable, "madness in children lies in the realm of the inconceivable", the famous Moreau de Tours supposedly stated in his classical treaty *La folie chez les enfants* (1888). Madness in children "can only exist exceptionally, as an acute transient phenomenon or the expression of some neurological disorder, such as epilepsy" (Misès, 1969, p. 10).[14]

In the early twentieth century, when Sancte de Sanctis (1908) described the most precocious cases found until then, he created an autonomous morbid entity, *dementia praecocissima*, the characteristics of which are close to precocious dementia of adults, characterised by Kraepelin in

1899. Misès highlighted, with regard to this new nosographical entity, the frequent observation "how a clinical picture in children which associated delirium, hallucinations and catatonia in children as a simple projection of adult pathology seemed artificial" (Misès, 1969, p. 11).

It was only very gradually that child disorders gained a specific place. Around 1912, researching children between the ages of eight and thirteen, Chaslin "sensed a particular meaning of certain morbid developments in retarded patients, epileptics, wayward children, wondering whether they should not be considered as hebephrenics" (Aubin, 1975, p. 14). It was nevertheless Bleuler who suggested the notion of schizophrenia without the implication, present in Kraepelin's precocious dementia, of loss of affectivity and of fatal evolution towards dementia. This, says Aubin, "opened the doors to child psychosis, the future of which is not one of inevitable despair [...]" (idem).

Even though child psychiatry had established itself as a specific field of study, a tendency remained to observe and understand child disorders, or those prior to puberty, in accordance with the parameters constructed for adult psychopathology. In the article "Psychoses and child care" (1953a), Winnicott mentions M. Creak's book *Psychoses in Childhood*, published in 1951, as an example of this. The author described a psychotic picture, without making an effort to research situations of immaturity in children, in which an organised introversion occurred, with consequent bizarre behaviour patterns and secondary physical disorders; he then applied this framework to a type of child undoubtedly familiar to child specialists. If matters were this simple, Winnicott argued, it would be possible to apply any type of adult nosological entity to countless childhood situations: states of melancholy, manic-depressive psychoses, hypomanic agitation, confusional states, etc.

Despite all of the advances in psychoanalytic research and its influence on general psychiatry, Winnicott observed major resistance among the latter to considering, firstly, the existence of a disorder of schizophrenic type which was entirely psychological, that is, which could be prevented and cured; secondly, to regarding schizophrenia as a disorder which established itself in the earliest stages of childhood, and consequently, which should be studied within the categories of child psychiatry, psychoanalytically oriented by the theory of maturational processes. Psychiatrists remained and are still averse to a study which shows that the aetiology of the illness is not entirely dependent on heredity, even if heredity and constitutional factors may often be important. Winnicott nevertheless points out that even in the case of progressive general palsy, a disease caused by an organic disturbance in the brain, it is possible to find in the psychology of the patient, "an illness which belongs specifically to that patient and his personality and character, and the details relate to the patient's early history" (1989q, p. 123). It is this conviction that leads Winnicott to assert that *the psychic diseases* to which a hereditary or constitutional character is usually attributed *are not diseases in the usual sense of the term*. This aetiological hypothesis is not acceptable even when constitution is considered in psychological terms, as is the case with traditional psychoanalysis. *Psychosis is not defined by the heritage of a family degenerative process and neither is it the fruit of an unbalanced constitution of the pulsional forces*. The aetiology is not that simple:

> For those psychiatrists who are interested not so much in people as in diseases—diseases of the mind, they would call them—life is relatively easy. But for those of us who tend to think

of psychiatric patients not as so many diseases but as people who are casualties in the human struggle for development for adaptation, and for living, our tasks is rendered infinitely complex. (1961a, p. 72)

Winnicott evidently acknowledges the existence of psychological disorders related to physical abnormalities. Lesions or chemical alterations may occur in the brain, which is the organ on which the mind depends in order to function. Malfunctions which affect the apparatus may be hereditary, congenital, caused by infectious disease, by a tumour or by degenerative processes, such as arteriosclerosis. The problem consists of failing to draw a distinction between psychiatric disorders, that is, those which present psychological manifestations deriving from physical diseases or lesions and which must be considered as such, and those which are fundamentally psychic, that is, which relate to failures in the maturational processes. It is not a question of denying the existence of hereditary factors, but rather of supplementing them with aspects that may prove more vital to the life of the individual than the disorder itself (cf. 1965n, p. 58). When the psychiatrist fails to pay attention to this distinction and an organic disorder is detected, all of the individual's difficulties are attributed to it, everything is due to the "nosological framework", with no consideration of the environmental factor. It follows from this, and this is the worst consequence, that the psychological approach is abandoned in favour of a biochemical and neurological one. Even with regard to tuberculosis, Winnicott said that much was lost when the treatment for this condition became purely chemical, with the long period of special care humanely provided to the patient being dismissed as unnecessary.

According to the author, however, at the time, psychiatry drew a distinction between the two classes of disorders, which could present similar and confluent symptomatology but which were nevertheless radically different in nature.[15] What could indeed occur was the conjugation of these two factors, since a mother who was capable of being good enough to a physically healthy baby, might not stand the tension of taking care of a baby with cerebral complications.

Generalising to the whole of psychoanalysis what was in fact the theoretical perspective of his own contribution, Winnicott asserted that the psychoanalysis tended to understand schizophrenia as a reversion of the maturational process of early childhood. That is, if every individual is endowed with an innate tendency towards maturation, disease consisted of the reversal of this tendency, in its paralysis at a point when absolute dependence was already a fact. Instead of developing, the baby came to a halt. If this perspective became widely accepted, this could bring

> [...] schizophrenia into the realm of the universal human struggle and would take it out of the realm of specific disease process. The medical world urgently needs this bit of sanity in so far as it is true, because disorders arising out of the human struggle should not be housed along with disorders secondary to degenerative processes. (1965f, p. 178)

Winnicott left no room for doubt: he was interested in people and not in things endowed with properties, which carried intrinsic determinations in themselves; his question was the suffering or the imprisonment of people due to their inability to live, and not the entities, mechanisms or forces operating inside people, despite themselves, which could be studied as natural and quantifiable entities. It is always possible to clarify mechanisms of functioning of living matter, but in so doing, we will make specific structures of this matter explicit and this in no way reveals the essence of life itself.

Winnicott's discussion with traditional psychoanalytical theory

Even though he has always declared that he could only think and write from his own experience, and in his own language, Winnicott did not abstain from discussing with his contemporaries. On the contrary, spread all over his work and correspondence, there are comments and appreciations on almost everything that has been written in psychoanalysis in his time and prior to it. From Jung to Lacan, from Anna Freud to the Kleinians, among whom Meltzer, Esther Bick, Susan Isaacs, and Joan Rivière, from Spitz to Erick Erickson, from Hartmann and other authors in ego psychology to Balint and Bowlby, from Virginia Axline to Harold Searles, Winnicott debated with almost all authors who, from different lines, sought to extend the theoretical field of psychoanalysis.

His main interlocutors were, however, Freud and Melanie Klein. It was especially to the work of these two authors that Winnicott referred when, while formulating his ideas, he tried to distinguish his own original contribution. For this reason, this is the debate that we are interested in resuming here, since while there have been developments in the psychoanalytical theory and even new lines (such as Lacan), we may say that no divergence or significant alteration was traced regarding the basic theoretical assumptions formulated by Freud that would justify what is now justifiable, namely, the assertion that Winnicott's contribution constitutes a new paradigm for psychoanalysis. The modifications introduced by Klein (or Lacan) are not really revolutionary in the specific sense of Thomas Kuhn, since they do not really alter, as we saw in the Introduction, the oedipal paradigm which guides the research in the traditional theory.

Just like other analysts and commentators of Freud, Winnicott also considers the existence of two different types of theorisation in the Freudian work, which leads his discussion with Freudian psychoanalysis to develop in two interdependent levels: the first level concerns the metapsychology as theoretical supra-structure; the second one refers to Freud's dynamic psychology, that is, the empirical-descriptive theory that interprets individual clinical phenomena. The latter, more pertinent to the theme under examination here, shall be detailed as it appears in the course of this study. I shall approach especially the structural differences, which are important to characterise the theoretical framework to which this study belongs.

For Winnicott, Freudian psychoanalysis undoubtedly went beyond the organicist hypothesis of psychiatry and the environmental positions of academic psychologists. The psychoanalysts were the ones who drew attention to the internal conflict which lies at the basis of psychoneurosis, and it was, above all, under the influence of psychoanalysis that psychiatry started to consider the psychogenesis of psychic phenomena in addition to the somatogenesis. Always affirming his filiation to psychoanalysis and the inestimable value of Freud and Melanie Klein's contributions to the understanding of psychic disorders, what Winnicott certainly appreciates and maintains of the psychoanalytical tradition is both the conception that psychic illnesses are fundamentally of a psychological origin and the fact that psychoanalysis, in the hands of Freud, has established itself as a method of research and treatment oriented by the scientific spirit, which means that the theories and practices are permanently subjected to revision. For this reason and precisely in order to advance the psychoanalytical knowledge, Winnicott sees no inconsistency in remaining a psychoanalyst while, at the same time that supported by his parallel experience with babies and psychotic patients, he proposes a radical questioning of the Freudian meta-psychological super-structure. Imposed by the new clinical phenomena, this questioning aims to raise the issue of theoretical differences in the conception of psychic illness and health which, in turn, were founded on the conceptual differences regarding the psyche and the human nature.

A first and more general point refers to the fact that Freudian psychoanalysis was built along the lines of a natural science and that Freud has never abandoned the idea of settling his findings on biology, having maintained a close connection to this science in many aspects of the theory. As Laplanche and Pontalis have well observed (1967, p. 126), it is the biological functions which provide the basic model for the functioning of the primitive psyche and this is showed, for example, in the way how the progression of the erogenous zones which mark the phases of sexuality was formulated.

The difficult and complex articulation between body and psyche was resolved by Freud by means of the concept of pulsions, understood as psychic representatives of physical forces, with the dualism of the pulsional forces setting the psyche in motion.[16] By the very definition of pulsion, one can affirm that Freudian psychoanalysis remains tied to the physical model of the psyche, with force as its central concept. Although Freud's interpreters differ as to which principle fundamentally rules the elaboration of the Freudian metapsychology, the fact is that the whole discussion remains in the ambit of forces or of libidinal investments. According to Loparic, the central methodological principle in the elaboration of the metapsychology is the dynamic viewpoint.[17] For Richard Simanke, the economical point of view is primordial, assuming the character of a necessary principle, albeit not sufficient, for the Freudian explanation of the psyche; and particularly in moments of impasse in the theory, says Simanke, when it is necessary to reformulate it, Freud relies on the quantitative criterion.[18] Also Laplanche and Pontalis affirm that it would not be possible for the father of psychoanalysis, the complete description of the psychic process without the appreciation of the economy of the investments.[19]

Winnicott shows that he is perfectly aware of the theoretical foundations on which the general ideas of Freudian psychoanalysis were developed:

> Freud is here dealing with human nature in terms of *economics*, and deliberately simplifying the problem for the purpose of founding a theoretical formulation. There is an implied determinism in all this work, an assumption that human nature can be examined objectively and can have applied to it the laws that are known to apply in physics. (1958e, p. 16)[20]

In addition, given his debt to the German philosophical tradition of the nineteenth century and the development of neurophysiology, Freud was led to build a model of mental functioning on the lines of a machine. Recognising the limits of this key to the understanding of human nature, Masud Khan states that:

> One has to admit the fact that the climate of neuro-physiological research at the end of the 19th century biased Freud to conceptualise human psyche and its functioning on the model of the machine: hence his theories of the psychic apparatus, energic cathexes and intrapsychic structures, where he diagrammaticaly traced out as the ego, the id and the super-ego; plus the topografical schema of the conscious, the preconscious and the unconscious. (Khan, 1958, p. xxxvi)

Loparic points to the affiliation of the basic notions of Freudian psychoanalysis, the mind and the psychic apparatus, to the "project of mechanising the image of the world and of the human being, which began in Ancient Greece and was made explicit by Nietzsche, as the will to power" (Loparic, 1997c, p. 99). He also notes that "in Freud, the mind makes use of an instrument [*Instrument*] or device [*Apparat*] in order to execute its actions or performances [*Leistungen*]. The mind also makes use of the energy termed libido, which drives the device" (ibid., p. 98).

As a result of this theoretical position, illnesses as described by the Freudian metapsychology are disorders of the functioning of the forces within an "apparatus" which, while psychic, belongs to the same context as the objects of the physical sciences: it is driven by forces and mechanisms. Health is also only describable in metapsychological terms. In "Finishable and unfinishable analysis", Freud says that

> It is impossible to define health except in metapsychological terms: i.e. by reference to the dynamic relations between the agencies of the mental apparatus which have been recognized—or (if that is preferred) inferred or conjectured—by us. (Freud, 1937c, vol. 23, p. 226, note 2)

Starting from another conception, in which abstract categories are absent and which includes the refusal to objectify life, Winnicott does not accept that the foundation of human nature may rest on the causal deterministic principle of the intensities of pulsional forces or any other quantifiable entity. It is not the conflicting pulsional forces that set life in motion; the baby lives from the fact that it "is alive" and has someone who responds to this fact in a satisfactory way; it develops since it is endowed with an innate tendency towards maturation and because there is someone facilitating the accomplishment of that tendency. A psyche where fantasies, mental mechanisms and repressed contents coexist is not given, but acquired; it is itself an achievement of the maturational process. "The psychoanalyst, more than any other type of careful observer, finds himself in the position of being certain from clinical experience that the individual's psychological life is not exactly adjusted to the time of birth" (1987c, p. 54). In addition to the fact that this position, averse to the concept of pulsional forces, is fully inferable from Winnicott's thought as a whole, it is clarified in a letter to Roger Money-Kyrle, in which he comments that it is unfortunate that Melanie Klein had made such an effort to reconcile her opinion with the pulsions of life and death, "which are perhaps Freud's one blunder" (1987b, p. 42). Likewise, in another article, "A personal view of the Kleinian contribution", after listing Klein's "positive contributions", he alludes to the "*doubtful* contributions", one of which is "retaining a use of the theory of the Life and Death Instincts" (1965g, p. 178).

Regarding the metaphysical framework within which Freud moves, it is possible to distinguish two aspects of Winnicott's criticism of Freudian psychoanalysis. On the one hand, there is the mode of theorisation. Loparic, who has dealt extensively with the theme, indicates that the considerations of a metapsychological type

> [...] prohibit access or even disfigure essential moments of the maturational process of human nature [...]. This is a question of opposing what is manifested to what is merely thought, observations to constructions, phenomena to fictions, in short, description to metapsychological speculation. (Loparic, 1995b, p. 44)

The fact is that the process which derives from the innate tendency towards maturation has nothing to do with biology or with any other physical substratum; it has to do with human nature and the capacity for existence.[21] This does not mean that the author has ignored the biological aspect. On the contrary, Winnicott takes it into account as it is, without trying to humanise it and this is why he uses the word "instinct" instead of "pulsion". Considering something which is a condition, that is, without which no human relation can be achieved, nevertheless does not mean taking the condition as the cause or foundation. For him, with regard to instinctuality, human beings are not radically different from animals; what makes them different is the fact that all of their bodily functions, including the instincts, go via the strictly human route of imaginative elaboration.[22] The brain is also the condition for the functioning of the psyche, but this does not entail that the psyche may be conceived on the basis of the categories governing the study of the brain.

Another of Winnicott's objections to Freud was that the latter had thought his theory on the nature and dynamics of neuroses could be the key to understanding all psychic disorders, and furthermore, that the study of neurosis could lead to a deep understanding of human nature. Even when, in an attempt to respond to the theoretical impasses presented by his theory of narcissism, Freud became interested in psychoses, the questions which he formulated derived from the same field that he had demarcated for understanding neuroses. For Winnicott, however, "a claim that the healthy child can be completely understood on the basis of a study of neurosis and its origins in childhood would be absurd" (1988, p. 37). Winnicott's argument rests on the conviction that the bases of psychic health are established at the beginning of life, the moment when the cornerstones of personality are being established. In this way, for a child to reach the point of a disorder of a neurotic type, we must assume that he has successfully completed the more primitive stages, with the basic achievements which, once the child has integrated into a unity and separated the me from the not-me, render him vulnerable to the type of conflict which is inherent to the triangular relationships.[23] For the psychotic individual, the interpersonal problem within the neurotic disorder simply does not make sense and he does not reach the point of being emotionally affected by it.[24] From Winnicott's perspective, neurosis in this very specific sense means health and this is the meaning of his claim that if primitive development is disturbed, then the child will not be "healthy enough" to reach neurosis (cf. 1988, pp. 38–39).

All of these questions relating to the establishment of the bases of personality could not even have been formulated within the theoretical horizon of classical psychoanalysis. Having founded his field of reflection on the internal dynamics of the psyche and taking for granted the feeling of real and the capacity for establishing relations with external reality, all that was left to do was to analyse the pulsional quality of the relations and not their existence or reality, or the existence and reality of the baby and the external world.[25] In this way, when the psychoanalyst becomes a specialist in obtaining the history, it still remains to be asked *which history* and what scope does it have for understanding phenomena, for example, of a psychotic type. In traditional psychoanalysis, the history is the development of the sexual functions, with the Oedipus complex as the basic plot. For Winnicott, however, *there is a pre-history in which the little individual, who already is a human being capable of being affected by the environment, has not yet reached himself;* the baby is only beginning the process of maturation which leads to the integration into a unitary me and if the process fails, this baby may never achieve a me with a history to tell.[26] Achieving the point of having a history depends on processes that do not belong to the domain of sexuality and largely antecede it, such as, for example, the constitution of a personal memory related to a process of temporalisation of the baby. The gradual integration of the baby into a time and a space cannot possibly be understood in terms of pulsions. Time and space are not objects; and neither are they goals or forces. Without time and space, however, one cannot find objects and even less desire them.

Another even more specific aspect derives from this, the difference between Winnicott's thought and traditional theory: since the latter conceives of health and illness in terms of categories constructed in order to understand neuroses, illness can only be conceived in terms of the pulsional conflicts regarding the Oedipus complex and, as a result, health consists of the state of defences of the ego. It is the rigidity of these defences which are erected against the anxiety resulting from the pulsional conflict that constitutes an indication of disease. A healthy individual is one who is relatively free from a massive repression and inhibition of instinctual impulses.

Despite the fact that for the author, these criteria remain valid in cases of neurosis which offer no doubt as to the integration of the personality—which is not easy to diagnose quickly—they do not permit an understanding of cases in which the personality was not established in integrated form, notably since after Winnicott's formulation of the defensive formation of the false self type, in which there is a psychosis underlying the neurotic symptomatology, we must be alert to the basic aspects of the personality, which *are not instinctual in nature*. For all of these reasons and given the knowledge now available, it is no longer acceptable to continue to access health in terms of what is traditionally termed the positions of the id, that is, instinctuality. Researchers and analysts must be prepared to examine the process of personality structuring from the outset. While it is certainly easier to describe the maturation in terms of instinctual functioning than in terms of the ego and its complex evolution, there is no longer any way to avoid the second alternative (cf. Winnicott, 1971f, p. 21).

One aspect of the question regarding the structuring of the ego may illustrate the way in which Winnicott makes ego achievements prevail over sexual functions, as well as how the development of the ego is seen as a condition for the possibility of instinctual life. According to the author, the initial hypothesis of Freudian psychoanalytical theory referred both to the id, active since the beginning, and the defence mechanisms of the ego, especially repression. The ego mechanisms organise themselves in order to avoid the anxiety deriving from object loss or from instinctual tensions, which are already felt as belonging to the me. This necessarily presupposes a separation from the self, an ego structure and perhaps a personal body scheme, meaning that the child has reached a sophisticated degree of maturation, having already achieved some independence and a defensive personal organisation. From the perspective of Winnicott's theory of maturational processes, however, *this can no longer be assumed* and a central aspect of the discussion, which derives from the observation of psychoses, consists precisely of this point: it is not the instinctual tension and the resulting formation of defences which force the structuring of the ego, but on the contrary, it is this structuring which, facilitated by good environmental conditions, generates the anxiety of instinctual tension or of loss of the object. It is only insofar as the instinctual phenomena can be experienced, catalogued, and interpreted by the functioning of the ego that the instinctual anxiety may make any sense. There is no id before the ego, says Winnicott, and it is only on the basis of this premise that an exhaustive study of the ego is justifiable. At the point when the constitution of the self is taking place, the anxiety is not that of castration or of separation but of the possibility of annihilation of the incipient self. In this respect, Winnicott considers that Melanie Klein added a great deal to the Freudian theory. By emphasising the earliest childhood, she clarified the interrelation between primitive anxieties and defence mechanisms. Winnicott nevertheless finds the Kleinian premise that the relation to external objects is already established as soon as the baby is born to be unacceptable, since it cuts off any possibility of a discussion on the origin of psychoses at the root.[27]

One of the consequences of this position of traditional theory is that health is again conceived in negative terms. This point of Winnicott's objection constitutes a blind spot in psychoanalytical theory, with the author clearly stating that when, as is generally the case, we start from the defences of the ego against the anxiety arising from instinctual life, health is conceived in terms of the state of defences of the ego, whether or not they are rigid, etc. "But we seldom reach the point at which we can start to describe what life is. That is to say, we have yet to tackle the question of *what life itself is about*" (1967b, p. 133).

The conception of health as the absence of illness and, in this case, as the absence of neurotic symptoms, ignores the fact that a state of good health must have a quality of its own, which cannot be described in merely negative terms, and that there is a "health" which is symptomatic, defensively constructed, and infused with fear of the various madnesses which traverse the life of every individual. It is thus of paramount importance to acknowledge openly, says Winnicott, "*that absence of psychoneurotic illness may be health, but it is not life*" (1967b, p. 134; my italics). The place from which psychoanalysts research human experience is thus a partial one which eludes the primordial issues of existence; this is the meaning of Winnicott's claim that:

> [...] psychoanalysts who have rightly emphasized the significance of instinctual experience and of reactions to frustration have failed to state with comparable clearness or conviction the tremendous intensity of these non-climactic experiences that are called playing. (1967b, p. 132)

Health includes the capacity for playing, which is the prototype of creative living; it refers to the possibility of inhabiting the potential space and of surrendering oneself there to an experience which is sustained by the basic illusion; it also refers to the freedom to transit via the various worlds created during maturation, which embraces the capacity for establishing relations with the world objectively perceived without a major sacrifice of personal spontaneity.

In conceiving of health in terms of ego defences, traditional theory ignores the fact that there are individuals who fail to establish egoic defences since an ego capable of defending itself has not been formed. The problem here lies not in rigid defence organisations, but in a failure *of formation of egoic type defences*. Psychoses refer to "not so much the individual's organized defences as [to] the individual's failure to attain the ego-strength or the personality integration that enables defences to form" (1963c, p. 220). In psychoses, there are indeed defences. In fact, psychoses are themselves defensive organisations, but not of a repressive type, in which the individual, who has already achieved a unitary identity with an already established internal psychic reality, suffers from conflicts both of instinctuality—which is already endowed with personal sense and relates to interpersonal relations—and the restrictions imposed by censorship. In psychoses, defences are of a nature which paralyses the innate tendency towards maturation, preventing the constitution of the self. For all of these reasons and in particular, since in Winnicott's view, neuroses were not the paradigm for psychic illness, the theory of the development of the sexual functions, which forms the basis for the theory of neuroses, ceased to be the theory *par excellence* of the constitution of the individual.[28]

Winnicott's debate with Melanie Klein reiterates these points, in that while she had made significant modifications to the Freudian theory of the most primitive stages of life, I do not perceive any significant difference in the field of theoretical foundations between her and Freud. Having examined primitive pre-oedipal anxieties at length, Klein did not modify but instead stressed their alleged oedipal character, extending the Oedipus complex backwards in time and resolving the theoretical impasses through abstract constructions such as the symbolic equations. Among Winnicott's objections to Melanie Klein, two, of a general character, stand out. The first one goes against Klein's resorting to the constitutional factor, with pulsional intensities determining fundamental aspects of human nature and maturation. By this route, the dynamics of development is predetermined and moves along phylogenetically traced paths. The endogenous is reduced to the regressive tendency and the only difference separating neurosis from psychosis is the radical and deep character of the regressions.

The second objection relates to the fact that Klein formulated the individual development of the human baby in exclusively intrapsychic terms, without reference to the environment. These differences in premises led to radically different theoretical and clinical paths: while Winnicott concerned himself with describing the personal needs of the infant and the various types of failures of the environment in responding to these needs, Melanie Klein continued to describe the baby's primitive mental mechanisms and to configure the psychic internal and phantasmatic conflicts, with a total contempt for external reality.[29]

Winnicott considered the theory of the depressive position as Klein's most valuable contribution to psychoanalysis, above all appreciating the fact that this achievement was conceived as an acquisition of normal development, which was a sign of health. For this reason, he had reservations about the term "*depressive* position", which led to thinking in terms of a disorder when it was a gain in maturity and health. By incorporating it into his theory of maturational processes, calling it the achievement of the capacity for guilt and responsibility at the stage of concern, Winnicott indicated that his description of this achievement, formulated in his own language, was the result of his own work, in the knowledge that Klein would certainly disagree with various details. This redescription was nevertheless necessary since Klein's formulation of the depressive position was based on a conception of aggression incompatible with Winnicott's own. When, in 1945, Klein formulated the schizo-paranoid position and above all, the postulation of innate envy, it became clear to him that he could not accept her theoretical framework: the constitutional factor is present in full force, providing easy explanations of manifestations that would demand an accurate study of the infinite and subtle details of the *sui generis* relations of the baby with the environment during the initial stages.

In this way, the discussion of many highly complex problems was discarded when, for example, Klein claimed with regard to the roots of aggression that there was an innate quantity of death pulsion. Winnicott could not accept any such theses. He is undoubtedly referring to her and to the Kleinians when he speaks of researchers who cannot conceive of a maturational process in which the baby is a being already capable of experiences at the outset and that the quality of these experiences depends on the encounter with the facilitating environment. For those researchers who do not take the environment into account, the phenomenon of babies who are very difficult and startled at birth can only be explained by the constitutional factor; in this case, a paranoid one (cf. 1988, p. 150). From Winnicott's perspective, this line of argument ignores the baby's pre-history, his immaturity and initial environment. Since a human being capable of experiences is already present, even in the uterus, he may have suffered several interruptions to the continuity of being while *in utero*, during the birth process, or immediately afterwards and may have reacted to these intrusions, leading to a paranoid state which, no matter how precocious, is due to the environmental factor and not to constitutional inheritance.

In his scientific practice, Winnicott was also intolerant and almost merciless to "anyone who treats psychoanalytic theory as if it were a religion, or a political view with religious overtones" (Rodman, 1987, p. xxv). There was something dogmatic, proselytising, and even religious in what might be called the Kleinian movement, which he particularly disliked. In 1956, after listening to the reading of Melanie Klein's article on envy, Winnicott wrote to Joan Rivière "the only thing that can happen is that those who like to support Melanie produce, as we could all do, clinical material or quotations from the Bible which support her theme" (1987b, p. 95). One of the problems related to scientific communication and his complaint, repeated on several occasions, was that the Kleinian group used terms which should have been descriptive but which ultimately became partisan slogans, the use of which was mandatory. In a letter to Bion from 1955, he stated that

> [...] the Society gets awfully bored with the plugging of terms. In the last six months the words "projective identification" have been used several hundred times. Of course we are in for a few months in which the word "envy" will be brought in everywhere. [...] There is something wrong here and I believe and hope that you will take part in the attempt we must make if the Society is to survive to get behind these disruptive tendencies, which are of the nature of a plugging of theme-songs. (1987b, p. 92)[30]

Winnicott glimpsed a religious bias not only in the group's stance but also in the Kleinian conceptualisation, which, in some aspects, made this theory a reaffirmation of the principle of original sin.[31] This situation introduced a certain sectarian politics into the British Psycho-Analytical

Society, which became an obstacle to freedom of thought, communication and to progress in psychoanalytical science.[32]

The debate with traditional psychoanalysis did not end there; on the contrary, it could form the object of an entire book. Although this theme falls outside the scope of this study, I would like to mention in broad terms Winnicott's theoretical rapprochement to the psychoanalytical school termed ego psychology. What often leads us to believe that his thought lies in this theoretical direction is that he was genuinely interested in some of the propositions of this school, particularly those stressing the importance of the environment in the constitution of the individual. This nevertheless does not mean that the general orientation of American ego psychology was akin to his own thinking.

For example, Winnicott appreciates Hartmann's concept of "average expectable environment", which, he affirms, is approximately the same thing that he himself termed the "ordinary devoted mother". Other analysts have also used similar terms in order to describe an environment whose qualities made the child's maturational process effective (cf. 1984e, p. 187), but Winnicott seems to have a particular liking for Hartmann, since he includes the term "expectable", the meaning of which approximates it to the central characteristic of the good enough environment, which is that of being reliable in the sense of being predictable.

Despite the different theoretical foundations on which they are based, there are several other theoretical affinities between Winnicott and ego psychology. One of them consists of the idea that the ego cannot possibly derive from the id. According to Hartmann, mental development is not simply the result of the struggle with impulses, objects, with the super-ego, etc. We must assume that this development "is served by a psychic apparatus which functions from the start of life" (Hartmann, 1958, p. 15). These are the "primary autonomous apparatus" or "innate ego apparatus", which would supposedly develop into functions, such as perception, object comprehension, intentionality, thought, language, memory, all of which are potentialities of the organism, in a "conflict-free zone". The conception of innate ego apparatus is very close to Glover's concept of "ego nuclei", which suggested to Winnicott the state of non-integration regarding the stages of absolute dependence. Despite the affinity of the general idea, Hartmann's theory nevertheless fails to draw the distinction between the mental and the psychic which is essential to Winnicott's thought and is based on the idea of apparatus, which is entirely foreign to Winnicott.

Hartmann's idea that the ego cannot possibly derive from the id relates to another one, that a theory of instincts is incapable of explaining the access to reality, with which Winnicott agreed. Hartmann's hypothesis nevertheless includes a concept of adaptation, primarily defined as a reciprocal relationship between organism and milieu. It is not difficult to grasp, however, that Winnicott did not see the baby as an organism and that in the initial stages, we cannot think in terms of a reciprocate relation, since the baby is not yet a unity capable of relating and is merely a part of the mother–baby unit; the adaptation derives exclusively from the mother.

The authors also agreed on the autonomous development of the egoic functions with regard to the id; Winnicott certainly accepts the sense of Hartmann's concept that the ego develops in a "zone free from conflicts", since he also held that the structuring of the ego is not subjected to the vicissitudes of instinct. In Hartmann's view, on the other hand, the conflict-free ego sphere was linked to inherited tendencies, whereas in Winnicott's, it depended on the quality of environmental care.³³ These differences are substantial and if a few modifications to the traditional theory, introduced by the psychology of the ego, were in line with Winnicott's positions, this does not mean that his thought can be regarded as ego psychology.

Notes

1. Referring to his work at the Paddington Green Hospital, Winnicott points to the fortunate influence of Guthrie, a paediatrician who despite failing to make a significant theoretical contribution, created a special atmosphere for exercising a type of paediatrics that was not merely organicist, but which considered psychological factors. Winnicott subsequently learned that his nomination as Guthrie's replacement in order to continue the work of his department was due to his own manifest interest in psychology.
2. In this same lecture of 1967, Winnicott remembers that around 1935 he could not find an interlocutor for his question on primitive emotional difficulties, unless they were interpreted as regressions and mentions having thought: "I'm going to show that infants are ill very early, and if the theory doesn't fit it, it's just got to adjust itself. So that was that" (1989f, p. 575).
3. Cf. Winnicott, 1955c, p. 262.
4. Cf. in the article "A note on normality and anxiety" (1931b) the case of Veronica, who started to wet her bed every night, after her mother had been away in hospital for a month, as well as the case of Francis, who presented episodes of violence associated with his mother's depression.
5. Winnicott was not entirely alone in this perspective. Some years before the war, another psychoanalyst, John Bowlby, working at the Child Guidance Clinic, had researched the history of disturbed children and, in a formal study of 150 cases with varied problems, had established a direct link between theft and deprivation, with the latter primarily understood as separation from the mother during the first years of childhood. Both men conducted a broad campaign in the UK to alert the health authorities to the serious problems resulting from the evacuation of children during the Second World War as well as the need to ensure emotionally safe conditions for them.
6. Cf. "A note on normality and anxiety" (1931b) and "Fidgetiness" (1931a); cf. also Winnicott, 1969a, Chapters Thirteen, Fourteen, Nineteen, Twenty, Twenty-one, and Twenty-two.
7. Winnicott warned on many occasions of the way in which doctors and nurses hindered the healthy mother and failed to assist the sick mother to deal with her baby. An example of this may be found in Winnicott, 1965c.
8. The question referring to the distinction between psyche and mind will be resumed in Chapter Two, sub heading "Psycho-somatic existence: the soma, the psyche and the mind". Cf. also Winnicott, 1954a and 1988 (part I).
9. Despite an entire current that asserts the heuristic fecundity of this conception and which remains extremely active and confident of its hypothesis, its very authors admit that the genetic derivation of the psychic phenomena from body sources remain scientifically problematic. Kronfeld, for example, states that one can already see that "certain psychic modifications depend on certain physical modifications, but it is not possible to explain them" (Kronfeld, 1927, cited in Tellenbach, 1961/1980).
10. L. Kanner, creator of the term "autism", states that the curiosity of psychiatrists was directed toward the mental illnesses of individuals rather than mentally ill individuals (cf. Kanner, 1935).
11. This is not due only to Freud. Also Jaspers, in his *General Psychopathology*, observed that the fundamental theme of psychiatry was man as man and that "Not everything that hapens in a psychic illness can be explained by using the criteria of science. Human beings are creators of

culture, they develop beliefs and moral standarts and constantly transcend their own empirical human self which is the only self that scientific research can recognise and grasp [...]. The most vital part of the psychopatologist's knowledge is drawn from his contact with people. What he gains from this depends upon the particular way he gives himself and as therapist partakes in events, whether he illuminates himself as well as his patients" (Jaspers, 1959/1997, pp. 8 & 21).

12. Much has changed since then in psychiatry and it is probable that psychoanalysis is reaping the fruits of its own contribution. With regard to the old question of putting the disease before the patient, Henri Aubin, a psychiatrist of the Solliès-Pont Hospital, specialist of the World Health Organization, affirms in his book *Les psychoses de l'enfant*, that "Our concern will never be to place a label on a patient, to classify him, to submit to a kind of botanical study but to take a first step towards the *understanding* of a case and towards a therapeutic treatment. I think that the vast majority of practicing psychiatrists see things in this way" (Aubin, 1975, p. 10).

13. According to some historians of child psychiatry, the first occasion for which it is possible to discern retroactively the first incursion in the field of child psychosis was the so-called "wild boy of Aveyron", who seems to have been "the first significant observation of a psychotic child" (Aubin, 1975, p. 13). According to Misès, this observation and the essay of the re-education of little Victor by Dr. Itard, a doctor at an institution for deaf-mutes, imposed "the notion of evolving personality disorders and retroactively raised the question of psychosis in children as a manifestation of a deficit" (Misès, 1969, p. 10).

14. Cf. also Misès, 1969, p. 11. Some historians of psychiatry consider the frequent attribution of this assertion to Moreau de Tours to be a mistake. Aspects of this polemic, which go beyond the limits of this present work, may be found in Aubin, 1975, p. 12.

15. Cf. for example, Winnicott's review (1963e) of the book *Childhood Schizophrenia*, by William Goldfarb, in Winnicott, 1996a, Chapter Twenty-four. In these cases, it may be necessary to medicate the patient in order to neutralise the inertial physical-chemical imbalances of the organism, but it is still left to psychotherapy to take care of the disorders that resulted from the environmental failure in promoting the maturational processes, failures that might imply the mother's difficulty in taking care of a child with physical problems satisfactorily.

16. For a detailed exam of the concept of pulsion (*Trieb*) in philosophy and in psychology, cf. Loparic, 1999a.

17. Already in his article from 1985, "Resistances to psychoanalysis", Loparic shows that Freud's inference, starting from the phenomenon of resistance to the affirmation of the existence of forces of repression, presupposes the additional methodological thesis that all causal explication in psychology must be dynamic. The philosopher says: "It may be clearly understood that this was the Freudian conception of scientific explanations, on the basis of the following extract from *Conferences*: 'We seek not merely to describe and to classify phenomena, but to understand them as signs of an interplay of forces in the mind, as a manifestation of purposeful intentions working concurrently or in mutual opposition. We are concerned with a *dynamic view* of mental phenomena. On our view the phenomena that are perceived must yield in importance to trends which are only hypothetical' (1916–1917, p. 86)" (Loparic, 1985, p. 32).

18. Simanke highlights section IV, of "The unconscious" (Freud, 1915e, AE, vol. 14, p. 178), as one of the passages of the Freudian work in which the prevalence of the economic principle over the topical and the dynamic is made clearer. (cf. Simanke, 1994, p. 171).

19. Cf. Laplanche & Pontalis, 1967, p. 125.

20. This appreciation is entirely in agreement with Heidegger who, having read Freud at Medard Boss's insistence, saw that "Freudian metapsychology is the application of Neo-Kantian

philosophy to the human being" (Heidegger, 1987/2001, p. 207). According to the philosopher, the Freudian theory is supported on one hand on the natural sciences and on the other, on the Kantian theory of objectivity; it is based on the postulate of "the complete explanation of psychical life", which is "not derived from the psychical phenomena themselves but is a *postulate* of modern natural science" (Heidegger, 1987/2001, p. 208).

21. An example of this stance may be found in the article "Primary maternal preoccupation" (1958h), in which Winnicott initially salvages some of the references to the nature of the relation between mother and baby in the work of other psychoanalysts. In addition to mentioning Anna Freud's studies, he discusses Margaret Mahler's expressions "homeostatic equilibrium" and "symbiotic relationship" (1952 & 1954), noting that: "I think that these various concepts need joining together and the study of the mother needs to be rescued from the purely biological. The term symbiosis takes us no further than to compare the relationship of the mother and the infant with other examples in animal and plant life—physical interdependence. The words homeostatic equilibrium again avoid some of the fine points which appear before our eyes if we look at this relationship with the care it deserves" (1958h, p. 301). In other words, both the term "symbiosis" and the expression "homeostatic equilibrium" are not specific to the nature of the human relationship and may be used for human or feline babies.
22. A detailed examination of Winnicott's conception of human instinctuality and of imaginative elaboration of the bodily functions is made in Loparic, 2000b.
23. For Winnicott, the term "deep", which refers to unconscious fantasy or repressed contents is not a synonym for "early", because "an infant needs a degree of maturity before becoming gradually able to be deep" (1958i, p. 111).
24. With regard, for example, to the jealousy between siblings, which is updated in the analytical situation as hate for other patients, Winnicott says that those individuals who suffer from a psychotic problem and regress to dependence "either have no objection to there being other patients or else they cannot conceive of there being another patient" (1955b, pp. 288–289).
25. Certain authors maintain that this position stems from the fact that for classical psychoanalysis, which falls within the metaphysical tradition of Cartesianism, reality, whether external or internal, has only one meaning: something already given, peopled by objects, the access to which, also unique, occurs via representation. From this perspective, there is no idea of a constitution of the senses of reality, inherent to the modes of being which unfold during development and throughout life (cf. Loparic, 1997a).
26. For more detail on this point, cf. Loparic, 2001b.
27. Melanie Klein, at the beginning of her famous article "Notes on some schizoid mechanisms" states: "I have often expressed my view that object relations exist from the beginning of life" (Klein, 1946, p. 2).
28. Cf. Loparic, 1997a.
29. Cf. Winnicott, 1989a, Chapter Fifty-three, part two.
30. Winnicott was extremely cautious with regard to this tendency, which we might call media-oriented. He was extremely cautious when proposing terms to designate a number of phenomena which became visible in the light of his theory, fearful that they would eventually be used as clichés, as "Winnicott's things", emptied of the experiential meaning that they should contain. For example, in distinguishing "object-mother" from "environment-mother", he warned that these expressions should not become empty slogans and "develop a rigidity and an obstructive quality" (1963b, p. 102).

31. Cf. Winnicott, 1971g, p. 95. Winnicott is not alone in this assessment. Pontalis also asserts that the Kleinian theory of envy and guilt attributed to the most primitive childhood, "was no more than a psychoanalytical transcription of the myth of original sin" (Pontalis, 1981, p. 95).
32. Cf. Winnicott's letter to Melanie Klein, of November 1952, in Winnicott, 1987b.
33. For Masud Khan, there is a bridge between Winnicott's work and Hartmann's research on this sphere of the ego free from conflicts (Khan, 1975, p. xviii) in the concept of "the period of hesitation" described by Winnicott in his article "The observation of infants in a set situation" (1941).

CHAPTER TWO

Basic concepts of the theory of maturational processes

Maturation as an innate tendency towards integration

Winnicott's theory of maturational processes is founded on two basic conceptions or, in other words, the personal maturacional process fundamentally depends on two factors: the innate tendency towards maturation and the continuous existence of a facilitating environment. We shall start with the first one.

According to Winnicott, every human being is endowed with an innate tendency towards maturation. This conception is based on another one, that man is essentially a temporal being. A human being, the author says, "is a time-sample of human nature" (1988, p. 11).[1] All human phenomena are an unfolding in time of human nature, in such a way that they cannot be described, at any level, as something substantial, under penalty of distorting the fundamental nature of man: of being a form of temporalisation. Winnicott's theory of personal maturational processes is the explanation in time, in the form of phases or stages, of the various tasks imposed by the innate tendency towards maturation on the individual throughout his life.

What does Winnicott understand by human nature? Human nature, which is "almost all we have" (ibid., p. 1), consists essentially of *an innate tendency towards integration into a unit* throughout a maturational process. As a time-sample of human nature, each human being is endowed with a *tendency* towards *maturation*, that is, a *tendency towards integration into a unitary whole*. This is her most important inheritance. "The individual inherits a maturational process" (1974, p. 89; 1984f, p. 62). Every individual is *destined to mature* and that means: becoming unified and bearing responsibility for a me. As a function of this, what fails in the process and is not integrated through experience is not just a nothing, but a perturbation.

The notion that maturation is governed by the tendency towards integration into a unit resulted from a long evolution in Winnicott's thought. The idea that development is always in progress was already established in the 1940s, as was the fact that there are difficulties relating to maturation itself. In a text from 1959, we find the statement that what is most important in heredity "is the individual's inherent tendency to grow, to integrate, to relate to objects, to mature" (1965h, p. 137); we may perceive that at this point, the fundamental direction of maturation as a tendency towards integration into a unity is still vague. It is in a late text, from 1968, that Winnicott spells out that *the state of unity is the basic human achievement for health in the emotional development of every human being* (cf. 1984f). In 1969, he reaffirmed the existence of something *"universal* in the emotional development of the individual, namely, the integrative tendency that can bring the individual to a *status* of unity" (1989i, p. 244; my italics).[2]

We should not attribute an essentialist character to Winnicott's thesis that human nature consists of an innate tendency towards integration into a unity. This is not an eternal essence, says Loparic,

> [...] for Winnicott understands that "human nature evolved, just as human bodies and beings evolved, in the course of hundreds of thousands of years". He does not dispute the *phylogenesis* of the human species, that is, of the tendency towards integration itself, even if he has nothing to say about this subject. At the same time, however, Winnicott notes that "there is very little evidence that human nature has altered in the short span of recorded history" [...]. Winnicott's concept of human nature may therefore be understood as designating the fixed structure of our *ontogenesis* or, in a less biologising language, more characteristic of Winnicott, of our personal or emotional development, which is governed by the innate tendency towards integration. (Loparic, 2000b, p. 355)[3]

In order to arrive at this final formulation, that the unitary status is the basic achievement for health in the emotional maturation of every human being, Winnicott had to overcome two ideas established by traditional psychoanalysis: first, the one which assumes that the constitution of the primitive me and the capacity for contacting reality are already given. Second, the idea that division, the essential "dynamic" of humans, could be described in terms of pulsions. Attentive to babies and psychotics, Winnicott introduced an initial phase in which there is not yet an established me, but rather, a non-integrated being who emerges from a state of essential aloneness. This aloneness, which will be partly overcome, remains throughout life in the depths of every individual. There is indeed an essential splitting, but it is not related to pulsions; inherent to human nature, it consists of the gap between the tendency to open up to relations with the other and the world, and the primordial isolation of the human being.[4] A successful process of integration will lead to the coexistence and transit between these two extremes within the individual: the essential aloneness, on the one hand, and the communication and encounter with the other and with external reality, on the other.

Maturation and the facilitating environment

Despite being innate, the tendency towards integration does not happen automatically, as if the mere passage of time were enough. This is a tendency, not a determination. In order for it to be achieved, *the baby depends fundamentally on the presence of a facilitating environment which provides good enough care*. The fact of dependence, which is absolute in the initial stages, is essential to Winnicott's theory: "Human infants cannot start to *be* except under certain conditions" (1960b, p. 43). No baby, no child can become a real person, *unless it is under the care of an environment that provides support and facilitates maturational processes*. Babies who do not receive this good enough care "do not fulfil themselves, even as babies. Genes are not enough" (1968d, p. 94). Since the absolute outset, the fundamental need of the human being is to be and to go on being. The individual must not only arrive at a beginning, so that entry into life may occur, but he must also keep himself alive throughout life: "It is a constant struggle to get to the starting point and to keep there" (1965j, p. 192). There are physically healthy babies who die because they do not find a basis for being from the outset. Others do not necessarily die; they are persuaded into "feeding and living, although the basis for living is feeble or absent" (1988, p. 107).

All this means that becoming unified and real and reaching the unitary identity (which implies the separation between the me and the not-me, demarcating the end of the initial stages) may never occur. For psychotics, whose disorders derive from the most primitive stages of life, this is precisely what they were unable to achieve. For this reason, their difficulties and problems are particularly afflicting, since these are "not so much a part of life as a part of the struggle to reach a life [...]" (ibid., p. 80). Such patients, permanently hovering between living and not living, force us to face this kind of problem, which actually relates to all human beings and which boils down to the following question: what is life about and what makes it worth living? (cf. 1967b & 1971g).

Hence, in *personal maturation* it is not isolated functions that are at stake, whether biological, mental or sexual, but human life itself, in what is strictly personal to it: the feeling of being, of being real, of existing in the real world as a self. None of this is given by biological conception or birth. Even when the cerebral and biological structures are intact, the fact of having been born does not guarantee the achievement of the feeling of being alive, of feeling real and of being able to have experiences that are felt as real. Throughout maturation, all of the human dimensions must be gradually integrated into the personality, but always starting from the personal sense of existence, a sense that, initially, is the mere continuity of being. Moreover, the drive to live, to stay alive and to develop is not described in terms of forces: it is not the libido that passes through various phases or object fixations, but human nature which temporalises itself as a result of its innate tendency towards growth, and gradually generates a self that is integrated both internally and with the environment.

General characteristics of maturational processes

The maturational process begins at some point after conception and continues throughout the individual's life until his natural death, with this being the last event to be integrated, the last task of health.

The process unfolds in stages, or steps, that can be briefly and generically enumerated as follows.[5] The primitive stages of absolute dependence include: (1) the essential aloneness, the experience of birth and the stage of the theoretical first feed. The initial stages of relative dependence include: (2) the stage of disillusion and beginning of mental processes; (3) the stage of transitionality; (4) that of object usage; and (5) the stage of I AM. After this, the baby moves on "towards independence": (6) the stage of concern. Next, are the stages of relative independence: (7) the oedipal stage; (8) the latency stage; (9) adolescence; (10) the beginning of adulthood; (11) adulthood; (12) old age and death. In old age, something of absolute or relative dependence returns.

The chronological age to which these stages correspond cannot be located accurately, but only approximately, for which reason, we refer much more to stages than to ages. To the different stages correspond tasks and achievements of different natures, which are imposed on the individual throughout development by the innate tendency towards integration itself. If the baby succeeds in accomplishing the task which corresponds to the phase, this fact becomes an achievement of maturation. As development proceeds, tasks become more complex, and if the individual is healthy, he is able to become involved and deal naturally with the tasks specific to his age group. Gradually, over time,

> […] the infant becomes the man or the woman, not too early, not too late. Middle age arrives in due course, with new appropriate changes, and eventually old age curbs the various functions till natural death follows as the final seal of health. (1988, p. 12)

From a global perspective, maturation can be described as a journey that starts with *absolute dependence*, passes through a period of *relative* dependence, reaches the stages which move *towards independence*, until it reaches *relative independence*, the stage at which the healthy individual remains regularly throughout life. It should be noted that the terms are relational, always implying the existence of another human being. At the beginning of the process, however, the "relation" has a *sui generis* character, due to the fact that the baby is not yet a unity. The unity is the mother–baby pair, with the mother being felt by the baby as part of himself, that is, as a subjective object.

The essential tasks and achievements of emotional development take place during the most primitive stage of life, when the baby lives in a state of absolute and then relative dependence on the mother's care. This results not only from the precocity of the moment, but also from the nature of the tasks and achievements that are inherent to it. These primitive stages may therefore be called fundamental in the literal sense that it is during this period that the fundamental bases of existence are being established, that is, the foundations of personality and of psychic health. This is achieved through the resolution of three tasks in which the baby is involved: integration in time and space; gradual indwelling of the psyche in the body and the beginning of object relation or of contact with reality. As these tasks are being achieved, there is a fourth one in progress: the self is being constituted through the continuous repetition of small experiences of integration; gradually, the integrated state becomes increasingly more stable in such a way, that the baby moves towards integration into a unit.[6]

It is also possible to describe development in terms of the sense of reality that the individual is able to create at each stage and of the nature of the relation that he establishes with the environment at a given moment in development. The baby initially lives in a world which is conceived subjectively; he then moves on to an intermediary form of reality, that of transitionality, which is halfway between the subjective and the objective; after that, he moves towards constituting the me as an integrated identity, separate from the not-me, being then able to start to perceive the external or shared world objectively.

> At first the relationship is to a subjective object, and it is a long journey from here to the development and establishment of a capacity to relate to an object that is objectively perceived and that is allowed a separate existence, an existence outside the omnipotent control of the individual. (1963c, p. 224)

If it is possible to say that the human individual has a beginning, this must be thought of as a sum of beginnings (cf. 1969e). In the above quotation, the achievement of the me as an identity separated from the not-me demarcates a beginning of the individual, probably the main one, when he becomes able to relate to external reality; however, everything depends on other previous beginnings having been successful. When speaking of psychic health, Winnicott is referring, above all, to the fact that a child has accomplished the initial tasks satisfactorily and has managed to reach a unitary status, which is the basic condition for the beginning of the establishment of relative independence. From this point onwards, with the foundations established, the individual may suffer psychic disorders but he does not run the risk of becoming a psychotic.

The achievement of unity in an integrated *me* occurs around the age of one year to eighteen months, in the stage rather appropriately termed "I AM". The me that is achieved is the initial self itself, which, after becoming integrated in various levels and aspects throughout the initial stages, has now separated from the mother. This unitary status is not a cohesive whole, without fractures or exempt from conflicts, but a state of spatio-temporal integration, in which "there is one self containing everything instead of dissociated elements that exist in compartments, or are scattered around and left lying about" (1971g, p. 90). In this achievement, there is a completion and a beginning, since the I AM state, the feeling of being real and of existing as an identity, "is not an end in itself, it is a position from which life can be lived" (1989h, p. 435).

We must not think of a baby in his "long journey", as a car that starts from a pre-existing point to arrive at another equally pre-existing one. There is no ready-made place from which he can start or at which he may arrive, that of objectively perceived reality, which is waiting to be discovered, nor is there an already determined path. Despite the limitations and dangers of such images, the baby is much more like the road, which builds itself, without losing the previous sections. The individual who develops progressively establishes his self like a path.[7]

Since the sequential presentation of the stages of the maturational processes[8] and the very term "stage" may lead to the idea of separate steps, each one following the other, it is necessary to highlight that despite being so presented, *the process is not linear*. Firstly, because in life, the different stages with their respective tasks partially overlap; secondly, because in Winnicott's conception, development is not a synonym for progress: developing includes the possibility of regression, whenever life demands rest, in moments of overloading and tension, or in order to return to points which have been lost. This is due to the fact that no achievement provides a guarantee: once reached, it may be lost, then reached again and then lost again.[9] This is why it is possible to find all kinds of needs in a person of any age, from the most primitive to the latest ones. People are not exactly their age; "they are to some extent every age, or no age" (1984c, p. 81).

The incompleteness of the maturational achievements is especially true with regard to the tasks at the start of life. These fundamental tasks are never left behind as completed or sorted out; they are never established as definitive achievements, since "they are matters which are and which go on being the basic task of every human being throughout life" (1988, p. 83).

However, despite the non-linearity of the process, we cannot neglect the fact that some achievements (and this refers, above all, to the primitive ones) can only be reached after others have been, which are their prerequisite, their condition of possibility.[10] That means that, achieving the tasks of each stage depends on having successfully achieved the tasks of the previous ones. If there is failure, new tasks will keep emerging, but the individual, having missed the previous acquisition, will lack the maturity required to address the new ones; he may even sort them out intellectually, but they will stand on false ground and will not become an intrinsic part of him or herself as personal acquisitions. Regarding the achievement pertinent to the stage of concern, for example, Winnicott says:

> [...] the earlier stages must have been successfully negotiated either in real life or in the analysis, or in both, if the depressive position is to be reached. To reach the depressive position a baby must have become established as a whole person, and be related to whole persons as a whole person. (1955c, p. 264)[11]

That is, for a child to be able to take responsibility for his instinctual impulsiveness, he must already be a me; only a me is capable of being concerned and worried about the consequences of instinctuallity. If this does not happen, then the child cannot achieve the capacity for guilt. He will simply go on without it, albeit with a distorted personality. It is probable that schizoid individuals, whose problems derive from very primitive stages, prior to the one in which they already have sufficient maturity to achieve the capacity for guilt and responsibility, will make no significant achievement regarding concern, and, for them, "magical re-creation has to be exploited in default of what is described as reparation and restitution" (ibid., p. 264).

When there is failure in the achievement of one or another stage of development, an emotional disorder is established. *The nature of the disorder relates to its point of origin on the line of development, that is, to the nature of the task in which the baby, or child, was involved at the time of the environmental failure.*

The theory of maturational processes thus constitutes the necessary theoretical horizon for the consideration and understanding of human phenomena that we encounter in clinical practice. According to this theory, any phenomenon that we wish to consider, be it in illness or in health, can only be duly appreciated if we consider the entire development process of the individual, starting from the most primitive stages, and if we can locate the stage at which the phenomenon originated, in other words, if we are alert to *the emotional age relating to the phenomenon or disorder* which arises. Only in this way, can we understand the "nature" of the problem with which the individual is involved, arrive at the classification of the disorder and provide specific care according to his needs. We must "always think in terms of the *developing individual.*

This means going back very early and looking to see if the point of origin can be determined" (1984c, p. 81).

It follows from this that in a particular clinical case, there is always a dominant difficulty, which refers to a task which was not resolved at a specific stage. This is the reason why diagnosis is so important. One of the main difficulties with the analytical technique, says Winnicott, is to know *the age of the patient at a specific moment of the analytical relationship,* so that we may provide care concerning the specific need that he or she presents and which varies with the emotional age of the patient (cf. 1958f).

Regarding the initial stages, if the baby does not resolve the task relating to his current maturational stage, there is an interruption to the process of personal maturation. Everything built from this point on will be distorted at the root, will acquire a defensive character and will have no personal value for the individual.

Psycho-somatic existence: the soma, the psyche, and the mind

Winnicott distinguishes personal maturation from bodily growth. The former is related to life experiences which, facilitated by the environment, permit the constitution of the unitary personality; the latter depends largely on genetic factors. However, even in this latter case, the environment factor is decisive, in so far as physical growth may be seriously affected by problems related to maturation.

Whatever human phenomenon is being considered, we must take account of the *total person*, in which the *soma* and *psyche* exist. Human nature, writes the author, "is not a matter of mind and body—it is a matter of inter-related psyche and soma" (1988, p. 26). Mind "is of an order special to itself, and must be considered as a special case of the functioning of the psyche-soma" (1988, p. 11). Although there are operational differences between psychic and bodily functions, on account of their very nature and the tendency towards integration, psyche and *soma* are closely interconnected. *Human existence is essentially psycho-somatic.*

It is always possible for an external observer to distinguish the physical, the psychic and the mental aspects in a human being, but this means looking from a certain point of view at the total, psycho-somatic, person, aiming at the consideration of one of the elements. This distinction is nevertheless superfluous for an individual whose mother took care of him as a whole, as a potentially psycho-somatic existence, during the initial stages. When the baby is held properly, he

> […] does not have to know about being made up of a collection of parts. The baby is a belly joined on to a chest and has loose limbs and particularly a loose head: all these parts are gathered together by the mother who is holding the child, and in her hands they add up to one. (1969e, p. 568)

The soma is the *living body*, which is gradually personalised as it is *imaginatively elaborated by the psyche*. This living body is undoubtedly physical but not merely physiological or anatomical; it is certainly not the physical machine, autonomous with regard to the psyche, with which classical medicine deals; in this way, it is not a body that may be studied through corpses. The living body is an aspect of the individual's "aliveness"; breathing, temperature, motility are an intrinsic part of his vitality, in addition to the vitality of tissues, since as a living body, "the tissues are alive and they are part of a whole animal, and are *affected* by the varying psyche states of that animal" (1988, p. 26; my italics).[12] There are situations of anxiety in which the child's metabolism is practically reduced to zero and, in this case, "sores sometimes do not heal simply as a result of a general lack of interest on the part of the child, and of the tissues, in living" (1931b, p. 17).

The psyche encompasses everything that, in the individual, is not the *soma*, including the mind, understood as a specialised mode of psycho-somatic operation. The psyche starts as "the *imaginative elaboration of somatic parts, feelings, and functions*, that is, of physical aliveness" (1954a, p. 244).[13] The psyche, *without ever losing this original function*, develops throughout maturation into ever more advanced functions, which include all of the mental operations that can be covered by the different meanings of the word *to think*. The central task of the psyche is nevertheless the gradual constitution of human temporality and hence, the manifestation of the sense of history in human life. Starting from the baby's primitive temporality, which is that of the body itself, at the start of life, the psyche is responsible for both the imaginative elaboration of bodily experiences of all kinds, and the storage and gathering of the memories of those experiences. As development proceeds, these become increasingly more sophisticated and the psyche gradually interconnects "past experiences, potentialities, and the present moment awareness, and expectancy for the future" (1988, p. 19). It is this operation that gives sense to the feeling of self and justifies "our perception of an individual there in that body" (ibid., p. 28).

The first task of the psyche is, as mentioned before, the imaginative elaboration of bodily functions. The body that is imaginatively elaborated is the living body of someone that breathes, moves, searches for something, suckles, kicks, sucks its thumb, rests, is cuddled, changed, surrounded by the bathwater, etc. Whatever is being experienced, and everything is initially experienced in the body and through the body, *is being personalised by the imaginative elaboration*. Since from the time of birth, the baby already has a life that, while restricted, is already personal, any experience is lived not as an anodyne and simple physical sensation, but with a *sense*.[14] That is, *the direct experience that a baby has of the functioning, of the sensations and of the movements of the body* has for him a sense, because of the fact that it is imaginatively elaborated. Despite the fact that this sense cannot be directly observed, it will become manifest later, in playing and/or in clinical situations of regression to dependence.

This "creation of meaning"[15] as Loparic states, and this is the central point for the understanding of the concept of imaginative elaboration, *precedes the mental operations of representation, verbalisation and symbolisation*, operations for which the baby is still too immature. Referring to the fact that one of the various forms of integration in the human being in development is "a satisfactory working arrangement between the psyche and the soma", Winnicott adds: "This starts prior to the time when it is necessary to add the concepts of intellect and verbalisation" (1971d, p. 270).

It is because of the concept of imaginative elaboration that Winnicott is able to make many statements, such as the following ones: We already have good evidence that in intrauterine life, both the movement phase and the rest phase are significant (cf. 1988, p. 21). Or that when it is a full-term birth, the baby feels that it was his impulse "that produced the changes and the physical progression, usually head first, towards an unknown and new position" (ibid., p. 144). He also notes that "the *imaginative* feeding experience is much wider than the purely physical experience", demanding "something more in infant life than sleeping and getting milk, and something more than getting instinctual gratification from a good feed taken in and kept down" (1993e, p. 17). It is precisely the things that the baby does while suckling, and that are not those which makes it gain weight, that corroborate the fact that it "is feeding and not just *being fed*, is living a life and not just responding to the stimuli we offer" (idem). Sucking the thumb is also a highly elaborated action for the human baby, since it means "being in control of the thumb which stands for all other objects which are gathered together in this way and put into relationship with the mouth, etc., etc." (1987b, p. 122). It also consists of the attempt by the baby to situate the object (breast, thumb, etc.), keeping it halfway between the inside and the outside, which constitutes "a defence against loss of object in the external world or in the inside of the body, that is to say, against loss of control over the object" (1945d, p. 156).[16]

In a definition of the concept of imaginative elaboration which is still vague, Winnicott says this is "a crude form of what later we call the imagination" (1993e, p. 17). In the earlier texts he sometimes uses the term fantasy to refer to what he will later more specifically term imaginative elaboration. We must nevertheless highlight that this "imagination" which elaborates the somatic functions from the outset and is responsible for the mutual interrelationship of psyche and soma *is not yet a fantasy* in the traditional sense of the term, as we shall see below. In a letter from 1954 to Betty Joseph, Winnicott writes: "I am trying to draw attention to the very early stages, quite apart from the fantasy" (1987b, p. 59).

Winnicott's substitution of the traditional concept of psyche, understood in the same sense as mind, for a psyche in which the mind is only one aspect of this psyche has the same character as his substitution of the concept of "fantasy" for that of imaginative elaboration, with regard to the early stages. The reasons are as follows: in the traditional theory, fantasy is a *mental* function that develops into mental mechanisms, such as introjection and projection, which, according to this theory, are in full operation since the beginning of life. For Winnicott, however, the baby's extreme immaturity does not allow us to suppose such a sophisticated operation. He pleads for an entire initial period when the work of the psyche, through imaginative elaboration, leads to a *schematisation* of the body, to a personal appropriation of the sense of anatomy, sensations, movements and the body functioning in general, without the participation of the mind.[17] In Winnicott's perspective, fantasy as a mental operation developing in an inner world that has already been constituted, *belongs to a later moment in development* and is not a direct elaboration from reality like imagination, but rather a creation from memory; it thus requires that a certain temporalisation has already been established, which has not yet occurred at the start of life.

Furthermore, the term "imagination" may itself lead to the wrong idea that images participate in imaginative elaboration, which would make it another mental mechanism. A clarification on this point is contained in a footnote in which Winnicott makes explicit his use of the term "fantasy", highlighting its peculiarity when it refers to the initial stages:

> It occurs to me that I may be using the word "fantasy" in a way that is not familiar to some of you. I am not talking about fantasying, or about contrived fantasy. I am thinking of the whole

> of the child's personal or psychic reality, some of it conscious, but mostly unconscious, and *including that which is not verbalized or pictured or heard in a structural way because it is primitive and near the almost physiological roots from which it springs.* (1989p, p. 69; my italics)

It is possible to say that the primary psychic function, the imaginative elaboration of bodily functions, which includes what is neither verbalised *nor pictured* and is close to "the physiological roots from which it springs"—is the necessary basis so that fantasy, in the sense of a mental mechanism, may become a later acquisition in the development of the individual. This moment, starting from which the individual becomes capable of fantasising, in the traditional sense, is clearly indicated by the author: at the stage of object usage, when the baby starts to destroy the mother as subjective object, in order to expel her from the area of omnipotence, in other words, into the externality of the world; if the mother survives, the child will find "a new meaning to the word love, and a new thing turns up in the baby's life which is fantasy" (1969b, p. 31).[18]

It is nevertheless important to emphasise that the imaginative elaboration does not disappear with the advent of the capacity to fantasise. This function remains so throughout life at the same time as it becomes "infinitely complex" as mental functions are included and both growth and maturation impose new tasks, deriving from anatomical transformation and from new forms of functioning, organisation and sensitisation of tissues, organs and the brain. In a text from 1958, Winnicott provides a list, ordered chronologically according to the successive stages of development, of the tasks incumbent on imaginative elaboration, clarifying that the primary psychic function plays an essential role in the main achievements of the process (cf. 1958j).

Imaginatively elaborated since the start of life, all of the bodily functions of the baby, motor, sensory and instinctive, are simultaneously *organised*, in other words, they are articulated and integrated by the "functioning of the ego". The result is the "experience of ego". It is by virtue of this organising function, in which the imaginative elaboration of the bodily functions participates, that the experiences of the id, that is, instinctive ones, are not lost, but brought together in all of their aspects. And it is because of this that Winnicott affirms: "There is thus no sense in making use of the word 'id' for phenomena that are not covered and catalogued and experienced and eventually interpreted by ego-functioning" (1965n, p. 56).[19]

For this same reason, Winnicott was able to affirm that in theory and in normality, the baby's ego is based on a bodily ego. The ego nevertheless only develops from the bodily ego if the baby is getting good enough maternal care, which favours the integrative tendency of the indwelling of the psyche in the body. Recalling that Freud, decades previously, had also stated that the ego was based on a corporeal ego, Winnicott comments: "Freud might have gone on to say that *in health* the self retains this apparent identity with the body and its functioning" (1966, p. 112). In this way, for Winnicott, unlike for Freud, the integration of the psyche in the body does not happen automatically, as an inevitable *a priori* of the maturational processes but requires the facilitation of the supporting environment. Since this latter is an imponderable element, the achievement may or may not happen. Neither the concepts of hysterical conversion and somatisation grasp the issue of the difficulty of establishing the psycho-somatic relation and the threat of breaking it.

The differences between Freud and Winnicott regarding this question nevertheless do not end there. Having conceived the body as the place from where the sensations both internal and external may arise, Freud was able to affirm that "the ego is first and foremost a bodily ego; it is not merely a surface entity, but is itself the projection of a surface" (Freud, 1923b, vol. 11, pp. 364–365). In a footnote, specifically added to this sentence, in the English translation of the text, *Ego and id*, Freud also explains that

> the ego is ultimately derived from bodily sensations, chiefly from those springing from the surface of the body. It may thus be regarded as a mental projection of the surface of the body, besides, [...] representing the superficies of the mental apparatus. (Freud, 1923b, vol. 11, note 2, p. 365)[20]

Commenting on this note, Loparic concludes:

> Like the ego and the id, Freud's corporeal ego, a speculative entity, related to the *surface of the body*, is essentially different from Winnicott's, which is based on the effectively experienced imaginative elaboration of the *whole body*. (Loparic, 2000b, p. 382)

Winnicott's thesis that human existence is essentially psycho-somatic does not imply a monism that obscures the specific features of soma and psyche, assimilating one with the other.[21] In fact, what we have is a dualism. He states: "There are the soma and the psyche" (1988, p. 11); or also: "There is no inherent identity of body and psyche" (ibid., p. 123). We must distinguish these two contexts, not only in order to be able to consider that both are intimately interconnected and tend towards integration. From the point of view of the developing individual,

> [...] the self and the body are not inherently superimposed, the one on the other, and yet it is necessary for health that such a superimposition should become a fact, so that the individual can become able to afford to identify with what is, strictly speaking, not the self. (1988, p. 123)

However, Winnicott's dualism, which tends towards integration, can in no way be approximated to the Cartesian mind/body dichotomy. First, because, in the latter, mind and body are understood as substances and not aspects of being. Furthermore, these substances are of an irreconcilable nature; between the *res cogitans* and the *res extensa* there is no possible association or integration. This is the meaning of Winnicott's statement that the terms mental and physical "are not descriptive of opposed phenomena. *It is the soma and the psyche that are opposed*" (1988, p. 11; my italics). Second, because from the Cartesian perspective, mind assimilates and dominates the whole of the psyche. For Winnicott, however, the psyche is far from being restricted to the functioning of the mind. With regard to Winnicott's preservation of dualism, in terms other than those of Descartes, Loparic says:

> In Winnicott's thought, the *substantial difference* between mind and body, introduced by Descartes, is not denied for the sake of reductionism, whether materialistic or spiritual; it is replaced by the *operational difference* between bodily functions and psychic ones. By analogy, the *problem of the union* of mind and body is replaced by the *problem of the integration* of the

bodily functions by the psychic ones, with each one of these two groups of functions being treated as irreducible to the other. (Loparic, 2000b, p. 360, note 20)[22]

At the same time, as the living body is in some way an element of the external world and has its own modes of growth and its own temporality, it must be said that there is always something of the physical body left that is not integrated and that when it sickens, it reveals its autonomy and opacity, as something that escapes the individual's omnipotence and cannot be fully covered by the work of the psyche.[23] It is thus always important to examine "the infant's original mix-up of the body itself with the feeling and ideas about the body" (1988, p. 95). If Winnicott had not preserved the body autonomy, he would not have been able to affirm that "it is distressing that healthy persons may have to live in deformed or diseased or old bodies, or may be starving or in great pain" (1971f, p. 29).

Where does the mind fit into the psycho-somatic existence? The mind, says Winnicott, "means something quite distinct from psyche" (1958j, p. 7); It constitutes an order special to itself (cf. 1988, p. 11). When environmental care facilitates the psycho-somatic partnership, the mind does not exist as a separate entity, being merely a *special way of functioning of the psyche-soma*, a specialisation for intellectual functions, its culminating point, "as a flourish on the edge of psycho-somatic functioning" (1988, p. 26).

The mental functions span the different meanings of the word "thinking". At the very outset, they exert the functions of cataloguing, comparing and classifying: "It is a function of mind to catalogue events, and to store memories and classify them" (1958j, p. 7). As these develop, they make use of time as a measurement, to measure space, relate cause and effect and to make predictions.[24] In health, the baby's mind is driven to exert its specialised functions as a natural development of the increasing psycho-somatic cohesion, starting from the stages where the de-adaptation of the mother begins, that is, when dependence shifts from absolute to relative. Intellectual processes equip the baby for dealing with the gaps in adaptation, for understanding and anticipating the environmental failures characteristic of this period, with this enabling him to continue in the direction of independence. This development occurs in its own time and while it has a defensive function, it is not pathological since it does not arise as a reaction to invasions which exceed the maturational capacity.

At the right moment, when the mental functions begin, the baby, by virtue of repeated experiences of adaptive care, already "knows" many things *through non-mental ways*. It is absolutely vital, for the psychic health of the little individual that this pre-cognitive knowledge is already established at the stage when intellectual processes effectively begin to function; this knowledge constitutes an essential basis for existence. Throughout life, above all at crucial moments, it is on this that the individual draws when he requires reassurance about himself or the world in which he lives.

Despite the fact that the right time for the beginning of mental functioning, which will not overwhelm the baby is the passage from absolute to relative dependence, it is already possible to observe the use of some mental functions at the start of the maturational process in a sort of "precognitive ordering of incipient thought" (1989s, p. 154), of which very little is yet known. We may thus speak of a "rudimentary mind", which is pre-representational and which is still not sufficiently mature for perception.[25] This kind of rudimentary mental functioning belongs to this moment of development; being natural and not impelled by pressure or invasion, it does not overload the baby. It must not be mistaken for the phenomenon consisting of the baby's mind being made to function prematurely as a result of his defensive need for alertness, preventing failures that may derive, for example, from environmental instability. The good enough mother, in spite of delighting in the "intelligence" or "cleverness" of her baby, always takes his emotional immaturity into account, so that she does not prematurely exploit the ability that he certainly has to understand and tolerate failure. If the mother abandons her protective function and neglects her adaptive behaviour to the infant's needs and begins to count on his intelligence for failing beyond that which is tolerable to a particular baby, a premature development of the ego may occur, which, as we shall see, is pathological and in these cases, the mind becomes an entity in itself.

Conceived as an operation mode of the psyche-soma and not as an entity in itself, the mind is not localised in the body. In popular thinking, however, people tend to place mental activity inside the head, or even outside of it, albeit in some special relation to the head.[26] Winnicott states that he cannot answer why the head is the place where individuals tend to situate the mind, but sees in this common understanding the fruit of one of the imaginative elaborations characteristic of the psyche itself regarding somatic functioning. Perhaps this is due to the fact, he suggests, that since the human baby has an absurdly huge head, this is affected and compressed during birth, exactly when the still rudimentary mind starts to function in "furiously active" fashion, cataloguing and memorising the many discontinuities that the process of birth entails.[27] Despite the fact, however, that it depends on the functioning of the brain, in terms of psycho-somatic existence, the mind is not necessarily linked to a given point in the body. We nevertheless indulge

> in a fantasy that there is a place, which we call the mind, where the intellect works, and each individual places the mind somewhere, and there feels muscular straining or experiences vascular congestion when trying to think. (1988, p. 53)

We all know that sometimes the mind knows things "in its gut" and that it is without doubt at the fingertips of the virtuoso pianist at the moment of the concert.

Heritabilities

The word "heritability" is used by Winnicott in two senses, which must be rigorously distinguished from each other: firstly, the innate tendency towards maturation, which in his view is the main inheritance of the human being; second, biological inheritance. My purpose in this section is to examine his position regarding the participation of genetics in the maturational process, in the constitution of the individual and in the aetiology of psychic disorders, and to examine how the two senses of heritabilities relate to each other.

On the one hand, we thus have the innate tendency towards integration. Having stated in a text from 1954 that there is a biological drive behind the progression contained in the tendency towards integration (cf. 1955b, p. 280), Winnicott never elucidated whether, due to this participation of biology, we are authorised to think of variable degrees of tendency towards integration.

It is nevertheless possible to affirm that this tendency is not reducible to any genetic inheritance. On the other hand, we have hereditary or congenital factors that are organic: lesions or acquired illnesses[28] which determine certain psychological disorders or tendencies of the personality: "There are genes which determine patterns and an inherited tendency to grow and to achieve maturity" (1969c, p. 187). In the same sense is the affirmation that "inheritance of personality traits and tendencies towards psychiatric types and disorders belongs to the physical, and limits are set to psychotherapy by inheritance" (1988, p. 19). We must thus distinguish between *genetic patterns*, which determine anatomical and biological patterns and the innate tendency to grow and to mature, which may or may not occur naturally, *within these patterns*. The meaning of this is not "to deny the existence of hereditary factors, but rather to supplement them in important respects" (1965n, p. 59).

An accurate examination of any psychic disorder must take all of the factors into account, both the inherited and the environmental ones. First, however, we must recall that, from a purely psychological perspective, "inherited *factors are environmental, i.e. external to the life and experience of the individual psyche*" (1989q, p. 124; my italics). People in general are surprised, the author says, when they hear that a baby's inherited tendencies are factors that are external to him, but they are just as clearly external or alien to the baby as is, for example, the capacity of the mother for being good enough or her tendency to become depressed (cf. 1968d).[29] They will only become part of the baby's personality if he appropriates them through experience.

Moreover, what Winnicott observes, on the basis of his clinical experience with psychotics, is that in the majority of cases, the hereditary factor is non-existent or irrelevant. There are cases of schizophrenia, says he, in which "a hereditary tendency to psychosis is strong, whereas in others it is not a significant feature" (1965l, p. 62). In a case in which the hereditary factor is active, we will be dealing with secondary psychological complications resulting from a disorder that is physical. We must nevertheless distinguish these psychological disorders, with a somatic basis, from *psychic disorders*, a term reserved by the author for disorders of the development process, which may also manifest themselves.

What must be considered is that somatic disorders, with their inevitable psychological complications, may (and usually are) accompanied by disorders relating to the development process. This occurs due to the additional difficulty of the parents in performing their role with a child whose development is arduous and impaired by organic-cerebral problems.

In this way, although it is necessary to consider the participation of physical heredity, it should not be regarded as a decisive factor. When studying, for example, the use that a specific individual makes of his mind, we generally carry out routine intelligence tests, that is, an assessment of his or her intellectual capacity, with regard to the quality of the cerebral tissue, which is hence basically hereditary. Such tests are useful and necessary, but, the author says, are "no basis, however, for the assessment of a personality or of personal emotional growth" (1988, p. 140).

This issue, relating to intellectual function, is a good example of how to include organic heredity in the consideration of disorders without attributing to them an exclusive aetiological meaning: when intellectual capacity is restricted, due to a cerebral tissue with a poor genetic endowment, in addition to the possible difficulty of the parents mentioned above, there is a reduction in the capacity that the baby generally has for converting an unsatisfactory environmental adaptation into a good enough one. As a result, some psychoses are more common in mentally defective persons than in the normal population. On the other hand,

> [...] exceptional brain-tissue endowment may enable an infant to allow for a severe failure of adaptation to need, but in such a case there can be a prostitution of mental activity so that one finds clinically a hypertrophy of intellectual processes related to a potential schizophrenic breakdown. (1953a, p. 225)[30]

The possibility of deficit exists both in the case of poorly endowed cerebral tissue (which is a case of organic deficiency) and an exceptionally endowed one. *What counts is the mother's adaptive care of that singular baby*, for even when an individual's cerebral capacity is restricted (e.g., with an IQ of 80), if the special conditions of the facilitating environment are present, this individual may present a healthy emotional development and may even become an interesting and valuable person, "of good character and of reliable disposition, even capable of becoming a good marriage partner and parent" (1988, p. 13). On the other hand, if a child with an exceptional cerebral endowment (e.g., with an IQ of 140) suffers serious perturbations to his development, due to poorly satisfactory environmental care, he may become extremely ill, subject to psychotic crises, lacking a trustworthy character and with little chance of one day being able to take care of himself. Such children, instead of using their intelligence, frequently fall into a state of helpless confusion, or show difficulties that are ultimately diagnosed as mental deficiency (cf. 1954a).[31] The inherited potential is different in the two cases, but this is not what determines the person that the individual will be.

A few consequences emerge for the study of the maturational process: since the brain is the essential basis for the development by both the psyche and the mind of what is specific to them, this implies that in order to study the development of the psyche-soma, we must assume that lesions or primary physical illnesses are absent.[32] In order to study a developing person, it is necessary that he is physically healthy. It is only in the absence of primary body disease that such a complex study may be made. In this case, we examine the gradual integration of a person's body and psyche, allowing the formulation of certain basic principles (cf. 1988, p. 28).

In the case of the investigation of the mind, for example, we must be able to presume an intact cerebral tissue. We cannot learn anything, in terms of development, if the brain is damaged or mutilated by some lesion or physical illness. Supposing that the brain is intact, we cannot apply to the mind the same concepts that we attribute to the soma or to the psyche, in other words, we cannot say of the mind that in itself, it is healthy or ill. Mental functioning depends on the quality of brain tissue, but this can only be described in terms of better or worse, of a higher or lower IQ. The expression "mental health" makes no sense at all, says Winnicott and the same is obviously true of the expression "mental illness", since "in fact there is no direct link between the concepts of health and of intellect. In health the mind works at the level of brain functioning *because the emotional development of the individual is satisfactory*" (1988, p. 14; my italics).

The psyche may become ill, despite not having any brain problem, and it becomes ill if environmental insecurity does not allow it to dedicate itself to its task of imaginative elaboration, forcing it, on the contrary, to use its mental resources prematurely in order to remain on the lookout for the unexpected. In this case, the psyche becomes "mentalised". When this happens, says Winnicott, mental functioning becomes "a thing in itself" (cf. 1954a). This does not mean that the mind itself has become ill, but that it has started to work autonomously, being precociously hyper-activated, detached from what would be the experiences of the individual, which, in order to exist as such, should necessarily be psycho-somatic. There can be no experiences because the mind anticipates itself in state of alert, occupied with preventing any threat of environmental invasion. There is the emergence of a precocious consciousness (which is purely mental), a sort of premature me, a self that is not sufficiently developed for proper states of conscience. When this occurs, the psycho-somatic cohesion weakens, and may even be obstructed, establishing an opposition between soma and psyche, with the latter being dominated by the mind.

What is at stake from the perspective of development and of disorders relating to development is not, therefore, the physical or psychic *constitution*. A baby "is not what one may postulate by assessing that baby's potential. A baby is a complex phenomenon that includes the baby's potential *plus* the environment" (1970b, p. 253). In order to understand this, we need only observe a two-year-old child and perceive that she is no longer the same after the birth of a new baby in the family. In many cases, an illness is diagnosed which requires treatment. At the same time, Winnicott says:

> [...] the existence of illness patterns must not be allowed to obscure the reality that the child in question is a child *with a younger brother or sister*. With the same potential, this child would be different if he or she were the youngest child or the only child, or if a baby had been born but had died. (1970b, p. 253)

Whatever the inherited potential of the infant, the environmental care that he receives is a part of the process of his constitution as a person. If the adaptation to the needs is good enough, there is a chance that the individual will develop his hereditary potential almost to the maximum extent; in some cases, it will perhaps be necessary for the environment to compensate for and balance, as far as possible, the baby's tendency to illness or, even be able to cope with diseases that are already established.

In Winnicott's theory of maturational processes nothing is determined beforehand. There is only the virtuality of a tendency towards integration, which, in health, leads to the constitution of a unitary identity and the establishment of relations with the world and external objects. The individual may or may not fulfil his inheritance in the direction of integration, *depending* on what happens in the encounter with the facilitating environment. Furthermore, his form of fulfilling or of failing to fulfil it is entirely indeterminate and depends on imponderable elements, such as environmental care and to a large degree, on chance.[33] Existence is not based on any prior positivity that carries in itself causal determinations that the maturational process would only complete. There are no forces endowed with goals that are intrinsic to them, nor is there a pulsional conflict already at the beginning, which would set life in motion independently of the individual and of the circumstances in which this individual is launched. What drives the psyche is the very fact that the baby is alive and carries in himself the innate tendency towards integration. The integrating tendency is conceived not as the result of work done by the psyche, but is itself the foundation for the emergence of the psyche. The maturational process is the manifestation of the creative potential of human nature. It can only take place in a time and space of its own, which are not the linear time and space of natural processes in physical and biological terms.

Integration via personal experience

One of the basic thesis of Winnicott's theory of personal development is that for the individual to reach the point of feeling alive and become able to appropriate his inherited or congenital potentialities, all states of being must be experienced; otherwise, these states will remain unintegrated in the personality. This refers both to physical conformations and personality tendencies and to states and facts of life: birth, the continuity of being, the states of quietness or excitation, hits and misses, the aloneness of pre-dependence, the state of amorphousness of the beginning, unthinkable agonies, etc. Winnicott rejects the idea that elements belonging to an individual may be considered independently of his own experience of them.[34]

What does Winnicott understand by "experience"? The concept is not clearly defined in his work; it is one of those concepts, the meaning of which should become intelligible in itself, on the basis of the use which Winnicott makes of it throughout his work. First, experience varies according to the moment in the maturational process. We must hence differentiate the meaning of the term "experience" when it refers to these initial stages, from the one used when some experience of the unitary self and of the world is achieved, which will include a beginning of integration in time and space as well as the lodging of the psyche in the body. Second, gathering the several passages on the theme, we can affirm that "experience" and the "feeling of real" are mutually interwoven: only what is given in experience is real for the individual. But one can also say that something, a state of being, a fantasy, a dream or an event, is an experience only if it is felt as real. The "real" that is implied here has nothing to do with external reality, in the sense of a representable, perceptible reality that can be visualised and is sayable. Freud's so-called "reality principle", which in Winnicott's redefinition, "is the fact of the existence of the world whether the baby creates it or not" (1986h, p. 40) is, for Winnicott, the "arch-enemy of spontaneity, creativity and *the sense of Real*" (1984d, p. 236; my italics).

A man approximately forty years old, who suffers from a disbelief that corrodes any reality told me: "I was socialised before I had become a person. I know quite well what is expected from me and I fulfil my duties precisely, but nothing has ever made any sense. I don't feel real, I don't feel the world or the others as real. I don't have a history. I don't know why I live or go on living". This man does not have problems with the reality principle, but suffers from the lack of feeling of real.

One of the few references to the general character of what is experience is in a letter from 1952, to Money-Kyrle:

> Experience is a constant trafficking in illusion, a repeated reaching to the interplay between creativity and that which the world has to offer. Experience is an achievement of ego maturity to which the environment supplies an essential ingredient. It is not by any means always achieved. (1987b, p. 43)

It is the environment that early in life provides the indispensable ingredient for establishing the capacity for experience. This ingredient consists of the baby having the possibility to inhabit, for as long as necessary, a subjective world, which is ruled by the "illusion of omnipotence", with this being the only solid basis for the belief that will gradually be established in the reality of the self and of the world.[35] The limits of the subjective world are traced by the omnipotence scope of the baby. Everything that happens there becomes an experience of the infant, because, being dictated by the baby's rhythm and deriving from spontaneous gesture, it happens in such a way that it does not disrupt the personal sense of existence which, at this point, is the continuity of being. The capacity for experience is thus related to spontaneity and primary creativity and to the root of the true self, in short, to *being*.

In summary, according to Winnicott, the baby is already a human being since intra-uterine life, with this defined by his innate capacity for experiences. Despite being innate, this capacity must be exercised, made real and integrated into the personality and this will only happen if, during the initial stages, the baby is provided with facilitating care, otherwise the capacity will wither or be paralysed. The capacity for experience is hence an acquisition of development, which depends on an imponderable element: environmental facilitation. In this way it may not be achieved. For this reason, while:

> It is possible to seduce a baby into feeding and into the functioning of all the bodily processes, but *the baby does not feel these things as an experience* unless it is built on a quantity of *simple being* which is enough to establish the self that is eventually a person. (1987e, p. 12; my italics)

There are people who did not initially find a basis for being because they were not permitted the illusion of omnipotence; in them, the sense of real is so debilitated that no matter how many times they undergo certain situations, everything always falls apart and they must always start again as if nothing had happened. They record the fact in an archive of memories, but nothing in them was affected or changed. In general, it is said that these people do not learn with experience, but perhaps it would be even more accurate to say that they are incapable of having experiences. Instead of being there, in the present event, they are absent, defending themselves from some invasion, some kind of imprisonment, or preventing some distress which may arise; everything that occurs is hence external to them, in such a way that nothing lasts.

The irreplaceable value of experience seems to have been a conviction that permeated not only the theory but also Winnicott's own life. Having started to write his biography shortly before his death, the title of which was to be *Not Less than Everything*,[36] Winnicott wrote a prayer, in which he asked to God to be alive at the moment of his death, so that this would also be an experience, the last one.[37]

His well-known aversion to any kind of abstract theoretical construction detached from experience probably derives from this same conviction. It is as a function of this aversion that the term "experience" is not defined but simply used, so that it is understood not merely by the intellect, but by another type of precision, that of the specifically human context. Concepts must reach the reader in the field of experience, placing her directly in the situation. In order to indicate that maternal care happens through the identification of the mother with the baby and not via a deliberate mental act, Winnicott says: "we find that she does not have to make a sort of shopping list of things she must do tomorrow; she feels what is needed at the moment" (1965e, p. 71). Or also, while trying to show to mothers that they must not expect that babies will start to suckle as soon as they are born: "A period of time is needed for many babies before they begin to search, and when they find an object they do not necessarily want immediately to make a meal of it" (1968f, p. 64).

There are significant theoretical consequences deriving from the conceptions of experience, from the capacity of having experiences and from the fact that the baby, from the outset, is already a human being capable of having experiences. Certain difficulties presented by a specific infant, such as an expectation of persecution, instead of being attributed to heredity or to the unconscious of the species, may perfectly well be related to the birth process which was excessively slow or to other precocious experiences of environmental invasion. Researchers who so easily attribute some primitive manifestations in a baby to the heredity factor, do not take into account his pre-history and the fact that dependence is significant as soon as something such as a state of being initiates. It is very simple, says Winnicott, to affirm that paranoid babies have a hereditary tendency or are manifesting a constitutional factor, but what the argument of this line of reasoning does is to disregard and sidetrack "the very interesting and important phenomenon of the development of the individual, and the memory of personal experiences" (1988, p. 149).

It is true that since the body is always included, the biological hereditary factor (if it can clearly be isolated) is always present: while some newborn babies show an intense sensitivity to clarity and need shade; others have a thermal, tactile, or auditory sensitivity. Indeed, some are actually startled by noises, while others seem simply not to hear them. There are babies who are extraordinarily affected by the emotional atmosphere of the environment, while others are more isolated and meditative. Some are very quick or perhaps more sensitive to discomfort and pain and as soon as an impulse emerges, they are already screaming. There are others who are slow and need time to conclude an experience, resenting very much if the environmental rhythm is accelerated. There are babies whose sensitivity is more evenly distributed; in others a specific sensitivity is exacerbated. The fact is that there are babies of all kinds, and an accentuated sensitivity will probably predispose them to an extraordinary specific ability (sometimes responsible for genius) or to a disease: a baby with such sensitivity is highly susceptible to be affected and traumatised. Furthermore, as has already been mentioned, when considering these aspects, we must include the baby's pre-history and the fact that he has already had several experiences during intrauterine life.

A very sensitive child will certainly demand more of the mother. However, when we speak of active adaptation, we think precisely of the ability that leads the mother to adapt to a singular *certain baby*, and not of a technique for raising babies. Although, as already stated, genetics determines some individual patterns and characteristics, such as being taller or shorter, having more or less muscle mass, having better or worse brain tissue, more or less vitality or sensitivity, none of these are decisive in terms of development. When we attribute certain characteristics or disorders to the constitution of the individual, we are not paying due attention to the mother's adaptive technique.[38] The most important thing of all is that the baby has a mother who adapts to him and accompanies him as he is and can be, that is, developing his inherited potentialities in his maturational process in the best possible way. We must also include the factor of chance, contributing to the mother carrying out her function well: a fortunate conjunction, for example, would be the fact that a slow child has a mother who is also slow and not one that is too fast and who becomes bored by or impatient with the baby's slowness.

The fact is that, if we include the essential participation of the environment in the constitution of human psyche—a participation which precedes and is also a condition that makes the constitution of object relations possible—there is no escape: we have to scrutinise and take into account the extremely subtle details of the mother–baby relationship in the more primitive stages.

The state of unintegration of the primitive stages

If the entire maturational process moves towards integration, in what state is the baby when this process starts? Winnicott postulates that at the beginning and throughout all of the primitive stages, most of the time the baby lives in a state of unintegration:

> This bit of theory is needed if one is to reach to the place where infants live—a queer place—where *nothing has yet been separated out as not-me,* so there is *not yet a* ME. […] rather that no mother, no object external to the self, is known; and even this statement is wrong because there is not yet a self. It could be said that the self of the infant at this very early stage is only potential. (1965c, p. 17)

Although there is a baby for the observer and for the mother, for the baby there is still no himself, no mother and no world. The baby is not yet a unit; the many aspects that will be integrated into the whole person that he will be are still disconnected. Before integration, it is as if the baby is spread out; "unorganized, a mere collection of sensory-motor phenomena, collected by the holding environment" (1965k, p. 148).

The unintegration, which is accompanied by a non-conscience (cf. 1988), is not a deficit. It is the baby's natural state of extreme immaturity and it means a lack of cohesion in a self, of integration in space and time, of psycho-somatic integration and ultimately of *wholeness*. The only temporality that the baby initially has, other than biological time, is the diffuse sensation of being able to go on being. The negative term, unintegration, has its raisons d'être: it refers to a *not-yet*, to a state prior to any integration and hence prior to the establishment of a me and of a psyche. This "negative" state has no pathological connotation, nor does it refer to what would be a state of chaos, since in the beginning, there is neither chaos nor order (cf. 1988). In addition, *unintegration* must be distinguished from *disintegration*, which has a defensive character and can only occur after some integration has been achieved.

When the infant is receiving good care, the unintegration

> […] is the natural state and there is no one there to mind about it. Good care produces a state of affairs in which integration begins to become a fact, and a person starts to be there. In so far as this is true, so far does failure of care lead to disintegration instead of to a return to

unintegration. Disintegration is felt to be a threat because (by definition) there is someone there to feel the threat. (1958d, p. 98)

The important point of the theory is as follows: *it is only from unintegration that the several forms of integration may be produced*. If integration were a given, human beings would not be the way they are, since health as well as difficulties and disorders, which are characteristic of human beings, are states relating to the success or failure in the integrative tasks of the initial stages, as achievements of development. On this point, Winnicott's position demonstrates a significant advance over the traditional theory, conceived on the basis of neuroses, which are disorders of a personality which is already integrated; this theory has no way of approaching the particular nature of these founding achievements and as such, does not allow us to assess the consequences of failure in these achievements.[39]

Starting from unintegration, small experiences of integration take place during states of excitation and immediately afterwards, the baby returns to the unintegrated state in order to rest. The state of integration gradually becomes more stable and consistent. However, it will never be a safe territory to which the individual has title of ownership. There will always be the risk of him losing himself, but for a healthy baby, this will increasingly depend on situations of extreme overload. The healthy individual is not constantly concerned with his psychic survival.

The mother–baby relation: absolute dependence

During the initial stages, the baby lives most of the time in a state of unintegration, a situation of absolute dependence, which is only possible by virtue of the adaptation of the mother, which is also absolute. While still in the uterus and during the first months after birth, dependence is so extreme that it is not possible to think about the new individual as a unit. "The unit is the *environment-individual set-up* of which unit the new individual is only a part" (1988, p. 131). This is the meaning of Winnicott's famous statement *"this thing such a baby does not exist"*. If this is so, there is no way of describing a baby, or a small child, without including the care that he is receiving in the description. It is only gradually that environmental care is incorporated as an aspect of the baby's self, at the same time as the facilitating environment gradually becomes something external and separate from the baby (cf. 1987c). The environment, initially the mother, or more precisely, the mother's way of being, *is a part of the baby and is indistinguishable from it*. We do not have two individuals, but a *sui generis* relation, which may be called *two-in-one*.[40]

The state of absolute dependence is not founded only on the fragility of the baby or on its inability to survive without help. Nor does it refer to what would be a massive influence from the environment that would "produce" the baby, from himself, as a *tabula rasa*. Nor even is it a question of affective dependence, since the baby is not mature enough to have feelings. The absolute dependence refers to the fact that the baby is entirely dependent on the mother in order to *be*—in the way that he *is* or *can be* at this initial moment—and in order to fulfil his innate tendency towards integration into a unit. The peculiar relationship with the mother during the initial stages of absolute dependence provides a pattern for the relations that the baby will develop with external reality. It is within this relationship that the illusion of contact with the external world is being built, as well as the trust that inter-human communication is possible and that life makes sense.

Although the word "dependence" implies the existence of another human being, this other is not yet an object in the classical sense of the term, since the baby is not sufficiently mature to have, to perceive or to desire objects. The mother is not an external object and nor an internal one, because the sense of externality, as well as that of inner world have not yet been constituted. From the baby's point of view, "there is, at this very early stage, no external factor; the mother is part of the child" (1965n, p. 61). Despite this, maternal care intrinsically participates in the gradual constitution of the self; with the baby being immediately affected by the kind of care that he receives.

The Winnicottian concept of initial "environment" must be understood in accordance with its two essential aspects: (a) it is neither external nor internal; (b) it is an instance which supports and responds to dependence: the baby is entirely dependent on another person *who is not yet another* separate or external to him.[41] We find here the embedded idea, the psychological and philosophical scope of which remains to be fully appreciated, that the reality of the self and that of the world are established during the development process, *within the mother–baby relation*. The constitution of the me, at the same time as the constitution of intrapsychic reality and external reality, only takes place within the relation with the other; the baby's self necessarily emerges from within the baby–mother unity. The "me" as an identity separate from the not-me is a surpassing of the primary identification that occurs within the initial fusional unity. This is the meaning of Winnicott's statement that the I AM status "[…] *means nothing unless I at the beginning am along with another human being who has not yet been differentiated off*" (1987e, p. 12; my italics). The ambit in which development takes place is not an intrapsychic space, but an inter-human one, something *in between* the mother and the baby.[42] This space is also pre-personal, since there are not yet two persons; each one is part of the other in the two-in-one unity. Despite this, it must be pointed out that, since the very outset, there is already a small detachment, a small gap between them, since "in the most intimate contact there is a lack of contact so that essentially each individual retains absolute isolation always and for ever" (1988, p. 157).[43] However, at the same time that this space already exists and will always exist, separating mother and infant and forever isolating the individual from the external world, *it does not yet exist* as such; achieving it is a conquest of development that will only start to be effective during the stage of transitionality.[44]

We can find something analogous to this fundamental isolation in biology: the "egg" is a guest in the mother's body and not a part of it. Throughout pregnancy it remains enveloped by substances that have been constituted to protect it, at the same time as they "separate" it from the mother. When the baby is born, this set of substances is lost; but neither the baby nor the mother loses anything of their own. From the viewpoint of the human person who is being constituted, this "space", which allows for the basic isolation, has always been and always will be there; at the same time, it will become, in due course, the first real distance between the mother and the baby, a distance that both separates and unites. The analogy of the "egg" hence evokes the essential aloneness, which is the original condition in which the baby finds himself at the most absolute beginning, when being emerges from non-being, an aloneness that will be preserved forever, no matter how communicative or well-related to external reality the individual may become. It is from this fundamental isolation that the basic illusion of contact will emerge and at a later stage, the potential space. In due course, this space will be filled with transitional phenomena and transitional objects that are simultaneously part of the baby and of the environment.

Additional characterisation of the facilitating environment: the good enough mother and the baby's father[45]

The facilitating environment is initially the "good enough mother". The expression "good enough" refers to the mother who is capable of acknowledging and responding to the infant's dependence, as a result of her identification with him, which enables her to know what his needs are at a given moment and to meet them. The *"enough"* goodness encompasses the mother's spontaneity and personal presence in her care of the baby, as well as her capacity for believing that the baby is an on-going maturational process and hence, it is not she (i.e., her care or control of the situation) that will give life to the baby. The mother merely facilitates a process which belongs to the baby. She is good enough because she attends to the baby to the precise extent of his needs, and not to her own, such as the need to be good or very good. What the baby needs is the concern and effective care of a real mother, who continues being herself consistently, fallible since human, but reliable precisely because she is fallible.[46]

From the outset, the good enough mother proceeds towards an absolute adaptation, and a little later, to a relative adaptation to the baby's needs. Winnicott insists that it is a question of "adaptation to *needs*" and not of satisfaction of desires. By so doing, he clearly characterises the specificity of the initial stages: the baby is not yet an individual with desires, but an immature being in a state of absolute dependence. With regard to this period, a source of misunderstandings

> [...] is the idea (that some analysts have) that the term "adaptation to need" in treatment of schizoid patients and in infant-care means meeting id-drives. In this setting it is not a question of meeting id-drives or of frustrating id-drives. There are more important things going on, and these are of the nature of giving ego-support to ego processes. (1965d, p. 241)

In a letter to Lili Peller of 1966, Winnicott mentioned that, having left paediatrics with a conscience alerted to child dependence, he found it exasperating that the only dependence which his psychoanalyst colleagues could consider was that related to instinctual needs. He then added: "In my more recent writings you have noticed that I have tried to enumerate the psychotic-type anxieties which cluster round the word need. These have nothing to do with instincts" (1987b, p. 156). In another text, he stated that in the most primitive initial stages,

> [...] the word "need" has significance here just as "drive" has significance in the area of satisfaction of instinct. The word "desire" is out of place as it belongs to sophistication that is not to be assumed at this stage of immaturity that is under consideration. (1970b, p. 256, note 7)

The environment adapts "to need arising out of being and arising out of the processes of maturation" (1965j, p. 183). That is, it is from the need to go on being that all the other needs emerge, and all of them largely prevail over any pleasure principle. That is the reason why the development of human instinctuality is thought by Winnicott within the more comprehensive line of the maturational processes.

The absolute adaptation of the mother to the baby's needs is temporary, but while it lasts it implies full involvement. A baby needs nothing less than a full person, that is, entirely surrendered or devoted to him, even if for a brief period of time at each day. This is generally possible because when the mother is healthy, she enters a state of "primary maternal preoccupation", which starts at the last months of pregnancy and lasts for some time after birth. This is a very special psychological condition, of heightened sensitivity that

> [...] could be compared with a withdrawn state, or a dissociated state, or a fugue, or even with a disturbance at a deeper level such as a schizoid episode in which some aspect of the personality takes over temporarily. (1958h, p. 302)

It is the baby and the totality of the baby's care that occupy the mother's life. By virtue of this state, which implies a partial regression, the mother becomes able to identify with the baby and know what he needs. At the same time, she retains her adult place, so that she is in a position not only to understand but also to take care of the infant effectively, providing what he needs. Being mature, the mother is not narcissistically wounded for having her personal life emptied in order to dedicate herself to caring for the baby. The good enough mother is devoted to the infant. The term "devotion", which implies the total involvement of the mother and her capacity for taking care of the baby, has nothing to do with sentimentality. Any kind of sentimentality, says the author, is worse than useless, for it contains an unconscious denial of hate and aggressiveness, which underlie all constructive effort, even when it is a question of raising a child.

Maternal care is frequently thought of in terms of indulgence, but the love or kindness of the good enough mother is not usually indulgent. If, as a result of some kind of deprivation, the infant presents a special period of need and the mother is capable of understanding the need that is thus communicated, she may become indulgent and "pamper" the child for a certain time, but this indulgence is actually a therapy that has become necessary by virtue of some failure of ordinary maternal care. "Therapy by the mother may cure, but this is not mother-love" (1958c, p. 128).

The adaptation of the mother to the child's need is not related to her intelligence, nor does it arise from knowledge that may be obtained from books or lectures. Her knowledge is of a nature that enables her to provide for the infant successfully, regardless of any intellectual appreciation of what is happening, nor of the need to understand everything. What orients her is her ability to identify with the infant. Such ability comes from her own experience of having been a baby and of having been taken care of; she retains bodily memories of comfort and safety as well as experiences of personal intimacy. Moreover, the mother knows what the baby's needs are, because she is alive and has an imagination. She is able to wait for the spontaneous gesture to emerge, because she "knows" of many subtle things such as, for example, that in order to be moved from one place to another, a baby needs to be prepared, and that the overall movement requires time. She also knows that it is more important to respect the baby's refusal to nurse, than to force him, due to discipline or fear of malnutrition, since in terms of development, "the basis of *feeding* is *not feeding*" (1968f, p. 64).[47]

Although primary maternal preoccupation is a state that arises naturally with maternity, there are women who fear it and resist the regression that it contains. They cling to their adult occupation and are unable or cannot bear to identify with the baby. This kind of mother will tend to take care of the baby mentally; her acts will be deliberate, governed by rules that are intellectually established. She may succeed in providing him with a few basic things, but she will not be capable of having the deep and silent communication which comes with intimacy. She will take care of the baby "as one is supposed to take care of babies", that is, providing impersonal care. This is typically the case of the mother who *does* but *is* not.[48] The good enough care required by a baby is not the care devised by thinking, which is deliberate or delivered mechanically; this care can only be provided by a human being, the mother or a substitute, who is alive and able to put herself in the place of another person, at the same time as she remains an adult and is continuously herself. It is surprising how babies seem to come endowed with a quality control of the communication we try to establish with them. When the mother, because of her identification and preoccupation with the baby, is alert in the sense of preventing and avoiding the occurrence of unpredictable events that may frighten or even traumatise the baby, such attention does not arise from an intellectual deliberation, but almost always occurs in her body. She is completely alert and this is reflected in her posture; her movements, her gaze are directed towards the baby and are naturally protective.

Even when she surrenders herself to the complete, psycho-somatic involvement with the baby, the mother, whose spontaneity is preserved, is able to be herself consistently. Starting from this, what has to be done takes place naturally, because "children always take the best from us."

For this reason,

> In order to be consistent, and so to be predictable for our children, we must be *ourselves*. If we are ourselves our children can get to know us. Certainly if we are acting a part we shall be found out when we get caught without our make-up. (1993b, p. 123)

With time, and according to the increasing maturational capability of the infant, the good-enough mother makes the adaptation progressively less absolute and in this way, she allows the baby to move gradually towards relative dependence and then towards independence. If the mother is healthy, de-adaptation occurs naturally, since it coincides with a moment when she is already tired of the demands that absolute adaptation requires. This passage is essential for the baby's development; if the mother is not able to abdicate from absolute dependence, it can generate serious difficulties for the child.

In describing the good-*enough* care of the *ordinary* devoted mother, Winnicott avoids any idealisation of the maternal or paternal figure.[49] Parents are not altruistic angels, nor is the world surrounding the baby a paradise. Children do not draw any benefit from mechanical perfection. If it were possible to make a choice, the author confesses, he would greatly prefer a mother who is capable of having doubts about her behaviour and of thinking that some things are going wrong due to something which she did or did not do, than a mother who "turned to an outside thing to explain everything", without assuming responsibility for anything (cf 1993d, p. 103). Moreover, if the mother is healthy, she will often hate her baby *much earlier than he has acquired the capacity to hate her.* Winnicott lists the good reasons that she has for so doing: the baby represented a danger to her body during pregnancy and birth; he interferes with her private life; he hurts her breast; she has to love him despite his excretions and everything else, even though he still shows his disappointment with her; his excited love is self-interested; he has no idea of what she does or sacrifices for him, etc. The mother naturally has to endure her own hate, without denying it to herself, but also without being able to do anything about it. She cannot manifest it directly towards the baby, except by means of songs or malicious expressions that she utters tenderly.[50] One of the most remarkable things in the ordinary mother is precisely, "her ability to be hurt so much by her baby and to hate so much without paying the child out" (1949f, p. 202).

There is yet another question: women who have just given birth are themselves necessarily in state of dependence.[51] It may even be said that mothers are as helpless with regard to the baby's helplessness as the baby is himself. In order to perform her task well, she needs to feel loved in the relationship with the child's father, and accepted both within the family circle and in the wider circles which constitute society (cf. 1958j). At this point, the father's role is extremely important, especially the function of protecting the mother and providing for the home. If adequately protected by her man, the mother is spared from having to concern herself with worldly things and to dedicate herself entirely to the inside of the circle formed by her own arms, at the centre of which is the baby. The father is also extremely necessary for helping the mother to feel well in her body and happy in spirit. Since, especially with regard to the first child, the mother tends to exaggerate her care, effectively wanting to become magical so as to guess the infant's need in advance, the father's help "makes human something in the mother, and draws away from her the element which otherwise becomes magical and potent and spoils the mother's motherliness" (1961a, p. 73). The effective presence and help of the baby's father provides moral support to the mother and a buttress for the order and security that she is trying to implant in the child's life. From a very early stage, children are sensitive to the atmosphere that is created in the home and to the stability that they feel in their parents, even when they still do not know that the parents exist as persons separate from them and with regard to each other.

At the same time, with regard to what refers directly to the baby that which is "paternal" necessarily comes after what is "maternal".[52] The father does not yet exist as a father, as the third party, since the baby does not even know of the existence of the mother and only establishes contact with the care that is offered to him. Since the baby does not yet even have a dual relationship, he is even less capable of having a triadic one. The father can nevertheless be very useful as a duplicator of the mother's care and, in this role, he has something of his own to add to the baby, as we shall see later.[53] Despite this, it is not good for the father to come onto the scene prematurely. The baby is not prepared for the inevitable differences in the ways of handling and holding. There are nevertheless cases of men who are more maternal than women and there are clinical reports of cases in which the father's aptitude for maternal care has minimised the environmental failure resulting from a pathology of the mother, saving the child from disorders that could have been much more severe than the ones that actually arose.[54]

If a little while later, the father begins to participate directly and actively, even if still in the maternal function, a certain paternal element is ultimately included in the constitution of the baby's self: from the child's perspective, the father is lived as an aspect of the mother "which is hard and strict and unrelenting, intransigent, indestructible" and who, when all goes well, gradually becomes the man who is transformed into a human being, "someone who can be feared, hated, loved and respected" (1986d, p. 131). This element contributes to a feeling of security of the home and to establishing the meaning of what a family is for a particular child (cf. idem).[55] Naturally, the way in which the child uses or does not use this father is determined by the way of being of the latter.

In a late text from 1969, reflecting on the innate tendency towards integration and the symbolism of this unitary status in monotheism, Winnicott adds another element to the participation of the father: regardless of whether or not the father has replaced the mother, at some point he appears to the baby as the first *glimpse of personal wholeness and totality* and in this way is used as a model for the baby's own integration. If the father is not present, the baby will somehow have to achieve integration, but this will be much harder to do, unless he can use another very stable relationship with a total person (cf. 1989i).

The paternal figure becomes especially significant when the baby reaches the stage at which, having achieved a unitary me, he is grappling with dealing the task of integrating instinctual life. At this stage of maturation, that of concern,[56] the child is conquering the capacity to take responsibility for the destructiveness inherent to primitive instinctual drives. Having started to appropriate the drives as belonging to the self, the child realises the harm that his instinctual impulsiveness does to the mother. He then begins to count on the father (his presence, firmness, ability to intervene and set limits) to protect the mother from his own drives. If the father does not play his part, the child will lose the freedom to move, act, and become excited, developing a self-control which paralyses his spontaneity and inhibits his instinctuality in general.[57]

As the baby achieves greater maturity, dependence slowly decreases. As a result of continuously adapting to the process of mutation and development of the child, the mother facilitates the gradual de-adaptation by progressively failing to adapt to the need, so as to help the child separate from her and to allow him to experience a relative dependence, so that he makes the transition that will lead to independence. The mother, then the father, and even later the family, the school, social groups, and increasingly wider circles provide the care relative to the needs of the new phase which is beginning.

The place of the parents implies *responsibility with their children*. It is up to the parents to keep the family and the home as a place of stability for the growth of the children, having to survive the various forms of destruction to which their children will expose them in order to grow up. This requires a few abdications. It is possible that the parents have kept themselves spontaneous and creative, which naturally is vital to them as persons and, to a certain extent, to their babies. When a child is present, however, they must be able to give up their place. The mother's spontaneity is highly necessary to the baby; being consistently herself is one of the sources which the infant needs to gain confidence. However, the adult mother does not expose the baby to her own drives. In addition, there are children who find themselves forced to live in an atmosphere of intense creativity, which nevertheless, belongs to the parents or the nanny and not to the child. "[…] this stifles them and they cease to be. Or they develop a technique of withdrawal" (1986h, p. 52). In order to raise children so that they may live in a world of real facts, remaining creative, "we do have to be uncreative and compliant and adaptive [...]" (idem). The same evidently holds for the analytical setting.

Winnicott's concepts of ego, self, and me

Since the terms "ego", "self", and "me" form part of the basic vocabulary of the theory of maturational processes and their meaning is far from being unambiguous, as may be proven by the diversity of meanings with which they are invested in different philosophical, theological, or psychological theories, it is appropriate to clarify their use in Winnicott's work.

In texts prior to 1962, Winnicott frequently used the terms "ego" and "self" indiscriminately, leading to conceptual inaccuracies. It was Fordham, a Jungian analyst and his personal friend, who made him recognise, probably at the start of the 1960s, that he

> was using the words "self" and "ego" as if they were synonymous, which of course they are not; they cannot be, since "self" is a word, and "ego" is a term to be used for convenience with an agreed meaning. (1964b, p. 490)

Winnicott realised that the two terms were not of the same semantic type. "Ego" is a theoretical term, the meaning of which is open to a consensual decision within a certain group of researchers, while the word "self" is a descriptive term in everyday language which "naturally knows more than we do; it uses us, and can command us" (1960a, p. 158).

The clearest statement by the author about the "ego" is in a text from 1962: "The term ego can be used to describe that part of the growing human personality that tends, under suitable conditions, to become integrated into a unit" (1965n, p. 56). The term "ego" is not used, as we can see, to designate an instance of the psychic apparatus, since Winnicott does not work with the heuristic concept of psychic apparatus, but to designate the tendency towards organisation and integration of the various psycho-somatic aspects which are not initially integrated and when everything goes well, gradually gather into a me. It does not have the same meaning as in traditional psychoanalysis; it was suggested to him by the psychology of the ego and by Edward Glover's concept of ego nuclei. In fact, in the traditional theory there is no concept equivalent to that of Winnicott's "ego", since neither in Freud, nor in Klein is there the conception of a tendency towards maturation. We must also bear in mind, in order to avoid the confusions which arise from this intricate terminological question, that the term "ego" is not one of Freud's: it was introduced into psychoanalytical literature by the English translation of Freudian works made by Strachey. When referring to the instance of the psychic apparatus which makes contact with reality, Freud spoke of the *Ich*, that is, "I" in German. It is most likely that Winnicott, in his readings of Freud, used Strachey's translation and when referring to this point in the Freudian theory, started to use the term "ego". In his own theory, he adopted the term "ego" in a modified sense, using "me" as well and giving different meanings to the two terms: one thing is the "ego", as a tendency towards maturation and another is the "me" (*I* from *I am*), as the result of the integrative task, the achievement of unitary identity.

In Freudian theory, at least in its initial formulation, the ego (*Ich*) emerges from the id, as a transformation, produced through the contact with the reality principle. The ego (*Ich*), says Freud, is that part of the id which was modified by the direct influence of the external world.[58] On the basis of this point, which is debatable even for Freudians, since it is difficult to understand how a given structure can give rise to another of a totally different nature, Winnicott welcomed the theoretical modifications introduced by E. Glover, based on his conception of nuclei or primitive unorganised ego structures, in order to formulate the primary state of unintegration, which is characteristic of the initial stages of development.[59]

Examples of the use of the concepts of ego and self may help to clarify the meaning of both terms. At a certain point, the author highlights that the ego is both weak and strong; all depends on the capacity of the mother to give ego support.

> [...] The infant's reinforced and therefore strong ego is able very early to organise defences, and to develop patterns that are personal [...]. It is this infant whose ego is strong *because of the mother's ego support* that early becomes himself or herself, really and truly. (1965c, p. 17)

In another text, Winnicott affirms that the baby's ego (its tendency towards integration):

> [...] is feeble in the extreme if there is no satisfactory facilitating environment. However, the mother or mother figure supplies the ego support, and if she does this well enough the infant's ego is very strong and has its own organization. (1989m, p. 101)

We should note the difference between the senses of "ego" and "self": the innate tendency towards maturation (integration) depends on the support provided by the environment. The ego support of the mother, or the mother's auxiliary ego, as Winnicott says in other texts, makes the baby's *ego* strong and facilitates integrative experiences, guiding the child more easily towards possessing his own organisation, towards *becoming himself*, that is, becoming a *self* integrated into a me. In terms of nomenclature, we should say that it is the *ego* which guides the integrative tendency towards a unitary *self*.[60] The self is the result of the integrative tendency, but it is necessary that the tendency is in operation. This is why Winnicott says "the ego offers itself for study long before the word self has relevance" (1965n, p. 56).

The term self was in turn used in two different ways as Winnicott's thought evolved. In the central and more general meaning, self refers to the unitary status achieved by the individual at the stage when the baby, if he could speak, would say I AM. If we adopt the term in this sense, the self is the result of a series of achievements of the integration process and is only established in a consistent manner in the stage when the infant achieves an identity, a unitary self. At this point, a healthy baby, operating on the basis of the true self, has already even integrated as an aspect of his personality an instrumental false self, which enables him to deal with social demands. As a synonym for the self, in this same sense, Winnicott also uses the term "*me*" or "*I*". The "me" is therefore, the self that separates from the mother, achieving unitary identity and integrating into it both the true and the false self. When the term "self" is used in this sense of the integrated personality, Winnicott will say that prior to this achievement, there is no self.

This can be illustrated by an excerpt in which, describing the more primitive phases, he states that

> rather that no mother, no object external to the self, is known; and even this statement is wrong because there is not yet a self. It could be said that the self of the infant at this very early stage is only potential. (1965c, pp. 17–18)

At the same time, in *Human Nature*, there are passages in which he uses the term "self" for the *result of any* momentary *integrative experience* prior to reaching unitary integration into a me. For example, when mentioning the little moments of integration, in the excited states of the most primitive stage, he says that both the instinctual demand and the drive towards motility are preceded "by a gathering together of the whole self. Awareness becomes possible at such moments, because *there is a self* to be aware" (1988, p. 117; my italics).

This use of the term "self" for any integrative experience, even prior to the achievement of the unitary self, is corroborated later in his work, when he proposes a new formulation for his concepts of world and of subjective objects: in the excited encounter with the object (subjective), the baby is momentarily united and, through a *primary identification* with the object (the baby *is* the object) he lives the first experience of *being* as an *identity*. Using new terminology, which shall be clarified later in Chapter Three, Winnicott affirms that "when the girl element in the boy or girl baby or patient finds the breast it is the self that has been found" (1971i, p. 180). From then on, the author uses the term "self" increasingly frequently for any degree or form of integration, starting from unintegration, even when this integration is incipient and purely momentary.

Winnicott deals more explicitly with the concept of self and its difference with regard to the ego in an article from 1970, in which he states that,

> [...] the self, which is not the ego, is the person who is me, who is only me, who has a totality based on the operation of the maturational process. At the same time the self has parts, and in fact is constituted of these parts. These parts agglutinate from a direction interior-exterior in the course of the operation of the maturational process, aided as it must be (maximally at the beginning) by the human environment which holds and handles and in a live way facilitates. [...] It is the self and the life of the self that alone makes sense of action or of living from the point of view of the individual [...]. (1971d, p. 271)

J. B. Pontalis observed that in French psychoanalytical circles, Winnicott's concepts of being and self were received with hesitation and suspicion, as a result of them being wrongly approximated to Guntrip's notion of self. Aligned with a certain tradition in phenomenology, Guntrip had tried to introduce into psychoanalysis, together with the concept of self, the idea of a unified and unifying subject, who can recognise himself, who is unity and continuity, "whose being would be liable to escape from the *irreducibility* of conflict, the *otherness* of the unconscious, the *irreconcilability* of representations [...]" (Pontalis, 1981, p. 127). Pontalis is certainly right when he argues against Guntrip that "three quarters of a century of analytical experience undermines the illusion of a totally monadic subject, of a person totally sure of belonging to himself" (Pontalis, 1981, p. 127). It is nevertheless a mistake to pair Guntrip's self with that of Winnicott: the Winnicottian notion of tendency towards integration into a unitary self does not refer to the pulsional field, or to unconscious conflicts that would be overcome or annulled by it. It instead refers to all of the aspects of the individual, to his potentialities, which are initially unconscious, but not in the sense of the repressed unconscious: his body, his bodily memories, his temporality and spatiality, initially subjective and then, objective, the states of quietness and of excitation, instinctuality, fantasy, the externality of the world, etc., etc., etc., which, starting from unintegration will gradually integrate into a unity, being part of the whole person of the individual. According to Pontalis, this unitary status does not resemble the cohesion without fissures, or the self-possession intended by Guntrip. On the contrary, it is precisely because of the integration into a unity and the development of an internal psychic reality that the individual can then suffer unconscious conflicts.

Some philosophical and epistemological characteristics of the theory of maturational processes

The abandonment of causal determinism

The central question for the understanding and classification of psychic disorders is the establishment of the aetiology, a term which means, etymologically, a theory of the causes. This meaning was historically established from the conception of science, based on the principle of causality, and from the deterministic view regarding the nature of entities, which are object of scientific study. In view of what has been said before, Winnicott does not share that conception of human nature, nor does he defend a deterministic science. When describing the origin of the human being, he resorts to a series of expressions that do not admit a causalist interpretation: the passage from the potential baby to the actual one cannot be understood in a causal manner. This is not an updating of given properties already embedded in the individual and which would develop and manifest over time. To begin with, there are no intrinsic "determinations" in a baby, either somatic or psychic. With the sole exception of the tendency towards integration and of primary creativity, all possible characteristics of the baby still have to be created. Genetic determinations provide some organic limits, but not the orientation of what the person of the individual will be. The process of emergence of an individual, as a person with an identity, does not occur automatically, depending fundamentally on an imponderable internal factor, which is the baby's creativity, and on other equally imponderable factors, such as the psychic health of the mother and good fortune. In 1960, referring to the fact that the stages of development have a certain period for taking place, which varies from child to child, Winnicott affirms that *"even if they were known in advance* in the case of a given child, [these dates] could not be used in predicting the child's actual development because of the other factor, maternal care" (1960b, p. 43; my italics).

Although the inherited characteristics of the individual provide a pattern and a certain configuration of possibilities and limitations, the human being cannot be thought of as a predetermined product, either by his biological or psychic constitution, or by the external environment, which would mould him, as has been postulated by academic psychology. Once development has initiated, the human being is thrown into the indetermination of hits and misses which may happen, and it is these imponderable factors which determine how his potentialities will be realised. This is why Loparic, approximating Winnicott's conception to that of Heidegger, sees the "ongoing" of the human being in the personal growth described by Winnicott.

On the other hand, although depending fundamentally on environmental care, it is necessary to say that the environment, "does not make the infant grow, nor does it determine the direction of growth" (1963c, p. 223). When good enough, the environment does not determine the baby in a causal way; it merely supplies the facilitating conditions for the action of the maturational process. It is frequently thought, Winnicott affirms, that we make our children and that we teach them everything. The truth is precisely the opposite, since "we cannot even teach them to walk, but their innate tendency to walk at a certain age needs us as supporting figures" (1987b, p. 186).

The same holds for the emergence of psychic disorders. It is certain that the child's psychic health cannot be established without good enough environmental care. However, says Winnicott, "we also know that a corrective environmental experience does not cure the patient directly, more than a bad environment directly causes the structure of the illness" (cf. 1963a). The neurotic disorder, for example, is not caused by the parents.

Throughout Winnicott's work, we find many examples of non-causality. In a text dedicated to fathers, Winnicott discusses each person's responsibility regarding the choice of a marriage partner in terms of *anatomical and physiological* inheritance. In this text, he says that after the spermatozoid has penetrated the ovum, things start to operate by themselves, and what is necessary is the parents' shelter for the innate tendency towards maturation of the foetus so generated. It is very helpful for the parents to know that there is *nothing to be done* for a baby to be converted into a child, for a child to grow up, for the growing child to be good and clean, to grow up generous and for the generous child to know how to make a thoughtful choice of the appropriate presents for the appropriate people. "No-one has to make a child hungry, angry, happy, sad, affectionate, good or naughty. *These things just happen*" (1993b, p. 123; my italics). There are nevertheless many things that can be done indirectly: one of them being that "the mother often prevents schizophrenia by ordinary good management" (1987b, p. 45).

The origination of the human being or his maturation is not, therefore, an event that can be viewed as the effect of a cause. The power from which human existence emerges is not of the type that produces effects. It is rather permitting that *what does not yet exist comes into being*, that what is not present achieves presence, that the possibilities of being come to light, launched into the indeterminacy of life.[61] The non-causal character of Winnicott's theory is also revealed in the fact that there is not, despite the importance attributed to environmental care in the constitution of the individual, *any rule which may be stipulated* that the mother should follow, nor any legislation on maternal behaviour that guarantees that mothers will be successful in their task. On the contrary, any standardisation of how the "good-enough mother" should be would be the same as destroying her. The "knowledge" of the mother, which has been working well for thousands of years, does not admit to being categorised or taught; it is the fruit of an entirely personal understanding, which must be recreated with each new infant, even in the case of twins.

Here the question may emerge regarding the cognitive, and hence therapeutic gain, in distinguishing the non-causality of Winnicott's theory. A possible answer is as follows: a non-causal theory allows for the highlighting of the essential precariousness of human life and its fundamentally uncontrollable character. For Winnicott, it is essential to acknowledge this fact and remain close to something that can be called the "mystery" of the human being, although this should not lead us to any kind of mysticism. On the contrary, it is precisely due to the scientific task, to the rigour which characterises it, in the obedience to the specific nature of its object of study, that life's indeterminacy must be preserved as it is. We must not, and that is one of the methodological principles of the science of man practised by Winnicott, attempt to thematise man at the cost of distorting his nature. For this reason, it is often necessary to admit "obscurity to have a value that is superior to false clarification" (1989k, p. 240). This seems to be exactly the sense of the question raised by Winnicott in the letter to Anna Freud of 1954, already mentioned in the Introduction, when, after expressing his profound suspicion regarding the terms of metapsychology, he asks: "Is it because they can give the appearance of a common understanding when such understanding does not exist?" (1987b, p. 58).

A non-causal conception of human development may be considered as revolutionary not only to psychoanalysis, but for the philosophy of science itself. This is one of the points which fundamentally distinguishes Winnicott's thought from Freud's libidinal theory and from the Kleinian theory as well as from any other conception founded on the notion of forces, in which human development is understood according to laws governing natural entities.

Negativity

In Winnicott's conception of the human being, there is an intrinsic negativity, which cuts across all positivity of life and maintains a permanent tension between being and not being. This negativity is the furthest possible from the psychoanalytic conception of the death pulsion. What the study of babies and psychotics clearly reveals is that the human being has always been committed to being and not being. In other words, all *ability to be* starts from not being and *being* is never completely given to the human being. It is always a precarious achievement, which, as such, is not always achieved: "Some must spend all their lives not being, in a desperate effort to find a basis for being" (1984b, p. 112).

Because he conceives of human nature in this way, it seems entirely artificial and unnecessary to Winnicott to resort to speculative constructions of a naturalistic or energetic type, such as death pulsion. The concept of death pulsion or of destruction *enthrones evil as an entity operating in itself*, neglecting the full implication of human dependency, whether absolute or not, and hence, of the environmental factor, which can cause considerable damage.

What lies at the origin of man is not a positivity. The human being is not inferable from his genes, nor is he the result of a given constitution. "Genes are not enough", says Winnicott. Nor does he derive from the mother's desire.[62] To the question that Winnicott asks himself—"What is the state of the human individual as the being emerges out of not being?" he answers: "At the start, there is an essential aloneness". For the human being, he continues, "the emergence has been not from an inorganic state but from aloneness" (1988, p. 133). The "state prior to that of aloneness is one of unaliveness" (ibid., p. 132). Emerging from not-being, he is thrown in life and there is no discernible foundation for his existence. His only determination, which is structural and devoid of content, is being alive and the tendency towards maturation, towards integration into a unit. This tendency nevertheless depends on what happens, and may even fail. Moreover, the tendency towards integration carries in itself a negative "operator", and must always integrate not-being, which permanently crosses and accompanies its unfolding. Human life is conceived as an interval between two states of not-being-alive; the basis of human nature is a space between being and not-being. The fact that existence is open at its two extremities to nothingness provides the matrix for all manifestations of human life and of its possibilities: "In the development of the individual infant living arises and establishes itself out of not-living, and being becomes a fact that replaces not-being, as communication arises out of silence" (1965j, p. 191).

Health, in particular, may be viewed as the surpassing of the original state of not-being, and a slow appropriation of being, which, however, may always evade. As it is for Heidegger, also for Winnicott, life occurs as an appropriation that takes place against the background of the original negativity. Psychic illness, of which psychosis is the prototype, occurs if the tendency towards integration is *not* allowed to follow its course. That is, psychosis results from the fact that what *should have come to terms* in the beginning of the maturational processes—the baby's structural tendency towards integration and relation with all that is not-me—*did not happen*. This means, according to Winnicott, that life's positivity must be constituted so as to enclose the negativity of the origin, without denying it. It is on the original negativity that the fabric of presence is woven, thereby veiling the abyss of absence. It is only in this way that being and presence may occur: "*Only out of non-existence can existence start*" (1974, p. 95).

This is true for all achievements covered by the label of health, such as the ability to feed oneself and to communicate:

> The only real eating has as its basis *not* eating. It is out of not being creative, out of being isolated, that the creation of objects and of the world comes to have meaning. There is no enjoyment of company except as a development from essential isolation, the isolation that reappears as the individual dies. (1984b, p. 111)

Finally, all achievements are precarious and even what has been achieved may be lost. This is the reason why the "potential space" of playing and cultural life is identified as "the place where we live" (cf. 1971g). Playing is the experience of precariousness itself, of finitude, the area of illusion, which is only valid for a certain time, which opens and closes. This is why playing serves as a paradigm for creative life, the only one that is worth living. Precariousness means that the thread that ties man to life and to life's meaning may always break up, or may never be constituted:

> The link can be made, and usefully made between creative living and living itself, and the reasons can be studied why it is that creative living can be lost and why the individual's feeling that life is real or meaningful can disappear. (1971g, p. 93)

There is no possible *foundation* for this basic question in the metapsychologies that are available to us. The existence of the individual, her ability to be, is not at stake in traditional psychoanalysis. This is what Pontalis (1977) refers to when he states in the preface to his French translation of *Playing and Reality*:

> Even if Winnicott used classical concepts, it seems they were not quite adequate for what he wanted to clarify, it seems that the very idea of an unconscious, imposed on Freud by the psycho-neurotic functioning, does not appear to Winnicott to account for the dimension of *absence*, which he sees as a necessary void in the subject. I shall willingly suggest that if the Freudian topography of the agencies and the psychical places can describe the intrasubjective conflict, for Winnicott, this appears as secondary, as a construction where the self—the subject—is already mutilated. Our entire conception of psychic reality has been modified by this. (Pontalis, 1981, p. 152)

We have here the main reason why very early in his career as a psychoanalyst, Winnicott acknowledged the non-essential character of neuroses with regard to an understanding of human nature. In neuroses, engaging with life is not called into question. The *no* that concerns neuroses is one that occurs *within* life, being part of the individual's history. In psychoses, the *no* denies the possibility of being itself; it is not therefore part of a history, because a history is only constituted on the basis of being. The fundamental questions, of life or death, which afflict psychotics cannot even be formulated within the framework of traditional metapsychology:

> We seldom reach the point at which we can start to describe what life is like *apart from illness or absence of illness*. That is to say, we have yet to tackle the question of *what life itself is about*. Our psychotic patients force us to give attention to this sort of basic problem. (1967b, p. 133; my italics)[63]

Language and the descriptive categories of the theory of maturational processes

Winnicott usually starts the description of the process of emotional development with the later stages, those studied by traditional psychoanalysis, and then presents the more primitive ones, "into the unknown of the earliest moments at which the term human being can be applied to the foetus in the womb" (1988, p. 34). This is what he does, for example, in *Human Nature*.

The choice of this order of presentation is due to the fact that he knows that the vast majority of his presumed readers are psychoanalysts, used to thinking of the already established individual. They are also accustomed to the *language* of metapsychology, which does not refer to a "person", but to a "psychic apparatus", composed of forces, intensities of forces and mental mechanisms, intended to describe pulsional disorders and conflicts.

Since his conception of human nature and of the initial stages also substantially differs from that formulated by metapsychology and traditional psychoanalysis in general, Winnicott is especially careful with the language that he uses to express himself when approaching this theme, precisely in order to deal with the peculiarity of what is happening to the baby at the start of life. He repeatedly underlines that the description of each stage requires a new method of presentation and a specific language (cf. 1988). The language used for the description of human phenomena, he says, "grows up, so to speak, with the growing child" (1964e, p. 9), so that the language adequate for describing the achievements of a stage becomes "wrong" for another stage (1988, p. 34). In particular, it is wrong to describe the initial stages in the same terms as those used for the description of the oedipal phase, when it is assumed that personal identity and wholeness have been achieved; and when an internal life already exists with the presence of unconscious conflicts resulting from instinctual life and interpersonal relationships.

The insistence on changing language is far from being a caprice or an idiosyncrasy, as has been indicated in the Introduction. It reflects the demands imposed on theorisation by the initial phenomena of life themselves. Winnicott strives to communicate what happens, directly and without misrepresentations, in the "magic of intimacy", between the baby and the mother, and between the patient and the analyst in the clinical situation. He knows that in the experiential field, involving babies and psychotics, understanding does not occur in an exclusively intellectual or mental way but demands a type of proximity and communication with the patient, similar to the contact between mother and baby. To this language, essentially, belong silence, pre-verbal and pre-representational communication. In addressing the communication between mother and baby, Winnicott points out that the reader is being led "to a place where verbalization has no meaning" (1968d, p. 91). What connection can there possibly exist between all this and traditional psychoanalysis, which has based itself on the process of verbal interpretation of thoughts and verbalised ideas?

The theory of personal maturational processes not only opens the question of appropriately understanding the initial states, for which an entirely new language becomes necessary, but imposes new conditions on the descriptive language of the later stages. Although Winnicott's approach to the later stages retains a good deal of what is already configured by the classical literature on neurotic disorders, Winnicott indeed makes a *redescription* of phenomena relevant to the oedipal stage and, consequently, of the corresponding theory of neurosis. This redescription, carried out in its own terms, on the basis of the theory of maturational processes, has become necessary as a result of the new paradigm which underpins the whole of his theory.

Notes

1. The implications of the temporal character of human nature are central to the Winnicottian theory of psychoses.
2. In this text, Winnicott indicates that this tendency in his thought was already present, without him realising it, in articles of a decade earlier, that is, approximately from the end of the 1950s and the start of the 1960s. He cites as examples the title of his book *The Maturational Processes and the Facilitating Environment* and the article "Roots of aggression" (1964c), included as the only new chapter in *The Child, the Family, and the Outside World* and also published as an addendum to the article of 1939, "Aggression and its roots", in *Deprivation and Delinquency*.
3. The cited excerpts from Winnicott are in Winnicott, 1963d, p. 93.
4. On the essential split, cf. Winnicott, 1988, part four, Chapter Six.
5. The stages of development, with their respective tasks, will be detailed in Chapters Three and Four.
6. Cf. Chapter Three, section titled "The constitution of the primary self".
7. In many religions, this feature of human life is expressed through the metaphor of the pilgrim. On the wall of a thirteenth century convent in Toledo, Spain, one can read: "*Peregrino, no hay*

caminos, hay que caminar" [Pilgrim, there are no paths, you must walk]. The contemporary Italian composer Luigi Nono (1924–1990) used this line in one of his later compositions, dedicated to the film director A. Tarkovsky, in which the music has a slowness that is frequently unsustainable, almost subversive. Heidegger characterises this same feature by the term *Wanderer*, borrowed from the title of Hölderlin's poem.

8. It is only in Winnicott's book *Human Nature* that we find a sequential presentation of the stages of maturation; throughout Winnicott's work, we can nevertheless find several affirmations that allow us to corroborate this ordering.

9. In any case, achieving something and then losing it is entirely different from never having achieved it.

10. In this point resides one of Winnicott's central arguments for refusing, as inacceptable, Melanie Klein's theory of innate envy. It is not reasonable to attribute this kind of feeling to the infant as far as it presupposes an assessment of the external object in a moment when, given his extreme immaturity, he is not capable of knowing the existence of the external object, and even less, of its attributes. The feeling of envy can only be attributed to the individual who has already achieved the sense of externality.

11. In this same text, Winnicott introduces, *in his own terms*, what he considers to be Melanie Klein's most important contribution to psychoanalysis: the "depressive position". There he affirms: "the term 'depressive position' is a bad name for a normal process, but no one has been able to find a better" (1955c, p. 264). My suggestion is to call this stage, and its corresponding achievement, "concern". On this point, see footnote 31, Chapter Four of this book.

12. On the meaning of the expression "human animal" in Winnicott, cf. Loparic 2000b. In this article, clarifying an aspect of the paradigmatic shift of Winnicott's theory with regard to traditional psychoanalysis, Loparic observes that, while the latter neglected and even expurgated the body in favor of desire and other psychic manifestations, in Winnicott the body become *soma*, is permanently considered. "Freud", says the philosopher, "was not concerned with psychosomatic existence, but with gaps in consciousness, that is, in the psyche. [...] the body was at most included as a physical source of pulsions, regarded as its psychic representatives" (ibid., p. 393).

13. Loparic explains in the same previously mentioned article: "Essential to Winnicott, the term 'psyche' is not current in traditional psychoanalysis. In order to refer to the same domain of phenomena, it prefers the term 'soul', 'mind', 'psychic apparatus', 'subject', among others. Winnicott has never made explicit the reasons for his choice. It is due, at least partially, to etymology. In common Greek, *'psyche'* firstly means life, including animal life, and only secondarily does it mean immaterial or immortal soul, conscious self or the person as center of emotions, desires and feelings. In any case, according to Winnicott, in a certain sense and to a certain degree, the psyche is in the baby since the beginning of life. [...] Winnicott's use of the word *'psyche'* does not suggest anything that may be connected to the spirit, an entity that, according to the traditional interpretation, has the property of existing independently of the body. For the same reason, Winnicott excludes the word 'soul' from his vocabulary, except when designating 'a property of the psyche', which also depends, ultimately, on the brain's functioning and can be healthy or ill" (cf. Loparic, 2000b, p. 361).

14. A mere physical sensation becomes experience because the imaginative elaboration gives sense to it. In 1952, answering to a letter from Money-Kyrle, in which the latter mentioned the utility of drawing a distinction between ideas and sensations, Winnicott agrees but observes that "I would rather say the difference between ideas and experience" (1987b, p. 40).

15. On imaginative elaboration as creation of meaning, cf. Loparic, 2000b, section 7.
16. Cf. 1987b, letter 74. See also Chapter Four, footnote 4.
17. An illustrative example of how imaginative elaboration leads to the schematisation of the body is to be found in the book *Coordination Motrice et Psychomotrice du Tout Petit* (1992), by the experts in psychomotricity, M. M. Béziers and Y. Hunsinger. The proximity to Winnicott's theory was pointed out to me by Maria Emília Mendonça. In the item on changing clothes, the authors say that, when placed on the changer, the baby will push his feet against the person who is changing him. This pressure by the feet is important in many aspects, one of them being that "from the point of view of the static body, the entire extension of the back will be supported in this way by the changer. The baby stretches himself and opens the hip joints (extension) and presses with the feet, which provides him the *image of straightening up,* preparing the 'straightening up in the standing position'" (Béziers & Hunsinger, 1992, p. 49; my italics). There is reason to believe that this "image" is not a visual one, as if the baby saw himself in a standing position. It is rather a schematisation of how he feels to be totally stretched, erect and supported by the feet.
18. Cf. also Winnicott, 1969d.
19. Sometimes, as is the case in this quotation, Winnicott, when referring to any of the aspects of instinctual life, uses the classical terminology and speaks of "id" and "ego". This use has a communicative function, and the sense he gives to such terms in his own theory does not correspond to that attributed to them in traditional theory, ruled by other theoretical assumptions. Here, for example, "id" and "ego" are not instances of the psychic apparatus; the id is not constituted of pulsions. It is the general denomination, already recognised, for human instinctuality: "The instinctual life has to be considered both in terms of the bodily functions and of the imaginative elaboration of these functions. (By instinctual one means what Freud called sexual, i.e. the whole range of local and general excitements which are a feature of animal life; [...])" (1965h, p. 130). The term "ego", in its turn, is used by Winnicott to designate the innate tendency towards development, in the sense of integration.
20. For a clarification of the use of the term "ego" in Freud and Winnicott, see section 10 of this chapter. Beyond the difference between the theories, regarding the "ego", the essential point in the question presented here is the fact that Winnicott conceives existence as psycho-somatic and constituted by experience, which is equally psycho-somatic, and not merely representational.
21. If, for centuries, medicine only considered the organic, psychoanalysis contributed to a perspective, which is nowadays widespread, in which everything is credited to the psychic aspect, with a complete disregard for the body autonomy, including the temporal one.
22. An interesting fact on the eternal discussion of the relations between body and psyche (or mind) is to be found in the item "psychoses" of the *"Enciclopedia de psiquiatria"* of Editorial "El Ateneo": the term "psychosis" was first used in a strictly psychiatric sense in the nineteenth century, by Ernst von Feuchtersleben (1806–1848), dean of the Medical Faculty of Vienna. "He used the terms psychoses and psychopathy indistinctly to mean mental illness, as a different thing from 'neurosis', or 'nerve infirmity'. According to Feuchtersleben, *the notion of infirmity does not derive from the mind, nor from the body, but from the relation of one to the other.* What is important is the interplay between both instances, and the way such process is configured, either as a unity or as 'body-soul' duality. The author limited himself to describing this situation and did not intend to explore its 'real complexity'" (Resnik, 1977 *apud* Vidal, Bleichmar, & Usandivaras (orgs.), 1977, p. 539; my italics).
23. In these cases, in general, it may occur that the imaginative elaboration gives a persecutory sense to the pain or distress.

24. For the detailing of the functions of child thinking, cf. Winnicott, 1989s.
25. "Rudimentary" here has nothing to do with the baby's mental capacity, which may even become exceptional if he is allowed to develop naturally.
26. According to Winnicott, this constitutes one of the important sources of headache as symptom.
27. Cf. Winnicott, 1954a.
28. It is important to mention here the distinction between hereditary and congenital factors. Heredity, in any of its meanings, relates to factors which existed before conception. The term "congenital" refers to two sets of disorders: those that include illnesses and deficiencies which existed prior to birth (during pregnancy) and those resulting from sequels of birth (cf. 1988, p. 38).
29. An eloquent example of how a child with a hereditary physical deformity may reach the sense of being a healthy self is offered in Winnicott, 1971d, pp. 262–265.
30. This picture configures one of the defensive organisations of schizophrenic type in which a split is present, designated by Winnicott as "split-off intellect".
31. States of mental confusion and serious learning difficulties have almost always been diagnosed, within a psychiatric context, as mental deficiency. Apart from cases of organic lesion, according to Winnicott, these are emotional disorders of the development process, related to environmental failure in the provision of care to these children. (Cf., for example, the case of Ashton, Chapter Twenty-five (1996c), by Winnicott, 1996a).
32. This category refers to those illnesses that are unquestionably physical, such as polio and scurvy.
33. We can thus say that Winnicott conceives a non-causal theory of psychic disorders, which will be addressed below, in this same chapter. This is why Loparic calls the Winnicottian baby "ongoing", attributing to him the sense of being that Heidegger gives to *Dasein*.
34. This will hence be one of the central aspects of therapeutic work: to provide the conditions for the experiencing for the first time, under the special conditions of the analytical setting, of what has not been experienced.
35. The concepts of subjective world, area of illusion of omnipotence and capacity for illusion, central to Winnicott's thought, will be detailed in Chapter Three.
36. This is a line from T. S. Eliot's last "quartet".
37. Cf. Clare Winnicott, 1989.
38. The importance of the environment for the shaping of the individual's personality is not new. Already in 1946, the publication of Anna Freud's book *The ego and the mechanisms of defence* (1946/1968), provoked a reassessment of the role of maternity and environmental care in the primitive development of the infant. The works of Dorothy Burlingham and Anna Freud (1942), during the war, resulted in the development of the study about the external condition and its effects. Before the war, John Bowlby studied the backgrounds of disturbed children and, in a formal study of 150 children with various types of problems, discovered a direct link between theft and privation, with this later related in particular to separation from the mother during the early years of childhood (cf. Bowlby, 1951; Winnicott, 1951a). An important and detailed study on environment in Winnicott's work was developed by Serralha, C., 2007.
39. It is worth noting that in Winnicott, all achievements and capacities, that is, everything that the individual appropriates, starts from a non-capacity, an absence, a negative from which something emerges. This negativity, which is at the origin, is never entirely surpassed. It remains as the mark of precariousness of all life's achievements. Everything that comes into being may subsequently cease to be. This is one of the possible approximations of Winnicott's thought, without him knowing it, to M. Heidegger's ontology of finitude. This point will be resumed at the end of Chapter Four, in the section referring to death and the return to the beginning.

40. This expression was proposed for the first time, by Z. Loparic. Cf. Loparic, 1997a.
41. The conception of an environment that, at the outset, is not external to the baby, but a part of him, is entirely original not only to traditional psychoanalysis, but to psychology in general, and can only be understood in its peculiarity from the theory of personal development. This is the reason why, when we try to compare Melanie Klein and Winnicott, via the internal/external polarisation, we consider it a badly formulated question, and a fruitless debate, since when either of them mentions environment, they are not referring to the same thing.
42. In some passages of his work, as is the case in the following one, Winnicott asserts that, at the initial moment, what we find is "the complete merging of the individual in the environment, that which is implied in the words primary narcissism" (1988, p. 157). In the same work, he explains what he understands by primary narcissism: "Primary narcissism, or the state *prior to* the acceptance of the fact of an environment, is the only state out of which environment can be created" (1988, p. 130). In another text, referring to the immaturity and dependence that characterise this initial moment, we read: "I have never been satisfied with the use of the word 'narcissistic' in this connection, because the whole concept of narcissism leaves out the tremendous differences that result from the general attitude and behavior of the mother" (1972, p. 191).
43. This point of the theory will be explained in Chapter Four, section titled "The return to the origin".
44. The transitional stage and the phenomena of transitionality will be presented in Chapter Four, titled "Transitionality".
45. Psychoanalysts of Freudian and Kleinian orientation find it difficult to accept the idea that, initially, the relationship is exclusively with the mother, that is, purely dual, since this discards the conception of the Oedipus complex as structuring the individual.
46. The good-enough mother is the model of the analyst in Winnicottian clinical practice. Having preserved the differences, what is valid for the former is applicable for the latter. Regarding the mother's need to be "very good", I recall a young man who had been suffocated by such necessity in his mother. When entering the room in my practice for the first time, he said: "Why so many cushions? Do I have to use them all?"
47. This is another example of how Winnicott starts from negativity, from not-being-yet, in order for any achievement to make sense. In other passages, noting that the only real eating has not-eating as a basis, Winnicott observes that this point makes a formidable contribution to the issue of anorexia. Cf., for example, Winnicott, 1963d, p. 95 and 1965j, p. 182.
48. The distinction between "being" and "doing", between the breast that "is" and the breast that "does", will be examined in greater detail in Chapter Three, section titled "The constitution of the primary self".
49. In the preface of the book *Talking to Parents* (1993a), the editors mention that Winnicott, supported and stimulated by Isa Benzie during the long series of radio lectures for the BBC, reported that it was she, who, in his words, "pulled the phrase 'the ordinary devoted mother' out of what I had talked about […]. This immediately became a peg to hang things on, and it suited my need to get away from both idealization and also from teaching and propaganda. I could get on with a description of child care as practised unselfconsciously everywhere" (1993a, p. xiv).
50. Winnicott points out again and again for the danger of sentimentality, which, according to him, is the denial of the natural hate from the part of the parents for being so affected by their children. Some lullabies are the expression of the parent's need to express their hate, preventing them from retaliating, which then would indeed be unbearable for the baby. One of these songs says:

> "Rockabye baby, on the tree top,
> When the wind blows the cradle will rock,
> When the bough breaks the cradle will fall,
> Down will come baby, cradle and all".

Some of the Brazilian lullabies also go in this direction:

> "Boi, boi, boi
> Boi da cara preta,
> Pega esse menino
> Que tem medo de careta".
> [Bull, bull, bull,
> Bull with a black face,
> come and catch this boy
> who's afraid of grimaces]

51. On the role of the father in environmental facilitation and possible paternal failures which hinder personal development, see the complex and exhaustive work of Claudia Dias Rosa, 2011.
52. Sometimes Winnicott is criticised for attributing an excessive responsibility to the mother and for the fact that this responsibility falls upon the mother and not the father. Feminists in general do not accept these ideas. Elisabeth Badinter, for example, cites WinnIcott's concept of the good-enough mother with extreme irony and equal incomprehension (1980). Winnicott however, describes and addresses the needs of the baby and not theories and/or ideologies. Regarding the fact that, in relation to the foundations of personality, the main responsibility lies with the mother, this duty does not seem to be excessive when we think that the period of absolute adaptation takes only a few months, two, three or four, and what the mother is doing is to avoid that her child is psychotic. Moreover, in the event that she was able to regress to the natural condition of primary maternal preoccupation, this will not be an overload but a need of the mother herself.
53. On this contribution by the father during the initial stages and on a few theoretical additions to this question, cf. Chapter Four, sub-section titled "The stage of concern".
54. Cf. the case of Sally, seventeen months, in Winnicott, 1996c, p. 207.
55. Winnicott reports the unprecedented case of a child who gave the name "Family" to his transitional object, noting how incredibly early this child tried to repair his parents' failure to provide a feeling of family cohesion. Thirty years later, this individual is still struggling with his incapacity for accepting his distance from his parents and the definitive disintegration of the family (cf. 1986d).
56. The stage of concern will be developed in Chapter Four.
57. This subject, as well as that of the place of the father in the Oedipus complex, will be addressed in Chapter Four, respectively in the description of the stage of concern and of the oedipal stage.
58. This conception naturally has theoretical consequences, one of which is the fact that the ego structuring is related to pulsional vicissitudes. On Winnicott's comment to this question, cf. Winnicott, 1964b.
59. Cf. Winnicott, 1989j.
60. In "Creativity and its origins" (1971g), Winnicott affirms that both schizoids and personalities of false self type ("extroverts") "have a sense that something is wrong and that there is a

dissociation in their personalities, and they would like to be helped to achieve unit status [...]" (1971g, p. 90).

61. Winnicott is not the only thinker, in the context of the theory of psychic disorders, to refuse the causal conception of man. Tellenbach, a psychiatrist influenced by phenomenology, also points to the difference between causality in the strict sense and of "having an origin". In his interpretation of the aetiology of melancholy, the causality principle is replaced by the principle of correlation. He resorts to analogy in order to express the difference: we cannot affirm, holds Tellenbach, that "trees blossom *because* it is spring". As regarding anything that flourishes from itself, we must say: "Trees blossom now that is spring even hibernation goes along with winter, and animal rut with autumn" (Tellenbach, 1980, p. 198).

62. It is quite common, and must be considered normal, the author says, that the child is the result of a little accident and "it is sentimental to put too much stress on the idea that the child was conceived in relation to any conscious wish" (1987c, p. 52).

63. There is also no way that we can find support for this question in philosophies of metaphysical type, in which the field of reflection is being as presence in its full positivity. We need Heidegger here. Rooted in non-being, there is, in the individual, an original split, essential and insurmountable. Juliano Pessanha, in his text on temporality in Freud and Heidegger, observes: "To break into the world, to give in to the temptation of existing, is to fall into scenes that distribute to each one a 'name', 'reality', 'duration', etc. This entry is a cut; a split between the strangeness of exile (*das Unheimliche*), the space of the night, where I am not yet, and the clear day of history (the house) which weaves me and speaks my name" (Pessanha, 1992, p. 82). Reaching life, endowing it with consistence and sense is an achievement. It is the work of forgetting, through the adhesion to the world's positivity, the primordial void that creeps in everywhere. Man, "thrown into the possibilities of the world, has already engaged in the fabric of meanings, having achieved a 'being' and a 'duration'. This duration is nevertheless always ultimately gnawed away, and marked by impossibility. To persist in the duration, to watch over the maintenance of the big factory of the world is to forget about the end, to escape, turning one's back on the great exile" (Pessanha, 1992, p. 82).

CHAPTER THREE

The primitive stages: absolute dependence

The prenatal stage: spontaneity and reactivity[1]

After presenting some general aspects of the theory of maturational processes, I shall now move on to the *description of the initial stages*, starting in this third chapter with the most primitive ones: intrauterine life, birth, the period immediately after birth, and the stage of the theoretical first feed, covering the entire period during which the baby lives in a state of absolute dependence on the mother.

When does the maturational process begin? In other words, at what point during gestation is it possible to consider that there is already a human being capable of having experiences? According to Winnicott, it is neither possible nor relevant to determine the exact point at which the foetus may start to be regarded as a human being who can be studied from a psychological viewpoint. Probably, he says that the only certain date is that of conception (cf. 1988, p. 29).

At some point after conception, a "first awakening" occurs, after which there is "a simple state of being, and a dawning awareness of the continuity of being and of the continuity of existence in time" (1988, p. 135). It is difficult, if not impossible, to observe this state directly: "It belongs to the infant and not to the observer" (1988, p.127).[2] Having reached the state of being, what the baby needs is *to go on being*. All other needs arise from the fact that the baby *is* and *has to go on being*. Throughout life until death, the continuity of being will remain as the fundamental problem; its preservation is equivalent to health.[3]

At a certain point during gestation, babies begin to move inside the uterus, and it is most likely that sensations begin during this phase. Clinical evidence allows us to assume that both the movement and the calm experienced in intrauterine life are meaningful to the babies and are somehow recorded. This is also due to the fact that cerebral development has reached a certain level, enabling the foetus to retain body memories. It is therefore likely that the storage of experience begins at that time, as does a central organisation of them, so that "body memories which *are personal* begin to gather in order to form a new human being" (1988, p. 21; my italics). This means that from a point before birth, nothing that a human being experiences is lost (cf. 1988, p. 127).

In terms of the personal maturation, the fundamental question, even at this initial stage, refers to the *opposition between spontaneity and reactivity*, an opposition that will be present in increasingly complex fashion throughout life. Searching for the appropriate language to describe this initial moment, Winnicott resorts to an analogy suggested to him by a patient:[4] the baby or the foetus is like a bubble. If outside pressure is adapted to internal pressure, the bubble can go on "existing". In the case of the human baby, we say that he goes on "being". If, on the other hand, pressure outside the bubble is bigger or smaller than inside, the bubble will react to the intrusion (impingement): it will be modified in reaction to a change in the environment, and not from an impulse of its own. For human beings, this means *an interruption of being, produced by a reaction to intrusion*. Once the intrusion ceases, the reaction also disappears, and the continuity of being may thence be re-established.

The decisive question is: where does the movement that generates contact start? Does the movement derive from demands arising from the baby's "aliveness", or is it a reaction to a change in the environment, a reaction that interrupts the continuity of being? In the former case, the baby is sleeping or quietly withdrawn and the mother preserves his isolation undisturbed, waiting for the moment when he will again make a movement, when he once again discovers the environment. The mother who follows this toing-and-froing of the baby from quietness to movement and vice-versa without interfering, based on the baby's needs, establishes a certain relationship pattern. In this case, the experiences and the body memories of the experiences *are personal*.

In the latter case, the initiative of movement arises from the environment. If it repeatedly anticipates the baby's movement, a pattern of relationship is established that may be called *intrusive*. During intrauterine life, the baby is more protected from invasive environmental movements, such as the oscillations in mood of an unstable mother. Even the conditions of intrauterine life are far from being the ideal ones, as is commonly assumed. There is growing empirical evidence that the foetus can feel sudden changes in the mother's cardiac rhythm, sharp movements or the effects of toxic or disorganised eating. Winnicott already knew that the mother's rigidity or inability to adapt, resulting from anxiety or from a depressive state, could affect the baby even before birth (cf. 1988). Environmental invasions force the baby to react and in this case, may establish a premature state of alertness, which has nothing to do with the perception of something, but with a certain tone of vigilance due to the potential threat of invasion (cf. 1974). The opposition between spontaneity and reactivity shows that "environmental influences can start at a very early age to determine whether a person will go out for experience or withdraw from the world when seeking reassurance that life is worth living" (1988, p. 128).

All of this becomes clearer after birth, when the baby must deal more directly with the mother's modes of being and with her emotional states. If she tends to act according to her own needs or anxiety and not to the changing needs of the baby, there is an intrusion, and the baby reacts. The reaction to invasion breaks the baby's *continuity of being*, since it bears no relationship to the vital process of that individual: "the infant that is disturbed by being forced to react is disturbed out of a state of 'being'. This state of 'being' can obtain only under certain conditions. *When reacting, an infant is not 'being'"* (1958f, p. 185; my italics).

If the contact is made on the basis of the spontaneous gesture of the baby, both the fact that he is alive and his own experience are felt as real and the accumulation of these personal experiences begins to integrate into personality; when, on the other hand, the reaction to the intrusion subtracts something from the sensation of true living, this may only be recovered by means of a return to isolation and quiet.

The experience of birth

Whatever the moment of the "first awakening", the fact is that at some point close to birth, the "great awakening" occurs, when "the baby, already alerted for the high dive" (1968d, p. 91). The effectiveness of the great awakening may be demonstrated by the perceptible difference that exists between a baby who is born prematurely and a post-term baby. The former is not yet ready for extra-uterine life, appearing poorly prepared for that condition, whereas the latter shows signs of having stayed too long in the uterus, being subjected to a sort of "state of frustration" for having been kept waiting when he was ready.[5]

The birth process is not traumatic in itself; it will only be so due to problems that may arise during birth.[6] Birth is considered normal when the foetus is able to cope with the reaction to the inevitable invasions on the occasion. The birth process evidently causes a discontinuity, even when everything goes well, although this can be tolerated, since the baby has already had several experiences of interruption of the continuity of being during intrauterine life, since he has not only accumulated body memories but has also organised defences against possible traumas.

The condition characterising normal birth is the baby being born at the right time, a full-term birth, that is, after nine months of life in the uterus, a deadline on which both physiology and psychology agree. For normal births, physiology coincides with "the readiness of the baby to abandon the uterus", so that he can feel the whole process as something natural, something which emerges from his own impulse. The birth process may nevertheless be traumatic and this will happen if, due to problems during birth, *delay* or *anticipation* occurs. These are the conditions, of a *temporal* nature, which characterise abnormal birth.[7] Difficulties and accidents of this type occur and are traumatic to various degrees, depending on the baby's capacity for tolerating intrusion, but they need not necessarily be decisive, unless a physical injury occurs. Apart from cases of physical injuries, which have their own psychological consequences, we may observe the differences which exist between the needs of a baby born in due time and those of the individual whose birth was traumatic as a result of being delayed or premature. It is precisely here that the "adaptation to the needs" of the good enough mother gains significance: it is up to her to understand and to adapt to the differences of the singular baby.

When everything goes well, birth constitutes an experience of great value for the future individual. The proof of this is the pleasure which almost all children and some adults extract from activities and games involving the dramatisation of one or another aspect of the birth process. This is why, if a baby is born by Caesarean section or is in a state of deep anaesthesia because the mother has been anaesthetised, he will have missed something very important, since from the baby's point of view, in the normal birth process "it was the infant's impulse that produced the changes and the physical progression, usually head first, towards an unknown and new position" (1988, p. 144). Hence, for the baby, the birth took place as a result of his own impulse; he was thus the one who made it happen.

At the same time, there is no reason to overestimate this experience. It is one of a series of factors, which are favourable for the development of reliability, stability, safety, etc. In cases in which everything went well during the birth process, it is unlikely that the birth experience will emerge as an important point in analysis. It is only when the complications of the birth process exceed the limits which the baby can tolerate, when unbearable degrees of invasion occur with their consequent reactions, that it becomes traumatic and a serious distortion may result, related to the premature and forced start of mental functioning. When this happens, the experience will be resumed several times in analysis, which is frequent in the treatment of psychotics.[8]

First moments of extra-uterine life

It is not as soon as the baby is born that he needs nourishment, or is completely ready to search for it. What he certainly needs is some time to recover from the discontinuities inherent to the birth process and to return to the feeling of continuity of being. This usually leads him into a state of quiescence. Crucially, he also needs the mother to establish contact with him. In addition to this, the development of the brain, combined with "the great awakening" and the experience of birth keep the baby busy with his new condition, at the same time as the primitive mind is cataloguing impressions and the series of small reactions to inevitable invasions of the new environmental situation.

In general, the newly born baby is extremely susceptible to all sensations relating to touch, temperature conditions, light, texture, etc., but, above all, there are two new facts with which he must deal: the start of breathing and the first experience of the action of gravity. We often assume that the inaugural experience of breathing is traumatic in itself. In Winnicott's view, however, what may be traumatic is not the start of breathing but a significant *delay* in it, associated with a prolonged birth. The start of breathing almost always occurs without major problems and is hardly significant (traumatic), except for inaugurating the sensation of something coming in and going out. At subsequent stages, difficulties involving breathing, such as asthma, will be linked to this first experience, which becomes a prototype for the "comes in and goes out". For babies who have suffered excessive invasions, "the to and fro of breathing is found to be intolerable", since the sensations related to breathing, which are "intolerably real", represent a total lack of defence and control over what moves in and out (cf. 1988). In addition to breathing, there is also the fact, unprecedented for the baby, of the action of gravity, which had not yet entered into play during intrauterine life. Accustomed to being contained all around, the baby now feels after birth that he is "pushed up from below". An alteration occurs, therefore, "from being loved from all directions to being loved from below only" (1988, p. 130).[9] This is why maternal care in physically "holding" the baby is not only that of holding, but of enveloping him from all sides.

The recovery of the continuity of being after delivery requires the reconnection with certain conditions which precede birth; in intrauterine life, the baby was used to feeling the mother's breathing, her abdominal movements, her body noises or her rhythmic changes of pressure, and it is likely that he needs to re-establish contact with these physiological functions of the mother. All of these experiences initiate communication with the mother, in addition to facilitating the constitution of time, a time that is necessarily primitive, subjective and pre-chronological. These are very subtle experiences, says Winnicott, which only human contact can provide.

A mother who is capable of identifying with the baby from the beginning will wait until he is ready for contact. Only in this way will contact not be felt as invasion, with the baby able to start having drives again and even to seek nourishment. If the mother is too anxious to play her part as provider, she will be incapable of letting the baby explore the breast with the mouth or with his little hands before feeding, or to hold it with his gums. Each baby has his own way of making his approach to the breast, and the mother knows that it will take time to understand the ways of her baby. What she needs is the opportunity to be natural and to find her own way with her baby (cf. 1988, p. 105). It is these aspects which appear to be simple but which involve highly complex issues that characterise the nature of the absolute dependence of the infant and the task incumbent on the mother.

The stage of the theoretical first feed: the fundamental tasks

In order to avoid the idea that the first concrete feed is the great inaugural moment of nursing, Winnicott uses the expression "theoretical first feed" to refer to the sequence of first concrete experiences in feeding. The stage that receives this name covers approximately the first three or four months of the infant's life. As its name states, during this period, the activity of breastfeeding is central, but this does not mean that feeding as satisfaction of hunger corresponds to what is essential. Nor does it mean that orality, in terms of libidinal contact, is the main aspect to be observed. Since the emphasis is on personal maturational processes and not on the development of sexual functions, the issue is not the configuration of the initial erogenous zones or the nature of the pulsional manifestation, but the beginning of contact with reality and of the constitution of a self which will gradually integrate into a unity. Instinctuality and erogeneity belong to and participate in the maturational processes, but do not constitute them. Alluding to the fact that traditional psychoanalysis has dealt almost entirely with instinctual needs (ego and id), neglecting the needs of the maturing being in a personal sense, Winnicott affirms:

> we are more concerned with the environmental provision which makes all the rest possible; that is to say, we are more concerned here and now with the mother *holding* the baby than with the mother *feeding* the baby. (1965k, pp. 147–148)

In Winnicott's theory, breastfeeding is the privileged situation during which, when everything goes well, the *beginnings of the relation to external reality are established*, of which the mother is the first representative. What is most important here is the quality of the human contact, the reality of the experiences that are being provided to the baby *through the act of breastfeeding*: the encounter with something which he does not know is an object, and the beginning of a very special communication with the mother, verbally unrepeatable and also the beginning of mutuality. This is why:

> [...] when the mother and the baby come to terms with each other in the feeding situation this is the initiation of a human relationship. This sets the pattern for the child's capacity for relating to objects and to the world. (1968f, p. 64)

The mother is thus the baby's first "object", with the following proviso: in this context, the term "object", as well as the expression "object relating" have a very peculiar condition; they should not be understood in the sense in which they are used both in traditional psychoanalysis and in common sense, presupposing the perception, from the start of something external to the baby, a capacity which, according to Winnicott, cannot be admitted at this point.[10]

At the stage of the theoretical first feed, the baby is involved in three tasks: (1) from the state of unintegration, carrying out the experiences of integration into space-time, that is, the temporalisation and spatialisation of the baby (*integration*); (2) the gradual indwelling of the psyche in the body (*personalisation*); (3) the beginning of object relations, which will later culminate in the creation and acknowledgement of the independent existence of objects and of an external world (*realization or having reality*), "that is, making real the infant's creative impulse" (1965s, p. 19). Winnicott refers to these fundamental tasks in numerous passages in his work, presenting them in varied orders. In *Human Nature*, he states that there is no obvious sequence that may determine the order of the description. However, in the 1962 text, "Ego integration in child development" (1965n), where central aspects of the theory of personal development are introduced, he states that the main tendency of the maturational processes is integration into space and time, beginning his description with this task, followed by that of the indwelling of the psyche in the body and finally by the beginning of contact with reality. In the article "Fear of breakdown" (1974), it is this same order that presides over the enumeration of the tasks: "In such a facilitating environment, the individual undergoes development which can be classified as *integrating*, to which is added *indwelling (or psycho-somatic collusion)* and then *object-relating*" (1974, p. 89). This is the order to which priority shall be given in this text.

The three basic tasks are mutually interdependent and none of them can be fully achieved without the others. Their discrimination has the function of clarifying a certain degree of specificity of these fundamental achievements. When all goes well, the baby faces these tasks more or less simultaneously, since, in order to initiate a sense of real and to be able to inhabit a real world, which is initially subjective, the baby must be gradually introduced into the order of time and space. Spatialisation begins with the gradual process of indwelling of the psyche in the body, making this body, which is held in the mother's arms, the first home. Dwelling in the body, the baby can start to occupy space, make presence concrete, establish distances and proximities and access the transitory nature of what ages and dies. Space and time are not objects to be found; they are, insofar as they are articulated with each other and constitute worlds, the condition for the possibility of finding any object. The three basic achievements form the foundations of an existence, which, because of the innate tendency towards development, moves towards integration into a unitary self.

As these tasks are being performed and the achievements are being organised with each other through the functioning of the ego, another task is being processed: *the constitution of the self as identity*. This fourth task was only mentioned together with the others after the mid-1960s.

It would only be made explicit in 1966, when, on finishing his theory of the subjective object, Winnicott introduced the concept of primary identification: during the excited experience of breastfeeding, the baby *becomes the object*, having his first experiences of identity.[11]

All these tasks are fundamental and express the basic needs of the baby, which stem from the primordial need to continue to be. They will have a certain degree of resolution concerning this initial stage; the establishment of the basis of personality and psychic health depends on that resolution. They nevertheless remain as tasks which, while growing in complexity in the subsequent stages, *will never be fully abandoned*.

In order for the basic tasks to be successfully accomplished, to become achievements of maturation, specific maternal care is required: integration in time and space corresponds to holding; the indwelling of the psyche in the body is facilitated by handling, which is a more specific aspect of holding, related to physical care; contact with objects is provided by object presenting. At the same time as the mother facilitates each of the baby's tasks in a specialised manner, the series of care actions by the mother constitutes the *total environment*, and the mode of being of the totality of care shapes a *world* for the baby. The first world that the baby inhabits is necessarily a *subjective world*, with the central characteristic of being reliable. Above all, environmental reliability means predictability: the mother prevents something unexpected from startling the baby, interrupting his continuity of being; the mother is reliable when, in the midst of the ever changing needs of the baby, who is sometimes quiet and sometimes excited, she maintains both herself and the environment constant and consistent so that, over time, the baby is gradually temporalised, becoming able, through the repetition of experiences, to recognise things and anticipate events.

I highlight here the distinction that Winnicott draws between world and objects. The world inhabited by the baby is one thing; the objects which may be encountered (created) within this world are another. *In order to encounter objects, a world, a context in which these objects may be found, must exist.* It is of great importance to note that besides being the object to be encountered (object-mother), the mother is initially also the context, the environment in which the encounter with the object may happen (environment-mother). Since she maintains the environment constant, regular, simple, monotonous, and predictable and since she allows the baby to create the object that he encounters, she provides him with the *illusion of omnipotence*, which, as we shall see, is the basis for *believing in ...* This is not a question of believing in this or that, but about the capacity for "believing in ..." Winnicott says: "I cling to this ugly, incomplete phrase, belief in ..." (1963d, p. 94). The sentence tends to be completed, over time, with the belief that the world can be found and is reliable, that there is something somewhere which makes sense or someone who understands and responds to the need. The most important environmental care to be provided to the child in order to establish the capacity for "belief in ..." is that he may "live for an adequate period in a subjective world in which the world of external reality does not impinge" (1989n, p. 286). The world that is initially constituted is the *subjective world*, that is, a reliable ambience, made of the totality of maternal provision.

Primary creativity

In order to accomplish the tasks of the initial stage, the baby relies on his *own* innate tendency towards maturation and on *primary creativity*. The baby nevertheless cannot create the world in a vacuum with only his own resources; a good enough provision of care is required so that he can realise his creative potential, making it real. Creativity is finite and must be exercised in order to stay alive.

Winnicott's concept of primary creativity is unprecedented in the context of psychoanalysis. Thoroughly altering the idea that the psyche, from its beginning, is constituted on the basis of mental mechanisms of projection and introjection[12] and that human creativity is a tributary of sublimated pulsions, Winnicott formulates the idea of a primary psychic creativity, which is inherent to human nature and is present from the onset: "The world is created anew by each human being, who starts on the task at least as early as at the time of birth and of the theoretical first feed" (1988, p. 110). It is the baby, says Winnicott, who "creates the breast, the mother and the world" (1989e, p. 457). Intimately related to basic spontaneity and opposed to reactivity, primary creativity participates in the constitution of what will be the unitary self, since "it is only in being creative that the individual discovers the self" (1971k, p. 73).

Both at this initial moment and during any subsequent phase, creativity is not about making something or an original or artistic output, but about how the individual relates to the sense of reality that characterises a given moment of the maturational processes; in time, the capacity to transit through the various senses of reality is added to this, without losing contact with the personal and imaginative world. Throughout life, and while developing, the healthy individual will go on exercising creativity in increasingly complex ways, but it is on the basis of *primary creativity* that any creative life can be constructed: creativity, then, "is the retention throughout life of something which belongs properly to the experience of the infant: the ability to create the world" (1986h, p. 40).

As is the case with other human potentialities, primary creativity, which creates the world and the various senses of real, must be exercised from the start of life; otherwise, it will wither away, and the individual will not become able to provide a personal meaning to the world. In order for the baby to be able to exercise it, the presentation of objects must initially be made in such a way that, at the same time as the infant establishes a relation with these objects, he is kept under the illusion of omnipotence, that is, he creates what he needs without any awareness of the assistance which makes this action possible. We shall see how this happens when all goes well.

On the occasion of the theoretical first feed, being endowed with primary creativity and provided with the necessary care, the baby already has "a personal contribution to make" (1988, p. 110). Supported by an instinctual tension (which he cannot yet acknowledge as emerging from himself), the baby reaches out with his hand or mouth towards an alleged object (he does not even suspect the existence of something). It is a "spontaneous gesture", since it arises from a "personal" need derived from the baby's aliveness. At this point, says Winnicott, *"the baby is ready to be creative"*. His spontaneous gesture announces: *I need ..., I am searching for something ...* and, at this very moment, the facilitating mother places the breast in a position where it can be found, or turns the baby on the side, or provides what he needs to make him feel more comfortable. A feeling may then occur, which would be formulated as follows: *this is what I needed*. The baby will be able to complete the sentence "*I need ...*" with "*... a turn-over, a breast, a nipple etc*" (1968d, p. 100).

When the mother responds adaptively to the spontaneous gesture, the baby feels as if the nipple and the milk were the result of his own gesture: he experiences *creating what he encounters*. The mother knows that what the baby created in accordance with his need was actually found. She nevertheless has a commitment to the baby, consisting of never asking him whether he found or created the object. The paradox is inherent, says Winnicott; it is not there to be resolved, but to be sustained and endured. Through her absolute adaptation, the mother accomplishes what may be her most important task: to introduce the baby to *the illusion* that he is the one who creates the world that he needs. This is a necessary illusion since "each child must be enabled to create the world (the mother's adaptive technique enables this to feel to be a fact) else the world is to have no meaning" (1984b, p. 111).

We could consider, as in traditional theory, that the baby "hallucinates" the object; as this is the initial moment, however, this cannot be affirmed, since hallucination will only be possible shortly afterwards, when through repeated experience, mnemonic material exists which is sufficiently well installed to be used in hallucination, that is, in creation, now enriched with the details drawn from experiences. Initially, *the baby's condition is only that of creating the object*. The motive is "the personal need" (1988, p. 102).

For a baby who has never had a feed, hunger arises and, even though he is "ready to conceive of something" (1947b, p. 90), he does not know what to expect, since he has no previous experience. If at this point the mother places the breast where the baby reaches out for something and if he is given enough time to explore with his mouth, hands, and the sense of smell, "the baby 'creates' just what is there to be found" (idem). With the repetition of experiences, the baby forms "the illusion that this real breast is exactly the thing that was created out of need, greed, and the first impulses of primitive loving" (idem). Since every part of the experience is recorded somewhere, over time, the baby "may be creating something like the very breast that mother has to offer" (cf. 1947b, p. 90). Prior to weaning, on the thousands of occasions when the mother offers this peculiar experience of introduction to external reality to the baby and, since the breast is there to be created/found, the baby feels repeatedly that he creates what he needs. As a result, the hope and subsequently the belief will be established that "there is a live relationship between inner reality and external reality, between innate primary creativity and the world at large which is shared by all" (1947b, p. 90).

Providing the baby with the possibility of creating that which he encounters is an extremely delicate act of care, not contained in any specific action by the mother, but rather in "how" she presents the baby with the small samples of the world that he is apt to experience in the context of his omnipotence.[13] With regard to the constitution of the capacity for object relations, the baby depends entirely on *how* each fragment of the world is presented to him. It is these "modes of being" of the care, that is, the totality of the care making up the world created by the mother which, in a given way, update or also hinder the baby's tendency to be and his gradual integration into a unity. Firstly, the world must be presented to him in small doses, in a comprehensible way, which makes sense, that is, which does not surprise him. It is also necessary to avoid coincidences that would overburden the baby: the baby should not be moved to another room when he has chicken pox or earache, in order not to abuse his limited comprehension. Furthermore, if he is withdrawn into isolation or quietness, the mother understands that he *is not there to be found*; interacting with him on that occasion, imposing outside needs will interrupt his continuity of being at that moment, since when the creativity of the baby is absent, the samples of world that the mother presents him do not make sense. On the other hand, if the baby makes a gesture and the mother is absent, distracted, or self-absorbed, the gesture will be stalled in space, waiting for something that does not come.[14] In any of these cases, the result is not frustration, since there is not yet any desire, which is a highly sophisticated feeling characteristic of a unitary self, but breakdown in the continuity of being. If this is the pattern of the environmental attitude, then, annihilation may occur.

The paradox contained in the illusion of omnipotence lies in the fact that what the baby created was actually found by him (from the perspective of the observer) and was already there before he created it. However, *what the baby created is not exactly what the mother offered*, in the same way that *we never find in reality what we imagine*. This disparity will never be solved. It is inherent to human nature, and we will always have to deal with it throughout life.[15] Initially, however, the baby does not know anything about this, and it is vital not only for his psychic health but also for the richness of his personality, that the mother is able to allow the illusion to be established. Initiating the baby into the capacity for illusion is the essential task of the good-enough mother. She does this by keeping him for the adequate amount of time in a subjective world, presided over by the illusion of omnipotence: she protects his continuity of being, preventing an unpredictable outburst of a type of reality (which is external for the observer) that is not comprehensible to the baby during this primitive moment. Through the very paths of maturation, in his own time, the baby will have to create the externality of the world and achieve the capacity to relate to external reality without this representing a threat to his personal self; this capacity nevertheless depends on the fact that he was initially taken care of in such a way that the inaugural presentation of the world offered to him did not imply the loss of reality of the subjective world.

> For the lucky infant the world starts off behaving in such a way that it joins up with his/her imagination, and so the world is woven into the texture of the imagination, and the inner life of the baby is enriched with what is perceived in the external world. (1949a, pp. 73–74)

Excited states and quiet states

Before examining each of the fundamental tasks, we must distinguish between two states of the baby which are in permanent alternation with each other: excited and quiet. The two states and the delicate transition from one to the other represent something with which the individual will have to contend throughout his life; how he does this is determined by the way in which, with the help of the mother, this is initially done. What the baby needs at this point follows the guidelines described in the previously mentioned metaphor of the bubble and relates to the opposition between spontaneity and reactivity. While the quiet states are more clearly the occasion for tasks of integration in time and space, as well as the indwelling of the psyche in the body, the excited states are more directly related to the beginning of the establishment of contact with reality (when sucking and grasping objects), in addition to being the privileged moment for the observation of the roots of aggression.

The excited states

The emergence of an excited state in the baby may be described as follows: while he is in a quiet state, whether sleeping or simply resting, a drive emerges, almost always on the crest of an instinctual wave. A tension develops which quickly becomes urgency; the motor drive "hitches a lift" on it. The baby is filled with an indefinite expectation, since he knows nothing of his need or of what may be expected; in fact, the baby does not know of his own existence, or of the existence of objects, whether external or internal. The expectation, manifested through a spontaneous gesture, could be thus made explicit: the baby reaches out "to find something somewhere" (1988, p. 100).

The drives that lead the baby to excitement derive from two sources: instinctuality and motility. Both instinctual and motor drives are manifestations of the baby's "aliveness". Instinctuality is the field in which sexuality will develop as a significant aspect of the personal maturational process. Inherent to the instinctual impulsiveness of early life, in which sexuality takes root, is a destructiveness which also constitutes one of the roots of aggression. Another root of aggression is found in motility. Although these two types of drives, instinctual and motor, have their own specificity, it is to be expected that, in health, they merge into a global experience and, over time, act in an integrated way.

We shall initially examine the instinctual root of the drive and the excitement that derives from it. It is, however, important that we first clarify what Winnicott understands as instinctuality and how he sees it in the most primitive phases.

Winnicott uses the term "instinctual" to refer to the set of local and general excitations, which, for him, are an aspect of animal life. Instincts are "powerful biological drives which *come and go* in the life of the infant or child, and which *demand action*" (1988, p. 39; my italics). I highlight three aspects. First, as instincts *come and go*, they *do not constitute* the life of the baby, child or adult individual. When these return to a state of tranquillity, instincts also rest and, nevertheless, the continuity of being goes on. Second, with regard to what is strictly biological, the way instincts act on human beings does not differ from the way in which they act on animals. In general, instinctual excitation leads the child, the adult or any other animal to an expectation of satisfaction; a drive derives from this for acting and achieving a climax as well as a post-climax period. What is fundamentally different in human beings is that all bodily functions, including instinctual ones, go through imaginative elaboration and *it is to the imaginatively elaborated body that the individual relates*. For this reason, when speaking of instinctive excitation, it is always necessary to distinguish between the body itself and the ideas and feelings that the individual has of that body. From this perspective, there is no major difference either among the various types of instinctive demand. There is no reason for classifying instincts or for deciding whether there is only one instinct, if two or several of them exist.

Third, what characterises instincts is *the demand for action*. Since, however, in Winnicott's view, the core of the issue—even in the case of a biological drive—is the individual and not a pulsion, and since the meaning of the instinctual experience varies according to the stage of maturation, we must take into account the degree of immaturity of the baby: he knows nothing of the need that afflicts him or which type of action would effectively placate it; he does not even know of the existence of objects, and even less whether a certain object is the adequate one for the need which is affecting him. Making use of an object is also an achievement that can only be accomplished in due course. In this way, the action demanded by the instinctual drive is initially only a gesture with no definite goal, which does not focus on a particular object. For this reason, when referring to the instinctuality of the most primitive phase, Winnicott does not properly speak of instincts, but of *tensions or instinctual excitations*. He reserves the term "instinct", or "instinctual life", for when instinctuality is integrated and given a meaning by the individual as something that concerns him, which is lived as a personal experience with all its consequences; this achievement will only occur later, at the stage of concern. At this point, the baby will also be capable of *doing* something to the object, in an attempt to solve the instinctual urgency.

Initially, however, the baby is an immature, non-integrated being, who still does not inhabit the body, and has no knowledge of the fact that the instinctual tensions concern him. These are as "external" to him as the world is, with this also true of the anatomy of the body and of other biological functions. In reality, they are not even external, since the infant does not yet have the sense of internal or external. This does not mean that instinctual tensions are reduced to mere bodily sensations. Despite the fact that the infant does not yet have enough maturity to endow them with meaning, or to appropriate them as belonging to his or her own instinctual impulsivity, they are endowed with meaning since they are permanently elaborated imaginatively by the psyche. At the moment when the baby is hungry, he is stricken by something that hits, invades and threatens him—being hungry "is like being possessed by wolves" (1949d, p. 81)—but the baby does not know where the unease comes from, or how to distinguish the unease which emerges out of hunger from the unease resulting, for example, from a thunderstorm, a door slamming or from a sudden drop in temperature.

When the mother, who is identified with the baby, responds to him promptly, what she avoids is not yet a frustration, but an *interruption in the continuity of being*, since "instinctual demands can be fierce and frightening, and at first can seem to the infant like threats to existence" (idem). When the total environment provides global experiences, including mutuality and communication, and the mother gives ego support, the whole trajectory launched by instinctual tension becomes an experience that strengthens the ego and promotes the psycho-somatic cohesion of the child. Without this support, instead of being gradually integrated and personalised, instinctual tensions remain external and are felt as intrusions, and may even become persecutory, establishing a paranoid disposition.[16]

As integration becomes more consistent, the baby becomes increasingly capable of acknowledging instinctual drives as an aspect of the living self and not as environmental. When this development takes place, instinctual satisfaction will become an important reinforcing element of the self. Later still, after reaching unitary identity, the child will feel the instincts as his own; he will be startled and concerned with their manifestations and effects, both on him and on the mother. For the time being, however, the baby still knows nothing about this.

We can find all kinds of excitations in the baby, whether local or general. When the excitation is generalised, it may either be contributing to an experience of integration or may itself be the result of a greater integration along the path of maturation. If the excitation is local, we must consider the body function which is involved and which becomes the goal for imaginative elaboration. Some structures of excitation prove to be dominant in the successive stages of instinctual development (pre-genital, phallic and genital), both in terms of the functions involved and the imaginative elaboration of those functions. Excitation tends to occur in terms of the dominant instinct. According to Winnicott, the only pre-genital zone of excitation that is clearly prevalent during the primitive stages is the oral one. Although one may already find localised genital excitations in the baby, these should not be differentiated as such, since there are neither specific body functions nor the typical genital fantasy. This means that distinction between the sexes at this point is artificial and forced. The difference between male and female will only become significant in the phase of sexual development that Freud termed phallic. Winnicott considers this phase in his re-description of the sexual development as an aspect of the maturational processes, the most important one after the oral phase, taking place along this process, during the stage of concern.[17]

In the initial stages, instinctual excitation leads the child to prepare for the climax, for the satisfaction of instinctual tension, especially when the call reaches the peak of demand:

> If satisfaction can be provided at the climax of demand, then there is a reward of pleasure and also a temporary relief from instinct. Incomplete or ill-timed satisfaction results in incomplete relief, discomfort, and an absence of a much-needed resting period between waves of demand. (1988, p. 39)

This quotation shows that Winnicott distinguishes pleasure from satisfaction. Driven by instinctual urgency, what the individual seeks is to satisfy this urgency; but it is only when satisfaction takes place at the culminating moment of the demand, that is, when the mother is well synchronised with the baby, that the "reward of pleasure" arises. In terms of the need to go on being, however, satisfaction does not reduce to placating the instinct but requires a global experience, which implies being well held, being seen by the mother, engaging in communication with her, creating the object which he encounters and being able to exercise full motility during the instinctual experience. The previous citation also considers the two prerequisites which permit the period of rest, which is so necessary between two waves of demand: the first is that the child must have good experiences during the quiet states described below, so that he or she, for example, will not feel alarmed in the absence of excitation.[18] The second condition is that the instinctual satisfaction must form part of a wider experience, which includes communication and mutuality.

All of this leads us to the theme of the capacity for adaptation of the good-enough mother. At the beginning of psychoanalysis, the author notes, maternal adaptation merely meant satisfying the instinctual needs of the baby, regardless of the global context of safety and reliability, in which and from which instinctual drives *"whether satisfied or frustrated, become experiences of the individual"* (1965d, p. 241; my italics). In Winnicott, the prevalence of the reality of the experience as such over the pleasure or displeasure that resulted from it is clear. Firstly, it is necessary to guarantee the conditions for the experience to be real, by means of the environmental provision that makes everything else possible, so that afterwards, as the maturational process continues, this experience may come to be satisfactory or frustrating. Winnicott affirms that:

> [...] with good-enough mothering at the beginning the baby is not subjected to instinctual gratifications except in so far as there is ego-participation. In this respect it is not so much a

question of giving the baby satisfaction as of letting the baby find and come to terms with the object (breast, bottle, milk, etc.). (1965n, pp. 59–60)

The surprising affirmation that *with good-enough care*, the baby is not *"subject to instinctual satisfactions"* means that if disconnected from a total experience, instinctual satisfaction may constitute a traumatic invasion:

> It is indeed possible to gratify an oral drive and by so doing to *violate* the infant's ego-function, or that which will later on be jealously guarded as the self, the core of the personality. A feeding satisfaction can be a seduction and can be traumatic if it comes to a baby without coverage by ego-functioning. (1965n, p. 57)[19]

From this perspective, it is easy to understand why Winnicott cannot accept that a libidinal connection to the breast or a search for satisfaction related to pulsional forces is seen in the breast-feeding situation. The needs of the baby are not dictated by the pleasure principle, but by the need to *be*, which includes reaching out and creating an object.[20] Satisfaction of instinctual tension is certainly necessary, but it only becomes an *experience* within a global experience of the encounter with the mother. Traditional psychoanalysis has accustomed us to think of the baby in terms of oral pulsions, but it is not adequate, says Winnicott, "to refer to a first feed as an instinctual experience taking place and ending with no reference to the human being in whom the excitement is taking place" (1988, p. 113). Clearly, the baby must satisfy the instinctual urgency, but the main quality of the experiences of the theoretical first feed is not defined by the pleasure/displeasure polarity, but by the communication and intimacy that they provide and achieve, by the possibility of exercising primary creativity, since "a good object is no good to the infant unless created by the infant" (1965j, p. 181). Furthermore, if the mother understands that breastfeeding the baby consists solely of satisfying his hunger, without considering the needs of the ego, or in technical terms, if, for her, breastfeeding consists of an instinctual discharge, in the manner of the pleasure principle, there is a real risk of establishing a fear of satisfaction, since this becomes associated with the disappearance of the object. This risk can be avoided when we think in terms of a global situation: in addition to the object, there is an entire ambiance in which it is possible to let oneself be carried by the excited drive and to which one can return later for rest. The mother, in her function of total environment, remains there independent of her function as food provider.

Having said all this, it is almost superfluous to point out that Winnicott cannot accept that feeding is understood as a reflex act either. His insistence on this point results from his familiarity with common paediatric practice. He never lost an opportunity to address nurses who, thinking that they were doing their job well, picked up a baby wrapped in swaddling clothes, with trapped arms, pushing the breast into the baby's mouth and declaring their determination to force the baby to feed (cf. 1988, p. 104). In this case, he says, the best way to inhibit a baby from sucking the breast is to push the breast into the mouth "without giving any opportunity for the baby to be the creator of the object which is to be found" (1988, p. 104). Winnicott never tires of warning experts, whose work puts them in direct contact with women in labour and babies, that their main task is not to interfere with what the mother knows better than anyone else how to do, even when she is weak. The mother who has just given birth may be too weak even to lift the baby out of the cot without being helped, but she is still the only person actually suited to adapting to the needs of the infant, "needs which are indicated in ways that call specifically on the actual mother's subtlety of understanding" (ibid., p. 113). What she needs is physical help from doctors and nurses, but there is no reason for these professionals to take away from her the task which she is capable of doing better than anyone else: initiating the relationship with her baby.[21]

In addition to the instinctual tensions, the other source of drives for the excited states is *motility*, which, in Winnicott's theory, is one of the roots of aggression. Motility expresses itself even before birth, in the movements of the foetus, including the sudden and vigorous movements of the legs, leading some mothers to say that the baby is kicking. After birth, while moving and exercising the vitality of muscles and tissues, the child encounters something and in this way, the environment is constantly discovered and rediscovered. In this case, discovering the environment does not mean that the baby begins to "perceive" the existence of the environment and external things, but that through the repeated experiencing of the qualities of permanence, consistency, texture, etc., a growing "knowledge" gradually starts to accumulate in him, which is not mental and which is based on familiarity, a knowledge which is previous to the perceptive awareness of the external world.

Under favourable conditions, motility merges with instinctual tension, and the baby expends as much as possible of his primitive motor drive, or muscle eroticism, in instinctual experiences. Even so, there is always a surplus which has its specificity and which must be experienced as such. In this way, motility must find opposition, that is, "it needs something to push against, unless it is to remain unexperienced and a threat to well-being" (1958b, p. 212). This opposition, which exercises the baby's muscular strength, is necessary in order to give reality to the drive. Aggressive (i.e., spontaneous) drives, states the author, does not generate any satisfactory experience unless they encounter opposition (cf. ibid). Furthermore, what gradually changes the baby's vitality into a capacity for aggression is the contact with the object that resists and offers opposition; according to Winnicott, the so-called "aggressive potential" of a baby depends on the amount of opposition that he has encountered until that point.[22] It becomes clear here that in the first encounters, the baby not only needs a libidinal object, but also an external and consistent object: "*It is this impulsiveness, and the aggression that develops out of it, that makes the infant need an external object*, and not merely a satisfying object" (1958b, p. 217). The problem here is to provide the adequate amount of opposition, since excessive opposition inhibits the drive and prevents motility from merging with the instinctual experience.[23]

If, during the excited states, the mother allows the baby's aliveness to be expressed through both the instinctual voracity and the free movement accompanying excitation, motility gradually merges with the instinctual tension; this favours the imaginative elaboration of bodily functions and, as a consequence, the task of the indwelling of the psyche in the body is facilitated. Furthermore, when the mother allows the baby to explore and enjoy intimate contact with her body while he is feeding, she facilitates the acquisition of a feeling of ease with his own excited body and instinctual urgencies in the presence of the other. Winnicott says:

> In psychoanalysis, where there is time for a gathering together of all the early roots of the full-blown sexual experience of adults, the analyst gets very good evidence that in a satisfactory

breast feed the actual fact of taking from part of the mother's body provides a "blue-print" for all types of experience in which instincts are involved. (1957c, pp. 53–54)

The sense of real, said Winnicott in 1950, originates in particular from the motor roots (and the corresponding sensorial ones), and when, in instinctual experiences, there is a weak infusion of the motor element, these experiences do not strengthen the sense of reality or the sense of existing. As a consequence, on many occasions, instinctual experiences are avoided precisely because they lead the person to a sensation of not existing.

As we have already seen, when the movement derives from the baby, the contact with the environment is an experience of the individual. However, if it is the environment that repeatedly has the initiative, instead of a series of individual experiences, a series of reactions to invasions occurs. In this event, motility is ultimately experienced only as a reaction to invasion. If this pattern remains in effect, an illness will arise. To a greater or lesser degree, the individual will then require opposition, not to give reality to his, but as a root of movement, and he will only be able to open the path to the important source of motility when something opposes him. In an extreme case, when *the drive is only experienced as a reaction to invasion*, the me is not established, since in the absence of personal impulsiveness, the primitive experiences of integration of the self, specific to the excited states, do not occur. In this situation, "the infant does indeed live, because of being seduced into erotic experience; but separately from the erotic life, which never feels real, is a purely aggressive reactive life, dependent on the experience of opposition" (1958b, p. 217). This unfavourable situation may be at the origin of one of the forms of paranoid disposition: the individual is always in search of the persecution which will trigger movement and only feels real when reacting to it. This represents a false mode of development, and he or she will need continuous persecution in order to feel alive.

These considerations lead to the question of the roots of aggression.[24] As early as 1939, in his first article devoted to the subject, Winnicott named the "aggressive" impulsiveness which some babies manifest as soon as they are breastfed, as "theoretical greed", "primary-love-appetite", stating that it originally forms part of the appetite and expresses itself in the act of eating and devouring. This impulsiveness, he says, may seem cruel, dangerous, but it is so only *by chance*. The term *greed*, the author continues, may express better than any other the idea of the original merging of love and aggression (cf. 1964c). Indeed, the instinctual tension generates a pressing need in the baby, a state of urgency which asks for immediate relief. With the participation of motility, in the nursing situation, vigorous activity of the gums may occur which could hurt the breast and cause cracks in the nipple. We cannot affirm, however, that the baby is trying to hurt, "because there is not enough baby there yet for aggression to mean anything" (1969b, p. 31). The term "aggression" only makes sense when an action is driven by a purpose, an intention, and the baby, at this point, is not yet in possession of reasons or intentionality. There is a great deal of confusion on that point, says Winnicott, because the term "aggression" is frequently used when what is meant is spontaneity. Aggression, in the beginning, is motility and part of the appetite, its manifestation resulting from the baby's aliveness. It is equally from his "aliveness" and from his absolute immaturity, particularly regarding time and the inability to wait, that his voracity derives. What would be called aggression is seen more as "evidence of life" (1965h, p. 127). The drive is part of the search for instinctual relief. The baby's goal "is gratification, peace of mind and body" (1964c, p. 88).

In the article "Aggression in relation to emotional development" (1958b), Winnicott admits the existence of a destruction that is inherent to the primitive love drive. This destructiveness must not be seen as a manifestation of aggression, since it is only incidental, forming part of the search for instinctual satisfaction. It must be studied completely separately from the aggressive reaction that results from the frustration caused by the non-satisfaction of instinctual needs or in face of the reality principle.[25]

At this point of the theory, Winnicott introduces a concept of maturation which is fundamental for understanding the aggressiveness and destructiveness contained in human nature: during the initial stages, the baby, unaware of the existence of the self and the environment, has no concern or compassion regarding the consequences of his excited love. The baby is a primitive *ruthless* self. It is thus convenient to say, Winnicott states, "that the primitive love impulse (id) has a destructive quality, though it is not the infant's aim to destroy since the impulse is experienced in the pre-ruth era" (1958b, p. 211).

This is one of the points for which it is possible to observe clearly the difference between Winnicott's conception of personal maturation and the theory of the development of sexual functions. For Winnicott, it is the individual who develops towards integration, and not the libido in terms of phases related to erogenous zones. So-called "aggressive" manifestations— eating, devouring, biting—are not successive results of sexual development, the progression of which is determined intra-psychically in accordance with the biological model. It is not a matter of saying that the oral zone is initially erotic and then sadistic or destructive. It is the baby, who, as he matures, becomes more potent and integrated into the body, increasingly needing to experience his strength and to deal with his growing capacity to recognise events and objects. Since the *baby is ruthless* during the initial stages, he continues to exercise his impulsivity at moments of excitation, without concern and with increasing strength and boldness.

There will be a long way to go before the ruthless baby gradually becomes concerned and compassionate, that is, he starts to feel responsible for the consequences of instinctual impulsiveness on the mother and on himself. All of this is nevertheless a work of growing integration, a gradual achievement which can only be effectively elaborated at the stage of concern, the moment when primitive "aggression"—which, in fact, is not yet aggression but incidental destructiveness belonging to the primitive love drive—will be integrated as part of the me and will then have a personal meaning. This nevertheless necessarily requires another achievement, described later in the text, even if in incipient form: the integration into a unitary self at the stage of the I AM, so that the baby becomes capable of relating as a whole person to a whole mother, and then, *because of being an I*, is able to feel concerned and worried about the effects of his own thoughts and actions on her.

The ruthless exercise of the instinctual drive, besides being the most primitive of the experiences of integration, is highly gratifying for the baby. The way it is received by the mother interferes crucially with the possibility and with the way in which aggression in increasing development will or will not be integrated to the total personality. With regard to the initial stages, what must not be forgotten is the situation of dependence. The baby depends entirely on how the mother receives the manifestations resulting from the fact that he is alive, has needs and completely occupies her; he depends on the way in which the mother responds to the spontaneous gesture. A mother who takes very good care of a baby in the quiet states may be startled and may react to him in the excited ones. She may become frightened or adopt a moralistic attitude or, perhaps, be of the type who resents the baby's attack as if it were one more of the attacks which life has inflicted on her. The mother's reaction may sometimes contain a kind of disapproval of what is alive or what appears to be aggressive precisely because it is alive. It may also be the case that she is emotionally ill. A mother's depression, for example, may traumatise the baby in a specialised way: full of vitality, the baby moves towards the breast and is dampened by the contact with a lifeless object. There is also the case of the mother who retreats, terrified of the pain, or of the supposed "aggression" of the baby; if vigorous and hungry, he will cling even more to the breast in order to hold it and keep it. In these cases, the baby is left with few alternatives, all of which are unfavourable: (1) to hide his impulses since the environment does not tolerate or accept "aggression" (spontaneity, vivacity); (2) to inhibit instinctual impulsiveness and develop a premature and defensive self-control; (3) to split the drives, which become then dissociated; and (4) to develop an anti-social tendency.

If instead of voracity, there is greediness, then this is no longer a manifestation of vitality. Greediness is a kind of imperative eagerness which is accompanied by suffering and which appears to be insatiable. In this case, we must assume that the child is suffering from some degree of deprivation. This type of deprivation results from the fact that some personal primordial need is not being acknowledged or met; in any of its variations, greediness means a compulsive search for a special care, one that we could call a "therapy", to be provided by the mother who caused the deprivation. If the mother can acknowledge the signal made by the child without becoming frightened and if she is willing to meet the need that is being communicated in this way, then in most cases, the compulsion will disappear (cf. 1958c). This greediness, which may manifest itself in various ways, including inhibition of appetite, dirtiness (abundant defaecation and urinating), or excessive destructiveness, is already a manifestation of the anti-social tendency and a precursor to theft. It can certainly be met and "cured" by the special, therapeutic adaptation of the mother, above all since, by being able to tolerate and understand the communication, she allows the baby's "hate" to be expressed at a moment when the deprivation complex is still close to the origin.

The deprivation that is revealed in greediness, even when related to nursing, does not concern instinctual needs, but the needs of the ego.[26] If the mother is "absent" while breastfeeding, or if nursing is carried out in an impersonal way, which is deficient in communication, intimacy, and mutuality, instinctual experiences become boring and, in this case, it may be "quite a relief to cry with anger and frustration, which at any rate can feel real and must involve the total personality" (1969b, p. 29).

In addition to instinctual motility and impulsiveness, Winnicott identifies a third root of aggression that was not perceived by traditional theory, since it did not consider the situation of dependence of the baby: it consists of the fact that the aggressive potential of certain children derives from the traumatic reactions provoked in them by environmental invasions. Traumas deriving from environmental failures, which frequently result from the mother's emotional state or psychiatric abnormalities,[27] inhibit the baby's spontaneity, prevent him from simply being, relaxing, living instinctual experiences; they leave a sort of alarm which is incorporated into him. Embedded in this is an anger, arising from the loss of being which results from those traumatic experiences. This feeling of anger, which is neither instinctual nor a development of motility towards aggression, cannot, however, be configured and felt as such at the original moment, on account of the baby's immaturity, which includes his total unawareness of the existence of an environment against which he must revolt.[28] When, at a later stage, the individual seeks therapeutic help and finds reliability (especially, in this case, when he finds a psychoanalyst capable of surviving what emerges), anger may start to manifest itself, in particular when the analyst fails and when, by acknowledging his own failure, this analyst provides the opportunity for the anger to be updated in the clinical context.[29]

This important root of aggression only became conceptually precise in the final phase of Winnicott's thought. It is presented very clearly in a written passage of 1969, added to the second version of the article "Transitional objects and transitional phenomena", of 1971. In this addendum, Winnicott states that there is a moment at the beginning of life when the baby is elaborating the capacity to keep people alive in his psychic reality, in the subjective world, and needs the concrete presence of the mother so that the memory and reality of presence as such do not fade away:

> Before the limit is reached, the mother is still alive; after this limit has been overstepped she is dead. In between is a precious moment of anger, but this is quickly lost, or perhaps never experienced, always potential and carrying fear of violence. (1953c, p. 29)

Anger is "lost or is never experienced" not because of a superego censorship, but as a consequence of the fact that the baby is not yet a me, does not know of the existence of the environment and that, for him, feeling has not yet sense or configuration. The identification of this important root of aggression led the author, who already disagreed with Freud on this theoretical point, to declare the insufficiency of the Freudian theory regarding the roots of aggression. Indeed, in Freud's view, unlike Winnicott's, the excited primitive love is not destructive in itself, and aggression is awakened in the individual by the anger provoked by frustration concerning the reality principle. Because it disregards dependence, says Winnicott, the Freudian theory of the roots of aggression,

> [...] becomes false because it avoids two vitally important sources of aggression: that which is inherent in the primitive love impulse (at the pre-ruth stage, apart from reaction to frustration) and that which belongs to the interruption of the continuity of being by impingement that enforces reaction. (1988, p. 133)

The quiet states

Since the quiet states of the baby have not been considered in traditional theory, Winnicott opens up an unusual field of reflection for the study of human nature and psychic disorders with the theoretical formulation of this theme. Where and how is the baby when he is not breastfeeding or reaching out for something, Winnicott asks. This is an invaluable area for investigation; first, because it focuses on the human need, which is never extinguished in the healthy individual, to abandon the world momentarily, withdrawing into solitude, remaining in quietness within the subjective world or protected from pragmatic objectivities within the potential space of art and culture. Second, because it shows that particularly in the initial stages, the *reality* of the excited *experience* in the encounter with the object depends on the fact that the drive that originated the search emerged from a state of rest, typical of non-integration. Third, because the difference between excited and quiet states provides the basis for the important distinction between two ambits which are generally confused: the *world* which the baby inhabits, and the *objects* that may be found (created) within this world.

During the quiet states of the theoretical first feed, the baby's need is to remain in the non-integrated state, in the relaxation characteristic of someone who feels well sustained. The baby surrenders himself to "contemplation", imaginatively elaborating the physiological states of digestion, or wrapped in the noises, smells, and movements of the environment. If the mother is holding him, he looks at her at length, she speaks to him or sings a song, he withdraws to a place where she has no access or he goes to sleep. The mother remains there, *sustaining the situation in time*, waiting for the baby to resume any search: when he wakes up and makes a gesture of communication, she is there, presenting him with a fragment of the world or handling which confirms to him that the world continues to be present and alive. It is the monotonous and regular repetition of this experience that gradually creates the capacity for trust in the baby. When this belief is established, which could be formulated as follows: "As soon as I need her, she will be there", the baby shifts very easily from the excited experience to the quiet one and vice-versa. The accumulation of such experiences becomes a pattern and forms the basis for the baby's expectations and for his capacity to "believe in ...":

> The mother's capacity to meet the changing and developing needs of this one baby enables this one baby to have a line of life, relatively unbroken; and enables this baby to experience both unintegrated or relaxed states in confidence in the holding that is actual, along with oft-repeated phases of the integration that is part of the baby's inherited growth tendency. The baby goes easily to and fro from integration to the ease of relaxed unintegration and the accumulation of these experiences becomes a pattern, and forms a basis for what the baby expects. The baby comes to believe in a reliability in the inward processes leading to integration into a unit. (1968d, p. 97)

The isolation into which the baby withdraws to rest is not defensive; it is the natural place of quietness to which he surrenders, since he feels safe, relaxed, non-integrated, without taking any notice of the environment. This is the basis for the capacity of the child and of the healthy adult to withdraw from the world momentarily in order to rest, as well as the basis for the ability to be alone in someone else's presence, which will be acquired a little later. Furthermore, *it is only starting from the state of rest that any drive may be felt as real and may become a genuinely personal experience*. If this does not happen, the other alternative, which is not healthy, is the false life founded on reactions to external stimuli. There are babies who were never allowed, even in the initial stages of infancy, simply to lie down, to be left to their own ramblings or even to be taciturn. Their mothers make them jump up and down or smile permanently, or do any other thing that provides reassurance that they are still alive. These babies, says Winnicott, "lose a great deal and may altogether miss the feeling that they themselves want to live" (1949b, p. 28). If the child is given the opportunity of gradually discovering his own personal life, he becomes able "to flounder, to be in a state in which there is no orientation, to be able to exist for a time without being either a reactor to an external impingement or an active person with a direction of interest or movement" (1958g, p. 34).

When, instead of reliability, there is a pattern of invasions to which the baby must react, the sense of being is lost and can only be recovered by a return to isolation. Once this state of things is established, isolation no longer benefits the individual, since it increasingly becomes a defensive organisation and no longer a possibility of rest which arises from reliability. If invasions are excessive, there will not even be a place of rest for individual experience: in this event, the conditions permitting the individual to become an integrated unit in due course are lacking:

> The "individual" then develops as an extension of the shell rather than of the core, and as an extension of the impinging environment. What there is left of a core is hidden away and is difficult to find even in the most far-reaching analysis. The individual then *exists by not being found*. (1958b, p. 212)

This point is essential for the understanding of certain psychotic pathologies, since, according to the author, studying the material of the unexcited states brings us nearer to a study of psychosis (cf. 1965i, p. 27). A possible interpretation of this statement is that the basic difficulty in psychoses is contact with reality, and this is associated with failure in the task of initiating object relations, a task characteristic of the excited states. In order for the drive and the encounter with the object to be felt as real, however, they must arise from a state of rest. In other words, *the return to the relaxation of non-integration is the necessary condition for whatever happens in the excited states to be felt as real and may promote integration into a self that is also felt as real*. If what is established is an impossibility of rest, the gesture will be alienated already at the foundation.[30]

This is where the third point mentioned above comes in. As we have seen, the baby needs the mother to remain present and consistently herself, at the same time as she keeps the characteristics of the environment regular, by *holding in time* the passage from one state to the other. It is the mother, says Winnicott, who being capable of concerning herself with her task, "is able *to provide the setting* for the start of excited relationships" (1988, p. 100; my italics). Maternal concern opens up a context, a *medium* in which something may happen.[31] Constituted by the totality of the mother's care, this place is the world that the baby can inhabit, the place to which he withdraws to rest, the background for excited experiences. In it, a type of relationship occurs between the baby and the mother which differs from the one established with the object during the moments of excitation. The distinction between world and objects thus corresponds to a difference between two types of maternal care. In order to describe this "duality", Winnicott draws a difference between the "mother-object", which is the target of the excited drives, and the "mother-environment", which provides total environmental care, keeping the baby's world stable and reliable.[32]

This distinction is important in many senses. First, in order to examine the implications of dependence, bearing in mind the many attributions of the mother in her condition as facilitator of maturational processes. Second, in order to configure one of the baby's primary dissociations, which will only be "healed", that is, integrated into the personality, as he develops. The baby does not initially know that he is the same individual who is now quiet, with his world reassured by the mother and then, excited, grasping the breast excitedly; nor is he aware that the mother who lets herself be sucked voraciously, is the same person who takes care of him during his quiet states. The integration of the quiet and the excited states concerning the same baby, and of the "two" mothers into a single person will be an achievement of maturation that will take place in the stage of concern.

All of these conceptual elements relating to the gradual integration into a unity are decisive contributions of Winnicott's theory. If, as is the case with traditional theory, the constitution of the me and the capacity for perception of external objects are taken for granted, and if the mother has been regarded as an external object, or even an erotic object from the start then, there is no room for considering the constitution of reality, when it is precisely the constitution of the sense of reality of the world and of the very individual that may fail in the case of psychotics.

For the infant whose mother always left open the path of return to the quiet states of non-integration and kept his moments of quietness undisturbed, the capacity to absent himself and rest becomes a source of personal wealth, a place of protection where he can always return throughout his life, whenever he feels the need to rest from the world and momentarily release himself from the task of existing. This state of absence, disconnection or "introspective" isolation is not a sign of illness; on the contrary,

> a sign of health, that the child can use relationships in which there is maximal trust, and in such a relationship at times disintegrate, depersonalise and even for a moment abandon the almost fundamental urge to exist and to feel existent. (1971d, p. 261)

If, instead of this pattern, the quiet states do not have their own positive value, being no more than the negative of the excited states, it may be that a great anxiety develops in the individual with regard to tranquility and, over time, a permanent avoidance of quietness or even of the intervals in which there is absence of tension or excitation. The absence of tension appears to him or her to be stagnation, which resembles death.

As integration becomes more consistent, regression to non-integration as a natural primitive condition is no longer possible. If the maturational process continues and a further step is taken towards independence, *there is the definitive loss of the capacity for non-integration* (cf. 1988, p. 139). This experience may perhaps be repeated but very rarely and under very special conditions: a healthy individual may be capable of losing all references for a moment, entering a state of detachment from the world, comparable only to that sought by mystics. This state of non-integration may also occur under the specialised conditions provided by psychotherapy, and even physiotherapy.[33] For an individual who has achieved a certain stable degree of integration, however, the necessary rest shall be carried out by other, more complex means: he will know how to absent himself from the shared world, momentarily withdrawing into the subjective world, surrendering himself to an imaginative activity, to playful or artistic concentration and even to creative work.

From a certain degree of integration onwards, the opposite of this integration is no longer unintegration, but a state of "maddening" disintegration. When the person of the baby begins to emerge, "failure of care leads to disintegration instead of to a return to unintegration" (1958d, p. 98). Since transitions are gradual, however, there is an intermediate state in which a well cared for baby, in full development, may still relax in unintegration and tolerate, *but merely tolerate*, says Winnicott, feeling "mad" in the non-integrated state (cf. 1988, p. 118). If, however, the environment repeatedly fails to provide safety to the baby beyond his tolerance limit, the threat of disintegration becomes permanent, and the individual will carry with himself the feeling of an unnameable danger, which must be avoided at any cost. As a result of a withheld feeling of environmental insecurity, he may also establish an exaggerated form of self-care, a sort of automatic self-preservation, which is a defence against the disintegration which environmental failure, now turned into potential failure, threatens to provoke.[34]

The basic tasks

Integration in time and space

In the theory of maturational processes, the term "integration" is used both to designate the innate tendency towards development, which leads to the unitary status, and the various partial integrations which gradually take place along the journey, starting from the state of unintegration. The task of *integration in time and space* is the most basic and fundamental of the maturational tasks. In fact, there is no possible sense of reality, of body, of world or of self outside space or time; there is no individual if there is no memory of oneself, which maintains the identity amid the transformations; there is no encounter of objects if there is no *world* where objects may be found and if there is no *self* who can find them. The whole integrative process is based on the temporalisation and spatialisation of the baby, beginning at the start of life. For this reason, "the main trend in the maturational process can be gathered into the various meanings of the word *integration*. Integration in time becomes added to (what might be called) integration in space" (1965n, p. 59).

Temporalising and spatialising the baby does not mean inserting him into the time and space of the external world, since he is not mature enough for the sense of externality. The newborn lives in a sort of *continuum*, in a mere extended duration. Although a few small temporal markings have already been experienced in intrauterine life, such as the mother's breathing or the alternation of states of movement and quietness, his temporality is limited to his continuity of being. Since the baby initially inhabits a subjective world, initiating him into the sense of time and space means making sure that the time and space that rule this world are also subjective.

The first sense of time in the subjective world is that of the continuity of presence, established through the repeated experience of the mother's presence and permanence, of the continuity of the care which the world constantly presents to him. The baby does not know of the permanent existence of the mother, but feels the effects of her presence and slowly, while creating a memory of this presence, comes to count on it. In order to preserve the continuity of being and to keep alive the subjective world, the baby must be permanently reassured by this continuing presence, since

> [...] the innate creative impulse withers unless it is met by external reality ('realized'). Each infant must re-create the world, but this is only possible if, bit by bit, the world arrives at the moments of the infant's creative activity. The infant reaches out and the breast is there, and the breast is created. (1958j, p. 12)

The baby is consolidating the state of being which has emerged from non-being. The negativity of the origin is still very near, ready to emerge from each hole of mother's absence, which lasts long enough to erase the incipient memory of the presence, which is still unconscious. The mother who is capable of identifying with the baby is only absent for the time interval during which the baby can maintain the memory of her presence. The feeling that the mother exists lasts for "x" minutes. If the mother is away longer than "x" minutes, the image of her presence fades away. The baby is distressed, but if the mother returns within "x + y" minutes, the affliction is corrected. We can say that within "x + y" minutes, the continuity of being of the baby did not alter but, if the mother's absence lasts for "x + y + z" minutes, he is traumatised and the return of the mother no longer corrects his altered state. If the memory of the presence is erased, the sensation is that of annihilation, of madness. "Madness here simply means a *break-up* of whatever may exist at the time of *a personal continuity of existence*" (1967b, p. 131). After recovering from the trauma, the baby must *start everything again*, being permanently deprived of the root that could provide continuity with the personal beginning. The personal beginning, that is, the basis of existence, "implies the existence of a memory system and an organisation of memories" (idem). The erasing of the memory of the presence is one of the specific traumas that appear in the aetiology of psychotic pathologies. It is an unthinkable agony.[35] What prevents this agony from happening, in this specific case, the agony of losing all sense of real, is the fact that the mother weaves her presence permanently, continuously presenting herself and the world to the baby in small doses at the moment of the spontaneous gesture.

From the start of the maturational process, with the baby still in uterus, personal body memories start to come together to form a new human being. This means that having experiences and having memories of them is what marks the beginning of the human being. At the very outset, body memories are sparse but gather gradually and form a stock of experiences. From then on, expectations become increasingly more configured. If the baby feels that the continuity of being is guaranteed, that is, if he does not find himself forced to develop a state of alertness against potential environment invasions, he is in the condition, without being startled, of living the various experiences which are repeated according to a certain pattern. With time, he begins to have some "knowledge" of himself, of the environment and of what will happen, which is not mental but is based on increasing familiarity with the body sensations that are imaginatively elaborated and with the state of things surrounding him. This is the foundation of the baby's temporalisation, which is initially subjective: on the basis of present experiences, the baby begins to constitute a "past", a "place" to store experiences, from where he can anticipate the future, due to the fact that some things and some events have become predictable. A history begins. This is the basis for establishing the capacity for experience in an increasingly wider sense, since a real experience "is not so much a matter of a single happening as a build-up of memories of events" (1988, p. 100). Throughout this originary process of temporalisation, the psyche is working towards connecting together the past which has already been experienced, the present and the expectation of the future, providing the feeling of the me and justifying the perception that an individual exists inside that body (ibid., p. 46).

Together with the constitution of the sense of presence, a special type of *temporal marking* begins to occur, which, in health, comes necessarily prior to the perception of chronologies. This marking is made in natural and specifically human ways, of the intimacy with the mother's body (the rhythm of her breathing, her heartbeats); it is also ruled by the rhythms of the baby's body, to which the environment adapts: hunger, breastfeeding, excretion, sleep, waking up, sounds, light, and smells. The dating of time, therefore, is carried out by the maternal care which initially adjusts to the rhythm of physiological functioning, which has its own timing, and by the imaginative elaboration of this functioning and of bodily sensations. By so doing, the mother provides that the baby is initiated into the periodicity of time, having as matrix his own rhythm, the rhythm of the body. With the repetition of the experience, a sense of "future" begins to be constituted: the baby becomes *capable of anticipating what will come, based on his own needs*, made real through the mother's responses and attention. If the mother imposes a rhythm on the baby that is external to him, either a chronological one or one that follows her own needs instead of his, subjective temporality and psycho-somatic cohesion are impaired, if not prevented. In order to guarantee that external time does not interfere with the natural processes of subjective temporalisation, the baby's natural rhythm must prevail. Feeding must take place "exactly when the baby wants it, and ceases as he ceases to want it. This is the basis", says Winnicott (1945c, p. 33). The mother initially obeys the baby's rhythm and only gradually adjusts this rhythm to regular intervals which seem to be convenient and adequate to his needs, while also contemplating her needs as a woman and mother. Only then, can a baby, over time, compromise with the mother and *reach an agreement* regarding the regularity of breastfeeding. The baby may adjust to this interval and be hungry regularly every three hours, feeling this as his own need. This is the kind of "agreement" to which Winnicott refers when he states that it is only during the initial stages, when the baby does not yet know of the dependence, and when a creative relation to the object is permitted to him, that he can gradually learn to comply "without losing face" (1968d, p. 103). In other words, because of his primary creativity, the baby has a dignity even before he is a unitary me.

An interval of waiting that is too long, however, leads to distress; often "if the coming of the feed is delayed more than X minutes, then when it comes it is meaningless for the baby" (1984f, p. 58). The easiest way for the mother to regain the baby's trust is to breastfeed him as and when he demands for a while and then, only gradually, to resume the attempt to establish regularity. On many occasions, however, the mother who was taught to train her baby to acquire regular habits, starting with regular feeding at each three hours, "feels actually wicked if told to feed her baby just like a gipsy" (1945c, p. 33). The main difficulty with mothers allowing themselves to follow the rhythm of the babies stems from the fact that the responsibility of bringing up a child hangs over them and they readily accept the rules of scheduled feeding, the medical regulations and prescriptions that make life less risky, even if a little monotonous. A part of this difficulty must also be attributed to paediatric orientation. When the relation between mother and baby is developing naturally, says Winnicott, techniques, quantities and timetables may be left to nature's criterion.

There is no doubt that many difficulties in maternal adaptation are precisely related to time. One of them arises when mother and baby fail to establish or lose contact due to lack of synchronisation, since by temperament some babies are slower than their mothers, while others are more rapid. It may be particularly tedious for a quick mother to adapt to a slow baby, but it is not easy either if the opposite is the case. In any case, the mother must have the time and spend it on the task of caring for the infant. When she is good-enough, she knows that in order to lift him from the cradle and move him somewhere, he must be prepared for the movement: the baby must *receive a warning* and be lifted at the right time, with the mother holding all of the various parts of the body. In addition, the mother's act starts, continues, and ends, for the baby is being carried, from one place to another, for example, from the cot to the mother's shoulder (cf. 1988, p. 117). That is to say, the mother assists the baby in having *total experiences*. She must thus have *enough time to wait*, at the baby's pace, for him to go from the beginning to the end of the experience, with this experience having a beginning, a middle, and an end.[36] When we are in a hurry or worried, we cannot ensure total events and the baby is impoverished.

> Total happenings enable babies to catch hold of time. They do not start off knowing that when something is on it will finish. The middle of things can be enjoyed only if there is a strong sense of start and finish. (1949c, pp. 77–78)

The central aspect of adaptive care is related to time. Its basic characteristic is reliability and this means *predictability*. When we say that a child is well cared for, that means that his parents protect him from unexpected events, from being taken by surprise by something that he does not or cannot expect. Regular experiences, repeated thousands of times, create *a sense of predictability* in the infant. As the unitary self builds up, with environmental care being incorporated as a quality intrinsic to it, integration becomes an increasingly consistent state and the individual starts to be able to take care of him. In this way, dependence is gradually reduced. The development of the autonomy of the child in relation to the environment has to do with his growing capacity to make predictions (cf. 1987d, p. 95).

Although the purpose of this study is not to arrive at the *clinical implications* of Winnicott's theory of maturational processes and of psychoses, I believe it appropriate to mention that these very basic issues concerning the constitution of time serve as a guide for the analyst in her therapeutic task. The care in ensuring that one is guided by the needs of the baby or of the patient and in avoiding abrupt events calls into question the issue, for example, of the ending of each analytical session, which is relevant in any type of case, but especially with patients for whom the central aspect of personality is psychotic. Whatever problems we are dealing with, we cannot end the session abruptly by relying on the fact that the patient has an adult side and that the time schedule has been agreed. Often, especially during a phase of regression to dependence, the person is not in contact with objective time, nor is he sufficiently emotionally mature to benefit from a real manifestation of hate from the analyst, one of which consists of ending the session at the scheduled time,[37] which would be important in other types of disorders, It is necessary to help the patient, signalling with some kind of movement or gesture that the session is about to end. Sometimes, as in the case of babies, a few more minutes are enough for the patient to reach his own end and to prepare to leave. This care applies not only on this specific occasion, but also for reassuring the patient that we will ensure that nothing will happen abruptly. It is nevertheless possible that he will effectively need more time, longer sessions; for a certain period of time, we will have to extend the duration of the session on a regular basis, knowing in advance that the conclusion of the session, even if extended, will require equal care. It is only in this way, that the patient, like the baby, over time, will be able to comply "without losing face".

More time, however, is not always what a patient needs; it is not even certain that he will benefit from the fact that the ending of the session depends on his subjective time. Some patients are in therapy precisely in order to succeed in establishing a subjective time; at the originary moment, when this should have been established, there was only chaos in the environment, and these individuals had to cling rigidly to an objective time, serving as a reference for them and without which they immediately feel lost, in order not to succumb to complete disorganisation of personality. There are people who cannot tolerate any situation of an indefinite duration. I had a patient who had been seriously affected with regard to these basic achievements relating to temporality and spatiality. In addition to being born in an unstable and chaotic environment, his birth had been delayed and he had always felt imprisoned in any situation without a rigorously scheduled end. Winnicott says that among the typical characteristics of genuine birth memories is the feeling of being in the clutches of some external thing, causing the newborn to feel completely vulnerable and helpless. Inherent to this feeling of helplessness "is the intolerable nature of experiencing something without any knowledge whatever of when it will end" (1958f, p. 184). In addition to this, the patient had had no experience of personal communication and even though this was what he needed most, any proximity was felt as a potential invasion. At the start of the analysis, the session could sometimes be too long, and he stuck rigidly to the scheduled time. For this patient, the idea of a session without a predictable end or with an end that depended on a subjective time, which simply did not exist, was unbearable. There was yet another aspect: always attentive to the only compass that he had, his watch, he knew very well when the formal time of the session ended, but would wait for me to take the initiative. I noticed that both for him and for some other patients, the ability of the analyst to finish the session within the agreed time provides reassurance and the question here is not one of hate, since for this type of person, the fact that the analyst assumes the task of monitoring time means that the same analyst has adopted the position of the person providing care and who, by being undertaking to maintain contact with external reality, releases the patient to go on constituting his subjective world.

One of the characteristics of defensive organisations of a psychotic type is the impossibility that the individual presents of "having time", of being able "to rely on the duration of time", of allowing some time for the development of an event or an experience. In the face of an unexpected event, despair or lack of resources arises *immediately*. This gives the impression that this individual is always on the edge of an abyss. Subjective time has not been established and, consequently, the subsequent development of internal time which would enable a parenthesis for reflection and prevent him from being dragged by external requests, has not occurred either. This lack of time manifests itself in different ways. An adult patient reports how he eats: he does not have a meal, instead, he swallows the food. The feeling is one of being exposed to an urgency which he must rapidly bring to an end, because all of the food will be finished before he satisfies his hunger. During analysis, it was revealed that for his mother, breastfeeding or even at a later stage, feeding her children was a difficult task, from which she had to free herself as soon as possible. While she was breastfeeding, she was not there and had already moved on to her next task, seeking to rid herself of it as soon as possible.

Another example is that of a girl whose subjective world was rich and full of precious details, with a very peculiar personal time, entirely incompatible with external time, which was felt as unbearable and oppressive. She had had a fairly good start, when she had been able to commit herself to imaginative life. At a certain point, her mother became a widow and, overloaded with daily chores, which included financial management of the household and of life in general, could no longer adapt to the rhythm of her little daughter and frequently hurried her. The patient became an excellent professional in her area, which required creativity and imagination, but could not deliver her work without feeling oppressed by her deadlines and could not arrive at her appointments on time either. "Obedience" to shared time was an unbearable submission that offended her.

At the same time as the acquisition of the sense of time, the *spatialisation* of the baby is taking place, with both achievements intimately intertwined. This is a question of allowing the baby to gradually acquire the feeling, which is far from being innate or acquired automatically, of having *a place where he can dwell* and "feel at home", to which he can return to rest and which is "a basic place to operate from" (1986h, p. 39). The sense of dwelling is built on many levels but the baby must primarily dwell in his own body. It is no coincidence that the second basic task is termed "residence" or "indwelling of the psyche in the body".[38] Since his own body is the first dwelling, we should add that this body is not loose in space, but is being held and brought together within the mother's arms, or tucked up in the cradle; the mother's lap and the details of the environment, which initially are indistinguishable from the baby himself, are constituent parts of this dwelling and of the inaugural experience of dwelling. If the baby is left for a long time without being held, he loses contact with his own body, which remains unrealised and it is this that characterises the states of depersonalisation, which are at the root of psycho-somatic disorders.

Time and space are articulated in such a way that some temporal factors must be guarded for the baby's dwelling to be consistent and reliable; one of these is the regularity and predictability of the environmental conditions. It is not advisable, for example, to move the cradle constantly from place to place, since in a particular position, the baby becomes used to finding the ray of light that comes through the window and traces a luminous line on the bedroom wall. The baby's place must also be simple and protected from confusion, turmoil, and excesses: in the small "enclosure" opened and maintained by the mother, fragments of the world are presented to the infant in small doses and in a comprehensible way. In addition, when the mother lingers attentively and without haste on the details presented by the baby, she enables him to create and inhabit a niche made of *time and concentration*, within which something that belongs to the here and now may be experienced. This has important implications for clinical practice, especially with patients who are regressed to dependence. Winnicott says, for example, that "one of the main principles of the psycho-analytic technique is that a setting is provided in which the patient can deal with one thing at a time" for *"two or more factors spell confusion"* (1958f, p. 192).

The small circle protected by the patient attention of the mother gradually establishes the basis for the individual's capacity at a later stage to inhabit the incommensurable world of external reality, without losing the sense of being at home. When the safety of the small world is established, the maturing baby is "too glad to find mother behind the breast or bottle, and to find the room behind mother, and the world outside the room" (1945a, p. 22). The totality of maternal care enables the infant to live in a *subjective world*, populated by imaginative life with regard to body functions and the environmental atmosphere, the main characteristic of which is that of being protected from the invasion by any sample of external reality. This is the first world the infant inhabits and throughout his life will be his main refuge for resting. The chaotic mother repeatedly alters not only the emotional climate but also the concrete environmental conditions of the baby, so that he cannot build the "habit", familiarity and feeling of safety, which are characteristic of feeling at home. Instead of concentration, there will be dispersion and confusion. Even worse, there will always be the threat hanging over the baby that something incomprehensible may suddenly arise and drag everything with it. It should be noted that the term "invasion", which is used to designate the general character of the environmental failure, has a *spatial sense*. The invasion of the "sacred" territory suddenly pulls aside the curtain of the cloister and makes him glimpse the outward immensity prematurely. One characteristic of the state of panic is the fear of enormous open spaces without contours, as well as the feeling of losing all references. At several points in her diary, Renée, the schizophrenic girl treated by M. A. Sechehaye, mentions some elements of her feelings of unreality: she saw herself in an "illimitable vastness", or "the street became infinite" or "my eye encountered a field of wheat whose limits I could not see".[39] By contrast, Forrest Gump took his "house" with him wherever he went.[40]

At a later stage, after having lived for long enough in the subjective world, the baby will inhabit the potential space, the area of which will initially be filled with transitional phenomena and then, gradually and successively, with play and cultural and artistic activities, that is, with everything that is free from the judgment ruled by objectivity. When there is health, says Winnicott, this is the place where we live. One of the characteristics of play and of activities relevant to the potential space is the state of alienation, which can only occur if the feeling of safety has been incorporated, that there is someone taking care of the permanence of things out there, which is the basis for concentration in the older child and in the adult. If these first experiences of dwelling are guaranteed by the good-enough care, the individual will arrive at the external world with the foundation which, despite what is objectively immense, unfathomable and inhospitable, will allow him to create a niche where he can feel at home.

In the same way that integration in time and space is the most basic of tasks, *holding*, the specific maternal care which corresponds to it, is equally the prototype of all good-enough maternal care. This holding, which is simple and refers to the handling of the baby and all of the physical care related to his well-being, gradually extends as the baby grows up and his world becomes more complex. Encompassing care in general, including the atmosphere of calmness and regularity of the environment which the mother is able to sustain, "holding" extends to "holding a situation", which is a serene availability that remains, that slowly extends over time and *does not demand that anything happen*; she merely awaits the baby's movements and follows him in his innumerable comings and goings. When the baby is awake, the mother is there, offering the samples of the world according to the need which he expresses and she understands: breastfeeding, handling, a bath, a song or simply being together and looking at each other. The person who takes care of the regularity and vivacity of the place and holds the situation is the good-enough mother and, like her, the analyst or the therapist.[41]

As a consequence of this care, very basic pre-representational experiences are favoured, constituting the beginning of the baby's familiarity with certain aspects of the ambience, and which, in health, *must precede the perception of the same phenomena*. Because the mother maintains the regularity, simplicity, and monotony of the environment and the care, events are repeated and the baby becomes capable of some predictions: *if* there is this particular smell or noise, *then* that particular thing is going to happen. The baby is being temporalised, he is acquiring a sense of future in a subjective sense; this increases his ability to wait.

Integration into a self is never complete and neither relates to a state which is unequivocal or closed in itself; on the contrary, it is precisely the gradual integration into the globality of space-time what allows the experience of incompleteness. When the baby *is integrated in time* and begins to be dated, to have a present, a past, and a future, he starts to exist in a finite way, that of the essential human incompleteness: at the same time that *he is something*, part of this *being something* necessarily and simultaneously is also an already-not (past) and a not-yet (future). Because they have not been temporalised in the subjective sense, psychotics suffer precisely from immediacy and at the same time, from infinitude.

Dwelling of the psyche in the body: personalisation

For the task of the dwelling of the psyche in the body, Winnicott also uses the term "personalisation". This designation is due to the fact that the word "depersonalisation" is the term already consecrated in adult psychiatry for the various clinical states in which the patient complains about not having a relation with his own body or feeling that his body, or part of it, does not belong to him, etc. (cf. 1988, p. 145).

The task of the dwelling of the psyche in the body only makes sense if we accept the idea that initially, body and psyche are not yet united and will only constitute a unity *if everything goes well in the maturational process*. At the outset, *soma* and psyche are undifferentiated. Differentiation takes place gradually, at the same time as the tendency towards integration acts to gather them into a unit. This psycho-somatic partnership is not guaranteed however, nor should it be taken for granted. It is not self-evident that the baby's psyche and *soma* will operate as a unit in every case, in such a way that the baby will live in his body, which will function in accordance with the baby's use of it. This may or may not be achieved and once it is, it may be lost, even in health. Psycho-somatic cohesion is an achievement and may not be established unless there is the active participation of a human being who holds the baby and takes care of him, so that the baby is brought together in her arms and gaze. A baby who is not brought together by the mother feels spread: "In psychology it must be said that the infant falls to pieces unless held together, and physical care is psychological care at these stages" (1988, p. 117).[42]

Much has already been clarified regarding the task of personalisation in the section about the quiet and excited states. Feeling well held and brought together in the body, especially during excited experiences, the infant surrenders confidently to the care of the mother and under these conditions, the psyche may carry out its work of imaginative elaboration of the body functions and sensations. Gradually, the body becomes *soma* and an intimate connection of increasing complexity between *soma* and psyche is established, with the potentially psycho-somatic character of existence becoming real. The psyche begins to inhabit the body, making it its dwelling.

The gradual achievement of dwelling in the body is hence intimately connected to the process of spatialisation of the baby. For the entire time that psycho-somatic cohesion is in the process of being achieved, the mother's arms and the baby's body are one and the same thing, so that one may say that *the baby's first dwelling is his very body in the mother's lap*.[43]

The maternal care that corresponds to the task of dwelling of the psyche in the body is the handling. Handling is part of the holding, but refers specifically to physical holding. Handling-holding must include all of the necessary sensory experiences: being involved from all sides in a lively embrace which has temperature and rhythm and which makes the baby feel both the mother's body and his own; being tucked in his cradle in such a way that he will still be in contact with the covers and cushions instead of loose in space; the countless tactile sensations on being handled in every way during bathing, while being caressed, cuddled, smelt, etc.; subtle and graduated differences in luminosity, texture, and temperature; the necessary opposition for the baby to exercise movement; the active and concrete response to the excited states both with regard to reaching out for something and to instinctual and motor satisfaction. All these experiences enable the baby to inhabit the body, even if momentarily, facilitating a psycho-somatic association and contributing to the sense of "real"—of the reality of the self—as opposed to the "unreal": the fact of being alive and existing gradually gains consistency, weight, gravity. Through the growing connection that is established between psyche and *soma*, whatever experience the infant lives, the body functioning and the body sensations go together, being equally affected. Clumsy or hesitant holding acts against psycho-somatic union, prevents the development of muscular tonus and "coordination", and goes against the child's capacity for enjoying the experience of body functioning and of *being*. When there is safety, two things are taking place: at the same time as the mother facilitates the general tendency towards integration, especially the indwelling of the psyche in the body, she provides the conditions for the return to the relaxed rest of the non-integrated state.

In the initial stage, the mother's love is expressed through *physical care*, which ultimately is what the baby needs and what he is capable of integrating into the subjective world. To hold the infant properly and to handle him is a way of loving and, possibly, "the only way in which a mother can show the infant her love" (1960b, p. 49). The insistence on this point relates to the demystification of the intense network of mental mechanisms and feelings with which traditional psychoanalysis has endowed the baby in his relationship with the breast. Even when referring to later stages of development, Winnicott affirms that "children need more of their parents than to be loved; they need something that carries over when they are hated and even hateful" (1961b, p. 43). The mother, while she takes care of the body, knows that there is a person in this body. She takes care of its physical well-being, but in such a way that she addresses the *total person* of the baby, which he has not yet become, but will. She is the one who puts the baby together, not only in her arms but in her conception of the baby as a total human being. As Winnicott nevertheless observes, there are mothers who, although they have good natural conditions for physical care of babies, seem to ignore that there is a human being dwelling in the body which they bathe and feed. If this is the case, the baby cannot integrate into a whole and the foundations are laid for a psycho-somatic splitting. When maternal care promotes psycho-somatic cohesion, the personal me is felt as being contained within the boundaries given by the limits of the skin. At around six months, a baby already uses the circle or the sphere as a diagram of the self. The baby becomes used to occupying space, to having a visible presence, to being seen and recognised. In the absence of this, he will never achieve the reality of the self or an effective contact with external reality; he will never be able to perceive clearly what comes from within and what comes from without. Even in health, however, psycho-somatic cohesion cannot be considered to be fully established and not only at the beginning but throughout life, it will show its precariousness in situations of tiredness and in the passage between waking and sleep.

Babies are highly sensitive to differences in the way in which they are held. This is one of the main reasons why Winnicott insists that the good-enough care should be provided by the same person. When several people hold the baby (father, aunts, nannies), he is subjected to varied techniques, losing, at least in part, the familiarity that forms the basis of predictability. Even when only the mother takes care of the baby, he is sensitive to changes in her mood, which naturally have an impact on the body. Winnicott observed that during air raids in World War II, babies were not scared of the bombs that fell, but were immediately affected if their mothers panicked.

Provided that the mother spares the baby from outbursts dictated by emotional instability, it is good for him to feel her various moods, meaning that she is alive and is affected by events. It is a good thing that the mother is transparent and not opaque. At best, the opaque mother leads to an endless need to dismantle all toys and machines in order to find out how they operate. A patient of mine reports that her mother had always had an unalterable expression, eternally placid; she was never irritated or manifested any other type of emotion. She remembers peeking at her mother's face at a very early date, desperately trying to know what happened inside her. At about this time, she felt entirely lost and was gripped by the fear that her mother would die suddenly; she then thought, but did not have the courage to ask, that it would be a good thing if her mother left her a full list of everything that she should or could do, and everything that she could not. This girl developed a high degree of sensitivity to and a sense of being threatened by any type of alteration in people's physiognomy or in her environment.

Babies also feel the difference between tense holding, which is uncomfortable for the mother, and relaxed holding which is a natural part of her tasks and which costs her nothing. The same patient once told me that she was now aware that she had never sat fully on her buttocks; her mother could not bear physical contact, and since a very young age she had always felt that she was a burden on her mother, with this being excessively painful. In moments of anxiety, she would go to the bathroom to smell the towel that her mother had used and this would calm her.

From the sensitivity of babies in relation to the mother's moods emerges the issue of the mother's consistency, of her capacity to be herself. The baby feels the difference between studied gestures, in which the soul is not present, and other, spontaneous ones, which indicate that the mother is really there: all of her and not just her mind. It is often the case that the mother is suffering from anxiety or is excessively controlling due to her fear of dropping the baby, or has warm skin and a fast heartbeat due to anxiety and in these cases, the baby cannot allow himself the luxury of relaxing, which will only take place as a result of pure exhaustion. When, after the experience of integration, returning to rest is made systematically difficult, the situation may become more serious than we would normally expect, since it is only from the non-integrated state that the experience of integration may be felt as real. If the mother acknowledges her own difficulties and wants to preserve the baby carefully, she places him in the cradle, which is a very welcome alternative, or asks for the help of a good nanny. In fact, the baby needs both experiences. Even mothers who feel confident and enjoy holding their babies, may sometimes feel drowsy or may be experiencing a period of depression. If they are good-enough, they will put the baby in the cradle, because they know "that your sleeping state is not alive enough to keep going the infant's idea of a space around" (1957e, p. 20). When the act of holding the baby is adequate, however, he gains confidence, returning to non-integration *while he is being held*. This, according to Winnicott, is the richest experience.

The beginning of the contact with reality: object relations

At the beginning of life, the baby is not sufficiently mature to know of the existence of external reality, to perceive the objects that belong to it, and even less to relate to them effectively. He still has not developed a sense of externality or the capacity for perception, characteristic of relations to objects that are perceived objectively. Separating the self from objects (which is a very sophisticated achievement and depends on other previous achievements) will only begin later, from the stage of object use onwards, when the baby himself creates the sense of reality that is specific to externality. After this, he will still have to complete the achievement, separating the self from the total environment, which will only take place at the I AM stage.[44]

As soon as the baby is born, he has neither the sense of externality nor any other sense of reality. In order for some sense of reality to be initiated, the baby must be provided with the only one that is possible for him at this point of development: *the reality of the subjective world*. Without establishing a subjective reality, the baby cannot proceed with the gradual achievements of maturation, which include the sense of real that is specific to transitionality and then the sense of external and shared reality. As Loparic has showed (1995a), the different senses of reality correspond to different "worlds", which differ according to a space and a time that are peculiar to each one. In each of these worlds, objects may be found, the mode of presence (or "reality") of which differs from the others in spatio-temporal terms; the mode of presence of the subjective object, for example, is not the same as that of transitional objects and is radically different from that of objects which are objectively perceived that belong to external reality.[45] The relation of the human individual to subjective objects is characterised by the fact that it excludes any separation between subject and object, since this sense of reality "is prior to action and to representation, conditions of life under the aegis of the principle of reality, to be understood as: of the external reality which characterises the objects of the external world" (Loparic, 1995a, p. 52). It is also important to note that the reality of the subjective world not only leaves nothing to be desired in terms of the feeling of real, to the reality of the objective world, which will follow it later but, in some cases, will continue, throughout life, to be always more real than objective reality itself.[46]

The main characteristic of subjective objects is that of being reliable.[47] The character of reliability was clarified earlier when the excited states of the baby were being examined: it refers to the fact that the good-enough mother provides the baby with the experience of creating what he encounters and also protects him from the irruption of anything unpredictable that may interrupt his continuity of being. Encountering a subjective object thus means that the baby finds, that is, creates what he needs at the moment when he needs it. The object comes to the baby at the *exact moment* when the need arises, and it is of the exact size of the baby's possibility of receiving and assimilating it *as part of him at that precise moment*. Subjective objects "exist as immediate, unconditioned presences" (Loparic, 1995a, p. 54). Their nature is such that the baby is not confronted with something that he cannot embrace in experience; they do not surprise or startle him, that is, they are not untimely, in the sense of being unpredictable. Their form of presence is of a kind that does not denounce the external character of their existence and in this way, does not extrapolate the scope of the baby's subjective experience. For all these reasons, the subjective object is reliable and, in this sense, real.

The beginning of the object relation (with subjective objects) takes place during the baby's moments of excitation. The maternal provision which is specific to this task is that of object-presenting. The baby nevertheless only creates from what he finds. For the subjective world to stay alive and for the infant to go on creating the objects that he needs, someone must make a continuous effort to present samples of the world to him in a way that is comprehensible and appropriate to the maturational capacity of the moment. An insufficient presentation of objects blocks the child's path towards feeling real and relating to the real world of objects and phenomena (cf. 1965c). There are environments that simply abandon the baby to his own resources and provide no material for creation:

> But someone has to be there if that which is created is to be realised, actual. If no one is there to do this, then, in the extreme, the child is autistic—creative into space—and boringly compliant in relationships (childhood schizophrenia). (1986h, p. 49)

The sense of the real of subjective reality, which will be the foundation for all others, rests on reliability, as has been already said.[48] It is this which actually constitutes the subjective world and it is only because the baby inhabits a subjective world that he can find subjective objects. In this world, the baby experiences total control over objects. This is thus a magical world in which the demands of the objective world have not been registered. The breast appears when hunger emerges, and disappears when the tension ceases. The absolute adaptation of the mother maintains the baby in the area of the illusion of omnipotence; and only there can he begin to be.

Sustaining the illusion of omnipotence and preserving the subjective world entails ensuring that the baby is not surprised with a sense of reality for which he is not yet prepared. If the mother insists on breastfeeding the baby or on exciting him when he has already gone to rest, and if, instead of corresponding to the baby's gesture, the mother replaces it with her own, the existence of something outside the infant's sphere of omnipotence emerges before he is prepared for such reality. An intrusion then occurs. This nevertheless does not mean that the baby perceives the object confronting him; he does not perceive it, because he is not capable of perception. He feels, nevertheless, the presence of something strange and incomprehensible, which falls upon him, so to say, and which he cannot embrace in the scope of his experience.

In due time, the baby will have to accept the fact of the external existence of the world, over which he will have no control; however, if he is initially provided with a creative and subjective relation to the world, he will gradually be able to submit himself to the evidence of this other reality "without losing face" (cf. Winnicott, 1968d, p. 103). According to Winnicott, it is entirely wrong to think that the sense of reality of a child depends on the mother's insistence on the external and objective nature of the things of the world. It is only starting from the illusion that a child can be expected to become able gradually to accept the independent existence of the external world and to assimilate disillusions: "Adaptation to the reality principle arises naturally out of the experience of omnipotence, within the area, that is, of a relationship to subjective objects" (1965j, p. 180).

When illusion is well installed, there gradually emerges "an intellectual understanding of the fact of the world's existence prior to the individual's, but feeling remains that the world is personally created" (1988, p. 111). Winnicott speaks of *intellectual* understanding. This means that after the capacity for illusion has been installed, the child *learns*, over time, of the separate existence of external reality, now understanding that the world has always been there, independently of the individual. The feeling that the world is created and will continue to be created personally nevertheless does not disappear. If the individual stays alive, his personal root is set in the imaginative world, and it is only from this place that the acceptance of the external world does not equal annihilation.

Throughout life, the central problem of the relation to reality remains the same: the world which is objectively real and shared has a lot to offer as long as its acceptance does not mean the loss of the reality of the personal imaginative world (cf. 1949m, p. 70). We can never be too careful when the preservation of the bonds which link external reality to subjective reality is at stake. If an older child, who is three or four years old and lives simultaneously in the shared world and in his own imaginative world, tells us that he wants to fly, we must not hit him head-on with the weight of objective reality, answering that children do not fly. On the contrary, we must pick him up and make him swirl high up the room, so that he really feels that he is flying like a bird.

> Only too soon the child will find that flying cannot be done magically. Probably in dreams magical floating through the air may be retained to some extent, or at any rate there will be a dream about taking rather long steps. [...] At ten years or so child will be practicing long-jump and high-jump, trying to jump farther and higher than the other. That will be all that remains, except dreams, of the tremendously acute sensations associated with the idea of flying that came naturally at the age of three. (1949m, p. 70)

The constitution of the primary self

The considerations of the previous section refer to the beginning of access to the senses of reality (through the reality of the subjective world) and to object relations with subjective objects.

According to Winnicott, however, the baby does not exist as a unitary individual yet, as a me. *Who* is it then, who, being in a world, encounters objects?

The unitary self is the result of the integrative tendency and reaches a more consistent and stable state at the stage when the individual, if he could talk, would say: I AM. We know, however, that integration does not occur all at once, or once and for all. *From the state of unintegration*, brief moments or periods of integration take place, and it is only gradually that the general state of integration is established on a stable basis. These moments of vivacity and of excitation are preceded by "a gathering together of the whole self" (1988, p. 117); this experience of being gathered together into a unitary self, even if momentarily, but from the creative drive, is felt as real. The encounter with the object "gives reality" to being alive, and also to the need, not only in the sense of satisfaction, but in the sense of *giving reality* to the need, the drive, the gesture which "reaches out ..." and the something that is found. What the immature self of a very young baby feels as real is this self-expression of the self (cf. 1993e, p. 25). We may well affirm, briefly, that in Winnicott, emotional health is related to the preservation of the creative drive throughout life: the experience initiated on the basis of it is integrative and is felt as real; it is the accumulation and integration of those experiences which gradually constitute the primary self in the direction of a unitary identity. Shortly after finishing breastfeeding, the baby's self falls apart, and he returns, at rest, to the state of non-integration.

In a later formulation of this same issue (cf. 1971i), Winnicott would say that the experiences of integration, which take place during the theoretical first feed, are the first and inaugural *experiences of the self*, of being as *identity*. That is, on encountering the subjective object, the baby has an experience of *primary identification* with the object, the baby *becomes the object: he is the breast*. This constitutes an experience of *being*, which has a new sense beyond that of the continuity of being: that of *being as identity*. Winnicott names this experience of being, which is present in men and women, the "pure female element". While the pure female element concerns *being*, the "pure male element" relates to *doing*. This distinction between being and doing is a new way of formulating the difference between subjective object and object objectively perceived:

> In this relatedness of pure female element to "breast" is a practical application of the idea of the subjective object, and the experience of this paves the way for the objective subject—that is, the idea of a self, and the feeling of real that springs from the sense of having an identity. (1971i, p. 177)[49]

What interests us here is the relation between the constitution of the initial self and the experience of the "pure female element". Winnicott says: "When the girl element in the boy or girl baby or patient finds the breast it is the self that has been found" (1971i, p. 180). *Being* is the most simple of all experiences and perhaps because of this, the most difficult to be conceived by means of reflection. Besides being the most simple, it is also the most important of all experiences, the basis for all subsequent ones, including the subsequent experiences of identification. For this reason,

> complex the psychology of the sense of self and of the establishment of an identity eventually becomes, as a baby grows, no sense of self emerges except on the basis of this relating in the sense of BEING. (1971i, p. 177)

Since Winnicott uses the term "breast", as we shall see, to designate the totality of the maternal care, we must say that in the primary experience of integration, the baby becomes identical to the care that he receives: he *is* that care, more precisely: the baby becomes the reliability of that care. Indeed, through the regular repetition of the experience, he will incorporate this environmental care as a part of the self. Although this question of identity is only completely formulated in the text of 1966, already in 1963, Winnicott writes that since the baby is merged with the mother, not having separated yet the "me" from the "not-me", "what is adaptive or 'good' in the environment is building up in the infant's storehouse of experience as a self quality, indistinguishable at first (by the infant) from the infant's own healthy functioning" (1963d, p. 97).

It is this sense of being that makes the baby feel not only real, but also integrated into an incipient identity, which is the primary self. In order to achieve this, however, it is essential that the drive emerges from a state of rest, in non-integration, and that it is hence personal, creative: the searching comes from the baby; it is not the environment that imposes something. If, as has already been mentioned, the initiative comes from the environment, what is left for the baby is to react and not to be. Furthermore, the baby must encounter a breast that "is", the breast of a mother who is capable of being, and not a breast that "does". The breast that "does" is a breast of the "pure male element", which is not satisfactory for the initial experience of identity.[50] During the time when the baby and the mother are a unity, if the mother has a breast that *is* then the baby can also be. The adaptation of the mother allows the baby, as he creates the breast, to create himself as someone who is. If the mother is not capable of making this contribution, the baby must develop without the capacity for being, or with a weakened capacity for being. In this case, "Instead of 'being like', this baby has to 'do like'" (1971i, p. 179).[51] When the mother is of the type that does, and imposes her mode of functioning on the baby, if she *makes him nurse*, instead of *allowing him to be, as he nurses* (thus, becoming the breast), an alert and a reaction occurs. The reaction breaks the continuity of being and exacerbates the split between spontaneity and reactivity or submission. If this is the environmental pattern, the baby will still build an identity, but this will be false and artificial, since it will be built defensively, aiming at protecting the true and spontaneous self; this self is isolated in order not to be traumatised. When spontaneity is isolated, however, being deprived in this way of opportunities for real experiences, the creative impulse is inhibited and the *true self loses expression and the opportunity to become a reality that is alive*. Without the ballast of being, the false identity must be permanently doing something, endlessly and uselessly trying to find being in doing.

Two other points must be noted here. First, the difference between being and doing must not be understood in terms of active and passive. The basis for everything is being, with the dichotomy between active and passive making sense only in relation to doing, which should only emerge from being. Second, we must bear in mind that the sense of "*being* the subjective object" of primary identity, precedes the idea of being-with-something or with someone. Two separate persons, Winnicott says, may *feel* that they are one, but in the question that is being examined here, "the baby and the object *are* one" (1971i, p. 177). In this latter case, therefore, there is no actual object relation, but a relation of "being". The relation with objects, the basis of which is *to have been the object*, will take place later, if everything goes well, and if the baby can, in due time, create the externality of the world and begin to relate to objects objectively perceived. In order for a relation to exist, there must be two individuals. There is a curious relation here that cannot rigorously be called a relation, because there are not yet two, but *two-in-one*. This is why, having already formulated the final version of his theory of the primary identity, Winnicott affirms: "it is axiomatic that there is no relating to a subjective object" (1989n, p. 187).

With regard to the term "breast", Winnicott uses it in a different sense from that of traditional psychoanalysis, especially in Kleinian psychoanalysis: "This language involving 'the breast' is jargon" he says (1969d, p. 225). It misleads us into thinking that the baby can make contact with an object which, even if understood as a partial one, is external to him (from the baby's own perspective), in that the immature baby still has not established a sense either of the external or of the internal. The word "breast" does not therefore refer to any object either external or internal, not only because there is not yet an individual capable of perceiving objects, but also because from the baby's perspective, no object is detached from the total environment.

Taking into account the totality of his thought, we can say that in Winnicott, the term "breast" has two fundamental meanings. Firstly, the breast is a *subjective object*; it is the first subjective object that the baby encounters, on the plane of *object relations*, the special character of which has just been mentioned. The mother who is there, available as breast, is the object-mother, that is, the mother who is the target of the baby's excited love and who provides the breast in such a way as to allow him to have the experience of creating the object. The experience of object relation, in the specifically Winnicottian sense, is nevertheless only possible against the background of a subjective world, which is permanently reassured by maternal reliability. In a second sense, "breast" is the name given by Winnicott to the *totality of care* with which the environment-mother provides the baby, a totality that includes the care relative to the three basic tasks.[52] Considering that the central characteristic of the care is reliability, when the baby encounters the breast, he encounters not the care itself, but the *way of being* of the care, that is, the environmental reliability. In other words, he encounters the *subjective object* (breast-object) in a *subjective world*, made of the totality of the care (breast-environment). We are now able to complete both the concept of subjective object and the full meaning of dependence. An object is subjective when, on encountering the object (which is presented by the mother in such a way that it does not detach from her, being external only to the observer), this object is created by the baby, and at the same time that he creates the object, he creates himself as identity, becoming, in this experience of primary identification, the object itself. At this precise point, the deep character of dependence emerges clearly. The mother supports the baby in three fundamental ways through the care that she offers. First, by preserving the area of illusion of omnipotence, as environment-mother, she opens and maintains a reliable subjective *world* (space and time) in which an encounter with an object may occur, and to which the baby can return to rest. Second, she enables him to reach the self, promoting an experience of *identity*, in which he becomes the object. That is to say, the mother aids in establishing "who" encounters objects. Finally, she is herself the object (subjective), the breast, the warmth, the milk, etc., which is encountered (mother-object).[53]

The mother does all of this because of her identification with the baby; because she accepts and is willing to respond to his immaturity and dependence. Her knowledge of the baby's needs is not intellectual, in the same way that the care is not really deliberate. If she is good enough, her understanding comes "from a deeper level and not necessarily from that part of the mind which has words for everything" (1968f, p. 61). Her communication with the baby, which takes place from a deep understanding, is silent: "The main things that a mother does with the baby cannot be done through words" (idem). Winnicott affirms:

> Acts of human reliability make a communication long before speech means anything—the way the mother fits in when rocking the child, the sound and tone of her voice, all communicate long before speech is understood. (1968b, p. 147)

The mother may or may not speak to the baby. This, however, is not the main issue, since when it comes to human communication, "the language is not important" (1968d, p. 95). What matters is that *through the experience of effective care*, the mother is always telling the baby that she is reliable, not because she is a machine, but because she knows, at each moment, what he needs. The baby, says Winnicott, "does not know about the communication except from the effects of *failure* of reliability" (ibid., p. 98). Either communication is silent and reliability is guaranteed, or it is traumatic, causing the experience of an unthinkable or primitive agony (cf. 1970b, p. 201).[54] If the mother needs to show her reliability and to guarantee the baby's acknowledgement of it, she will fail precisely there, since she will be imposing her external existence on him and calling for an understanding for which he is still too immature. In this case, this mother lacks confidence in the baby's maturational process in progress.

An essential aspect of this silent communication, within the strange form of "relation" which provides the baby with the primary identity is the mother's gaze.[55] Often, while nursing, the baby looks around and it is probable that he does not look at the breast, but at the mother's face. What does the baby see when he looks at the mother's face? He sees himself, affirms Winnicott; not as an *image*, since he is not yet capable of perception. What emerges in the mother's gaze is her own vision of the baby and the satisfaction that it contains. In other words, the mother is looking at the baby, and her face and gaze reflect what she sees, that is, *her vision of the baby*. To be seen by the mother's gaze is one of the fundamental bases of the feeling of existing: "When I look I am seen, so I exist" (1967a, p. 154). There is, however, the case of the baby, whose mother has an opaque gaze, herself trapped in her own interior; in this case, it is not the baby who is reflected there, but her own mood, or even worse, the rigidity of her defences. In this case, what does the baby see? There are babies, says the author, who have already become used to not receiving what they are seeking. They look and they do not see themselves. This has consequences:

> First, their own creative capacity begins to atrophy [...]. Second, the baby gets settled in to the idea that when he or she looks, what is seen is the mother's face. The mother's face is not then a mirror. So perception takes the place of apperception. (1967a, p. 151)

Winnicott uses the term "apperception" as opposed to "perception". It refers to the creative gaze, characteristic of the subjective world. It is linked to the word "to create", in the sense of "to bring into existence", to the fact that someone is able to go on "seeing everything afresh all the time" (1986h, p. 41). When there is health, this ability to look creatively at the world does not disappear. Even later, when the individual is able to relate to the world of objectively perceived objects, this gaze will never be entirely subject, as perception is by definition, to the objective outlines of external reality. If the mother's gaze does not reflect the baby, but what he sees is the mother's own face, then a fact from external reality violates the baby's legitimate experience of omnipotence.

When the mother protects the area of illusion of omnipotence at the same time that, in small doses, she presents the world to the baby, he makes the experience of creating the world and himself continuously and of having a place to inhabit. In this way, the mother provides her own person as raw material for the child to create, so that eventually the subjective mother is very similar to the mother who is objectively perceived. For Winnicott,

> In the course of time the individual becomes able to forgo the *actual* presence of a mother or mother-figure. This has been referred to in such terms as the establishment of an 'internal environment'. It is more primitive than the phenomenon which deserves the term "introjected mother". (1958g, p. 34)[56]

Establishing an "internal environment" does not mean *to introject* imagos or maternal functions, but to incorporate maternal care and the sense of reliability.[57] The baby is not a dynamics in search of content, he does not relate yet to objects and possesses neither an inside nor an outside for a mechanism such as introjection to make sense. When primary creativity is considered, it is not necessary to postulate that the human being, as a baby, becomes an individual and has a world only because he is able to project what has been previously introjected; that is, "excreting what has been incorporated" (1988, p. 110). On the basis of the Winnicottian conception of the human being, it is not difficult to understand why human psychic life cannot be seen in the terms of body symbolism. There is no way of reconciling the concepts of creativity on one side, and those of introjection and projection on the other. The author is keen to emphasise "the concept of primary creativity, and of absolute originality, as against the projection of previously introjected (digested and worked over)" (1988, p. 112).

Notes

1. The book *Human Nature* is taken as the basis for the analysis presented in this section.
2. With this sentence, Winnicott highlights the fact that essential things happen to the baby, which are inaccessible to the observer. It follows from this that the study of severe pathologies of schizophrenic type, which originate in the most primitive phases, is especially fruitful if carried out by observing and treating older children and adults who regress to dependence and not through observing babies. He says: "My experiences have led me to recognise that dependent or deeply regressed patients can teach the analyst more about early infancy than can be learned from direct observation of infants [...]" (1965m, p. 141).
3. On this point, Loparic says: "As in Heidegger, the inner difficulty of life does not come from its finitude, from having-to-die, but rather from *having to go on being*. According to Winnicott, it is from this having-to-be that all other human needs originate" (Loparic, 2000b, p. 359).
4. Cf. Winnicott, 1958f, p. 182.
5. Winnicott uses the word "frustration" here in the common and not in the technical sense, since for him, "such words as *frustration* begin to have meaning in the sense that the infant is able to hold in his mind the idea that something was expected but the expectation was not completely

fulfilled" (1987c, p. 54; my italics). This condition evidently cannot be affirmed at such a primitive moment, with a long maturation process being required before frustration may exist, that is, before it may be experienced as such.

6. Winnicott emphasises the need to distinguish birth experience from birth trauma (cf. 1958f). Like Freud, he considers Otto Rank's thesis that birth would be traumatic in itself because it causes a dramatic separation from the mother, to be entirely unfounded. The newly born baby is not sufficiently mature even to feel connected to the mother; he merely feels either security and continuity or insecurity and discontinuity; he thus cannot experience any separation (cf. 1958f).
7. Cf. Winnicott, 1958f. Trauma at this point is related to delivery and birth. I highlight its temporal character since, according to Winnicott, this is the specific character of traumas which form the basis of psychotic pathologies. The question will be developed in a future book on schizophrenic psychoses in Winnicott's work.
8. On birth and trauma experience, and on the importance of this issue in the analysis of psychotics, cf. Winnicott, 1958f.
9. We should note the meaning that Winnicott gives to the word "love" at this beginning of life. He associates it with contact and physical care, which are the only manifestations of love that the baby is capable of receiving.
10. I shall clarify the sense in which Winnicott uses the term "object" when referring to the mother later in the text.
11. Winnicott clarifies the concept of primary identification, which forms the basis of the experience of primary identity, by distinguishing being from doing, one of the most complex points of Winnicott's theory, which shall be addressed later.
12. In reviewing the book *Psychoanalytical Studies of the Personality* (1952), by Fairbairn, Winnicott criticises the fact that the former does not take primary creativity into account and says: "In his theory, primary psychic creativity is not a human property; an infinite series of introjections and projections form the infant's psychic experience. Fairbairn's theory here lines up with the theory given us by Melanie Klein, which also allows no tribute to be paid to the idea of primary psychic creativity" (1953b, p. 420).
13. The word "omnipotence", used for this primitive stage, describes a special characteristic of dependence and means that the baby does not know anything about his own existence or that of the external world. We must not confuse this specific meaning of the *experience of omnipotence*, in the area of illusion, characteristic of the subjective world, with the *feeling of omnipotence*, which relates to a power which knows no limits and precisely "belongs to hopelessness about dependence" (1971h, p. 40).
14. This configures the trauma of the non-event, which will be retained, not in the repressed unconscious, which already presumes a high degree of maturation, with an already established internal psychic reality, but in the not-happened unconscious, which is the negative form of the Winnicottian originary unconscious. To name a type of unconscious that does not consist of repressed material (Freudian unconscious), but the very primitive one, proceeding the advent of representations, which retains the lost memory of the breakdown, I will use the expression "not happened unconscious", coined by Zeljko Loparic for this purpose. This "not happened" unconscious is merely the negative side, so to speak, of the primary unconscious, the content of which can only be reached in dreams and "contributes fundamentally to all significant experiences of human individual" (1963c, p. 218).

The phrase was inspired by a phrase by Winnicott in the 1974 text, "Fear of breakdown". Referring to the breakdown which occurs when environmental intrusion is of the type leaves the baby's gesture without a response, Winnicott says, "To understand this it is necessary to think not of trauma [in the sense of something imposed] but of nothing happening when something might profitably have happened" (1974, p. 93).

What "did not happen" was the experience which, from rest or motivated by an impulse, would have been completed and would have provided continuity to the maturation process due to the environment adapting to the needs and rhythm of the baby and which was lost due to lack of environmental favour: the environment did not respond, was hasty or intervened in the baby's gesture. His reaction to this environmental failure interrupts his continuity of being, which constitutes a breakdown. While it occurs, the breakdown is not actually experienced, since the baby is not yet a unitary person able to experience and record what exceeds his area of omnipotence; even so, he suffers the consequences of this "disaster" which occurs to him, even before an "I" has been established.

15. The issue of illusion and, initially, the illusion of omnipotence is one of Winnicott's basic contributions to the theme of the constitution of the self and of the senses of reality. It is an issue of utmost complexity and a central theme in philosophy. Within the context of psychoanalysis, Winnicott is one of the only thinkers to attach due weight and status to it. This contribution, central to an understanding of his thought, has nevertheless been the target of distortions and/or improper assimilations by/to psychoanalytical tradition. For example, Michael Jacobs (1995), after stating that Winnicott is undoubtedly an original thinker, primarily because of the concepts which are clearly "his output", such as the transitional object and the squiggle game [sic], notes that there is a second sense in which Winnicott may be considered original: the "ability to adapt and adopt the concepts and aspects of clinical practice which others invented". Here, Jacobs continues, "we may cite the significant change which he made in Freud's concept of illusion, which in Winnicott became a means of perceiving [sic] the present, more than as an indication, as in Freud, of the child's desire" (Jacobs, 1995, p. 27).

16. Depending on its moment of origin, some cases of denial or inhibition of the instinctual source may be understood not in terms of censorship of undesirable content, but as retreat as a reaction to intrusion. The instinctual tension is intrusive and interrupts the continuity of being if there is not an active facilitation by the mother. Before the indwelling of the psyche in the body, the body is as foreign to the baby as the things in the external world, so that instinctual tensions are as intrusive as anything intrusive deriving from the environment.

17. Cf. Chapter Four, section titled "The stage of concern".

18. In a text from 1957, Winnicott states that the lack of instinctual tension may generate anxiety, but if there is integration of the sense of time within the personality, this will enable the baby to wait for the natural return of instinctual demand (cf. 1958g, p. 33). For a more extensive development of this question, cf. Winnicott 1958b and 1958g. See also the case described in Winnicott 1986a, in addition to the introduction to the same book by Masud Khan.

19. It should be noted that this quotation offers a good example of the Winnicottian use of the terms "ego" and "self". Oral satisfaction may be traumatic if it violates the "ego function", that is, what is already integrated in the baby and exists as an incipient self. The trauma affects the person of the baby, whatever is the existing degree of integration and affects the maturational process.

20. The idea that the baby is not driven mainly by the principle of pleasure/displeasure, but by the search for the object had already been proposed by Fairbairn. Despite the fact that Fairbairn developed this point in a different direction from that of Winnicott, the latter affirmed in a text of 1969: "I am obviously near to Fairbairn's statement made in 1944 that psycho-analytic theory was emphasizing drive-satisfaction at the expense of what Fairbairn called 'object-seeking'. And

Fairbairn was working, as I am here, on the ways in which psycho-analytic theory needed to be developed or modified if the analyst could hope to become able to cope with schizoid phenomena in the treatment of patients" (1970b, p. 256).

21. Winnicott cites Merrill Middlemore who, in the book *The Nursing Couple* (1941), describes how immensely careful she had to be in order not to interfere with this extremely delicate situation of the mother and the baby at the beginning of the relationship. "She took care", says Winnicott, "not be expecting successes or afraid of failure. There must be very few who are equipped to make this type of observation of intimacy" (1988, p. 105).

22. In their fine book *Le bébé et la coordination motrice* [The baby and motor coordination] (1994), the experts on psychomotricity, M. –M. Béziers and Y. Hunzinger, affirm that one of the caring actions which can promote well-being and safety in the baby, facilitating motor coordination, consists of the mother ensuring, while handling or breastfeeding the baby, that his feet are supported, so that they can exert pressure against the armrest of the armchair, the mother's hands or against her body.

23. The experts cited in the previous note remind the reader that for the baby, life is movement and that since the beginning, we must be careful to "avoid any obstacle to the expression of his or her movement" (Béziers & Hunzinger, 1994, p. 32).

24. Winnicott dedicated much of his theoretical effort to elucidating the aggressiveness and destructivity inherent to human nature. It should be noted that the two concepts, aggressiveness and destructivity, are necessary for distinguishing two forms of "aggression" that are radically different. This will become clearer throughout this book, especially in Chapter Four, in the sections referring to the stages of use of an object and of concern. This question runs through the whole of Winnicott's work and his formulations change as his thought evolves. It took him a long time to arrive at a more finished formulation, which only occurred, according to him, in one of the latest and more important articles, "The use of an object", of November 1968. In *Human Nature*, in a footnote added in 1970, he points out that with regard to the lack of a satisfactory formulation for the roots of aggression "this is the reason why I could not publish this book" (1988, p. 79).

25. It is not difficult to perceive that Winnicott's conception of the roots of aggression is completely at odds with the theories of Freud and Klein. With regard to Freud, the central point of discord is the fact that he conceives of aggression as a reaction to frustrations in contact with the reality principle, assuming a high degree of development in the baby, which is inconceivable during the initial moments. With regard to Melanie Klein, the motives are well known: in order to explain aggression, especially in the primitive stages, she invokes a constitutional destructiveness in the individual. In relation to both them there is another objection: the two theories fail to consider the baby's dependence and the fact that he reacts to the kind of care he receives.

26. On this question cf. Winnicott, 1965n and 1965r.

27. The theme of the invasive and traumatic environmental pattern deriving from psychiatric abnormalities of the mother, will be developed in another study, which aims to clarify Winnicott's theory of psychoses.

28. The existence of this non-instinctual anger, actually related to the loss of being became clear to me as a finding of clinical practice. Guided by this phenomenon, I searched for some observations by Winnicott which would provide a basis for it. As in other cases, I found a number of extremely interesting affirmations scattered throughout his work. It is the results of this search which are presented here.

29. For a more extensive study of the therapeutic use of failure by the analyst, see Dias, 2011b, text 3.

30. This theme is of great importance for the configuration of schizoid pathologies.

31. In the clinical case presented in the article "Withdrawal and regression", Winnicott points out to the patient who withdraws and snoozes during the session that his withdrawal at that moment is an escape from the painful experience of being precisely between the states of waking and sleeping, or between speaking to the analyst and withdrawing. The patient then says that although he remained lying on the couch, he had had the idea of being curled up. At this point, Winnicott made a highly significant interpretation: "In speaking of yourself as curled up and moving round, you are at the same time implying something which naturally you are not describing since you are not aware of it; you imply the *existence of a medium*." The patient showed he had grasped the idea of a medium that provided him with *holding*, saying: "Like the oil in which wheels move" (1955a, p. 257). It is this medium that may be called *the mother's lap*.
32. By proposing the terms "object-mother" and "environment-mother" in order to distinguish two aspects of maternal care, Winnicott proceeds with great caution, afraid that these terms may become empty *slogans* and "develop a rigidity and an obstructive quality" (1963b, p. 102).
33. In her book *Ginástica holística: história e desenvolvimento de um método de cuidados corporais* [Holistic gymnastics: history and development of a method of bodily care] (2000), Maria Emília Mendonça, who sought in Winnicott a greater understanding of certain phenomena occurring in her clinical practice, discusses the subtle details of her method of bodily care and reflects upon the importance of the teacher–student relationship. She states that she always noticed that in group classes, some students "disconnected" from the class for a few moments; perhaps due to the silence, or perhaps because they were rocked by the teacher's voice; these students reached a state of quietness, departing from the objective action that was taking place. She intuitively perceived the importance of not interfering in an abrupt manner with these states which, according to her, were not a manifestation of disinterest, but, on the contrary, of trust. After a while, the student would return with an enhanced sensation of presence in class. It is only from this moment on, the author observes, that class may effectively start for that student (Mendonça, 2000, p. 205).
34. Fear of disintegration is one of the central aspects of psychotic pathologies of a schizophrenic type.
35. The unthinkable agonies constitute the core concept of psychotic pathologies in Winnicott's work. They will be studied in detail in a forthcoming book.
36. An important example of total experience, on the occasion of the activities of excretion of the infant, is found in Winnicott, 1949e.
37. Cf. Winnicott, 1949f.
38. The theme of the dwelling in the body will be developed next, when the task specific to it is described: the indwelling of the psyche in the body.
39. M. Sechehaye, 1994, respectively pp. 22; 30; 22.
40. Forrest Gump is the name of the character and the title of the film by director Robert Zemeckis (1994).
41. Referring to the care to the patient that regresses to dependence, Winnicott says that "'holding', like the task of the mother in infant-care, acknowledges tacitly the tendency of the patient to disintegrate, to cease to exist, to fall for ever" (1965d, p. 241). Hence, the need to sustain the presence and vivacity of the world.
42. The already cited M. –M. Béziers and Y. Husinger corroborate this point and show that the position of well-being, for the baby, is the one in which he is "rolled up". When feeling safe, the baby naturally adopts this rolling up position. Under pathological conditions or "if the baby is suffering from some discomfort, this 'rolling up' will not occur on being taken in the mother's arms. On the contrary", the authors state, "what we will observe is the reverse position 'in extension':

head and arms pulled back, the back arched and the extensor muscles pulled taut" (Béziers & Hunsinger, 1994, p. 20).

43. I recommend to the reader the excellent work by Vera Regina F. de Laurentiis (2016) regarding the process of indwelling of the psyche in the body, starting from the initial moments and through every stage of maturation.
44. On the distinction between separating objects and separating the environment from the self, Winnicott, 1964d.
45. For Winnicott, an essential aspect of the issue of the access to reality is that there is not a single sense of reality, but several. Human development can be seen as the process by means of which the many senses of reality with their different types of object are gradually established, along with the constitution of various possibilities of object relation of the human individual. In traditional psychoanalysis, there is only one sense of reality. For a development of this issue, cf. Loparic, 1995a.
46. This is true above all in the cases of schizoid pathologies.
47. We should note here that the expression "subjective object" is not the most fortunate. First, because the very etymology of the term "object" leads us to think of an object of perception (*ob-jectum*), which is not specifically the case at this point. Second, because the term "subjective" can easily lead us to think about the subject/object polarity, which belongs to a certain lineage of Western thought, in which the subject is above all a thinking being, endowed with consciousness and filled with representations and feelings. In addition to the fact that Winnicott's thought does not belong to this lineage, at this point of maturation, the baby is not a self-conscious being and does not yet have objects of mental representation. We must thus bear in mind the specific sense which Winnicott attributed in his theory to the expression "subjective".
48. Winnicott uses the term "reliability" to name the central characteristic of the faciliting environment. In Webster's Encyclopedic Unabriged Dictionary (1996), the verb "rely", deriving from the Latin *religare*, means "to depend confidently, put trust in". The adjective "reliable" means "that may be relied on, trustworth [...] that can be dependent upon with confident certainty". Winnicott could have used "trustworthness", which also contemplates the idea, in the sense of confidence, of dependability, but predominantly used reliability. It is likely that he preferred this term, since it was used more in common language, or also, as it seems to me, since the term includes, due to its etymological root, the sense of linkage, contact, recontact, reconnection, referring not only to the initial contact of mother and baby, which is what causes the engagement of the baby with life, but also due to the idea that what is reliable is the thing with which one can always restore links, to which one can always reconnect. This question is of such importance in Winnicott, that the breakdown of reliability during the initial stages constitutes a traumatic experience and results in disorders of a schizophrenic type. In Winnicott's classification of traumas according to the moment of maturation, the breakdown of reliability is described as the first sense of trauma. Cf. Winnicott, 1989d. On environment reliability as participating in the constitution of the self, cf. Dias, 2011b, text 1.
49. In a text dating from 1968–1969, which is a response to comments on his 1966 article "The split-off male and female elements to be found in men and women", Winnicott affirms that as a result of the clinical work described in this article, he saw himself in condition to compare *being* and *doing*. "I discovered myself looking at an essential conflict of human beings, one which must be operative at a very early date; that between being the object which also has the property of being, and by contrast a confrontation with the object which involves activity and object-relating that is

backed by instinct or drive. This turned out to be a new statement of what I have tried to describe before in terms of the subjective object and the object that is objectively perceived" (1972, p. 191).

50. In Winnicott's proposition, "being" and "doing" are two forms of object relation, with the difference between them to be understood on the basis of the line of maturation. While the first one is based on the need to be, the second already presupposes a separation between me and not-me and is based on instinctual drives. This last question, already related to doing, will be implicitly examined in sections "The stage of concern" and "The oedipal stage" of Chapter Four.

51. This point has important implications for the understanding of psychotic defences and for clinical work with schizophrenic patients who regress to dependence and whose central problem lies in an absence of the experience of *being*, which was replaced by a defensive organisation supported by *doing*.

52. In the article "Transitional objects and transitional phenomena", referring to the repeated creation by the baby of the mother's breast as a "subjective phenomenon", Winnicott introduces a note, in which he states that the term "breast" includes "the whole technique of mothering. When it is said that the first object is the breast, the word 'breast' is used, I believe, to stand for the technique of mothering as well as for the actual flesh" (1953c, p. 15, note 3). In another article, he notes that he has made it very clear that "the word *breast* and the idea of breast-feeding is an expression that carries with it the whole technique of being a mother to a baby" (1969b, p. 26). He also points out in another text: "The part-object is a whole object from the infant's point […]" (1989g, p. 431).

53. Maternal failures only become traumatic when they establish a pattern of failure. With regard to this pattern, the mother may fail in the totality of the care, which includes these three modes of favouring, or she may fail in a more specific way, being able to provide certain aspect of the care, but failing in another. Without taking into account other factors that may play a role, such as the presence of an aunt or nanny, it can be said that the difficulties or disorders of the individual will assume different configurations according to the nature of maternal failure.

54. On unthinkable agonies, central for the understanding of psychotic pathologies, cf. Winnicott, 1968d; 1974, and 1989q. The issue will be examined in detail in another study in the process of conclusion.

55. Cf. Winnicott, 1967a.

56. In this citation, we note the distinction, emphasised by Winnicott, between "internal environment", which is no object, but rather the reliable (or unreliable) modes of being of the mother and the total environment, and the Kleinian expression "introjected mother", which supposes an inside, with the mother as an internal object. Emphasising the difference between his theory and Melaine Klein's, Winnicott notes that the expression "internal object" is a mental concept (cf. 1953c). He also says: "'The good mother' and 'the bad mother' of the Kleinian jargon are internal objects and are nothing to do with real women" (1987b, p. 38).

57. On the difference between incorporation and introjection in Winnicott, see Dias' study, 2011b, text 7.

CHAPTER FOUR

The stages of relative dependence and independence

The stage of disillusion, weaning, and beginning of mental functions

The stages in which the baby gradually moves from absolute to relative dependence on the mother's care still form part of the early phases of development; since they precede the structuring of the me as a unity, if a pattern of environmental failure is established, there is still risk of psychosis. During this period, the tasks of integration in time and space, of indwelling of the psyche in the body and of contact with reality (still subjective), parallel to the constitution of the primary self, which began during the stage of the theoretical first feed, continue along the maturational process, requiring new resolutions, which will constitute new tasks. Throughout life, these tasks will set the individual before new challenges to be faced and experienced. The description provided here does not cover the features assumed by these initial tasks in the later stages of life, being limited to the aspects concerning the initial stages.

What characterises this stage, during which disillusion begins, as well as the subsequent ones, is the fact that, unlike the stages described in the previous chapter, a gradual de-adaptation of the mother is initiated regarding the needs of the baby. If healthy, the mother emerges naturally from the state of "primary maternal preoccupation", already tired of the limitation of her world and of the extreme demands imposed by the baby's absolute dependence. Small failures begin to occur, which, because they occur as the baby progressively matures, still form part of the adaptation agenda. This coincides with the baby's need to continue with the maturational process; the mother's de-adaptation is vital for initiating the break up of the undifferentiated mother–baby unit, in order to set in motion the long and slow process of separation which will lead the little individual to the integration into a unitary and separated me, capable of establishing relations with the not-me or the external world.

The mother's de-adaptation triggers the process of disillusion of the baby. But disillusion, with its own acquisitions, *can only take place on the basis of a well-founded capacity for illusion*. It is often thought that in Winnicott's theory, as is the case in common sense, disillusion is a merely negative process of breaking an illusion, but this is not entirely correct. According to the author, what the baby leaves behind as he matures *is not the basic illusion*, which will remain if the baby is healthy, but rather the illusion of *omnipotence*. Over time, the child will progressively understand that he is not the one who effectively creates the world; that its existence is prior to and independent from him. The child will learn that the world has always been there and will continue to be there after his death. However, the *feeling* that the world was created personally and may continue to be created does not disappear. Despite an intellectual understanding, the individual retains the capacity for illusion, exercising creativity naturally, which is, as we have already seen, "the retention throughout life of something that belongs properly to infant experience: the ability to create the world" (1986h, p. 40).

Among the various aspects of the total process of disillusion, weaning is a particularly significant achievement. When the baby himself does not promote it, it is the mother who must carry it out; for this purpose, she needs her aggressiveness, she must count on some capacity for hating, whether actively or passively, which may be triggered when necessary. If, however, the mother is depressed, she will fear her hate, which may not be within reach of her consciousness; in this way, she will not be in a condition to fulfil her role in the disillusionment process, of which weaning is an aspect. In addition to being able to hate the overload which the baby represents, she must also be capable of facing the baby's wrath or hate, caused by the de-adaptation.[1] In other words, the mother who is healthy can face ambivalence in object relating and use it appropriately (cf. 1989d, p. 146). As Edna Vilete puts it, the mother must be able to

> [...] acknowledge and endure the child's hate, as well as accept that, for sometime, she will become the mean mother for him. Accepting means surviving as the strong mother, who is able to take care without the resources of omnipotence with which she was invested by the child until then. (Vilete, 2000, p. 158)

It is during this period that mental functioning and intellectual processes begin to be exercised specifically, helping the baby to deal with the gap existing between the complete and the incomplete adaptation. It is the flaws in maternal care that drive forward the use of the mind; it is by means of the incipient intellectual understanding that environment failures start to be taken into account, becoming understandable, bearable, and even predictable (cf. Winnicott, 1953a). If, until then, everything went well and the baby was spared a precocious and defensive mind functioning due to the good-enough adaptation, he is already capable, at this point, of using a type of knowledge *which is not mental* but stems from the *growing familiarity* with the bodily sensations and things of the environment. The baby already recognises rhythms, sounds, smells, emotional moods on a pre-intellectual plane and is already in possession of a certain pre-representational "if ... then" scheme.[2] When the baby is healthy, it is on this basis of a non–mental understanding that intellectual functioning begins to operate, without being a pathological defence aimed at controlling potential intrusions. From that moment onwards, the baby starts to use his intellect to know that the noises in the kitchen indicate that food is about to turn up. The "if … then" scheme becomes more refined and can now be properly thought out; instead of simply becoming more excited and impatient with the noises, the baby uses these new resources to be able to wait. Furthermore, in this phase of de-adaptation, there is a first glimpse of dependence: the infant learns, *in his mind*, that the mother is necessary. This, naturally, leaves him very exposed and no care is enough to avoid hurting the baby's dignity.

There are two general environment attitudes which are especially important in facilitating the individual's natural tendency towards maturation. They must be present at all stages, those prior and those subsequent to this one, but are particularly significant at the point when the baby is moving towards relative dependence: on one hand, the continuous existence of the conditions for a high degree of dependence, which may be again necessary, depending on the circumstances; on the other, the provision of opportunity for the individual to separate gradually from the mother and connect to the family, and from the family to the social unit closest to it and so on in ever wider circles. In this last sense, the mother's love, or the therapist's, means not only meeting the needs of dependence, but giving the opportunity which, at the appropriate time, will allow the child or the patient to move gradually from dependence to autonomy. As infants grow and develop, they acquire an increasing capacity to signal their needs; there are mothers who, because they have become excessively good and skilled in the technique of taking care of their children, do not always pay attention to the countless signs of communication and continue to guess and meet their needs as if they were still merged in with the environment. In this way, very often,

> […] the mother, by being a seemingly good mother, does something worse than castrate the infant. The latter is left with two alternatives: either being in a permanent state of regression and of being merged with the mother, or else staging a total rejection of the mother, even of the seemingly good mother. (1960b, p. 51)

On the other hand, the process of separation must be gradual. The child must break free from the mother's arms and lap, "but not to go into space"; the child moves away to a wider area, albeit still under control, "something that is symbolical of the lap from which the child has broken away" (1965p, p. 90). This movement of going away and releasing oneself, which will effectively start at the stage of transitionality, will remain real throughout life. Life, says the author, "is a long series of coming out of enclosures and taking new risks and meeting new and exciting challenges" (1965q, p. 115). In a text on the importance of the family as the thing which gives continuity to the mother's lap, which one must leave, Winnicott notes that each individual must walk the long path from being merged with the mother to being separate yet still related to her, and then, to mother and father together; the journey continues through the larger group known as the family, with the father and the mother as the main features. The family has its own growth […]. The family protects the child from the world, but gradually the world finds its way in via the aunts and uncles, the neighbours, the earliest schoolmates. "This gradual environmental seeping-in is the way by which a child can best come to terms with the wider world, and follows exactly the pattern of the infant's introduction to external reality by the mother" (1961b, p. 40).

Despite often being a burden and a hindrance, the family never ceases to be important throughout the individual's life. It is responsible for many of our journeys, since we escape, emigrate, change address because of the need to break away; then, we return periodically because we need to renew contacts with family (cf. 1961b).

In order for the explorations outside the fence to continue to be challenging and exciting it is necessary, however, that above all at the beginning, the path of return to the more primitive stages, of regression to dependence, is always open, since "coming out of the enclosure is very exciting and very frightening; and that once out, its awful for the child not being able to get back" (1965q, p. 115).

A central aspect of environment reliability consists in *always keeping the possibility of return open, a need that lasts forever*. The older child, the adolescent, the healthy young person and adult have various immaturities to fall back upon either for fun or during a period of need, whether in secret auto-erotic experiences or in dreaming (cf. 1965p). These immaturities indicate health, being "the residues of the healthy states of dependence that are characteristic of all the earlier phases of growth" (1954b, p. 181). Healthy individuals have this ability because the foundation was given to them at the initial stages, through the experience of countless returns to unintegration and, during the period described here, through the mother's capacity for allowing the baby to return to dependence and to the subjective world, whenever this proved necessary.

The stage of transitionality

The description of the phenomena of transitionality was undoubtedly the most rapidly accepted of Winnicott's contributions and was the reason why he became known and famous. Indeed, for a long time, the majority of the articles and comments on his work were predominantly devoted to this theme. The indisputable originality of the phenomenon, which had never been conceptualised before by traditional psychoanalysis, made it easy to assimilate into the already established body of theory, without further questions regarding the conceptual appropriateness of such assimilation. In addition to the fact that its particular place in the maturational process was ignored by analyses of the issue, the apparent simplicity of the phenomenon lent itself to such popularisation, that Winnicott felt obliged, in *Playing and Reality*, to re-issue a slightly modified version of the original article "Transitional objects and transitional phenomena", in which he tried to correct some distortions in the interpretation. He pointed out, for example, that what interested him was "not so much the object used as the use of the object" (1971e, p. xvi). That is, what is important for the psychoanalytical knowledge is not the description of new objects (internal, external, bizarre, *petit a*, etc.) but rather, the modes of being and relating of the human being.

From the perspective of the totality of Winnicott's work, the transitional phenomena are fundamental for the human maturational process, since they inaugurate one of the stages, and one of the achievements of maturation, leading the individual to a new sense of reality which, in the healthy individual, will establish a specific area of experience. The capacity for what is specific to transitionality, however, depends on the successful resolution of the tasks of the previous stages, since the experiences that take place within the transitional area and the new sense of reality which results from them are necessarily rooted in the subjective world of the baby. It is the reality based and experienced in his subjective world that provides a foundation for this transitional sense of reality. If the subjective sense of real has not been established, the transitional phenomena will not have meaning and the individual will not be able to enjoy their rewards. A baby who has not been provided with a sense of safety which is incorporated as a belief cannot "absent himself", being distracted with the transitional object; on the contrary, he can only remain alert, preventing possible invasions.

Transitional phenomena do not belong to the instinctual line, but to the ego line, of the maturational process; they are in the direct line of the achievement of the task of establishing contact with external reality, which began with the theoretical first feed. At the outset, the task of contact with reality is facilitated by the fact that the mother presents the world to the baby in such a way that, initially, the infant does not have to know that the object was found instead of being created by him. The baby thus begins to relate to reality, which is external from the perspective of the observer, via creativity and not via submission. At a subsequent moment in development, the I AM stage, he will have to start dealing with the fact of the separate existence of the world, and the great challenge will be to relate to the objectivity of the external world without the loss of personal spontaneity and primary creativity. Transitional phenomena are precisely halfway, as an intermediary and facilitating passage, in this "long journey", which goes from reality conceived subjectively to reality perceived objectively.[3] The "third area of experience" must therefore be preserved at every stage of the maturational process and in any sector of life, so that external, naked, and raw reality has a personal meaning. Over time, it must also be exercised on its own terrain, the arts and culture in general. But even when the individual has already accessed the shared world and even when, through talent, he becomes capable of artistic creation, creativity continues to be primarily a phenomenon of life; it has to do with the way in which the person becomes capable of relating to external reality, *without the loss of the personal sense of existence.*

Transitional phenomena emerge from the area of the illusion of omnipotence, within which the reality of the subjective world has been constructed. When they start to occur, at around eight to ten months, the process of disillusion has already started. They are responsible for giving continuity to the illusion, with gradual changes to omnipotence. They are characterised by the clinging to the transitional object and constitute the beginning of the capacity for symbolisation; they subsequently develop into the capacity for play and, as development continues, extend themselves to the entire cultural field. Transitional objects and then play are the precursors of the adult's capacity for using the field of culture, religion, and art for the necessary and salutary rest from the eternal task of separating facts from fantasy. What lies at the beginning of everything, however, is the illusion, since the child needs to start living "in a subjective state, being the creator of all" (1986c, p. 16).

How do transitional objects come about and in what way do they promote the passage to the reality of objects that are perceived objectively? It is an observable fact that, shortly after birth, babies suck their fingers and wrists, adopt some technique of touching their face or mutter sounds. These activities, which are normally seen as an oral autoerotic exercise are in part already transitional, being precursors of the subsequent adoption of a beloved object by the baby: the teddy bear, the edge of a blanket or a nappy. In order for the pre-transitional sense of these activities to become explicit, we must be able to see more than excitation and oral satisfaction in these primitive phenomena; we must acknowledge the baby's drive to reach an object, his capacity for creating, inventing, originating an object, his increasing ability to recognise a not-me object, the beginning of an affectionate type of object relation, etc. (cf. 1953c).[4]

In due time, as a result of the baby's increasing maturity, during the mother's de-adaptation, this phenomenon occurs, which had not yet received attention from analytical research but which had been noticed by mothers: the attachment of the baby to certain objects which he, so to speak, elects.[5] Invested with a very special importance, transitional objects are treated with great affection by the baby, but also with brutality, requiring them to be durable. For quite some time, they become indispensable, irreplaceable, particularly during moments of tension, unease, and anxiety such as the passage from wakefulness to sleep or during prolonged absences of the mother, who knows that the object cannot be replaced, not even by an equivalent one and that it must not be washed, however dirty it may be, since this would introduce a break in the continuity of the baby's experience, and that it must be taken on the family travels. If the baby is permitted this experience then over time, the object will lose the meaning that it had at that time, being "not so much forgotten as relegated to limbo" (1953c, p. 7).

During the period of absolute adaptation of the mother, object presenting, that is, the provision of raw material for the creation of subjective objects, was carried out in such a way that the external reality of the object did not confront the reality of the subjective world. The nature of object relation was that of primary identification with the object: the baby *is* the object. As integration becomes more consistent, maturation demands that something of the external world gradually interferes in the area of omnipotence of the infant. Being able to adopt a transitional object already announces that this process is underway and, from then on, some changes are introduced. A small break occurs in the omnipotence. With the transitional object, some characteristics of external reality start to enter into experience: the transitional object adapts itself but not as absolutely as the mother does. From *being* the object, the baby changes to *possessing* the object and, by means of this possession, he postpones the abandonment of magical control over the world, prolonging for some time the omnipotence which was originally satisfied by the mother's adaptation (cf. 1988). During the phase ruled by transitionality, the baby will abandon the omnipotent magical control which characterises the relation to subjective objects, gradually assuming control via manipulation, involving the pleasure of muscular exercise and coordination. Shortly afterwards, another achievement will be made, when the baby can already know that a particular object was given to him and he is be able to say "ta", "thereby acknowledging a limitation of magical control and acknowledging dependence on the goodwill of people in the external world" (1988, p. 107).

Many other acquisitions are occurring while the baby uses transitional objects; some of them show the intimate connection between the functioning of the body and personal maturation. In parallel with the development of coordination, a gradual enrichment of bodily sensitivity takes place, with the sharpening of the senses and corresponding imaginative elaboration of sensory experiences. The sense of smell, for example, reaches a peak which perhaps is never repeated with this intensity, except in psychotic episodes; texture and temperature, dryness and humidity have a tremendous meaning; palate becomes much more refined and one frequently observes the baby drooling. It is also possible to observe, during this phase, the beginning of the capacity for feelings of affection. Since all of this adds up to the voracious appetite which emerges with hunger, the baby reminds us, Winnicott jokes, of the lion in its cage, with tender feelings for the bone which is about to be destroyed.

At the beginning of the passage from absolute to relative adaptation, transitional objects play an indispensable supporting role, since they replace the mother who is de-adapting and hence disillusioning the baby. Transitionality marks the beginning of the distinction, of the breaking of the mother–baby unit. The infant, who is a creator of worlds, creates the first region, the first distance, the inaugural area of separation between him and the mother: the potential space.[6] Gradually, from the *two-in-one* fusional unit, two individuals will emerge, permitting the initiation of what is properly called a relationship, the bases of which are provided by the *sui generis* experience with the subjective object.[7] The transitional object enters the precise space between mother and baby, which is both separation and the symbol of the union with what is being separated; it represents the mother or the breast, or even the child's self, as it exists at this point of maturation. The symbolic activity which starts here brings a great breadth of experience, since "the symbol of union gives wider scope for human experience than union itself" (1986d, p. 135). I believe that this is the meaning of Winnicott's polemical assertion that over time, the transitional object becomes as indispensable or more indispensable than the mother herself.

It may occur that the same concrete object—the teddy bear, the blanket, the dummy—which initially is subjective, becomes transitional. It is thus not a question of one particular object being subjective and another one transitional. What changes is not the object, but its *sense of reality*, and it is to this that Winnicott refers when he affirms that this phenomenon enables us to observe something of the *nature of the object* (cf. 1953c), that is, of the change in the nature of object relation within the maturational process, specifically because

> it is not the object, of course, that is transitional. The object represents the infant's transition from a state of being merged with the mother to a state of being in relation to the mother as something outside and separate. (1953c, pp. 19–20)

In order for this transition to take place, for transitionality to be configured as such, the baby must gradually create a new space, a new "world". What maturation promotes is the capacity, inherent to every human being, to create worlds and transit between them. At this point, the potential space is being created, the third area of experience, the place where, if we are healthy, we may live (cf. 1971g), temporarily spared from the task of separating facts from fantasy. If the baby enjoys the satisfactory environmental conditions which enable him to create this new world, in which the continuity of the basic illusion is preserved, this area will be available for the creation and exercise of the capacity for symbolising and playing, extending itself over the course of life to the arts and to culture in general. Everything that subsequently happens in the potential space maintains the characteristics of the original transitional phenomena: it is neither inside nor outside; it belongs neither to the "internal" personal psychic reality, nor to external and shared reality; it is neither delirium, nor objectivity. In this way, transitional objects and phenomena initiate human beings into what will always be most important to them: "a neutral area of experience which will not be challenged" (1953c, p. 17).

But where is this space? What is the nature of this space and of playing? In an article on the various senses of reality in Winnicott's work, Loparic notes that:

> [...] more primitive than use and representation, while subsequent to the experience of contact, is play. This type of access to reality is a way of being of the baby, which can only be realised in its own *space*, termed potential. This space differs from that of representation by an essential characteristic: it is not exterior, internal or external, but is a component of the baby's being. The baby is not "inside" potential space, in the way that we say that a tree is in a garden, it *is* this space. (Loparic, 1995a, p. 53)

The baby hence does not transit from one object to another, but from one world to another. More precisely: since he is himself this space, we should say that he transits from one sense of reality to another within himself, as modes of his being, and that he may inhabit the different worlds which he creates, in which new objects may emerge. The baby can only accomplish this, however, if he has inhabited a subjective world for a sufficient period of time and continues to inhabit this world, the reality of which is not doubted. Winnicott asserts that where there is trust and reliability, there will also be a potential space "that can become an infinite area of separation", which may be creatively filled with play by babies, children, adolescents and adults, which in time becomes enjoyment of cultural heritage. "The special feature of this place where play and cultural experience have a position is that it *depends for its existence on living experiences*, not on inherited tendencies" (1971j, p. 146).

The passage from the subjective world, which is never lost, to the transitional world only occurs in time and takes time to establish itself as an achievement. Even if the process of separation and symbolic activity have been initiated, this does not guarantee that the image and meaning of the transitional object are kept alive, unless concrete maternal care continues to sustain the process. That is, the baby may use the transitional object to serve as mother, *while the subjective object is alive, real, good-enough and not very persecutory*. This subjective object, in turn depends, with regard to its qualities and duration, on the existence, vitality and behaviour of the external object, that is, on the concrete care of the real mother:

> Failure of the latter in some essential function indirectly leads to deadness or to a persecutory quality of the internal object. After a persistence of inadequacy of the external object the internal object fails to have meaning to the infant, and then, and then only, does the transitional object become meaningless too. (1953c, p. 13)

Before going any further, I would like to clarify the use of the expression "internal object" cited above. At the time when this article was written (1951), Winnicott had not yet formulated the concept of subjective object, which he only did in 1962. Although this text was revised for the publication of *Playing and Reality* (1971), and Winnicott did not make alterations regarding this point, I understand that in it, "internal object" refers to the "subjective object". The arguments are as follows: first, from the perspective of the theory of maturational processes, it is only possible to speak of an internal object when we refer to a point of maturation at which there is already an internal world or reality, and this achievement only occurs after the baby has reached a unitary identity in the I AM stage, with transitionality prior to this. In 1963 (1965j), referring to the more primitive versions of what Klein denominated "internal", Winnicott stated that when we refer to the beginning of life,

> [...] the word internal cannot be used in the Klein sense since the infant has not yet properly established an ego boundary and has not yet become master of the mental mechanisms of projection and introjection. At this early stage 'inner' only means personal, and personal in so far as the individual is a person with a self in process of becoming evolved. (1965j, p. 185)

Second, Winnicott maintains the expression "internal object" in order to emphasise the point which really interests him, namely, that "the transitional object is *not an internal object* (which is a mental concept)" (1953c, p. 13); it does not therefore have a life of its own and depends for its survival on the relation, communication, and ultimately on the maintenance of continuity of environmental care. In Winnicott's theory, the constitution of the internal world supposes that the separation me/not-me has occurred, with the existence of a system of fantasies, including everything resulting from the repressed unconscious; as soon as the internal world already exists, the real experiences, satisfactory and unsatisfactory—and this refers to the reality of the global experience and not only to the pleasure principle—lead respectively to the existence of things felt as good or as bad in the child's internal reality. Although the objects and conflicts of the internal world are influenced by the relationships occurring in real life, internal life has a certain autonomy which allows it to be examined as something in itself. None of this is already established in the transitionality phase.

We must hence point out that the reality and symbolic character of the transitional object depend on the vivacity and reliability of the subjective object, which in turn depends on the permanence and vitality of the external object. The loss of the subjective object is "a great catastrophe", something that belongs to the order of things which Winnicott's theory terms unthinkable agonies. If the child "loses" the mother, if the mother disappears for too long a period, "the subjective object dies" and the symbolic capacity of the transitional object dissipates. For this reason, despite the importance of the symbolic character of the transitional object, Winnicott pointed out that what is initially important is not so much its symbolic value, but *its reality*.

What happens if a pattern of environmental failure is established during this phase, and the baby starts to lose reliability? When deprivation is not excessive, a compulsive use of the transitional object itself may occur, such as a dummy, with this use being a communication of the same sort as greediness. If the deprivation is serious and prolonged, the baby loses the capacity for sucking. At this stage, when the baby has just started to differentiate from the mother, the loss is not only of the object, but of a part of himself, for example, the mouth. Indeed, the very capacity for play, sucking the tip of the blanket, playing with the mouth or the fists, tickling the nose, loses meaning.[8] If the baby loses the transitional object, which is sustained by the corresponding subjective ones, he loses the mouth and the breast at the same time, creativity and the path to objective perception.

Contact with reality depends fundamentally on creativity, without which no reality, not even the external one—and perhaps above all the external one—can be reached or have meaning. The reality with which we are concerned here is not that of the reality principle, as formulated by

Freud, but rather that of the feeling of real that is founded on an illusion. It is only by means of this feeling of real that the sense of external reality is reached.[9] However, the transitional object "is one of the bridges that make contact possible between the individual psyche and external reality" (1965k, p. 192). Losing the transitional object as a consequence of the mother's failure to keep the subjective world alive results in disbelief and hopelessness regarding the capacity for relating to objects: interest in the object fades, with the baby knowing nothing about what has happened. He only feels that something very important has been lost, that something has died even though this something may be there, now devoid of meaning.[10]

Creativity is thus in the service of the contact with reality; it relates to being alive and to feeling real, it refers to the way in which the individual allows reality to emerge, to the way he welcomes events, that is, the way in which any person, whether a baby, a child, an adult, or an elderly person, looks at or accomplishes something. No special talent is required for this creativity. Creativity is also originary and is not a sublimation of the pulsional conflict.[11]

The potential space, as third area of experience, maintains open the permanent, insuperable tension between creating and discovering. Due to this tension, there is an excitement that is particular to the transitional phenomena and hence to playing, albeit which is not of an instinctual character; it refers essentially to the ego organisation, being a question here of a

> [...] part of the ego that is not a body-ego, that is not founded on the pattern of body *functioning* but is founded on body *experiences*. These experiences belong to object-relating of a non-orgiastic kind, or to what can be called ego-relatedness. (1967b, pp. 135–136)

Playing is exciting in itself, especially because of the precariousness that is inherent to it. Its territory is the interplay between personal psychic reality and the experience of controlling real objects. Because of spontaneity, because of what it lacks of form, because of the absence of rules, (which makes Winnicott insist on the difference between game and play), playing provides a limited experience of the emergence of something frightening, because it is unpredictable. It is easy to see how much the author differs from the Kleinian theory, on the basis of the new paradigm in which he is moving. In the former, the importance of playing lies not in itself but in the fact that by means of playing, unconscious and repressed phantasms come to light; for Klein, therefore, playing has the function of a masturbatory discharge, of controlling anxiety or fulfilling desire. In Winnicott's theory, on the other hand, the importance of playing lies not in the content, but in playing itself, in the type of concentration which characterises it, in the fact that the child is able to "lose himself" there, being plunged into a state of virtual detachment, which is related to the concentration in older children or in adults.

The stage of the use of an object

The topic of the development of capacity for using objects is entirely original in psychoanalytic literature. While much has been said about object relations based on mechanisms of projection and introjection, the ability to *use an object* and the requirements needed for this have never been considered. The formulation of this achievement derives naturally from the theory of maturational processes and is considered by the author to be one of the most complex and difficult points of his thought.

Any consideration regarding the capacity for using objects requires that we start from the conception that this capacity initially does not exist. In the maturation process, this achievement, as well as that of transitionality, continues that initiated at the stage of the theoretical first feed, which concerns the establishment of relations with external reality; it is only at this stage, however, that objects may start to be perceived and used as external ones. In order to achieve this, the mother must have been able, from the outset, to present the world to the baby in small doses and in a comprehensible manner, so that he has had the opportunity, through primary identification, to *be* the object (subjective). Subsequent to this, already during the de-adaptation period, the "mixed" reality of transitional objects (part of the baby and part of the world) leads the infant to *possess* the object. During the transitional phase, he continues to live in a subjective world, but the omnipotence characterising the basic illusion is shattered, and some small aspects of external reality are included in experiences. From a certain point onwards, these two senses of reality no longer suffice and the tendency towards maturation pushes the baby towards another sense of reality: that of external and shared reality, in which he can use objects, which are now seen from the perspective of objectivity.

Even during the primitive stages, while living in an entirely subjective world, the baby is being provided with experiences of contact with objects which, since they arrive as subjective objects, are small samples of external reality (from the observer's perspective). Repeated experiences with these objects, not only become part of the baby through primary identification, but also gradually render the object meaningful, even though he does not yet know of his separate existence.[12] This will emerge with full clarity when the baby elects and attaches himself to the transitional object. Until this point is reached, we are still in the field of what is termed "object relating", although at this stage, the expression is inaccurate, since there is no actual relation with subjective objects as there are not yet two entities. From this point onwards, if all goes well, the baby can move from *relating to the object* to *using the object*. In order for this to occur, there must be a change for the baby regarding the *"nature of the object"*, that is, a change in the sense of reality of that object, which implies the creation of a world other than the subjective one or the potential space. According to Winnicott, this change is one of the most difficult and significant achievements of maturation, in addition to constituting, when it fails to be accomplished, "the most irksome of all the early failures that come for mending" (1969d, p. 222).

What exactly is the point to which Winnicott draws attention when he distinguishes "object relating" from "object usage"? In terms of the maturational processes, object relating is prior to and the basis for the development of the capacity for using objects. While *object relating* is a kind of experience that allows us to think the individual as an isolated being, living in a world which consists of a bundle of projections[13] and communicating with subjective objects within the context of the illusion of omnipotence, *object usage* may only be described, in the same way that the capacity for *using objects* itself can only be effected, if the independent external reality of the object is considered. Since psychoanalysis has always preferred to eliminate all environmental factors, unless these could be considered in terms of projective mechanisms, it is much easier for analysts to examine object relating than object usage. When examining usage, however, there is no other way: the analyst "must take into account the nature of the object, not as a projection, but as a thing in itself" (1969d, p. 221).

This change in the *sense of reality of the object,* from object relating to object usage, does not occur with the mere passage of time. In order to use an object, the baby must develop the *capacity* for using objects, which implies him beginning to consider the object as a "thing in itself", external and separate from himself, in its property of having always been and continuing to be there independently of him and hence, outside his omnipotent control. In order for the object to be used, it "… must necessarily be real in the sense of being part of shared reality, not a bundle of projections" (1969d, p. 221). In this way,

> [...] between relating and use is the subject's placing of the object outside the area of the subject's omnipotent control; that is, the subject's perception of the object as an external phenomenon, not as a projective entity, in fact recognition of it as an entity in its own right. (1969d, p. 222)

It should be noted, from the quotation, that it is the infant who gives the object an external character. He does so by expelling the (subjective) object to outside the ambit of omnipotence: something (someone) which is part of the self or of the subjective world is detached or expelled, in order to be examined and/or attacked. Winnicott terms this operation of expulsion of the object as something that no longer belongs to the subjective world the *"destruction"* of the object. *The object which is destroyed by the baby is the subjective object.* In other words, it is the subjective character of the object that is being destroyed. The destructiveness that is implied here is not of an instinctual character, although it is supported by the experiences of primitive instinctual impulsiveness, which, at this point, has not yet been integrated as part of the self, and does not derive either from anger stemming from frustration. It is a destructiveness *without anger*, which refers to the individual's need, characteristic of maturation, to begin to inhabit a world which is not his projection and in which there are objects which, having their own existence, may be used. If the capacity for relation and communication of the little individual is restricted to the communication with subjective objects, which was indispensable during the stages of absolute dependence, over time, it becomes a dead end (cf. 1965j, p. 184).

How does the destructiveness which leads to the capacity for using objects manifest itself? In many different forms, which naturally come mixed with aggression of another nature such as the instinctual one. The baby who by now is physically stronger, begins, for example, to kick the mother or to effectively bite the breast; or makes an effort to wear it out; or even to reject it while observing the mother's reaction; or simply to stop needing it.[14] However a particular baby begins to destroy the object, which is still subjective, what characterises the phenomenon is that being neither hungry nor angry, the baby *needs to destroy* the object. That is to say, there is a *real drive to destroy* which must be experienced.

Winnicott's thesis is hence that there is a destruction, which is prior to the functioning of the reality principle, a destruction that *has a particular role in the creation of reality*, with the baby placing the object outside of the self, that is, outside the subjective world. What the individual is creating at this stage is not properly an object, but a new sense of reality, that of externality. "It is the destructive drive that creates the quality of externality" (1969d, p. 226). The destructive urgency has, therefore, a vital positive function, that of objectifying the object.[15] In 1970, the author wrote that we would not get anywhere with the study of aggression if we were to think of it as irrevocably connected to jealousy, to envy, to anger from frustration or to the instinctual functioning habitually termed as sadistic. (cf. 1989n, p. 287). For him, human aggressiveness and destructiveness are phenomena related to the issue of the constitution of reality: "More nearly basic is the concept of aggression as part of the exercise *that can lead to the discovery of objects that are external*" (1989n, p. 287).[16]

What must be highlighted here is that the conquest which is being achieved by *the experience of destruction depends on the survival of the object*.[17] Surviving, in this context, means not retaliating, not changing attitude, remaining reliably the same. The word "destruction" is required, affirms Winnicott, not so much because of the baby's drive to destroy, "but because of the object's liability not to survive, which also means to suffer change in quality, in attitude" (1969d, p. 225). The baby's drive to destroy is real, and he must experience it but can only do so if there is safety, that is, if there is no risk that the object will succumb. *In the event that the object survives*, the drive changes into the *capacity* for using the object which has survived. At the same time as it releases the baby to continue exercising the destructive drive, which is real, the survival of the object releases him to destroy objects in the unconscious fantasy. In other words, the survival of the object leads to the usage of the object, and the usage leads to the separation of two phenomena: the destruction in the unconscious fantasy and the placing of the object outside the area of projection. Winnicott illustrates how events would unfold and what the baby would tell the object in the circumstance of the destruction:

> "I destroyed you", and the object is there to receive the communication. From now on the subject says: "I destroyed you". "I love you". "You have value for me because of your survival of my destruction of you". "While I am loving you I am all the time destroying you in (unconscious) *fantasy*". (1969d, p. 222)

It should be noted that it is only from this moment onwards that fantasy starts for the individual,[18] inasmuch as it is here that the separation between fact (survival of the object) and fantasy (the destruction of the object in unconscious fantasy) takes place. After this achievement of maturation is accomplished, the subjective object will always be destroyed in the unconscious fantasy.

This accomplishment, the creation of the sense of external reality and the achievement of the capacity for using objects and for unconscious fantasy is so important for maturation and so difficult to describe conceptually that before we go any further, it is worth examining some differences and additions which were made to the theory as Winnicott's thought evolved. Even before 1968, when he arrived at the most complete formulation of this type of aggression, as destructiveness which leads to the creation of externality and to the capacity for using objects, Winnicott already stated that human aggression "is always linked in this way with the establishment of a clear distinction between what is the self and what is not the self" (1964c, p. 94). In this text of 1964, he still related aggression to the primitive instinctual drive and made no reference to the value of object survival. Aggression is exercised by the child, he observed, in the form of a magical destruction, which is hence of the same nature as magical creation, albeit in the opposite direction. Through this child's magic, the world can be annihilated in the twinkling of an eye and recreated through new eyes. The primitive or magical destruction of all objects is necessary for the object to cease to be part of the "me" and become "not-me", *from being subjective phenomena to being perceived objectively*" (1964c, p. 98, emphasis added). Allowing time for the maturational process, the child "becomes able to be destructive and becomes able to hate and to kick and to scream instead of magically annihilating that world" (1964c, p. 98). In this formulation, the beginning of the achievement takes place with the child carrying out a magical destruction (that is hence not effective) which changes, over time, and with the development of the capacity for accepting that hate and love live together in human nature, into the real possibility for aggression. In this way, the author asserts, "*actual aggression is seen to be an achievement*. As compared with magical destruction, aggressive ideas and behaviour take on a positive value, and hate becomes a sign of civilization" (1964c, pp. 98–99).

What is new in the 1968 formulation is that this achievement starts with a *real drive* to destroy. That is, the baby, who is still ruthless, has by now a new muscular power and improved motor coordination and in order to continue with development, must expel the subjective objects from within the ambit of omnipotence. In order to achieve this, it effectively bites its mother, throws objects forcefully and is prepared to treat the transitional object brutally. All of this, which the mother must be capable of surviving, is accompanied by the still remorseless idea of having destroyed the object. If the object survives, meaning that it has an independent existence, the baby discovers that it may continue to destroy objects, albeit now within the realm of unconscious fantasy, because the object that it needs to use remains unscathed, which may thus be used.

The assumption underlying the concept of the destructiveness that creates the externality "goes right to the base of the existence of the human individual, and to the most fundamental aspect of object-relating". The axiom, postulates the author, is "[…] *what is good is always being destroyed*" (1986e, p. 262). In terms of the maturational process, what is the meaning of the need to destroy what is good? An answer to this question, says Winnicott, must point to the *actual qualities* of the good thing, that is, to the fact that the good thing *can survive because of its own real qualities*. That is, the object survives by itself and not because it is protected from destruction by the baby, since, after surviving destruction, the good thing will be loved, valued, and almost adored in a new way. This, notes the author, "has come through the test of being ruthlessly used and of having been the object, unprotected by us, of our most primitive impulses and ideas" (1986e, p. 263). If the baby has to protect the object due to its fragility, he will not make the necessary experience of destruction and will not come to relate to the external object, will not be able to use it, or to love or hate it. While initially referring to the mother, this will subsequently extend to the father and at a later stage, to all objects that are loved and cherished.[19]

In the theory of maturational processes, the capacity for love only emerges after destruction, the survival of the object and the advent of the capacity for destroying in the unconscious fantasy. It is true that Winnicott also speaks of primitive *love*, referring to the baby's excited states, charged with instinctual tension, but this "love" consists of needs and knows nothing of the external existence of the other. Love for the object that survives destruction is something completely different and is now the feeling of a me who, while incipient is whole and separate, directed at another individual, who is whole and separate. The prerequisite for this love is the same as for the exercise of mature genitality, not just a solitary exercise; in this case as well, the object must be perceived as external and separate from the individual. That is, love is also constituted within the maturational process.[20]

It follows from this that both objective reality and love depend on the fact that there is always destruction. This becomes the unconscious backdrop for the love for a real object, situated outside the area of omnipotent control of the subject. In order to demonstrate the fundamental character of this destructiveness which creates the externality and leads to the achievement of the relation to external reality, Winnicott reflects on the place of the Monarchy among British people, since they realise that "it is in the personal inner psychic reality that the thing is destroyed" (1986e, p. 263). It becomes clear that things survive due to their own properties independently of our dreams of destruction. This brings a great sense of relief into waking life and a new sense of confidence; "the world now begins to exist as a place in its own right; a place to live in, not as a place to fear or to be complied with or to be lost in [...]" (1986e, pp. 263–264).

The capacity for using an object, which includes its destruction as a subjective object, is perhaps the most difficult and painful achievement of the maturational process. If the mother succumbs to the destruction, the child will not be able to complete this passage. If she survives, assisting the child in the difficulties specific to that stage, the child will have the necessary time to acquire ways for dealing with the shock of realising the existence of a world situated outside of the child's control. In general, the passage from the subjective to the objective takes place through subtle gradations which accompany the changes characteristic of development, but without the participation of the mother, these changes occur abruptly and in ways that are unpredictable to the child (cf. 1964c, p. 98).[21] Instead of the child being the one who creates the world's externality, this bursts into his world. In this way, whilst the process of objectification of reality is taking place, the good enough mother will spare the child external changes. Thus protected, he will be free to play and experience everything within his personal psychic reality, both destructiveness and love; he will dream and in these dreams, there will be destruction and murder. Such dream activity, accompanied to some degree of bodily excitation, will constitute a concrete experience and not just an intellectual exercise. Destructiveness thus has a positive value, which is the paradoxical fact of being related to the creation of the externality of the world. Something is nevertheless lost; some subjective object has to be sacrificed as subjective, even though its subjective meaning does not disappear. Those who were nevertheless fortunate enough to succeed in creating a rich subjective world will always have a wealth of subjective objects which may be destroyed in favour of the shared reality which enriches experience.

In order to illustrate what happens when children cannot make the experience of destruction, Winnicott uses Jung's account of his early childhood in an autobiographical book.[22] Everything suggests, the author maintains, that Jung had no contact with his basic destructiveness. At the age of four, a framework of child schizophrenia was already installed: around a pathological split between the true and the false self, a defensive organisation was built against the danger of disintegration of the falsely integrated personality. At the basis of this split was a precocious external factor, his mother's depression, which was apparently compensated by his father's maternal attitude. When Jung was three years old, he suffered a psychotic breakdown relating to his parents' separation. The point emphasised by Winnicott, however, arises from Jung's account of the way in which he used to play; his play consisted of concrete and constant construction and destruction, with the building up of an edifice always followed by an earthquake that would destroy it. What does not appear in the material is the imaginative destruction followed by a feeling of guilt and then by construction. In other words, Jung does not describe himself playing constructively in relation to the fact of his *having destroyed* in his unconscious fantasy. This is understandable, observes Winnicott, since it is indeed extremely difficult for a child to achieve primitive destructiveness if he is cared for by a clinically depressed mother.[23] Since this had been his situation,

> [Jung] spent his life looking for a place to keep his inner psychic reality, although the task was indeed an impossible one. By the age of 4 he had adopted the sophisticated theory of the underground of the dream [...]. He went down under and found subjective life. At the same time he became a withdrawn person, with what was wrongly thought at the time to be a clinical depression. (1964b, p. 488)

In other words, the issue for Jung was not depression related to guilt or to responsibility for the aggression contained in instinctual impulsiveness, which is characteristic of the stage of concern as we shall see below. The question was a more primitive and basic one: the origin of Jung's difficulty is located, in terms of maturational processes, in the incapacity for the *destructiveness which creates externality*, which concomitantly establishes the self as a me separated from the not-me. The capacity for this destruction depends on the feeling of confidence that the object will survive. Jung could not destroy the mother in his fantasy, or expel her from his omnipotent control in order to constitute her as a separate person, in exteriority, since she had no chance of surviving. This difficulty undoubtedly gives rise to a depressive disorder, albeit of a nature which does not refer to the problems typical of the stage of concern, but which is linked to the despair, typical of personalities of the false self type, of achieving a personal reality which permits the establishment of real relations with the world and external objects.

Despite having demonstrated the need for the destruction of the good object in order to continue with the process which leads to the capacity for establishing relations with the reality objectively perceived, Winnicott did not make clear what it is, in terms of human nature, which requires that the good object, precisely the one created by the individual, is always destroyed.[24] I believe that this question refers to a fundamental problem, glimpsed but not developed by the author, the examination of which would require the assistance of a philosopher, a poet or, maybe, a schizoid in the Winnicottian sense.[25] We may perhaps believe that the good must be destroyed because what is important is creating and not the object that is created. The object, even the good one, must be destroyed, because after having been created, it becomes something of the world, an engagement, an attachment, something to which the identity remains linked or even imprisoned. The good must be destroyed to avoid the objectification of the human being, even with regard to his creations. What matters, what is vital and what makes life worth living is to be able to continue creating *ex nihilo*, from the essential aloneness, from primary creativity, as always.

The stage of I AM

It is at this stage, appropriately termed I AM, that the achievement of unity in an integrated *me* takes place. While it is not possible to determine the exact ages for the maturational achievements, the author suggests that around the age of eighteen months, children begin to establish the integration of the personality. This integration only achieves greater stability around the ages of two or three years. In any case, there is a well-defined point in the life of any child when he realises that he is a unitary existence, with some kind of established identity. If the child could talk, he would say: I AM.

The me which is achieved at this point is the result of a long process of integration which began with the primitive non-integrated self: throughout the initial stages, the various aspects of the personality were gradually integrated, including the instrumental false self, meaning that the me of unitary identity includes the true and the false self. Now, after having repeated experiences of expelling the mother from the ambit of omnipotence, during the previous stage, that is, after having objectified the mother and hence separated from her, at this stage of I AM, the child can separate from the total environment.

The unitary status of the me is not a cohesive whole, without fractures or free of conflicts, but a state of spatial-temporal integration, where "there is one self containing everything instead of dissociated elements that exist in compartments, or are scattered around and left lying about" (1971g, p. 90). With this achievement, we reach an end and a beginning, since the state of I AM, the feeling of being real and of existing as identity "is not an end in itself, it is a position from which life can be lived" (1989h, p. 435).

At this point, the child inhabits the body more firmly; he perceives himself as having a contour, with a limiting membrane, the skin, which separates him from everything that is not-me. Any not-me is repudiated as external; at the same time, the child now has an inside, a personal psychic reality, where memories from experiences may be collected and related, including all the formations of the repressed unconscious, which, added to the originary unconscious that is not repressed, but simply forgotten, enrich the infinitely complex structure belonging to the human being (cf. 1965k, p. 191; 1965q, p. 112).

The integration of the personality in a one-year-old child points to a remarkable change in the sense of independence. This is evidently not always true, but, at certain moments and in some relationships, it can be said that he already has an established identity. The child is already able to keep alive both the feeling of the presence of the mother and by incorporation, the memory of the care to which he is accustomed for far longer than the few months which was previously the case. With regard to personalisation, for most of the time, he remains firmly rooted in the body; when this is the case, not only does the use of the body reinforce the development of the unitary personality, but reinforces bodily functioning as well, promoting muscular tone, coordination, adaptation to temperature changes, etc. Integration is never a guaranteed state, however, either in a healthy adult or even less in a recently integrated baby. Everything is extremely variable at this age; not just from one child to another, but in the same child at different moments. It may well occur that in a healthy child the psyche loses contact with the body and there are circumstances in which it is not easy to restore this. If he is awakened and taken from the cradle in a moment when he is immersed in deep sleep, he will be startled and scared because of the abrupt change in body position at a moment when the psyche was absent from it.

In addition to the questions involving the daily routine of a one-year-old child, there are those related to the scope of integration itself. The moment when a sense of integration begins is an extremely difficult and vulnerable one. The baby sees the world and itself from a new position, the me. The daring of being a self, which now has boundaries marking a territory necessarily includes the repudiation of the not-me. The integration into a self is thus an act of hostility towards the not-me and brings along the expectation of an attack. The new individual feels himself to be "infinitely exposed" and will only be able to face and endure the struggles of this achievement at this point, "if someone has her arms round the infant at this time" (1965k, p. 148). This is the meaning of the affirmation that:

> [...] the most aggressive and therefore the most dangerous words in the languages of the world are to be found in the assertion I AM. It has to be admitted, however, that only those who have reached a stage at which they can make this assertion are really qualified as adult members of society. (1986d, p. 141)

For a certain amount of time, the experiences related to the achievement of unitary identity generate a state that could be called paranoid, and which constitutes one of the roots of the tendency towards paranoia.[26] In this situation, the protection provided by the mother is essential, since it lies "between the repudiated external world and the newly integrated individual" (1988, p. 121). The paranoid state, when refering to this achievement, is smaller when integration occurs at the original time specific to the achievement and potentially greater when the individual reaches integration at a late stage, as for example, in the case of an adult patient who is retracing the maturational path in psychoanalysis. Furthermore, since integration depends both on environmental provision and personal factors such as the pattern of personal impulsivity, of motility, sensibility, intelligence, etc, it may be favoured more by one of the factors involved than by another. Ultimately, the expectation of persecution is more frequent if integration occurs with the support, above all, of personal factors, some of which are hereditary. When the baby achieves integration basically due to environmental care, so that one could say that the self was somehow impelled to agglutinate, then a relative absence of expectation of persecution may occur and unlike in the previous alternative, there is a basis here for naïvety, for a certain incapacity to expect persecution and for an almost irrevocable dependence on good environmental provision (cf. 1988, p. 124).

In order to express the precarious situation of the recently integrated I AM, Winnicott alluded to the figure of Humpty Dumpty, the short round character of the traditional English song, the personification of an egg which falls from the wall, breaking itself into pieces. Winnicott says, the wall on which Humpty Dumpty is precariously perched, is like the mother who has ceased to offer her lap. The child needs time to explore this changeover stage thouroughly. He advances in certain directions but often needs to return and regress to situations which already appeared to have been overcome. He must be given the opportunity to experience several types of object relations during the same day and at times, simultaneously. A child may be entertained by playing with an aunt or a dog at the same time as he has some objective perceptions and makes creative discoveries. The next moment, he may merge into the cradle or the mother or with familiar smells and re-establish himself in a subjective environment. Throughout life, it is these familiar patterns of the child, those of the subjective world which, more than anything else, nourish him for all other types of relations with reality so that "when the child discovers the world there is always the return journey that makes sense" (1986d, p. 135).

Advancing towards the future and independence is also a "return journey", to one's origins. In the healthy individual, regardless of the degree of objectivity that he has been able to achieve, the subjective world remains the source of personal wealth and inalienable singularity. Despite the fact that the subjective and the objective never coincide, *it is possible to keep bridges open which allow for a transit between the various senses of reality.* The mature adult is capable of objectivity without losing touch with the personal imaginative world. He makes concessions to society via an instrumental false self without losing the thread which connects him to himself, that is, without the loss of primary spontaneity and creativity.

The maturational tasks continue. Achieving I AM status does not yet make the baby a whole person. It is nevertheless the platform, the position from where life may be lived. More specifically, it is the condition of possibility for the next stage, that of concern, in which the baby begins to feel concern regarding his instinctual impulsiveness and to worry about the results of the primitive love drive on itself and on others.

The stage of concern

Having achieved the status of a unitary me to some degree, the child is now capable of accomplishing the task of integrating instinctual life. When this integration is achieved more consistently, the child will become a whole person, capable of relating to whole persons. At the beginning of this stage, drives, which until now have been external to the person of the baby and invasive if the baby was not assisted in dealing with them, begin to be integrated, to have meaning and to be accessed with regard to their consequences. From ruthless, the baby now starts to feel *concerned* with the impulsiveness which dominates him during the excited moments, as if saying: "This has to do with me, this concerns me, this is my business"; the baby also becomes *anxious* since he begins to perceive that this impulsiveness affects and may hurt the other; he thus realises that he is the one who, with his own hands, makes "a hole, where previously there was a full body of richness" (1955c, p. 268) in the mother. The anxieties characteristic of this period are extremely complex, since concern relates not only to the effects of the voracious impulsiveness towards the object of excited love, but also to the consequences on the self of the experience of excitation (cf. 1988, p. 79). From then on, a feeling of guilt and of responsibility arises with regard to the destructiveness inherent to instinctual impulsiveness.

One of the most important things which occurs during this stage is that the child begins to perceive that not only is he one and the same person, whether he is excited or quiet, but also that the mother who takes care of him, changing and pampering him during the quiet states is the same person whom he vigorously attacks during the excited states. The mother has been and for some time will continue to be environment-mother and object-mother simultaneously; while the former was and continues to be tenderly loved and caressed, the latter is repeatedly damaged and destroyed. During the time when the child is combining the environment-mother and the object-mother into one person, the real mother must continue to play two roles, in each one playing her part in the task of caring for the baby. The mother is responsible for maintaining the environment safe and reliable and offering herself as the object to be used, consciously sucked, destroyed and a cause for concern:

> The object-mother has to be found to survive the instinct-driven episodes, which have now acquired the full force of fantasies of oral sadism and other results of fusion. Also, the environment-mother has a special function, which is to continue to be herself, to be empathic towards her infant, to be there to receive the spontaneous gesture, and to be pleased. (1963b, p. 76)

Up to this point, an enormous growth has taken place: from the mother–baby unit to the relation of a me to an external and separate not-me; from pre-ambivalence to ambivalence, from primary dissociation between quiet and excited states to a discrimination between these two states and an integration of both into the self. Even now, however, the baby can only relate to *one* other: the mother. All of the elaboration of the capacity for concern, guilt and responsibility for the damage provoked by instinctual impulsiveness occurs in an exclusively dual plane, within the relation of the baby to the mother, who only gradually becomes one only person to the child.

The task of integrating instinctuality, with all of its inherent aggressiveness, requires time and an on-going personal environment; in the lack of understanding on the part of the environment, of what is happening and of a certain type of care, this achievement cannot be made. Winnicott's argument is as follows: the human baby cannot cope with the weight of the guilt and fear resulting from the full realisation that the "aggressive" ideas and acts contained in the primitive ruthless love drive are directed towards the same person who takes care of him and on whom he continues to depend, now in a relative form. Since all this takes place within the dual relation and is elaborated with regard to the mother, the child must face these issues alone, since he "is not yet advanced enough to make use of the idea of a father intervening, and by intervening making the instinctual ideas safe" (1988, p. 70).

The tendency of the child who begins to face the fact that aggression is part of his nature is to project this aggression outwards, onto the world, which becomes populated with threats, establishing a vague and magical feeling of fear which spreads everywhere. It is the mother's receptive and protective availability that neutralises the retaliatory and magical character of these fears:

> As each infant begins to collect a vast experience of going on being in his or her own sweet way and to feel that a self exists, a self that could be independent of the mother, then fears begin to dominate the scene. These fears are primitive in nature, and are based on the infant's expectation of crude retaliations. The infant gets excited, with aggressive or destructive impulses or ideas, showing as screaming or wanting to bite, and immediately the world feels to be full of biting mouths and hostile teeth and claws and all kinds of threats. In this way the infant's world would be a terrifying place were it not for the mother's general protective role which hides these very great fears that belong to the infant's early experience of living. The mother (and I'm not forgetting the father) alters the quality of the small child's fears by being a human

being. Gradually she becomes recognized, by the infant, as a human being. So instead of a world of magical retaliations the infant acquires a mother who understands, and who reacts to the infant's impulses. But the mother can be hurt or become angry. When I put it this way, you will see immediately that it makes an immense difference to the infant if the retaliatory forces become humanised. (1993c, pp. 105–106)

The resolution of this crucial difficulty, which consists of accepting that destructiveness is personal and coexists with love, depends on the child developing the capacity for repairing or, mending, to use the preferred expression of the author. The child has an urgent need to know that the damage may be fixed and repaired, that the hole can be mended, that even destructive ideas and actions may be balanced with some gifts. Only then will he feel free and safe to continue to exercise his own impulsiveness. This capacity will nevertheless only be developed

> [...] *if the mother holds the situation*, day by day, then the infant has time to sort out the rich imaginative results of instinctual experience, and to rescue something that is felt to be "good", supportive, acceptable, unhurting, and with this imaginatively to repair the damage done to the mother. (1988, p. 70; my italics)

The essential element here is the continuous presence of the mother, her survival for the entire period when the baby or the child is integrating the destructiveness which is a part of his own nature. First, for holding the situation: the mother remains there, alive and available, that is, accessible both physically and in the sense of not being preoccupied by something else during the necessary interval of time between the baby's aggressive attack, the advent of guilt and the gesture of repairing or mending. Second, for her survival value, which means not retaliating, not changing her attitude, not withdrawing because of feeling personally offended by any cannibalism of the baby, not adopting a moralistic attitude aiming at providing precocious education or training of the baby in civility. Surviving is not remaining indifferent or immune to what is happening; it does not mean permissiveness. The child now knows that he is hurting or wounding someone when he is excited; he knows and needs the mother to know it as well. The latter does not pretend that "it was nothing"; she does not play the martyr who endures the attack because, after all, this is her place as mother. No. If she is alive, she feels and defends herself: without tension, without fears regarding the cruel nature of the son, without reviving old stories of violence suffered. Surviving thus means that the mother does not renounce her role in the disillusionment process: she *can bear being hated*.[27]

The fact is the child must exercise his impulsiveness and faces the fear that the damage is irreversible. When the mother provides the opportunity for the "benign circle" of "hurting-made-good" to repeat itself countless times, the baby gradually comes to believe in the possibility of a remedy, in the constructive effort, and if good conditions for enduring the guilt are provided, he has more freedom for instinctual love.

> The result of a day-after-day reinforcement of the benign circle is that the infant becomes able to tolerate the hole (result of instinct love) Here then is the beginning of *guilt* feeling. This is the only true guilt, since implanted guilt is false to the self. (1955c, p. 270)

If several and alternating people take care of the baby, as in the case of an institution, the child loses the opportunity for mending (which must be done to the same person who was hurt) and the benign circle cannot be established. Nor are there conditions for these dynamics to take place when, even if they derive from the mother, care is impersonal and mechanical.

It is during the achievement of the capacity for concern that the child's temporalisation is established more consistently. His new awareness regarding the damage that he causes during moments of excitation is both retroactive and is projected into the future: he not only comes to know that he is now the one who, in the excitement of the moment, sucks, devours, wears out, in brief, causes damage to the mother, but also knows that he *has always done so, will continue to do so*. There is no remedy, the drive to live implies grasping, using, and devouring whatever is needed to stay alive. If, due to growing confidence in the act of repair, the child feels free to exercise his impulsiveness and, shortly afterwards, having felt guilty, makes the gesture: a smile, a caress, a cuddle, signaling that he has mended the mother's body, then the day's work is completed. When the benign circle fits entirely into a single day, "tomorrow's instincts can be awaited with limited fear. Sufficient unto the day is the evil thereof" (1988, p. 72). The achievement of the capacity for concern is thus followed by a more complete sense of time, since it is at this point that present, past, and future articulate themselves (cf. 1988, p. 34). Integration at the level of the whole person means responsibility, conscience, "the collection of memories, and by the bringing of the past, present and future into a relationship, it almost means the beginning of human psychology" (ibid., p. 119).

It should be noted that it is only at this point that a psychic life inhabited by internal conflicts begins: the child now has an inside and an outside; a personal and complex internal world, with fantasies and anxieties in opposition to the external world. The life that takes place in this internal world, in the manner of a soap opera, with plots and characters, is endowed with such autonomy that the growing complexity and richness of this internal world may be an object of consideration in itself; a terrible dispute takes place there between the destructive and the constructive tendencies of the personality, in addition to a special type of anxiety, the feeling of guilt derived from the idea that the destructive drive emerges precisely when love is operating. In this way, what is "good" is constantly threatened by what is "bad".[28] It is nevertheless this anxiety which, under favourable conditions, leads the child to constructive or actively loving behaviour, resurrecting the object and repairing what was damaged. It is this which later will form the foundation of every personal initiative or constructive work. The task of the good enough mother is to remain there, available to *acknowledge and receive the repairing gesture*. The baby's capacity for repair is very limited and he depends on someone acknowledging his "symbolic gift". If the child realises the damage and "no person can be found to accept a gift or to acknowledge effort to repair" (1958b, p. 207) then he will despair. In this event, the change from ruthlessness to concern and guilt is undone and aggressiveness reappears, sometimes implacably.

The child's tolerance of his own destructive drives, a tolerance constituted by the experience of the survival of the mother, results in the ability to enjoy ideas (even destructive ones) and the bodily excitement corresponding to them. Such development makes room "for the experience of concern, which is the basis for everything constructive" (1984c, p. 87). Without destructiveness, says Winnicott, there is no true love. For a long period of time,

[...] the small child needs someone who is not only loved but who will accept potency (whether it be boy or girl) in terms of reparative and restitutive giving. In other words the small child must go on having a chance to give in relation to guilt belonging to instinctual experience, because this is the way of growth. There is dependence here of a high order, but not the absolute dependence of earliest phases. (1955c, p. 271)

In Winnicott's theory, it is in this way that the foundation of a *personal* morality is established, which is not imposed from outside or taught, which is not merely intellectual and apprehended, but which emerges naturally from the experience of the "original goodness", that is, of environmental reliability (cf. 1963d, p. 94). It is this experience that, by sustaining personal growth, leads to the awareness of the existence of the other and to the capacity for cross-identification, of putting oneself in another's place.[29] Living with the construction and destruction inherent to human nature is also the foundation for the capacity for play and later, for working and finding joy and fulfilment in work. It is also with regard to this achievement, where there is failure, that disorders may arise which may be covered by the term active depression or a certain type of paranoia and sometimes, the anti-social tendency.[30]

We should note that, in Winnicott, morality is established in a non-oedipal context and does not refer to a law or prohibition; what is essential to it is not defined in terms of adequacy or transgression, except secondarily, for the individual who is already socialised, but in terms of ensuring that the child can be him so that he also acquires the capacity of letting the other be as a self. Winnicott regarded morality as innate, in the sense that a tendency exists in every human being to develop a feeling of responsibility for one's own actions, although this achievement remains to be integrated into the personality via personal experience. As with all other aspects of human nature, the tendency is only realised if the environment facilitates it, initially providing the baby with the experience of original goodness, of being the object of understanding, concern, and respect.[31]

The elaboration of the capacity for concern is a long process. It is difficult to determine a starting date, other than the requirement of already possessing some degree of integration into a me, which will assume the blame. As a result of this, Winnicott does not agree that the task and achievements of this stage can be dated to the early days, weeks, or months of life, as Melaine Klein did in her theory of the "depressive position", since achieving this capacity requires "the development of a sense of time, on an appreciation of the difference between fact and fantasy, and above all on the fact of the integration of the individual" (1955c, p. 274). Since, however, between the initial condition of ruthlessness and the subsequent capacity for feeling concern and responsibility there is an entire period during which this capacity is in the process of being established, it is possible to find scattered signs of guilt around the age of six months[32] or before one year. With regard to the task specific to the stage, however, the process reaches its peak of elaboration around the age of two and a half, albeit without ever establishing itself consistently before the age of five. The difficulties at the beginning of the stage are evidently different from those arising at the end of it.

One of these differences consists of the fact that at some point starting from the second half of the elaboration of concern, the father enters the picture in the role of father, that is, as the third person and his existence and real presence become extremely important. At the start of the maturational process, the father existed only as a duplication of the maternal role. As we have already seen, even in this role, something of him was added, an aspect "which is hard and strict and unrelenting, intransigent, indestructible" (1986d, p. 131), which was experienced by the baby as an aspect of the mother. As the child accedes to the mother's separate and external existence, this aspect differentiates itself and becomes part of the father, who then becomes significant as a man, "who turns out to be a human being, someone who can be feared and hated and loved and respected" (1986d, p. 131).[33]

When the child realises that the father is a person other than the mother and glimpses the family triangle, he begins to see or imagine the exciting relationship which exists between the parents. This is crucial for his security, since the stability of the parental relationship, expressed by the parents' interest in each other, allows the child to begin to dream of taking the place of one of them, without the risk that this might actually become true. At a certain point, there is a shift in the way the child perceives the triangle: now it is he who is the third person. Winnicott terms this discovery—the perception of the triangle with the child at its vertex—the "primal scene".[34] If healthy, the child is capable of dealing with the anger resulting from this new awareness and to use it for masturbation, taking responsibility for the conscious and unconscious fantasies that accompany it.

It is with the father in this position, in relation to the mother, but in a situation which is still prior to the oedipal one, that a sense of family begins to be shaped for the child. It is the mother and the father together and the relationship between them plus the atmosphere that they both imprint on their home that provides the basis for the first circle beyond the mother's arms. This circle gradually widens to include grandparents, aunts and uncles, old friends, and even neighbours, but the central characteristics continue to bear the mark of the parents, some of which they bring from their own families. This sense of family includes that of a family history to which the small individual child very slowly comes to belong. This belonging to the family group provides the individual with the feeling of having roots, a lineage and provides the foundation for customs and traditions to be preserved. Family consistency and continuity also provide a second chance for the grown-up individual, when a return is needed: for the adolescent who, for example, needs to re-enact his primitive experiences, or even for a young person who goes out into the world, becoming increasingly independent, "though retaining the hole for creeping back into" (1989n, p. 288). In any such case, however, Winnicott says: "the precondition is clear. The precondition has to do with the mother, and with two parents together, and the family, and the extended family and the local social setting including the school, and so on" (1989n, p. 286).

Again with regard to the child's discovery of the place that he occupies in family life, we should point out that the capacity for dealing with the feelings generated by the primal scene leads to the establishment of another achievement of the utmost importance: the capacity for being alone. There are several studies in the psychoanalytic literature on the fear of being alone, or on the desire to be alone, but little has been said about the capacity for being alone. Although this capacity is only established in a consistent manner after the experience of the primal scene,[35] *"this experience is that of being alone, as an infant and small child, in the presence of mother"* (1958g, p. 30). That is to say, while still very young and before knowing of the existence of the environment, the baby could be alone, in quietness or close to essential aloneness, due to the reliability on the mother's continuous presence and care. "In the course of time the individual introjects the ego-supportive mother and in this way becomes able to be alone without frequent reference to the mother or mother symbol" (1958g, p. 32).

The child now begins to *count on the father* to do his part, consisting of protecting the mother from the attacks of the child himself during the moments of the excited drive. It is here that the intransigent and indestructible element of the father helps the child to release himself to instinctual life and its consequences. The presence of a strong, intervening father, who provides this type of security makes the instinctual ideas and actions safer, allowing the child to run the risk of moving, acting, and getting excited, since the father is present, ready to remedy the damages or, with his strength, to prevent them from happening (cf. 1989l, p. 184). The father becomes the necessary support in the search for instinctual satisfaction without much danger. If this kind of assistance cannot be provided due to the father's absence or to the mother's depression, the child will become inhibited and will lose the capacity for excited love. He will have to adopt a precocious self-control of drives, before he is capable of doing so on the basis of a paternal strength that would have been gradually incorporated as his. In these cases, there is inhibition of the spontaneity and of the drive, in addition to a permanent fear that some aspects of the destructiveness escape control. The result may be depression or one form of anti-social tendency.

What is more, without the experience of counting on the father to place limits on the instinctual drive, the child is later unable, at the oedipal stage, to rival the father, to have the experience of a confrontation which is highly necessary for his development. The child's need, specific to this stage, is to count on the availability and survival of the mother and on the firmness of the father. This becomes especially clear in the study of anti-social tendencies, when it is possible to distinguish two types of deprivation:

> One is in terms of loss of object and the other is in terms of loss of frames, loss of controls. In a sense you could say loss of mother and loss of father—the paternal father, not the standing-in-for-mother father. The thing is the frame, the strength—the deprivation in terms of that. (1989f, p. 578)

The lack of frame for containing the picture and the resulting non-incorporation of limits becomes evident in cases of fully developed delinquency, especially when it involves theft and destruction. What stands out in these cases, says the author, "is the child's acute need for the strict father, who will protect mother when she is found. The strict father that the child evokes may also be loving, but he must first be strict and strong" (1946, p. 116).[36]

Throughout the whole of the stage of concern, while the child is trying to deal with the aggression contained in instinctual life, instinctuality is being integrated, along with a growing sense of the parts of the body, thus strengthening personalisation and spatialisation. It is approximately at this point that an important aspect of sexual development occurs. Excitations become increasingly localised. Both phallic erection and clitoral excitation begin to take on an importance of their own. Until then these excitations were possible, but did not have the sexual and gender character that they now acquire; prior to now, they were associated with the excitation of food or the thought of food and, shortly afterwards, with the activities of excretion. As has been already indicated, in these pre-genital phases, despite the emergence in the baby of all sorts of excitation, including those of a genital character, there was still insufficient maturity for the imaginative elaboration of the genital function.

At some point during the elaboration of the stage of concern, probably around the age of two, the child enters what Winnicott termed the exhibitionist or ostentatious phase, approximately the same as the one denominated by Freud as the phallic phase. This is the moment, in terms of the maturational process—and in terms of the development of gender and sexual identity as aspects of this process, in which the distinction between boys and girls starts to become meaningful. The central feature of the exhibitionist or phallic phase, relates to the obvious quality of the male organ, as opposed to the hidden quality of the female organ. Male genitals are thus central and sightly, with their erections and periodic sensitisations, whereas "the female state is a negative matter". The existence of this stage "marks the parting of the ways between the boy and girl infant" (1988, p. 41).[37] At the beginning of this phase, erection is the most important element. Both erection and the sensitisation of the clitoris arise in direct relation to a person who is actively loved or through ideas of rivalry with the loved person as background. Later, in the second phallic phase, there will be "a more open aim of penetration and impregnation, and here a real person is likely to be the object of love" (1988, p. 44). Since the excited experience is one of the ways through which the child inhabits his or her own body and relates to others, children who experience erections or vaginal contractions in relation to other people or to bodily functions are in a diferent and healthier position than boys and girls who do not have these integrative experiences (cf. 1986g, p. 145).

From the phallic phase onwards, along with the distinction of gender, we must also consider the fact of bisexuality: there is always a boy inside a girl and a girl inside a boy and this is especially undeniable in the case of girls. At this point, the evidence emerges that boys have something that girls do not; in addition to erection, they can, for example, urinate in a way that girls cannot. To varying degrees, they may feel inferior or mutilated and, in this case, "penis envy is a fact" (ibid., p. 186). The trauma that this may represent nevertheless varies, affirms Winnicott, and depends very much on external factors, such as the atitude and expectations of the parents, the nature and the position of the brothers in the family, etc. The frequent phenomenon of delusion among girls that there was a penis in them which no longer exists or that they have one which has yet to develop; the delusion among boys that girls have a penis, aiming to avoid the castration anxiety; in brief, the denial of the diference between being a male and being a female during the phallic stage is, for the author, a universal phenomenon, which belongs to this stage and which requires a good deal of healthy growth in order to be achieved as such. If the individual carries the burden of previous stages, such things may undoubtedly cause psychic disorders of varying degrees of severity, such as perversions or sadomasochist configurations.[38] In any case, experiences relating to gender difference, characteristic of this phase, are complex and difficulties arise both in health and in illness. The difference is that when there is a disorder, fantasy or play, which could help with the self-expression and integration of these aspects into the structure of personality, are prevented due to repression, which is a sophisticated defence mechanism for those who already have an inner life and instinctual conflicts connected to interpersonal relations. The difficulties of the phallic phase only assume an exaggerated importance, however, for those who on reaching it have already suffered previous deprivations of another nature.[39]

The examination of the tasks of this stage, in light of personal development, is especially important in order to relativise the seriousness of the difficulties of this period, as is supposed in traditional theory. Freud probably attributed the origin of psychoses to the threat of castration, which belongs to this period, due to the fact that, there was no place in his theory for the consideration of the previous stages in which the constitution of reality is processed. In order to account for psychoses, which he understood as a loss of reality or a disruption of the connection to reality, assuming that this was established, he chose the reality of castration as the paradigm of reality to be avoided.[40]

The oedipal stage

If the child truly achieves the capacity for experiencing the anxieties of the oedipal situation, this means that he is already established as a unitary identity. Being firmly integrated and having become a whole person as a result of having integrated the instincts and taken responsibility for the effects of instinctual impulsiveness, it may be said that he is no longer subject to the risk of psychosis.[41] He has now sufficient psychic health to be able to experience the difficulties inherent to instinctual life within the frame of triangular and interpersonal relations. In clear and explicit opposition to the Kleinian theory, Winnicott states that it only makes sense to speak of triangular relations or of the Oedipus complex when referring to the whole person:

> I cannot see value in the use of the term Oedipus Complex where one or more of the trio is a part object. In the Oedipus Complex, for me at least, each of the three of the triangle is a whole person, not only for the observer but also and especially for the child. (1988, p. 49)

Difficulties relating to the oedipal stage do not result from environmental failures or negligence, although these may complicate the resolution of the phase, but from difficulties of life and interpersonal relations and cannot be prevented by means of adequate care. During this period of life, even the healthiest child may present various neurotic symptoms: despite being vitally active, he suddenly looks pale and withered; he is sweet and affectionate but may suddenly be filled with rage, behaving cruelly towards animals or anything else; he has nightmares and drives away the mother who comes to console him; is very daring and, at the same time, manifests all kinds of fears; from time to time, he is suspicious of the food served to him, refusing to eat at home, but devouring anything at his grandparents' or neighbour's house. There is now an *internal world*, in which a whole life of intense and violent fantasies and feelings develop; instincts and bodily excitation are present in play, and identification occurs with either of the parents.

Mixed with the feelings which have been recently integrated and have become meaningful, it is the moments of excitation clearly determined by instinctuality which are most important; much of what is occurring between one excitation and the next relates either to the preparation for instinctual satisfaction or to the attempt to keep instincts under control or also, to the task of keeping them alive indirectly through play, through healthy masturbation (which is not compulsive) or through the dramatisation of a fantasy (cf. 1988, p. 54). When the child is healthy, he is in acute state of attraction towards the parent of the opposite sex, with tensions regarding the parental figure of the same gender, due to the ambivalence, that is to say, to the coexistence of love and hate. A major part of the child's emotional life remains unconscious and even in the most satisfactory of environments, the child has drives, ideas, fantasies, and dreams in which the unbearable conflict between love and hate unfolds, between the desire to preserve and that of destroying and in a more complex way, between the heterosexual and homosexual positions with regard to the identifications with the parents.[42] All of this indicates that the child is alive and elaborating the difficulties inherent to life.

Through the birth of another baby, for example, the child may nevertheless need to regress to patterns which have already been overcome, and even to dependence. If the child had a good start and his personality is structured, he loses nothing of his previous achievements. He may even exhibit regressed behaviour, but these are defences against anxiety arising from instinctual conflict. The main defence is repression, since, by now, a special type of unconscious has already been developed: *the repressed unconscious*. Maintaining repressed contents under control requires a huge amount of energy, due to the tendency they have to reappear in dreams, fantasies or to be projected onto external phenomena. A particular result of repression is the inhibition of instincts: there is loss of a part of the instinctive drive in the object relation and this may result in a serious impoverishment of the child's vital experience (cf. 1989p, p. 69).

If, on reacting to the arrival of his little brother, a child loses the phallic and genital characteristics of fantasy and of excited playing to the point even of losing achievements of integration such as psycho-somatic cohesion and the capacity for object relations, then this is no longer neurosis and an accurate observation will reveal that the child's development has in some sense been forced, having left important immaturities which now reveal themselves by means of a regression.[43] There are cases in which the child does not achieve any oedipal complex whatsoever; his development has been paralysed at a previous stage, so that "the true and full-blooded triangular relationships never became a fact" (1963c, p. 219). While they are not frequent, it is also possible to find cases in which a mixture occurs, of normality, insofar as the child is capable of experiencing the Oedipus complex, and psychosis, in the sense of immaturity, which remains restricted to a particular aspect (cf. 1963c, p. 219).

After the perception of the family triangle, the child begins to have *loyalty* problems. He is still inexperienced with feelings, especially those involving the triangular relationship, and needs a situation in which there is tolerance regarding what may seem disloyal, but which is merely an experiment forming part of his development (cf. 1986d, p. 138). He begins, for example, to establish a relationship with the father and in so doing, gains a new perspective; he comes to see things from the point of view of the father, thus developing a new attitude with regard to the mother:

> Not only can the mother be seen objectively from where the father is, but also the child develops an in-love type of relationship to the father which involves hate of the mother and fear of the mother. It is dangerous to go back to the mother from this position. There has been a

gradual build-up, however, and the child returns to the mother and in this familiar orientation sees father objectively and the feelings of the child contain hate and fear. (1986d, p. 138)

If the father does not ensure this other perspective for the child, the child will have to deal with the need to move away from the mother on his own; he will have to exercise self-control and will experience considerable difficulty in elaborating the oedipal situation. A good example of this situation is found in a clinical note by Winnicott (1989o), regarding a patient whose problems, at the time described in the analysis, related to his sexual identity, which had been considerably hindered as a result of the type of relationship established with him by his mother during the initial stage and the absence of an effective father who would play his part. In addition to this difficulty mentioned above, the result for this young man of the primary relations was *complete inexperience regarding a certain position with regard to the father,* in other words, his ability to see the mother from the father's perspective. In analysis, this manifested itself in his impossibility to place and use the analyst in this position. As we shall see, this obstacle was particularly acute for the oedipal question. In the relevant passage, Winnicott states:

> [...] the whole hour was a muddle and no interpretation of mine was of any use. The patient was exasperated. What eventually did do some good was my interpreting that the analysis has continued in his relationship to his wife but here now, whatever it may have been at other times, he was working out his exasperation with his mother and his absolute hopelessness about dealing with her [...]. Eventually he felt that I had really met the situation when I said the home relationship is so much like your relationship to your mother that there is no man and therefore you cannot come to me because it is no use, there is no man to come to. There is no question of there being a father on whose knee you could sit looking at your mother, etc. (1989o, p. 186)

This toing and froing of the child must take place within the context of the mother–father relationship, although it is not necessarily restricted to it: it may also occur with the child going to the nanny and coming back to the mother, or going to the grandmother, aunt or older sister. These possibilities may be experienced within the family and the child may gradually be reconciled with the fears associated with them. These fears include instinctuality and the child may enjoy excitation in relation to these conflicts, provided that it is permitted and contained by the adults and may be elaborated in play. Perhaps, Winnicott observes, "the tremendous interest that children have in playing fathers and mothers derives from a gradual widening out of the experiencing of the experimentation with disloyalties" (1986d, p. 138).

What is the role of the environment at this stage? The more we advance in maturation, the less important the environment becomes for the structuring of personality. It nevertheless continues to be important in another way: the child needs a stable domestic environment in which he feels safe, in order to play and dream and elaborate his internal life, which is convulsed by the coexistence of love and hate, without having to worry about the stability of home. For this purpose, the family structure must remain solid and survive the constant tests caused by internal turbulence. It is within the family that the child can move forward step by step, from the relationship between three people to other, ever more complex circles. The author nevertheless points out "it is the simple triangle that presents the difficulties, and the full richness of human experience" (1988, p. 39).

The nature and behaviour of the parents, the place of the child within the family, among other factors, affect the classic picture known as the Oedipus complex. If, for example, the father is at the table during breakfast, the child will feel safe to dream that he will be run over by a car or that someone's husband is shot during a robbery. If, however, the father is absent, the dream will be terrifying, causing feelings of guilt or a state of depression (cf. 1989p, p. 68). There is a huge difference in the nature of the difficulties of a child according to the history of his development and the type of problem which must be confronted at this point. A father who is weak or incapable of playing his part is one thing; the collapse of the family due to discord or even the separation of the parents is another. When the family proves to be solid and enduring, it functions as a frame of reference which gives the child the feeling that it is safe to have feelings and even aggressive actions. This allows the child to explore crudely destructive activities which are related to movement in general and more specifically those activities which take place within the fantasy formed around hate. On this couse, due to environment safety, with the mother supported by father, etc., the child becomes capable of doing something very complex, namely, of integrating his destructive and love drives; with the result that the child acknowledges

> the reality of the destructive ideas inherent to living and to loving, and finds a way of protecting himself and the people and the objects that he loves. […]. In order to achieve this in his development, the child *absolutely requires an environment that is indestructible in essential respects.* (1968e, p. 94)

When there is deprivation, for example, in terms of breakdown of the family, something very serious happens to the psychic organisation of the child. He becomes insecure about his ideas and aggressive impulses. Immediately,

> […] the child takes over the control that has been lost and becomes identified with the framework, the result being that he loses his own impulsiveness and spontaneity. There is much too much anxiety now for experimentation which could result in his coming to terms with his own aggression. (1968e, pp. 94–95)

To an ever increasing degree, we must be able to deal with the fact that nowadays, families break up more easily than when Winnicott formulated his theory. The theory of maturational processes nevertheless remains essential for parents who, while they dissolve their marital life, want to maintain the emotional stability and development of their children. It is no certainty that children will suffer more from the concrete, emotional, and geographical separation of their parents than they do when the parents stay under the same roof without having an emotional relationship or real communication. Since the parents have a perfect right to seek what they feel to be better for themselves, it is in any case important that each one of them continues to perform his role with regard to the child. They may need to be even more present and not neglect the care and orientation required by their children, for whom some form of explanation of what happened, accessible at their level of maturity, is vital, and that the parents, no matter how disappointed and angry, do not begin to denigrate each other's parental image.

The child's sexual life now reaches the primacy of genitality. When this is achieved, fantasy is already enriched with the typical masculine and feminine acts of penetrating and being penetrated or impregnating and being impregnated (cf. 1988, p. 41). The important fact continues to be erection as a part of a relationship, but it is now associated with the idea of provoking irreversible changes to the body of the beloved person.[44] The child is capable of genital sexual experiences with all of the fantasies and excitation which accompany it and this constitutes a new potency, even if physical immaturity obliges him or her to postpone the capacity to proceed with the genital act which potentially leads to procreation until puberty. When, at a much later stage, puberty arrives bringing with it another level of potency, the experiences and fantasies realised during childhood will be of immense help to the new condition.

Any study on instinctuality which requires action, that is, an act of doing, especially with regard to the genital phase, is more adequate for the description of the male than of the female.[45] On the male side, it is possible to distinguish accurately between the fantasy of the phallic experience and that of the genital experience, both in the boy and in the boy-in-the-girl. Whereas during the phallic phase, the boy's performance is in line with his fantasy, in the genital phase, his performance is deficient with regard to his fantasy; this gap calls the boy's potency into question and as we shall see, this will have a meaning in the oedipal situation, as is redescribed by Winnicott. Furthermore, differently from the girl, the boy is "complete" in the phallic phase, whereas, in the genital phase, he *depends on the female in order to complete himself*.

Even if it is not as evident as in the male, feminine genitality cannot be defined only in negative terms: the woman is not a castrated male. The penis envy experienced during the phallic phase does not necessarily establish itself as the determinant of feminine sexuality, unless there is already a split masculine component in the girl, triggered previously. When in an adult woman, this split pure masculine element[46] has been potentialised by a painful experience of penis envy, in the exhibitionist phase, a defensive organisation is established which may be regimented and put at the service of the ideological aspect of a social struggle such as the feminist movement. A significant example of this situation is found in a letter by the Bulgarian psychoanalyst and linguist Julia Kristeva to the French essayist Catherine Clément.[47] Writen while her son was in a Paris hospital for a surgical operation, Julia wrote to Catherine that a popular saying kept running through her head: "Nothing is more sacred for a woman, than the life of her child" (p. 56). After commenting that this sentence constitutes one of those banal pieces of popular wisdom that has always held true and which may lend itself to mockeries such as "what a shame that women stick to children, don't you find?", she writes:

> The great, subtle pediatrician, the English psychoanalyst Winnicott has a curious idea I like, namely, that the mother's primordial connection to her child stems from "being", and is distinguished from "doing", which occur only later, with the drive, desire, and acts. Like you, it occurred to me that the "serenity of Being" imagined by Heidegger may be rooted in these zones of experience, if one chooses to see such things with an anthropologist's eye. *She is* simply *there*, the mother, with a part of her that is already an *other*. *Being there with*: the dawn of difference. Peace, recognition, devotion. It is not that she "does" nothing, but the eagerness

> for action is suspended in a capable tenderness. Seduction, affect, drive, desires—the assets of the lover she was, barely nine months earlier, are not destroyed but deferred, "inhibited regarding the goal" (as my colleagues, the female psychoanalysts who have read their Freud, would say). I distrust that suggestion of inhibition; I prefer to speak of waiting. The serenity of maternal love is a deferred eros, desired in waiting. [...] It is truly at the dawn of the mother's connection to the child that a miraculous alchemy occurs: the "object" of erotic satisfaction, the father (or some relationship, profession or gratification) is slowly resored into a loved, and only loved, "other". Love-tenderness takes the place of erotic love: the "object" of satisfaction is transformed into an "other"—to care for—to nourish. (Clément & Kristeva, 2001, pp. 56–57)

Despite being infused by the traditional psychoanalytic perspective, the above citation demonstrates that Kristeva-as-mother understands well the distinctive character of maternal love and the distinction between "being" and "doing" proposed by Winnicott, in addition to drawing an interesting connection to the issue of the serenity of the second Heidegger, referring it to this peculiar region of human experience. This serene maternal love, which is typically feminine, anything but phallic and is constituted by the identification with the mother herself and to the women's lineage, nevertheless seems to stifle her, since later in the letter she herself states:

> [...] it is here that I take my distance somewhat from the kindly Winnicott. Even though I find that serenity of the mother–baby being seductive, I only half-believe in it. Per female narcissism, that "other me" of the child is a "me me" all the same: the mother is never short on the tendency to annex the cherished other, to project herself onto it, to monopolize it, to dominate it, to suffocate it. [...] Moreover, the mother also remains a woman, with her desires and her erotic or professional "doing", and that tension of existence (that bisexuality, if you prefer) is continually interfering with her serenity and her connection to the child. A warm, conflictual connection, laden with all the noise of the world. And fortunately so! Without that pulsating, active, phallic share of maternal love, where would the call of language come from, the thrill of breaking free, that erection (yes, I say the word and insist upon it), which allow the mother and baby to stand up, to move beyond each other toward third parties? (Clément & Kristeva, 2001, pp. 57–58)

This citation not only demonstrates a vigorous reassertion of femininity constituted in the masculine line of penis envy, but also a suspicion about the possibility of a woman entirely surrendering herself to maternity, even if only temporarily and also, of being able to let the child be.[48]

For Winnicott, however, the imaginative elaboration of genital functions shows that genitality incorporates much of what is pre-genital, with this being truer for the feminine side of human nature. There is a basic feminine fantasy and sexuality which have their origins in the earliest childhood, founded on the girl's identification with the feminine side of human nature: identification with the mother and through her with the female lineage. This means that the elements pertaining to girls participate more in the category of *woman* than do those of the boys in the category of *man*. The fantasies relating to complete genitality, being penetrated, pregnancy, breastfeeding etc., which are still concretely remote, appear associated, in games and in dreams, with the girl's capacity to identify herself with the mother and the woman. In girls, ideas about genitality:

> [...] find fullest expression through identification with mother or with older girls who are able to experience and to conceive. The little girl's play, in so far as she is *truly female*, is of type that shows a mothering tendency [...]. (1988, p. 46; my italics)

The identification of the girl with what could be termed a "feminine lineage" is a recurrent theme in Winnicott's work. According to him, even if we can see that the vagina of a little baby becomes active and excitable on the occasion of breastfeeding and anal experiences, in fact, "the true female genital functioning tends to be hidden, if not actually secret" (1988, p. 46). When, at a later stage, genital eroticism is intensified and appears, for example, in compulsive masturbation, normally, "the type of fantasy is of collecting and of secrecy and of hiding" (1988, p. 46). That is why any description of feminine sexuality must include the girl's fantasies regarding her insides and those of her mother. Unlike boys, girls are led to think and to feel the inside of the body very early and throughout their lives. The ability to keep a secret, for example, is a characteristic which typically belongs to the feminine side of human nature; if a girl cannot keep a secret she will not become pregnant. From the masculine side, the tendency is to fight and to push things into holes. If the boy cannot develop this aggressive aspect of his nature, he will subsequently be incapable of deliberate impregnation of a woman.

Winnicott's central thesis that every woman has always belonged to the female lineage means that, unlike men, who are one and become increasingly more unified, the woman is always a trio. It is this trio that is often represented in the famous figuration, the painting of the Three Graces. There are always three women in every woman: girl baby, woman female/mother, and mother's mother (cf. 1986g, p. 192). Or, in another formulation: female infant, veiled bride, and old woman (cf. 1988, p. 47). They are always all three from the start: when the mother takes care of the little baby, she does so in accordance with the care that she has received, that is, by the hand of her own mother, so that something of the grandmother becomes part of the girl; when, shortly afterwards, the girl plays and generally does so by taking care of a doll, putting a little house in order, cooking, etc., this is the mother herself and the grandmother. During adolescence and in youth, the woman blossoms as a female and, there is a lot of the fragile cuddly girl in her as well as of the seductive woman who attracts the male both for sexual relations and to make her a mother. In the elderly woman, as the female withers away, the little baby increasingly installs herself, requiring care from the grown up children, at the same time as she continues to be the mother who now takes care of the grandchildren.

> Whether a woman has babies or not, she is in this infinite series; she is baby, mother and grandmother [...]. This enables her to be very deceitful. She can be a sweet little thing to catch her man, and then become a dominating wife–mother, and later gracious grandmother. It's all the same because she starts off three, while man starts off with a tremendous urge to be one. One is one and all alone, and ever more shall be so. (1986g, p. 192)

In any case, with regard to the constitution of sexual identity, we must also consider bisexuality, especially in the context of fantasy and in relation to the capacity for identification with any of the parents. Leaving aside other aspects which may intervene in this particular case, the main factor which determines this identity is the gender of the person with whom the child is in love at the critical age, that is, between weaning and the latency period (cf. 1988, p. 48). Although it is easier and more convenient for the individual to develop in a way that is largely congruent with the characteristics of his or her physical constitution, "society gains much if it can tolerate the homosexual as well as the heterosexual in the emotional development of children" (1988, p. 48). If the development of the boy's personality is going well from other perspectives, a strong identification with the mother, including effeminate behaviour, may be valuable for exploring many potentialities. In girls, a certain masculinity is not only tolerated, but also expected and valued.

In healthy instinctual and emotional development, in addition to these identifications, girls effectively pass through a moment when they feel inferior because they do not have a penis, so that the male-in-the-female is always present and is always important, albeit not necessarily decisive. Penis envy must not be ignored as a source of powerful motivations in girls and in women, with this becoming clear, above all, in the analysis of neuroses in women. Conversely, femininity in the boy, to the same extent as his masculinity, is fundamental, albeit variable, as a function of several hereditary characteristics, environmental influences, identification with parents and wider cultural patterns. With regard to the boy's identification with his mother, we must distinguish between his capacity to identify with the woman in terms of her female genitality and his identification with her in her role as mother. This latter is more accepted within the culture and less problematic for the male genitality of the boy, since it is more closely related to the type of fantasy than to the localisation and the imaginative elaboration of bodily functions.

With regard to girls, however, even when they develop their femininity including some element of penis envy, which belongs to the masculine aspect of the development of sexual identity, correcting the "defect" is not as in Freud, in having a son by the father, but by acknowledging the dependence on the other. Winnicott describes the sequence through which, under normal conditions, the envy of the penis is overcome. In order to face the superiority of boys, the girl imagines having a penis growing in her. She then thinks that she already had one, which was taken from her as a punishment for excitation. This is then followed by the idea that since she does not have a penis, she may use one by proxy, that is, some male may act on her behalf. She will then say something like: "I shall let the male use me. In this way I get a deficiency made up but acknowledge a dependence on the male for completeness" (1988, p. 45). This, says Winnicott, is how the girl discovers "the true female genital" (1988, p. 45).

It should be noted that, while the "true genital" refers to the female, to the wreathed and veiled bride of the trio of women, in the strict line of elaboration belonging to the phallic phase of sexual development, true femininity, including genitality, belongs to the line of personal maturation and necessarily combines the female-woman with the potential mother through the girl's identification with the mother and the female lineage. This means that although the male-in-the-female is always present and penis envy is a fact at a certain point of the development of sexuality, this kind of resolution fails to account for true feminine sexuality and if the sexual identity of the woman is built on the problem of penis envy, the path will be precarious.

The constitution of sexual identity, as well as gender differences, are elaborated by Winnicott within a theory of sexuality belonging to the theory of instinctuality, which is in turn a part of the maturational process. At a later stage in his thought, more precisely in 1966, and driven by his clinical work, the author was led to perceive another aspect of bisexuality and to formulate the concepts of "pure female element" and "pure male element", both present in girls and boys, men and women.[49] I understand that the term "pure" specifically seeks to mean that while refering to the bisexuality present in the human individual and in each case, interfering with the constitution of the sexual identity, the pure female and male elements are not in themselves of an instinctual or sexual character, nor do they relate to the individual's biological gender. Furthermore, due to their nature, they are not repressed and, instead, it may occur that they are split off from the total personality.

These elements constitute a new way of formulating the two modes of object relation: the relation with subjective objects (pure female element) and the relation with objects perceived objectively (pure male element). The "pure female element" relates to *being*, to the experience of primary identity, in which one *is* the same as the other (the baby *is* the object), an experience that takes place within the context of the illusion of omnipotence, with subjective objects. In normal development, the pure female elemento presides over the relation of both girls and boys with their mother. The "pure male element", which occurs only later in the maturational process, relates to *doing*; it is based on instinctual drive and already presupposes the establishment of a me, as an integrated identity, separated from the not-me and the world, as external reality. If everything goes well, *doing* only arises at the point when instinctuality is being integrated as part of personality. In brief, while the female element *is*, the male element *does*. *Doing*, says Winnicott, must come after and on top of *being*.

It is only in terms of the pure male element that the distinction between active and passive makes sense, that is to say, between an active relationship (doing something with the object), or a passive allowing oneself to relate to (allowing to be done to oneself), with each of these atitudes being supported by the instinctual drive. It nevertheless must be noted that, while based on instinct, which demands action, the *doing* of the pure male element is not instinctual in itself.

According to the author, this new approach greatly enriched his understanding both of bisexuality and of the constitution of identity, including sexual identity, since it led him to clarify an essential dilemma of the human being, which must operate at a very early date, namely the conflict "between being the object which also has the property of being, and by contrast a confrontation with the object which involves activity and object-relating that is backed by instinct or drive" (1972, p. 191).

The insight which led Winnicott to this new level of theoretical understanding, by the realisation of the phenomenon consisting of the presence, both in men and women, of a pure female or male element, of the other sex, which is not biological, split off from the total personality, occured to him during the analysis of a middle-aged man, who was married, had a family, and was professionally successful (the patient FM)[50]. This man had already undergone a long analysis following a traditional line, but continued seeking help, since he felt that something very important had not been achieved. At a moment prior to the stage of analysis at which he was able to formulate the question in terms of a split-off pure feminine element, Winnicott already knew, because of the patient's frequent compulsive fantasies about being a woman, that a complete exploration regarding the feminine self which inhabited him would be necessary. The previous analysis of this patient had also required regression to a state in which "at the centre there is nothing" (cf. 1989r, p. 51). On this occasion, it was found that his entire life had been built as reactions to invasions which he, so to speak, collected, since this was how he managed to feel active and potent in different areas and at different levels. While in regression, he had to set aside many things, including his potency, since this proved to be entirely reactive. After achieving and managing to remain as nothing for a few sessions, the only tolerable state after acknowledging that it was the only real one in his life, the patient began to reveal himself in a positive manner. At the end of one session in which the theme was thouroughly elaborated, he spoke of the sensation of being tightly wrapped between the legs and the effect that this had on his genital organs and on his ability to urinate. In view of the material that he already had, Winnicott interpreted that while he was a baby, his mother had probably arranged his nappies in way that would be appropriate for a girl; with the possible result that he had never been free to urinate as a boy, pointing out that it would have been very different had he been born in a cabin in the forest and lived freely with nature. The patient immediately captured the meaning of what it would be to urinate freely. In a subsequent session, the patient told him that from what he could remember, that was the first time he felt that his penis was his own. "It looks", said Winnicott, "as if this is the beginning of his potency which he has never had although in fact he has a family" (1989r, p. 52).

The way in which the case unfolded and in which Winnicott dealt with the trasference enabled him to formulate a new aspect of the same problem: the-girl-in-the-boy, or the feminine self, in that man, could be seen as a *split-off pure female element*, which, despite being part of his sexual identity, was not properly sexual and had been dissociated from personality at a very primitive stage. This condition, the author pointed out, had nothing to do with homosexuality. The basis of this split-off pure female element, as we have seen, resided in the fact that when he was a baby, the patient had been the object of a delirious cross-identification: his mother had seen a girl in him and had treated him physically as such, making him ajust to the mother's idea that her baby was a girl. The point here is not so much how the mother saw him or whether she had wished for a girl, but the fact that she had translated this conception into a type of care that suited a girl and not a boy. The imaginative elaboration of the sensation did the rest.

The analytical situation which made possible the new understanding was that, at a certain point after the elaboration mentioned above, the man started to mention something that could be understood as penis envy (cf. 1971i, p. 170). Winnicott told him:

> I am listening to a girl. I know perfectly well that you are a man but I am listening to a girl, and I am talking to a girl. I am telling this girl: 'You are talking about penis envy'. (1971i, p. 170)

After a break, the patient said: "If I were to tell someone about this girl I would be called mad" (ibid.). The issue could have ended there, but Winnicott decided to take it further and made the observation which surprised himself and which, with regard to transference, touched the core of the problem. Winnicott observed: "It was not that *you* told this to anyone; it is *I* who see a girl and hear a girl talking, when actually there is a man on my couch. The mad person is *myself*" (1971i, p. 171). It was not necessary to elaborate it, the author wrote, because he hit the target.

The patient then said that now he felt sane in a mad environment. That is, he had been released from his dilemma. Winnicott observed: "This madness which was mine [when he took on the madness of the mother who saw a girl where there was a boy] enabled him to see himself as a girl *from my position*. He knows himself to be a man, and never doubts that he is a man" (1971i, p. 171). The patient said later: "I myself could never say (knowing myself to be a man) 'I am a girl'. I am not mad that way. But you said it, and you have spoken to both parts of me" (1971i, p. 171).

In a case such as this one, the analyst must be able to accompany, tolerate, and even provide the patient with the full experience of delirious identification. "It could be said", says the author, "that the patient was in search of the right kind of mad analyst and that in order to meet his needs I had to assume that role" (1971i, p. 189). With regard to this new understanding, he noted that

> [...] Here was no new theoretical concept, here was no new principle of technique. In fact, I and my patient had been over this ground before. Yet we had here something new, new in my own attitude and new in his capacity to make use of my interpretative work. [...] I found myself with a new edge to an old weapon. (1971i, pp. 172–173)

Returning to the more general questions concerning the oedipal stage, it must be said that although the child is capable of having genital experiences, he must wait until puberty in order to be capable to realise his fantasy, which means that at the genital phase the child's ego is able to deal with a tremendous quantity of frustration (cf. 1988, p. 44). The focal point here, and this is one of the aspects presiding over Winnicott's redescription of oedipal themes and the anxiety of castration, is that the child *must deal with impotency*. As a result, from this perspective, the presence of an intervenor father brings great relief; "fear of castration by the rival father becomes welcome as an alternative to the agony of impotence" (1988, p. 44).

Assuming there was a good start, it is possible to examine the different defences used by the child to deal with the anxieties resulting from the Oedipus complex. In the triangular relation, the child "is overtaken by instinct and loves. This love involves physical and fantasy changes and is violent. It leads to hate. The child hates the third person" (1988, p. 54). The boy may be in love with the mother and, as we have already seen, the existence of the intervening father provides relief for the agony of real impotence. This is nevertheless only one side of the story. The other one is that he lives the painful conflict of ambivalence in which he perceives himself to hate, wishing to castrate or kill the father and fearing retaliation regarding fear of castration by the father whom he loves and trusts, because he is in love with his wife.

If the child is healthy and the foundations of the home are solid, anxiety stemming from this situation can be tolerated and he eventually recovers from the moments of high instinctual tension. The fact is that hate may now appear freely, since "[...] what is hated is a person, one who can defend himself, and one who is already loved"; and someone "[...] who can survive and punish and forgive" (1988, p. 54). If this is actually experienced, as a result of the father doing his part, then he begins to be used as "prototype of conscience". Incorporating the father whom he knows, the boy reaches an agreement with him: on one side, he loses something of his instinctual potential capacity, renouncing part of what he had been claiming; on the other side, he shifts the love object to a sister, aunt, nanny, that is, someone who is less involved with the father. At best,

> [...] the boy enters into a homosexual pact with the father, so that his potency becomes not entirely individual but instead (through identification) a new expression of the father's potency that has been taken in and adopted. [...] By identification with the father or father-figure the boy gets a potency by proxy, and a postponed potency of his own, which can be recovered at puberty. (1988, p. 55)

If, due to absence or incapacity, the father does not intervene during the oedipal phase, this is perceived by the boy as a non-acknowledgement and a non-legitimation of his potency and also deprives him of the experience of rivalry. The central issue in the oedipal situation described by Winnicott is not just the threat of castration but, due to the establishment of rivalry, the legitimation of the child's potency. In other words, there are more and other ambivalences in the oedipal situation than those indicated by traditional theory. The rivalry between the boy and the father, regarding the oedipal question, does not necessarily include deadly hatred and the boy, who needs the experience of rivalry, under reliable conditions does not necessarily want to kill the father.[51] Child aggression in the traditional psychoanalytical lexicon has assimilated with destruction, hatred, hostility, anger, and a similar confusion, resulting from the use of these terms as synonyms, led to no few consequences with regard to the analytical work.

There are cases in which the difficulties of the oedipal phase already derive from the stage of concern, with the child having had to inhibit his instinctual drives since he could not depend on the active presence of a father who would protect the mother from his impulsiveness. This was the case of patient B, the protagonist of the book *Holding and Interpretation* (1986a). His main issue during the second period of his analysis, related to the problems of the stage of concern (cf. 1986a, p. 21), in addition to him showing a split in the mind with regard to the psyche-*soma*. The achievements relating to the capacity for concern had been made difficult not only due to the difficult relationship established with the mother, but also as a result of the fact that his father had been more maternal than paternal, and could not play his role when the boy needed him to do so.[52] At a certain point, when patient B embarked on an intellectual digression on the prohibition of incest, Winnicott told him:

> You are using society's prohibition of incest between son and mother because you cannot find the man who will get in between you and your mother, which means that father did not play his part here, and so you have no hate and no fear of man and you are back in the old position of either being frustrated by the woman or else developing an internal inhibition. (1986a, p. 82)

On another occasion, while mentioning a dream, the patient said: "To sum up, my own problem is how to find a struggle that never was. In the dream it was the struggle that was missing". Winnicott answered: "You were not able to get the relief that the triangular situation brings when a child is in a clash with father; relief from the struggle with mother alone" (1986a, p. 165).

In addition to the difficulties arising from the impossibility for the father to play his part, this young man could not develop the necessary homosexual relation with the father during the phallic phase and could not identify with him. At a certain moment in analysis, when it became clear that his affective and sexual choices had always been directed towards "the girl with the penis of adolescent dreams" the patient observed: "I might be looking for a man, which would be a kind of homosexuality, which would imply that I'm an effeminate type of man". Winnicott replied:

> No, I don't think so. The fact is you are looking for father, the man who prohibits intercourse with mother. Remember the dream in which the girl friend originally appeared and this was about a man, one who was ill. (1986a, p. 77)

The patient noted:

> This would account for my lack of grief or of feeling when my father died. He had not met me as a rival and so left me with the awful burden of making the prohibitions myself. (Ibid)

The analyst observed:

> Yes, on the one hand he never did you the honour of recognizing your maturity by banning intercourse with mother, but also he deprived you of the enjoyment of rivalry and of the friendship that comes out of rivalry with men. So you had to develop a general inhibition, and you could not mourn a father you have never "killed". (Ibid)

Instinctual tension, which is characteristic of this period, reaches its peak at some point between the ages of three and five or six, when it is either resolved or shelved, also on account of the endocrinological phenomenon of suspension of instinctual tension during the latency period. During this period, when the child is healthy, the child experiments with play, dreams, and fantasies, deriving a benefit from the identification with the parents and other adults. The immature pre-genital and genital experiences, which are within the child's reach, include the body and bodily pleasures which do not depend on the help of others. If there is reliable family support, if someone remains present and calm, the child begins to realise that the passage of time, sometimes hours or perhaps minutes, brings relief for practically everything, however intolerable it might seem. Child sexuality, says Winnicott, is something very real. It may or may not be mature by the time the transformations of latency appear, bringing relief. If sexuality is "immature or distorted or inhibited at the end of this first period of interpersonal relationships, so will it reappear as immature or distorted or inhibited at puberty" (1988, pp. 57–58).

Puberty and adolescence

If, at the age of puberty, sexuality is not mature, the individual will not be able to face the important and difficult physical changes associated with this phase and personal maturation itself, which emerges during adolescence. Even for the healthy youngster, there is no escape from the anxieties which result from this passage; however, the way the individual will deal with them depends essentially on the pattern, which was previously established, during childhood. The child who was well cared for is able to tolerate, to a certain extent, the new feelings and strangeness which arise from body changes and which do not depend on him, as well as to avoid, refuse, or defend himself from situations involving unbearable anxiety. Of this acquired pattern, which is largely unconscious, also make part residues of some inevitable early failures. On the other hand, it is of great help for the individual when puberty provides a potential for male potency, and its equivalent for girls, that is, when full genitality has already become a characteristic since it has been achieved in the reality of playing during the phase preceeding the latency period. However,

> boys and girls at puberty are not deceived into thinking that instinctual drives are all, and in fact they are essentially concerned with being, with being somewhere, with feeling real, and with achieving a degree of object constancy. (1971f, p. 25)

Yet nothing ensures the absence of problems. There is no cure for puberty or adolescence and the only thing to do is give time and survive the turbulence, which may even be greater, the better the start, since the sense of freedom and of personal richness do not make things any simpler.

During puberty, to the important alterations resulting from physical growth and the development of sexuality are added the physical capacity for genital experience and for actually killing (cf. 1965c). In other words, an overwhelming and frightening potency arises, since what once belonged to the realm of fantasy can now become concrete reality: the power to destroy and even to kill, the possibility of prostituting oneself, being impregnated, going mad on drugs, commiting suicide.

Another point to be mentioned—and in that, the psychology of the adolescent may greatly help to understand the nature of psychotic suffering—are the typical anxieties of adolescence, which repeat those of the primitive stages: the adolescent, like the baby, is essentially isolated. Furthermore, like the baby, it is only from this isolation that he may launch himself and come to establish some relation which is felt as real. The group phenomenon in adolescence is that of a collection of isolated individuals who attempt to form an aggregation around some common interest or preoccupation, albeit with the personal self receded and protected. Isolation is also associated with a feature of sexuality, more precisely, with sexual indefinition: the child does not know yet if he will be heterosexual or homosexual, unless environmental patterns force definition. There is a long period of uncertainty during which, in general, an unstoppable masturbatory activity occurs, which should be understood not so much as sexual activity, but rather as a way of *getting rid of sex*. The same may occur to heterosexual or homosexual experiences which, far from being a form of union between complete human beings, are rather a way of discharging tension. When there is immaturity in instinctual life, "then there is danger of ill health in the individual, in personality or character or behaviour" (1971f, p. 26). In this case, we must remember "that sex can operate as a part–function so that, although sex may seem to be working well, potency and its female equivalent can be found to deplete, instead of enrich, the individual" (1971f, p. 26).

What indicates that the adolescence repeats the patterns of the primitive stages is the fact that the child suffers from the feeling of irreality, with the main struggle relating to feeling real. There exists in the adolescent a rigid morality not in terms of what was socially established as good and bad, which is precisely what he despises and rebels against, but in terms of what is felt as real and what is felt as false: the adolescent does not accept false solutions. What is worst, what is intolerable is to betray oneself. Like the psychotic, the adolescent cannot compromise. Some acquiescence, which is a part of health and necessary for conviviality, becomes a threat of personal extinction (cf. 1962). This is a particularly difficult period for the individual who, having not had a good start, bears with him the threat of disintegration, since adolescence drags him close to collapse. On the contrary, for the individual who had a good start, time will take care of many things, in case the family environment survives and remains reliable. In anyway, throughout adolescence, there will certainly be acute management problems and the need for firm support and reliability, since growing up means occupying the place of the genitor: "In the unconscious fantasy, growing up is inherently an aggressive act [...]. If the child is to become adult, then this move is achieved over the dead body of an adult" (1969a, pp. 169–170).

Adult age

Having emerged relatively unscathed from adolescence, it is possible to discriminate at least four tasks, which, interdependent of each other, await the individual in adult life. Even for those who had a good start, the first task is to continue to develop and staying alive, even in old age, until death. Naturally, this depends on the preservation of primary creativity, on the capacity to allow oneself to be hit by events and to continue to surprise oneself:[53] "Each member of the adult community is growing, and continues to grow, we hope, throughout life" (1961b, p. 44). At the same time, if the individual was able to experience omnipotence at the appropriate time, with maturity, he gives up being the steering wheel and adopts a more comfortable position of being a piece in the gear, even because, at this point, it is not the place that he has in society which tells him who he is. If, however, he did not have the opportunity to begin life with the small experience of being omnipotent, he may become someone who needs to exacerbate omnipotence, creativity, and control; something like "trying to sell unwanted shares in a bogus company" (1986h, p. 50). The mature adult, on the contrary, is capable of creativity without losing contact with the richness of the subjective world; the adult can make concessions without feeling robbed of spontaneity. Health is related to condescendence and imposture and when maturation elapses favourably,

> the individual becomes able to deceive, to lie, to compromise, to accept conflict as a fact and to abandon the extreme ideas of perfection and an opposite to perfection that make existence intolerable. Capacity for compromise is not a characteristic of the insane. (1988, pp. 137–138)

The second, more specific task would be the fact that, once personal maturity is achieved, which includes the idea of value and that there are people and things which deserve to be preserved, there gradually emerges social maturity and what booms and flourishes with it is the capacity for valuing and promoting, when possible, the democratic way of life (cf. 1950a,

p. 243, note 3). Democracy is one of the most important achievements and, simultaneously, a remarkable contribution of the healthy adult to society, but it can only become possible with the existence of a good proportion of individuals who have been successful in their personal maturational process. Winnicott resumes this point several times in his work: society depends essentially on its healthy members, since it is precisely those individuals who have achieved maturity who are capable of establishing and ensuring the "[…] *innate tendency towards the creation and re-creation and maintenance of the democratic machinery*" (1950a, p. 243). Viewed from this perspective, it necessarily involves having to ensure the family institution: "In this way, democracy (in one meaning of the word) is an indication of health because it airses naturally out of the family, which is in itself a construct for which healthy individuals are responsible" (1971f, p. 38).

> Society depends on the integration of family units, but I think it is important to remember that these family units in turn depend on the integration which takes place in the growth of each individual member. In other words, in a healthy society, one in which democracy can flourish, a proportion of the individuals must have achieved a satisfactory integration *in their own personality development*. The idea of democracy and the democratic way of life arises out of the healthy and the natural growth of the individual, and can be maintained in no way except by the integration of the individual personality, multiplied of course many times according to the number of healthy or relatively healthy individuals […] to carry the unintegrated personalities who cannot contribute in, otherwise society degenerates from democracy. (1961b, p. 47)

The same position is corroborated in *Human Nature*:

> In a community in which there is a sufficiently high proportion of mature individuals there is a state of affairs which provides the basis for what is called democracy. If the proportion of mature individuals is below a certain number, democracy is not something which can become a political fact since affairs will be swayed by the immature, that is to say, by those who by identification with the community lose their own individuality or by those who never achieve more than the attitude of the individual dependent upon society. (1988, p. 152)[54]

We shall see now the third task, which consists of the acceptance of impotence and of imperfection. People, the author observes, have to

> […] accept what they are and the history of their personal development along with the local environmental attitudes and influences, and they have to get on with life and living, attempting to interweave with society in such a way that there is a cross-contribution. (1986g, p. 188)

Having to face imperfections of the me and of the world, as they are, often causes depression. When it is not mutilating, or linked to psychotic disorders, however, depression is a state of spirit proper of truly responsible people, of those who are really valuable. They get depressed precisely because they are able to see and to accept the precariousness of human condition and the fact that the world is never the way we imagine it; and also because they clearly realise that their capacity for loving and for constructing coexists with their own hate, wickedness, and destructiveness. Depression is thus inherent to life and to maturity. This may be terrible, but not being able to doubt or to suffer perturbations is a condition which is even worse (cf. 1965o, p. 52). "The fact is that the sense of *doubt* is very close to its opposite which is *belief*, and to a sense of values, and to the feeling that *there are things worth preserving*" (1965o, p. 52). Most likely, the greatest suffering in the human universe is the suffering of the normal, healthy, or mature person: "Unhappy is a you or a me who, over a phase, is conscious of the lack of what is essential to the human being, much more important than eating or than physical survival" (1986h, p. 44).

All this is linked to the fourth, and perhaps, most important and difficult task of adulthood: to be able to age and to die. At this point, the fact that integration can never be fully achieved emerges thoroughly. What always lacks, to man is his own end. In October of 1970, shortly before his death in January 1971, while addressing an association of social workers for maladjusted children, Winnicott mentioned a type of growth "to becoming smaller": "If I live long enough I hope I may dwindle and become small enough to get through the little hole called dying" (1984g, p. 220). Learning to die, however, is only possible for someone who has lived and has had experiences. It is only possible to have lived and to continue to live having achieved the unitary status which makes it possible to say I AM. Only from this condition is it possible both to live and to die. "There is no death", says Winnicott, "except of a totality" (1984f, p. 61). When there is a sense of wholeness in personal integration, this brings with it

> [...] the *possibility* and indeed the *certainty of death*; and with the acceptance of death there can come a great relief, relief from fear of the alternatives, such as disintegration, or ghosts—that is the lingering on of spirit phenomena after the death of the somatic half of the psycho-somatic partnership. (1984h, pp. 61–62)[55]

Fearsome is the internal death. Even when healthy, no one is safe from losing that which links them to life and to the meaning of life. The question always remains: why is it that creative living can be lost and why the individual's feeling that life is real or meaningful can disappear? (cf. 1971g, p. 93). Grateful to one of his patients for the expression "phenomenal death", Winnicott affirms: "many men and woman spend their lives wondering whether to find a solution by suicide, that is, sending the body to death which has already happened to the psyche" (1974, p. 93).

The return to the origin

The maturational process begins with "the first awakening". We can now ask: where and how does it end?

In *Human Nature*, Winnicott tries to bring together these two extreme moments of human existence. Refering to the beginning of maturation, he asks:

> What is the state of the human individual as the being emerges out of not being? [...] What is the fundamental state to which every individual, however old and with whatever experiences, can return in order to start again? (1988, p. 131)

His answer is as simple as it is unexpected: *if the individual were to re-start, he or she would have to return to the state of essential aloneness*. Since, "at the start is an essential aloneness" (1988, p. 132).

Perhaps we should understand that human life constitutes an attempt to forget this aloneness. An attempt that is always frustrated, since the essential aloneness remains throughout life as an occult backdrop, untouchable and unspeakable, shadow of nothingness, inscribed in the very bosom of the origin and with which "there is no communication with the not-me world either way" (1965j, p. 189). Winnicott does not tire from emphasising the need which we have […]

> to recognize this aspect of health: the non-communicating central self, for ever immune from the reality principle, and for ever silent. Here communication is not non-verbal; it is, like the music of the spheres, absolutely personal. It belongs to being alive. And in health, it is out of this that communication naturally arises. (1965j, p. 192)

Astonishing affirmation, which points to a dimension of isolation, elusive for any mundane event, yet inherent to being alive. Winnicott also says that,

> Except at the start there is never exactly reproduced this fundamental and inherent aloneness. Nevertheless throughout the life of an individual there continues a fundamental unalterable and inherent aloneness, along with which goes unawareness of the conditions that are essential to the state of aloneness. (1988, p. 132)

What can we understand from this? The sentence "[…] except at the start […]" refers to the affirmation that "at the start is an essential aloneness". The essential aloneness of the beginning will be, therefore, overcome, transposed, in some sense, since "there is never exactly reproduced this fundamental and inherent aloneness" (1988, p. 132). At the same time, however, that the inherent state of aloneness is altered, *something of it remains and there continues to be a fundamental aloneness*. It is thus, a split, a basic split which lies at the very root of human existence and remains "uncurable": while something remains as an untouchable background, forever lonely, another part of the individual is launched into the light of the world, in order to inhabit it, so that life, which includes living close to things and with the other, may establish itself and happen.

The individual only "knows" of essential aloneness when, through the experience of the "first awakening", life enters the extreme quieteness of the beginning: "The experience of the first awakening gives the human individual the idea that there is a peaceful state of unaliveness that can be peacefully reached by an extreme of regression" (1988, p. 132). Although the baby or the foetus has no capacity to worry about death, "there must be, however, a capacity in every infant for concern about the aloneness of pre-dependence since this has been experienced [… .]" (1988, p. 133).

What does all this have to do with the final moment of the maturational process? Winnicott has another surprising answer: it is the same as the initial state. "Most of what is commonly said and felt about death is about this first state *before aliveness*, where aloneness is a fact and long before dependence is encountered" (1988, p. 132).

Winnicott identifies the end of the maturational process with the initial moment. In this way, maturation as a whole is characterised as a process of return to the origin, as a *circular* movement which goes back to the place where it started. He leaves no doubts: the state prior to the essential aloneness is a state of not-being-alive. It is to this state, which T. S. Eliot called "pure simplicity, costing not less than everything", that the human individual necessarily returns: "The life of an individual is an interval between two states of unaliveness. The first of these, out of which aliveness arises, colours ideas people have about the second death" (Winnicott, 1988, p. 132).

Second death? The first one is prior to the beginning, whence being emerges from not-being and, from there on, the path is a journey towards the second one. There is a nothingness prior to the start and a nothingness after the end. Life consists of the interval between these two nothingnesses. Life does not rule absolutely, however, as an event immune to these two nothingnesses. They traverse it from end to end. It is by means of this fundamental link that "there is no enjoyment of company except as a development from essential isolation, the isolation that reappears as the individual dies" (1984b, p. 111).

In death, which is the great return, the essential aloneness will close onto itself, completing the life cycle. While the individual is still alive, it will remain as a background, as a non-configurable reserve which delivers man to the task of existing as unprecedented and personal history, without the support of any determination, sustained only by the illusion of the power to create. It will also remain as a matrix for all possibilities of return, of retreat by the individual who, when healthy, needs to rest from the task of existing and of permanently having to separate fantasy from reality, of what is perceived subjectively from what is perceived objectively. Essential aloneness is the only true and unknowingly desired quietness, which comes closest to the condition of pure simplicity that costs nothing less than everything.

On the inside cover of the notebook where Winnicott started to write his autobiography, which would be entitled *Not Less Than All*, there is a fragment from T. S. Eliot's *Four Quartets*:

> What we call the beginning is often the end
> And to make an end is to make a beginning
> The end is where we start from. (Eliot, 1980, pp. 144–145)

Brief comparison of the theory of maturational processes with the traditional psychoanalytic theory of the development of sexual functions

Elaborated from the author's experience of babies and psychotics, Winnicottian psychoanalysis is based on the theory of maturational processes, meaning a process of integration starting from a state of unintegration, which gives special emphasis to the primitive tasks of constitution of the self and access to the senses of reality. The issue here is the baby in the mother's lap. Traditional psychoanalysis, developed from the study and treatment of neurosis, is based on the theory of the development of sexuality in terms of object relations oriented by the pleasure principle, which privileges the Oedipus complex, that is, the child in the mother's bed.[56] There are fundamental differences between these two theoretical frameworks of psychoanalysis. With regard to the theoretical premises, some of these differences were cited at the end of Chapter One. I shall point out here some differences between the Winnicottian theory of maturational processes and the traditional theory of the development of sexual functions.

According to Winnicott, the theory of the development of sexual functions ignores the initial stages of maturation, taking for granted certain acquisitions regarding the structuring of personality: the constitution of the reality of the self and of the external world. These initial achievements should on no account be presumed or regarded as an automatic result of growth. It is the experience of dealing with these tasks of maturation and their successful resolution which constitute the foundations of psychic health. Psychosis is precisely the failure to achieve them and in this case, there will not even be an individual there, who, answering for a me, may become entangled in intrapsychic conflicts to the point of suffering from the vicissitudes characteristic of instinctual life and interpersonal relationships.

Another distinction between Winnicott's maturational paradigm and the oedipal paradigm of traditional psychoanalysis lies in the fact that at the basis of Freud's understanding of neuroses is the psychic conflict, the theoretical foundation of which is pulsional duality. Freud could not change this concept, since he ran the risk of losing the entire theoretical construction of psychoanalysis.[57] For Winnicott, however, moving along another theoretical horizon, there is no need to conceive of pulsional forces in conflict in order to set life in motion and provide theoretical support for the difficulties, impasses, and disorders, even the most primitive ones. What drives life and the psyche is the very fact that the baby is alive and carries within him the innate tendency towards integration; it is from this that the tasks and vital needs derive. Having to go on being and to develop already places the individual in the face of enough challenges and difficulties, bearing in mind, in particular, his situation of extreme dependence on environmental care, which may humanly fail at any time. It is thus not necessary to postulate instinctual and affective conflicts in order to explain the baby's primitive anxieties.

Freudian theory conceives of development in terms of the development of *sexual functions*. This derives from Freud's central thesis that neuroses are disorders which relate to a sexual conflict. The central theme of the conflict is the Oedipus complex, and it is within the resolution of the complex that the constitution of the subject occurs. Even when Freud becomes interested in psychoses, in attempting to respond to the theoretical impasses created by his theory of narcissism, the questions that he formulates derive from the same field configured for the understanding of neuroses. The inadequacy of his theory of psychoses is already established in his premises: Lacking the means to accept a domain of problems, which falls outside the pulsional conflict, Freud must fit psychotic pathologies into this domain. According to Winnicott, however, maturation does not refer to isolated functions, but specifically to integration into a wholeness and to the tendency to live as a unit. Even though personal maturation includes the gradual integration of instinctuality and the development of sexuality, it is not within this domain that the individual is constituted. There are people who, because their development was interrupted during primitive phases, will never attain sufficient maturity to suffer from problems inherent to the oedipal situation. In Winnicott's theory, there must be first an individual so that something like human sexuality may occur.

These are some of the reasons why Winnicott affirms that although it is much easier to describe the maturational processes with regard to instinctual functions than in terms of the ego and its complex evolution, this latter alternative can no longer be avoided. We may illustrate how, in the theory of maturational processes, Winnicott makes the achievements of the ego prevail over sexual functions, as well as how these achievements are considered as a condition for the possibility of instinctual life. Returning to an aspect of the development of instinctuality within the maturational process, that of the progression of instinctual dominance in accordance with the functions involved and the imaginative elaboration of these functions, Winnicott lists the pre-genital, phallic, and genital phases as the only important ones to be considered; in his view, the subdivision of phases, proposed by K. Abraham (erotic oral, sadistic oral; erotic anal, sadistic anal, etc.), are essentially unsatisfactory, since it consists of the application to the primitive stages, of the model of progression, ranging from the pre-genital to the genital and implying seeing the infant from what we already know about the child who walks, instead of seeing the baby in his immaturity.

Winnicott's central objection, however, is the fact that it is not the fantasy of oral activity that is initially erotic, that is, non-sadistic, pre-ambivalent, and only then, sadistic, destructive, and ambivalent. "It's better to say that is the infant who changes, starting ruthless and then becoming concerned" (1988, p. 42). The establishment of ambivalence is related to maturational changes of the self and not to the development of instinctual functions. Regardless of the phase of the process, the character of personal development remains. In the oedipal stage, for example, instinctual life, coupled with the achieving of genitality, will cause sexuality to gain prominence. This position, however, is not structural, but characteristic of this stage. Neurotic disorders are, as Freud described them, of a sexual character, but because the individual orbits the oedipal question and is stricken by the instinctual turbulence which accompanies it, he does not become an eminently instinctual or sexual being. His issues as a person remain as issues and, just as before, sexuality does not define or constitute him. In the clinical situation, the therapist must keep in mind the question of knowing whether someone is already there, a me who is there to be found, who feels alive and capable of giving meaning to instinctual life and sexuality, or whether, regardless of the content with which the individual cloaks his immaturity, for example, a false family soap opera, this therapist must be alert to the conditions which facilitate the constitution of the primary self.

Unlike in traditional psychoanalysis, the achievements of maturation do not occur automatically. The human baby depends, even in order to reach the point of being a baby, on the concrete and continuous presence of a facilitating environment. The process is not initially intrapsychic, but interpersonal, albeit, in the beginning, in a very peculiar sense. The dynamics of development, since they are taking place within a relationship of absolute dependence of the baby with regard to the environment, does not exclusively or mainly result from internal or constitutional factors, but from environmental facilitation. Furthermore, the primary relation with the environment mother is not initially object related. The baby is not yet a unitary me, who already has an internal world, within which the conflict between good and bad internal objects occurs; he is neither aware of the existence of an external world or of external objects. At the very outset, the "relation" with the mother is not even dual and must be described as a baby–mother unit of two-in-one. It is within this *sui generis* relationship, the reality of which is subjective, that the contact with external reality begins, albeit without the baby realising that is external. Since it is not even dual, the relationship is even less triangular. Nor can it be said to be erotic, since the baby is not governed by the pleasure principle, but by the need to be, to feel real, and to achieve existence in a real world. For this purpose, what he needs is the mother's reliability, personal communication with her, intimacy, and the opportunity to create the world.

With regard to the roots of aggression, it is easy to perceive Winnicott's disagreement with Freudian theory. For Freud, in the first topic, human aggression begins as a reaction to frustrations in the contact with the reality principle. In Winnicott's view, this theory fails to cover these roots, since "this anger at frustration does not go early enough" (1988, p. 79). That is to say, the baby is not mature enough to have desires, or to be frustrated or to feel angry about something that is external to him, since he does not have a sense of externality. Precisely because it did not examine the questions governing the initial stages of maturation, Freudian theory ignores two significant roots of aggression: the destructiveness inherent to the primitive instinctual drive (as early as 1939, Winnicott said that the babies "bite chiefly when they are excited, and not chiefly when frustrated" (cf. 1957b, p. 87) and the reactions to environmental invasions which interrupt the continuity of being.

In Freud's view, the mental mechanisms of projection and introjection are active from the outset and drive the psyche. According to Winnicott, the foundations of psychic health do not rest on mental mechanisms, nor do the initial tasks and their resolutions refer to mental processes. Many achievements are required before these processes enter into action. On the contrary, if mental processes were led to operate precociously, before some psycho-somatic integration is established and prior to the establishment of some "knowledge" of an experiential and non-mental nature, this will have a pathological defensive character and will lead to the establishment of a disorder of a schizophrenic type.

Furthermore, mental mechanisms are conceived by traditional theory according to a bodily model of incorporation and excretion. Winnicott's conception of primary creativity excludes the idea of a human psyche built on the basis of the projection of objects previously introjected, that is to say, digested, reprocessed, and expelled. An important theoretical element at the basis of this difference lies in the fact that for Freud and, to an exaggerated degree, for Melanie Klein, the judgment of attribution (good and bad) precedes that of existence. It follows that the constitution of the *Lust-Ich*, the originary pleasure-ego, may be thought of in terms of the projection of what is bad (not pleasurable) and the introjection of what is good (pleasurable), which also means that an inside and an outside would precede the existence of an individual. In Winnicott, the existence, the sense of real (subjective), necessarily precedes any judgment of attribution, which assumes the perception of the existence of the object. Furthermore, at the beginning, the "good" and the "bad" are articulated precisely with the existence, or non-existence, of something real in the subjective sense. Good is the experience which is real, even when it is frustrating; bad is the false experience, in which something seems to happen but does not.

Nor can Winnicott accept the recourse to phylogeny, on which Freud drew so extensively when, discovering the error in his first theory of seduction, he had to account for the effectiveness of fantasies of seduction. From then on, protofantasies (*Urphantasien*) were introduced into the theory, which consisted of typical phantasmatic structures, such as the originary scene, castration, seduction, which would organise psychic life, whatever the personal experiences of the individuals. Freud legitimated them through the argument that they constituted a phylogenetically transmitted inheritance. In Winnicott's view, only what the individual experiences may be considered as belonging to him; otherwise, it remains external.

Finally, for traditional psychoanalysis, culture, sociability, morality, and art are products which derive from the pulsional conflict via sublimation. Pulsions form their foundation, that is to say, transformed instincts. According to Winnicott, however, instincts are instincts, biological drives, and in this, there are no differences between human beings and animals, except insofar as in human beings, all bodily functioning is imaginatively elaborated, which does not occur even to the most interesting of animals. Moreover, if the individual begins by introjecting objects and then by projecting them, as the traditional theory states, then he is made of the world and there is no room for primary creativity. All creativity, including artistic creativity in general, is understood in terms of the sublimation of the libido. This is why the phenomenon of transitionality could not be conceived within traditional psychoanalysis. Winnicott sees the individual as creative not because he sublimates: he is creative because he is human. Creativity is primary and refers to the capacity which all human beings have for recreating the world.

This point may be illustrated by the difference between Freud and Winnicott in their approaches to artistic production and to art in general. According to the latter, the attempts by Freudian psychoanalysis to analyse artwork loses sight of the essentials. It may be possible to relate the work of artists to their childhood or to link themes in their work to their sexual inclinations, as, for example, was done for Leonardo da Vinci. Besides irritating artists and creative people in general, these studies circumvent the central question of creativity, giving the impression that it is possible to explain and determine the reasons why a particular person is capable of artistic realisation. The question which moves Winnicott on this point becomes even clearer if we examine the difference between his concept of play and that of Melanie Klein. When she observes children's play, she asks herself the question: which fantasies are expressed in this play? In Klein's view, play demonstrates the inhibitions and performs many *functions*: the fulfilling of desires, control of anxiety, masturbatory discharge, etc. Klein is not interested in play itself, but only in the symbolic *use* which the child makes of it; that is, the purposes served by play are more important than play itself. For Winniccott, this perspective not only ignores the essential aspect of play, but causes it to lose something of its clinical meaning: play is therapeutic, not because it expresses unconscious conflicts, but because it is a natural form of life and creativity in itself.

Many of the points cited above relate both to Freud and to Melanie Klein. More specifically with regard to Klein, the differences, on the one hand, are more complex and on the other, simpler. They are more complex because, while both Winnicott and Klein were seeking answers for the same primitive period, the differentiating line is more delicate and simpler because the foundations of Klein's theory are so clearly antagonistic to Winnicott's that in a sense, it is easier to trace their frontiers. I shall limit myself to point out the following differences:[58]

1. In order to explain certain primitive phenomena (such as precocious paranoia), Melanie Klein resorts to the constitutional factor, in this way putting an end to any discussion on the role of the environment. That is to say, she disregards the fact of dependence and the nature of the care that the baby receives. If we accept the initial situation of absolute dependence, however, a phenomenon such as precocious paranoia need not be attributed to heredity; we do not need to assume the existence of an evil entity operating in isolation; we can see in it a reaction of the baby to a pattern of environmental intrusions or to some sort of failure which leads to privation.
2. In Klein's view, what goes on with the baby is intrapsychic; she does not take into account the real interpersonal experience, which takes place in the subjective plane, except in terms of fantasy.

3. Klein's theory takes for granted that the baby is capable of establishing relations with *external* objects at the very start of life. Since, in Winnicott's view, this capacity is an achievement of the maturational process, which, in the event of failure, is specifically responsible for psychoses, this means that, from the author's perspective, the Kleinian assumptions in principle eliminate any possibility of an effective consideration by Kleinian theory of the initial stages of development and, as a consequence, of psychoses, particularly of those of a schizophrenic character.
4. According to Klein, these primary object relations occur with objects that are still partial, but in her view, the subject of the relation is already present; there is an *initial unit of the mind* which may be actively split by the destructive action of the death pulsion. This changes the whole perspective of research on the initial stages which could be considered as acceptable to Winnicott.[59]
5. In describing the phenomena of the primitive stages as pre-oedipal, Klein intended to elucidate psychoses by pushing back the same elements present in the theory of neuroses: she postulates the precocious Oedipus and introduces the father's penis into the dual baby/breast relationship, reconfiguring the triangle. For Winnicott, what happens in the primitive stages is not pre-oedipal, but non-oedipal; the tasks of the constitution of the self and of access to reality do not refer to pulsional issues, but to the baby's need to go on existing and take place in an exclusively dual plane. Furthermore, for Winnicott, it is not possible to speak of Oedipus, except with regard to whole persons and on no account to partial objects.
6. The type of disruption which Melanie Klein studies, concerning the depressive position, refers to the handling of weaning which, according to Winnicott, takes place approximately between the ages of nine and eighteen months. For him, however, *prior to weaning, there is the wider question of disillusion*. It is the mother who performs the role of disillusioning the baby. This can only be accomplished, however, on the basis of a previous stage in which the mother, because of her special adaptation, provides the baby with the illusion of omnipotence. It is only on the basis of illusion that disillusion may occur.

"Weaning", says Winnicott, "implies successful feeding and disillusionment implies the successful provision of opportunity for illusion" (1953a, p. 221). Failures relating to weaning cannot cover schizophrenic phenomena, which are related to more primitive stages, the tasks of which are of a primordially different nature from those belonging to this moment of maturation. In order to arrive at psychoses of schizophrenic type it is indispensable to refer to the stages in which dependence is absolute:

> To make progress towards a workable theory of psychosis, analysts must abandon the whole idea of schizophrenia and paranoia as seen in terms of regression from the Oedipus Complex. The aetiology of these disorders takes us *inevitably* to stages that precede the three-body relationship. The strange corollary is that there is at the root of psychosis an *external factor*. It is difficult for psychoanalysts to admit this after all the work they have done drawing attention to the internal factors in examining the aetiology of psycho-neurosis. (1989i, p. 246)

7. According to Winnicott, death does not make sense until the capacity for hating is achieved, implying the perception of the other as a complete human person; in addition to the others,

this is one of the reasons why the so-called death pulsion, or destruction, is unacceptable in the description of the basis of destructiveness.
8. In Klein's view, the psyche is constructed on the basis of bodily models of incorporation and expulsion; introjection and projection. This presupposes an inside and an outside which are already constituted, which, in Winnicott's view, is not possible for the baby in a state of non-integration.

In summary, these are Winnicott's reasons for affirming that the theory of libidinal development does not explain or provide treatment for the type of disorder affecting psychotics. Consequently, it cannot understand the basic problems of human nature revealed by psychosis.

Notes

1. If the mother is healthy and manages to be aware of her feelings, she will certainly hate the baby circumstantially and, as we saw in Chapter Two, she will do something such as complain under her breath, albeit without taking any revenge on the baby. The mother's *unconscious* hate, is something completely different, for which two different situations should be distinguished, which affect the baby differently: if the mother is depressive or depressed, on the whole, she does not have conscious access to her hate since she fears this feeling which would put her in contact with her destructiveness. In this event, the unconscious hate may occasionally fall on the baby, but, here, it is not his existence with all the discomforts accompanying it that is at the basis of her impossibility of being destructive but rather the fact that she had not sufficiently integrated this aspect of her personality at the time. The mother may nevertheless harbour an unconscious hatred for the baby, which does not refer to a depression in the mother, but to *the very fact that the baby exists*, to the interference that he causes in her life. This unconscious hate leads to massive reactive formations constituting, according to Winnicott, one of the basis for the establishment of an autistic pathology in the child. This phenomenon will be addressed in another study, which is being prepared.
2. I believe that it is to this phenomenon of a pre-representational and without a doubt, pre-linguistic knowledge that Gilberto Safra draws attention in his article "A vassoura e o divã" [The broom and the couch] (1996). Safra approximates this phenomenon to Suzanne Langer's concept of "presentational symbols", which she created in order to distinguish a semantics of sensoriality from a semantics of discursive forms. Since Suzanne Langer belongs to a line of thought which, together with Cassirer, approaches human phenomena from the point of view of a philosophy of representation, I believe that it is more useful to approximate this phenomenon to what Heidegger names "pre-understanding". Winnicott heads in this direction when he describes the pre-verbal, pre-symbolic and pre-representational nature not only of the communication between mother and baby, but also of the growing non-mental knowledge that the latter acquires because of the repeated experiences of environmental reliability. Cf. Winnicott, 1968d, and in the current study, Chapter Three, heading "Integration in time and space".
3. According to the theory of maturational processes, inhabiting a subjective world and relating to subjective objects are prerequisites for achieving transitionality, an *intermediary* passage to relating to the shared world and to objects perceived objectively. Cf., for example, the article where, enumerating the tasks that preside over the beginning of life, Winnicott refers to "the

baby's initial steps in object-relating, which lead to the ability to adopt symbolic objects and to the existence of an area in between the baby and persons in which play is meaningful" (1996c, p. 216).

4. In a text from 1945, in which Winnicott sketches out ideas on transitional phenomena, which eventually came to light in 1951, he alludes to the universal practice of thumb sucking or sucking a dummy, assuming that all agree that the finger is sucked not only for pleasure, but as a consolation. As he developed the subject and in a still rudimentary formulation of it, he mentions that having no doubts that these phenomena, such as normal finger sucking, are "an attempt to localize the object (breast, etc.), to hold it half-way between in and out. This is either a defence against loss of object in the external world or in the inside of the body, that is to say, against loss of control over the object" (1945d, p. 156). This "half-way between in and out" was a "between" and was what he would eventually call potential space in a 1951 article.

5. An allusion to these objects had already been made, in the analytical literature, by M. Wulff, in terms of fetish objects. For Winnicott, this approach is unsatisfactory and leads to misunderstandings: first, because he does not accept that these objects primarily have the nature of fetish, except in pathology; second, because he does not agree with the traditional interpretation of fetish, followed by Wulff, who transforms a phenomenon which is universal, the attribution of a penis to the mother, into pathology. For a thorough discussion of the theme, cf. Gurfinkel, 1996.

6. As we have seen in chapter III, this space already exists potentially, on the basis of the fundamental isolation of the individual. Cf., also, chapter II, section 8.

7. It should be pointed out that at this moment, the expression "internal object" may not yet be used. The baby still does not have an "inside" in which he can store images, representations, a territory where the fight between the constructive and destructive aspects of human nature takes place (cf. 1986d, p. 133]. This fight with his inner objects can only take place after the baby reaches the I AM unitary status and begins to feel concerned with his destructive drives.

8. Cf. Winnicott, 1993e.

9. Winnicott goes so far as to assert that the illusion with which the bridges between subjective and objective reality are built "may be the essential basis for all true objectivity" (1951b, p. 391).

10. The fear of losing the capacity for relating to objects, the origin of which may be located in the loss of the subjective object, is one of the traumatic experiences, unthinkable agonies, which form the basis of psychotic pathologies.

11. Winnicott's concept of creativity is not easy to grasp, maybe as a result of trivialisation by the media, or because it usually refers to artistic and/or original creation, or even because psychoanalysis understands it in the sense of sublimation. Pontalis himself, who, in many articles, strongly criticised the misunderstandings derived from Winnicott's theory of creativity, replies a question by Anne Clancier (1987) on the notion of creativity as follows: "I don't care for the word, still less for its promotion, here there and everywhere. Trying to get everybody to believe that there is a treasure inside him is a false scent. To say, as Winnicott does, even with humour, that one can be as creative in frying eggs as Schumann composing a sonata, don't you find that rather excessive?" (Pontalis, in Clancier: 1987, p. 143). It appears that Pontalis did not understand Winnicott's concept of creativity accurately, since the feeling of being able to create and of creating, which is closely related to spontaneity, does not depend on the output that is created. Creativity relates to the phenomena of life, to the reality of the experience, and not merely to bold creation or to artistic creation; creativity should be acknowledged, says Winnicott, but not so much by the originality in the production "as by the individual's sense of the reality of the experience" (1988, p. 109). Cf., also in the same text, p. 109.

12. It is known that during moments of pain or anxiety, the baby only accepts the mother's lap and knows how to discriminate this lap from all others, including the father's, even when he frequently plays the mother's part.
13. When referring to the initial stages, Winnicott often uses the term "projection" to designate a creation, by the baby, of the object or the world. In a text from 1960, for example, he notes that the baby can only receive what comes from the external world if theses things are included in "the infant's omnipotence and sensed as projections". At this point, he adds the following footnote: "I am using the term 'projections' here in its descriptive and dynamic and not in its full metapsychological sense" (1960b, p. 46, note 2).
14. Refering to this theme, in a text written in 1963, and hence before his complete formulation of the question in 1969, Winnicott affirms, alluding to the clinical work, that there is an intermediate state in normal development, in the passage between what is subjectively and what is objectively perceived, when "the patient's most important experience in relation to the good or potentially satisfying object is the refusal of it. The refusal of it is part of the process of creating it" (1965j, p. 182). I would add: it is part of its creation as external reality, inasmuch as this type of aggression as refusal and the ideas linked to it "lends itself to the process of placing the object, to placing the object separate from the self, in so far as the self has begun to emerge as an entity" (1965j, p. 181).
15. It would be interesting to distinguish between two possible meanings of the term "objectify", with the first being the one described above, and a second meaning in which "objectify" means treating what belongs to personal relations as relating to objects.
16. The destructiveness which creates the sense of externality is, according to the author, one of his most difficult concepts. After reading the article on object usage at the New York Society of Psychoanalysis, in 1968, his work was subject to considerable criticism. At a later stage, he made comments on that criticism, which resulted in some addenda gathered afterwards in Chapter Thirty-four of *Psychoanalytical Explorations*. The theme certainly caused perplexity in the psychoanalytical milieu: if in traditional psychoanalysis, reality is given and not created during the maturational process; if destructiveness is always related to envy or sadism, or to anger deriving from frustration, which comes precisely from the reality principle, then, what kind of destructiveness is it that is non-instinctual and *without anger*?
17. This is the meaning of the affirmation that we cannot describe the usage of the object without considering the nature of the object, in this case, the external one or, in other words, we cannot characterise a given relation without taking into account the features and the behaviour of the object.
18. Although in previous texts, the word "fantasy" sometimes appears as a synonym for imaginative elaboration, which has thus occurred since the beginning of life, it should be noted that, according to Winnicott's last writings, fantasy as something pertaining to the inner world only begins for the individual when he achieves object usage, that is, when he achieves a sense of external reality. Cf. Winnicott, 1969d, especially pp. 222–223.
19. In adult relationships, the destruction of the object in its subjective character takes the form of a sudden estrangement with regard to someone who is so close, intimate, and familiar that he or she was not seen for him- or herself and in some cases had never been seen in his or her exteriority.
20. This is why it is so important to know how to detect the emotional age of the individual in clinical practice, since for people who regress to dependence, we must account for the fact that in many cases, the word "love" may not yet make any sense.

21. On aggressiveness and destructiveness in Winnicott, see also the study by Dias E. 2011b, text 4. I also refer the reader to two other studies, in the same book, on object usage (text 5) and on Theodore Kaczynski, the Unanomber terrorist (text 10).
22. Cf. Jung, 1963. Cf., also, the review by Winnicott of this book (1964b).
23. Cf. Winnicott, 1964b, p. 490. For these statements, Winnicott based himself on Fordham's book on the work by Jung. Cf. M. Fordham, 1962, Lecture number 119.
24. In an article dedicated to Winnicott, Marion Milner (1987) recounts that after her first reading of "The use of an object", she telephoned Winnicott with the following question: "Yes, but just why does the good object have to be destroyed?" Winnicott took some time before answering: Because it is necessary (Milner, 1987, p. 284).
25. The peculiar sense that Winnicott gives to the schizoid personality will be examined in the next book on Winnicott's theory of psychoses, which is in preparation.
26. Shortly after having made this statement, Winnicott adds, without doubt referring to the Kleinian hypothesis of the innate paranoid disposition: paranoid tendency "very early yet not inherited or truly constitutional" (1988, p. 124). It should also be noted that the tendency to feel persecuted, related to the achievement of the unity in an I AM, is entirely different from the paranoid disposition resulting from a pattern of environmental invasions or from the one, the origin of which is the discovery of personal destructiveness.
27. On the value of the mother's survival and that of the analyst, cf. Dias, E. 2011b, text 6.
28. Good and bad are placed in inverted commas, since although they are in common use, as a general rule, their meaning in psychoanalytical literature is interpreted on the basis of Kleinian theory. I believe that this is also the reason why in a text on the depressive position, Winnicott added a footnote referring to these terms, in which he stated that "The words good and bad are an inheritance from the dim past; they are also suitable words for description of the extremes that every infant feels about inside matters—whether these be forces, objects, sounds or smells. I am not referring here to the use of the terms good or bad by parents and nurses who wish to implant morality on the infant" (1988, p. 71).
29. A detailed consideration of Winnicott's concept of "cross-identification", that is to say his re-description of the mechanisms of projection and introjection, lies outside the scope of this study. In rough terms, this is the ability to put oneself in the place of another and to allow for the reverse; "to enter imaginatively and yet accurately into the thoughts and feelings and hopes and fears of another person" (1986f, p. 117). While this capacity, which is a sign of health, belongs to a rather advanced maturational stage, its basis is established in the originary experience of having had someone identify with your needs, which were incommunicable at a verbal level.
30. Winnicoot's approach to the achievement of the capacity for concern is largely based on Melanie Klein's theory of the depressive position, considered by him as the greatest of her contributions to the psychoanalytical thought. A few differences should nevertheless be highlighted. Winnicott cannot agree, for example, with the conception of aggressiveness which is involved in the phenomenon, or with the precocity with which these achievements take place, according to Klein; nor does he agree with the pre-conditions or causes of "depression": he cannot see Oedipus in the baby's attack on the mother's breast. In addition, the expression "depressive position" is not entirely adequate for him, since despite the fact that Klein has described the phenomenon as an achievement of normal maturation, her term suggests that when normal babies reach this stage, they fall into a state of clinical depression.
31. For a more detailed analysis of the origin and nature of morality in Winnicott, cf. Loparic, 2000a.

32. If, as a result of conditions of environmental unreliability, a precocious me emerges, therefore immature for states of awareness and "perception" of external objects, this "precocious me" will have a premature awareness of its existence, dependence, and impulsiveness and may be stricken by guilt and responsibility, which, due to the basic immaturity, cannot be integrated into the personality. In these cases, guilt is devastating.
33. An in-depth investigation, in Winnicott's view, on the role of the father in the child's maturational process and the possible failures which interfere with it is to be found in Rosa, 2011.
34. Winnicott considered that if a child is exposed to the sight of his parents having sexual relations, which is the last thing he needs in emotional terms with regard to them, he will experience a maximum tension, which may be traumatic (cf. Winnicott, 1988, p. 59).
35. Cf. Winnicott, 1958g, p. 33.
36. The distinction between the two types of deprivation is extremely important in the diagnosis and treatment of the several types of anti-social tendency. With regard to this distinction and father failures in general, I refer the reader to the meticulous work of Claudia Dias Rosa, 2011.
37. It is worth noting the moment and sense in which gender distinction becomes significant for Winnicott, in order to highlight conceptual differences relative to Freudian psychoanalysis, particularly for the theory of psychosis, cf. Freud, 1924b, 1924e, and 1925h.
38. Perversions may be seen, for example, as an "elaborate attempt to bring about some kind of sex union in spite of the delusion that the girl has a penis" (1986g, p. 187). In this same generalised delirium that there is a penis in the woman, both in men and in women, Winnicott finds one of the roots of feminism. At one extreme, he says, "it is woman's protest against a male society dominated by phallic-phase male swank; and at the other extreme it is a woman's denial of her true inferiority *at one phase* of physical development" (1986g, p. 188).
39. Freud insisted until the end of his life on the importance of the effect of the inferiority trauma of women, derived from the phallic phase (Cf. Freud 1925j, 1931b, and 1933a). According to Winnicott, this insistence was understandable, since it was on the denial of the lack of a penis in girls that he based the etiology of psychoses, a denial which aimed to prevent the anxiety of castration.
40. Cf. Freud, 1924b, 1924e, and 1925h.
41. It is clear that even if individuals begin well, they may subsequently develop a psychosis, if they are exposed to traumatic situations beyond their capacity for tolerance at that time or which exceed their capacity for tolerance over time. For example, Winnicott mentions the case of prisioners, who are victims of cruel political persecution, etc. (cf. 1971g, p. 91). In any case, this psychosis will differ from one established during the more primitive stages as a result of traumatic environment failures, notably because a failure of maturation is one thing and its achievement and subsequent loss another. It may also happen that in situations of overload, or because the child did not elaborate the conflict between love and hate adequately, regression to previous stages occurs, with the loss of past achievements. The extent of this regression will depend on the consistency of achievements preceding the oedipical complex (cf. 1988, end of Chapter Two, Part II and 1989p, p. 68).
42. It should be noted that in order to refer to the identifications made by children with the parent of the same gender, Winnicott uses the term "homosexual". This identification and proximity constitute a necessary phase of maturation.
43. To illustrate this situation, see the case of the little Piggle in Winnicott, 1977/1987.
44. Traditional psychoanalysis dealt predominantly with the satisfaction of desire and not with the genital capacity and act in themselves. It did not develop the issues relating to the body

strictly speaking. For the same reason, the issue of the initial genitality is ultimately linked to the consequences deriving from the prohibition on touching forbidden fruit and not, as Winnicott states, to the fear of provoking irreversible changes in the other person's body. For Winnicott, the question of loving is personal and takes into account the imaginative elaboration of the result of the impulse in the body of the loved person.

45. This issue in Winnicott's work became clearer in a subsequent formulation of 1966, in which sexual identity is was conceived by Winnicott in non-instinctual terms, as we shall see later.
46. The Winnicottian concepts of "pure female element" and "pure male element" will be made explicit later in this same chapter.
47. This letter is in the book *The Feminine and the Sacred* (2001) with the collected correspondence between Julia Kristeva and Catherine Clément from November 1996 to September 1997.
48. Kristeva's position is closely in line with that of Lacan. According to the French psychoanalyst, the mother never wants the baby for himself; what satisfies her in the baby is what he represents, the phallus. According to Lacan, the child is not merely the child, since he is also the phallus (cf. Lacan, 1956–1957, p. 57). In another passage of the same seminar, Lacan also notes that the woman only achieves satisfaction with her baby because the baby contains something which calms her, since it fulfils her need for a phallus.
49. This new formulation was already made explicit in Chapter Three of this study, since it is also the most complete with regard to the issue in question, the constitution of identity as such; it serves here to clarify the issue of bisexuality in non-sexual terms.
50. In order to refer to Winnicott's clinical cases without having to describe them each time, I shall use an acronym to make them recognisable. I shall refer to this case as FM, since it is the clinical example which illustrates pure female and male elements (1971i).
51. The article by Ricardo Rodulfo was originally a lecture delivered at the IV Winnicott Coloquium, promoted by PUC-SP, in 1999, and not yet published.
52. This patient was in analysis for two periods, with some of the sessions being clinically reported by Winnicott. From the first period of analysis, we have only the introduction to his clinical annotations, inserted by Khan in the Introduction to the book *Holding and Interpretation* (1986a). From the second period, there are two groups of annotations: the first dates from 1954 (1955a) and is composed of annotations referring to six episodes of analysis; the second one comprises the book *Holding and Interpretation*, which encompasses six months of the second period of analysis. Referring to the first period of analysis, Winnicott says that the young man, at the time "a schizoid case", had looked for him saying that "he could not talk freely, that he had no small talk or imaginative or play capacity, and that he could not make a spontaneous gesture or get excited" (1986a, p. 20).
53. For this purpose, it is necessary to preserve sensitivity. Winnicott tells that when he worked as a paediatrician at the ambulatory of the Paddington Green Hospital, he was promoted to task of taking care of beds, which meant *status*. He said that not knowing quite well the reason, he did not accept it. He managed to get a permission to use beds when necessary, but passed on the interned patients to his assistant. He subsequently understood why he did that: "[…] the distress of babies and small children in a hospital ward, even a very nice one, adds up to something terrific. Going into the ward disturbs me very much. If I become an in-patient doctor I shall develop the capacity not to be disturbed by the distress of the children, otherwise I shall not be able to be an effective doctor. I will therefore concentrate on my O. P. work and avoid becoming callous in order to be efficient" (1987b, p. 168).

54. Regarding the relation between maturity and democratic machinery, I refer the reader to Roseana Moraes Garcia's excellent work on aggression in Winnicott's work (2009).
55. Winnicott did not have children and, at the end of his life, knowing that he was very ill and had very few time left, "he then goes to discuss the difficulty that a man has dying without a son to imaginatively kill and to survive him—to provide the only continuity that men know" (*apud* Clare Winnicott, 1989, p. 4).
56. The "baby in the mother's lap" and the "child in the mother's bed" are expressions created by Z. Loparic in order to define the paradigmatic exemplars of the Winnicottian and the Freudian theories respectively (cf. Loparic, 1997a).
57. On pulsional duality and the dynamic viewpoint in Freud, cf. Loparic, 2001b and 2006. See also Simanque, 1994, Chapter Three.
58. Details of the differences between Winnicott and Klein are provided in the following texts by Winnicott: 1965g; 1988, Part II, Chapter One; 1989c, and 1989e.
59. In the attempt to establish a dialogue with the Kleinians, by various means, Winnicott wrote a letter to Joan Rivière in 1956: "My trouble when I start to speak to Melanie about her statement of early infancy is that I feel as if I were talking about colour to the colour-blind. She simply says that she has not forgotten the mother and the part the mother plays, but in fact I find that she has shown no evidence of understanding the part the mother plays at the very beginning" (1987b, pp. 95–96). In the same letter, commenting on the essay "A study of envy and gratitude", presented by Klein to the British Society of Psychoanalysis (cf. Klein, 1984), he distinguised three themes contained in the essay, stating that, with regard to the third one, namely, "[…] the interesting attempt Melanie is making all the time to state the psychology of the earliest stages" (1987b, p. 94), he felt that "she has let herself down badly by making a statement which it is very easy to pull to pieces, and which can easily hold up the study of the development of Ego stability and the researches which are going on in various parts the world into the treatment of psychosis" (1987b, p. 95).

FINAL CONSIDERATIONS

The aim of this book has been to present the conceptual assumptions of the theory of maturational processes, in an articulate and unified manner, describing the various stages of the process with their different tasks and achievements.

Its primary motivation was the central position occupied by this theory in Winnicott's *opus* and also because it constitutes the necessary theoretical horizon from which Winnicott's theory of the psychic disorders can be explained, although this is a topic for a future book which will deal with psychoses in particular. Third, observing that to date and as far as I am aware, Winnicott's work has not been the focus of an analysis that would clarify its internal unity, there was a need to emphasise the central place of the theory of maturational processes and its status as the frame of reference for the study of human phenomena, demonstrating not only the conceptual articulations of his thought as a whole, but the important theoretical and clinical developments resulting from the connection between the stages of maturation and the various types of psychic disorder. Fourth, this study was motivated by the acknowledgement of the richness, relevance, and efficiency of Winnicott's contribution to the therapeutic task, reflected in the author's own clinical cases and illustrations, which are confirmed both in my own experience and by that of other analysts who have permitted themselves to be oriented by this perspective.

Carrying out the plan for this research project as it was conceived, soon proved to be a rather solitary task. In addition to finding poor bibliographic support in the secondary literature, this author encountered a series of difficulties since the conceptual and descriptive elements underlying the basic assumptions of the theory of maturational processes, as well as the characterisation of the various stages, are scattered throughout Winnicott's work. By applying the methodological principle of reading the parts starting from the whole and understanding the whole from the parts, all of Winnicott's work was carefully deployed with regard to the theme of maturation against the background of psychoses, in other words, of the problems relating to the continuity or discontinuity of maturational process and to success or failure in constituting the unitary identity. Having also considered the author's own suggestion that both psychoanalysis in general and his own work should be read from a historical perspective, this author was obliged to follow the evolution of each concept. This aspect of the research also revealed the remarkable progress which occurred throughout Winnicott's scientific career, particularly during the 1960s. This latter task, which permeated the whole of the work, has been given a special emphasis in Chapter One.

In order to open and sustain the course of the research, this author was obliged to consider objections to this sort of project, entailing the questioning of various established ideas about Winnicott himself. I shall point out two of them: first, the idea that a conceptual organisation of Winnicott's work would be contrary to its spirit, the unsystematic nature or alleged lack of theoretical unity of which supposedly constitutes the principal characteristic to be preserved; second, the idea that the articulation of Winnicott's thought and the demonstration of its unity would kill its inherent poetry. Even though I consider the fear upon which these objections are partly based, of creating an orthodoxy, of petrifying his thought, to be a valid one, I nevertheless believe that I have succeeded in showing that the key to averting this danger derives from the careful and organised study of his theory, since Winnicott the theorist knew how to protect the various dimensions of the human in his conceptions, emphasising and securing, without mystification, the many and varied aspects of human existence, including creativity, wherever it may be exercised, on the basis of tradition. Regarding the risk of destroying its poetry, I start from the position that the poetic aspect of Winnicott's work results not from its lack of a systematic character but from the fact that he knew how to preserve the specific nature of human phenomena by using different languages, appropriate to each stage of development. This was his precise procedure when he illuminated the poetic and almost unutterable character of the phenomena characterising the initial stages, such as the subtlety of the pre-verbal relation and communication between mother and baby, at the initial moment of his life, describing them in a language which does not injure their essential nature, which, after all, is a poet's approach. The complexity and internal articulation of Winnicott's thesis nevertheless clearly demonstrates that his writing, whether addressed to mothers or to psychoanalysts and to the scientific public in general, far from being restricted to poetic evocations, offers an impressive body of concepts which, even if they do not constitute a closed "system", may legitimately be characterised as "theoretical", a status which Winnicott himself reserved for his contribution.

I thus believe that I can affirm that the main challenges to the set task have been overcome. In the light of historical-hermeneutic analysis, it proved possible to reconstitute the central theme of Winnicottian psychoanalysis, the theory of personal maturational processes, briefly showing that this theory:

a. is based on a set of assumptions and recurrent ideas in Winnicott's work which, with the evolution of his thought, were endowed with increasing depth and cohesion;
b. is founded, in particular, on a theory of human nature, characterised as a mode of temporalisation which, at each stage, represents a certain form of integration of the human person;

c. is the horizon from which the psychic phenomena of health and sickness in general may be accessed;
d. presupposes various philosophical theses which are not commonly found in theories of the human sciences in general.

The characterisation of the theory of maturational processes in this book also demonstrates that in order to set forth his theoretical viewpoint and the new phenomena illuminated by his theory, Winnicott abandoned abstractions or speculations of a metaphysical character. In describing the various stages of maturation, he used terms of ordinary language as frequently as he could, linked to lived experience, which were sometimes raised to the category of technical terms. Throughout his work, he highlighted that the terms intended to describe one stage would be incorrect for describing another.

In addition to demonstrating, in this way, the breadth of Winnicott's contribution, in the last section of Chapter Four, I have also listed some basic differences between Winnicott's theory of maturational processes and traditional psychoanalytic theory regarding the development of the sexual functions. This comparison not only served to highlight the innovation of Winnicott's conceptions, but also to raise another issue, namely, deciding on the precise nature of the change in psychoanalytic theory caused by Winnicott's work. Since this latter question is essentially epistemological in nature, despite permeating the whole of the study, it was only indicated, but not developed, since it falls outside the scope of this study.

Since the theory of maturational processes is the theoretical horizon from which it is possible to explain the nature of the various psychic disorders, a study of this theory allows us to glimpse what will be studied in detail in my next work. Broadly speaking, it may be said in advance that according to Winnicott, *psychoses* are related to the environmental failure in facilitating the tasks of the initial stages, which start at some point during intrauterine life and last until the stage of I AM. If the environment fails repeatedly, in the form of an established pattern, to adapt to the needs of the baby during the stage of absolute and even relative dependence, the process of personal maturation will be interrupted (at this primitive moment, in which the foundations of personality are being constituted) giving rise to a psychotic disorder. There will evidently be different types of psychotic disorders depending on the point, within the initial stages, at which the baby was traumatised by environmental failures.

If everything goes well until the achievement of the unitary identity (at the milestone in the maturation process represented by the I AM stage), the child, who is now one or two years old, will then have to confront the integration of the instinctual drives during the stage of concern. If the environment does not favour this achievement, there will be the risk of *depression*, the central problem of which consists of the difficulty in accepting and integrating the destructiveness relating to human nature, arising precisely with regard to the loved object.

In favourable cases when this achievement is also realised, the child, who may be said to have seeded the bases of personality (in this sense being whole and healthy), will have to grapple with the anxieties resulting from interpersonal relations, now possible because of the maturity that has been reached; in particular, with the situation in which the Oedipus complex may be effectively experienced, that is, between whole persons. All this mobilises anxieties relating to instinctuality, to feelings and to the fantasy taking place in the internal psychic reality. Here, the facilitation of the environment does not have the same importance as during the previous stages, although it should remain consistent enough for the small individual to deal with his personal internal problematic and to avoid succumbing to *neurosis*.

Psychosis, depression, and neurosis are the main diagnostic categories of Winnicott's classification of psychic disorders, with their different natures defined in terms of their aetiologies, that is, their point of origin in the line of maturation, according to the task with which the baby was involved at the time of the trauma and to the nature of this trauma. In addition to these disorders cited above, there are three others which do not constitute diagnostic categories in themselves, since they always appear in conjunction with the previous ones. These are: the anti-social tendency, psycho-somatic disorders, and paranoias. These disorders are also characterised according to their point of origin; the last two have multiple meanings which vary according to this same criterion.

Winnicott always emphasised the existence of gaps in his understanding of the maturational processes, particularly with regard to the initial stages, encouraging analysts to observe and describe their analytical experiences, in order to develop the theory further. There is also still much to be done in order to understand the results already achieved by Winnicott in his study and theory. This account is also far from representing a complete analysis of what already exists. Each aspect discussed in a section could constitute a theme for future research in itself. This is true both of the initial stages and of all the subsequent ones.

Several points relating to the main theme presented here have only been outlined and also require additional treatment. The most important of these consists of the relevance of the results obtained here to psychoanalytic practice. Indeed, this study will only achieve its full psychoanalytic meaning when the clinical implications deriving from this new understanding of the primitive stages of maturation and the role of the environment in the facilitation of the innate tendency towards maturation become clear, with this meaning, for the initial stage, the participation of environmental care in the constitution of the self and personal identity. This will imply a new vision of the therapeutic task, in the light of Winnicott's theory of human nature and of the mishaps of its circular temporalisation.

REFERENCES

Abram, J. (1996). *The Language of Winnicott: A Dictionary of Winnicott's use of Words*. London: Karnac.
Abram, J. (2013). *Donald Winnicott Today*. London: Routledge.
Amado, G. (1979). *De l'enfant à l'adulte*. Paris: Press Universitaires de France.
Aubin, H. (1975). *Les psychoses de l'enfant*. Paris: P. U. F.
Badinter, E. (1980). *L'amour en plus*. Paris: Flammarion.
Béziers, M. -M. & Hunzinger, Y. (1994). *O bebê e a coordenação motora*. São Paulo: Summus.
Bogomoletz, D. (2001). Resenha de Jan Abram 2000: A linguagem de Winnicott: dicionário das palavras e expressões utilizadas por Donald W. Winnicott. *Natureza Humana, 3(1)*: 177–186.
Bowlby, J. (1951). *Maternal Care and Mental Health*. Geneva: W. H. O.
Burlingham, D., & Freud, A. (1942). *Young Children in Wartime: A Year's Work in a Residencial War Nursery*. London: Allen & Unwin.
Chaslin, Ph. (1912). *Eléments de sémiologie et clinique mentales*. Paris: Asselin et Houzeau.
Clancier, A., & Kalmanovitch, J. (1987). *Winnicott and Paradox: From Birth to Creation*. London: Tavistock.
Clément, C., & Kristeva, J. (2001). *The Feminine and the Sacred*. New York, NY: Columbia University Press.
Davis, M., & Wallbridge, D. (1981). *Boundary and Space: An Introduction to The Work of D. W. Winnicott*. London: Mark Paterson.
Dias, E. O. (2001). Resenha de Jan Abram: A linguagem de Winnicott: dicionário das palavras e expressões utilizadas por Donald W. Winnicott. *Psychê, 5*: 163–169.
Dias, E. O. (2003). *A teoria do amadurecimento de D. W. Winnicott*. São Paulo: Imago.
Dias, E. O. (2011b). *Sobre a confiabilidade e outros estudos*. São Paulo: DWW editorial.
Dias, E. O. (2014a). *A teoria do amadurecimento de D. W. Winnicott* (3ª ed.). São Paulo: DWW editorial.
Eliot, T. S. (1980). *The Complete Poems and Plays 1909–1950*. New York, NY: Harcourt Brace & Company.
Fairbairn, W. R. D. (1952). *Psychoanalytic Studies of the Personality*. London: Routledge, 1994.

Fordham, M. (1962). An evaluation of Jung's work. *Guild of Pastoral Psychology*, Conference 119.
Freud, A. (1966). *The Ego and the Mechanisms of Defense*. London: Karnac.
Freud, S. (1915e). The unconscious. In: J. Strachey (Ed.), *The Standard Edition of the Complete Works of Sigmund Freud* (vol 14, pp. 153–213). London: Hogarth and the Institute of Psychoanalysis, 1989.
Freud, S. (1923b). The ego and the id. In: J. Strachey (Ed.), *The Standard Edition of the Complete Works of Sigmund Freud* (vol 19, pp. 1–66). London: Hogarth and the Institute of Psychoanalysis, 1989.
Freud, S. (1924b). Neurosis and psychosis. In: J. Strachey (Ed.), *The Standard Edition of the Complete Works of Sigmund Freud* (vol 19, pp. 151–159). London: Hogarth and the Institute of Psychoanalysis, 1989.
Freud, S. (1924e). The loss of reality in neurosis and psychosis. In: J. Strachey (Ed.), *The Standard Edition of the Complete Works of Sigmund Freud* (vol 19, pp. 189–197). London: Hogarth and the Institute of Psychoanalysis, 1989.
Freud, S. (1925h). Negation. In: J. Strachey (Ed.), *The Standard Edition of the Complete Works of Sigmund Freud* (vol 19, pp. 249–257). London: Hogarth and the Institute of Psychoanalysis, 1989.
Freud, S. (1925j). Some psychical consequences of the anatomical distinction between the sexes. In: J. Strachey (Ed.), *The Standard Edition of the Complete Works of Sigmund Freud* (vol 19, pp. 259–276). London: Hogarth and the Institute of Psychoanalysis, 1989.
Freud, S. (1931b). Female sexuality. In: J. Strachey (Ed.), *The Standard Edition of the Complete Works of Sigmund Freud* (vol 21, pp. 223–244). London: Hogarth and the Institute of Psychoanalysis, 1989.
Freud, S. (1933a). New introductory lectures on psycho-analysis. 33ª lecture: Feminity. In: J. Strachey (Ed.), *The Standard Edition of the Complete Works of Sigmund Freud* (vol 22, pp. 104–125). London: Hogarth and the Institute of Psychoanalysis, 1989.
Freud, S. (1937c). Analysis terminable and interminable. In: J. Strachey (Ed.), *The Standard Edition of the Complete Works of Sigmund Freud* (vol 23, pp. 211–254). London: Hogarth and the Institute of Psychoanalysis, 1989.
Freud, S. (1940b). Some elementary lessons in psycho-analysis. In: J. Strachey (Ed.), *The Standard Edition of the Complete Works of Sigmund Freud* (vol 23, pp. 279–288). London: Hogarth and the Institute of Psychoanalysis, 1989.
Gadamer, H.-G. (1976). *Verité et méthode*. Paris: Éditions du Seuil.
Garcia, R. M. (2009). *A agressividade na psicanálise winnicottiana*. São Paulo: Tese de Doutorado em Psicologia Clínica, Pontifícia Universidade Católica.
Geets, C. (1981). *Winnicott*. Paris: Jean-Pierre Delarge.
Glover, E. (1932). *On The Early Development of Mind*. London: Imago, 1956.
Graña, R. B. (1997). Apresentação à edição brasileira. In: D. W. Winnicott, *Pensando sobre crianças* (pp. xi–xii). Porto Alegre: Artes Médicas.
Green, A. (1976). The borderline concept. In: *On Private Madness*. London: Karnac, 1997.
Green, A. (1977). La royauté appartient à l'enfant. *L'Arc, 69*: 4–12.
Greenberg, J. R., & Mitchell, S. A. (1983). *Object Relations and Psychoanalytic Theory*. Cambridge: Harvard University Press.
Grolnick, S. (1990). *The Work & Play of Winnicott*. London/NewYork: Jason Aronson.
Gurfinkel, D. (1996). O carretel e o cordão. *Percurso, 9*: 56–68.
Hartmann, H. (1958). *Ego Psychology and the Problem of Adaptation*. New York, NY: International Universities Press.
Heidegger, M. (1974). *El ser y el tiempo*. México: Fondo de Cultura Econômica.
Heidegger, M. (1987). *Zollikon Seminar*. USA: Northwestern University Press, 2001.
Home, H. J. (1966). The concept of mind. *International Journal of Psychoanalysis, 47*: 42–49.

Jacobs, M. (1995). *D. W. Winnicott*. London: Sage.
Jaspers, K. (1959). *General Psychopathology (vol. 1)*. London: Johns Hopkins Paperbacks, 1997.
Jung, C. G. (1963). *Memories, Dreams, Reflections*. New York, NY: Pantheon.
Kanner, L. (1935). *Child Psychiatry*. USA: Charles C Thomas, 1972.
Khan, M. (1975). Introduction. In: D. W. Winnicott. *Through Paediatrics to Psychoanalysis* (pp. xi–1). London: Karnac, 1992.
Klein, M. (1946). Notes on some schizoid mechanisms. In: *Envy and Gratitude and Other Works 1946–1963*. London: Virago, 1988.
Klein, M. (1957). Envy and Gratitude. In: *Envy and Gratitude and Other Works 1946–1963*. London: Virago, 1988.
Knobloch, F. (Org.). (1991). *O inconsciente: várias leituras*. São Paulo: Escuta.
Kuhn, T. S. (1970). *The Structure of Scientific Revolutions*. Chicago, IL: The University of Chicago Press.
Lacan, J. (1956–1957). *La relation d'object—Le séminaire, livre IV*. Paris: Éditions du Seuil, 1994.
Laplanche, J., & Pontalis, J. -B. (1967). *Vocabulaire de la psychanalyse*. Paris: Presses Universitaires de France.
Laurentiis, V. R. F. (2016). *Corpo e psicossomática em Winnicott*. São Paulo: DWW editorial.
Lins, M. I. A. (1997). História e vida na obra de Winnicott. In: A. Podkameni & M. A. Guimarães (Orgs.), *Winnicott 100 anos de um analista criativo* (pp. 13–22). Rio de Janeiro: Nau.
Loparic, Z. (1983). Heurística kantiana. *Cadernos de história e filosofia da ciência, 5*: 73–89.
Loparic, Z. (1985). Resistências à psicanálise. *Cadernos de história e filosofia da ciência, 8*: 29–49.
Loparic, Z. (1995a). Winnicott e Heidegger: afinidades. *Boletim de novidades, 69*: 53–60.
Loparic, Z. (1995b). Winnicott e o pensamento pós-metafísico. *Psicologia USP, 6*: 39–61.
Loparic, Z. (1997a). Winnicott: uma psicanálise não-edipiana. *Percurso, 9*: 41–47.
Loparic, Z. (1997b). A máquina no homem. *Psicanálise e Universidade, 7*: 97–113.
Loparic, Z. (1998). Psicanálise: uma leitura heideggeriana. *Veritas, 43(1)*: 25–41.
Loparic, Z. (1999a). O conceito de *Trieb* na psicanálise e na filosofia. In: J. Machado (Org.), *Filosofia e psicanálise: um diálogo* (pp. 97–157). Porto Alegre: Edipuc.
Loparic, Z. (1999b). Heidegger and Winnicott. *Natureza humana, 1(1)*: 103–135.
Loparic, Z. (1999c). É dizível o inconsciente? *Natureza humana, 1*: 323–385.
Loparic, Z. (2000a). A moralidade e o amadurecimento. *Anais do IX Encontro Latinamericano sobre o pensamento de D. W. Winnicott* (pp. 300–316).
Loparic, Z. (2000b). O "animal humano". *Natureza humana, 2*: 351–397.
Loparic, Z. (2000c). *A semântica transcendental de Kant*. Campinas: UNICAMP, CLE.
Loparic, Z. (2001a). Além do inconsciente. *Natureza humana, 3(1)*: 91–140.
Loparic, Z. (2001b). Esboço do paradigma winnicottiano. *Cadernos de história e filosofia da ciência, 11*: pp. 7–58.
Loparic, Z. (2005). Elementos da teoria winnicottiana da sexualidade. *Natureza humana, 7*: 311–358.
Loparic, Z. (2006/2011). De Freud a Winnicott: Aspectos de uma mudança paradigmática. In E. Dias & Z. Loparic, (Orgs.), *Winnicott na Escola de São Paulo* (pp. 29–58). São Paulo: DWW editorial, 2011.
Loparic, Z. (2013). From Freud to Winnicott. In: J. Abram (Ed.), *Winnicott Today* (pp. 113–156). London: Routledge, 2013.
Luz, R. (1989). O espaço potencial: Winnicott. *Percurso, 2*: 25–32.
Machado, J. A. T. (Org.). (1999). *Filosofia e psicanálise: um diálogo*. Porto Alegre: Edipuc.
Mello Filho, J. (1989). *O ser e o viver*. Porto Alegre: Artes Médicas.

Mendonça, M. E. (2000). *Ginástica holística: história e desenvolvimento de um método de cuidados corporais*. São Paulo: Summus.
Meyer, L. (1994). O que faz fracassar uma formação? *Percurso, 12*: 83–88.
Middlemore, M. P. (1941). *The Nursing Couple*. London: Hamish Hamilton.
Milner, M. (1987). Winnicott and overlapping circles. In: *The Suppressed Madness of Sane Men* (pp. 279–286). London and New York: Routledge.
Misès, R. (1969). Origines et évolution du concept de psychose chez l'énfant. *Revue Confrontations Psychiatriques—Psychoses de L'Enfant , 3*: 9–29.
Outeiral, J. O. (1991). A tendência antissocial. In: J. Outeiral & R. Graña (Orgs.), *Donald W. Winnicott: estudos* (pp. 129–135). Porto Alegre: Artes Médicas.
Outeiral, J. O. (1994). Apresentação à edição brasileira. In: D. Winnicott, *Explorações psicanalíticas* (pp. vii–xv). Porto Alegre: Artes Médicas.
Outeiral, J. O. (1997). Sobre a concepção de pai na obra de D. W. Winnicott. In: I. F. Catafesta (Org.), *A clínica e a pesquisa no final do século: Winnicott e a universidade* (pp. 91–104). São Paulo: Instituto de Psicologia da USP.
Outeiral, J. O., & Graña, R. (Orgs.). (1991). *Donald W. Winnicott: estudos*. Porto Alegre: Artes Médicas.
Pessanha, J. G. (1992). O ponto K: Heidegger e Freud. *IDE—Revista da Sociedade Brasileira de Psicanálise, 22*: 80–89.
Phillips, A. (1988). *Winnicott*. London: Fontana.
Podkameni, A., & Guimarães, M. A. (Orgs.). (1997). *Winnicott 100 anos de um analista criativo*. Rio de Janeiro: Nau.
Pontalis, J. -B. (1981). *Frontiers in Psychoanalysis: Between the Dream and Psychic Pain*. London: Hogarth.
Rodman, R. (1987). Introduction. In: D. Winnicott, *The Spontaneous Gesture: Selected Letters of D. W. Winnicott* (pp. xiii–xxxiii). London: Karnac, 1999.
Rosa, C. D. (2011). *As falhas paternas em Winnicott*. São Paulo: Tese de Doutorado em Psicologia Clínica, Pontifícia Universidade Católica.
Rycroft, C. (1985). *Psychoanalysis and Beyond*. London: Chatto and Windus.
Safra, G. (1996). A vassoura e o divã. *Percurso, 17*: 69–74.
Sechehaye, M. A. (1947). *Autobiography of a Schizophrenic Girl: The True Story of "Renée"*. London: Penguin, 1994.
Serralha, C. A. (2007) . *Uma abordagem teórica e clínica do ambiente a partir de Winnicott*. São Paulo: Tese de doutorado em Psicologia Clínica, Pontifícia Universidade Católica.
Shepherd, R., Johns, J., & Robinson, H. T. (1997). Introduction. In: D. Winnicott, *Thinking about Children* (pp. xix–xxxii). London: Karnac, 1996.
Simanke, R. T. (1994). *A formação da teoria freudiana das psicose*. Rio de Janeiro: Editora 34.
Tellenbach, H. (1961). *Melancholy: History of the Problem, Endogeneity, Typology, Pathogenesis, Clinical Considerations*. Pittsburgh: Duquesne University Press, 1980.
Vidal, G., Bleichmar, H., & Usandivaras, R. J. (Orgs.). (1977). *Enciclopedia de psiquiatria*. Buenos Aires: El Ateneo.
Vilete, E. P. (2000). Sobre "O homem morto que caminha". *Natureza humana, 2(1)*: 149–164.
Webster's Encyclopedic Unabridged Dictionary of the English Language (1996). New York/Avenel: Gramercy Books.
Winnicott, C. (1984). Introduction. In: D. Winnicott, *Deprivation and Delinquency* (pp. 1–5). London: Routledge, 1994.
Winnicott, C. (1989). D. W. Winnicott: a reflection. In: D. Winnicott, *Psychoanalytic Explorations* (pp. 1–18). London: Karnac, 1989.

Winnicott, C., Shepherd, R., & Davis, M. (1984). Introduction, parts 1 (pp. 9–12), 2 (pp. 81–83), 3 (pp. 161–162), 4 (p. 231). In: *D. Winnicott, Deprivation and Delinquency*. London: Routledge, 1994.

Winnicott, D. W. (1931a). Fidgetiness. In: *Collected Papers: Through Paediatrics to Psychoanalysis* (pp. 22–30). London: Karnac, 1992.

Winnicott, D. W. (1931b). A note on normality and anxiety. In: *Collected Papers: Through Paediatrics to Psychoanalysis* (pp. 3–21). London: Karnac, 1992.

Winnicott, D. W. (1941). The observation of infants in a set situation. In: *Collected Papers: Through Paediatrics to Psychoanalysis* (pp. 52–69). London: Karnac, 1992.

Winnicott, D. W. (1945a). Getting to know your baby. In: *The Child, the Family and the Outside World* (pp. 19–24). London: Penguin, 1985.

Winnicott, D. W. (1945b). Towards an objective study of human nature. In: *Thinking about Children* (pp. 3–12). London: Karnac, 1996.

Winnicott, D. W. (1945c). Infant feeding. In: *The Child, the Family and the Outside World* (pp. 30–34). London: Penguin, 1985.

Winnicott, D. W. (1945d). Primitive emotional development. In: *Collected Papers: Through Paediatrics to Psychoanalysis* (pp. 145–156). London: Karnac, 1992.

Winnicott, D. W. (1946). Some psychological aspects of juvenile delinquency. In: *Deprivation and Delinquency* (pp. 113–119). London: Routledge, 1994.

Winnicott, D. W. (1947a). The child and sex. In: *The Child, the Family and the Outside World* (pp. 147–160). London: Penguin, 1985.

Winnicott, D. W. (1947b). Further thoughts on babies as persons. In: *The Child, the Family and the Outside World* (pp. 85–92). London: Penguin, 1985.

Winnicott, D. W. (1948). Paediatrics and psychiatry. In: *Collected Papers: Through Paediatrics to Psychoanalysis* (pp. 157–173). London: Karnac, 1992.

Winnicott, D. W. (1949a). The world in small doses. In: *The Child, the Family and the Outside World* (pp. 69–74). London: Penguin, 1985.

Winnicott, D. W. (1949b). The baby as a going concern. In: *The Child, the Family and the Outside World* (pp. 25–29). London: Penguin, 1985.

Winnicott, D. W. (1949c). The baby as a person. In: *The Child, the Family and the Outside World* (pp. 75–79). London: Penguin, 1985.

Winnicott, D. W. (1949d). Weaning. In: *The Child, the Family and the Outside World* (pp. 80–84). London: Penguin, 1985.

Winnicott, D. W. (1949e). The end of the digestive process. In: *The Child, the Family and the Outside World* (pp. 40–44). London: Penguin, 1985.

Winnicott, D. W. (1949f). Hate in the countertransference. In: *Collected Papers: Through Paediatrics to Psychoanalysis* (pp. 194–203). London: Karnac, 1992.

Winnicott, D. W. (1951a). The foundation of mental health. In: *Deprivation and Delinquency* (pp. 168–171). London: Routledge, 1994.

Winnicott, D. W. (1951b). Critical notice of *On Not Being Able to Paint* (Marion Milner). In: *Psychoanalytic Explorations* (pp. 390–392). London: Karnac, 1989.

Winnicott, D. W. (1953a). Psychoses and child care. In: *Collected Papers: Through Paediatrics to Psychoanalysis* (pp. 219–228). London: Karnac, 1992.

Winnicott, D. W. (1953b). Review of psychoanalytic studies of the personality (W. R. D. Fairbairn). In: *Psychoanalytic Explorations* (pp. 413–422). London: Karnac, 1989.

Winnicott, D. W. (1953c). Transitional objects and transitional phenomena. In: *Playing and Reality* (pp. 1–34). London: Routledge, 2005.

Winnicott, D. W. (1954a). Mind and its relation to the psyche-soma. In: *Collected Papers: Through Paediatrics to Psychoanalysis* (pp. 243–254). London: Karnac, 1992.

Winnicott, D. W. (1954b). Needs of the under-fives. In: *The Child, the Family and the Outside World* (pp. 179–188). London: Penguin, 1985.

Winnicott, D. W. (1954c). Two adopted children. In: *Thinking about Children* (pp. 113–127). London: Karnac, 1996.

Winnicott, D. W. (1955a). Withdrawal and regression. In: *Collected Papers: Through Paediatrics to Psychoanalysis* (pp. 255–261). London: Karnac, 1992.

Winnicott, D. W. (1955b). Metapsychological and clinical aspects of regression within the psychoanalytical set-up. In: *Collected Papers: Through Paediatrics to Psychoanalysis* (pp. 278–294). London: Karnac, 1992.

Winnicott, D. W. (1955c). The depressive position in normal emotional development. In: *Collected Papers: Through Paediatrics to Psychoanalysis* (pp. 262–277). London: Karnac, 1992.

Winnicott, D. W. (1957a). The mother's contribution to society. In: *Home is Where We Start From* (pp. 123–127). London: Penguin, 1990.

Winnicott, D. W. (1957b). Aggression and its roots. In: *Deprivation and Delinquency* (pp. 84–99). London: Routledge, 1994.

Winnicott, D. W. (1957c). Breast feeding. In: *The Child, the Family and the Outside World* (pp. 50–57). London: Penguin, 1985.

Winnicott, D. W. (1957d). The contribution of psycho-analysis to midwifery. In: *The Family and Individual Development* (pp. 106–113). London: Routledge, 1995.

Winnicott, D. W. (1957e). Knowing and learning. In: *Babies and Their Mothers* (pp. 15–22). London: Free Association, 1988.

Winnicott, D. W. (1958a). *Collected Papers: Through Paediatrics to Psychoanalysis*. London: Karnac, 1992.

Winnicott, D. W. (1958b). Aggression in relation to emotional development. In: *Collected Papers: Through Paediatrics to Psychoanalysis* (pp. 204–218). London: Karnac, 1992.

Winnicott, D. W. (1958c). The antisocial tendency. In: *Deprivation and Delinquency* (pp. 120–131). London: Routledge, 1994.

Winnicott, D. W. (1958d). Anxiety associated with insecurity. In: *Collected Papers: Through Paediatrics to Psychoanalysis* (pp. 97–100). London: Karnac, 1992.

Winnicott, D. W. (1958e). Psycho-analysis and the sense of guilt. In: *The Maturational Processes and the Facilitating Environment* (pp. 15–28). London: Karnac, 1990.

Winnicott, D. W. (1958f). Birth memories, birth trauma, and anxiety. In: *Collected Papers: Through Paediatrics to Psychoanalysis* (pp. 174–193). London: Karnac, 1992.

Winnicott, D. W. (1958g). The capacity to be alone. In: *The Maturational Processes and the Facilitating Environment* (pp. 29–36). London: Karnac, 1990.

Winnicott, D. W. (1958h). Primary maternal preoccupation. In: *Collected Papers: Through Paediatrics to Psychoanalysis* (pp. 300–305). London: Karnac, 1992.

Winnicott, D. W. (1958i). On the contribution of direct child observation to psycho-analysis. In: *The Maturational Processes and the Facilitating Environment* (pp. 109–114). London: Karnac, 1990.

Winnicott, D. W. (1958j). The first year of life: Modern views on the emotional development. In: *The Family and Individual Development* (pp. 3–14). London: Routledge, 1995.

Winnicott, D. W. (1958k). Paediatrics and childhood neurosis. In: *Collected Papers: Through Paediatrics to Psychoanalysis* (pp. 316–321). London: Karnac, 1992.

Winnicott, D. W. (1960a). Counter-transference. In: *The Maturational Processes and the Facilitating Environment* (pp. 158–165). London: Karnac.

Winnicott, D. W. (1960b). The theory of the parent-infant relationship. In: *The Maturational Processes and the Facilitating Environment* (pp. 37–55). London: Karnac, 1990.

Winnicott, D. W. (1961a). The effect of psychotic parents on the emotional development of the child. In: *The Family and Individual Development.* (pp. 69–78). London: Routledge, 1995.

Winnicott, D. W. (1961b). Integrative and disruptive factors in family life. In: *The Family and Individual Development* (pp. 40–49). London: Routledge, 1995.

Winnicott, D. W. (1962). Struggling through the doldrums. In: *Deprivation and Delinquency* (pp. 145–155). London: Routledge, 1994.

Winnicott, D. W. (1963a). Dependence in infant-care, in child-care, and in the psycho-analytic setting. In: *The Maturational Processes and the Facilitating Environment* (pp. 249–259). London: Karnac, 1990.

Winnicott, D. W. (1963b). The development of the capacity for concern. In: *The Maturational Processes and the Facilitating Environment* (pp. 73–82). London: Karnac, 1990.

Winnicott, D. W. (1963c). The mentally ill in your caseload. In: *The Maturational Processes and the Facilitating Environment* (pp. 217–229). London: Karnac, 1990.

Winnicott, D. W. (1963d). Morals and education. In: *The Maturational Processes and the Facilitating Environment* (pp. 93–105). London: Karnac, 1990.

Winnicott, D. W. (1963e). Review of *Childhood Schizophrenia* (William Gooldfarb), part of three reviews of books on autism. In: *Thinking about Children* (pp. 193–194). London: Karnac, 1996.

Winnicott, D. W. (1964a). *The Child, the Family and the Outside World*. London: Penguin, 1985.

Winnicott, D. W. (1964b). Review of *Memories, Dreams, Reflections* (C. J. Jung). In: *Psychoanalytic Explorations* (pp. 482–492). London: Karnac, 1989.

Winnicott, D. W. (1964c). Roots of aggression, part of aggression and its roots. In: *Deprivation and Delinquency* (pp. 92–99). London: Routledge, 1994.

Winnicott, D. W. (1964d). The value of depression. In: *Home is Where We Start From* (pp. 71–79). London: Penguin, 1990.

Winnicott, D. W. (1964e). Introduction. In: *The Child, the Family and the Outside World* (pp. 9–11). London: Penguin, 1985.

Winnicott, D. W. (1965a). *The Family and Individual Development*. London: Routledge, 1995.

Winnicott, D. W. (1965b). *The Maturational Processes and the Facilitating Environment*. London: Karnac, 1990.

Winnicott, D. W. (1965c). The relationship of a mother to her baby at the beginning. In: *The Family and Individual Development* (pp. 15–20). London: Routledge, 1995.

Winnicott, D. W. (1965d). Psychiatric disorder in terms of infantile maturational processes. In: *The Maturational Processes and the Facilitating Environment* (pp. 230–241). London: Karnac, 1990.

Winnicott, D. W. (1965e). Providing for the child in health and crisis. In: *The Maturational Processes and the Facilitating Environment* (pp. 64–72). London: Karnac, 1990.

Winnicott, D. W. (1965f). The price of disregarding psychoanalytic research. In: *Home is Where We Start From* (pp. 172–182). London: Penguin, 1990.

Winnicott, D. W. (1965g). A personal view of the kleinian contribution. In: *The Maturational Processes and the Facilitating Environment* (pp. 171–178). London: Karnac, 1990.

Winnicott, D. W. (1965h). Classification: Is there a psycho-analytic contribution to psychiatric classification? In: *The Maturational Processes and the Facilitating Environment* (pp. 124–139). London: Karnac, 1990.

Winnicott, D. W. (1965i). Growth and development in immaturity. In: *The Family and Individual Development* (pp. 21–29). London: Routledge, 1995.

Winnicott, D. W. (1965j). Communicating and not communicating leading to a study of certain opposites. In: *The Maturational Processes and the Facilitating Environment* (pp. 179–192). London: Karnac, 1990.

Winnicott, D. W. (1965k). Group influences and the maladjusted child: The school aspect. In: *The Family and Individual Development* (pp. 146–154). London: Routledge, 1995.

Winnicott, D. W. (1965l). The effect of psychosis on family life. In: *The Family and Individual Development* (pp. 61–68). London: Routledge, 1995.

Winnicott, D. W. (1965m). Ego distortion in terms of true and false self. In: *The Maturational Processes and the Facilitating Environment* (pp. 140–152). London: Karnac, 1990.

Winnicott, D. W. (1965n). Ego integration in child development. In: *The Maturational Processes and the Facilitating Environment* (pp. 56–63). London: Karnac, 1990.

Winnicott, D. W. (1965o). The family affected by depressive illness in one or both parents. In: *The Family and Individual Development* (pp. 50–60). London: Routledge, 1995.

Winnicott, D. W. (1965p). The family and emotional maturity. In: *The Family and Individual Development* (pp. 88–94). London: Routledge, 1995.

Winnicott, D. W. (1965q). Now they are five. In: *Talking to Parents* (pp. 111–120). Cambridge/Massachusetts: Perseus, 1993.

Winnicott, D. W. (1965r). From dependence towards independence in the development of the individual. In: *The Maturational Processes and the Facilitating Environment* (pp. 83–92). London: Karnac, 1990.

Winnicott, D. W. (1965s). The relationship of a mother to her baby at the beginning. In: *The Family and Individual Development* (pp. 15–20). London: Routledge, 1995.

Winnicott, D. W. (1966). Psycho-somatic illness in its positive and negative aspects. In: *Psychoanalytic Explorations* (pp. 103–114). London: Karnac, 1989.

Winnicott, D. W. (1967a). Mirror-role of mother and family in child development. In: *Playing and Reality* (pp. 149–159). London: Routledge, 2005.

Winnicott, D. W. (1967b). The location of cultural experience. In: *Playing and Reality* (pp. 128–139). London: Routledge, 2005.

Winnicott, D. W. (1968a). The aetiology of infantile schizophrenia in terms of adaptive failure. In: *Thinking about Children* (pp. 218–223). London: Karnac, 1996.

Winnicott, D. W. (1968b). Children learning. In: *Home is Where We Start From* (pp. 142–149). London: Penguin, 1990.

Winnicott, D. W. (1968c). The concept of clinical regression compared with that of defence organization. In: *Psychoanalytic Explorations* (pp. 193–199). London: Karnac, 1989.

Winnicott, D. W. (1968d). Communication between infant and mother, and mother and infant, compared and contrasted. In: *Babies and Their Mothers* (pp. 89–103). London: Free Association, 1988.

Winnicott, D. W. (1968e). Delinquency as a sign of hope. In: *Home is Where we Start From* (pp. 90–100). London: Penguin, 1990.

Winnicott, D. W. (1968f). Environmental health in infancy. In: *Babies and Their Mothers* (pp. 59–68). London: Free Association, 1988.

Winnicott, D. W. (1969a). Death and murder in the adolescent process. Part of contemporary concepts of adolescent development and their implications for higher education. In: *Playing and Reality* (pp. 169–176). London: Routledge, 2005.

Winnicott, D. W. (1969b). Breast-feeding as communication. In: *Babies and Their Mothers* (pp. 23–34). London: Free Association, 1988.

Winnicott, D. W. (1969c). Contemporary concepts of adolescent development and their implications for higher education. In: *Playing and Reality* (pp. 186–203). London: Routledge, 2005.

Winnicott D. W. (1969d). The use of an object and relating through indentifications. In: *Psychoanalytic Explorations* (pp. 218–227). London: Karnac, 1989.

Winnicott, D. W. (1969e). Physiotherapy and human relations. In: *Psychoanalytic Explorations* (pp. 561–568). London: Karnac, 1989.

Winnicott, D. W. (1969f). A link between paediatrics and child psychology: Clinical observations. In: *Thinking about Children* (pp. 255–276). London: Karnac, 1996.

Winnicott, D. W. (1970a). Dependence in child care. In: *Babies and Their Mothers* (pp. 83–88). London: Free Association, 1988.

Winnicott, D. W. (1970b). The mother–infant experience of mutuality. In: *Psychoanalytic Explorations* (pp. 251–260). London: Karnac, 1989.

Winnicott, D. W. (1971a). *Playing and Reality*. London: Routledge, 2005.

Winnicott, D. W. (1971b). *Therapeutic Consultations in Child Psychiatry*. London: Karnac, 1996.

Winnicott, D. W. (1971c). Introduction (part one). In: *Therapeutic Consultations in Child Psychiatry* (pp. 1–11). London: Karnac, 1996.

Winnicott, D. W. (1971d). Basis for self in body. In: *Psychoanalytic Explorations* (pp. 261–271). London: Karnac, 1989.

Winnicott, D. W. (1971e). Introduction. In: *Playing and Reality* (pp. xv–xviii). London: Routledge, 2005.

Winnicott, D. W. (1971f). The concept of a healthy individual. In: *Home is Where we Start From* (pp. 21–34). London: Penguin, 1990.

Winnicott, D. W. (1971g). Creativity and its origins. In: *Playing and Reality* (pp. 87–114). London: Routledge, 2005.

Winnicott, D. W. (1971h). Dreaming, fantasying and living: a case-history describing a primary dissociation. In: *Playing and Reality* (pp. 35–50). London: Routledge, 2005.

Winnicott, D. W. (1971i). The split-off male and female elements to be found in men and women. In: *Psychoanalytic Explorations* (pp. 169–182). London: Karnac, 1989.

Winnicott, D. W. (1971j). The place where we live. In: *Playing and Reality* (pp. 140–148). London: Routledge, 2005.

Winnicott, D. W. (1971k). Playing: Creative activity and the search for the self. In: *Playing and Reality* (pp. 71–86). London: Routledge, 2005.

Winnicott, D. W. (1972). Answer to comments (part III of Chapter Twenty-eight). In: *Psychoanalytic Explorations* (pp. 189–192). London: Karnac, 1989.

Winnicott, D. W. (1974). Fear of breakdown. In: *Psychoanalytic Explorations* (pp. 87–95). London: Karnac, 1989.

Winnicott, D. W. (1977). *The Piggle: An Account of the Psycho-Analytic Treatment of a Little Girl*. London: Penguin, 1991.

Winnicott, D. W. (1984a). *Deprivation and Delinquency*. London: Routledge, 1994.

Winnicott, D. W. (1984b). The absence of a sense of guilt. In: *Deprivation and Delinquency* (pp. 106–112). London: Routledge, 1994.

Winnicott, D. W. (1984c). Aggression, guilt and reparation. In: *Home is Where We Start From* (pp. 80–89). London: Penguin, 1990.

Winnicott, D. W. (1984d). Varieties of psychotherapy. In: *Deprivation and Delinquency* (pp. 232–240). London: Routledge, 1994.

Winnicott, D. W. (1984e). Freedom. In: *Home is Where We Start From* (pp. 228–238). London: Penguin, 1990.
Winnicott, D. W. (1984f). *Sum*, I am. In: *Home is Where We Start From* (pp. 55–64). London: Penguin, 1990.
Winnicott, D. W. (1984g). Residential care as therapy. In: *Deprivation and Delinquency* (pp. 220–228). London: Routledge, 1994.
Winnicott, D. W. (1986a). *Holding and Interpretation. Fragment of an Analysis.* New York, NY: Grove, 1986.
Winnicott, D. W. (1986b). *Home is Where We Start From.* London: Norton, 1990.
Winnicott, D. W. (1986c). Psychoanalysis and science: Friends or relations? In: *Home is Where We Start From* (pp. 13–18). London: Penguin, 1990.
Winnicott, D. W. (1986d). The child in the family group. In: *Home is Where We Start From* (pp. 128–141). London: Penguin, 1990.
Winnicott, D. W. (1986e). The place of the monarchy. In: *Home is Where We Start From* (pp. 260–268). London: Penguin, 1990.
Winnicott, D. W. (1986f). Cure. In: *Home is Where We Start From* (pp. 112–120) London: Penguin, 1990.
Winnicott, D. W. (1986g). This feminism. In: *Home is Where We Start From* (pp. 183–194). London: Penguin, 1990.
Winnicott, D. W. (1986h). Living creatively. In: *Home is Where We Start From* (pp. 35–54). London: Penguin, 1990.
Winnicott, D. W. (1986i). The pill and the moon. In: *Home is Where We Start From* (pp. 195–209). London: Penguin, 1990.
Winnicott, D. W. (1987a). *Babies and Their Mothers.* London: Free Association, 1988.
Winnicott, D. W. (1987b). *The Spontaneous Gesture: Selected Letters of D. W. Winnicott.* London: Karnac, 1999.
Winnicott, D. W. (1987c). The beginning of the individual. In: *Babies and Their Mothers* (pp. 51–58). London: Free Association, 1988.
Winnicott, D. W. (1987d). Preliminary notes for "Communication between infant and mother, mother and infant, compared and contrasted". In: *Babies and Their Mothers* (pp. 107–109). London: Free Association, 1988.
Winnicott, D. W. (1987e). The ordinary devoted mother. In: *Babies and Their Mothers* (pp. 1–14). London: Free Association, 1988.
Winnicott, D. W. (1988). *Human Nature.* London: Free Association, 1992.
Winnicott, D. W. (1989a). *Psychoanalytic Explorations.* London: Karnac, 1989.
Winnicott, D. W. (1989b). Roots of aggression (part of Chapter Fifty-three). In: *Psychoanalytic Explorations* (pp. 458–461). London: Karnac, 1989.
Winnicott, D. W. (1989c). Contribution to a symposium on envy and jealousy. In: *Psychoanalytic Explorations* (pp. 462–464). London: Karnac, 1989.
Winnicott, D. W. (1989d). The concept of trauma in relation to the development of the individual within the family. In: *Psychoanalytic Explorations* (pp. 130–148). London: Karnac, 1989.
Winnicott, D. W. (1989e). The beginnings of a formulation of an appreciation and criticism of Klein's envy statement. In: *Psychoanalytic Explorations* (pp. 447–457). London: Karnac, 1989.
Winnicott, D. W. (1989f). D. W. W. on D. W. W. In: *Psychoanalytic Explorations* (pp. 569–582). London: Karnac, 1989.
Winnicott, D. W. (1989g). Discussion of "Grief and mourning in infancy" (John Bowlby). In: *Psychoanalytic Explorations* (pp. 426–432). London: Karnac, 1989.

Winnicott, D. W. (1989h). Character types: the foolhardy and the cautions (Michael Balint). In: *Psychoanalytic Explorations* (pp. 433–437). London: Karnac, 1989.
Winnicott, D. W. (1989i). The use of an object in the context of "Moses and Monotheism". In: *Psychoanalytic Explorations* (pp. 240–246). London: Karnac, 1989.
Winnicott, D. W. (1989j). Fragments concerning varieties of clinical confusion. In: *Psychoanalytic Explorations* (pp. 30–33). London: Karnac, 1989.
Winnicott, D. W. (1989k). Comments on my paper "The use of an object". In: *Psychoanalytic Explorations* (pp. 238–239). London: Karnac, 1989.
Winnicott, D. W. (1989l). Clinical illustration of "The use of an object". In: *Psychoanalytic Explorations* (pp. 235–237). London: Karnac, 1989.
Winnicott, D. W. (1989m). The importance of the setting in meeting regression in psycho-analysis. In: *Psychoanalytic Explorations* (pp. 96–102). London: Karnac, 1989.
Winnicott, D. W. (1989n). Individuation. In: *Psychoanalytic Explorations* (pp. 284–288). London: Karnac, 1989.
Winnicott, D. W. (1989o). Clinical material (part II of Chapter Twenty-eight). In: *Psychoanalytic Explorations* (pp. 183–188). London: Karnac, 1989.
Winnicott, D. W. (1989p). Psycho-neurosis in childhood. In: *Psychoanalytic Explorations* (pp. 64–72). London: Karnac, 1989.
Winnicott, D. W. (1989q). The psychology of madness: a contribution from psycho-analysis. In: *Psychoanalytic Explorations* (pp. 119–129). London: Karnac, 1989.
Winnicott, D. W. (1989r). Nothing at the centre. In: *Psychoanalytic Explorations* (pp. 49–52). London: Karnac, 1989.
Winnicott, D. W. (1989s). New light on children's thinking. In: *Psychoanalytic Explorations* (pp. 152–157). London: Karnac, 1989.
Winnicott, D. W. (1993a). *Talking to Parents*. Cambridge/Massachusetts: Perseus.
Winnicott, D. W. (1993b). The building up of trust. In: *Talking to Parents* (pp. 121–134). Cambridge/Massachusetts: Perseus.
Winnicott, D. W. (1993c). The development of a child's sense of right and wrong. In: *Talking to Parents* (pp. 105–110). Cambridge/Massachusetts: Perseus.
Winnicott, D. W. (1993d). Feeling guilty. In: *Talking to Parents* (pp. 95–104). Cambridge/Massachusetts: Perseus.
Winnicott, D. W. (1993e). What do we know about babies as cloth suckers? In: *Talking to Parents* (pp. 15–20). Cambridge/Massachusetts: Perseus.
Winnicott, D. W. (1996a). *Thinking about Children*. London: Karnac.
Winnicott, D. W. (1996b). The association for child psychology and psychiatry observed as a group phenomenon. In: *Thinking about Children* (pp. 235–254). London: Karnac.
Winnicott, D. W. (1996c). Autism. In: *Thinking about Children* (pp. 197–217). London: Karnac.
Wulff, M. (1946). Fetishism and object choice in early childhood. *Psychoanalytic Quarterly, 15*.
Zemeckis, R. (1994). *Forrest Gump*. Paramount Pictures: USA.

INDEX

Abram, Jan xvii, xxix, xlviii, xlix
academic psychology l, 1, 7, 57
acquiescence or complacency 155, 283
aetiology (of psychic disorders) xxvii, 3, 11, 39, 57, 92, 176
aggression/aggressiveness 83–87, 126–127, 132, 134–136, 144, 155, 161, 171
    inherent to the primitive love drive 79–82, 85–86, 124–125, 133–134
    motor drive (motility) 34, 56, 79, 81, 83–84, 86, 99, 132
    roots of 78–79, 86
aloneness 28–29, 43, 48, 59, 130, 157, 159
ambivalence 116, 127–128, 132, 142, 144, 151
    of the mother 52, 116
    pre-ambivalence 161, 169 note 41
anger 86–87, 141
    at the loss of being as a result of environmental invasion 86
    resulting from frustration 87, 126–127, 162, 167
    resulting from the perception of the primal scene 138
annihilation of the self 18, 78, 92, 103
anti-social tendency 3, 86–87, 137, 139–140, 176
    aetiology xxx, 3, 11, 39
    delinquency xliv, 3, 139

anxiety xxxiii, 2–3, 5, 17–19, 34, 49, 70, 90, 100–101, 110, 120, 124, 133, 136, 140–142, 144, 151, 154, 160, 163, 167, 169, 175
apperception 107
artistic experience xliii
Aubin, Henri 11, 23 note 12
average expectable environment (Hartmann) 21

basic tasks of the maturational process 29–30, 32, 115
belief xxvii, xxxix, 44, 75, 77, 88, 119, 157
    believe in (see also reliability, trust) 75, 88
    disbelief 43, 124
benign circle 135–136
Béziers, M. Madeleine 64, 111–113
biology 16, 39, 48
birth 5, 35, 39, 45, 71–72
    birth trauma 45, 71, 95, 109 note 6
    experience of 71–72, 95
    memories of 39, 71, 95
bodily memories 69, 71, 91–92
body (soma) 28, 64, 35–36, 38, 80, 93, 120, 124, 131, 139, 157, 164
    as soma (imaginative elaboration) 35, 41, 80, 94, 99

190   INDEX

as the dwelling of the psyche 30, 36, 43, 74–75, 78, 83, 96, 98–99, 115, 131
bodily experiences 44, 116, 141, 153
bodily memories 50–51, 80, 94, 99, 147–148
body–mind dichotomy 1, 4, 8–9, 33, 37
body scheme 18, 35
external (part of the external world) 38, 40, 80
living body 33, 38
of the mother 48, 51–52, 99, 133, 155
physical growth 120, 139
somatic temporality 34, 57, 72
Bogomoletz, Davi xlix note 12
Bowlby, J. 13, 22, 65 note 38
breast 105–106
    object of excited attacks 73, 85–86, 90–91, 126, 133, 135
    psychoanalytical jargon 106
    subjective object 104, 106, 126
    totality of the maternal care 105
breastfeeding 35, 73–74, 82, 85, 114 *see also* theoretical first feed, good enough care, excited states),
    first contact with reality 59, 101
    is not a reflex act 82
    is not just a search for instinctual satisfaction 49, 73, 81–82
    refusal of breastfeeding 51, 60, 126, 167 note 14
    rhythm of feeds 93
breathing 34–35, 72
    of the mother 72, 91

capacity to age and die 157
capacity to be alone 88, 139
capacity to believe in 88, 135, 138
capacity to doubt 51, 157
care provided to the infant 30, 42, 47, 52, 57, 111, 132, 160, 163
    are gradually incorporated 47, 94, 108, 114
    are not subject to rules 58
    participate in the establishment of the self 42, 47, 58, 176
castration anxiety xxxv, 18, 140–141, 151–152
    fear of castration xxxv, 18, 151
    threat of castration 141, 152
character disorders 3, 10
circle
    as diagram of the self 100
    benign 135–136
Clancier, Anne xxxi–xxxii, lix, 166
Clément, Catherine 145
communication xli, 28, 47–48, 60, 80, 88, 117, 123, 144
    between mother and infant xliii, 48, 60, 62, 73–74, 81–82, 86, 88, 106–107, 123, 161, 165 note 2
    dead end xxxiii, 126
    in the squiggle game xxxiii
    non-communication (essential aloneness) 157–158
    pre-verbal, pre-representational 62, 73–74, 81, 107, 174
    silent 51, 74, 106–107
    with subjective objects xliii, 107, 117, 126–127
communication between scientists 20–21, 64
communication with the patient 62, 95
concentration 97, 124
    in playing 90, 124
    of the mother when taking care of the infant 96
concern 32, 53, 85, 133, 136–137, 142
    capacity for 134–135, 137
    concerned 32, 85, 133
    mending 3, 135, 137, 139
    of the mother 49, 89
    participation of the father in 137, 139
    ruthless 85, 128, 133, 136–137, 161
    stage of 27, 29, 32, 53, 63 note 11, 80– 81, 85, 90, 130, 133–141, 176
continuity of being xliii–xliv, 20, 29, 43–44, 69–72, 75, 78–79, 87, 92, 110, 120, 161
control xliii–xliv, 35, 49, 72, 101, 103, 117, 124, 129–130, 141, 144, 156
    magical 35, 102, 120, 126, 166
    omnipotent 31, 126, 129–130
    self- 53, 86, 139, 143
Creak, M. 11
creative apperception (or gaze) 107
creativity xxviii, xxxvii–xxxviii, xli, xlvii, 43, 75–78, 96, 108, 116, 124, 155, 162, 166 note 11, 174
    loss of 60, 119–120, 123
    of parents 54

primary xxvii, 44, 57, 75–78, 82, 93, 108, 119, 130, 133, 155, 161, 163
culture 23, 88, 119, 121, 148, 162

Darwin, Charles xxix, xlix note 10
Davis, Madeleine xxvii, xlviii note 7
de-adaptation of the mother 51, 53, 115–117, 120, 125
death xxiii, xxxviii, 29–30, 90, 155, 157–159
defences 17, 19, 55, 107
    against anxiety 151
    against environmental intrusion 116
    against loss of control of the object 35
    against trauma 71
    as split-off intellect 65, 152
    ego defence 17, 19
defensive organisation 19 *see also* defences
delinquency xliv, 3, 139 *see also* character disorders
    aetiology of 3
    theory of 3
democracy 156
dependence xxlx, 29, 38, 44, 48–49, 59, 86, 89–90, 106, 117–118, 120, 133, 142, 163
    absolute 12, 21, 28–30, 38, 47, 69, 73, 87, 161–162
    pre-dependence 43, 115, 158
    relative xxix, 29, 53, 117, 137
depersonalisation 90, 96, 98
depression 137, 139, 157, 176
depressive position 19, 32, 137, 168
deprivation 50, 86, 123, 139, 144, 169
    related to anti-tendency 50, 86, 123, 139, 144, 169
    two types of deprivation 139
destructiveness 53, 79, 111 note 24, 126, 129–130, 135, 137, 139, 167, 175
    constitutional to M. Klein 111 note 25
    difference of aggressiveness 85, 127
    inherent to the primitive love drive 53, 85, 130, 133, 162, 167
    integration as inherent to human nature 135
    manifestation of antisocial tendency (resulting from deprivation) 86
    no anger xxviii, 126
    of the mother 116
    which creates externality xxviii, 127–130

devotion 50
Dias, E. O. xlix, 111 note 29, 113 note 48, 114 note 56, 168 note 27
disillusionment 29, 115–116, 135, 164
disintegration 46–47, 91, 188, 241
    family disintegration 3, 67
    threat of 91, 155
dissociations 31, 50, 86, 150
    primary 90, 134
distinction between subjective world and objects 75, 90

ego 17–19, 36, 39, 80, 82, 86, 123–124, 151, 161
    bodily ego 29
    difference between the terms "self" and "ego" 54–56
    meaning of the term 54
    of the infant xlvi
    of the mother (auxiliary support) xlvi, 80, 139
ego psychology 13, 21–22
    differences regarding 21
Eliot, T. S. 65 note 36, 158–159
environment (in the earlier stage)
    as a subjective world 75
    concept of 48–49, 117
    consists of the whole of maternal provision 75, 78, 89, 97, 105
    during the Oedipal stage 143–144
    facilitating 20, 28, 42, 55, 144, 176
    failures of 90, 114, 116
    in the constitution of the individual 21, 42, 45
    in the establishment of health 7
    is not external, but subjective 8
environment (as wider circles) 53, 117, 138, 144
environmental failure 38, 86, 91, 97, 106, 115, 123, 125, 141, 163–164, 175
    as an aetiological factor of psychic disorders xxv, xxx, 12, 23 note 15, 41, 58, 65 note 31, 91, 106, 114 note 53, 115, 176
environmental pattern of care
    good enough (facilitating) 29, 36, 41–42, 49–53, 244–245
    invasive (or intrusive, not facilitating) 8, 70
environmental retaliation 134–135
envy 127, 167

innate(Klein) xlix, 19–20, 25, 63 note 10, 171 note 59
  of the penis 145–146, 148, 150
essential aloneness 28, 48, 59, 130, 138, 157–159
excited states 79–87
  genital 140–141, 148
  primitive (pre-genital) 43, 47, 56, 78–79, 81, 83, 85, 87, 89, 99, 102, 124, 128, 134–135
exhibitionistic or phallic phase 140–141, 145
external object 18, 42, 46, 55–56, 63, 74, 79, 83, 90, 101, 127, 130
  need to find the external object 83
external, objective or shared reality (or world) xvi, xxiii, xlvi, xlix note 15, 8, 17, 19, 28, 31, 35, 43, 47, 55, 57, 74, 77–78, 83, 91, 95, 97, 100–101, 103, 107–108, 110, 119, 121, 124, 128, 130, 134, 159, 161–162
  repudiated 131–132

Fairbairn, W. Ronald D. 109–110 note 20
false self xxvii–xxviii, xlix, 17, 55, 67 note 60, 129–131, 133
false solutions 155
family 52–53, 117–118, 138, 143–144, 153, 155–156
family triangle 142, 144
fantasy xxvii–xxviii, xxxi, 35, 119, 123, 135, 138, 141, 145, 148, 161–162
  beginning of the capacity for 127, 167
  female (girl's fantasy) 146–147
  genital 144, 151
  proto- xlii, 162
  unconscious 24 note 24, 127–128, 130, 138, 155
father 138–140, 143–144
  acts as mother 52–53, 142
  child's pact with 152
  glimpse of integration 53
  humanises the mother 52
  maternal 52, 129
  paternal 52, 137–138, 143–144
  protects the mother from the child's instinctual impulsiveness 134, 139
  prototype of conscience 151
  rivalry of the boy with the 152–153
  supports the mother during primary maternal preoccupation 52
  the child counts on the 139
  within the family triangle 138–139, 142
  within the Oedipal triangle 126, 142, 151–152
feeling of real 17, 29, 31, 43, 101–102, 104, 107, 124, 131, 155
first awakening 69, 71, 157–158
  great awakening 71
freedom 16, 18, 21, 53, 97, 117, 129, 135, 143, 150, 154
  free to play 129
  obstacles to freedom 1, 21
Freud, Anna xlii, 13, 24 note 21, 59, 65 note 38
Freud, Sigmund,
  Freud as scientist xxxviii
  Freudian metapsychology xli–xlii, 13–16, 23 note 20
  Freudian theory xli–xlii, xlvii, 2, 4, 13–16, 18, 23 note 20, 55, 87, 160–162
frustration 71, 78, 80, 86, 151
  as the origin of aggression in Freud 87, 126–127, 162
  reaction to 18, 85, 87
fundamental tasks of the initial stages xxxiv, 29–30, 32, 74, 91, 115
  beginning of contact with objects 30, 45, 101–103, 161
  establishment of the primary self (primary identity) 56, 75, 103–108, 115, 161
  personalisation: indwelling of the psyche in the body 36, 74, 98–101, 110, 131, 139
  primitive spatialisation: inhabiting the body (in the mother's lap) 74, 91, 96–97, 99, 112 note 31, 117, 132, 139
  temporalisation 44, 73–74, 91–96, 98, 106, 115
  see also subjective time

Garcia, Roseana M. 171
Geets, Claude xxvii–xxviii, xxxii–xxxiii
Glover, Edward 21, 54–55
good and bad objects 130, 161
good enough care 29, 36, 41, 51–52, 58, 75, 82, 97, 105
  as devotion 50
  handling 99
  holding 72, 75, 88, 97, 99–100
  holding the situation 135
  is reliable 21, 48, 75, 102, 107, 113 note 48

object-presenting xxvi, xlvi, 75, 78, 102, 120
    totality of (makes up the world of the infant) 75–76, 78, 89, 97, 105
goodness (of the mother, of the environment) 49–50, 137
Graña, Roberto xxxvi
gravity
    action of 72, 99
greed 83–84, 86
greediness 86, 146
Green, André xxx, xxxii
Greenberg, Jay R. xxxiv
Grolnick, Simon xxvii
group loyalty xxxviii, l
growing smaller/ downwards 157
guilt 3, 19, 32, 133–137, 144
Guntrip, Harry 56–57

hallucination 77
handling 52, 97, 99
Hartmann, Heinz xxxiii, 13, 21, 25
hate 50, 53, 66 note 50, 142, 152, 156
    felt by the child 86, 99, 128, 135, 143–144, 151
    felt by the mother for the baby 52, 116, 165 note 1
health xvi, xxiii, 1–2, 4, 19, 116
    as maturity 156
    foundations of psychic health 6, 160
healthy individual 17–18, 29–30, 41, 91, 132, 148, 153, 176
    healthy infant or child 5, 12, 17, 141, 151, 153
    healthy mother 22, 50–51, 115, 165
Heidegger, M. xlviii, l–li, 23–24, 58, 60, 63, 65, 68, 108, 145–146
heredity 7, 11, 28, 40, 45
    as an innate tendency towards integration into a unity 27, 39
    constitutional psychic (Klein) 162
    genetic 22, 33, 39–40, 45, 57, 162
hermeneutic method xxv, xlviii note 4
historical analysis of Winnicott's work xxvi, xlviii note 6
Home, H. J. xlii–xliii, xlvi
human animal 16, 34, 63, 79
human nature xlvi, l, 14, 28–29, 43, 85, 137, 176
    as tendency towards integration xxxv, 17, 27–28, 39, 42, 47, 57, 60, 85, 98–99, 104, 157, 159
    feminine side of 146–147
    human being as time- sample of 27
    intuitive understanding xli
    study of xxii, xxix, xxxix, xliv, 87
    theory (science) of xxxix, 174, 176
Humpty Dumpty 132
Hunsinger, Yva 111, notes 22–23

identification 107, 169
    cross- 137, 168 note 29
        delusional [delirious] 150
    of the analyst with the patient xlv
    of the mother with the infant 44, 48–49, 51, 137
    primary 56, 75, 103–108, 106, 109 note 11, 115, 120, 125, 161
    projective (Klein) 20
    with the father 152
    with the mother and the female lineage 146–147
    with the parents 141–142, 148, 153
    with the parent of the same sex xxxv, 146, 151–153
    with society 156–157
identity 48, 55, 104–106, 131
    constitution of 74, 105–106
    primary 104, 107, 149
    unitary (me) xxiii, xxix, 17, 19, 28–29, 31, 33, 42–43, 54–56, 74, 76, 78, 80, 91, 93–94, 104, 110, 115, 123, 131–133, 141, 157, 161, 166, 174–175 *see also* unitary self
illusion of omnipotence 18, 44, 47–48, 75–78, 102–103, 106, 108, 116, 119, 122, 124
    is not the same as the feeling of omnipotence 109
imaginative elaboration 16, 33–34, 41, 79, 81, 99, 127, 140, 146, 162
immaturity 10, 39, 142, 154, 161
    of the infant xxiv, 20, 35, 46, 63, 79, 85, 87, 106
imponderable factor (luck or chance) 42, 45, 57
imposture 155
impotence of the child (during the Oedipal stage) 151
incorporation 47, 139, 151

of care (see also internal environment) 47, 94, 108, 114
of trust/reliability 97, 108, 119 *see also* trust, capacity to believe in
infants (babies) 5, 10, 29, 45, 51, 88–89, 94, 100, 107, 162
    are like a bubble 70, 78
    can became ill early 2, 6
    paranoid 45
    similar to psychotics xxiv, 14, 59, 62, 159
infant's reaction to environmental intrusion 65, 88, 116
inhibition of the drive 17, 53, 110, 139, 148, 153
initial stages of maturation xxiii, 31, 58, 173
    as pre-history 17, 20, 45
    birth experience 20, 39–40, 45, 72–75, 95
    disillusionment, weaning 115–120, 135, 164
    first moments of extra uterine life 20
    intrauterine life 27–28
    theoretical first feed 73, 82, 87, 104, 117, 126
    transitionality 31, 48, 87, 96, 105, 122, 163 *see also* transitional object and transitional phenomena
    use of the object 124–130
initial state of being 69
innate personal morality 137
    original goodness 137
    mother's identification with the baby 44, 48–49, 51, 137
innate tendency towards maturation (towards integration) 15, 19, 27–29, 39, 42, 55, 58, 73, 76, 88, 91–92, 98–99, 105
instinctual satisfaction 81–82, 99
    is never entirely instinctual 82
    may be traumatic 82
instinctuality 16–18, 64, 79–81, 83, 127, 135, 149, 154, 161
    concept of instinct 79–80
    development of 139, 144–145
    during puberty and adolescence 153–154
    during the initial stages (instinctual tensions or urgencies) 83, 86, 110, 128, 131, 153
    during the Oedipal stage 141–143, 145
    during the stage of concern 133–135
    female 145–146, 148
    instinctual experiences (excited) 56, 79–81

    instinctual impulsiveness 79, 85, 127, 133, 141, 176
    instinctual satisfaction 81–82, 99
    male 145, 148
    pre-genital 80, 146, 161
    primitive instinctual (love) drive 127, 162
integration 90–91, 99, 101, 103, 131, 157
    as the general direction of maturation 27–29
    false (false identity) 32, 105
    from unintegration 46–74, 55, 74, 88, 101, 104, 131
    into a unitary me (I AM) 42, 104
    late 132
    of instinctual impulsiveness 134
integration in time and space 91–97
    spatialisation 96–97
    temporalisation 91, 136
    the most basic task 74, 90–91, 97
internal conflicts 3, 19, 136
internal environment 99
    incorporation of care 94, 97, 105, 108, 114
    incorporation of safety 97, 119
    incorporation of trust (of belief) 88, 119
internal object 123, 166
interpersonal relations (between whole persons) 19, 62, 140, 160
interruption of the continuity of being 70–71, 80, 87
intrapsychic 3, 8, 15, 19, 160–161, 163
    constitution of intrapsychic reality 48
intuition xliv, xlvi
invasion (or intrusion) 44–45, 71, 92, 97
    reaction to 70, 84
    threat of 42, 70, 82, 95
isolation 28, 48, 54, 60, 70, 77, 88–89, 154, 159, 166

Jacobs, Michael xxix, xxxiv, 110 note 15
Jung, Carl G. 13, 54, 129–130

Kalmanovitch, Jeannine xxvii, xxxi, xlix
Khan, Masud xxxiii, xl, xlix, 14, 25, 110, 170
Klein, Melanie 2, 4, 13, 19–20, 163–165
    contribution to psychoanalysis 13, 15, 63, 168 note 30
Kleinian theory xlix note 10, 2, 4, 16, 18–20, 111, 114, 124, 132, 137, 141, 163–165, 168 note 26

constitutional factor 19–20, 45, 85, 111 note 25, 132, 163, 168 note 26
depressive position 19–20, 32, 63, 137, 164, 168 note 28
innate envy 20, 25 note 31, 63 note 10, 171 note 59
intrapsychic (disregard for the environmental factor) 11, 119, 85, 145, 148, 162
Kraepelin, Emil 9–11
Kristeva, Julia 145–146, 170
Kuhn, Thomas xxviii, xxxv–xxxvi, 13

Lacan, Jacques xxxii, xxxiv, 13, 170
Laing, Ronald 51 note 31
language xxxvii, xxxiii, xl–xlii, 13, 19, 28, 61–62, 70, 107, 174–175
  different to describe each stage xxvii, xl, 62, 174
  in Freud xlii–xliii, xlvii
  in theory xxxii, 12–13, 54, 62, 133
Laplanche, J. & Pontalis J. -B. 14, 23
Laurentiis, Vera de, 113 note 43
life (living)
  is difficult in itself 5, 7
  to be alive 15, 29, 34, 42, 44, 50, 59, 70–71, 79, 83, 85–86, 99, 157–158, 160
  to feel alive xxviii, 1, 5, 29, 43, 84, 161
  to stay alive 5, 7, 29, 89, 103, 136, 155
Lins, M. Ivone xliv, li
lobotomy 9
Loparic, Zeljko xxxiv–xxxv, xlii–xliii, xlvii, 14–16, 24, 28, 34, 37, 63 note 12, 65, 101–102, 108 note 3, 109 note 14, 122, 168 note 31
love
  capacity to love 156
  love object 77, 128, 134, 136
loyalty/disloyalty 143–144
Luz, Rogério xxxii, xxxvii

management xv, xlvi, 7, 58, 96, 155
manic-depressive psychoses 11
masturbation 124, 138, 142, 154
maternal (or environmental) adaptation to needs xlv, 38, 42, 45, 47, 50, 71, 77, 81, 86, 94, 102, 105, 116, 121, 164 *see also* good enough care

de-adaptation of the mother 51, 53, 115–117, 120, 125
during absolute dependence 42, 45, 48, 67, 77, 163
during relative dependence 29–30, 38, 51–52, 54, 117, 124 *see also* de-adaptation of the mother
during the stage of concern 133–140.
during the stage of I AM 131–133
failure of xxv, 41, 46, 52, 65, 86, 91, 97, 107, 110 note 14, 115, 124, 141
passage to relative dependence 38, 48, 51, 54 117, 120
maternal love
  initially, is expressed through the physical care for the infant 90, 109 note 9, 199
  is not indulgent 50
maturational processes xxiv–xxv, 28, 29–35, 47 note 1 *see also* basic tasks of the maturational process
  as tendency towards integration into a unity xxiii, 15–16, 19, 27–30, 33, 37, 39, 42, 46–47, 53, 55, 57–58, 75, 85, 88, 91–92, 98, 105, 117, 125, 160, 176
  depends on a facilitating environment xxviii, 28, 33, 41, 48, 55, 58, 98, 104, 161
  general characteristics of 20, 29–35
  study of—depends on the brain being intact 42
maturational processes theory
  assumptions of 27–29
  back-bone of the Winnicott's thought xvi, xxiii, xlviii note 2
  include negativity li note 30, 5, 10, 18, 46, 59–61, 65 note 39, 66 note 47, 109 note 14, 116, 140, 145
  language appropriate to the phenomenon xxxvii, xlii–xliii, xlvi, 19, 61–62, 106, 174
  non-causal 58–59, 65 note 33
  need to study and improve the xlv, l note 24, 41, 60, 87, 173.
me/I
  I AM 131–132 *see also* unitary identity
  premature 39, 42, 169
  unitary xxiii, xxix, 17, 19, 28–29, 31, 33, 42–43, 54–56, 74, 76, 78, 80, 91, 93–94, 104, 110,

115, 123, 131–133, 141, 157, 161, 166, 1175
    see also unitary identity
Mello Filho, Julio xxx–xxxi
Mendonça, M. Emília 112
mental functioning 14, 36–39, 41–42, 72, 115–116
    split-off-intellect 65 note 30, 150
mental mechanisms xxxvi, 19, 35–36, 61, 76, 99, 123–124, 162
    projection and introjection 76, 108, 123–124, 137, 162, 168 note 29
Meyer, Luiz xxxi, 1
Milner, Marion 168 note 24
mind 33–34, 37–38, 41–42
    different from brain 7–9
    different from psyche 7, 33, 101
    mental functions (representation and symbolisation) 34, 38, 119, 121–123, 166 note.
    rudimentary mind 39, 65 note 25
    split from psycho-somatic existence (split-off intellect) 86, 100, 152
Misès, Roger 10–11, 23
Mitchell, Stephen A. xxxiv
Money-Kyrle 15, 63 note 14
mother
    anxious 70, 73, 100
    as subjective object 30–31, 36, 75, 104, 106, 108, 125–126
    capable of hating the baby 52, 116
    depressed 1, 22, 40, 86, 101, 116, 129–130, 139, 165 note 1
    environment- 75, 89, 106, 134, 161
    good enough xl, 49–51, 58, 66–67 note 52, 81–82, 84, 94
        is reliable, 21, 48, 75, 102, 107, 113 note 48
    helpless 52
    incapable of regression 51, 117
    is neither an external nor an internal object 47–48
    mirror role 107
    non-adaptability of the mother 70
    object- 24 note 30, 75, 89, 106, 112, 133–134
    prevents schizophrenia 58
    sane (normal) 115
    takes care only of the body or only of the person of the infant 99–100

    therapist, if there is deprivation 50
mother–infant relationship
    dual 52, 66 note 45, 134, 163
    pre-verbal xlvi, 62, 165 note 2, 174
    two-in-one 47–48, 106, 121, 161
motility 34, 56, 79, 81, 83–84, 86–87, 132
mutuality 74, 80–81, 86

narcissism 66 note 42, 160
needs of the baby (of dependence) 39, 42, 48, 50, 70, 75, 83, 88, 106, 117, 176
    and not desires 49
    instinctual needs 49–50, 76, 79, 81, 86
    of being 29, 50, 70, 81, 92, 105, 114 note 50
    of communication and non-communication xl, xliii, 28, 51, 60, 62, 81
    of ego support 55, 80, 82, 86
needs of the mother 49–50, 52, 73, 93–94
neurosis 6, 16–17, 19, 62, 159, 164
    in Winnicott 16–17, 62, 142
    related to the Oedipal stage 62, 141
non-mental knowledge 38, 165 note 2
not being 59–60, 66 note 47, 92, 157–159
nurses 4, 22 note 7, 82, 168 note 28

object
    external xxiii, 18, 42, 46, 63 note 10, 79, 83, 90, 106–107, 123, 127, 164, 169
    internal 79, 114 note 56, 166 note 7
    need to find the external object 83, 127
    subjective xxvi, xxx, xxxiii, xlix note 10, 30–31, 36, 56, 74–75, 101–106, 113 note 45, 114 note 50, 121–122, 128, 167 note 19
    transitional 49, 87, 101, 118–125, 128, 165 note 3
object relating (object relation) xxvii, xxxvi, 24 note 27, 30, 46, 74, 77, 89, 101–103, 105–106, 113 notes 45 and 49, 114 note 50, 116, 120–121, 124–126, 128, 132, 142, 149, 159, 161, 164, 166 note 3
objectivity xxxix, xl, xliv, 14, 88, 97, 119, 121, 125, 133, 166 note 9
oedipal
    situation 137, 143, 145, 151
    stage 141–153
Oedipus xxx, xxxv, 17, 19, 141, 151, 163
    complex 17, 141–142, 144, 151, 163–164

feminine 145, 148
non-centrality of complex xxxv, 13, 17–18, 48, 62, 159–160
precocious 137, 163
omnipotence of the baby (subjective) 44, 107, 126, 155–156
organicist theories 4, 6–7, 13, 64 note 21
Outeiral, José Ottoni xxxiii

paediatricians 4–6, 22 note 1
paradigm xxxiv–xxxvi, 13, 62, 124
paradigmatic revolution xxxv–xxxvi, 13, 59
paradox xxxvii, 77–78, 129.
paranoia 20, 45, 80, 132, 137, 164, 168 note 26, 176
    disposition 20, 80, 84, 132, 168 note 26
    precocious 163
    tendency to 168 note 26
parents (family, home) 6, 40, 51–53, 58, 67 note 55, 94, 99, 130, 138, 140, 142, 144, 148, 151, 153
    good enough without idealisation 52
    responsibility for the children 54
personal experience 43–44, 80, 88, 137
    capacity for experience 44, 92
    global experience 79, 82–83, 123
personal psychic reality 57, 130, 144
perversions 140, 169 note 38
Pessanha, Juliano 68, note 63
Phillips, Adam xxviii, xxix, xxxiv, l–li
philosophy xxxvii, xlii, xlv–xlvii, 8, 41 note 31, 57–59
    of science 59, 110 note 15
physical (somatic) 3, 11–12, 23
physiotherapy 90
playing 34, 60, 119, 124, 137, 166 note 3
    capacity 34, 122, 127, 153
    of the boy 147
    of the girl 147
pleasure 81–82, 120, 153
    Freudian pleasure-ego 162
pleasure/displeasure principle 50, 81–82, 110 note 20, 123, 159, 161
poetry 49
    poetical truth xliii
Pontalis, J.-B. xxxii, 14, 56–57, 61, 166
potency 135, 137, 145, 149–150, 152–153
    during adolescence 154

    during the Oedipal stage 151–152
    impotence 151–152
    male 154
    muscle 128
    omnipotence 44, 107, 155–156
    (illusion of, or experience of) 36, 44, 65, 75, 77–78, 102–103, 106, 108–109 note 13, 110, 116, 119–120, 125–126, 128, 131, 149, 155, 163–164, 167 note 13
potential space 18, 49, 60, 88, 97, 121–122, 124–125, 166 note 4
pre-dependence aloneness 43
prevention of psychic health vii, xx–xxi, xxiii–xxiv, 6, 11, 58
primal scene 142–143, 169
primary maternal preoccupation 50–51, 67, 89, 115
privation
    primary (lack of initial maternal care) 86, 163
projection
    as creation 167
    (and introjection) defensive mental mechanism 35, 76, 108, 123, 162, 165
psyche 9, 14–16, 22, 30, 33–35, 37, 41, 46, 80, 93, 99, 124, 131–132, 157, 160, 162
    different from mind 7–9, 22, 38, 41
    indwelling in the body 30, 36, 43, 74–75, 78, 83, 96, 98, 110, 112, 115
    originary as imaginative elaboration 16, 24, 34–37, 39, 41, 63–64, 79–81, 83, 93, 99, 120, 140, 146, 150, 160, 167, 170 note 44
psychiatry/psychiatric 1, 5, 8–13, 22 note 11, 98
    child xxxviii, 2, 4, 6, 8, 10–11
    disorder 7–8, 10
psychic (emotional or maturational) disorders xxi, xxiv–xxvii, xxix–xxx, xxxvi–xxxvii, 2, 4, 8–11, 13, 16, 31, 39–40, 57–58, 68, 87, 156, 162, 173, 175–176
    aetiology xxvi–xxvii, xxx, 3, 8, 11, 39, 57, 92, 164, 176
    classification xxvi, 4, 10, 32, 57, 176
    diagnostic xv, 9, 17, 41, 65 note 31, 169 note 36, 176
    importance of biography (history of the patient) 10, 17
    theory of xxi, xxiv, xxvii, 7, 65, 173
psychoanalysis

as art xliv–xlv
as religion xxxvii, xxxix, 20, 119
as science xxxvii–xxxviii–xl, 13–14
contribution of Freudian xxxvi, xxxix, xli, 10, 13–14
differences regarding Freud (see also Freudian theory) 12, 13–19, 137, 159–163
differences regarding Klein 19–20, 137, 163–165
different psychoanalyses 4
theoretical differences regarding 2–3, 56, 82, 127, 137, 159–165
traditional (Freud and Klein) xx, xxxi, xxxv, xxxviii, xlvii–xlviii note 5, xlix note 15, 2–3, 7, 13–19, 21, 28, 35, 47, 54, 60, 62, 73–74, 77, 82, 86–87, 90, 106, 118, 152, 159–165
psychoses xxv, xxvii, xxxvii, 1, 6, 17–19, 29, 61, 71, 89, 115, 141, 160, 164
child 10–11
hereditary tendencies 40–41
prototype of psychic illness 60
study of xxvi–xxvii, 4, 89, 94, 111 note 27
psycho-somatic disorders 96, 176, 184
psycho-somatic existence (see also total person) xxx, 7, 33, 37–39, 63 note 12, 98, 100, 142, 157, 162
mind 4, 7–9, 11, 15, 33, 34–42, 72, 106
psyche (imaginative elaboration) 16, 24, 34–37, 39, 41, 63–64, 79–81, 83, 93, 99, 120, 140, 146, 150, 160, 167, 170 note 44
soma 33–35, 37, 39, 41–42, 63 note 12, 98–99
puberty 11, 145, 151, 153–154
pulsion(s) (Freud and Klein) xxx, xxxv–xxxvi, xlii, 11, 14–17, 19, 23, 28, 42, 57, 61, 63 note 12, 76, 79, 82, 160, 162
death xli, 20, 59, 164–165
pure female element (being) and pure male element (doing) 104–105, 145, 149–150

quiet states (quietness) 43, 57, 70–71, 75, 78–79, 81, 86–91, 133–134, 138, 158

Rank, Otto 109 note 6
reactivity 69–70, 76, 78–79, 105
real
feeling of xl, 17, 29, 31, 43, 101–102, 104, 124, 131, 155 *see also* feeling of real
senses of 29, 43–44, 71, 83, 88, 92, 99–100, 124, 154 *see also* sense of real
reality (or world)
external, objective or shared xvi, xxiii, xlvi, xlix note 15, 8, 17, 19, 28, 31, 35, 43, 47, 55, 57, 74, 77–78, 83, 91, 95, 97, 100–101, 103, 107–108, 110, 119, 121, 124, 128, 130, 134, 159, 161–162
personal psychical (called inner or internal) 19, 57, 62, 77, 123, 176
senses of realities (internal and external) xxxviii, 77
subjective 101–103, 107, 109 note 13, 162
reality principle 44, 55, 85, 87, 124, 127, 161
regression 31, 43, 90, 117, 142, 150, 158
natural, as a part of life 51, 67 note 52, 118, 132–133, 142
of the mother 50–51
to dependence xliii, xlv, 34, 93, 96, 94, 114 note 50, 118
to previous stages 133, 141
relative independence 18, 30–31, 38, 51, 115, 132
reliability 72, 75, 81, 87–89, 94, 102, 107–108, 113 note 48, 122, 155
as predictability 75, 94, 96, 100
environmental 75, 81–82, 106, 118, 137, 165
incorporated by the baby 88, 105
is silent 51, 62, 107
loss of 123
of the mother 106–107, 112 note 33, 138, 161
religion xxxix, 21, 44, 62 note 7, 119
repression 17, 23, 123, 140, 142
responsibility of the child with instinctual impulsiveness 32, 53, 130, 133–134, 137, 141
responsibility of the parents 52, 58, 67 note 52, 93
rivalry of the boy with the father 139, 152–153
Rivière, Joan xxxviii, 13, 20, 171
Rodman, Robert xlvii, 20
roots of aggression 62 note 2, 78–79, 87, 83, 87, 111 note 24, 161
motility 83–84, 86
primitive love drive 84–86, 139, 144, 175

reaction to environmental invasions 72, 84, 105, 110 note 14, 150, 162
roots of the anti-social tendency 86
Rosa, Claudia 67, 169
ruthless, 85, 128, 133–134, 136–137, 161
Rycroft, Charles xxxiv

Safra, Gilberto 65 note 2
Sancte de Sanctis 10
Sartre, Jean-Paul li note 31, 51n
satisfaction 49, 73, 79–82, 85, 99, 104, 107, 110 note 19
    fear of 82
    search for instinctual 85
schizophrenic psychoses vii, xxiv, xlv, 4, 9, 11–12, 40–41, 58, 113 note 48, 162, 164
    as defensive organisations 40–41, 58, 113, note 48, 114 note 51, 162, 164
    child (or autism) 11, 58, 102, 129
    schizoid disorders 32, 49–50, 111 note 20, 130
science xxxiv, xxxvi–xxxix, xli, xliv, xlvi, xlviii, l, li, 6, 8, 14–15, 21–22, 24, 57
Sechehaye, M. A. 97
self 19, 31, 37, 44, 54–56, 80, 85, 91, 126–127, 132, 134, 161, 176
    false xxvii–xxviii, 17, 55, 67 note 60, 84, 88, 105, 129–131, 133, 155
    primary (primitive) 56, 75, 103–107, 115, 120, 125, 149, 161
    true 44, 55–56
    unitary xxiii–xxiv, 17, 19, 27–29, 31, 33, 42–43, 56, 74, 76, 78, 93, 130, 141, 157
    use of the term 54–55
self-control or inhibition of impulsiveness 53, 86, 139, 143
sense of externality (of the world) 48, 57, 63, 78, 80, 101, 105, 119, 124, 127, 162
sense of real 29, 43–44, 71, 83, 88, 92, 99–100, 124, 154
senses of reality xxviii, 24, 48, 80, 84, 90–91, 103, 113, 118–119, 121–122, 125–126, 159
    of being 65, 89
    of internal/external 80, 106
    personal psychical (or inner or internal) 57, 62, 123, 109 note 14, 129–130, 167 note 18
    subjective 101–103, 107, 109 note 13, 162

sentimentality 50, 66, note 50, 68 note 62
separation from the mother 22, 65, 109, 117
Serralha, Conceição 65 note 38
sexual identity (gender) 148–150
    boys (men) 148
    girls (women) 145–148
sexual(ity) 17, 64 note 19, 79, 83, 85, 160–161
    as a partial function 154
    beginning of gender distinction 81, 140
    bisexuality (non-instinctual) 140, 146, 149
    development of 19, 85, 139, 154, 160,
    difference between the sexes 81, 140, 145
    during puberty and adolescence 147, 153–155
    exhibitionist phase 140
    feminine 140, 145, 147–148
    Freudian theory of xxxviii, xxix, xxxv, 14, 17, 81, 159–161
    genital phase xxix, 129, 142, 145, 147, 154, 161
    heterosexuality 142, 148, 154
    homosexuality 150, 152–153, 169 note 42
    identity 140, 142–143, 148–150
    indefinition 154
    male 140, 144–148, 153
    pre-genital phase 80–81, 140, 146, 151, 153, 161
shock therapies 9
Simanke, Richard 14, 23
split 105, 149
    between male and female elements 113 note 49, 129, 145, 150
    essential 28, 62 note 4, 65 note 30, 68 note 63, 158
    -off intellect 152
    pathological 149
    psycho-somatic 100
spontaneity xvi, xli, 18, 43–44, 84, 86, 124, 133, 155, 166 note 11
    and reactivity 69–70, 76, 78, 105
    as a source of personal drives 84, 86
    inhibition or loss of 53, 86, 105, 119, 139, 144
    of the mother xli, 49, 51, 53, 139
spontaneous gesture xxxiii, xlix, 44, 50, 71, 76–80, 86, 89, 110 note 14, 134, 170 *see also* spontaneity
squiggle game xxxiii, 110 note 1

stages of maturation after the achievement of I AM
  adolescence 153–155
  adulthood 155–157
  Oedipal stage 141–153
  of concern 133–141
  old age and death 285–286
stages of maturation xxiv, xxvii–xxviii, xxxviii, 27, 29, 36, 38, 57, 63 note 8, 175
state of aliveness 34, 70, 76, 79, 83–84, 86
  state of unaliveness 59, 158–159
state of withdrawal 54, 70, 77, 80, 89–90, 112 note 31
  in play 97, 124
  mystical 90
Strachey, James 2, 6, 54
subjective object(s) xxvi, xxx, xxxiii, xlix note 10, 30–31, 36, 56, 74–75, 101–106, 113 note 47, 114 note 49, 121–122, 128, 167 note 19
  are reliable 102
  destruction of 126, 130
  different from the Kleinian internal object 123–124
subjective reality (or world) 30, 99, 102
subjective time 44, 73–74, 91–93, 96, 98, 106, 115
  clinical issues related to subjective time 94
sublimation 124, 162–163, 166
submission 195, 105, 119
survival of the object (mother, parents, analyst, environment) 123, 127–128, 135–136, 139, 168 note 27
  during adolescence 153–154
  during the Oedipal stage 144, 152
  during the stage of concern 134, 13
  during the stage of object usage 36, 124, 12
  in primitive instinctual impulsiveness 52, 133–134, 136, 154
  of family 154
symbol(s) 121, 165 note 2
  beginning of symbolic capacity 119, 121–122
  symbolic function of the transitional object (acting as mother) 121–123, 139
  use 117, 122, 139

theoretical first feed 69, 73–74, 76, 82, 88, 104, 119

theory of maturational processes
  core ("backbone") of xvi, xxiii, xlviii note 2
  encompasses negativity 59–60, 65 note 39, 66 note 47
therapeutical use of the analyst's failure 87, 111 note 29
total person 33, 53, 85, 99
transitional object 49, 87, 101, 118–125, 128, 165 note 3
transitional phenomena xxvii, 30, 49, 66, 87, 97, 101, 118–124, 163, 166 note 4 *see also* transitionality
transitionality xxxiv, 29–30, 34, 48–49, 97, 101, 117–125, 128, 163, 165
trauma 7, 45, 51, 71–72, 82, 86, 92, 107, 109 notes 6–7, 14, 110, 113 note 48, 114 note 53, 140, 166 note 10, 175
  birth (Rank) 45, 71–72, 109 note 6
  from the infant's reaction to environmental invasion 38, 70–72, 84, 105, 110 note 14, 150, 162–163
triangular relation (Oedipal situation) 16, 141–142, 151–152, 161
  with loyalty, l note 23, 142–143
trust, confidence, reliability 53, 88, 90, 93, 112–113 note 48, 122–123, 129–130, 136
  capacity to trust (believe in) 49, 75, 88
  incorporation of (by the infant) 47, 88, 97, 101, 105, 108, 119, 131, 135, 139
  loss of (by the infant) 89, 92–93, 123
two-in-one xlvi, 47–48, 106, 121, 161

unconscious xxix, xlii, 15, 23 note 18, 36, 61, 109, 138, 142, 154, 165
  conflict 3, 50, 57, 62, 163
  fantasy 24, 36, 127–130, 138, 155
  not-happened 109 note 14
  of species 45
  originary 92, 109, 154
  repressed 57, 109, 123–124, 131, 165
unintegration 46–47, 56–57, 88, 91, 159
  loss of the capacity for 91
unthinkable agony xxx, 43, 92, 107, 112, 114, 166 note 10
  of losing the sense of real 92

use of an object 29, 111 note 24, 124–125, 167 note 17
    different from object relation 125–126

Vilete, Edna xx, 116

Wallbridge, David xxvii
weaning 77, 115, 148, 164
whole person xlix note 13, 32–33, 35, 46, 57, 128, 133, 160
Widlöcher, Daniel xxxiv, xlix
Winnicott, Clare xlviii, 3, 171 note 55
Winnicott, D. W.
    absence of speculations 59, 175
    as paediatrician xxiv, xxvi, xlviii, note 6, l note 21, 1–2, 4, 6, 22 note 1, 170 note 53
    as a psychoanalyst xxiv, xxxviii, 13–14, 61
    as a scientist xxxviii, xxxix, l note 26
    autobiography 2, 44, 159
    aversion to dogma xxxiv, xxxvii, xxxvii, xlvii
    death 44
    freedom of thought xxxvii, xli, 21
    indebted to Freud and Klein xxxviii–xxxix
    phases of his thought xxvi
    philosophical themes xlvi–xlvii, 8, 54, 57–61, 130, 175
    refusal of organicist hypotheses for psychic disorders 1, 4, 7, 13, 22 note 1
    refuses becoming callous 170 note 53
    rejection of objectification xxxviii, xlvii, 130
    rejection of the Freudian metapsychology xli–xlii, xlvi–xlvii, 14–16, 23 note 20, 61
    supervision with Klein 2, 4
Winnicott's clinical cases
    boy (two years old, who reacts to the birth of a brother) 5
    patient B (from *Holding and Interpretation*) 112 note 31, 152–153, 170 note 52
    patient FM (man with a split-off pure female element) 149–151, 170
    Veronica (bed wetting after the absence of the mother) 22 note 4
world xxxviii, 74–78, 92, 101, 121, 125, 129, 149, 163
    difference and relation between world and objects 75, 88–89, 105
    external, shared, perceived objectively 18, 31, 83, 103, 106, 119
    internal 35, 77–78, 80, 123, 136, 141, 143, 161
    presentation by the mother xxvii, xlvi, 75–76, 78, 102, 117
    reality of 17, 36, 90–92, 101, 129, 132
    subjective 31, 44, 46, 56, 75, 78, 91, 97, 102, 119, 122, 125, 133
    various (as are the senses of reality) 76, 101, 122
Wulff, M. 166

STANDARD LEVEL
HIGHER LEVEL

PEARSON BACCALAUREATE

Biology

ALAN DAMON • RANDY McGONEGAL • WILLIAM WARD
SERIES EDITOR: CHRISTIAN BRYAN

Supporting every learner across the IB continuum

essentials

Published by Pearson Education Limited,
80 Strand, London, WC2R 0RL.

www.pearsonglobalschools.com

Text © Pearson Education Limited 2016

Edited by Judith Shaw
Proofread by Eva Fairnell and Judith Shaw
Typeset by Ken Vail

Original illustrations © Pearson Education 2016
Illustrated by Ken Vail
Cover design by Pearson Education Limited

The rights of Alan Damon, Randy McGonegal and William Ward to be identified as authors of this work has been asserted by them in accordance with the Copyright, Designs and Patents Act 1988.

First published 2016

19 18 17 16

IMP 10 9 8 7 6 5 4 3 2 1

British Library Cataloguing in Publication Data
A catalogue record for this book is available from the British Library

ISBN 978 1 4479 9068 0
eBook only ISBN 978 1 4479 9069 7

Copyright notice
All rights reserved. No part of this publication may be reproduced in any form or by any means (including photocopying or storing it in any medium by electronic means and whether or not transiently or incidentally to some other use of this publication) without the written permission of the copyright owner, except in accordance with the provisions of the Copyright, Designs and Patents Act 1988 or under the terms of a licence issued by the Copyright Licensing Agency, Saffron House, 6–10 Kirby Street, London EC1N 8TS (www.cla.co.uk). Applications for the copyright owner's written permission should be addressed to the publisher.

Printed in Slovakia by Neographia

Acknowledgements
The authors and publisher would like to thank Pat Tosto for the inspiration provided by material which appears in *Pearson Baccalaureate Biology*.

The authors and publisher would like to thank Ellen Vriniotis of ACS Athens, Rizma Rizwan of City and Islington College, Ellen Dittmar of Western Academy of Beijing, Susanna Joachim of Nymphenburger Schulen, Kania Grazyna of 33 Liceum IMM Kopernika, Sami Sorvali of Kannas School, Diane Howlett of Szczecin International School, Brian Hull of AIS Kuwait, Jacques Weber of British International School of Jeddah, Adrianna Anderson of International Community School, and Michael Ashleman of Wellington, for their invaluable help in the development of this series by piloting the concept material.

With thanks to the EAL reviewer Baljit Nijjar and the subject specialist Graham Mallard, for their helpful and constructive advice that greatly improved the clarity and accuracy of the text.

With thanks also to IB Biology guru Paul Billiet for his fact checking and diplomatically constructive suggestions.

We are grateful to the following for permission to reproduce copyright material:

Text, tables and figures
Figure 3.6 from http://biomed.emory.edu/PROGRAM_SITES/PBEE/pdf/sherman1.pdf, reproduced with permission from Dr. Stephanie Sherman; Figure 4.4 adapted from http://www.esrl.noaa.gov/research/themes/carbon/, U.S. Department of Commerce | National Oceanic and Atmospheric Administration Earth System Research Laboratory; Figure 4.7 from Temperature change and carbon dioxide change, https://www.ncdc.noaa.gov/paleo/globalwarming/temperature-change.html (National Oceanographic and Atmospheric Administration), NOAA/National Climatic Data Center; Figure 4.8 from http://sofia.usgs.gov/sfrsf/rooms/coastal/flbay/genedustbigs/geneco2concx.gif, U.S. Department of the Interior; Figure 11.10 from *Cell and Molecular Biology*, 6th ed., John Wiley & Sons (Karp, G. 2009) Fig. 9.57 (b) p.361, copyright (c) 2009 Wiley. Reproduced with permission of John Wiley & Sons, Inc., Cell and Molecular Biology by BIANCHI, DONALD E. ; SHEELER, PHILLIP Reproduced with permission of JOHN WILEY & SONS, INCORPORATED in the format republish in a book via Copyright Clearance Center; Figure 12.5 adapted from Cosmic Evolution website, v 7, 2013, copyright Eric J. Chaisson, Harvard University https://www.cfa.harvard.edu/~ejchaisson/cosmic_evolution/docs/splash.html; Figure 12.6 adapted from the article 'Brain Gyrification and its Significance' *Trends in Cognitive Sciences* 2005 May; 9(5):250-7 http://white.stanford.edu/teach/index.php/Brain_Gyrification_and_its_Significance#References Roth G1, Dicke U.2005, copyright © 2005 Elsevier Ltd. All rights reserved; Figure 12.13 adapted from Journal of Comparative Psychology from the article 'Experimental evidence for spatial learning in cuttlefish (*Sepia officinalis*)' http://www.ncbi.nlm.nih.gov/pubmed/12856785, Karson MA1, Jean GB, Hanlon RT. 2003 Jun; 117(2):149-55 American Psychological Association; Figure 12.16 adapted from *Ion channels of excitable membrane*, 3rd ed., Sinauer Associates, Inc. (Hille, B. 2001) fig. 7.1, p.202, copyright © 2001, Sinauer Associates, Inc.; Figure 12.18 from Repeated administration of MDMA causes transient down-regulation of serotonin 5-HT2 receptors *Neuropharmacology*, 31 (9), pp. 881–893 (Scheffel, Ursula Lever, J.R. Stathis, M., Ricaurte, G.A. 1992), with permission from Elsevier, copyright © 1992, published by Elsevier Ltd.

Text extracts relating to the IB syllabus and assessment have been reproduced from IBO documents. Our thanks go to the International Baccalaureate for permission to reproduce its intellectual copyright. This material has been developed independently by the publisher and the content is no way connected with or endorsed by the International Baccalaureate (IB). International Baccalaureate® is a registered trademark of the International Baccalaureate Organization.

Photographs
DK Images: Zygote Media Group Figure 15.6; **Science Photo Library Ltd**: Astrid & Hanns-Frieder Michler Figure 9.6, Biophoto Associates Figure 9.7, CNRI Figure 3.2.

All other images © Pearson Education.

Websites
Pearson Education Limited is not responsible for the content of any external internet sites. It is essential for tutors to preview each website before using it in class so as to ensure that the URL is still accurate, relevant and appropriate. We suggest that tutors bookmark useful websites and consider enabling students to access them through the school/college intranet.

Dedications
Alan Damon:
To Angèle, Lucas, Anna and Lysa for their support.

Randy McGonegal:
For my father, who taught me why the word 'gentle' is found within the word, 'gentleman'.

William Ward:
I dedicate this book to all my students in 41 years of teaching. Each one has helped make my career enjoyable and fulfilling.

Contents

Introduction   iv

Core

1	Cell biology	2
2	Molecular biology	24
3	Genetics	54
4	Ecology	78
5	Evolution and biodiversity	98
6	Human physiology	119
7	Nucleic acids	143
8	Metabolism, cell respiration, and photosynthesis	157
9	Plant biology	178
10	Genetics and evolution	197
11	Animal physiology	211

Options

12	Option A: Neurobiology and behaviour	234
13	Option B: Biotechnology and bioinformatics	276
14	Option C: Ecology and conservation	302
15	Option D: Further human physiology	325

Internal Assessment   352

Extended Essay   359

Index   365

Glossary: Command terms

Introduction

Welcome to your Essentials guide to Biology. This book has been designed to solve the key problems of many IB Diploma students:

- relating material you have been taught to the syllabus goals and outcomes
- remembering it from one lesson to the next
- recalling it months later in an exam situation
- demonstrating your understanding of it in an exam situation within a strict time limit.

Who should use Essentials guides?

Essentials guides serve as highly effective summaries and have been carefully designed with all IB students in mind.

However, the guides also deal with the particular interests of IB students whose first language is not English, and who would like further support. As a result, the content in all Essentials guides has been edited by an EAL (English as an additional language) expert to make sure that:

- the language used is clear and accessible
- key terms are explained
- essential vocabulary is defined and reinforced.

Key features of an Essentials guide

Reduced content: Essentials guides are not intended to be comprehensive textbooks – they contain the essential information you need to understand and respond to the Understandings in the IB Biology Guide. This allows you to understand material quickly and still be confident you are meeting the essential aims of the syllabus. We have reduced the number of words as much as possible to ensure everything you read has clear meaning, is clearly related to the IB Biology Guide, and will help you in an exam.

Format and approach: The content of the book is organized according to the Understandings in the IB Biology Guide. Each Understanding is looked at separately so that you can study each one without having read or understood previous sections. This allows you to use the book as a first text, or a revision guide, or as a way to help you understand material you have been given from other sources.

Main ideas: Most sub-topics start with a main idea, which gives a simple introduction to the topic and an idea of the main learning point.

> ### Main idea
> Chromosomes carry genes in a **linear** sequence that is shared by members of a species.

Model sentences: These summarize key concepts so that you gain a clearer understanding of them. They are examples of the sort of sentences you could use in an exam. For example:

> **Model sentence: It is possible to find out the gender of an unborn child or determine if there are any chromosomal anomalies by preparing a karyogram.**

Applications and skills: These relate to the applications and skills in the IB Biology Guide, and show how you can apply the Understandings in a more practical way; they illustrate how theory can be used in practice in real situations.

> Skill: **Use of a database to determine differences in the base sequence of a gene in two species**
>
> Application: **Use of karyograms to deduce sex and diagnose Down syndrome in humans**

Vocabulary and synonym boxes: Useful words and phrases are colour coded in the text and given matching colour-coded explanations in the margins. There are three different sets: vocabulary related to the topic, synonyms, and general vocabulary. These are included to help identify and support your understanding of academic and difficult words. In order to make the text more accessible to students whose first language is not English, we have avoided using a highly academic tone. However, at the same time we have ensured that the complexity of the content is at the level required by successful IB Diploma students.

> **Subject vocabulary**
>
> **hypothesis** possible explanation for a set of observations or possible answer to a scientific question
>
> **ratio** a relationship between two numbers
>
> **nutrient** chemical material a cell or organism needs
>
> **excretion** process in which a cell rids itself of waste products

> **Synonyms**
>
> **rid**................ remove

> **General vocabulary**
>
> **squaring** process of multiplying a number by itself
>
> **cubing** process of taking a number times itself twice

Internal Assessment and Extended Essay sections: These are intended to help you design, research, and write your own investigations and essays. They provide useful guidance on how to complete your investigation or essay, and explain what is required to achieve the top marks.

eText and audio: In the accompanying eText you will find a complete digital version of the book. There are also links to spoken audio files of the vocabulary terms and definitions to help with comprehension and pronunciation. In addition, all the vocabulary lists are located together as downloadable files.

Above all, we hope this book helps you to understand and consolidate your Biology course more easily than ever, helping you to achieve the highest possible result in your exams.

How to use your enhanced eBook

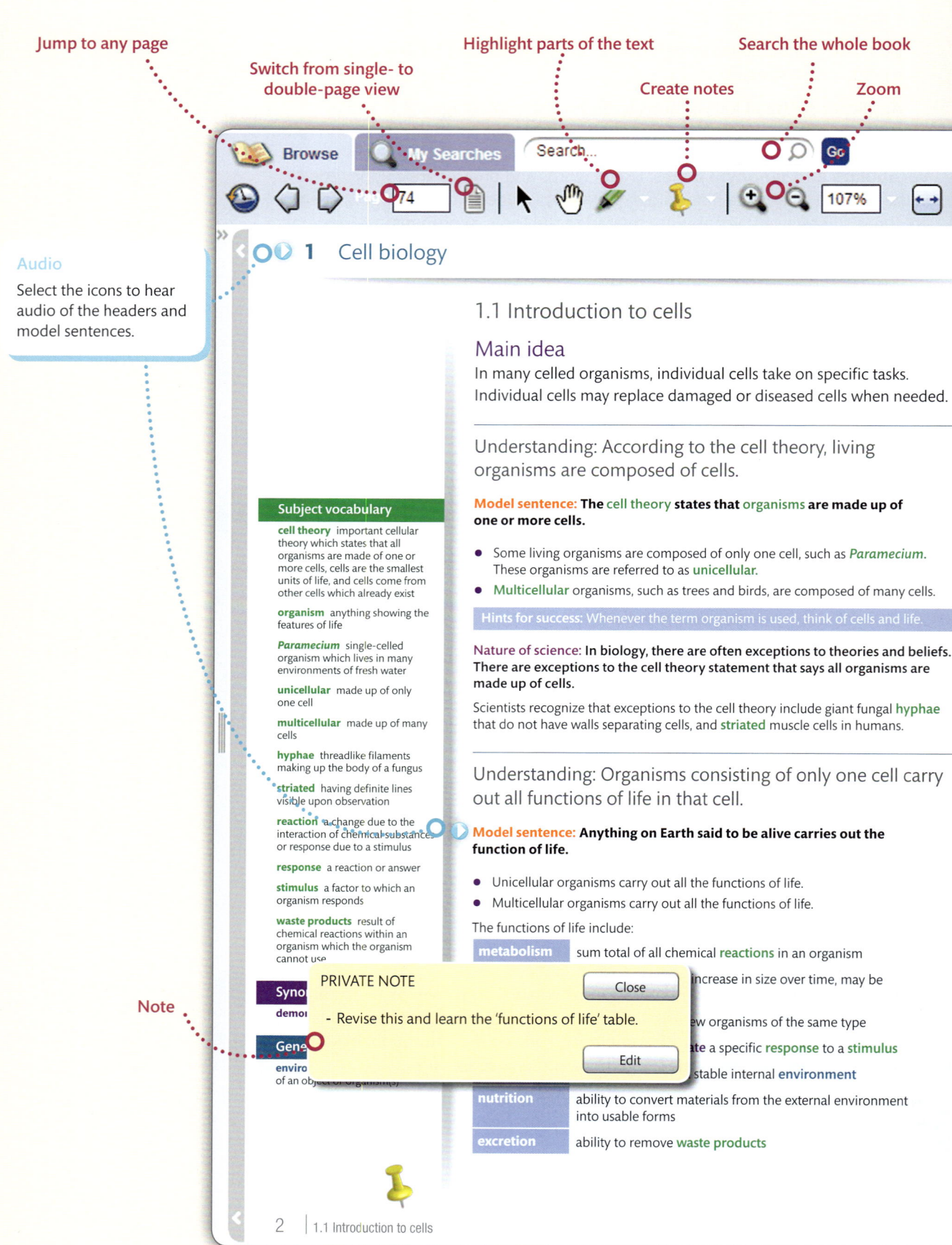

See the definitions of key terms in the glossary

Switch to whiteboard view

Create a bookmark

Hints for success: When asked how one would know if something was alive, state that anything alive would have to demonstrate all the functions of life listed in the table.

Any living organism may be observed over a period of time to recognize the functions of life mentioned in the table. *Paramecium* and *Chlorella* are unicellular organisms which when grown in a lab culture will allow the observation of most of the functions of life mentioned in the table.

Nature of science: A hypothesis is often produced by scientists before any observations or experiments are carried out.

Understanding: Surface area to volume ratio is important in the limitation of cell size.

Model sentence: When a cell becomes too large there is not enough surface area to rid the cell of all the waste produced by metabolism.

- Large cells also have problems bringing in enough materials for cell metabolism to occur.
- The surface area of a cell is that area of the cell which makes contact with its external environment.
- The surface area controls the movement of materials in and out of the cell.
- When the cell grows, the thin surface layer increases by a factor involving squaring the cell radius.
- The volume of a cell includes everything inside the thin surface layer.
- It is in the interior of the cell, the volume area, where most of the chemical reactions of the cell occur.

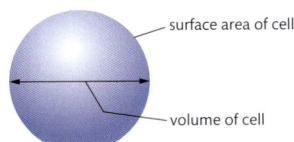

Figure 1.1 *General cell diagram*

- When the cell grows, the volume of the cell increases by a factor involving cubing the cell radius.
- If the ratio between the surface area and the volume is low, not enough nutrients can enter the cell to keep the necessary chemical reactions of life occurring.
- If the surface area to volume ratio is high, such as 11:1, the cell will be healthy and may continue to grow.
- If the surface area to volume ratio is low, such as 2:1, the cell will not grow. It may even die because not enough nutrients may enter the cell and excretion of waste is slowed.

Hints for success: Remember that a large cell has less surface area compared to its volume than a small cell. The larger a cell is, the less it will continue to grow. Larger organisms are composed of many small cells, not larger cells.

Subject vocabulary

hypothesis possible explanation for a set of observations or possible answer to a scientific question

ratio a relationship between two numbers

nutrient chemical material a cell or organism needs

excretion process in which a cell rids itself of waste products

Synonyms

rid .... remove

General vocabulary

squaring process of multiplying a number by itself

cubing process of taking a number times itself twice

Definitions with audio
Click on highlighted terms to see the definition and hear the audio.

Vocabulary lists
Select the icons at the back of the book to see complete vocabulary lists.

1 Cell biology

1.1 Introduction to cells

Main idea
In many celled organisms, individual cells take on specific tasks. Individual cells may replace damaged or diseased cells when needed.

Understanding: According to the cell theory, living organisms are composed of cells.

Model sentence: The cell theory states that organisms are made up of one or more cells.

- Some living organisms are composed of only one cell, such as *Paramecium*. These organisms are referred to as unicellular.
- Multicellular organisms, such as trees and birds, are composed of many cells.

Hints for success: Whenever the term organism is used, think of cells and life.

Nature of science: In biology, there are often exceptions to theories and beliefs. There are exceptions to the cell theory statement that says all organisms are made up of cells.

Scientists recognize that exceptions to the cell theory include giant fungal hyphae that do not have walls separating cells, and striated muscle cells in humans.

Understanding: Organisms consisting of only one cell carry out all functions of life in that cell.

Model sentence: Anything on Earth said to be alive carries out the function of life.

- Unicellular organisms carry out all the functions of life.
- Multicellular organisms carry out all the functions of life.

The functions of life include:

metabolism	sum total of all chemical reactions in an organism
growth	ability to change or increase in size over time, may be limited in amount
reproduction	ability to produce new organisms of the same type
response	ability to demonstrate a specific response to a stimulus
homeostasis	ability to maintain a stable internal environment
nutrition	ability to convert materials from the external environment into usable forms
excretion	ability to remove waste products

Subject vocabulary

cell theory important cellular theory which states that all organisms are made of one or more cells, cells are the smallest units of life, and cells come from other cells which already exist

organism anything showing the features of life

Paramecium single-celled organism which lives in many environments of fresh water

unicellular made up of only one cell

multicellular made up of many cells

hyphae threadlike filaments making up the body of a fungus

striated having definite lines visible upon observation

reaction a change due to the interaction of chemical substances or response due to a stimulus

response a reaction or answer

stimulus a factor to which an organism responds

waste products result of chemical reactions within an organism which the organism cannot use

Synonyms

demonstrate... show

General vocabulary

environment the surroundings of an object or organism(s)

Hints for success: When asked how one would know if something was alive, state that anything alive would have to demonstrate all the functions of life listed in the table.

Any living organism may be observed over a period of time to recognize the functions of life mentioned in the table. *Paramecium* and *Chlorella* are unicellular organisms which when grown in a lab culture will allow the observation of most of the functions of life mentioned in the table.

Nature of science: A hypothesis is often produced by scientists before any observations or experiments are carried out.

Understanding: Surface area to volume ratio is important in the limitation of cell size.

Model sentence: When a cell becomes too large there is not enough surface area to rid the cell of all the waste produced by metabolism.

- Large cells also have problems bringing in enough materials for cell metabolism to occur.
- The surface area of a cell is that area of the cell which makes contact with its external environment.
- The surface area controls the movement of materials in and out of the cell.
- When the cell grows, the thin surface layer increases by a factor involving squaring the cell radius.
- The volume of a cell includes everything inside the thin surface layer.
- It is in the interior of the cell, the volume area, where most of the chemical reactions of the cell occur.

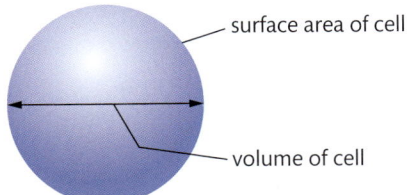

Figure 1.1 *General cell diagram*

- When the cell grows, the volume of the cell increases by a factor involving cubing the cell radius.
- If the ratio between the surface area and the volume is low, not enough nutrients can enter the cell to keep the necessary chemical reactions of life occurring.
- If the surface area to volume ratio is high, such as 11:1, the cell will be healthy and may continue to grow.
- If the surface area to volume ratio is low, such as 2:1, the cell will not grow. It may even die because not enough nutrients may enter the cell and excretion of waste is slowed.

Hints for success: Remember that a large cell has less surface area compared to its volume than a small cell. The larger a cell is, the less it will continue to grow. Larger organisms are composed of many small cells, not larger cells.

Subject vocabulary

hypothesis possible explanation for a set of observations or possible answer to a scientific question

ratio a relationship between two numbers

nutrient chemical material a cell or organism needs

excretion process in which a cell rids itself of waste products

Synonyms

rid .... remove

General vocabulary

squaring process of multiplying a number by itself

cubing process of taking a number times itself twice

Subject vocabulary

magnification the ratio of the image size to the actual object size

field of view what is visible when looking through the ocular/eyepiece of a microscope

scale bar line added to a micrograph or drawing to show the actual size of an object or structure

micrograph visual representation of a microscopic image

functions specific actions or jobs

emergent coming into existence, arising through an evolving process

specialized having a specific function or action

differentiation series of changes which transforms unspecialized cells into specialized cells and tissues in multicellular organisms

unspecialized without specific function, general in function

Synonyms

accomplish..... achieve

General vocabulary

emerge to come from, as a result of

interaction the process of having an effect on other objects or organisms or being affected by other objects or organisms

Skill: Use of a light microscope to investigate the structure of cells and tissues, with drawing of cells

You are expected to be able to:

- Name the parts of a typical light microscope.
- State the major function of each part of the light microscope.
- Determine the total **magnification** when making observations with the light microscope.
- Calculate the diameter of the **field of view** when looking through the eyepiece/ocular of the light microscope.
- Use the diameter of the field of view to determine the approximate size of cells.
- Use **scale bars** on a **micrograph** to determine the actual size of cells or cell parts.
- Make proper drawings of cells when observing with the light microscope that include correct labelling.

Understanding: Multicellular organisms have properties that emerge from the interaction of their cellular components.

Model sentence: Cells working together can **accomplish** more than cells working individually.

- Multicellular organisms have specific cells carrying out unique **functions**.
- Usually, no single cell in a multicellular organism carries out all the functions to keep the organism alive.
- Multicellular organisms are able to carry out more functions than the sum of the functions of the individual cells they contain.
- These increased properties of the multicellular organism over the sum of its individual cells are called **emergent** properties.

Hints for success: Remember that the whole is greater than the sum of the parts. This relates to the organism compared to the cells it is composed of. The greater properties of the organism **emerge** from the **interaction** of the organism's cells.

Understanding: **Specialized** tissues can develop by cell differentiation in multicellular organisms.

Model sentence: Groups of cells in a multicellular organism may go through similar changes over time to produce a mass of similar cells called a tissue.

- A group of cells with similar structure and function within a multicellular organism is called a tissue.
- **Differentiation** is a process cells may go through over time to bring about change in their structure and/or function.
- Differentiated cells are specialized to carry out functions more efficiently than undifferentiated or **unspecialized** cells.
- Differentiation of cells to perform specific functions is important to the overall success of the multicellular organism.
- Differentiation of cells allows emergent properties to develop within the multicellular organism.

1.1 Introduction to cells

Hints for success: Think of differentiation of cells as being important in bringing about greater **efficiency** in multicellular organisms. Greater efficiency results in a greater chance of survival.

General vocabulary
efficiency level of production

Subject vocabulary
genome the complete DNA sequence of an organism

hereditary passed from generation to generation by genes

chromosomes structures on which DNA occurs within a cell

species a group of organisms which are structurally similar and able to pass their genetic traits on to their offspring

gene section of DNA molecule which codes for a particular trait/protein in an organism

Synonyms
segment .... part

Understanding: Differentiation involves the expression of some genes and not others in a cell's **genome**.

Model sentence: When not all the genes of a cell's DNA become active, the genes which do become active cause the cell to differentiate.

- DNA is the **hereditary** material of the cell and is present on structures called **chromosomes**.

The complete line represents a chromosome

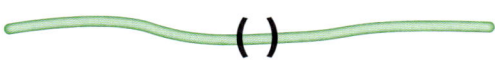

The small area in parentheses would be a gene.
Many, many genes exist on a single chromosome.

Figure 1.2 *Representation of a gene on a chromosome*

- All of the DNA within a cell is called the cell's genome.
- Cells of different **species** of organisms will have different numbers of chromosomes in their genome.
- A **gene** is a **segment** of DNA on a chromosome which controls a particular structure or function in the cell.
- Not all genes of a cell are active at the same time. When certain genes become active, the function, and even structure, of cells may change.
- Cells become specialized according to which DNA segments become active.

Hints for success: Think of DNA as the controlling material within the cell. Also, keep in mind not all the DNA of a cell is active at any one time. The activities and properties of a cell will change depending on which genes are active at a particular time.

Example: flowering plants

The form and structures of a flowering plant go through great changes over the life of the plant. The DNA of all the cells stays the same during the plant's life. However, at different times in the life cycle of the plant, sections of the DNA in specific cells become active and non-active. Different areas of DNA activity cause the changes in form and structures of the plant.

Synonyms

capacity	ability
retain	keep
significant	large
derived	taken
controversy	disagreement/debate

Subject vocabulary

therapeutic relating to the treatment of disease

bone marrow soft tissue which fills the inner, hollow spaces of certain types of bones

disease change or condition, other than injury, that affects the normal functioning of the organism

umbilical cord structure which attaches the embryo to the mother in mammals

eukaryote organism composed of a cell or cells which are complex in structure and always include organelles

prokaryote organism composed of a cell which does not contain most of the known cell organelles

---

Understanding: The **capacity** of stem cells to divide and differentiate along different pathways is necessary for embryonic development and also makes stem cells suitable for **therapeutic** uses.

Model sentence: Stem cells are non-specialized cells which may go through the process of differentiation to become cells needed in the multicellular organism's future.

Stem cells have a function in the development of the embryo of an organism. A multicellular organism is an embryo during the stages it goes through before it is able to live on its own.

The undifferentiated stem cells may also be used therapeutically. Stem cells are cells within an organism which **retain** their ability to divide and differentiate into various cell types. These stem cells are relatively large in number in an organism's embryo stages. As the embryo develops, the undifferentiated stem cells specialize to become certain types of tissue necessary for the function of the adult organism. Most tissues in adult multicellular organisms retain a **significant** number of stem cells. The large stem cell number allows possible repair of damaged or diseased cells in that tissue.

The use of stem cells in therapeutic situations is largely in the experimental stage at present. Their use in the treatment of disease and trauma seems very promising. **Bone marrow** stem cells have been successfully used in human therapeutic instances.

Application: Use of stem cells

The use of stem cells is very promising for the possible treatment of Stargardt's **disease** and diabetes. Stargardt's disease is due to a genetic condition which eventually results in blindness. Diabetes results in a problem metabolizing sugars within the organism's cells.

The use of stem cells **derived** from specially created embryos has created ethical concerns amongst some groups of people. There are also questions of right or wrong in using stem cells obtained from an organism's tissues or from **umbilical cord** blood in humans.

Nature of science: Research involving stem cells has not been without **controversy**. Many religions and cultures have questions about the ethics of stem cell research.

1.2 Ultrastructure of cells

Main idea

Cells of organisms known as **eukaryotes** have a more complex structure than cells of organisms known as **prokaryotes**.

Understanding: Electron microscopes have a much higher resolution than light microscopes.

Model sentence: Electron microscopes allow a clearer image of cells and their structures.

- Electron microscopes provide greater magnification than light microscopes. Electron microscopes may enlarge objects over 500 000 times. Light microscopes can enlarge objects only 2000 times.

- Electron microscopes use electrons to produce high-resolution images. Resolution refers to the clarity of an image. Light microscopes use light to produce images. Resolution is not nearly as high in light microscopes as in electron microscopes.
- One advantage light microscopes have over electron microscopes is that light microscopes can allow observation of living cells or specimens. Electron microscopes are only able to provide images of non-living cells or specimens.

Scale bars are often used with micrographs or drawings so that the actual size may be determined. One may calculate magnification or enlargement of an object by using the following formula:

Magnification = size of image ÷ actual size of specimen

Understanding: Prokaryotes have a simple cell structure without compartmentalization.

Model sentence: The lack of **compartments** within the prokaryotic cell leads to their simple structure.

General vocabulary

compartment area separated from other areas

Subject vocabulary

plasma membrane membrane which surrounds the cell

bacterium (bacteria) organism which is an example of a prokaryotic cell

nucleoid region of a prokaryotic cell where the DNA exists

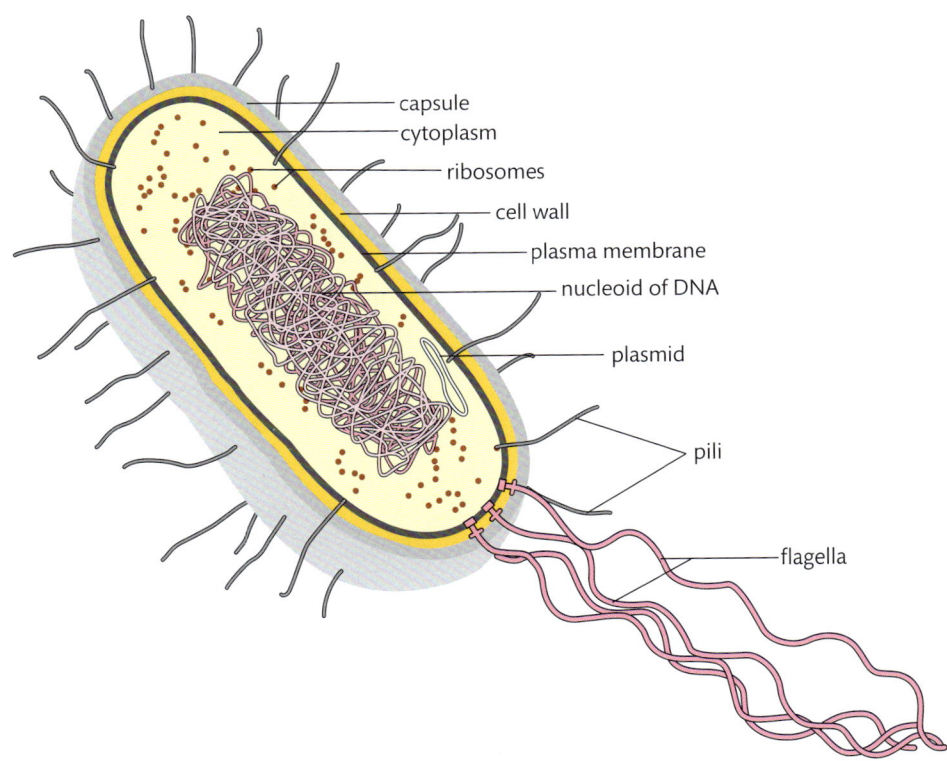

Figure 1.3 *Drawing of the ultrastructure of a prokaryotic cell*

- As you examine the drawing of the ultrastructure of a prokaryotic cell, notice there are no internal compartments. All the structures within the **plasma membrane** are mixed together.
- Bacteria are examples of prokaryotic cells. The drawing is of a type of **bacterium**.
- Note the **nucleoid** region containing DNA. The nucleoid region contains the DNA which is the material that controls the cell.
- The prokaryotic DNA also allows characteristics to be passed to offspring of prokaryotic cells.

1 Cell biology | 7

Subject vocabulary

binary fission simplified form of cell division in bacteria

ultrastructure detailed structure of a cell not visible with light microscope

cell wall outermost layer of bacterial and plant cells

pili hairlike growths on bacterial cells which function in attachment and DNA exchange between bacteria

flagella (singular: flagellum) whip-like structure which allows movement of cells

cytoplasm region of the cell within the plasma membrane in which the cell organelles exist

ribosome organelle within cells where polypeptides are formed

General vocabulary

compartmentalization division into separate areas or groups

complexity the state of being complicated

- Prokaryotic cells divide by **binary fission**. Binary fission is a simple form of cell division which produces two cells or organisms from one.
- Many prokaryotes reproduce by carrying out binary fission. Binary fission is why many types of bacteria can increase in numbers very rapidly.
- Prokaryotic cells contain ribosomes, just as more complex cell types do. However, the ribosomes of prokaryotes are simpler in structure than those of more complex cells.

Skill: Drawing the ultrastructure of a prokaryotic cell

When asked to draw the **ultrastructure** of a prokaryotic cell in an exam, be certain to include the following structures and their labels: **cell wall**, **pili**, **flagella**, plasma membrane, **cytoplasm**, and **ribosomes**. These structures must be clearly drawn and their relative size and position must be correct. The drawing provided should be studied carefully and used as a model when making drawings.

Application: The division of prokaryotic cells by binary fission is a simple process

The simplicity of binary fission is partly due to the DNA of the nucleoid region of the prokaryotic cell being pure. The DNA is not attached to any other compounds or proteins as it is in more complex cells.

Understanding: Eukaryotes have a **compartmentalized** cell structure.

Model sentence: Eukaryotic cells have compartments within an outside membrane to produce greater interior **complexity** than prokaryotic cells.

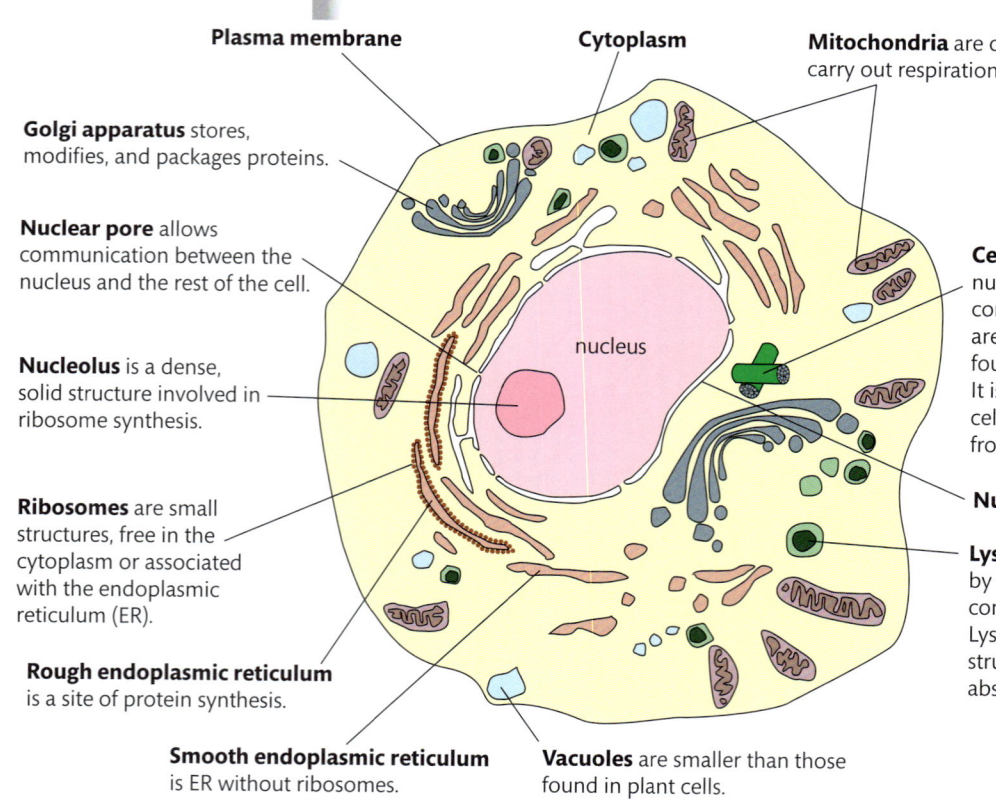

Figure 1.4 *Generalized animal eukaryotic cell*

8 | 1.2 Ultrastructure of cells

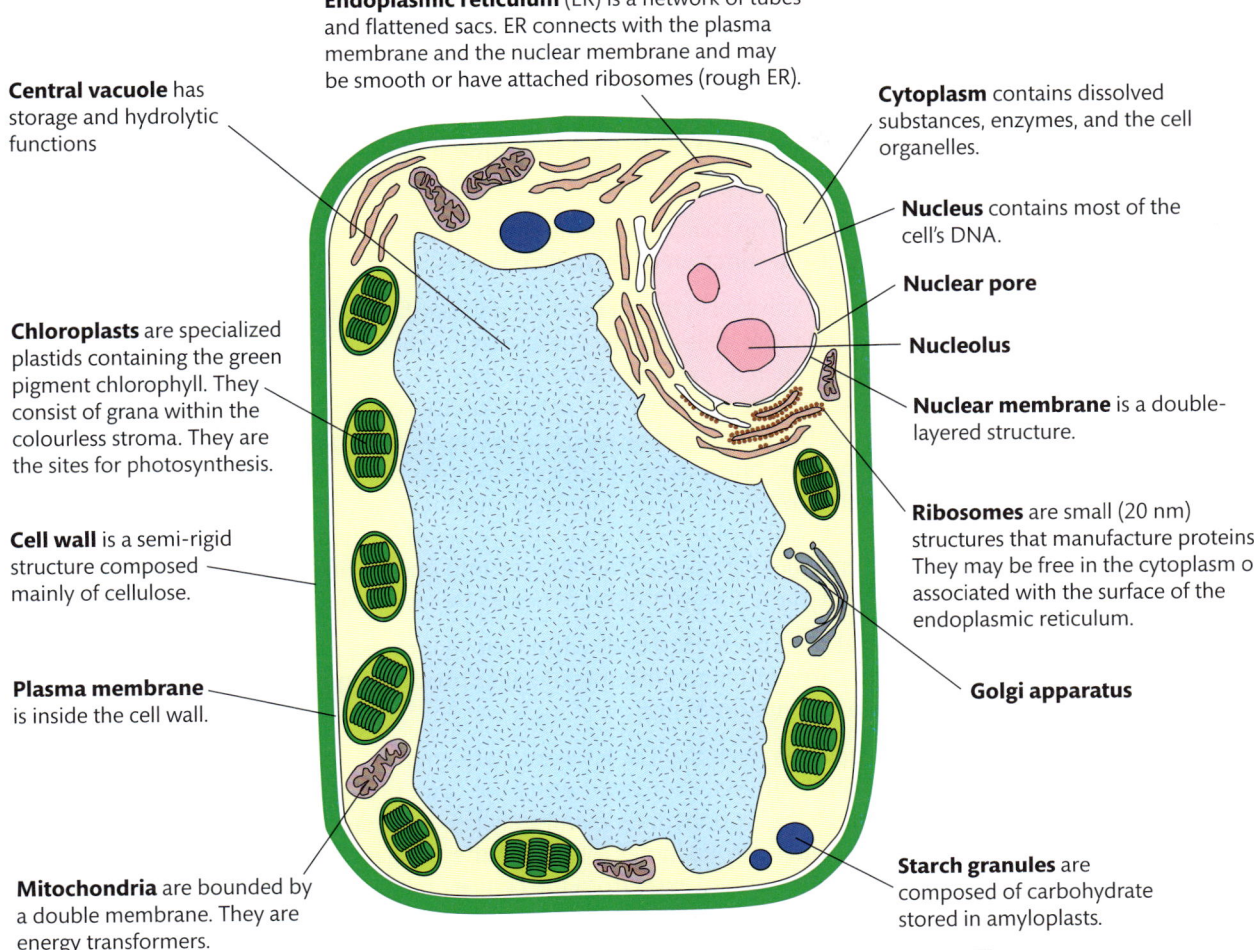

Figure 1.5 *Generalized plant eukaryotic cell*

- The compartments formed in eukaryotic cells are separated from the cell cytoplasm and other structures of the cell by at least one plasma membrane.
- The structures formed by these compartments are called **organelles**.
- The plasma membranes which form compartments are very similar to the plasma membrane which occurs on the outside of the eukaryotic cell. Plant cells are eukaryotic. Most plant cells have a cell wall outside their plasma membrane. Animal cells are also eukaryotic cells. They do not have a cell wall.
- Compartmentalization allows greater efficiency for chemical reactions which occur in specific regions of the eukaryotic cell.
- Ribosomes are unique structures which occur in both prokaryotic and eukaryotic cells. The ribosomes of eukaryotic cells are greater in mass than the ribosomes of prokaryotic cells. Ribosomes of prokaryotic cells are 70S. Ribosomes of eukaryotic cells are 80S.
- The figures above represent the ultrastructure of animal and plant eukaryotic cells. Most of the ultrastructure of a eukaryotic cell is visible only with an electron microscope.
- The DNA of the eukaryotic cell's nucleus is combined with protein. The DNA of prokaryotic cells is not combined with any other compound.

Subject vocabulary

organelles non-cellular structures within a cell which carry out organ-like processes

Skill: Drawing the ultrastructure of eukaryotic cells

Study both the plant and animal cell figures so you can draw each with all structures properly labelled. The structures and organelles in these drawings must be of correct relative size. They must also be in the correct cell position.

1 Cell biology

Subject vocabulary

exocrine gland a gland that secretes a substance into a duct for transport

enzyme a protein that acts as a catalyst

duct a small tube

intestine digestive system part involved in breakdown of food

Golgi apparatus cell organelle involved in the storage, modification, and packaging of proteins

endoplasmic reticulum organelle involved in transport within the cell

mitochondrion (plural: mitochondria) cell organelle(s) involved in cell respiration

palisade mesophyll cells cells in the middle section of leaves specialized for carrying out photosynthesis

chloroplasts organelles involved in carrying out photosynthesis

photosynthesis process which converts light energy into chemical energy

vacuoles cell storage structures especially visible in plants

starch large molecule made up of many sugars chemically bonded to one another

Synonyms

modifications . changes/alterations

Skill: Interpretation of electron micrographs to identify organelles and deduce the function of specialized cells

Study electron micrographs of both plant and animal cells. Practise correctly labelling the structures and organelles shown in these micrographs.

Nature of science: It took the development of the electron microscope to form an understanding of the ultrastructure of the cell.

Application: The pancreas is able to act as an **exocrine gland** due to the structure and function of certain cell parts

The pancreas has cells which produce and send chemicals called **enzymes** into specialized tubes called **ducts**. These enzymes help in the digestion of food in the **intestine**. Pancreas exocrine cells have the following **modifications** to accomplish this task: increased number and activity of ribosomes, increased development and activity of the **Golgi apparatus**, more extensive **endoplasmic reticulum** within the cytoplasm, and a larger number of **mitochondria**. The mitochondria provide the energy necessary for the increased production of enzymes which occurs in the ribosomes. The Golgi apparatus is very active in the final preparation and packaging of the enzymes for release from the cell into ducts. The endoplasmic reticulum is important in the transportation of necessary raw materials within the cell.

Application: Specialized cells within the leaf called **palisade mesophyll cells** are able to carry out high amounts of sugar production which is necessary for plant growth and maintenance

These palisade mesophyll cells contain large numbers of **chloroplasts** which carry out **photosynthesis**. Photosynthesis is the plant process which uses light energy to produce the carbohydrate commonly known as sugar. These plant cells will also have few, but large, **vacuoles** for storing these sugars as **starch**. In these plant cells, the nucleus is pushed away from the centre of the cell by the large vacuole(s).

Hints for success: Use a pencil to practise drawing plant and animal cells. Your drawing must include the following structures and organelles in their proper cell position and their proper relative size: 80S ribosomes, nucleus, mitochondria, plasma membrane, cell wall (if a plant cell), chloroplast (if a plant cell), endoplasmic reticulum, Golgi apparatus, lysosomes (if an animal cell), and centrioles (if an animal cell). It is very important to know the internal parts and function of all the structures and organelles of the cell. Use the following summary table to study the parts and functions of eukaryotic cells.

Organelle or location name	Major function	Organism type
cytoplasm	contains the organelles	plant and animal
endoplasmic reticulum (ER)	transportation	plant and animal
rough ER	protein transportation, processing, and packaging, along with cell support	plant and animal
smooth ER	lipid synthesis, transportation, and packaging, along with cell support	plant and animal
ribosomes	protein synthesis	plant and animal
lysosomes	intracellular digestion	animal and some plants

Organelle or location name	Major function	Organism type
Golgi apparatus	storage, packaging, and transport	plant and animal
mitochondria	ATP generation	plant and animal
nucleus	control centre containing chromosomes	plant and animal
chloroplasts	photosynthesis	plant
centrosome	region that aids in cell division	plant and animal (but no centrioles in plants)
vacuole	storage	most obvious in plants
		similar smaller structures in animal cells are called vesicles and tend to be temporary

1.3 Membrane structure

Main idea
All cellular membranes have a structure that allows them to be flexible and active in cellular activities.

Understanding: **Phospholipids** form **bilayers** in water due to the **amphipathic** properties of phospholipid molecules.

Model sentence: Phospholipids form the foundation of cellular membranes and have regions of different solubility properties with water.

- Phospholipids are made up of three parts: a phosphate group, a glycerol molecule, and two fatty acids.
- The phosphate region of the phospholipid is **polar**, while the fatty acid region is **non-polar**.
- In the figure notice the polar region is said to be **hydrophilic**. The hydrophilic region associates freely with water.
- The fatty acid region of the molecule shown in the figure is **hydrophobic**. This region does not associate freely with water.
- Two layers of phospholipids form the foundation of cellular membranes. The hydrophobic regions of each phospholipid bilayer attract one another when placed in water.

Subject vocabulary

ATP a molecule used for a source of chemical energy

phospholids lipids formed from two fatty acids, a phosphate group, and glycerol; important component of cell membranes

amphipathic molecule with both hydrophobic and hydrophilic regions

polar having a region of electrical charge

non-polar region of no electrical charge

hydrophilic 'water loving', substances that dissolve in water

hydrophobic 'water fearing', substances that do not dissolve in water

General vocabulary

bilayer structure composed of two layers

solubility ability of a substance to dissolve

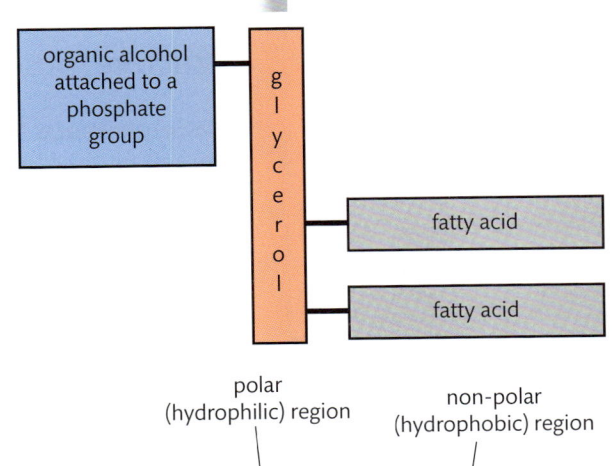

Figure 1.6 *This is a model of a phospholipid*

1 Cell biology

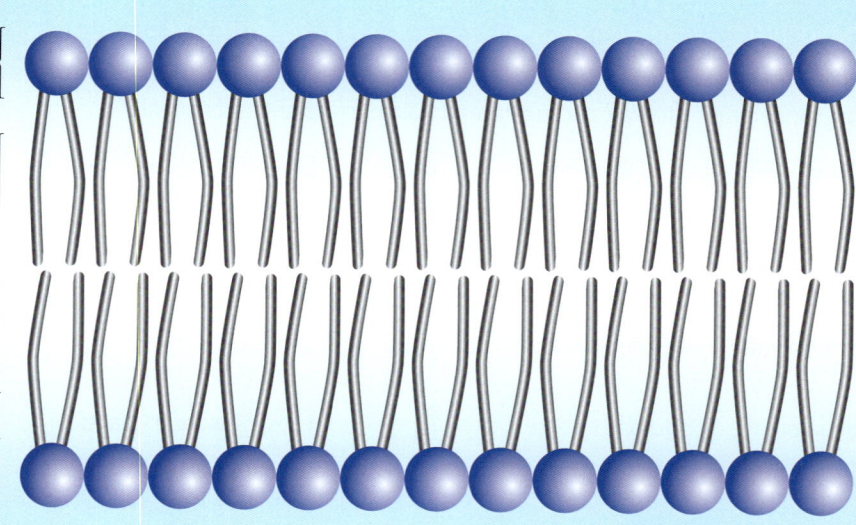

Figure 1.7 *A model of the phospholipid bilayer in cellular membranes*

- The hydrophilic parts of the two layers face outward where there is water present.
- Since the phospholipid molecule has both hydrophobic and hydrophilic regions, it is said to be amphipathic.

> **Hints for success:** Remember when it comes to solubility, hydrophilic compounds and regions associate freely with other hydrophilic compounds and regions. The same is true for hydrophobic compounds and regions. Hydrophobic and hydrophilic compounds and regions do not associate freely with one another. Because most cellular membranes are surrounded by water, the hydrophilic portions of the amphipathic phospholipids are positioned toward water, while the hydrophobic portions are positioned toward each other and away from water.

Understanding: Membrane **proteins** are diverse in terms of structure, position in the membrane, and function.

Model sentence: Various kinds of proteins occur at different positions within the cell membrane and carry out many different functions.

There are two major types of proteins seen when observing their position in membranes. **Peripheral** proteins occur on the external or internal surfaces of the phospholipid bilayer and are hydrophilic. **Integral** proteins occur completely through the phospholipid bilayer and have amphipathic properties. Observe these two types of proteins in the following diagram.

Each of the different proteins in the membrane has a specific function. Some of the functions of these proteins are cell **adhesion**, enzyme action, **active transport**, **passive transport**, communication between cells, and **hormone** interaction. Some of these proteins have carbohydrate chains attached to them. When proteins are attached to carbohydrates the combined structure is called a **glycoprotein**.

Subject vocabulary

proteins biochemical compounds composed of large numbers of amino acids connected by peptide bonds

active transport cellular transport requiring energy from the cell

passive transport cellular transport not requiring cellular energy to occur, occurs along a concentration gradient

hormone chemical messenger produced in very small amounts in one area, used to send messages to other areas

glycoprotein combination of a carbohydrate and a protein

General vocabulary

peripheral at the edge

integral membrane protein present in both layers of the membrane

adhesion process where two different substances stick together or attach to one another

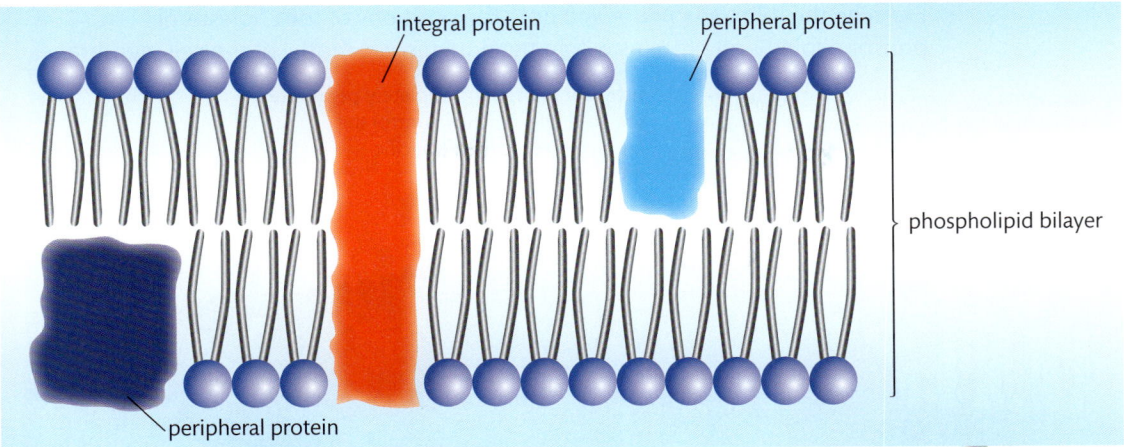

Figure 1.8 *Positions of proteins in the cell membrane*

Skill: **Analysis of evidence from electron microscopy led to the proposal of the Davson–Danielli model**

Early studies of the cell membrane indicated they were largely made up of proteins and phospholipids. Using this information, Davson and Danielli produced the first model of the cell membrane, the Davson–Danielli model. These scientists used relative amounts and solubility properties of proteins and phospholipids to form a model with a phospholipid bilayer on the inside surrounded by a thin protein layer on both surfaces. It was simply a protein–phospholipid–protein sandwich.

Singer and Nicolson modified the Davson–Danielli model of the cell membrane. They based their modified model on:

- Electron microscope observations of the cell membrane.
- Cell membranes differ in their composition.
- Cell membranes are asymmetrical.
- Membranes with different functions have different structure and composition.
- Proteins do not form a layer. They are only found at certain locations within the phospholipid bilayer.
- Evidence from freeze fracture studies shows proteins often occur inside the membrane.

Singer and Nicolson used the modifications of the Davson–Danielli model to produce the Singer–Nicolson model. This model has been slightly changed over recent years to produce the present cell membrane model, which is known as the fluid **mosaic** model.

Understanding: Cholesterol is a component of animal cell membranes.

Model sentence: Animal cell membranes contain cholesterol in their structure. Plant cell membranes do not contain cholesterol in their structure.

The cholesterol component of animal cell membranes allows these membranes to work effectively over a wide range of temperatures. The cholesterol contributes to the fluid or flexible characteristic of the membrane. The cholesterol acts as a fluidity **buffer** in which it keeps the fluidity of the cell membrane within proper limits for *optimum* function. The cholesterol molecules occur at various locations within the hydrophobic region of the animal cell membrane.

General vocabulary

mosaic structure made up of visible smaller pieces

buffer something that prevents or slows change

Subject vocabulary

cholesterol a lipid steroid found in animal membranes

Examine the following figure and note the positions of the cholesterol, phospholipids, and proteins within the fluid mosaic model of the cell membrane.

Glycoproteins are composed of carbohydrate chains attached to peripheral proteins. They play a role in recognition of like cells and are involved in immune responses.

Integral proteins completely penetrate the lipid bilayer. They control the entry and removal of specific molecules from the cell.

phospholipid bilayer

Cholesterol helps to regulate membrane fluidity and is important for membrane stability.

Some polar substances, particularly ions and carbohydrates, are transported across the membrane via the channel proteins.

Some non-polar substances are transported directly through the lipid bilayer.

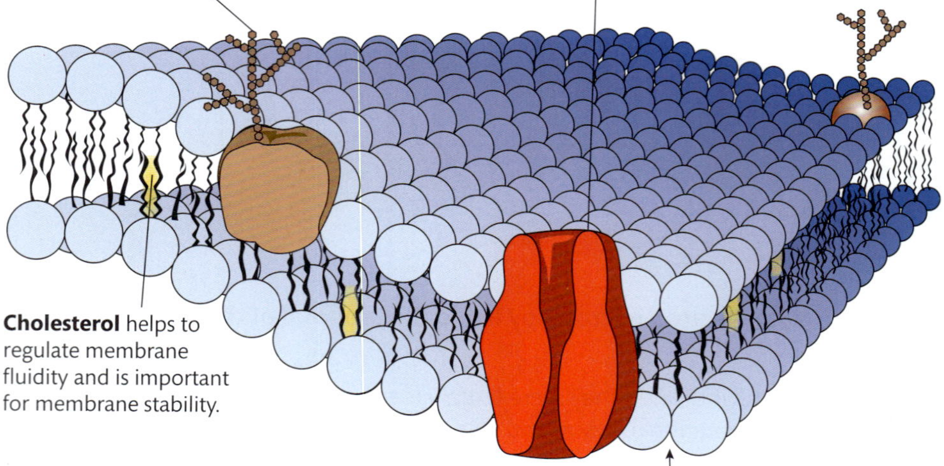

Figure 1.9 *In the fluid mosaic model of the cell membrane there is a double layer of lipids (fats) arranged with their tails facing inwards. Proteins are thought to 'float' in the lipid bilayer*

Plant cells do not have membranes containing cholesterol. The membranes of plant cells depend on modifications of their phospholipid fatty acid tails to maintain a fluid or flexible characteristic.

> **Hints for success:** Recognize that it is because of detailed analysis that we now recognize the best representation of cell membranes is the fluid mosaic model. This model is named fluid mosaic because:
>
> Fluid – this term is used because phospholipid molecules allow a flexible or fluid basic structure. Animal membranes have cholesterol which helps in maintaining their optimum flexibility. Plant membranes do not.
>
> Mosaic – proteins occur in patches or as single proteins 'floating' in the phospholipid bilayer producing a mosaic appearance.
>
> Remember that carbohydrates can be attached to both proteins and lipids. Carbohydrates are sometimes found attached to membrane lipids and proteins as short, branched chains. When carbohydrates are attached to lipids, **glycolipids** are formed. When carbohydrates are attached to proteins, glycoproteins are formed.

Subject vocabulary

glycolipid combination of a carbohydrate and a protein

Skill: Drawing of the fluid mosaic model

Study the diagram of the fluid mosaic model. Practise drawing it with the following structures correctly labelled: phospholipids, integral proteins, peripheral proteins, glycolipids, glycoproteins, and cholesterol. All structures must be properly positioned within the drawing to earn marks in the exam. Always show the structure of a phospholipid as a circle with two parallel tails attached.

1.4 Membrane transport

Main idea
Membranes control **homeostasis** and functions within the cell.

Understanding: Particles move across membranes by simple diffusion, facilitated diffusion, osmosis, and active transport.

Diffusion and **osmosis** are types of passive transport. Passive transport does not require energy from the cell when it occurs. Passive transport is movement of particles from an area of high concentration to an area of low concentration of the same type of particles. These two areas of different concentrations of the same particles produce a **concentration gradient**. Study this table.

Type of passive transport	Description of movement at the membrane	Example
simple diffusion	Particles of substances other than water move between membrane phospholipid molecules or through integral proteins which possess **channels**.	oxygen moving through plasma membrane along a concentration gradient
facilitated diffusion	Proteins of the membrane form an attachment to the particles and move them through the membrane. The proteins which attach to the particles are called **carriers**. Facilitated diffusion does not describe water movement.	glucose moving into cells involving a carrier **potassium channels** allowing potassium to move along a concentration gradient in **nerve cells**
osmosis	Osmosis allows movement of water molecules through membranes. Water may move through aquaporins which are proteins with specialized channels. Water may also move directly through the membrane.	water moving in and out of the cell to keep the proper water concentration in the cell

The **sodium–potassium pump**, **endocytosis**, and **exocytosis** are types of active transport. For active transport to occur, the cell must provide energy in the form of ATP. Active transport does not require a concentration gradient to occur. Study this table.

Type of active transport	Description of movement at the membrane	Example
sodium–potassium pump	A protein binds with sodium and potassium to move them through a membrane against a concentration gradient. Sodium is transported out of the cell and potassium is transported into the cell.	functions in nerve cells and allows their continual action

Subject vocabulary

homeostasis steady or controlled state

diffusion movement along a concentration gradient not requiring cell energy

osmosis movement of water through a membrane along a concentration gradient

concentration gradient(s) change(s) in a chemical concentration between two areas of chemical concentrations

carrier substance which helps in the movement of another material, usually involving proteins in the plasma membrane

potassium channels transmembrane proteins that allow potassium ions to move in or out of a cell

nerve cells neurones

sodium–potassium pump process carried out by membrane proteins which keep sodium and potassium at proper levels

endocytosis active transport in which substances are brought into the cell

exocytosis active transport in which substances are lost from the cell

General vocabulary

channels openings in a larger object

Type of active transport	Description of movement at the membrane	Example
exocytosis	A membrane from a **vesicle** fuses with a plasma membrane to allow release of the vesicle's contents to the cell exterior.	release of **insulin** from **pancreas** cells into the bloodstream
endocytosis	The plasma membrane forms around a substance forming a vesicle or vacuole and allowing the substance to enter the cell interior.	fluids and small particles brought into the cell by **pinocytosis**; larger particles and substances are brought into the cell by **phagocytosis**

A change in membrane shape is visible in both pinocytosis and phagocytosis. Pinocytosis involves a small **deformation** of the membrane called invagination in which a small channel forms and material from the cell exterior flows into the channel. Pinocytosis results in the temporary formation of smaller storage structures. Phagocytosis involves a much more obvious change in membrane shape. The membrane will actually flow around a substance on the cell exterior to form a larger temporary storage structure.

Subject vocabulary

vesicle smaller storage structure surrounded by a membrane in cells

insulin hormone produced and released by exocytosis from the pancreas which controls glucose absorption by cells

pancreas an organ within the body that has many functions including production of three important digestive enzymes

pinocytosis active transport in which fluids and small particles are brought into the cell

phagocytosis active transport in which larger particles and substances are brought into the cell

sterile free of disease-causing organisms and viruses

isotonic solutions solutions with equal concentrations of solutes and solvents

solute(s) molecules dissolved in a solvent (water)

General vocabulary

deformation a change in shape

irrigating applying water

Synonyms

fusing .... merging

Understanding: The fluidity of membranes allows materials to be taken into cells by endocytosis or released by exocytosis. Vesicles move materials within cells.

Model sentence: Endocytosis and exocytosis require membrane fluidity to occur.

Membranes may change shape. The fluidity, which gives them the ability to change shape, allows them to form vesicles transporting substances from outside the cell into the cell interior. The property of fluidity also allows the **fusing** of vesicles with the plasma membrane. The fusing of vesicles with the plasma membrane allows materials produced inside the cell to be released to the cell exterior.

Application: Irrigating the eye

A **sterile** solution of 0.9% sodium chloride in water is best to use when irrigating the eye. This concentration is very similar to the concentration of water and chemicals inside the cells of the eye exterior. Because the concentrations are very similar there will be no significant fluid loss or gain in the cells of the eye during the irrigation. This allows the eye cells to maintain homeostasis. A similar solution may be used to irrigate skin wounds so that little damage will be done to exposed cells due to fluid gain or loss. The gain or loss of water in cells when not using the proper concentration of irrigating solution would be due to osmosis.

Skill: Investigating differing concentrations of solute

A required lab for this section involves the effect of differing concentrations of solute in water on living cells. Potato cells are often used for this lab. In the lab, several key observations are required:

- In **isotonic solutions** (solution has same concentration of **solutes** as are in the potato cells), potato cell mass remains the same. This indicates homeostasis between the cell and the surrounding solution with no net gain or loss of water.

- In **hypotonic solutions** (solution has a lower concentration of solutes in water than that inside the potato cells), potato cell mass will increase. This increase in mass is because water moves from outside to inside the potato cells.
- In **hypertonic solutions** (solution has a higher concentration of solutes in water than the solute concentration inside the potato cells), the mass of the potato cells will decrease. This decrease in mass is because water moves from inside the cell to outside the cell.

Knowing these principles, one can estimate the **osmolarity** (solute concentration) in cells using solutions of known osmolarity. The solution concentration with the least gain or loss of mass in the cells used is the most accurate osmolarity of the cells.

Application: **Structure and function of sodium–potassium pumps for active transport and potassium channels for facilitated diffusion in axons**

The sodium–potassium pump has several features which maintain proper sodium and potassium ion concentrations within nerve cells at rest.

These are that:
- An integral protein exists in the nerve cell membrane which is involved in the sodium–potassium pump.
- Three sodium ions attach to the open protein on the interior surface of the membrane.
- When ATP attaches to the protein, the protein changes shape and opens to the exterior of the cell membrane.
- When this happens, the three sodium ions are released to the exterior of the cell. Then two potassium ions attach to the open end of the protein.
- Next, the phosphate from ATP is released from the interior of the protein. The result of this is the protein now opens on the inside of the cell membrane. The potassium ions are then released to the interior of the cell.

Hints for success: The sodium–potassium pump transports three positively charged sodium ions to the outside of the cell. Immediately after, it transports two positively charged potassium ions to the inside of the cell. The result of this is a slightly negative charge inside the cell.

> **Subject vocabulary**
>
> **hypotonic solution** a solution with a lower concentration of solute and a higher concentration of solvent
>
> **hypertonic solution** a solution with a higher concentration of solute and a lower concentration of solvent
>
> **osmolarity** solute concentration

1.5 The origin of cells

Main idea
The cells we see in organisms today have arisen from the first cells which appeared on Earth.

Understanding: **Cells can only be formed by division of pre-existing cells.**

Model sentence: **The cell theory states that new cells only come from already existing cells by a process of division.**

One reason for saying all cells are related by a common ancestor is the similarity of the genetic code in cells. There are 64 code terms (codons) observed in all studied cells today. Each of these codes in all cells observed has the same meaning. There are only minor changes in this code in some cells. These minor changes indicate a common beginning for all cells.

The slight changes in the DNA code are explained by mutations. Mutations are structural changes which occur to DNA.

> **Hints for study:** The hereditary material of life is DNA. It is a molecule which does not often change. When it does change, a mutation is said to occur. These changes occur at a relatively constant rate. The longer the time between the first cells on Earth and the present cells, the more changes will be in the DNA. Very closely related cells or organisms will show very little difference in their DNA.

Understanding: The first cells must have arisen from non-living material.

Model sentence: A major part of the cell theory is to explain how the very first cells formed on Earth.

- We have not observed non-living materials giving rise to living cells. The production of living cells from non-living sources is called **spontaneous generation**.
- The first cells on Earth were most likely very simple. However, these simple cells had to have demonstrated the functions of life.

Application: Evidence from Pasteur's experiments that spontaneous generation of cells and organisms does not now occur on Earth

Louis Pasteur used nutrient broth in different types of flasks to show spontaneous generation of cells and organisms does not occur today.

Understanding: The origin of eukaryotic cells can be explained by the **endosymbiotic theory**.

Model sentence: The endosymbiotic theory is an explanation of how a compartmentalized, complex cell may result from a non-compartmentalized simple cell.

Major points of the endosymbiotic theory:
- Very simple, non-compartmentalized cells existed 2 billion years ago.
- A smaller prokaryote cell was **engulfed** by a larger existing cell and survived.
- The two cells formed a symbiotic relationship in which both were helped. **Symbiosis** refers to a close relationship between two unrelated organisms.
- As time proceeded, the cells changed resulting in an even stronger positive relationship between them. The beneficial symbiotic relationship between two organisms is referred to as **mutualism**.

Evidence for the endosymbiotic theory:
- Organelles such as mitochondria and chloroplasts are about the same size as bacterial cells.
- Mitochondria and chloroplasts divide by fission as do bacterial cells.
- Mitochondria and chloroplasts divide independently of the overall cell.
- Mitochondria and chloroplasts have their own DNA which is very similar in code to bacterial DNA.
- Mitochondria and chloroplasts have two membranes on their exterior.

Subject vocabulary

spontaneous generation the disproven idea that living organisms can arise from non-living sources

endosymbiotic theory a theory which attempts to explain the formation of a complex cell from simple cells

symbiosis condition in which two or more species have a close relationship

mutualism a type of symbiotic relationship where two different species benefit from a relationship they have with each other

Synonyms

engulfed .... surrounded

Nature of science: There is a need to replicate how the first cells formed on Earth. This will most likely be done when scientists can assemble all the non-living components of life in the laboratory and produce a living cell. It is possible that some other explanation than spontaneous generation for the first cells on Earth will be found. This explanation would have to be based on proper scientific observation and experimentation.

1.6 Cell division

Main idea

Cell division is an essential process. However, it must be controlled or a condition called **cancer** may occur.

Understanding: Cell division involves both **mitosis** and **cytokinesis**.

Model sentence: For controlled cell division to occur, mitosis and cytokinesis are both necessary.

- Mitosis refers to division of the nucleus.
- Cytokinesis involves division of the cytoplasm.

Hints for success: If a cell is to successfully divide, it must include division of the nucleus and the cytoplasm. Controlled and proper division of both cell parts is essential for the continuation of the cell and the well-being of the organism. If cell division becomes uncontrolled, large numbers of abnormal cells may be produced. This condition is called cancer.

Understanding: Mitosis is division of the nucleus into two genetically identical daughter nuclei.

Model sentence: The DNA of the two nuclei produced by mitosis is an exact copy of the original nucleus.

DNA replication in the process of mitosis is very accurate. Rarely, changes occur in the process of copying DNA in mitosis. These changes are called mutations. Most of the time mutations are bad for the cell and organisms. Mutations are often **lethal**.

Hints for success: It is important to remember that mitosis only occurs in eukaryotic cells. Since prokaryotic cells do not have a nucleus, they cannot go through mitosis.

Synonyms

replicate .... copy/repeat

Subject vocabulary

cancer disease involving uncontrolled abnormal cell growth

mitosis cell division where one diploid cell becomes two diploid cells

cytokinesis division of the cytoplasm in cell division

General vocabulary

lethal causing the end of life functions, death

Subject vocabulary

condense process of shortening and thickening

chromatid the identical parts of a doubled chromosomes held together by a centromere

centromere region where sister chromatids attach

sister chromatids the two identical structures of a doubled chromosome

mitotic spindle microtubules which form in the cell division process

General vocabulary

equator middle region of an object

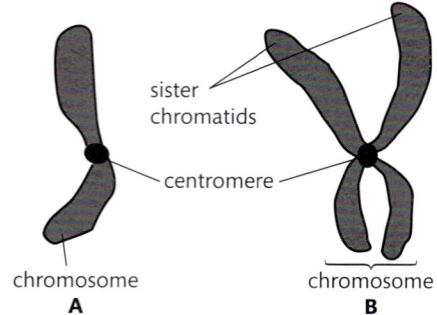

Figure 1.10 *Comparison of a non-doubled and doubled chromosome*

Understanding: Chromosomes **condense** by supercoiling during mitosis.

Model sentence: Chromosome condensation by supercoiling is necessary for mitosis to occur efficiently.

- Supercoiling is the wrapping process DNA goes through to become condensed enough for mitosis to proceed. DNA is first coiled around spherical proteins called histones. Then it continues to be folded, coiled, and condensed enough to form a chromosome. It is the movement of chromosomes that is described in mitosis.
- DNA that is not supercoiled into chromosomes represents active DNA. Active DNA is DNA carrying out the life activities of the cell. If chromosomes are not present in the nucleus of a cell, that cell is not going through mitosis.
- Before mitosis may occur, two things must happen to the DNA:
  - DNA must be replicated or doubled.
  - DNA must supercoil to form chromosomes.
- In the diagram both **A** and **B** represent chromosomes. Example **A** is a chromosome in which the DNA has not been replicated. Example **B** is a chromosome in which the DNA has been replicated. Example **B** is often referred to as a doubled chromosome. Each identical part of a doubled chromosome is called a **chromatid**. The chromatids are attached to one another by the **centromere**. These attached chromatids are often called **sister chromatids**. Example **B** is the doubled chromosome which enters the process of mitosis. Example **A** represents a chromosome at the conclusion of mitosis.
- The stages of mitosis with their major events are:

Stage of mitosis	Major events
prophase	Chromosomes condense and become visible with the microscope, nuclear membrane disappears, **mitotic spindle** forms.
metaphase	Mitotic spindle fibres line the centromere of the chromosomes along the **equator** of the cell.
anaphase	Doubled chromosomes which are composed of two sister chromatids split at the centromere, the separated chromatids are now called chromosomes, these separated chromatids move toward opposite poles of the cell.
telophase	Mitotic spindle disappears, nuclear membrane reforms, chromosomes go through a process of uncoiling to produce the active form of DNA called chromatin, and two identical nuclei are produced.

Hints for success: Condensed DNA in the form of chromosomes can be efficiently managed during mitosis to produce two daughter nuclei which are genetically identical. Mitosis involves four stages. These stages represent the major changes chromosomes go through in nuclear division.

Skill: Identification of phases of mitosis in cells viewed with a microscope or in a micrograph

Identify the stages of mitosis while viewing squashes made of living plant root cells. These stages can be viewed by using a light microscope. Roots of plants grow relatively rapidly. Squashes of plant root cells may be performed to view the location of chromosomes in the various stages of mitosis.

You may also use micrographs to practise identifying the various stages.

Understanding: Cytokinesis occurs after mitosis and is different in plant and animal cells.

Model sentence: In cell division, mitosis occurs first and is followed by cytokinesis.

Cytokinesis involves division of the cytoplasm in the cell division process. Cytokinesis occurs immediately after mitosis. Cytokinesis occurs differently in plant and animal cells.

- In plant cells, the cell wall is involved in the process of cytokinesis. A **cell plate** forms about **midway** between the two groups of chromosomes. These two identical groups of chromosomes are the result of mitosis. The cell plate begins to form in the central area of the cell. It then continues to form towards both sides of the cell. This proceeds until the cell with two nuclei is separated into two halves. Each half is now a cell with one nucleus and is called a **daughter cell**.
- In animal cells, there is no cell wall and a cell plate is not involved in cytokinesis. Cytokinesis in animal cells occurs when the plasma membrane pinches inward from the outside. The pinching inward continues until the cytoplasm of the one cell with two nuclei is separated into two halves. Each half is now a cell with one nucleus and is called a daughter cell.

Subject vocabulary

cell plate structure which forms in plant cells to allow cytokinesis to occur

daughter cells cells produced as a result of cell division

General vocabulary

midway halfway through

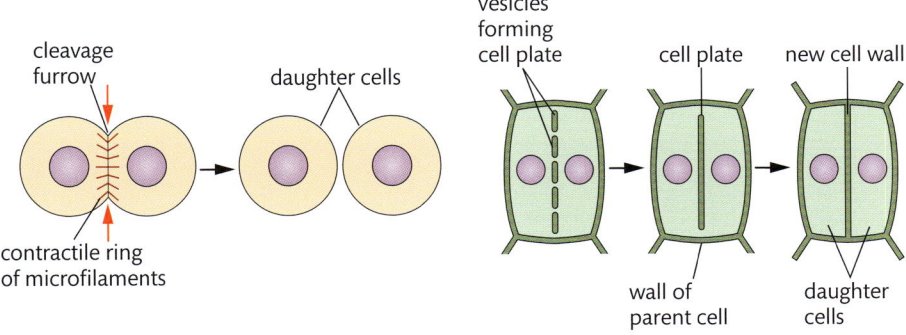

Cleavage of an animal cell

Cell plate formation in a plant cell

Figure 1.11 *Cytokinesis in animal and plant cells*

Hints for success: The process of cytokinesis in cell division is different in plant and animal cells because plant cells have a cell wall and animal cells do not. The formation of the cell wall must be explained in questions involving plant cell cytokinesis. Animal cell cytokinesis is explained by only describing the action of the plasma membrane.

Subject vocabulary

interphase stage in the life of a cell in which it is carrying out activities other than cell division

cell cycle the stages in the life of a cell

parent cell cell which gives rise to daughter cells in cell division

cyclin group of proteins which control the cell's progression through the cell cycle

kinase enzymes which may activate or deactivate other proteins by catalyzing a chemical reaction in which phosphate is added to these proteins

G_0 cell cycle stage, some cells are said to be in when they do not progress beyond the G_1 phase

Understanding: Interphase is a very active phase of the cell cycle with many processes occurring in the nucleus and cytoplasm.

Model sentence: The cell goes through a series of phases called the cell cycle in its life with the most active phase called interphase.

- The cell cycle includes three major parts. They are:
  - interphase
  - mitosis
  - cytokinesis.
- Mitosis and cytokinesis together are referred to as cell division. They involve the production of two daughter cells by division of the nucleus and the cytoplasm of a **parent cell**.
- Interphase is usually the longest lasting phase of the cell cycle. Interphase is the phase when the cell carries out all the cell functions other than cell division. Interphase is a very active phase in which the following occurs:
  - Organelles increase in number.
  - The cell increases in overall size.
  - In multicellular organisms, the cell carries out functions necessary for the well-being of the organism.
- Study the figure closely noting that interphase makes up most of the cell's life.
- Interphase of the cell cycle is divided into three shorter phases as shown in the figure. Each phase has specific actions occurring. The following table relates interphase phases to main actions.

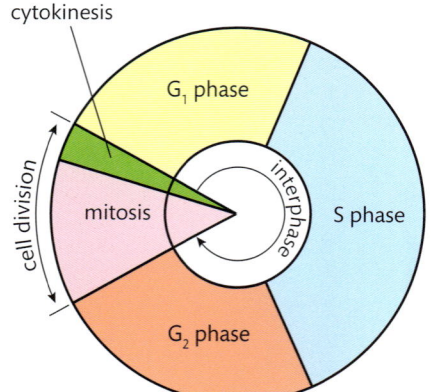

Figure 1.12 *The eukaryotic cell cycle*

Phase of interphase	Major action of phase
G_1	Overall growth of cell occurs in this phase.
S	DNA of the cell is replicated.
G_2	Cell continues to grow with organelles increasing in number. Preparations are occurring for mitosis to begin. DNA begins to condense into chromosomes.

Hints for success: Study the cell cycle diagram and the table of the phases of the cell cycle. Be aware of the major occurrences within each phase. Note that during interphase the cell carries out its specialized functions which are necessary for the well-being of the organism.

Understanding: Cyclins are involved in the control of the cell cycle.

Model sentence: Cyclins are proteins which control the progress of the cell through the cell cycle.

- **Cyclins** bind to other proteins called **kinases** at specific points of the cell cycle.
- When the binding of a cyclin with kinase occurs, the cell moves into the next phase of the cell cycle.
- Some cells never progress past G_1 of interphase. Human nerve and muscle cells remain in G_1 throughout their life. These cells grow very little in their lifetime. These cells are said to be in a phase referred to as **G_0**.

Understanding: Mutagens, oncogenes, and metastasis are involved in the development of primary and secondary tumours.

Model sentence: Many factors may be involved in causing a cell to begin going through uncontrolled cell division; this may result in a cancerous tumour.

- A **tumour** is a mass of abnormal cells in an organism. The cells in a tumour do not carry out tasks necessary for the well-being of the organism.
- A **primary tumour** occurs at the original site of the cancer. A **secondary tumour** is produced when cells from a primary tumour move to a different site resulting in an additional tumour or tumours.
- The spreading of cancer cells is called **metastasis**.
- **Oncogenes** are sections of DNA in a normal cell which may become active and contribute to the development of a cancer cell. These oncogenes may become active through a change or mutation caused by an outside agent. The outside agent which **activates** the oncogene is called a **mutagen**.
- Cigarette smoke shows a **positive correlation** with the occurrence of certain types of cancers.
- Components of cigarette smoke appear to have a high positive correlation in the occurrence of cancers of the **trachea**, **bronchi**, and **lungs**. These components of cigarette smoke are considered mutagens.

Skill: Determination of a mitotic index from a micrograph

The **mitotic index** is an important tool in predicting the success of **chemotherapy** in the treatment of a cancer. The mitotic index is determined as follows:

- Obtain a micrograph or microscope slide of a tumour section.
- Count the number of cells showing chromosomes in the four stages of mitosis.
- Count the number of cells in which chromosomes are not visible. These cells are not going through mitosis.
- Determine the ratio of the number of cells undergoing mitosis compared to the number of cells not going through mitosis. This is the mitotic index.
- A high mitotic index (ratio) indicates a low success in the chemotherapy treatment of the cancer.

Hints for success: Uncontrolled cell division is not good for the well-being of the organism. It may result in the development of cancers. Oncogenes present in the nucleus of a cell may be acted upon by mutagens to bring about uncontrolled cell division and primary tumours. Primary tumours may go through metastasis to produce secondary tumours.

Subject vocabulary

tumour mass of cancerous cells

primary tumour first site of a cancer

secondary tumour sites of cancer in an organism which originated at a primary site

metastasis spreading process of the cells of a tumour

oncogenes segments of DNA which when active may contribute to the development of a cancer

mutagens chemicals capable of causing changes in DNA

positive correlation two factors that both increase together or decrease together

trachea section of the respiratory system which carries air to the bronchi

bronchi respiratory structure which carries air from the trachea into the lungs

lungs major respiratory organs in many organisms

mitotic index ratio of the number of cells undergoing mitosis to cells not undergoing mitosis in a tumour section

chemotherapy treatment of cancer involving chemicals

General vocabulary

activates makes active

2 Molecular biology

2.1 Molecules to metabolism

Understanding: The chemistry of living organisms is called molecular biology.

Model sentence: Molecular biology can be thought of as all of the chemical reactions within a living cell.

Living organisms must do many activities to stay alive. Cells of living organisms must do the following chemical processes:

- **Replicate** their DNA.
- Use sugars and other substances as fuels for energy (**cell respiration**).
- **Synthesize** their own proteins.
- Produce sugars using the energy of sunlight (**photosynthesis**).

All of the molecules and reactions involved in the above processes are part of the metabolism of the organism. Think of metabolism as being the sum total of all chemical reactions in an organism.

Understanding: Carbon atoms form four covalent bonds leading to organic compounds of great diversity.

Model sentence: Many different types of organic compounds can form because the element carbon forms four covalent bonds.

The element carbon exists in all **organic substances**. Each time an atom of carbon bonds with another atom, the two atoms share electrons. This type of bond is known as a covalent bond:

- Carbon always forms four covalent bonds.
- Carbon frequently forms covalent bonds with other carbon atoms, oxygen atoms, nitrogen atoms, and hydrogen atoms.

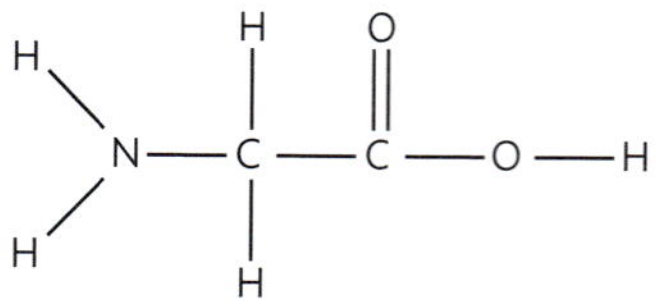

- C = carbon
- H = hydrogen
- O = oxygen
- N = nitrogen

Figure 2.1 *A diagram of a relatively small molecule important to cells. Notice that the two carbon atoms are surrounded by four covalent bonds each. Notice also that carbon is bonded to another carbon. In addition, carbon is bonded to nitrogen, oxygen, and hydrogen*

Synonyms

replicate .... copy/repeat

Subject vocabulary

DNA the molecule that determines which polypeptides are produced within cells

cell respiration chemical process used by cells to gain energy from sugars and other substances

photosynthesis process which converts light energy into chemical energy

covalent bond chemical bond in which electrons are shared

compound a molecule that contains at least two different kinds of elements

element a substance that is impossible to break down further by chemical means

organic substances a collection of carbon-based compounds found in living organisms

General vocabulary

synthesize produce from smaller building block units

diversity existing in many different types or forms

Understanding: Living things are made up of carbon compounds, including carbohydrates, lipids, proteins, and nucleic acids.

Model sentence: Carbohydrates, lipids, proteins, and nucleic acids are the four organic compound types found within living things.

Carbon compound	In brief	Common example
carbohydrates	molecules often referred to as sugars	glucose
lipids	fat when a solid, oil when a liquid	triglyceride
proteins	diverse functions	proteins making up muscles
nucleic acids	molecules most often used in genetics	DNA

Skill: Identification and drawings of common biochemically important molecules

Practise drawing and recognizing the following molecules. You will learn more about their functions and terminology in later units of study:

- alpha-D-glucose
- beta-D-glucose
- D-ribose
- a saturated fatty acid
- a generalized amino acid.

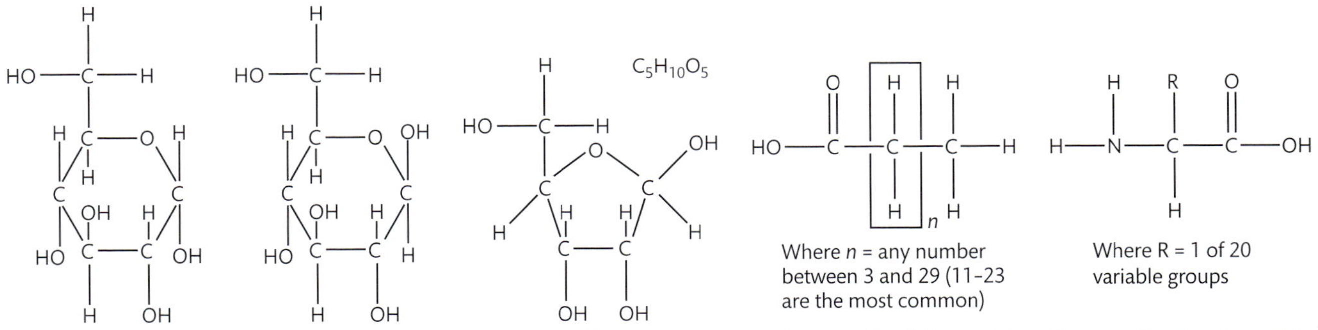

Alpha-D-glucose Beta-D-glucose D-ribose A generalized fatty acid A generalized amino acid

Figure 2.2 *Common molecular structures to practice*

Understanding: Metabolism is the term used for all of the enzyme-catalysed reactions in a cell or entire organism.

Model sentence: A cell's metabolism is very complex, as metabolism includes all of the reactions in the cell, with each reaction catalysed by an enzyme.

A catalyst is a substance that increases the rate of a reaction, but the catalyst is not considered a reactant or a product. A catalyst was there before the reaction began and it will still be there after the reaction is over. Thus, catalysts are reusable for many reactions.

When a catalyst is a protein molecule, the catalyst is called an enzyme. Each enzyme only catalyses one reaction. Many times the product of one reaction is catalysed

Subject vocabulary

glucose a simple sugar produced by photosynthesis and used for cell respiration

triglycerides fats or oils formed from three fatty acids and a glycerol molecule

genetics transfer of traits from parents to children

fatty acid one of the components of a lipid molecule

metabolism sum total of all reactions in a cell or organism

enzyme a protein that acts as a catalyst

catalyst molecule that increases the rate of a reaction without being consumed by the reaction

reactant one or more molecules that are used in a reaction to create one or more products

product those molecules that are formed as a result of a reaction

General vocabulary

terminology related technical words

reusable can be used many times for the same purpose

by another enzyme to create a second product. The second product may then be catalysed by a third enzyme and so on. This is called a 'chain of reactions'.

There can be many chains of reactions going on within a cell all at the same time. The sum total of all of these reactions is that cell's metabolism. The sum total of the metabolism of all of the cells is the metabolism of the organism.

> **Subject vocabulary**
>
> **anabolism** type of metabolism in which smaller compounds are used to build larger compounds in organisms
>
> **synthesis** constructing complex molecules from smaller, simpler ones
>
> **macromolecules** large, complex organic molecules
>
> **monomer** a 'building block' unit of a macromolecule
>
> **condensation reaction** a chemical reaction in which two monomers are bonded together to form a larger molecule
>
> **synthesized** chemically created
>
> **catabolism** type of metabolism in which larger compounds are broken down with the release of energy
>
> **hydrolysis** a chemical reaction in which a larger molecule is split into two smaller molecules

Understanding: **Anabolism** is the **synthesis** of complex molecules from simpler molecules, including the formation of **macromolecules** from **monomers** by **condensation reactions**.

Model sentence: Anabolism is the part of metabolism where larger molecules (macromolecules) are formed from smaller molecules (monomers) by reactions called condensation.

Living organisms must be able to form their own large complex organic molecules known as macromolecules. They often form these from smaller, simpler molecules known as monomers. The reaction that bonds one monomer to another monomer is known as a condensation reaction. The part of an organism's metabolism where monomers are bonded together to create macromolecules is known as anabolism.

> **Hints for success:** In examinations, be sure to include the water molecule that is always one of the products of a condensation reaction.

Application: Organic molecules are frequently formed within living organisms, but many can be produced artificially as well

The first organic molecule to be produced in a laboratory setting was urea. Urea is produced in the liver tissue of many animals and becomes a component of urine. In 1828, a German physician by the name of Friedrich Wohler **synthesized** urea from inorganic compounds in his laboratory. This showed that organic substances can be artificially synthesized.

Understanding: **Catabolism** is the breakdown of complex molecules into simpler molecules including the **hydrolysis** of macromolecules into monomers.

Model sentence: Catabolism is the part of metabolism where smaller molecules (monomers) are formed from larger molecules (macromolecules). These reactions are called hydrolysis.

Organisms often ingest foods that contain macromolecules. As part of digestion, the organism must be able to breakdown the large molecules into smaller molecules. This chemical reaction is an example of catabolism. Notice that catabolism is the opposite of anabolism. In catabolism, macromolecules are turned back into monomers by a reaction type known as hydrolysis.

> **Hints for success:** During examinations, be sure to include a water molecule as a reactant during a hydrolysis reaction. Notice that this is the opposite of condensation where a water molecule was formed as a product.

2.2 Water is the medium of life

Understanding: Water molecules are polar and **hydrogen bonds** form between them.

Model sentence: Each water molecule has a positive and a negative end permitting hydrogen bonding between water molecules.

Covalent bonds are bonds between atoms formed by the sharing of electrons between those two atoms. Sometimes that sharing is equal and sometimes it is not equal. Here are two examples:

H———H

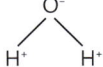

Figure 2.3A *Notice that when two hydrogen atoms share a pair of electrons between them, neither takes on a charge. This is because the sharing is equal. This is called a non-polar covalent bond*

Figure 2.3B *Notice that when hydrogen atoms share electrons with an oxygen atom, the oxygen atom takes on a negative charge and each hydrogen atom takes on a positive charge. This is because the sharing of the negative electron is not equal. This is called a polar covalent bond*

Notice that:
- Both hydrogen and oxygen take on a slight and opposite charge because they are not sharing their pair of electrons equally.
- Molecules that contain these types of covalent bonds where the electrons are not shared equally are called **polar molecules**.

A single drop of water contains millions of moving polar water molecules. As each water molecule comes near another water molecule, the positive end of any one is attracted to the negative end of another. This attraction is called a hydrogen bond. Each hydrogen bond is very weak and short-lived. The many millions of hydrogen bonds that occur within water at the same time lead to many of the important properties of water. Some of those properties will be discussed in the upcoming section.

Remember that oxygen atoms do not share electrons equally when they form a covalent bond with some other atoms. One of those atoms is hydrogen. Because electrons are negatively charged, an oxygen atom will take on a slight negative charge and the hydrogen will take on a positive charge when the two atoms are bonded together.

Subject vocabulary

hydrogen bond a weak bond that forms between positive and negatively charged areas of two molecules

covalent bond chemical bond in which electrons are shared

polar molecules molecules that contain one or more unequally shared electrons

dipolarity having two oppositely charged ends

solvent the liquid portion of a solution (solution = solvent + solute(s))

cohesion attraction of one water molecule for another

General vocabulary

adhesion process where two different substances stick together or attach to one another

---

Understanding: Hydrogen bonds and **dipolarity** explain the cohesive, adhesive, thermal, and **solvent** properties of water.

Model sentence: Each water molecule has both a positive and negative end (dipolarity) giving rise to many of the important properties of water.

Hydrogen bonding between nearby water molecules explains the following properties:
- **Cohesion** – term used when water molecules attract other water molecules.
- **Adhesion** – term used when water molecules attract another polar substance besides water.

2 Molecular biology | 27

General vocabulary

thermal related to/caused by heat

Subject vocabulary

hydrophilic 'water loving', substances that dissolve in water

hydrophobic 'water fearing', substances that do not dissolve in water

soluble a substance that will dissolve

non-polar region of no electrical charge

insoluble a substance that will not dissolve

immiscible two substances that when mixed together will tend to separate from each other in layers

cytoplasm region of the cell within the plasma membrane in which the cell organelles exist

haemoglobin a protein found in red blood cells used to carry oxygen in the blood

Synonyms

transport .... movement

- **Thermal** properties:
  - High specific heat – water can absorb and give off a great deal of heat without changing its temperature much.
  - High heat of vaporization – water requires a great deal of heat in order to convert it from the liquid phase to the gas phase.

Hints for success: Have you ever thought about why sweating cools your body? The cooling is due to the body heat that is absorbed by the (sweat) water. The heat that is taken from your body is used to evaporate the water from your skin. For an examination, this would be a good example to remember for the importance of high heat of vaporization.

Water is an excellent solvent for other polar (charged) substances. The following are a few examples of substances that are polar and thus dissolve well in water:

- ions
- glucose
- amino acids.

Understanding: Substances can be **hydrophilic** or **hydrophobic**.

Model sentence: The polarity of a substance determines whether that substance is hydrophilic 'water loving' or hydrophobic 'water fearing'.

Polar substances like glucose are 'water loving'. This is because of their numerous alcohol (-OH groups). They easily dissolve in a water solution. We say that these molecules are water **soluble**.

Non-polar substances, like lipids, are 'water fearing'. This is because of their lack of polar covalent bonds. They do not mix with water very well. We say that these molecules are water **insoluble** or the two substances are **immiscible**.

The following tables show common molecules and their solubility in water solutions. These solutions could represent the **cytoplasm** of a cell or perhaps blood.

Polar molecules (hydrophilic)	Mode of **transport** in blood
glucose	easily dissolves in plasma
amino acids	easily dissolve in plasma
sodium chloride (salt)	easily dissolves in plasma

Non-polar molecules (hydrophobic)	Mode of transport in blood
cholesterol	attaches to polar proteins
lipids	attaches to polar proteins
oxygen	carried by **haemoglobin**

2.3 Carbohydrates and lipids

Understanding: **Monosaccharide** monomers are linked together by condensation reactions to form larger **carbohydrate** molecules.

Model sentence: Single carbohydrate units are covalently bonded together to make disaccharides and polysaccharides.

Fundamentals of carbohydrates:
- The smallest carbohydrates are monosaccharides.
- Two monosaccharides bonded together form a disaccharide.
- Many monosaccharides bonded together form a polysaccharide.

Examples of carbohydrates:
- monosaccharides – glucose and fructose
- disaccharides – sucrose and maltose and lactose
- polysaccharides – starch and cellulose.

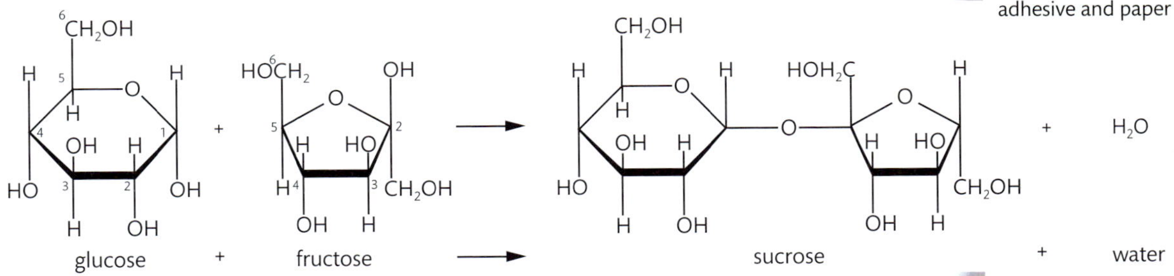

> **Subject vocabulary**
>
> **monosaccharide** smallest (monomer) unit of carbohydrates
>
> **carbohydrates** any of a group of molecules often referred to as 'sugars'
>
> **disaccharide** two monosaccharides bonded together by a condensation reaction
>
> **polysaccharide** many monosaccharides bonded together by many condensation reactions organized into a linear or branched shape
>
> **amylose** type of starch that is the most common storage form of carbohydrates in plants
>
> **amylopectin** type of starch produced by plants that has adhesive and paper uses

Figure 2.4 *The condensation reaction between glucose and fructose to form the disaccharide sucrose and a water molecule. Each corner of the sugar rings has an 'unshown' carbon atom. Each carbon atom is numbered in the reactants. Glucose and fructose are isomers of each other because they have the same chemical formula, $C_6H_{12}O_6$*

Application: Common uses and structure of polysaccharides

Name of polysaccharide	Structural form (shape)	Common use
cellulose	linear	used by plant cells within plant cell walls
starch	highly branched	used by plants to store glucose for later use
glycogen	highly branched	used by humans to store glucose for later use

Note: starch is composed of two types of polysaccharide, **amylose** and **amylopectin**.

Understanding: Fatty acids can be saturated, monounsaturated, or polyunsaturated.

Model sentence: Fatty acids are classified into one of three categories depending on the presence of double bonds within the molecule.

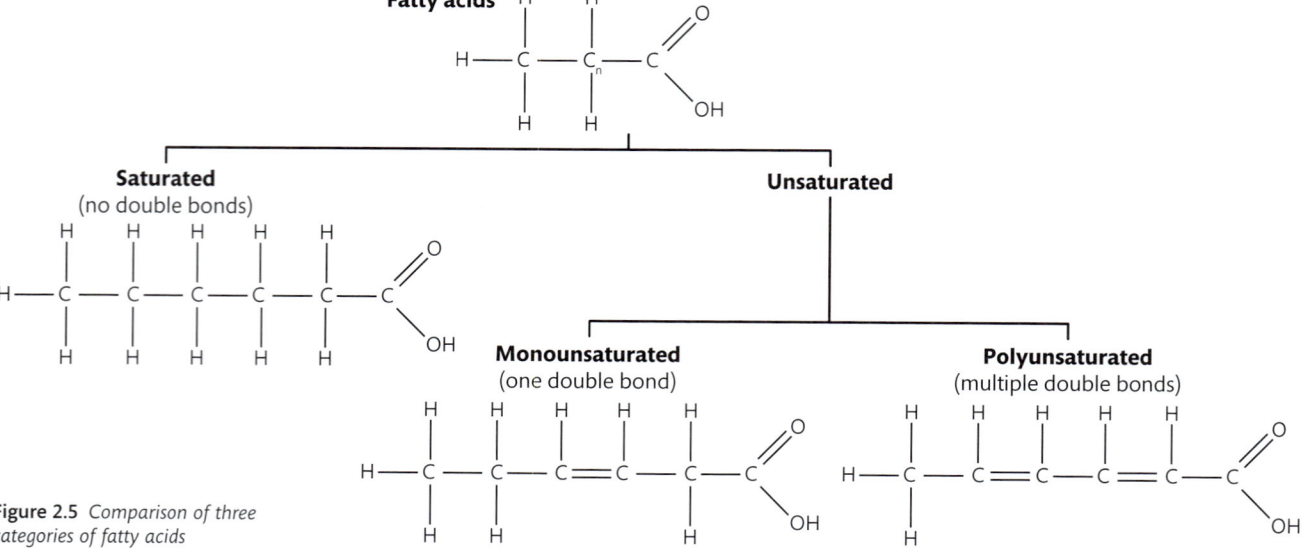

Figure 2.5 Comparison of three categories of fatty acids

Understanding: Unsaturated fatty acids can be **cis** or **trans** **isomers**.

Model sentence: Food-processing companies often modify unsaturated fatty acids converting them from a cis form to a trans form.

When polyunsaturated (generally healthy) fatty acids are used in packaged foods, the food product has a relatively short **shelf life**. Many food-producing companies modify the fatty acids they use to a form with fewer double bonds. This extends the shelf life of the product.

Subject vocabulary

cis term used to describe a natural form of an unsaturated fatty acid

trans a chemically modified fatty acid sometimes used by food-processing companies

isomers two molecules that have the same chemical formula but differ in structure

General vocabulary

shelf life how long a food product can remain without becoming spoiled

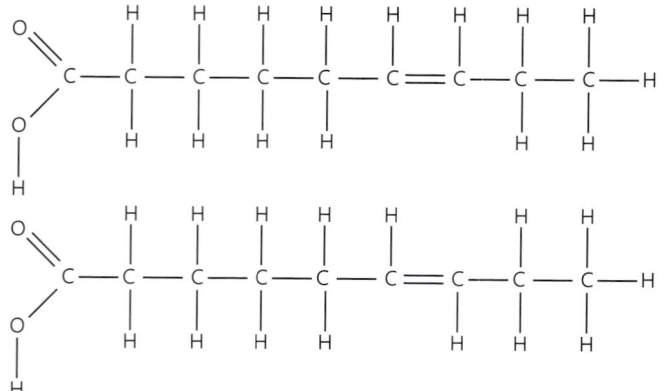

'Cis' bonded unsaturated fat, notice both hydrogens of the double bond are on the same side of the molecule.

'Trans' bonded unsaturated fat, notice both hydrogens of the double bond are on different sides of the molecule.

Both molecules have the same chemical formula and thus are isomers of each other.

Figure 2.6 When food companies attempt to modify unsaturated fatty acids the remaining double bonds are often converted from a cis form to a trans form. The cis form is considered relatively healthy and the trans form is unhealthy as part of your diet

- The relatively healthy, original form of the fatty acid is called the cis form.
- The unhealthy, modified form of the fatty acid is called the trans form.
- Foods that are made with the modified trans fatty acids are said to contain trans fats.
- Most polyunsaturated fatty acids found in nature are in the cis form.

Understanding: Triglycerides are formed from one **glycerol** and three fatty acids by condensation reactions.

Model sentence: The 'building block' molecules of triglycerides are one glycerol molecule and three fatty acid molecules.

- Several types of molecules can be classified as lipids.
- Triglycerides are one type.
- Triglycerides are most often used for energy storage within cells.
- The subcomponent (building block) units are bonded together by condensation reactions.

> **Subject vocabulary**
>
> **glycerol** a three-carbon molecule found within lipids
>
> **General vocabulary**
>
> **online calculator** a website designed to do mathematics

Application: Lipids are better for long-term energy storage in humans as compared to carbohydrates

Imagine a kilogram of lipid in one container and a kilogram of carbohydrate in another container. Next imagine that each is burned and the energy release from each was measured. There would be approximately twice as much energy released from the container with lipid as compared to the container with carbohydrate.

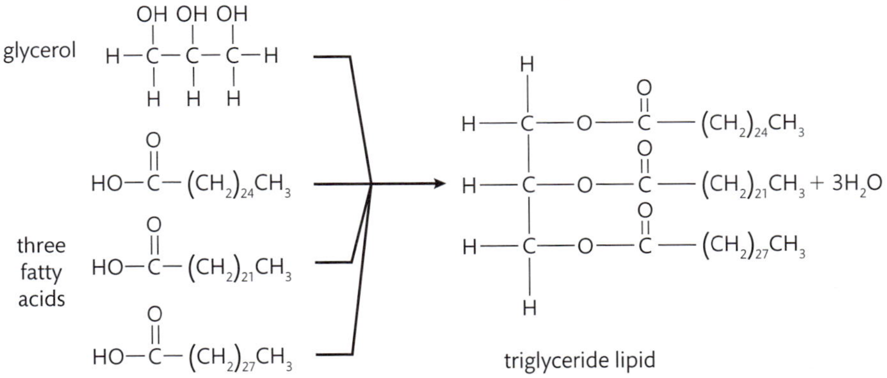

Figure 2.7 Condensation reaction showing the four reactants necessary to form a triglyceride lipid. Notice that there are four products: the three water molecules as well as the triglyceride

- This shows that lipids are much more efficient at storing energy as compared to carbohydrates.
- This also demonstrates why long-term energy storage is done by way of lipids.

Skill: Determination of body mass index by calculation or use of a nomogram

A determination of one's weight compared to one's height can be done by calculation of a value known as the Body Mass Index (BMI).

A BMI can be determined by a formula with one's known mass and height. The BMI can also be determined by consulting a graph or using an **online calculator**. The BMI value is then compared to a published chart to show relative health.

BMI	Description category
below 18.5	underweight
18.5–24.9	normal weight
25.0–29.9	overweight
30.0 and above	obese

2.4 Proteins

Subject vocabulary

polypeptide polymer of many amino acids joined by peptide bonds

ribosome organelle within cells where polypeptides are formed

R-group the portion of each of the 20 amino acids that is different from one another

Understanding: Amino acids are bonded together by condensation reactions to form **polypeptides**.

Model sentence: A polypeptide forms when amino acids become linked together by condensation reactions.

Building block molecules often bond together to form the larger molecules important to living organisms. This is true for molecules called polypeptides. A polypeptide is formed when many amino acids bond together in a chain. A condensation reaction has occurred each time one amino acid bonds to another in the chain. Each new covalent bond that forms is called a peptide bond.

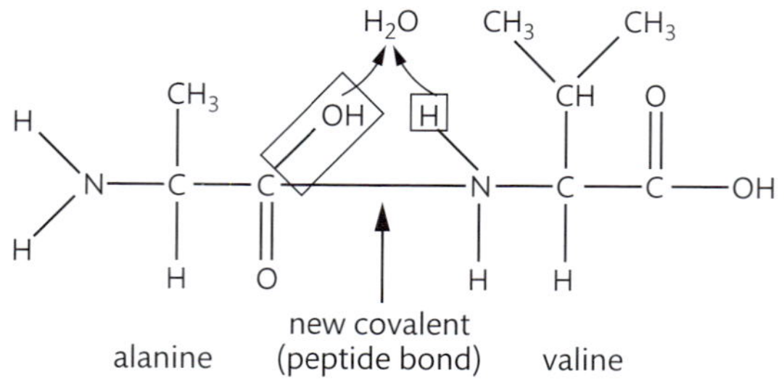

Figure 2.8 Condensation reaction between the amino acids alanine and valine. Note that for simplicity the amine and carboxyl groups are being shown in a non-ionized form. This reaction looks the same for any two amino acids, as the only change would be to the R (variable) groups

Hints for success: Practise drawing two or more amino acids undergoing a condensation reaction. You will need to be able to do this in an examination.

Understanding: There are 20 different amino acids in polypeptides synthesized on **ribosomes**.

Model sentence: When a polypeptide is created, as many as 20 different types of amino acids may be used at the ribosome where this occurs.

Each of the 20 amino acids is very similar in overall structure. The exception is the one part of each amino acid that is called its **R-group**. The chart on the following page shows the structure of all 20 amino acids with a box around the R-group of each. You do not need to memorize all of these structures.

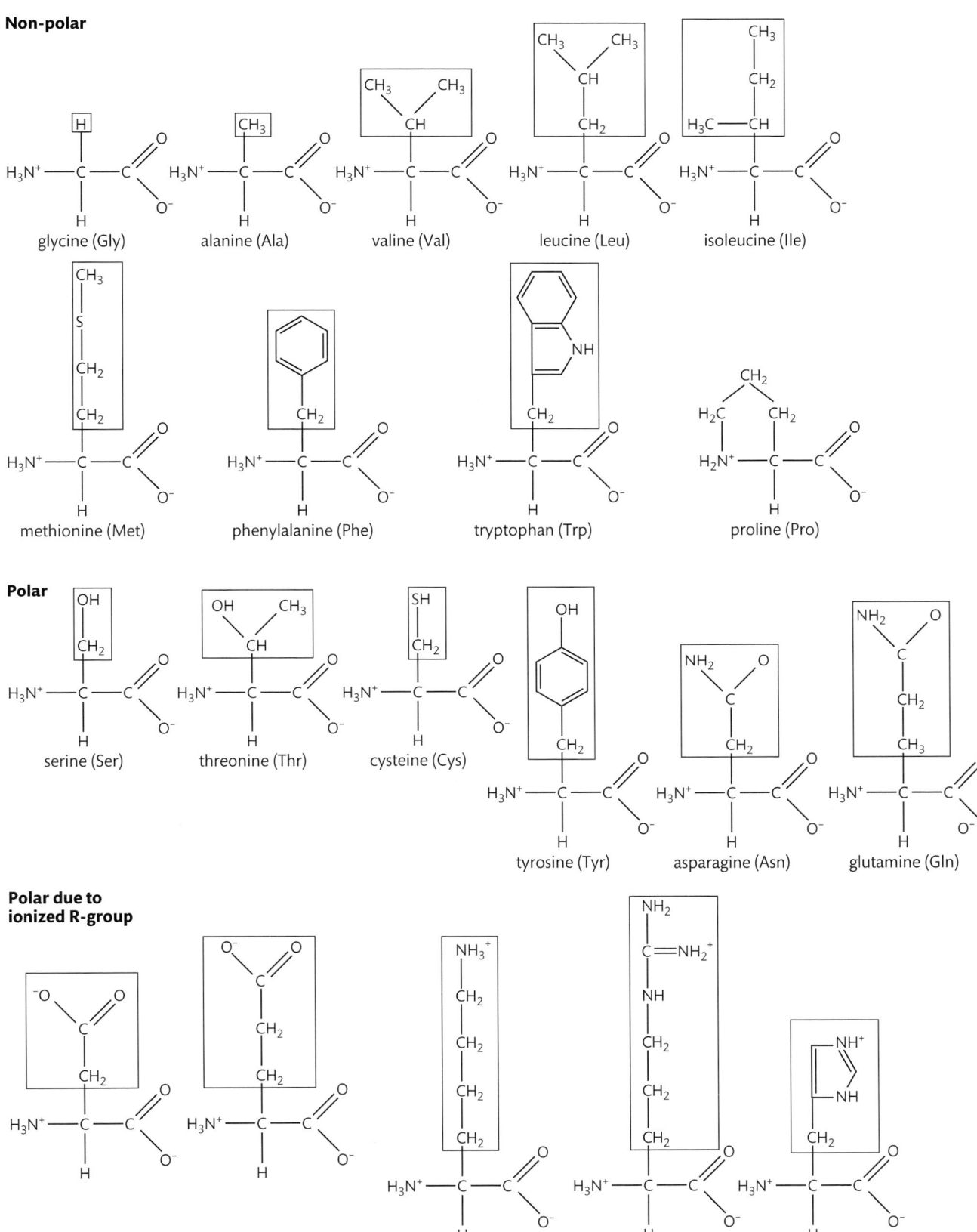

Figure 2.9 *A chart showing the structures of the 20 amino acids. The boxed areas shown are the R-groups of the amino acids. Note how each amino acid is identical except for the variable R-group*

Understanding: Amino acids can be linked together in any sequence, giving a huge range of possible polypeptides.

Model sentence: The many kinds of polypeptides are explained by the 20 types of amino acids being bonded together in any possible order and number.

Consider a very short polypeptide that has only four amino acids of four different types. Imagine those four types of amino acids to be glycine, alanine, serine, and threonine. Here are eight possible sequences in which they could be arranged:

1. glycine – alanine – serine – threonine
2. alanine – glycine – serine – threonine
3. serine – alanine – glycine – threonine
4. alanine – glycine – threonine – serine
5. serine – alanine – threonine – glycine
6. glycine – serine – alanine – threonine
7. glycine – threonine – serine – alanine
8. alanine – serine – glycine – threonine

Now imagine a polypeptide that has 50 or more total amino acids. Some of the 20 types of amino acids would have to be used more than once. The number of possible sequences is incredibly large.

Understanding: The amino acid sequence of polypeptides is coded for within our genes.

Model sentence: The DNA of living organisms contains sections called genes each coding for a different polypeptide.

- Each DNA is a very long molecule containing a great deal of genetic information.
- A single DNA molecule may contain a thousand or more sections called genes.
- Each gene is enough genetic information to code for a polypeptide.
- The coding information is for the sequence of amino acids that make up the polypeptide.

Subject vocabulary

gene section of DNA molecule that codes for a particular trait/protein in an organism

protein one or more polypeptides that has a defined function

Understanding: A protein may consist of a single polypeptide or two or more polypeptides linked together.

Model sentence: Some proteins are made up of a single polypeptide, whereas other proteins are made up of two or more polypeptides bonded together.

A protein is a molecule that has a function within a living organism. A single polypeptide that begins its function soon after being synthesized can also be called a protein. In some instances, a single polypeptide is not functional until it combines with one or more other polypeptides. Only then is the molecule called a protein. In short, a single polypeptide is a protein only when it does not require one or more other polypeptides to begin its function.

Examples of proteins are:

- **Myoglobin** is a single polypeptide that is found within muscle cells. Myoglobin's single polypeptide is capable of binding to an oxygen molecule that is only released when you exercise very hard. It functions as a single polypeptide and is a protein.
- Haemoglobin is composed of four polypeptides and is found within red blood cells. Haemoglobin can bind to and release as many as four oxygen molecules. Its function does not begin until all four polypeptides are bonded to each other. Haemoglobin is a protein only when all four polypeptides are present and working together.

Subject vocabulary

myoglobin a protein found within muscles that bonds to an oxygen molecule

hormone a chemical messenger produced by an endocrine gland

tendons tissue used to connect muscles to bones

Synonyms

regulating …… controlling

Understanding: The amino acid sequence determines the three-dimensional shape of a protein.

Model sentence: Each type of protein has a unique three-dimensional shape that is a result of its amino acid sequence.

When a polypeptide is first formed, the amino acids that it is made up from begin to interact with each other. Through a series of positive and negative charges, amino acids either attract or repel one another. The polypeptide settles into an overall three-dimensional shape that is repeated every time that same polypeptide is synthesized. Remember that some proteins do not function until two or more polypeptides join together. The joining that they do is also due to forces between charges they contain. Every time a protein forms it will automatically take on the exact same shape.

Understanding: Living organisms synthesize many different proteins with a wide range of functions.

Model sentence: The proteins found within any one living organism are numerous and serve a number of different functions.

Application: This table shows just a few examples of the incredible variety of proteins in nature:

Protein	Function
rubisco	enzyme used in photosynthesis
insulin	**hormone** involved in **regulating** blood sugar
immunoglobins	helps fight viruses and bacteria
collagen	component of skin and **tendons**
spider silk	used for making webs
rhodopsin	pigment found in retina cells of the eye

Subject vocabulary

proteome the unique collection of proteins within a cell, tissue type, organ, or organism

genetic determined by DNA and passed on from parents to offspring

active site the area of an enzyme to which the substrate(s) attach(es)

substrate substance which begins a chemical reaction or process

reaction a change due to the interaction of chemical substances or response due to a stimulus

catalysed the action of a catalyst, such as an enzyme, whereby the enzyme increases the rate of reaction

catalysis the action of a catalyst such as an enzyme

General vocabulary

collision two things moving toward and eventually impacting each other

Understanding: Every individual has a unique **proteome**.

Model sentence: The genetic makeup of each individual is slightly different and thus the collection of proteins in every individual is also slightly different.

Researchers have known for years that each individual organism has unique DNA. This explains why humans are all a little different from each other. The same is true for all other species as well. Each member of a species is genetically different from all other members of that species.

DNA is the genetic code for proteins. It makes sense that if every organism has unique DNA, then every organism also has a unique set of proteins as well. The unique collection of proteins within any one organism is called the proteome of that organism.

2.5 Enzymes

Understanding: Enzymes have an **active site** to which specific **substrates** bind.

Model sentence: Each enzyme molecule has a specific area called its active site where the substrate(s) of that enzyme attach.

- Each enzyme is a protein with a very specific three-dimensional shape.
- Part of that three-dimensional shape is an area called an active site.
- The molecule or molecules that enter the active site are called the substrate(s) of that enzyme.
- When the substrate(s) are within the active site a **reaction** is **catalysed**.

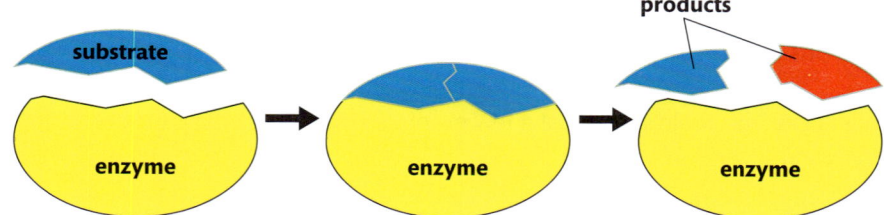

Figure 2.10 *An enzyme and substrate are specific for each other*

Understanding: Enzyme **catalysis** involves molecular motion and the **collision** of substrates with the active site.

Model sentence: The ability of an enzyme to act as a catalyst depends on the substrate(s) colliding with the active site.

Reactions require energy. This energy is called the activation energy of a reaction. Activation energy is most often in the form of heat. An increase in heat results in molecules moving faster. When molecules move faster they collide with other molecules with greater energy. The function of an enzyme is to provide an active site where the collision that occurs has a better chance of the reaction being successful.

Understanding: Enzymes can be denatured.

Model sentence: The three-dimensional shape of an enzyme can be altered in a process called **denaturing**.

Each specific enzyme has its own ideal conditions in which it best catalyses reactions. Altering those ideal conditions leads to a change in the shape of the enzyme. This is called denaturing the enzyme. The same denaturing happens to all proteins. The most important part of an enzyme that must be perfectly shaped is the active site of the enzyme.

Understanding: Temperature, pH, and substrate **concentration** affect the rate of activity of enzymes

Model sentence: Each enzyme has an **optimum** temperature, pH, and concentration of substrate that ensures the maximum **reaction rate**.

Factors affecting an enzyme reaction that are not optimum will lower the rate of reaction as compared to the ideal.

Factor	What does condition do?	Why?
temperature below ideal	molecules in a reaction move relatively slowly	Even when an active site helps, a minimum activation energy is required.
temperature above ideal	molecules in a reaction move relatively fast	Enzyme begins moving fast as well. Enzyme becomes denatured.
pH below ideal	reaction becomes more **acidic** than ideal	Acidic environment modifies the structure of the enzyme leading to denaturing.
pH above ideal	reaction becomes more **basic** than ideal	Basic environment modifies the structure of the enzyme leading to denaturing.
substrate concentration below ideal	reaction does not have enough reactant(s)	Enzyme can provide more available active sites but there is not enough substrate to fill those 'openings'.
	Note: if substrate concentration is above ideal, the reaction rate is not increased nor is it decreased.	Each active site of each enzyme is **saturated** and is thus working as fast as is possible.

Subject vocabulary

denature to cause a molecule to lose its natural three-dimensional shape

pH a measure of the acidity or alkalinity of a solution

concentration a measurement of the density of a substance in a solution

reaction rate number of successful reactions per unit of time

acidic a fluid that has a pH measured at less than 7.0

basic a fluid that has a pH measured at more than 7.0

saturated all four iron atoms within a single haemoglobin are bonded to an oxygen molecule

Synonyms

optimum .... best/ideal

2 Molecular biology | 37

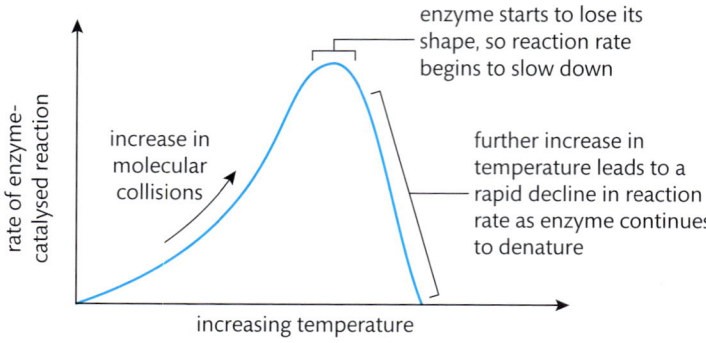

Figure 2.11 *The effect of increasing temperature on the rate of an enzyme-catalysed reaction*

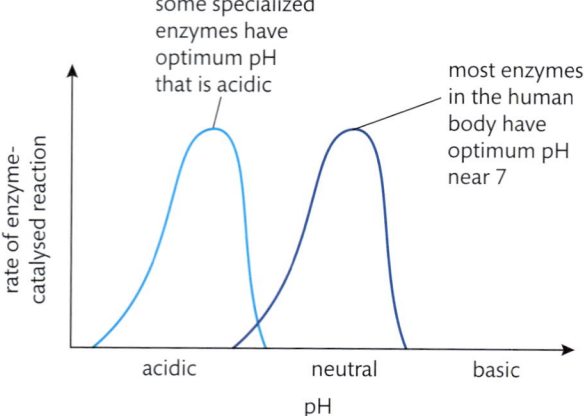

Figure 2.12 *The effect of pH on the rate of an enzyme-catalysed reaction. This illustrates that there is no single pH that is best for all enzymes*

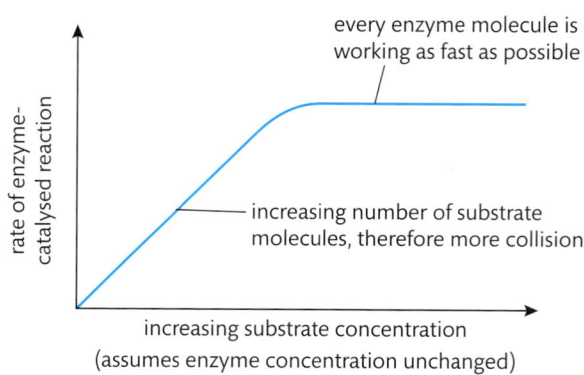

Figure 2.13 *The effect of increasing the substrate concentration on the rate of an enzyme-catalysed reaction*

Understanding: Immobilized enzymes are widely used in industry.

Model sentence: Commercially used enzymes are often embedded into a permanent substance in order to avoid losing the enzymes.

Using enzymes in industry is an expensive process. One of the most expensive parts is acquiring and purifying the enzyme needed. The solution is to make sure that the enzyme used does not get wasted and is recycled. One way this is done is to trap the enzyme molecules in small beads called alginates. The enzyme molecules are said to be immobilized in the small beads. When the factory uses the enzyme the small beads are recovered from any product formed and can be reused many times.

Application: Methods of production of lactose-free milk and its advantages

Lactose-free milk can be produced by adding the enzyme lactase to milk. The lactase is trapped within small alginate beads that are then mixed with milk. The lactase converts the lactose to two monosaccharide sugars. Those people that cannot digest their own lactose (lactose intolerance) have milk products 'pre-digested' by this method.

Subject vocabulary

immobilized to contain something so that it remains trapped

alginates chemicals derived from a seaweed (algae)

lactose a disaccharide sugar composed of glucose and galactose

General vocabulary

embedded positioned firmly and deeply

Synonyms

purifying .... cleansing/cleaning

2.6 Structure of DNA and RNA

Main idea
DNA has a structure which allows genetic information to be stored efficiently.

Understanding: The nucleic acids DNA and RNA are polymers of nucleotides.

Model sentence: DNA and RNA are nucleic acids made up of large numbers of nucleotides.

- **Nucleic acids** are one of the major organic groups. DNA and RNA are classified as nucleic acids.
- DNA and RNA are made of **polymers** or large chains of **nucleotides**. These nucleotides are connected by chemical bonds. A **generalized** nucleotide is shown to the right.
- Parts of a DNA nucleotide:
  - one **phosphate group**.
  - one deoxyribose – a 5-carbon sugar.
  - one nitrogenous base – adenine (A), thymine (T), cytosine (C), or guanine (G).
- Parts of a RNA nucleotide
  - one phosphate group
  - one ribose – a 5-carbon sugar
  - one nitrogenous base – adenine (A), uracil (U), cytosine (C), or guanine (G).
- **Covalent bonds** attach the parts within a nucleotide. Covalent bonds also attach individual nucleotides together to form a polymer (chain).
- It is the sequence of bases in a DNA or RNA molecule which provides the genetic code.

> **Hints for success:** Organisms are quite complex. The base sequence in nucleic acids must be quite long to code for this complexity. When asked to draw a nucleotide for IB, always show the phosphate group as a circle. Always show the pentose (5-carbon sugar) as a pentagon. Always show the nitrogenous base as a rectangle.

Skill: Drawing simple diagrams of the structure of single nucleotides of DNA and RNA, using circles, pentagons and rectangles to represent phosphates, pentoses, and bases

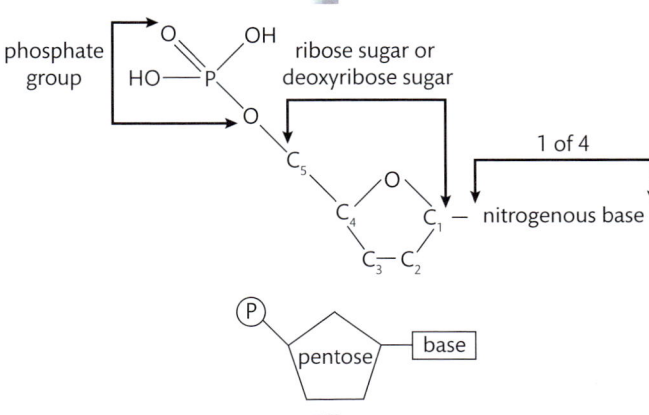

Figure 2.14 The first diagram represents the structure of a nucleotide showing bond locations. The second diagram represents the structure of a general nucleotide using the symbols suggested by the IB

Subject vocabulary

nucleic acids one of the major organic groups which includes DNA and RNA

polymer large molecules composed of smaller units (monomers) connected by covalent bonds

nucleotides smaller units chemically bound to form nucleic acids

phosphate group chemical group composed of phosphorus and oxygen

covalent bond chemical bond in which electrons are shared

General vocabulary

generalized not specific, relates to a group

2 Molecular biology | 39

Understanding: DNA differs from RNA in the number of strands present, the base composition, and the type of pentose.

Model sentence: DNA is double-stranded while RNA is single-stranded. DNA has a difference from RNA in bases present. DNA has a different 5-carbon sugar than RNA.

The sugar of DNA is deoxyribose. The sugar of RNA is ribose. Both these sugars are made up of five carbons. DNA is composed of two strands of nucleotides. These two strands are connected to one another by **hydrogen bonds** between the bases. RNA is composed of only one strand of nucleotides.

RNA contains the nitrogenous bases A, U, C, and G. DNA contains the nitrogenous bases A, T, C, and G.

> Hints for success: Use a table or t-chart to represent the main characteristics of DNA and RNA. In your table or t-chart include similarities and differences.

Subject vocabulary

hydrogen bond a weak bond that forms between positively and negatively charged areas of two molecules or within a single molecule to help shape the molecule

complementary base pairs nitrogenous bases which pair together in nucleic acids, A–T, A–U, C–G

double helix three-dimensional shape of DNA involving a double spiral

Understanding: DNA is a double helix made of two antiparallel strands of nucleotides linked by hydrogen bonding between complementary base pairs.

Model sentence: The structure of DNA is a double helix made up of two strands connected by hydrogen bonds.

- DNA has a double helix shape. This is because there are two strands and each is in a spiral form.
- Relatively weak hydrogen bonds connect the two DNA strands. These hydrogen bonds occur between complementary bases. A and T are complementary bases and are connected by two hydrogen bonds. C and G are complementary bases and are connected by three hydrogen bonds
- The two strands of DNA are antiparallel because they occur in opposite directions. On one strand the number 5 carbon is on top. On the other strand the number 3 carbon is on top.

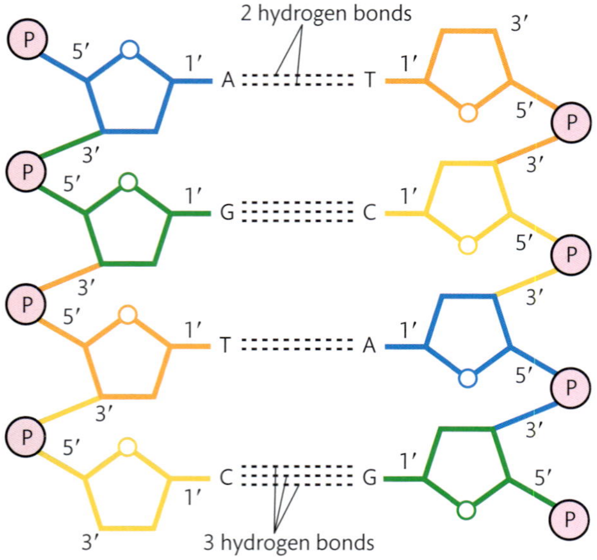

Nature of science: Watson and Crick worked with models to discover the actual structure of DNA. They used information from many sources to construct their final actual model.

> Hints for success: When drawing the structure of DNA a ladder structure shown to the left is required. It is not necessary to show the actual number of hydrogen bonds between complementary bases.

Figure 2.15 The ladder structure of DNA is represented in this figure. Note the two strands have carbons numbered in the opposite direction. Also note the hydrogen bonds between complementary bases. All other bonds in this molecule are covalent bonds

2.6 Structure of DNA and RNA

2.7 DNA replication, transcription, and translation

Main idea
DNA **transcription** and **translation** allow the production of the proteins necessary to the cell.

Understanding: The replication of DNA is semi-conservative and depends on complementary base pairing.

Model sentence: DNA replicates based on complementary base pairing. The replication process is said to be **semi-conservative**.

- DNA in the nucleus of the cell must replicate before cell division occurs.
- DNA replication is referred to as semi-conservative.
- Semi-conservative means that each of the two molecules of DNA formed in replication has one strand of the original DNA molecule. The other strand of the new DNA molecule is new. This new strand is formed from free nucleotides in the nucleus.
- The two strands of DNA are chemically bound by hydrogen bonds between adenine (A) and thymine (T), and between cytosine (C) and guanine (G).

Hints for success: Because of complementary base pairing, two identical copies of DNA are produced from one. Each molecule of DNA produced in replication has one strand from the original DNA molecule.

Subject vocabulary

transcription the process of creating RNA from DNA

translation process of protein production which occurs at the ribosome in cells, DNA language is changed into the language of proteins

semi-conservative type of replication in DNA in which each new DNA molecule has one original strand of the parent molecule

helicase enzyme which opens the DNA double helix in the replication process

General vocabulary

unwind to loosen from the original shape

unzipping to open a zipper-like structure, to open a closed structure

Synonyms

replicate .... copy

Understanding: Helicase unwinds the double helix and separates the two strands by breaking hydrogen bonds.

Model sentence: Helicase is an enzyme which causes the DNA double helix to **unwind** and breaks the hydrogen bonds between complementary base pairs.

Initial steps in the replication of DNA:
- First, the double helix of the DNA molecule must unwind.
- Next, the hydrogen bonds which connect the two strands of the DNA must be broken. This is often referred to as an **unzipping** process.
- Helicase, an enzyme, allows these two steps to occur very rapidly.

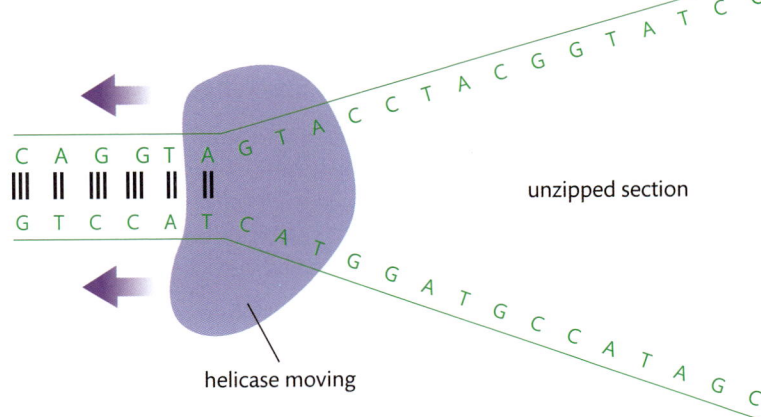

Figure 2.16 The first steps of DNA replication is helicase catalysing the unwinding and unzipping of the double-stranded DNA molecule, forming a section with two single strands

helicase moving

unzipped section

Hints for success: Remember the enzyme helicase allows the unwinding and unzipping of DNA to occur very rapidly so that replication can efficiently occur.

Understanding: DNA polymerase links nucleotides together to form a new strand, using the pre-existing strand as a template.

Model sentence: DNA polymerase is an enzyme which catalyses the linking of nucleotides in the new DNA strand.

- When DNA unzips, free nucleotides in the nucleus pair with the exposed bases of the existing strands.
- Each strand of the unzipped DNA acts as a template for the formation of a new complementary strand.
- Nucleotides with the nitrogenous base A always pair with nucleotides with the nitrogenous base T. The same is true for C and G.
- A type of DNA polymerase catalyses the formation of a covalent bond between adjacent nucleotides as complementary bases line up.
- The result of this is two molecules of DNA which are exact copies of one another. Study the figure below:

Subject vocabulary

DNA polymerase group of enzymes which are involved in DNA replication

Taq DNA polymerase enzyme stable at high temperatures which is used to produce large numbers of copies of DNA in the laboratory

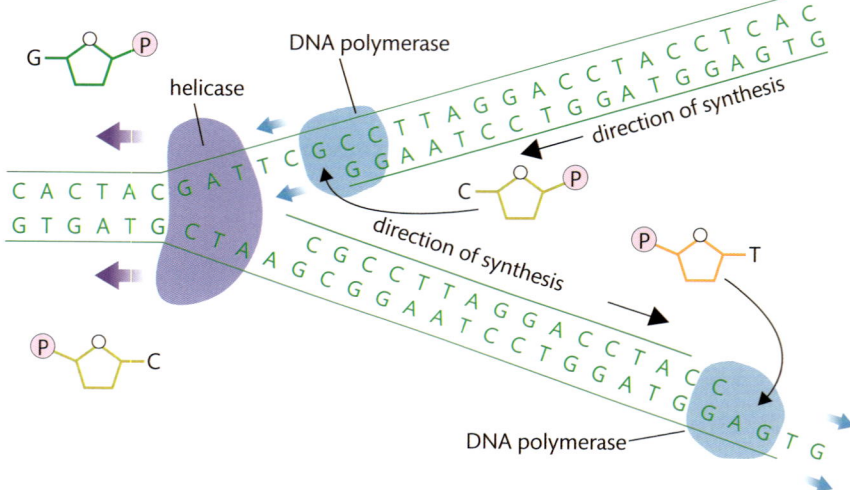

Figure 2.17 DNA replication

Hints for success: Study the figure carefully. Note the two molecules of DNA being formed from the original one molecule. Notice the locations where both helicase and DNA polymerase carry out their functions. A is always paired with T, and C is always paired with G in both new molecules.

Skill: Analysis of Meselson and Stahl's results to obtain support for the theory of semi-conservative replication of DNA

Meselson and Stahl carried out a beautifully designed experiment to provide evidence for the semi-conservative method of DNA replication. They used bacterial cultures of *Escherichia coli* and an isotope of heavy nitrogen to tag DNA. Percentages of DNA strands composed of heavy nitrogen to DNA strands composed of 'lighter' nitrogen were then analysed. Their findings provided support for semi-conservative replication.

Application: There is a special type of DNA polymerase called **Taq DNA polymerase**. Taq DNA polymerase is relatively stable at high temperatures. It can be used in laboratory settings to artificially create large numbers of small segments of DNA by the DNA replication process. These replicated copies of DNA are exact copies and may be used for analysis and study. This technique is often used to increase small amounts of DNA found at some crime scenes so that a potential source may be found. Taq DNA polymerase has also allowed great advances in the field of gene technology.

Understanding: Transcription is the synthesis of mRNA copied from the DNA base sequences by RNA polymerase.

Model sentence: RNA polymerase is an enzyme which catalyses the copying of the DNA base sequence onto mRNA by the process called transcription.

DNA controls almost all the cellular activities through the process of protein synthesis. Many of the proteins produced in the cell are enzymes. It is the sequences of bases on the DNA molecule which determine the specific proteins to be made. Specific regions of the DNA molecule code for specific proteins. Each of these regions is called a **gene**. The first steps in the formation of proteins in the cell are:

- A region of the DNA molecule, the gene, becomes unzipped. The unzipping process is similar to that which occurred in DNA replication.
- Only one strand of the unzipped DNA molecule is used as a template to form mRNA. mRNA is single stranded.
- RNA polymerase is the enzyme involved in unzipping of the DNA region. RNA polymerase is also needed to bring about the complementary base pairing of RNA nucleotides with the exposed DNA bases in the unzipped region of the DNA molecule.

Subject vocabulary

RNA polymerase enzyme involved in the transcription process

gene section of DNA molecule that codes for a particular trait/protein in an organism

This table summarizes the differences between DNA and RNA.

DNA	RNA
composed of two strands of covalently bonded nucleotides in a double helix	composed of one strand of covalently bonded nucleotides
each nucleotide contains the 5-carbon sugar called deoxyribose	each nucleotide contains the 5-carbon sugar called ribose
each nucleotide may contains one of four nitrogenous bases: adenine (A), thymine (T), cytosine (C), and guanine (G)	each nucleotide may contain one of four nitrogenous bases: adenine (A), uracil (U), cytosine (C), and guanine (G)

Hints for success: Study the figure below to be able to explain the process of transcription.

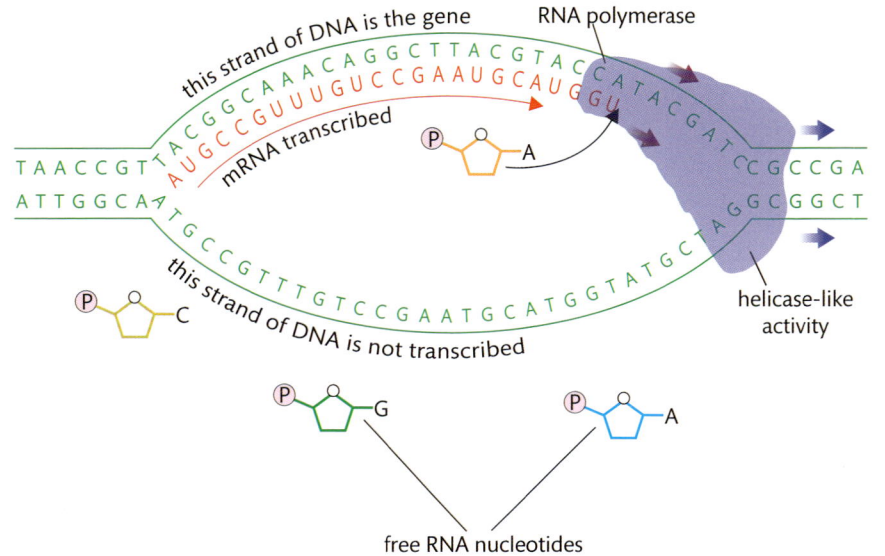

Figure 2.18 Transcription (synthesis of an RNA molecule). RNA polymerase has helicase-like activity as it plays a role in opening the DNA double helix. It also catalyses the addition of free RNA nucleotides to the growing mRNA strand

Understanding: Translation is the synthesis of polypeptides on ribosomes.

Model sentence: The production of the **polypeptides** necessary for cell activities occurs at the ribosomes and is called translation.

A polypeptide is a polymer of many amino acids. A protein may include more than one polypeptide and has a complex three-dimensional shape. Polypeptides are produced at the ribosomes which then form proteins needed for the cell's activities. Translation requires an mRNA, a ribosome, many tRNAs, amino acids and enzymes. There are three types of RNA and all play a role in translation. Study this table comparing the three RNA types.

RNA type	Function
mRNA or messenger RNA	carries the DNA code from the nucleus to the ribosomes in the cytoplasm
rRNA or ribosomal RNA	provides a large percentage of the ribosome composition
tRNA or transfer RNA	carries one of 20 possible amino acids to the mRNA-ribosomal complex

The sequence of actions in translation are:

1. mRNA moves out of the cell nucleus and forms a complex with a ribosome. This complex is called the **mRNA–ribosomal complex**.

2. tRNAs bring specific amino acids to the mRNA-ribosomal complex. The amino acids brought to the complex are coded for by mRNA.

3. The amino acids are lined up in a sequence indicated by the mRNA.

4. Bonds called **peptide bonds** occur between adjacent amino acids. These bonds result in the formation of the specific polypeptide molecule.

> **Hints for success:** The DNA in the cell nucleus carries the code for almost all the activities of the cell. This code is transcribed onto mRNA. mRNA carries the code for the specific polypeptide needed for a ribosome in the cytoplasm. Translation then occurs at the ribosome to produce the needed polypeptide. Once the polypeptide is produced the mRNA–ribosomal complex breaks apart. The ribosome is then able to combine with a different mRNA to produce a totally different polypeptide. The tRNA moves to a different cytoplasm location to pick up the same type of free amino acid. It then can become active in the translation process of another polypeptide.

Subject vocabulary

polypeptide polymer of many amino acids combined by peptide bonds

mRNA–ribosomal complex structure formed when a mRNA is combined with a ribosome in the cytoplasm

peptide bonds covalent bond which occurs between the amino group of one amino acid and the carboxyl group of another

Understanding: The amino acid sequence of amino acids of polypeptides is determined by mRNA according to the genetic code.

Model sentence: It is the sequence of bases on the DNA molecule which is the genetic code. This code is transcribed onto an mRNA so that translation of the proper polypeptide may occur at the ribosome.

Hints for success: It is the sequence of the bases, A, T, C, and G, in a cell's DNA which determines what polypeptides will be produced at the ribosomes of that specific cell. This genetic code is passed through cell division from one generation to the next after DNA replication, mitosis, and cytokinesis occur.

Understanding: Codons of three bases on mRNA correspond to one amino acid in a polypeptide.

Model sentence: Each three-base sequence of nucleotides along an mRNA molecule is called a codon and codes for a specific amino acid.

The mRNA molecule produced by transcription represents a complementary copy of one gene of DNA. The genetic code is written in triplets. The region of DNA called a gene is made up of many, many bases. These bases of the DNA are organized into 'genetic words' called DNA triplets. Transcription allows the formation of the mRNA codons from DNA triplets. Each mRNA codon corresponds to one amino acid in a polypeptide. Some mRNA codons act as 'punctuation marks' starting or stopping the production of a polypeptide.

DNA triplet → transcription → mRNA codon

gene (many DNA triplets) → transcription → mRNA molecule (many mRNA codons)

The mRNA molecule formed by transcription is quite large. The fact that mRNA is single-stranded allows it to carry the DNA code from the nucleus to the ribosomes in the cytoplasm. Translation then occurs at the ribosome to produce the needed polypeptide.

Skill: Use a table of mRNA codons and their corresponding amino acids to deduce the sequence of amino acids coded by a short mRNA strand of known base sequence

Use these bases in mRNA to determine the sequence of amino acids which would be produced by translation at the ribosome.

A-U-G-A-A-A-G-C-U-C-C-U-U-A-U-U-A-G

Skill: Use a table of the genetic code to deduce which codon(s) corresponds to which amino acid

Use the table on the next page to determine the codons corresponding to the following amino acids:

methionine (start) – asparagine – alanine – proline – tyrosine – stop

---

Subject vocabulary

transcribed the production of an mRNA molecule from a DNA template

mitosis cell division where one diploid cell becomes two diploid cells

cytokinesis division of the cytoplasm in cell division

codon a group of three bases that together code for a single amino acid

DNA triplets three bases of DNA making up a 'word' in the genetic code

General vocabulary

triplets groups of three

The genetic code. The first, second, and third positions represent the base location in the codon. Twenty amino acids are coded for. Note AUG is the start codon. Also, note the three stop or termination codons. These start and stop codons are the punctuation marks referred to above

First position		Second position				Third position
		U	C	A	G	
U		phenylalanine	serine	tyrosine	cysteine	U
						C
				stop	stop	A
		leucine		stop	tryptophan	G
C		leucine	proline	histidine	arginine	U
						C
						A
				glutamine		G
A		isoleucine	threonine	asparagine	serine	U
						C
						A
				lysine	arginine	
		*methionine				G
G		valine	alanine	aspartic acid	glycine	U
						C
						A
				glutamic acid		G

*and start

Understanding: Translation depends on complementary base pairing between codons on mRNA and anticodons on tRNA.

Model sentence: Codons of mRNA go through complementary base pairing with anticodons of tRNA in the process of translation.

The genetic code of DNA is carried by the codons of mRNA to the ribosomes of the cell cytoplasm. tRNA molecules are present within the cell cytoplasm. Each tRNA has a region called the **anti-codon** which pairs with the complementary mRNA codon. There are 20 different amino acids which make up polypeptides and 61 different tRNA molecules. The difference in tRNA molecules is based on the anticodon present. Each of the different tRNA molecules attaches to a specific amino acid. Both the codon and the anticodon have three bases. These three bases of codons and anticodons complementary base pair, A with U, and C with G. By the complementary pairing of bases between codons and anticodons, amino acids are lined up in the exact sequence called for in the genetic code. This allows the proper polypeptide to be produced.

Application: Production of human insulin in bacteria as an example of the universality of the genetic code allowing gene transfer between species

The process of producing polypeptides/proteins uses a DNA code that is **universal** in most organisms on Earth. This universal nature of the genetic code has allowed scientists to insert the gene from humans that produces **insulin** into bacteria. This gene transfer between species allows the bacteria to actually produce human insulin. This insulin may then be successfully used to treat many humans who have **diabetes**.

Subject vocabulary

anti-codon group of three nucleotides on tRNA which base-pair with the complementary codon of mRNA

insulin hormone produced and released by exocytosis from the pancreas which controls glucose absorption by cells

diabetes disease which creates problems in the metabolism of sugars

General vocabulary

universal common, the same

2.8 Cell respiration

Main idea
The energy necessary to maintain the functions of life is provided by cell respiration.

Understanding: Cell respiration is the controlled release of energy from organic compounds to produce ATP.

Model sentence: **ATP is produced from the breakdown of organic compounds by cell respiration.**

- **Cell respiration** is a cellular process which occurs in a controlled series of **oxidation reactions**. Each step in the oxidation reaction of cell respiration is controlled by enzymes.
- It is the breakdown or oxidation of **covalent bonds** in organic compounds which provides the energy to produce **ATP**.
- The breakdown of covalent bonds occurs one bond at a time so small amounts of energy are released. The small amounts of energy released are used to produce the ATP molecules.
- The small amounts of energy released at a time allow the efficient production of ATP. Large amounts of energy release would result in increased heat within the cell. The increased heat is because not all the energy released would be converted to ATP. The increased heat produced could very well damage the cell.
- ATP is the molecule which provides the energy for all the life processes of the cell to occur.

Hints for success: **Glucose** is the organic molecule cells most prefer for cell respiration. If no glucose is present, other organic molecules may be used. The release of energy in cell respiration is due to a specific sequence of enzymes. This sequence of enzymes results in a very controlled release of energy. The sequence of enzymes and intermediate compounds bringing about the breakdown of a particular organic compound makes up a **metabolic pathway**.

Understanding: ATP from cell respiration is immediately available as a source of energy in the cell.

Model sentence: **The ATP produced in cell respiration is the form of energy used by the cell to carry out the life functions.**

ATP contains three **phosphate** molecules. The last two phosphates are bonded to the ATP molecule by **high energy bonds**. These high energy bonds are easily broken by the cell. The released energy is then used by the cell to carry out the necessary functions of the cell.

Hints for success: ATP is the essential source of energy for the cell to carry out all of its functions. Cell life ends when ATP is no longer available.

Subject vocabulary

cell respiration chemical process used by cells to gain energy from sugars and other substances

oxidation reaction a chemical reaction in which electrons are lost

covalent bond chemical bond in which electrons are shared

ATP a molecule used for a source of chemical energy

glucose a simple sugar produced by photosynthesis and used for cell respiration

metabolic pathway a chemical pathway in which a series of enzymes produces intermediate compounds on the way to producing a final product needed by the organism

phosphate group chemical group composed of phosphorus and oxygen

high energy bonds the chemical bonds which allow bonding of the last two phosphate molecules in ATP

ADP cellular energy compound which contains two phosphate molecules and one high energy bond

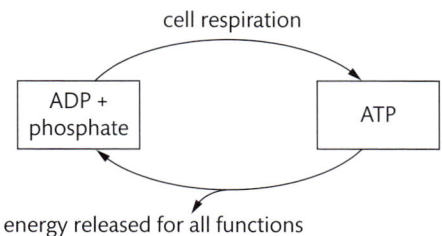

Figure 2.19 The diagram shows ADP has a phosphate added to it by the process of cell respiration to produce ATP. The energy contained in the high energy bonds of ATP may then be used by the cell to carry out the cell functions

Understanding: Anaerobic cell respiration gives a small yield of ATP from glucose.

Model sentence: Anaerobic cell respiration brings about **partial** breakdown of glucose. Anaerobic cell respiration results in a small number of ATP molecules.

Subject vocabulary

anaerobic cell respiration cellular breakdown process of organic molecules which does not require oxygen, produces a net gain of two ATP molecules

pyruvate 3-carbon compound formed by the breakdown of glucose in glycolysis, the first stage of cell respiration

glycolysis first stage of cell respiration in which oxygen is not required and glucose is broken down into 2 pyruvate molecules

fermentation process where sugar is changed to alcohol

General vocabulary

partial part of, not the whole

net gain increase after consideration of the amount used to obtain increase

- Anaerobic cell respiration does not require oxygen to occur.
- Anaerobic cell respiration occurs in the cell cytoplasm.
- Anaerobic cell respiration is the first stage in the breakdown of glucose. If glucose is not present, another organic molecule will be substituted for it.
- Anaerobic respiration breaks glucose down into two 3-carbon compounds called **pyruvate**.
- When the covalent bonds of glucose are broken in anaerobic respiration, energy is released. The released energy is used to produce a small number of ATP molecules.
- Two ATP molecules are needed to begin the process of anaerobic cell respiration.
- A total of four ATP molecules are produced from glucose anaerobic cell respiration.
- The results of the first portion of anaerobic cell respiration from the breakdown of glucose are:
  - two molecules of 3-carbon pyruvate
  - a **net gain** of two ATP molecules.
- This first part of anaerobic cell respiration is also called **glycolysis**.

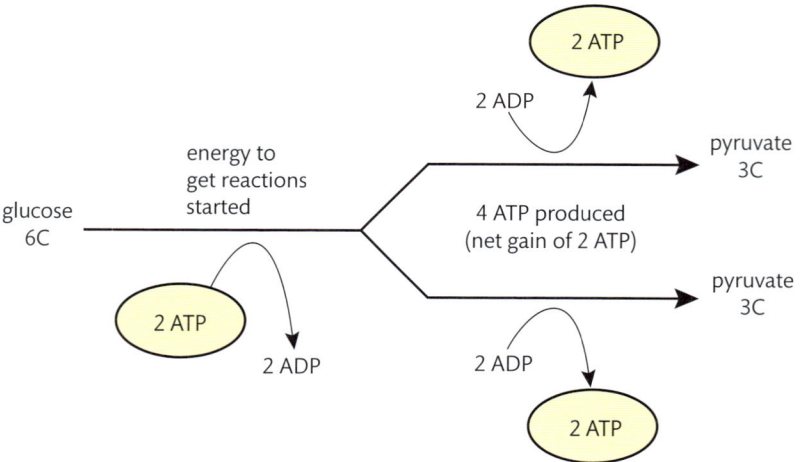

Figure 2.20 *A simplified version of the events of glycolysis*

If no oxygen is present after the first part of anaerobic cell respiration called glycolysis, a process called **fermentation** will occur. Fermentation is often described using yeast cells and human cells.

Yeast cells	Human cells
occurs in the cell cytoplasm	occurs in the cell cytoplasm
occurs in the absence of oxygen	occurs in the absence of oxygen
begins with pyruvate	begins with pyruvate
end products are ethanol and carbon dioxide	end products are lactic acid (lactate)
no gain in ATP number after glycolysis	no gain in ATP number after glycolysis

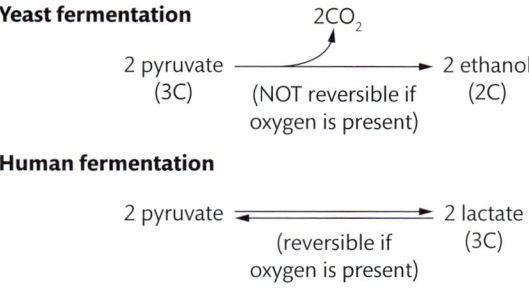

Figure 2.21 *A comparison of fermentation in yeast and human cells*

> **Hints for success:** Study the table and diagrams carefully to understand the similarities and differences between yeast and human cell fermentation. Note that if oxygen becomes available in human cells, the lactic acid (lactate) produced may be changed back to pyruvate. This is referred to as a **reversible reaction**. If oxygen becomes available in yeast cell fermentation, a reversible reaction to reform pyruvate will not occur.

Subject vocabulary

reversible reaction reaction which produces products from raw materials and also raw materials from products

Application: Use of anaerobic cell respiration in yeasts to produce ethanol and carbon dioxide in baking

The carbon dioxide produced by yeast in the fermentation process is valuable in baking. This gas causes bread to rise.

Application: Lactate production in humans when anaerobic respiration is used to maximize the power of muscle contractions

Lactate production in humans occurs during intense muscle activity. Due to the intensity of the activity not enough oxygen can be delivered to the muscles. The result of this lack of oxygen delivery is maximum muscle contraction. However, the lactate produced will seriously limit the number of maximum muscle contractions.

Understanding: Aerobic cell respiration requires oxygen and gives a large yield of ATP from glucose.

Model sentence: Aerobic respiration produces a much larger number of ATP molecules than anaerobic respiration when glucose is broken down.

- When oxygen is present, the two pyruvate molecules produced by glycolysis from one glucose molecule move into the mitochondrion.
- Once inside the mitochondrion, the two pyruvates enter the Krebs cycle one at a time and are completely broken down.

Aerobic respiration:

> Pyruvate → enters the mitochondrion → becomes part of the Krebs cycle → completely oxidized → final products are water, carbon dioxide, and a large number of ATP molecules

> **Hints for success:** Notice the final products of aerobic respiration include the production of a large number of ATP molecules. Organisms with cells containing mitochondria are capable of aerobic cell respiration.

Subject vocabulary

respirometers devices used to measure the rate of cellular respiration by analysing oxygen usage

invertebrate living creature with no backbone

photosynthesis process which converts light energy into chemical energy

visible light spectrum that portion of the light spectrum which is visible to the human eye, includes wavelengths of 400 nm to 700 nm

Skill: Analysis of results from experiments involving measurement of respiration rates in germinating seeds or invertebrates using a respirometer

It is possible to use devices called **respirometers** to measure cell respiration rates. The respirometer measures the oxygen rate of exchange. By analysing the oxygen usage when seeds germinate or as **invertebrates** carry out the life functions, one can determine the rate of cell respiration. Analysis of oxygen usage data will show changes in cell respiration rate when factors such as temperature and pH are changed.

2.9 Photosynthesis

Main idea
Photosynthesis is a cell process which converts the energy in sunlight to chemical energy.

Understanding: Photosynthesis is the production of carbon compounds in cells using light energy.

Model sentence: Photosynthesis allows the production of carbon compounds using the energy present in light.

- Photosynthesis uses the energy of light to produce carbohydrates.
- The most common carbohydrate produced by photosynthesis is glucose.
- Glucose is then broken down by cell respiration to produce ATP.

Understanding: Visible light has a range of wavelengths with violet the shortest wavelength and red the longest.

Model sentence: Photosynthesis uses energy from the visible light spectrum which has increasing wavelengths from violet to red.

- Sunlight includes all the colours of the visible light spectrum. Sunlight is said to be white light.

  violet (400 nm) → blue → green → yellow → orange → red (700 nm)

  The wavelength of each colour increases from violet to red (400 nm to 700 nm). The energy of each colour decreases from violet to red.

- Violet of the visible light spectrum has the shortest wavelength (400 nanometres). Red of the visible light spectrum has the longest wavelength (700 nanometres).
- The colours with the shortest wavelengths possess the highest energy.

Understanding: Chlorophyll absorbs red and blue light most effectively and reflects green light more than other colours.

Model sentence: **Chlorophyll** is the main **pigment** of photosynthesis and it absorbs red and blue light most efficiently.

Photosynthesis depends largely on the pigment called chlorophyll to absorb light energy. This absorbed light energy in then used to convert carbon dioxide and water into carbohydrates such as glucose.

Red and blue are the colours of the visible light spectrum that are most efficiently absorbed by chlorophyll. The energy of the red and blue colours is then used in the production of glucose.

Green light from the visible spectrum is not absorbed by chlorophyll. It is reflected and is the reason plant parts with chlorophyll appear green in colour.

> **Hints for success:** Remember that red and blue colours play a large role in the process of photosynthesis. Wavelengths producing green colours are reflected by chlorophyll and not used in photosynthesis. This is why plants with chlorophyll appear green.

Skill: Separation of photosynthetic pigments by chromatograph

Chlorophyll is not the only pigment active in photosynthesis in most plants. Pigments in different types of plants may be isolated and studied by using a **chromatograph**. Key concepts of this required practical include:

- Producing a chromatograph so that paper chromatography or thin layer **chromatography** may be carried out.
- Different pigments have different solubilities in the solvent used.
- Different pigments have different molecular masses.
- Different solubilities and different pigments will cause the pigments to separate on the chromatogram.
- Varying colours in different areas of the **chromatogram** with different R_f values indicate separate pigments.

The more pigments a plant has, the more light wavelengths may be absorbed. More light wavelengths absorbed may increase the rate of photosynthesis.

Understanding: Oxygen is produced in photosynthesis from the photolysis of water.

Model sentence: **An early stage of photosynthesis is the splitting of water to produce oxygen.**

- **Photolysis** is the process in which energy from light is used to split water.
- When photolysis occurs oxygen gas is produced. Most of the oxygen is released into the atmosphere. Hydrogen is also produced. The hydrogen is used in later stages of photosynthesis.

Application: Changes to the Earth's atmosphere, oceans, and rock deposition due to photosynthesis

Much of the oxygen produced when photolysis occurs is released into the atmosphere. This allows a continual supply of oxygen for those organisms dependent on aerobic cell respiration for their ATP.

Subject vocabulary

chlorophyll main pigment involved in the process of photosynthesis, absorbs light energy

pigment a substance with colour, able to absorb light energy in the process of photosynthesis

chromatograph instrument used to carry out chromatography

chromatography process used to separate the components of a chemical mixture

chromatogram pattern, usually of colours, formed as a result of chromatography

R_f distance moved of separate pigments compared to distance moved of the solvent, expressed as a decimal

photolysis process in photosynthesis where water molecules are split using the energy from light

General vocabulary

abundant existing in large numbers

Subject vocabulary

action spectrum a graph showing photosynthetic rate in relation to light wavelength

absorption spectrum a graph showing absorption of light at various wavelengths in the process of photosynthesis

Figure 2.22 *This action spectrum of photosynthesis indicates that most photosynthesis occurs in the blue and the red wavelength areas. Note the lower rate of photosynthesis with the green wavelength*

Understanding: Energy is needed to produce carbohydrates and other carbon compounds from carbon dioxide.

Model sentence: The energy from the absorbed colours of the visible light spectrum is used to build carbon compounds which include carbohydrates.

- In photosynthesis plants combine carbon dioxide from the atmosphere with water to produce carbon compounds such as carbohydrates.
- Glucose is commonly referred to as the carbohydrate produced by photosynthesis.
- When red and blue wavelengths are **abundant**, photosynthetic activity is at its highest.

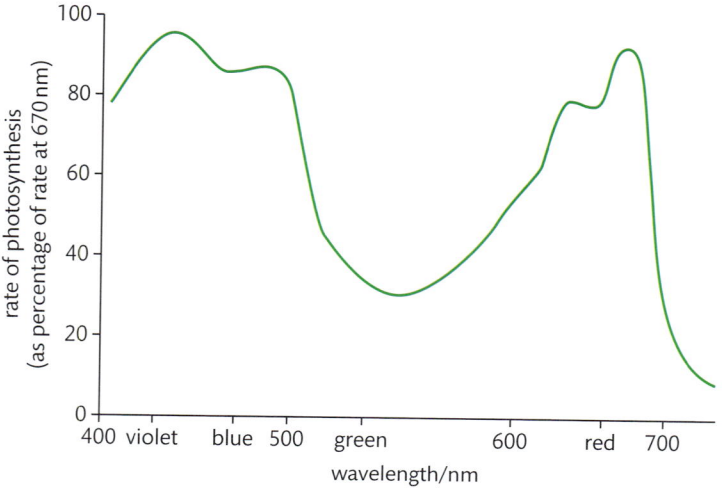

- The above figure represents an **action spectrum** for photosynthesis. Chlorophyll is the key pigment in photosynthesis. Where photosynthetic activity is highest on the graph is also the areas where the most visible light wavelengths are absorbed.

Skill: Drawing an absorption spectrum for chlorophyll and an action spectrum for photosynthesis

A visible light **absorption spectrum** drawn for chlorophyll would have similar peaks and valleys as the action spectrum for photosynthesis. An absorption spectrum for chlorophyll would show very little light absorbed at the green wavelength. Action spectrums show lesser rates of photosynthesis at the green wavelength.

Application: Changes to the Earth's atmosphere, oceans, and rock deposition due to photosynthesis

Carbon dioxide is removed from the atmosphere by photosynthesis. This causes a decrease in the overall carbon dioxide levels of the atmosphere. Also, when photosynthesis occurs there are increased carbon compounds produced from plants. The increase in plant matter may result in rock-like deposits of coal over long periods of time. When photosynthesis rates are relatively low, carbon dioxide levels rise. High levels of carbon dioxide in our atmosphere may add to an increase in overall temperatures of our planet. High carbon dioxide levels may also increase the acidity of our rain and our oceans. Higher rain and ocean acidity levels may harm existing organisms.

Hints for success: Practise drawing absorption and action spectrums for photosynthesis. Both graphs should show highest light wavelength absorption and highest rates of photosynthesis at the same blue and red wavelengths. Both graphs should show little absorption and low photosynthetic rates at the green wavelengths.

Understanding: Temperature, light intensity, and carbon dioxide concentration are possible limiting factors on the rate of photosynthesis.

Model sentence: Varying the temperature, light intensity, and carbon dioxide concentration all affects the rate of photosynthesis.

- A **limiting factor** is a factor that most directly affects the rate of a process such as photosynthesis.
- A limiting factor is often the factor which is in shortest supply. When low light intensity is present, the rate of photosynthesis is decreased even if all other factors are present in **adequate** supply. If light intensity is adequate, low levels of carbon dioxide will decrease the rate of photosynthesis.
- A limiting factor may also be an environmental factor such as temperature. If temperatures are lower than normal, photosynthetic rates will be decreased. Lower rates of photosynthesis due to low temperatures are due to decreased enzyme activity.

Skill: Design of experiments to investigate the effect of limiting factors on photosynthesis

Be certain to vary only one potential limiting factor at a time. All other photosynthetic factors should be in adequate amounts. The rate of photosynthesis may then be determined by measuring oxygen production, carbon dioxide absorption or usage, or plant biomass increase. This method allows you to say for certain whether a factor is a limiting factor or not.

Subject vocabulary

limiting factors environmental factors that determine the maximum rate of a process

General vocabulary

adequate satisfactory or sufficient for a particular requirement

3 Genetics

3.1 Genes

Main idea
Every living thing inherits **genetic** material from its parents.

Understanding: A gene is a heritable factor that consists of a length of DNA and influences a specific characteristic.

Model sentence: A gene is a sequence of DNA that controls a genetic **trait** such as blood type.

The genes which you possess are organized into chromosomes.

Examples of genetic traits include: eye colour, the ability to digest lactose, wet or dry earwax, and blood type.

> **Hints for success:** Whenever a definition is given for a major concept in biology – in this instance, the term 'gene' is defined in the heading – be sure to memorize its definition word for word. Such definitions have been phrased carefully in such a way that all important details are included.

Understanding: A gene occupies a specific position on a chromosome.

A gene for a specific trait occupies a corresponding place, called a **locus** (plural, **loci**), on a chromosome.

For example, the gene controlling a protein called transducin that allows for colour vision is found on chromosome 1. A difference of one **base** (T instead of C at position 235) in the gene's **sequence** causes an error in the production of the transducin protein and the person cannot perceive any colours.

Application: Comparison of the number of genes in humans with other species

Organism	Scientific name	Number of bases	Genes
virus	T2 bacteriophage	160 000	269
bacterium	*Escherichia coli* (type K-12)	4 639 000	4 377
human	*Homo sapiens*	3 000 000 000	21 000
fruit fly	*Drosophila melanogaster*	122 654 000	13 918
Japanese canopy plant	*Paris japonica*	150 000 000 000	unknown

---

Subject vocabulary

genetic determined by DNA and passed on from parents to offspring

heritable a genetic trait which can be passed on to offspring

trait a characteristic that distinguishes one individual from another, such as blood type

locus (plural: loci) the specific place where a gene is found on a chromosome

base the basic unit of the DNA code, represented by A, T, C, or G

sequence a series of bases in the genetic code in a particular order

Understanding: The various specific forms of a gene are alleles.

Model sentence: Variations or versions of a gene are called alleles.

In the example of transducin above, a single base pair difference between the most common allele and the rare mutated allele affects the ability to distinguish colours.

Example: cystic fibrosis

A gene called *CFTR*, found on chromosome 7, plays a key role in the production of mucus.

The standard allele allows a person's mucus-producing cells to function properly, but there is an allele generated by a mutation of the *CFTR* gene that causes cystic fibrosis.

People with this genetic condition produce abnormally thick and sticky mucus in various organs. They have difficulties with their respiratory and digestive systems, among other complications.

Understanding: Alleles differ from each other by one or only a few bases and new alleles are formed by mutation.

Model sentence: A mutation is a random, rare change in genetic material.

Mutations can be beneficial, detrimental, or neutral. A beneficial mutation is one that improves chances for survival.

Beneficial mutations contribute to an organism's success. For example, LRP5 is a rare mutation that can block infection by certain types of HIV. People with this mutation are more resistant to AIDS.

Detrimental (or harmful) mutations make survival more difficult. For example, the inability to distinguish colours could make it more challenging for an animal to find food or to see predators in time to escape.

Neutral mutations do not have an effect on survival. A mutation from GAG to GAA would not make any difference in the production of the protein concerned because both codons code for the same amino acid: glutamic acid.

The type of mutation which results in a single letter being changed is called a base substitution mutation; for example, sickle cell disease.

Application: The causes of sickle cell disease

Sickle cell disease gives a different shape to the haemoglobin molecule responsible for giving red blood cells their shape. The mutation GAG to GTG causes the haemoglobin to clump together to make the cells elongated and curved instead of disc shaped. This is due to the fact that valine replaces glutamic acid at a key point in the sequence.

The disease causes weakness, fatigue, and shortness of breath. Oxygen cannot be carried as efficiently by the irregularly shaped red blood cells. In addition, the haemoglobin tends to crystallize within the red blood cells, causing them to be less flexible. The affected red blood cells can get stuck in capillaries so blood flow can be slowed or blocked, a condition that is painful for the person. When the malformed cells are removed from the blood, the person's red blood cell count gets low and causes anaemia.

However, having the disease can be beneficial in regions where malaria is a problem because the mutation gives a person resistance to *Plasmodium*, the parasite in the blood that causes malaria.

Subject vocabulary

allele version of a gene, differing by one or more bases

mucus a slimy, protective secretion

mutation an accidental change in a genetic sequence

cystic fibrosis a genetic disease causing the overproduction of mucus in the body

HIV human immunodeficiency virus, the virus that causes AIDS

AIDS a viral infection caused by HIV and resulting in weakening of the immune system

predator an organism that hunts and eats other organisms

base substitution mutation an accidental change in one base of a genetic sequence

anaemia a low number of red blood cells in the blood

parasite a plant/animal that lives on/in another plant/animal and feeds from it

Synonyms

beneficial.......	helpful
detrimental....	harmful
neutral	neither good nor bad
fatigue...........	tiredness

General vocabulary

elongated longer than normal

crystallize form a hard solid

Subject vocabulary

sequence the order of bases in a fragment of DNA

sequencer machine that determines the order of bases in a fragment of DNA

codon a group of three bases that together code for a single amino acid

base pair a matching pair of nucleotides (A-T or C-G)

General vocabulary

linear organized along the shape of a line

Understanding: The genome is the whole of the genetic information of an organism.

To **sequence** a genome (meaning to locate each A, T, C, and G in all the genes of the organism), researchers use highly specialized laboratory equipment including **sequencers** to locate and identify the sequence of bases.

Here is an example of a fragment of a genome sequence: GTGGACCTGACTCCTGAGGAG. This short fragment contains 7 **codons** with a total of 21 bases represented by letters. The human genome possesses 3 billion **base pairs**.

Only a very limited number of organisms have had their genomes fully sequenced: baker's yeast, the fruit fly, and humans are among them.

Understanding: The entire base sequence of human genes was sequenced in the Human Genome Project.

Started in 1990, an international cooperative venture called the **Human Genome Project** set out to sequence the complete human genome. In 2003, the Project announced that it had succeeded in achieving its goal. Now, scientists are working on which sequences represent genes and which genes do what.

Skill: Use of a database to determine differences in the base sequence of a gene in two species

You are expected to be able to analyse a sequence and compare the same sequence between species in order to be able to recognize mutations and changes that have lead to evolution.

Retrieve the PDF file from the following web link: www.indiana.edu/~ensiweb/lessons/molb.ws.pdf

Or do a search for 'Cytochrome c Comparison Lab on www.indiana.edu' and you should find it. Follow the instructions to compare the genetic sequences for various organisms for the gene that makes cytochrome *c*, a protein all living things need.

The uses of genetic comparisons

The number of mutations a species has in that gene compared to another species gives insight into how closely they are related to each other.

Example: biologist Carl Woese proposed the domain Archaea to distinguish certain single-celled organisms from bacteria (prokaryotes) and eukaryotes

It took decades for Woese's proposal to be accepted but the overwhelming evidence in Archaea's favour made it very difficult for opponents of the idea to resist it.

3.2 Chromosomes

Main idea

Chromosomes carry genes in a **linear** sequence that is shared by members of a species.

Understanding: Prokaryotes have one chromosome consisting of a circular DNA molecule.

Instead of a membrane-bound nucleus, **prokaryotes** have a **nucleoid** region containing one molecule of DNA in a loop.

These single-celled organisms (bacteria and archaeans) reproduce **asexually** by **binary fission** – the chromosomes are not in pairs the way **eukaryote** chromosomes are.

Application: Cairns' technique for measuring the length of DNA molecules by autoradiography

How do we measure the length of a DNA molecule? In 1962, John Cairns used a technique called **autoradiography** to capture an image of a DNA molecule in order to measure its length. Autoradiography consists of first getting a bacterium to absorb a **radioactive marker** called ^{3}H-thymidine so that it can build its DNA with it. When placed on a photographic film in a dark room, the radioactive marker exposes the film, tracing an outline of the DNA. The outline of the DNA on the film can be used to measure the length of the loop, making it possible to know how long the DNA molecule is.

Understanding: Some prokaryotes also have plasmids but eukaryotes do not.

Plasmids are small circles of DNA consisting of segments of a prokaryote's genome.

Plasmids are not found in eukaryotes so plants, animals, fungi, and protists do not have them in their cells.

Plasmids can be used by prokaryotes to transfer some of their genetic information from one individual to another. Plasmids can also be used in laboratories to genetically modify a prokaryote. More about this in section 3.5.

Understanding: Eukaryote chromosomes are linear DNA molecules associated with histone proteins.

Model sentence: Bacteria and Archaea have a single circular chromosome in their cells, whereas eukaryotes have multiple linear chromosomes.

Eukaryotes have a membrane-bound nucleus containing chromosomes made of DNA that is not in the form of loops. Instead of circular DNA, eukaryotes have linear DNA.

The DNA is wrapped around protein molecules called **histones**. Histones stacked together form structures called **nucleosomes** that act as a packaging system to keep the DNA organized. As in eukaryotes, archaeans also have histones associated with their DNA.

The process of wrapping DNA around these proteins again and again is called **supercoiling**. Supercoiled DNA cannot be **transcribed** or worked on by enzymes – it must be **unwound** before such things can happen.

Subject vocabulary

prokaryote single-celled organism whose organelles are not bound by membranes

nucleoid region of a prokaryotic cell where the DNA exists

binary fission a method of reproduction whereby a single-celled organism makes a copy of itself and splits in two

eukaryote single-celled organism that contain organelles bound by membranes

autoradiography technique of capturing images of radioactive substances on photographic film

radioactive marker a radioactive isotope of an element introduced into an organism and used to follow how the organism uses that element

plasmid small ring of DNA separate from the bacterial chromosome often used in genetic modification

histones proteins associated with DNA in eukaryotic chromosomes

nucleosome structure found in eukaryotic chromosomes consisting of a strand of DNA wrapped around eight histone molecules

supercoiling a process in which intense folding and coiling of a structure occurs

transcribed the production of an mRNA molecule from a DNA template

General vocabulary

asexually without sexual association

unwound loosened from the original shape

Understanding: In a eukaryote species there are different chromosomes that carry different genes.

Typically, eukaryotes have many different chromosomes (see the table opposite) and each chromosome will have different genetic information controlling the various traits of the organism.

Example: wild wheat plants

A wild wheat plant (*Triticum baeoticum*) that can be used to produce flour for bread has 14 chromosomes arranged in 7 pairs. In each pair, one chromosome is from the plant's father and the other from the plant's mother. Some chromosomes will carry information about the plant's height or its colour, other chromosomes will have DNA that codes for its root system or for producing sex cells.

Skill: Use of databases to identify the locus of a human gene and its polypeptide product

Students are expected to be able to use a database to identify the locus of a human gene and its **polypeptide** product. One example of such a database is the National Center for Biotechnology Information (NCBI). Search for it online and see if you can find the gene sequence that codes for human insulin; the gene is found on chromosome 11, its name is *INS* and its ID number is 3630.

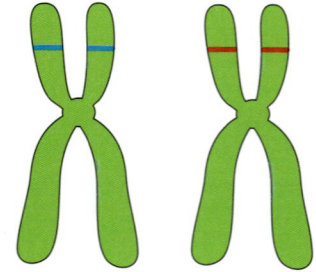

Figure 3.1 *Homologous chromosomes. Although these are the same size and shape, and carry the same genes, the different coloured bands on the short arms of each chromosome reveal that they do not carry the same allele of the gene at the locus shown*

Understanding: Homologous chromosomes carry the same sequence of genes but not necessarily the same alleles of those genes.

When referring to similar chromosomes, the term **homologous** means having similar size and shape and it means that the two chromosomes carry the same genes. For a chromosome, shape usually refers to the position of the **centromere**.

Since genes can come in different forms (alleles), the information on two homologous chromosomes will not necessarily be identical.

Example: homologous chromosomes and alleles

For a given gene with the alleles **B** or **b**, a child could receive the allele **B** from her mother and the allele **b** from her father, the maternal chromosome in the child's homologous pair will have a **B** and the paternal chromosome will have a **b**.

Understanding: Diploid nuclei have pairs of homologous chromosomes. Haploid nuclei have one chromosome of each pair.

The term **diploid** is used to describe a nucleus in which the chromosomes are organized into pairs.

Most cells in the human body, for example, are diploid with 46 chromosomes organized into 23 pairs. Some cells have no nucleus, such as red blood cells.

The letter n indicates the number of sets of chromosomes a nucleus can have. In humans, $n = 23$ because humans have 23 different chromosomes. Diploid human cells are $2n = 46$.

Haploid cells contain only one of each chromosome, instead of containing pairs of chromosomes.

Subject vocabulary

polypeptide polymer of many amino acids combined by peptide bonds

homologous chromosome pairs that occur at fertilization, one from the female parent and one from the male parent

centromere region where sister chromatids attach

diploid a cell which has chromosomes in homologous pairs

haploid a cell that has only one chromosome of each homologous pair

Sex cells (sperm cells and egg cells) are haploid. For example, in humans, sex cells contain $n = 23$ chromosomes. When a sperm cell encounters an egg, the newly formed cell becomes diploid.

It is rare for adult eukaryotes to contain only haploid cells, but adult male bees, wasps, and ants are haploid.

Understanding: The number of chromosomes is a characteristic feature of members of a species.

One aspect that makes a species different from others is the number of chromosomes it possesses.

Example: number of chromosomes in different species

The fruit fly (*Drosophila melanogaster*) used in genetics experiments has four pairs of chromosomes ($n = 4$) and the first organism whose genome was sequenced, *Caenorhabditis elegans*, has six pairs of chromosomes ($n = 6$).

The table below shows more examples.

	Types of cells and chromosome numbers	
Species	Haploid (n)	Diploid ($2n$)
human, *Homo sapiens*	23	46
chimpanzee, *Pan troglodytes*	24	48
domestic dog, *Canis familiaris*	39	78
rice, *Oryza sativa*	12	24
roundworm, *Parascaris equorum*	2	4

Skill: Comparison of diploid chromosome numbers

Compare the chromosome numbers of the organisms in the table above. Also, have a look at the table in Section 3.1 comparing the number of bases and genes in various organisms.

Understanding: A karyogram shows the chromosomes of an organism in homologous pairs of decreasing length.

Model sentence: It is possible to find out the gender of an unborn child or determine if there are any chromosomal **anomalies** by preparing a karyogram.

A **karyogram** is a diagram used to arrange the chromosomes of a cell into pairs in order of their size, shape (position of their centromere), and banding patterns (lines across the **chromatids**).

It is usually made from the cells of an unborn baby and uses images of the chromosomes taken during **mitotic metaphase**.

A karyogram is used to determine a person's **karyotype**, which can reveal various kinds of genetic information such as the number of chromosomes they have and the kinds of sex chromosomes they have.

Synonyms
anomalies ...... differences

Subject vocabulary
karyogram a diagram showing the chromosomes of an organism

chromatid the identical parts of a doubled chromosomes held together by a centromere

mitotic metaphase a stage of meiosis during which homologous chromosomes line up and the nuclear membrane disintegrates

karyotype the number and appearance of chromosomes within the cell of an organism

When interpreted correctly, a karyogram can indicate whether or not the unborn baby is a boy or a girl and whether or not the child has any chromosomal disorders such as extra or missing chromosomes.

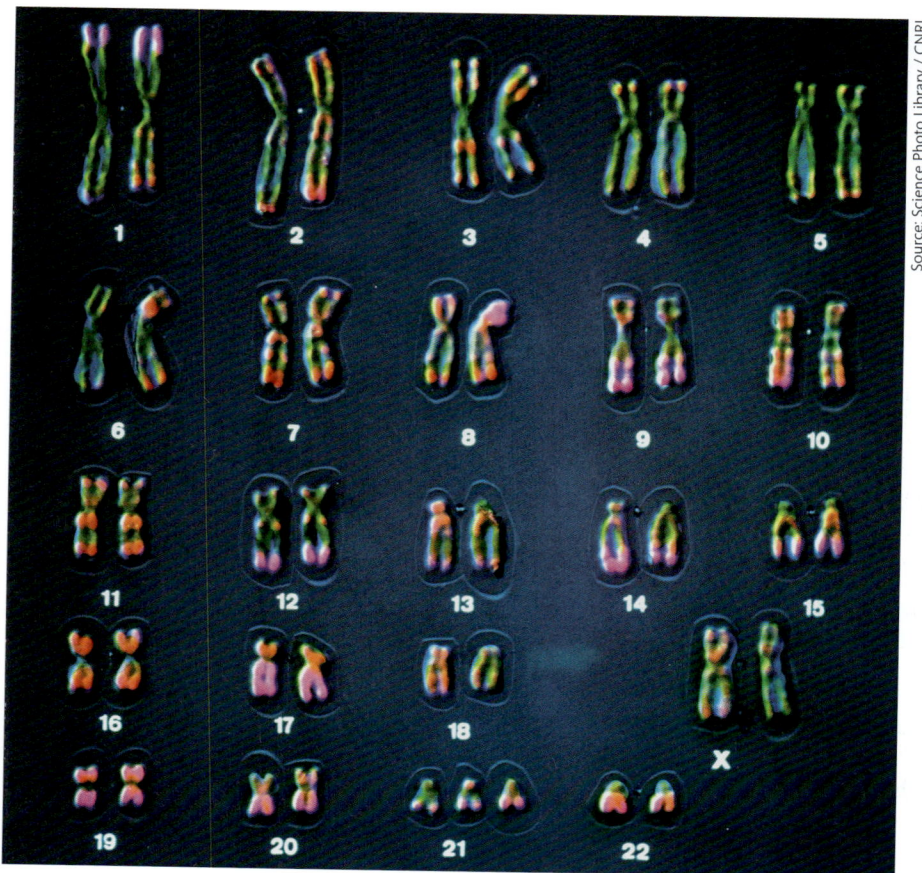

Figure 3.2 *This is a karyogram showing all 23 pairs of chromosomes. What can we learn about the individual's karyotype from this figure? This karyogram was prepared using false colour imagery*

Application: Use of karyograms to deduce sex and diagnose Down syndrome in humans

By looking at the 23rd set of chromosomes in the karyogram above, doctors are able to determine the sex of this child: XX means it is a girl (see next section). Also, by looking at the 21st pair, a specialist is able to see if the child has **Down syndrome**. The image above shows that this girl has three chromosomes in the 21st pair (**trisomy**) and therefore has Down syndrome.

Understanding: Sex is determined by sex chromosomes and **autosomes** are chromosomes that do not determine sex.

The gender of humans is determined by the last set of chromosomes, the 23rd pair.

There are two types of sex chromosomes: X and Y.

X chromosomes are big, with long chromatids, whereas Y chromosomes are easy to recognize by their very small size and short chromatids.

Typically, one of two configurations can happen: XX for a girl and XY for a boy. Mothers donate one of their two X chromosomes and fathers can donate either an X (found in half the sperm cells he produces) or a Y chromosome (found in the other half of the sperm cells he produces).

The other chromosomes, numbers 1 to 22, are called autosomes. Any traits whose genes are found on these 22 chromosomes are called autosomal traits.

Subject vocabulary

Down syndrome a chromosomal anomaly characterized by 3 chromosomes in the 21st pair

trisomy presence of three copies of a chromosome in a cell rather than the usual pair

autosomes chromosomes that do not determine sex

3.3 Meiosis

Main idea
Alleles **segregate** during **meiosis** allowing new combinations to be formed by the **fusion** of gametes.

Understanding: One diploid nucleus divides by meiosis to produce four haploid nuclei.

Gametes, otherwise known as sex cells, are haploid. In humans, this means there are 23 chromosomes present in sperm cells or in egg cells.

A special type of cell division called meiosis is needed for the production of gametes. Whereas most cells in the body divide using **mitosis**, sex cells are the only ones to use meiosis.

Meiosis is known as a **reduction division** because the number of chromosomes in the cell is reduced from $2n$ to n. The number of nuclei that can be produced by meiosis is four.

For example, inside the testes, a cell that uses meiosis to divide will produce four sperm cells, each containing half the information from the parent cell.

Understanding: The halving of the chromosome number allows a sexual life cycle with fusion of gametes.

Model sentence: In order to ensure that the chromosome number is maintained from generation to generation, meiosis produces sex cells with half the total number of chromosomes per cell that the individual possesses.

Genetic information is precious to a species so it might seem **contradictory** to eliminate half of it when producing gametes.

The reason for putting only half of the genetic information into a sperm cell or egg cell is to maintain the same chromosome number generation after generation.

If a woman donated all of her 46 chromosomes and a man donated all of his 46 chromosomes to their future baby, the child would receive a total of 92 chromosomes. This would generate too much conflicting genetic information and the baby's cells would not form correctly.

Instead, the mother donates 23 chromosomes and the father donates 23, producing a baby with a number of chromosomes that is characteristic to humans: 46.

The fertilized egg, called a **zygote**, is now diploid. The sexual life cycle is complete.

Understanding: DNA is **replicated** before meiosis so that all chromosomes consist of two sister chromatids.

As with mitosis, meiosis requires two copies of all the DNA in a cell before it can begin. This copying happens during the **S phase** of a cell's **life cycle**.

Synonyms
segregate .... separate
contradictory . inconsistent
replicate .... copy/repeat

Subject vocabulary

meiosis cell division where one diploid cell becomes four haploid cells

fusion two cells that join together as one

gamete a sex cell, either a sperm cell or an egg cell

reduction division meiosis, so called because the number of chromosomes in the daughter cells is half the original number in the parent cell

zygote diploid fertilized egg

S phase the stage in the cell cycle when DNA is replicated before division begins

life cycle the repeating pattern of cell growth, reproduction, and death that allows a species' DNA to be passed on generation after generation

Subject vocabulary

sister chromatids the two identical structures of a doubled chromosome

condensation in DNA, the coiling of chromatin to form chromosomes; in chemical reactions, the joining of two organic molecules during which a water molecule is produced

meiosis I first part of meiosis during which homologous chromosomes separate to produce two diploid cells

meiosis II second part of meiosis during which sister chromatids separate to produce four haploid cells (gametes)

prophase I a stage of meiosis during which homologous chromosomes line up and can perform crossing over

crossing over a process during meiosis I involving the exchange of genetic material between non-sister chromatids

Synonyms

offspring........ young/children

When DNA replication is complete, each chromosome has two identical **sister chromatids**. They are joined together at the centromere, giving the chromosome the 'X' shape we are familiar with.

Later, these two sister chromatids will separate so that each one will become a distinct chromosome. For now, however, they must be considered sister chromatids of the same chromosome.

Understanding: The early stages of meiosis involve pairing of homologous chromosomes and crossing over followed by **condensation**.

Meiosis consists of two parts: **meiosis I** and **meiosis II**. There are four stages in each part: prophase, metaphase, anaphase, and telophase.

Prophase I: homologous chromosomes pair up and **crossing over** happens

Crossing over involves sections of two non-sister homologous chromatids breaking at the same point, twisting around each other, and then connecting to the other's initial position.

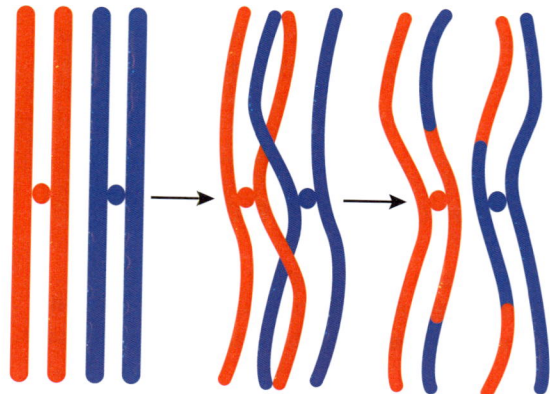

Figure 3.3 Crossing over occurring in a pair of homologous chromosomes

Crossing over is one way to increase genetic variety in the gametes by creating some chromosomes that are a mix of the person's maternal and paternal chromosomes. We will see later why variety in **offspring** is so important to evolution.

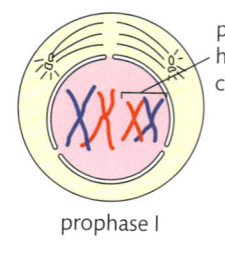 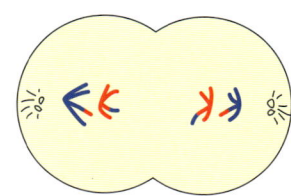

prophase I — pair of homologous chromosomes — metaphase I — cell's equator — anaphase I — telophase I

Figure 3.4 The stages of meiosis I

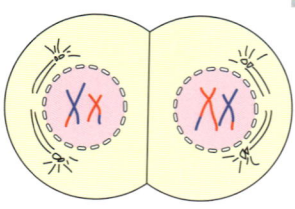 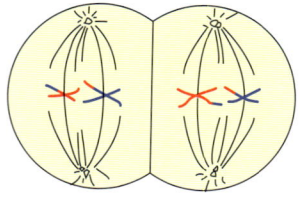 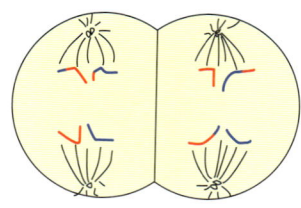 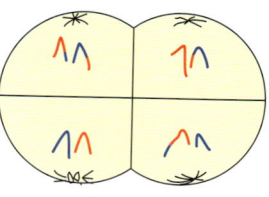

prophase II — metaphase II — anaphase II — telophase II

Figure 3.5 The stages of meiosis II

Skill: Drawing diagrams to show the stages of meiosis resulting in the formation of four haploid cells

You are expected to be able to draw the eight stages of meiosis shown in the diagram above starting with a parent diploid cell and resulting in four haploid daughter cells.

> **Hints for success:** To be sure you are ready for an exam question asking you to draw a diagram, take out a blank sheet of paper and try to draw what is asked for without looking at your notes or at the original diagrams. Remember: for drawings, always use pencil and always label or annotate using arrows that touch the details concerned.

Understanding: Orientation of pairs of homologous chromosomes prior to separation is random. Crossing over and random orientation promotes genetic variation.

Model sentence: Two effective ways of increasing variety in offspring are random orientation and crossing over.

Metaphase I: the way in which the homologous pairs line up along the cell's equator is random.

In humans, there are 2^{23} ways in which chromosomes can be randomly aligned. That's over 8 million different possible orientations.

Like crossing over, **random orientation** also helps to increase the genetic variety in the gametes, making it very unlikely for any two of a woman's eggs to be identical or any two of a man's sperm cells to carry the same combination of alleles.

Understanding: Separation of pairs of homologous chromosomes in the first division of meiosis halves the chromosome number.

Anaphase I: one of each of the homologous chromosomes in a pair is pulled to one side of the cell and the other is pulled to the other side. At this point, the chromosomes still are composed of two chromatids connected at the centromere.

Telophase I: usually, the chromosomes **uncoil** and a new nuclear membrane forms around each of the two nuclei.

By the end of meiosis I, the chromosome number has been halved. It has gone from 2*n* to *n*.

In humans, that means 23 chromosomes (one per pair) are present in each of the two cells instead of 46. In the figure, it means four chromosomes (two pairs) from the parent cell have become two chromosomes in the daughter cells.

Application: Non-disjunction can cause Down syndrome and other chromosome abnormalities.

If two homologous chromosomes got pulled over to the left side instead of being separated to opposite parts of the cell, the resulting nucleus on the left would have an extra chromosome and the one on the right would be missing one. This kind of event is called a non-disjunction and it produces chromosome abnormalities

Synonyms

orientation ..... location/position
uncoil .... unwind/untwist

Subject vocabulary

metaphase I the stage of meiosis when homologous chromosomes pair up along the equator of the cell

random orientation a process during meiosis involving the lining up of chromosomes in an order determined by chance

anaphase I the stage in meiosis where homologous chromosomes separate

telophase I the stage in the cell cycle where chromosomes uncoil and a new nuclear membrane forms

chromosome abnormalities condition where cells contain too many or too few chromosomes, usually caused by non-disjunction during cell division in which children can be born with 45 chromosomes or 47 instead of 46. As seen in the previous section, in the case of trisomy of the 21st chromosome, non-disjunction leads to Down syndrome.

Application: **Studies showing age of parents influences chances of non-disjunction**

Scientists wanted to know what factors influenced the occurrence of Down syndrome. Below is a graph of the results of frequency of the syndrome compared to the mother's age at the time of birth of the child. Not surprisingly, it was concluded that after the age of 35, as the age of the mother increases, the chances of having a baby with Down syndrome increase dramatically.

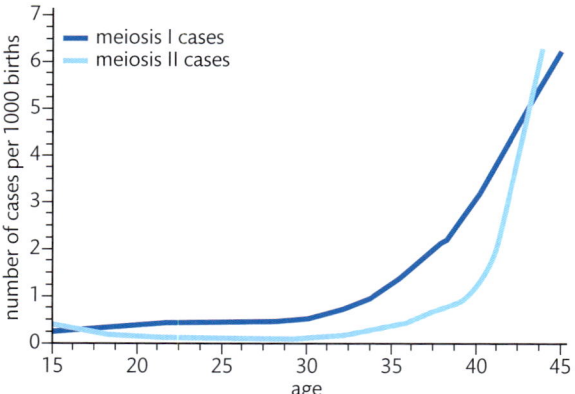

Figure 3.6 *Correlation of age of mother and occurrence of Down syndrome in children*

Source: reproduced with permission of Dr. Stephanie Sherman

Application: **Description of methods used to obtain cells for karyotype analysis**

One way to find out if an unborn child has a chromosome abnormality is to prepare a karyogram. One way of doing this is by **amniocentesis**. This involves removing some **amniotic liquid** that surrounds the baby. A long needle is used to collect the liquid through the mother's abdomen. **Ultrasound** technology is used to see where the baby is to ensure its safety. **Chorionic villus sampling** is another technique and is preferred earlier in the pregnancy. Here, tissue from the **placenta** is collected and cells are analysed.

Understanding: Fusion of gametes from different parents promotes genetic variation.

Meiosis II: the next four steps are to pull the chromatids apart and make a total of four nuclei, each with *n* number of chromosomes.

At the end of **telophase II**, each chromosome now consists of a single copy and the cells produced by meiosis are ready to become gametes.

The next step for gametes is to find their **complementary** partner: a sperm cell must meet an egg cell.

In determining which sperm cell will **fuse** with which egg, there is a certain amount of randomness (which egg or which sperm cells happen to have been produced at the time of fertilization) as well as a certain amount of chance (which man meets which woman and at what time fertilization happens).

The zygote, which is the first cell of what may become a new child, is unique.

The three main factors influencing variation in offspring are: (1) crossing over during prophase I, (2) random orientation during metaphase I, and (3) some of the randomness and chance involved in the process of fertilization.

Subject vocabulary

amniocentesis a test used to determine the genetic make-up of a foetus using cells collected from amniotic liquid

amniotic liquid the fluid surrounding the developing foetus

ultrasound a method used to produce an image of a baby in the uterus

chorionic villus sampling a test used to determine the genetic make-up of a foetus using cells collected from the placenta

placenta a structure found in the uterus that allows exchanges of gases, nutrients, and waste products between mother and foetus

telophase II the second telophase stage in meiosis where chromosomes uncoil and a nuclear membrane forms around the haploid nucleus to produce a gamete

fuse join together

Synonyms

complementary ..... balancing/matching

3.4 Inheritance

Main idea
The **inheritance** of genes follows patterns.

Nature of science: Making **quantitative** measurements with **replicates** to ensure reliability. Mendel's genetic crosses with pea plants generated numerical data.

Understanding: Mendel discovered the principles of inheritance with experiments in which large numbers of pea plants were crossed.

In 1865, an Austrian monk named Gregor Mendel published the results of his experiments on how garden pea plants (*Pisum sativum*) passed on their characteristics.

Gregor Mendel used **artificial pollination** in a series of experiments in which he carefully chose the pollen of various plants to fertilize other individuals of the same species.

He used a small brush to place the pollen on the reproductive parts of the flowers, thus replacing the insects that do it naturally. This technique allows the experimenter to decide exactly which plants are fertilized by which pollen, instead of leaving it up to chance encounters with insects.

Some of the characteristics, or traits, he examined were whether the peas were yellow or green, round or wrinkled, or if the plants were tall or short.

For the genetic trait of height, one allele is dominant (**T**) for tall, and the other is recessive (**t**) for short. The table shows Mendel's results. (See last row of table for Mendel's results for height.)

Characteristics in parents	First generation produced	Second generation produced	Ratio of results seen in second generation
round × wrinkled seeds	100% round	5474 round 1850 wrinkled	2.96:1
yellow × green seeds	100% yellow	6022 yellow 2001 green	3.01:1
green × yellow pods	100% green	428 green 152 yellow	2.82:1
tall × short plants	100% tall	787 tall 277 short	2.84:1

Understanding: Gametes are haploid so contain only one allele of each gene.

When the male parts of a flower produce pollen, the sex cells inside the pollen contain only one copy of each pair of genes; gametes are haploid.

Subject vocabulary

inheritance passing on a trait from one generation to the next

artificial pollination process where humans control plant fertilization by transferring pollen from one specific flower to another

gene section of DNA molecule that codes for a particular trait/protein in an organism

General vocabulary

quantitative a numerical measurement

Synonyms

replicate .... copy

As a result, if the parent plant had a genotype of **Tt**, half the gametes would contain only **T** and the other half would contain only **t**. Each sex cell contains only one allele in the pair that the parent had.

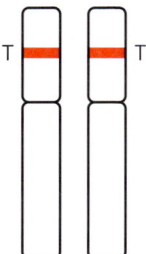

Figure 3.7 *This drawing shows you a pair of chromosomes showing a homozygous state,* **TT**

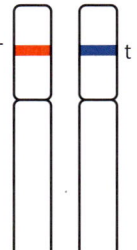

Figure 3.8 *This drawing shows you a pair of chromosomes showing a heterozygous state,* **Tt**

Understanding: The two alleles of each gene separate into different haploid daughter nuclei during meiosis.

The reason why there is only one allele in each gamete is because of meiosis.

During anaphase I, the two chromosomes in each homologous pair are separated so that the daughter cells only contain one of each chromosome in the pair. Remember that meiosis is considered a reduction division for this reason.

The result: the two alleles for any given trait are separated between gametes.

For example, some children from the same mother and father can be born with different hair colour or blood type. It depends on which alleles were present in the sperm cell that fertilized the egg.

Understanding: Fusion of gametes results in diploid zygotes with two alleles of each gene that may be the same allele or different alleles.

When a sperm and an egg cell meet during fertilization, the two nuclei fuse.

For example, if the egg contained a **T** and the sperm contained a **t**, the resulting zygote's genotype would be **Tt**. (Remember to read it 'big T little t'.)

The zygote is diploid. Its genotype may be the same as one or both parents but it could also be different from both parents. This is demonstrated below.

- Both parents are **Tt**. This genotype has one dominant allele and one recessive allele. It is said to be **heterozygous**. To see what kind of offspring these parents have, we can draw a table called a Punnett grid in which the alleles in one parent's set of gametes are shown on the side and those of the other parent are shown on top.
- Notice how some of the offspring (the four genotypes in the centre) are also heterozygous, like their parents. However, there is a 1 out of 4 chance that the genotype turns out **TT**. This is called **homozygous dominant**. The third possibility (which also represents one chance in four) is **tt**. This is called **homozygous recessive**.
- This type of cross is called a **monohybrid cross**. It shows how one trait can be passed on.

Subject vocabulary

heterozygous possessing two different alleles of a gene at a particular locus

homozygous dominant having the same two dominant alleles for a particular gene

homozygous recessive having the same two recessive alleles for a particular gene

monohybrid cross a cross between two heterozygous parents to show how a single trait is passed on to the offspring

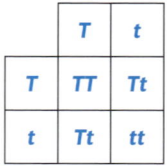

Figure 3.9 *A monohybrid cross showing the possible offspring of two heterozygous parents*

Understanding: Dominant alleles mask the effects of recessive alleles but co-dominant alleles have joint effects.

The rules of dominance: in garden peas, **TT** (homozygous dominant) results in a tall plant. Only the allele for being tall is present.

tt (homozygous recessive) results in a short plant. Only the allele for being short is present.

Tt results in a tall plant because the dominant allele **T**, masks the recessive allele **t**. The result is that the recessive allele **t** is neither transcribed nor translated.

The steps to setting up a Punnett grid to determine the offspring of a given set of parents are as follows:
- Step 1: Choose a letter. Use capital and small case versions of the same letter to show alleles. An example is: **T** = allele for tall plants, **t** = allele for short plants.
- Step 2: Determine the parents' genotypes. It is best to write all possibilities (**TT**, **Tt**, or **tt**) and proceed by elimination. A short plant cannot be **TT** or **Tt** so it must be **tt**. A tall plant cannot be **tt**, but could be **TT** or **Tt**.
- Step 3: Determine gametes.
- Step 4: Draw the Punnett grid.
- Step 5: Work out the chances of each genotype and phenotype occurring.

Here are some further examples: first cross: **TT** × **tt**, second cross: **tt** × **Tt**.

	t	t
T	Tt	Tt
T	Tt	Tt

	T	t
t	Tt	tt
t	Tt	tt

Analysis and interpretation:	
Genotypes of offspring:	**Genotypes of offspring:**
TT: 0% chance	**TT**: 0% chance
Tt: 100% chance	**Tt**: 50% chance
tt: 0% chance	**tt**: 50% chance
Phenotypes:	**Phenotypes:**
100% chance of being tall	50% chance of being tall
0% chance of being short	50% chance of being short

Figure 3.10 *Analysis of the two Punnet grids above*

Hints for success: Be careful when choosing letters. Nearly half the letters of the alphabet should be avoided because they are too similar in their capital and lower case forms. Don't use Cc, Ff, Kk, Oo, Pp, Ss, Uu, Vv, Ww, Xx, Yy, Zz. If the person grading your work cannot tell the difference between the two letters, they cannot give you the marks.

A **test cross** can be done if a plant is tall and we need to know if it is **TT** or **Tt**. It is impossible to determine the genotype just by looking at the plant.

To perform a test cross, a known homozygous recessive individual is crossed with the individual that has the unknown genotype.

Subject vocabulary

test cross crossing with a homozygous recessive individual to determine the alleles of the test individual

The two possible results are shown below – if the unknown parent was **TT**, all offspring will be tall, whereas if the unknown parent was **Tt**, only half should be tall.

	t	t
T	Tt	Tt
T	Tt	Tt

	t	t
T	Tt	Tt
t	tt	tt

Figure 3.11 *Two possible outcomes of a test cross*

Sometimes one allele does not mask another but rather both alleles are expressed. This is called **co-dominance** and will be explored below.

Understanding: Many genetic diseases in humans are due to **recessive** alleles of autosomal genes although some genetic diseases are due to **dominant** or co-dominant alleles.

Model sentence: Some traits are caused by alleles that have a dominant/recessive relationship, whereas other traits can show co-dominance.

The vast majority of genetic diseases are caused by genes found on chromosomes numbered 1 to 22 (the autosomes).

It is more common for genetic diseases to be caused by recessive alleles.

Examples of **recessive autosomal genetic diseases** or conditions are:
- Albinism – a lack of **pigmentation** in skin, eyes, and hair.
- Cystic fibrosis – production of excessively thick, sticky mucus, resulting in respiratory and digestive difficulties.
- Tay–Sachs disease – causes damage to nerve cells and early death in children.

It is less common for genetic diseases to be caused by dominant alleles.

Examples of **dominant autosomal genetic diseases** are:
- Huntington's disease – causes the degeneration of neurones, often not showing up until the age of 40 years old and causing difficulty walking and uncontrollable movements.
- Polydactyly – causes the growth of more than five fingers or toes on a hand or foot.

A small number of genetic diseases result from co-dominance. Sickle cell disease is one example (see the third example below).

Example: cystic fibrosis

If a couple wants to know what the chances are that their next child will inherit cystic fibrosis, it is important to determine the **genotypes** of the parents. Consider a couple in which the woman does not have cystic fibrosis but her father did. The man in the couple has cystic fibrosis. Use the five steps:
- Step 1: Use **A** to represent the allele for healthy mucus production, and **a** for the allele for cystic fibrosis. The allele that causes the disease is recessive so the only way to get it is to have the genotype **aa**.
- Step 2: There are three possible genotypes: **AA**, **Aa**, and **aa**. The mother must have at least one **A** since she does not have cystic fibrosis. She must have at least one **a** since her father was **aa** (he had cystic fibrosis). We can eliminate the possibility that she is **AA** so she must be **Aa**. In order to have cystic fibrosis, the man in the couple cannot possess an **A** allele. He can only be **aa**.

Subject vocabulary

co-dominance alleles that have joint effects, both alleles are expressed in the organism's phenotype

recessive an allele that is only expressed when no dominant allele is present to mask it, notably when an individual is homozygous recessive

dominant an allele that is expressed in preference to another (recessive) allele

recessive autosomal genetic diseases a condition which only occurs when two recessive alleles on non-sex chromosomes are present

dominant autosomal genetic diseases diseases caused by the presence of a particular dominant allele on non-sex chromosomes

genotypes genes of an organism for a particular trait

Synonyms

pigmentation . colour

- Steps 3 and 4: Gametes (**A** and **a** for the woman, **a** and **a** for the man) are placed in the side and top boxes of the Punnett grid, which is then filled in:
- Step 5: There is a 50% chance that their child will be **aa** and have cystic fibrosis.

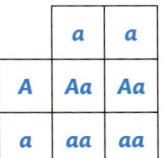

Figure 3.12 *A Punnett grid showing a heterozygous woman and a man with cystic fibrosis*

Hints for success: When answering questions about genetic outcomes for offspring, it is sometimes tempting to go straight to the Punnett grid and forget about steps 1–3. The problem is that if you do not think carefully about the information going into the Punnett grid, you could put in the wrong information.

Example: Huntington's disease – use of a pedigree chart

The diagram to the right is called a **pedigree chart** and it allows genetic experts to follow a trait from one generation to the next.

Symbols used: filled shapes show the trait is present in the **phenotype** (in this case, Huntington's disease), whereas empty shapes show individuals who do not have the trait. Circles show females and squares show males. The children (the second row in this example) are presented in order from oldest on the left to youngest on the right. Each new row is a new generation.

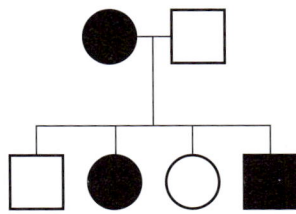

Figure 3.13 *A pedigree chart showing an affected woman, a non-affected man, and their four children*

This family has six individuals. The mother, the second son, and the first daughter have Huntington's disease. The father, the second daughter, and the eldest son do not.

Pedigrees are useful for establishing the genotypes of members of a family. In the case of Huntington's, **H** = the allele for the disease and **h** = the allele for healthy nerve functions.

It can be concluded that the mother must be heterozygous (**Hh**) because she had some children without Huntington's. A parent who is **HH** could produce only children with the disease so this is definitely not her situation.

Only the first daughter or youngest son, who are both **Hh**, could pass on to the next generation the allele that causes Huntington's (with a 50% chance).

Example: sickle cell disease – co-dominance

Sickle cell disease is caused by a mutation of a gene that helps to make haemoglobin. The result is a misshaped haemoglobin molecule, which also causes a change in shape of the red blood cells. Instead of disc-shaped cells, elongated, curved cells with a boomerang shape are formed.

People who inherit two mutated alleles (one from the father, one from the mother) have high numbers of sickle-shaped cells and suffer severe symptoms such as fatigue and pain because the blood vessels get blocked.

People who inherit only one mutated allele but receive a healthy allele from the other parent do not have the symptoms of the disease but they are resistant to malaria.

Someone who is heterozygous is said to have **sickle cell trait**. This condition shows co-dominance or incomplete dominance. Some of the characteristics of the mutated allele are **masked** by the dominant allele but others are not.

Subject vocabulary

pedigree chart a diagram showing how a genetic trait is passed on from generation to generation

phenotype visible result of an organism's genotype

sickle cell trait the heterozygous condition where an individual has one healthy allele and one mutated allele coding for sickle cell disease

Synonyms

masked .... covered/hidden

Example: the ABO blood type system – multiple alleles and co-dominance

Until now, the examples have all been with only two alleles. The ABO blood type system is different – it has three alleles. They are written as follows:

- I^A = the allele that produces proteins for type A antigens, giving type A blood. This allele is dominant to *i* and co-dominant with I^B.
- I^B = the allele that produces proteins for type B antigens, giving type B blood. This allele is dominant to *i* and co-dominant with I^A.
- *i* = the allele that produces neither A nor B antigens, giving type O blood. This allele is recessive to both I^A and I^B.

These three alleles can produce four possible phenotypes: type A blood, type B, type AB, and type O.

There are six unique combinations of these three alleles to produce the four phenotypes:

- $I^A I^A$ or $I^A i$ = type A blood
- $I^B I^B$ or $I^B i$ = type B blood
- $I^A I^B$ = type AB blood (this is where co-dominance comes in)
- ii = type O blood.

Notice with the fifth combination that both alleles for A and B are present. The person will produce both A and B antigens. One allele does not mask the other – there is no such thing as recessive between A and B. The two alleles are co-dominant. Both alleles are transcribed and translated.

Understanding: Some genetic diseases are sex linked. The pattern of inheritance is different with sex-linked genes due to their location on sex chromosomes.

Model sentence: Not all genetic traits are passed on equally to males and females – sex-linked traits are distributed unequally between men and women.

When the gene responsible for a genetic disease is found on the 23rd set of chromosomes, the X or Y sex chromosomes, the disease is said to be **sex linked**.

Sex-linked traits affect one gender more frequently than another.

Examples: haemophilia and colour blindness (both found on the X chromosome) affect more males than females.

- **Haemophilia** prevents the production of certain blood-clotting proteins (factor VIII or factor IX, depending on the type of haemophilia). As a result, the person is at risk of excessive bleeding and haemorrhaging.
- **Red–green colour blindness** (affecting about 1% of males) causes deficiencies in certain types of **photoreceptors** of the retina. People with this condition have difficulty distinguishing red from green. There are several other types of colour blindness.

The allele is represented by the letter h but is written as a superscript X^h to show that it is on the X chromosome. The Y chromosome cannot carry an allele for this gene so the notation is Y. A man with haemophilia has a genotype $X^h Y$. Note the absence of a dominant allele to mask the trait.

If a woman was $X^H X^h$, she would not have haemophilia. However, she would be a carrier.

Only females can be carriers for sex-linked traits whose genes are found on the X chromosome.

Subject vocabulary

sex linked a trait that is controlled by alleles located on the sex chromosomes

haemophilia a condition where certain blood clotting factors are not produced, so the blood does not clot

red-green colour blindness a sex-linked trait that affects the ability to distinguish between red and green

photoreceptors receptors in the eye that respond to light by beginning a nerve impulse

Understanding: Many genetic diseases have been identified in humans but most are very rare.

Thanks to natural selection, genetic disorders and diseases are rare, most affecting far less than 1% of the population.

There are thousands of genetic diseases and disorders.

One of the most common genetic diseases is cystic fibrosis, which affects about 1 birth in 3000 in the United States and Europe. The most rare genetic diseases only affect a limited number of people worldwide.

Do not confuse genetic diseases with chromosomal anomalies caused by **non-disjunction**. The first is caused when a mutated allele is passed on from one generation to the next but does not change the number of chromosomes. The second is caused by a new event (the non-disjunction) changing the number of chromosomes.

Understanding: Radiation and mutagenic chemicals increase the mutation rate and can cause genetic diseases and cancer.

DNA can be damaged by certain chemicals and by certain types of radiation.

These are said to be **mutagenic**, meaning they can cause mutations in DNA.

Some mutations might become new alleles that could produce a genetic variation or disease, other mutations are capable of causing **cancer**. Chemicals that can cause cancer are called **carcinogens**.

Two factors that determine how likely it is that radiation or chemicals will cause a mutation are:
- their concentrations or strength
- the length of exposure.

Mutations are more likely to be produced by high concentrations and long exposure to a mutagenic radiation or carcinogens. However, small concentrations over long time periods or very high concentrations over a short period of time can sometimes cause a mutation.

Example: results of exposure to radiation

The nuclear bombs dropped on Hiroshima and Nagasaki in Japan in 1945 killed over 100 000 people on impact but killed thousands more people in the decades to follow. Radiation sickness affected Japanese citizens in the weeks following the bombings. Symptoms show cellular damage such as gastrointestinal problems, a drop in the number of blood cells, and neurological damage.

The Chernobyl nuclear power plant accident in Ukraine in 1986 killed about 30 people immediately but exposed about 200 employees to dangerous doses of radiation. The spread of radioactive material around the explosion was extensive and hundreds of thousands of people were exposed, including citizens of the nearby city of Pripyat. It is difficult to estimate the number of radiation-related deaths in the decades since the accident, but a UN agency specializing in such exposure puts the number at approximately 4000. As for the number of people who will develop cancer from the exposure in the coming decades, estimates are in the tens of thousands.

> **Subject vocabulary**
>
> **non-disjunction** the process where two homologous chromosomes do not separate during anaphase I of meiosis, resulting in a daughter cell with one too many chromosomes and a daughter cell with one too few
>
> **mutagenic** causing a mutation
>
> **cancer** disease involving uncontrolled abnormal cell growth
>
> **carcinogen(s)** a chemical that causes cancer

3.5 Genetic modification and biotechnology

Main idea
Biologists have developed techniques for artificial manipulation of DNA, cells, and organisms.

Nature of science: **Assessing risks associated with scientific research – scientists attempt to assess the risks associated with genetically modified crops or livestock.**

Understanding: Gel electrophoresis is used to separate proteins or fragments of DNA according to size.

One technique used for identifying DNA is called **gel electrophoresis**. Here is how it works:

- A DNA sample is cut into fragments using specialized enzymes.
- Some of the fragments are small, some are bigger, some are highly charged, and others do not carry much of an electrical charge.
- All the fragments are put into wells at one end of a block of gel.
- An electric current is run through the gel.
- The particles are separated between the two ends of the gel by their size and electrical charge.
- This separation process leaves a pattern of bands that is different for each unique sample of DNA.

Gel electrophoresis can be used on protein molecules in the same way.

The banding patterns of a person's DNA or protein (from their hair, for example) can be used to identify that person.

> **Subject vocabulary**
>
> **gel electrophoresis** process of passing electricity through a gel matrix to separate fragments or molecules of proteins or nucleic acids

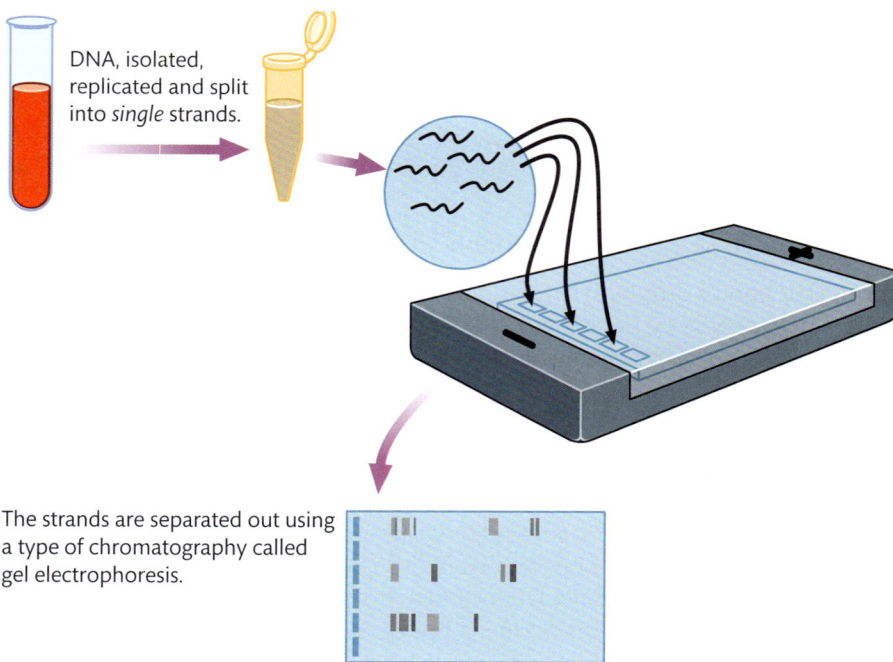

Figure 3.14 *Gel electrophoresis is used to separate DNA fragments so that they can be analysed*

Understanding: PCR can be used to **amplify** small amounts of DNA.

Model sentence: Before a DNA sample can be identified, a sample needs to be collected and amplified using PCR, and then gel electrophoresis is used to separate DNA fragments.

Gel electrophoresis is only possible if there is a certain quantity of DNA to analyse. However, sometimes at a crime scene or other situation where DNA needs to be analysed, there is only a limited quantity available.

It is possible to make millions of copies of DNA using a technique called PCR: polymerase chain reaction. Here's how it works:

- A sample of DNA is collected and isolated.
- The DNA is placed in a **thermocycler** which contains free nucleotide phosphates (containing A, T, C, and G nucleotide phosphates).
- Through a series of modifications of the temperature of the DNA fragments in the presence of enzymes, new strands of DNA are made.
- From one copy, two are made. From those two, four copies can be made. Then 8, then 16, 32, 64, and so on. Very quickly, millions of copies are being made and they are all identical to each other.

Now there is enough to analyse using other techniques such as gel electrophoresis above.

Understanding: DNA profiling involves comparison of DNA.

At a crime scene, a forensics investigator collects blood or other human tissue.

The DNA in the nuclei of the collected cells can be used to identify the victim or the attacker. Here's how:

- DNA is collected and isolated then put through PCR to make enough copies for analysis to be possible.
- The samples are put through gel electrophoresis to obtain the banded patterns characteristic of each individual's DNA.
- Comparisons are made between the banding patterns of DNA found at the scene with those on record in the police files or those prepared from suspects' DNA (see below).

If the bands from a suspect's DNA match those from DNA found at the crime scene, it suggests that the police are dealing with the same person. If no match is found, this indicates that it is unlikely to be the same person.

In addition to crime scenes, DNA profiling (sometimes called DNA fingerprinting) can be used for paternity cases (finding out who the real father of a child is) or ecological studies (constructing family connections within a population under study).

How can DNA profiling be used in paternity and forensic investigations?

- Perform gel electrophoresis on the DNA samples from the father and the child. In a criminal case, DNA found at the crime scene is compared to samples of DNA taken from various suspects.
- Line up the banded patterns to see which ones connect.

Subject vocabulary

thermocycler a machine used to produce many copies of DNA from a sample

General vocabulary

amplify make louder/stronger or increase in number

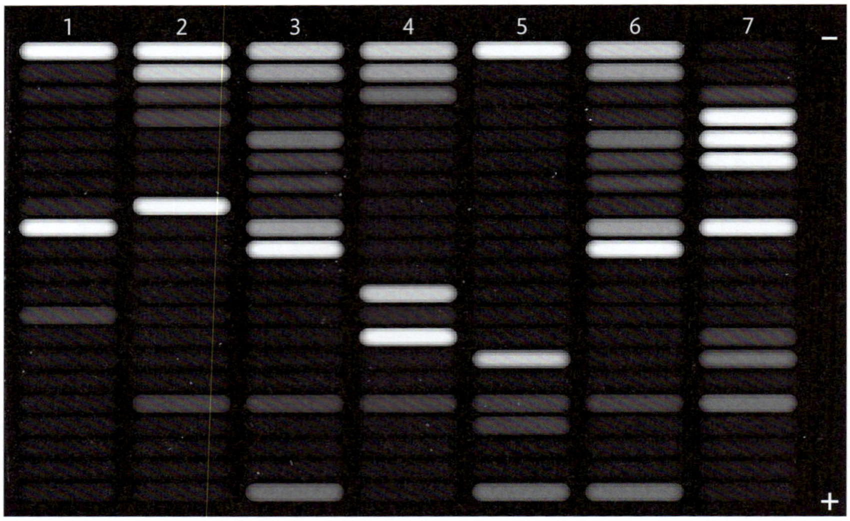

Figure 3.15 *This gel electrophoresis shows six samples – the seventh column on the right is made of known DNA fragments and is used to estimate the lengths of the unknown fragments. Samples 3 and 6 match*

- Examination of the lines in the diagram above clearly shows that rows 3 and 6 have the same banding patterns. This would suggest a match. If track 1 was the father and 6 was the child, it is unlikely they are related. However, if 3 was the DNA sample found at a crime scene and 6 was the sample of a suspect, that person has a lot of explaining to do.

Understanding: Genetic modification is carried out by gene transfer between species.

Model sentence: Because the DNA code is universal, it is possible to place a gene from one species into another and have it expressed in the host organism.

In the 1970s, scientists first developed techniques that allowed a gene from one species to be placed in another species' genome to allow the host species to express a trait that is new to it.

This is possible because DNA is **universal** – the code works for all living organisms.

One example of a **genetically modified organism (GMO)** is *Bt* corn. Here is how it works:

- Corn is often attacked by **pests** such as the corn earworm, *Helicoverpa zea*.
- Farmers do not like pests because they cannot sell corn that is **infested** and half-eaten.
- A certain soil bacterium called *Bacillus thuringiensis* has a gene that allows it to make a protein that poisons and kills pests when they eat the protein.
- The gene from the bacterium was isolated and inserted into a corn kernel. The plant that grew was in every way exactly like a regular corn plant except that it could now produce the **pesticide** protein that the bacterium makes.
- This **transgenic** species is the product of human laboratory work and is called *Bt* corn, named after the bacterium that helped it.
- Farmers can increase their **yield** because the corn is not attacked by the pests that used to eat it.

Skill: Analysis of data on risks to monarch butterflies of *Bt* crops

Monarch butterflies, *Danaus plexippus*, eat milkweed plants, *Asclepias syriaca*, on their long migration between Mexico, the United States, and Canada. Along

Subject vocabulary

universal common to all living organisms

genetically modified organism (GMO) an organism that has had a gene from another species inserted into its genome allowing it to express a new trait

transgenic having one or more genes from a different plant/animal

strain a type or variety of organism

General vocabulary

pest small animal/insect that destroys crops

infested covered in pests

pesticide poison used to treat pest infestations

resistant not affected by

Synonyms

yield............. crop/harvest
negligible....... small
emergence..... appearance

their route, many fields are planted with genetically engineered *Bt* corn. Scientists are worried about the decline in the number of butterflies in recent decades. They wanted to find out if the pollen from the *Bt* corn, which can be blown by wind from the corn to the milkweed, was harmful to the butterflies.

These data suggest that nearly half the butterflies die after 4 days of eating milkweed leaves dusted with *Bt* corn pollen and that those that survive eat less.

However, it is difficult to reproduce natural environments in a laboratory. This study has been challenged for several reasons, including the fact that sprinkling pollen on a leaf will put many more grains of pollen on it than wind in a field could and the fact that the butterflies were not given any other choice of food. Also, one variety of *Bt* corn that showed negative results has been removed from the market. In the end, the US Department of Agriculture determined that in the field, the impact of *Bt* corn on monarch butterflies is **negligible**. So what is causing the decline in their population? Probably a combination of factors including deforestation, parasites, and the reduction of habitats where milkweed can grow.

Application: **How genetic engineering is being used today**

The most commonly found genetically engineered food crops in the world today are corn, soybeans, and canola (all three of whose seeds are used for oil and animal feed).

Some animals and bacteria have alsoee been genetically engineered.

- Transgenic goats are able to produce medication in their milk for people with haemophilia.
- One **strain** of *E. coli* bacteria has had the human insulin gene inserted into it so that it can make insulin to help treat people with type I diabetes, thus saving millions of lives.

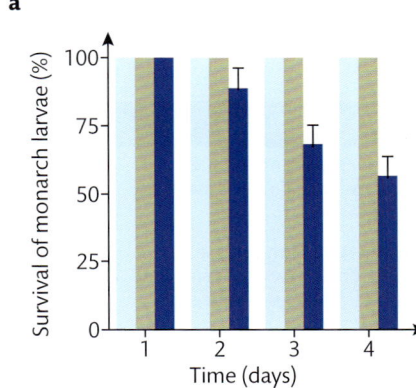
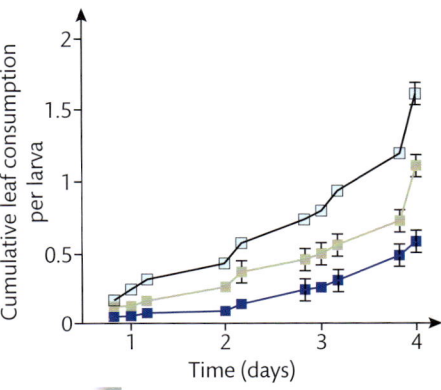

Figure 3.16 *Table of results from 1999 study.*
Legend for both graphs a and b:
Light blue = no pollen on milkweed leaves
Green = traditional corn pollen on leaves
Blue = Bt corn pollen on leaves

Understanding: transgenic crops have potential benefits and potential risks.

Model sentence: **Like many technologies, genetic engineering has generated much debate about whether or not it is safe and worthwhile to use.**

Transgenic crops – good or bad?

Potential benefits	Potential risks
increased yields – farmers can get more food from the same land	higher yields increase the problems of overproduction of crops and excess crop waste, and can drive crop prices down
improve nutritional quality, such as inserting genes for beta carotene (for vitamin A) in GM golden rice	unknown health risks to consumers such as possible allergies
pesticides grown in plants directly so fewer pesticides need to be sprayed on the crops	unknown ecological risks of the introduced genes on other organisms in the environment
some foods could be saved from viral infections by being genetically engineered, such as the GM papaya	pesticide made by *Bt* corn is consumed not only by pests but by humans and animals who eat the corn
herbicide-**resistant** crops reduce the need for mechanized weed removal and therefore reduce fossil fuel consumption on farms	**emergence** of resistant strains of pests that adapt to the new crops

3 Genetics

Subject vocabulary

clone an organism that has exactly the same genetic make-up as its parent cell

reproductive cloning the production of new organisms that are genetically identical to the parent organism

therapeutic cloning the process of making copies of cells

stolons runners from a plant that produce cloned daughter plants

budding a type of asexual reproduction where new individuals develop from outgrowths of the original individual

wounding damaging

girdling removal of a strip of bark from around a branch or trunk

Understanding: Clones are groups of genetically identical organisms derived from a single original parent cell.

The definition of a **clone** is an organism or a group of cells that are genetically identical to the parent cell they came from.

Cloning occurs when there is no mixing of genes and DNA. In other words, the form of reproduction must be asexual (no meiosis, no gametes, no fertilization).

A clone's DNA must come directly from one parent.

This chapter deals with **reproductive cloning**, which should not be confused with **therapeutic cloning**, discussed earlier. Using stem cells to grow new tissue is considered therapeutic cloning because the objective is not to produce a new organism, only to make new copies of cells.

Understanding: Many plant species and some animal species have natural methods of cloning.

Clones are all around us.

- Bacteria clone themselves during binary fission.
- Identical twins are formed by natural cloning.
- Plants grown from the same plant material such as potato plants grown from their tubers cut into pieces are a clone. Strawberry plants send out **stolons**, also known as runners, which are horizontal projections that have new plants on the end that can grow into cloned daughter plants.
- Ginger and bamboo spread underground and grow new copies of themselves as they spread out over an area. The new plants are a clone of the old plant.
- Under certain conditions, hydra (*Hydra vulgaris*) use **budding** to make a clone.

Skill: Design of an experiment to assess one factor affecting the rooting of stem-cuttings

You are expected to be able to design an experiment to assess one factor affecting the rooting of stem cuttings.

Stem cuttings from plants can become new plants in the right conditions. In the lab, using a plant that responds well to propagation by stem cutting, set up an experiment to find out how one of the following can influence how well roots form:

- abiotic factors (light, water, temperature)
- type of medium (soil, agar, water)
- horticultural techniques such as **wounding** or **girdling**
- the presence of plant hormones such as auxins.

Understanding: Animals can be cloned at the embryo stage by breaking up the embryo into more than one group of cells.

Model sentence: Cloning has existed in nature since the beginning of life, whereas human-generated cloning of animals has been done for a century, most notably with the invention of the laboratory technique called **somatic cell nuclear transfer** used to make Dolly the sheep in 1996.

Scientists have been cloning embryos for decades.

It is possible to cut an embryo into smaller parts and grow them into new embryos.

The new embryos, which are all identical to one another, can be placed into the **uterus** of the animal that the original embryo came from.

If more than one of the animal embryos survive, they will form identical twins, triplets or quadruplets, depending on how many embryos were used and how many are successful.

Understanding: Methods have been developed for cloning adult animals using differentiated cells.

Here's how Dolly the sheep was made in 1996 using somatic cell nuclear transfer:

- A somatic cell (non-gamete cell) from the **udder** of the original donor sheep to be cloned was collected and cultured. The nucleus was removed from the cultured cell.
- An unfertilized **oocyte** was collected from another sheep and its nucleus was removed.
- Using an electrical current, the egg cell and the nucleus from the cultured somatic cell were fused together. This sets the cell cycle back to G_0 (see page 22).
- The new cell developed in vitro in a similar way to a zygote, and started to form an embryo.
- The embryo was placed in the womb of a **surrogate** mother sheep.
- The embryo developed normally.
- Dolly was born, and was presented to the world as a clone of the original donor sheep. One thing set her apart from her genetic mother: only the nuclear genome was copied, not the mitochondrial DNA. The mitochondrial DNA in Dolly's cells came from the surrogate mother.

Subject vocabulary

somatic cell nuclear transfer a process used in cloning where the nucleus from a non-sex cell is put into a sex cell that has had its nucleus removed and is then cultured to produce a zygote

uterus muscular organ of females where the embryo develops

oocyte the large cell that is the female's gamete

surrogate a substitute

General vocabulary

udder milk-producing structures of many mammals

4 Ecology

4.1 Species, communities, and ecosystems

Main idea
The continued survival of living organisms including humans depends on sustainable communities.

Nature of science: Looking for patterns, trends, and **discrepancies** – plants and algae are mostly **autotrophic** but some are not.

Understanding: **Species** are groups of organisms that can potentially interbreed to produce **fertile** offspring.

Definition of species: a group of organisms that can **interbreed** and produce fertile offspring.

Species is the basic unit used to classify organisms. Members of a species are distinct from all other species, they have similar **morphology** and they share a common **phylogeny** (family tree).

As an example, there is only one species of humans currently living on Earth: *Homo sapiens*.

Challenges to the definition: what about bacteria or other organisms that reproduce **asexually**? In this case, morphology and phylogeny are used. What about **hybrids** such as mules (when a horse and a donkey mate) or a liger (when a lion and a tiger mate)? Since these organisms are **infertile**, no new species has been produced.

Understanding: Members of a species may be reproductively isolated in separate populations.

Through natural circumstances or through the intervention of humans, **populations** can sometimes be separated and therefore cannot interbreed anymore.

For example, a volcanic eruption might produce a lava flow or mud flow that could cut through a forest, separating a population of snails that once interbred. The construction of a major railway or a canal through the countryside could cut in two a population of **mosses** that can no longer interbreed.

Understanding: Species have either an autotrophic or heterotrophic method of nutrition (a few species have both methods).

Model sentence: Heterotrophs are organisms that cannot make their own food, whereas autotrophs are capable of **synthesizing** their food from sources of energy such as sunlight.

Autotrophs are capable of making their own food from **inorganic** substances. For example, photosynthetic organisms such as cyanobacteria, algae, or plants are capable of making sugar from carbon dioxide and water by using the energy from sunlight.

Synonyms
discrepancies . differences/inconsistencies

Subject vocabulary
autotrophic organisms capable of producing their own food

fertile capable of reproducing

species a group of organisms which are structurally similar and able to pass their genetic traits on to their offspring

interbreed mate to produce fertile offspring

morphology the structure and shape of an organism

phylogeny family tree showing evolutionary relationships of species

asexually reproduction without fertilization and the fusion of gametes

hybrid something that has the properties of two things

infertile not capable of reproducing

populations a group of interbreeding members of a species living at the same time in the same place

synthesize a chemical reaction (or series of reactions) leading to the formation of a molecular substance

inorganic substances that do not contain carbon and are not produced by a living organism

General vocabulary
mosses small plants with no roots or water conducting vessels, often seen growing on rocks and tree trunks

Heterotrophs are organisms that need to get their food from the environment; they cannot make their own food. They need to consume organic molecules that have been made by other organisms. For example, a dolphin needs to eat fish, alpaca need to eat grass, and bees need to eat nectar.

A very small number of organisms can be considered both autotrophs and heterotrophs. For example, *Euglena* feed on microscopic aquatic organisms but they also contain chlorophyll and can **photosynthesize** as well.

Understanding: Consumers are heterotrophs that feed on living organisms by **ingestion**.

- Organisms that eat other organisms are called **consumers**.
- Consumers that eat plant material are considered **herbivores**.
- Consumers that eat plant and animal material are considered **omnivores**.

Understanding: Detritivores are heterotrophs that obtain organic nutrients from detritus by internal digestion.

An organism that feeds on dead organic material is called a **detritivore**. For example, the organisms that transform dead leaves into soil, such as earthworms and soil mites, are detritivores.

These organisms play a vital role in the recycling of nutrients within an ecosystem. Without them, the return of valuable molecules to the soil would stop and the growth of plants and trees would be impossible.

Understanding: Saprotrophs are heterotrophs that obtain organic nutrients from dead organisms by external digestion.

Instead of eating food and digesting it internally, some organisms use external digestion.

How do they do this? They **secrete** digestive enzymes onto the dead organic material they consume and then absorb the digested nutrients.

Organisms that do this are called **saprotrophs**. For example, mushrooms on the forest floor can secrete enzymes onto dead wood and then absorb the nutrients that are released from the wood.

Organisms such as detritivores and saprotrophs are considered **decomposers**, since they play a vital role in the decomposition of dead organisms.

Skill: Classifying species by their mode of nutrition

You should be able to classify species using knowledge of their mode of nutrition.

What am I? Indicate 'autotroph', 'consumer', 'detritivore', or 'saprotroph' for each of the descriptions of species.

1. I move around the ocean floor looking for dead organisms to eat.
2. I sit in the sun and make food using my **chlorophyll**.
3. I swim in rivers hunting for small fish to catch and eat.
4. I secrete digestive juices onto dead organisms, then I absorb the nutrients that are released. [1]

[1] Answers: 1 detritivore, 2 autotroph, 3 consumer, 4 saprotroph

---

Subject vocabulary

heterotroph an organism not capable of producing its own food, requiring preformed organic compounds from other sources

photosynthesize convert light energy into chemical energy

ingestion the taking of food/ substances into the body

consumer an animal that eats plants or other animals

herbivore an animal that only eats plants

omnivore an organism that eats plants and animals

detritivore an organism that eats non-living organic waste matter

saprotroph an organism which uses detritus as its energy and nutrient source

decomposer an organism that feeds on and breaks down waste organic material

chlorophyll main pigment involved in the process of photosynthesis, absorbs light energy

Synonyms

secrete .... produce/release

Subject vocabulary

community all of the living organisms in an ecosystem

intertidal zone between the low and high tide water mark

quadrat an area of land marked off in order to count or study the organisms within

random sampling selecting study areas chosen by chance rather than a particular pattern

chi-squared test a statistical test to determine if two factors show independence or to show if expected values differ from observed values by chance or not

frequency how often an event happens in a fixed time

null hypothesis a default statement in statistics saying that two things are independent of each other or that there are no differences between them; the null hypothesis is challenged then rejected or not rejected

degrees of freedom the number of values in the chi-squared calculation that can vary

contingency table a reference table used to check whether a chi-squared value is significantly different from the expected value

critical value in statistical tests, a number used to determine if the null hypothesis is rejected given a certain level of statistical significance

General vocabulary

incubate keep eggs warm until the young hatch

Understanding: A community is formed by populations of different species living together and interacting with each other.

Sometimes biologists are interested in studying a group of populations. Such a study would be at the **community** level rather than the individual or population level. Examples include a soil community, an **intertidal** community, or the community of microorganisms living in your large intestine.

Within a community, organisms depend on each other. For example, many insects depend on trees for their habitat, vampire bats depend on warm-blooded mammals for food, and cowbirds never raise their own chicks - they depend on other species of birds to **incubate** their eggs and to feed and raise their young

Skill: Testing for association between two species using the chi-squared test with data obtained by quadrat sampling

You should be familiar with the idea of sampling an ecosystem using a **quadrat** and **random sampling**. One question that might come up when studying an ecosystem is 'Is the presence of these two species together determined solely by chance?' In other words, is the fact that two species, such as a species of fern and another of moss, are often found together just a coincidence or is there something other than chance bringing them together?

A statistical test called the **chi-squared test** (χ^2) can be used to determine connections between **frequencies**. Chi is a Greek letter and it is pronounced like 'sky' without the s.

You are expected to be able to do the following:

- State the **null hypothesis** (H_0) in the given situation. The general null hypothesis is 'there is no statistically significant difference between the frequencies – they are determined by chance' and should be modified to the specific situation.
- Determine the number of **degrees of freedom** in this calculation. This is done by setting up a **contingency table** of expected and observed values as shown:

	Observed values	Expected values
first category of data		
second category of data		

Then take the number of categories minus 1. In this case, with two categories, the number of degrees of freedom is 1.

- Determine the **critical value** in order to obtain a 95% certainty that there is a statistically significant difference between these two sets of numbers. This is done by looking up the value in a table (critical value tables for the chi-squared test can be found online or in textbooks).
- Calculate the chi-squared value for these data. The general formula is below where *O* represents the observed values and *E* is for the expected values.

$$\chi^2 = \sum \frac{(O - E)^2}{E}$$

- Interpret the value calculated. Does it mean we can reject the null hypothesis or not? (See Skill below.)

Skill: Recognizing and interpreting statistical significance

If the chi-squared value is larger than the critical value, the null hypothesis is rejected. This means that the distributions in the frequencies are not due to chance.

It means that there is a **statistically significant** difference in the distribution of the populations. The calculation does not say what the reason is for this. It simply lets the investigator know with some certainty that something other than chance is influencing the data.

Understanding: A community forms an ecosystem by its interactions with the **abiotic** environment. Autotrophs obtain inorganic nutrients from the abiotic environment.

Model sentence: A group of populations interacting with each other is a community but once their non-living environment is considered, it is an ecosystem.

The term **ecosystem** refers to a community plus its abiotic (non-living) environment.

In a marine ecosystem such as a coral reef, the temperature, **salinity**, and pH of the water are going to have an impact on the communities living there. It is important that phytoplankton have access to dissolved minerals in the water so that they can grow.

On land, rainfall, air temperature, and soil chemistry will also impact the communities present. The water and inorganic substances present in an ecosystem influence the types of organisms that live there.

In the savannah, **shrubs** absorb inorganic materials such as nitrogen from the soil. If the quantity of nitrogen available in the soil becomes too low, plants will not be able to grow.

When plants stop growing, the organisms that rely on the plants suffer as well. It is vital for there to be organisms in the soil capable of transforming nitrogen gas from the air into usable nitrogen-rich compounds. One example of this is some types of bacteria that live in the soil or in compartments of the roots of certain plants and that transform N_2 into nitrates that plants can absorb (see Figure 14.11 on page 321).

Understanding: The supply of inorganic nutrients is maintained by nutrient cycling.

If plants, **phytoplankton**, and consumers are constantly taking in the inorganic substances from their environment, why is it that these materials never run out?

The answer is **nutrient cycling**, something ecosystems have been doing for a long time.

Nutrient cycling means that any inorganic material taken from the environment (such as nitrogen or calcium) will be returned to the environment sooner or later. Sometimes the nutrients are returned in the form of waste, other nutrients are only released back into the environment once the organism is dead and has **decomposed**.

Understanding: Ecosystems have the potential to be sustainable over long periods of time.

Thanks to nutrient cycling, it is possible for an ecosystem to provide inorganic substances indefinitely.

Subject vocabulary

statistically significant said of statistical tests, it means that the null hypothesis can be rejected (or not) with a certain degree of confidence, usually 95%

abiotic pertains to non-living

ecosystem the plants and animals in a region plus the non-living components of the environment

phytoplankton aquatic photosynthetic organisms that are usually microscopic

nutrient cycling the movement of nutrients through the ecosystem

General vocabulary

salinity amount of salt a substance contains

shrubs bushes

Synonyms

decomposed .. decayed

All the atoms in an organism came from the environment surrounding it. All the carbon, oxygen, and hydrogen in your body, as well as all the other atoms, came from something you ate or from the time early in your life when your mother ate something and passed on the nutrients to you.

If humans ever tried to live for a long time outside the planet Earth, such as on a space station, the Moon, or another planet, they would most likely have to take with them a sustainable ecosystem that would provide them with food, water, and air to breathe.

Until then, it is important to maintain a healthy balance in the current ecosystems that surround us on this remote space station we call Earth. If we throw the ecosystems here too far off balance, we may destroy the very thing that is keeping us alive: the **biosphere**.

Skill: Setting up sealed mesocosms to try to establish sustainability

You are asked to demonstrate that a long-term closed ecosystem can be setup and maintained without feeding it, as long as certain conditions are respected: raw materials must be introduced in the beginning along with a community of organisms that are capable of recycling the raw materials. A sealed **mesocosm** is an example of such a system and it consists of a transparent sealable container with water, nutrients, and living organisms inside that is placed in a sunny window to allow light energy to be used by the autotrophs inside. This should be set up early enough in the year to give it time to prove its **sustainability**. One version to try is called a Winogradsky column – there are lots of resources available online for how to set one up.

4.2 Energy flow

Main idea

Ecosystems require a continuous supply of energy to fuel life processes and to replace energy lost as heat.

Nature of science: Use theories to explain natural **phenomena** – the concept of energy flow explains the limited length of food chains.

Understanding: Most ecosystems rely on a supply of energy from sunlight.

Model sentence: Sunlight is essential to ecosystems because it provides the initial energy that will be transformed into organic molecules that will nourish the organisms.

In the previous section, we saw how nutrients are cycled so that ecosystems never run out of raw materials. In this section, we will see that it is impossible to do the same with energy.

In ecosystems, energy can be transformed but cannot be recycled. A constant supply of energy needs to enter ecosystems on Earth's surface or else they will not function.

The supply of energy for the most familiar and best-studied ecosystems on Earth is sunlight. Sunlight allows **photosynthetic** autotrophs to produce sugars and they feed the rest of the ecosystem. If the sun were to be blocked out, such ecosystems would not be able to continue at their current levels of productivity.

Subject vocabulary

biosphere all areas on and in Earth where living organisms exist

mesocosm a closed container in which a small functioning ecosystem exists

photosynthetic converts light energy into chemical energy

General vocabulary

sustainability how easy or difficult it is for an activity to continue over a long time

nourish provide food/substances needed to live and grow healthily

Synonyms

phenomena.... events/ happenings

Understanding: Light energy is converted to chemical energy in carbon compounds by **photosynthesis**.

Photosynthesis allows for a very important transformation of energy from light energy to chemical energy.

The kind of energy found in carbohydrates such as sugar is called **chemical energy**. Chemical energy in organic substances is stored in the form of bonds between carbon, hydrogen, and oxygen.

Sunlight energy is needed by photosynthetic organisms to build the energy-rich bonds in sugars. The chemical energy is stored in the sugar until the bonds are broken during other chemical reactions such as cellular respiration.

Understanding: Chemical energy in carbon compounds flows through food chains by means of feeding.

Model sentence: In a food chain, the producers make chemical energy available in the food they make, the herbivore consumers eat it, and the carnivore consumers eat the herbivores.

Organic molecules such as sugar or lipids have many hydrogen and oxygen atoms bonded to their carbon atoms. The energy, measured in **calories** or in **joules**, depends on the number of bonds. More bonds mean more energy. Since lipids have long **hydrocarbon chains**, they contain many bonds and are therefore energy-rich compounds.

Hungry organisms will seek out energy-rich organic compounds such as sugars, starches, lipids, or proteins in order to meet their energy needs. Mayfly larvae, for example, will eat algae growing on rocks in a river. The energy flows from the algae (the producer) to the larvae (the consumer). A small fish might come along and eat one of the mayfly larvae. The energy flows to the fish. The energy will continue to flow – a kingfisher might swoop down and eat the fish and later the kingfisher might be eaten by a fox.

This flow of energy can be traced using a food chain. A **food chain** is a representation of which organisms depend on which other organisms as a source of food. The arrows between the organisms show how energy is passed on.

> **Subject vocabulary**
>
> **photosynthesis** process which converts light energy into chemical energy
>
> **chemical energy** energy stored in the bonds of organic molecules
>
> **calories** a unit of measurement of energy
>
> **joules** a unit of energy measurement
>
> **hydrocarbon chains** long organic molecules formed from linked carbon atoms, hydrogen and oxygen
>
> **food chain** one possible set of feeding relationships starting with a producer
>
> **trophic levels** the position of an organism in a food chain

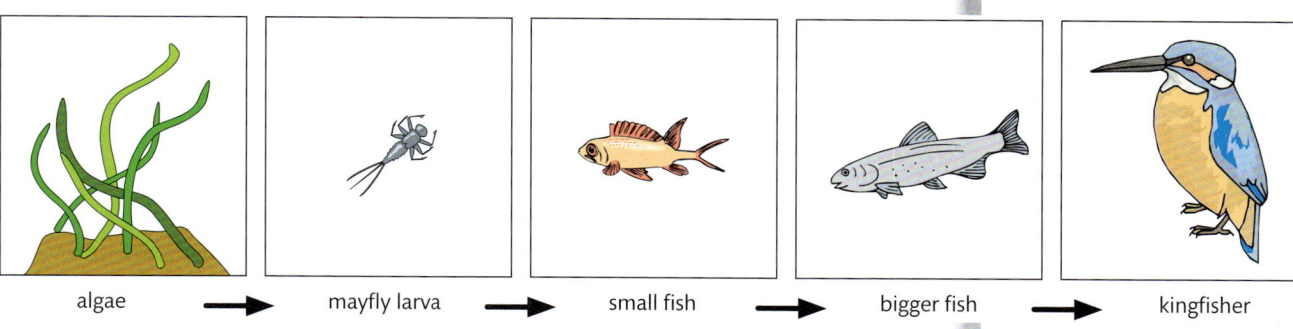

algae → mayfly larva → small fish → bigger fish → kingfisher

Notice how the food chain starts with an autotroph. If the photosynthetic organism at the beginning is removed or is in short supply, all other organisms afterwards are affected.

The levels between the arrows in a food chain are called **trophic levels**.

Figure 4.1 *A food chain shows the flow of energy from one organism within a community to the next*

Subject vocabulary

producer a photosynthetic organism that starts a food chain

exergonic energy releasing

There are names for each trophic level of a food chain starting from the beginning:
- First trophic level = **producers**, made up of autotrophs.
- Second trophic level = consumers that are herbivores.
- Third and subsequent trophic levels = consumers that are carnivores.

Understanding: Energy released from carbon compounds by respiration is used in living organisms and converted to heat.

Some of the chemical energy from the plant and animal materials that are eaten is transferred to the organism that ate them. However, the process of transforming organic compounds into usable energy is not a very efficient process, and much of the energy is transformed into heat energy. In effect, cellular respiration is an **exergonic** reaction, a biochemical reaction that releases energy.

For example, a cow gets chemical energy from grass and the organic molecules from the grass can be used in cellular respiration in the cow. Cellular respiration generates heat, which is transferred to the environment around the cow.

Understanding: Living organisms cannot convert heat to other forms of energy.

The heat that is produced by living organisms enters the surrounding environment. Unlike light energy or chemical energy which can be useful to autotrophs, heat energy generated by cellular respiration cannot be absorbed and used by other life forms as a source of energy.

As a result, heat energy produced by living organisms is said to be lost. This means that it goes into the surrounding environment and cannot be converted into another useful source of energy by living organisms.

Understanding: Heat is lost from ecosystems.

Model sentence: Unlike minerals that can be recycled indefinitely, energy is constantly being lost from ecosystems and new energy needs to enter the system in order for it to continue.

The heat that is lost is not only considered to be unavailable for individual organisms, it is lost from the whole ecosystem. Heat will go into the water, soil, or the air and eventually will be released into space.

Again, as we have seen before, nutrients must be recycled because they are stuck within a closed cycle. Energy, on the other hand, is constantly leaving the biosphere in the form of lost heat. It cannot be recycled.

Fortunately, this is not a problem because new energy arrives every day in the form of sunlight.

Understanding: Energy losses between trophic levels restrict the length of food chains and the **biomass** of higher trophic levels.

Let us re-examine a food chain:

algae → mayfly larva → small fish → bigger fish → kingfisher → fox

Recall that the arrows represent the passage of chemical energy from one trophic level to the next.

At each passage of chemical energy, only about 10% of that energy is passed on. The vast majority of energy is lost due to various things:

- Heat from cellular respiration, as seen above.
- Some parts of organisms cannot be eaten.
- Some parts of food cannot be digested.
- Not all individuals in a population become food, some die without their organic molecules being passed on to the next trophic level.

This can be illustrated in an energy pyramid (see Skill).

Skill: Using pyramids of energy as quantitative representations of energy flow

Students should be able to draw a pyramid of energy based on numbers given. An example is below: the base of the pyramid shows the energy that producers require. The subsequent levels show the energy values for the consumers starting with the herbivores and the carnivores up to the top predator in the food chain concerned.

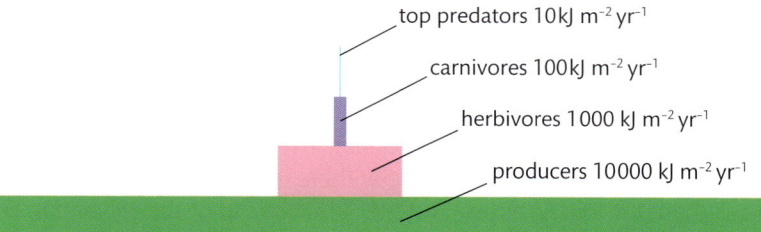

Subject vocabulary

biomass the mass of all organisms of a particular category of organisms, e.g. the mass of all producers for a food chain

methane a biogas composed of carbon and hydrogen

General vocabulary

quantitative a numerical measurement

Figure 4.2 A pyramid of energy showing a 90% loss of energy at each trophic level. Notice the units used are kilojoules of energy per metre squared per year

4.3 Carbon cycling

Main idea

Continued availability of carbon in ecosystems depends on carbon cycling.

Nature of science: Making accurate, quantitative measurements – it is important to obtain reliable data on the concentration of carbon dioxide and **methane** in the atmosphere.

Understanding: Autotrophs convert carbon dioxide into carbohydrates and other carbon compounds.

Photosynthesis generates glucose. The carbon atoms found in glucose come from the CO_2 molecules they absorb. Autotrophs can convert some of the sugars they make into complex carbohydrates such as starch and cellulose.

4 Ecology | 85

General vocabulary

terrestrial living on land

aquatic living/growing in water

flammable burns easily

Subject vocabulary

hydrogen carbonate ions a negatively charged ion made of hydrogen, carbon, and three oxygen atoms

concentration gradient change in a chemical concentration between two areas

diffuse movement of a substance from an area of high concentration to an area of low concentration

natural gas methane found in petroleum deposits underground and used as fuel

archaeans members of the prokaryotic domain Archaea

anaerobic said of processes or organisms that do not require oxygen

Synonyms

accumulate .... build up

Understanding: In aquatic ecosystems carbon is present as dissolved carbon dioxide and hydrogen carbonate ions.

In **terrestrial** photosynthetic organisms, the CO_2 that is needed comes from the air.

In **aquatic** photosynthetic organisms, the CO_2 that is needed comes from carbon-rich substances in the water. The main sources are:

- carbon dioxide, which can dissolve in water, especially cold water
- **hydrogen carbonate ions** (written as HCO_3^-).

Understanding: Carbon dioxide diffuses from the atmosphere or water into autotrophs.

In the cells of terrestrial plants, as the CO_2 gets used up during photosynthesis, the concentration of this gas inside the cells of the autotroph decreases. This provides a **concentration gradient** allowing CO_2 to **diffuse** from the air to the cells.

Aquatic autotrophs can absorb the CO_2 from the water in order to build sugars using photosynthesis. Again, a concentration gradient forms with a low concentration inside the cells and a higher concentration outside the cells. Diffusion from outside the cell into the cell allows for the supply of CO_2 to the cell to be maintained.

Understanding: Carbon dioxide is produced by respiration and diffuses out of organisms into water or the atmosphere.

Some of the sugars that are produced by photosynthesis will be used to make ATP.

Cellular respiration produces CO_2 as a waste product. The build-up of CO_2 inside the cells creates a concentration gradient whereby there is a higher concentration of CO_2 inside the cell than outside. As a result, CO_2 will diffuse out of the cell and into the environment (surrounding air or water).

Understanding: Methane is produced from organic matter in anaerobic conditions by methanogenic archaeans and some diffuses into the atmosphere or accumulates in the ground.

Methane, CH_4, is an organic gas that is energy rich and highly **flammable**. It is called **natural gas** when used for industry or homes for heating or cooking. The blue flame of a Bunsen burner is made by methane.

Some microbes, notably certain **archaeans**, can produce CH_4 in **anaerobic** (oxygen free) conditions. One place such anaerobes live is inside the digestive tracts of animals. Cows, for example, host large colonies of anaerobic microbes in their guts.

Understanding: Methane is oxidized to carbon dioxide and water in the atmosphere.

During combustion, methane, CH_4, combines with oxygen gas, O_2, from the atmosphere to yield water vapour, H_2O, and carbon dioxide gas CO_2.

$$CH_4 + 2O_2 \rightarrow 2H_2O + CO_2$$

This is an **oxidation reaction**. The reaction is accompanied by light energy and heat energy in the form of a blue flame.

Apart from O_2, all three of the other gases in this equation are considered greenhouse gases, meaning they can retain heat in Earth's atmosphere. More about these later.

Understanding: Peat forms when organic matter is not fully decomposed because of acidic and/or anaerobic conditions in waterlogged soils.

Soil is made of decomposed plant material mixed with water, inorganic minerals from rock particles and air.

When the amount of organic material in soil is high, the amount of chemical energy in it can be used as a fuel to burn.

One type of soil that has such properties is called **peat**. Peat is a dark, thick soil that forms in waterlogged areas. At least 30% of its dry mass is organic material.

The high water content of the soil prevents air from circulating and prevents decomposers from doing their work. As a result, many of the energy-rich organic molecules from the dead plant material in the soil do not get broken down.

Another effect of the high water content is that the soil becomes acidic. The high acidity levels also prevent soil organisms from decomposing. Decomposers are killed by the acidic conditions.

If peat is dug up and dried out, it can be burned as fuel. Humans in many different parts of the world have been using peat as a fuel source for generations.

Understanding: Partially decomposed organic matter from past geological eras was converted either into coal or into oil and gas that accumulate in **porous** rocks.

Coal or petroleum products, such as **crude oil** or natural gas, take millions of years to form.

All of these fuel sources, otherwise called **fossil fuels** (because of their ancient once-living origins), **originated** from photosynthetic organisms.

Just like with peat, wet **sediments** of partially decomposed photosynthetic organisms accumulated in certain regions of the world. In anaerobic conditions, full decomposition was not possible so many energy-rich compounds remained in the layers.

Subject vocabulary

oxidation reaction a chemical reaction in which electrons are lost

peat an accumulation of partially decayed plants found in wet areas that can be dried and used as a fuel

coal an organic hard, black rock formed deep below the earth from fossil remains and used as a carbon-based fuel

crude oil a thick, black petroleum-based liquid which is formed deep underground from fossilized material and which can be used to make fuels and plastics

fossil fuels a non-renewable fuel source formed by the compression of plant and animal materials in the Earth's crust over millions of years

sediments matter deposited by wind or water that has settled in an area, often forming layers

General vocabulary

porous having many small holes that liquids can slowly pass through

Synonyms

originated (from)   started/came (from)

Subject vocabulary

hydrocarbons organic molecules made of carbon, hydrogen, and oxygen atoms

crust the Earth's hard outer layer

non-renewable energy energy from resources, such as fossil fuels, that cannot be replaced

fermentation process where sugar is changed to alcohol

biofuels a renewable fuel resource usually based on plants or waste materials

renewable resource molecules used by humans that are able to be regenerated or recycled on a long-term basis

These layers accumulated and were packed down over long stretches of geological time. The layers were pushed underground under the weight of new layers and water was squeezed out. Heat and high pressure caused molecules to rearrange and form long chains of **hydrocarbons**.

These hydrocarbon chains are rich in energy and that is what makes them valuable fuels. Remember that the more bonds an organic molecule has, the richer it is in chemical energy.

Coal is formed deep below the surface and needs to be mined from underground.

Crude oil accumulates in domes formed when porous rock layers fold due to the movements of the **crust**. Oil companies search for these deposits and drill down into the earth to pump them out.

Since gas is less dense than liquid, natural gas can accumulate above the crude oil deposits. These are also drilled for and extracted.

Fossil fuels are called **non-renewable energy** sources because once we burn them all they are gone. It is unrealistic to consider using them on a long-term basis because it takes too long for new ones to form.

Understanding: Carbon dioxide is produced by the combustion of biomass and fossilized organic matter.

As we saw with the methane equation, when organic substances are burned in oxygen gas, carbon dioxide is released as a waste product.

Such is the case every time we burn fossil fuels for cooking, heating, or transportation. The human activity that produces the most carbon dioxide in the world is transportation: cars, trucks, airplanes, and ships that burn fossil fuels.

There are some sources of organic fuel that can be considered renewable. Two examples are methane, produced by biomass, and ethanol, produced by the **fermentation** of plant material.

Biomass in the context of fuel refers to things such as farm waste in the form of animal waste or plant material that cannot be eaten. Such materials are placed in a large container and special microbes (including archaeans that produce methane gas as a waste product) transform the organic material into useful fuel.

Some countries in the world, such as Brazil and the United States, have reduced their dependence on fossil fuels by mixing gasoline for cars and buses with ethanol made from the fermentation of crops such as corn.

The idea is that uneaten corn is still an energy-rich substance but not rich enough to be used as fuel. By fermenting the corn and extracting the ethanol that results from fermentation, the alcohol is rich enough in energy to be useful in combustion engines.

Biofuels are considered a **renewable resource** because the plants that provide the raw materials can be grown in a few months.

Understanding: Animals such as reef-building corals and Mollusca have hard parts that are composed of calcium carbonate and can become fossilized in limestone.

Photosynthesis is not the only way organisms pull carbon out of the environment. Reef builders or molluscs use a carbon compound called calcium carbonate to make shells or other body parts.

Coral reefs are made from **calcium carbonate**, $CaCO_3$. Coral polyps, the organisms that build reefs in the ocean, use two dissolved ions found in seawater to make the calcium carbonate:

$$Ca^{2+} + 2\,HCO_3^- \rightarrow CaCO_3 + CO_2 + H_2O$$

The first ion is dissolved calcium, Ca^{2+}, the second should be familiar to you from earlier in this chapter: hydrogen carbonate, HCO_3^-. As shown in the equation, the two types of ions are combined to yield calcium carbonate, carbon dioxide gas, and water.

Calcium carbonate has chemical properties that make it as hard as rock. The coral polyps secrete it to build up the reef.

Other organisms, such as snails and clams, use calcium carbonate to make shells. Since it is a strong solid, it is a good protection.

Limestone, a rock often used by humans as a building material (such as the Ancient Egyptian pyramids or Notre Dame Cathedral in Paris), is full of fossil shells. These shells, often made by molluscs such as bivalves (i.e. clams, mussels, or oysters) are sometimes visible in stone steps and building facades made of limestone.

Model sentence: The carbon cycle shows how carbon atoms are recycled on Earth from photosynthesis to cellular respiration or burning of fossil fuels.

Subject vocabulary

Mollusca/mollusks land/sea animals with a soft body and hard shell

calcium carbonate ($CaCO_3$) a chemical used by organisms to make hard structures such as shells and reef-forming corals

carbon cycle the way carbon atoms circulate through the environment

Skill: Construct a diagram of the carbon cycle

A diagram showing the various chemical reactions in which carbon plays a role, such as photosynthesis or cellular respiration, can be used to represent the **carbon cycle**.

Practise drawing the diagram opposite and fill in the following missing terms: carbon in decomposers, carbon in the atmosphere, carbon in producers, carbon in fossil fuels, carbon in consumers.[1]

Application: Estimation of carbon fluxes due to processes in the carbon cycle

Climatologists are interested in how the carbon cycle works and in the ways in which humans are changing the carbon cycle.

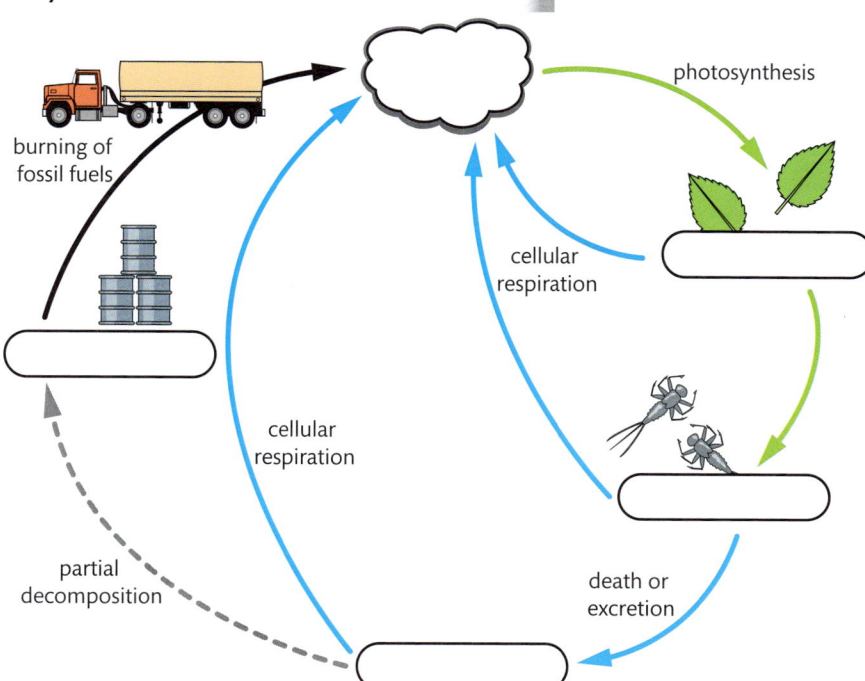

Figure 4.3 *The carbon cycle*

---

[1] Answers: clockwise from the top: carbon in the atmosphere, carbon in producers, carbon in consumers, carbon in decomposers, carbon in fossil fuels

One way to study this is to measure and monitor carbon dioxide levels in the atmosphere and oceans and to estimate the amounts of carbon in each part of the carbon cycle.

When carbon changes from one place to another, such as going from the atmosphere to being dissolved in the ocean, this change is called a **flux**.

Carbon fluxes are measured or estimated in **gigatons of carbon per year**, GtC yr^{-1}.

Carbon fluxes	Quantity of carbon (GtC yr^{-1})
Examples of fluxes into the atmosphere	
respiration of terrestrial organisms	120
respiration of marine organisms at the surface of the ocean	92
burning of fossil fuels (such as transport)	7.7
changes in land use (such as deforestation)	1.5
Examples of fluxes out of the atmosphere	
absorption of carbon dioxide into the water at the surface of the ocean	90
gross primary production (GPP), photosynthesis of terrestrial organisms	90
photosynthesis of marine organisms	40
changes in land use (such as growing crops in prairies)	0.5
weathering, carbon dioxide being incorporated into rocks and soils	0.2

In the diagram below replace the letters with the numbers from the table. Note: the last item in the table is not shown in the diagram.[1]

Subject vocabulary

flux the process of flowing from one place to another

gigatons of carbon per year unit of measurement of carbon fluxes

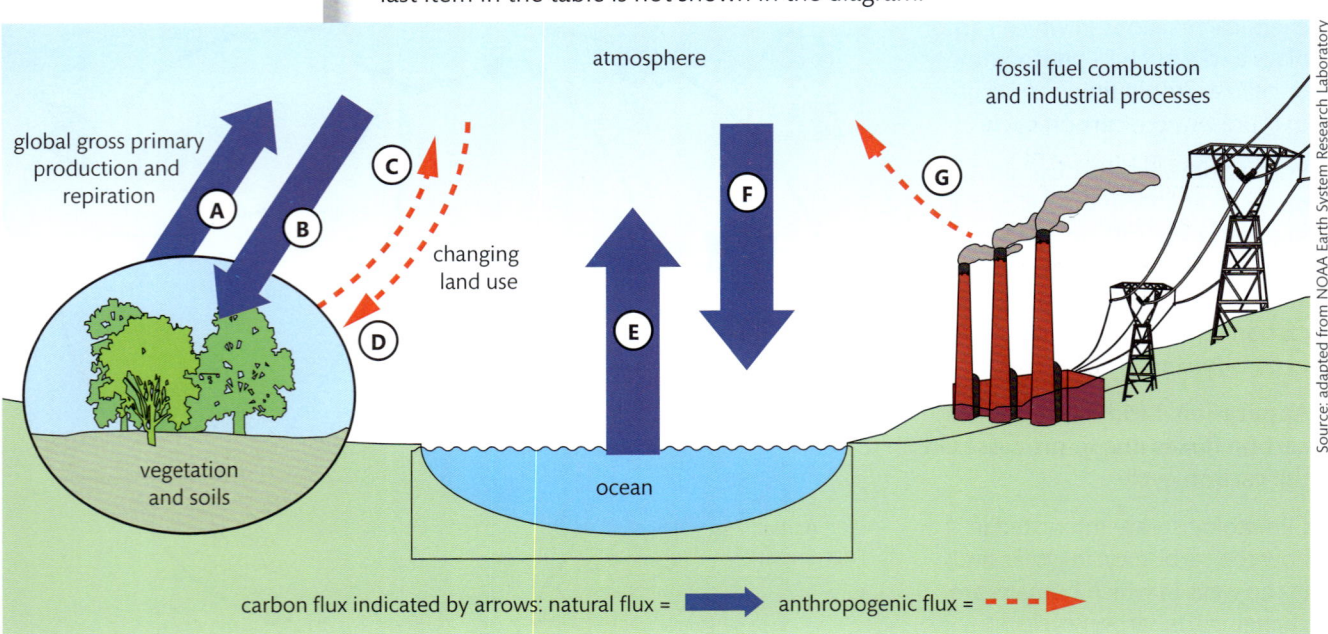

Figure 4.4 *Carbon fluxes into and out of the atmosphere*

---

[1] Answers: A = 120, B = 90, C = 1.5, D = 0.5, E = 92, F = 90, G = 7.7. All units are GtC yr^{-1}.

Application: **Analysis of data from air monitoring stations to explain annual fluctuations**

The graph below shows measurements made by climatologists concerning atmospheric carbon dioxide from the beginning of 2011 to the first quarter of 2015. You could probably find a more recent one at the NOAA website.

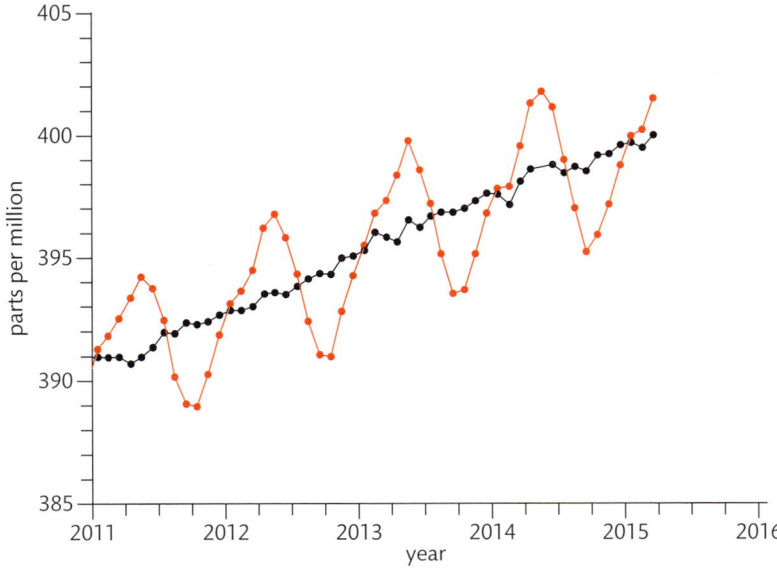

Figure 4.5 *Recent monthly CO_2 at Mauna Loa in the northern hemisphere. The red line shows direct measurements and the black line shows the average for each season*

Analysis of this graph:

- The red line **fluctuates** from season to season.
- In the coldest months of year in the northern hemisphere (January, February, March), the graph is increasing.
- In the warmest months of the year (July, August, September), the graph is decreasing.
- The cause of the seasonal increase in atmospheric carbon dioxide is due to the reduction of photosynthetic activity in the northern hemisphere in winter.
- The cause of the seasonal decrease in atmospheric carbon dioxide is due to the increase in photosynthetic activity during the summer. In effect, carbon dioxide is removed from the air by photosynthetic bacteria, phytoplankton, plants, algae, and trees during the warmer months of the year.
- The black line shows the average which has been corrected for these seasonal changes.
- This part of the graph shows an increase from 391 ppm (parts per million) at the beginning of 2011 to 400 ppm at the end of March 2015.
- That's a 2.3% increase in this 51 month period.
- As a percentage, 391 ppm is 0.00391%.

General vocabulary

fluctuate move back and forth

4.4 Climate change

Main idea
Concentrations of gases in the atmosphere affect climates experienced at the Earth's surface.

Nature of science: Assessing claims – assessment of the claims that human activities are producing climate change.

Understanding: Carbon dioxide and water vapour are the most significant greenhouse gases.

The **greenhouse effect** is a naturally occurring **phenomenon** in Earth's atmosphere. It helps the planet maintain a temperature that provides ideal conditions for life as we know it.

Like a glass greenhouse for growing plants, Earth is surrounded by a transparent material that lets light in, but prevents too much heat from escaping. A greenhouse uses glass or plastic, whereas Earth uses its atmosphere.

We will see later in this section how, in recent decades, certain human activities have changed the composition of the atmosphere and altered the greenhouse effect.

Many gases in the atmosphere contribute to the greenhouse effect, but two have the biggest effect:
- carbon dioxide
- water vapour.

Gases that contribute to the warming effect of the atmosphere are called **greenhouse gases**, GHGs.

Understanding: Other gases including methane and nitrogen oxides have less impact.

A gas's ability to contribute to the greenhouse effect depends on several factors including:
- the concentration of the gas in the atmosphere
- its ability to retain heat
- how long it stays in the atmosphere.

Gases such as methane and nitrous oxides are also GHGs that have an effect on global climate change. However, they contribute less to the greenhouse effect than carbon dioxide. We will find out why next.

Understanding: The impact of a gas depends on its ability to absorb long-wave radiation as well as on its concentration in the atmosphere.

Methane does not stay in the atmosphere as long as other GHGs because it tends to react with other substances present in the atmosphere and be transformed.

Subject vocabulary

greenhouse effect atmospheric trapping of heat that helps to maintain Earth's temperature

greenhouse gases gases, such as carbon dioxide, in the atmosphere that contribute to the greenhouse effect

Synonyms

phenomenon . event/happening

In addition, methane is much less concentrated in the atmosphere (approximately 1700 parts per billion, ppb) than gases such as carbon dioxide (400 000 ppb).

With an ability to retain heat 100 times stronger than that of carbon dioxide, nitrous oxides might be considered to have a major impact on the greenhouse effect. Instead, since they are present in very small quantities (320 ppb), they are not as much of a worry as carbon dioxide, which is present in concentrations 1000 times that of oxides of nitrogen. One characteristic of nitrous oxides is that they can stay in the atmosphere for a long time.

Scientists focus on the kinds of GHGs that are not only present in larger concentrations but can also stay longer in the atmosphere. These are two of the main reasons carbon dioxide gets the most attention.

Water vapour is an important GHG but we are not seeing the same kinds of dramatic fluctuations in its concentration in the atmosphere that we are seeing in carbon dioxide's concentrations.

> **Subject vocabulary**
>
> **nitrous oxides** greenhouse gases formed from nitrogen and oxygen with the general formula NO_x
>
> **visibility** ability to be seen
>
> **General vocabulary**
>
> **emits** sends out

Understanding: The warmed Earth emits longer wavelength radiation (heat).

As we have seen, energy arrives on Earth in the form of sunlight. Some of that light bounces off the surface and back into space.

On the electromagnetic spectrum, light waves have a relatively short wavelength.

The gases in the atmosphere are transparent to light waves – they have no way of trapping light waves and storing their energy.

Some of the light energy from the sunlight hitting Earth, however, is transformed into heat. Heat has longer wavelengths than light and therefore has different properties concerning visibility and temperature, to name just two.

The idea of transformation from short-wave energy to long-wave energy is a key concept in understanding the greenhouse effect. You have experienced such a transformation when you wear dark-coloured clothing on a sunny day or when a car is parked in the sunshine with the windows closed and it warms up inside.

Model sentence: Energy arrives on Earth as short-wave light energy and some of that energy is converted to long-wave heat energy which can remain trapped in greenhouse gases in the atmosphere.

Understanding: Longer wave radiation is absorbed by greenhouse gases that retain the heat in the atmosphere.

One property of heat energy that makes it different from sunlight is that, unlike light, heat can be trapped and stored by GHGs.

As the heat from Earth's surface (rocks, water, vegetation) radiates upwards, it warms up certain gases in the atmosphere: water vapour, carbon dioxide, methane, and nitrous oxides (the GHGs).

This is another key step in understanding the greenhouse effect: GHGs trap some heat before they escape to space.

This is what helps keep Earth's surface warm even at night when there is no more sunlight.

Figure 4.6 *A summary of the greenhouse effect: short-wave radiation (shown in yellow) hits the surface and some is converted into long-wave radiation (shown in orange). Some of this infrared heat escapes into space but some (shown in red) is radiated back by greenhouse gases*

4 Ecology | 93

Hints for success: The greenhouse effect is not a simple phenomenon to explain. To be able to explain the step-by-step process on an exam, be sure to take time to practise with drawings and text or try to explain it to a friend or family member. Remember: be concise and precise.

Understanding: Global temperatures and climate patterns are influenced by concentrations of greenhouse gases.

There is a direct **correlation** (and **causality**) that is observable in the concentrations of GHGs and global temperatures and climate.

Climate refers to long-term changes in temperature, rainfall, and cloud cover. It can be thought of as being similar to weather except instead of being on a scale of hours or days the way weather is, climate is on a scale of decades, centuries, or even millennia.

Climatologists study climate and try to understand how it works. When they look at changes in concentrations of GHGs they see that the gases can influence the kinds of climate found.

For example, sampling deeply buried layers of ice that trapped air bubbles in the past, makes it possible to measure the concentrations of gases such as CO_2 going back thousands, tens of thousands or even hundreds of thousands of years.

Analyses of these ice cores reveal interesting patterns. The colder periods correspond to the times when there were the lowest concentrations of GHGs such as CO_2. The hottest periods of Earth's past correspond with the highest concentrations of CO_2 in the atmosphere.

Getting measurements from sources such as ice cores is an example of measurement by **proxy**. Proxies are used when direct measurements are not possible.

Subject vocabulary

correlation relationship between two occurrences

causality that one event is a direct result of another

climate the long-term pattern of weather (temperature, precipitation, and winds) of a region

proxy an indirect measurement or estimation

Application: Correlations between global temperatures and carbon dioxide concentrations on Earth

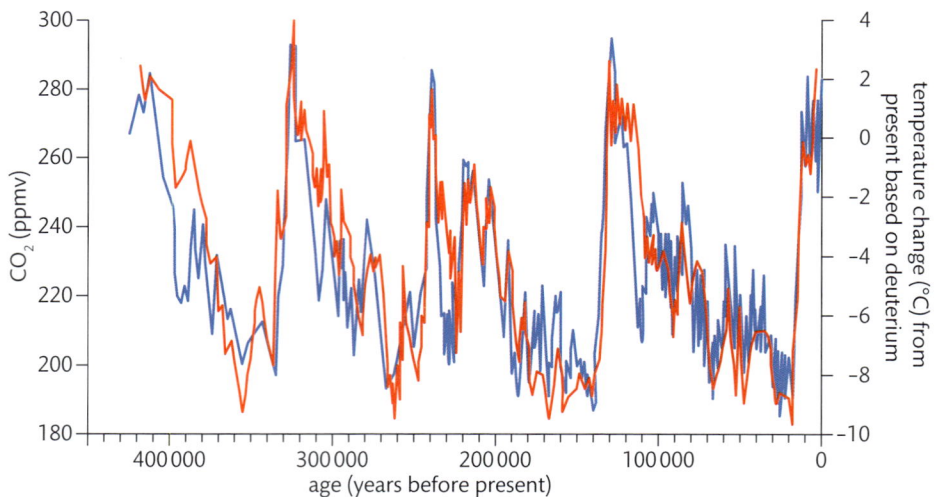

Figure 4.7 Atmospheric CO_2 levels and atmospheric temperatures over the last 400 000 years show a correlation

Source: NOAA National Climatic Data Center

This graph from the National Oceanographic and Atmospheric Administration (NOAA) shows data going back more than 400 thousand years and was made from proxy data gained from ice core samples.

Temperature change (°C) compared to modern temperature is in blue and CO_2 levels (ppm) are in red.

The graph shows that, in general, as CO_2 levels go down, temperatures decrease, and as CO_2 levels increase, temperature increases.

This graph is mostly for palaeo (ancient) data. Current CO_2 levels are closer to 400 ppm, which would be distinctly above the line shown in the graph.

Understanding: There is a correlation between rising atmospheric concentrations of carbon dioxide since the start of the industrial revolution 200 years ago and average global temperatures.

The industrial revolution, which began in the 1800s, brought with it great advances in machinery but increased society's need for a fuel supply to keep the machines running.

Coal was a main source of fuel for many decades but little by little, other fossil fuels were exploited as well, including petroleum products, such as crude oil and natural gas (methane).

The burning of these fossil fuels produces CO_2 as a waste product. Colourless and **odourless**, CO_2 was thought for a long time to be harmless.

In recent decades, climatologists have collected enough data worldwide to see that CO_2 levels have been increasing for the last 200 years and these increases coincide with two things: increased industrialization and increases in global temperatures. In other words, there is a clear correlation between human activities such as burning fossil fuels and an increase in CO_2 levels on Earth.

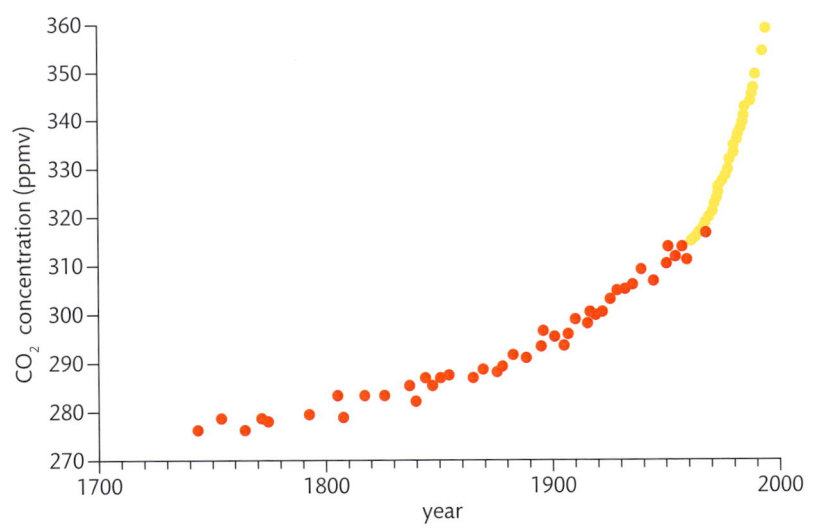

Source: US Geological Survey

General vocabulary

odourless having no smell

Subject vocabulary

runaway greenhouse effect increasing global temperature rise due to the release by human activity of high levels of greenhouse gases into the atmosphere

Figure 4.8 Graph from the US Geological Society showing CO_2 concentrations in the atmosphere in ppmv (parts per million by volume)

The red data points are from indirect measurements (proxy data) and the yellow points are direct measurements.

This intensification of Earth's natural greenhouse effect is called the **runaway greenhouse effect** and it causes the temperature of the atmosphere to increase.

Hints for success: Sometimes students as well as adults confuse the problem of a runaway greenhouse effect with another environmental problem: the thinning of the ozone layer. Although both are caused by human pollution, they are not the same thing. Avoid wasting time explaining the ozone layer – it is off topic for this section.

Understanding: Recent increases in atmospheric carbon dioxide are largely due to increases in the combustion of fossilized organic matter.

These three increases (industrialization, burning of fossil fuel, and CO_2 levels in the atmosphere) have a connection and are more than just correlations. There is a causality, and the workings explaining the causality are explained in the following way by climatologists:

- Increased use of combustion engines for industry and transportation in recent decades has increased the consumption of fossil fuels.
- When fossil fuels are burned, CO_2 is released into the atmosphere. This explains the increase in atmospheric concentrations of CO_2 in recent decades.
- The higher CO_2 concentrations in the atmosphere are causing **climate change** as seen in increased temperatures in many parts of the world, more **drought**, more extreme weather such as severe storms, and rising sea levels.
- Statistical analysis of the data shows that climatologists are 95% sure that the atmospheric changes and therefore climate change is due to human activity rather than due to natural fluctuations.

Model sentence: The increase in the levels of atmospheric carbon dioxide from about 270 ppm before the industrial revolution to about 400 ppm today are due to human activities such as the burning of fossil fuels and deforestation.

Application: Threats to coral reefs from increasing concentrations of dissolved carbon dioxide

Coral polyps, the organisms that make reefs in the ocean, are sensitive to changes in the water that surrounds them, notably the pH.

The increase of CO_2 in the atmosphere causes a concentration gradient to form between the air and the oceans, and CO_2 diffuses into the water. When water absorbs CO_2, it becomes more acidic due to the formation of carbonic acid.

If the pH of the water goes too low, it kills the coral polyps and the reef dies.

Coral reefs support a rich concentration of communities and killing them has similar consequences to deforestation of tropical rainforests – once the habitat is gone, the other organisms are no longer supported.

When reefs die, their rich colours are lost and they turn white as bone – this process is called **coral reef bleaching** and it is happening in many places all over the world at alarming rates.

Application: Evaluating claims that human activities are not causing climate change

Critics of climate change, sometimes referred to as climate change deniers or doubters, challenge the climatologists' view that humans are causing climate change.

You are expected to be able to evaluate statements such as the ones in the following list. To evaluate in this context means to judge their validity by weighing the 'for' arguments and the 'against' arguments.

Subject vocabulary

climate change an alteration of the weather patterns experienced in a region

coral reef bleaching the death of a coral reef due to the surrounding water becoming more acidic

General vocabulary

drought shortage of water due to dry weather

Climate change critics' claims: true or false?

- **Claim 1:** Yes, the climate is changing now but it always has in the past and will continue to do so – it's a natural phenomenon and is not due to human activity.
- Counterclaim to explore: Have the changes ever happened this fast?
- **Claim 2:** There is a lot of disagreement in the scientific community – many scientists do not agree with the idea that climate change is caused by humans and can explain it in other ways such as measuring the increased output of the Sun.
- Counterclaim to explore: in recent decades, how many studies by climatologists have been published supporting the idea that climate change due to human activity is not true?
- **Claim 3:** Warmer temperatures have been due to higher solar output – it's the Sun's fault, not ours.
- Counterclaim to explore: How does the trend in solar energy output over the past 200 years compare with that of the last few decades?
- **Claim 4:** Tackling climate change would require reducing carbon emissions and that would ruin the economy. Besides, we don't have realistic alternative solutions to fossil fuels.
- Counterclaim to explore: many sustainable energy sources can be implemented to reduce carbon emissions – what role does politics play in encouraging or discouraging these technologies?

One way to evaluate the claims is to see if they are based on evidence or based on belief. Also, are the criticisms driven by economic or political concerns rather than scientific evidence?

5 Evolution and biodiversity

5.1 Evidence for evolution

Main idea
There is overwhelming evidence for the evolution of life on Earth.

Nature of science: Looking for patterns, trends, and discrepancies – there are common features in the bone structure of vertebrate limbs despite their varied use.

Understanding: Evolution occurs when heritable characteristics of a species change.

Model sentence: Evolution is the process of cumulative change in the heritable characteristics of a population and the process by which evolution happens is natural selection.

Charles Darwin and Alfred Russell Wallace presented the theory of evolution by natural selection in 1858.

Evolution is the process of cumulative change in the heritable characteristics of a population. The characteristics referred to here are genetic ones (coded in DNA).

When the combinations of alleles present in a population change over time, we say the population is evolving. Evolution within a population often occurs when the population's environment changes.

Understanding: The fossil record provides evidence for evolution.

Fossils are traces of parts of organisms (bones or leaf imprints) or their activities (footprints or burrows) left in layers of rock.

When palaeontologists dig up fossils, they try to determine the age of the fossil and the type of organism that made it.

When fossils are arranged by age, some clear patterns emerge:

- Most of the history of life on Earth was in the oceans in the form of single-celled organisms.
- Life existed on land starting about 475 million years ago (meaning that over 90% of the time that life was on Earth, it was only in the oceans).
- Life only evolved hard parts (such as shells) starting about 500 million years ago.
- Living things that are familiar to us today are relatively recent in evolutionary or geological time – such as the first flowers 130 million years ago or the first songbirds 55 million years ago. These seem like ancient events but 130 million years represents less than 4% of the existence of life on Earth.
- The majority of all species that ever inhabited Earth are extinct, such as the trilobites or stegosaurs – it is difficult to quantify, but the percentage of life forms that have gone extinct is much greater than 99.99%.

We can conclude that life forms are constantly changing due to evolution. We are living on a planet where staying the same is not a long-term option for most species.

Synonyms
discrepancies . differences/inconsistencies

Subject vocabulary
vertebrate living creature with a backbone

limb arm or leg

heritable a genetic trait which can be passed on to offspring

theory of evolution by natural selection idea that the frequency of characteristics in a population changes due to the survival advantage they give an individual that has those traits

evolution cumulative change in the heritable characteristics of a population

allele version of a gene, differing by one or more bases

fossils petrified remains of plants or animals

extinct no longer existing

General vocabulary
cumulative gradually increasing

burrows holes

Understanding: Selective breeding of domesticated animals shows that artificial selection can cause evolution.

A way to see evolution on a more familiar time scale is to look at the breeding of domesticated animals. Domesticated animals such as farm animals are produced using a process called **selective breeding**.

To obtain animals with the most wanted traits, farmers often do not let nature decide which males will breed with which females. The farmer chooses animals that will give **offspring** that possess the traits chosen by the farmer.

If a cattle farmer sees that certain individuals in the herd are more resistant to disease, those cows will be chosen for reproduction. The same can be said for milk production or body shape. Having a straight back, for example, instead of a curved back makes birthing less problematic for cows, and having longer legs makes it easier for mechanical pumps to be placed under the cow for milking.

Racing dogs, such as greyhounds, have been bred to have very long legs and thin, streamlined bodies. Like all domestic dogs, these dogs never existed in nature. They are a product of human intervention called **artificial selection** in the form of selective breeding.

The following are examples of animals that are in the form they are in today thanks to artificial selection: cows, sheep, pigs, chickens, camels, llamas, turkeys, and alpaca.

Understanding: Evolution of homologous structures by adaptive radiation explains similarities in structure when there are differences in function.

Model sentence: Homologous structures in different species such as the pentadacyl limb seen in bats, whales, and humans are evidence that these species had a common ancestor.

Homologous structures are **anatomical** features of organisms that show a similar structure but do not necessarily have a similar function.

Example: the pentadactyl limb

The **forelimbs** of many animals show the following pattern starting from the body and moving outwards – one bone, two bones, many bones, five **articulated digits**.

Humans have this pattern in their arms: one bone (the humerus in the upper arm), two bones (the ulna and radius in the forearm), many bones (the carpals in the wrist), and five bony articulated digits (metacarpals and phalanges in the fingers).

Bats have this pattern in their wings, dolphins in their fins, and horses used to have it but they lost all but one digit on each limb.

Notice how the anatomy shows a similar structure but the functions are different: flight for bats, swimming for dolphins, and running for horses.

The name for an arm or leg that ends in five digits is a **pentadactyl limb**. 'Penta' means five and 'dactyl' means digit or finger.

Evolution explains this with two ideas: speciation and adaptive radiation.

Adaptive radiation is the evolution of many different species from one species or a small number of species.

Subject vocabulary

selective breeding choosing organisms with particular traits to reproduce so that their offspring share these traits

artificial selection selective breeding for particular traits

homologous structures structures which have similar genetic and structural origin that now show obvious differences

anatomical relating to the structure of the body

forelimbs front limbs (arms, legs, or flippers) of an animal

articulated jointed

pentadactyl limb an arm or leg with five jointed digits

adaptive radiation the emergence of many diverse species from a single or small number of species

Synonyms

offspring .... young/children
digits .... finger

General vocabulary

terrestrial living on land

colonized moved into a new geographical area

diverge develop in different ways so they are no longer similar

Subject vocabulary

fertile capable of reproducing

speciation process by which one species splits into two species which can no longer interbreed

predator an organism that hunts and eats other organisms

hybrid something that has the properties of two things

Synonyms

accumulated .. built up

It is hypothesized that some of the first animals to crawl onto land from the sea were quadrupeds (four-legged). They had a new habitat unoccupied by no other **terrestrial** animals except insects.

These animals had pentadactyl limbs.

With no pre-existing competition, they were able to spread out and occupy a wide range of habitats. Each habitat had a slightly different influence on which alleles were favoured.

Over hundreds of millions of years of evolution by natural selection, organisms with pentadactyl limbs have **colonized** vast territories and become many different species that occupy the land (both over- and underground), the trees, the skies, and the waters. In effect, some pentadactyl land creatures have returned to the oceans as marine mammals – whales and dolphins are two examples.

Understanding: Populations of a species can gradually diverge into separate species by evolution.

Model sentence: When a population evolves in a different way to other members of the species to an extent that it can no longer produce **fertile** offspring with members of the original population, a speciation has occurred, meaning that a new species has evolved.

When two populations of a similar species evolve in different ways, sometimes enough differences have **accumulated** over time to make it impossible for members of the two populations to interbreed anymore. When this happens, we say that **speciation** has occurred.

Example: speciation as seen in Darwin's finches

When Charles Darwin studied birds in South America, notably finches in the Galapagos Islands, he proposed that the similarities in the birds suggested a common ancestor. And yet, the birds were different enough to constitute different species.

The 13 species of finches must have come from one species that arrived on the islands long ago. As the birds spread out over the islands, different populations adapted to different habitats. With little competition and no **predators**, the process of adaptive radiation can happen relatively quickly.

Finch populations that had larger beaks were better adapted for eating seeds, whereas those that ate insects were more successful if they had finer, more pointed beaks. If the two populations tried to mate today, fertile offspring would not be produced. Some **hybrids** might arise but, generally speaking, if they are separate species, they should not be able to produce offspring. When fertile offspring cannot be produced, we say that speciation has occurred separating two groups that once had a common ancestor. The same can be said for all 13 species of Darwin's finches.

Understanding: Continuous variation across the geographical range of related populations matches the concept of gradual divergence.

How fast does evolution happen? There are two main theories: gradualism and punctuated equilibrium.

- The theory of **punctuated equilibrium** states that populations do not evolve much over long stretches of time and then suddenly, due to a significant change in their environment, they evolve quickly over a short period.
- The theory of **gradualism** states that evolution is a steady, slow, ongoing process with no sudden changes in populations.

If major differences were found between closely related species across a geographical area, this would suggest that speciations are sudden and dramatic. If, on the other hand, the variations change by small **increments** from one geographical area to another, this would give credibility to the gradualism theory.

For example, various species of conifer trees can be found ranging from warmer climates in southern China and Japan all the way up to the much colder climates near the Arctic Circle in Siberia, with **incremental** changes in tolerances to colder temperatures as the geographical range stretches northward. This gives credibility to the idea of gradual change over long periods of time as conifer species spread out to colonize different zones.

Application: Development of melanistic insects in polluted areas

Different degrees of **pigmentation** can exist in organisms, from total lack of pigmentation (white) to extreme pigmentation (black). Genes determine the degree of pigmentation, although the environment can sometimes have an influence. When individuals possess unusually dark pigmentation, it is called **melanism**. The ability of a species to have more than one appearance is called **polymorphism**.

One insect has shown some remarkable changes in the frequency of dark and light members of its population: the peppered moth in England.

During the industrial revolution, the percentage of all-black moths was high, and when the soot and smoke were removed from the air in the 1950s, the number of melanistic moths dropped significantly and the lighter-coloured moths were seen in high percentages again.

This can be explained in the following way:

- Thrushes are birds that eat moths. When they see a dark-coloured moth on a light background such as a clean tree branch, they eat it.
- This **predator**/**prey** relationship keeps the number of dark-coloured moths low in the population.
- In the 1800s, soot and smoke from the industrial revolution darkened many surfaces, making tree branches and trunks near cities dark in colour.
- This allowed the dark moths to hide well and made it easier for birds to see the light-coloured moths.
- During the industrial revolution, the light-coloured moths were seen against the darker background and eaten, so they did not pass on their genes to the next generation. This caused a change in the population: unusually high numbers of dark-coloured moths were present. This **phenomenon** is called **industrial melanism**.
- Their numbers stayed low until the Clean Air Act removed smoke and soot from the air and trees. Now the dark-coloured moths are low in number.

Subject vocabulary

punctuated equilibrium evolution by big jumps with periods of no change in between

gradualism evolution by slow, continuous small changes

pigmentation pattern of coloration

melanism dark colouring

polymorphism having several different forms

predator an organism that hunts and eats other organisms

prey animal that is food for another animal

industrial melanism production of dark-coloured form of organism, well camouflaged in areas polluted with soot

General vocabulary

increments gradual and regular increases

incremental increasing in gradual and regular amounts

Synonyms

phenomenon . event/happening

Application: Comparison of the pentadactyl limb of mammals, birds, amphibians, and reptiles with different methods of locomotion

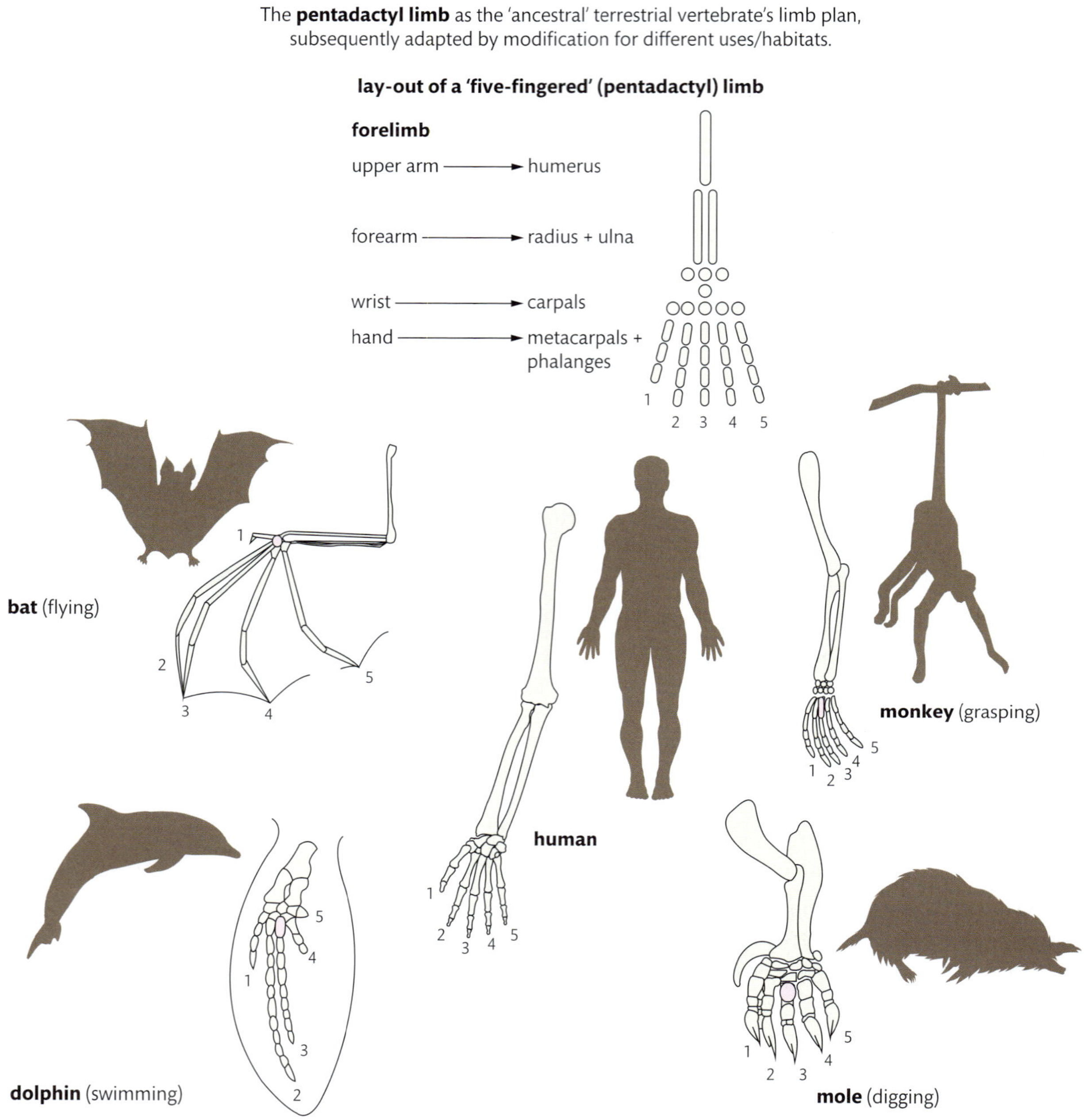

The **pentadactyl limb** as the 'ancestral' terrestrial vertebrate's limb plan, subsequently adapted by modification for different uses/habitats.
lay-out of a 'five-fingered' (pentadactyl) limb
forelimb
upper arm → humerus
forearm → radius + ulna
wrist → carpals
hand → metacarpals + phalanges
1 2 3 4 5
bat (flying)
1 2 3 4 5
human
1 2 3 4 5
monkey (grasping)
1 2 3 4 5
dolphin (swimming)
1 2 3 4 5
mole (digging)
1 2 3 4 5

Figure 5.1 *Similarities in pentadactyl limbs are used as evidence of common ancestry*

Compare each of these organisms and identify what they do with their pentadactyl forelimbs. Which pentadactyl limbs are for swimming, flying, **grasping**?

General vocabulary

grasping holding something firmly

5.2 Natural selection

Main idea
Natural selection explains how life on Earth has become so **diverse** and how it continues to evolve.

Understanding: Natural selection can only occur if there is variation among members of the same species.

Model sentence: Natural selection is a theory to explain evolution through three main aspects: (1) overproduction of offspring that show variety, (2) a struggle for survival, and (3) the best-adapted organisms passing on their genes to the next generation.

If all the organisms in a species are identical, the species only has two options: survive or die out. It is better to have variation in the population so that some organisms survive even if others die. If and when the species' environment changes, variety in the population will help it to adapt to the changes.

Understanding: Mutation, meiosis, and sexual reproduction cause variation between individuals in a species.

There are three main sources of the variation found in a population:

1. Mutations – small changes in the genetic sequence can lead to changes in genetic traits. Mutations do not happen frequently. Examples of results of new variations that could be generated by such changes are better frost resistance in plants, changes in pigmentation that help with an animal's **camouflage**, changes in an alga's ability to grow in warmer waters.

2. Meiosis – both crossing over during prophase I and random orientation of the chromosomes during metaphase I allow for new combinations of genetic material. This makes it possible for a much greater variety in the production of sperm cells and egg cells. The more variety there is in the **gametes**, the more variety there will be in the offspring.

3. Sexual reproduction – there is a certain amount of chance involved in where and when a sperm cell can meet an egg cell. This element of chance produces new combinations and decreases the chances of the same offspring being produced twice.

Understanding: Adaptations are characteristics that make an individual suited to its environment and way of life.

The term 'adaptation' refers to characteristics of an organism's **morphology** or **innate** behaviour that improve its chances for survival.

Species that are well adapted to their environment have better chances in one or more of the following domains:
- finding resources such as food, shelter, and water
- escaping from predators

General vocabulary
camouflage way of hiding by looking like the surroundings

Subject vocabulary
gamete a sex cell, either a sperm cell or an egg cell

morphology the structure and shape of an organism

innate genetically determined, controlled by DNA

General vocabulary

mate organism of the opposite sex to reproduce with

appendages arms/legs/other body parts that extend outward from the body

larvae young immature stages of insects with soft bodies

migrate to change geographical locations from one season to another (said of populations when they change geographical locations from one season to another or said of neurones when they travel to new parts of the brain)

bioluminescent light up in the dark

nocturnal organisms that are active at night

aquatic living/growing in water

Subject vocabulary

parasite organism that uses another organism for resources and does harm to that organism

pollination transfer of pollen from the anther to the stigma of a flower, occurs before fertilization in angiosperms

- attracting a **mate**
- fighting off disease and **parasites**
- reproducing and providing for their offspring.

Examples include:

- hooks on their **appendages** that could improve the success of insect **larvae** living in fast-flowing rivers
- plant populations that can attract bees with colourful patterns on their flowers will be better adapted for successful **pollination**
- the instinct in some birds to **migrate** to a warmer climate, greatly improving survival during winter.

Some adaptations are not fully understood by biologists, such as **bioluminescent** fungi in the forest – although it is hypothesized that the light attracts **nocturnal** insects that would help spread fungal spores.

Understanding: Species tend to produce more offspring than the environment can support.

Model sentence: Because of an overproduction of offspring and limited resources, only some members of a population will survive.

Organisms tend to produce too many offspring.

For example:

- Fish produce hundreds or thousands of eggs but only a small number will survive.
- Fruit trees produce many more seeds than will ever be able to grow into new trees.
- Mushrooms produce millions more spores than will ever grow into new mushrooms.

There are not enough resources to allow all the offspring to survive. Examples of resources are water, sunlight, food, shelter, or dissolved oxygen (in **aquatic** systems).

Since there is variety in the population, some members of the population will be better adapted to survive. Some fish might hide well from predators or swim faster. A particular tree sapling might be better adapted to the soil conditions where its seed germinated.

Organisms with adaptations that help them to survive are considered fit for survival. High fitness, such as good camouflage, will improve the chances of survival. Low fitness, such as poor vision in a predator, will decrease chances of survival.

Hints for success: Avoid using human examples to illustrate the theory of natural selection. It is preferable to use plants, fungi, and non-human animals as examples. If you would like to use bacteria as an example, it is best to use the idea of resistance to antibiotics talked about later in the unit.

Understanding: Individuals that are better adapted tend to survive and produce more offspring while the less well adapted tend to die or produce fewer offspring.

Model sentence: Well-adapted organisms have a higher chance of passing on their successful genes to their offspring. Organisms with low fitness will have a greater chance of dying before being able to pass on their genetic characteristics.

Zebras have evolved to have black and white stripes and tend to gather in groups. The stripes confuse predators who try to attack the group. Female lions, for example, have difficulty determining where one zebra ends and the next one begins.

If by **mutation** or by natural variation through mixing of alleles, one zebra was all black, that individual would be easy to see in the herd. Its fitness, and therefore its chances for survival, would be greatly reduced.

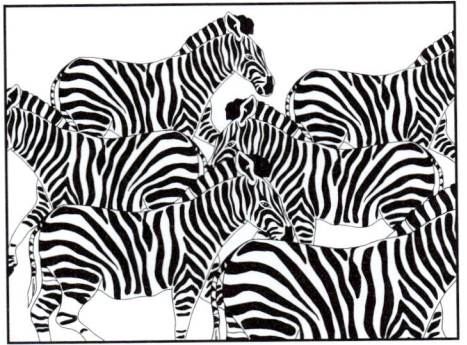 

Figure 5.2 When all zebra have stripes, it is difficult for a predator to isolate one individual from the herd. If a mutated zebra had all dark fur and no stripes, it would be at a disadvantage to the individual but also to the others since the dark fur provides a uniform background that makes the striped zebra stand out

When a young all-black zebra is killed by a predator, its ability to pass on its genes to the next generation is reduced to zero. The frequency of alleles for all-black zebras is greatly reduced in this process. In contrast, the frequency of alleles for striped zebra increases. If all the zebra in a group are striped, then other characteristics will be used for selection. For example, if a zebra is unable to fight off parasites, it could die young and not be able to pass on its genes.

Over many generations, the frequency of successful characteristics increases and the frequency of unsuccessful characteristics decreases. This explains why most unhealthy traits such as **debilitating** genetic diseases are very rare in a population.

Understanding: Natural selection increases the frequency of characteristics that make individuals better adapted and decreases the frequency of other characteristics, leading to changes within the species.

The giant leaf insect, *Phyllium giganteum*, has an effective way of hiding from predators such as birds: it looks just like a leaf. If a bird flies nearby hunting for an insect to eat, it will think it sees a leaf and it will keep flying. It will not think it sees an insect. Having an appearance of something else is called **mimicry**.

Mimicry is an effective way of tricking organisms in the surrounding habitat. Leaf insects that look more closely like leaves hide better than those who show variations that do not make them leaf-like. This gives them higher fitness and therefore an advantage for survival.

Subject vocabulary

mutation an accidental change in a genetic sequence

mimicry a type of adaptation that gives an organism advantages of the organism being imitated

General vocabulary

debilitating having a seriously weakening effect

Synonyms

imitate .... copy

Subject vocabulary

acquired traits characteristics that are learned not inherited

General vocabulary

drought shortage of water due to dry weather

In this type of insect, the alleles for colours and shapes that **imitate** leaves are found more frequently. On the other hand, alleles for colours and shapes that poorly imitate leaves are selected out of the population. For example, if a leaf insect has a white colour instead of a green colour, a predator would see it more easily. This low fitness would increase the insect's chances of being seen and eaten. That would make it impossible for the insect to pass on its genes for white colour to the next generation.

It is important to note that if there is a change in the environment, a green colour or leaf shape might not be such a useful adaptation. If climate change causes a thinning of the forest and reduces the leaf cover, the insect's camouflage is less effective because it will be more challenging to hide.

Understanding: Individuals that reproduce pass on characteristics to their offspring.

The two examples above illustrate the importance of reproductive success. If a population shows variety and has a large population size, the chances of some of the individuals possessing successful characteristics and being able to survive and pass on their characteristics increase.

On the other hand, small populations with fewer variations have a lower chance of survival and therefore less of a chance to pass on their genes.

One of the challenging concepts of evolution is that the changes in allele frequencies occur at the level of the population and yet those who are contributing to the changes are individuals. It is important to remember that evolution happens at the population or species level, and not at the individual level. Evolution is a group phenomenon over many generations.

Characteristics that an individual develops during its lifetime, called **acquired traits**, are not passed on genetically. If a cat gets into a fight and loses an eye, for example, its future kittens will not be born missing one eye. We will see in Chapter 7 that there are some interesting exceptions to this phenomenon.

Hints for success: Here is a way for remembering the key ideas in natural selection: **VISTA**. **V**ariation, **I**nheritance, **S**election, **T**ime, **A**daptations.

Application: Changes in beaks of finches on Daphne Major

In addition to being able to explain examples like the ones above, you should be able to use the theory of natural selection to explain how the beaks of Darwin's finches changed over time, notably on the Galapagos Island called Daphne Major. Decades of studies by evolutionary biologists Peter and Rosemary Grant at Princeton University have shown how food supply and **drought** that are influenced by El Niño can affect frequencies of different alleles through natural selection.

Do some research on this subject and explain what has happened to finches on that island in the past few decades. Be sure to use the ideas of overproduction of offspring, variety in the population, a struggle for survival, and whether or not genes are passed on to the next generation.

Application: Evolution of antibiotic resistance in bacteria

Model sentence: Because we expose bacteria populations to high doses of antibiotics, humans have accelerated the evolution of populations of bacteria that are resistant to antibiotics.

A patient sees a doctor and gets a treatment of antibiotics for a **strep throat**.
- The treatment kills most of the bacteria. The patient feels better and stops taking the antibiotic.
- One or more bacteria in the population were naturally **resistant** to the antibiotic. This resistance could be because of a mutation or because of receiving genetic material from another bacterium through **plasmid transfer**.
- Now without competition for resources from other bacteria, this resistant bacterium **thrives** and produces a new population of resistant bacteria.
- The patient gets sick again. This time, the antibiotic treatment will not work on him because the infection is caused by a resistant **strain**. Therefore, a new antibiotic must be used.

Methicillin-resistant *Staphylococcus aureus* (MRSA) is a type of bacteria that possesses such antibiotic resistance.

General vocabulary
strep throat a sore throat caused by a strain of bacterium

thrive grow/multiply well

Subject vocabulary
resistant unaffected by something

plasmid transfer a technique used by bacteria to share DNA

strain a type or variety of organism

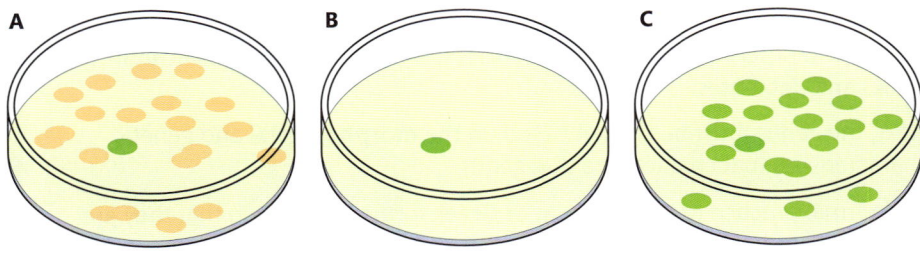

Figure 5.3 (A) Original population of bacteria being treated with antibiotics, (B) all bacteria killed except one that is resistant, (C) new population of resistant bacteria thrives

5.3 Classification of biodiversity

Main idea
Species are named and classified using an internationally agreed system.

Nature of science: Cooperation and collaboration between groups of scientists – scientists use the binomial system to identify a species rather than the many different local names.

Understanding: The binomial system of names for species is universal among biologists and has been agreed and developed at a series of **congresses**.

All known species on Earth are named using the **binomial nomenclature** system. The system was perfected and generalized by the Swedish naturalist Carolus (Carl) Linnaeus. It can be referred to as the **Linnaean system**.

Binomial = 'two names', nomenclature = 'naming system'. The plant *Pisum sativum* is the garden pea that Gregor Mendel used in his genetics experiments. *Pisum* is the **genus** name and *sativum* is the species name.

For modern humans, the genus and species names are *Homo sapiens*. Notice that most of the names are in Latin or Greek – sometimes the scientific name is called the Latin name.

General vocabulary
congresses formal meetings with members of different groups

Subject vocabulary
binomial nomenclature the naming system where all organisms are given two names

Linnaean system the binomial classification system, named after Linnaeus

genus (plural: genera) a group of species with shared characteristics

5 Evolution and biodiversity | 107

General vocabulary

zoologist scientist who studies animals

botanist scientist who studies wild plants

Subject vocabulary

morphological relating to structure and form

type specimen a sample displaying typical characteristics of a species

holotype a standard defining specimen of a species

taxonomist someone who classifies life into categories

hierarchical system classified in order of rank

taxa a level in the hierarchy of classifying living organisms, e.g. kingdom

phylum a taxon made up of many classes

kingdom a taxon made up of many phyla

families a group of related genera

taxonomy the study of classifying organisms

The genus name is capitalized but the species name is not. When typing, the two names are in italics, when writing by hand, they should be underlined.

To make the rules about how to classify organisms and to discuss new species, specialists hold congresses on a regular basis. Each group of specialists such as **zoologists** or **botanists** will have their own meetings and discussions.

These meetings ensure that a single species does not have two different names. They also take into consideration the possibility that some species might have to be moved to different categories if new information about how they are classified becomes available. When renaming an organism, the species name must remain the same.

Understanding: When species are discovered they are given scientific names using the binomial system.

Model sentence: In the binomial nomenclature system, there are certain rules that must be followed about publishing the name and making an example of the organism (a holotype) available for study.

The discoverer of a new species must first prove that no one else has already named and described the organism. This is done by checking classification books and databases.

Next, the genus must be chosen based on the **morphological** and genetic characteristics that characterize that genus.

It is normal practice to use the Latin or Greek forms of words so that they are universally understood and so that there is some stability in the system worldwide.

The new name must be published in a way that is available for others to see and an example of the organism, called a **type specimen** or **holotype**, must be made available for inspection in a place such as a museum or a university collection.

What if two scientists identify the same species independently? In such as case, the first name that was given is adopted.

Understanding: Taxonomists classify species using a hierarchy of taxa. The principal taxa for classifying eukaryotes are kingdom, phylum, class, order, family, genus, and species.

Organizing things by having categories inside other categories (like folders inside other folders) is called a **hierarchical system**.

Such is the case for **taxa**, the word we use to describe categories of organisms that are similar to folders. Bigger categories such as a **phylum** or a **kingdom** contain many sub-categories such as **families** or genera (the plural of genus).

Taxonomy is the science of classifying organisms and a taxonomist is a specialist who classifies life into categories. They use a hierarchical system of categories and sub-categories to make sense of the natural world.

Here is what it looks like:

Kingdoms contain many phyla (plural of phylum), a phylum contains many classes, etc., until you get to a genus which will contain many species.

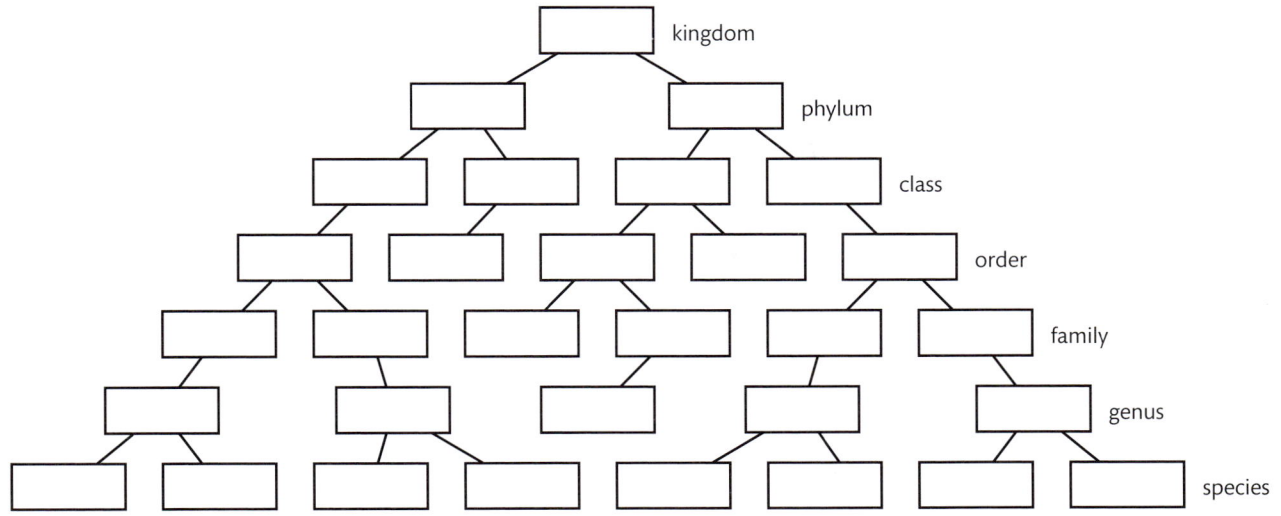

Figure 5.4 *This diagram is a very simplified way of showing the relationships between eight species from two phyla in one kingdom. It would be impossible to show the relationships of the hundreds of thousands of species in each of the kingdoms in this way. If this diagram was flipped upside down, can you see how it could be thought of as a tree? Also, remember that kingdoms can be classified under one of three domains*

Understanding: All organisms are classified into three domains.

There is one more over-arching category: a **domain**. All organisms can be placed into three domains: the Archaea domain, the Eubacteria domain, and the Eukaryote domain.

Archaea are prokaryotic single-celled organisms that have some similarities with bacteria but have very different molecular properties. For example, one type of archaean can use methane as a food source, something neither one of the other domains can do.

Eubacteria are also prokaryotes. They are the true bacteria – they are single-celled and have no membrane-bound **organelles**.

Eukaryotes have cells that possess membrane-bound organelles such as a nucleus or mitochondria. They can be single-celled such as yeast or paramecia or they can be multicellular such as plants and animals.

Subject vocabulary

domain the highest category that living things are classified into

Archaea a domain of single-celled organisms similar in size to bacteria but significantly different in biochemistry

organelles non-cellular structures within a cell which carry out organ-like processes

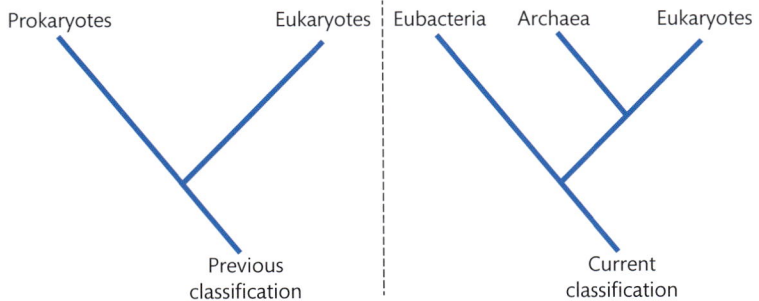

Figure 5.5 *The classification of Archaea*

Subject vocabulary

natural classification system a way of grouping organisms based on their biological similarities

morphology the structure and shape of an organism

circumscription the process of defining the characteristics of a classification group

Synonyms

ornamental.... decorative

Understanding: In a natural classification, the genus and accompanying higher taxa consist of all the species that have evolved from one common ancestral species.

The binomial nomenclature system is a **natural classification system** based on biology and ancestry.

Linnaeus was not able to use genetics because it had not yet been discovered. But by placing organisms together based on similar **morphologies**, naturalists in the 18th and 19th centuries often, without meaning to, put organisms together by how closely they were related.

With the invention of gene sequencing tools, it is now possible to confirm whether the original classifications under the Linnaean system did, in fact, group organisms by common ancestry.

On the other hand, if there are enough differences, taxonomists may choose to remove one or more species from a taxon.

Understanding: Taxonomists sometimes reclassify groups of species when new evidence shows that a previous taxon contains species that have evolved from different ancestral species.

Some classifications have had to be adjusted based on new genetic evidence. Defining (or in this case re-defining) the characteristics for groups of taxa is called **circumscription**.

Example: circumscription

Flowering plants in the genus *Costus* are found in tropical regions and include plants used for medicinal purposes or as **ornamental** flowers.

As with many organisms, these plants were originally classified by their morphology such as the characteristics of their flowers. In *Costus*, some species have long tube-like flowers that are well adapted for hummingbirds to feed from, and others have flatter, more open flower structures for bee pollination.

DNA analysis has more recently shown that the tube-like flower structure evolved more than once along different evolutionary lineages. Using this characteristic to group species together does not conform to a natural classification because it would mean putting organisms together that have differing ancestries.

In 2006, Dr Chelsea Specht proposed breaking up up the *Costus* genus into four genera: *Cheilocostus*, *Chamaecostus*, *Paracostus*, and the original *Costus*. In addition to the flower morphology contradiction mentioned above, one of the issues this new classification resolved is that it took into account DNA differences showing that the species that evolved in Asia are on different evolutionary lineages than those found in the Americas.

Understanding: Natural classifications help in identification of species and allow the prediction of characteristics shared by species within a group.

Model sentence: Taxonomists use a natural classification system (one based on ancestry) rather than an arbitrary one (such as one based on how a plant tastes to humans).

There are several reasons to adopt a natural classification system:
- to make sense of the biosphere – to see that there are connections between species of living organisms
- to show how species are related to each other
- to predict characteristics shared by a group.

For this last one, imagine a specialist who has just discovered a new species of spider. It has an exoskeleton and four pairs of articulated legs. Without watching the spider's behaviour, the specialist can predict that this organism produces spider silk because all spiders produce it (although it is true that not all spiders use the silk to make webs).

Application: Classification of one plant and one animal species from domain to species level

Research your favourite plant and animal – can you find out how they are classified? Here are two examples:

	Ginger	Gray wolf
Domain	Eukaryote	Eukaryote
Kingdom	Plantae	Animalia
Phylum	Angiospermophyta	Chordata
Class	Liliopsida	Mammalia
Order	Zingiberales	Carnivora
Family	Zingiberaceae	Canidae
Genus	*Zingiber*	*Canis*
Species	*officinale*	*lupus*

Hints for success: To help remember the order of the taxa, a memory trick is helpful. Make a sentence using the first letters of each level, such as 'King Philip Came Over For Good Soup'. The human brain is very poorly adapted for remembering lists of words but very highly adapted for remembering stories. Transforming lists into stories is a good way to remember them.

Application: Recognition features of Bryophyta, Filicinophyta, Coniferophyta, and Angiospermophyta

Characteristics of organisms in the phylum Bryophyta:
- non-vascular
- very short in stature
- do not produce flowers
- reproduction by spores
- examples: mosses, liverworts.

Subject vocabulary

biosphere all areas on and in Earth where living organisms exist

exoskeleton a skeleton of some material that is found on the outside of an animal

vascular related to the tubes that carry liquid in animals/plants

Synonyms

stature .... size/height

General vocabulary

fronds leaves of a fern or palm

Subject vocabulary

radial symmetry body plan where any line through the centre of the organism produces two similar halves, e.g. sea anemone

invertebrate living creature with no backbone

bilateral symmetry one side of an organism is a mirror image of the other side

segmentation having separate parts that are joined together

Characteristics of organisms in the phylum Filicinophyta:
- no flowers
- reproduction by spores
- ferns have triangular **fronds** – made up of multiple smaller blade-like leaves
- examples: besides ferns, horsetails are also filicinophytes.

Characteristics of organisms in the phylum Coniferophyta:
- woody stems
- leaves are needle-like or in the form of scales
- cones hold the seeds
- examples: pine, spruce, cedar, juniper.

Characteristics of organisms in the phylum Angiospermophyta:
- flowers
- fruit holding a seed (or seeds) inside
- examples: rose, wheat, apple.

Application: Recognition features of Porifera, Cnidaria, Platyhelmintha, Annelida, Mollusca, Arthropoda, and Chordata

Characteristics of organisms in the phylum Porifera:
- aquatic and sessile (do not move around)
- no digestive system – food filtered out of water
- no muscle, nerve tissue, or clear internal organs
- example: sponges.

Characteristics of organisms in the phylum Cnidaria:
- no bones or shell
- **radial symmetry**
- stinging cells
- examples: coral polyps, sea jellies, hydra.

Characteristics of organisms in the phylum Platyhelmintha:
- **invertebrate**, long flat body
- **bilateral symmetry**
- two-way digestive system (only one opening)
- no **segmentation**
- examples: flatworms, such as tapeworm.

Characteristics of organisms in the phylum Annelida:
- invertebrate
- bilateral symmetry
- long thin body with one-way digestive tube (two openings)
- segmentation
- examples: earthworm, leech.

Characteristics of organisms in the phylum Mollusca:
- invertebrates, but can produce hard shells
- bilateral symmetry
- rarely segmented (exception: chitons)
- one-way digestive tube
- examples: snail, clam, octopus.

Characteristics of organisms in the phylum Arthropoda:
- invertebrates
- bilateral symmetry
- segmented
- hard exoskeleton made of chitin
- jointed limbs
- examples: insect, crab, spider.

Characteristics of organisms in the phylum Chordata:

- **vertebrates**, most produce a bony spinal column
- bilateral symmetry
- segmented
- notochord (line of cartilage going down the back)
- examples: lizard, fish, human.

Application: Recognition of features of birds, mammals, amphibians, reptiles, and fish

Characteristics of birds:

- wings with feathers (although not all birds can fly)
- **bipedal**
- very short tail
- eggs with hard shells
- hollow bones for a lightweight skeleton
- complex breathing system
- beaks or bills instead of teeth
- **endothermic**
- examples: pigeons, penguins, chickens, gulls.

Characteristics of mammals:

- hair
- females produce milk
- usually have four limbs, mostly land-dwelling
- **thermoregulation**
- specialized teeth
- examples: polar bear, dolphin, platypus, bat, human.

Characteristics of amphibians:

- **larval** stage in water (using gills), adult stage in air (using lungs)
- most have four legs
- teeth
- ectothermic (do not maintain body temperature)
- examples: frog, salamander.

Characteristics of reptiles:

- amniote egg (egg with protective membrane around it)
- **scales**
- **ectothermic**
- examples: lizard, turtle, snake.

Characteristics of fish:

- aquatic, possess gills
- limbs in the form of fins
- ectothermic
- most have bony spinal cord, some (such as sharks) have cartilaginous spines
- examples: sharks, tilapia, carp.

Skill: Construction of dichotomous keys for use in identifying specimens

A dichotomous key is a tool used for identification of unknown specimens. It starts with a pair of statements (1a and 1b, for example) that can either be true or false about the specimen. If 1a is false ('1a: feathers present', for example), then 1b must be true ('1b feathers not present').

If statement 1a is true, the investigator looks at the end of the line to find a number that refers to the next pair of statements to look at.

If statement 1a is false, the investigator looks at 1b. The end of the line will indicate which pair of statements to go to next. If the end of a line contains the name of an organism instead of a number, it is indicating the type of the specimen being identified.

You should be able to construct a dichotomous key for a set of organisms. Use the list of characteristics shown above to practise making a key.

Subject vocabulary

vertebrate living creature with a backbone

endothermic warm blooded, body maintained at a constant temperature

thermoregulation ability to maintain a certain body temperature

larva (plural: larvae) an immature form of an insect species

ectothermic cold blooded, constant body temperature not maintained

General vocabulary

bipedal can walk using two legs rather than four

scales type of skin found on snakes, fish, and reptiles

5.4 Cladistics

Main idea

The **ancestry** of groups of species can be determined by comparing their base or amino acid sequences.

Nature of science: Falsification of theories with one theory being superseded by another – plant families have been reclassified as a result of evidence from cladistics.

Subject vocabulary

ancestry how groups of species were related in the past

ancestor individual from which an organism is descended

cladistics the study of evolutionary relationships

clade a group of organisms that share the same ancestor

primitive traits ancient traits observed in the earliest common ancestor, also called plesiomorphic traits

plesiomorphic traits ancient traits observed in the earliest common ancestor, also called primitive traits

ancestral trait a characteristic inherited from an ancestor

apomorphic or derived traits characteristics that have evolved fairly recently

anatomy the study of the structure of the body

molecular systematics classifying organisms by genetic sequences or protein sequences

---

Understanding: A clade is a group of organisms that have evolved from a common **ancestor**.

- **Cladistics** is the study of **clades**. Organisms that show more recently evolved characteristics (such as the ability to produce milk) are classified differently from organisms that show a characteristic that evolved from another ancestor (such as the ability to grow feathers).
- **Primitive traits**, also called **plesiomorphic traits** or **ancestral traits**, are the traits that evolved from the earliest ancestor in the species being studied.
- **Derived traits**, also called **apomorphic traits**, are the traits that evolved more recently. In plants, flowers evolved after vascular tissue, for example.

Understanding: Evidence for which species are part of a clade can be obtained from the base sequences of a gene or the corresponding amino acid sequence of a protein.

Although traditionally biologists have used **anatomy** and morphology to help classify organisms, more recently, gene sequencing and protein analysis have been implemented.

Using genetic information or amino acid sequences in proteins to classify organisms into clades is called **molecular systematics**.

If two organisms show similar sequences in their DNA or similar patterns of amino acids in certain proteins, it suggests that they are closely related species. If there are many differences, it can be assumed that they are more distantly related.

Since large quantities of data are involved, computers often help biologists by comparing thousands, if not millions, of data points.

As an example, compare the imaginary sequences of three species below showing four codons and the amino acids that would be coded for (in parentheses).

Species X: GGGAAATTTCCC (proline – phenylalanine – lysine – glycine)

Species Y: GGGA**T**ATTTCCC (proline –**tyrosine** - lysine – glycine)

Species Z: **C**GGA**T**A**T**ATCC**G** (**alanine** – **tyrosine** - **isoleucine** - glycine)

Notice that compared to species X, species Z has four times as many mutations (shown in red) as species Y. If the corresponding mRNA sequences are translated, we see that they code for different amino acids. This is what researchers can look at when deciding how closely related species are: species X and Y are the most closely related and species X and Z are the least closely related.

Note also that often a change in letters of the code will result in a different amino acid showing up in the polypeptide sequence, but not always. Glycine is coded for in species Y and Z even though they have different base sequences. This phenomenon is expressed in the term **degenerate code**.

Understanding: Sequence differences **accumulate** gradually so there is a positive correlation between the number of differences between two species and the time since they **diverged** from a common ancestor.

Model sentence: When analysed over millions of years, alterations in the genetic code can be used as a kind of molecular clock to estimate times when speciation events occur.

By studying mutations in DNA sequences or by causing them to happen in laboratory experiments, it has been determined that mutations are infrequent and their accumulation in a species is therefore slow.

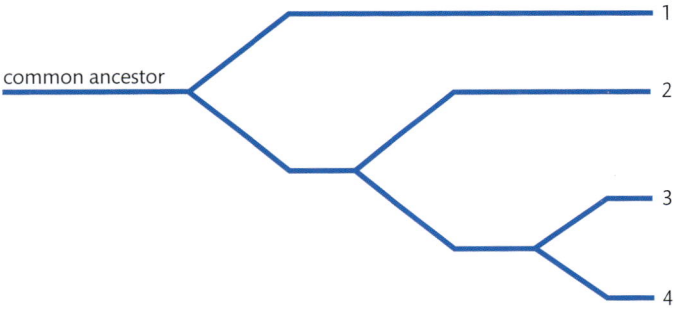

Figure 5.6 *A cladogram showing three speciation events and four species of which 3 and 4 are the most closely related to each other*

In the figure, species 3 and 4 are the most closely related, meaning that they show the most recent modifications. A speciation happened earlier to separate the species that became 3 and 4 from species 2. The first split shows how species 1 has continued to live but that subsequent speciation events (shown by the splits) have resulted from variations on the original species. The horizontal line at the left of the figure shows the common ancestor from which all four species in the diagram **descended**.

Using the idea of a biological clock, if species 2 shows ten differences in its DNA sequence compared to the original common ancestor, and species 1 shows only five differences compared to the original species and assuming that mutations happen at a steady pace, the following can be hypothesized: species 1 has existed for twice as long as species 2.

Understanding: Traits can be analogous or homologous.

Analogous traits are those that have a similar function but not necessarily a similar structure. They are found in species which do not have a recent common ancestor. Such anatomical features have different embryological origins.

Many analogous traits are the result of **convergent evolution**.

Subject vocabulary

degenerate code more than one codon coding for a given amino acid

analogous traits two traits are analogous if they have similar functions but dissimilar ancestries, for example, insect wings and bird wings

convergent evolution process by which different structures in different species develop to perform the same function

Synonyms

accumulate .... build up

General vocabulary

diverged developed in different ways so they are no longer similar

descended came from

Subject vocabulary

homologous traits two traits are homologous if they have similar ancestries but dissimilar functions, for example, pentadactyl limbs used for swimming or flying

divergent evolution process by which the same structure in different species develops to perform the different functions

cladogram branching diagram showing relationships amongst a group of organisms

node point in a cladogram where lines meet at a common ancestor showing a speciation event

sister groups groups in a cladogram that are closely related, with a recent common ancestor

outgroup a group that is not closely related to others

parsimony the principle by which the simplest and least convoluted explanation is chosen

General vocabulary

grasping holding something firmly

camouflage way of hiding by looking like the surroundings

divergence development in different ways so as to be no longer similar

Synonyms

pigments .... colours

Homologous traits are those that have a similar structure but not necessarily a similar function. They are evidence that the two species share a common ancestry. Such anatomical features have the same embryological origins.

Examples:

Analogous	Homologous
bird wings for flight and insect wings for flight	pentadactyl limbs in bats for flight evolved from a common ancestor that also gave rise to the pentadactyl limbs in monkeys for grasping objects
flippers in dolphins for swimming and fins in sharks for swimming	eyes with lenses in fish evolved from a common ancestor that also gave rise to eyes in birds
spots of pigments on moths for camouflage and spots of pigments on mammal fur for camouflage	brains in lizards evolved from a common ancestor that also gave rise to brains in primates

Homologous traits that look different are the result of **divergent evolution**.

Homologous characteristics are useful for cladistics, whereas analogous characteristics are not. Taxonomists would not put into the same taxon all organisms that have stripes, for example, zebra, certain insects, certain flowers.

Understanding: **Cladograms** are tree diagrams that show the most probable sequence of **divergence** in clades.

Model sentence: Cladograms allow for the visualization of how species emerged from common ancestors.

To visualize the genetic similarities between species in clades, diagrams called cladograms are used.

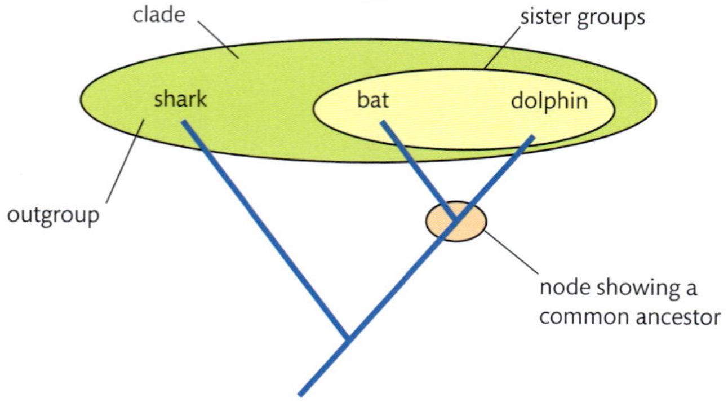

A cladogram is made up of lines showing lineage (ancestry) and each **node** (each Y-shaped branch) represents the common ancestor after which a speciation event occurred. Everything above a node is a clade.

Groups that are very closely related are called **sister groups**. The group that is the most distantly related to the others is considered an **outgroup**.

All cladograms are to be considered as proposed hypotheses. There is no one single 'correct' cladogram. Depending on the characteristics chosen, more than one cladogram could be proposed for the organisms being considered.

Figure 5.7 A cladogram showing three taxa organized into a clade, of which two are sister groups and one is an outgroup. Nodes show a common ancestor for the descendants that appear above them in this cladogram

However, there is a rule to be followed: the principle of **parsimony**. Parsimony is the practice of adopting the simplest and most probable explanation while rejecting more complex and less probable explanations.

Hint for success: Do not overinterpret these diagrams. Cladograms are only supposed to show more ancient ancestors towards the base of the diagram and more recently developed species towards the ends of the branches. When analysing cladograms, you should not talk about 'progress', 'improvement', or 'more highly evolved species'. Evolution works by natural selection rather than following some kind of path towards perfection. All species alive today have evolved for the same number of years.

Understanding: Evidence from cladistics has shown that classifications of some groups based on structure did not correspond with the evolutionary origins of a group or species.

Some cladograms have been proved false. A cladogram that does not show the similarities and differences in genetic sequences correctly cannot be accepted. Putting two distantly related species next to each other above the same node on a cladogram when other species are clearly more closely related does not follow the principle of parsimony.

In the past, some organisms were wrongly classified as being closely related due to their similar morphologies. Later it was shown that the two species were more distantly related than originally thought. In this case, a new cladogram and therefore a new classification are proposed.

The opposite can also happen: birds have always been placed in a class of their own but the more we study them and study dinosaurs called theropods, it is clear from a cladistics point of view that birds are, in fact, theropods. The features that they share include backward-pointing knees, fused clavicle bones (the Y-shaped 'wishbone'), and eggs with hard shells.

Application: Cladograms including humans and other primates

Example of a cladogram including humans and chimpanzees. The numbers represent the following: (1) vertebrates, (2) **quadruped**, (3) hair, (4) **opposable thumb** (thumb that can be used to grasp), (5) **bipedalism** (ability to walk on two legs).

Application: Reclassification of the figwort family using evidence from cladistics

There is a family of flowering plants called figworts which have traditionally been classified in the family called Scrophulariaceae. This classification was based on the morphology of parts of the plants such as the nectaries (where sweet nectar is produced) or the type of aestivation. **Aestivation** in plants refers to how the flower's petals are arranged before the bud opens.

Taxonomists have analysed zones of DNA markers such as the nuclear ribosomal **internal transcribed spacer** (ITS) and found that figworts with the morphological similarities listed above did not show expected similarities in their DNA sequences. This means that plants that were originally thought to be **monophyletic** (sharing a recent common ancestor) were in fact **polyphyletic** (on a different lineage).

One example of a figwort that has been reclassified is the foxglove. These flowering plants are now in the family called Plataginaceae, which is the same family as plantains.

> **General vocabulary**
> **quadruped** an animal with four legs
>
> **Subject vocabulary**
> **opposable thumb** a digit arranged opposite the other digits which allows objects to be grasped
>
> **bipedalism** ability to walk on two legs
>
> **aestivation** the arrangement of flower petals within a bud
>
> **internal transcribed spacer** a marker in DNA used to check similarities between species
>
> **monophyletic** having one common ancestor
>
> **polyphyletic** said of two or more clades that have different common ancestors

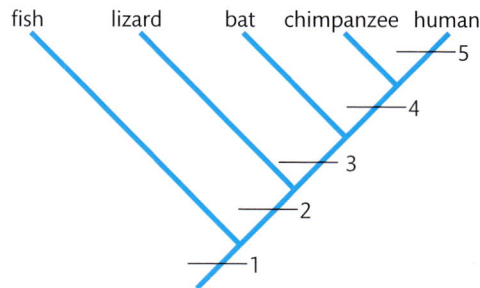

Figure 5.8 A cladogram showing the relationship of humans to four other vertebrates. Cladograms are helpful in showing that we are more closely related to chimpanzees than to fish. But notice that there is no judgement of how evolved an organism is. Fish are just as highly evolved as humans, only they have adapted well to living underwater whereas we have not

5 Evolution and biodiversity

Figure 5.9 *Rearranging a cladogram based on new DNA evidence. The clade that included species C, D, and E on the left was moved from the branch that included species A, and placed on the branch with species B instead, because C, D, and E show a common ancestry with species B. In the old cladogram on the left, B, C, D, and E are shown as being* paraphyletic, *whereas the new cladogram on the right is showing them as monophyletic*

Subject vocabulary

paraphyletic a group containing some but not all of the descendants of a common ancestor

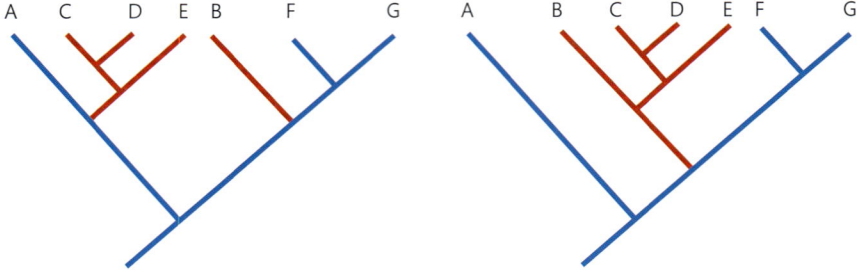

Skill: Analysis of cladograms to determine evolutionary relationships

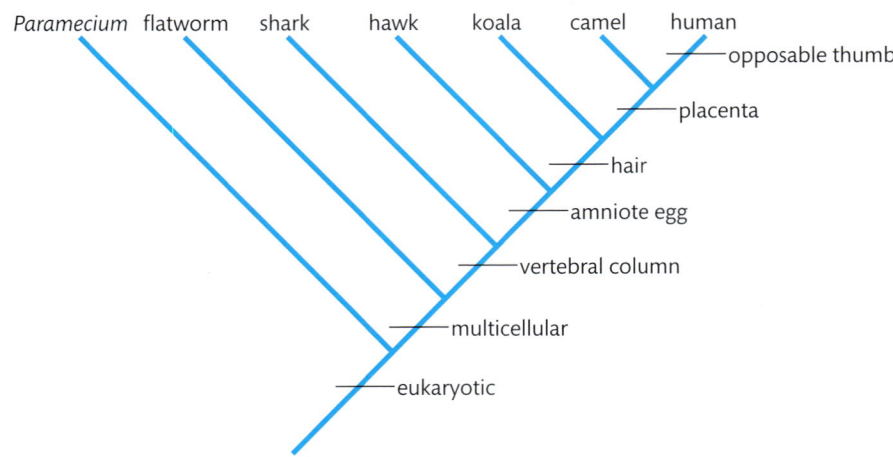

Figure 5.10 *A cladogram showing the evolutionary relationships between seven organisms*

1 What is the primitive characteristic in the cladogram shown in Figure 5.10?

2 Name the members of the mammal clade in this cladogram.

3 What is the outgroup when considering the clade of multicellular organisms?

4 Do shark eggs have a protective membrane (the amnios) around them?

5 Explain why there are no bacteria shown in this diagram.

> **Hints for success:** To help you remember the difference between analogous and homologous, remember that these terms refer to anatomy (the flesh and blood) and that an analogy is used to compare very different things. The term 'homo' means 'same', so homologous refers to anatomically similar things.

Answers:
1 Being eukaryotic is the primitive characteristic shared by all.
2 koala, camel, human
3 *Paramecium*
4 No. Sharks are not amniotes.
5 Because the primitive characteristic requires the organisms to have a nucleus. If bacteria were to be added to this cladogram, a new primitive characteristic would need to be chosen.

6 Human physiology

6.1 Digestion and absorption

Understanding: The **contraction** of circular and longitudinal muscle of the small intestine mixes the food with **enzymes** and moves it along the **gut**.

Model sentence: Food within the small intestine is mixed with enzymes and is kept moving due to contractions of two layers of intestinal muscles.

Ingested food moves along a 'tube' called the **alimentary canal**.

The interior **cavity** of the alimentary canal is called the **lumen**.

The small intestine is the longest part of this tube.

Enzymes needed for **digestion** are added to the food at various places along the tube.

Two layers of muscle that make up the wall of the tube contract in order to:
- mix the food with the enzymes
- keep the food moving from beginning to end.

Food moves by way of a process called **peristalsis**. Peristalsis is muscle contractions just behind the food mass so that the food mass continues moving in one direction.

The two layers of muscle are called the **circular muscle layer** and the **longitudinal muscle layer**. Both of these muscle layers are controlled by areas of the brain that control activities at the subconscious level. The type of muscle controlled at the subconscious level is called **smooth muscle**.

Skill: Drawing the digestive system

You should be able to draw a diagram of the human digestive system and give the functions of each major part. The figure to the right would be good practice for doing this. Add functions as you learn them from various sections of this part of the text.

Skill: Identifying tissue layers from a sectioned view of the small intestine.

The following figure will help you to learn these layers.

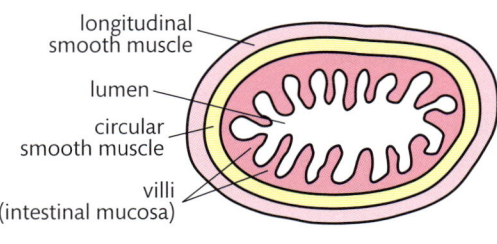

Figure 6.1 This drawing shows a sectioned view of a part of the small intestine. Notice that the outer layer of muscle is called the longitudinal layer and under that layer is the circular layer. You will learn about the villi in an upcoming section

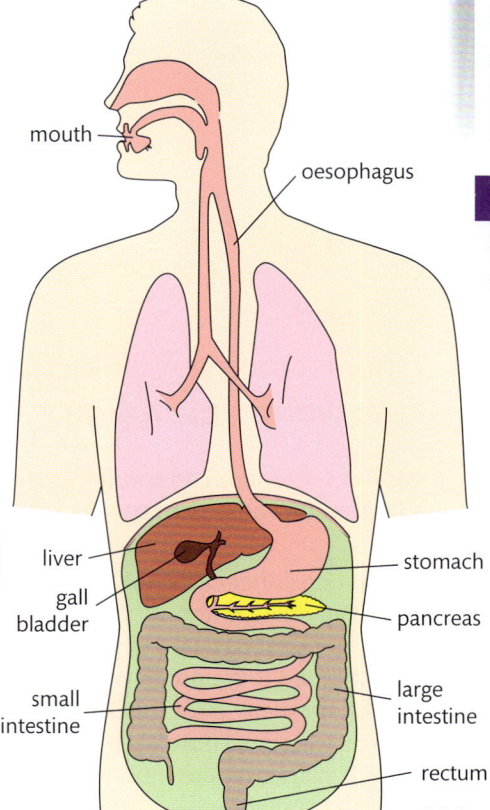

Figure 6.2 The human digestive system

General vocabulary

contraction tightening and narrowing

sectioned 'cut-away' view

Subject vocabulary

enzyme a protein that acts as a catalyst

ingested food/substances taken into the body

alimentary canal the tube that carries food while it is being digested

lumen area within surrounding walls or membranes; usually used for the cavity of a tubular structure such as a blood vessel

digestion a chemical process whereby large molecules undergo reactions in order to become a molecular size that can be absorbed into the blood

peristalsis contractions of smooth muscle in the alimentary canal that moves the food from mouth towards anus

circular muscle layer the inner layer of smooth muscle of the alimentary canal

longitudinal muscle layer outer layer of smooth muscle of alimentary canal

smooth muscle muscle that contracts to move something in the body besides a bone or heart chamber

Synonyms

gut .... alimentary canal

cavity .... space (within)

Subject vocabulary

pancreas an organ within the body that has many functions including production of three important digestive enzymes and production of two hormones that regulate glucose

substrate substance which begins a chemical reaction or process

hydrolyses splits a larger molecule into two smaller molecules through a chemical reaction

digest a reaction that hydrolyses or splits a molecule into a smaller form

macromolecules large, complex organic molecules

monomer a 'building block' unit of a macromolecule

villus (plural: villi) a small finger-like projection that extends into the lumen of the small intestine

epithelium cell layer that often forms a covering or outer cell layer of a structure (formed of epithelial cells)

capillary smallest blood vessels; all substances moving in or out of the bloodstream pass through the walls of these small vessels

Synonyms

secrete .... produce/release
absorption ..... taking in

General vocabulary

projection something that extends outward from a surface

Understanding: The **pancreas** **secretes** enzymes into the lumen of the small intestine.

Model sentence: Digestive enzymes are sent into the cavity of the small intestine from the pancreas.

The table shows three enzymes that are produced by the pancreas and sent to the small intestine.

Enzyme	Substrate	Action
lipase	lipids (fats and oils)	hydrolyses lipids into glycerol and fatty acids
amylase	starch	hydrolyses starch into smaller carbohydrates
trypsin	proteins	hydrolyses proteins into smaller sections

Understanding: Enzymes **digest** most **macromolecules** in food into **monomers** within the small intestine.

Model sentence: The large molecules found in food are digested into smaller molecular forms by enzymes in the small intestine.

Most people think of foods as meats, breads, fruits, and vegetables. Each of these foods is made up of very large molecules called macromolecules. The macromolecules are too large to be absorbed into our blood. The function of enzymes is to digest the macromolecules into smaller forms called monomers. The small intestine can then absorb the monomers into the bloodstream.

Food example	Macromolecule form	Monomer form
meat (chicken)	protein	amino acids
bread	starch	glucose
cooking oil	triglycerides	fatty acids and glycerol
fruit (orange)	nucleic acids	nucleotides

Understanding: **Villi** increase the surface area of **epithelium** over which **absorption** is carried out.

Model sentence: The small intestine contains many small projections called villi that increase the surface area for absorption.

The lumen (inner cavity) of the small intestine is lined by cells called epithelial cells. This lining is not smooth. Instead, it is composed of a great many finger-like projections called villi. Each villus creates a great deal of surface area for absorption as compared to a smooth walled surface. In addition, the cells that make up each **villus** have many even smaller projections that also greatly increase surface area. These projections from each cell are called microvilli. After the food monomers enter a villus, they are most often taken into the smallest of all blood vessels called a **capillary**.

Understanding: Villi absorb monomers formed by digestion as well as **mineral ions** and **vitamins**.

Model sentence: Vitamins and mineral ions are absorbed by villi in addition to food monomers.

Here is a partial list of the important substances that are absorbed from the small intestine into our bloodstream:
- water
- glucose
- amino acids
- mineral ions (e.g. sodium, potassium, calcium)
- vitamins (e.g. vitamin B, vitamin C).

Subject vocabulary

mineral ions the charged form of inorganic substances like sodium (Na^+)

vitamins organic compounds needed in small amounts in our diet

Understanding: Different methods of membrane transport are required to absorb different nutrients.

Model sentence: The nutrient monomers absorbed through the villi membranes use a variety of membrane transport methods.

Each villus that extends into the lumen of the small intestine is made up of many epithelial cells. The epithelial cells have plasma membranes that the food monomers must pass across in order to reach a capillary. The figure illustrates three of the common transport methods.

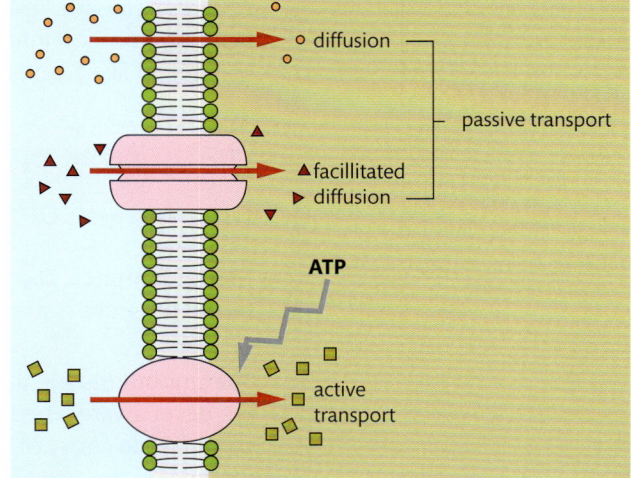

Figure 6.3 Schematic view of three of the more important mechanisms used by cells of the villi epithelium to absorb nutrients from the lumen of the intestine. The mechanism used depends on the size and polarity of the molecule transported. Not shown is endocytosis where a portion of the plasma membrane invaginates to take in many molecules at one time

6.2 The blood system

Understanding: Arteries convey blood at high pressure from the **ventricles** to the **tissues** of the body.

Model sentence: Ventricles are the heart chambers that pump high pressure blood through arteries to tissues in the body.

- The heart is **composed** of four chambers.
- The upper two chambers collect incoming blood and are called **atria**.
- The lower two chambers pump blood out and are called ventricles.
- Any blood vessel that takes blood away from the heart is an artery.
- The ventricle on the left side of the heart pumps blood to the body tissues.
- The ventricle on the right side of the heart pumps blood to the lungs.

Subject vocabulary

ventricles the lower two chambers of the heart

tissues a collection of cells in the body that serve a common purpose

artery any blood vessel that carries blood away from the heart

atria the upper two chambers of the heart (singlular - atrium)

Synonyms

composed (of) made up (of)

General vocabulary

coronary relating to the heart

rigid stiff/not moving or bending

contract tighten and narrow

permeable allows one or more substances to pass through

Subject vocabulary

plaque build-up of cholesterol and other substances on the inner wall of arteries or biofilm on the surface of teeth

occlusion a condition where a blood vessel no longer carries enough blood due to plaque build-up

elastic fibre a protein found in the wall of arteries that can expand and contract

blood pressure the pressure exerted by blood on the inner wall of a blood vessel

lumen area within surrounding walls or membranes; usually used for the cavity of a tubular structure such as a blood vessel

capillary smallest blood vessels; all substances moving in or out of the bloodstream pass through the walls of these small vessels

nutrient chemical material a cell or organism needs

Application: Causes and consequences of occlusion of the coronary arteries

Some of the most important arteries in the body are the arteries that feed blood directly into the muscle tissue of the heart. These arteries are called coronary arteries. Over a long period of time substances can build up in the inner walls of the coronary arteries. These substances are called plaque. Eventually plaque begins to block blood from flowing freely through one or more coronary arteries. This block is called an occlusion. Occlusions can lead to the heart muscle experiencing a lack of oxygen and may result in a heart attack.

Understanding: Arteries have muscle cells and elastic fibres in their walls.

Model sentence: An artery is not a rigid tube carrying blood as its walls have muscle cells and elastic fibres that allow the wall to move and be flexible.

Arteries must have the strength to withstand the high blood pressure provided by the pumping action of each ventricle. Thus, the wall of an artery is relatively thick. Much of this thickness is made up of a type of muscle called smooth muscle.

Arteries also have flexible fibres made of protein that stretch when a ventricle first pumps blood into an artery. These flexible proteins are capable of stretching something like a coiled spring.

Understanding: The muscle and elastic fibres assist in maintaining blood pressure between pump cycles.

Model sentence: During the brief time period when ventricles are not pumping, blood pressure is maintained with the help of smooth muscle and elastic fibres.

The smooth muscle that makes up the wall of an artery does contract at times. You are never aware when this is happening. The contraction causes changes in the size of the inside cavity of the artery. This inside cavity is called the lumen of the artery. Changes in the size of the lumen help control blood pressure.

Arteries also have flexible fibres made of protein that stretch when a ventricle first pumps blood into an artery. Between pumps these elastic fibres return to their original length. This action helps maintain blood pressure even when the ventricle is not pumping.

Understanding: Blood flows through tissues in capillaries. Capillaries have permeable walls that allow exchange of materials between cells in the tissue and blood in the capillary.

Model sentence: Capillaries are the only blood vessels that have walls permeable to materials entering or leaving the blood.

- Blood enters a capillary from a very small branch of an artery.
- Each capillary wall is only one cell layer in thickness.
  - This makes the capillary permeable to many molecules.
  - Oxygen and nutrients typically leave the blood and move into surrounding cells.

- Carbon dioxide and sometimes other **wastes** leave the cells and move into the blood.
- Blood cells are not able to leave from the capillary.
- Blood leaves the capillary and goes into a very small **vein**.

> **Subject vocabulary**
>
> **wastes** molecules produced by body cells that need to be carried away
>
> **vein** a blood vessel that collects blood from capillaries and returns that blood to the heart
>
> **pumping cycle** the muscular contractions of both atria and then both ventricles
>
> **valves** structures that allow a one-way fluid flow
>
> **atrioventricular valves** valves located between each atrium and ventricle
>
> **semilunar valves** valves located where blood exits each ventricle

Understanding: Veins collect blood at low pressure from the tissues of the body and return it to the atria of the heart.

Model sentence: Blood is returned to the atria of the heart through veins that carry low-pressure blood leaving the capillaries of the body.

When blood leaves the ventricles of the heart through an artery it is under high pressure. This pressure is a result of each ventricle acting as a pump. When the blood enters capillaries it must slow down as the blood cells move through the small capillaries one cell at a time. As a result, much of the blood pressure is lost while in the capillaries.

When this low-pressure blood enters a vein it is still under low pressure. It is this blood that makes its way back to the heart through larger and larger veins. The slow-moving blood is carried back to the atria of the heart to begin another **pumping cycle**.

Understanding: **Valves** in veins and the heart ensure circulation of blood by preventing backflow.

Model sentence: The heart and veins have valves to keep blood moving in a single direction.

Veins have one-way valves that stay open when blood is moving back towards the heart. The valves close if the blood attempts to move in the other direction. The heart has four internal valves that prevent backflow of blood. This keeps blood moving in a single direction.

Skill: Identification of blood vessels as arteries, capillaries, or veins from the structure of their walls

As described in the previous sections, arteries will have the thickest walls. Veins will have thin walls, but not thin enough for substances to enter or leave. Capillaries will have extremely thin walls composed of a single cell layer.

Inside of the heart there are four valves that keep blood moving in a single direction. There are valves located between each atrium and ventricle. These two valves are called the **atrioventricular valves**. There are also valves located where blood is pumped out of the ventricles. The valve on the left side is called the left **semilunar valve**. The valve on the right side is called the right semilunar valve.

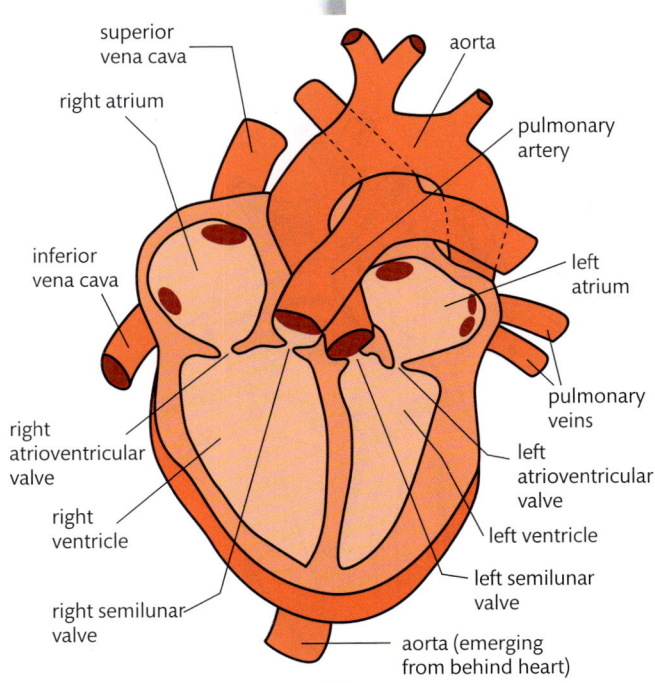

Figure 6.4 *Human heart anatomy*

6 Human physiology | 123

Subject vocabulary

cardiac involving the heart

aorta the largest artery in the body, taking oxygenated blood away from the left ventricle of the heart

pulmonary artery large artery leaving the heart taking blood to the lungs

pulmonary associated with the lungs

pulmonary veins veins that return blood to the heart from the lungs

cadaver a dead human body

General vocabulary

circulation a pathway that leads back to a starting point

dissection to cut up the dead body of an organism to study it

Synonyms

oxygen-rich .... oxygenated

oxygen-poor .. deoxygenated

Skill: Recognition of the chambers and valves of the heart and the blood vessels connected to it in dissected hearts or in diagrams of heart structure

You may want to study the names and positions of the chambers and valves of the heart from a dissected animal heart. If not, you can learn this information from many heart diagrams including the figures provided in this text.

Application: Pressure changes in the left atrium, left ventricle, and aorta during the cardiac cycle

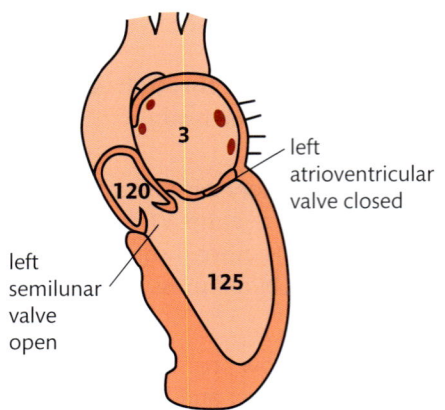

'Late' ventricular systole

Figure 6.5 *Blood pressure produced by the left ventricle. The numbers shown in this figure are pressure readings in mm Hg. The left ventricle exerts enough pressure to open the semilunar valve sending blood out of the aorta. This pressure also keeps the atrioventricular valve closed*

The numbers shown in this figure are pressure readings in millimetres of Hg (mm Hg). The left ventricle exerts enough pressure to open the semilunar valve sending blood out into the aorta. This pressure also keeps the atrioventricular valve closed.

Understanding: There is a separate circulation for the lungs.

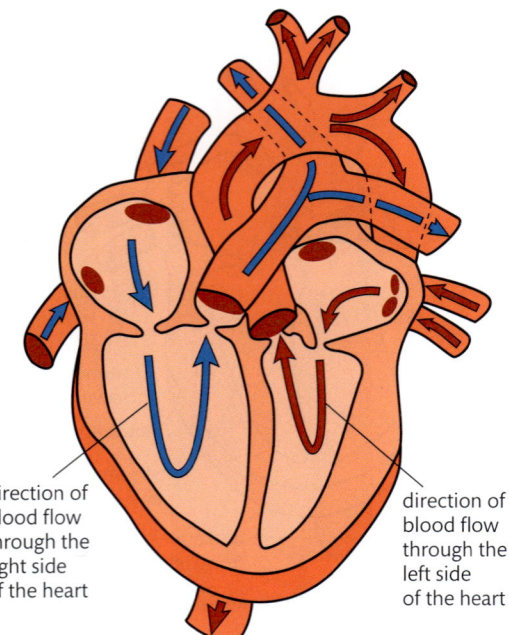

Model sentence: The heart acts as two pumps with one of the two pumps sending blood to the lungs.

The left side of the heart pumps **oxygen-rich** blood out to the body. This blood leaves the left ventricle and flows through the **aorta**. The aorta then branches into many smaller arteries.

The right side of the heart pumps **oxygen-poor** blood to the lungs. This blood leaves the right ventricle and flows through the **pulmonary artery**. Since you have two lungs the **pulmonary** artery branches into two large arteries. Oxygenated blood is returned to the heart through the **pulmonary veins**.

Application: William Harvey's discovery of the circulation of the blood with the heart acting as a pump

It was not until the 17th century that people learned that blood was being pumped through the body by the heart. William Harvey showed this by **dissection** of many human **cadavers** and living animals.

Figure 6.6 *Blood flow through the human heart. Blue arrows show oxygen-poor blood and red arrows show oxygen-rich blood*

Understanding: The heart beat is **initiated** by a group of specialized muscle cells in the right atrium called the **sinoatrial node.**

Model sentence: The sinoatrial node is composed of specialized muscle cells in the right atrium that begin each heart beat.

The cells that make up the sinoatrial node have features that make them muscle cells. They also have features that make them nervous system cells.

The sinoatrial node is often abbreviated as SA node.

Understanding: The sinoatrial node acts as a **pacemaker.**

Model sentence: By acting as the pacemaker, the sinoatrial node sets the rate at which our heart beats.

A single heart beat is when both atria contract at the same time followed by both ventricles contracting at the same time. These two sets of contractions are followed by a brief rest period until the next heart beat occurs. When a person is 'at rest' (not being physically active) the sinoatrial node initiates each heart beat at its own pace.

Understanding: The sinoatrial node sends out an electrical signal that stimulates contraction as it is **propagated** through the walls of the atria and then the walls of the ventricles.

Model sentence: The electrical signal initiated by the sinoatrial node results in contraction of both atria and then is transferred to the walls of both ventricles.

Synonyms
initiated......... started/begun

Subject vocabulary
sinoatrial node a specialized group of cells in the heart that send out spontaneous electrical signals leading to a resting heart rate

pacemaker something that determines a rate for one or more events

General vocabulary
propagated caused to spread out

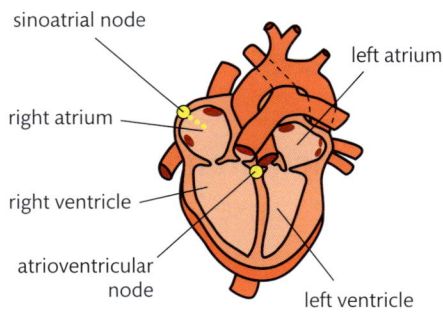
The sinoatrial node initiates an impulse. Both atria contract.

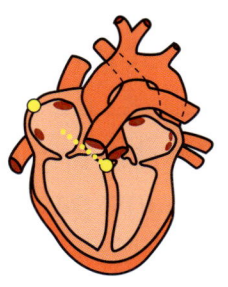
A second node receives the impulse from the SA node.

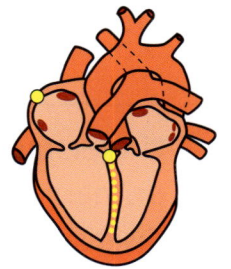
After a short delay, the second node sends an impulse down the wall separating the two ventricles.

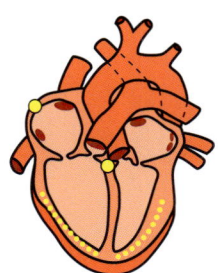
This impulse spreads throughout the ventricles. Both ventricles contract.

Figure 6.7 *Electrical activity of the heart initiated by the atrioventricular node*

Synonyms

medulla of the brain........ medulla oblongata

General vocabulary

subconscious mental activities that one is not aware of

vigorous done with great energy

Subject vocabulary

accelerans nerve nerve that carries impulses from the medulla to SA node in order to increase heart rate

vagus nerve nerve that carries impulses from the medulla to the SA node in order to decrease heart rate

epinephrine hormone secreted from the adrenal glands

secretion release of a substance from a cell, tissue, or gland

adrenal glands glands located on top of each kidney

mucous membrane living tissue that secretes a mucous protection

pathogens disease-causing agents such as viruses and bacteria

infectious capable of causing an infection

Understanding: The heart rate can be increased or decreased by impulses brought to the heart through two nerves from the **medulla of the brain.**

Model sentence: The medulla of the brain can increase or decrease heart rate by sending impulses through two nerves that connect to the sinoatrial (SA) node of the heart.

- The medulla of the brain is part of the brainstem.
- The medulla controls many physiological factors in the body that occur at the **subconscious** level.
- During exercise, the medulla sends impulses through a nerve called the **accelerans nerve** to increase heart rate.
- After exercise, the medulla sends impulses through a second nerve called the **vagus nerve** to decrease heart rate.
- Both nerves connect into the SA node.
- The SA node stills sends impulses to the atria but the rate is being controlled by the medulla of the brain.

Understanding: **Epinephrine** increases the heart rate to prepare for **vigorous** physical activity.

Model sentence: Humans are capable of increasing their heart rate through **secretion** of the hormone epinephrine.

Epinephrine is a hormone secreted by two glands in the body called the **adrenal glands**. When needed the adrenal glands secrete epinephrine into the bloodstream. This can result in a dramatic increase in heart rate above the resting rate.

6.3 Defence against infectious disease

Understanding: The skin and **mucous membranes** form a primary defence against **pathogens** that cause **infectious** disease.

Model sentence: Most pathogens never get a chance to enter the body and cause disease because of the actions of skin and mucous membranes.

The outer layer of human skin is a layer of dead waterproofed cells. This helps protect us from many infectious diseases that can only infect living cells.

Mucous membranes line the openings of many body openings like the mouth and nose. This living tissue produces a layer of mucus. This mucus helps trap and eliminate many pathogens.

Understanding: Cuts in the skin are sealed by **blood clotting**.

Model sentence: Blood loss is kept to a minimum by blood clotting when blood vessels in the skin are cut.

Capillaries and other small blood vessels are opened whenever one accidently cuts through their skin. Our blood system has a response to that situation called clotting. Clotting involves both cells and chemicals that are found in our bloodstream.

Understanding: **Clotting factors** are released from **platelets**.

Model sentence: Small **fragments** of blood cells, called platelets, release chemicals called clotting factors in response to a cut.

- Platelets are blood cell fragments.
- Platelets are regularly produced in **bone marrow**.
- In response to a damaged blood vessel, platelets release chemicals.
- These chemicals are called clotting factors.
- Clotting factors are needed in order to clot blood at the cut area.

Understanding: The **cascade** results in the rapid **conversion** of **fibrinogen** to **fibrin** by **thrombin**.

Model sentence: A blood clot is a result of a cascade of reactions ultimately changing fibrinogen to fibrin by the enzyme thrombin.

A blood clot is accomplished by a set of reactions called a cascade. This is because one step of the reaction leads to another, then another, and so on. Fibrinogen and the inactive enzyme prothrombin are always circulating in the blood waiting to be used if needed to form a clot.

The clot is the fibrin **mesh** that acts somewhat like a spider web in that it traps blood cells to help seal the cut area.

Application: Causes and consequences of blood clot formation in coronary arteries

Note: the coronary arteries are the blood vessels that feed oxygenated blood directly into the heart muscle.

Causes of blood clot formation	Consequences of clots in coronary arteries
Deposits of cholesterol and fat build up over time inside the arteries. These deposits are called plaque.	Blood being provided to specific areas of the heart becomes limited.
Plaque narrows the inside opening of the blood vessel.	The areas with limited blood supply become weak.
Plaque in one area can break off and become **lodged** in another area where the vessel is smaller.	If enough **blockage** occurs a heart attack may result.

Subject vocabulary

blood clotting a body response to minimize blood loss from small blood vessels

clotting factors chemicals that help the clotting process

platelets cell fragments in the blood that release clotting factors

bone marrow soft tissue which fills the inner, hollow spaces of certain types of bones

fibrinogen the inactive form of the blood-clotting protein called fibrin

fibrin the active form of fibrinogen that forms the mesh of a blood clot

thrombin the enzyme that converts fibrinogen to fibrin

Synonyms

fragments ...... pieces
lodged .... stuck

General vocabulary

cascade a sequence of events, each one causing the next

conversion change from one form to another

mesh a structure that works like a net

blockage something that stops movement

Subject vocabulary

phagocytic a cell capable of phagocytosis

non-specific immunity actions by the immune system based on the pathogen only being identified as 'not self'

phagocytosis active transport in which larger particles and substances are brought into the cell

not self a foreign invader to the body such as a virus or bacterium, often called an antigen

antibody a protein produced by our immune system in response to an antigen

lymphocytes white blood cells capable of producing antibodies, often referred to as B lymphocytes or B cells

antigen substance which stimulates the production of antibodies in vertebrates

specific immunity actions by the immune system based on a specific pathogen having been identified

Understanding: Ingestion of pathogens by **phagocytic** white blood cells gives **non-specific immunity** to diseases.

Model sentence: The human body contains white blood cells that ingest disease-causing agents (pathogens) by identifying the agent as foreign to the body.

White blood cells are also called leukocytes. There are many types of leukocytes in the body.

Some leukocytes are capable of **phagocytosis** (phagocytic white blood cells). Some phagocytic white blood cells recognize molecules making up pathogens as being '**not self**' or foreign to the body. If a pathogen is recognized as 'not self' it is ingested by phagocytosis and destroyed. This type of immunity is called non-specific as the pathogen is not identified, it is only determined to be 'not-self'.

Understanding: Production of **antibodies** by **lymphocytes** in response to particular **antigens** gives specific immunity.

Model sentence: Specific immunity is provided by white blood cells known as lymphocytes when they recognize antigens and produce antibodies.

Lymphocytes are another type of leukocyte. They are capable of producing specifically shaped proteins called antibodies. Each type of antibody is a molecule that recognizes specific molecules found on pathogens called antigens.

For example:

- A specific virus infects an individual.
- The protein coating of the virus acts as the antigen(s).
- Lymphocytes produce and secrete antibodies that bond to the virus antigen(s).
- The virus is more readily eliminated from the body.

This is called specific immunity because the pathogen has been identified and a specific response (the antibody) has been used to fight the infection.

Application: Effects of HIV on the immune system and methods of transmission

HIV is a virus that infects specific white blood cells of a person's immune system. Those cells are important for cellular communication to other white blood cells. When HIV kills enough of the communicating cells, a person's immune system stops functioning properly.

HIV is transmitted when a body fluid of an infected person is transmitted to someone else. This can happen when:

- Body fluids are exchanged during sex.
- Hypodermic needles are used on an HIV patient and then someone else uses the same needle.
- Donated blood products are used without testing for the presence of HIV.

Understanding: **Antibiotics** block processes that occur in **prokaryotic cells** but not in **eukaryotic cells**

Model sentence: Chemicals called antibiotics help fight bacterial infections by blocking cellular processes that are unique to prokaryotic cells.

It is common for people to receive an antibiotic from a doctor when they have an infection. Antibiotics are chemicals that selectively target cell processes that occur only in prokaryotic cells (bacteria). The antibiotic will then either kill the pathogenic bacteria or at least stop their growth. The antibiotic has no harmful effect on body cells as body cells are eukaryotic.

Application: Florey and Chain's experiments to test penicillin on bacterial infections in mice

In the first half of the 20th century, Howard Florey and Ernst Chain tested the antibiotic **penicillin**. They infected eight mice with a deadly **strain** of bacteria and then injected four of them with penicillin. The four not injected with penicillin died within a day. The four injected with penicillin lived for several days.

Understanding: Viruses lack a **metabolism** and cannot therefore be treated with antibiotics.

Model sentence: Antibiotics are not useful treatments against viruses as viruses are not prokaryotic cells and lack their own metabolism.

- Viruses are made up of a protein coat surrounding either DNA or RNA.
- Viruses are not cells and are not alive.
- Viruses do not have their own metabolism.
- Antibiotics do not work against infections caused by viruses.

Understanding: Some strains of bacteria have evolved with genes that confer resistance to antibiotics, and some strains of bacteria have multiple resistance.

Model sentence: There are some strains of bacteria that have developed a resistance to one or more types of antibiotics.

A single species of bacteria can exist in different strains. Each strain has a slightly different metabolism. Those bacteria that have a natural **variation** that give them some resistance to a specific antibiotic have a better chance of surviving when that antibiotic is used. Those that do survive reproduce in large numbers, where all of the bacteria now are resistant. There are some strains of bacteria that have evolved a resistance to many antibiotics. These strains are very difficult to treat with antibiotics.

> **Hints for success:** On examinations, avoid using the term immunity as a synonym for resistance. The term immune or immunity refers to protection given by an organism's immune system. Resistance to an antibiotic by a bacterial strain is due to natural selection of existing genes.

Subject vocabulary

antibiotic chemical used to kill or stop the growth of bacteria

prokaryotic cells bacterial cells

eukaryotic cells all cells that are not bacteria

penicillin an antibiotic

strain a type or variety of organism

metabolism sum total of all reactions in a cell or organism

variation a form of a gene that makes one organism different than another

6.4 Gas exchange

Understanding: Ventilation maintains **concentration gradients** of oxygen and carbon dioxide between air in **alveoli** and blood flowing in adjacent capillaries.

Model sentence: The correct concentration gradients of oxygen and carbon dioxide are maintained between the air in alveoli and blood in nearby capillaries by the continuous action of ventilating the lungs.

- The lungs are composed of numerous tiny air sacs called alveoli.
- Each alveolus has one or more nearby capillaries.
- Air is continuously refreshed in each alveolus when we breathe in and out. Breathing in and out is called ventilation.
- The air we breathe in has a higher concentration of oxygen as compared to the oxygen level in the nearby capillary. Thus, oxygen will **diffuse** from the alveolus into the capillary.
- The blood in the capillary has a higher concentration of carbon dioxide as compared to the carbon dioxide level in the alveolus. Thus, carbon dioxide will diffuse from the blood to the alveolus. Blood is continuously refreshed in the lung capillaries.

Hint for success: In an examination, remember that oxygen and carbon dioxide concentrations and movements are the reverse of those shown above when the blood gets to the body tissues.

Understanding: Type I pneumocytes are extremely thin alveolar cells that are adapted to carry out gas exchange.

Model sentence: Each alveolus is composed of two types of cells, one of those types is the type I pneumocytes that are very thin and are used for the exchange of gases.

A single alveolus is a very small **spherical** structure that is composed of two types of cells. The most numerous of those cell types are the type I pneumocytes. These cells form most of the spherical shape and are thin and flat. This helps with the diffusion of oxygen and carbon dioxide between the air in the alveolus and the blood in a nearby capillary.

Understanding: Type II pneumocytes secrete a solution containing surfactant that creates a **moist** surface inside the alveoli to prevent the sides of the alveolus **adhering** to each other by reducing **surface tension.**

Model sentence: A second type of cell making up alveoli are the type II pneumocytes that secrete a solution that prevents alveoli from sticking to each other by reducing surface tension.

Subject vocabulary

ventilation the act of breathing in and out to refresh air in the lungs

concentration gradient change in a chemical concentration between two areas of chemical concentrations

alveoli the many tiny air sacs making up each lung

diffuse movement of a substance from an area of high concentration to an area of low concentration

type I pneumocytes cells of the alveoli that aid in gas exchange

surface tension attraction forces that exist at the surface of a liquid

Synonyms

spherical .... round

General vocabulary

moist slightly wet

adhering sticking to

All alveoli also contain a less numerous type of cell. These cells are called type II pneumocytes. Their function is to produce and secrete a solution called a **surfactant** to the outside of the alveolar cells. This is helpful when cells of one alveolus touch cells of another alveolus during ventilation. The surfactant prevents the two alveoli from sticking to each other by reducing the surface tension of each.

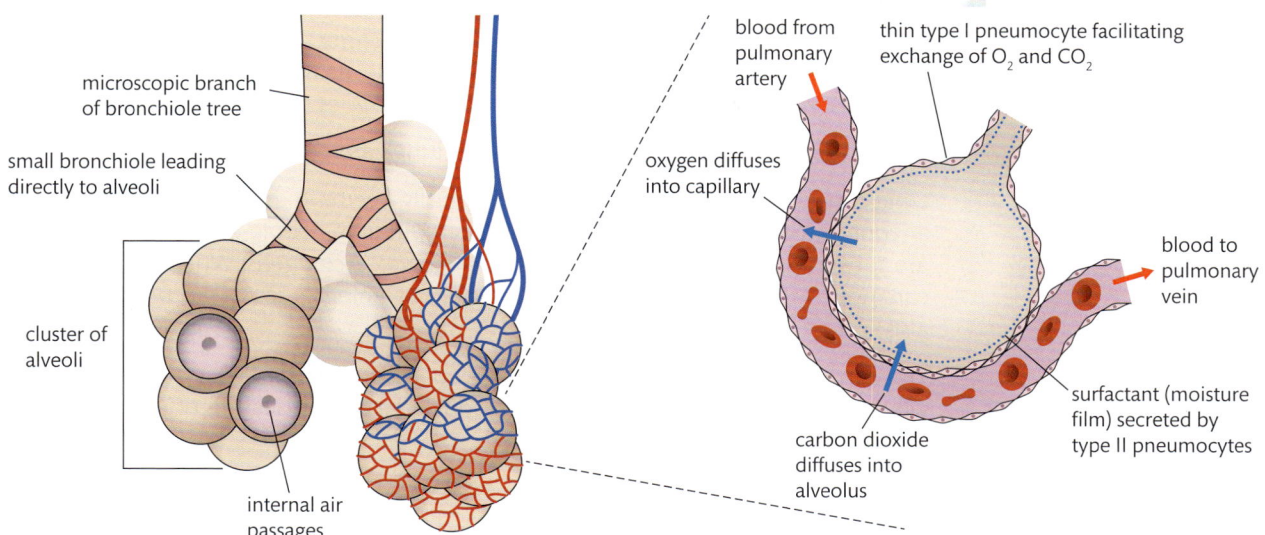

Hint for success: In examinations, you should be able to draw and label the structure of an alveolus and a nearby capillary. This view is being shown on the right side of figure above.

Figure 6.8 Microscopic view of a small area inside a human lung. Each cluster of alveoli is surrounded by a capillary bed for efficient gas exchange. The inset shows a sectioned drawing of a single alveolus and the structures that make gas exchange efficient

Understanding: Air is carried to the lungs in the **trachea** and **bronchi**, and then to the alveoli in **bronchioles**.

Model sentence: When you breathe in, the air passes down your trachea to a right and left bronchi and is eventually carried to the alveoli by small bronchioles.

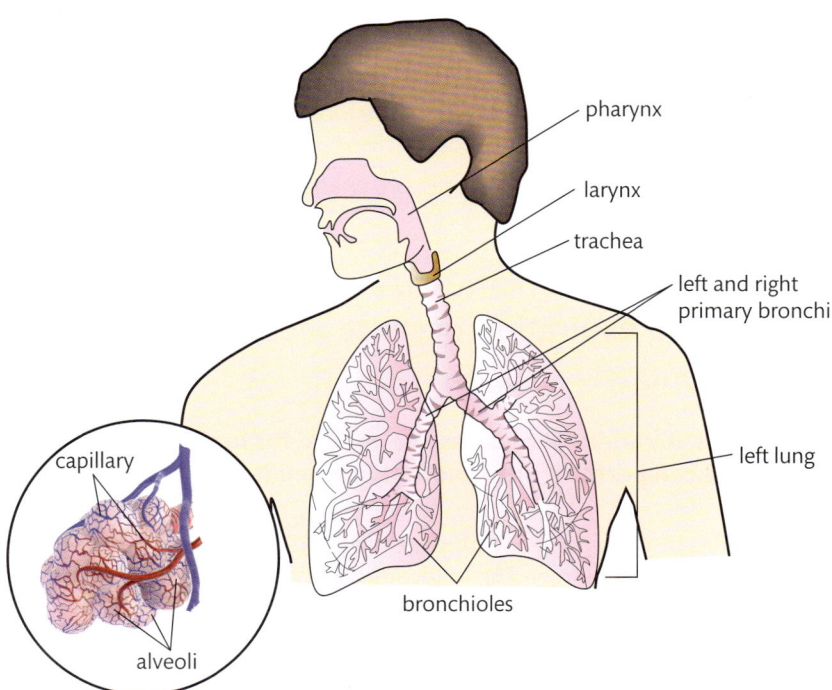

Subject vocabulary

surfactant a solution that reduces surface tension

trachea tube of the respiratory system that carries air to both lungs

bronchi (bronchus singular) respiratory structures (branches of the trachea) which carry air from the trachea into the lungs

bronchioles microscopic sized branches of the bronchi

microscopic too small to be seen without magnifying

Figure 6.9 Air is taken in by your mouth or nose. This air goes down the trachea to either the left or right bronchus. The left or right bronchus branches many times until the branches become **microscopic**. These very small branches are called bronchioles. The bronchioles lead to the alveoli surrounded by capillaries

6 Human physiology | 131

Subject vocabulary

emphysema a lung disease where alveoli become damaged, typically due to smoking

muscular composed of muscle

inspiration the act of breathing in

expiration the act of breathing out

inspire breathe in

rib cage the collection of all ribs that form a shape around the lungs

diaphragm the muscle below the lungs that rises and lowers

General vocabulary

fatal causes death

elastic able to stretch

deflate lose air

inflate gain air

Synonyms

thorax .... chest cavity

Application: Causes and consequences of emphysema

Emphysema is a slowly progressing disease where the alveoli of the lungs become destroyed. What is left behind are huge holes where alveoli used to be. This greatly decreases the surface area for oxygen and carbon dioxide to diffuse. The most common reason people develop emphysema is long-term smoking of cigarettes.

The consequences of emphysema take time to become serious. A person would first experience 'shortness of breath' when they exercise. As the disease progresses, the 'shortness of breath' will occur at all times. As time goes on, the disease is **fatal**.

Application: Causes and consequences of lung cancer

Lung cancer is a cancerous growth that typically begins in the lungs. Although anyone can develop lung cancer, it is most frequent in people who smoke. There are substances in cigarette smoke that are known carcinogens. When inhaled, a carcinogen can result in an internal lung cell becoming cancerous. Lung cancer can also spread to other parts of the body.

The consequences of lung cancer largely depend on how early it is detected and whether the cancer has spread to other body areas. The disease is often fatal unless detected and treated early.

Understanding: Muscle contractions cause the pressure changes inside the thorax that force air in and out of the lungs to ventilate them.

Model sentence: Pressure changes inside the chest cavity caused by muscle contractions result in air being forced into and out of the lungs resulting in ventilation.

- The lungs are not **muscular** and cannot move themselves.
- The lungs are **elastic** and will tend to **deflate** themselves (a little like a balloon deflates).
- The lungs are inside the chest cavity, also known as the thorax.
- When pressure in the thorax is high, the pressure pushes on the lungs and makes them smaller. This will force air out of the lungs
- When pressure in the thorax is low, the lungs are able to **inflate** to their full size. This creates a low pressure area inside of the lungs. Air enters the lungs to fill this low pressure area.
- Muscles of the thorax create these pressure changes.

Understanding: Different muscles are required for inspiration and expiration because muscles only do work when they contract.

Model sentence: A variety of muscles are needed for breathing in and out as any one muscle can perform only one action when it contracts.

When you **inspire** (breathe in), your **rib cage** rises and moves somewhat outward in order to make your thorax larger. The following muscles are involved in this action:
- The **diaphragm** (under your rib cage) contracts and flattens out.

- A group of muscles between your ribs contract (these are called the external intercostal muscles).
- One set of muscles in your abdomen contract.

When you expire (breathe out), your rib cage lowers and moves somewhat inward in order to make your thorax smaller. The following muscles are involved:
- The diaphragm relaxes and forms the shape of a dome.
- A different group of muscles between your ribs contract (called the internal intercostal muscles).
- A second set of muscles in your abdomen contract.

Subject vocabulary

intercostal muscles muscles surrounding your ribs: external intercostal muscles contract when breathing in; internal intercostal muscles contract when breathing out

expire breathe out

antagonistic performing opposite actions

Synonyms

abdomen .... lower/hind body cavity

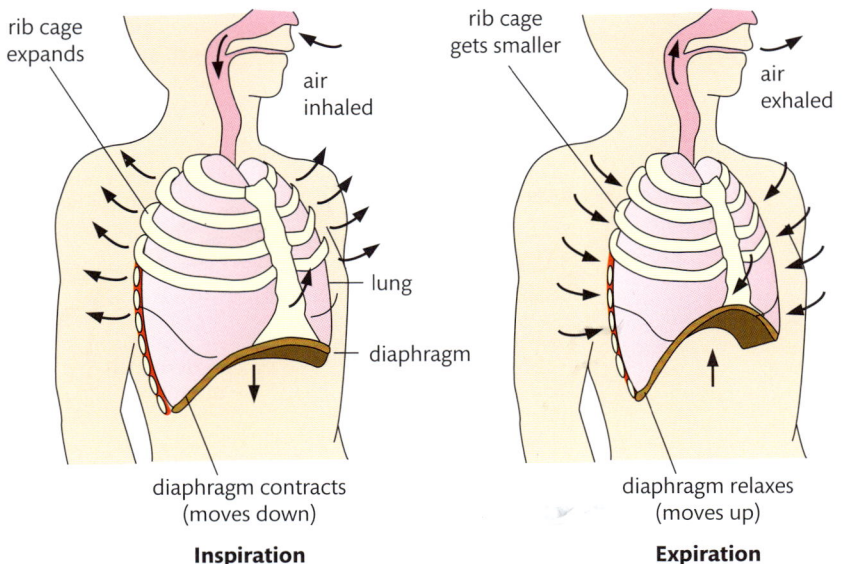

Figure 6.10 *The mechanisms for inspiration and expiration (ventilation)*

Application: External and internal intercostal muscles, and diaphragm and abdominal muscles as examples of antagonistic muscle action

Muscles can only perform one action when they contract. For that reason, they typically exist in pairs. Each of the pair of muscles achieve the opposite actions. This is often described as being antagonistic to each other. This is illustrated in the pairs of muscles involved in breathing in and breathing out.

6.5 Neurones and synapses

Understanding: Neurones transmit electrical impulses.

Model sentence: The nervous system cells that transmit electrical impulses are called neurones.

Neurones are often very long cells. This helps to transmit impulses long distances when necessary.

Neurones have three main areas:
- **Dendrites** – receive electrical impulses from other neurones.
- **Cell body** – contains nucleus and other organelles.
- **Axon** – long extension from cell body that gives length to a neurone.

Subject vocabulary

neurones cells of the nervous system that transmit electrical impulses

impulse an electrical signal

dendrites short extensions from the neurone cell body which receive impulses

cell body area of neurone that contains a nucleus and other organelles

axon long extension of a neurone that carries an impulse away from cell body

6 Human physiology

Neurones carry electrical impulses in a single direction. The impulse begins at a dendrite, then continues to the cell body, and finally down the axon to the terminal buttons.

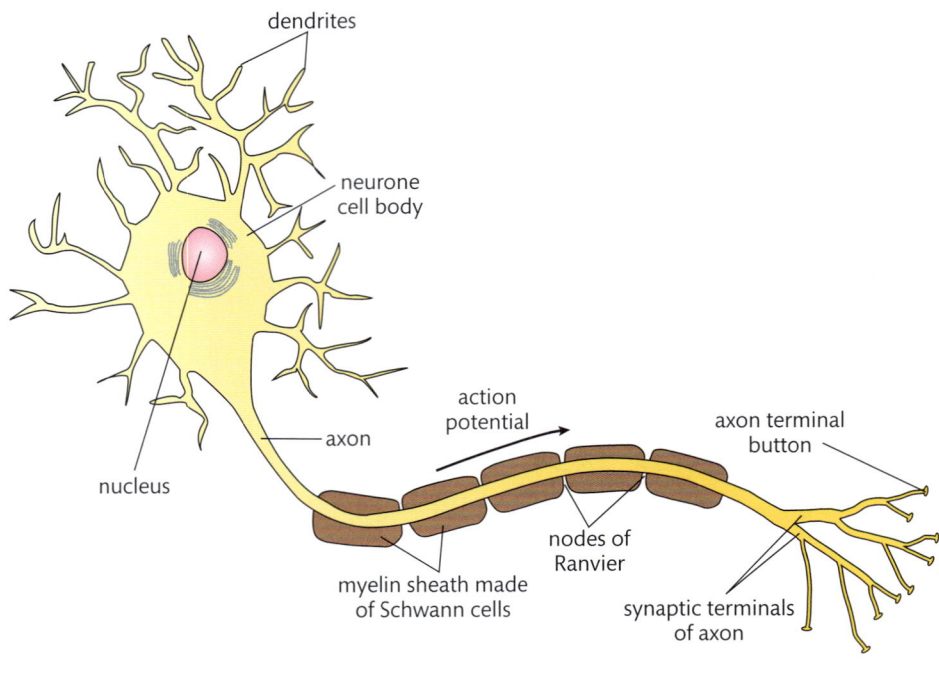

Figure 6.11 *The structure of a neurone. Some structures shown in this figure will be described in the upcoming sections*

Subject vocabulary

myelination production of myelin sheath around an axon

saltatory conduction impulse skipping from one node of Ranvier to the next

myelin sheath an insulation layer around the axon of neurones composed of multiple layers of Schwann cells

Schwann cell one of the cells helping to form a myelin sheath

node of Ranvier the gap area between Schwann cells of a myelin sheath

resting potential a neurone that is ready to send an electrical impulse

actively transporting moving substances through a membrane using energy in the form of ATP

Synonyms

nerve fibres .... axons (of neurones)

General vocabulary

insulation the addition of a material to keep an electrical impulse from going in or out

Understanding: The myelination of nerve fibres allows for saltatory conduction.

Model sentence: Neurones that have a myelin sheath are capable of faster transmission of the electrical impulse called saltatory conduction.

The figure of a neurone above shows several cells that wrap themselves around the axon of the neurone. These cells are called Schwann cells. Each Schwann cell wraps itself around the axon many times. This creates an insulation where the electrical impulse cannot occur. There are gaps between Schwann cells. Each gap is called a node of Ranvier. The entire area of the axon wrapped many times by Schwann cells is called the myelin sheath.

An electrical impulse is able to jump from one node of Ranvier to the next node of Ranvier when it travels down the axon. This greatly increases the speed at which an impulse is able to travel. When an impulse travels from one node of Ranvier to the next it is called saltatory conduction.

Understanding: Neurones pump sodium and potassium ions across their membranes to generate a resting potential.

Model sentence: Neurones prepare themselves to send an electrical impulse by actively transporting sodium and potassium ions across their membranes.

A neurone that is ready to send an impulse is said to be at its resting potential. The resting potential is achieved by pumping sodium ions out of the neurone and potassium ions into the neurone through the cell membrane. Pumping sodium and potassium ions is an **active transport** mechanism.

Understanding: An **action potential** consists of **depolarization** and **repolarization** of the neurone.

Model sentence: An electrical impulse is also called an action potential and consists of a depolarization followed by repolarization of the neurone membrane.

- An electrical impulse starts when sodium ions diffuse through channels in the neurone membrane.
- Sodium ions diffuse from outside the cell membrane to inside the cell membrane. This is called a depolarization.
- This is followed by potassium ions diffusing in the opposite direction (from inside to outside the cell membrane) through their own channels in the axon.
- In order for this neurone to send another impulse the sodium and potassium ions must be actively transported back to their resting potential positions. This is called repolarization.

Understanding: Nerve impulses are action potentials propagated along the axons of neurones.

Model sentence: Action potentials travel from one end of a neurone to the other starting with the dendrites and then along the axon.

Any one neurone can only send impulses in a single direction. The action potentials are propagated along the neurone starting at the dendrite end and moving towards the end of the axon.

Understanding: Propagation of nerve impulses is the result of **local currents** that cause each **successive** part of the axon to reach the **threshold potential**.

Model sentence: Specific areas of a long axon are being affected by an action potential at slightly different times and are successively stimulated to depolarize by reaching their threshold potential.

The long axon of a neurone does not depolarize all at the same time. Each area of an axon that may currently be depolarized is affecting the next area of the membrane to soon depolarize. This is known as a 'local current'. The entire movement of the nerve impulse is a series of **chain reactions**. A membrane will stay at its resting potential until an event causes it to reach a threshold potential. Then and only then will that area of the membrane begin an action potential. The event that does this is the area of the neurone nearby that is going through an action potential.

Subject vocabulary

active transport cellular transport requiring energy (ATP) from the cell

action potential the depolarization of a neurone membrane

depolarization sodium ions diffusing from outside to inside the neurone membrane

repolarization pumping of sodium and potassium ions back to their resting potential positions

local current an area of a neurone that is undergoing an action potential

threshold potential the minimum intensity signal needed to begin a nerve impulse

General vocabulary

successive following in order with no break between

chain reaction one event leading to the next event

Subject vocabulary

synapse an area where one neurone comes close to another cell in order to send a chemical message

receptor specialized structure in an organism which allows response to a stimulus

effector cell a muscle cell

presynaptic neurone neurone sending a chemical communication to postsynaptic neurone

postsynaptic neurone neurone receiving a chemical communication from a presynaptic neurone

receptor cell a cell that begins an impulse by being stimulated by an external factor, e.g. a touch receptor stimulated by pressure

neurotransmitter a chemical released from a presynaptic neurone into a synaptic gap

synaptic gap the fluid-filled space between a presynaptic neurone and a postsynaptic neurone

acetylcholine a common neurotransmitter

cholinergic synapse a synapse that uses acetylcholine as the neurotransmitter

neonicotinoid insecticides insecticides that work by blocking receptor proteins that normally bind acetylcholine

paralysis inability to use muscles

General vocabulary

junctions area where two things join or come close to joining

insecticide chemical used for killing insects

Synonyms

binding.......... attachment
bind.............. attach

Understanding: Synapses are junctions between neurones and between neurones and receptor or effector cells.

Model sentence: Neurones communicate with other cells by chemical connections called synapses.

The following are examples of neurone to cell communications:
- one neurone sending a communication to another neurone along a chain of neurones
  - the neurone sending the communication is called the presynaptic neurone
  - the neurone receiving the communication is called the postsynaptic neurone
- a receptor neurone cell sending a communication to the second neurone of a chain of neurones
- a neurone sending a communication to an effector (muscle) cell.

Understanding: When presynaptic neurones are depolarized they release a neurotransmitter into the synapse.

Model sentence: The chemical communication released by a presynaptic neurone is called a neurotransmitter.

There is always a narrow, fluid-filled space between the end of a presynaptic neurone and the dendrites of a postsynaptic neurone. This space is called a synaptic gap.

The presynaptic neurone releases a chemical into the synaptic gap. This chemical is called a neurotransmitter.

The neurotransmitter affects the postsynaptic neurone causing it to begin an action potential.

Application: Secretion and reabsorption of acetylcholine by neurones at synapses

One of the more common neurotransmitters used in the body is called acetylcholine. Acetylcholine is released by a presynaptic neurone and diffuses across the synaptic gap. Acetylcholine binds to receptor proteins on the postsynaptic neurone. This causes the postsynaptic neurone to begin a nerve impulse. An enzyme in the synaptic gap degrades acetylcholine. Finally, the neurotransmitter 'pieces' are released and reabsorbed back into the presynaptic neurone.

Application: Blocking of synaptic transmission at cholinergic synapses in insects by binding of neonicotinoid insecticides to acetylcholine receptors

When acetylcholine is released into a synaptic gap it must bind to a receptor protein on the postsynaptic neurone. Synapses that use acetylcholine as a neurotransmitter are called cholinergic synapses. If acetylcholine does not bind, the nerve impulse is not continued.

Researchers have recently come up with a new type of insecticide. These insecticides are called neonicotinoid insecticides. Neonicotinoid molecules fit the receptor proteins on the postsynaptic neurones that normally fit and accept acetylcholine. Thus, the insecticide molecules prevent the synapse from working correctly and the insect dies of paralysis.

Understanding: A nerve impulse is only initiated if the threshold potential is reached.

Model sentence: Each neurone has a minimum strength stimulus, called a threshold potential, that is needed to begin an impulse.

Each type of receptor neurone responds to a different type and intensity of a stimulus. For example, there are **photoreceptors** in your retina that only begin a nerve impulse if they receive red light. In addition, the intensity of that red light must be high enough to **initiate** the action potential. This minimum intensity of a particular stimulus type is called the threshold potential of that stimulus.

If the threshold stimulus is not reached no nerve impulse is sent. A nerve impulse from any one receptor is an 'all or nothing' event. In other words, an impulse is either sent or not.

6.6 Hormones, **homeostasis**, and reproduction

Understanding: Insulin and glucagon are secreted by β cells and α cells in the pancreas, respectively, to control blood glucose concentration.

Model sentence: The pancreas contains beta (β) cells that produce insulin and cells called alpha (α) cells that produce glucagon to help regulate the glucose concentration in the blood.

The pancreas is an **endocrine gland**. An endocrine gland produces hormones. These hormones are distributed to body cells by the bloodstream.

One hormone produced by the pancreas is insulin. Insulin is produced by beta (β) cells in the pancreas. Insulin results in body cells taking in glucose from the blood. This lowers the concentration of glucose in the blood.

A second hormone produced by the pancreas is glucagon. Glucagon is produced by α cells in the pancreas. Glucagon results in the liver releasing a stored form of glucose. This increases the concentration of glucose in the blood

Application: Causes and treatment of type I and type II diabetes

Diabetes is a disease where the body does not effectively regulate the level of glucose in the bloodstream and the amount of glucose provided to body cells. There are two types of diabetes:

- **Type I diabetes** – people are born with type I diabetes. This is a genetic disease where the cells that produce insulin are destroyed by one's own immune system. Treatment is regular injections of insulin when appropriate.
- **Type II diabetes** – this is a type of diabetes that develops during one's lifetime. Insulin is being produced but body cells do not respond. Treatment is control of one's diet and a healthy lifestyle.

Subject vocabulary

photoreceptors receptors in the eye that respond to light by beginning a nerve impulse

homeostasis steady or controlled state

beta (β) cells cells in the pancreas that produce and secrete the hormone insulin

alpha (α) cells cells in the pancreas that produce and secrete the hormone glucagon

endocrine gland a gland that produces a hormone

type I diabetes a genetic disease where insulin is not being produced by the pancreas in sufficient amounts

type II diabetes a form of diabetes where one develops a resistance to the normal function of insulin

Synonyms

initiate .... start/begin

Subject vocabulary

thyroxin hormone that results in an increase in cell metabolism

thyroid gland endocrine gland that produces thyroxin

metabolic rate sum total of all cell and organism chemical reactions including cell respiration

leptin hormone produced by body fat that lowers the appetite

adipose tissue body fat

hypothalamus a region of the brain that controls pituitary gland secretions and other autonomic functions

melatonin hormone produced by the pineal gland

pineal gland small gland located within the brain

circadian rhythm a cycle of something based on a 24-hour time period

Synonyms

secreted .... produced/released

inhibit .... prevent/reduce

General vocabulary

regulate to adjust the degree or rate of something

obesity being overweight in an unhealthy way

Understanding: Thyroxin is secreted by the thyroid gland to regulate the metabolic rate and help control body temperature.

Model sentence: The thyroid gland produces a hormone called thyroxin that helps regulate body metabolism including the control of body temperature.

The thyroid gland is an endocrine gland located in the neck area. It produces the hormone thyroxin.

Thyroxin increases the metabolic rate of all cells. Increased metabolic rate will generally increase internal body temperature:
- To lower body temperature – body decreases thyroxin production.
- To raise body temperature – body increases thyroxin production.

Hints for success: In an examination, you should know that humans have a nearly constant internal body temperature of 37 °C.

Understanding: Leptin is secreted by cells in adipose tissue and acts on the hypothalamus of the brain to inhibit appetite.

Model sentence: Adipose tissue secretes leptin, a hormone that targets the hypothalamus of the brain to help lower one's appetite.

Leptin is a hormone produced by fat stored in the body.

The production of leptin is high after eating. Leptin travels in the bloodstream to the brain, where it affects cells in the hypothalamus of the brain. The effect is to lower the appetite.

Application: Testing of leptin on patients with clinical obesity

Leptin is a hormone produced by adipose tissue (body fat). Leptin should decrease appetite. Logic says that obese people should have lowered appetites. This has not been shown to be the case. One theory says that the function of leptin is only evident in those people with very low body fat. The theory says that those people produce very little leptin and increase their appetite in order to gain body fat.

Understanding: Melatonin is secreted by the pineal gland to control circadian rhythms.

Model sentence: The pineal gland secretes a hormone called melatonin that helps regulate our 24-hour sleep-wake cycle.

The pineal gland is a very small gland located within the interior of the brain. It secretes the hormone melatonin.

Levels of melatonin change over a 24-hour time period. A repeating pattern that occurs over a 24-hour time period is called a circadian rhythm.

The changes in melatonin help us to fall asleep and wake up.

Application: **Use of melatonin to alleviate jet lag**

Jet lag is the term used when someone flies a long distance and their destination is a time zone that is far different from where they started. This upsets the circadian rhythm and the sleep–wake cycle. Some people report that taking pills with melatonin help lessen the symptoms of jet lag.

Understanding: A gene on the Y chromosome causes embryonic gonads to develop as testes and secrete testosterone.

Model sentence: **The Y chromosome of male embryos has a gene that results in formation of testes that soon begin secreting testosterone.**

Females have the chromosome pattern of XX and males XY. Thus, females do not have a Y chromosome. The Y chromosome contains a gene that causes embryonic gonad tissue to become testes. This gene is called the *SRY gene*. The *SRY* gene produces a protein that helps to regulate other genes that are important in becoming a male. The testes soon begin producing and secreting the hormone testosterone.

Understanding: Testosterone causes prenatal development of male genitalia and both sperm production and development of male secondary sexual characteristics during puberty.

Model sentence: **Before birth testosterone results in the formation of male sex organs; at puberty, testosterone results in sperm production and formation of secondary sex characteristics.**

Testosterone is a hormone that causes male reproductive structures to form. The male reproductive structures are often called the male genitalia. The development of male genitalia is called prenatal as it happens before birth.

When a young man becomes a teenager he enters a stage of life called puberty. At this time, the testes begin a higher secretion of testosterone. This leads to sperm production and development of male secondary sexual characteristics.

Some male secondary sex characteristics are:
- increase in muscle growth
- increase in height
- deeper voice
- body hair in armpits and **pubic** region.

General vocabulary
alleviate to make something less severe

Subject vocabulary
jet lag disruption of the sleep–wake cycle

Y chromosome a chromosome only found in males

embryonic early development after fertilization

gonads the tissue that produces sperm in males and eggs in females (testes and ovaries)

testosterone hormone produced by the testes of males

testes male organs where spermatogenesis occurs

SRY gene a gene located on the Y chromosome that leads to an embryo becoming male

prenatal before birth

genitalia sex organs such as the penis

secondary sexual characteristics body characteristics that begin at puberty

puberty age in males and females where reproduction is first possible

Synonyms
pubic............ groin

6 Human physiology

Skill: Annotate a diagram of the male reproductive system to show names of structures and their functions

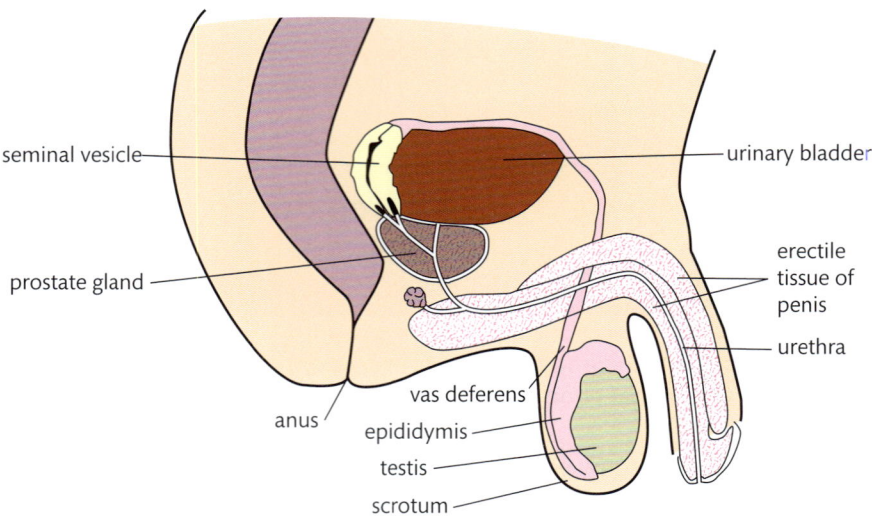

Figure 6.12 *Male reproductive structures and their functions*

Structure	Function
testis	sperm are produced here and testosterone is produced here
epididymis	area where sperm are stored
scrotum	sacs that hold the testes outside of the body
vas deferens	a tube that carries sperm
seminal vesicle	small glands that add fluid to the sperm
prostate gland	another gland that adds fluid to the sperm
penis	a structure capable of becoming erect during sex
urethra	the tube in which semen leaves the body during sex

Subject vocabulary

oestrogen one of two hormones produced by the ovaries of a female

progesterone hormone produced initially by ovaries / signals endometrium of uterus to remain ready to receive an embryo

Understanding: **Oestrogen** and **progesterone** cause prenatal development of female reproductive organs and female sexual characteristics at puberty.

Model sentence: Before birth, oestrogen and progesterone result in the formation of female sex organs; at puberty, these two hormones result in the formation of female sex characteristics.

Oestrogen and progesterone are hormones produced during the prenatal development of females. These two hormones are responsible for the formation of the female genitalia.

At the age of puberty the increased levels of these two hormones result in the formation of the female secondary sex characteristics. Some female secondary sex characteristics are:
- development of breasts
- body hair in armpit and pubic region
- increase in height
- **menstrual cycle** begins.

Skill: Annotate a diagram of the female reproductive system to show names of structures and their functions

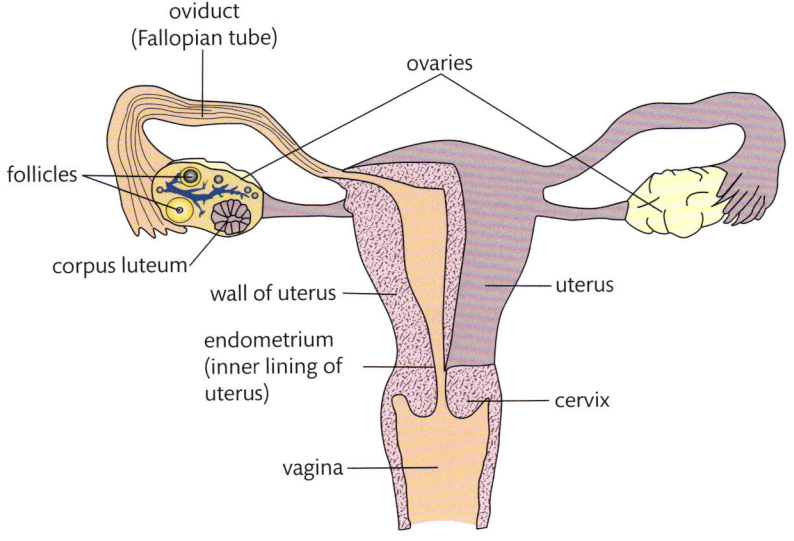

Subject vocabulary

menstrual cycle a cycle of events in females that results in release of an egg from an ovary

ovarian hormones hormones produced by an ovary (oestrogen and progesterone)

pituitary hormones those hormones produced by the pituitary gland (FSH and LH)

Figure 6.13 *Female reproductive structures and their functions*

Structure	Function
ovaries	organ that produces and releases ovum and hormones
Fallopian tubes	ducts that can carry an early embryo to the uterus
uterus	muscular organ where an embryo can develop
endometrium	inside lining of the uterus
cervix	opening from vagina to inside of uterus
vagina	semen is deposited here during sex

Understanding: The menstrual cycle is controlled by negative and positive feedback mechanisms involving **ovarian** and **pituitary hormones**.

Model sentence: The pituitary gland and the ovary both secrete hormones that control the timing of the menstrual cycle by negative and positive feedback mechanisms.

The female menstrual cycle is a series of events that lead to the release of an egg from an ovary. At the same time, the uterus must be prepared to receive a young embryo if the released ovum is fertilized. Many of these events are controlled by the release of specific hormones at specific times.

6 Human physiology

Here is a summary of the hormonal events of the menstrual cycle:

Hormone	Secreted from	Effect of hormone
FSH	pituitary gland	prepares ovum within a **follicle** for release (**ovulation**)
LH	pituitary gland	prepares ovum for release (ovulation)
oestrogen	follicle cells of the ovary	prepares female uterus to receive young embryo if a fertilization occurs
progesterone	**corpus luteum** of ovary (only after ovulation)	maintains the uterus to receive a young embryo if a fertilization occurs

Subject vocabulary

follicle an egg surrounded by numerous follicle cells

ovulation release of a follicle from the ovary

corpus luteum a gland that forms in the ovary in the location where an ovum is released

IVF a technique for fertilization of eggs outside of the body

oocyte the large cell that is the female's gamete

Positive feedback is when one event increases the level of another event. An example of this in the menstrual cycle is the effect that oestrogen increase has. When oestrogen is secreted at relatively high levels from the ovary this increases the amount of FSH secreted by the pituitary gland.

The menstrual cycle also shows negative feedback control. Negative feedback is when one event decreases the level of another event. An example of this is when the ovary increases levels of progesterone. This leads to decreased FSH and LH secreted by the pituitary.

Application: The use in IVF of drugs to suspend the normal secretion of hormones, followed by the use of artificial doses of hormones to induce superovulation and establish a pregnancy

Some people make use of a reproductive technique abbreviated as **IVF** in order to have children. IVF stands for 'in vitro fertilization'. The technique requires an **oocyte** to be taken from a female. This oocyte is then placed into a glass dish where it is fertilized by the father's sperm. After the fertilized egg develops into a young embryo, the embryo is placed into the mother's uterus for development.

IVF has a much higher success rate if several embryos are produced at the same time. Thus, it is common for the mother to be treated with hormones that will cause what is called a superovulation. This is where the ovaries produce and ovulate many eggs during one menstrual cycle. Many eggs can then be collected to be fertilized for the IVF procedure.

Application: William Harvey's investigation of reproduction in deer

William Harvey was most famous for his experimental work that showed how blood circulates in the body. He also did many dissections on deer. This work showed many of the developmental stages of mammals. He was not able to study the early embryonic stages as the microscopic was not yet in use in the early 1600s when he was carrying out his investigations.

7 Nucleic acids

7.1 DNA structure and replication

Main idea
The functions of DNA are possible because of its structure.

Understanding: **Nucleosomes** help to supercoil the DNA.

Model sentence: Structures called nucleosomes allow DNA to fit within the nucleus of a cell.

A single **chromosome** is a molecule of DNA. This molecule of DNA may be as long as 4 cm.

Each **species** of organism with **eukaryotic cells** has a specific number of chromosomes. The human species has 46 chromosomes normally.

Coiling is necessary for all the chromosomes of a eukaryotic cell to fit in the cell nucleus. This coiling is **extensive** and is referred to as **supercoiling**. The supercoiling occurs around **spherical** molecules of a group of proteins called **histones**.

A section of DNA coiled around a core of eight histone molecules is called a nucleosome.

A ninth histone molecule holds the DNA coiling in place around the core histone molecules.

Nucleosomes are connected by **linker DNA**. Linker DNA is a short section of DNA.

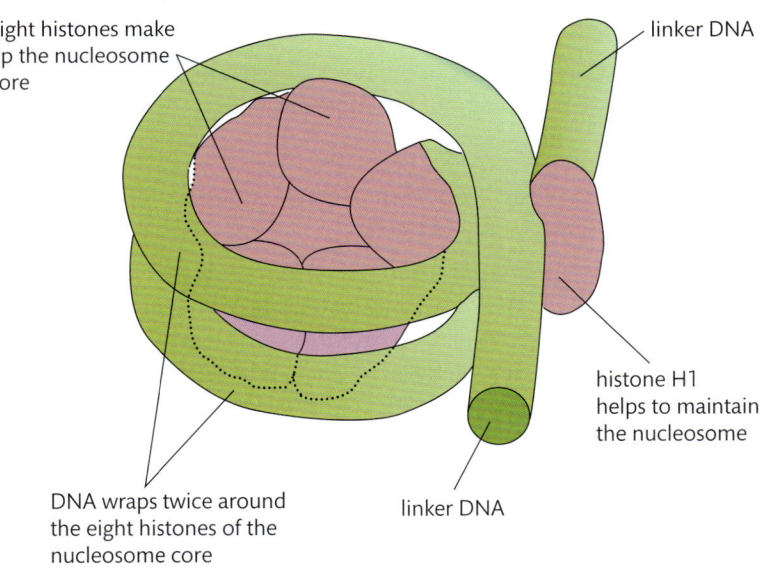

Figure 7.1 *Histones and DNA together form nucleosomes*

Skill: Utilization of molecular visualization software to analyse the association between protein and DNA within a nucleosome

There are many sites on the internet where a model of a nucleosome can be seen. Observe some of these to gain an understanding of how the folding of DNA occurs. Watch videos from several different sites showing examples of the DNA folding process.

Subject vocabulary

nucleosome structure found in eukaryotic chromosomes consisting of a strand of DNA wrapped around eight histone molecules

chromosomes structures on which DNA occurs within a cell

species a group of organisms which are structurally similar and able to pass their genetic traits onto their offspring

eukaryotic cells all cells that are not bacteria

supercoiling a process in which intense folding and coiling of a structure occurs

histones proteins associated with DNA in eukaryotic chromosomes

linker DNA short section or strand of DNA which occurs between adjacent nucleosomes

General vocabulary

extensive wide ranging

Synonyms

spherical........ round

Synonyms

mechanism .... way/process
conducted ...... undertook

Subject vocabulary

replication process of producing a copy of a molecule or structure

X-ray diffraction bending of X-rays as it passes through a substance

nitrogenous containing nitrogen

base pairing process in DNA replication and protein synthesis in which nitrogenous base pairing is very specific

semi-conservative type of replication in DNA in which each new DNA molecule has one original strand of the parent molecule

replication process of producing a copy of a molecule or structure

double helix three-dimensional shape of DNA involving a double spiral

radioisotope an isotope which is radioactive

radiation particles given off by a substance which allow its tracking

radioactive element or isotope which gives off energetic particles

virus infectious particle composed of protein and nucleic acid not able to replicate itself outside a cell

bacterial cultures a laboratory collection or association of bacteria maintained for study

General vocabulary

strands single thin pieces of matter

Understanding: DNA structure suggested a mechanism for DNA replication.

Model sentence: With the finding of the structure of DNA came a logical way to explain how DNA may make copies of itself.

Many scientists from all over the world were involved in the early studies of DNA. Findings of these studies led to the explanation of the detailed structure of DNA.

Research done by Alfred Hershey and Martha Chase provided evidence that DNA was the actual genetic material of the cell.

Rosalind Franklin and Maurice Wilkins conducted X-ray diffraction studies of DNA.

Erwin Chargaff analysed data involving the nitrogenous bases of DNA.

Francis Crick and James Watson used information provided by Franklin, Wilkins, Chargaff, and other world scientists to produce the model of the structure of DNA we recognize today.

The base pairing between the two strands which make up the DNA model was a major factor in the semi-conservative explanation of DNA replication.

Application: Rosalind Franklin's and Maurice Wilkins' investigation of DNA structure by X-ray diffraction

Rosalind Franklin and Maurice Wilkins provided some key findings concerning the structure of DNA. They used X-ray diffraction studies of DNA. Their investigations gave the following results:

- The distance between the two DNA strands is consistent all through the molecule.
- The DNA molecule is a double helix.
- The distance between the twists of the helix was determined. This distance was found to be consistent throughout the molecule.
- The DNA molecule is made up of repeating units.

Skill: Analysis of results of the Hershey and Chase experiment providing evidence that DNA is the genetic material

Alfred Hershey and Martha Chase carried out experiments that helped confirm that DNA is the genetic material. They used radioisotopes of sulfur and phosphorus in their experiments. Radioisotopes give off radiation which can be detected. These radioisotopes are said to be radioactive. Hershey and Chase used viruses labelled with these radioisotopes to infect bacterial cultures in their work. Study the figure below which summarizes their experiment:

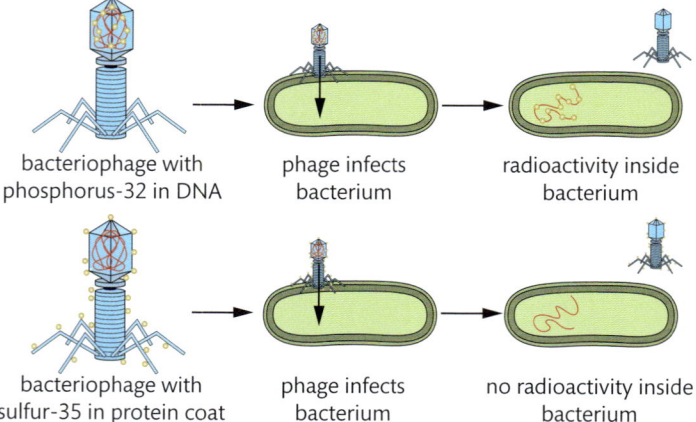

Figure 7.2 *The Hershey–Chase experiment used radioisotopes as markers to label the DNA and protein of T2 bacteriophages. The basic procedure and findings are shown here*

Key points from the experiment:
- When the virus, a **bacteriophage**, was labelled with the radioisotope phosphorus-32, radioactivity was measureable within the bacterium.
- When the virus was labelled with the radioisotope sulfur-35, no radioactivity was measureable within the bacterium.
- Radioactive phosphorus was found in the region of the bacterial cell where the genetic material was known to exist. Radioactive sulphur was not.
- Since DNA contains phosphorus and not sulfur, DNA was shown to be the genetic material.

Subject vocabulary

bacteriophage a type of virus which infects bacteria

nucleotides smaller units chemically bonded to form nucleic acids

primer some process or structure needed to begin a specific task

Understanding: DNA polymerases can only add **nucleotides** to the 3′ end of a **primer**.

Model sentence: The strand produced during DNA replication is lengthened by adding nucleotides to the 3′ end only.

DNA is a double stranded molecule. The strands are anti-parallel to one another.

The 5′ and 3′ refer to which carbon of the nucleotide deoxyribose is on the end of the strand.

The strand being produced in semi-conservative replication always has nucleotides added to its 3′ end. A type of **DNA polymerase** is the enzyme that causes nucleotides to be added only on the 3′ end. DNA replication, therefore, occurs in the 5′ to 3′ direction.

Prokaryotic DNA is a single, relatively short, and circular chromosome. Prokaryotic DNA has only one site which serves as the **origin of replication**. Replication in the prokaryotic chromosome proceeds in both directions around the loop from the origin of replication.

Eukaryotic DNA is not circular. Eukaryotic DNA involves multiple chromosomes of relatively large size. Each eukaryotic chromosome has many sites serving as origins of replication. This allows for a much faster replication process.

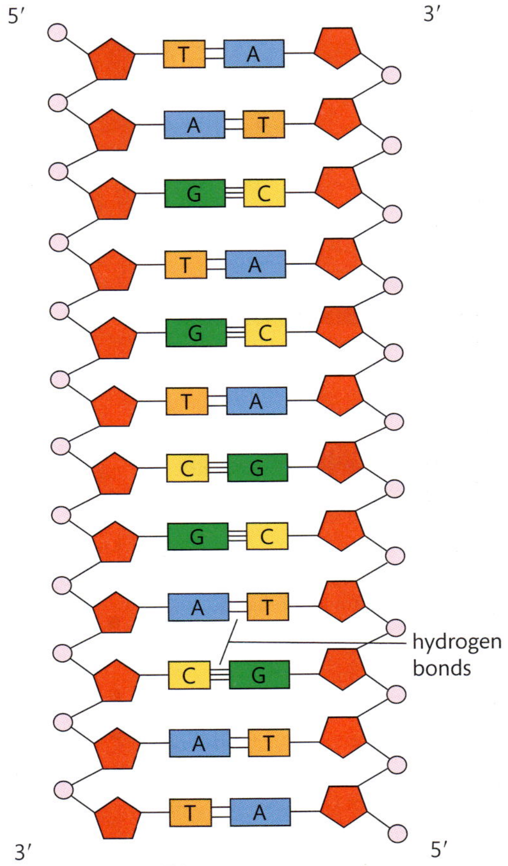

Figure 7.3 *The antiparallel strands in DNA run in opposite directions*

Hints for success: To understand the position of growth of a DNA strand, draw a single DNA nucleotide including its three major parts. It should look similar to the following diagram.

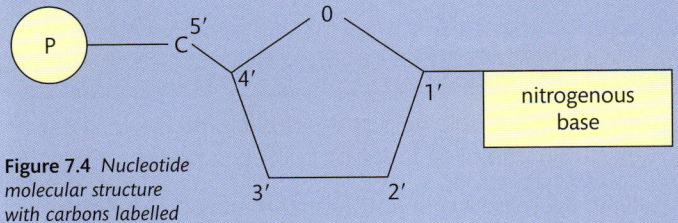

Figure 7.4 *Nucleotide molecular structure with carbons labelled*

Nucleotides are added to the carbon of deoxyribose labelled 3′ in DNA replication. DNA polymerase can only bring about the addition of nucleotides at the 3′ end of the DNA chain.

Nucleotides are added to the 3′ end of an existing DNA chain by a **covalent bond**. This covalent bond is specifically called a **phosphodiester bond**.

Subject vocabulary

DNA polymerase group of enzymes which are involved in DNA replication

prokaryotic bacterial cells

origin of replication point on a DNA molecule which opens to begin the replication process

covalent bond chemical bond in which electrons are shared

phosphodiester bond type of covalent bond in DNA and RNA which involves two hydroxyl groups and one phosphate group

Understanding: DNA replication is continuous on the leading strand and discontinuous on the lagging strand.

Model sentence: The two strands of DNA are different in how they are replicated because they are antiparallel to one another.

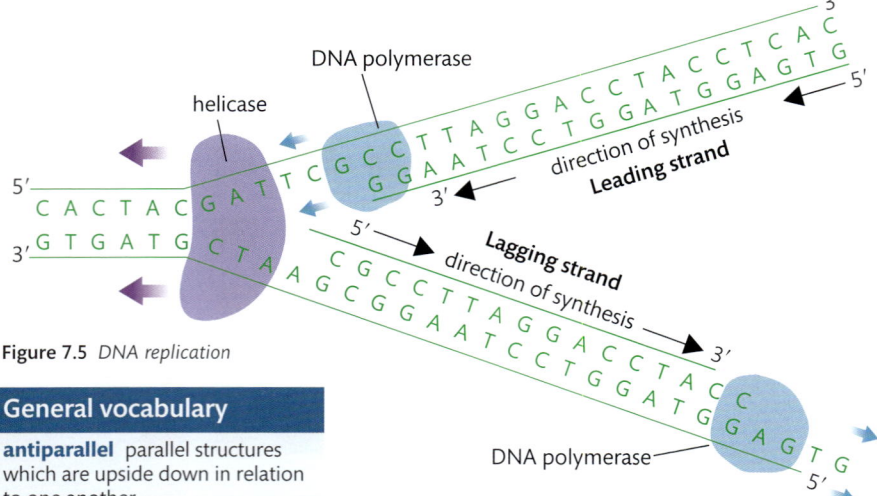

Figure 7.5 DNA replication

Both strands of DNA must be replicated to produce two molecules of DNA from the original DNA molecule.

These strands are **antiparallel**. Antiparallel means the two strands of DNA are upside down when compared to one another. One strand of the DNA molecule has the 5′ carbon on the top of the chain and the 3′ carbon on the bottom. The other strand has the 3′ carbon on top and the 5′ carbon on the bottom. Each strand may only be built in the 5′ to 3′ direction due to DNA polymerase.

General vocabulary

antiparallel parallel structures which are upside down in relation to one another

Subject vocabulary

leading strand in DNA replication the strand produced continuously

lagging strand in DNA replication the strand produced in segments called Okazaki fragments

helicase enzyme which opens the DNA double helix in the replication process

replication forks the point at which the helix of DNA unwinds to allow replication

DNA gyrase (DNA topoisomerase) enzyme which lessens the strain of the DNA helix just ahead of helicase activity

primase synthesizes RNA primer which is necessary to begin the synthesis of a DNA strand or fragment in DNA replication

RNA primer a short length of RNA that forms the starting point for DNA synthesis

synthesis constructing complex molecules from smaller, simpler ones

Okazaki fragment segments of DNA produced on the lagging strand in DNA replication

Synonyms

fragments ...... pieces

One strand is built continuously from the origin of replication site. This strand is called the **leading strand**. The other strand is not built continuously. It is built in **fragments**. This strand is called the **lagging strand**. Study the diagram above.

Note: there are several reasons for a leading and a lagging strand in DNA semi-conservative replication. These reasons include:

- DNA polymerase may only allow nucleotide additions to a DNA strand at the 3′ end.
- The two strands of DNA are antiparallel to one another.
- The leading strand requires fewer steps to completion and will finish replicating before the lagging strand.

Understanding: DNA replication is carried out by a complex system of enzymes.

Model sentence: There is a large number of enzymes involved in the control of DNA replication.

Enzyme	Role
helicase	unwinds the double helix at the **replication forks** (sites of replication origin) by breaking hydrogen bonds
DNA gyrase (DNA topoisomerase)	acts to decrease the helical strain just ahead of helicase activity, stabilizes the single strands
primase	synthesizes **RNA primer** which is necessary to begin the **synthesis** of a strand (leading strand) or **Okazaki fragment** (lagging strand)

Enzyme	Role
DNA polymerase III	allows the building of the new DNA strand by adding DNA nucleotides onto RNA primer or onto the 3' end of the existing DNA segment
DNA polymerase I	removes the RNA primer and replaces it with DNA nucleotides
DNA ligase	joins the ends of DNA segments and Okazaki fragments

Single-stranded binding proteins are not enzymes. However, they are involved in the replication process by keeping the DNA strands apart until these strands are copied.

Hints for success: The diagram below shows the location and function of each of the enzymes involved in DNA replication in prokaryotic cells. DNA gyrase would be placed **adjacent** to the helicase on the unopened DNA double helix.

Subject vocabulary

DNA polymerase III enzyme which adds DNA nucleotides to the RNA primer or the 3' end of the DNA strand

DNA polymerase I enzyme which removes the RNA primer and replaces it with DNA nucleotides in DNA replication

DNA ligase enzyme which joins the ends of Okazaki fragments to produce a continuous strand

General vocabulary

adjacent next to

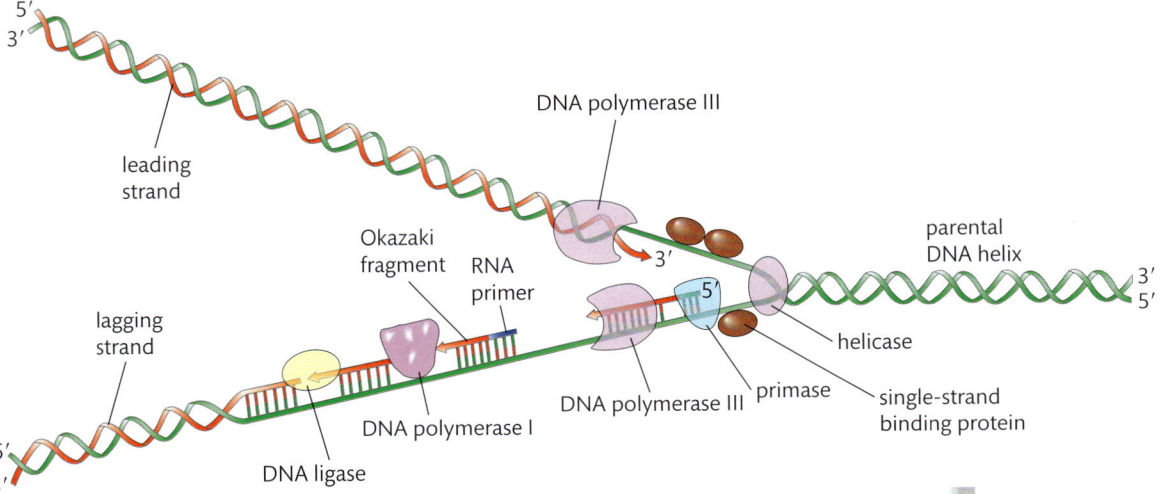

Figure 7.6 *DNA replication in prokaryotic cells*

Understanding: Some regions of DNA do not code for proteins but have other important functions.

Model sentence: Many nucleotide sequences within a DNA molecule have functions other than coding for protein production.

Most of the DNA nucleotide sequences in eukaryotic cells do not code for protein formation. These non-protein coding sequences include:

- **Telomeres** which occur on the ends of chromosomes and have a protective function. Telomeres also shorten with each chromosomal replication. They seem to play a role in the number of reproductive cycles a cell may go through.
- Areas which act as regulators of gene expression.
- Areas which code for **tRNA** molecules.
- **Highly repetitive sequences** of nucleotides which include transposable elements capable of changing their position within a chromosome. The **centromere** region and the telomeres of chromosomes are actually examples of highly repetitive sequences. However, these two regions of highly repetitive sequences are not transposable.

Subject vocabulary

telomeres repeated DNA sequences which occur at the tip of chromosomes which shorten with cell divisions

tRNA transfer RNA, the molecule that carries an amino acid to the ribosome in protein production

highly repetitive sequences short DNA nucleotide repeats typically not transcribed

centromere region where sister chromatids attach

Subject vocabulary

short tandem repeats repeating sequence of 1–5 nucleotides which varies in number of repeats for different individuals

locus (plural: loci) the specific place where a gene is found on a chromosome

tandem repeats segments of DNA composed of particular sequences of repeating DNA nucleotides

DNA profiling method of studying DNA using restriction enzymes and gel electrophoresis

restriction enzymes enzymes which cut DNA at particular nucleotide sequences

gel electrophoresis process using electricity passing through a gel matrix to separate fragments or molecules of proteins or nucleic acids

DNA fragment bands DNA bands of different size produced by restriction enzymes which migrate at different rates in gel electrophoresis

dideoxyribonucleic acid component in nucleotides used to stop DNA replication at specific locations

base sequencing process in which the exact sequence in a DNA fragment or molecule is produced

fluorescent marker used to allow identification in DNA studies

mRNA messenger RNA carries the DNA code from the nucleus to the cytoplasmic ribosomes for specific production of proteins

transcription the process of creating RNA from DNA

complementary base pairs nitrogenous bases which pair together in nucleic acids, A–T, A–U, C–G

template strand DNA strand, also known as the antisense strand, where complementary base pairing occurs to produce mRNA

antisense strand DNA template strand in transcription

sense strand DNA strand not transcribed in the production of mRNA, contains the same code as the mRNA which is produced on the template strand

promoter region non-coding DNA region which binds with RNA polymerase to begin the transcription process

RNA polymerase enzyme involved in the transcription process

terminator sequence sequence of DNA which stops the transcription process for a particular protein

Synonyms

encountered..... met/reached

- **Short tandem repeats** are chromosomal regions of variable numbers of repeats of nucleotide sequences. These short tandem repeats occur in specific loci of a species' chromosomes.

Application: Tandem repeats are used in DNA profiling

These short tandem repeats are unique for each individual. Analysing regions of short tandem repeats allows identification of family relationships, possible criminal activity, and identification of disaster victims. DNA analysis involves the use of restriction enzymes and gel electrophoresis. DNA fragment bands are produced when restriction enzymes and gel electrophoresis are used. The unique position of these fragment bands on the gel is then analysed to determine relationships.

Application: Use of nucleotides containing dideoxyribonucleic acid to stop DNA replication in preparation of samples for base sequencing

Special nucleotides containing dideoxyribonucleic acid are used to stop DNA replication in preparation for base sequencing in DNA profiling. There are four different nucleotides with each containing a dideoxyribonucleic acid. Each of these four special nucleotides have a different fluorescent marker attached to them. Observing the position of these florescent markers allows the sequencing of a segment of DNA since they stop the DNA replication process at the exact position they are added.

7.2 Transcription and gene expression

Main idea

The DNA code must be copied onto mRNA if it is to be involved in protein synthesis.

Understanding: Transcription occurs in a 5′ to 3′ direction.

Model sentence: mRNA produced by transcription is formed by adding RNA nucleotides to the 3′ end of the existing chain.

mRNA is a single-stranded molecule produced by complementary base pairing of the template strand of DNA. This template strand of DNA is also known as the antisense strand. The sense strand of DNA is not used to produce mRNA. However, the sense strand does contain the same code as the mRNA produced on the template strand.

Application: The promoter as an example of non-coding DNA with a function

DNA has promoter regions on the template strand. The promoter is a non-coding region of the DNA molecule which binds with RNA polymerase to begin the process of transcription of a particular DNA segment (gene).

The enzyme known as RNA polymerase starts transcription by attaching to the DNA strand at a promoter. RNA polymerase aids the addition of the 5′ end of a free RNA nucleotide to the 3′ end of an existing mRNA molecule. Transcription then continues in a 5′ to 3′ direction until a terminator sequence is encountered. The RNA polymerase detaches from the template strand at the terminator sequence. This ends the transcription process at this DNA location.

Understanding: Nucleosomes help to regulate transcription in eukaryotes.

Model sentence: The packaging of DNA that occurs at nucleosomes serves as a regulator of transcription in eukaryotic cells.

DNA wrapped around histones in nucleosomes is inaccessible to transcription enzymes. This wrapping prevents transcription of this part of DNA from occurring.

DNA wrapped around the histones of a nucleosome is also subjected to chemical changes that affect its ability to be transcribed. These chemical changes often involve the addition of acetyl or methyl groups.

Skill: Analysis of changes in the DNA methylation patterns

Analysis of changes in the DNA methylation patterns has produced some very interesting observations. Many cancer cells have either a larger amount of methylation or a lower amount of methylation than non-cancerous cells. The presence of methyl groups also seems to play a role in the maternal or paternal expression of a gene. The analysis of methylation patterns has shown changes in an organism's amount of methylation as they go through the ageing process.

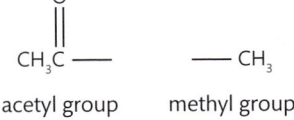

Figure 7.7 *Molecular groups involved in DNA regulation*

Understanding: Eukaryotic cells modify mRNA after transcription.

Model sentence: The mRNA produced by transcription in eukaryotic cells goes through several changes before it leaves the nucleus to enter the cytoplasm.

Changes to mRNA produced by transcription before exiting the nucleus:
- Segments of non-coding mRNA called **introns** are cut and removed from the original mRNA strand produced. The original mRNA strand is known as the **pre-mRNA strand**.
- **Small nuclear RNAs (snRNAs)** known as **spliceosomes** bring about this cutting and removal. This process is called **splicing**.
- The mRNA segments remaining after splicing are called **exons**.
- The exons are then chemically connected to one another.
- A **cap** is added to the 5′ end of the mRNA segment.
- The 3′ end of mRNA segment then has a **poly-A tail** added.
- The final product is called **mature mRNA**. It then leaves the nucleus to enter the cytoplasm.

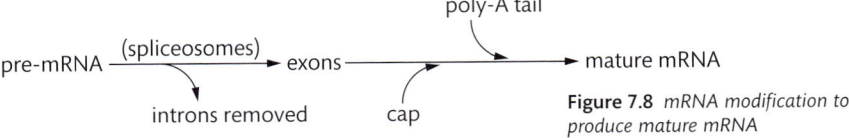

Figure 7.8 *mRNA modification to produce mature mRNA*

Hints for success: The modification of the original strand of mRNA is necessary for many reasons. The intron portions are not involved in protein synthesis at the ribosomes and must be removed by the splicing process. The cap and poly-A tail serve to protect mature mRNA as it moves through the **pores** of the nuclear membrane into the cytoplasm. The cap and poly-A tail also seem to enhance or help the translation process at the ribosome.

Subject vocabulary

methylation patterns refers to the methyl groups which occur on DNA of organisms

cancerous of or involving cancer

introns non-coding regions of DNA which are transcribed onto the mRNA molecules, they are removed before leaving the nucleus

pre-mRNA strand original, unprocessed strand of mRNA produced in transcription

small nuclear RNAs snRNAs also known as spliceosomes

snRNAs small nuclear RNAs involved in the cutting of pre-mRNA strands to remove introns

spliceosomes also known as snRNAs which remove introns from pre-mRNA

splicing the removal of introns from mRNA

exons sections of mRNA containing the protein coding nucleotide sequences

cap protective structure added to the 5′ end of mRNA after processing before the mRNA leaves the nucleus

poly-A tail protective structure added to the 3′ end of mRNA after processing before the mRNA leaves the nucleus

mature mRNA final product of mRNA processing which occurs in the nucleus and will be translated at the ribosome

General vocabulary

maternal relating to being a mother

paternal relating to being a father

Synonyms

pore .... hole/opening

Understanding: Splicing of mRNA increases the number of different proteins an organism can produce.

Model sentence: The modification of mRNA in the splicing process allows a larger number of proteins to be produced at the cell's ribosomes.

The splicing process allows a gene to produce several different proteins. Different proteins are produced when exons are **removed** in the splicing process. It is also possible for exons to change position in the splicing process. This will allow the production of different proteins. In some higher eukaryotes, different sections of a gene may act as introns at different times. Again, this will result in the production of different proteins.

Understanding: Gene expression is regulated by proteins that bind to specific base sequences in DNA.

Model sentence: Proteins which bind to DNA have a controlling factor in gene expression.

There are several types of proteins which have an effect on gene expression in the cell. These proteins bind to certain base sequences of DNA to cause their effect. Examples include:

- Proteins which assist the binding of RNA polymerase at the **promoter region** to bring about a higher rate of transcription.
- **Transcription activators** are proteins which cause looping of DNA. The looping of DNA may result in a shorter distance between the **activator** and the promoter regions of a gene. This will increase the expression of that gene.
- **Repressor proteins** may bind to segments of DNA known as **silencers**. This prevents transcription and gene expression.

Enhancers are sections of DNA which proteins may combine with to increase the rate of transcription of a particular gene. Silencers are sections of DNA to which proteins may attach. This decreases the rate of transcription of a gene.

Understanding: The environment of a cell and of an organism has an impact on gene expression.

Model sentence: The environment of an organism has an effect on the expression of genes of that organism's cells.

Organisms with the same **genotypes** often express different **phenotypes** when in different environments.

Identical twins are often used in studies to prove the effect of different environments.

Examples of this include:

- The gene which produces fur **pigmentation** in Himalayan rabbits is only active at temperatures between 15 and 25 °C.
- When the larval form of the *Vanessa urtica* butterfly is placed in red light, it produces intensely coloured wings. When a larva of the same species is placed in green light, dark colourless wings are produced.

General vocabulary

removed taken away

Subject vocabulary

sequence a series of bases in the genetic code in a particular order

promoter region non-coding DNA region which binds with RNA polymerase to begin the transcription process

transcription activator proteins which cause looping of DNA and increase expression of a gene

activator transcription factor which causes transcription of a gene

repressor proteins bind to segments of DNA and prevent transcription and gene expression

silencer segment of DNA to which a repressor protein binds

enhancers parts of DNA that speed up transcription by binding to certain proteins

genotype genes of an organism for a particular trait

phenotype visible result of an organism's genotype

pigmentation pattern of coloration

7.3 Translation

Main idea
Translation involves the transfer of the DNA code into an amino acid sequence.

Understanding: Initiation of translation involves assembly of the components that carry out the process.

Model sentence: Translation begins with the binding of a mature mRNA strand with the two subunits of a ribosome.

The process called translation occurs at the ribosome. Translation uses the base sequence of the DNA code to produce a specific **polypeptide** which may become a protein. A protein has a much more detailed structure than a polypeptide. Proteins may be made up of one or more polypeptides. Proteins differ from one another by the number and the sequence of amino acids of which they are composed. The sequence of the steps involved in cellular protein synthesis is:

DNA (gene) → transcription (mRNA) → translation → protein

Translation involves the following components:
- ribosome
- mature mRNA
- tRNA
- amino acids.

A **ribosome** must bind with a mature mRNA strand before tRNA can begin bringing amino acids to the **complex**. The complex is the combination of the ribosome and the mRNA strand. This formation of the **ribosome–mRNA complex** is the initiation or beginning of the translation process.

The sequence of events to initiate translation is:
- The mature mRNA strand attaches first to the small subunit of the ribosome.
- A tRNA carrying the amino acid **methionine** attaches to an mRNA binding site.
- The large ribosomal subunit then attaches to these parts.

Skill: The use of molecular visualization software to analyse the structure of eukaryotic ribosomes and a tRNA molecule.

Utilizing websites which show the molecular structure of eukaryotic ribosomes is essential to understand their function. Examining a website showing the molecular structure of a eukaryotic ribosome will show the following key points:
- Ribosomes are composed of protein and rRNA molecules.
- Ribosomes are composed of one larger subunit and one smaller subunit.
- Each ribosome has three binding sites to which tRNA may attach.

Subject vocabulary

translation process of protein production which occurs at the ribosome in cells, DNA language is changed into the language of proteins

polypeptide polymer of many amino acids combined by peptide bonds

ribosome organelle within cells where polypeptides are formed

ribosome–mRNA complex combination of ribosome and mRNA which must occur for translation to begin

methionine particular type of amino acid which begins the production of a polypeptide in translation

Synonyms

components … parts

General vocabulary

complex a larger structure made up of smaller parts

Subject vocabulary

anti-codon group of three nucleotides on tRNA which base-pair with the codon of mRNA

polysomes group of ribosomes attached to a single strand of mRNA all producing the same polypeptide

tRNA binding sites the A, P, and E sites on the small subunit of ribosomes that connects with the amino acid carrying tRNA molecules

polypeptide chain large sequence of amino acids chemically combined by covalent bonds called peptide bonds

Synonyms

discharged ..... released

cavity .... space (within)

General vocabulary

sequentially in order

Utilize websites to view the molecular structure of tRNA. Some key points of your observations should include:
- tRNA includes areas where base pairing creates a double strand.
- Loops are apparent in three areas.
- One loop contains the **anti-codon** of the molecule.
- Has a single-strand 3′ end with the base sequence CCA which is the amino acid attachment site.

Skill: Identification of polysomes in electron micrographs of prokaryotes and eukaryotes

Observe the cytoplasm in electron micrographs of prokaryotic and eukaryotic cells. Structures which appear as a number of beads attached to a single string are called **polysomes** or polyribosomes. Each bead is a ribosome. The single string is one mRNA molecule. The polysome produces many copies of the same polypeptide.

Understanding: Synthesis of the polypeptide involves a repeated cycle of events.

Model sentence: There is a repeated cycle of events in the production of polypeptides at the ribosome.

There are three **tRNA binding sites** on the small subunit of the ribosome. They are labelled A, P, and E. The following table explains the action at each binding site.

Ribosomal binding site	Function
A (entry site)	holds the tRNA carrying the next amino acid to be added to the polypeptide chain
P (peptide bond formation site)	holds the tRNA carrying the growing polypeptide chain
E (exit site)	site at which tRNA that has lost its amino acid is **discharged** from the ribosome

Polypeptide chains are assembled in the **cavity** between the two ribosomal subunits. tRNAs carrying specific amino acids move **sequentially** through the three ribosomal binding sites; first the A site, then the P site, and finally the E site.

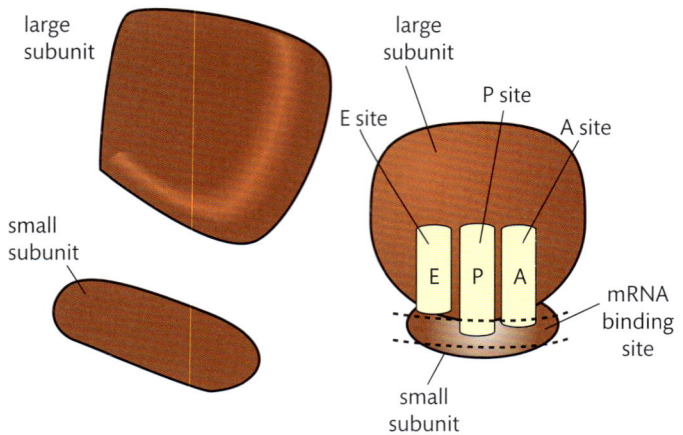

Figure 7.9 *This model shows the arrangement of subunits and binding sites in a ribosome*

tRNAs come to the A site so that base pairing of their anti-codon with the mRNAs **codon** occurs. This base pairing creates the exact sequence of amino acids called for in the cell's genetic code. **Peptide bonds** between the amino acid and the growing polypeptide chain occur at the P site. A continuous repetition of the cycle of events occurs at the A, P, and E sites until the full polypeptide chain is assembled. The ribosome moves from the 5′ to the 3′ end of the mRNA strand to build the polypeptide.

The polypeptide chain produced at the ribosome is assembled by a repeated cycle of events. Amino acids are added one at a time as a result of base pairing between mRNA codons and tRNA anticodons. The initiation of a polypeptide chain assembly occurs with the combining of a tRNA carrying the amino acid methionine with the mRNA codon AUG. This methionine carrying tRNA has the anticodon, UAC. The growth of the polypeptide chain continues until a stop codon is **encountered**. The polypeptide is then released.

Application: tRNA-activating enzymes illustrate enzyme–substrate specificity and the role of phosphorylation

Certain enzymes work with certain **substrates** and this is demonstrated by the enzymes necessary to allow the attachment of an amino acid to its specific tRNA. There are 20 different amino acids. Therefore, there are 20 different tRNAs. There are also 20 different enzymes needed to aid in the attachment of each different amino acid to the proper tRNA. The addition of a phosphate and its accompanying energy from ATP is also necessary for the attachment of an amino acid to its proper tRNA. This is known as **phosphorylation**. The tRNA attached to a specific amino acid is now said to be activated. It may then be involved in translation. The energy in the bond connecting the amino acid to the tRNA is used in the attachment of the amino acid to the growing polypeptide chain in the translation process at the ribosome.

Translation is a two-step process:
- tRNA-activating enzymes attach the appropriate amino acid to the correct tRNA (based on the tRNA anticodon)
- the tRNA anticodon binds with the correct complementary mRNA code.

Understanding: **Disassembly** of the components follows termination of translation.

Model sentence: The polypeptide is released and the mRNA–ribosomal complex splits apart once the stop codon is encountered during translation.

Polypeptide synthesis ends at a ribosome when that ribosome comes to the 3′ end of an mRNA strand. The mRNA-ribosomal complex involved in the translation process breaks into its individual parts. The polypeptide produced goes free to be used for cellular needs. The mRNA is released into the cytoplasm. The ribosome splits into its two subunits. This ribosome is then available to attach to a different mRNA strand coming from the nucleus so that a new translation process may occur.

Subject vocabulary

codon a group of three bases that together code for a single amino acid

peptide bonds covalent bond which occurs between the amino group of one amino acid and the carboxyl group of another

substrate substance which begins a chemical reaction or process

phosphorylation process of adding a phosphate group to a molecule, usually includes the addition of energy as well

disassembly breaking something down into the parts of which it is made

Synonyms

encountered… met/reached

Subject vocabulary

endoplasmic reticulum organelle involved in transport within the cell

free ribosomes ribosomes in the cytoplasm of the cell which are not connected to the endoplasmic reticulum

signal sequence group of amino acids coded by mRNA which controls whether a ribosome is attached to the endoplasmic reticulum or not

secretion release of a substance from a cell, tissue, or gland

lysosome eukaryotic cell organelle involved in hydrolytic or breakdown processes within the cell

bound ribosomes ribosomes which are connected to the endoplasmic reticulum

General vocabulary

interior the inner part or inside of something

Understanding: Free ribosomes synthesize proteins for use primarily within the cell.

Model sentence: Ribosomes in the cytoplasm which are not attached to the endoplasmic reticulum usually produce proteins which are used within the cell.

The polypeptides produced by translation at free ribosomes in the cell usually become proteins or become parts of proteins needed within the cell. Free ribosomes are not attached to the endoplasmic reticulum. Whether a ribosome is attached to the endoplasmic reticulum or not seems to be determined by a signal sequence of specific amino acids called for on the mRNA strand coming from the nucleus.

Understanding: Bound ribosomes synthesize proteins primarily for secretion or for use in lysosomes.

Model sentence: Bound ribosomes are attached to the cell's endoplasmic reticulum and produce proteins most often used for secretion from the cell or for use in lysosomes.

Ribosomes will become attached to the membrane of the cell's endoplasmic reticulum when a certain signal sequence of amino acids is present in a polypeptide or protein being assembled. These ribosomes are then called bound ribosomes. Polypeptides or proteins produced by these bound ribosomes then enter the interior of the endoplasmic reticulum. Once inside the endoplasmic reticulum, transport occurs of these polypeptides or proteins through the cell's membrane system. The membrane system includes the endoplasmic reticulum, the Golgi apparatus, vesicles, lysosomes, and the plasma membrane. Most often these polypeptides or proteins will be secreted outside the cell or will be used in the cell's lysosomes.

Understanding: Translation can occur immediately after transcription in prokaryotes due to the absence of a nuclear membrane.

Model sentence: Translation occurs more rapidly after transcription in prokaryotes because there is not a nuclear membrane present.

The speed of protein synthesis in prokaryotic cells is faster than in eukaryotic cells. This is due to two factors:
- Non-coding sequences do not exist in prokaryotic DNA. Therefore, there is no need to process the mRNA produced by transcription to remove introns.
- Prokaryotic cells do not have a nucleus. Therefore, in these types of cells mRNA does not have to move through the nuclear membrane to attach to a ribosome.

Hints for success: Prokaryotic cells will start the translation process immediately after transcription. Eukaryotic cells have a delay between transcription and translation. This delay is due to the need for mRNA to be processed and to move through the nuclear membrane.

Understanding: The sequence and number of amino acids in the polypeptide is the **primary structure**.

Model sentence: The primary level of protein structure refers to the unique sequence of amino acids present.

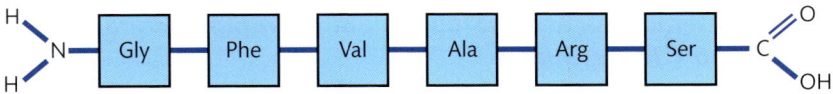

The figure shows the primary structure of a protein. The primary structure refers to the unique sequence of amino acids present. There are 20 different amino acids which make up proteins. These 20 different amino acids vary in the R-groups which they contain. The **R-group** is often called the side chain. The figure shows the general formula of an amino acid.

> **Hints for success:** The primary structure of proteins produced in a cell by translation is determined by the cell's DNA code. The primary structure of a protein determines the secondary, tertiary, and quaternary levels of protein structure. Only **covalent bonding** is involved in primary structure.

Figure 7.10 *This figure represents a primary structure. Each blue box represents a particular amino acid. The lines connecting these amino acids represent a covalent bond called a peptide bond. The peptide bond is formed between an amino group of one amino acid and the carboxyl group of the other amino acid*

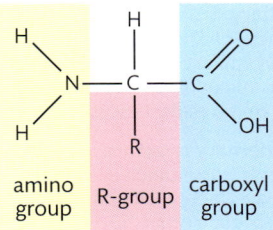

Figure 7.11 *General structure of an amino acid*

General vocabulary
stabilized made stable

Subject vocabulary
primary structure sequence of amino acids forming the polypeptide chain of a protein

R-group the portion of each of the 20 amino acids that is different from one another

covalent bond chemical bond in which electrons are shared

carboxyl group -COOH

amino group -NH_2

secondary structure alpha helices and beta-pleated sheets which are produced in polypeptides due to interactions between carboxyl and amino groups

alpha helix secondary structure possible for polypeptide chain involving a helical structure

beta-pleated sheet one of the possible shapes formed in the secondary structure of a polypeptide

Synonyms
regions .... particular parts

Understanding: The secondary structure is the formation of alpha helices and beta pleated sheets **stabilized** by hydrogen bonding.

Model sentence: Hydrogen bonding produces the secondary structure of proteins which includes alpha helices and beta pleated sheets.

Hydrogen bonds occur between oppositely charged polar regions of the **carboxyl** and **amino groups** of amino acids in a polypeptide. The result of these hydrogen bonds is the **secondary structure** of proteins. The secondary structure takes two major forms.
- The **alpha helix** is a coiled form.
- The **beta-pleated sheet** is a folded form.

The hydrogen bonds form between the relatively positively charged hydrogen **regions** of the amino groups and the relatively negatively charged oxygen regions of the carboxyl group.

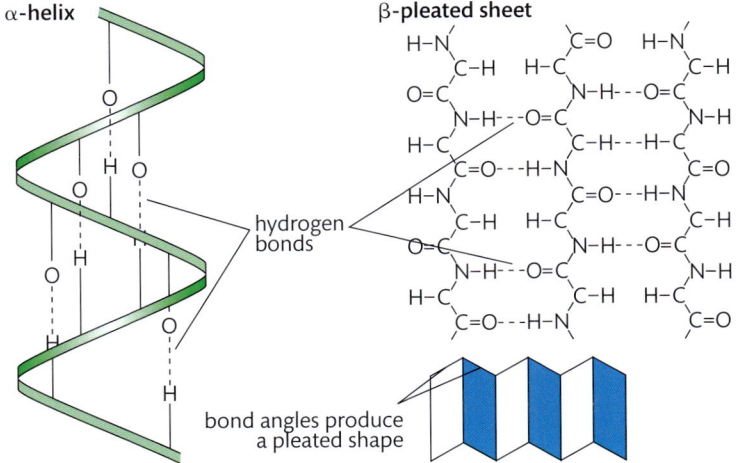

Figure 7.12 *Protein secondary structure*

Understanding: The tertiary structure is the further folding of the polypeptide stabilized by interactions between R-groups.

Model sentence: The tertiary structure of proteins is due to the complex folding of the polypeptide as a result of **disulphide bridges**, weak hydrogen bonds, ionic interactions, and hydrophobic or hydrophilic interactions between amino acid R-groups.

The folding of a protein to create the **tertiary structure** is quite specific based on interactions of the amino acid R-groups present.

Amino acids with non-polar R-groups are hydrophobic. Amino acids with polar R-groups are hydrophilic.

Hydrophobic amino acids will move to the interior of the folded molecule where contact with water is less likely. Hydrophilic amino acids will move toward the exterior of the folded molecule where contact with water is more likely.

Polar and non-polar amino acids are important in determining the tertiary structure of a protein. The tertiary structure of proteins is especially important when the protein is an enzyme. The active site of an enzyme is mostly due to tertiary structure. Substrates which 'fit' specific active sites must have a similar shape and proper polar and non-polar charges.

A protein's primary and secondary structures do not change when it folds to form the tertiary structure. This folding is three dimensional and is quite specific. The same sequence of amino acids will always produce the same tertiary structure.

Understanding: The quaternary structure exists in proteins with more than one polypeptide chain.

Model sentence: Proteins with a quaternary structure have multiple polypeptide chains combined to form a single structure.

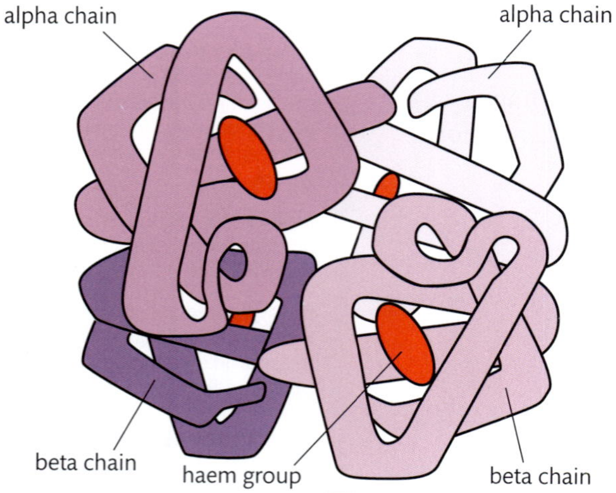

Only proteins with more than one polypeptide chain are said to have **quaternary structure**.

Bonding to create quaternary structure involves all the bonds present in the primary, secondary, and tertiary structures.

Proteins with quaternary structure often include non-polypeptide components. These non-polypeptide groups are also called **prosthetic groups**. Proteins with prosthetic groups are called **conjugated proteins**. An example of a conjugated protein is haemoglobin. Haemoglobin contains two alpha polypeptide chains, two beta polypeptide chains, plus four haem groups which contain iron atoms for oxygen attachment. The adjacent figure shows a 'sausage' model of haemoglobin.

Figure 7.13 *This 'sausage' model of haemoglobin contains four polypeptide chains. Each polypeptide chain has a haem group associated with it*

Hints for success: The function of a protein in an organism is directly related to its primary, secondary, tertiary, and quaternary structure. Environmental factors such as temperature and pH may permanently alter the shape of a protein. This shape change will result in the loss of that protein's function. The protein is then said to be **denatured**.

Subject vocabulary

disulphide bridges covalent bond which occurs between two sulfur atoms of the same or different molecules

tertiary structure three-dimensional folding of a polypeptide chain due to multiple interactions amongst the parts of the amino acids present

quaternary structure protein level of organization which includes more than one polypeptide chain

prosthetic group non-protein group which occurs in the quaternary structure of some proteins

conjugated protein a protein which contains at least one prosthetic group

denatured protein protein to which a permanent shape change has occurred with loss of original function

8 Metabolism, cell respiration, and photosynthesis

8.1 Metabolism

Main idea
The metabolic activities of the cell are maintained to meet the needs of the cell.

Understanding: Metabolic pathways consist of chains and cycles of enzyme-catalysed reactions.

Model sentence: Enzymes catalyse each step of all metabolic pathways within cells.

Metabolism includes all chemical reactions which occur within a cell or an organism.

General types of metabolism include:
- **Anabolism** – uses energy and smaller compounds to build complex molecules useful to the cell or organism.
- **Catabolism** – breaks down complex molecules and releases energy in the process.

Metabolism usually occurs in a series of small steps with each step catalysed by a particular enzyme.

The small steps which occur in a single metabolic process make up a **metabolic pathway**.

Metabolic pathways take two forms:

1. Chain – a straight-line series of small reactions in which several **intermediate** products are formed between the initial substance or reactant and the final product.

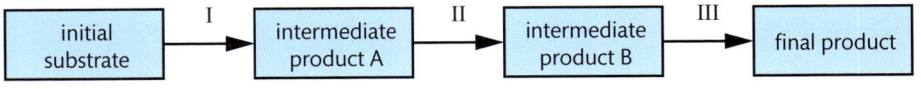

I, II, and III represent different enzymes

Figure 8.1 *General representation of a chain metabolic pathway*

2. Cycle – circular type of metabolic pathway in which an initial substance or reactant is also the final product of the pathway.

Each step in both forms of metabolic pathways is catalysed by a unique enzyme.

Subject vocabulary

anabolism type of metabolism in which smaller compounds are used to build larger compounds in organisms

catabolism type of metabolism in which larger compunds are broken down with the release of energy

metabolic pathway a chemical pathway in which a series of enzymes produces intermediate compounds on the way to producing a final product needed by the organism

General vocabulary

intermediate between

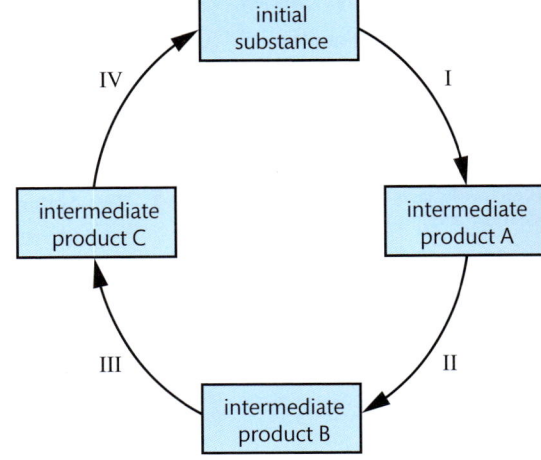

I, II, and III represent different enzymes

Figure 8.2 *General representation of a cycle type of metabolic pathway*

Understanding: Enzymes lower the activation energy of the chemical reactions that they catalyse.

Model sentence: Enzymes catalyse reactions by lowering activation energy.

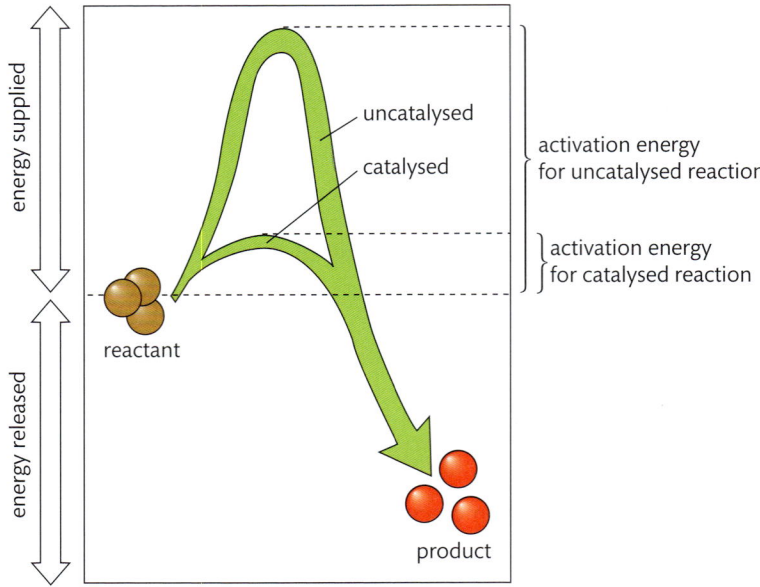

Figure 8.3 *Enzymes accelerate reactions by lowering the activation energy required for a reaction to occur*

Key points:

1. **Activation energy** is needed to **destabilize** the chemical bonds in the reactant or initial substance.

2. The upper curve shows the activation energy needed when no enzyme is present.

3. The lower curve shows the activation energy needed when an enzyme is present.

The material on which an enzyme acts is referred to as the **substrate**.

Mechanism of the **induced-fit model** of enzyme action:

1. The surface of the substrate contacts the active site of the enzyme.

2. The enzyme's active site and the substrate **conform** so that a close fit occurs between the two. The result is a **temporary** complex called the **enzyme–substrate complex**.

3. The activation energy necessary to change the substrate is lowered. The reaction occurs more rapidly.

4. The changed substrate or product is released from the active site.

The induced-fit model of enzyme action is a more accurate description of enzyme action than the more simple lock-and-key model.

Subject vocabulary

activation energy energy needed to begin a chemical reaction

substrate substance which begins a chemical reaction or process

induced-fit model the idea that enzymes change shape to better match the shape of the substrate when they come into contact making the reaction more efficient

enzyme-substrate complex combination of enzyme and substrate which occurs at the active site of the enzyme

General vocabulary

destabilize to make less stable

conform matching of shape

temporary continuing for only a limited period of time

Understanding: Enzyme **inhibitors** can be competitive or non-competitive.

Model sentence: Enzyme inhibitors decrease enzyme activity and are grouped as either competitive or non-competitive.

The following table compares competitive and non-competitive enzyme inhibitors.

Competitive enzyme inhibitor	Non-competitive enzyme inhibitor
decreases enzyme activity	decreases enzyme activity
decreases substrate's encounters with the enzyme's active site	prevents the substrate's ability to fit and combine with the enzyme's active site
attaches to the active site of the affected enzyme and blocks substrate attachment	usually attaches to a site of the enzyme other than the active site, called the **allosteric site**
increasing the substrate concentration will increase the rate of enzyme activity	increasing the substrate concentration will not increase the rate of enzyme activity
active site does not change shape	active site does change shape

An example of a competitive enzyme inhibitor is sulphanilamide which attaches to the active site of the enzyme which converts paraminobenzoic acid (PABA) to folic acid in certain types of bacteria. This prevents the formation of folic acid. These bacteria will die when folic acid is not present.

Examples of non-competitive enzyme inhibitors are some nerve gases which prevent the action of an enzyme to break down a neurotransmitter at the junction of two neurones. These types of nerve gas attach to an allosteric site of the enzyme. This changes the shape of the enzyme's active site. The result is a continuous action of the muscle to which a nerve attaches. This may cause death in humans due to heart or lung **malfunction**.

Skill: Calculating and plotting rates of reaction from raw experimental results

You should develop the skill of producing graphs for enzyme reaction rates from raw data. Hydrogen peroxide breaks down over time to produce water and oxygen. This reaction is shown below:

$$2H_2O_2 \rightarrow 2H_2O + O_2 \text{ (gas)}$$

The enzyme known as catalase will significantly increase the rate of this reaction. Raw data from this reaction showing the amount of oxygen produced over time or amount of hydrogen peroxide broken down over time may be used to calculate the reaction rate of catalase. These raw data collected over a series of times may also be used to produce a graph representing the enzyme's reaction rate over the full time period.

Skill: Distinguishing different types of inhibition from graphs at specified substrate concentration.

You must be able to **distinguish** different types of enzyme inhibitors from graphs which indicate specific substrate concentration. Competitive and non-competitive inhibition produce characteristic graphs of substrate concentration and enzyme activity.

Subject vocabulary

inhibit to lower

competitive enzyme inhibitor substance which decreases enzyme activity by directly competing with a substrate for an enzyme's active site

non-competitive enzyme inhibitor substance which affects an enzyme's activity by combining with an allosteric site of the enzyme and altering the enzyme's active site shape

allosteric site a site that is not the active site on an enzyme to which a non-competive enzyme inhibitor attaches

General vocabulary

malfunction failure to function well

distinguish to recognize the difference

Synonyms

raw .... unprocessed

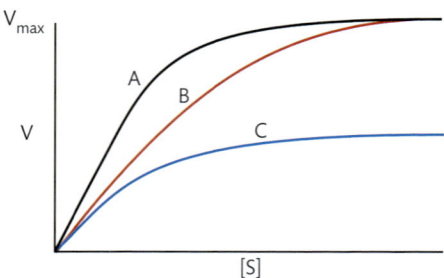

Figure 8.4 Enzyme inhibition. [S] = substrate concentration; V = reaction rate; V_{max} = maximum reaction rate

Study the following example:

Curve A in the example is the curve showing the reaction rate of an enzyme as substrate concentration increases. For curve A, there is no inhibition of the enzyme occurring.

Curve C in the example represents **non-competitive inhibition**. This is because:

- Curve C shows a lower maximum reaction rate due to attachment of the product to the enzyme's allosteric site.
- Curve C shows the reaction rate of the enzyme does not increase as the substrate concentration increases.

Curve B in the example represents **competitive inhibition**. This is because:

- Curve B shows the reaction rate of the enzyme increasing as the substrate concentration increases.
- Curve B will reach the maximum reaction rate if the substrate concentration becomes high enough.

Subject vocabulary

non-competitive inhibitor a substance which changes the shape of an enzyme's active site by combining with an allosteric site on the enzyme

competitive inhibiton reaction in which inhibition occurs due to competition for an enzyme's active site

General vocabulary

inhibition the slowing or prevention of a process, reaction or function

Understanding: Metabolic pathways can be controlled by end-product **inhibition**.

Model sentence: End-product inhibition is a common way by which metabolic pathways in cells may be controlled.

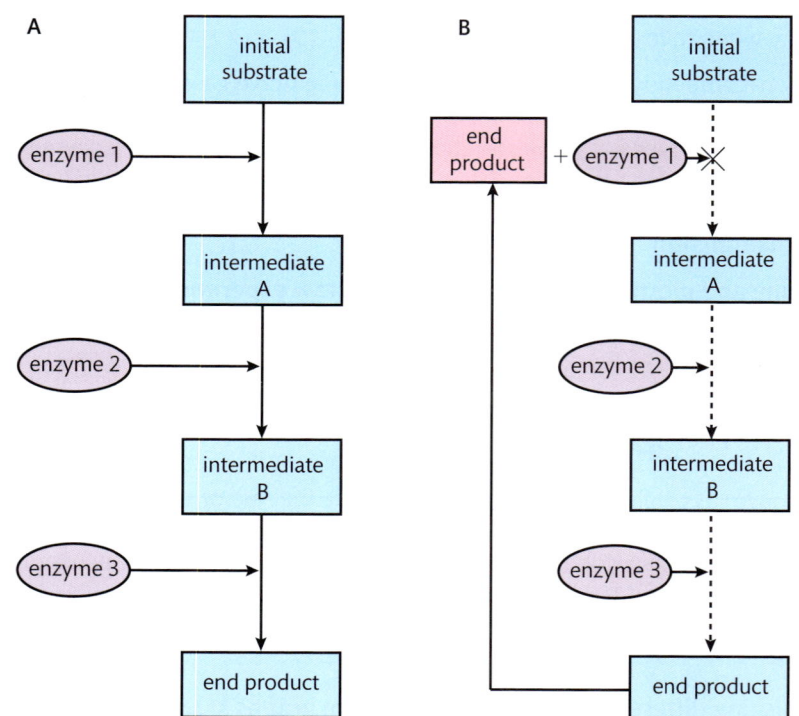

Figure 8.5 A short pathway of metabolic reactions with a specific end product that, when in sufficient quantity, causes end-product inhibition. This is also a form of negative feedback. The intermediates are essential molecules produced in the step-by-step pathway to achieve the end product. **A** represents a normal pathway with several enzymes producing intermediate compounds along the way. **B** represents feedback inhibition. In this condition a large amount of end product is present. The end product inhibits enzyme 1 in the pathway. The result is that the pathway is halted

Hints for success: End-product inhibition is an example of negative feedback. Inhibition of a pathway occurs when the concentration of the pathway's end-product is high. This inhibition occurs when the end product binds to the enzyme catalysing the first reaction in the metabolic pathway. The inhibition of the first enzyme in the pathway prevents the production of more of a product than is needed. Also, inhibition of the first enzyme prevents a build-up of pathway intermediates.

Application: End-product inhibition of the pathway that **converts** threonine to isoleucine

Escherichia coli, a type of bacterium, has a pathway which allows the conversion of threonine to isoleucine. Isoleucine is necessary for growth in this bacterium. The generalized pathway is presented in the figures.

In this example, isoleucine attaches to an allosteric site of enzyme 1 in the pathway. This attachment prevents the formation of intermediate A. The result is that the pathway will no longer occur. This is a negative feedback system. Higher concentrations of isoleucine will result in more combinations of isoleucine with enzyme 1. The result of increasing concentrations of isoleucine will be lesser amounts of isoleucine being produced by the pathway.

Application: Use of databases to identify potential new anti-malarial drugs

Scientists are using a relatively new field of biology called **bioinformatics** to determine potential new anti-malarial drugs. Bioinformatics uses databases contributed to by multiple researchers to search for unique events and patterns. This approach has led to the discovery of a group of compounds which may be successful in treating or preventing malaria in the future.

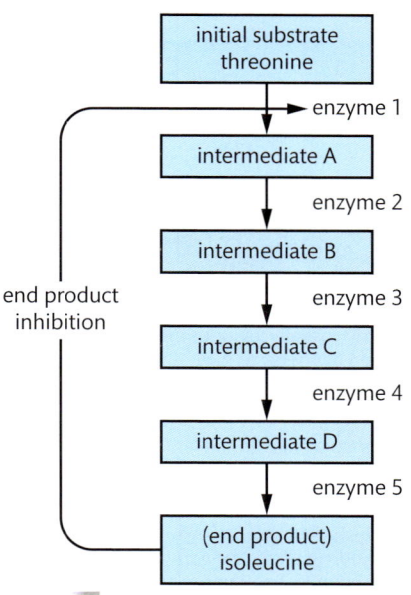

Figure 8.6 *End-product inhibition of the threonine to isoleucine pathway*

General vocabulary

converts changes something into a different form

conversion change from one form to another

Subject vocabulary

bioinformatics branch of biology which uses computers in an effort to understand biological processes

oxidation reaction a chemical reaction in which electrons are lost

reduction reaction a chemical reaction in which electrons are gained

electron carriers specialized chemicals with the ability to form temporary bonds with freed electrons

8.2 Cell respiration

Main idea

Cell respiration allows the **conversion** of energy into a usable form in cells and organisms.

Understanding: Cell respiration involves the **oxidation** and **reduction** of electron carriers.

Model sentence: Oxidation and reduction of electron carriers occurs in cell respiration to produce usable energy for the cell and organism.

Oxidation	Reduction
loss of electrons	gain of electrons
gain of oxygen	loss of oxygen
loss of hydrogen	gain of hydrogen
results in many carbon to oxygen covalent bonds	results in many carbon to hydrogen covalent bonds
results in a compound with lower potential energy	results in a compound with higher potential energy

The major **electron carriers** of cell respiration which are oxidized and reduced are NAD and FAD.

Understanding: Phosphorylation of molecules makes them less stable.

Model sentence: Molecules which have a phosphate chemically added to them are more likely to break down.

Phosphorylation is the process by which a phosphate group (PO_4^{3-}) is added to a molecule.

Phosphorylated molecules are more likely to enter into reactions than non-phosphorylated molecules.

ATP is very often the source of the phosphate group when phosphorylation occurs in cells.

$$ATP \rightarrow ADP + phosphate + energy$$

The energy released when ATP splits away a phosphate may be used to aid in the phosphorylation of a molecule.

> **Hints for success:** Most phosphorylated molecules are more likely to enter into chemical reactions than non-phosphorylated molecules.

Subject vocabulary

phosphorylation process of adding a phosphate group to a molecule, usually includes the addition of energy as well

phosphorylated molecules molecules to which phosphate groups have been added resulting in a decrease of stability of the molecules

glycolysis first stage of cell respiration in which oxygen is not required and glucose is broken down into two pyruvate molecules

pyruvate 3-carbon compound formed by the breakdown of glucose in glycolysis, the first stage of cell respiration

triose phosphate 3-carbon carbohydrate with a phosphate group attached produced in the glycolysis pathway

Understanding: In glycolysis, glucose is converted to pyruvate in the cytoplasm.

Model sentence: Glycolysis results in the formation of pyruvate in the cytoplasm.

- The first series of reactions in cell respiration is called glycolysis.
- Glycolysis usually begins with the monosaccharide known as glucose.
- Glycolysis occurs in the cytoplasm of the cell. Glycolysis does not require organelles.
- Glycolysis occurs in prokaryotic and eukaryotic cells.
- The reactions of glycolysis are controlled by enzymes.
- 6C in the diagram means a 6-carbon compound. 3C in the diagram means a 3-carbon compound.

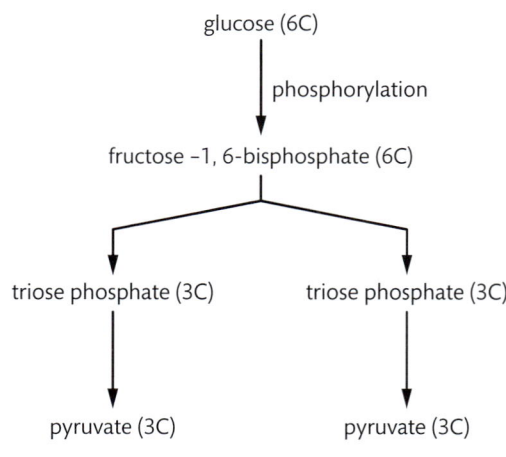

Figure 8.7 *General diagram of glycolysis*

> **Hints for success:** Phosphorylation of glucose makes it an unstable molecule. The result of the instability is the formation of two **triose phosphates**. Each triose phosphate goes through a series of reactions to produce one pyruvate molecule. Two pyruvate molecules are produced from one glucose molecule in the process of glycolysis.

Understanding: Glycolysis gives a small net gain of ATP without the use of oxygen.

Model sentence: There is a net gain of two ATP molecules in the process of glycolysis.

Glycolysis does not require oxygen to occur. Study the general diagram of glycolysis with ATP usage and gain.

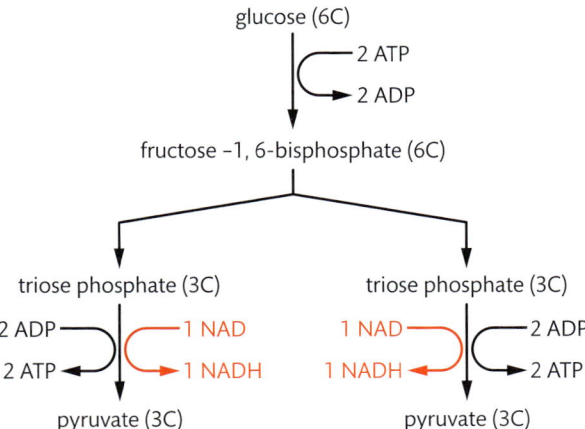

Figure 8.8 *Overview of glycolysis*

Notice from the diagram that two ATP molecules are necessary to phosphorylate glucose so it becomes reactive. Each triose phosphate (three carbon molecules) goes through a series of reactions to produce two ATP molecules. Two ATP molecules are used in glycolysis but four ATP molecules are directly produced. Therefore, there is a net gain of two ATP molecules due to glycolysis. Note the red NAD and NADH molecules. Be aware you will often see the reduced form of NAD written as $NADH^+ + H^+$. They will be discussed in a later part of cell respiration.

Understanding: In aerobic cell respiration pyruvate is decarboxylated and oxidized, and converted into acetyl compound and attached to coenzyme A to form acetyl coenzyme A in the link reaction.

Model sentence: The first stages of aerobic cell respiration involve the **decarboxylation** and oxidation of pyruvate in the **link reaction** to form an acetyl compound.

The presence of oxygen in the cell allows aerobic cell respiration to occur.

Aerobic cell respiration occurs in the **mitochondria** of cells. Prokaryotic cells do not have mitochondria. Therefore, the process of aerobic cell respiration does not occur in prokaryotic cells.

The presence of oxygen brings about the active transport of pyruvate into the matrix of the mitochondrion.

Subject vocabulary

decarboxylation process of removing a carbon from a compound

link reaction aerobic cellular respiration pathway in which a carbon is removed from pyruvate and acetyl CoA is formed

mitochondrion (plural: mitochondria) cell organelle(s) involved in cell respiration

Subject vocabulary

mitochondrial matrix region of a mitochondrion within the inner membrane filled with a cytosol-like material

acetyl group 2-carbon organic compound group formed in the link reaction

coenzyme A molecule which combines with and carries the link reaction acetyl group into the Krebs cycle

acetyl CoA compound moving from the cellular respiration link reaction to the Krebs cycle

Krebs cycle cyclic metabolic pathway of aerobic cellular respiration occurring in the mitochondrial matrix producing ATP, carbon dioxide, and reduced NAD and FAD

Synonyms

coupled to...... joined with/paired with

liberating....... freeing/releasing

Enzymes are present in the **mitochondrial matrix** to control the link reaction. The link reaction is a series of reactions which begins aerobic cell respiration. The major events of the link reaction are:

1 Pyruvate loses a carbon atom. This loss is referred to as decarboxylation. This carbon atom combines with oxygen to form carbon dioxide. The carbon dioxide is released from the cell.

2 When pyruvate loses a carbon atom, it forms an **acetyl group**. The acetyl group contains two carbons.

3 The acetyl group then combines with **coenzyme A** (CoA) to form **acetyl CoA**.

4 The acetyl CoA then enters the next stage of aerobic cell respiration called the **Krebs cycle.**

Oxidation in the link reaction occurs with the loss of hydrogen atoms/high energy electrons from pyruvate to form NADH from NAD. The NADH produced then enters the electron transport chain of the aerobic cell respiration process.

Hints for success: Study the following representation of the major steps of the aerobic cell respiration's link reaction:

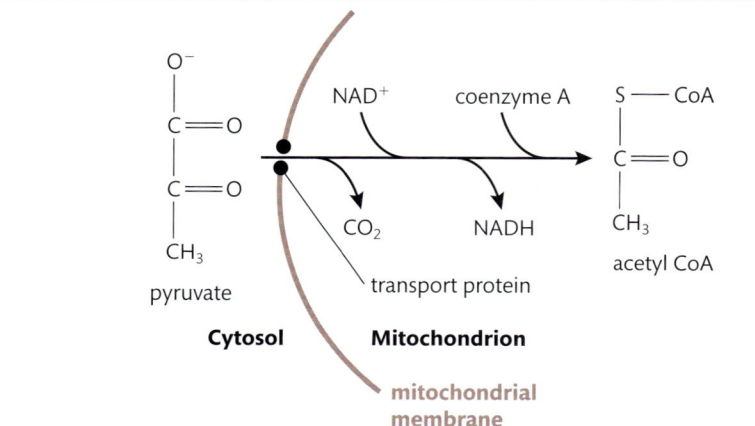

Figure 8.9 Link reaction of cell respiration

- Notice the loss of CO_2 from the pyruvate which occurs inside the mitochondrion.
- Also, notice the loss of hydrogen/electrons from pyruvate to form NADH from NAD.

The loss of CO_2 is referred to as decarboxylation. The loss of hydrogen and energized electrons to form NADH from NAD is referred to as oxidation.

Understanding: In the Krebs cycle, the oxidation of acetyl groups is **coupled to** the reduction of hydrogen carriers, **liberating** carbon dioxide.

Model sentence: The Krebs cycle involves the decarboxylation and oxidation of acetyl groups to form reduced hydrogen carriers and carbon dioxide.

Study the following overview of the Krebs cycle.

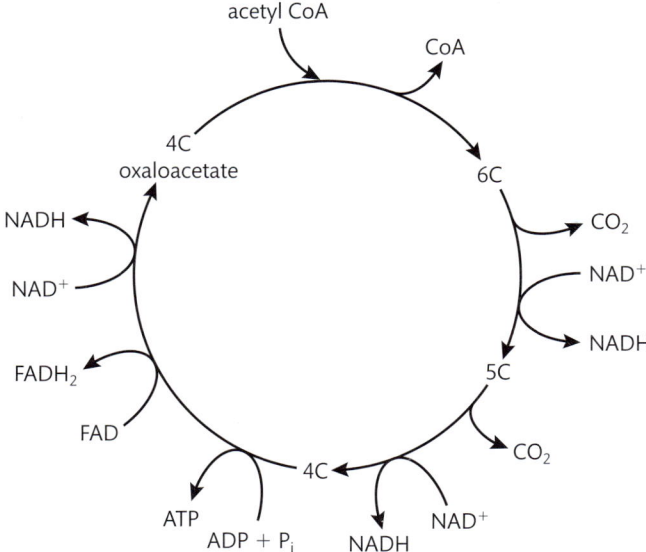

Figure 8.10 *Overview of the Krebs cycle*

Notice the following from the above figure.
- Each acetyl CoA which enters the Krebs cycle results in the formation of three NADH molecules and one $FADH_2$ molecule. The acetyl group is oxidized to form these reduced molecules. The formed NADH and $FADH_2$ molecules move to the aerobic cell respiration electron transport chain.
- Two molecules of carbon dioxide are produced. These two molecules of CO_2 are due to the decarboxylation of the acetyl group which enters the Krebs cycle.
- One molecule of ATP is produced as oxidation of the acetyl group occurs.

Skill: Analysis of diagrams of the pathways of aerobic respiration to deduce where decarboxylation and oxidation reactions occur

You must be able to work out where **decarboxylation** and oxidative reactions occur from a diagram showing the pathways of aerobic respiration. Look at the figure above.

1 Where does decarboxylation occur?

2 Where is oxidation occurring?

Decarboxylation is occurring just prior to the release of CO_2 from the 6-carbon (6C) and the 5-carbon (5C) compounds in the cycle. Oxidation of the cycle compounds is occurring just before the three reductions of NAD to NADH, just before the reduction of FAD to $FADH_2$, and just before the production of ATP from ADP.

Hints for success: A glucose molecule entering glycolysis results in two pyruvate molecules. Therefore, the two pyruvates produced from a single glucose molecule results in the following products when the Krebs cycle occurs twice, once for each pyruvate molecule:

- Two ATP molecules.
- Six molecules of reduced NAD (NADH).
- Two molecules of reduced FAD ($FADH_2$).
- Two molecules of reduced NAD (NADH), produced in the link reaction before the Krebs cycle began.
- Four molecules of carbon dioxide, which are released from the cell as waste.

Subject vocabulary

pathways means of getting from one substance or position to another

decarboxylation process of removing a carbon from a compound

Subject vocabulary

mitochondrial cristae inner membranes of the mitochondria with a shelf-like appearance

pumping active means of changing a particle's or substance's position

electron transport chain chain involving specialized molecules used to transport electrons due to different attractions for the electrons

cytochromes type of proteins which act as carriers in many electron transport chains

oxidative phosphorylation process of adding a phosphate group to ADP using energy received from an electron transport chain

---

Understanding: Energy released by oxidation reactions is carried to the cristae of the mitochondria by reduced NAD and FAD.

Model sentence: NAD and FAD carry the energy released by oxidation reactions to the mitochondrial cristae in cell respiration.

- Oxidation of one glucose molecule in glycolysis results in the reduction of two NAD molecules to form NADH.
- Oxidation of two acetyl groups occurs in the link reaction and results in the reduction of two NAD molecules to form NADH.
- Oxidation of two acetyl CoA molecules in the Krebs cycle results in the reduction of six NAD and two FAD molecules to form NADH and $FADH_2$.
- The NADH and $FADH_2$ molecules move from the mitochondrial matrix to the mitochondrial cristae.
- These reduced forms of NAD and FAD molecules are high in energy as they move to the cristae.

Understanding: Transfer of electrons between carriers in the electron transport chain in the membrane of the cristae is coupled to proton pumping.

Model sentence: Transfer of electrons paired with proton pumping occurs between carriers of the cristae's electron transport chain.

The transfer of electrons and the pumping of protons occur together at the mitochondrial cristae. These two processes are said to be coupled. This transfer of electrons and the pumping of protons is known as the electron transport chain.

The electron transport chain utilizes specialized molecules called carriers in the cristae membrane to produce ATP from ADP. These carriers are mostly types of proteins called cytochromes.

Electrons are passed from carrier to carrier based on the specific amount of energy they possess. A small amount of energy is released at each electron passage or exchange from one carrier to the next. This released energy is used to pump protons across membranes.

These small released amounts of energy along with the proton pumping are used to add a phosphate to ADP to produce ATP. Producing ATP from ADP using an electron transport chain is called oxidative phosphorylation.

> **Hints for success:** The pumping of protons across membranes using the energy released from electron transfers from carrier to carrier allows the formation of ATP from ADP in the electron transport chain.

Understanding: In chemiosmosis protons diffuse through ATP synthase to generate ATP.

Model sentence: **Chemiosmosis** is the process in which ATP production occurs as a result of protons **diffusing** through an enzyme of the cristae membrane called **ATP synthase**.

Study the following drawing of a mitochondrion to understand the location of the major processes of chemiosmosis.

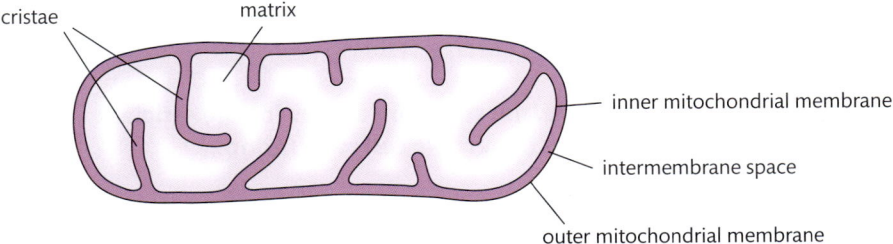

Figure 8.11 *Structure of a typical mitochondrion*

Key points of chemiosmosis:
- Small amounts of energy are released as electrons move from carrier to carrier in the electron transport chain. These carriers are present in the inner mitochondrial membrane which projects inward to form the cristae.
- This released energy is used to pump hydrogen ions by active transport out of the mitochondrial matrix into the space between the membranes of the cristae. In the figure above, this space is labelled the intermembrane space. Note the relatively small volume of the intermembrane space. This low volume is important in allowing a high hydrogen ion volume to develop.
- This hydrogen pumping creates a higher concentration of hydrogen ions in the **intermembrane space** than in the matrix. This is a concentration **gradient** involving hydrogen ions.
- The concentration gradient of hydrogen ions results in the passive flow of hydrogen ions from the intermembrane space into the mitochondrial matrix. The passive flow of hydrogen ions across the cristae membrane occurs through channels of the enzyme ATP synthase.
- The passive flow of hydrogen ions through ATP synthase results in energy available to allow the formation of ATP. ATP is formed by the phosphorylation of ADP. This form of phosphorylation by chemiosmosis is called oxidative phosphorylation.

Subject vocabulary

chemiosmosis process in which ATP is produced due to protons diffusing through ATP synthase in thylakoid and cristae membranes

ATP synthase enzyme of thylakoid and cristae membrane which allows phosphorylation of ADP to form ATP

intermembrane space space between membranes such as between the membranes of the cristae and the thylakoids in which a build-up of hydrogen ions occurs

acceptor receiver of particles or substances

water of metabolism water produced when the de-energized hydrogens of the aerobic cellular respiration electron transport chain combine with available oxygen

Synonyms

diffusing .... spreading

General vocabulary

gradient 'area of difference' involving a factor

Understanding: Oxygen is needed to bind with the free protons to maintain the hydrogen gradient, resulting in the formation of water.

Model sentence: The final **acceptor** of protons and electrons at the end of chemiosmosis is oxygen resulting in the formation of water.

The electrons which move down the electron transport chain in chemiosmosis combine with oxygen at the very end of the chain. The energy that these electrons carried from the earlier phases of aerobic cell respiration has been removed.

This electron-enriched oxygen immediately combines with the free hydrogen ions in the mitochondrial matrix to form water. Water formed in this way is referred to as **water of metabolism**.

The free hydrogen ions in the mitochondrial matrix are the result of the passive flow of these hydrogen ions through ATP synthase. It is essential these free hydrogen ions combine with oxygen to form water. The formation of water of metabolism in the mitochondrial matrix keeps the hydrogen ion concentration relatively low. The low hydrogen concentration in the matrix maintains the hydrogen ion concentration gradient between the intermembrane space and the mitochondrial matrix. This allows the **maintenance** of the passive flow of hydrogen ions through ATP synthase and the continued production of ATP in chemiosmosis.

General vocabulary
maintenance the act of making a state or situation continue

Subject vocabulary
cytosol the fluid part of the cell that surrounds and supports organelles

Understanding: The structure of the mitochondrion is adapted to the function it performs.

Model sentence: The mitochondrial structure allows for the efficient formation of ATP in the process of aerobic cell respiration.

Mitochondrial structure or feature	Function
outer mitochondrial membrane	a membrane which separates the contents of the mitochondrion from the rest of the cell
matrix	an internal *cytosol*-like area that contains enzymes for the link reaction and the Krebs cycle
cristae	tube-like projections of the inner membrane into the mitochondrial matrix which allow added membrane surface area for oxidative phosphorylation
inner mitochondrial membrane	a membrane that contains the carriers for the electron transport chain and ATP synthase for chemiosmosis
intermembrane space	space into which hydrogen ions are pumped using energy from the electron transport chain

Skill: Annotation of a diagram of a mitochondrion to indicate the adaptations to its function

Students must be able to label and add notes to a mitochondrial diagram to show the relationship of structure to function. Obtain several electron micrographs or drawings of mitochondria. Annotate these with the names and functions of the mitochondrial parts.

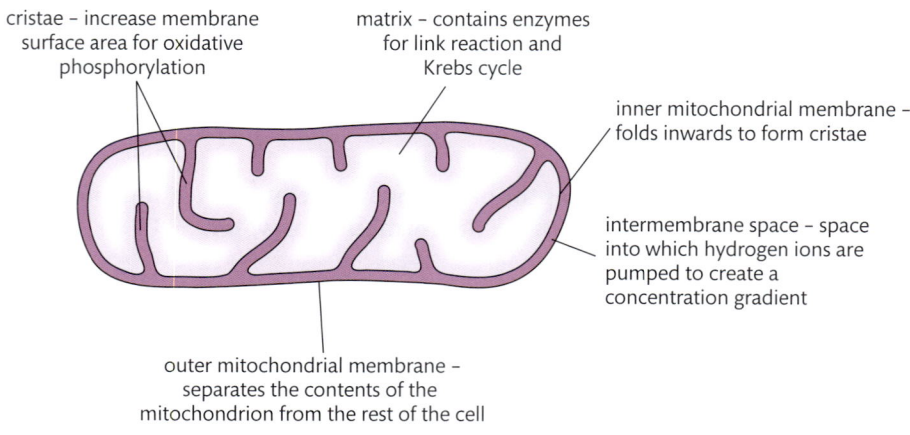

Figure 8.12 *General functions of the parts of a mitochondrion*

Application: **Electron tomography used to produce images of active mitochondria**

Electron tomography studies are being used by scientists to help determine the detailed internal structure of an active mitochondrion. This technique is similar to **CAT (computerized axial tomography) scans** which are used for medical purposes to study internal organs and body structures. Scientists study computerized images of mitochondria produced by this method at various times to develop a better understanding of the internal structure and actions of this essential organelle to aerobic cell respiration.

8.3 Photosynthesis

Main idea
Photosynthesis is a process which converts light energy into chemical energy.

Understanding: Light-dependent reactions take place in the intermembrane space of the **thylakoids**.

Model sentence: **The light-dependent reactions of photosynthesis occur on the thylakoid membrane and within the thylakoid intermembrane spaces.**

Review the parts of a chloroplast presented in the figure below.

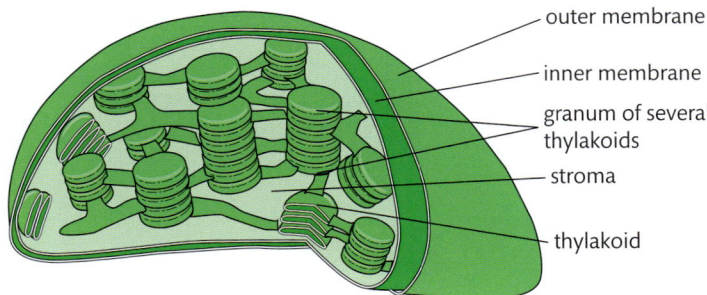

Figure 8.13 *Basic structure and parts of a chloroplast*

Photosynthesis includes two separate, yet connected, reactions. They are:

1 light-dependent reaction

2 light-independent reaction.

These two reactions occur in different parts of the chloroplast.

The light-dependent reaction occurs in the thylakoids of the chloroplast. Notice in the drawing above a thylakoid looks like a flattened sac. A membrane provides the outer most part of the thylakoid. A space known as the intermembrane space occurs within the membrane.

It is important to note from the drawing that thylakoids usually occur in stacks called **grana** (**granum** is singular). The thylakoid membranes contain **pigments** which are involved in the absorption of light energy.

Subject vocabulary

electron tomography studies computerized images of active mitochondria to determine the reactions taking place

CAT (computerized axial tomography) scans computerized internal scans used in medical tests to determine body structures

thylakoids flattened sacs which, when stacked, form grana within chloroplasts

light-dependent reactions reactions of photosynthesis in which light energy is directly needed

granum (plural: grana) stack of thylakoids in the chloroplast

Synonyms
pigments .... colours

Subject vocabulary

light-independent reactions reactions of photosynthesis in which light energy is not directly needed, this reaction uses the products of the light-dependent reactions

photosystems complexes of pigments and a protein matrix occurring on the thylakoid membranes involved in the light-dependent reactions of photosynthesis

photosystem I photosystem of the light-dependent reaction of photosynthesis involved in production of NADPH

photosystem II photosystem of the light-dependent reaction of photosynthesis involved in production of ATP and photolysis

General vocabulary

corresponds is very similar or the same

Understanding: Light-independent reactions take place in the stroma.

Model sentence: A chloroplast's stroma is where the light-independent reactions of photosynthesis occur.

Notice the location of the stroma in the drawing of the chloroplast presented in the previous understanding. The stroma is the cell cytosol-like region of the cell. It corresponds to the matrix of the mitochondrion.

The light-independent reaction of photosynthesis occurs in the stroma of the chloroplast. There are no pigments involved with light absorption in the stroma. The products of the light-dependent reaction are involved in the light-independent reaction.

Understanding: Reduced NADP and ATP are produced in the light-dependent reactions.

Model sentence: The products of the light-dependent reaction which are important to the overall process of photosynthesis are reduced NADP and ATP.

The overall equation representing both reactions of photosynthesis is:

$$6CO_2 + 12H_2O + \text{light energy} \rightarrow C_6H_{12}O_6 + 6H_2O + 6O_2$$

Molecules called pigments are present in specialized regions of the thylakoid membrane. These specialized regions are called **photosystems**. The pigments of the photosystems are quite efficient at absorbing light energy.

The light-dependent reaction of photosynthesis first involves the absorption of light energy. The absorbed light energy is then used to produce these products:

- reduced NADP or NADPH
- ATP.

These two products are necessary for the light-independent reaction of photosynthesis to occur.

Understanding: Absorption of light by photosystems generates excited electrons.

Model sentence: Energized electrons are produced when photosystems on the thylakoid membranes absorb light energy.

There are two types of photosystems which occur on thylakoid membranes. They are:

- **photosystem I**
- **photosystem II**.

Bacteria have only one type of photosystem, photosystem I. Most modern-day plants have both types of photosystems.

Both types of photosystem are composed of the following:
- a protein supporting region or matrix
- a pigment called **chlorophyll *a***
- pigments other than chlorophyll *a* involved in light absorption.

Chlorophyll *a* and the other pigments are **embedded** in the protein matrix of the photosystem. The pigments of the photosystems are involved in the absorption of light. Light is absorbed in packets of energy referred to as **photons**.

Steps in the light-dependent reaction involving the production of excited electrons:

1. One of the pigments of the photosystem absorbs a photon.
2. The energy of a photon is passed to chlorophyll *a* which is present in the **reaction centre**.
3. Electrons of chlorophyll *a* become excited. The chlorophyll *a* is now said to be **photo-activated**.
4. These excited electrons move to a higher energy electron shell. There is one photon of light necessary for each electron energized.
5. The excited electrons are then received by the **primary acceptor** of the reaction centre.

Both types of photosystems follow the same steps in the absorption of light energy to produce energized electrons.

Understanding: Photolysis of water generates electrons for use in the light-dependent reactions.

Model sentence: Electrons from the photolysis of water are used in the light-dependent reaction of photosynthesis.

Water is split by an enzyme to produce free electrons, hydrogen ions, and an oxygen atom.

$$H_2O \rightarrow 2H^+ + 2e^- + \tfrac{1}{2}O_2$$

The splitting of water is driven by the energy provided by light, and is called photolysis. The free electrons are taken up by the chlorophyll *a* molecules which lost their electrons when they were energized. Oxygen is also a product of photolysis and leaves the chloroplast as a waste gas. The hydrogen ions or protons, which are a product of photolysis, add to the protons which exist in the thylakoid space. These protons are also available for reduction reactions occurring in the area.

The presence of light allows two processes to occur in the light-dependent reaction:

1. Electrons of chlorophyll *a* are excited and captured by the primary acceptor of the reaction centre.
2. Photolysis of water occurs resulting in replacement of electrons in chlorophyll *a*. The **splitting** of water due to light occurs over and over so that chlorophyll *a* can continuously have electrons available to be excited or energized.

It is important to note that photolysis only occurs with photosystem II. This indicates that the structures and chemicals necessary for the photolysis process are not present in photosystem I.

Subject vocabulary

chlorophyll *a* type of chlorophyll often found in the reaction centre of a chloroplast

photons units or packets of light energy

reaction centre specific part of a photosystem which has electrons energized to a higher level and moved to an electron transport chain

photo-activated process in which light causes electrons to be energized and moved to a higher level

primary acceptor compound of the reaction centre which receives the energized electrons of chlorophyll *a* and passes them to an electron transport chain

photolysis process in photosynthesis where water molecules are split using the energy from light

General vocabulary

embedded positioned firmly and deeply

splitting dividing or separating something

Understanding: Transfer of excited electrons occurs between carriers in thylakoid membranes.

Model sentence: Energized or excited electrons pass through an electron transport chain involving carriers which exist in the thylakoid membranes.

Electrons of chlorophyll *a* excited by light are transferred to the primary acceptor in the reaction centre known as plastoquinone.

Plastoquinone carries the excited electrons from the reaction centre to the electron transport chain. The electron transport chain is outside the reaction centre. This chain consists of a series of carriers in the thylakoid membranes which includes a centre region referred to as the **cytochrome complex**.

The electron transport chain allows energy to be released in small amounts from the excited electrons as the electrons are transferred from one carrier to another.

These steps occur in photosystem II. The steps of photosystem I will be discussed later.

Subject vocabulary

plastoquinone compound which carries excited electrons from the reaction centre to the electron transport chain in photosystem II

cytochrome complex centre group of carriers in the photosystem II electron transport chain involved with the generation of ATP

proton (H⁺) gradient concentration gradient involving protons inside an intermembrane space and outside the membrane which occurs in chemiosmosis

Understanding: Excited electrons from photosystem II are used to contribute to the generation of a proton gradient.

Model sentence: The excited electrons of photosystem II which move through a thylakoid membrane electron transport chain provide the energy to produce a concentration gradient of protons.

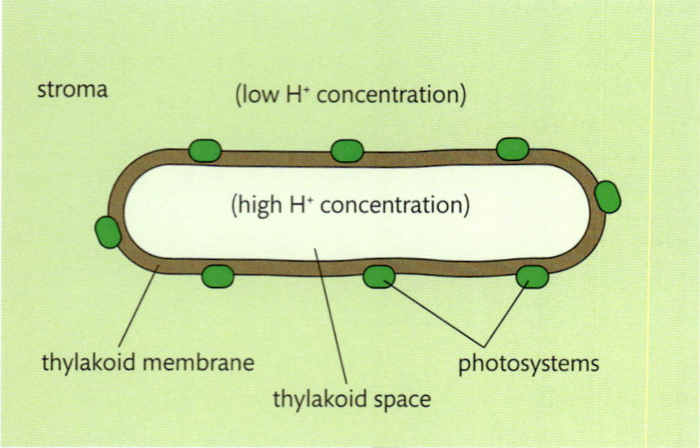

The figure shows a single thylakoid surrounded by stroma in a chloroplast. Notice that many photosystems are present on the thylakoid membrane. The photosystems are embedded in the phospholipid bilayer of the membrane.

Note the **proton (H⁺) gradient** between the thylakoid space and the stroma that surrounds the thylakoid. This gradient is the result of the pumping of protons (H⁺) from the stroma into the thylakoid space. Energy for this pumping action comes from the release of energy in small amounts as excited electrons move down the electron transport chain. Photolysis occurs in the cytosol-like fluid of the thylakoid space and also provides protons (H⁺) to the space.

Figure 8.14 *The structures and conditions needed for chemiosmosis in the light-dependent reaction*

This proton (H⁺) gradient is essential to the next process of the light-dependent reaction called chemiosmosis which allows the generation of ATP.

Understanding: ATP synthase in thylakoids generates ATP using the proton gradient.

Model sentence: The proton (H⁺) gradient between the thylakoid space (intermembrane space) and the stroma allows the passive transport of protons (H⁺) through ATP synthase to generate ATP.

Chemiosmosis occurs and generates ATP when a gradient of protons exists between the thylakoid space (intermembrane space) and the stroma just outside the thylakoid membrane. The small volume of the thylakoid intermembrane space allows a high concentration of protons to be achieved quickly.

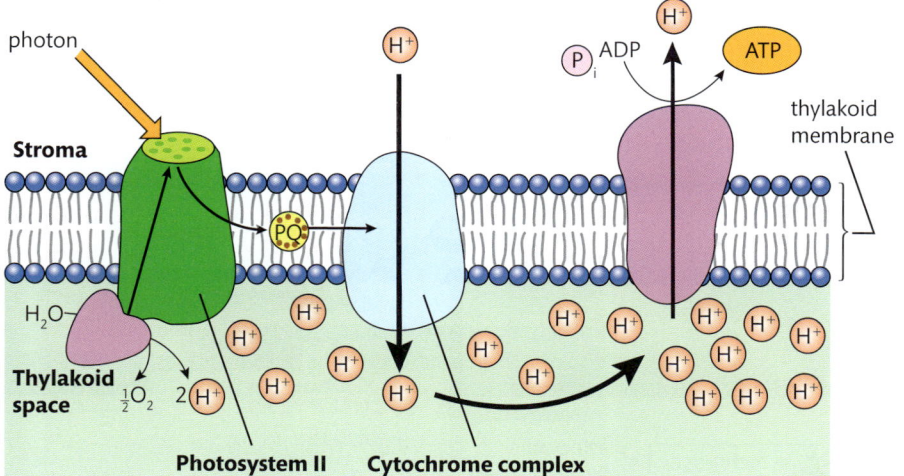

Figure 8.15 *Chemiosmosis at the thylakoid of a chloroplast*

The chemiosmosis which occurs at the thylakoid is very similar to the chemiosmosis which occurs at the mitochondrion. Note that in the diagram above hydrogen ions (protons) move passively from the thylakoid intermembrane space through ATP synthase into the stroma of the chloroplast. The passive transport occurs due to the concentration gradient of hydrogen ions (protons) between the inside thylakoid and the surrounding stroma. As the hydrogen ions pass through the ATP synthase, energy is made available which is used to phosphorylate ADP to form ATP. This type of phosphorylation is referred to as **photophosphorylation** since light is the actual energy source.

The energized electrons which enter the electron transport chain release all the extra energy they received from a photon of light. At the end of the chain they are received by an electron carrier called **plastocyanin**. The plastocyanin will carry these de-energized electrons to photosystem I. The plastocyanin, carrying de-energized electrons from the electron transport chain of photosystem II to photosystem I, allows a connection between the processes which occur in these two photosystems.

Subject vocabulary

photophosphorylation process of adding phosphate to a molecule using the energy from light

plastocyanin compound which carries de-energized electrons from photosystem II to photosystem I

ferredoxin final carrier of the photosystem I electron transport chain of the photosynthesis light-dependent reaction

NADP reductase enzyme which catalyses the transfer of electrons from ferredoxin to NADP to allow formation of NADPH in the photosystem I electron transport chain

Understanding: Excited electrons from photosystem I are used to reduce NADP.

Model sentence: Photons of light in photosystem I are used to excite electrons in order to reduce NADP.

The following events occur in the thylakoid involving photosystem I:

1. A photon of light is absorbed by a pigment in photosystem I.
2. This energy is transferred to a chlorophyll *a* molecule.
3. Electrons of chlorophyll *a* are moved to a higher energy level.
4. These higher energy level electrons are transferred to a primary electron carrier.
5. From the primary electron carrier, the electrons move down a short electron transport chain combining with **ferredoxin** at the end.
6. An enzyme known as **NADP reductase** catalyses the transfer of the electrons from ferredoxin to NADP to allow the formation of NADPH.

The energized (excited) electrons of photosystem I which move away from chlorophyll *a* are replaced by the de-energized electrons carried by plastocyanin from photosystem II. The de-energized electrons of photosystem II replacing the energized (excited) electrons of photosystem I links these two photosystems together.

Hints for success: Study the following figure showing the major processes of photosystems II and I. Notice the linking of the two photosystems by the passing of electrons from photosystem II to photosystem I.

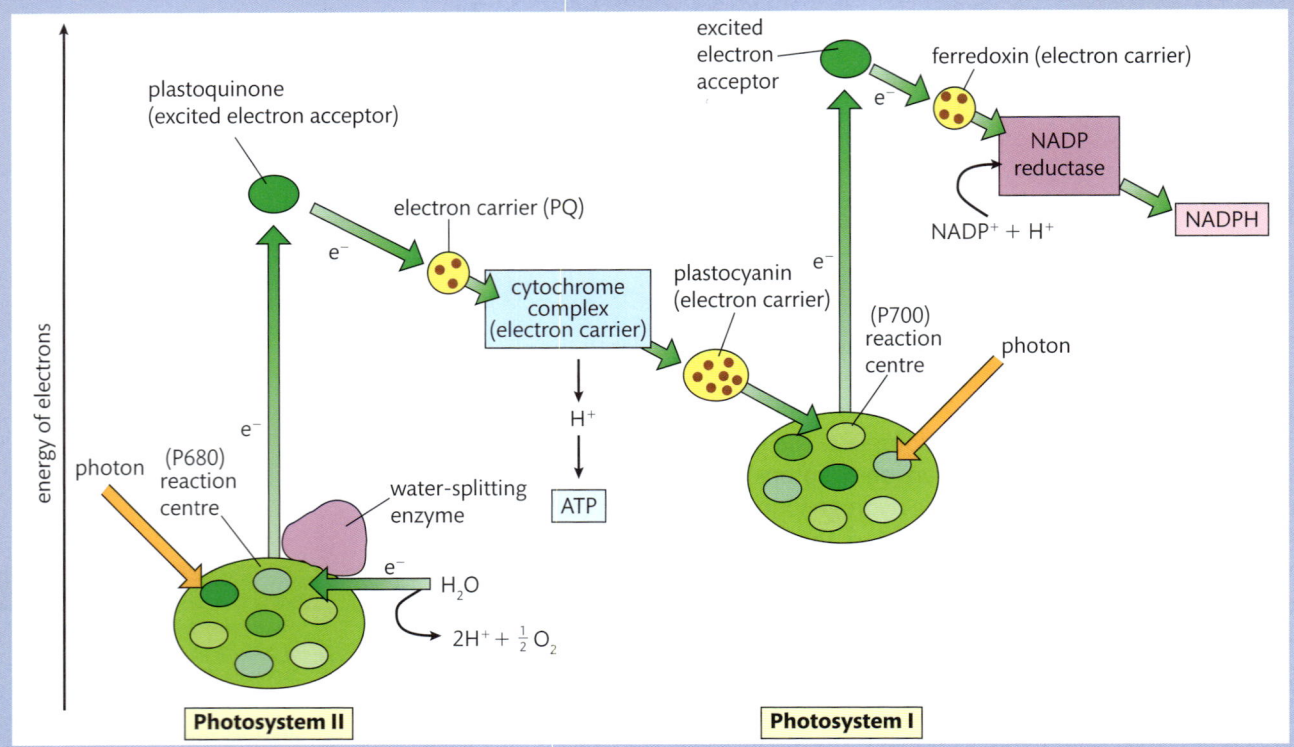

Figure 8.16 *The light-dependent reaction of photosynthesis*

This figure represents the light-dependent reaction of photosynthesis. It is especially important to note the two major products of this reaction: ATP and NADPH. These two products are essential to the light-independent reaction of photosynthesis.

Subject vocabulary

ribulose bisphosphate first compound of the Calvin cycle of the light-independent reaction, also known as RuBP

Understanding: In the light-independent reactions a carboxylase catalyses the carboxylation of ribulose bisphosphate.

Model sentence: The light-independent reaction begins with the addition of carbon to **ribulose bisphosphate**.

The light-independent reaction of photosynthesis occurs within the stroma of the chloroplast. The ATP and NADPH produced by the light-dependent reaction provide the energy and reducing power for the light-independent reaction to occur.

Oxygen was released from the chloroplast as a result of photolysis in the light-dependent reaction. The light-dependent reaction did not produce glucose ($C_6H_{12}O_6$). The ATP and NADPH from the light-dependent reaction is used to produce glucose in the light-independent reaction.

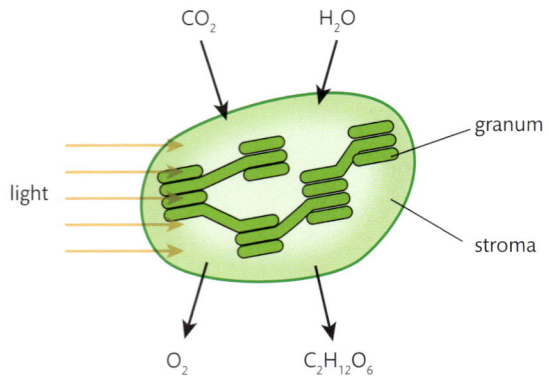

Figure 8.17 *The process of photosynthesis*

174 | 8.3 Photosynthesis

The light-independent reaction involves the Calvin cycle. The Calvin cycle begins and ends with the same substance, ribulose bisphosphate.

The first reaction of the Calvin cycle is the addition of carbon to ribulose bisphosphate. Ribulose bisphosphate is often abbreviated as **RuBP**. This process of adding a carbon to a compound is called **carboxylation**. A carboxylase enzyme, **RuBP carboxylase**, catalyses the carboxylation of the ribulose bisphosphate. RuBP carboxylase is usually referred to as **rubisco**. The carbon used in the carboxylation reaction comes from carbon dioxide, which along with water are the raw materials of photosynthesis. This is shown in the diagram below.

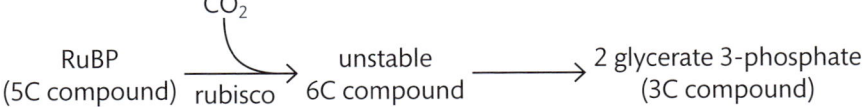

RuBP is a 5-carbon (5C) compound. Adding one carbon from carbon dioxide to RuBP produces an unstable 6-carbon compound. This addition of carbon to RuBP is called carboxylation. Rubisco is the enzyme which catalyses the carboxylation process. The unstable 6-carbon compound immediately breaks down into two compounds of glycerate 3-phosphate. Glycerate 3-phosphate is a 3-carbon compound.

> **Subject vocabulary**
>
> **RuBP** ribulose bisphosphate
>
> **carboxylation** process in which a carbon is added to another compound
>
> **RuBP carboxylase** enzyme which catalyses the addition of carbon from carbon dioxide onto RuBP in the Calvin cycle, also known as rubisco
>
> **rubisco** RuBP carboxylase
>
> **glycerate 3-phosphate** 3-carbon compound formed immediately after splitting of the unstable 6-carbon compound formed after carboxylation of RuBP in the Calvin cycle
>
> **triose phosphate** 3-carbon carbohydrate with a phosphate group attached produced in the glycolysis pathway

Understanding: Glycerate 3-phosphate is reduced to triose phosphate using reduced NADP and ATP.

Model sentence: NADPH and ATP from the light-dependent reaction are used to reduce glycerate 3-phosphate to triose phosphate in the Calvin cycle.

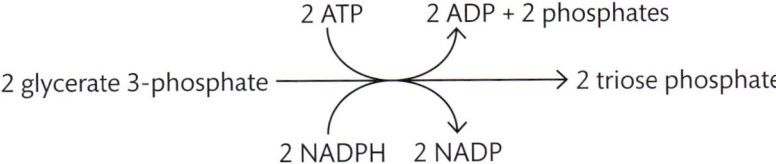

The two **glycerate 3-phosphate** molecules formed from the carboxylation of RuBP are reduced to form two **triose phosphate** molecules in the Calvin cycle. ATP provides the energy for this reduction to occur. NADPH provides the hydrogen which is needed to convert glycerate 3-phosphate to triose phosphate. The ATP and NADPH come from the light-dependent reaction of photosynthesis.

The importance of this reduction process is to get the hydrogen to oxygen ratio in triose phosphate to 2:1. This will allow the production of a carbohydrate from triose phosphate molecules.

Understanding: Triose phosphate is used to regenerate RuBP and produce carbohydrates.

Model sentence: The production of triose phosphate in the Calvin cycle allows for the regeneration of RuBP and the formation of carbohydrates.

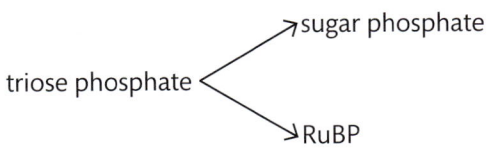

8 Metabolism, cell respiration, and photosynthesis | 175

Subject vocabulary

hexose 6-carbon monosaccharide

Triose phosphate formed in the Calvin cycle may be used to produce sugar phosphate or RuBP. The sugar phosphate produced is a **hexose**. It may be used to form a more complex carbohydrate such as starch. The sugar phosphate also allows the formation of the most recognized product of photosynthesis which is glucose.

Understanding: Ribulose bisphosphate is reformed using ATP.

Model sentence: Triose phosphate from the Calvin cycle allows the reformation of RuBP using ATP.

Any metabolic pathway which is a cycle must begin and end with the same compound. The Calvin cycle begins and ends with RuBP. Most of the triose phosphate molecules produced in the Calvin cycle are used to reform RuBP. Triose phosphate molecules must go through a series of enzyme-catalysed reactions to reform RuBP. ATP is essential to provide the energy necessary for these catalysed reactions.

Study the figure below to understand the Calvin cycle. The figure also shows how RuBP is reformed from triose phosphate. In the figure, circles represent carbon atoms.

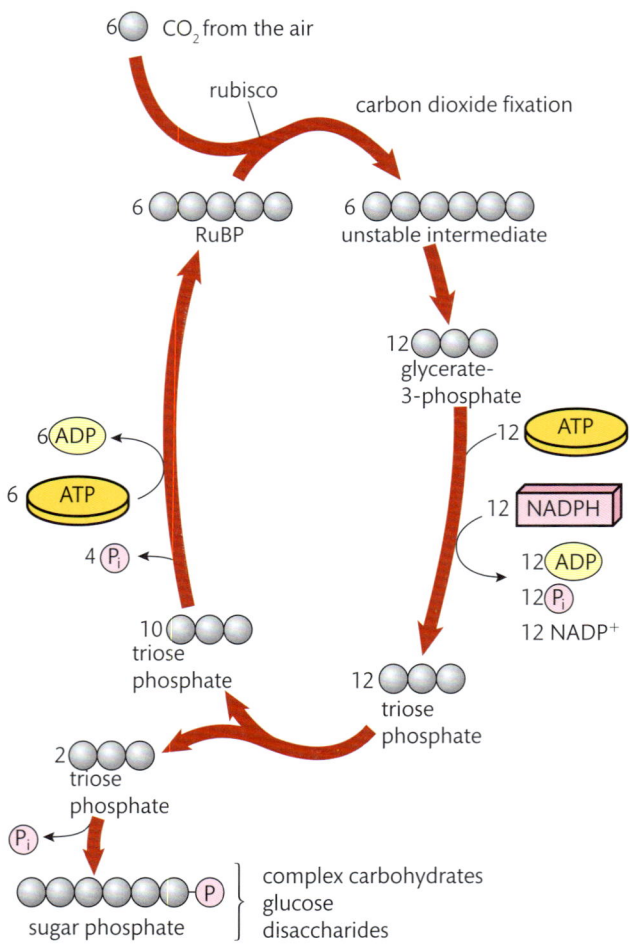

Figure 8.18 *The Calvin cycle*

Notice in the figure that most of the triose phosphate molecules are used to reform RuBP. This allows the Calvin cycle to continue over and over again. Only 2 out of 12 triose phosphates are used to produce the sugar phosphate. Careful observation of the figure will show that it takes six turns of the Calvin cycle to produce one sugar phosphate.

Application: **Calvin's experiment to elucidate the carboxylation of RuBP**

Melvin Calvin and his team used chromatography, radioactive tracers, and autoradiography to discover the details of the cycle which produced carbohydrates in the light-independent reaction of photosynthesis. He and his team used a 'lollipop' apparatus and a type of green alga to determine the compounds produced at various stages of the cycle. Techniques developed by his team and earlier researchers were applied to allow the determination of these compounds. Because of his work, the carbon fixation cycle of the light-independent reaction of photosynthesis was named the Calvin cycle.

Understanding: The structure of the chloroplast is adapted to its function in photosynthesis.

Model sentence: **The functions of the various parts of the chloroplast in photosynthesis are directly related to their structure.**

The following table summarizes the relationship of chloroplast structure to function.

Chloroplast structure	Function allowed
extensive membrane surface area of the thylakoids	allows greater absorption of light by photosynthesis, also allows more surface area for the photosystems and the electron transport chains
small space (lumen) within the thylakoids	allows for faster accumulation of protons (H⁺) to create a concentration gradient
stroma region similar to the cytosol of the cell	allows an area for the enzymes necessary for the Calvin cycle to be stored and to work in
double membrane on the outside	isolates the working parts and enzymes of the chloroplast from the surrounding cell cytosol

Skill: **Annotation of a diagram to indicate the adaptations of a chloroplast to its function**

Add notes to the following diagram of a chloroplast explaining the adaptations of the chloroplast to its function.

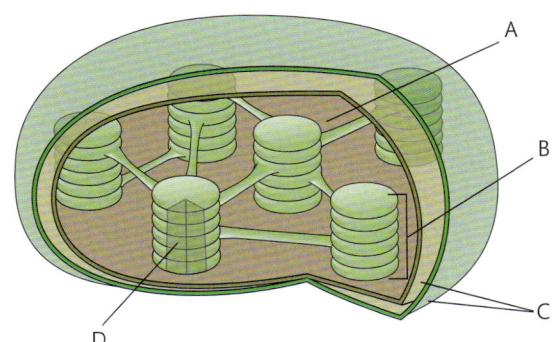

Figure 8.19 Basic structure of a chloroplast

Answers: A Stroma allowing for the storage and function of enzymes involved in the Calvin cycle
B Granum or stack of thylakoids allowing more membranes and thylakoid spaces for the light-dependent reaction to occur
C Double membrane to isolate the working parts and enzymes of the chloroplast from the surrounding cell cytosol
D Small lumen within thylakoid allowing for a more rapid build-up of H⁺ so that chemiosmosis may occur to generate ATP

Subject vocabulary

radioactive tracers elements or compounds giving off radioactivity and are used in studying organism reactions

autoradiography study of radioactive substances and images produced from them

carbon fixation cycle Calvin cycle in which carbons are fixed to RuBP

lumen area within surrounding walls or membranes; usually used for the cavity of a tubular structure such as a blood vessel

Synonyms

accumulation . build up

General vocabulary

adaptation(s) change(s) which make(s) something more suitable for a situation

9 Plant biology

9.1 Transport in the xylem of plants

Main idea
The **xylem** is able to carry out its functions efficiently due to its structure.

Understanding: Transpiration is the inevitable consequence of gas exchange in the leaf.

Model sentence: The exchange of carbon dioxide and oxygen between the leaf interior and the surrounding environment includes transpiration.

Transpiration is the loss of water vapour from leaves and other parts of the plant that are above the ground. Most transpiration occurs through leaf structures called **stomata** (singular: **stoma**). Most of the leaf stomata are on the underside of the leaf. The underside of the leaf receives less light. Less light results in a lower temperature. Lower temperatures result in decreased transpiration. The positioning of stomata on the leaf underside is one plant **adaptation** which decreases water loss. **Guard cells** are a second plant adaptation which decreases water loss. Note the drawing of a stoma and its two accompanying guard cells.

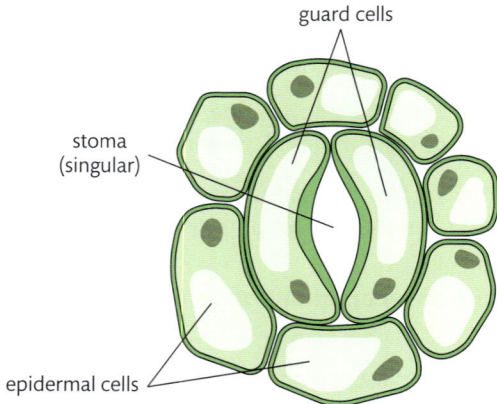

Figure 9.1 *A leaf stoma and its guard cells*

The guard cells control the size of the stoma. When the guard cells are enlarged due to increased amounts of water, the stoma gets larger. Guard cells with little water result in a small opening or stoma. Stomata which are smaller or closed decrease water loss from the leaf. In many plants, guard cells close stomata during the warmer parts of the day to decrease water loss.

A disadvantage of plants having stomata is loss of water through transpiration. The water movement in transpiration is good for the plant because it allows **solute** distribution throughout the plant. These solutes were initially absorbed by the roots. However, the stomata are essential for the exchange of gases between the inside and the outside of the leaf. Carbon dioxide and oxygen are the two gases of **photosynthesis** that are maintained at the correct level for photosynthetic activity due to movement through the stomata.

Subject vocabulary

xylem tissue which conducts water and minerals in plants

transpiration loss of water vapour from leaves and other aerial parts of the plant

stoma (plural: stomata) opening, usually on the underside of leaves, through which gas exchange and transpiration occur

guard cells specialized leaf cells involved in transpiration control

solute molecules dissolved in a solvent (water)

photosynthesis process which converts light energy into chemical energy

General vocabulary

adaptation change which makes something more suitable for a situation

Skill: Design of an experiment to test hypotheses about the effect of temperature or humidity on transpiration rates

You need to know how to measure transpiration rates using a **potometer**. A potometer is a rather simple device used to measure transpiration rates in plants. There are several ways a potometer may be constructed. One way is presented in the following figure.

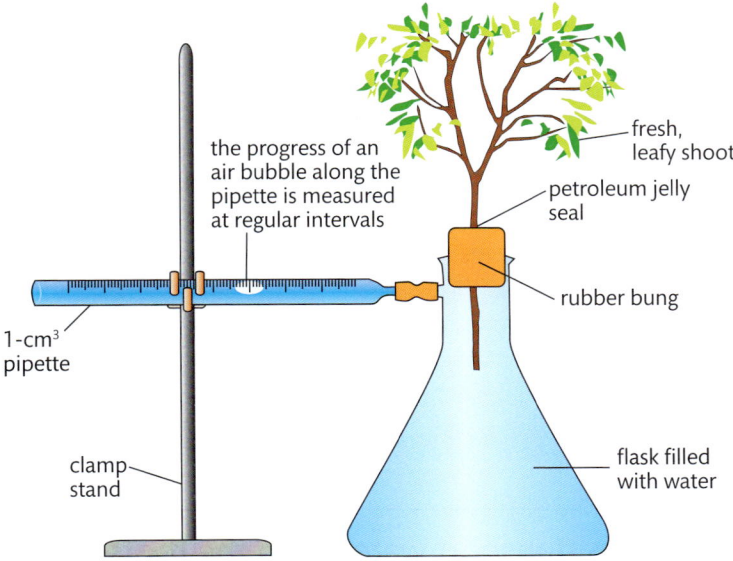

Figure 9.2 *An example of a potometer used to measure transpiration rate*

You are to design an experiment to measure the effects of temperature or humidity on transpiration rates in a plant species using your constructed potometer. Some findings you would expect from carrying out this procedure should include:

- The rate of transpiration increases as the surrounding temperature rises.
- The rate of transpiration increases as the surrounding **humidity** decreases.

Other environmental factors which usually affect transpiration rates include:

- Wind usually increases transpiration rates by carrying humid air away from the stomata.
- Low soil water content may result in more water lost by transpiration than the water brought in by the roots. This will result in less water in the guard cells and stomata closing.
- High carbon dioxide levels around the plant leaves usually cause the guard cells to close due to loss of water pressure (**turgor**) in the guard cells.

Application: Adaptations of plants in deserts for water conservation

Plants that survive in the desert have adaptations for water conservation. Plants that survive in the desert are referred to as **xerophytes**. These adaptations include:

- Smaller leaves which brings about a decrease in the number of stomata.
- Stomata located in pits or crypts on the leaf to increase humidity near the opening and minimize transpiration.
- Thick, waxy leaf coverings called a **cuticle**.
- A period of **dormancy** or even a **shedding** of leaves during the driest months.
- Hair-like structures on the leaf near stomata which trap water vapour. This maintains a higher humidity near the stomata.
- Using a different photosynthetic pathway in which the stomata are open at night and closed during the day. These are called **CAM plants**. They use a unique 4-carbon compound to attach to and release carbon dioxide in the photosynthesis process.

Subject vocabulary

potometer specialized device used to measure transpiration rates in plants

turgor water pressure within a cell

xerophytes plants with specialized adaptations to survive in the desert

cuticle waxy, protective, water-conserving layer on some leaves

dormancy inactivity

CAM plants plants carrying out a type of photosynthesis that is an adaptation to arid environments

General vocabulary

humidity the amount of water in the air

Synonyms

shedding........ dropping/loss

Subject vocabulary

halophytes plants with specialized adaptations to survive in high saline areas

succulents plants which possess fleshy, water-storing leaves

vacuoles cell storage structures especially visible in plants

General vocabulary

cohesion attraction of one water molecule for another, two like materials stick together or attach to one another

adhesion process where two different substances stick together or attach to one another

Application: Adaptations of plants in saline soils for water conservation

Plants which survive and grow in saline soils are referred to as **halophytes**. These adaptations include:

- Plants store large amounts of water in their tissues becoming **succulents**. This large store of water serves to dilute the salt concentration.
- Storing the salts present in **vacuoles** stops the salts from negatively affecting the functions of the plant.
- Leaf surface area is reduced.
- Stomata are sunken into the surface of the leaf in pits or crypts.
- Thickened cuticles.
- Plants possess structures which allow excretion from the cells of the salts brought in from the soil.
- A period of dormancy or loss of leaves when environmental conditions would result in high transpiration rates.

Hints for success: It is extremely important for a plant to have adaptations to minimize loss of water through its stomata. The stomata may pose a problem in water loss from the plant. However, they are essential for gas exchange in the process of photosynthesis.

Understanding: Plants transport water from the roots to the leaves to replace losses from transpiration.

Model sentence: Water lost from the plant by transpiration is replaced by water supplied from the roots.

Transpired water has to be replaced by the intake of water at the roots. There is a continuous stream of water from the roots to the upper parts of a plant. This upward, continuous stream of water through the plant provides both the water and the minerals necessary for the life of the plant.

The stream of water from the roots occurs in the xylem of the plant. **Cohesion**, **adhesion**, and the active uptake of minerals allow the maintenance of this stream of water in the xylem.

Understanding: The cohesive property of water and the structure of the xylem vessels allow transport under tension.

Model sentence: Two features that allow water transport in plants are cohesive properties between water molecules and the structure of xylem vessels.

Two features which allow water transport in plants are:
- cohesion
- structure of xylem vessels.

Cohesion in this case involves water molecules. Water is a polar molecule. The oxygen regions of the water molecule have a relatively negative charge. The hydrogen regions of the same molecule have a relatively positive charge.

Opposite electrical charges attract. In water the negatively charged regions are attracted to the positively charged regions of other water molecules. This attraction helps maintain the continuous columns of water in plants which occur in the xylem vessels.

Xylem vessels are formed when living cells arranged in long columns die and the contents break down. The ends of the cells which connect to one another develop large **pores** or perforations. This creates continuous, relatively uninterrupted tubes for water. The xylem vessel cell walls are thickened due to the addition of a material called **lignin**. The lignin is combined with the existing **cellulose** of the cell walls of the xylem to create a strong supporting part of the plant. The thick xylem walls are also necessary to withstand a negative pressure due to tension, which occurs within them due to water loss from transpiration.

There are regions of these xylem cell walls that are **hydrophilic**. The water of the xylem is attracted to these regions. This attraction between different molecules due to electrical charge differences is called adhesion. Adhesion also plays a role in the passage of water upward in a plant.

Skill: Drawing the structure of primary xylem vessels in sections of stems based on microscope images

You should be able to draw xylem vessels as they would appear in plant stem microscopic images.

Subject vocabulary

xylem vessels columns of dead xylem forming cells without cytoplasm and with pores on their ends

lignin complex polymer combined with the cellulose of xylem cell walls which provides strength

cellulose complex carbohydrate present in plant cell walls

hydrophilic 'water loving', substances that dissolve in water

Synonyms

pore .... hole/opening

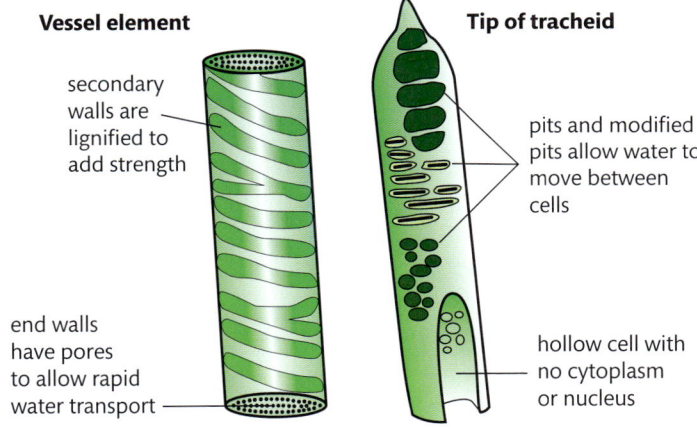

Figure 9.3 *Representation of plant xylem*

Understanding: The adhesive property of water and evaporation generate tension forces in leaf cell walls.

Model sentence: The evaporation of water and the polar attraction of water to surrounding structures create forces of tension within leaf cells.

The **intercellular spaces** in leaves normally have a high concentration of water molecules. It is the water molecules of the leaf intercellular spaces that have the potential to move to the leaf stomata. Molecules of water lost by evaporation through the stomata are replaced by water moving out of the xylem vessels and into the leaf intercellular space. This is partly due to the cohesion forces which exist between water molecules. However, there are adhesion properties at work as well. Water is attracted to polar regions of the leaf cell walls. A molecule of water lost by evaporation will **initiate** adhesion forces between water molecules and the cell walls to bring the next water molecule to the location. This adhesion force that

Subject vocabulary

evaporation water changing from a liquid to a gaseous state

intercellular space space between cells

Synonyms

initiate .... start/begin

Subject vocabulary

transpirational pull pull or tension exerted on xylem columns of water as a result of transpiration

ion charged atom or group of atoms

osmosis movement of water through a membrane along a concentration gradient

epidermal of, or related to, the outer surface or epidermis

root hairs specialized extensions of root epidermal cells which increase the surface area of these cells for added water and mineral uptake

protein pumps proteins of the cell membrane involved in the transport of specific materials with the use of energy

plasma membrane membrane which surrounds the cell

mutualistic relationship relationship between two organisms in which both are helped

nutrient chemical material a cell or organism needs

capillary tubing glass tubing with small lumen used to demonstrate adhesion and cohesion

Synonyms

absorption ..... taking in
specific .... particular

General vocabulary

continuous continuing to happen or exist without stopping

absorbent able to easily take in liquids

---

pulls the next molecule into position is referred to as tension. The pull of the water molecules towards the stomata creates a tension called **transpirational pull**. This transpirational pull exists in the xylem and the leaf intercellular spaces all the way from the stomata of the leaves to the very lowest root structures. The column of water in the xylem is maintained by cohesion amongst the water molecules.

> **Hints for success:** Cohesion and adhesion are both at work in order to allow a continual supply of water necessary for the plant to carry out photosynthesis and remain alive. These forces are strong enough to ensure continuous columns of water in the plant xylem vessels all the way from the deepest root structures to the tallest stem and leaf structures. Root pressure is also involved in maintaining these columns of water.

Understanding: Active uptake of mineral **ions** in the roots causes **absorption** of water by **osmosis**.

Model sentence: The osmosis of water from the soil into a plant's root cells is due to the active uptake of mineral ions into the root.

A major function of roots is the uptake of water and mineral ions. Roots are efficient at this uptake function because of an extensive branching pattern and because of specialized **epidermal** structures called **root hairs**. The extensive branching pattern and the root hairs increase the surface area over which water and mineral ions may be absorbed.

Water moves into the root hairs from the soil because root cells have a higher mineral ion concentration and a lower water concentration than the surrounding soil. The build-up of the mineral ion concentration within the root hairs is due to active transport of the various ions from the soil into the root cells. This active transport involves very **specific protein pumps** for each ion in the root cell **plasma membranes**.

There is a **mutualistic relationship** between some plants' roots and a fungus. The fungus helps the plant by moving some mineral ions into the root. The plant helps the fungus by providing sugars and possibly other **nutrients**.

Water moves into the root cells by osmosis because of the high mineral ion concentration within the root cells.

Note that both active and passive transport are involved in the movement of water from the soil into the root system of plants. Active transport occurs when mineral ions are moved into the cell through protein carriers. Passive transport occurs when water moves by osmosis into the root cells.

Application: Models of water transport in xylem

Use all the available information to produce a model which represents water transport in the xylem of plants. **Capillary tubing** could be used in your model to represent the xylem with **continuous** columns of water in plants. Both adhesion and cohesion may be demonstrated using the capillary tubing. You could use a container of a measured amount of water into which one end of the capillary tubing is placed. Filter paper or some other type of **absorbent** paper could be used to draw the column of water out of the container and upward into the capillary tubing. The construction of your model will depend on the materials you have available. A model constructed correctly will provide a very good demonstration of how water moves upward in plants.

Hints for success: Study the following figure which provides an overview of the mechanism for upward movement of water in land plants.

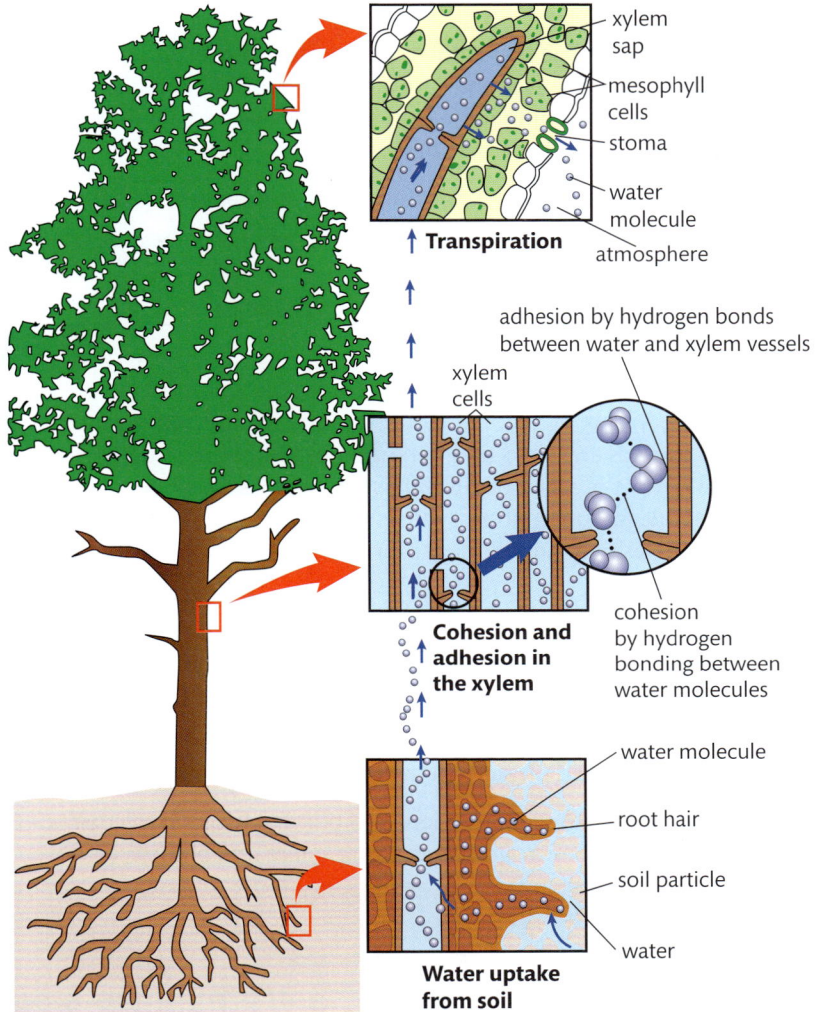

Figure 9.4 *Upward movement of water in land plants*

9.2 Transport in the phloem of plants

Main idea
The phloem is able to carry out its functions efficiently due to its structure.

Understanding: Plants transport organic compounds from sources to sinks.

Model sentence: The **phloem** of plants transports organic compounds such as sugars and amino acids from **source** areas to **sink** areas.

Xylem and phloem are the two major types of transport tissue in plants. Xylem transports water and minerals. Phloem transports organic **compounds**. Phloem is mostly made up of **sieve tube members**, also known as sieve tube elements, and

Subject vocabulary

phloem vascular tissue type in plants involved with transport of organic substances from sources to sinks

source area of high organic substance concentration in the pressure-flow hypothesis of phloem transport

sink area of low organic substance concentration in the pressure-flow hypothesis of phloem transport

sieve tube members cells of the phloem connected to one another by sieve plates to form sieve tubes

General vocabulary

compounds a combination of two or more parts, substances, or qualities

9 Plant biology | 183

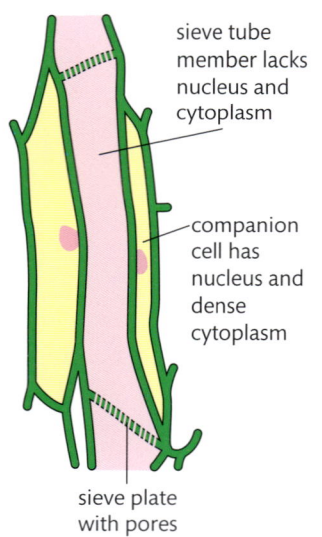

Figure 9.5 *The structure of phloem, including the sieve tube member and accompanying companion cell*

their **companion cells**. Sieve tube members are connected to one another by sieve plates to form **sieve tubes**. Study the figure.

Notice the **sieve plates** have pores at the ends of sieve tube members. These **pores** allow the movement of water and dissolved organic molecules from one sieve tube member to another. The sieve tube members lack nuclei and have only small amounts of **cytoplasm**. However, they are alive and are able to maintain a functional cell membrane. The companion cells are also alive and aid in the transport process which occurs in the sieve tubes.

Phloem tissue transports organic compounds from sources to sinks within the plant.
- A source is a plant organ or region that is a net producer or storage area of a particular organic compound.
- A sink is a plant organ or region that uses or stores a particular organic compound.

Sugars, usually sucrose, are among the most common organic compounds transported from source to sink by phloem tissue. It is possible for some plant structures to be both sources and sinks at different times. **Bulbs** are structures which are associated with the roots of some plants. Bulbs often act as a sink in the summer as they store sugar produced during photosynthesis. These same bulbs may act as a source in the early spring as they provide sugar for stem and leaf development.

The movement of organic compounds in plants is called **translocation**. These organic compounds are dissolved in water. The combination of water and organic compounds in phloem sieve tubes is called **phloem sap**. Sugars and amino acids are the most common compounds of phloem sap. Other compounds found in the phloem **sap** are plant hormones and small RNA molecules.

Skill: Identification of xylem and phloem in microscope images of stem and root

It is essential for you to be able to identify xylem and phloem tissue in microscope images of plants. Below are two micrographs showing xylem and phloem tissue.

Subject vocabulary

companion cells living cells in the phloem involved in maintaining phloem functions

sieve tubes functional columns of the phloem through which the phloem sap flows, also known as sieve elements

sieve plates structures with pores connecting adjacent sieve tube members

cytoplasm region of the cell within the plasma membrane in which the cell organelles exist

bulb storage region of nutrients in the plant root region, serving as a source of nutrients in seasons with early growth

translocation movement of organic compounds in plants

phloem sap contents of the fluid within the phloem sieve elements often containing sugars and amino acids as well as water

Synonyms

pore .... hole/opening

General vocabulary

sap the watery substance that carries food through a plant

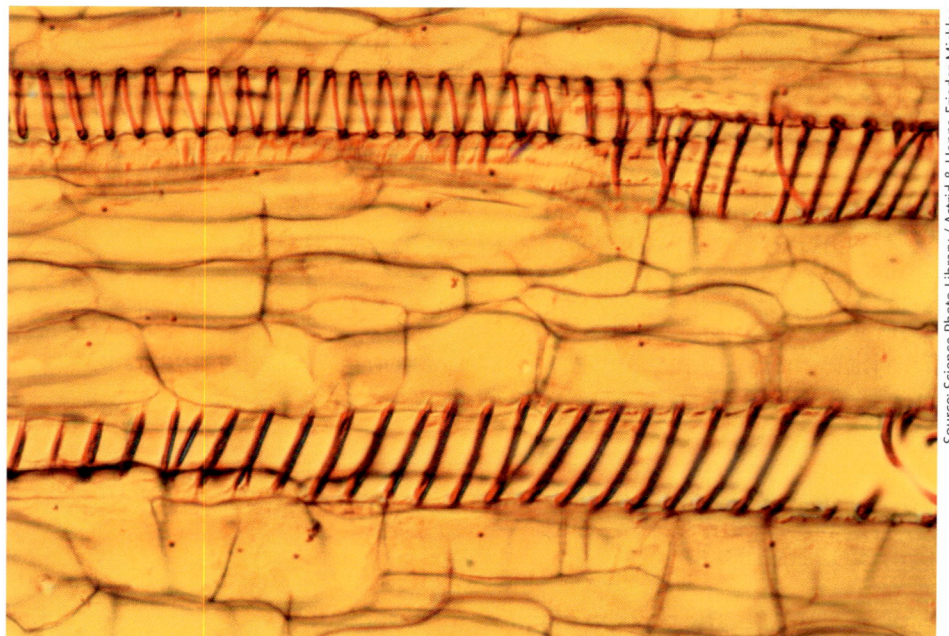

Figure 9.6 *Light micrograph of pumpkin tissue showing the lignin of the xylem vessel elements*

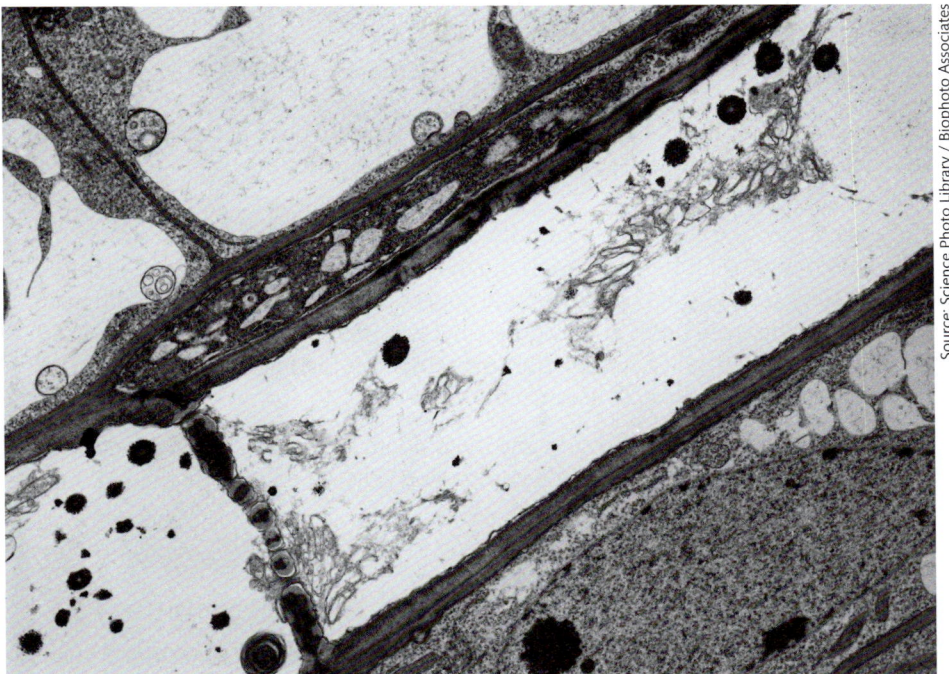

Figure 9.7 *TEM of a phloem sieve tube and its companion cell*

Study the examples above and search for other micrographs on the internet to develop your skills in identifying xylem and phloem tissue.

Microscopic cross-sections of stems and roots will usually show xylem cells are larger than phloem cells. **Vascular bundles** will usually have phloem cells closer to the outside of the plant than xylem cells. Analyse microscope cross-sections of roots and stems to verify these statements.

Understanding: Incompressibility of water allows transport along hydrostatic pressure gradients.

Model sentence: Phloem sap moves from areas of high pressure to areas of low pressure within the plant.

Water has many properties which makes it essential to the everyday functions of life. One property is that it is relatively **incompressible**. Two factors especially important in causing this incompressibility are:

- Water has a rather dense molecular structure as a liquid. Even when water is cooled to form ice, the ice has a lower density than liquid water.
- The numerous interactions amongst the water molecules. An example of the interactions are hydrogen bonds, which form between oppositely charged regions of the individual molecules.

It is this incompressibility which allows water to easily flow through tubes. The incompressibility of water also allows water to flow from areas in the plant of high water pressure to areas in the plant of low water pressure.

The **hydrostatic pressure** of water in a plant refers to the pressure water and its dissolved contents places on its confining structure such as the phloem sieve tubes. A **hydrostatic pressure gradient** in a plant's phloem refers to areas in the sieve tubes having different pressures pushing against the walls. Water movement in plant phloem occurs along hydrostatic pressure gradients.

Subject vocabulary

vascular bundles groups of vascular cells found together in stems and roots of some plants

hydrostatic pressure pressure of water and its dissolved contents on their confining structures such as on the cell walls of the phloem sieve tubes

hydrostatic pressure gradient two areas connected in which one area has a higher hydrostatic pressure than the other, fluids will flow from the high pressure area to the low pressure area

General vocabulary

incompressible not able to be pressed together any closer

Understanding: Active transport is used to load organic compounds into phloem sieve tubes at the source.

Model sentence: Source areas in phloem sieve tubes use active transport of sucrose to produce high hydrostatic pressure regions.

The sugar **sucrose** is the form of carbohydrate most often carried from source to sink in phloem sieve tubes. Sucrose is the major organic compound loaded into phloem sieve tubes by active transport at source areas of a plant. The loading of sucrose into the sieve tubes at the source involves **proton pumps** and specialized membrane proteins called **cotransport proteins**. This loading is an example of **chemiosmosis**, a type of active transport.

The companion cells which accompany the phloem sieve tubes are involved with this active transport process. It is the companion cells which provide the **ATP** for the loading to occur.

Understanding: High concentrations of **solutes** in the phloem at the source lead to water uptake by osmosis.

Model sentence: The active transport of sucrose creates a hypertonic solution at the phloem source areas which causes passive water flow into these areas.

Study the following sequence of events which occur at the phloem source:
- **Active transport** of sucrose into the phloem source area occurs.
- A **hypertonic solution** in the phloem results from this active transport with a relatively lower water concentration than the surrounding fluid.
- Water then moves from the surrounding fluid into the phloem source area attempting to equalize the water concentration inside and outside the phloem sieve tubes.

The water moving in this system from an area of higher water concentration to an area of lower water concentration is a passive process. The movement of water is an example of osmosis.

> **Hints for success:** Water moves by osmosis from a **hypotonic solution** across cell membranes to a hypertonic solution without the need of energy from the cell. This **passive transport** of water into the source only occurs after sucrose has been actively transported into the same source area.

Understanding: Raised hydrostatic pressure causes the contents of the phloem to flow towards sinks.

Model sentence: Movement along hydrostatic pressure gradients in the phloem sieve tubes results in the flow from source to sink.

Both active and passive transport occurs at phloem sources to cause increased hydrostatic pressures. Sucrose is removed from the phloem sap in the sink areas. This sucrose may be used for metabolic needs in the sink area or it may be stored in the form of starch in the vacuoles of surrounding cells. The continuous removal of sucrose from the sink results in the maintenance of a relatively low hydrostatic

---

Subject vocabulary

sucrose disaccharide of glucose and fructose

proton pumps protein in the cell membrane which uses ATP to transport hydrogen ions out of a cell against a concentration gradient

cotransport proteins proteins of the cell membranes which aid in the transport of compounds across the cell membrane

chemiosmosis process in which ATP is produced due to protons diffusing through ATP synthase in thylakoid and cristae membranes

ATP a molecule used as a source of chemical energy

solute molecules dissolved in a solvent (water)

active transport cellular transport requiring energy (ATP) from the cell

hypertonic solution a solution with a higher concentration of solute(s) and a lower concentration of water (the solvent)

hypotonic solution a solution with a lower concentration of solute(s) and a higher concentration of solvent (water)

passive transport cellular transport not requiring cellular energy, occurs along a concentration gradient

pressure at this location. It is this hydrostatic pressure gradient which results in the flow of phloem sap from source to sink.

The relatively pure water left after the removal of sucrose at the sink is moved along a concentration gradient into xylem vessels to enter the xylem transpirational stream or to be used at another plant source site.

This complete process explaining the movement of phloem sap through plants is known as the **pressure-flow hypothesis**.

The following figure provides an overview of the pressure-flow hypothesis of phloem sap movement.

Application: Structure–function relationships of phloem sieve tubes

There are several structural features of phloem tissue which allow it to carry out its functions. The table below summarises the functions of the structures.

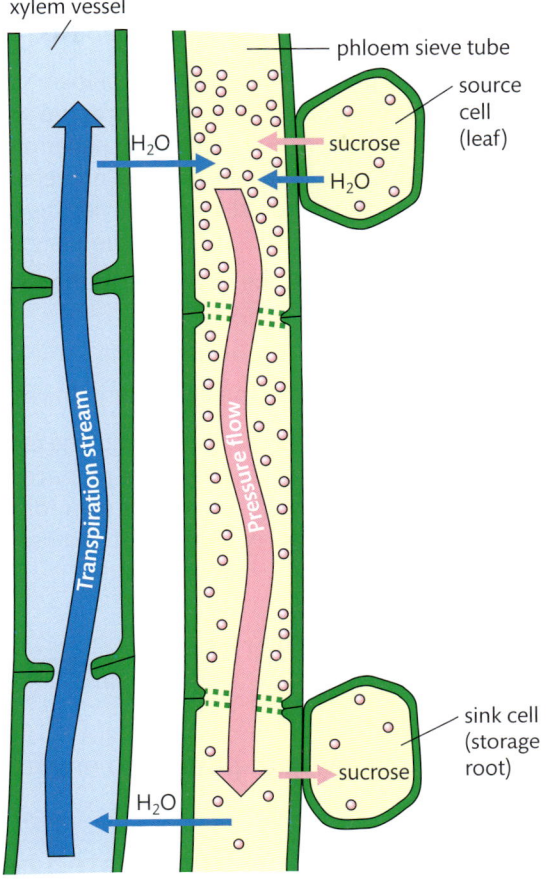

Figure 9.8 *The pressure–flow hypothesis*

Subject vocabulary

pressure-flow hypothesis presently most accepted hypothesis of water and content movement within the phloem of plants

mitochondrion (plural: mitochondria) cell organelle involved in cell respiration

General vocabulary

rigid stiff/not moving or bending

Synonyms

pore .... hole/opening

Phloem structure or feature	Function allowed by structure or feature
living sieve tube cells	ensures the presence of a cell membrane to allow osmosis and the active transport of organic compounds, mostly sucrose, into the sieve tube source areas
companion cells	have numerous **mitochondria** to produce the ATPs necessary for active transport in sucrose loading at the source areas
	help in the maintenance of the sieve tube cells
proton pump proteins and cotransport proteins in the sieve tube cell membranes	help in the loading of sucrose and other organic compounds into the phloem sieve tubes which occurs at the source
rigid cell walls of the sieve tube cells	allows the development of the hydrostatic pressures essential to the pressure-flow hypothesis for plant phloem sap transport
pores in the ends of the sieve tube cell walls	allows increased flow between the connecting sieve tube members (elements) in a sieve tube
decreased cytoplasm in the sieve tube members	allows increased flow between the connective sieve tube members (elements) in a sieve tube

9 Plant biology | 187

Subject vocabulary

aphid stylets extensions of an aphid's mouth which penetrate and obtain nutrients from a source

radiation particles given off by a substance which allow its tracking

undifferentiated cells cells without specific structure or function

meristem region in plants which allows growth

determinate growth growth occurring to definite limits involving stage, size, or age

indeterminate growth growth which continues throughout the life of an organism, such as in plants

primary growth growth in length of a plant or plant structure

secondary growth plant growth involving increase in width

apical meristems/primary meristems regions of growth at the tips of plants

cork cambium meristematic tissue which produces new cork/bark cells

Synonyms

penetrate .... go through

Skill: Analysis of data from experiments measuring phloem transport rates using aphid stylets and radioactively labelled carbon dioxide

Evidence for the pressure–flow theory of phloem sap movement can be provided by analysis of data from procedures involving **aphid stylets**. Stylets are extensions from an aphid's mouth which the insect uses to **penetrate** a single sieve tube in a plant. The stylet inserted into the sieve tube provides nutrients to keep the animal alive. If the aphid is **anaesthetized** and removed from the stylet, the contents and the pressure of the fluid continuing to come out of the stylet may be analysed. Data analysis should show:

- Pressure decreases in the sieve tube as the stylet is inserted further from the source.
- The lowest pressure is nearest the sink.
- Sucrose levels are substantially lower in the sink than in the source.

Analysing fluid from the stylets coupled with the use of radioactively labelled carbon dioxide demonstrates how carbohydrates produced in photosynthesis are transported throughout the plant to multiple areas for many different uses. The radioactively labelled carbon dioxide can be tracked in the plant because it gives off traces of **radiation**.

9.3 Growth in plants

Main idea

Plant growth shows **adaptation** to environmental conditions.

Understanding: **Undifferentiated cells** in the meristems of plants allow indeterminate growth.

Model sentence: Cells of meristem regions of plants allow growth throughout a plant's life.

Types of growth in organisms include two major types:

- **Determinate growth** occurs in most animals and in some plant organs such as flowers. Organisms with this type of growth stop growing at a particular stage, size, or age.
- **Indeterminate growth** occurs in most plants. Organisms with this type of growth show continued growth throughout their life.

Meristems are regions of plants which contain specialized cells allowing continual growth. **Primary growth** is growth in length of a plant or plant structure. **Secondary growth** is growth in width of a plant or plant structure. Stems and roots show primary growth due to meristematic tissue at their tips. Meristems occurring at the tips of plants are called **apical meristems** or **primary meristems**. Lateral meristems allow growth in the thickness of plants or plant structures. Examples of lateral meristems are **vascular cambium** and **cork cambium**. These lateral meristems are common in trees and shrubs known as woody plants.

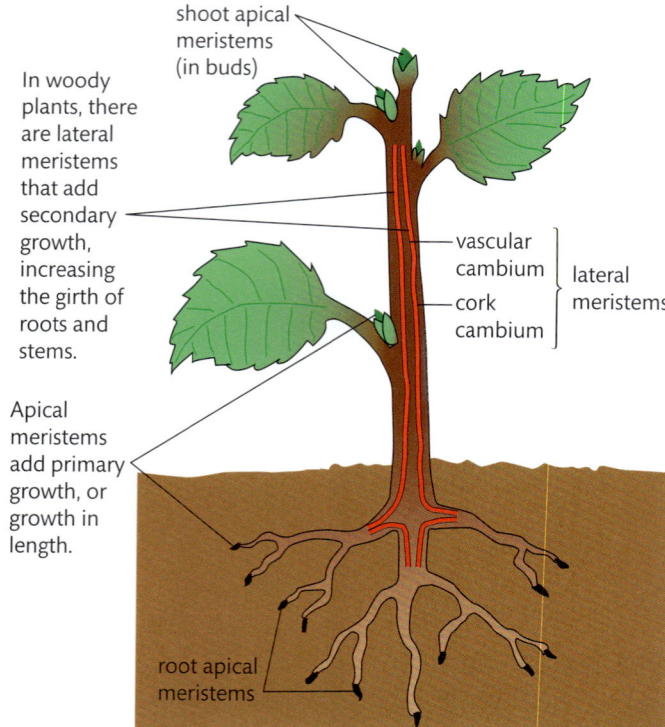

Figure 9.9 *An overview of primary and secondary growth*

Understanding: **Mitosis** and cell division in the **shoot apex** provide cells needed for extension of the stem and development of leaves.

Subject vocabulary

mitosis cell division where one diploid cell becomes two diploid cells

shoot apex apical meristem and its surrounding developing plant tissue at the tip of a stem

Model sentence: The shoot apex of plants carries out rapid and continuous cell division to provide the cells needed for primary stem growth and leaf development.

The **meristematic tissue** at the tips of roots and stems is composed of many small cells which are continuously going through mitosis and **cytokinesis** cell division. These small cells show no **differentiation** into a particular plant cell type. When a **meristematic cell** divides the result is the following:

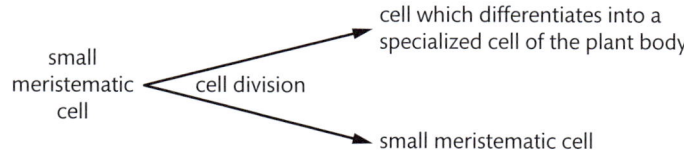

Figure 9.10 *Division of a meristematic cell*

meristematic tissue tissue of the meristem which allows continual growth

cytokinesis division of the cytoplasm in cell division

differentiation series of changes which transforms unspecialized cells into specialized cells and tissues in multicellular organisms

meristematic cell undifferentiated cell of plant meristems

protoderm early shoot apex area which becomes the mature plant epidermis

leaf primordia early shoot apex area which become the leaf

hormone chemical messenger produced in very small amounts by an endocrine gland

target cell cells that respond to a particular hormone

The products of this meristematic cell division produce cells for plant growth while maintaining the meristematic tissue necessary for future and ongoing growth.

The apical meristem and its surrounding developing plant tissue at the tip of a stem is known as the shoot apex. Differentiation of cells produced by cell division of meristematic tissue allows the production of all the different cells necessary for plant elongation or growth. This cell differentiation from the shoot apex also allows the formation of the cells necessary to form new leaves in the plant growth process. The table below shows what early shoot apex structures become in the mature plant.

Shoot apex structure	Mature plant part
protoderm	epidermis
leaf primordia	leaf
procambium	vascular tissue and **lateral** meristem

General vocabulary

anaesthetized given a drug to prevent the feeling of pain

adaptation change which makes something more suitable for a situation

lateral related to the sides or movement to the side

Understanding: Plant hormones control growth in the shoot apex.

Model sentence: Growth and cell division within the shoot apex are controlled by chemical messengers called plant hormones.

Factors which affect plant development and growth include:
- environmental factors, such as day length and water availability
- receptors, which allow the plant to detect certain environmental factors
- the genetic make-up of the plant
- **hormones** of several types produced in various plant regions.

Plant hormones are produced in very small amounts. They have the potential to bring about effects in many parts of the plant. The plant hormones normally move through the phloem transport system or from cell to cell. The cells upon which hormones have an effect are called **target cells**.

9 Plant biology

A plant hormone will have varying effects depending on the target cell's location within the plant. It is also common for various plant hormones to interact with one another to produce a particular response within a plant.

Auxins are a group of plant hormones which have a very large effect on shoot apex growth and development. These auxins may also affect leaf and fruit development. Other common plant hormones and their general effect are shown in the table below.

Hormone	General effect
gibberellin	promotes seed germination and stem growth
cytokinin	promotes root growth and maintains leaf health
abscisic acid	closes stomata, maintains seed dormancy
ethylene	promotes fruit ripening

Hints for success: It is especially important to note the role of auxins in promoting shoot apex growth and development.

Application: Use of micropropagation for rapid bulking up of new varieties, production of virus-free strains of existing varieties, and propagation of orchids and other rare species

Scientists are using the present understanding of plant meristems and plant hormones in **micropropagation** procedures to produce large numbers of plant offspring which have desired characteristics. Micropropagation uses cells from the shoot apex of desired plants. The propagation of new plants from these cells involves sterile cultures grown on nutrient gels. The addition of specific plant hormones such as an auxin or cytokinin to the sterile cultures is necessary to obtain the new plants from the shoot apex cells. Scientists are making use of the fact that plant cells retain the ability to differentiate into any plant part in this procedure.

This method also allows them to obtain plants which are virus-free or which are new varieties of an existing plant. Orchids and other rare species of plants are produced in laboratories by micropropagation.

Understanding: Plant shoots respond to the environment by tropisms.

Model sentence: Plant tropisms occur in response to environmental stimuli.

Tropisms refer to plant growth or movement in response to directional stimuli in the immediate environment. **Positive tropisms** bring about growth or movement toward environmental stimuli. **Negative tropisms** refer to growth or movement away from environmental stimuli. Common stimuli for plant tropisms are:
- chemicals
- light
- gravity
- touch.

Growth or movement in plants due to gravity is called **gravitropism**. Most plant roots show **positive gravitropism**. The stems of most plants show **negative gravitropism**. **Phototropism** is growth or movement of a plant towards or away from light. In general, roots are **negatively phototropic**. Stems are usually **positively phototropic**.

Subject vocabulary

auxins group of plant hormones affecting plant growth and development

gibberellin plant hormone which promotes seed germination and stem growth

cytokinin plant hormone which promotes root growth and maintains leaf health

abscisic acid plant hormone which closes stomata and maintains seed dormancy in some plant species

ethylene plant hormone involved in promoting fruit ripening

micropropagation process of culturing cells from the shoot apex of plants on nutrient gels to produce desired plants

tropism plant growth or movement to directional stimuli in the immediate environment

positive tropism plant growth toward a specific environmental stimulus

negative tropism plant growth away from a specific environmental stimulus

gravitropism growth or movement in plants due to gravity

positive gravitropism plant growth toward gravity such as roots show

negative gravitropism plant growth away from gravity

phototropism plant growth or movement towards or away from light

negatively phototropic plant growth away from light

positively phototropic plant growth toward light

Understanding: Auxin efflux pumps can set up concentration gradients of auxin in plant tissue.

Model sentence: Auxin efflux pumps **move auxins out of plant cells in a region which is closest to light creating cells with different auxin concentrations.**

The figure opposite shows the effect of sunlight on a typical stem shoot. There is a higher concentration of auxin on side B. The higher concentration of auxin on side B causes increased elongation of the cells on this side compared to side A. As shown, the result is growth towards the light.

This figure demonstrates positive phototropism. Auxin is actually being produced in all cells of the region of plant shown. It is specialized membrane proteins called auxin efflux pumps that move the auxins out of the cells closer to the light to cells which are further from the light. The specialized proteins of the auxin efflux pumps are known as PIN3 proteins. ATP is the energy source that allows the auxin efflux pumps to function. The position of the PIN3 proteins (auxin efflux pumps) may be altered to affect the direction of auxin movement.

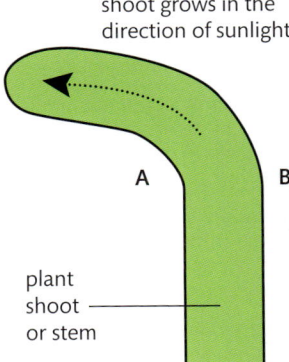

Figure 9.11 *Effect of auxin on some plant stems*

Sequence of events in plant phototropism:

1. Auxin is produced by all cells in the plant shoot region exposed to light.
2. Auxin efflux pumps move auxin out of cells on the shoot side closest to the light and into the intercellular space.
3. Auxin is moved to the intercellular space of the shoot cells further away from the light.
4. The auxin activates proton pumps in the cell membranes of the shoot cells further from the light.
5. The proton pumps cause a build-up of hydrogen ions in the intercellular space.
6. Increased hydrogen ions in the intercellular space causes a decrease in pH.
7. A decrease in pH breaks hydrogen bonds in the cellulose of the cell walls of cells away from the light.
8. The result of breaking cellulose hydrogen bonds is elongation of cells on the darker side and bending toward the light.

The particular auxin involved in this elongation process of phototropism is called indole-3-acetic acid (IAA).

Subject vocabulary

concentration gradient difference in chemical concentrations between two regions

auxin efflux pump PIN3 proteins of plant cell membranes involved in moving auxins in plant tissues

PIN3 proteins proteins making up auxin efflux pumps

phototropism plant growth or movement towards or away from light

indole-3-acetic acid specific plant auxin involved in elongating plant stems in response to light

transcription the process of creating RNA from DNA

transcriptional repressors protein which binds to DNA and prevents transcription of a particular region or gene

General vocabulary

elongation to grow longer

Understanding: Auxin influences cell growth rates by changing the pattern of gene expression.

Model sentence: **The hormones known as auxins are able to alter** transcription **in certain plant cells and alter growth rates.**

Current research shows that auxins combine with specific plant cell receptors which target transcriptional repressors of genes that respond to auxins in the plant cell

DNA. There are repressors in certain plant stem cells that **inhibit** the transcription of growth-stimulating genes. Growth is very slow when these repressors are present. The ways auxins affect gene expression and plant growth are as follows:

1. When auxin comes into contact with receptors on the nuclear membrane of these repressor-containing cells, an **auxin-receptor complex** is formed.
2. This complex moves to and binds with the repressor of the DNA that codes for growth-stimulating genes.
3. The binding with the repressor results in the breakdown of the repressor.
4. Growth-stimulating genes are transcribed when the repressor is no longer present.
5. The transcription of the growth-stimulating genes causes growth.

9.4 Reproduction in plants

Main idea

The living and non-living environment of flowering plants greatly affects reproduction in the plants.

Subject vocabulary

auxin-receptor complex combination of an auxin and a transcriptional repressor which leads to breakdown of the repressor and transcription occurring

angiosperms largest taxonomic group of plants in which flowers are involved in their reproductive process

pollination transfer of pollen from the anther to the stigma of a flower, occurs before fertilization in angiosperms

pollen produced by the anther of the stamen and carries the male gametes in angiosperms

stigma upper most part of the flower's female structure which receives the pollen

vegetative non-reproductive, non-flowering

repression the act of preventing or decreasing the chances

Understanding: Flowering involves a change in gene expression in the shoot apex.

Model sentence: A change in gene expression must occur in the shoot apex to cause flowering in an angiosperm.

Plants which produce flowers are known as **angiosperms**. The flowers produced by different species of angiosperms differ greatly. A typical flower is shown in the figure.

This flower has features which allow **pollination** by animals. There are differences in flower structure when pollination is by wind or water. Pollination involves the placing of **pollen** (containing male sex cells) on the **stigma** of the carpel (female flower part).

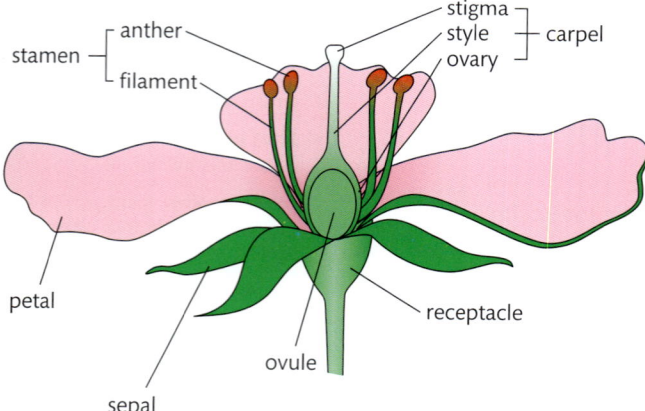

Figure 9.12 Half-views of animal-pollinated flower

The flower develops from the shoot apex. The shoot apex usually allows a **vegetative** or growth mode in the plant. At certain times the vegetative or growth mode of the shoot apex switches to a reproductive mode. Environmental factors which may be involved in the change from vegetative to reproductive mode in flowering plants include:

- day/night length
- temperature.

Some flowering plants seem to have an 'internal clock' which **initiates** the production of flowers.

Whatever the cause of the switch to the reproductive mode, the result is a **cascade** of changing gene expression. **Repression** of vegetative-focused genes and initiation of reproductive-focused genes occurs. Even the flower organs are formed in an exact order and location based on which genes are being expressed at certain times in the shoot apex.

Synonyms

inhibit(s) .... prevent(s)/reduce(s)

initiate(s) .... start(s)/begin(s)

General vocabulary

cascade a sequence of events, each one causing the next

Skill: **Drawing of half-views of animal-pollinated flowers**

You must be able to draw and label a half-view of a typical animal-pollinated flower, such as the one opposite. Be certain the flower parts are in the correct location in relation to one another. Also, make sure the flower parts are scaled correctly. You may also be asked to label a drawing of a flower. Observe several examples of flower half-views on the internet to develop your skill. Be certain the flowers you look at are animal-pollinated flowers.

Understanding: The switch to flowering is a response to the length of light and dark periods in many plants.

Model sentence: Many plants switch from vegetative to flowering mode in response to length of light and dark periods.

Photoperiodism is the response of a plant to light involving the relative lengths of day and night. Day and night length control flowering in many plants. There are two categories of plants which flower according to the lengths of day and night. They are:

- **Long-day plants,** which flower when days are longest and nights are shortest.
- **Short-day plants,** which flower when days are shorter and nights are longer.

Flowering in plants known as day-neutral plants does not depend on day length. Long-day and short-day plants are actually responding to night length and not day length.

Photoperiodism depends on the presence of a blue-green pigment called **phytochrome**. Phytochrome occurs in the leaves of the plant. There are two forms. They are:

- P_r – an inactive form of phytochrome
- P_{fr} – an active form of phytochrome.

The following figure shows the **interconversion** of the phytochrome molecule and its two possible forms. This mechanism promotes or inhibits flowering in many plants.

Subject vocabulary

photoperiodism response of a plant to light involving the relative lengths of day and night

long-day plants plants which flower when days are longest and nights are shortest

short-day plants plants which flower when days are shorter and nights are longer

phytochrome blue-green pigment occurring in plant leaves and involved in photoperiodism

P_r inactive form of phytochrome involved in photoperiodism

P_{fr} active form of phytochrome involved in photoperiodism

interconversion the way a molecule changes between its possible forms

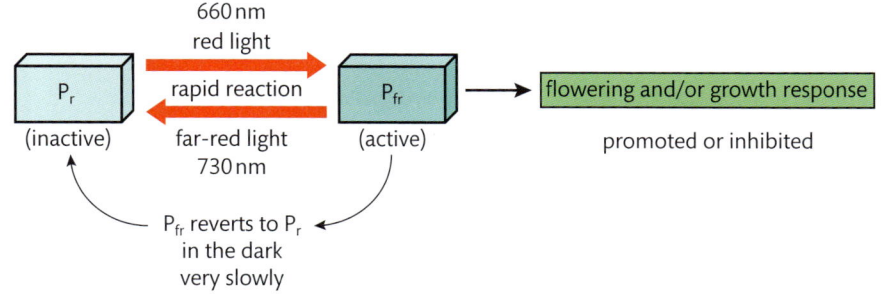

Figure 9.13 *Interconversion of phytochrome*

Notice that P_r is converted to P_{fr} in the presence of red light which has a wavelength of 660 nm. This is a relatively rapid conversion. P_{fr} may be converted to P_r in two ways:

1. When P_{fr} is exposed to far-red light which has a wavelength of 730 nm, it is rapidly converted to P_r.
2. Darkness causes the very slow conversion of P_{fr} to P_r.

In long-day plants the remaining P_{fr} at the end of a short night stimulates the plant to flower by acting as a promoter to genes which bring about flowering.

In short-day plants the P_{fr} acts as an inhibitor to the genes which bring about flowering. For these short-day plants, enough P_{fr} has to be converted to P_r for inhibition of the flowering genes to stop. This conversion can only happen with long nights.

> **Hints for success:** P_{fr} is referred to as the active form of phytochrome since it is the form that may either inhibit or promote flowering. It inhibits flowering in short-day plants. It promotes flowering in long-day plants. Night length which allows the slow conversion of P_{fr} to P_r is the actual cause of photoperiodism.

Application: Methods used to induce short-day plants to flower out of season

Scientists apply photoperiodism in *Euphorbia pulchemrrima*, the poinsettia plant, to produce large numbers of the plant with colourful displays commercially. Poinsettia plants are short-day plants in which P_{fr} acts as an inhibitor of flowering. These plants are grown in large **greenhouses** in which light is controlled. Plants kept in the dark for at least 14 hours will produce the brightly coloured displays consumers want. The bright displays of colour are not actually due to the flowers. The coloured structures are **bracts** (a form of leaf) which are produced at the same time as the plant's tiny flowers. Many other plants can be stimulated to flower by altering periods of darkness **artificially**.

Understanding: Success in plant reproduction depends on pollination, fertilization, and seed dispersal.

Model sentence: Pollination, fertilization, and seed dispersal are all essential for success in plant reproduction.

Pollination

Pollination is the process by which pollen is transferred from the male **stamen** to the female stigma in flowering plants.

Pollen contains the male sex cells and is produced in the **anther** part of the stamen.

The first step in successful sexual reproduction in a flowering plant is the transfer of pollen from the anther to the stigma of the same plant species.

Locate the anther and the stigma in the drawings below:

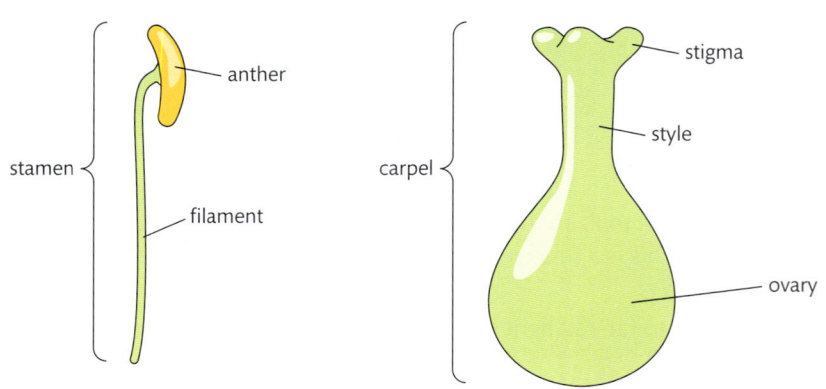

Figure 9.14 *The reproductive structures of a flowering plant: the stamen and the carpel*

In **self-pollination**, pollen is transferred from anther to stigma of the same flower or another flower of the same plant.

General vocabulary

greenhouse a glass building used for growing plants needing warmth, light and protection

artificially not in a real way

Subject vocabulary

bracts unique structures produced in some plants which are a form of leaves

stamen male reproductive structure of the flower

pollen produced by the anther of the stamen and carries the male gametes in angiosperms

anther stamen structure in which pollen is produced and matures

self-pollination pollen is transferred from anther to stigma of the same flower or of the same plant

Subject vocabulary

cross-pollination pollen transferred from anther to stigma of flowers on different plants

haploid a cell that has only one chromosome of each homologous pair

diploid zygote fertilized egg with the diploid chromosome condition

stigma upper most part of the flower's female structure which receives the pollen

pollen tube growth structure from a germinating pollen grain which contains the male gametes

Cross-pollination occurs when pollen is transferred from anther to stigma of flowers on different plants.

There are three major factors called vectors involved in pollination. They are:
- wind
- water
- animals.

Animals are the most commonly involved vector in pollination. Water is the least commonly involved.

Fertilization

Fertilization occurs after pollination. It is the **union** of **haploid** male and female sex cells to form a **diploid zygote**.

Pollen which falls on the **stigma** of a flower produces a **pollen tube** which grows through the **style** of the **carpel** to the ovary.

The growing pollen tube carries the male **gametes** to the **ovules** (the female gametes) of the ovary.

Fertilization in flowering plants is actually a **double fertilization**. One sperm combines with an ovule egg nucleus. Another sperm from the same pollen tube combines with two **polar nuclei** in the ovule to produce the **endosperm**. The endosperm is 3n, triploid, and provides the nutrients for the new plant that develops from seed germination.

Fertilization in flowering plants results in the formation of a **seed**.

Seed dispersal

The final factor in the successful sexual reproduction of flowering plants is **seed dispersal**.

Seeds must have some means to move from the parent plant. Successful seed dispersal lessens competition for resources around the parent plant. It also allows the species to spread from a single location.

Some common factors which allow seed dispersal include water, wind, or animals. Seeds have specific **adaptations** that allow them to be successfully dispersed by one of these three means.

Seeds must go through **germination** to produce new plants. Seeds contain an **embryonic plant** which goes through development as a result of germination. There are many factors which may affect seed germination. These factors are investigated in the Skill activity below.

Skill: Drawing internal structure of seeds

You should practise drawing and labelling the structures of seeds. Adjacent is a figure showing a bean seed and its structures.

Cotyledons are seed leaves which contain the nutrients of the bean seed. Bean seeds have two cotyledons and are said to be **dicotyledonous**. Some seeds have one cotyledon and are said to be **monocotyledonous**.

Subject vocabulary

style structure which connects the stigma to the ovary in the carpel of a flower

carpel female sex organ of a flower

gamete(s) a sex cell, either a sperm cell or an egg cell

ovules female gametes which occur in the ovary of the carpel, will become seeds when fertilized by male gametes

double fertilization plant fertilization when one male gamete combines with an egg nucleus of an ovule and another combines with two polar nuclei

polar nuclei occur in an ovule and form the endosperm when a male gamete combines with them

endosperm part of the seed which provides the nutrients for the developing plant after seed germination

seed structure produced after fertilization in plants which allows the formation of a new plant

seed dispersal transport of seed from the parent plant to a new location

germination early growth or sprouting of a seed

embryonic plant early plant which occurs inside the seed

cotyledons seed leaves which provide nutrients early in a plant's life

dicotyledous plant seed with two seed leaves

monocotyledous plant seed with one seed leaf

General vocabulary

union the act of joining things together

adaptation change which makes something more suitable for a situation

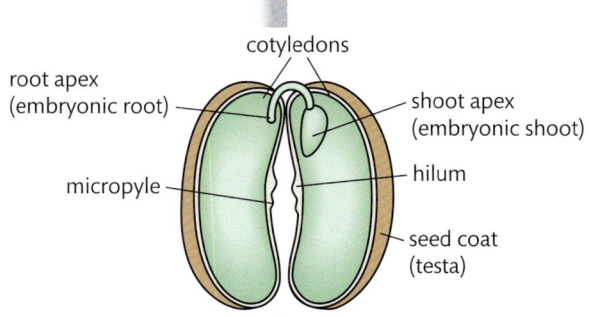

Figure 9.15 *Structure of a typical dicotyledonous seed*

Skill: Design of experiments to test hypotheses about factors affecting germination

Design an experiment to test a hypothesis about a factor which affects seed germination. Water amounts, periods of seed dormancy, oxygen levels, temperature, and pH are possible factors to investigate. You will need to decide on a particular seed type. Rapidly germinating seeds will produce results sooner. With rapidly germinating seeds, there will also be less chance of fungal growth. Be certain to keep all factors constant in your procedure except for the one factor you are investigating. Vary the factor you want to examine. It is essential to plan the collection of data so that a correct and meaningful conclusion may be obtained.

Understanding: Most flowering plants use mutualistic relationships with pollinators in sexual reproduction.

Model sentence: Most flowering plants have developed mutualistic relationships with pollinators to bring about successful sexual reproduction.

Common **pollinators** of flowering plants include bats, birds, and, especially, insects. A **mutualistic relationship** often develops between the pollinator and the flowering plant. In a mutualistic relationship, both of the organisms involved benefit. Pollinators gain food in the form of **nectar** when they carry out pollination of many flowering plants. An example of this is the honey bee. The honey bee gains food in the form of nectar while carrying out pollination of a flower. Both honey bee and plant are helped by this association.

It is important to maintain our pollinator populations in order to allow the continued existence of our flowering plants. Much of our food supply comes either directly or indirectly from these plants.

Subject vocabulary

pollinators organisms which are involved in the process of pollination

mutualistic relationship relationship between two organisms in which both are helped

nectar high sugar substance produced by plant flowers which is beneficial to pollinators

10 Genetics and evolution

10.1 Meiosis

Main idea

Meiosis leads to independent **assortment** of chromosomes and unique composition of alleles in daughter cells.

Nature of science: Making careful observations – careful observation and record keeping turned up **anomalous** data that Mendel's law of independent assortment could not account for. Thomas Hunt Morgan developed the notion of linked genes to account for the anomalies.

Understanding: Chromosomes **replicate** in **interphase** before meiosis.

To prepare for meiosis, the chromosomes replicate while they are still in interphase. This causes single chromosomes to develop a sister chromatid resulting in two identical sister chromatids attached at the centromere.

The extra copies of DNA will ensure that the desired quantity of genetic information gets to the daughter cells that will be produced in the various phases of meiosis.

> **Hints for success:** When looking at chromosomes in the early stages of meiosis, do not confuse two sister chromatids as two chromosomes. Be sure to learn to identify the difference between sister chromatids and homologous chromosomes.

Understanding: Crossing over is the exchange of DNA material between non-sister **homologous chromatids**.

Homologous chromosomes are matched in pairs. One in each pair is from the person's father and the other is from the person's mother.

The first pair contains the longest homologous chromosomes, for example. Remember that homologous chromosomes are similar but not necessarily identical because they can possess different **alleles** for the same genes.

When the homologous pairs pair up during **prophase**, crossing over can occur. This allows for the exchange of alleles between non-sister homologous chromatids. In other words, the maternal chromosome 1 could exchange a piece of one of its chromatids with the equivalent piece of the paternal chromosome 1.

Understanding: Crossing over produces new combinations of alleles on the chromosomes of the **haploid** cells.

Model sentence: Without the process of crossing over, paternal chromosomes and maternal chromosomes would remain unchanged and would not show as much variety.

Crossing over can increase the genetic variety of the sperm cells and egg cells that will be produced. Because the exchange happens between maternal and paternal chromosomes, there is a possibility of introducing alleles that were present in the

---

Subject vocabulary

meiosis cell division where one diploid cell becomes four haploid cells

interphase stage in the life of a cell in which it is carrying out activities other than cell division

homologous chromatids chromatids of the same shape and size that carry corresponding alleles in the same positions

alleles versions of a gene, differing by one or more bases

prophase a stage of the cell cycle during which the nuclear envelope breaks down and chromatin fibres coil to form chromosomes which form and attach to the mitotic spindle

haploid a cell that has only one chromosome of each homologous pair

Synonyms

assortment..... variety
anomalous..... different/ unexpected/ unusual
replicate........ copy/repeat

Synonyms

vice versa....... the opposite of

Subject vocabulary

bivalent/tetrad a pair of homologous chromosomes lined up during metaphase I of meiosis

chiasma (plural: chiasmata) the point at which two chromosomes cross each other during crossing over

meiosis I first part of meiosis during which homologous chromosomes separate to produce two diploid cells

diploid a cell which has chromosomes in homologous pairs

anaphase I the stage in meiosis where homologous chromosomes separate

paternal line but never present in the maternal line or **vice versa**. When the sperm and eggs form, they will possess combinations of alleles that were not present in their original chromosomes.

Understanding: Chiasmata formation between non-sister chromatids can result in an exchange of alleles.

When two homologous chromosomes line up during meiosis, they form what is called a **bivalent** or **tetrad**. This pairing up is unique to meiosis and not seen in mitosis.

Once they are matched up, crossing over can take place. The chromosomes do this by twisting around each other in such a way that a cross shape can sometimes be seen under an electron microscope.

The word **chiasma** (plural **chiasmata**) is used to refer to this formation.

Skill: Drawing diagrams to show chiasmata formed by crossing over

You should be able to draw the process of crossing over. An example can be found below. In examinations, drawings without labels or annotations do not earn any points.

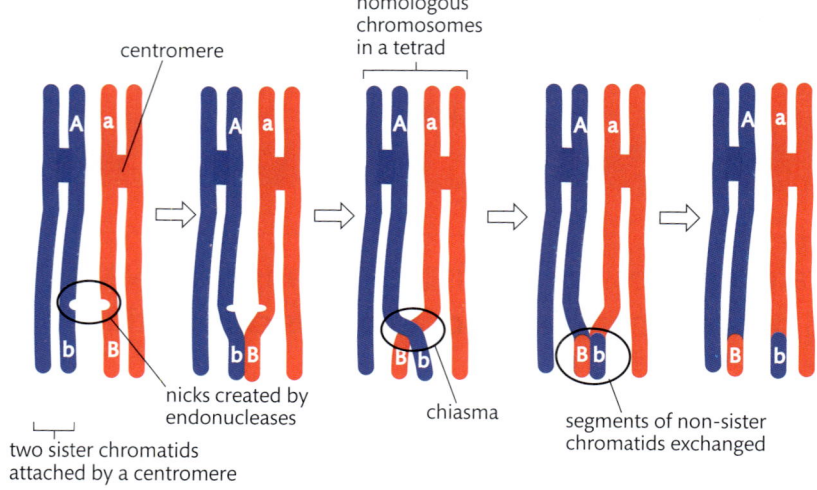

Figure 10.1 How an allele **B** from a maternal chromosome (in red) can be switched with an allele **b** on a paternal chromosome (in blue)

Understanding: Homologous chromosomes separate in meiosis I.

Model sentence: During meiosis I, the number of chromosomes is halved and the diploid nucleus of the parent cell becomes two haploid nuclei in the daughter cells.

Once crossing over is complete, the homologous chromosomes can separate. This is done during **anaphase I**. Each chromosome of the pair is pulled to opposite ends of the cell and two daughter cells can now be formed.

Note that at this phase (during meiosis I), the chromosomes are still carrying copies of themselves. In other words, two sister chromatids are attached at the centromere.

What is different is that some of the sister chromatids are no longer identical copies due to crossing over.

During meiosis I, the cells are converted from diploid to haploid.

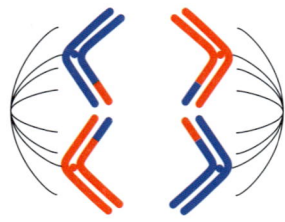

Figure 10.2 Anaphase I, during which homologous chromosomes (bivalents) are separated. Notice the swapped tips of chromosomes where crossing over has happened

Understanding: Sister chromatids separate in meiosis II.

Model sentence: In meiosis II, the two attached chromatids of the single chromosomes in the haploid cells are pulled apart so that any gametes produced will have a single copy of each chromosome.

To complete meiosis, a second division occurs. This second division pulls apart the sister chromatids so that they can each occupy one of four daughter cells.

It is important to notice that when the two sister chromatids become separated, they change names. We can now call them individual chromosomes. Before separation, they are sister chromatids, whereas after separation (thanks to anaphase II), they are considered individual chromosomes.

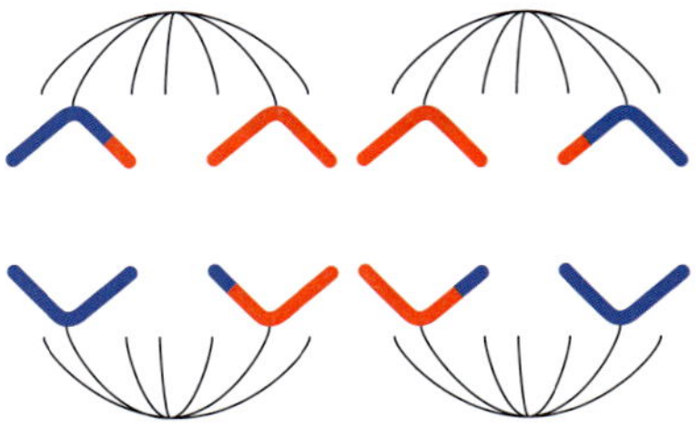

Figure 10.3 Anaphase II, during which sister chromatids are pulled to opposite poles of the cells

Understanding: Independent assortment of genes is due to the random orientation of pairs of homologous chromosomes in meiosis I.

Increasing the ways in which genetic variation can be introduced will increase a population's ability to survive and adapt to new situations.

An interesting phenomenon ensures the maximization of variation in gametes and therefore in the population: random orientation.

Random orientation refers to the way in which chromosomes align by chance along the equator of the cell during metaphase I. Like rolling dice, the chromosomes can align in a different way each time a cell gets ready for metaphase I.

Imagine an organism with six pairs of chromosomes ($n = 6$, $2n = 12$). Although it is relatively unlikely, there is a possibility that the chromosomes could line up in order of their size: 1, 2, 3, 4, 5, and 6. In fact, mathematically there are 2^n possible combinations, or 2^6 in this case, which is 64 possible combinations. So for six pairs of chromosomes there is a 1 in 64 chance that they could line up in this order. Others could show the following random orientations:

- 6-1-3-2-5-4
- 3-6-1-4-2-5
- 2-4-6-1-3-5.

The orientation of each of the maternal and paternal halves of the pair of homologous chromosomes determines the combination of the alleles. This sends different combinations to the gametes.

Humans have 23 pairs of chromosomes so the total number of combinations is much greater. Mathematically there are 2^n, or 2^{23}, which is over 8 million, possible combinations. But that number does not take into account crossing over, which makes the calculation more difficult but certainly guarantees a much greater number than 8 million.

The law of independent assortment states that when gametes are formed, the separation of one pair of alleles between the daughter cells is independent of the separation of another pair of alleles. This means that just because one allele is passed on to the next generation does not mean that another one must follow it. Each allele has an equal chance of being passed on or not.

Subject vocabulary

meiosis II second part of meiosis during which sister chromatids separate to produce four haploid cells (gametes)

gamete(s) a sex cell, either a sperm cell or an egg cell

anaphase II the stage in meiosis where sister chromatids separate

random orientation a process during meiosis involving the lining up of chromosomes in an order determined by chance

law of independent assortment the idea that the way one pair of alleles separates into daughter cells does not depend on the way any other pair separates

Synonyms

align............. line up
orientation..... location/position

10.2 Inheritance

Main idea

Genes may be linked or unlinked and are inherited accordingly.

Nature of science: Looking for patterns, trends, and **discrepancies** – Mendel used observations of the natural world to find and explain patterns and trends. Since then, scientists have looked for discrepancies and asked questions based on further observations to show exceptions to the rules. For example, Morgan discovered non-Mendelian ratios in his experiments with *Drosophila*.

Understanding: Gene **loci** are said to be linked if on the same chromosome.

Until now, the only kinds of genes that have been discussed have been ones that determine **traits** that are passed on independently. There are some traits, however, that can be passed on together. In humans, the genes for haemophilia and for red–green colour blindness are linked genes and get passed on together more frequently than predicted in Punnett grids.

Linked genes are ones whose loci are on the same chromosome. In the example above, haemophilia and red–green colour blindness are determined by genes found on the X chromosome. So if a mother possesses alleles for both conditions on one of her two X chromosomes, she will pass both traits to any of her sons who receive that chromosome. Two traits caused by linked genes can be passed on together and both will be seen in the **phenotype** of the **offspring**.

Model sentence: A dihybrid cross is one that considers two genetic traits and the Punnett grid used to show it can use up to 16 squares to show the possibilities for the offspring.

Application: Completion and analysis of Punnett squares for dihybrid traits

A **dihybrid cross** is one that examines two genetic traits at a time. The calculation in a dihybrid cross is a little more complicated than in a monohybrid cross, but the rules are not much different.

Let us examine two traits in an organism. The alleles can be written as follows:

A = dominant allele for trait 1

a = recessive allele for trait 1

B = dominant allele for trait 2

b = recessive allele for trait 2

The dihybrid cross is between the following parents who are **heterozygous** for both traits: *AaBb* × *AaBb*.

A dihybrid cross is a 4 × 4 cross showing 16 possibilities for the offspring. The female parent's eggs are shown across the top (see following table). Notice that instead of one allele shown in each box (as for monohybrid crosses), there are two alleles. Similarly, the contents of the male's sperm cells are shown along the left-most column, each box showing alleles for both traits being studied.

A systematic way of setting up the alleles must be used so that no combinations are left out. One way to write the letters in the boxes is to use the 'FOIL' rule: write the First letters of each genotype, then the Outside letters, then the Inside letters and

---

Synonyms

discrepancies . differences/inconsistencies

offspring........ young/children

Subject vocabulary

locus (plural: loci) the specific place where a gene is found on a chromosome

trait a characteristic that distinguishes one individual from another such as blood type

phenotype visible result of an organism's genotype

dihybrid cross a cross that considers the inheritance of two different traits

heterozygous possessing two different alleles of a gene at a particular locus

finish with the Last letters. This has been done on the top row and left column of the dihybrid Punnett grid below.

	AB	Ab	aB	ab
AB	AABB	AABb	AaBB	AaBb
Ab	AABb	AAbb	AaBb	Aabb
aB	AaBB	AaBb	aaBB	aaBb
ab	AaBb	Aabb	aaBb	aabb

Analysis of the **genotypes** above can lead us to the phenotypes shown below. Count how many there are of each. When looking at two traits, do you get a 3:1 ratio the way we did for a monohybrid cross? What about if you only look at one trait?

	AB	Ab	aB	ab
AB	dominant trait 1, dominant trait 2	dominant trait 1, dominant trait 2	dominant trait 1, dominant trait 2	dominant trait 1, dominant trait 2
Ab	dominant trait 1, dominant trait 2	dominant trait 1, recessive trait 2	dominant trait 1, dominant trait 2	dominant trait 1, recessive trait 2
aB	dominant trait 1, dominant trait 2	dominant trait 1, dominant trait 2	recessive trait 1, dominant trait 2	recessive trait 1, dominant trait 2
ab	dominant trait 1, dominant trait 2	dominant trait 1, recessive trait 2	recessive trait 1, dominant trait 2	recessive trait 1, recessive trait 2

Subject vocabulary

genotypes genes of an organism for a particular trait

autosomal all chromosomes except the sex chromosomes

Synonyms

deviation .... difference

Skill: Calculation of the predicted genotypic and phenotypic ratio of offspring of dihybrid crosses involving unlinked **autosomal** genes

Using the example above, we can see the following pattern in the results for the possible genotypes:

- Four out of the 16 possibilities are *AaBb*, like their parents.
- There are two each of the following: *aaBb*, *Aabb*, *AaBB*, and *AABb*.
- And there are four unique genotypes: *AABB*, *AAbb*, *aaBB*, and *aabb*.

This gives the following results for the phenotypes:

- **9** out of 16: dominant phenotype for both traits
- **3** out of 16: dominant trait 1, recessive trait 2
- **3** out of 16: recessive trait 1, dominant trait 2
- **1** out of 16: recessive phenotype for both traits.

A dihybrid cross predicts the ratio of offspring to be **9:3:3:1**. It is perfectly acceptable for there to be slight **deviations** from this ratio but if there are significantly different proportions found in offspring, it can be concluded that something else is influencing the distribution of the alleles. One possible cause of this could be that the traits being studied are genetically linked.

Synonyms

segregate .... separate

Subject vocabulary

mutation an accidental change in a genetic sequence

reciprocal cross a pair of crosses of a male of type A with a female of type B and a male of type B with a female of type A

sex linked a trait that is controlled by alleles located on the sex chromosomes

Understanding: Unlinked genes segregate independently as a result of meiosis.

Most genes are not linked because any two genes picked at random are likely to be on separate chromosomes. As a result, when they are passed on to the next generation, they do so without depending on each other.

Genes found on different chromosomes follow the law of independent assortment. As a result, they follow the patterns of inheritance that are mathematically predicted by Punnett grids. In such cases, when considering any two traits *A* and *B*, we would expect to find that *AaBb* × *AaBb* will give a ratio of offspring showing the 9:3:3:1 ratio.

Application: Morgan's discovery of non-Mendelian ratios in *Drosophila*

Model sentence: Thomas Hunt Morgan was able to make multiple discoveries about genetics by breeding fruit flies and finding exceptions to Mendel's law of independent assortment.

What if the ratio obtained in a breeding experiment does not give the expected ratio of 9:3:3:1 in a dihybrid cross or 3:1 in a monohybrid cross? Remember that Gregor Mendel's work breeding peas showed clear patterns of proportions of offspring with specific characteristics such as tall or short plants. Heterozygous tall parents produced a 3:1 ratio of tall to short offspring, for example.

In the early 1900s, following the work of William Bateson, Edith Saunders, and Reginald Punnett, Thomas Hunt Morgan did similar breeding experiments with *Drosophila* fruit flies. One of the traits that is easy to observe is eye colour. Flies with naturally occurring traits are said to be 'wild-type' flies and their natural eye colour is red. In 1910, Morgan's team found a **mutation** never seen before in the wild-type flies: white eyes.

For some crosses with eye colour, his team of researchers found Mendelian ratios such as the 3:1 ratio mentioned above. But for other crosses, they got some unexpected results.

When breeding a mutant white-eyed female fly with a wild-type male fly that had red eyes (in a cross called a **reciprocal cross**), Morgan got a surprising result: 50% had red eyes, which is a 1:1 ratio. Stranger still, all the male offspring had white eyes and all the females had red eyes.

When an unexpected ratio is found in one gender compared to another, it can be explained by the fact that the trait is **sex linked** (see Section 3.4). This means that the gene that determines the trait is found on the sex chromosomes. In fruit flies, the eye colour gene is found on the X chromosome but absent from the Y chromosome.

When a male fruit fly receives a mutant allele from his mother for white eye colour, he has no second allele on his Y chromosome, so he inherits only the information for white eyes. When a female fly receives a white-eyed allele from one parent, she will have a good chance of receiving a red-eyed allele from the other parent. In Morgan's experiment above, the females all got one allele for red eyes from their red-eyed fathers.

Morgan's team discovered sex linkage in *Drosophila* and also used the frequency with which certain combinations occur to show how frequently crossing over events happen. This information was used in 1913 to make the first maps of chromosomes by working out how close or far genes were to each other by how often certain unexpected combinations of alleles occurred.

Model sentence: When two genes are found on the same chromosome they are said to be linked and they often do not follow the law of independent assortment.

Skill: Identification of recombinants in crosses involving two linked genes

Let us examine a cross with two linked genes in *Drosophila*: body colour (grey or black) and length of wings (short or long). Both genes are found on chromosome 2 of the fly. The alleles can be written as follows:

- *G* = dominant allele for grey-coloured body
- *g* = recessive allele for black-coloured body
- *L* = dominant allele for long wings
- *l* = recessive allele for short wings (also called **vestigial** wings)

The cross is between these two parents: *GgLl* × *ggll*.

Since the genes are on the same chromosome, the following notation is needed to indicate how they are linked:

$$\frac{G\ \ L}{g\ \ \ l} \text{ and } \frac{g\ \ \ l}{g\ \ \ l}$$

The horizontal bars are used to represent the chromosomes. In this example, they show that *G* and *L* are on the same chromosome.

Since the *ggll* parent can only give one allele for each trait, the Punnett grid does not need to be 4 × 4, it can be 1 × 4 as follows:

	GL	Gl	gL	gl
gl	GgLl $\frac{G\ \ L}{g\ \ \ l}$	Ggll $\frac{G\ \ \ l}{g\ \ \ l}$	ggLl $\frac{g\ \ L}{g\ \ \ l}$	ggll $\frac{g\ \ \ l}{g\ \ \ l}$
		Ⓡ	Ⓡ	

Notice that the genotypes are shown in two ways for each offspring: with and without linkage notation.

The two offspring in the middle have different configurations along the bars that represent the chromosomes. They are labelled Ⓡ because they are known as **recombinants**. You should be able to figure out the process that generates these new combinations: crossing over during meiosis.

> **Hints for success:** It is impossible to acquire skills from simply reading about them. Being able to set up a Punnett grid and analyse it can only be learnt by practice. You should be able to take the information about the parents and construct your own Punnett grid on a blank sheet of paper.

Subject vocabulary

vestigial said of body parts that are significantly smaller than normal and usually functionless

recombinant organism that posses a different combination of alleles to its parents

discrete variation distinct categories of phenotypes with no intermediate forms

continuous variation a range of different phenotypes for a trait, e.g. human height

Understanding: Variation can be discrete or continuous.

Discrete variation is when the variety of phenotypes that alleles can produce can be put in distinct categories. They are either one or the other and do not show intermediate or transitional variants in between. Blood type (A, B, AB or O) is a good example of a trait that shows discrete variation.

Continuous variation is when there is a wide variety of intermediate versions of a trait from one extreme to another. It is difficult to distinguish one phenotype from the other because of smooth transitions. The genetic aspects of human skin colour or height are examples of continuous variation. There is a wide range of possibilities rather than a small number of distinct categories. We often oversimplify by saying 'tall', 'short', 'black' or 'white', but in fact both traits have a wide variety of possible intermediate phenotypes.

Synonyms

arbitrary........ random

Subject vocabulary

polygenic traits characteristics that are controlled by several genes

chi-squared test a statistical test to determine if two factors show independence or to show if expected values differ from observed values by chance or not

---

Continuous variation can be plotted on a graph as a curve or histogram, often showing a bell-shaped distribution around a mean. The placing of the measurements along the x-axis is not **arbitrary** – items must go from one extreme to the other. Discrete variation, on the other hand, can be shown as a bar chart with no transitions between the bars. The items can be placed in an arbitrary way along the x-axis.

Understanding: The phenotypes of polygenic characteristics tend to show continuous variation.

One way to obtain continuous variation is by having the trait in question controlled by more than one gene. Remember that when there is only one gene with two possible alleles, the phenotype will either show the dominant or the recessive trait (assuming the alleles are not co-dominant).

As we saw with the ABO blood type system, however, a single gene can sometimes have multiple alleles. This gives greater variety in the phenotypes but it still does not give continuous variation.

If, on the other hand, several genes control the trait, the slight differences created by the numerous possible combinations can generate continuous variation. Multiple genes explain the wide variation in human skin colour, for example. Traits controlled by many genes working together are called **polygenic traits**.

Application: Polygenic traits such as human height may also be influenced by environmental factors

It is estimated that human height is about 80% genetic and 20% environmental. The environmental factors that promote height include good nutrition, physical activity, and healthy sleep patterns.

If identical twins had very different lifestyles, they might not grow to the same height even though their genes for height are identical. If one twin had poor eating habits and never got any exercise, there is less of a chance that he or she would reach his or her full height.

Understanding: **Chi-squared tests** are used to determine whether the difference between an observed and expected frequency distribution is statistically significant.

Often the results of an experiment are different from the predicted mathematical values. One difficulty researchers have is determining whether the difference between the expected values and the values obtained are due to chance or if they are due to something else. There is a mathematical test for this which we saw in Chapter 4: the chi-squared (χ^2) test.

To carry out the χ^2 test, the following are needed:
- The expected values (E), which are predicted using mathematical models. In this case, the expected values will be predicted by the Punnett grid.
- The observed values (O), which are the results of the experiment.
- The value for χ^2, as determined by this equation:
$$\chi^2 = \Sigma \frac{(O-E)^2}{E}$$
- The null hypothesis (H_0) is the result assuming that there is no unexpected factor acting on the experiment's results. In this case, H_0 = the results will follow the expected ratios and any deviation from the expected results will be due to

chance rather than due to an external factor.
- The **degrees of freedom (d.f.)**. To determine the degrees of freedom, take the number of classes into which the data can be categorized and subtract 1.
- Lastly, the critical values. These can be looked up on tables of critical values for chi-squared tests.
- Look at the skill below to see a worked example.

Subject vocabulary

degrees of freedom the number of values in the chi-squared calculation that can vary

Skill: Use of a chi-squared test on data from dihybrid crosses

A test cross with two traits: *GLgl* × *glgl*

	LG	Lg	lG	lg
lg	LlGg	Llgg	llGg	llgg

The phenotypes are shown in the four possibilities below. Notice how it is not necessary to repeat *lg* four times, since each line would be identical.

	LG	Lg	lG	lg
lg	long wings, grey body	long wings, black body	short wings, grey body	short wings, black body

The Punnett grid above predicts that the ratio of each type of offspring is 1:1:1:1. This means that there should be equal proportions of each. These are *E*, the expected values. The cross was performed by Morgan's team on fruit flies and *O*, the obtained values, are below:

283	grey long wing
1294	grey short wing
1418	black long wing
241	black short wing
3236	total

Using the total number of offspring, it is possible to calculate the number of flies that should have been produced: 3236/4 = 809.

Putting these results into the chi-squared test as explained in Chapter 4 gives the following:

	Grey body, long wings	Grey body, short wing	Black body, long wing	Black body, short wing	Total
Observed phenotypes (O)	283	1294	1418	241	3236
Expected proportions	1 out of 4	1 out of 4	1 out of 4	1 out of 4	
Expected phenotypes (E)	809	809	809	809	3236
Difference (O – E)	–526	485	609	–568	
Difference squared (O – E)^2	276 676	235 225	370 881	322 624	
(O – E)^2 / E	342	291	458	399	1490

- From the above table, we see that the value for χ^2 is 1490.
- The null hypothesis (H_0), is: 'The results will follow the expected 1:1:1:1 ratio and we should have approximately 809 of each type of fly.'
- There are three degrees of freedom (d.f.) since there are four classes of data.
- By looking at a table of critical values for χ^2 when $p = 0.05$ we get 7.815.
- The calculated value of χ^2 is greater than the critical value so we can confidently reject the null hypothesis. This means that something other than chance is influencing the data. We can formulate a new hypothesis: 'The ratios of traits are giving results that are statistically significantly different from the expected values because the two genes are linked.'

> **Hints for success:** You need to become comfortable with using the steps of the chi-squared test. You do not need to memorize the tables for *p* values. However, it is recommended that you practise with several different problems so that you understand how it works.

10.3 Gene pool and speciation

Main idea
Gene pools change over time.

Nature of science: Looking for patterns, trends, and discrepancies – patterns of chromosome number in some genera can be explained by speciation due to polyploidy.

Understanding: A gene pool consists of all the genes and their different alleles, present in an interbreeding population.

All the genes available within an interbreeding population is called a **gene pool**.
- A population that shows wide variety possesses a large gene pool.
- A population showing little variety possesses a small gene pool.

Understanding: Evolution requires that allele frequencies change with time in populations.

Model sentence: A key to quantifying how fast a population is evolving is to examine changes in allele frequency – no change suggests no evolution and significant change suggests significant evolution.

Examine the population in the following figure. Count the number of dominant alleles *T* in the population. What percentage is this? Of the 32 alleles present, 16 are *T* and 16 are *t*. Therefore, the **allele frequency** in this case can be expressed as 0.50 or 50%.

If this percentage remains stable over time, it means that the population is not evolving. On the other hand, if the allele frequencies change over time, the population is evolving.

Subject vocabulary

genus (plural: genera) a group of species with shared characteristics

speciation process by which one species splits into two species which can no longer interbreed

polyploidy having more than two sets of chromosomes per cell instead of the usual two (diploidy)

gene pool all of the alleles of all of the genes that exist in a population

allele frequency number of versions of a particular gene found in a population

Figure 10.4 *In this gene pool, the frequencies of each allele **T** and **t** is 50%*

The allele frequency can change due to several things, including the following:
- Mutations, which generate new alleles.
- Introduction of new alleles into the gene pool from contact with a new population or individuals that join the population (immigration).
- Loss of an old allele when the last members of the population that possess it die off by natural selection or leave the population (emigration).
- Mating choices.

One way of quantifying the changes in allele frequencies is by using the Hardy–Weinberg equation (see Skill below about comparing allele frequencies).

Understanding: Reproductive isolation of populations can be temporal, behavioural, or geographic.

- **Temporal isolation** happens when members of a population can no longer interbreed due to a timing issue. For example, if one subset of a population of flowers produces pollen at a different time than the optimal or best time for pollination, their alleles will not be passed on.
- **Behavioural isolation** happens when members of a population are prevented from breeding together due to differences in behaviour. For example, if a subset of a population of birds has a different mating call than other birds, only a small number of mates might be attracted by that call.
- **Geographic isolation** happens when members of a population are prevented from breeding due to physical barriers such as mountains or rivers. If a population of rats get onto a boat and are brought to a distant island, they will no longer be able to breed with members of their original population on the mainland.

Subject vocabulary

temporal isolation members of a population prevented from interbreeding by timing, e.g. flowering at different times

behavioural isolation making one subgroup of a population unavailable for breeding due to changes in the way they behave, e.g. being nocturnal

geographic isolation members of a population prevented from interbreeding by location, e.g. separated by rivers or mountain ranges

In all three cases, the isolation can lead to a speciation. How? If the isolated population breeds only with others in the isolated population, the gene pool is different since it is only a subset of the original population. As a result, the number of possible combinations is different and certain combinations of alleles in the new population will come up more often than in the original.

In addition, the isolated population sometimes occupies a different habitat, such as the rats on the distant island mentioned above. This new environment can have very different selective pressures and lead to **adaptations** that are very different from the original population.

If there are enough differences between the old and the new populations, speciation can happen. The two populations will no longer be able to breed together. They are now two separate species.

Speciation can be gradual or **abrupt**, as we will see next when we look at the two theories about speciation: gradualism and punctuated equilibrium.

Understanding: Speciation due to **divergence** of isolated populations can be gradual.

Model sentence: There are two theories about the rate of speciation and evolution: (1) gradualism, which states that changes were slow and steady and (2) punctuated equilibrium, which states that changes were sudden followed by long periods of no change.

Gradualism is a theory of speciation that states that evolution is a slow and steady process with changes happening constantly but in small **increments**.

For example, this theory explains that vision in animals is not something that evolved in a short period. On the contrary, it took many millions of years for photoreceptors to evolve little by little and then to develop into complex eyes with lenses.

Understanding: Speciation can occur **abruptly**.

Punctuated equilibrium is a theory of speciation that states that evolution is a process marked by very little change over long periods of time (**stasis**) followed by sudden evolution due to changes in the environment.

Some organisms have changed very little in hundreds of millions of years – sharks, horseshoe crabs, and cockroaches are three examples of organisms whose fossils are strikingly similar to modern-day individuals.

On the other hand, the mammals that are successful today have evolved more recently. The sudden mass extinction that destroyed the dinosaurs 65 million years ago changed the ecological balances of habitats in the oceans and on land. This allowed for an abrupt branching out, or **adaptive radiation**, of many new species, notably mammals.

General vocabulary

adaptation change which makes something more suitable for a situation

divergence development in different ways so as to be no longer similar

increments gradual and regular increases

Synonyms

abrupt............ sudden

Subject vocabulary

gradualism evolution by slow, continuous small changes

punctuated equilibrium evolution by big jumps with periods of no change in between

stasis no change over a period of time

adaptive radiation speciation by adjusting to conditions in a new area

Application: Identifying examples of directional, stabilizing, and disruptive selection

- **Directional selection** is when natural selection favours one extreme phenotype over the opposite extreme or over any intermediate forms, if they exist. Over time, a population that once had two extreme versions of a trait and perhaps one or more intermediate versions will show a higher frequency of one trait over another. For example, male peacocks (*Pavo cristatus*) and male Astrapian sicklebills (*Astrapia nigra*) are birds known for their unusually long tail feathers. Birds of these species born with more modest feathers would be selected against because female birds would not be attracted to them.

- **Stabilizing selection** is when natural selection favours an intermediate phenotype over one of the extremes. Human height is an example. Individuals who are extremely short or extremely tall do not have an advantage over individuals of average height. On the contrary, the rarity of exceptionally tall or short people shows that such extremes have a negative selective pressure.

- **Disruptive selection** is when natural selection favours two extreme phenotypes rather than an intermediate phenotype. In Darwin's finches, beak sizes vary dramatically. Since they all evolved from one or a small number of species of finches, there must have been a stage in their evolution when one population favoured two extreme beak sizes. Eventually the differences between the individuals were so great that a speciation split occurred. This happened multiple times generating the 13 species we find on the Galapagos today.

> **Subject vocabulary**
>
> **directional selection** selection for one extreme phenotype over the other extreme or intermediate phenotypes
>
> **stabilizing selection** selection for the intermediate phenotype rather than either of the extreme phenotypes
>
> **disruptive selection** selection for two extremes of phenotype rather than intermediate forms
>
> **strain** a type or variety of organism
>
> **triploid** having three sets of chromosomes

The following table summarizes the three types of selective pressures:

	One extreme phenotype	Intermediate phenotype	Both extreme phenotypes
directional	selected for	selected against	selected against
stabilizing	selected against	selected for	selected against
disruptive	selected for	selected against	selected for

Application: Speciation in the genus *Allium* by polyploidy

The genus *Allium* includes plants such as onions, shallots, leeks, and garlic, as well as some popular ornamental flowers.

When examining their chromosomes in karyograms, it is clear that hybrids have formed between species and some show polyploidy. Remember that haploid cells have a single set of the standard number of chromosomes for the species in question and diploid have a double set. Polyploid cells contain more than two sets. This is very rare in animals but quite common in hybrid plants.

The most commonly cultivated species of onion is *Allium cepa*, but this species can have many varieties and the varieties can have **strains**. For example, the vast majority of strains of the *viviparum* variety of *A. cepa*, known as the Egyptian walking onion, are diploid. However, there is a strain called Ljutika, grown in Croatia along the coast of the Adriatic Sea, that has been found to be **triploid**.

Analysis of various karyotypes has revealed that the Egyptian walking onion, *A. cepa* var. *viviparum*, is a hybrid between two *Allium* species: *A. fistulosum* and *A. cepa*.

This is an example of new varieties being formed by polyploidy. If the varieties are isolated and continue to evolve separately, they could completely split and become two distinct species, no longer able to produce fertile offspring.

Skill: Comparison of allele frequencies of geographically isolated populations

The Hardy–Weinberg equation can be used to calculate and compare allele frequencies between two populations. The equation is as follows:

$$p^2 + 2pq + q^2 = 1$$

Where:

- p = the frequency of the dominant allele (T)
- p^2 = the frequency of homozygous dominant phenotypes (TT) in the population
- q = frequency of the recessive allele (t)
- q^2 = the frequency of homozygous recessive phenotypes (tt) in the population
- $2pq$ = the frequency of heterozygous phenotypes in the population (Tt)

To determine frequencies, it is useful to know that $p + q = 1$. So if the frequency of T is 0.50, then the frequency of t must be 0.50. If p is 0.50, then p^2 is 0.25. This means that 25% of the population has a genotype TT. We can do the same for q to find that 25% of the population has a genotype tt. Knowing these two parts of the equation, the only part missing ($2pq$) can be solved because we know that all three parts of the equation must add up to 1. So $2pq$ must equal 0.50 to make 0.25 and 0.25 add up to 1. This means that 50% of the population is Tt. Notice how there is no need to split up $2pq$; just leave it as a single entity.

> **Hints for success:** When solving the Hardy–Weinberg equation, put in any of the values given in the question and any values you can calculate knowing that $p + q = 1$. The most advanced mathematics you need is squaring or taking the square root of a number. You do not need to do this in your head – use a calculator.

Example

Population 1 has the following characteristics. Of 301 flowering plants, 142 produce large flowers (F) and 159 produce small flowers (f). A subgroup, population 2, has split away and is now geographically isolated from the original population. Of 48 plants, 33 have small flowers. Use the Hardy–Weinberg equation to compare the allele frequencies for F and f in the two populations.

Answer: It is best to start with looking at the number of plants producing small flowers because we are certain of their genotype (ff). Once we know ff, we know q^2 and can work out q. In population 1, there are 159 out of 301 small-flowered plants, which is about 53%. The square root of 0.53 gives 0.73 meaning that q is 73%, or that 73% of the alleles in the gene pool are f. We can use what we have calculated so far to determine that p is 27% and therefore p^2 is 7%. When adding 53% and 7%, 40% is missing in order to add up to 100% so therefore $2pq$ must be 40%. Here is a table of the same types of calculations with population 2:

			%	Plants
allele frequencies	recessive f	q	57%	N/A
	dominant F	p	43%	N/A
genotype frequencies	homozygous recessive ff	q^2	69%	33
	heterozygous Ff	$2pq$	12%	6
	homozygous dominant FF	p^2	19%	9

Description of the changes in F and f between the two populations: F has gone from 27% to 43% and f has gone from 73% to 57%. This shows that there has been a change in the allele frequencies between the geographically isolated groups meaning that population 2 is evolving differently than population 1.

11 Animal physiology

11.1 Antibody production and vaccination

Understanding: Every organism has unique molecules on the surface of its cells.

Model sentence: The plasma membranes of the cells of each organism contain unique molecules.

Remember from your previous study of cell membranes that proteins are embedded into and sometimes through plasma membranes. These proteins serve a variety of purposes. One of those purposes is to provide identification for the cell. Each cell of any one organism has the same set of proteins that act as the identifying proteins. These proteins will identify a cell as being 'self' as opposed to 'not-self'. Many molecules that are found to be 'not-self' will be regarded as antigens. Antigens are molecules that stimulate the immune system to begin a response.

Application: Antigens on the surface of red blood cells stimulate antibody production in a person with a different blood group

Red blood cells have a variety of proteins on the surface of their plasma membranes. Three of the protein types must be matched if a person receives a transfusion of blood. Those three proteins are:

- A protein
- B protein
- Rh protein.

There are two different blood identification categories based on the presence or absence of these three proteins.

The first category is called the A–B–O blood group:

- A person who has only the A protein is type A.
- A person who has only the B protein is type B.
- A person who has both the A and B protein is type AB.
- A person who has neither the A or B protein is type O.

The second category is called the Rh blood group:

- A person who has the Rh protein is Rh$^+$.
- A person who does not have the Rh protein is Rh$^-$.

When receiving blood in a transfusion a person cannot receive a protein that they do not already have. A patient that does receive one of the proteins that is 'not-self' to them will regard the new protein as an antigen. They will begin a primary immune response using the new protein as an antigen. This will lead to agglutination problems within their blood. You can see how correct transfusions are done from the chart at the top of the next page.

Subject vocabulary

plasma membrane membrane which surrounds the cell

antigen substance which stimulates the production of antibodies in vertebrates

immune system the system within our body that protects us from diseases

antibody a protein produced by our immune system in response to an antigen

transfusion the blood of one person is transferred to another person

agglutination clumping of blood cells due to antibodies

General vocabulary

embedded positioned firmly and deeply

	You can receive							
If your type is	**O−**	**O+**	**B−**	**B+**	**A−**	**A+**	**AB−**	**AB+**
AB+	yes	yes	yes	yes	yes	yes	yes	yes
AB−	yes		yes		yes		yes	
A+	yes	yes			yes	yes		
A−	yes				yes			
B+	yes	yes	yes	yes				
B−	yes		yes					
O+	yes	yes						
O−	yes							

Figure 11.1 *Chart showing blood transfusion possibilities*

Subject vocabulary

pathogens disease-causing agents such as viruses and bacteria

B lymphocytes leukocytes that produce antibodies

activated a chemical notification sent from one leukocyte to another leukocyte

T lymphocytes leukocytes that can activate other types of leukocytes

Synonyms

leukocyte .... white blood cell

Understanding: Pathogens can be species-specific although others can cross species barriers.

Model sentence: Disease-causing agents typically infect only one species but a few can infect more than one species.

Pathogens are those things that are capable of causing a disease. Two of the most common types of pathogens are some viruses and some bacteria. Usually, a specific virus or bacterium are pathogens to only one type of organism. There are exceptions to this as shown in the table below:

Caused by a virus	Caused by a bacterium
influenza caused by H1N1	tuberculosis
SARS	salmonella

Hints for success: In an examination, remember that a virus is not a living thing. Viruses are not cells.

Understanding: B lymphocytes are activated by T lymphocytes in mammals.

Model sentence: White blood cells known as T lymphocytes activate other leukocytes called B lymphocytes in mammals.

There are many types of white blood cells (also known as leukocytes). Leukocytes have a variety of functions related to the immune system. Each type of leukocyte specializes in one of the functions.

One specialized type of leukocyte is called T lymphocytes. The T lymphocytes known as helper T lymphocytes recognize antigens on pathogens. Antigens are molecules that make up a pathogen. Each pathogen has its own unique set of antigens. Once a helper T lymphocyte recognizes a specific antigen it chemically communicates with (activates) another type of leukocyte. This type of leukocyte is called a B lymphocyte.

Understanding: Activated **B cells** multiply to form clones of **plasma cells** and memory cells.

Model sentence: B cells that have become activated will divide by **mitosis** many times and become clones called plasma cells and memory cells.

When cells divide by mitosis each resulting cell is a clone of the other. Imagine a cell that undergoes mitosis many times in a short period of time. A small army of clones would be formed. This is what happens when B cells become activated. The resulting army of cells is of two types:

1 Plasma cells – plasma cells are B cells that immediately begin producing molecules called antibodies.
2 Memory cells – memory cells are B cells that live for a very long period of time and are capable of producing antibodies. Memory cells typically wait for a second infection of the same pathogen before becoming active.

Understanding: Plasma cells **secrete** antibodies.

Model sentence: Antibodies are produced and secreted by plasma cells.

Each different type of B cell produces a single type of antibody. Each antibody is a protein that will bind to one antigen. The plasma cells that are cloned during an infection are cells that produce only one type of antibody. Each cell is like a protein factory as it produces many of that type of antibody.

Understanding: Antibodies aid the destruction of pathogens.

Model sentence: Antibodies are an important step in the immune response by helping to destroy a pathogen.

Each antibody is a 'Y' shaped protein molecule. At the two upper ends of the 'Y' are two identical **binding sites**. These binding sites stick to a specific antigen. Most likely the antigen is a protein molecule on the surface of a pathogen (like a virus or bacterium).

Antibodies help to destroy pathogens by:
- marking the pathogen for destruction by leukocytes
- sticking antigens together by using the two binding sites on different antigen molecules (this is called agglutination).

Understanding: White cells release **histamine** in response to **allergens**.

Model sentence: Certain antigens cause some leukocytes to release chemicals called histamines.

Histamines are chemicals that are released from leukocytes called mast cells. When the antigen is first encountered, B cells produce an antibody called **IgE**. The IgE antibodies bind to leukocytes called mast cells. Whenever that same antigen is encountered again, the antigen will find the IgE molecules on the mast cells. The mast cell will then release histamine into the surrounding area.

Synonyms
B cells............ B lymphocytes
secrete .... produce/release

Subject vocabulary
plasma cells B cells that immediately begin antibody production during an infection

mitosis cell division where one diploid cell becomes two diploid cells

binding sites the area of an antibody that can stick to an antigen

histamine chemicals released by leukocytes called mast cells

allergen a substance capable of initiating an allergic response

IgE a type of antibody produced by some B cells

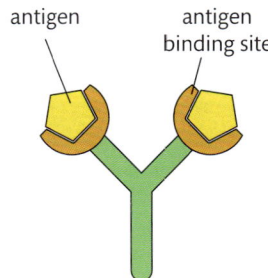

Figure 11.2 Antibody molecule showing two identical binding sites

11 Animal physiology

Subject vocabulary

allergic symptoms sneezing, itchiness, etc., that are common with an allergy

allergy reaction to an antigen as if it were part of a pathogen

mast cells leukocytes that release histamines during an allergy episode

dilate inner portion of a tube getting larger

Understanding: Histamines cause **allergic symptoms**.

Model sentence: Allergy symptoms are a result of mast cells releasing histamines.

Histamines have a variety of effects. Some of those effects are useful when a pathogen has infected the body. For example, small arteries and capillaries dilate when exposed to histamines. This brings more blood to the site of infection.

Histamine release is triggered from some people in response to antigens that do not cause disease. The resulting condition is called an allergy. One of the more common things that trigger histamine release is pollen. Antigens on pollen trigger mast cells to release histamines. Histamines lead to the uncomfortable allergy symptoms such as sneezing and itching.

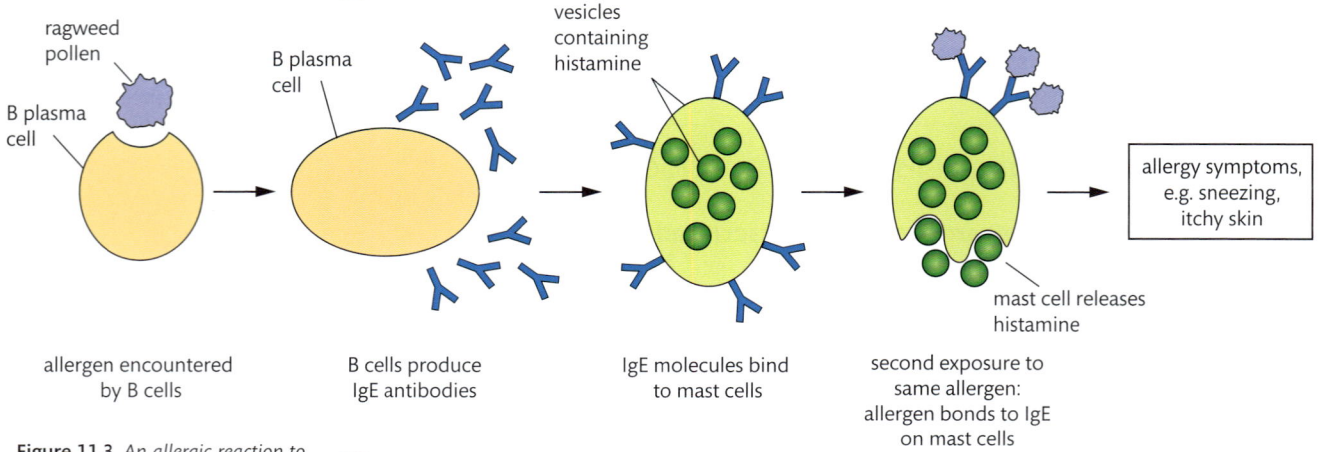

Figure 11.3 *An allergic reaction to an allergen*

General vocabulary

itching a feeling on the skin that makes you want to scratch

Subject vocabulary

immunity having a protection due to previous exposure

primary immune response immune response upon first infection

secondary immune response immune response from any infection of the same pathogen that is not the first infection

Synonyms

B cells .... B lymphocytes

Understanding: **Immunity** depends upon the continued existence of memory cells.

Model sentence: Memory cells from a previous infection give immunity from further infections of the same type.

The first time a person is exposed to a pathogen it results in a response called the primary immune response. There is a fairly long time period where:

- The pathogen is identified by T cells.
- Various cells including specific **B cells** undergo cloning.
- B cells produce large numbers of antibodies for that pathogen.

A person is likely to experience symptoms of the disease while completing the primary immune response.

The primary immune response leaves behind long-lived cells called memory cells. Memory B cells can be called into action to produce antibodies in a relatively short period of time. Thus, memory cells give the immune system a 'head start' if an infection occurs a second time. Often the second response is so rapid that symptoms of the disease do not have time to appear. Anytime we respond to the same infection after the first time it is called a secondary immune response. As you can see from the graph below, the production of antibodies occurs much quicker and produces many more antibodies as compared to the primary response.

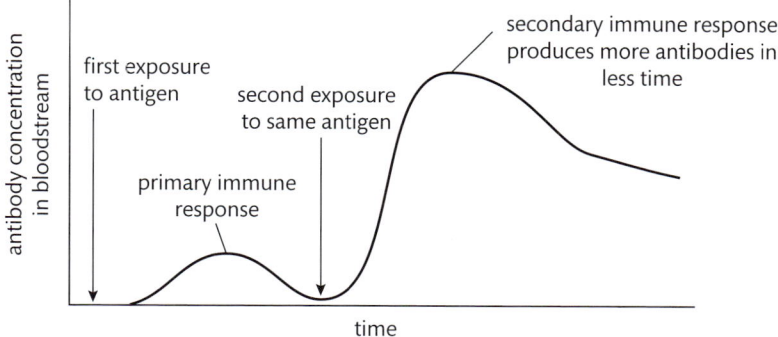

Figure 11.4 *Graph showing antibody production in a primary and secondary immune response. The secondary immune response may occur soon after the primary response, or occur months or years after it*

Understanding: Vaccines contain antigens that trigger immunity but do not cause the disease.

Model sentence: Immunity can be achieved by using a vaccine that contains antigens but does not result in the disease.

To understand how a vaccine results in immunity you will need to understand the difference between a pathogen and an antigen:

- A pathogen is a term used for the disease-causing agent. For example, a virus is a pathogen.
- An antigen is a molecule that makes up the pathogen. Most antigens are proteins. A virus typically has several different proteins making up its outer coating (called a **capsid**).

A vaccine is created by damaging the disease-causing agents of the pathogen so that it is just the non-pathogenic molecular parts. The antigens are still there but they are no longer in a form that can cause the disease. Our immune system recognizes the antigens as if they were still a part of the intact pathogen. A primary immune response will still occur. Memory cells will still be created. All of the benefits occur without the person having to suffer the symptoms of the disease. If the real pathogen ever infects the body, it will have a secondary immune response. If you remember, that response is quicker than a primary response and produces many more antibodies.

Application: Smallpox was the first infectious disease of humans to have been eradicated by vaccination.

In 1967, the World Health Organization began a campaign to 'vaccinate the world' against the deadly disease smallpox. The last reported case of smallpox was in 1977. The vaccination programme was so successful that people no longer need to be vaccinated.

Subject vocabulary

vaccine an injection prepared from the non-pathogenic antigens of a pathogen

capsid outer coating of a virus

vaccination a shot (inoculation) of an inactive pathogen that leads to a primary immune response

Synonyms

eradicated ..... eliminated/ removed

Subject vocabulary

fusion two cells that join together as one

tumour cell a cell that has a very long cellular life-span and divides rapidly

hybridoma cell a cell created by fusing a tumour cell with an antibody-producing plasma cell (B cell)

hybrid something that has the properties of two things

cell culture a container with liquid medium for growing cells outside of the body

monoclonal antibodies antibodies created by a single type of hybridoma cell

mitotic clones identical cells created by mitosis

HCG hormone produced by an early embryo which signals the ovary to secrete progesterone

Understanding: Fusion of a tumour cell with an antibody-producing plasma cell creates a hybridoma cell.

Model sentence: Hybridoma cells **are created by fusing a cancer cell with an antibody-producing B cell.**

Hybridoma cells are truly a hybrid between two types of body cells. The two types of body cells are made to fuse together in a cell culture. The resulting cell (the hybridoma) has properties of each of the two cells used to create it. The two cells that fuse together are:

1. A cancerous (tumour) cell.
   - This gives the hybridoma a very long cellular life.
   - The hybridoma will divide by mitosis many times.

2. An antibody-producing B cell.
   - A specific B cell is chosen for the type of antibody it produces.
   - The antibody can be purified from the cell culture.

The hybridoma cells can be grown in cell cultures. The cell culture can be kept healthy for a very long period of time.

Understanding: Monoclonal antibodies are produced by hybridoma cells.

Model sentence: Each hybridoma cell creates a single type of antibody called a monoclonal antibody.

Each hybridoma cell is created by using one antibody-producing plasma cell. This cell will only produce one type of antibody. A cell culture is created starting from a single hybridoma cell. All of the other cells in that cell culture will be mitotic clones of the original. They all produce only one type of antibody. All of the antibodies from one culture are called monoclonal antibodies.

Antibodies produced during an immune response are mixed into the blood with many other kinds of antibodies. Monoclonal antibodies are created in a laboratory and have specialized uses in medicine and research.

Application: Monoclonal antibodies to HCG are used in pregnancy test kits

HCG is a hormone that is produced only by a very young embryo. The hormone passes across to the mother's bloodstream. Monoclonal antibodies that recognize HCG as their antigen are used for pregnancy testing. If the monoclonal antibodies find HCG, a reaction occurs leading to a colour change that indicates that the female is pregnant.

11.2 Movement

Understanding: Bones and **exoskeletons** provide **anchorage** for muscles and act as **levers**.

Model sentence: The internal or external skeleton of an animal provides anchor points for muscles allowing parts of it to act as levers.

The type of skeleton most people think of is an internal skeleton (**endoskeleton**) made of bones. Some animals have another kind of skeleton. Their skeleton is located on the outside of the body and is called an exoskeleton.

Both types of skeletons provide support for the body and also:
- anchor muscles at both ends of the muscle
- act as levers in order to provide movement efficiency.

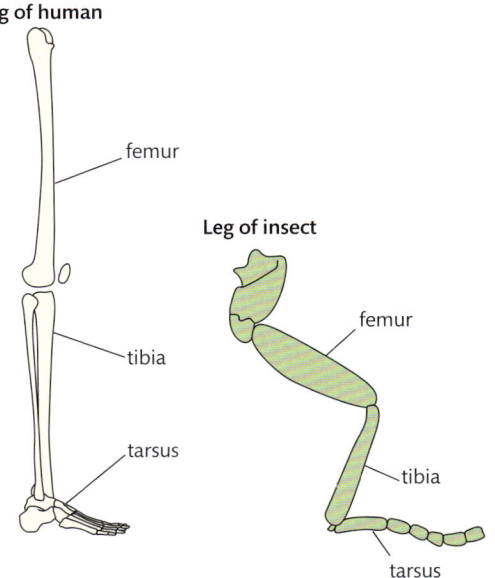

Figure 11.5 *The bones of the endoskeleton of a human and the segments of the exoskeleton of an insect are similar enough to be given many of the same anatomical names*

Understanding: **Synovial joints** allow certain movements but not others.

Model sentence: Bone to bone joints in the body, called synovial joints, permit only certain movements of the bones.

A joint is where one bone connects to another bone. These connections require structures called **ligaments**. If the joint allows movement there may be a fluid that helps **lubricate** the area. If so, the joint is called a synovial joint. Here are two examples of synovial joints and the movements they permit:
- Elbow joint – the elbow joint works like a **hinge**. The elbow allows your forearm to move up and down but it does not permit **rotation**. Your knee is similar to the elbow in its structure and in the movement allowed.
- Shoulder joint – the joint that connects each of your arms into your shoulders is called a ball-and-socket joint. This joint allows all kind of movements including rotation. Your hip joint is similar in structure and movements.

Subject vocabulary

exoskeleton a skeleton of some material that is found on the outside of an animal

endoskeleton a skeleton made of bones found on the inside of an animal

synovial joint a bone to bone connection where there is a chamber filled with a fluid that lubricates movement of the bones

ligaments structures in the body that help join bones together at a joint

General vocabulary

anchorage acting as an attachment point for something

lever a bar-shaped object used to transmit force efficiently

lubricate the use of a substance to reduce friction

hinge an adaptation that allows only a side-to-side or up-and-down movement

rotation movement in a circular motion

Skill: Annotation of a diagram of the human elbow

If given a figure showing a sectioned view of the human elbow, you should be able to label the parts and give their functions.

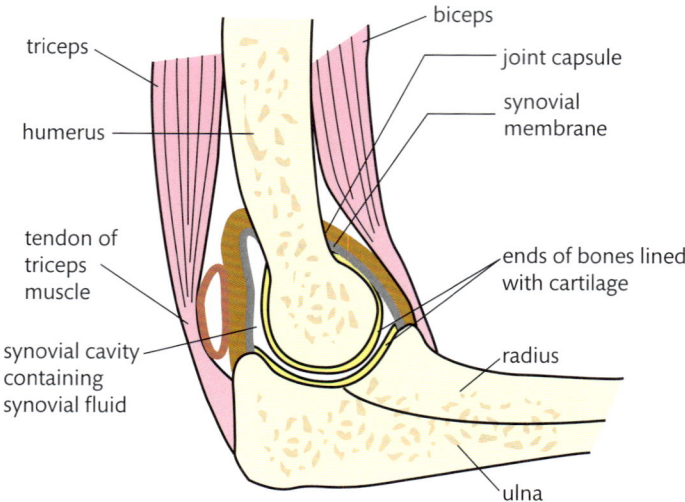

Figure 11.6 *The human elbow in section*

Joint part	Function
cartilage	reduces friction and absorbs compression
synovial fluid	lubricates to reduce friction and provides nutrients to the cells of the cartilage
joint capsule	surrounds the joint, encloses the synovial cavity, and unites the connecting bones
tendons	attach muscle to bone
ligaments	connect bone to bone
biceps muscle	contracts to bring about flexion (bending) of the arm
triceps muscle	contracts to cause extension (straightening) of the arm
humerus	acts as a lever that allows anchorage of the muscles of the elbow
radius	acts as a lever for the biceps muscle
ulna	acts as a lever for the triceps muscle

Understanding: Movement of the body requires muscles to work in antagonistic pairs.

Model sentence: Muscles provide movement by working in antagonistic pairs.

Every time a bone of your body moves into a new position at least one muscle contracts to cause that movement. Now, in order for that same bone to move back to where it started another muscle must be used. The muscles that work in pairs like that are called **antagonistic muscle** pairs.

Subject vocabulary

antagonistic muscles muscles that work in pairs to cause opposite movements

A good example of antagonistic muscle pairs is shown by the way your forearm **flexes** and straightens at the elbow. In order for your forearm to flex, you must contract a muscle called your **biceps**. Then, in order to straighten again you must contract a muscle called the **triceps**.

Synonyms
flex .... bend

Subject vocabulary

biceps muscle that causes the forearm to flex

triceps muscle that causes the forearm to straighten

skeletal muscle muscle that is used to move bones

multinucleate containing many nuclei

endoplasmic reticulum organelle involved in transport within the cell

muscle fibre term used for a muscle cell

sarcoplasmic reticulum the specialized ER in muscle cells

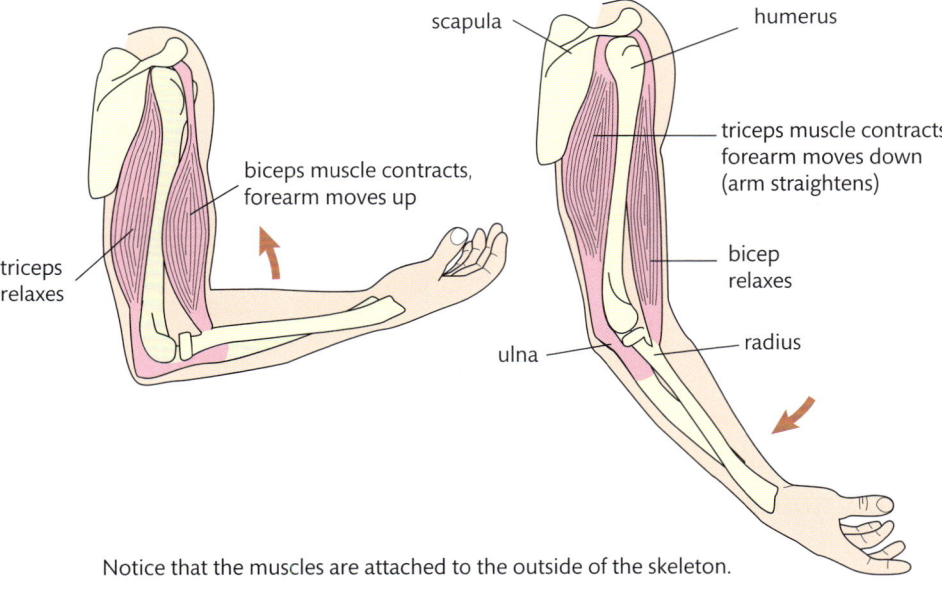

Notice that the muscles are attached to the outside of the skeleton.

Figure 11.7 The forearm of a human is moved up and down by the action of the triceps and biceps

Application: Antagonistic pairs of muscles in an insect leg

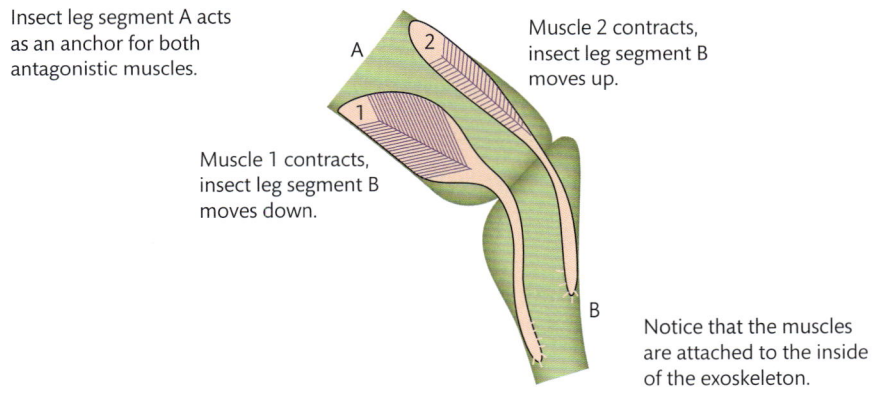

Figure 11.8 The segments of an insect's leg are moved up and down by the action of antagonistic muscle pairs

Understanding: Skeletal muscle fibres are multinucleate and contain specialized endoplasmic reticulum.

Model sentence: Each cell of a skeletal muscle, called a muscle fibre, has many nuclei and contains specialized endoplasmic reticulum.

Skeletal muscle is muscle that moves your bones. All muscle tissue is made of living cells. The cells are very thin and long. Thus, these cells are called muscle fibres. Unlike most cells, each muscle fibre has many nuclei within the cytoplasm. Muscle fibres are described as being multinucleate.

The endoplasmic reticulum of skeletal muscle cells is different from that in other cells. It is highly branched and has many folds. This specialized endoplasmic reticulum is called the **sarcoplasmic reticulum**.

11 Animal physiology

Understanding: Muscle fibres contain many **myofibrils**.

Model sentence: The interior of muscle cells (fibres) contains many contracting proteins organized into long strands called myofibrils.

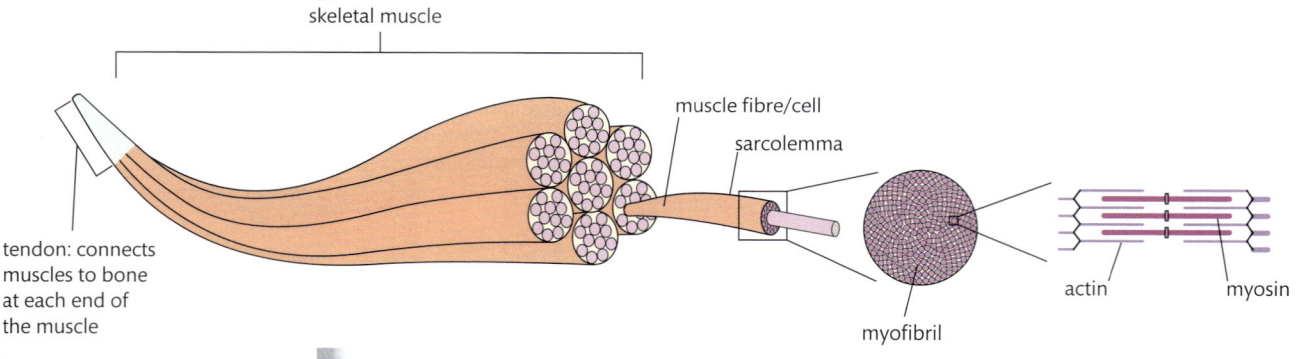

Figure 11.9 Each muscle fibre is a muscle cell. The entire muscle is composed of many muscle fibres all running in the same direction and thus all able to contract in unison when necessary

Subject vocabulary

myofibrils the filaments made up of actin and myosin inside muscle fibres

contractile sarcomeres the contracting sections of a myofibril

actin the protein in a sarcomere that slides during a contraction

myosin the protein in a sarcomere that does not move during a contraction

Z-lines the outside boundary of actin within a single sarcomere; each sarcomere has a Z-line on each side

General vocabulary

alternating occuring one after the other in a repeated pattern

Figure 11.10 This figure shows a single sarcomere. Notice that a sarcomere is composed of **alternating** actin and myosin proteins. The myosin is a set length and cannot move. The actin is able to slide over the top of the myosin. In this figure, imagine the two lines called the **Z-lines** both moving closer to each other as the actin slides. The entire sarcomere becomes shorter

Understanding: Each myofibril is made up of **contractile sarcomeres**.

Model sentence: The length of an individual myofibril is made up of many contractile sarcomeres.

A muscle gets shorter when it contracts. The shortening that occurs is because many thousands of individual sections all get shorter at the same time. Those sections are called contractile sarcomeres. The sarcomeres are all connected to each other.

Understanding: The contraction of skeletal muscle is achieved by the sliding of **actin** and **myosin** filaments.

Model sentence: The shortening of skeletal muscle occurs because the protein actin slides over another protein called myosin.

Skill: Drawing labelled diagrams of the structure of a sarcomere

Sarcomere

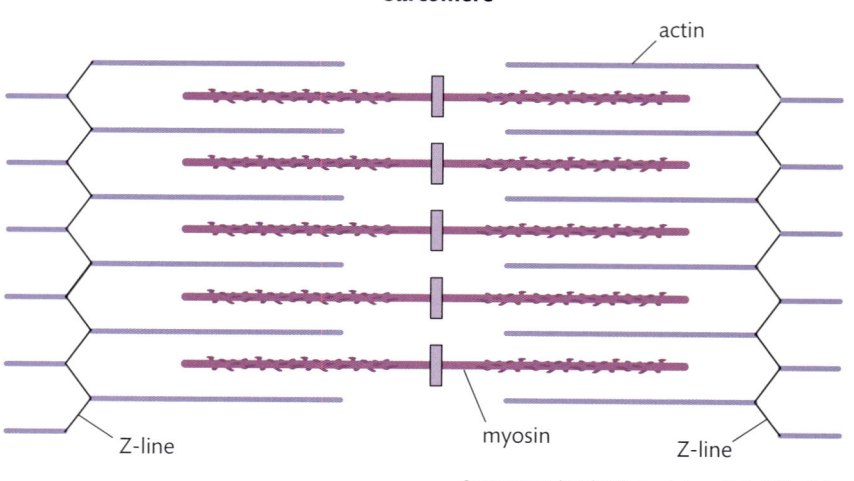

Source: reproduced with permission of John Wiley & Sons, Inc.

Understanding: ATP hydrolysis and cross bridge formation are necessary for the filaments to slide.

Model sentence: The sliding of actin over myosin requires myosin to form a bridge to actin and energy from ATP.

The myosin within a sarcomere has many protein extensions called 'heads'. The **myosin heads** make connections with or connect with actin. This is called cross bridge formation. An ATP molecule is required each time a myosin head forms a cross bridge with an actin. Notice in the figure below that the two Z-lines move closer to each other when a muscle contracts.

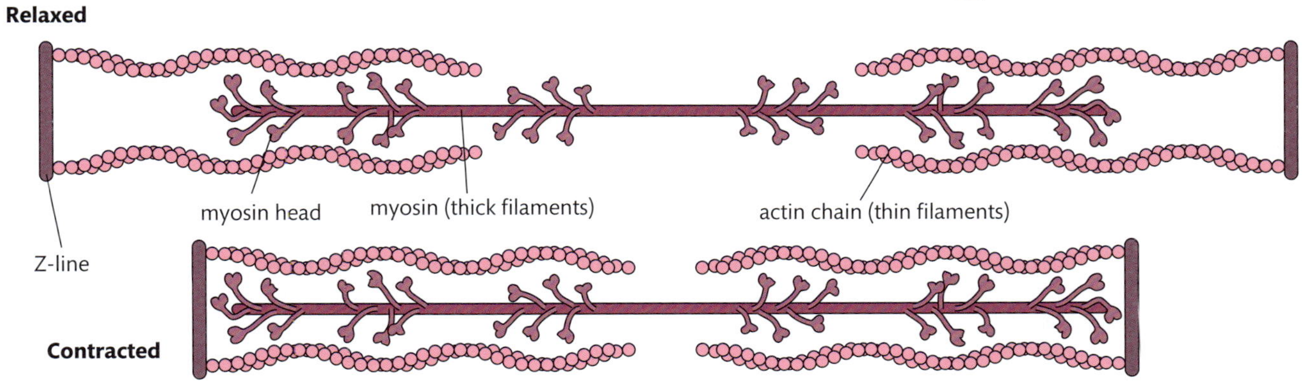

Relaxed

Contracted

Labels: Z-line, myosin head, myosin (thick filaments), actin chain (thin filaments)

Figure 11.11 Position of actin and myosin in a relaxed muscle and a contracted muscle. With the energy of ATP the myosin heads have moved the actin fibres toward the centre of the sarcomere

Skill: Analysis of electron micrographs to find the state of contraction of muscle fibres

Ask your instructor to show you photographs taken using an **electron microscope** that show:

- one or more sarcomeres in a relaxed position
- one or more sarcomeres in a contracted position.

Use your knowledge of how a sarcomere contracts in order to explain what you are seeing in the photographs.

Understanding: Calcium ions and the proteins tropomyosin and troponin control muscle contractions.

Model sentence: A muscle is signalled to contract by the interaction of calcium ions and the proteins tropomyosin and troponin.

When a muscle is relaxed the actin fibres prevent myosin cross bridging. The cross bridging is prevented by binding sites on the actin being covered up. Two proteins, called tropomyosin and troponin are used to cover the actin-binding sites.

Skeletal muscle only contracts when your brain sends an impulse to the muscle. The impulse triggers calcium ions to enter all of the sarcomeres. The calcium ions result in tropomyosin and troponin moving and uncovering the binding sites on actin. The myosin heads automatically bind to actin and cause actin to move toward the centre of the sarcomere. The result is a muscle contraction.

> **Subject vocabulary**
>
> **ATP** a molecule used for a source of chemical energy
>
> **hydrolysis** a chemical reaction in which a larger molecule is split into two smaller molecules
>
> **cross bridge** connections between myosin heads and actin
>
> **myosin heads** the protein extensions of myosin that connect to actin
>
> **electron microscope** a microscope capable of very high magnification
>
> **calcium ions** positively charged ions that enter sarcomeres when a nervous system impulse is received by muscle
>
> **tropomyosin** one of two proteins that blocks binding sites on actin to control muscle contractions
>
> **troponin** one of two proteins that blocks binding sites on actin to control muscle contractions

11.3 The kidney and osmoregulation

Understanding: Animals are either **osmoregulators** or **osmoconformers**.

Model sentence: Animals stay in osmotic balance in their environment by being either an osmoregulator or an osmoconformer.

Animals achieve water balance with their environments in two main ways:

1. Most animals are osmoregulators. These animals use mechanisms to make sure that they remain in water balance with their environment. They may **expel** or gain **solutes** (like salt ions) in order to remain in balance. They also may expel more or less water to their environment in differing situations. Osmoregulators respond to their environment in order to remain in water balance. You are an example of an osmoregulator.

2. Osmoconformers live in a water environment that is already in balance with the cells in their bodies. They neither gain nor lose water because they are already in osmotic balance. Osmoconformers are restricted to living in water environments that match their own tissues. A scallop is an example of an osmoconformer.

Understanding: The **Malpighian tubule** system in insects and the **kidney** carry out osmoregulation and removal of **nitrogenous waste**.

Model sentence: Water balance and removal of nitrogenous waste is done by the Malpighian tubules of insects and the kidneys in many other animals.

Nitrogenous wastes are nitrogen-containing molecules that are waste products traced back to proteins. Each organism must expel these wastes from their body before the waste becomes toxic.

Insects have numerous small tubes called Malpighian tubules within their body **cavities**. The Malpighian tubules are bathed and surrounded in the insect's blood within their body cavities. The tubules absorb the nitrogenous wastes from the blood. The waste is then taken to the animal's **gut** to be released with the **faeces**. Water can also be absorbed into the tubules if excess water needs to be **excreted**.

Mammals have kidneys that remove nitrogenous wastes from the blood. Blood is taken to the kidneys by large blood vessels. The blood is filtered in the kidney and nitrogenous waste and excess water is removed. These waste products become **urine**. Urine is stored in a **bladder** before it is released from the body.

Subject vocabulary

osmoregulator an animal that modifies its own tissues to stay in osmotic balance

osmoconformer an animal that lives in an environment where it is already in osmotic balance

osmotic balance two fluids that have equal solute and water concentrations

solute(s) molecules dissolved in a solvent (water)

Malpighian tubules small tubes located in the body cavities of insects that absorb nitrogenous waste to be taken to the gut

kidney the organ in some animals that filters blood to remove nitrogenous wastes and excess water

nitrogenous waste molecules that contain nitrogen that must be removed from an organism before they become toxic

faeces solid waste from our gut

excrete pass from the body

urine the liquid waste of an animal that has kidneys

bladder a storage sac for urine until it is excreted

Synonyms

expel .... force out/push out
cavity .... space (within)
gut .... alimentary canal

Subject vocabulary

renal artery large blood vessel taking blood into a kidney

renal vein large blood vessel taking blood out of a kidney

renal cortex the outer layer of tissue in a kidney

renal medulla the layer of tissue under the cortex in a kidney

renal pelvis collection chamber for urine in a kidney

ureter tube that takes urine from the kidney to the bladder

Understanding: The composition of blood in the **renal artery** is different from that in the **renal vein**.

Model sentence: Blood entering the kidney in the renal artery has a different chemical composition compared to the blood leaving the kidney in the renal vein.

Humans have two kidneys. Each kidney has a large blood vessel that takes blood into the kidney. That blood vessel is called the renal artery. The kidney then filters the blood to remove nitrogenous waste and excess water. The blood then leaves the kidney through a large vein called the renal vein.

Skill: **Drawing and labelling a diagram of the human kidney**

Practise drawing and labelling the human kidney, as shown in the figure.

Notice that a kidney has an outer layer called the **renal cortex**. The layer under the cortex is called the **renal medulla**. Under that is a collection chamber for urine called the **renal pelvis**. The tube that drains urine out of the pelvis is called the **ureter**.

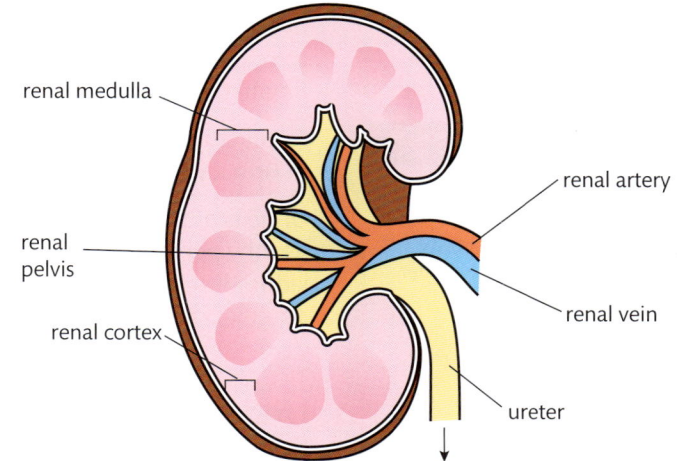

Figure 11.12 *Sectioned view of the human kidney*

Hints for success: In an examination, data may be presented to you showing the chemical make-up of molecules in the blood. The difference between the composition of blood in the renal vein as compared to the renal artery shows the chemical change made by the kidney. The molecules removed from the blood will be found in urine.

Subject vocabulary

ultrastructure detailed structure of a cell not visible with a light microscope

glomerulus (plural: glomeruli) the capillary bed inside of Bowman's capsule

Bowman's capsule surrounds the glomerulus capillary

ultrafiltration filtration under pressure

nephron a small filtering 'unit' of a kidney

General vocabulary

facilitate make easier

Understanding: The **ultrastructure** of the **glomerulus** and **Bowman's capsule** facilitate **ultrafiltration**.

Model sentence: The structural features of the glomerulus and Bowman's capsule are adapted for efficient filtration of the blood.

Each kidney is made up of about 1.25 million filtering units called **nephrons**. Each nephron filters a very small amount of the blood entering the kidney through the renal artery. The filtration process is under high blood pressure and is called ultrafiltration. Each nephron begins with a swollen area called Bowman's capsule. Inside Bowman's capsule is a capillary bed called the glomerulus. Ultrafiltration occurs through the glomerulus capillary bed.

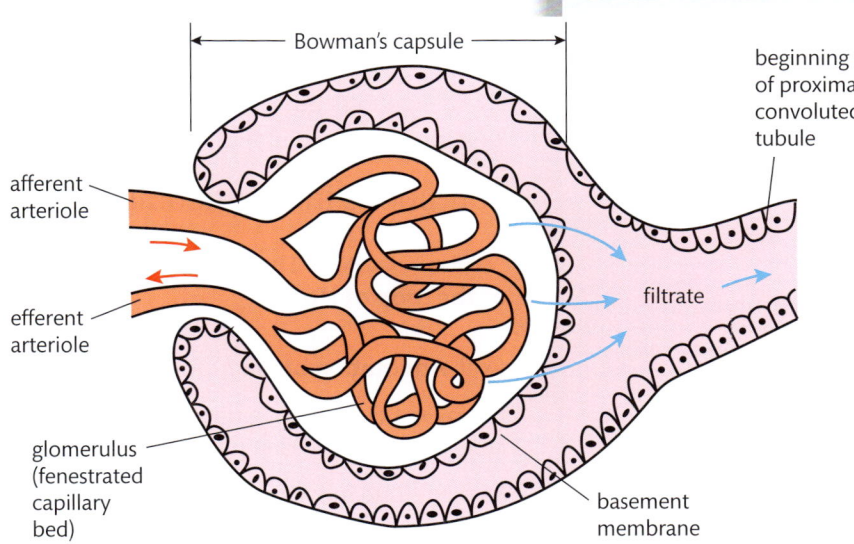

Figure 11.13 *Bowman's capsule is the site of the process called ultrafiltration*

11 Animal physiology | 223

General vocabulary

slits long, narrow openings

selectively some but not all of something

transplant to move from one person to another person

Subject vocabulary

filtrate the fluid that is being filtered out of the glomerulus

proximal convoluted tubule the portion of the nephron just after Bowman's capsule

active transport cellular transport requiring energy (ATP) from the cell

haemodialysis removal and cleansing of blood

loop of Henle portion of the nephron tubule that extends down into the medulla of the kidney

---

The glomerulus capillary bed contains very small **slits** called fenestrations. These slits open as blood moves through. The fenestrations are only big enough to let some molecules through but not others. Blood cells are much too large to fit through the slits, as are most protein molecules. This **filtrate** must next pass through a membranous structure called the basement membrane. The fluid that does pass through the fenestrations and the basement membrane is called the filtrate. The filtrate then enters a part of the nephron called the **proximal convoluted tubule**.

Application: Blood cells, glucose, proteins, and drugs are detected in urinary tests

Urine is often tested for the presence of substances that should not be there in a healthy person. The presence of blood cells and many proteins is a sign that the kidney is not functioning as it should. The presence of glucose in urine is often a sign that the level of glucose in the blood is too high.

Understanding: The proximal convoluted tubule **selectively** reabsorbs useful substances by **active transport.**

Model sentence: Active transport is used to recover useful substances from the filtrate through the walls of the proximal convoluted tubule.

The filtrate that is formed in Bowman's capsule has many substances that the body cannot afford to lose. A good example of this is glucose. Glucose is small enough to become a part of the filtrate. If this glucose were not recovered it would be lost from the body as part of urine.

Each nephron is capable of actively transporting useful molecules out of the proximal convoluted tubule to be recovered back into the bloodstream. This process is so efficient that no glucose is typically found in a healthy person's urine.

Application: Treatment of kidney failure by **haemodialysis** or kidney **transplant**

There are two options available when a patient has failing kidneys. One option is to filter the blood by the use of a machine. This procedure is called haemodialysis. The patient's blood is passed through a device containing a membrane and a fluid. Urea diffuses out of the blood and through the membrane into the fluid. The blood returned to the body has a lower content of urea. This procedure needs to be repeated every few days.

The second option is to receive a transplanted kidney by surgery. The kidney that is received must be 'matched' between the donor and receiving patient.

Understanding: The **loop of Henle** maintains hypertonic conditions in the medulla.

Model sentence: The medulla area of the kidney is hypertonic due to actions of the loop of Henle.

Skill: Annotation of diagrams of the nephron

If shown a diagram of a nephron similar to the one opposite, you should be able to label the parts and describe their function.

As the filtrate moves through the proximal convoluted tubule down and then back up through the loop of Henle further changes occur to the filtrate. One of those changes is that many ions are reabsorbed out of the filtrate. These ions remain for a period of time in the surrounding fluid. This makes that fluid hypertonic to most other fluids in the area.

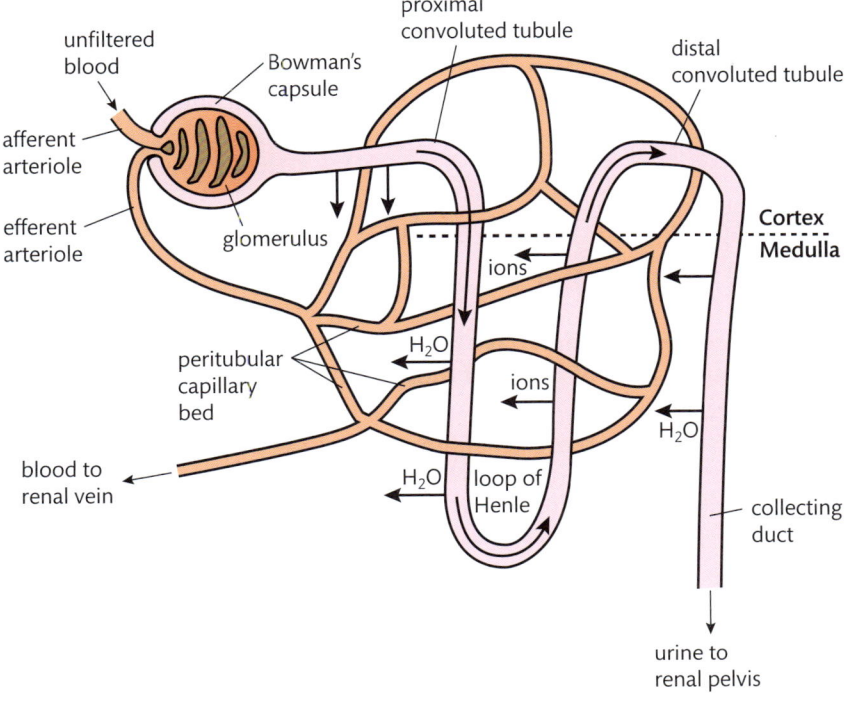

Figure 11.14 A single nephron of the mammalian kidney. Notice the dotted line showing the portion of each nephron in the renal cortex of the kidney and the portion of each that extends down into the renal medulla

Subject vocabulary

ADH the hormone that affects the collecting duct to make it permeable to water

reabsorption the return of molecules to the blood that were a part of the filtrate

collecting duct a duct that takes urine to the pelvis of a kidney

hypotonic a fluid that has a high water content compared to another fluid

osmosis movement of water through a membrane along a concentration gradient

General vocabulary

dilute make less concentrated

permeable allows one or more substances to pass through

Understanding: ADH controls reabsorption of water in the collecting duct.

Model sentence: The presence or absence of the hormone ADH determines whether water is reabsorbed out of the collecting duct.

As you can see from the figure above, the filtrate moves up the loop of Henle and into the distal convoluted tubule. From there it passes into a tube called a collecting duct. The filtrate by this time has been modified so that many of the molecules that were originally filtered have now been returned to the blood (reabsorbed).

The filtrate that enters the collecting duct is quite **dilute.** This means that its water content is quite high. This also means that the fluid in the collecting duct is **hypotonic** to the highly hypertonic fluid of the medulla of the kidney. If the collecting duct becomes **permeable** to water, that water will leave the collecting duct by **osmosis.** Any water that leaves the collecting duct is reabsorbed back into the blood.

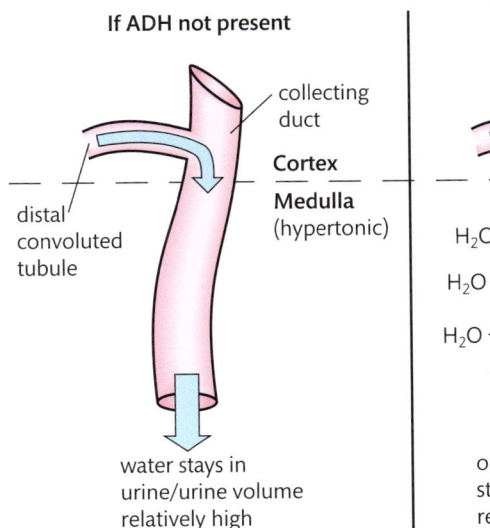

Figure 11.15 Control of water reabsorption in the kidney by ADH

11 Animal physiology | 225

General vocabulary

impermeable does not allow substances to pass through

Synonyms

conserve .... save/retain

Subject vocabulary

positive correlation two factors that both increase together or decrease together

desert an environment where little to no water is available

The collecting duct is sometimes permeable to water and sometimes it is not permeable. The permeability of the collecting duct is controlled by the hormone, ADH. If ADH is present, the collecting duct allows water to leave by osmosis. If ADH is not present, the collecting duct remains **impermeable** to water. In that case, water stays in the collecting duct and will be lost as part of the urine.

Your body produces ADH when you need to **conserve** water. Your body stops producing ADH when more water needs to be eliminated in urine. This is an example of negative feedback control.

Understanding: The length of the loop of Henle is **positively correlated** with the need for water conservation in animals.

Model sentence: Animals that have the greatest need to conserve water tend to have the longest loop of Henle of those animals that have kidneys.

The loop of Henle is the part of the nephron that creates a hypertonic fluid. This fluid surrounds the collecting duct. The longer the loop of Henle the more water can be drawn out of the collecting duct. This water is returned to the animal's blood and is not lost in the urine. Here are two examples to show this correlation:

1. Grass frog – the grass frog has virtually no loop of Henle. The urine of this animal is always very dilute. Grass frogs live in areas where there is high availability of water. Conserving water is not necessary.

2. Kangaroo rat – the kangaroo rat has a very long loop of Henle. There is very little water in the urine of this animal. Kangaroo rats live in **desert** areas. Almost all their water intake is from the food they eat.

Application: Consequences of dehydration and overhydration

Dehydration is an insufficient intake of water to keep up with water lost by the body. Overhydration is a result of an excess of water intake as compared to water lost. The symptoms of each are shown by this chart.

Dehydration	Overhydration
sleepiness	change in behaviour/confusion
constipation	blurred vision
dry mouth and skin	muscle cramps
dizziness and headache	nausea and vomiting

Understanding: The type of nitrogenous waste in animals is correlated with evolutionary history and habitat.

Model sentence: Evolutionary history and habitat largely determine the type of nitrogenous waste an animal produces.

Structure of nitrogenous waste	Example organism	Advantages	Disadvantages
ammonia	fish	requires very little energy to produce	very toxic in blood and tissues; must be diluted and removed from the body quickly by using a great deal of water
urea	mammals	requires less energy to produce compared with uric acid; toxic in blood and tissues but only at physiologically abnormal levels	requires more energy to produce compared with ammonia; requires some water for dilution and removal from the body
uric acid	birds	relatively insoluble in aqueous solutions such as blood and cytoplasm; can be stored within specialized structures within some animal's eggs; requires little to no water for dilution and removal from the body	its complex structure requires a great deal of energy to produce

11.4 Sexual reproduction

Subject vocabulary

spermatogenesis process of creating sperm cells

oogenesis process of creating egg cells

meiosis cell division where one diploid cell becomes four haploid cells

cell differentiation the development of specialized structures within a cell

diploid a cell which has chromosomes in homologous pairs

haploid a cell that has only one chromosome of each homologous pair

flagellum (plural: flagella) whip-like structure which allows movement of cells

organelles non-cellular structures within a cell which carry out organ-like processes

Synonyms

ovum (plural: ova) ... egg

Understanding: **Spermatogenesis** and **oogenesis** both involve mitosis, cell growth, two divisions of **meiosis**, and differentiation.

Model sentence: Production of both sperm and egg requires mitosis, cell growth, meiosis, and cell differentiation.

- Sperm production is called spermtatogenesis.
- Egg (or **ova**) production is called oogenesis.

Both of these types of reproductive cells require the following:

Process	Purpose
mitosis	Mitosis creates more cells that can become reproductive cells.
cell growth	Cell growth is necessary because the beginning cell will undergo two cell divisions to form four cells.
meiosis	Meiosis converts a single 2n (**diploid**) cell into four 1n (**haploid**) cells.
cell differentiation	Sperm cells are very small and develop a **flagellum**. Egg cells are very large and have numerous **organelles**.

Skill: Annotation of diagrams of a seminiferous tubule and ovary to show the stages of gametogenesis

The seminiferous tubules are the small tubes in the testes where sperm are produced by meiosis. The ovary is the structure where eggs are produced by meiosis in females. Using the two figures below, practise labelling and make sure that you understand the events being shown.

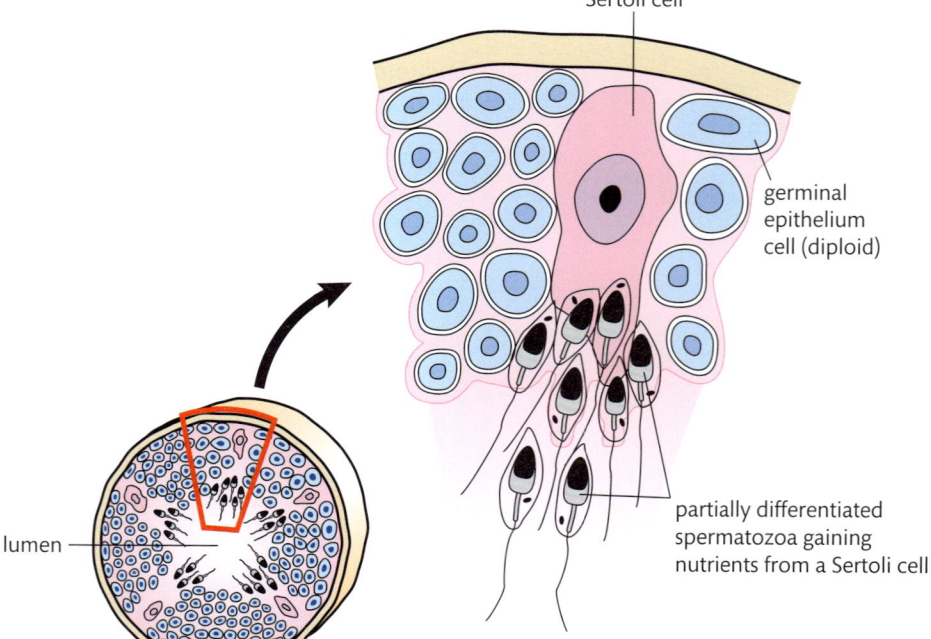

Figure 11.16 *A section view through a seminiferous tubule*

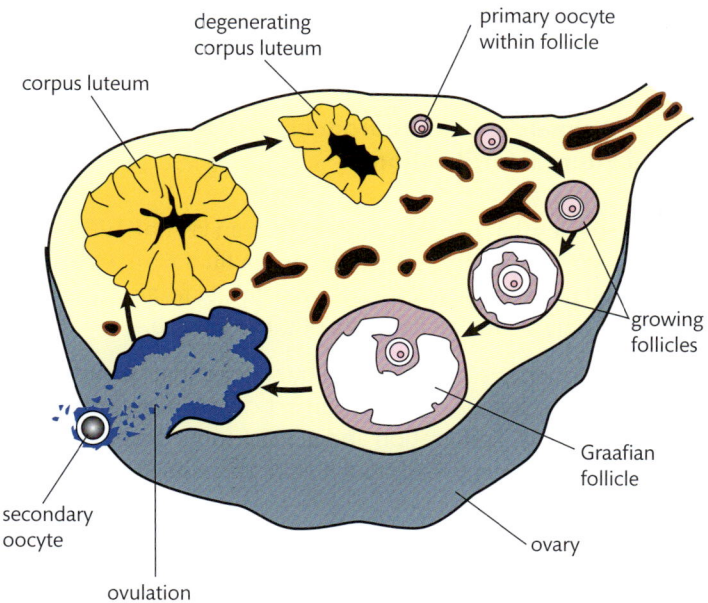

Figure 11.17 An ovary showing the stages in the production of a human Graafian follicle, leading to ovulation and the formation and degeneration of the corpus luteum. This diagram is like a time-lapse photograph of the ovarian events during a single menstrual cycle, as not all of these stages would be occurring at the same time

Understanding: Processes in spermatogenesis and oogenesis result in different numbers of **gametes** with different amounts of **cytoplasm**.

Model sentence: The production of sperm and eggs differs greatly in the number of cells created and the size of the cells.

Sperm cell production in a male's **testes** begins when a male reaches **puberty**. Millions of sperm cells are then produced each day. This continues for the rest of a male's life. In contrast, the number of ova produced in a female's **ovaries** is relatively small. Within a female's ovaries there are approximately half a million total cells that can become an ovum. These cells form during a female's **embryonic** development and will be more than enough to last her entire life.

Sperm cells are some of the smallest cells in the body. They have very little cytoplasm and very few organelles. In contrast, an ovum is the largest cell in the body. An ovum has a huge amount of cytoplasm along with many organelles and stored nutrients.

Skill: Annotation of diagrams of mature sperm and egg to indicate functions

Use the figure below to practise labelling and make sure that you understand the function of the structures being shown.

Subject vocabulary

gamete a sex cell, either a sperm cell or an egg cell

cytoplasm region of the cell within the plasma membrane in which the cell organelles exist

testes male organs where spermatogenesis occurs

puberty age in males and females where reproduction is first possible

ovary female organ where oogenesis occurs

embryonic early development after fertilization

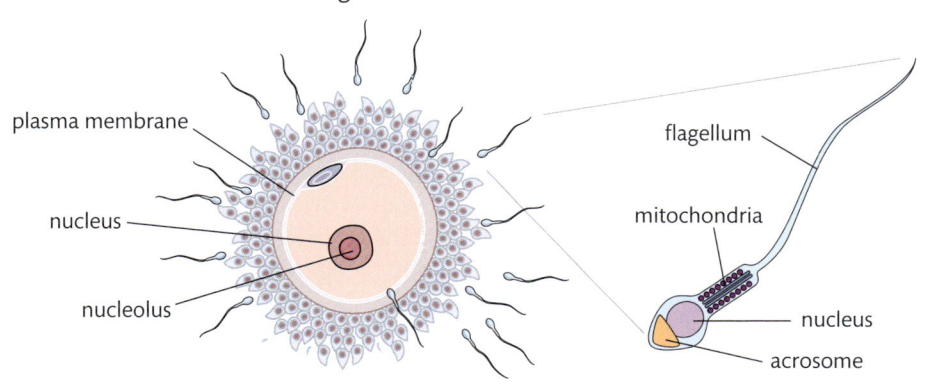

Figure 11.18 Figure showing an ovum and sperm. Notice how small the sperm are in comparison to the ovum. One sperm is shown enlarged for clarity

Subject vocabulary

external fertilization fertilization outside of the female's body

internal fertilization fertilization inside of the female's body

intercourse a reproductive act in which the male deposits sperm inside of a female

polyspermy an abnormal situation where more than one sperm fertilizes an ovum

cortical granules small organelles inside of an ovum that release a substance when the first sperm reaches the egg cell membrane

zona pellucida layer just outside of an ovum's plasma membrane

progesterone hormone produced initially by ovaries; signals endometrium of uterus to remain ready to receive an embryo

Fallopian tubes tubes that carry the ovum or embryo from the ovary to the uterus

endometrium inner portion of the uterus that has many small blood vessels

Synonyms

penetrate....... go through

Understanding: Fertilization in animals can be internal or external.

Model sentence: Animals use two reproductive strategies, external fertilization and internal fertilization.

Female animals of species that use external fertilization lay unfertilized eggs outside of their body. The male of the species then releases a fluid that contains sperm cells. Typically, only a small percentage of the eggs actually get fertilized. Out of the eggs that do get fertilized only a small percentage of those survive.

A more efficient reproductive strategy is used by species that use internal fertilization. The male and female engage in an act called **intercourse**. Sperm are deposited inside the female. Fertilization and at least some development also occur inside of the female. This strategy leads to a higher percentage of eggs fertilized.

Understanding: Fertilization involves mechanisms that prevent polyspermy.

Model sentence: There are mechanisms in place to make sure that more than one sperm does not fertilize the same ovum.

An ovum needs to be fertilized by one and only one sperm. Fertilization by more than one sperm is a condition called polyspermy. This condition will not result in a healthy embryo.

Inside of an ovum there are many small organelles called **cortical granules**. The contents of these cortical granules are released when the first sperm cell enters the membrane of the ovum. The release of the contents of these granules leads to a chemical change to the area just outside of the ovum's membrane called the **zona pellucida**. The end result is that no more sperm will be able to **penetrate** to the ovum membrane.

Understanding: HCG stimulates the ovary to secrete progesterone during early pregnancy.

Model sentence: Ovaries are stimulated to continue progesterone secretion under influence of the hormone, HCG.

A human egg is released from an ovary and becomes fertilized in a **Fallopian tube**. The new embryo does not wait long to begin development. As the embryo moves through the Fallopian tube it is also dividing by mitosis. It takes 7–10 days for an embryo to move into the cavity of the uterus.

During the time that the embryo is dividing and moving down the Fallopian tube, it is also producing a hormone. That hormone is HCG. The effect of HCG is to stimulate the ovaries to continue secreting progesterone. In turn, the continued secretion of progesterone keeps the **endometrium** of the uterus prepared to receive the embryo. The production of HCG by the embryo is a chemical signal to the mother's tissues that she is pregnant and to be ready to receive the embryo into the uterus.

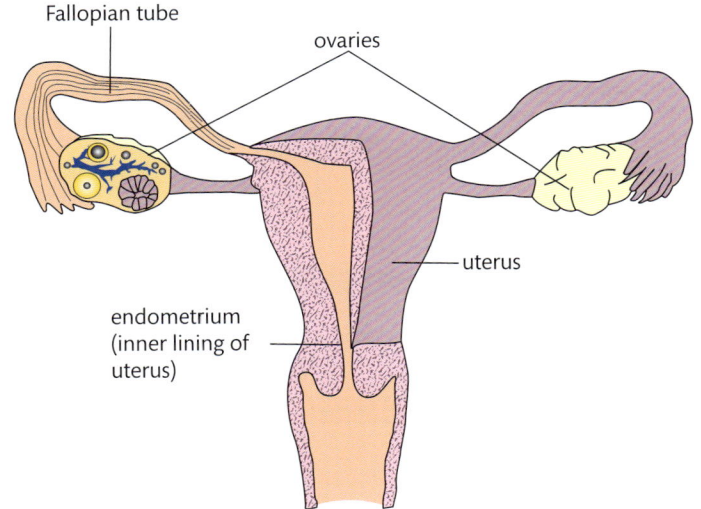

Figure 11.19 Section view of female reproductive system

Understanding: **Implantation** of the **blastocyst** in the endometrium is essential for the continuation of pregnancy.

Model sentence: A young human embryo must implant itself into the inner wall of the mother's **uterus** for pregnancy to be successful.

An ovum contains stored nutrients. This material is called yolk. The stored yolk provides enough nutrition for about the first 10 days of life after fertilization. In order to gain further nutrition an embryo must implant itself into the inner wall of the mother's uterus. This inner wall has many small blood vessels and is called the endometrium.

An embryo begins cell divisions soon after fertilization. It begins to form a hollow ball of cells. After about 10 days this ball of cells is called a blastocyst. The blastocyst enters into the uterus and settles into a location on the endometrium.

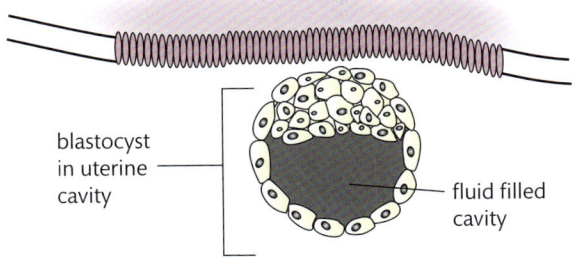

Figure 11.20 A human blastocyst shown in section. This blastocyst has reached the endometrium of the uterus and is going to implant itself through the cell layers shown in colour

When the embryo implants into the endometrium a structure called a placenta forms. The **placenta** will allow the mother's bloodstream to provide nutrients to the embryo.

Subject vocabulary

implantation process where a young embryo sinks into the endometrium

blastocyst stage of a human embryo about 10 days after fertilization

uterus muscular organ of females where the embryo develops

placenta a structure found in the uterus that allows exchanges of gases, nutrients, and waste products between mother and foetus

General vocabulary

facilitate make easier

Subject vocabulary

foetus term for an embryo once it forms recognizable features

concentration gradient change in a chemical concentration between two areas

Understanding: The placenta **facilitates** the exchange of materials between the mother and **foetus.**

Model sentence: Nutrients and waste products are exchanged between the mother and the foetus by way of the placenta.

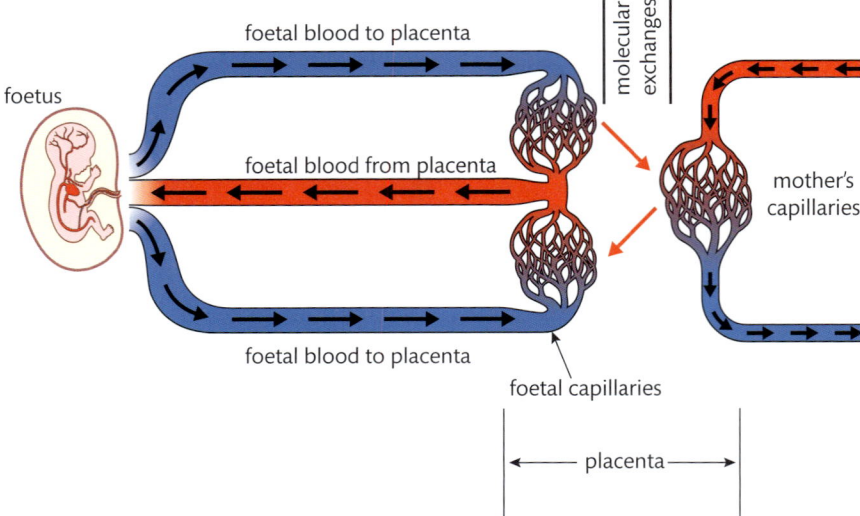

Figure 11.21 A schematic showing the blood flow pattern of the placenta. No blood is ever exchanged between the mother and foetus

The placenta is a structure where the capillaries of the mother and the capillaries of the foetus can exchange molecules. Blood does not get exchanged between mother and child. The exchanges that occur are molecules. The direction of the molecular exchange largely depends on the **concentration gradient** of each type of molecule. The direction of each molecule's diffusion is always from high concentration to low concentration. The table below shows some of the important molecules:

Molecule	Process that explains why and where the molecule becomes concentrated	Direction of diffusion across the placenta
oxygen	Only the mother is breathing. Oxygen concentration is higher in her blood.	Oxygen diffuses from mother's capillaries to foetal capillaries.
carbon dioxide	Both mother and foetus are using cell respiration. The foetus cannot breathe to expel carbon dioxide.	Carbon dioxide diffuses from foetal capillaries to mother's capillaries.
nutrients	Only the mother is eating and digesting. Nutrient concentrations are higher in her blood.	Nutrients, like glucose, diffuse from mother's capillaries to foetal capillaries.
urea	Urea is produced by both mother and foetus as a waste product. The foetus has no way to produce and eliminate urine. Urea is higher in foetal blood.	Urea diffuses from foetal capillaries to mother's capillaries.

Understanding: Oestrogen and progesterone are secreted by the placenta once it has formed.

Model sentence: Once formed, the placenta begins to secrete the two hormones oestrogen and progesterone.

The table below outlines some of the functions of progesterone and oestrogen during pregnancy.

Progesterone	Oestrogen
helps maintain large number of small blood vessels in the endometrium of uterus	encourages muscle growth and expansion of uterus as pregnancy continues
suppresses uterine contractions (until birth)	stimulates mammary gland development late in pregnancy (along with progesterone)

Understanding: Birth is mediated by **positive feedback** involving **oestrogen** and **oxytocin**.

Model sentence: Oestrogen and oxytocin are the two hormones that control the events of birth by way of a positive feedback mechanism.

The secretion of the hormone oestrogen begins at approximately a third of the way through pregnancy. Oestrogen secretion continues to regularly increase. Over time, uterine muscle begins to develop protein receptors for another hormone due to the influence of oestrogen. This second hormone is called oxytocin.

Very late in pregnancy the pituitary gland secretes a small amount of oxytocin. This hormone binds to the newly formed oxytocin receptors in the uterus muscle. The result is a light contraction of the uterus. This is the first labour contraction.

The stretching caused by the first contraction results in the pituitary gland releasing even more oxytocin. This causes a second more intense labour contraction. Once again this causes even more oxytocin to be released. As time goes on during labour, the uterine contractions become more and more intense as well as more frequent. Only birth will stop the positive feedback mechanism that these actions demonstrate.

General vocabulary

suppresses prevents something from growing or developing

Subject vocabulary

mammary gland milk-producing glands in a female's breasts

positive feedback a series of events controlled by one or more hormones that leads to a continuously increasing effect, e.g. contractions of the uterus

oestrogen one of two hormones produced by the ovaries of a female

oxytocin a hormone secreted from the pituitary

labour the series of events in mammals that lead to birth

12 Option A: Neurobiology and behaviour

A.1 Neural development

Main idea

Modification of **neurones** starts in the earliest stages of embryogenesis and continues to the final years of life.

Nature of science: Use models as representations of the real world – developmental neuroscience uses a variety of animal models.

Model sentence: Nerve cells start growing and specializing very early in the developing embryo and can continue to be modified throughout a person's life.

Subject vocabulary

neurones cells of the nervous system that transmit electrical impulses

chordates organisms that possess a notochord and (usually) a spinal column

embryogenesis process by which undifferentiated cells specialize to become the embryo

neural tube area in the embryo that develops into the central nervous system

ectoderm the outermost layer of cells of an embryo

endoderm the inner layer of cells in an embryo

mesoderm the middle layer of cells in the developing embryo

notochord a long thin part of the back of an organism developed from the mesoderm of the embryo which usually matures into the spine

General vocabulary

elongation to grow longer

sphere shaped like a ball

Understanding: The neural tube of embryonic **chordates** is formed by infolding of ectoderm followed by **elongation** of the tube.

Chordates begin their development as an embryo, a **sphere** of hundreds of undifferentiated cells. As the cells divide, they begin to specialize in a process called **embryogenesis**. This section will examine the cells that will specialize to become the nervous system.

Because experimentation on human embryos raises ethical and technical concerns, much of what we know about these early stages of development has come from the study of other chordates. In effect, we use animal models such as clawed frogs of the genus *Xenopus* to learn about embryogenesis. These frogs produce strong and healthy embryos that survive well during experimental manipulation and observation.

A key step in specialization towards a brain and neurones is the formation of the **neural tube**. This forms from the outermost layer of cells in the embryo called the **ectoderm**. There are two other main layers of cells found in the embryo: the **endoderm**, found in the centre, and the **mesoderm** in the middle.

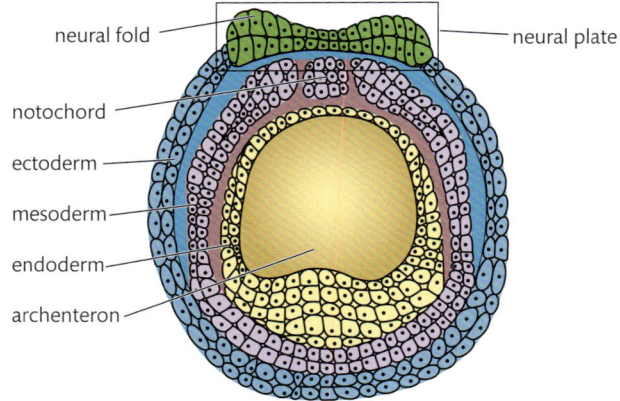

Figure 12.1 *Embryonic tissues in* Xenopus

One part of the mesoderm is called the **notochord**. All chordates have this zone of cells at one point in their development and it is where the phylum Chordata gets its name. In humans, the notochord leads to the formation of the vertebral discs of the spine.

In a process called **induction**, part of the ectoderm forms the **neural plate**, a flattened elongated disc of cells. As this block of cells grows, it develops a fold down the centre. The fold deepens and the sides grow up and around it forming a tube. This is the neural tube. This is where nerve cells will start to form.

Subject vocabulary

induction process that forms the neural plate

neural plate a flattened disc of cells that develops into the nervous system

spina bifida a condition where the embryonic neural tube does not close properly

neurogenesis formation of specialized neurones

neuroblasts immature nerve cells

glial cells cells which provided support and nutrition to neurones

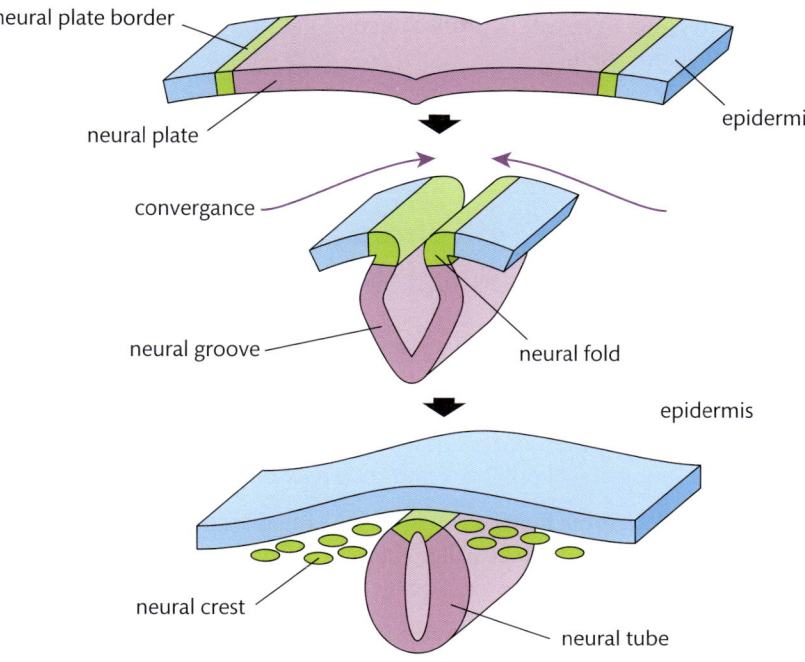

Figure 12.2 *Formation of the neural tube*

Application: Incomplete closure of the embryonic neural tube can cause spina bifida

It is important that the neural tube closes completely. If it does not, there is a risk that some nerve tissue would grow outside the protection of the spine. In humans, the spine forms around the spinal cord and so nerve cells growing outside of it would not be protected by its bony structure.

This can occur in children with a birth defect called spina bifida. The lower part of the neural tube, which forms the base of the spinal cord, does not close correctly. As a result, a little pocket of flesh can be seen at the base of the child's back. Consequences for the child can include learning disorders and difficulty walking.

Understanding: Neurones are initially produced by differentiation in the neural tube.

- The process of forming specialized neurones is called **neurogenesis**.
- **Neuroblasts**, immature nerve cells, are formed in the neural tube. These will mature into two types of cells: neurones and glial cells.
- Neurones carry nerve impulses, whereas **glial cells** are responsible for giving physical support and nutrition to the neurones. Glial cells represent 90% of all cells in your brain. They do not carry nerve impulses.

Synonyms

migrate .... travel

Subject vocabulary

glial fibres elongated structures along which nerve cells can travel to their destination

axon long extension of a neurone that carries an impulse away from cell body

growth cone structure at the tip of an axon which directs its growth

chemotrophic factors molecules that affect the growth of an axon

chemoattractive factors molecules that cause the growth cone of the axon to grow towards them

chemorepellant factors molecules that cause the growth cone of the axon to grow away from them

synapse an area where one neurone comes close to another cell in order to send a chemical message

synaptic cleft the gap between two synapses across which neurotransmitters must pass

cell adhesion molecules (CAMs) molecules that signal to the growth cone to form a synapase

peripheral nervous system the part of the nervous system outside of the brain and spinal cord

central nervous system (CNS) brain and spinal cord

sciatic nerve a long nerve cell that controls leg and foot movements; longest neurone in the body

General vocabulary

activated made active

facilitate make easier

Understanding: Immature neurones **migrate** to a final location.

One way glial cells physically help neurones is by providing a structure along which the neurones can migrate. In effect, neurones need to get from where they are formed to where they are useful.

The immature neurones attach to **glial fibres** and move to their final destination by moving along the fibres.

Understanding: An **axon** grows from each immature neurone in response to chemical stimuli.

Once the neurone has reached its final location, it is ready for the next step: the production of its axon. From the cell body of the nerve cell, an axon pushes forward, led by a **growth cone**. The growth cone will advance as long as it encounters favourable conditions. If it bumps into a surface that is not favourable to the passage of a nerve impulse, it will pull back and try a new direction.

Molecules called **chemotrophic factors** can influence the direction of the growth cone. **Chemoattractive factors** will pull the axon towards them, whereas **chemorepellant factors** will push the axon away.

When the axon has reached a target cell that is its final destination, it must make a connection with that cell. A **synapse** must be formed. The synapse is used to convert the nerve impulse into a chemical signal using neurotransmitters across the **synaptic cleft**.

One way to form the synapse is to have the target cell send out a chemical message indicating that it is available to link with other nerve endings. **Cell adhesion molecules** (**CAM**s) are used to inform the growth cone on the axon that this is a good location on the target cell for a synapse to form.

CAM-specific receptors on the growth cone are **activated** and enzymes **facilitate** the elongation of the axon.

Understanding: Some axons extend beyond the neural tube to reach other parts of the body.

Model sentence: Nerve cells that stay within the neural tube form the CNS, whereas nerve cells that extend beyond the neural tube will form the peripheral nervous system including sensory cells all over the body.

The neural tube is only going to form the **central nervous system** or **CNS** (the brain and spinal cord). The human body has many other nerve cells such as sensory neurones (for things such as sight, smell, or touch) or motor neurones (to tell the muscles to walk, pump blood, or blink).

To get out of the neural tube and into the other parts of the body, the growth cone of the axon leaves the neural tube and seeks out target cells that are more distant than the ones that will form the brain and spinal cord.

The longest neurone in the human body is the **sciatic nerve** which goes from the spinal cord all the way down to the big toe.

Understanding: A developing neurone forms multiple synapses.

A young neurone starts out with no synapses. It proceeds by pushing its axon forward looking for possible connections. Along the way, it will be attracted and repulsed by chemotrophic factors and eventually it will be encouraged to form a synapse with a cell. Many cells will surround the end of the axon and therefore many connections with many target cells can possibly be made at the end of one axon.

Just because a synapse forms, however, does not mean it will be useful. The axon will try to transmit signals to or from the target cells.

Understanding: Synapses that are not used do not persist.

Model sentence: Nerve cells that are used frequently for transmitting messages will maintain a strong connection with each other, whereas those that go unused will lose their connections.

If synapses are used frequently, they will be maintained. If they are not used, they will not be maintained.

In the cases where the signal is not passed from the axon to the target cell, the synapse weakens until any possible connection is lost. Only the most useful and efficient connections are maintained and the weaker or less used connections are eliminated.

Understanding: Neural pruning involves the loss of unused neurones. The plasticity of the nervous system allows it to change with experience.

'Use it or lose it' is a phrase commonly used to describe neurones in a developing brain.

Neural pruning or **synaptic pruning** refers to the process of elimination of synapses and axons that are not used.

For example, the neurones found in the part of the brain used for interpreting smell (the olfactory bulb) do not need to send axons out to the muscles. As a result, during neural pruning, any axons randomly extending from the olfactory bulb into muscle will not be useful and will be eliminated.

Likewise, any axons from the neurones in the part of the brain used for muscle contraction (such as the primary **motor cortex** – see Section A.2) that send axons to the nose to pick up odours would be useless. As a result, they are pruned.

Although this process is especially active during the growth of the brain until **adolescence**, it continues even in adulthood. The ability of the brain to modify connections based on experiences is referred to as the **plasticity** of the brain. This means that the brain can re-wire itself depending on the needs of the user.

Although there are limits to the plasticity of the brain, neuroscientists are often impressed with how the brain can adapt to new situations. For example, a person who has suffered brain damage due to an accident can often re-learn skills that were lost. Undamaged parts of the brain can sometimes take over from damaged parts to accomplish tasks such as speech.

Subject vocabulary

neural or **synaptic pruning** process of removing synapses and axons that are not used

motor cortex area of the brain that plans and carries out movement

plasticity the ability of the brain to form new connections to learn new skills or re-learn lost skills

General vocabulary

adolescence the time when a young person is becoming an adult (12–18 years old)

For example, former US Senator Gabrielle Giffords survived an assassination attempt in 2011 but was left with severe brain damage caused when she was shot in the head. Thanks to her inspiring willpower and hard work, as well as the plasticity of the human brain, she has been able to learn to walk and speak again.

Application: **Events such as strokes may promote reorganization of brain function**

One event that might require the rearranging of neural connections is a stroke. A stroke is caused in the brain when a blood vessel is blocked and blood circulation is cut off from a particular region of the brain. When blood can no longer flow, neurones and glial cells do not get oxygen or nutrients. Such cells can die and consequently a part of the brain is destroyed.

If the part of the brain that is affected by the stroke happens to be the zone in charge of speech, the person might have difficulty speaking. In some cases, other parts of the brain can take over for this damaged zone and the person can learn to speak again.

Model sentence: **Model organisms are species such as mice that are studied in detail because of their availability and how easy they are to breed and keep in a laboratory – things learned about the biological processes in model organisms are extrapolated to human biological processes.**

Skill: **Annotation of a diagram of embryonic tissues in *Xenopus*, used as an animal model, during neurulation**

Match the labels on the diagram below with the following:[1]

1. Neural folds. An indentation, called the neural groove, occurs along the neural plate between the neural folds
2. Neural crest. Many of the cells that were once along the folds **fuse** together to close off the neural tube, other cells detach from the top of the tube to form the neural crest which will later form the peripheral nervous system.
3. Neural plate. Part of the ectoderm above the notochord forms the neural plate
4. Neural tube. This closes all the way along its full length from the cranial end (head) to the caudal end (tail) and will form the central nervous system.
5. Neural groove. This forms as the neural folds push cells downwards.

Subject vocabulary

neurulation development of the neural tube in embryos

Synonyms

fuse............... merge

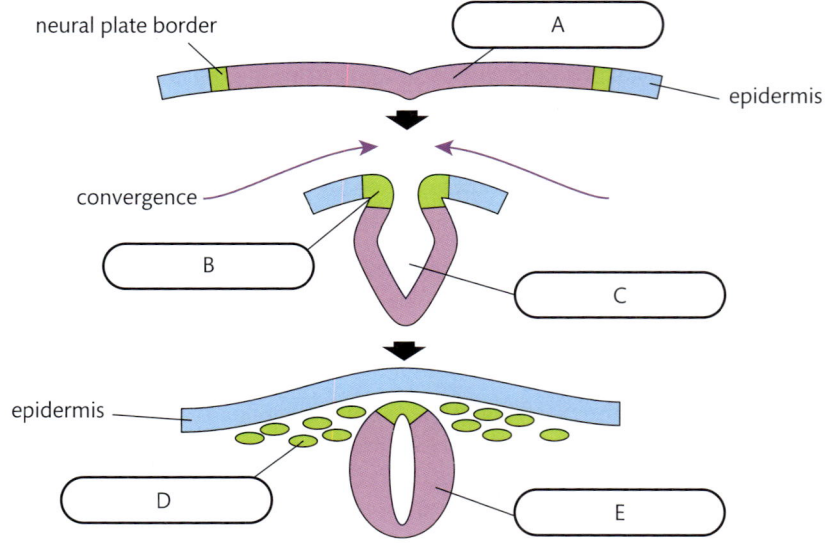

Figure 12.3 *Neurulation in Xenopus*

[1] Answers: A3, B1, C5, D2, E1

A.2 The human brain

Main idea
The parts of the brain specialize in different functions.

Nature of science: Use models as representations of the real world – the sensory homunculus and motor homunculus are models of the relative space human body parts occupy on the **somatosensory cortex** and the motor cortex.

Understanding: The **anterior** part of the neural tube expands to form the brain.

In the previous section, we saw how the neural tube closes and we learned that this collection of cells will become the central nervous system (CNS). The wider anterior (front) part of the neural tube, also referred to as the cranial end, will form the forebrain. The narrower **posterior** (back) end of the tube, also called the caudal end, will become the spinal cord and other parts of the brain.

For the brain to form, the anterior section of the neural tube expands as cells divide rapidly. By 7 weeks, the two hemispheres (right and left) begin to form.

Understanding: Different parts of the brain have specific roles.

Model sentence: Each part of the brain is adapted for specific activities from the lobes of each hemisphere (processing sensory impulses and memory) to the hypothalamus (coordinating the nervous and endocrine systems) and cerebellum (which is in charge of unconscious functions).

- The **cerebral hemispheres** are in charge of functions such as memory, emotions, and learning. The outer layer of grey matter makes up the **cerebral cortex**. The hemispheres can be divided into lobes:
  - The **parietal lobe**, located at the top of the brain, is in charge of processing sensory information such as touch or temperature.
  - The **occipital lobe** is the visual processing part of the brain. It is located at the back of the brain.
  - The **temporal lobe**, located on the side of the brain, is in charge of processing sensory input to make sense of the world around us. This includes transforming the sound of someone speaking into meaningful language or transforming shapes and colours into recognizable objects. Certain memories are also created and stored here, notably long-term ones.
  - The **frontal lobe** is at the front of the brain and is responsible for a wide variety of tasks including short-term memories, behaviour, learning, and motivation.
- The **corpus collosum** forms a bridge between the left and right hemispheres allowing them to communicate and share information with each other.
- The **hypothalamus** maintains **homeostasis**, coordinating the nervous and the endocrine systems. It is located slightly in front of the centre of the brain. It synthesizes hormones which are stored in the posterior pituitary and releases factors regulating the anterior pituitary.

Subject vocabulary

somatosensory cortex area of the brain that processes information about touch

cerebral hemispheres area of brain that deals with complex functions such as memory, learning, and emotions

cerebral cortex layer of grey matter covering the cerebral hemispheres

parietal lobe area at the top of the brain that processes touch

occipital lobe the part of the brain associated with sight

temporal lobe region on the side of the brain mostly concerned with processing speech and language

frontal lobe front of the brain that controls behaviour, learning, and short-term memory

corpus collosum the bridge between the two hemispheres of the brain

hypothalamus a region of the brain that controls pituitary gland secretions and other autonomic functions

homeostasis steady or controlled state

Synonyms

anterior .... front
posterior .... back

Vocabulary

cerebellum area of brain that controls unconcious actions such as movement and balance

medulla oblongata portion of the brainstem that controls many involuntary functions; also known as medulla of the brain

pituitary gland area just below the centre of the brain that secretes several types of hormone

spinal cord an elongated collection of nerve cells that run down the spine and form, with the brain, the central nervous system

brainstem medulla oblongata, area of brain that regulates vital body functions, e.g. breathing

central pattern generators a group of neurones that regulate repetitive actions, e.g. breathing

cardioaccelerator region area of the brain that increases heart rate

cardioinhibitory region area of the brain that decreases heart rate

Synonyms

protruding …. sticking out

- The **cerebellum**, found at the back of the brain below the hemispheres, is responsible for unconscious functions, such as balance.
- The **medulla oblongata** controls automatic and homeostatic activities, such as heartbeat, digestion, and breathing. It is found **protruding** out of the skull from the base of the brain down towards the body.
- The **pituitary gland**, found below the centre of the brain, has two lobes, the posterior lobe and the anterior lobe. Both are controlled by the hypothalamus, and both secrete hormones regulating many body functions.
- The **spinal cord** is below the brain extending into the spine and it connects the brain to the rest of the body.

Application: Swallowing, breathing, and heart rate as examples of activities coordinated by the medulla

From early experiments on the medulla oblongata, it became clear that this part of the brain is responsible for some very vital functions of the body. In the early 1800s, Pierre Flourens experimented on animals such as rabbits and pigeons. Removing some parts of the brain such as the cerebellum allowed the animals to live (with notable impairments) but removal of the medulla oblongata caused death.

Why? Because vital functions such as breathing are controlled by the medulla oblongata, otherwise called the **brainstem**. When a task requires a repetitive or rhythmical action, a network of neurones called **central pattern generators** can be used. The central pattern generators for breathing, for example, are found in the brain stem.

This is also true for swallowing, a complex task requiring the coordination of over 24 muscles. You do not have to think about swallowing because your brainstem uses a central pattern generator in the unconscious part of your nervous system to do it.

Another control centre exists in the medulla oblongata to regulate heart rate. This is made up of two cardiovascular centres, the **cardioaccelerator region** and the **cardioinhibitory region**. The first increases heart rate as part of the sympathetic nervous system, and the second decreases heart rate as part of the parasympathetic nervous system, communicating with the heart via the vagus nerve.

Skill: Identification of parts of the brain in a photograph, diagram, or scan of the brain

You should be able to identify the following parts of the brain:[1]

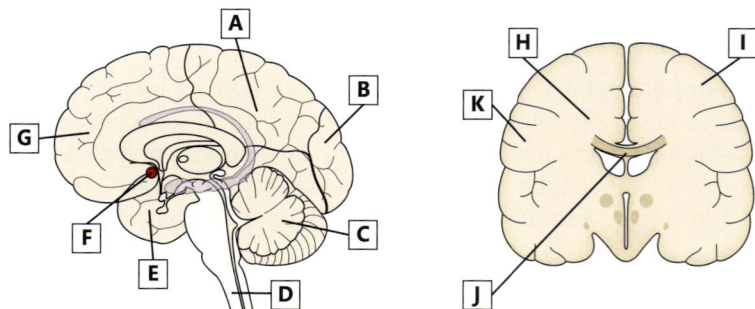

Figure 12.4 Identifying parts of the brain

See if you can do the same with a photograph or a scan of the human brain.

---

[1] Answers: A parietal lobe, B occipital lobe, C cerebellum, D spinal cord, E temporal lobe, F hypothalamus, G frontal lobe, H left cerebral hemisphere, I right cerebral hemisphere, J corpus collosum, K central cortex

Understanding: The autonomic nervous system controls involuntary processes in the body using centres located mainly in the brainstem.

Model sentence: The peripheral nervous system (PNS) is made up of the autonomic nervous system (ANS) and the somatic nervous system (SNS).

The somatic nervous system controls things such as the movement of your arms and legs, and manages the senses you have (touch, smell, hearing, etc.).

The autonomic system is in control of things you are usually not aware of such as heart rate or pupil dilation. The autonomic system is divided into the sympathetic and parasympathetic systems.

There are certain situations in which the brain and body need to function at a higher level of activity. Emergency situations require that your body and brain enter a 'fight or flight' mode. Your heart may beat faster, your brain might process information more quickly, and your breathing rate could increase, depending on the situation. The process of digestion is not a priority in such situations, so blood flows away from the gut and towards other more vital organs. In order to help gather more visual information about your surroundings, your pupils dilate allowing more light to enter the eye.

The part of the peripheral nervous system in charge of 'fight or flight' is the sympathetic system. It is associated with excitatory neurotransmitters such as norepinephrine (or noradrenaline).

There are other situations when your body needs to relax and calm down. Such situations are controlled by the parasympathetic system. The parasympathetic system returns the body to normal. Inhibitory neurotransmitters such as acetylcholine are associated with it.

In a relaxed state, the body can concentrate on things such as digestion, so blood flows back to the gut. Heartbeat and breathing rate return to normal and the pupils constrict back to normal size.

> **Hints for success:** Remember that peripheral is what is outside of the brain and the spinal cord. Somatic has to do with the body, and you know skeletal muscles are voluntary. Autonomic is similar to 'automatic', so you can remember that these functions are not voluntary. Sympathetic is when you are in 'sympathy' with your fear of a lion chasing you. Whereas, with the parasympathetic system, you are like a 'parrot' sitting up in a tree completely relaxed, because the lion is down on the ground. If you can take the complex terms of biology and relate them to something else, you will find it easier to remember them.

Application: Use of the pupil reflex to evaluate brain damage

Since the size of the pupil is controlled by the CNS, it can be used as a tool to test the proper functioning of a person's brain.

In a normally functioning eye, the pupil constricts when exposed to a bright light. Doctors test this during a physical checkup by shining a light into the patient's eye. The light stimulates the photoreceptors which send a signal to the pretectal nucleus of the brainstem. The action potential reaches the Edinger–Westphal nucleus, the axons of which run along ocular motor nerves back to the eye, telling the pupil to contract.

If the pupil does not contract, it could be a sign that the brain is not able to process the information or not able to tell the eyes what to do.

Subject vocabulary

autonomic nervous system that portion of your nervous system that controls unconscious activities

somatic nervous system the network of nerves that control movement and senses

sympathetic system part of the autonomic nervous system concerned with the 'fight or flight' response

parasympathetic system part of the autonomic nervous system responsible for returning the body to 'normal' levels after exertion, e.g. slowing heart rate

norepinephrine (or **noradrenaline**) an excitatory neurotransmitter

pretectal nucleus part of the brain that processes signals from photoreceptor cells

Edinger–Westphal nucleus part of the brain that controls pupil contraction

In modern hospitals, life-support systems can keep a patient breathing and keep their heart beating artificially even after many bodily functions have failed. Is such a person technically 'alive'? One way to determine this is to find out if the brain is still functioning. If there is no sign of brain activity, this suggests that the patient is no longer aware of his or her surroundings and cannot speak, think, or feel. The patient is brain dead.

One way of testing for **brain death** is to perform the **pupil reflex test**. If the pupils do not respond to bright light, this suggests brain death. The body is being kept alive by machines but the brain no longer functions.

Skill: Analysis of correlations between body size and brain size in different animals

Does a bigger brain mean a more intelligent animal? Analyse the graph below comparing brain mass to body mass. Notice that the scale for body mass is logarithmic: each line on the x-axis has a value ten times greater than the line before it.

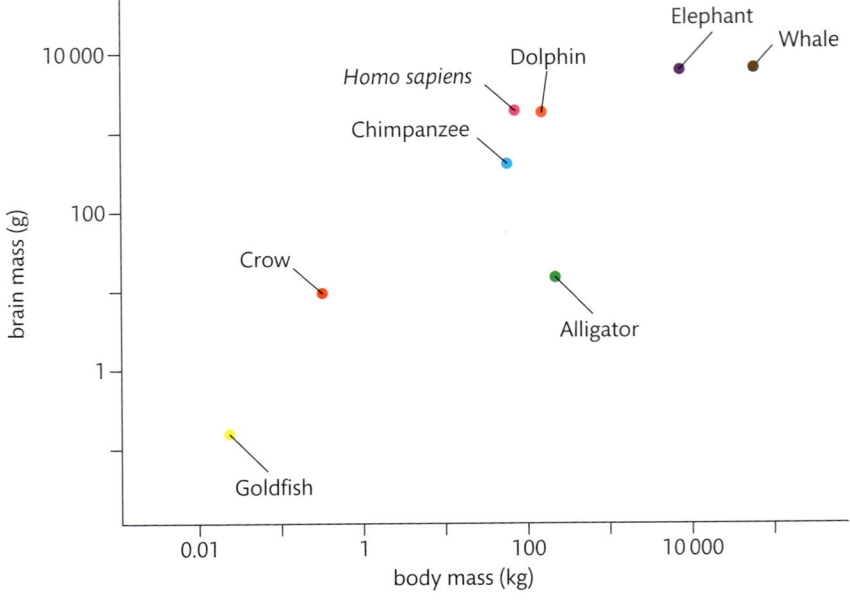

Source: adapted from Cosmic Evolution website, v7, 2013 © Eric J. Chaisson, Harvard University

Subject vocabulary

brain death abscence of any activity in the brain

pupil reflex test a check for brain death that looks to see if pupils contract in response to bright light

correlation relationship between two occurrences

grey matter the cerebral cortex

Figure 12.5 *A graph plotting brain mass against body mass for various species*

Understanding: The cerebral cortex forms a larger proportion of the brain and is more highly developed in humans than other animals.

Model sentence: The size of an animal's brain is not the only thing that is important for higher order thought processes; the thickness of the cerebral cortex and the number of folds it has also play an important role.

The outermost layer of nerve cells in the two hemispheres of the brain form the cerebral cortex. The cerebral cortex is made up of **grey matter**.

The cerebral cortex is where higher order thought processes happen, such as language, visual processing, reasoning, and complex thought such as problem solving.

Compared to other animals, this part of the brain occupies a high **encephalization quotient** (EQ). It is important to look at such a comparison because although an elephant has a large brain, it is smaller in proportion to its body mass than human brains. See the graph below.

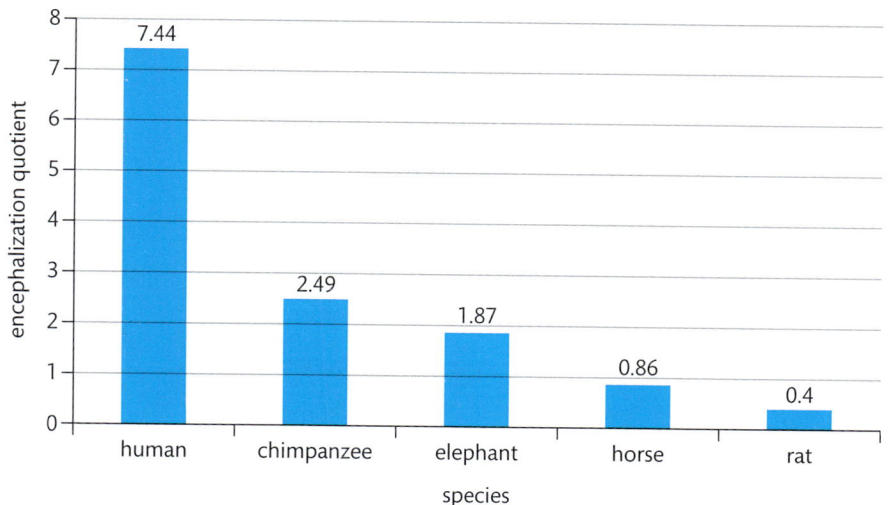

> **Subject vocabulary**
>
> **encephalization quotient** the relationship between brain size and body size

Figure 12.6 A bar chart of the encephalization quotient of five species

The EQ takes into consideration the mass of the brain, the mass of the body, an encephalization constant, and an exponential constant to ensure that small animals with comparatively large brains, such as birds, do not appear as outliers.

The EQ of humans is 7.44, that of elephants is 1.87, and rats is 0.40. In general, predators (carnivores) have higher EQs than their prey (herbivores).

We need to be careful about how we interpret graphs like the one above. Does a higher EQ automatically mean that one species is more intelligent that another? Intelligence is difficult to define and therefore difficult to measure and quantify. Intelligence is complex and cannot be reduced to a single number on a scale.

Understanding: The human cerebral cortex has become enlarged principally by an increase in total area with extensive folding to accommodate it within the cranium.

Because the brain is locked inside the skull, it cannot get much bigger. And yet, the total volume of the cerebral cortex has increased during evolution. How? By increasing its surface area thanks to multiple folds.

Examining a mammal brain's hemispheres, one of the most striking features is the complex pattern of indentations caused by folds. The more there are, the greater the surface area of the cerebral cortex. Because the thickness of the grey matter cannot change much, the best way to increase the total volume is to increase the number of folds.

Mice have few folds on the surface of their brains, whereas great apes such as chimpanzees have many.

Understanding: The cerebral hemispheres are responsible for higher order functions.

Region of the cerebral cortex	Function
prefrontal cortex	organizes thoughts, solves problems, and formats strategies
motor association cortex	coordinates movement
primary motor cortex	plans and executes movements
primary somatosensory cortex	processes information related to touch
sensory association cortex	processes sensory information of perceptions or multisensory information
visual association area	processes visual information
visual cortex	recognizes visual stimuli
Wernicke's area	understands written and spoken language
auditory association area	processes auditory information
auditory cortex	detects sound quality such as loudness or tone
Broca's area	produces speech and language

Application: **Visual cortex, Broca's area, nucleus accumbens as areas of the brain with specific functions**

In the second half of the 20th century, David Hunter Hubel and Torsten Wiesel did experiments on cats which led to breakthroughs in the understanding of how the visual system in animals works. They inserted electrodes into cats' brains in order to measure neural activity. By projecting black and white shapes in front of the cats, they were able to measure different levels of activity in the visual cortex depending on the images.

In the mid-1800s, Pierre Paul Broca dissected the brains of patients who could not speak and found **lesions** on the temporal lobe which is now called Broca's area. The inability to speak is called **aphasia**. One of his aphasic patients could only say one word: 'tan'.

A remarkable experiment was done in the 1950s with rats. Electrodes were placed in their brains and the rats would have that part of the brain stimulated with an electrical impulse if they walked over to a particular part of their cage. The researchers hypothesized that the electrical stimulation would be unpleasant and that the rats would avoid walking over to the part of the cage with the electricity. On the contrary, the rats seemed to fully enjoy the impulses and kept coming back for more. This part of the brain is called the **nucleus accumbens** or the pleasure centre of the brain. Further investigations allowing rats to push a lever to stimulate the nucleus accumbens had a somewhat disturbing result: rats preferred to push the lever again and again attaching no importance to food or water until they died of **starvation** and **exhaustion**.

Synonyms

lesion .... damage

Subject vocabulary

aphasia inability to speak

nucleus accumbens the part of the brain that detects pleasure

General vocabulary

starvation lack of food leading to suffering/death

exhaustion extreme tiredness

One way to help understand the complexity of the functions of the human brain is to represent it with a model.

The drawing below is called a **cortical homunculus**. It is a modified representation of the human body to show where the nerves in the brain are for the somatosensory cortex and the motor cortex.

Notice how the fingers and thumb occupy a disproportionately large area of the brain. This is because there are many more nerve endings in this part of the body.

> **Subject vocabulary**
>
> **cortical homunculus** a representation that relates areas of the brain to the parts of the body they control

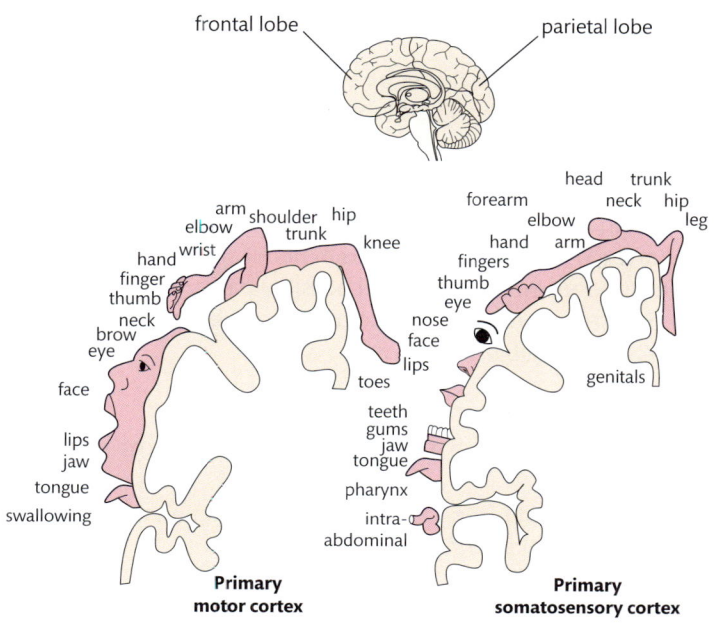

Figure 12.7 *This homunculus cartoon shows the relative importance of areas of the body in the primary motor cortex and the primary somatosensory cortex*

Understanding: The left cerebral hemisphere receives sensory input from sensory receptors in the right side of the body and the right side of the visual field in both eyes and vice versa for the right hemisphere.

The part of the somatosensory cortex found in the left hemisphere of the brain processes information coming from the right-hand side of the body. For example, if you touch a cold drinks glass with your right hand, the sensory neurones send signals to the left hemisphere to process the sensation of cold, the smoothness of the glass, and how heavy it feels.

The opposite is true for the left-hand side of the body. Sensory information picked up from stimuli exciting neurones on the left-hand side of the body send information to the right hemisphere.

As we will see in more detail in section A.3, the left hemisphere also picks up information from the right visual field. This happens in both eyes. It is important to understand that the right eye can see to your right as well as to your left. Consequently, sensory impulses arriving from the right visual field arrives at the left hemisphere and vice versa.

Understanding: The left cerebral hemisphere controls muscle contraction in the right side of the body and vice versa for the right hemisphere.

Model sentence: Senses and actions on the left-hand side of the body are dealt with by the right hemisphere of the brain and senses and actions on the right-hand side of the body are dealt with by the left hemisphere of the brain.

When an athlete swings a tennis racket or a musician presses a key on a piano with their right hand, it is the left side of the brain that is controlling the muscular movements. Likewise, the right side of the brain controls the muscles on the left-hand side of the body.

The part of the brain responsible for movement of muscles is the motor cortex and, like the visual cortex, there is one part on each hemisphere. As with vision, damage to the right hemisphere's motor cortex will possibly paralyse a patient's left side. This can be caused by a stroke and can make **locomotion** very difficult. In severe cases, the damage can be irreversible.

Synonyms
locomotion .... movement

Subject vocabulary
exocytosis active transport in which substances are expelled from the cell

ablation removal by surgery

General vocabulary
autopsy examination of a dead body to find the cause of death

Understanding: Brain metabolism requires large energy inputs.

One of the disadvantages of having a big and highly functional brain is that it demands a large amount of energy.

When the human body is at rest, roughly 20% of the energy being used up is consumed by the brain. Compared to other animals, that is exceptionally high.

Recall that exocytosis requires energy and that neurotransmitters are released by neurones using **exocytosis**. So to keep billions of brain cells sending messages constantly, large amounts of ATP are needed.

Brain cells need glucose in order to get enough ATP. Since neurones cannot store sugar, this glucose must come from the blood, which is why a healthy blood flow to the brain is so important and why a stroke is so dangerous.

Application: Use of animal experiments, autopsy, lesions, and fMRI to identify the role of different brain parts

How do we know what each part of the brain does? There are several techniques, all of which raise ethical issues.

1. Researchers experiment with or dissect animals. Vertebrates such as reptiles and mammals share similarly structured brains; so studying one can help understand the others. It is technically and logistically more practical to find animal subjects for tests and dissections than to find human subjects. By stimulating parts of the brain with electrical signals, for example, researchers can generate certain reactions such as muscle contractions in the body of the animal. **Ablation** (removal) of part of the brain while the animal is still alive can reveal what that part's function is because the animal will no longer be able to perform a certain task such as keeping balance or processing visual stimuli.

2. An **autopsy** on a person who has suffered from a problem can reveal what part of the brain was damaged. This is how Broca's area was found, for example.

3. During brain surgery, doctors can look for lesions (damaged tissue) of the brain that might explain certain problems. Also, stimulating zones of the brain can generate reactions. Although the patient is under anaesthesia, an electrical

stimulation of a certain part of the brain can make the patient laugh. The stimulation of other parts of the brain can make muscles contract.

4 **MRI (magnetic resonance imagery)** has shown itself to be very effective at obtaining images of soft tissue such as the brain. fMRI (the f is for functional) has the additional feature of being able to scan for blood flow in the brain in real time. It is thought that increased blood flow to an area of the brain means that part of the brain is being used for the task at hand.

A.3 Perception of stimuli

Main idea
Living organisms are able to detect changes in the environment.

Nature of science: Understanding of the underlying science is the basis for technological developments – the discovery that electrical stimulation in the auditory system can create a perception of sound resulted in the development of electrical hearing aids and ultimately cochlear implants.

Model sentence: The brain is locked in a dark and silent skull but it can learn about its surroundings by receiving and interpreting nerve impulses from the sensory neurones that pick up stimuli such as light, pressure, chemicals, or temperature.

Subject vocabulary

MRI (magnetic resonance imagery) an imaging technology that uses electromagnetic fields interpreted by computers in order to see both hard bones and soft tissue inside a person's body

sensory neurones cells that detect senses such as tastes or smells

mechanoreceptors nervous system receptor cells that are sensitive to pressure or mechanical force

chemoreceptors nervous system receptor cells that are sensitive to one or more chemicals

thermoreceptors nervous system receptor cells that are sensitive to temperature

photoreceptors receptors in the eye that respond to light by beginning a nerve impulse

---

Understanding: Receptors detect changes in the environment.

Your brain can only perceive what is around it by receiving electrical impulses. Such impulses are generated by your **sensory neurones** and the brain is in charge of processing and interpreting them so that you are able to observe the sights, sounds, and smells of the world around you.

Sensory neurones can be divided into several categories:

- **Mechanoreceptors** convert pressure or mechanical force into nerve impulses. When you write with a pen, important information about how hard you are pushing the pen (and in what direction) gives your brain the information it needs to decide where to go next in order to write the next word.
- **Chemoreceptors** generate nerve impulses when stimulated by certain molecules. Your ability to taste and smell are made possible by chemoreceptors in your mouth and nose.
- **Thermoreceptors** convert heat energy into nerve impulses. When you dive into cold ocean water at the beach, your skin's thermoreceptors feed signals to your brain allowing it to evaluate the sensation of cold.
- **Photoreceptors** convert light energy into nerve impulses. The retina at the back of your eye has specialized cells that respond to different coloured light. The brain interprets the signals sent by these cells to produce an image in your head of what is in front of you.

Application: Detection of chemicals in the air by the many different olfactory receptors

Sometimes when walking down the street, we are distracted by the smell of a coffee shop or bakery. In order for the smell to be recognized by your brain, it has to enter your nose first.

Subject vocabulary

olfactory receptor cells cells in the nose that detect certain volatile molecules associated with smells

glomerulus (plural: glomeruli) a capillary bed

olfactory bulb the part of the brain associated with smelling

retina the part of the eye containing rod and cone cells that detects light

rod cells cells in the eye that detect light intensity

cone cells cells in the retina that detect bright light and colours

How does this work? Volatile chemicals diffuse into the air and can be picked up by olfactory receptor cells in your nose. They send an impulse to the glomeruli in the olfactory bulb, which is a part of the brain located just above the nasal passages.

The impulses are now ready to be sent to the brain for processing and interpretation. It is the brain that recognizes the smell of coffee, not the nose. The nose prepares the nerve signal for the brain to interpret.

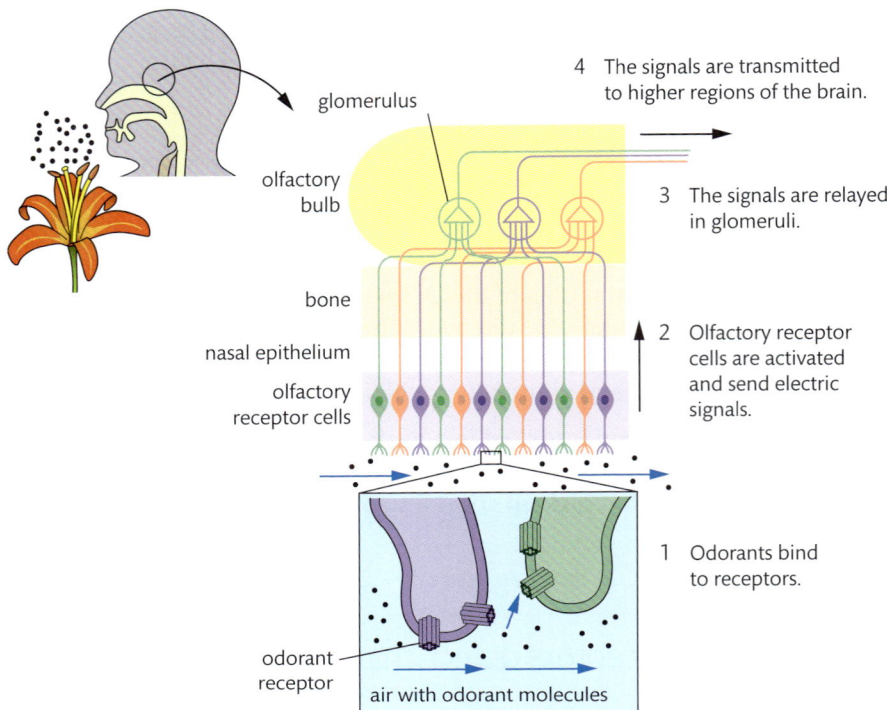

Figure 12.8 *How receptors function in the olfactory system*

Exactly how the olfactory receptors are able to pick up so many different smells is not fully understood. One thing is clear: humans have a much poorer sense of smell than many other mammals, notably dogs.

Understanding: Rods and cones are photoreceptors located in the retina.

Model sentence: Rod cells are well adapted for low light situations but are low resolution and cannot distinguish between colours, whereas cone cells are well adapted for bright light situations and allow for full colour and high resolution.

The part of the eye that senses light is the retina, found at the back of the eye. The retina has two categories of photoreceptors in it: rod cells and cone cells.

- **Rod cells** are adapted for low light vision and send signals to the brain about light and dark. They have a very limited range of wavelengths they can detect which peak at 498 nm.
- **Cone cells** are adapted for bright light and can send signals to the brain about a much wider range of wavelengths from just under 400 nm to about 750 nm. We perceive the different wavelengths as different colours.

Skill: Labelling a diagram of the structure of the human eye

You should be able to label the parts of the human eye shown below. Trace the outline and replace the names with letters or numbers. Once you have memorized them, use the letters or numbers to test yourself.

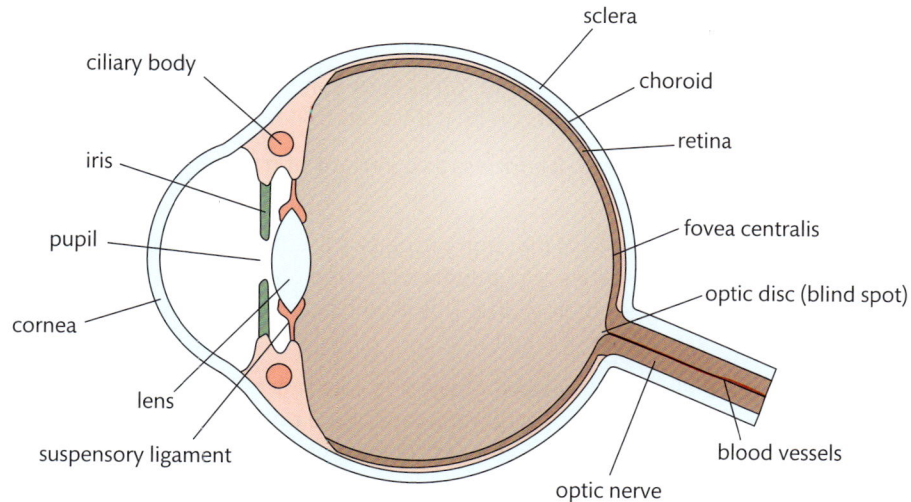

Figure 12.9 *Structure of the human eye*

Skill: Annotation of a diagram of the retina to show the cell types and the direction in which light moves

The diagram below is a close-up of one portion of the retina. You should be able to annotate a figure like this one. Just like for the eye diagram, practise testing yourself using a redrawn diagram with letters or numbers replacing the names.

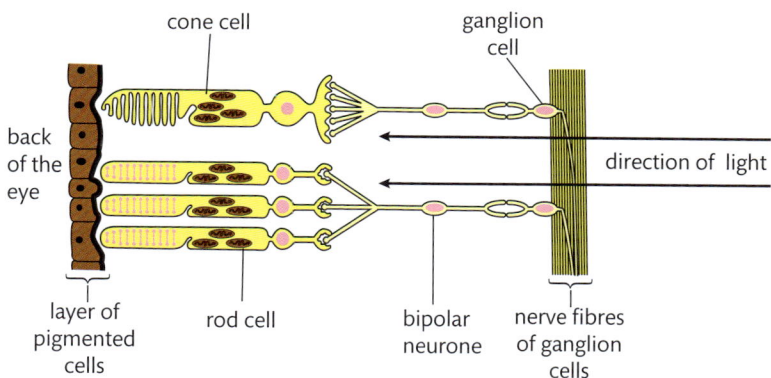

- Possible labels:
  - Rod cells receive the stimulus of light, even very dim light, and synapse with a **bipolar neurone**.
  - Cone cells are activated by bright light and synapse with a bipolar neurone.
  - Bipolar neurones carry impulses from a rod or a cone cell to a **ganglion cell**.
  - Ganglion cells synapse with the bipolar neurones and send the impulses to the brain via the **optic nerve**.

Figure 12.10 *Structure and function of the retina*

Subject vocabulary

bipolar neurone a type of sensory neurone with two extensions protruding from the cell

ganglion cells cells that receive impulses from the rod and cone cells via the bipolar neurone

optic nerve nerve that carries impulses from the eye to the brain

Understanding: Ganglion cells send messages to the brain via the optic nerve.

Ganglion cells have long axons that make up a network of fibres that line the retina.

The ganglion cells relay the nerve impulses along the optic nerve. The optic nerve sends the impulses to the part of the brain where vision happens.

Where the optic nerve leaves the eye, no rod cells or cone cells are present. In this zone, called the **blind spot**, no light can be converted to nerve impulses.

Application: Red-green colour-blindness as a variant of normal trichromatic vision

When all three types of cone cells function properly, full colour vision is possible. This happens when light hits special pigments inside the photoreceptors called **photopigments** and changes their shape. This modification signals to the photoreceptor that light has hit the cell.

Some people have **dichromatic vision**, where one category of cone cell does not function. For example, if the red cells do not work or are not present, the person cannot perceive the colour red. The same is true for green cone cells.

Red-green colour blindness is the most common form of colour perception **deficiency**. As we saw in Chapter 3, it is hereditary and is sex-linked.

What is wrong with the photoreceptors? It could be that there is no functional photopigment **synthesized** in the cone cells but in red–green colour blindness it can be because a **hybrid** pigment is synthesized that cannot discriminate between red or green objects. The photopigment would cause the same signal to be sent whether it was hit with red light or green light.

Understanding: The information from the right field of vision from both eyes is sent to the left part of the visual cortex and vice versa.

Model sentence: Contralateral processing happens when light entering from the left visual field of each eye is processed in the right visual cortex of the brain and vice versa.

Vision is a complex function of the brain. Here we will examine one aspect of vision: how the brain processes right and left visual fields. In reality, vision is more complex than this, but let us simplify the idea down to only right and left and ignore up / down as well as how three-dimensional vision works by mixing right and left visual fields.

In the figure below notice that the retina in each eye has a zone on which light from your **left visual field** enters. In other words, your left eye receives light from your left visual field and your right eye also receives light from your left visual field. Both eyes also have a zone where light from the **right visual field** enters. If you close your right eye, you can still see things both to the right and to the left.

Subject vocabulary

blind spot area of retina with no rod or cone cells so light cannot be sensed

photopigments molecules that react to specific wavelengths of light

dichromatic vision having only two functioning types of cone cell

synthesized chemically created

hybrid something that has the properties of two things

left visual field area which can be seen to your left when you are looking at a central point

right visual field area which can be seen to your right when you are looking at a central point

Synonyms

deficiency ...... shortage/absence

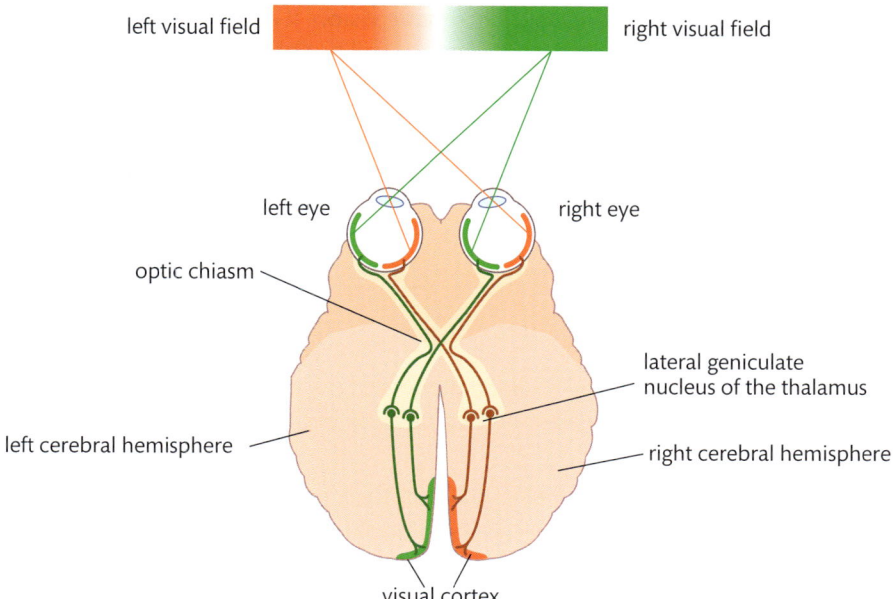

Figure 12.11 *How contralateral processing works to produce an image based on what your two retinas pick up*

Notice also that in each eye, the light from each visual field hits the opposite side of the retina. So light entering the eye from the left visual field touches the right side of the retina in both the right and left eyes.

Follow the green and red lines inside the brain on the diagram. They show the path taken by nerve impulses from the optical nerve to the back of the brain where vision is processed by the visual cortex in the occipital lobe. Along the paths, the optic nerves relay the impulses to other nerves at a zone called the **lateral geniculate nucleus** (LGN). Note: the red and green colours in the diagram have nothing to do with red/green cone cells.

Red represents signals from stimuli that are present in the left visual cortex. Green is for information about the right visual field. The visual cortex has a zone in the right hemisphere of the brain (shown in red), which processes information from the left visual field. Can you see what is happening for the left hemisphere?

As seen in the diagram, each eye sends some signals to the same side of the brain and some to the opposite hemisphere of the brain. The point where the nerves sending impulses to opposite sides of the brain cross is called the **optic chiasm**. The idea of sharing and interpreting information across the two hemispheres is called **contralateral processing**. The brain is remarkably skilled at **fusing** the two fields together to make a smooth and **seamless** image in the brain.

Hints for success: Practise drawing diagrams of the neural pathway for vision until you understand it thoroughly.

Subject vocabulary

lateral geniculate nucleus an area of the brain that relays nerve impulses from the optic nerves to other nerves

optic chiasm point where nerves cross between the two hemispheres of the brain

contralateral processing the sharing and processing of information by both hemispheres of the brain

Synonyms

fusing............ merging

seamless......... smooth/ unbroken

Understanding: Rods and cones differ in their sensitivities to light intensities and wavelengths.

The reason why rod cells are well adapted for dim light is that they are more sensitive to light than cone cells. In other words, they will produce a nerve impulse even in low light situations. But since there is only one type of rod cell, they do not generate any signals about colour. This is why night vision is not colour vision.

The cone cells, however, come in three types. One is specialized to respond to wavelengths in the red part of the spectrum, a second responds to green, and

Subject vocabulary

trichromatic vision normal colour vision involving three types of cone cells that detect blue, green, and red light

refraction the act of bending a ray of light as it passes through a liquid or a lens

auditory canal part of the outer ear through which sound waves enter

tympanic membrane or **eardrum** part of the ear that transmits sound waves to the bones of the middle ear

incus anvil; one of three bones that transmit vibrations through the middle ear

malleus hammer; one of three bones that transmit vibrations through the middle ear

stapes stirrup; one of three bones that transmit vibrations through the middle ear

oval window a part of the ear that vibrates when struck by the stapes

cochlea the part of the ear that detects sound waves

General vocabulary

blurry difficult to see clearly

amplify make louder/stronger or increase in number

Synonyms

relay .... pass on

---

a third to blue. This is referred to as trichromatic vision. If a cell specialized in detecting blue light receives a red wavelength, it will not produce a nerve impulse. Among the three types of cone cells, only the red ones will send information to the brain when red light enters the eye. This is how the brain recognizes colours. By mixing even slightly different combinations of these three signals, the brain can interpret intermediate colours between red, green, and blue.

Understanding: Bipolar cells send the impulses from rods and cones to ganglion cells.

Once the rod or cone cells are stimulated, they send their nerve impulses to bipolar neurones. They are called bipolar because of the two extensions protruding from the cell.

Look back at Figure 12.10, notice that cone cells have their own dedicated bipolar cell. This is to ensure that the brain receives information about the correct colour that the cone cell is detecting. It also ensures high-resolution vision.

On the other hand, multiple rod cells are connected to the same bipolar cell. This makes low-light vision a bit blurry since only one bipolar cell relays the information of three rod cells. In addition to this, the density of rods in the fovea is very low and the refraction of the light that rod cells detect is not so well focused as those of the cone cells.

The bipolar cells send their nerve impulses to the ganglion cells.

Understanding: Structures in the middle ear transmit and amplify sound.

Model sentence: The ear plays two roles in the sensory system: (1) it converts sound vibrations into nerve impulses for the sense of hearing and (2) it converts motion of the head into nerve impulses for the sense of balance.

In order to transmit nerve impulses to the brain about the sounds around you, the sound vibrations must be transformed into mechanical movement for mechanoreceptors deep inside your ear.

First, sound waves enter the outer ear through the auditory canal and cause the eardrum (or tympanic membrane) to vibrate. See the figure opposite.

Three small bones behind the eardrum work as levers to increase the vibrational movement by a factor of 20. This has the effect of amplifying the sound. The names of the bones, which are found in the middle ear and which are the smallest ones in your body, are the incus, malleus, and stapes.

The stapes transmits the amplified vibrations to the oval window, which is not a window at all, but another flexible membrane similar to the eardrum.

Now the amplified vibrations can enter the cochlea, which is the part of the ear that contains the mechanoreceptors.

Skill: Labelling a diagram of the structure of the human ear

Below are the parts of the ear referred to in this section. You should be able to label a blank version of this diagram. Why not practise right now?

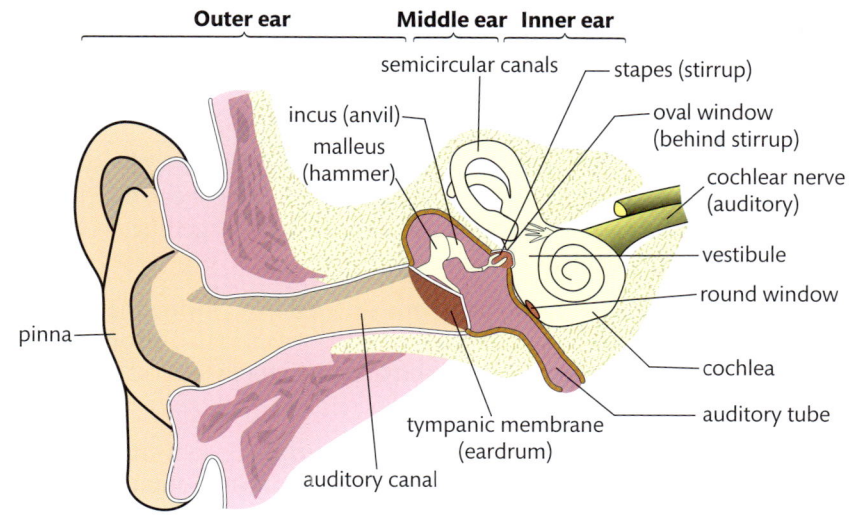

Figure 12.12 *Anatomy of the human ear*

Understanding: Sensory hairs of the cochlea detect sounds of specific wavelengths.

The cochlea, found in the inner ear, is filled with fluid through which vibrations travel.

Small **hair cells** that line the cochlea have hair-like **projections** called stereocilia that are pushed back and forth by the vibrations in the fluid. These hair cells are the mechanoreceptor cells that can convert the movement into nerve impulses.

Different cells are sensitive to different vibrations. **Frequency** refers to how rapid a vibration is and it is measured in **hertz**. One hertz (Hz) is one vibration per second. The human ear can hear sounds of low frequency vibrations (lowest notes on a bass musical instrument, 30 Hz), medium frequency (human voice, 200 Hz), or high frequency (high notes on a flute, 20 000 Hz).

Understanding: Impulses caused by sound perception are transmitted to the brain via the auditory nerve.

The nerve impulses leave the ear and are sent to the brain via the **cochlear nerve** (also called **auditory nerve**). At this point, we are not dealing with sound anymore, only electrical impulses generated by the hair cells.

The brain receives the nerve impulses and processes them to be able to recognize sounds. You hear with your brain, not with your ears.

Subject vocabulary

hair cells cells that detect vibrations in the ear and convert them to nerve impulses

frequency how often an event happens in a fixed time

auditory or **cochlear nerve** the nerve that carries impulses from the ear to the brain

General vocabulary

projections something that protrudes or projects outwards

hertz a unit of the frequency of a vibration defined as one cycle per second

General vocabulary

dissipate become less or weaker

profound complete

Subject vocabulary

round window part of the ear that helps to regulate sound intensity

cochlear implant a device that aids hearing by stimulating the auditory nerves

vestibular system the part of the nervous system that controls balance

semicircular canals part of the ear that detects movement

vestibular nerve the nerve that carries impulses from hair cells in the ear to the brain

Synonyms

oriented .... located/positioned

Back in the cochlea, the vibrations dissipate through the round window. This structure is also useful if sounds are too loud, because it can lessen the pressure in the fluid if necessary.

Application: Use of cochlear implants in deaf patients

If a person has mild to moderate hearing loss, a hearing aid can be used to improve their perception of sound. These are external devices that have a miniaturized microphone, battery, amplifier, and earphone to increase the volume of sounds.

If a person has severe to profound hearing loss, hearing aids will not be sufficient. If the eardrum is not functioning or there is damage to the middle ear, the vibrations cannot get to the cochlea. Fortunately, there is another way of getting nerve impulses to the brain: a cochlear implant.

This is an electronic device with two parts: one external and one internal. The internal part is an implant that must be surgically placed inside a person's skull that stimulates the cochlear nerves. The external part contains a microphone, processor, and battery.

The microphone picks up the sound vibrations, the processor converts the vibrations into electrical impulses and the implant transmits the impulses through electrodes to the cochlear nerve cells. These in turn generate their own impulses that are sent to the auditory nerve. The brain receives the signals and the person can hear. There are some inspiring videos online of people hearing for the first time thanks to this technology.

Because it requires delicate surgery and is an expensive solution, it is not available for all people with hearing loss.

Understanding: Hair cells in the semicircular canals detect movement of the head.

Your ears are also in charge of something else that has nothing to do with hearing: sensing balance. The part of the nervous system in charge of balance is called the vestibular system.

If you look back at the figure, you will notice in the middle ear three semicircular canals. These tubes are oriented in different directions so that various movements can be detected: up/down, side to side.

They are filled with liquid and, like the cochlea, they also have hair cells that act as mechanoreceptors. Only this time, instead of detecting vibrations from sound, they detect movements of the head.

When the head moves, the liquid tends to want to stay in one place, the way that sliding a glass of water across a table makes it splash out of the glass. The hair cells have cilia protruding into the liquid. The liquid being pushed against one extreme or the other of the semicircular canals pushes the cilia around the same way that ice cubes in the glass of water would be pushed around when it is moved.

The hair cells generate a nerve impulse which is sent to the vestibular nerve. The brain interprets these signals constantly to make sure we do not lose balance.

A.4 Innate and learned behaviour

Main idea
Behavioural patterns can be inherited or learned.

Nature of science: Looking for patterns, trends, and *discrepancies* – laboratory experiments and field investigations helped in the understanding of different types of behaviour and learning.

Model sentence: Behaviour can be divided into two categories: (1) innate behaviour, which is determined by genetics and is inborn, and (2) learned or acquired behaviour, which must be learned.

Understanding: Innate behaviour is inherited from parents and so develops independently of the environment.

Some animal behaviour is **innate**. This means that it is encoded in the animal's DNA. It is a mistake to think of DNA as being only for physical attributes. Some behaviour is determined by genetics.

When given a sour-tasting food, babies will instinctively make a face that communicates disgust. They did not learn this from others; it happens without having to *imitate* parents or siblings.

One way of measuring the effects of innate behaviour is to measure the movements of animals in different environments. The idea is that if they move towards something, it means they are attracted to it but if they move away they are repulsed by it. Likewise, they might increase their movement or they might change direction frequently. The types of movement are:

- **Taxis** – a directional response to a stimulus. Positive taxis is when the animal moves towards the stimulus and negative is when it moves away. There are several types of taxes:
  - **phototaxis** – movement towards or away from light
  - **gravitaxis** – movement towards or away from Earth's gravitational pull
  - **rheotaxis** – movement towards or away from water current
  - **thigmotaxis** – movement towards or away from touch
  - **chemotaxis** – movement towards or away from certain molecules.

- **Kinesis** – a non-directional response to a stimulus. The animal moves but not necessarily towards or away from the source of stimulus. Rather than depending on the direction it is coming from, the response of the animal depends on the intensity of the stimulus. Organisms slow down or turn less in favourable environments (so stay longer) and speed up and turn more frequently in less favourable environments to leave that zone more quickly. Stimuli can include things such as concentrations of gases in the surrounding atmosphere, humidity levels, and light intensity (but not direction). Examples of kineses:
  - **orthokinesis** – when an animal changes the speed at which it moves around (fast or slow) depending on the stimulus
  - **klinokinesis** – how often the organism changes direction in response to a stimulus.

Synonyms
discrepancies . differences/inconsistencies

imitate .... copy

Subject vocabulary
innate genetically determined, controlled by DNA

taxis directional movement in response to a stimulus

phototaxis movement in response to light

gravitaxis movement in response to gravity

rheotaxis movement in response to water current

thigmotaxis movement in response to touch

chemotaxis movement in response to particular molecules

kinesis movement in response to a stimulus

orthokinesis change of speed in response to a stimulus

klinokinesis change of direction in response to a stimulus

General vocabulary

opaque difficult to see through

Synonyms

mimic .... copy

Skill: Analysis of data from invertebrate behaviour experiments in terms of the effect on chances of survival and reproduction

One way of gathering data about how animals learn is to give them a task to do, such as putting them in a maze, and see if they improve how well they do the task. If the time it takes the animal to perform the task gets shorter and shorter or if the number of successful trials increases, it suggests that the animal is learning the best way to do the task. Although such experiments are often done with mice, they can also be done with marine invertebrates such as the cuttlefish, *Sepia officianalis*.

A study published in 2003 by a team lead by Miranda Karson showed that cuttlefish could learn how to escape from an unfavourable environment in a tank.

- The researchers built a tank that was separated by a vertical **opaque** wall with two 20 cm holes in it, one 10 cm from the bottom and the other 60 cm from the bottom.
- The side of the tank the cuttlefish were placed in was unfavourable to the cuttlefish because it had no horizontal surface to rest on. Cuttlefish are benthic invertebrates, meaning that they live on the ocean floor.
- The other part of the tank had more favourable conditions such as horizontal surfaces to rest on and artificial sea grass to **mimic** the animal's natural habitat.
- Ten trials were done and exit times were measured in seconds. If the cuttlefish did not escape, a maximum time of 1000 s was recorded. The results can be seen in the graph below.

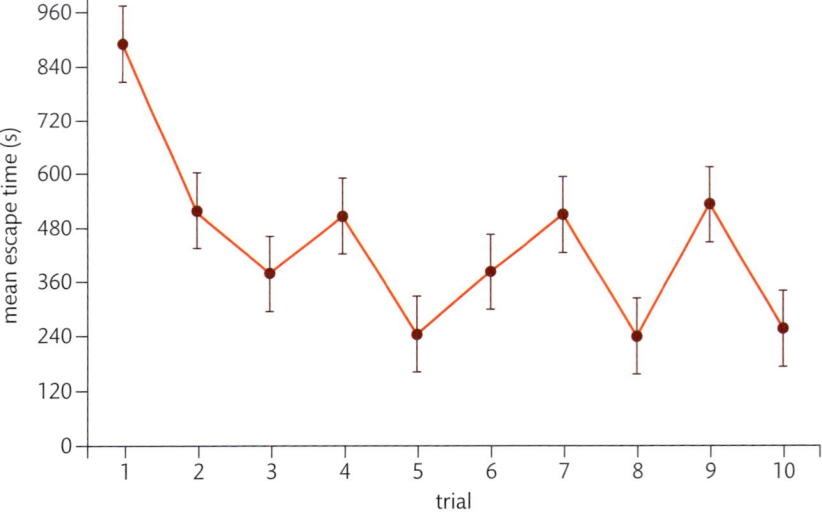

Source: adapted from American Psychological Association (APA)

Figure 12.13 *Mean escape times for cuttlefish over 10 trials. The error bars represent standard errors*

- Trial 1 has the highest mean time due to the fact that very few cuttlefish (3 out of 18) managed to escape and the rest were assigned the maximum escape times.
- The overall trend showing a reduction in mean escape times is, in fact, more of a result of increased success in completing the task rather than completing the task faster and faster.
- An animal that can improve performance at a skill such as escaping from an unfavourable environment will increase its chances of survival.

Understanding: Autonomic and involuntary responses are referred to as reflexes.

During a visit to the doctor, a swift tap on the knee with a reflex hammer should generate a kicking response that happens without you thinking about it. This is your **patellar reflex**. It is a surprising feeling because you have the impression that you did not make the decision to kick. This is because your spinal cord made the **kneejerk** decision for you.

In some circumstances, the brain is not needed to make a decision and take action. When there is a sudden loud noise, you are startled and various muscles flex suddenly to make you jump in surprise and your eyes blink. Like with the knee jerk reaction, this is an **involuntary response**. You did not make the conscious decision to tell your muscles to move or your eyes to blink.

Application: Withdrawal reflex of the hand from a painful stimulus

Have you ever touched a hot stove by accident? Pain receptors in your hand detect painful stimuli which, when painful enough, can cause a **withdrawal reflex**. This is when the hand is pulled away from danger without you thinking about it.

Anything that is innate is hereditary. Hereditary traits follow the laws of natural selection, so if we have this reflex today it is because it most likely gave our ancestors a survival advantage.

Reflexes are controlled by the autonomic nervous system, the part of the CNS found in the medulla oblongata and the spinal cord. In other words, the brain has no say.

Understanding: Reflex arcs comprise the neurones that mediate reflexes.

Model sentence: When a stimulus goes to the spinal cord and a reflex reaction is generated immediately without going to the brain, it is said to follow the path of a reflex arc.

Here is how the withdrawal reflex works:
- Pain receptors in the hand convert the pressure (or extreme heat) into nerve impulses
- The sensory neurone carries the signal up the arm and into the spinal cord.
- The signal is passed on to a **relay neurone** inside the spinal cord. This is where the 'decision' is made to move the hand away from danger. If the signal is weak, there will be no reflex. If it is strong, the reflex will pull the hand away.
- To move the hand, the relay neurone passes the signal to the motor neurone.
- The motor neurone signals to the **effector** (the muscle) it synapses with to contract and move the hand away from danger. This is the response to the original stimulus.
- The path of the message follows an almost complete loop. This shape – from the hand to the spinal cord back to the arm – is called the **reflex arc**.
- Note that the arc does not go through the brain. Other neurones send impulses to the brain where they can be recognized as pain. The sensation of pain comes from these impulses that reach the brain. This happens after the reflex response so you feel the pain after your hand has been pulled away.

Subject vocabulary

patellar reflex the automatic jerking of the leg when the knee is tapped

kneejerk automatic kicking reflex that does not require a conscious decision

involuntary response automatic reaction

withdrawal reflex the automatic reaction that causes an animal to quickly move away from a pain stimulus

relay neurone cell that passes impulses from sensory neurones to motor neurones

effector the organ that performs a response when stimulated by a motor neurone

reflex arc the chain of events from stimulus to spinal cord to response, involving a receptor cell, a sensory neurone, a relay neurone, and a motor neurone

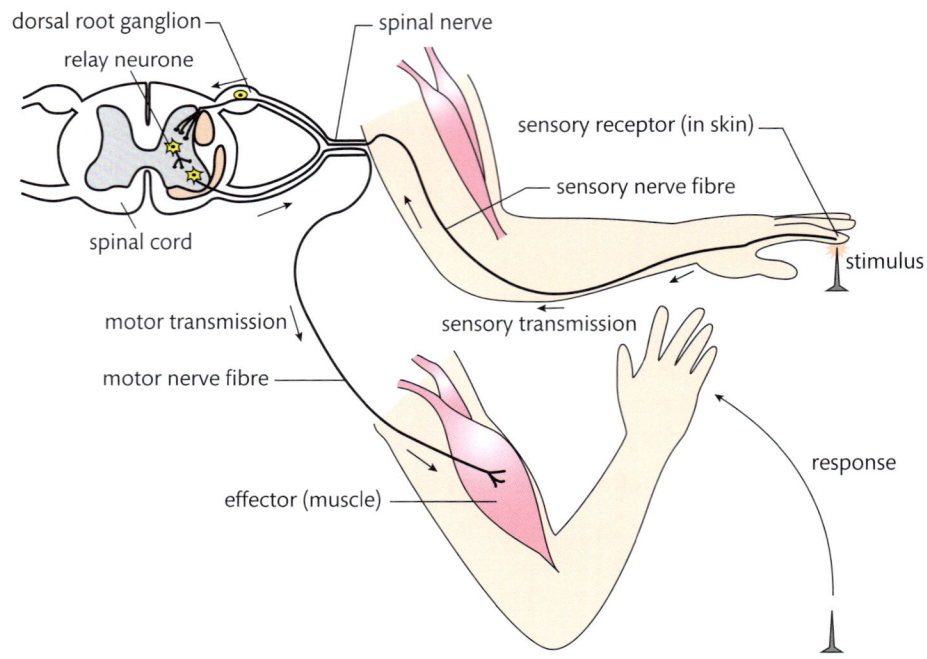

Figure 12.14 *A reflex arc showing the path of a spinal reflex*

Skill: Drawing and labelling a diagram of a reflex arc for a pain withdrawal reflex

You are expected to be able to draw the diagram above. After studying it, close your book, take out a blank sheet of paper and try drawing and labelling it. You should have the following five labels: receptor cell, sensory neurone, relay neurone, motor neurone, and effector.

Understanding: Reflex conditioning involves forming new associations.

Model sentence: Reflex conditioning, also known as classical conditioning, happens when an animal is trained to associate a once neutral stimulus with an unconditioned stimulus to generate a conditioned reflex that did not exist before the training.

Generally speaking, a reflex only happens with a specific stimulus. The withdrawal reflex should only happen in case of sudden pain. The sharp object or the hot surface is considered the **unconditioned stimulus**. No training or learning is necessary to cause the reflex.

Through special training, however, it is sometimes possible to produce a reflex response using a different stimulus. Before training, this stimulus, a **neutral stimulus**, does not produce a response.

During training, exposure to the neutral stimulus at the same time as the unconditioned stimulus can cause the nervous system to associate the neutral stimulus with the reflex. This pairing of the two stimuli during training is called **reflex conditioning** or **classical conditioning**.

After training is complete, the neutral stimulus will now produce the reflex response even without the unconditioned stimulus. Since it produces a response, it is referred to as the **conditioned stimulus**. The new response is the result of a **conditioned reflex** instead of an innate reflex.

Subject vocabulary

unconditioned stimulus a specific sensation or action which produces an automatic response

neutral stimulus an action that does not produce a response

reflex conditioning training an animal to respond to a neutral stimulus

classical conditioning association of a neutral stimulus with a reflex

conditioned stimulus a neutral action or sensation which, through training, produces a response

conditioned reflex a trained response

Such experimentation with animals and later with humans is one of the founding principles of the field of **behaviourism**. Conditioning was well illustrated in Pavlov's experiments with dogs.

Application: Pavlov's experiments into reflex conditioning in dogs

In 1903, Russian scientist Ivan Pavlov published his work experimenting with dogs.

First, he observed that hungry dogs had a natural reaction to the stimuli of the sight and smell of food: they salivated and the volume of saliva was proportional to the response. This was an easy response to measure because he could collect the saliva in tubes. The unconditioned stimulus was the food and the innate reflex was the production of saliva.

Next, he tested some neutral stimuli. The sound of a **metronome** and the ringing of a bell did not produce a response. No saliva was produced when the dogs heard these sounds.

Now the training began: Pavlov paired the sound of a metronome with the presentation of food. The food would be hidden from the dog until the sound was produced, at which point the food was presented to the dog. Repeating this systematically over time allowed the dogs to associate the sound with food. He repeated the method using other neutral stimuli, including the sound of a bell ringing.

Final result: when the conditioned stimulus (the sound) was produced, the conditioned response occurred (the dogs salivated), even when the unconditioned stimulus (the food) was completely absent. The volume of saliva that was produced with the conditioned stimulus was the same as that from the unconditioned stimulus.

> **Subject vocabulary**
>
> **behaviourism** a branch of psychology based on individual behaviour
>
> **learned behaviour** behaviour that is acquired rather than innate
>
> **General vocabulary**
>
> **metronome** an instrument which makes a repeated sound similar to a clock

Understanding: Learned behaviour develops as a result of experience.

The opposite of innate behaviour is **learned behaviour**. If an organism makes the same mistakes over and over, its chances for survival will be reduced.

Learned behaviour is not passed on genetically through DNA. It must be acquired through experience with the organism's surrounding environment. Chimpanzees like to eat termites but this kind of food is hard to get because termites live inside the tunnels of their mound. Chimpanzees can make tools for fishing out termites. They find a twig that is just the right length and diameter and, by passing the twig through their clenched teeth, the fibres separate to make a brush. When put into a termite tunnel, the twig is attacked by soldier termites which bite it. The chimp pulls the twig out and eats the nutritious termites. This tool-making behaviour is learned and takes time to perfect.

The table below summarizes the differences between innate and learned behaviour.

Innate behaviour	Learned behaviour
develops independently of the environmental context	is dependent on the environmental context of the animal for development
controlled by genes	not controlled by genes
inherited from parents	not inherited from parents
developed by natural selection	develops as a result of experience
increases the chance of survival and reproduction	may or may not increase chance of survival and reproduction

Be aware of the fact that the ability to learn is genetic. Whether or not an organism is capable of learning things (such as language acquisition) is a genetic trait. However the behaviours that are learned are not genetic. The ability to speak Spanish, for example, is learned, not innate.

Application: The role of inheritance and learning in the development of birdsong

Certain behaviours are a mix of innate plus learned behaviours. For example, some types of birds have an innate birdsong that is the same for all the members of their species. However, they can add to this song and improvise new melodies by inventing songs to add or by imitation.

Since birdsong is a key stage in the courtship process, it is important for the male birds to have a song that will attract a female. He will start out with a crude template song, which is the basic melody of his species. Birds hatched in captivity with no exposure to the sound of their species' birdsong still sing this template. This demonstrates that it is innate.

When exposed to other birds singing its species' song, a bird can listen and perfect the template. This is called the memorization phase and it lasts about 100 days.

Once he is sexually mature, he can add to the song during the motor phase. Here, he can improvise and add his personal touch.

Understanding: Imprinting is learning occurring at a particular life stage and is independent of the consequences of behaviour.

Model sentence: Imprinting is an example of an innate behaviour that requires an external stimulus to generate a behaviour.

The study of behaviour is called ethology. Ethologist Konrad Lorenz did some interesting experiments with graylag geese. He noticed that the baby geese (goslings) would follow their mother out of the nest and go wherever she went. He decided to have some goslings hatch in an incubator far from the mother and see what happened when they saw him. He found that they followed him around instead.

This is an illustration of imprinting. This is when one animal looks upon another animal as a parent figure or a figure of trust. It is a form of learning that must happen at a particular developmental stage. For graylag goslings, Lorenz discovered that it was 13 to 16 hours after hatching.

Understanding: Operant conditioning is a form of learning that consists of trial and error experiences.

Model sentence: A Skinner box, developed by behaviourist B.F. Skinner, can be used for operant conditioning, the process by which positive and/or negative reinforcement is used to shape behaviour.

Another behaviourist was B.F. Skinner, who did experiments in the 1930s with pigeons and rats. One of his most influential contributions to science was the invention of the Skinner Box or operant conditioning chamber. This is a small box into which an animal is placed. The box has one or more buttons or levers that the animal can activate. The box also contains a way of rewarding the animal, such as a system for delivering a treat.

General vocabulary

improvise do something without preparation

Subject vocabulary

template song a sample song that is copied

memorization phase the time during which a male bird listens to and perfects the template song of his species

motor phase the time during which a male bird can improve upon the template song and add his own improvisations

ethology study of behaviour

imprinting learning at a particular age that is independent of the consequences of behaviour

operant conditioning chamber or **Skinner box** apparatus used to train an animal to perform particular actions

Skinner observed that as the animal explores its cage, it eventually activates the lever. The act of unintentionally pushing the lever is an example of **operant behaviour**. The animal is simply acting by trial and error, not responding to a stimulus yet. If this action delivers a food treat, the animal quickly learns how to feed itself. Variations of this kind of experiment might include lights flashing in a certain sequence before the animal can reward itself, or the sound of a buzzer.

To make things more complex, multiple levers can be introduced. Some might produce a negative stimulus such as an electric shock. Again, the animal learns very quickly which lever does what. This is what Skinner called **shaping** of behaviour. For this to work, the process of **reinforcement** is key. Positively reinforced behaviour is favoured and negatively reinforced behaviour is avoided.

This was a breakthrough in behavioural science. Instead of merely talking about stimulus–response, Skinner saw a third important factor: stimulus–response–reinforcement. Skinner had pioneered the idea of **operant conditioning**. This comprised of multiple steps:

- an animal exploring its environment by trial and error
- its behaviour being shaped by positive and negative reinforcement
- a new behaviour is learned.

Understanding: Learning is the acquisition of skill or knowledge.

Learning is complex. Learning involves using your experiences in life to acquire knowledge or be able to perform skills.

Learning is measured by performance. If a student does well on a test, it suggests that she learned the material and had acquired the skills necessary to obtain a good grade.

In order to be able to perform, the knowledge and skills have to enter your memory, preferably your long-term memory. Then they have to stay there until you need them, and finally, they need to be available for recall when you want to use them.

Understanding: Memory is the process of encoding, storing, and accessing information.

Encoding is the process of placing ideas and skills into your memory. There are many ways of accomplishing this – think of the ways people study for a test:

- Sometimes you can use **visual encoding** to memorize images and keep a mental picture of something.
- Some students prefer to hear sounds such as a melody or the sound of a phrase. Making up a song about the subject or hearing definitions read out loud can help with **acoustic encoding**.
- Sometimes it helps to connect a new idea with an old idea that is already present in your memory. Analogies such as saying that enzymes and substrates are like a lock and key help this kind of memorization called **elaborative encoding**.
- **Sensation encoding** is memorizing the way things feel, smell, or taste. Performing a heart dissection might help a student learn about the chambers and blood vessels – being able to touch them and feel the different thicknesses of tissues in the heart helps encode the memory of the experience.

Subject vocabulary

operant behaviour in behavioural psychology, a type of behaviour encouraged by the consequences it produces

shaping in behavioural studies, the modification of behaviour of a test subject animal by positive or negative reinforcement

reinforcement a technique used in behavioural psychology that strengthens or encourages a desired behaviour

operant conditioning in behavioural psychology, a technique for generating desired behaviour by giving rewards; in contrast with classical conditioning

encoding processing of information to be remembered

visual encoding a way of remembering things by associating them with a picture or image

acoustic encoding using sound as an aid to remembering something

elaborative encoding adding new knowledge to memories that are already stored

sensation encoding remembering the smell, taste or feel of something

> **Subject vocabulary**
>
> **storage** the way memories are kept
>
> **short-term memory** type of memory that can remember small amounts of information for short periods of time
>
> **long-term memory** type of memory that can remember large amounts of information for long periods of time
>
> **accessing** reaching or retrieving
>
> **recognition** identify
>
> **recall** remember
>
> **excitatory neurotransmitters** chemicals that cause the postsynaptic neurone to produce an action potential
>
> **inhibitory neurotransmitters** chemicals that prevent the postsynaptic neurone from producing an action potential
>
> **dopamine** a neurotransmitter often associated with reward pathways in the brain

Storage of memories works by maintaining synapses.

- There are two types of memory: short term and long term.
  - **Short-term memory** is well adapted for small amounts of information for a few minutes, hours, or days.
  - **Long-term memory** is well adapted for larger amounts of information for months, years, or even a lifetime.
- The brain is good at remembering things but it is even better at forgetting. Your brain is constantly getting rid of information that is unimportant. How? Recall from earlier in this chapter that when a connection is weak and not used, it is not maintained.

Accessing memory: ideas you have put in your memory are useless if they are not accessible. There are two ways of accessing memory: recognition and recall.

- **Recognition** is the ability to connect an object or event with something you have already experienced and know. Examples include hearing a familiar melody, seeing a familiar face, or identifying the smell of apple pie in the oven.
- **Recall** is bringing to mind a fact, object, or event that is not currently present. Recall questions on exams are the ones that ask for definitions or the name of a famous scientist.

A.5 Neuropharmacology

Main idea

Communications between neurones can be altered through the manipulation of the release and reception of chemical messengers.

Nature of science: Assessing risks associated with scientific research – patient advocates will often press for the speeding up of drug approval processes, encouraging more tolerance of risk.

Understanding: Some neurotransmitters excite nerve impulses in postsynaptic neurones and others inhibit them.

In this section, keep in mind that the presynaptic neurone is the one that is attempting to pass on its message and the postsynaptic neurone is the one that needs to be 'convinced' to pass on the message.

There are two types of neurotransmitter: excitatory and inhibitory.

- **Excitatory neurotransmitters** are chemicals present in the synaptic cleft that encourage the postsynaptic neurone to produce an action potential.
- **Inhibitory neurotransmitters** are chemicals present in the synaptic cleft that attempt to block the postsynaptic neurone from producing an action potential.

The nature of the neurotransmitter does not determine if it is excitatory or inhibitory. Rather, it is the receptor it binds to and the resulting action which determine this. For example, the neurotransmitter **dopamine** can have an excitatory effect or an inhibitory effect depending on which receptors it binds to in different situations.

Understanding: Nerve impulses are initiated or inhibited in postsynaptic neurones as a result of summation of all excitatory and inhibitory neurotransmitters received from presynaptic neurones.

Model sentence: Summation is the process by which postsynaptic neurones receive a combination of excitatory and inhibitory neurotransmitters – if the excitatory neurotransmitters succeed in raising the positive charge above a certain threshold without being cancelled out by the inhibitory neurotransmitters, the cell will produce an action potential.

Just because neurotransmitters arrive at the postsynaptic neurone does not mean that the message will be relayed. A sort of 'voting' process determines whether or not the postsynaptic neurone will pass on the signal. If there is not a strong enough signal, it does not produce an action potential and the message stops being relayed from neurone to neurone.

The 'voting' process works by adding up the 'for' votes (excitatory neurotransmitters) and subtracting any 'against' votes (inhibitory neurotransmitters). The term used for this is **summation**. If the signals from excitatory neurotransmitters are stronger than the signals from all the inhibitory neurotransmitters, the postsynaptic nerve is depolarized and generates an action potential to keep transmitting the message. Otherwise, no signal is transmitted; the postsynaptic neurone does not produce an action potential.

When an action potential is produced:

- The receptors are like gates that allow ions to enter or leave when the neurotransmitter binds to them.
- Excitatory neurotransmitters increase the **permeability** of the postsynaptic membrane to positive ions. This is done by opening the **gated ion channels** that are **embedded** in the membrane.
- Positive sodium ions (Na^+) that are in the synaptic cleft **diffuse** into the postsynaptic neurone through the open channels.
- **Depolarization** occurs, meaning that the total net charge inside the neurone becomes more positive compared to the outside of the cell.
- As more and more excitatory neurotransmitter depolarize the cell, the positive charge increases, a bit like charging up a battery. In order for an action potential to be produced, a certain **threshold** must be reached. Once the charge arrives at the threshold, the action potential is generated and sent down the axon. The excitatory neurones have succeeded in getting the postsynaptic neurone to send the message. In the voting analogy, the 'for' vote has won.

In the case where an action potential is blocked, here is what happens:

- When the receptors receive inhibitory neurotransmitters, the inside of the cell becomes more negative than the outside. Negatively charged chloride ions (Cl^-) are pulled into the cell and positively charged potassium ions (K^+) are pushed out of the cell.
- This process, called **hyperpolarization**, has the effect of cancelling out some or all of the positive charges that the excitatory neurotransmitters are building up.
- The result is that it becomes very difficult or impossible to reach the threshold. The message is blocked.

Subject vocabulary

summation a combination of excitatory and inhibitory neurotransmitters that together either cancel each other out or trigger the further transmission of an action potential

gated ion channels transmembrane proteins that can be activated to let ions in or out of a cell

diffuse movement of a substance from an area of high concentration to an area of low concentration

depolarization sodium ions diffusing from outside to inside the neurone membrane

threshold some significant level which brings about some sort of change or shift in response

hyperpolarization process where the inside of the neurone becomes more negative

General vocabulary

permeability ability to allow one or more substances to pass through

embedded positioned firmly and deeply

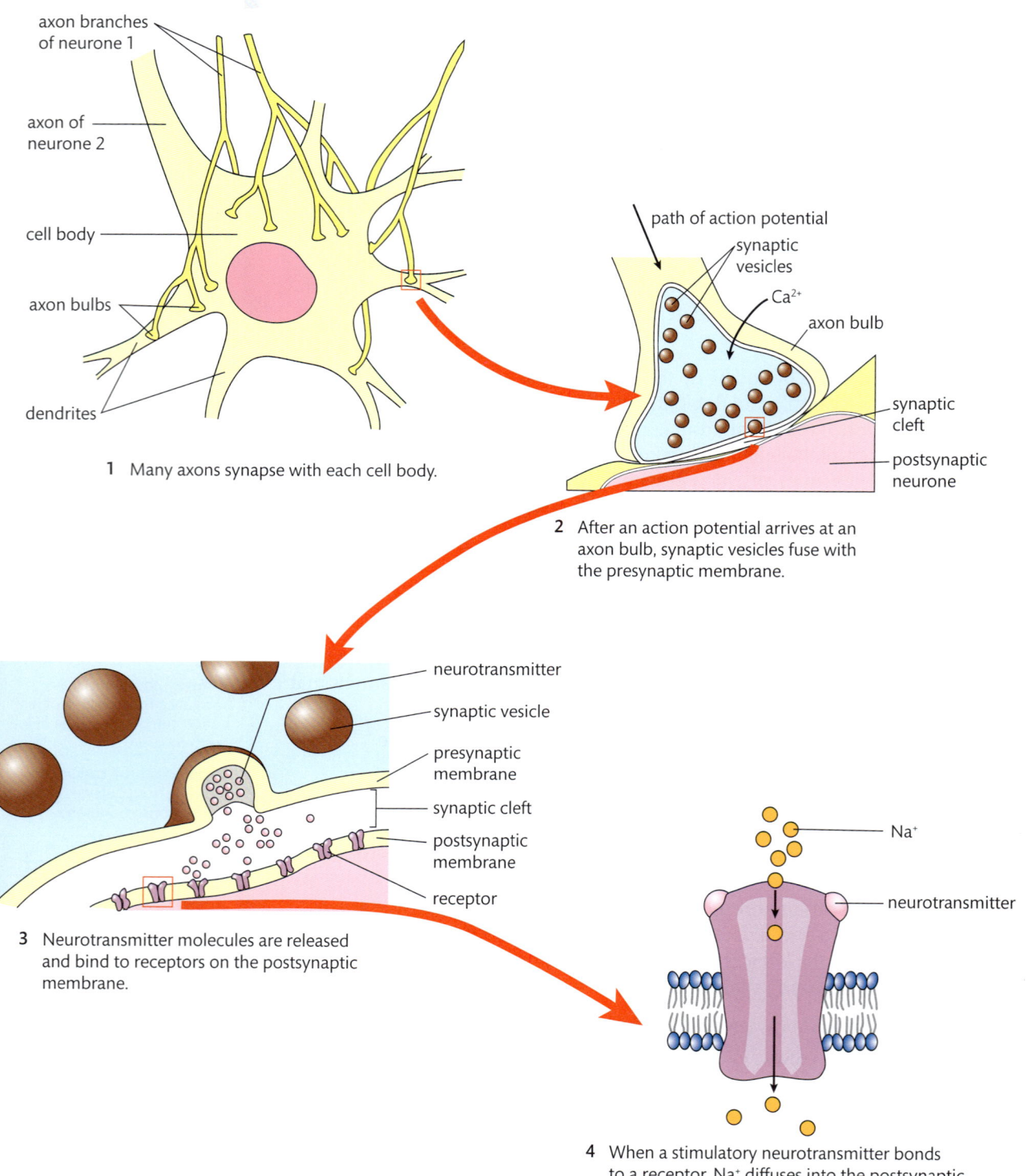

Figure 12.15 *Synaptic transmission*

Understanding: Many different slow-acting neurotransmitters modulate fast synaptic transmission in the brain.

Some neurotransmitters have a faster effect than others:
- **Fast-acting neurotransmitters** have an effect on the target cell within 1 millisecond of binding to a receptor.
- **Slow-acting neurotransmitter** have an effect on the target cell in hundreds of milliseconds or can take up to a minute.

As seen in the figure to the right, fast-acting neurotransmitters can open the gated ion channel directly without the help of other molecules. This is why they can act so quickly.

Slow-acting neurotransmitters, on the other hand, cannot open gated ion channels themselves. Instead, they bind to a receptor which in turn sends a second chemical messenger to open the gate. This slows down the process considerably. Examples of slow acting neurotransmitters include:
- dopamine
- serotonin
- acetylcholine.

Slow-acting neurotransmitters can have a **modulating effect** on the transmission of signals. This means they can change the rate at which the transmissions happen, a bit like traffic lights regulating the flow of cars. One way they do this is to regulate the efficiency of neurotransmitter release from the presynaptic neurone (the sender). Slow-acting neurotransmitters can also regulate the efficiency of the postsynaptic neurone (the receiver). Because of this ability, these types of neurotransmitters are called **neuromodulators**.

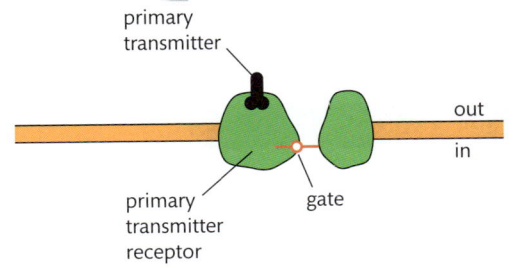
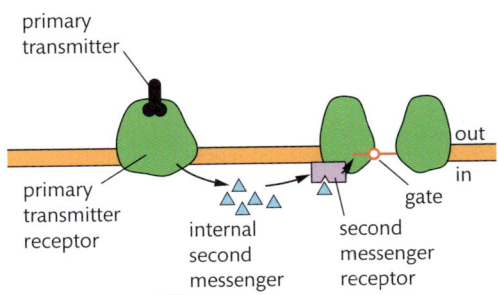

Figure 12.16 *Fast and slow transmission at the postsynaptic membrane. Adapted from Hille 2001*

Understanding: Memory and learning involve changes in neurones caused by slow-acting neurotransmitters.

Memory and learning at the level of neurones are **phenomena** that are not fully understood. One thing that appears to be clear is that when a new idea or skill is learned and encoded in memory, plastic changes occur in synaptic connections in the brain. These can be biophysical changes (involving the physical structure of the connections, or 'wiring') and/or biochemical changes (involving neurotransmitters and other molecules such as messenger molecules).

Since slow-acting neurotransmitters such as serotonin act as neuromodulators, they are good candidates for helping in the process of increasing neural transmission rates. In experiments, dopamine has been found to play a role in memory in the prefrontal cortex. Recall the 'use it or lose it' rule for synaptic connections. If a connection is used frequently (and slow-acting neurotransmitters can modulate this), then it is maintained. Hence, a connection that is encouraged by neurotransmitters to continue passing will be reinforced. The idea or skill that this connection is helping to encode is retained thanks to the reinforced connection.

Short-term memory tends to be more of a biochemical change in synaptic connections, whereas long-term memory also involves biophysical changes. In order for long-term memory to work, new axons are grown which makes necessary the switching on of the transcription of certain genes inside the neurone's nucleus.

Subject vocabulary

fast-acting neurotransmitters neurotransmitters that produce an effect within 1 ms of binding to a receptor

slow-acting neurotransmitters neurotransmitters that produce a delayed effect up to 1 minute after binding to a receptor

modulating effect controlling the speed of a process or the degree to which it occurs

neuromodulators a type of neurotransmitter that regulates postsynaptic neurones

Synonyms

phenomena.... events/happenings

These genes control the production of proteins such as the ones needed for axon growth, synaptic vesicle formation, and neurotransmitter receptor formation.

Understanding: Psychoactive drugs affect the brain by either increasing or decreasing postsynaptic transmission.

Model sentence: Psychoactive drugs can affect the process of summation, disturbing the natural system of determining whether or not a message will be sent by the postsynaptic neurone.

Certain drugs can have an effect on synaptic transmission:

- **Stimulants** are **psychoactive drugs** that increase alertness and wakefulness. They are sometimes referred to as 'uppers' for their ability to improve peoples' moods, increase heart rate, or sharpen mental focus. They can do this by:
  - promoting activity at excitatory receptors
  - inhibiting activity at inhibitory receptors.

- **Depressants** are psychoactive drugs that reduce stimulation of brain activity and calm down a person's mood. They are sometimes referred to as 'downers' for their ability to calm people by numbing the senses and slowing transmission of signals. They can do this by:
  - promoting activity at inhibitory receptors
  - inhibiting activity at excitatory receptors.

Because of these properties, psychoactive drugs can significantly affect the brain and produce changes in emotion, perception, or personality. Examples below include ones prescribed by doctors as medicine as well as drugs that are not, but are either illegal or controlled by the law.

Stimulants		Sedatives / Depressants	
Pharmaceutical	Non-pharmaceutical	Pharmaceutical	Non-pharmaceutical
analgesics/painkillers (such as paracetamol)	nicotine (notably in cigarettes)	benzodiazepines (as sedatives or anti-anxiety treatments)	alcohol
adderall (for attention deficit hyperactivity disorder (ADHD) management)	caffeine	antihistamines (against allergies)	cannabis
	ecstasy	morphine	heroin
	khat, a plant from East Africa		

Application: Endorphins can act as painkillers

Your brain produces natural analgesics (painkillers) called **endorphins**. These are small neuropeptides that bind to opiate receptors in the brain. **Opiates** occur naturally and can be found in plants such as the opium poppy plant, *Papaver somniferum*. It is from this plant that drugs such as opium, morphine, and heroin are made.

Endorphins can be released when the body does intense exercise such as running long distances. Athletes can get pain relief as well as a feeling of **euphoria** known as

---

Subject vocabulary

stimulants drugs that increase neural activity

psychoactive drugs drugs that affect postsynaptic transmission altering perception or mood

depressants drugs that reduce neural activity in the brain and produce a calming effect

endorphins chemicals produced by the body that act as painkillers

opiates naturally occurring painkillers found in the opium poppy plant

General vocabulary

euphoria feeling extremely happy/excited for a short time

'runner's high'. These neuropeptides can also be released in high-stress situations or in case of serious injury.

Endorphins are released by the pituitary gland and they work by blocking transmission of impulses relating to pain. When they bind to the opiate receptors, they prevent the pain-related neurotransmitters from delivering their message.

Understanding: Anaesthetics act by interfering with neural transmission between areas of sensory perception and the CNS.

Before surgery, doctors remove a patient's ability to feel pain by giving the patient **anaesthetics**. These molecules prevent any signals being produced by the sensory neurones from arriving at the central nervous system (CNS). They produce a numbing effect where the part of the body affected cannot feel heat, touch, or pain. Examples of drugs used as an anaesthetic are **lidocaine** or nitrous oxide (also known as laughing gas).

One way of blocking pain is to introduce molecules that will target the receptors on the surface of neurones in the CNS that interpret pain signals. The anaesthetic molecules can either block the receptors on the neurones or modify them so that the neurotransmitters that are supposed to bind there cannot do so.

Since the receptors are in charge of opening ion gated channels, the blocked channels stay shut and therefore the depolarization cannot happen. The action potential is not produced and the message of pain is blocked. Even though the sensory neurones are doing their job to relay pain signals to the brain, the person does not feel the pain because the message is blocked.

Another way anaesthetics can work is to occupy the ion channels so that Na^+ ions cannot get through.

Application: The effect of anaesthetics on awareness

There are two categories of anaesthetics:
- **General anaesthetics** – when the entire body is anaesthetized and the person is unconscious. This is for major surgery.
- **Local anaesthetics** – when only a part of the body is anaesthetized and the person remains awake. This is for minor surgery such as dental work or it can also be used during childbirth since the mother needs to be awake to help with the birthing process.

One characteristic of anaesthetic treatments is that they are reversible. When the drugs wear off, the person can feel again. After surgery, the patient will start to feel pain, at which point an analgesic (painkiller) is given.

> **Subject vocabulary**
>
> **anaesthetic** a drug which prevents the signals from sensory neurones reaching the central nervous system, producing a numbing effect
>
> **lidocaine** a drug used as an anaesthetic
>
> **general anaesthetic** medication given to a patient before surgery to provoke unconsciousness and take away reflexes and pain
>
> **local anaesthetics** drugs that cause numbness of a small part of the body

Understanding: Stimulant drugs mimic the stimulation provided by the sympathetic nervous system.

Stimulant drugs can mimic neurotransmitters found operating in the sympathetic nervous system. Nicotine, for example, mimics the neurotransmitter called acetylcholine. Acetylcholine can act as an excitatory neurotransmitter when dealing with muscles in charge of running or fighting. After acetylcholine delivers its message to the receptors, it is broken down by acetylcholinesterase. This enzyme cannot break down nicotine molecules that bind to the same receptors. This excites the postsynaptic neurone and it begins to release the neurotransmitter dopamine.

Subject vocabulary

dopamine a neurotransmitter often associated with reward pathways in the brain

reward pathways chemical reactions in the brain that give a feeling of satisfaction, encouraging the animal to repeat the action

cocaine a drug that acts as a stimulant

amphetamines a class of drugs that act as stimulants

diazapam a sedative

benzodiazepine a type of sedative

γ-aminobutyric acid or **GABA** a neurotransmitter that reduces the activity of neurones

opioids medications such as morphine that mimic the painkilling effects of opiates such as opium

μ-opiate receptors specific receptors that bind to opioids

General vocabulary

insomnia inability to sleep

amplify make louder/stronger

Dopamine plays an important role in the **reward pathways** of the brain. When a person is very hungry and then eats a meal, dopamine plays a role in producing the sensation of satisfaction. It is the brain's way of saying, 'Yes, that feels good. Keep going.' Reward pathways can be thought of as the opposite of pain.

Stimulant drugs can mimic this feeling of pleasure and satisfaction. But there are costs and disadvantages to the brain and body, which we will see later when we look at addiction.

Application: Effects on the nervous system of two stimulants and two sedatives

Stimulants:

- Illegal drugs such as **cocaine** stimulate alertness and can produce temporary feelings of euphoria. The feeling produced by cocaine comes from the fact that dopamine uptake receptors are blocked and dopamine neurotransmitters cannot be removed from the synaptic cleft as they usually are. Under normal conditions, the dopamine uptake receptors clean out the synaptic cleft by pulling back into the presynaptic neurone any dopamine neurotransmitters that have finished delivering their message. Because cocaine has blocked their passage, they stay and are able to repeatedly bind with the postsynaptic receptors to keep sending a reward pathway message: 'Yes, that feels good. Keep going.' Drug users fool their brains into thinking it feels good.

- Another class of drug, amphetamines, has a similar stimulating effect but for a different reason. **Amphetamines** mimic neurotransmitters such as dopamine or noradrenaline, a neurotransmitter that can increase heart rate or release more glucose to the muscles. Amphetamines enter the presynaptic neurone and are incorporated into vesicles just like the natural neurotransmitters. When they are released, they send the same message as the natural neurotransmitters. What is different is that unlike the natural neurotransmitters, which are attacked by enzymes and broken down after delivering their message, amphetamines are not broken down. The enzyme's active site does not fit. As a result, the amphetamines can continue to deliver their message and mimic the reward pathway. The person feels awake, alert, and euphoric until the drug eventually wears off.

Sedatives:

- **Diazapam**, a type of **benzodiazepine**, which can be found under the trade name Valium, is a prescription medication used to treat **insomnia** and anxiety. To understand how it works, you need to know about the neurotransmitter **GABA**. This neurotransmitter's full name is **γ-aminobutyric acid**. It plays an important role in reducing neurone activity by being able to control chloride ion (Cl^-) or potassium ion (K^+) channels. When a drug such as Valium is taken, the effect is that it **amplifies** the signal of the GABA neurotransmitter. More Cl^- ions are pumped into the postsynaptic neurone. The hyperpolarization effect will reduce the chances of the threshold being reached and the cell will be less likely to pass on the message. A patient suffering from anxiety will feel relaxed and relieved because the neural activity is reduced. They may also feel sleepy.

- **Opioids** such as opium, morphine, or heroin act upon the nervous system by binding to specific receptors called **μ-opiate receptors**. These receptors are only found in neurones in certain parts of the body and brain. Opioids contain opiate molecules, which bind to the opiate receptors. Inhibitory neurotransmitters that would normally stop the release of dopamine are blocked when the opiate receptors are activated. Dopamine can now be released in large quantities. The user feels the pain go away; they are sedated and can get a feeling of artificially induced euphoria. Undesirable effects of the use of opioids can include nausea, constipation, constricted pupils, or death.

Skill: Evaluation of data showing the impact of MDMA (ecstasy) on serotonin and dopamine metabolism in the brain

Serotonin is an important neurotransmitter related to many things including appetite, reproduction, well-being, and happiness. Imbalances can lead to symptoms such as digestive problems and depression.

The recreational drug MDMA, also known as ecstasy, has an effect on NTs such as serotonin and dopamine.

MDMA causes the release of extra serotonin by presynaptic neurones. The postsynaptic serotonin neurone's receptors are activated. A serotonin transporter vesicle, or SERT receptor, in the presynaptic neurone will remove excess serotonin from the synaptic cleft once the message has been delivered. The continued exposure to MDMA will cause more and more serotonin to be released. The user gets an artificial high as the brain is fooled by an artificially induced feeling of well-being. Eventually, all the cell's serotonin will be used up.

When the serotonin is used up, the SERT receptors are empty. Dopamine now enters the SERT receptors in place of serotonin. This is not supposed to happen. The nerve cells destroy the dopamine. The problem is that the products of the breakdown of dopamine are toxic to the nerve cell. This can damage or kill nerve cells, causing irreversible damage to the brain.

You should be able to analyse data about MDMA levels in laboratory tests. The data below are from an experiment with rats that were given ecstasy. A molecule labelled MIL was injected to label active serotonin receptors in the brains of the animals.

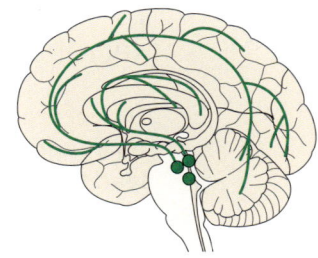

Serotonin neurones
● cell body
— axons

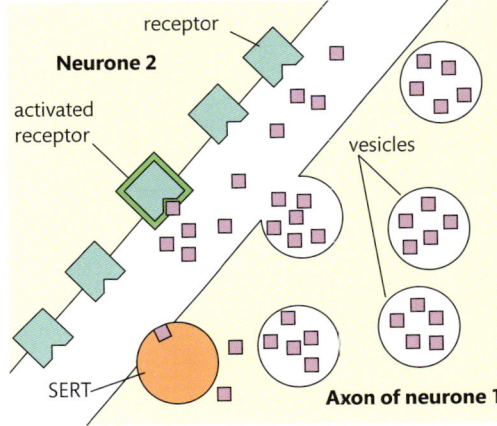

Figure 12.17 Serotonin neurones in the brain and in the synapse

Subject vocabulary

serotonin a slow-acting neurotransmitter associated with happiness, appetite, and reproduction

ecstasy or **MDMA** a psychoactive excitatory drug that is illegal in most countries

serotonin transporter (SERT) a vesicle that removes excess serotonin from the synaptic cleft once the message has been delivered

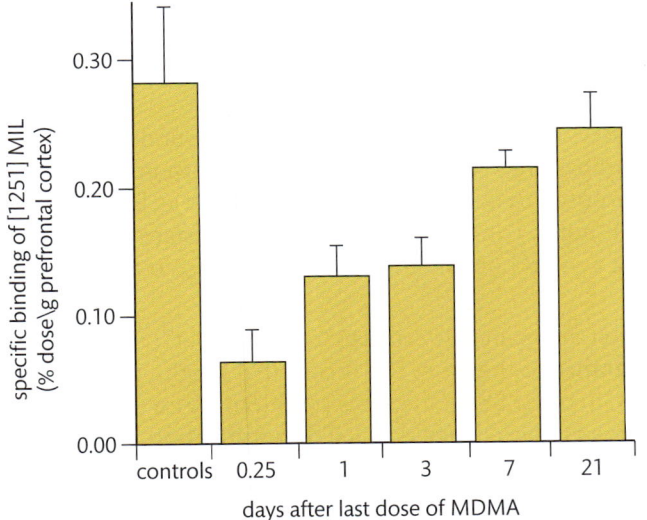

Source: Copyright © 1992. Published by Elsevier Ltd.

Figure 12.18 The effect of MDMA on the number of available serotonin receptors in the brains of a group of rats. MIL is a molecule used to label active serotonin receptors.

12 Option A: Neurobiology and behaviour

Understanding: Addiction can be affected by genetic predisposition, social environment, and dopamine secretion.

Model sentence: Addiction to a drug happens when a person is so dependent on a substance that they cannot stop taking it; stopping consumption would lead to physical and/or mental suffering.

Addiction is a difficult concept to define because of how complex it is. For psychoactive drugs, it refers to a state of such chemical dependency that if the user stopped consuming the drug, there would be symptoms of withdrawal. Withdrawal is a negative reaction to stopping a drug and can include anxiety, depression, or cravings. In extreme cases, there can be seizures or severe shaking. In the worst cases, withdrawal can be fatal.

Addiction is a serious problem in itself but the long-term consumption of drugs can lead to serious health problems:

- Cigarettes are linked to respiratory diseases including lung cancer.
- Alcohol is associated with car accidents and liver disease.
- Overconsumption of psychotropic drugs can lead to psychosis.
- Purchasing illegal drugs contributes to killings in drug trafficking circles.
- Consuming intravenous drugs can sometimes lead to needle sharing which is an effective way to spread HIV, the virus responsible for AIDS.

The causes of addiction are multiple and complex. It is difficult to say with certainty why any one user becomes addicted to the drug they are using. Here are some causes to possibly consider:

- Genetic predisposition. Some people are born with brains that are more sensitive to psychoactive drugs than others. There is a component of alcoholism that is genetic, for example. This does not mean, however, that someone born with a genetic predisposition to be addicted to alcohol will become an alcoholic. They can still choose whether or not to consume alcohol.
- Social factors. If a child grows up in a family or community surrounded by consumers of a particular drug, they have a higher chance of consuming that drug than a child never exposed to it. Peer pressure can play a role. In places where the cultural norm is not to consume alcohol, such as the state of Gujarat in India, alcoholism is not a social phenomenon the way it is in so many other parts of the world.
- Dopamine secretion. When the brain gets exposed to a drug over long periods of time, it develops a tolerance to the drug. This means that the drug no longer works at the current dose. In order to get the same sensation, more of the drug is needed. This neuroadaptive change is called desensitization, another term for tolerance to a drug. Increasing the dose to get the same sensation can lead to addiction.

Subject vocabulary

addiction extreme desire/need for something

withdrawal the negative effects often felt when regular drug use is stopped suddenly

psychotropic drugs that affect perception

psychosis a mental disorder involving a loss of connection to reality

tolerance being used to a drug and so needing more of that drug to produce an effect

desensitization development of tolerance to a drug that results in the drug having a reduced effect

A.6 Ethology

Main idea
Natural selection favours specific types of behaviour.

Nature of science: Testing a hypothesis – experiments to test hypotheses on the migratory behaviour of blackcaps have been carried out.

Understanding: Ethology is the study of animal behaviour in natural conditions.

Ethology is the study of animal behaviour in natural conditions. Ethologists go out into the field and observe the way animals behave in their habitat. Sometimes experiments are set up in labs to recreate a natural habitat if possible, but ideally the observations are in the field.

Jane Goodall went to the forests of Tanzania in the 1960s to observe chimpanzees and subsequently became the world's leading authority on chimpanzee behaviour.

Understanding: Natural selection can change the frequency of observed animal behaviour.

Scientists studying animal behaviour have observed that some populations of animals have changed the frequency of their behaviour. As is true for physical genetic traits, if the frequency of a behaviour changes in a population, there is evidence of evolution by natural selection. As we will see in this section, some birds may migrate earlier, some salmon may mature quicker, and some birds may develop more extreme courtship patterns.

Understanding: Behaviour that increases the chances of survival and reproduction will become more **prevalent** in a population.

Synonyms

prevalent .... common

Model sentence: Because of natural selection, if an innate behaviour helps a population survive better or produce more offspring, its frequency in the population will increase.

Whether or not it is innate or learned, behaviour that improves survival chances will be seen more frequently in a population.

For example, male emperor penguins (*Aptenodytes forsteri*) that need to keep warm in Antarctica do so during the cold winter by using a behaviour called huddling. They stand in large groups with their bodies pressed up against one another. Part of this behaviour includes a rotation system so that individuals take turns being on the outside of the formation.

Imagine if one penguin has the innate behaviour of standing on his own, away from the group. He will freeze to death. When he dies, the chances of passing on his free-standing genes to the next generation drop to zero. This is a behaviour that is not selected for – there is a selective pressure against it.

Understanding: Learned behaviour can spread through a population or be lost from it more rapidly than innate behaviour.

Because innate behaviour is passed on from generation to generation by genes, it does not change quickly. Learned behaviour, on the other hand, can be modified more rapidly.

Learned behaviour is acquired by observing and repeating what another individual does. This can happen between members of the same generation as well as from offspring to parents, or it can even miss a generation. The same is not true for innate behaviour, which must go from parents to offspring.

Unlike innate behaviour, which is built into the organism's DNA, learned behaviour can be lost in a population if it is no longer being observed and repeated.

Application: Feeding on cream from milk bottles in blue tits as an example of the development and loss of learned behaviour

The Eurasian blue tit (*Cyanistes caeruleus*) is a bird species common to Europe and Western Asia. For much of the 20th century, especially before the home refrigerator was introduced, it was common in Britain to have milk delivered to the door early in the morning. The glass bottles had foil caps on them to keep germs out and the foil was painted different colours depending on the type of milk in the bottle. At the time, milk was not homogenized the way it is today so the cream would float to the top.

Blue tits somehow figured out that the foil was thin enough to pierce with their beaks and be peeled away. Then they could drink the nutritious cream off the top. Birds see colours in a similar way to humans and they quickly recognized that some milk containers had higher fat content than others. They learned to peel open only the tops with the richest, thickest layer of cream and ignore the low-fat milk.

Other birds in the population watched the well-nourished birds and learned the behaviour. This bird's social communication allowed the learned technique to be spread all over the country.

Because bottles are not delivered to homes anymore, the learning in this population has been lost. If bottles were delivered to doorsteps again, the populations alive today would have to learn the technique all over again. It did not get passed down genetically, so it is gone from the population.

Application: Migratory behaviour in blackcaps as an example of the genetic basis of behaviour and its change by natural selection

Model sentence: Sometimes learned human behaviour can have an impact on innate animal behaviour – the case of migration patterns in the European blackcap is one example.

The European blackcap (*Sylvia atricapilla*) is a bird that usually migrates from Germany to Spain in the winter to escape the cold temperatures and lack of available food.

There are many bird watchers and bird lovers in the UK and it is a common practice to leave out bird feeders in the winter for birds that are having trouble finding food. Since the 1950s, it has been observed that some blackcaps do not go down to Spain in the winter but go to the UK instead, where they find enough food in feeders to survive the winter.

This offshoot population of birds returns to Germany 10 days earlier than the ones that go to Spain. This gives them an advantage of finding the best nesting spots and there is less competition for food. In addition, the journey is not as difficult.

Experiments have been done where eggs from each population were removed from nests and hatched away from the parents. The chicks that hatched could not observe other birds' migration patterns. When they grew up and were ready to migrate, the birds from the original population went southwest towards Spain and the ones from the UK-migrating population went northwest. This is evidence that it is innate rather than learned behaviour.

Application: Blood sharing in vampire bats as an example of the development of altruistic behaviour by natural selection

Vampire bats, notably the species *Desmodus rotundus*, demonstrate an uncommon behaviour among animals – they regularly share their food with other individuals close to them. This is an example of **reciprocal altruism**, the idea that 'if you help me now, I will help you later'. This is in contrast to **altruism**, in general, which is a way of helping another individual with a cost to oneself and without expectation of repayment.

As their name indicates, vampire bats are **sanguivorous** – they feed on blood from live animals including birds, pigs, goats, and cows.

To make flight efficient, they maintain low body masses by not storing large amounts of fat. As a result, they must eat a blood meal every 2 days to stay alive. They only hunt at night and each night about 30% of the bats come back to the group without success. The bats who have found blood will **regurgitate** some to the bats who ask for it. The following night, the situation might be the other way around.

It would be tempting to think that this is a good example of **kin selection** (helping individuals who are genetically related), but in fact, many groups of bats who help each other are not related.

Application: Foraging behaviour in shore crabs as an example of increasing chances of survival by optimal prey choice

Successful shore crabs (*Carcinus maenas*) have been naturally selected to invest their time and energy looking (**foraging**) for a type of food that will give them the most benefit. They eat mussels by breaking the shells with their claws. Although a bigger mussel will have more food inside it, the energy needed to crack the shell and the risk of damage to the crab's claws represents a high cost. So it is better to eat two medium-sized mussels than to try to break open and eat one large mussel.

Saving the claws has a reproductive advantage: when males fight to mate with the females, those with fully functioning claws will have an advantage. Crabs who have damaged their claws trying to break an oversized mussel shell will probably be less successful in competing for a female. Notice the role that natural selection has played in determining the preference of mussel size.

Application: Breeding strategies in coho salmon populations as an example of behaviour affecting chances of survival and reproduction

Model sentence: Innate behaviours are the result of natural selection so if an animal has a behaviour that seems atypical such as a fish swimming long distance against the current of a river, there must be a selective pressure that gives that animal a better chance of survival.

Coho salmon (*Oncorhynchus kisutch*) spend their adult lives in the Pacific Ocean but they are **spawned** in freshwater rivers and return to mate in the same river.

Subject vocabulary

reciprocal altruism performing a good act in the expectation that it will be repaid

altruism behaviour that benefits the receiver without reward to the giver

sanguivorous blood eating

kin selection helping closely related individuals in preference to unrelated individuals

foraging searching for food

General vocabulary

regurgitate bring back into the mouth food already swallowed

spawned large amounts of eggs produced at the same time

Subject vocabulary

redds a nest

courtship display a demonstration to attract a mate

Females lay their eggs in shallow, fast running zones of freshwater rivers. They build multiple nests, called **redds**, and lay thousands of eggs in each one.

Male coho salmon will fertilize the eggs by releasing sperm cells over the eggs. They then keep watch over the eggs and attack potential predators if they get too close. Most return after 3 years but some males, called jacks, return to the river at the age of 2 years.

Males go through some physical changes when they are in reproductive mode: their colour changes, they develop a hooked nose and jaw and their backs develop an arch. When they have completed their role, they do not return to the ocean; instead, they die.

Can you see how the behaviour of these fish increases the chances of survival of this species?

- First of all, spawning (laying eggs) in the river instead of the ocean reduces the chances that potential predators will eat the eggs. Shallow water will prevent larger fish from accessing the eggs. Fast-moving water will dissuade hungry predators that cannot fight the current.
- Fast-moving water is often well-oxygenated water and the fragile eggs will need a good supply of dissolved oxygen.
- Constructing redds instead of simply laying eggs directly on the riverbed keeps the eggs and sperm from being pulled away by the current.
- Laying thousands of eggs instead of just a few greatly enhances the chances of some surviving.
- Spreading the eggs out over several nests also increases the chances that some will not be found by predators.
- The fact that the males remain present to protect the nests also greatly enhances survival rates. The development of the hooked nose and jaw allows a male to have defensive behaviours such as ramming into predators, hitting them hard, or grabbing their tails.
- Even though they usually only represent a small percentage of the male population, the jacks show a behaviour (returning early) that is a sustainable one and therefore must have been selected for by natural selection.
- The change in colour can have multiple possible messages including signalling to females that they are ready to fertilize eggs or signalling to rivals or predators that they are ready to defend themselves and their offspring. The arching of the back could have similar meaning and could also help in making sure the fish do not wander into water that is so shallow it will not be favourable for spawning.
- The death of the male at the end of the spawning season suggests that this species, like many salmon, have adapted in such a way that they invest all their energy in ensuring that the next generation is off to a good start.

Application: Courtship in birds of paradise as an example of mate selection.

Why would a male blue bird of paradise (*Paradisaea rudolphi*) hang upside down? In addition to seeming to be useless, it would put the bird at a disadvantage in many ways including making it open to predators.

Why would another bird of paradise dance around in circles or sway its head back and forth in rhythm like a fan at a rock concert? Or hop backwards up a branch?

The answer to all of these is that each one is a **courtship display**. The male is trying to impress a female with such rituals. Male birds that do the most elaborate displays have a better chance of impressing a female. Displaying feathers by stretching them out demonstrates that the bird has undamaged wings and would make a good partner. Birds are often the victims of attacks by parasites and showing off his wings is a way of demonstrating that he is not infested. Swaying the head back and forth without getting dizzy and falling off the branch suggests strength, good health, and reliability. If the female is impressed (or hypnotized) she will be more willing to mate. Notice the steps of this process in which natural selection is acting and the importance of the role of sexual selection.

Application: Synchronized oestrus in female lions in a pride as an example of innate behaviour that increases the chances of survival and reproduction of offspring

Lions (*Panthera leo*) are social animals that live in groups called prides. The females raise the young together: all females can give milk to all the cubs and all females watch over all the cubs. The females within a pride are related – they are either sisters, aunts, or cousins.

When male lions take over a pride, they tend to kill all the cubs they find.

After the death of her cubs, a lioness will move into **oestrus** within 2 weeks. This means that her body will prepare her to have new cubs. She produces a scent that signals to the male lion when she is ready to mate.

Since all the females had their cubs killed at the same time, they are all synchronized in oestrus. This means that all the cubs in the next generation will be the same age.

This has some advantages for survival including less competition or bullying between the cubs and a shorter time during which the cubs are too young to be left on their own.

If they have increased chances of survival, they will have a much better chance of passing on the genes of that pride. Once again, natural selection has made it possible to favour adaptations that are the most successful.

> **Subject vocabulary**
>
> **oestrus** period of time when a female is fertile

13 Option B: Biotechnology and bioinformatics

B.1 Microbiology: organisms in industry

Main idea
Microorganisms have been modified for use in industrial processes.

Understanding: Microorganisms are metabolically diverse.

Model sentence: Different species of microorganisms show great variation in their metabolic pathways.

The term **microorganism** refers to any small organism which can only be seen with a microscope. Microorganisms may include bacteria, fungi, protozoans, and algae. These small organisms are very diverse in structure, ecological role, and in the metabolic pathways they possess. Microorganisms may occupy various roles in the ecosystems they are a part of. These possible roles include:

- **Autotrophs** – these microorganisms act as **chemoautotrophs** or as **photoautotrophs** and are able to produce the **nutrients** they need for survival from inorganic sources. Photoautotrophs use the energy from the Sun, water, and carbon dioxide to produce the organic nutrients they need. Chemoautotrophs use the energy from the oxidation of an inorganic source and carbon dioxide to produce the organic nutrients they need. Autotrophs are often referred to as **producers**.

- **Heterotrophs** – these microorganisms require preformed organic compounds as their nutrient source. A group of heterotrophic microorganisms known as **saprotrophs** uses **detritus** as their energy and nutrient source. Detritus is dead organic matter. The actions of saprotrophs free the nutrients in dead organic matter for use within the ecosystem. Another group of heterotrophic microorganisms called yeast is able to carry out anaerobic respiration of simple sugars to derive their energy and nutrients.

The diversity of microorganism metabolism provides many products that are very useful to us. These products include food, biofuels, industrial solvents, food additives, pharmaceuticals such as antibiotics, and valuable biochemicals such as enzymes and proteins.

Understanding: Microorganisms are used in industry because they are small and have a fast growth rate.

Model sentence: Small sizes and rapid growth rates are two characteristics of microorganisms which make them valuable for industrial use.

The small size of microorganisms is a great advantage for using them in industrial roles. They take up little space. Due to their size, it is easier to control their surroundings. They can also be cultured or grown in huge numbers allowing for more production of desired products. They have very fast growth rates as well. Many bacteria reproduce by **binary fission** every 30 minutes if their environment is **optimal**.

Synonyms

diverse .... different/varied

Subject vocabulary

metabolic pathway a chemical pathway in which a series of enzymes produces intermediate compounds on the way to producing a final product needed by the organism

microorganism any relatively small organism which requires a microscope to observe

autotrophs organisms capable of producing their own food

chemoautotrophs organisms which produce their own food by using energy from the oxidation from an inorganic source and carbon dioxide

photoautotrophs organisms which produce their own food using energy from the Sun, water, and carbon dioxide

nutrient chemical material a cell or organism needs

producer a photosynthetic organism that starts a food chain

heterotrophs organisms not capable of producing their own food, requiring preformed organic compounds from other sources

saprotrophs organisms which use detritus as their energy and nutrient source

detritus dead organic matter

binary fission simplified form of cell division in bacteria

General vocabulary

optimal the best or most suitable

Understanding: **Pathway engineering** optimizes genetic and regulatory processes within microorganisms.

Model sentence: Genetic engineering has been carried out to make the metabolic pathways of many microorganisms more beneficial to us.

Pathway or metabolic engineering is the practice of optimizing genetic and regulatory processes within microorganisms for our use. **Genetic engineering**, also known as **genetic modification**, is used to bring about this optimizing process. To achieve this optimization two things are necessary:

- a thorough knowledge of existing metabolic pathways in the microorganism of interest
- changes made at key points in the microorganism **genome** to bring about more efficient pathways to produce the desired product or products.

Genetic engineering may also be carried out to allow the use of more common **substrates** in a particular metabolic pathway. Sometimes, the pathways are altered so a group of products may be produced by a pathway rather than just one product.

Understanding: Pathway engineering is used industrially to produce **metabolites** of interest.

Model sentence: Industry uses genetic modification of metabolic pathways in microorganisms to produce desired products.

A bacterium called *Escherichia coli* has a natural metabolic pathway which allows it to produce a 2-carbon alcohol. Longer chain alcohols are important to us because they yield more energy especially when they are present in gasolines and jet fuels. Scientists introduced new genes into *E. coli* to modify the naturally existing metabolic pathway which produced a 2-carbon alcohol. The result of the genetic modification is that this bacterium can now produce industrial quantities of a 5-carbon alcohol. This 5-carbon alcohol is very important in increasing the efficiency of our gasolines and jet fuels and is the metabolite of interest in this case.

Understanding: Fermenters allow large-scale production of metabolites by microorganisms.

Model sentence: Scientists and industry have produced very efficient **fermenters** which allow microorganisms to produce large quantities of desired metabolites.

Structures referred to as fermenters have been developed by scientists and industry for large-scale production of a desired metabolite by specific microorganisms.

Subject vocabulary

pathway engineering modifying the chain of reactions in a metabolic process (usually within a microorganism) to produce a substance or perform an action that is useful to us

genetic engineering process of artificially altering the normal genome of an organism

genetic modification genetic engineering, process of artificially altering the normal genome of an organism

genome the complete DNA sequence of an organism

substrate substance which begins a chemical reaction or process

metabolite product of metabolism

fermenters structures in which fermentation occurs

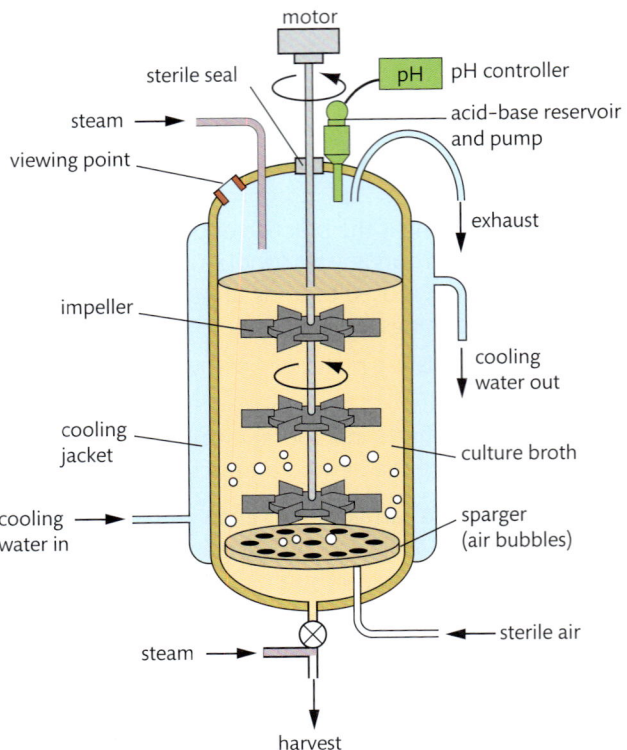

Figure 13.1 An industrial fermenter

Subject vocabulary

contamination process of being made unfit for further growth or development

toxic level concentration at which serious harm and death may occur to involved organisms

archaeans members of the prokaryotic domain Archaea

biogas gas produced by the anaerobic breakdown of organic matter which may be used for cooking, heating, or running engines

methane a biogas composed of carbon and hydrogen

methanogens bacteria group capable of producing methane

General vocabulary

broth nutrient mixture

agitation mixing

Fermenters, like the one above, allow effective control of the conditions surrounding and within the culture **broth**. The culture broth contains the microorganism which provides the desired metabolite. The maintenance of optimum growth conditions for the microorganism allows the recovery of large quantities of the product. One major feature of fermenters involves a design that prevents **contamination**. Contamination may occur as a result of the introduction to the fermenter of other microorganisms. The chance of this happening is decreased with the use of a stainless steel growth chamber which has closely monitored input and exit points. Contamination may also occur with the build-up of waste products. Many fermenters are designed with exit points. The exit points allow waste products to be removed so that their levels never reach a **toxic level**.

Most fermenters include some sort of device which allows mechanical agitation. This **agitation** helps maintain proper conditions throughout the culture.

Application: Biogas is produced by bacteria and archaeans from organic matter in fermenters

Fermenters containing cultures of bacteria and **archaeans** are being used to produce **biogas**. Biogas is the gas produced from the anaerobic breakdown of organic matter which may be used for cooking, heating, and running engines. Scientists apply the normal metabolic activities of bacteria and archaeans to bring about the production of methane from organic matter. **Methane** is the desired metabolite. The sequence of steps in the production of biogas in fermenters is:

- the splitting of long-chain organic compounds by bacteria to produce a liquid product
- the production of short-chain acetate, hydrogen, and carbon dioxide by bacteria
- the production of methane and carbon dioxide by archaeans or bacteria known as **methanogens**.

Skill: Production of biogas in a small-scale fermenter

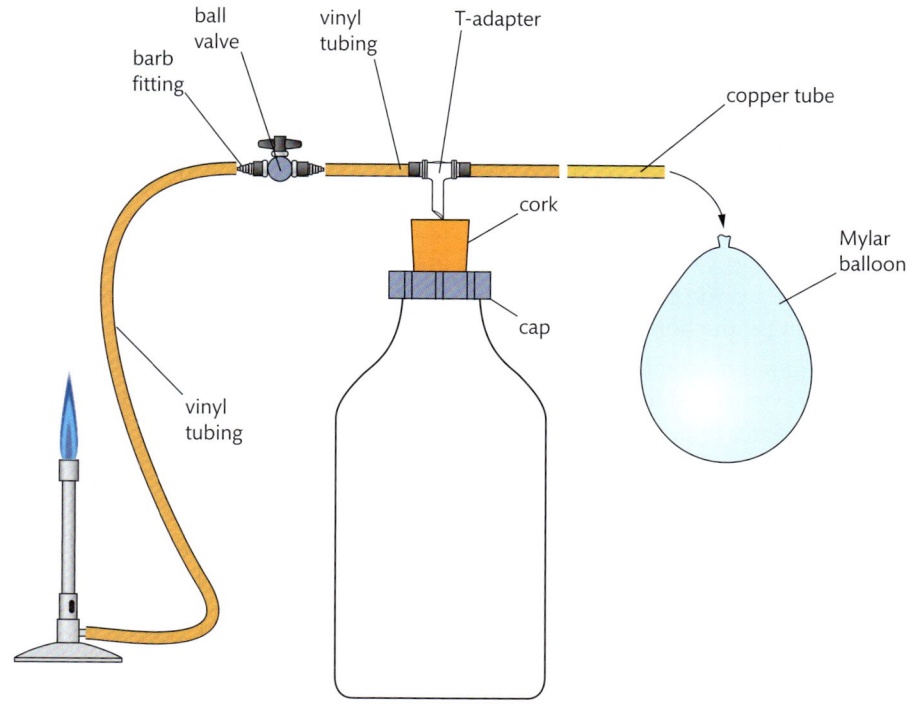

Figure 13.2 *Small-scale lab fermenter*

Understanding: Fermentation is carried out by batch or continuous culture.

Model sentence: Industry uses batch culture and continuous culture fermentation techniques.

Batch culture techniques in fermentation **utilize** a one-time introduction of a microorganism into the fermenter. The fermenter has all the nutrients necessary for the successful culturing of the microorganism. The microorganism is then allowed to reproduce to its maximum density level possible in the fermenter. The desired metabolite is removed from the fermenter once the **carrying capacity** for the microorganism in the culture broth has been reached.

Continuous culture techniques in fermentation utilize a continuous addition of nutrients and required substrates to the fermenter. This allows the desired metabolite to be continuously produced and recovered from the nutrient broth. This process can be maintained over a long period of time.

Hints for success: Batch culture techniques involve fermentation product extraction only when the concentration of the product is high. Continuous culture techniques allow a continuous extraction of the fermentation product over an extended period of time.

Subject vocabulary

batch culture technique way of fermenting microorganisms which involves a one-time introduction of the microorganism

carrying capacity an environment's ability to support an organism's population based on resource availability and other factors

continuous culture technique way of fermenting microorganisms which involves continuous addition of nutrients and required substrates

General vocabulary

utilize make use of

13 Option B: Biotechnology and bioinformatics

Application: Deep-tank batch fermentation in the mass production of penicillin

Science and industry have applied the principles of batch culture techniques to mass produce penicillin. Modifications of the usual batch culture techniques were necessary to produce large amounts of penicillin from a bacterium of the genus *Penicillium*. Some of the modifications include:

- Deep tank fermenters are used to allow increased yields compared to the usual shallow tanks.
- Bacteria of the genus *Penicillium* grow best when oxygen levels are relatively high. Oxygen is bubbled into the deep tanks and a stirring device is used to provide optimum conditions throughout the culture broth for penicillin production.
- *Penicillium* is most efficient at producing penicillin when glucose levels are low. This knowledge led to a reduction of glucose in the nutrients which are placed in the fermenter to begin the culture.
- pH and temperature are maintained at the optimum levels for *Penicillium* reproduction.

Penicillin is a **secondary metabolite** in this batch culture technique. Secondary metabolites are only produced in an organism if certain conditions occur. Large quantities of penicillin are only produced when the bacterium is stressed. Scientists have applied the natural ways the *Penicillium* is stressed to obtain the maximum amounts of penicillin possible.

Application: Production of citric acid in a continuous fermenter by *Aspergillus niger* and its use as a preservative and flavouring

Citric acid is a common food additive for flavour enhancing and preservation used by industry. Citric acid may be successfully produced by continuous culture techniques and the microorganism *Aspergillus niger*. Conditions under which this bacterium grows optimally have been applied in the continuous culture technique. pH, temperature, and nutrient levels kept at ideal levels allow large amounts of citric acid to be obtained over extended periods of time. There is a continuous input of nutrients and environmental conditions are continuously monitored to maintain the *Aspergillus* at its ideal growth conditions. The continued removal of the citric acid occurs during this culturing process. This culture occurs over an extended period because a **homeostatic system** is maintained.

Understanding: Microorganisms in fermenters become limited by their own waste products.

Model sentence: The build-up of microorganism waste products in fermenters is a limiting factor in microorganism growth and survival.

Common waste products of microorganisms which must be controlled in fermenters include:

- Heat – this is a by-product of metabolism and it may increase the temperature of the medium within the fermenter.
- Carbon dioxide – this a common product of metabolism and, in higher amounts, may alter the optimum pH within the fermenter.
- Various gases may be released in large enough quantities so that pressure within the fermenter may be raised to a harmful level.
- Alcohol may be one of the products of microorganism metabolism in the fermenter. Alcohol becomes toxic to the microorganism when it reaches certain concentrations.

Subject vocabulary

secondary metabolite products of metabolism produced in organisms only under specific conditions

homeostatic system environment in which all conditions are steadily maintained

- Oxygen levels may be affected by the metabolic actions of the microorganism.
- Secondary metabolites may reach toxic levels. Secondary metabolites are metabolites produced by a microorganism that are not used for energy.

These waste products must all be considered and controlled in the culturing of microorganisms in fermenters.

Understanding: **Probes** are used to monitor conditions within fermenters.

Model sentence: Conditions within a fermenter are monitored through the use of probes.

Many conditions within a fermenter must be monitored when continuous culture techniques are being used. Probes within the fermenter allow constant monitoring of these conditions so changes may be made to obtain maximum desired products. These probes are designed and located to prevent contamination of the culture broth. Usually, these probes are connected to computers to allow easier monitoring by technicians.

Subject vocabulary

probe a device used in a laboratory for data logging a specific measurement, e.g. temperature

Understanding: Conditions are maintained at optimal levels for the growth of the microorganisms being cultured.

Model sentence: Optimal conditions must be maintained to bring about the desired growth of microorganisms in industrial fermenters.

The maintenance of optimal conditions for a microorganism in a fermenter is especially important when using continuous culture techniques. Conditions to monitor and maintain at optimal levels in continuous cultures include:

- temperature
- pH
- oxygen and carbon dioxide levels
- pressure
- water concentrations of the culture broth
- foam or bubble amounts of the culture broth
- correct nutrient levels for the microorganism
- waste product concentration
- microorganism density.

Batch culture techniques do not require all these conditions to be monitored and maintained. This is because the desired product will only be extracted when the carrying capacity for the microorganism in the fermenter has been reached. Once the maximum number of microorganisms possible is achieved, they are removed. If more microorganisms are then necessary, a complete new setup would be produced and the process repeated. Batch culture techniques involve limited periods of time.

Subject vocabulary

zone of inhibition area of no bacterial growth in an area to which a bactericide has been introduced

bactericide chemical which kills bacteria

agar gelatin-like substance used to support growth of a bacterium or specific cell

Gram staining type of staining done with bacteria to determine their general grouping in classification

biotechnology science which uses knowledge to artificially alter organisms so they may be more useful

proteome the unique collection of proteins within a cell, tissue type, organ, or organism

transgenic having one or more genes from a different plant/animal

General vocabulary

pathogenic something that causes disease

disinfectant a chemical that destroys bacteria

incubator a container that maintains a specific temperature

Skill: Experiments showing zone of inhibition of bacterial growth by bactericides in sterile bacterial cultures

Bacterial cultures showing zones of inhibition using bactericides are easily produced in the classroom. Suggested materials for this skill development include:

- a safe, non-pathogenic strain of bacteria
- petri dishes
- proper nutrient agar for the bacterium being used
- a potential bactericide, such as a market disinfectant
- small, disc-shaped sections of a sterile absorbent filter paper dipped in disinfectant
- bacterial incubator.

Place the paper discs soaked with the bactericide being used on the agar to which the safe bacterium has been introduced. Incubate for sufficient time to allow visual bacterial growth. Do not remove the tops of the Petri dishes in your final observations. Zones of inhibition are areas of no bacterial growth where the disc is placed and a varying distance outward from the disc. The larger the zone of inhibition, the more effective the bactericide.

Skill: Gram staining of Gram-positive and Gram-negative bacteria

Gram staining should be done in the classroom to understand this important technique in bacteria identification. Bacteria with cell walls which accept the Gram stain are said to be Gram-positive and appear blue or violet in colour. Bacteria with cell walls which do not accept the Gram stain are said to be Gram-negative and will appear pink in colour. The Gram-staining process includes crystal violet, Gram's iodine, 95% alcohol, safranin stain, and water.

B.2 Biotechnology in agriculture

Main idea

Biotechnology in agriculture is being used to modify crops to increase crop yield and even the products harvested from crops.

Understanding: Transgenic organisms produce proteins that were not previously part of their species' proteome.

Model sentence: A genetically modified organism will produce proteins it did not produce before the modification.

A **proteome** is the set of proteins an organism can produce due to its genome. The genome of an organism is its complete DNA sequence. A genetically modified organism (GMO) is one in which a new gene or group of genes has been added to its genome. These genetically modified organisms are called transgenic organisms. The result of the changed genome could be the production of a protein or proteins that were not being produced before the modification occurred. Another result of the changed genome is that a protein or proteins which may have been produced naturally are no longer produced.

Understanding: Genetic modification can be used to overcome environmental resistance to increase crop yields.

Model sentence: Limiting factors in the environment for higher crop yields may be overcome by genetically modifying existing organisms.

Environmental resistance refers to limiting factors in the environment which limit an organism from reaching its growth and production potential. Environmental factors which may limit crop yields include both **biotic** and **abiotic** factors. Genetic modification is being used to overcome these limiting factors in many crops.

Possible abiotic limiting factors of the environment include **drought**, **frost**, high salinity soils, and low-nitrogen-containing soils. Rice has been genetically modified to produce a variety which is able to produce a higher yield and to survive extended dry spells. A gene known as *Arabidopsis HARDY* has been added to rice to produce a variety which has an increased photosynthesis rate and decreased water loss by transpiration. Another gene known as *DRO1* has recently been added to this transgenic rice which increases the root depth of the plant, making it more drought tolerant.

Possible biotic limiting factors of the environment include insects, viruses, and weeds. An example of overcoming a biotic environmental limiting factor is the introduction of a gene which brings about **glyphosate** resistance in soybean crops.

Application: Use of tumour-inducing (Ti) plasmid of *Agrobacterium tumefaciens* to introduce glyphosate resistance into soybean crops.

Scientists have applied genetic modification to produce a variety of soybeans which is resistant to a chemical used to control weed growth called glyphosate. Weeds create environmental resistance by taking water and nutrients away from desired crops. These weeds must be controlled. A bacterium normally pathogenic to plants called *Agrobacterium tumefaciens* contains a **plasmid** known as a Ti plasmid (tumour-inducing plasmid). This Ti plasmid can be genetically modified to carry a gene which brings about glyphosate resistance. *A. tumefaciens* with this modified plasmid will 'infect' soybean cells. The result is the growth and development of soybean plants with glyphosate resistance. Fields of these genetically modified soybean plants are then sprayed with glyphosate allowing control of weeds without damage to the soybean plants.

Skill: Evaluation of data on the environmental impact of glyphosate-tolerant soybeans

You should develop your ability to evaluate data to determine the environmental impact of adding glyphosate-tolerant genes to soybeans. In your evaluation, note the **gene flow** of the glyphosate-tolerant gene from the soybean plants to the wild plants (weeds) in the surrounding area. A high gene flow from the soybean plants to the weeds would indicate a risk involved with this example of genetic modification. On the other hand, data showing low gene flow between the soybean plants and weeds would indicate high benefits and low risks to this genetic modification.

Subject vocabulary

environmental resistance limiting factors in the environment which prevent an organism from reaching its full growth and production potential

biotic pertains to living

abiotic pertains to non-living

glyphosate chemical used to control weeds

plasmid small ring of DNA separate from the bacterial chromosome often used in genetic modification

gene flow movement of a gene from one population to another involving transfer by gametes

General vocabulary

drought shortage of water due to dry weather

frost very cold weather that causes water to freeze

Subject vocabulary

phenotype visible result of an organism's genotype

transgenic plants plants of one species which contain genes from plants of different species

pharmaceuticals medicines

hepatitis B antigen protein which is produced in organisms with hepatitis B

antibodies protective proteins produced in an organism in response to exposure to disease-causing antigens

amylopectin type of starch produced by plants that has adhesive and paper uses

amylose type of starch that is the most common storage form of carbohydrates in plants

bioinformatics branch of biology which uses computers in an effort to understand biological processes

General vocabulary

adhesive the ability to stick to/attach to another substance

Understanding: Genetically modified crop plants can be used to produce novel products.

Model sentence: New proteins or phenotypes may be produced in plants when they are genetically modified.

Genetic modification has led to the development of transgenic plants capable of producing very unique products. Some of these novel or unique products include vitamins, pharmaceuticals, enzymes, and even vaccines.

Application: Genetic modification of tobacco mosaic virus to allow bulk production of hepatitis B vaccine in tobacco plants

Scientists have genetically modified tobacco mosaic viruses to carry a gene which codes for the production of hepatitis B antigen. When these modified viruses are allowed to contact tobacco plants, the gene carrying the code for the production of the hepatitis B antigen is transferred to the tobacco plant. The tobacco plant then produces the hepatitis B antigen. This transgenic tobacco plant is then fed to an animal such as a mouse, which has an immune system which will respond to the hepatitis B antigen. The desired response of the animal is the production of antibodies. These antibodies may then be used to bring about passive immunity in organisms receiving them. Future plans are to modify the hepatitis B antigen into a non-pathogenic form which could be given to individuals in a vaccine to bring about active immunity.

Application: Production of Amflora potato (*Solanum tuberosum*) for paper and adhesive industries

Scientists at the company BASF have produced a variety of potato called the Amflora potato by genetic modification. This potato only produces starch of one type called amylopectin. Normally, 20% of the starch potatoes produce is amylose. In Amflora potatoes the gene to produce amylose has been modified so no amylose is produced. The 100% production of amylopectin by this modified potato allows more efficient paper and adhesive properties than non-modified potatoes. Another benefit of this modified potato is it allows conservation of energy and water in the production of paper.

Understanding: Bioinformatics plays a role in identifying target genes.

Model sentence: The use of computers in bioinformatics allows the identification of specific genes called target genes.

Bioinformatics uses computers in an effort to understand biological processes. Bioinformatics has been especially valuable in the sequencing of DNA so that particular genes of interest or target genes may be identified and located in an organism's genome. It has also been essential in the sequencing of whole organism genomes.

Understanding: The target gene is linked to other sequences that control its expression.

Model sentence: Specialized DNA sequences are necessary for the expression of a target gene in genetic modification.

A **target gene** must include more than just the DNA sequence necessary to produce a particular protein if it is to be expressed when placed into an organism's genome. The target gene is also called the transgene. DNA sequences that must be added to the target gene include:

- A **promoter DNA sequence** must be present to **initiate** transcription and the gene expression process.
- A **termination DNA sequence** is necessary to signal the end of the target gene sequence.

Often, a marker or a gene known as a recognition sequence is included. This recognition sequence allows scientists to see that the target gene has been taken up by the host DNA. All the parts for a functional target gene in genetic modification are called a **construct** and it often takes the form shown in the figure below.

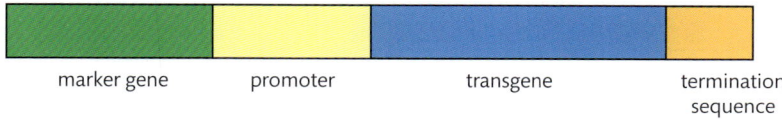

Figure 13.3 *General example of a functional target gene*

Understanding: An open reading frame is a significant length of DNA from a start codon to a stop codon.

Model sentence: The DNA base sequence from a start codon to a stop codon which codes for a polypeptide is called an open reading frame.

An **open reading frame** (ORF) is the DNA base sequence which codes for a particular gene. Once an organism's genome has been sequenced, the location of genes may then be determined from the database. Some key points about ORFs are:

- The DNA code occurs in base triplets.
- There are 64 possible base triplets. 61 of these base triplets code for an amino acid. There are three base triplets (TAG, TGA, and TAA) which signal the end of a gene or ORF. These three triplets are called stop codes. One base triplet (ATG) signals the start of a gene or ORF. The base triplet which signals the beginning of an ORF also codes for an amino acid and is called a start code.
- Most ORFs in DNA are over 100 base triplets and code for proteins which have at least 100 amino acids.

To find ORFs, scientists look for sequences of DNA base triplets which do not contain a stop code. The sequence of DNA base triplets would occur after a start code (ATG).

Skill: Identification of an open reading frame (ORF)

Develop your skill to recognize ORFs from a long DNA sequence. There is a public website presented by the National Center for Biotechnology Information (NCBI) which lists DNA sequences from various organisms. Visit the site, select a DNA segment of bases and find an ORF. Remember to look for a start code (ATG) in the

Subject vocabulary

target gene also called the transgene, the gene and all the sequences necessary to control its expression in genetic engineering

promoter DNA sequence section of DNA which initiates transcription of a gene

termination DNA sequence section of DNA which signals the end of a target gene sequence

construct all the parts for a functional target gene in genetic modification

open reading frame (ORF) DNA sequence which codes for a particular gene

Synonyms

initiate............ start/begin

DNA segment. Then look for a longer sequence of DNA base triplets without one of the stop sequences mentioned above. It is typical to find roughly 300 DNA bases separating the start code and the stop code.

Understanding: Marker genes are used to indicate successful uptake.

Model sentence: Marker genes are used in genetic modification to indicate the target gene has been taken up.

Marker genes are important to scientists since they confirm that a target gene or construct in a genetic modification attempt has been successfully incorporated into the desired host's genome. Some marker genes allow visual confirmation of the uptake. An example of this is the attachment of a marker gene which codes for the production of a green fluorescent protein. Other marker genes are called selectable markers. Selectable markers allow some sort of natural selection property. An example of this is a marker gene which brings about resistance to an antibiotic in a bacterium. A bacterium which has taken up a construct with this type of marker gene will not be affected if grown on agar which contains the antibiotic.

Understanding: Recombinant DNA must be inserted into the plant cell and taken up by its chromosome or chloroplast DNA.

Model sentence: The production of a transgenic plant requires that recombinant DNA be inserted into one of the plant's chromosomes in the nucleus or into the DNA of the plant's chloroplasts.

Recombinant DNA contains sequences of bases from two or more sources. Organisms with recombinant DNA are known as transgenic organisms. The first step in producing a transgenic plant is the introduction of the recombinant DNA into a plant cell. There are two general ways recombinant DNA may be introduced into a plant cell. These are:

- The recombinant DNA may be taken up into a plant cell's chromosomes, which occur in the nucleus of the cell.
- The recombinant DNA may be taken up by the DNA of the chloroplasts of the plant cell. Recombinant DNA taken up in this way will not be transferred in pollination. This method is often used when it is not desirable to spread the genetic modification to other plants.

The introduction of recombinant DNA into plant cells often utilizes a vector or carrier of some type.

Subject vocabulary

marker gene a gene which when present has an accompanying identification factor, such as a fluorescent colour

selectable marker genes a gene used for recognition by allowing some sort of natural selection property

recombinant DNA DNA which contains sequences of bases from two or more sources

vector carrier

Understanding: Recombinant DNA can be introduced into whole plants, leaf discs, or protoplasts.

Model sentence: Once introduced into a plant's cells, recombinant DNA can then be taken up by sections of that plant's leaves, protoplasts from the plant, and finally, the whole plant.

Protoplasts refer to the living parts of a plant cell including the cell membrane. They do not have cell walls. Vectors carrying recombinant DNA may be used to infect protoplasts from specific plants with desired traits. A common vector used is the bacterium *Agrobacterium*. The Ti plasmid of this bacterial genus may be genetically modified to carry the desired trait into the genome of the protoplasts.

Sections of plant leaves may also be incubated with the genetically modified *Agrobacterium* to allow introduction of a desired gene into a particular plant species. A selectable marker is used with this technique to confirm the uptake of the desired gene into the leaf cells. The selectable marker usually is a gene which gives resistance to a particular type of antibiotic.

Once the recombinant DNA is introduced into the protoplast or the leaf section, a whole plant may result in which all the cells have the desired trait or traits.

Understanding: Recombinant DNA can be introduced by direct physical and chemical methods or indirectly by vectors.

Model sentence: Both direct and indirect methods may be used to introduce recombinant DNA into an organism.

Direct physical methods of introducing recombinant DNA into plants include:
- **Electroporation** – a high voltage electrical field is produced by electrical pulses at the plant cell membrane. The resulting electrical field forms pores in the plant cell membranes to allow recombinant DNA to enter the cell and nucleus.
- **Biolistics** – tiny metal particles such as gold or tungsten are covered with the gene to be introduced into the plant. The coated particles are then propelled into the plant by a particle gun.
- **Microinjection** – a micro-needle is used to inject the desired gene into a cell. This usually includes the use of a micropipette to hold the target cell while the injection occurs.

Direct chemical methods of introducing recombinant DNA into plants include:
- **Liposomes** – liposomes are artificially prepared lipid sacs with an aqueous interior. The DNA to be introduced into a plant is placed into the aqueous solution of the liposome interior. The liposome with the desired DNA may then fuse with the plant cell membrane allowing the DNA to be transferred into the cell's nuclear DNA.
- **Calcium chloride** – the plant cells to be genetically modified are placed in a cold solution of calcium chloride containing the desired DNA for uptake. Addition of heat to the cell and calcium chloride solution allows the active transport of the desired DNA in the solution by endocytosis into the cell.

Subject vocabulary

protoplasts living parts of a plant cell including the cell membrane but not the cell wall

electroporation process by which a high voltage electrical field is produced by electrical pulses at the cell membrane

biolistics particles coated with a gene are propelled into a cell to bring about recombinant DNA

microinjection process by which a desired gene is actually injected into a cell

liposomes artificially created lipid sacs used to deliver a substance in a biological system

calcium chloride chemical used to increase the uptake of recombinant DNA into a cell

endocytosis active transport in which substances are brought into the cell

Synonyms

pore.............. hole/opening

General vocabulary

coated covered with a thin layer of something else

Vectors are biological agents used to carry recombinant DNA into cells. Vectors are viruses, plasmids such as the Ti plasmid, and other biological agents. Specific examples of commonly used vectors include:
- *Agrobacterium tumefaciens* – this bacterium includes a Ti plasmid commonly used as a vector.
- Tobacco mosaic virus – used to carry the hepatitis B gene into tobacco plants allowing the expression of hepatitis B antigens. These antigens may then be used with certain animals to produce a hepatitis B vaccine.

B.3 Environmental protection

Main idea
Potentially toxic wastes in our environment may be decreased or eliminated by the use of biotechnology.

Understanding: Responses to pollution incidents can involve bioremediation combined with physical and chemical procedures.

Model sentence: Bioremediation along with physical and chemical procedures may be used in the response to pollution incidents.

Pollutants are factors in the environment which affect the lives and health of living things in a negative way.

Bioremediation is the process where the normal metabolic processes of organisms are used to breakdown pollutants. Microorganisms are commonly used in the bioremediation process.

Phytoremediation is the use of plants in the removal of environmental contaminants. Bioremediation along with chemical and physical methods are utilized to treat areas where pollution occurs.

Chemical methods often used in treating environmental pollutants include:
- **Gelling agents**, which react with pollutants such as oil to form solids. The solids are then recovered and thrown away.
- **Oxidizing agents**, which may be injected into soil or added to water to accelerate the breakdown of organic pollutants.

Physical methods often used in treating environmental pollutants include:
- Removal of chemically contaminated soils followed by crushing, filtering, and mixing with water. If the pollutant is water soluble it will go into the solution with water. The water may then be **purified**.
- Detergents may be added to polluted areas to bring about quick **dispersal** of the pollutant.
- **Skimmers** may be used to remove pollutants which occur on the top of water.

Subject vocabulary
pollutants substances released into an ecosystem that have the potential to do harm

bioremediation process where the normal metabolic processes of organisms are used to breakdown pollutants

phytoremediation use of plants in the bioremediation process

gelling agents substances that react with certain pollutants to produce solids which can be disposed of

oxidizing agents agents used to accelerate the breakdown of organic materials

skimmers physical method used to remove pollutants from the top of bodies of water

Synonyms
purified .... cleansed/cleaned

General vocabulary
dispersal spreading out

Understanding: Microorganisms are used in bioremediation.

Model sentence: **Microorganisms are often very effective in the breakdown of pollutants.**

Many microorganisms are quite effective in bioremediation due to the enzymes they possess allowing them to break down long hydrocarbon chains present in organic pollutants. These microorganisms include prokaryotes such as bacteria and archaeans. These prokaryotes work well for several reasons:

- They have rapid reproductive rates.
- They possess quite variable metabolic pathways. The prokaryotes have metabolic pathways to break down many pollutants since they are such a diversified group.

Understanding: Some pollutants are metabolized by microorganisms.

Model sentence: **Certain microorganisms may remove some pollutants from the environment by actually using the pollutant in their normal metabolic pathways.**

Application: Degradation of benzene by halophilic bacteria such as *Marinobacter*

Scientists use an archaean of the genus named *Marinobacter* to remove a **carcinogenic** pollutant called benzene. Benzene occurs in the highly saline wastewater produced by drilling for oil in marine environments. This archaean is known as a **halophilic** bacterium due to its ability to survive in high saline environments. *Marinobacter* possesses the enzymes in a metabolic pathway which will break benzene down completely into carbon dioxide.

Application: Degradation of oil by *Pseudomonas*

Scientists found a species of bacterium within the genus *Pseudomonas* which naturally occurs on the bottom of ocean environments. This bacterium was observed to break down petroleum which seeped upward into the ocean water through cracks in the ocean floor. Scientists have now applied the naturally occurring metabolic pathways of this bacterium to break down oil pollutants in salt water. Chemicals such as rhamnolipid, glycerol, urea, and potassium are often added to the oil spill area to increase the growth and effectiveness of this bacteria in eliminating the oil pollutant.

Application: Conversion by *Pseudomonas* of methyl mercury into elemental mercury

Scientists have applied another bacteria from the genus *Pseudomonas* to remove methyl mercury from garbage dumps. Mercury is a component of some paints and is found in some types of light bulbs. A bacterium known as *Desulfovibrio desulfuricans* adds a methyl group to the mercury in rubbish. The result is methyl mercury which is potentially quite dangerous to many organisms due to **biomagnification** near the top of food chains. When the *Pseudomonas* bacterium is added to the garbage dumps with methyl mercury, it changes this dangerous chemical into insoluble elemental mercury. This insoluble elemental mercury sinks to the bottom of the garbage dump and does not become part of any food chain.

Subject vocabulary

carcinogenic having cancer-causing properties

halophilic organisms able to survive in high saline environments

biomagnification increasing concentration of a pollutant as the pollutant moves up through the trophic levels of a food chain

Understanding: Cooperative aggregates of microorganisms can form biofilms.

Model sentence: Biofilms are composed of large numbers of microorganisms working as a team to cover the surface of objects.

Biofilm key points:

- Biofilms are large groups or **aggregates** of microorganisms working together to cover a surface.
- Biofilms may include many different types of microorganisms including fungi, bacteria, and algae.
- Biofilms hold together by secreting **extracellular polymer-like substances (EPS)**. These EPS also allow the aggregate to **adhere** to a surface.
- Biofilms can develop in a short time, even in hours.

Examples of biofilms include the **plaque** which occurs on teeth, the layers of microorganisms which may contaminate the surfaces of materials used in food production, and the very thick layers of microorganisms which may lead to the blocking and **corrosion** of pipes.

Application: Use of biofilms in trickle filter beds for sewage treatment

Scientists have applied the properties of biofilms in a positive way to bring about the efficient treatment of sewage. Biofilms are used with **trickle filter beds** in treating sewage. An aerobic bacteria is used to produce biofilms on rocks or artificial particles which exist as a bed in a filter tank. Sewage water is sprayed onto the rock or particle bed with the biofilm. The spraying adds oxygen to the sewage. The biofilm of aerobic bacteria on the rocks or particles in the bed breaks down the sewage into carbon dioxide, which escapes into the atmosphere. The treated water is collected through a drainage system at the bottom of the tank.

Understanding: Biofilms possess emergent properties.

Model sentence: The properties of the biofilm community are greater than the properties of the individual components.

The self-organization of individual members of a biofilm into a complex structure or architecture is an **emergent property**. The complex structure or architecture which a biofilm may form is often referred to as a matrix. Common emergent properties of the biofilm include:

- complex matrix formation
- **quorum sensing**
- resistance to antimicrobial agents.

> **Hints for success:** Emergent properties are common in biology. We see them when all the individual parts of a cell work together to form a structure which has properties greater than the sum of the properties of the individual parts. The same is true of biofilms. The 'team' formed in the development of biofilms possesses many more properties than the sum of the properties of the individual members.

Subject vocabulary

biofilm large groups of microorganisms working together that cover a surface

extracellular polymer-like substances (EPS) substances which hold the microorganisms of a biofilm together and add in the adherence to a surface

plaque build-up of cholesterol and other substances on the inner wall of arteries or biofilm on the surface of teeth

trickle filter bed a bed of rock or other particles which allows fluid to pass through bringing about the removal of some substance, usually a pollutant

emergent property a property which is greater than the sum of the parts

quorum sensing process of communication when the population of a microorganism in a biofilm reaches a population level which brings about some change in response

General vocabulary

aggregates clumps

corrosion slow destruction

Synonyms

adhere........... stick

Understanding: Microorganisms growing in a biofilm are highly resistant to antimicrobial agents.

Model sentence: Antimicrobial agents have very little effect on the microorganisms which exist within a biofilm.

Many biofilms are resistant to antimicrobial agents such as antibiotics. Examples of problems due to this emergent property are:
- Biofilms are often found in hospitals and may cause secondary infections in patients during their stay.
- Biofilms often occur in the lungs of cystic fibrosis patients in which the bacterium *Pseudomonas aeruginosa* forms a biofilm which is very difficult to control.
- Biofilms may develop in the medical catheters or on implants of patients requiring their replacement. This replacement results in significant cost and trauma to the patient.

Causes of this resistant antimicrobial emergent property are being researched at present. One possible cause is the EPS produced by the individual members of the biofilm. Another possible cause is the fact that individual microorganisms of a biofilm have a much lower rate of cell division than when they occur alone. This presents a problem controlling biofilms because most antimicrobial agents act by controlling or inhibiting cell division.

Skill: Evaluation of data or media reports on environmental problems caused by biofilms

It is important for you to study data provided by studies in order to evaluate the environmental problems caused by biofilms. There are many studies available concerning biofilms. One study addresses the effects of biofilms which occur in ship ballast water. It has been shown these biofilms may become aquatic invasive species when released into the ocean. Read media reports of the effects in the environment of biofilms. Many media reports are available concerning the role of biofilms in quite varied instances of food poisoning. Certainly, this activity should bring about some concern about biofilms in the environment. However, many reports show their potential benefits to our environment.

> **Subject vocabulary**
>
> **antimicrobial** an agent which harms or kills microscopic organisms
>
> **secondary infections** infections developed during treatment for some other disease
>
> **species** a group of organisms which are structurally similar and able to pass their genetic traits onto their offspring
>
> **threshold** some significant level which brings about some sort of change or shift in response

Understanding: Microorganisms in biofilms cooperate through quorum sensing.

Model sentence: Quorum sensing allows the microorganisms of biofilms to work together.

Quorum sensing is an emergent property which occurs when the population of microorganisms in a biofilm reaches a certain (threshold) population level. Bacteria in biofilms will express different genes as their population changes. There appears to be signalling or communicating molecules and receptor-like molecules involved in quorum sensing. When population levels are higher more signalling molecules are present. These signalling molecules are detected by receptor molecules on the involved cells. Very often the result of this signalling and reception is the production of more EPS by the microorganisms involved. The EPS allows the further development of the biofilm.

Hints for success: Quorum sensing brings about greater communication and increased chances of success for the organisms involved. It only occurs when a particular level of population is achieved which is known as the threshold population. A threshold in biology is generally the level of some factor at which specific actions begin to occur.

Understanding: Bacteriophages are used in the disinfection of water systems.

Model sentence: Bacteriophages may be used to control biofilm-forming bacteria which occur on the equipment of water systems.

A **bacteriophage** is a virus which has the ability to attack and destroy a specific type of bacteria. There are many different types of bacteriophages. Each type of bacteriophage attacks a particular bacteria type.

Biofilms may cause serious damage to water systems. Uncontrolled biofilms may corrode or block the pipes of the system.

Treatment with a number of different bacteriophages has been shown to successfully reduce the biofilm which may develop in pipes of our water systems. The success of the bacteriophage treatment is increased when the addition of chlorine follows the addition of the bacteriophage mixture. The bacteriophage success is largely due to the ability of the virus to **penetrate** all the layers of the existing biofilm. Disinfectants are not as effective in treating water system biofilms because they are only effective on the outer most layer of the biofilm.

B.4 Medicine

Main idea

Biotechnology is allowing greater efficiency at finding, identifying, and treating disease.

Understanding: Infection by a **pathogen** can be detected by the presence of its genetic material or by its **antigens**.

Model sentence: Tests for a pathogen's genetic material or for the antigens it produces allows its detection in an infection.

Disease can be treated more effectively when the pathogen which is causing it is accurately and quickly identified. Identification of the pathogen involves an analysis of its genetic material or the observation of an antigen it produces. Present biotechnology tests commonly used in this pathogen identification process are:

- **PCR (polymerase chain reaction)** – tests for the actual genetic material of a pathogen
- **enzyme-linked immunosorbent assay (ELISA)** – tests for the antigens a pathogen directly produces or tests for the antibodies an organism produces in response to a disease (both antigens and antibodies are proteins)
- **DNA microarrays** – tests for the presence of particular sequences of DNA by using mRNA.

Subject vocabulary

bacteriophage a type of virus which infects bacteria

pathogens disease-causing agents such as viruses and bacteria

antigen substance which stimulates the production of antibodies in vertebrates

polymerase chain reaction (PCR) process which increases the amount of DNA of a specific type

enzyme-linked immunosorbent assay (ELISA) test for specific antigens or antibodies

DNA microarrays tests for the presence of particular sequences of DNA by using mRNA

Synonyms

penetrate .... go through

Skill: Interpretation of the results of an ELISA diagnostic test

ELISA stands for enzyme-linked immunosorbent assay. It was the first test used to successfully screen for the HIV antibody in blood. The presence of the HIV antibody indicated the potential presence in the system of the human immunodeficiency virus. In the ELISA test for HIV antibody, a sample of blood from the individual to be tested is **centrifuged** and placed in a small well. The well contains the HIV protein which will provide a positive result for the antibody in question. The **serum** is allowed to incubate in the well with the protein. The serum is removed after the incubation period. A series of buffer washes then occur. The final step is the addition of an enzyme substrate. The well will now show colour if the serum antibodies match the protein placed in the well for identification purposes. Follow these steps to interpret the results of an ELISA test:

- If colour is present in the well, the serum antibodies match the identification protein placed in the well for identification purposes.
- The amount or intensity of the colour of the well is directly proportional to the amount of serum antibody initially bound to the protein on the well bottom.

Application: Use of PCR to detect different strains of influenza virus

Scientists use polymerase chain reaction (PCR) to detect various types of influenza virus. PCR involves the production of multiple copies of DNA. Influenza virus is a **retrovirus**, which means it contains RNA but not DNA. The influenza RNA is purified from an infected patient. An enzyme called **reverse transcriptase** is then added to the RNA. The enzyme allows **cDNA** to be produced. Complementary DNA (cDNA) is DNA produced from mRNA by base pairing. Primer sequences for the influenza virus being tested are then added. More cDNA produced after the primer addition indicates this particular influenza virus is present.

Understanding: **Predisposition** to a genetic disease can be detected through the presence of markers.

Model sentence: The presence of specific genetic markers indicates a predisposition to a genetic disease.

Genetic markers are DNA sequences which are associated with a tendency to develop a particular genetic disease. A genetic marker may be of varying lengths of DNA sequences.

Single nucleotide polymorphisms (SNPs) often called 'snips' are DNA sequences that involve single nucleotides. SNPs serve as markers indicating a predisposition to certain genetic diseases.

Segments of DNA composed of repeats of particular sequences of DNA nucleotides called **tandem repeats** are also valuable as markers.

The most valuable markers are found close to the gene that is thought to be the cause of the genetic disease. Markers are also useful when they are associated with a single gene which is the cause of the genetic disease. Markers are less useful when multiple genes are the cause of a genetic disease. Markers also show less value when associated with genetic diseases strongly influenced by the environment.

Examples of genetic markers and the genetic disease they cause predisposition toward are:

- *melanocortin 1 receptor* (*MC1R*) – predisposition to melanoma skin cancers
- *BRCA 1* – predisposition to breast or ovarian cancer
- *BRCA 2* – predisposition to breast or ovarian cancer.

Subject vocabulary

centrifuged process of separating solids from a liquid by spinning the liquid at high speed

serum component of blood minus blood cells and clotting factors

retrovirus virus which contains RNA as its nucleic acid within a capsid

reverse transcriptase enzyme which allows the production of cDNA from mRNA

cDNA complementary DNA produced from mRNA by base pairing, single stranded

genetic marker DNA sequences which are associated with a tendency to develop a particular genetic disease

single nucleotide polymorphisms (SNPs) DNA sequences which involve changes in single nucleotides

tandem repeats segments of DNA composed of particular sequences of DNA nucleotides

General vocabulary

predisposition tendency to suffer from a certain illness

Understanding: DNA microarrays can be used to test for genetic predisposition or to diagnose the disease.

Model sentence: Markers and genetic diseases are capable of being identified by using DNA microarrays.

A DNA microarray is a collection of DNA probes attached to a solid surface which can be used to identify a genetic marker or disease. The steps in using a DNA microarray to identify specific genetic sequences are:

- Isolate mRNA from the patient in question.
- Carry out reverse transcription to produce complementary DNA (cDNA) which is single stranded.
- Label the cDNA with a type of florescent dye.
- Expose the cDNA to the microarray which contains DNA probes of the marker gene or the defective gene causing the disease.
- Rinse excess cDNA from the microarray.
- Base pairing of the cDNA and the microarray DNA probes which is called hybridization results in a recognizable colour.

Many microarray tests involve the use of green and red fluorescent dyes. Green dyes are added to normal or non-cancer control cell cDNA. Red dyes are added to cDNA of cancerous cells. Analysis using these two dyes and the colours observed on the microarray would be based on the following:

- green colour – high hybridization for normal cells or cDNA
- red colour – high hybridization for cancer cells or cDNA
- yellow colour – equal hybridization for both cell (cDNA) types.

The yellow colour indicates the gene is not involved in the cancer. A red colour indicates the gene is involved with the cancer. A green colour indicates the gene may be involved with prevention of the cancer.

Understanding: Metabolites that indicate disease can be detected in blood and urine.

Model sentence: Certain diseases produce products of unique metabolic pathways which are detectable in blood and urine.

Many genetic diseases include unique metabolic pathways often due to DNA which affects the enzymes controlling a normal pathway. The result of the defective pathway is a metabolite which is unique and detectable. These metabolites may be referred to as biomarkers due to their occurrence with specific diseases. Biotechnology is allowing detection of these metabolites so that early detection and treatment may occur. Several diseases produce these detectable metabolites in blood and urine.

- Prostate cancer is usually associated with high levels of the metabolite prostate-specific antigen (PSA).
- A significant number of breast cancer patients have a high level of a protein in their blood known as HER2 (human epidermal growth factor receptor 2).
- Lesch–Nyhan syndrome results in a large concentration of uric acid in the urine.

Subject vocabulary

reverse transcription process in which cDNA is produced from mRNA

hybridization in molecular genetics, the complementary base pairing between two segments of DNA such as between a strand of cDNA and microarray probes

metabolite product of metabolism

biomarkers a substance not normally produced by the body but produced by the metabolic pathway of a particular disease that can be used to indicate the patient has that disease

Synonyms

defective........ faulty

Understanding: Tracking experiments are used to gain information about the localization and interaction of a desired protein.

Model sentence: Proteins of interest may be modified to allow tracking within an organism.

Another type of biomarker is a protein to which a radioactive probe is attached allowing tracking of the protein's circulation and distribution within an organism. Some proteins can be tracked after attaching a green fluorescent protein (GFP) to them. Equipment recognizing radioactivity or fluorescent colouring is then used to study the actions of the protein.

Application: Tracking tumour cells using transferrin linked to luminescent probes

Scientists now **routinely** use fluorescent proteins also known as luminescent probes to track tumour cells. Transferrin is the fluorescent protein often used. Transferrin will seek out and attach to unique receptors which occur on cancer tumour cells. This allows detection of the cancer. It also represents a future means of attacking tumour cells by attaching anticancer drugs to the transferrin protein.

Understanding: Biopharming uses genetically modified animals and plants to produce proteins for therapeutic use.

Model sentence: Genetically modified plants and animals have been developed to produce proteins for the treatment of diseases.

The genetic modification of plants and animals has been developed to allow these plants and animals to produce therapeutic proteins which may be used in the treatment of diseases. This process is called **biopharming**. Genetically modified bacteria are used to produce human insulin and growth hormone which are simple proteins. However, bacteria are not able to produce the complexity of protein structure needed to form most therapeutic proteins. This complexity issue is why plants and animals with eukaryotic cells are now being developed for biopharming.

Application: Biopharming of antithrombin

Scientists are using goats and biopharming techniques to produce a protein called **antithrombin**, which decreases the occurrence of blood clots in surgery and in birthing. Excess **clotting** occurs in people with a hereditary antithrombin deficiency. Clotting is especially a problem in these people when they are having surgery or when they are birthing. Goats have been genetically modified to produce antithrombin in their mammary **glands**. The gene which is necessary for the production of antithrombin must be inserted into the goat's genome along with the proper **promoter** and signal sequences. The proper **signal sequence** is essential so that the antithrombin is produced by ribosomes attached to the ER. Ribosomes attached to the ER of the goat's mammary cells will produce antithrombin which is carried outside the cells and will become a part of the milk. Ribosomes free in the cytoplasm would still produce antithrombin. However, this antithrombin would remain in the cells and would not be able to be recovered. Goats were chosen because they have a high milk production rate. They also have a short generational time of 18 months. Antithrombin can be successfully retrieved from the milk of these genetically modified goats. This isolated and purified antithrombin may then be given to antithrombin-deficient patients to minimize the excess clotting problem.

General vocabulary

routinely done as a normal part of a process or job

clotting becoming thicker and more solid

gland an organ of the body which produces a substance

Subject vocabulary

therapeutic relating to the treatment of disease

biopharming genetic modification of plants and animals in order to produce therapeutic proteins or medicines

antithrombin protein which decreases the action of thrombin in blood clotting

promoter region of a target gene which initiates transcription and the gene expression process

signal sequence group of amino acids coded by mRNA which controls whether a ribosome is attached to the endoplasmic reticulum or not

13 Option B: Biotechnology and bioinformatics

Understanding: Viral vectors can be used in gene therapy.

Model sentence: Viruses may be used to deliver new genetic material into organisms in which gene therapy may be helpful.

The use of viruses to insert beneficial genes in gene therapy is usually called **somatic therapy**. This name comes from the fact that body or somatic cells are being altered, not reproductive cells. It is essential that the viruses used in gene therapy delivery cases are disabled in some way so they will only infect the cells that need to be modified.

Cystic fibrosis is a very serious genetic disease which is presently being treated with great promise by gene therapy. SCID is also being treated successfully in many cases with gene therapy. The steps of SCID gene therapy are explained in the application below.

Application: Use of viral vectors in the treatment of Severe Combined Immunodeficiency (SCID)

Scientists are using viruses as vectors to insert into cells a gene missing from patients with a disease known as Severe Combined Immunodeficiency (SCID). People with SCID do not have a gene which produces an enzyme known as **adenosine deaminase (ADA)**. The lack of ADA results in the build-up of a metabolite known as **deoxyadenosine**. This metabolite is toxic to the immune system's T and B **lymphocytes**. Loss of T and B lymphocytes results in a non-functional immune system. Any infection becomes a very serious problem to these people. A treatment involving genetic modification is now being used to treat many of these SCID patients. Steps in this treatment are:

- Remove ADA-deficient lymphocytes from a SCID patient.
- Culture these lymphocytes in the laboratory (*in vitro*).
- Infect the cultured lymphocytes with a genetically modified retrovirus which is carrying the normal ADA gene and the necessary promoter sequence. The retrovirus is disabled before being modified so it only affects target tissues which produce lymphocytes.
- Transfuse the modified lymphocytes back into the SCID patient.

Scientists have achieved beneficial effects with this procedure that have lasted 4 years.

B.5 Bioinformatics

Main idea

The use of computer-stored databases and other computer information sources to analyse biological research is known as bioinformatics.

Subject vocabulary

somatic therapy use of viruses to insert beneficial genes into body cells, not reproductive cells, in gene therapy

adenosine deaminase (ADA) enzyme which breaks down the metabolite deoxyadensine which adversely affects the immune system

deoxyadenosine metabolite which is toxic to B and T lymphocytes

lymphocytes white blood cells capable of producing antibodies, often referred to as B lymphocytes or B cells

Understanding: Databases allow scientists easy access to information.

Model sentence: Access to biological information has been made much easier due to structured collections of data on computers known as **databases**.

Databases have made the access to scientific information much easier. Databases need the following characteristics to be successful:

- an accessible, identifying code or name
- the name of the scientists contributing to the database
- indication of the time the data were entered
- literature information providing additional sources about the information being presented
- real data which were actually generated.

A few major biology databases in use today are:

- GenBank – lists a collection of DNA sequences of many, many sources
- OMIM (On-Line Mendelian Inheritance in Man) – lists the phenotypes for a series of disease-causing SNPs (single nucleotide polymorphisms)
- Swiss-Prot – lists a huge set of protein sequences from many sources
- Ensembl – provides complete genomes of humans and many other vertebrates.

Scientists may use databases to:

- extract information for a particular question or for further research
- add new data found by personal research.

Skill: Explore chromosome 21 in databases

You should develop your skill in using a biotechnology database by examining chromosome 21 of the human genome. The database known as Ensembl can be used for this. Chromosome 21 is suggested because it is the shortest of the human chromosomes. Its genetic sequence is also well known due to numerous studies associated with research involving Down syndrome, also known as trisomy 21. An Ensembl search involving this chromosome will show the genes present, their location on the chromosome, the proteins they express, and even centromere location relative to the genes present.

Subject vocabulary

database collection of data maintained on computers

General vocabulary

exponential getting faster as more is added

Understanding: The body of data stored in databases is increasing exponentially.

Model sentence: The amount of data available in databases is increasing at an **exponential** rate.

Biotechnology has added greatly to the data which are being added to databases. Every day more scientists are becoming even more involved with the generation of data using biotechnology and other modes of research. Increased access to these databases has also added to their size and value.

Understanding: BLAST searches can identify similar sequences in different organisms.

Model sentence: BLAST is a computer program which allows comparison of nucleotide and protein sequencing in different organisms.

BLAST is an acronym for Basic Local Alignment Search Tool. Similar protein amino acid and DNA nucleotide sequences exist in different organisms. BLAST is a computer program which can demonstrate these similarities by comparing nucleotide or protein sequences to sequence databases. Comparing sequences may lead to greater understanding of evolutionary and functional relationships amongst organisms. BLAST actually consists of a family of programs which allow specific queries to be made. Of all the BLAST programs, BLASTn and BLASTp are most used. The reason they are most used is that they allow direct comparisons between sequences.

Some other uses of BLAST are to aid in the identification of species, assist in the DNA mapping of an organism, and to identify common genes in different organisms.

Understanding: Gene function can be studied using model organisms with similar sequences.

Model sentence: Model organisms may be used to study gene functions in organisms with similar nucleotide sequences.

Model organisms are extensively studied to understand biological phenomena. The goal is that the studies will provide a better understanding of the functions within other organisms. Humans are not used as model organisms to avoid possible ethical issues and other difficulties in the studies.

There is great variety in model organisms. Several viruses have even been selected for detailed study. Some other organisms studied extensively as model organisms are the bacterium *Escherichia coli*, a green single-cell alga called *Chlamydomonas*, the fruit fly *Drosophila melanogaster*, the plant *Arabidopsis thaliana*, and the mouse *Mus musculus*. Most model organisms have had their entire genome sequenced allowing sequence sharing with other organisms.

Application: Use of knockout technology in mice to determine gene function

Scientists often use a process called knockout technology to determine gene function. This technology involves the substitution of functional gene sequence with a non-functional sequence. It is carried out using stem cells and embryos until an organism, for example, a mouse, is obtained which is pure for the non-functional gene sequence. The purebred 'knockout' organism may then be observed to see what phenotype or phenotypes are not expressed as a result of the change. A gene which expresses the hormone known as leptin in mice has been studied by knockout technology. Findings indicate leptin is essential in controlling energy metabolism and fat deposition.

Subject vocabulary

BLAST computer program which utilizes databases to compare biological sequences

model organisms organisms studied to understand biological phenomena

knockout technology technology in which a non-functional gene is substituted for a functional gene to determine the actions of the functional gene

General vocabulary

acronym a word made up from the first letters of the name of something

Synonyms

ethical .... moral

Understanding: **Sequence alignment** software allows comparison of sequences from different organisms.

> **Subject vocabulary**
>
> **sequence alignment** matching strings of nucleotides in different samples of DNA or amino acids in proteins to identify how similar organisms are
>
> **Synonyms**
>
> **align**............. line up

Model sentence: Sequence alignment software allows a way to identify similar regions between organisms involving DNA and protein sequences.

Short or similar sequences may be **aligned** manually. Most organism comparisons involve very long sequences. These long sequences require sequence alignment software. Sequence alignment software can compare sequences of DNA, RNA, and protein. Alignment may refer to the open reading frames (ORFs) of DNA being compared. Alignment may also refer to the translated protein of ORFs being compared. Alignment can involve the comparison of mRNA from ORFs as well. This software usually presents the aligned sequences of various organisms as rows within a matrix. The rows of similar sequences may then be compared to determine such things as evolutionary and structural similarity. If similar sequences from different organisms have few substitutions, then the region probably is involved with structural or functional importance to the organism.

There are many sequence visualization software programs available. These various programs allow queries of many different types to be addressed when looking at sequences from different organisms.

Skill: Use of software to align two proteins

You must be able to compare two proteins by using appropriate sequence alignment software. BLASTp or FASTA are databases that are often used to compare the amino acid sequences of two proteins produced by similar open reading frames. Selection of a protein common to two different organisms is the first step in this process. The beta haemoglobin chain in humans and rats can be compared using either of the two programs mentioned above. The algorithms of both programs will allow the sequence alignment of this protein in these two organisms.

Understanding: BLASTn allows nucleotide sequence alignment while BLASTp allows protein alignment.

Model sentence: BLASTn allows comparison of similar nucleotide sequences from different organisms. BLASTp allows comparison of similar protein amino acid sequences from different organisms.

BLASTn is a program into which a researcher may enter a particular DNA nucleotide sequence. The particular DNA nucleotide sequence entered most often represents an ORF. Once the sequence has been entered, the researcher then specifies which database the program should use to find any similar DNA sequences. Hopefully, the similar DNA sequences will allow the researcher to satisfy any queries they may have.

BLASTp is a program that works in the same way as BLASTn. However, BLASTp is used for protein amino acid sequences.

There are many other BLAST programs. Here are some:
- BLASTx – allows identification of potential protein products from a nucleotide query
- tBLASTx – allows location of a nucleotide sequence in an organism that produces a particular protein.

Understanding: Databases can be searched to compare newly identified sequences with sequences of known function in other organisms.

Model sentence: Databases are valuable in the comparison of DNA and protein sequences between organisms.

The various BLAST programs may be used to find comparable sequences or products from sequences in different organisms. These database searches are valuable in attempting to find comparable sequences in DNA, mRNA, or protein amino acids. These types of searches may also compare the products produced in different organisms from similar DNA sequences.

Understanding: Multiple sequence alignment is used in the study of phylogenetics.

Model sentence: Multiple sequence alignment is used to find out evolutionary relationships between or amongst different organisms.

Phylogenetics is the study of the evolutionary history of an organism or group of organisms. When carrying out multiple sequence alignment involving several different organisms, it is important to note similarities may occur due to structures which are homologous or analogous.

Homologous structures are more likely to have similar mutations or base substitutions at similar positions in the DNA sequence examined. Homologous structures in evolution have similar genetic and structural origin but may have over time developed different functions. This results in similar sequences and a possible common evolutionary history.

Analogous structures are structures with similar function at the present time. However, analogous structures may have had very different origins in both structure and genetics. The reason you may see similar sequences with analogous structures is that the DNA sequence may have significantly changed over time to produce common products.

ORFs are most often examined in these types of studies.

Skill: Use of software to construct simple cladograms and phylograms of related organisms using DNA sequences

It is important that you develop the ability to construct a simple **cladogram** and **phylogram** from related organisms using DNA or protein sequences. Both cladograms and phylograms show probable evolutionary relationships of a group of organisms. A phylogram has lengths of branches which indicate relative amounts of change. A cladogram does not have lengths of branches which indicate relative amounts of change. Use the database Swiss-Prot to compare the haemoglobin beta chains of the following eight organisms: domestic duck, Canada goose, rat, mouse, alligator, Nile crocodile, human, and rhesus monkey. This database will provide you with the differences among these organisms' haemoglobin beta chains. Organisms with the greatest differences in sequences are the farthest apart on the cladogram or phylogram. Programs are available to produce cladograms and phylograms of the differences in the sequences of the haemoglobin beta chains in these eight organisms using Swiss-Prot.

Subject vocabulary

phylogenetics study of the evolutionary history of an organism or group of organisms

homologous structures structures which have similar genetic and structural origin that now show obvious differences

analogous structures structures which have common functions but different origins genetically and structurally

cladogram branching diagram showing relationships among a group of organisms

phylogram branching diagram showing relationships among a group of organisms in which the branches represent proportional amounts of change or differences

Understanding: EST is an expressed sequence tag that can be used to identify potential genes.

Model sentence: An EST may be used to identify and locate an organism's potential gene from a database.

There is an EST database involving over 1000 organisms which is known as **dbEST**. An EST is a short segment of complementary DNA (**cDNA**) that is single stranded. The cDNA is produced using reverse transcriptase from messenger (mRNA). This cDNA does not have any **introns** since it comes from the mature mRNA which is translated to produce a protein at the ribosome. These ESTs are generally between 300 to 500 nucleotides long. A BLAST search involving the dbEST may then be done to see if there is a known gene for the protein the EST produces. The database may even provide the location of the gene in an organism's genome.

Application: Discovery of genes by EST data mining

Scientists use a technique known as EST data mining to match DNA sequences with the dbEST database. This allows them to determine if the EST in question matches a known gene and to find the gene's function.

Subject vocabulary

EST short segment of cDNA that is single-stranded used to see if there is a known gene for the protein the EST produces

dbEST database of short sequences of single-stranded cDNA

cDNA complementary DNA produced from mRNA by base pairing, single stranded

introns non-coding regions of DNA which are transcribed onto the mRNA molecules, they are removed before leaving the nucleus

14 Option C: Ecology and conservation

C.1 Species and communities

Understanding: The distribution of species is affected by **limiting factors**.

Model sentence: Species live in certain areas because of both non-living and living factors that affect their survival.

All species have certain requirements to stay healthy and alive. Those factors might be as simple as available water and sunlight. It is also possible that there is a wide range of factors including such things as food availability, **predators** in the area, maximum or minimum temperature, and many other possibilities. The factor or factors that determine whether a species can **inhabit** an area is called a limiting factor. Limiting factors can be subdivided into two main groups as shown by the following table.

Abiotic – limiting factors that are not created by something that is alive	Biotic – limiting factors due to one or more other living species
sunlight availability	**abundance** of a prey animal
water availability	abundance of a predator
soil type	abundance of a **competitor** for a resource
air or water temperatures	abundance of a **parasite**

Application: Distribution of one animal and one plant species to illustrate **limits of tolerance** and **zones of stress**

Example 1: animal species

Macropus giganteus lives in eastern Australia, where precipitation varies little seasonally or falls mainly in summer.

Macropus fuliginosus lives in southern Australia, where winter rainfall dominates.

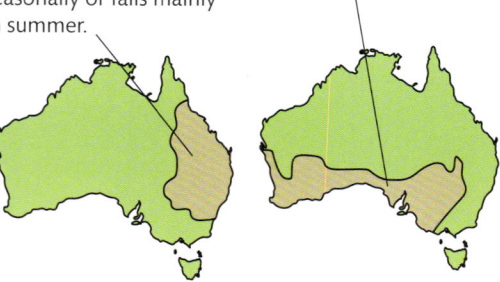

Macropus rufus lives in central and western Australia, where conditions are hot and dry.

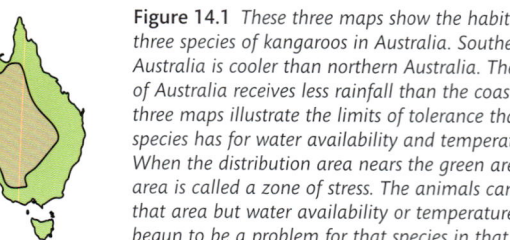

Figure 14.1 These three maps show the habitat of three species of kangaroos in Australia. Southern Australia is cooler than northern Australia. The interior of Australia receives less rainfall than the coasts. These three maps illustrate the limits of tolerance that each species has for water availability and temperature. When the distribution area nears the green area that area is called a zone of stress. The animals can live in that area but water availability or temperature has begun to be a problem for that species in that area

Subject vocabulary

limiting factors environmental factors that determine the maximum size of a population or the maximum rate of a process

predator an organism that hunts and eats other organisms

abiotic pertains to non-living

biotic pertains to living

competitor two organisms that compete for the same resource

parasite organism that uses another organism for resources and harms that organism

limits of tolerance the edges of the range for any one environmental limiting factor, e.g. if a species of fish can live in water temperatures between 18–26 °C, then 18 °C and 26 °C would be its limits of tolerance

zone of stress an area of a habitat where a species is nearing the limits of tolerance for any one limiting factor

Synonyms

inhabit .... live in/occupy

General vocabulary

abundance large quantity of something

Example 2: plant species

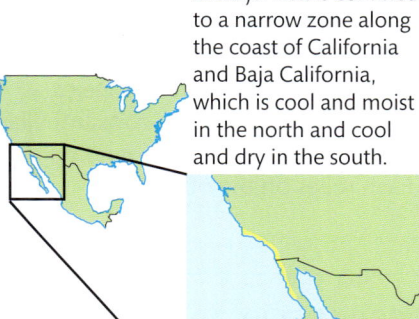

E. californica is confined to a narrow zone along the coast of California and Baja California, which is cool and moist in the north and cool and dry in the south.

E. actoni lives farther inland, where conditions are drier and warmer than the areas inhabited by E. californica.

E. farinosa and E. frutescens live still farther inland in areas that are much hotter. The geographic distributions of these two species overlap a great deal.

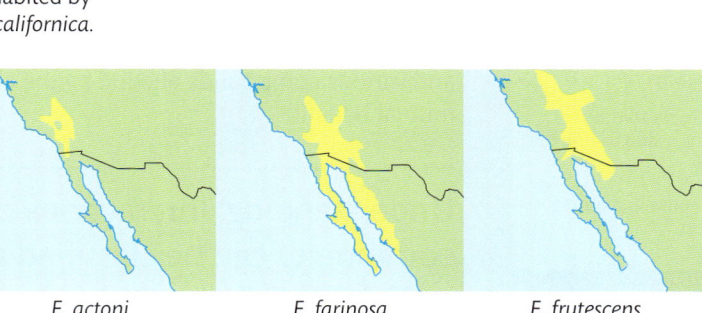

E. californica   E. actoni   E. farinosa   E. frutescens

Figure 14.2 *Plants of the genus* Encelia *are in the daisy family. Four different species of this genus live in different habitats in California and Baja California of North America. Each species has a habitat based on water availability and temperature. Each has different **adaptations** that allow it to survive according to their own limits of tolerance. Once again, when the distribution area nears the green area, that area is called a zone of stress. The animals can live in that area but water availability or temperature has begun to be a problem for that species in that area*

General vocabulary

adaptation change which makes something more suitable for a situation

Understanding: Community structure can be strongly affected by **keystone species**.

Model sentence: The health of a biological community is negatively affected if a keystone species is removed.

A keystone species in a biological community is one that is particularly important to the health of that community. Whether a species is a keystone species is not dependent on how many individuals of that species are present.

The test to determine whether a species is a keystone species is to remove that species from an area for a period of time. After removal, if the health of the community is not severely affected, then the species is not a keystone species.

Subject vocabulary

keystone species a species that has an unusually large impact on a community if that species is no longer present

spatial habitat the location where a species exists

nutrient chemical material a cell or organism needs

Understanding: Each species plays a unique role within a community because of the unique combination of its **spatial habitat** and interactions with other species.

Model sentence: Where a species lives and the interactions it has with other species are important to the role the species plays within its community.

A species' spatial habitat is simply the location that it lives in. Within that spatial habitat each species is likely to have many types of interactions with other species who share that spatial habitat.

No matter where a species lives it is likely to have many interactions with other species. Sometimes that interaction is very direct. An example would be one species eating another as a food source. Other times the interaction may be much less direct. An example would be a species of bacterium that provides **nutrients** that can be taken up by a species of plant.

Subject vocabulary

symbiotic a relationship between two species in which both benefit from their relationship with each other

mutualism a type of symbiotic relationship where two different species benefit from a relationship they have with each other

resource a factor within an ecosystem that is useful to one or more species

host the species that a parasite lives within or on

General vocabulary

dispersal spreading out

Application: The symbiotic relationship between zooxanthellae and reef-building coral reef species

One type of symbiotic relationship between species is called mutualism. This interaction is one in which both species benefit from the relationship. Coral reefs would not be possible without a mutualistic relationship between species. Zooxanthellae are single-celled algae that live inside coral tissues. The zooxanthellae photosynthesize and provide nutrients for the coral. The coral provides a home and various compounds needed by the algae. Each relies on the other for a mutual benefit.

Understanding: Interactions between species in a community can be classified according to their effect.

Model sentence: It is possible to classify species to species interactions based on the effect the interaction has.

This table summarizes some of those types of species to species interactions.

Category of interaction	Brief description	Example
competition	Two species competing for the same resource.	Two species of birds who both feed on the same species of insects.
predator / prey	One species that is a prey animal for another.	Apple snails are the only prey of a bird called the Everglades kite.
parasitism	One species acts as a host to another (the parasite). Parasite damages the host.	Leeches are parasites to many mammals. The leech gains blood as food and the host loses blood.
mutualism	Both species benefit from the interaction between species.	Some flowering plants are pollinated by insects. The insect gains nectar and/or pollen to eat. Plant gains dispersal of its sex cells.
commensalism	One species benefits and the other is relatively unaffected by the relationship.	Many 'air plants' (epiphytes) like Spanish moss in the southern United States simply use various trees as places to grow. The tree is not harmed or benefitted in any way.

Application: Local examples to illustrate the range of ways in which species can interact within a community

Look at the examples given of species to species interactions in the table above. See if you can come up with one or more examples of each category of interaction for species in your area of the world.

Understanding: Two species cannot survive indefinitely in the same habitat if their niches are identical.

Model sentence: One of two species that share an identical niche will eventually be forced out of the same habitat.

A well-studied principle in ecology is known as the **competitive exclusion principle**. This principle states that if two species share the same ecological niche, one of the two species will outcompete the other. The end result will be that one species will be excluded from the habitat by the other. This doesn't mean the excluded species will go extinct. The species that gets outcompeted in this habitat might flourish in another spatial habitat.

So, what is the niche of a species? A simple way to think of a niche is that it is the species' special role or function within its ecosystem. Frequently, an important component of a species' niche includes what it eats. Thus, if two species share a limited food source, the species that outcompetes the other is the one that will not be excluded.

Sometimes an organism's niche becomes modified over time. These modifications often occur because of human activities. Fundamental niche is the term used for a niche without any limitation from other organisms. A realized niche is the term used for a niche in reality. A realized niche takes into account the interactions of other organisms including humans.

For example, beaches have been in existence long before people started using them for leisure. Seagulls that live near a beach area used to make use of the natural food sources that the shoreline provides. Those natural food sources are an important part of their fundamental niche. Today, people often offer food to seagulls. This food is typically not healthy for the birds. The birds now spend their time 'begging' food from people. This unhealthy food is now a part of the realized niche of seagulls.

Skill: Use of a transect to correlate the distribution of plant or animal species with an abiotic variable

A transect is a method of sampling a type of organism along a straight line. The length of the line should vary in an environmental factor expected to be important to the organism sampled.

Subject vocabulary

niche a function within an ecosystem (an insectivore is an example)

competitive exclusion (principle) the ecological principle that states that two species who share an identical niche cannot both survive in the same spatial habitat

transect straight line along which measurements are made at regular intervals during an ecological study

General vocabulary

flourish survive and grow well

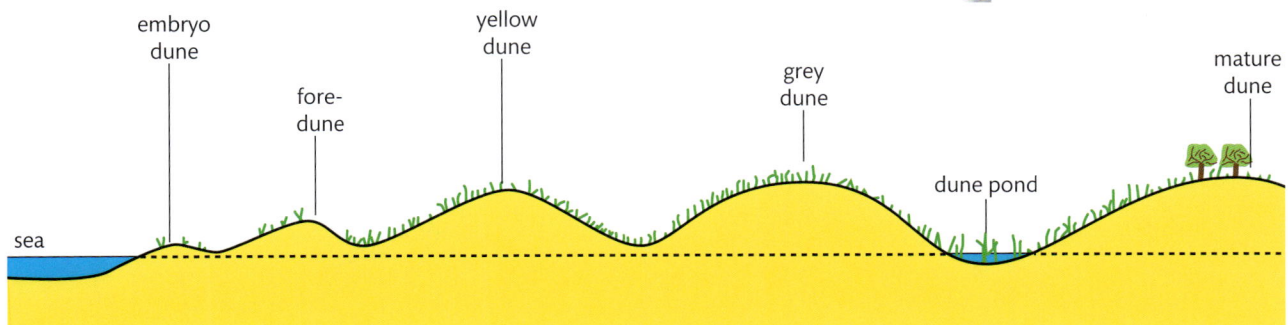

Figure 14.3 *The figure shown shows a possible transect line (dotted line) that starts at a shoreline and runs on top of the various dune types that eventually lead to a mature dune. One of the factors expected to vary amongst the various dune types is pH of the soil. In order to do this study, a researcher would choose length intervals along the transect line and then collect two pieces of data at each interval. One would be the pH of the soil at that location and the other would be a count of the number of a particular organism. A plant species would be an appropriate type of organism to study by this technique. Alternatively, a line of traps could be used to study the distribution of animal species along the transect*

C.2 Communities and ecosystems

Subject vocabulary

trophic levels the position of an organism in a food chain

food chain one possible set of feeding relationships starting with a producer

producer a photosynthetic organism that starts a food chain

food web a figure showing all of the feeding relationships in a community

Synonyms

trophic level 1 — producer
trophic level 2 — primary consumer
trophic level 3 — secondary consumer
trophic level 4 — tertiary consumer

Understanding: Most species occupy different **trophic levels** in multiple **food chains**.

Model sentence: Most species have a diet that includes many types of food and thus they fit into multiple food chains at different trophic levels.

A food chain shows a possible transfer of food (energy) along a single set of organisms. The following is an example food chain:

grass → rabbit → rattlesnake → eagle

The arrows within the food chain show the transfer of energy from one step of the food chain to the next. In this food chain each organism can be given a trophic (feeding) level. A photosynthetic organism (grass) is always **trophic level 1**. This level can also be called the **producer** for the food chain. The rabbit in this food chain is **trophic level 2** or primary consumer. The snake is **trophic level 3** or secondary consumer. Finally, the eagle is **trophic level 4** or tertiary consumer.

Each food chain only represents one possible set of events. For example, the eagle may directly eat the rabbit. In that shorter food chain, the eagle would be on trophic level 3 and would be a secondary consumer. This shows that real life is much more complicated than shown by a single food chain.

Understanding: A **food web** shows all the possible food chains in a community.

Model sentence: A more realistic view of the feeding relationships in a community is by way of interconnecting all possible food chains in a diagram called a food web.

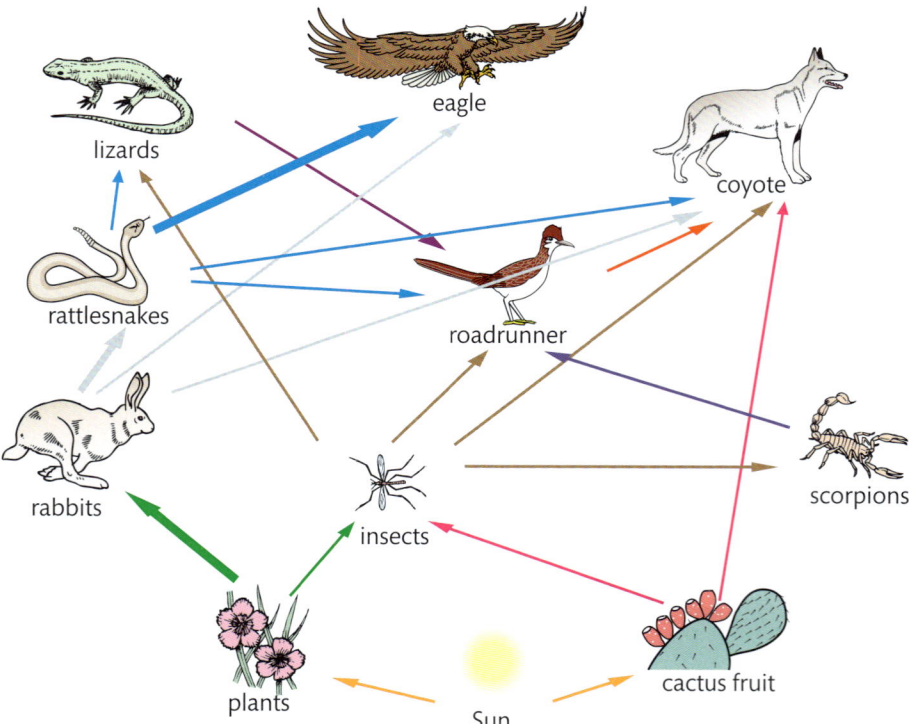

Figure 14.4 This figure shows a food web for a desert community. Notice that there is more than one food source for many of the organisms. Any one 'food path' that one follows starting at one of the producers will ultimately end at a top predator. The top predators shown in this food web are the eagle and the coyote. Notice that producers have no arrows leading to them (except energy from the Sun) and top predators have no arrows leading away from them

Understanding: The percentage of **ingested** energy converted to **biomass** is dependent on the **respiration rate**.

Model sentence: In living organisms, the amount of food that gets converted to biomass depends on how much energy is lost by cell respiration.

Food provides energy to animals. Animals use that energy for body movements and many physiological processes in their bodies. The specific process that provides energy for things like body movements is cell respiration.

Food chains always begin with a producer. The producer uses photosynthesis to store energy in the form of carbohydrates. Plants respire to produce energy for processes inside of their cells. Thus, for a plant we can use this simple formula to calculate their energy totals:

$$\text{energy from gross production} - \text{energy used for respiration} = \text{net energy production}$$

Where:
　gross production is the energy that plants create from photosynthesis

A similar idea is valid for animals when they eat food. The amount of energy used by cell respiration is subtracted from the energy from the food they eat. The difference can be used to add to the biomass of the organisms.

Each step of a food chain is not very efficient for transferring energy. Much of the food that is eaten is lost as energy or waste. A typical number used to estimate energy transfer from one step of a food chain to the next is 10%. In other words, 10% of the energy from food goes into increasing the biomass of the next step of a food chain. This idea is often represented by a **pyramid of energy** as shown below.

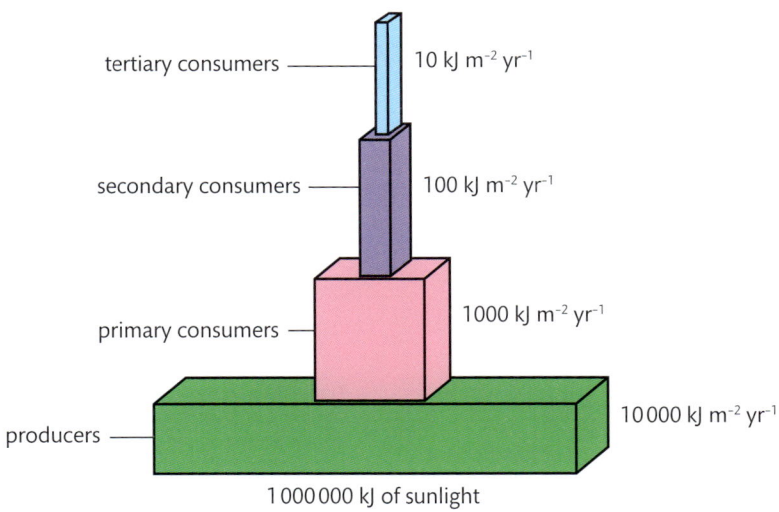

Figure 14.5 *A pyramid of energy (not drawn to scale)*

Subject vocabulary

ingested food/substances taken into the body

biomass the mass of all organisms of a particular category of organisms, e.g. the mass of all producers for a food chain

respiration rate a measurement of cell respiration per unit mass per unit time

gross production the total energy plants produce by photosynthesis

pyramid of energy a graphic representation of the energy flow through a food chain

feed conversion ratio a calculation of how efficient an animal is in converting food into body mass

Skill: Comparison of pyramids of energy from different ecosystems

When comparing two or more pyramids of energy, look for the efficiency of the transfer of energy at each step. As mentioned earlier, an estimate that can be used is a 10% energy transfer at each step. That estimate can vary based on the type of ecosystem and the trophic level that is being compared.

Application: Conversion ratio in sustainable food production practices

A **feed conversion ratio** is a mathematical calculation of how efficiently an animal converts food into body mass. This is especially important for farm animals that are raised for food. The lower the feed conversion ratio (FCR), the more efficient the animal is in converting its food into body mass.

Understanding: The type of stable ecosystem that will emerge in an area is predictable based on climate.

Model sentence: Stable ecosystems called **biomes** form based on climate differences in various parts of the Earth.

Subject vocabulary

biome an ecosystem that forms due to a combination of temperature and rainfall in that area

climograph a graph that plots annual precipitation versus annual temperature and shows the predictable biomes that exist based on those two factors

General vocabulary

coniferous having leaves like needles and producing seed-containing cones

temperate never very hot or very cold

Synonyms

mean............ average
precipitation .. rain, snow, dew
matter........... material

The major biomes on Earth

Biome	Type of climate
desert	high temperatures low rainfall
grassland	low elevations seasonal low and high temperatures varying rainfall
coniferous forest	slightly warmer than tundra low rainfall
temperate forest	seasonal low and high temperatures high rainfall
tropical forest	high temperatures high rainfall
tundra	high elevations low temperatures low rainfall

Skill: Analysis of a **climograph** showing the relationship between the temperature, rainfall, and the type of ecosystem.

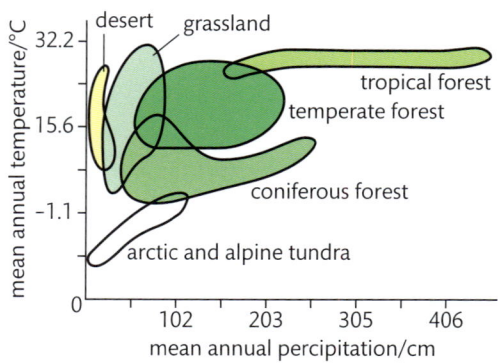

Figure 14.6 This graph is called a climograph. You can use it to predict the type of biome that will exist in an area based on *mean* annual temperature and mean annual *precipitation*

Understanding: In closed ecosystems energy but not **matter** is exchanged with the surroundings.

Model sentence: Ecosystems that are closed off to the outside world require an outside source of energy but do not exchange matter with their surroundings.

No natural ecosystem on Earth is completely closed off to the outside world. There are some that come close, as is the case with small islands, for example.

In a closed ecosystem there is still a need for an input of energy. This energy typically comes from light. The light energy is used for photosynthesis. This allows food chains in the closed system to have one or more producers.

Application: **Consideration of one example of how humans interfere with nutrient cycling**

One might consider the entire Earth to be a closed system. In fact, we refer to the parts of Earth where living organisms can live as the **biosphere**. Within this huge closed system, a variety of substances are constantly being recycled. One of those substances is carbon. Remember that carbon is the basis of all organic molecules and therefore is of great importance to living things.

Humans are currently causing serious problems for the cycling of carbon. Much of the harm caused is a result of mining carbon-based fuels and then burning them. This is resulting in a slow, but ever increasing amount of carbon dioxide in our atmosphere. The implications of this increase in carbon dioxide in the atmosphere are just beginning as Earth's global temperature rises as a result.

Skill: **Construction of Gersmehl diagrams to show the inter-relationships between nutrient stores and flows within and between biomes**

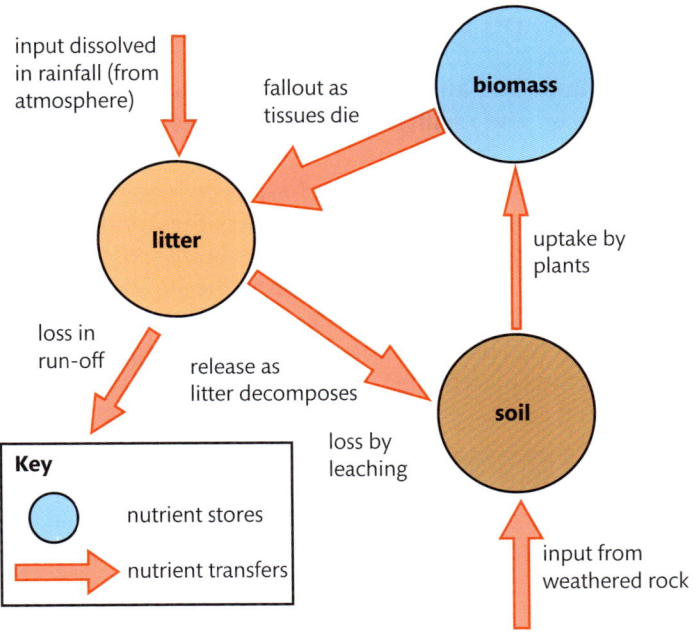

Subject vocabulary

biosphere all areas on and in Earth where living organisms exist

Gersmehl diagram diagram showing nutrient stores and cycling within or between ecosystems

mature ecosystem an ecosystem that has been in place for a very long period of time and is no longer undergoing major changes

Synonyms

disturbance.... interruption

General vocabulary

colonize organisms that first come to live in an area

Figure 14.7 This is a Gersmehl diagram showing mineral nutrient cycling of an ecosystem. The circles show the main storage of a nutrient that is being studied. The size of the circle shows how much of the nutrient is being stored in that form. The arrows show transfer or loss of the nutrients. The width of the arrow shows how much of the nutrient is being transferred or lost

Understanding: Disturbances influence the structure and rate of change within ecosystems.

Model sentence: **When an ecosystem is disturbed, the disturbance changes the structure and rate of change of the ecosystem.**

An ecosystem that has been in existence and reasonably stable for a very long period of time is called a **mature ecosystem**. A mature forested ecosystem will typically be dominated by a certain species of tree. The entire forest may be very similar because this tree species is dominating the available light and soil resources.

Occasionally, a mature ecosystem experiences a major disturbance such as a forest fire. If this is a major fire, all of the dominant trees may be burned off in a large area. Without those trees to dominate the available light and soil resources other species of plants begin to **colonize** the area.

14 Option C: Ecology and conservation | 309

Subject vocabulary

succession a series of changes that occur within an ecosystem as it progresses towards becoming a mature ecosystem

primary succession succession beginning with new land

lava rock in hot liquid form that emerges from volcanoes

secondary succession succession that occurs when an existing ecosystem is disrupted by a major disturbance and soil is already present

alien species a species that is introduced into an ecosystem

competitive exclusion (principle) the ecological principle that states that two species who share an identical niche cannot both survive in the same spatial habitat

Synonyms

diversity .... wide range

endemic species .... native species

The description above is called **succession**. Succession leads to a series of changes that eventually will give rise to the same mature ecosystem each time. There are two main categories of succession:

- **Primary succession** is the series of changes that occur when new land is formed. An example of this is when a volcano makes an island larger by flowing **lava** into the sea. This new land has no soil and will take a very long period of time to establish a **diversity** of life.
- **Secondary succession** is the series of changes that occur after a major disruption to an existing ecosystem. The situation described above with an area burned by a forest fire is an example. Because there is already soil and perhaps some remaining living things, this type of succession is much more rapid than primary succession.

C.3 Impact of humans on ecosystems

Understanding: Introduced **alien species** can escape into local ecosystems and become invasive.

Model sentence: Plants and animals that are not native to an area are sometimes introduced and result in a permanent breeding population.

There are numerous examples of species that have been brought to an area and have established a breeding population in that area of the world. Sometimes the introduction is done by accident and sometimes on purpose. For example, pet owners have released their pet python snakes in the Florida Everglades in recent times. It is thought that the pythons became too large to keep as pets. These pythons have formed breeding populations in the Everglades and thus have become an invasive species. They compete with the alligators and other top predators of the area for prey.

> **Hints for success:** You may be asked to describe a local example of an invasive species. Be sure to research a species of plant or animal that has been released in your area and has established itself.

Understanding: **Competitive exclusion** and the absence of predators can lead to reduction in the numbers of **endemic species** when alien species become invasive.

Model sentence: Invasive species can reduce the numbers of endemic species due to competition and absence of predators.

The pythons that are now breeding in the Florida Everglades have no natural predators. Ecological principles state that other top predators, such as the Florida alligator, will be in competition for food.

The description above is a classic example of the competitive exclusion principle. This principle states that two species that share a common niche cannot survive in the same ecosystem. One of the two will be eliminated from the ecosystem due to 'losing' the competition for a common resource.

Understanding: **Pollutants** become concentrated in the tissues of organisms at higher trophic levels by **biomagnification**.

Subject vocabulary

pollutants substances released into an ecosystem that have the potential to do harm

biomagnification increasing concentration of a pollutant as the pollutant moves up through the trophic levels of a food chain

DDT a non-biodegradable insecticide that has created problems in areas of the world in which it has been utilized

plankton small organisms at or near the bottom of marine food chains

calcium a mineral necessary for healthy bird eggs

General vocabulary

run-off water that makes its way into rivers, lakes, and other bodies of water

biodegradable able to be broken down by bacteria or in other natural ways

estuary a marine environment where a river also adds fresh water

incubate keep eggs warm until the young are born

Synonyms

trade-off .... balance

Model sentence: Biomagnification explains how pollutants become more concentrated in the tissues of organisms at the top of food chains.

Most pollutants that are released into an ecosystem are in very low concentrations. One example is the insecticide DDT. DDT use is primarily to kill mosquitoes, but at one time DDT was used to spray on crops to kill a wide variety of insects. Run-off from rainwater made its way into many rivers, lakes, and saltwater estuaries. DDT in the environment is very long lasting as it is not biodegradable.

The smallest living organisms in a food chain are often microscopic. In an estuary, these very small organisms are collectively called plankton. The water that the plankton were in only contained a very small amount of DDT. This was taken into the cells of the plankton. Larger plankton organisms eat smaller plankton organisms. This helped to concentrate the DDT in the larger plankton. Very small fish often eat the larger plankton organisms. When they do eat plankton, they eat many. This concentrates the DDT even more in the small fish. Larger fish eat many smaller fish, once again increasing the concentration. Finally, top predators, such as osprey, pelicans, and eagles eat many of the larger fish. These top predators receive the highest concentration of DDT.

Unfortunately for each of these birds, the effect was to damage their calcium metabolism. This resulted in thinner than normal eggs. These thin eggs often were crushed when the birds tried to incubate them. The ultimate effect was a severe population decline of these birds as very few young birds were hatched (born). It was not until many areas banned the use of DDT that these bird populations recovered.

This example shows how a pollutant makes its way through the trophic levels of a food chain. At each step, the pollutant becomes more concentrated. This effect of becoming more concentrated is called biomagnification.

Application: Discussion of the trade-off between control of the malarial parasite and DDT pollution

The parasite that results in the disease called malaria is spread from person to person by mosquitoes. The best way to prevent malaria is to control mosquito populations. Malaria kills over 1 million people each year worldwide.

Mosquito populations are most effectively controlled by the use of DDT. In areas of the world such as parts of Africa and Indonesia, there is on-going debate over the use of DDT to help control cases of malaria. There is no easy answer to this problem. If DDT is used, biomagnification will result in severe ecological damage. If DDT is not used, people will continue to die of malaria.

Hints for success: You may be asked to discuss a topic such as use of DDT to control malaria. When doing so, be sure to give points that support both possible sides of an issue. If you only give your opinion you will not receive full marks.

Subject vocabulary

macroplastics plastic items larger than 5 mm

microplastics plastic items smaller than 5 mm

ingesting taking food/substances into the body

indicator species an organism that is very sensitive to one or more changes in its ecosystem

Synonyms

debris............ rubbish/waste

accumulated .. built up

contaminate... pollute

General vocabulary

degrade break down into a simpler form

Understanding: Macroplastic and microplastic debris has accumulated in marine environments.

Model sentence: Large and small plastic items have accumulated in saltwater environments.

Any item that is made of plastic will not degrade in the environment for a very long period of time. It is estimated that a plastic bottle that is carelessly disposed of in an ecosystem will still be in one piece more than 400 years later. Ecologists classify plastic pollutants into two categories based on their size:

- Macroplastics are relatively large items made of plastic. This includes anything larger than 5 mm. Bottles, toys, dinnerware, etc., made of plastic are all considered a macroplastic item.
- Microplastics are plastic items smaller than 5 mm. Some of these are broken off from macroplastic items and some were originally created in a small form. Microplastics created in a small form are frequently from facial cleaning products.

Both macroplastics and microplastics are damaging to living organisms in marine environments.

Example 1: Laysan albatross

Adult birds often look for available food on the water surface. Sometimes they mistake floating plastic objects as food. In addition, the adult bird often returns to the nest and provides the plastics as food to the young birds on a nest. Both adult and young birds can die from ingesting items made of plastics.

Example 2: sea turtles

Sea turtles often eat jellyfish as a food source. When a sea turtle encounters a plastic bag floating in the water, they easily confuse it for a jellyfish. After swallowing the plastic bag the digestive system of the animal becomes blocked and death often occurs.

C.4 Conservation of biodiversity

Understanding: An indicator species is an organism used to assess a specific environmental condition.

Model sentence: An environmental problem is often first noticed when there is a decline in the population of an organism called an indicator species.

Many different types of organisms can act as indicator species. What all indicator species have in common is that they are all very sensitive to one or more changes in their ecosystem. When an environmental problem begins these organisms are some of the first to be affected by the change. Here are two examples:

Example 1: frogs

Frogs have many ways of taking chemicals into their bodies. They breathe air with possible pollutants. They eat prey animals that may already contain a pollutant. They drink water that may be contaminated. Additionally, they take chemicals directly through their moist skin. Biologists have learned to monitor frog populations for possible environmental problems associated with freshwater ecosystems.

Example 2: lichen

A lichen is a **mutualistic relationship** between an algae and a fungus. Lichens grow best in areas with good air quality. It is very rare to see lichen growth in large cities with air pollution problems. For this reason, lichens are good indicator organisms for air quality problems.

Understanding: Relative numbers of indicator species can be used to calculate the value of a **biotic index**.

Model sentence: A biotic index is a number that can be calculated by using relative numbers of indicator species in one area.

One ecosystem may contain many indicator species. Each indicator species may be sensitive to one or several environmental problems. Each species may also have its own sensitivity to an environmental problem.

A good example is a freshwater stream. In some freshwater streams, these three organisms can be used to calculate a biotic index:

- mayfly larvae – very sensitive to water quality problems
- dragonfly larvae – reasonably sensitive to water quality problems
- blackfly larvae – not very sensitive to water quality problems.

To create a biotic index, one would first count the number of each of these organisms in an area. Each type of organism would be given a number based on its sensitivity to water quality. The mayfly larvae would receive the highest number because they are the most sensitive to water pollution. Dragonfly larvae would receive the second highest number and blackfly larvae the lowest number. The count of each organism is then multiplied by its sensitivity number. A sum of all the resulting numbers is then made.

The sum is a type of biotic index. The higher the biotic index, the better the water quality. The biotic index has two ways of becoming high:

- having larger numbers of organisms counted
- having larger numbers of the sensitive organisms counted.

Understanding: *In situ* **conservation** may require active management of nature reserves or national parks.

Model sentence: Maintaining natural populations in nature reserves or national parks is called *in situ* conservation and sometimes requires human intervention.

There are large and small nature reserves and national parks all over the world. Most of these are areas of land set aside for plants and animals to live a life with minimal human intervention. A few reserves and national parks have been set up in marine environments.

Plants and animals cannot live as nature intended if humans are building roads, homes, and businesses. The type of conservation that sets aside natural areas for plants and animals to live is called *in situ* conservation. In most instances these areas are not large and independent enough to remain completely untouched from humans. For that reason, they require human intervention at times.

> **Subject vocabulary**
>
> **lichen** a growth that is composed of a fungus with algae growing within
>
> **mutualistic relationship** relationship between two organisms in which both are helped
>
> **biotic index** a calculation based on numbers of environmentally sensitive organisms in an ecosystem
>
> *in situ* **conservation** maintaining populations of plants and animals in their natural setting with minimal human intervention

Subject vocabulary

ex situ conservation preservation of a species outside of its natural environment

captive breeding animals bred while being kept in a zoo or other wildlife facility

seed banks facilities designed for long-term storage of seeds

biogeographic term indicating both location (geography) and living (bio) organisms

species diversity a measurement of the number of different species

General vocabulary

elevation height above sea level

mid-range at or near a half-way point

Understanding: *Ex situ* **conservation** is the preservation of species outside their natural habitats.

Model sentence: Where species are kept alive outside of their natural habitats this is called *ex situ* conservation.

There are situations where it is not possible to maintain a species in its natural environment. The following situations often lead to *ex situ* conservation:

- habitat destruction may have already occurred to the point where a species cannot survive in its natural environment
- a population may be so small that breeding is either unlikely or genetic diversity cannot be maintained
- protection of the species can best occur in an environment outside the natural environment of that species.

The following are examples of *ex situ* conservation methods:

- **captive breeding** of some species of animals
- growing of plant species in botanic gardens
- long-term storage of seeds in **seed banks**.

Application: Case study of the captive breeding and reintroduction of an endangered animal species.

The California condor (*Gymnogyps californianus*) is a very large species of vulture that is native to the southwestern area of the United States. California condor numbers dramatically declined in the early 1900s due to habitat destruction, hunting, and chemical poisoning. By 1987 the population had declined to a total of 22 birds. All 22 birds were captured and added to birds held at two zoos in California where captive breeding programmes were underway. Thus, in 1987, California condors became extinct in the wild.

The captive breeding programme proved successful and by 1991 condors were being reintroduced back into wild habitats.

Understanding: **Biogeographic** factors affect **species diversity**.

Model sentence: The number of species and the relative abundance of each is affected by both biological and geographic factors.

The following geographic factors have an influence on species diversity:

- Distance from equator: land areas near the equator tend to have the highest species diversity. This simply means that there will be a greater number of species in areas near the equator. As you move north or south of the equator species diversity tends to decrease.
- **Elevation**: the greatest number of species tends to be at a **mid-range** of elevation. Species diversity increases until a midpoint in elevation is reached and then it declines after that.
- Size of habitat: larger habitats can support more organisms and they can also support greater species diversity. Some habitats are true islands and others can sometimes be thought of as islands. If a habitat is physically separated from other habitats (like lakes and ponds) then the ecosystems they support work like a true island. Since larger habitats have greater biodiversity, larger 'islands' also tend to have greater biodiversity.

- Edge effect: the edge effect is due to areas where two different kinds of habitat border each other. A classic example is where a forest borders a grassland area. Some species specialize in using this 'edge area' as habitat or as a source of food. The edge effect tends to increase biodiversity as it increases the number of species in an area.

In summary, the greatest species diversity would be found in a relatively large area, near the equator, and at a midpoint in elevation within that area.

Understanding: Richness and evenness are components of biodiversity.

Model sentence: Biodiversity is a combination of how many species live in an area and the relative abundance of each species.

There are two components of biological diversity:

1 **Richness** – this is the number of different species that live in an area.

2 **Evenness** – this is the relative abundance of each species in an area.

The table below compares the number of species of larvae at two ponds.

Larva species	Number of individuals in sample 1*	Number of individuals in sample 2*
caddisfly larvae	200	20
dragonfly larvae	425	55
mosquito larvae	375	925
total	1000	1000

*Sample 1 and sample 2 are larvae counts taken at two different ponds.

Notice that both ponds have three species of larvae. Thus, the two ponds would have the same richness of larvae. Also notice that the two counts are identical in total number of larvae. Note that the sample taken from pond 2 is dominated by mosquito larvae. This shows that pond 2 has very low evenness. A community is not considered diverse if it is dominated by one species.

Skill: Analysis of the biodiversity of two local communities using Simpson's reciprocal index of diversity

The biodiversity of an ecosystem can be calculated through a formula called the **Simpson's reciprocal index of diversity**. The formula takes into account both the richness and evenness of species. The formula is:

$$D = \frac{\text{sum of } n(n-1)}{N(N-1)}$$

Where:

D = Simpson reciprocal index of diversity

N = total number of organisms in the ecosystem

n = number of individuals of each species

Subject vocabulary

richness a measurement of the number of different species living in an area

evenness a measurement of the relative abundance of each species in an area

larva (plural: larvae) an immature form of an insect species

Simpson reciprocal index of diversity a calculation that indicates biodiversity of an ecosystem taking into account both richness and evenness

C.5 Population ecology

Subject vocabulary

sampling technique counting a sample of a total number of organisms in order to calculate an estimate of a total population

quadrat an area of land marked off in order to count or study the organisms within

density number of organisms per area

random number generator a mathematical tool that will pick random numbers from a set

sample part of a whole

Synonyms

stationary ...... non-moving/ sendentary

General vocabulary

disperse spread out

humane showing compassion or consideration

Understanding: **Sampling techniques** are used to estimate population size.

Model sentence: Populations of organisms that are too large or difficult to directly count can be estimated by sampling techniques

Two common types of sampling technique are:
- quadrat counting
- capture–mark–release–recapture.

Quadrat counting works well for **stationary** organisms such as plants. The organism chosen should show a fairly equal **density** throughout the area to be counted. The entire area to be counted is marked off and subdivided into many equal sized parts. These equal sized parts are called quadrats. A reasonable number of quadrats is decided upon in order to count the number of organisms within. A **random number generator** is used in order to decide the identity of the quadrats to count. After the **sample** quadrats are counted, the mean number of organisms per quadrat is calculated. The mean number of organisms per quadrat is then multiplied by the total number of quadrats. The resulting number is an estimate of the total population in the area.

Example: quadrat counting

A landowner wants to estimate how many black cherry trees are found on his very large forested property. The trees are reasonably equally **dispersed** and quite plentiful. The property is a rectangle measuring 12 km long and 10 km wide. Using GPS co-ordinates, the property is divided into 120 equal sized quadrats. The landowner decides to count the number of trees in 8 of the 120 quadrats. A random number generator is used to identify the 8 quadrats and they are counted. The total number of trees in those 8 quadrats turns out to be 176 black cherry trees.

Mean of 22 trees per quadrat × 120 total quadrats = 2640 estimated trees

Application: Use of the capture–mark–release–recapture method to estimate the population size of an animal species

This capture–mark–release–recapture method of estimating the size of a population works well for some animals. The technique involves capturing a sample of the animal population to be estimated. The animals are temporarily marked in a **humane** way in order to be identified later. The animals marked are released back into their habitat. Time is given for the animals to disperse. After that period of time, a second sample of animals is captured. It is expected that some, but not all, of this second capture will be marked. The following formula is then used:

$$N = \frac{n_1 \times n_2}{n_3}$$

Where:

N = estimated population size

n_1 = number marked in the first capture

n_2 = number caught in the second capture

n_3 = number marked in the second capture

Example: capture–mark–release–recapture method

An estimate is needed for the number of soft-shell turtles in a pond. A researcher uses a net to capture 10 turtles. Each of the turtles is marked with a small amount of fingernail polish on their shell. The turtles are all released back into the pond. A day later, the researcher nets 15 turtles. Of those 15 turtles, 4 of them have marked shells. The estimate would be:

$$\text{Estimate of turtles} = \frac{(10 \times 15)}{4}$$
$$= 38 \text{ turtles (rounded to nearest whole number)}$$

Understanding: The **exponential growth** pattern occurs in an ideal, unlimited environment

Subject vocabulary

exponential growth growth of a population in which the number of individuals being added is proportional to the number already present

Model sentence: An organism introduced into a suitable environment will show an exponential growth pattern if an environment is ideal with unlimited resources.

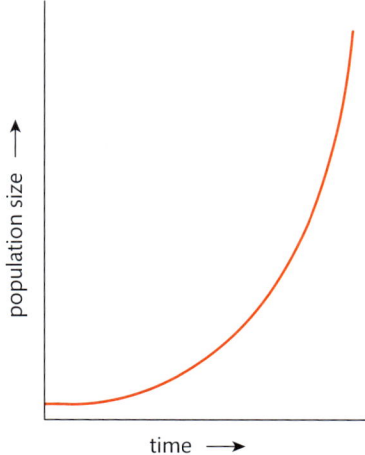

Figure 14.8 *This graph shows a population of organisms that is experiencing exponential growth. The population was introduced into a new environment at time = 0. No slowing of the rate of growth is evident*

The exponential growth pattern is only shown in nature under a rare set of conditions. First, this must be an organism introduced into a new and ideal environment. The environment must have plenty of resources for the organism. Resources may include food, sunlight, locations to live, and many other possibilities. The resources must be so plentiful that the organism itself is not competing for any of the needed resources.

This ideal situation is not sustainable forever. Some organisms may show exponential growth for a long period of time, but eventually one or more limiting factors will begin to slow the rate of growth. You will explore what happens when limiting factors do influence the growth rate in the following section.

Subject vocabulary

carrying capacity an environment's ability to support an organism's population based on resource availability and other factors

sigmoid having a shape like the letter 'S'

logistic growth a pattern of population growth that follows a sigmoid shape due to increasing density of the population

Synonyms

scarce............ limited

General vocabulary

fluctuates a value that rises above and falls below a set value

Understanding: Population growth slows as a population reaches the **carrying capacity** of the environment.

Model sentence: Rate of growth of a population will begin to slow as conditions begin to approach the carrying capacity of the environment.

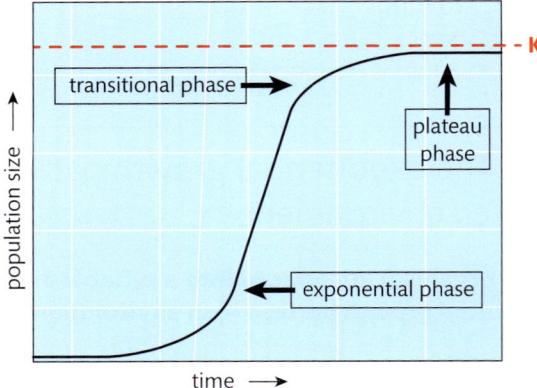

Figure 14.9 *Graph showing the overall pattern and phases of logistic growth. Imagine an organism introduced into an ideal environment at time = 0. Notice that the overall pattern has the shape of the letter 'S'. This graph shape is called* sigmoid. *The three phases and the line shown at 'K' will be explained in following sections*

The logistic growth curve has three phases:

- Exponential phase: the first phase of **logistic growth** is called the exponential phase. This phase begins when an organism first enters a new and suitable environment. The conditions and circumstances for this phase were described in the previous section of this text. Population rate of growth is very high due to ideal conditions.

- Transitional phase: one or more resources is beginning to become **scarce** as the population increases. One or more predators may be slowing the population rate of growth. Population density is becoming high enough that spread of disease may have become a problem. Notice that growth is continuing, but the rate of growth has slowed during this phase.

- Plateau phase: competition for resources and possibly other limiting factors have led to a zero growth rate. Notice that the number of organisms is as high as ever, but the rate of growth is zero. This does not mean that no new individuals are being produced. The graph simply shows that the total number of individuals in this environment is stable.

When a population is within their plateau phase of logistic growth, it is said that they have reached the carrying capacity of that environment. The carrying capacity is shown by the dotted line in the figure above labelled as 'K'. There are enough resources to support that number of individuals, but no more. In reality, a population that has reached the carrying capacity of an environment **fluctuates** a little above or below the carrying capacity as time progresses.

Skill: Modelling the growth curve using a simple organism such as yeast or species of *Lemna*

Start a population of yeast growing in a suitable culture medium. Alternatively, you could start with a small sample of duckweed (*Lemna*) in a container of water under light. Either approach should show population numbers characteristic of logistic growth over a suitable period of time.

Understanding: The phases shown in the sigmoid curve can be explained by relative rates of natality, mortality, immigration, and emigration.

Model sentence: Relative rates of natality, mortality, immigration, and emigration explain the various phases of the logistic growth curve.

As described in the previous section, logistic growth has three phases:
- exponential – very high growth rate in population
- transitional – growth rate beginning to slow
- plateau – growth rate has slowed to zero (population has peaked).

The rate of growth in each of these phases is ultimately determined by the rate of these four factors:
- natality – the birth/hatching rate
- mortality – the death rate
- immigration – the rate of organisms moving into an area
- emigration – the rate of organisms moving out of an area.

Application: Discussion of the effect of natality, mortality, immigration, and emigration on population size

Natality and mortality have an opposite effect on a population's growth rate. Immigration and emigration also have an opposite effect on a population's growth rate. One way a population can reach its plateau phase is for natality and mortality to be equal and immigration and emigration to also be equal. Your class might want to have a discussion on what happens to a population when one or more of these factors increase or decrease.

Population growth rate = (natality – mortality) + (immigration – emigration)

Understanding: Limiting factors can be top down or bottom up.

Model sentence: Limiting factors determine the carrying capacity of an environment and can be top down or bottom up.

Consider a population of organisms that shows a population growth curve as shown below.

General Vocab
fluctuate move back and forth

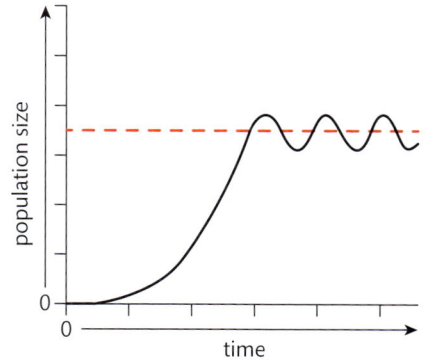

Figure 14.10 *Population showing logistic growth. Notice that when the population begins its plateau phase the population size begins to* **fluctuate** *a little above and below the carrying capacity*

This population shows logistic growth. Notice that once the population has reached the plateau phase (carrying capacity of that environment), the population size does not typically follow a perfect straight line for number of individuals. A pattern begins where sometimes the population is slightly above the carrying capacity and sometimes below. The reason is the top-down and bottom-up limiting factors that are influencing the population size at any given time.

Top-down limiting factors affect food chains by determining mortality rates due to predation and disease. For example, if a population of mice was to exceed the carrying capacity, this would attract more predators of mice. In addition, disease spread among the mice would be more likely.

Bottom-up limiting factors are due to limitations placed on resources when populations begin to exceed the carrying capacity. These resources may be food or habitat availability.

Application: Bottom-up control of algal blooms by shortage of nutrients and top-down control by herbivory

In some locations, grass fertilizers containing nitrogen and phosphate run off into lakes and ponds. This often begins what is called an algal bloom. An algal bloom is when the growth of algae in a body of water becomes very rapid. This leads to an unhealthy body of water for the other organisms. The control of algal blooms can be achieved in two ways:

1. Limit the amount and timing of fertilizers applied to lawns and shrubs. For example, some locations ban the sale and use of fertilizers during their 'rainy seasons' in order to limit the fertilizer run-off.

2. Stock the body of water with fish species that eat algae. This will help keep the algae under control through herbivory.

Application: Evaluating the methods used to estimate the size of commercial stock of marine resources

Marine resources are all of those foods and other useful items that humans take from our oceans. This includes many species of fish and also other marine organisms that we eat and use for a variety of purposes. These resources are not unlimited. There are many species of marine organisms that humans have already had an impact on n a negative way. One approach is to determine a **maximum sustainable yield** (MSY) for each species that is harvested. The MSY is the maximum number of each population that can be removed without impacting on the population size for the future.

Because the oceans are so massive, a variety of methods are used to estimate the current size of each organism at any given time. These estimation methods include:
- asking fishermen to collect data on their catch
- direct observation by government agents on fishing vessels
- monitoring fish populations by **sonar devices**
- **tagging** fish for capture–mark–release–recapture data
- studies on ages of fish that are caught:
  - too few young fish may mean problems with **spawning**
  - too few old fish may mean overfishing is occurring.

Each of these techniques gives nothing more than an estimate of the current state of a population's size.

Subject vocabulary

yield maximum number of each (fish) population that can be removed without affecting the yield for the future

tagging applying a tag (sometimes electronic) that allows an animal to be identified at a later time

General vocabulary

sonar device a device that works by way of a sound echo

spawning producing large amounts of eggs at the same time

C.6 Nitrogen and phosphorus cycles

Understanding: Nitrogen-fixing bacteria convert atmospheric nitrogen to ammonia.

Model sentence: Some bacterial species convert nitrogen from the atmosphere into ammonia.

Like many other substances, the element nitrogen is cycled through ecosystems. At any given time most nitrogen on our planet is found in the atmosphere. This form of nitrogen is N_2, also known as **diatomic** nitrogen gas. The forms of nitrogen that are useful to plants are ammonia (NH_3) and nitrates (NO_3^- compounds). The conversion of N_2 into compounds such as ammonia and nitrates is called nitrogen fixation.

Many of the conversions of one form of nitrogen substance to another is achieved by specific types of bacteria most often found in soil. The first step in converting N_2 in the atmosphere into another form is accomplished by nitrogen-fixing soil bacteria and results in the formation of ammonia. Some plants can take in ammonia and further metabolize it to make useful nitrogen-containing organic compounds.

Other bacteria can convert ammonia into compounds known as nitrites. Still other soil bacteria can then convert the nitrites into nitrates. This process of converting ammonia into nitrites and nitrates is called nitrification. The process of **nitrification** requires oxygen and occurs best in soils that are well **aerated**. Often, it is these nitrates that plants use as their source of nitrogen in order to synthesize amino acids, nucleotides, and other nitrogen-containing compounds.

Understanding: *Rhizobium* **associates** with roots in a mutualistic relationship.

Model sentence: In some plants, the bacterium *Rhizobium* forms a mutualistic relationship with the plant.

Some plants form a mutualistic relationship with a bacterium known as *Rhizobium*.

One group of plants known to form this relationship are the **legumes** that include beans, peas, and clover. The *Rhizobium* bacteria live in outgrowths on the roots of the plant. These outgrowths are called **nodules**.

Rhizobium are nitrogen-fixing bacteria and provide nitrates to the plant. In turn, the plant provides carbohydrates and a suitable environment for the bacteria to grow. Thus, both species benefit. Other plants also benefit as the nitrates often remain in the soil when the legume dies and **decomposes** into the soil.

Subject vocabulary

diatomic molecule consisting of two atoms of the same element

nitrification bacterial process of converting ammonia into nitrites and nitrates

Rhizobium type of nitrogen-fixing bacteria that forms a mutualistic relationship with legumes

mutualistic relationship relationship between two organisms in which both are helped

legumes a plant grouping that includes beans, peas, and clover

nodules growths on the roots of legumes where *Rhizobium* bacteria live

General vocabulary

aerated containing air

associates forms a relationship with

Synonyms

decomposes… decays

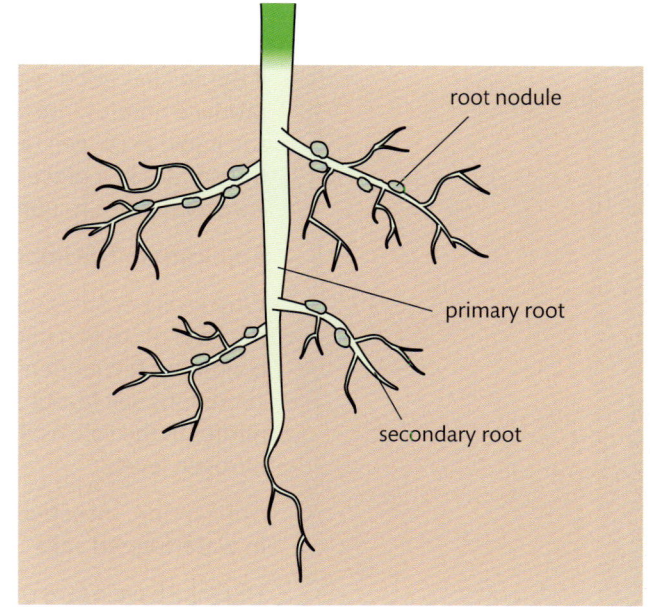

Figure 14.11 *The root of a legume showing the enlargements known as nodules. It is within these nodules that* Rhizobium *lives*

Subject vocabulary

denitrifying bacteria bacteria that reduce nitrates back into atmospheric nitrogen under low oxygen conditions

aerobic an environment with good oxygen availability

anaerobic an environment with poor (or no) oxygen availability

denitrification the process of converting nitrates into nitrites and atmospheric nitrogen

waterlogged soil soil where all of the air spaces are filled with water

General vocabulary

insectivorous insect eating

adaptation(s) change(s) which make(s) something more suitable for a situation

Understanding: In the absence of oxygen, **denitrifying bacteria** reduce nitrate in the soil.

Model sentence: If there is no or little oxygen present, denitrifying bacteria convert nitrates in the soil to nitrites and atmospheric nitrogen.

Hints for success: Be able to draw and label a flowchart showing the major events of the nitrogen cycle as shown in the figure below.

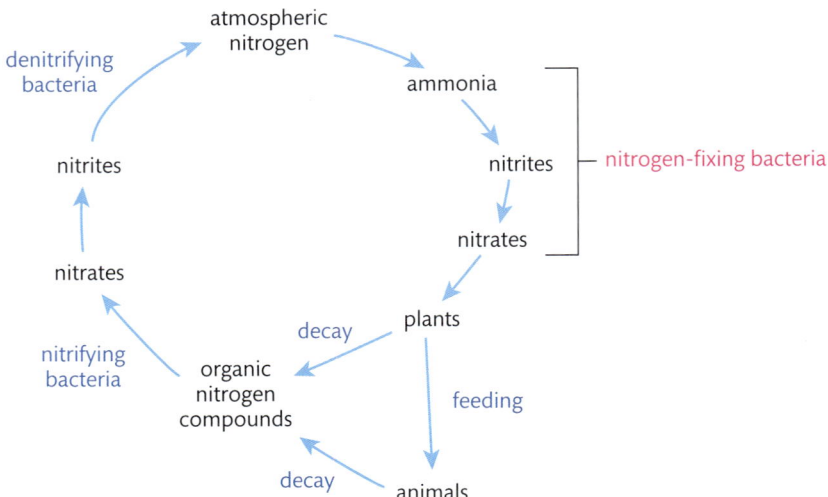

Figure 14.12 *Flow chart showing the nitrogen cycle. Notice that nitrogen truly does follow a cycle. The majority of nitrogen at any given time is within the atmosphere. Any nitrogen that becomes 'fixed' into nitrogen compounds useful for living organisms will eventually be returned to the atmosphere*

Plants use nitrates as a source of nitrogen for a variety of molecules including amino acids and nucleic acids. These nitrogen-containing molecules then either become a part of a food chain if an animal eats the plant (or an animal eats an animal that ate the plant) or the plant dies and decays into the soil. Eventually, the animals in the food chain will also die and decay. Either way, this returns the nitrogen compounds back into the soil.

If the soil has good oxygen availability (**aerobic** conditions), nitrifying bacteria will produce nitrates from the organic nitrogen compounds released from decay. If the soil is low in oxygen (**anaerobic** conditions), another group of bacteria will act on the nitrates in a process called **denitrification**. The process of denitrification will convert nitrates to nitrites and finally return the nitrogen back to the atmosphere.

Application: The impact of waterlogging on the nitrogen cycle

When soil becomes too wet and stays that way for an extended period of time, the level of oxygen in the soil becomes very low. As you have seen, anaerobic conditions favour denitrification of the nitrogen cycle. This means the low oxygen conditions will favour the production of atmospheric nitrogen from nitrates and nitrites in the soil. As a result **waterlogged soils** tend to have very low useful nitrogen levels.

Application: Insectivorous plants as an adaptation for low nitrogen availability in waterlogged soils

You may have heard of a plant called the Venus flytrap. This plant was named because of its ability to trap insects. The plant uses the insects as a source of nitrogen as the plant often grows in nitrogen and phosphorus poor soils. The Venus flytrap is a plant and photosynthesizes like any other plant. The trapping of insects is simply an **adaptation** for life in a soil that cannot support most plant species.

Understanding: Phosphorus can be added to the phosphorous cycle by application of fertilizer or removed by the harvesting of agricultural crops.

Model sentence: Fertilizers containing phosphorus are frequently made from phosphorus removed from ground deposits, and when agricultural crops are harvested that phosphorus is effectively removed from future use.

Although phosphorus does cycle through ecosystems, the cycle is extremely slow. Almost all reserves of phosphorus are contained within **marine sediments**. There are only a few places on Earth where these sediments can be economically mined from ground deposits.

The most common use for mined phosphorus is to make fertilizers for agricultural use around the world. The phosphorus is removed from the soil by plants in order to make phosphorus containing organic molecules such as DNA, RNA, ATP, and phospholipids. When the plants are harvested the phosphorus is removed as molecular parts of the plant. A farmer has no choice but to add additional phosphorus fertilizer in order to grow a new crop.

Understanding: The rate of **turnover** in the phosphorous cycle is much lower than the nitrogen cycle.

Model sentence: The phosphorus cycle is a much more time consuming cycle as compared to the nitrogen cycle.

As mentioned in the previous section, most phosphorus is contained within marine sediments. These sediments become buried under further sediments for incredibly long periods of time. The only economical way that large quantities of phosphorus can be mined is when a previous ocean floor area becomes uplifted to become dry land.

The nitrogen cycle in comparison can be a relatively fast cycle. The change from atmospheric nitrogen to the various forms of nitrogen produced by nitrogen-fixing bacteria is a wide-scale and ongoing process.

Understanding: Availability of phosphorous may become limiting to agriculture in the future.

Model sentence: Growing of agricultural crops relies on availability of limited phosphorus and this may become more of a problem in the future.

Because so much of Earth's phosphorus is contained within hard to access marine sediments, the availability of phosphorus is a limited resource at any given time. The **United States Geological Survey (USGS)** currently estimates that we will run out of phosphorus available in currently known **reserves** in about 80 years.

Subject vocabulary

marine sediments the slow deposit of a variety of substances on the ocean floor

United States Geological Survey (USGS) a science organization that provides impartial information on the health of Earth's ecosystems and environment

General vocabulary

turnover the continuous process of loss and replacement of something

reserves a location where something is kept for future use

Subject vocabulary

leaching removal of mineral nutrients such as phosphorus and nitrogen compounds from soils by dissolving in rainwater and run-off

eutrophication term used to describe a body of water that has experienced an algal bloom due to fertilizer run-off and the resulting oxygen depletion

algal bloom very rapid increase in the algae population of a body of water

biological oxygen demand the oxygen required by aerobic organisms in a body of water, for metabolism

Understanding: Leaching of mineral nutrients from agricultural land into rivers causes **eutrophication** and leads to increased biochemical oxygen demand.

Model sentence: Rainwater run-off dissolves mineral nutrients from agricultural land leading to eutrophication and increased biochemical oxygen demand in rivers and other bodies of water.

Farmers need rain to provide water for their crops. One of the negative consequences of rain is the leaching of mineral nutrients from the soil. Leaching is where phosphate and nitrogen compounds become dissolved in the rainwater. This rainwater does not always stay in the soil, sometimes it runs off into nearby bodies of water. The phosphate and nitrogen compounds are taken with the water run-off. This not only lessens the mineral nutrients in the soil, but it also may greatly increase the mineral nutrient content of the river, lake, or sea, negatively affecting water quality.

This is what happens when phosphate and/or nitrogen mineral nutrients leach into a body of water:

- High nitrates and phosphates fertilize the algae in the body of water.
- There is a rapid increase in growth of algae (called an **algal bloom**).
- This rapid increase is not sustainable for long.
- Aerobic bacteria begin to decompose the overgrowth of algae using up much of the available oxygen in the water (this is called a high **biological oxygen demand** or high BOD).
- The body of water becomes very low in oxygen and organisms such as fish die as a result.

The term used to describe this effect of fertilizer run-off on bodies of water is eutrophication.

15 Option D: Further human physiology

D.1 Human nutrition

Understanding: Essential nutrients cannot be synthesized by the body, therefore they have to be included in the diet.

Model sentence: Those nutrients that cannot be synthesized by the body are called essential nutrients and must be part of our diet.

The term essential is often used for something that is important. When it comes to our diet, the term 'essential' has a very specific meaning. Something essential in our diet must be a part of our diet or a health problem will eventually result. Your body has a metabolism that allows it to make (or synthesize) some nutrients from other nutrients when needed. That is not true for all nutrients, however. Those that cannot be synthesized and must be within the foods that we eat are called essential nutrients.

Understanding: Dietary minerals are essential chemical elements.

Model sentence: Minerals in the diet are chemical elements that are essential.

Perhaps you have read on a food product **nutrition label** the percentage of daily iron, calcium, or magnesium contained in a serving of that food. These three are examples of the **essential minerals** we must include in our diet. Each essential mineral is used for specific biochemical purposes. The body is very good at **recycling** minerals, but that recycling is not perfect. Therefore, we always need to include small amounts of essential minerals in the foods that we eat.

Some common minerals and some of their uses within the body:
- calcium – bone growth and repair
- magnesium – activation of many enzyme reactions
- iron – important component of **haemoglobin**.

Understanding: Vitamins are chemically **diverse** carbon compounds that cannot be synthesized by the body.

Model sentence: Vitamins are a diverse group of organic molecules that are essential in our diet.

Unlike minerals, vitamins are organic compounds. Like minerals, we only need very small quantities of vitamins on a daily basis. There are many different types of vitamins and each is used for one or more specific purposes. A well-balanced diet should include all of the vitamins necessary for good health. Vitamins are synthesized by living organisms and a diet with numerous fruits and vegetables should provide all one needs.

Subject vocabulary

essential nutrient nutrient that must be included in our diet

nutrition label a packaging label found on many food products listing amounts of a variety of ingredients

essential mineral elemental substance needed in our diet

haemoglobin a protein found in red blood cells used to carry oxygen in the blood

vitamins organic compounds needed in small amounts in our diet

General vocabulary

recycling make use of something more than once

diverse showing a great deal of variety

Application: Production of ascorbic acid by some mammals, but not others that need a dietary supply

Ascorbic acid is also known as vitamin C. Many animals can produce their own vitamin C as part of their metabolism. This is not true for humans and just a few other animal species. Thus, ascorbic acid is an essential vitamin for humans. It is not an essential vitamin for those animals that can synthesize it. Humans who do not consume any source of vitamin C for a long period of time develop a serious disease caused scurvy. At one time, scurvy was a common disease among sailors who went on **voyages** for many months and did not carry foods containing ascorbic acid.

Understanding: Some fatty acids and some amino acids are essential.

Model sentence: There are some fatty acids and some amino acids that cannot be synthesized by the body.

In Chapter 2, you learned that there are a variety of types of fatty acids within **triglycerides** and **phospholipids**. Two fatty acids are essential in our diets. Remember that the term essential does not imply importance; essential means that our body cannot synthesize the molecule from another molecule. The two that are essential are called **omega-3** and **omega-6 fatty acids.**

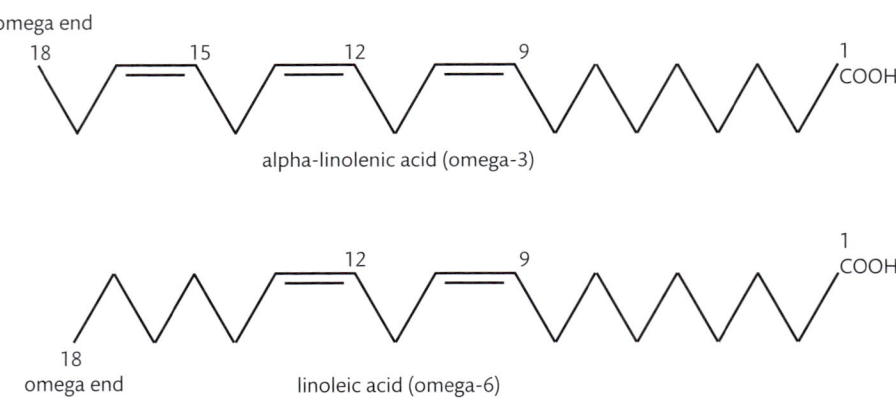

Application: Cholesterol in blood as an indicator of the risk of coronary heart disease

Cholesterol is a lipid substance needed in the body for a variety of reasons. Unfortunately, many people have cholesterol levels circulating in their blood stream that are too high. This can create long-term health problems within their blood vessels.

Over time, many people develop deposits on the inside of their arteries called **plaque**. One of the components of plaque is cholesterol. As these deposits begin to get larger, the inside of the blood vessel has less room to carry blood. One of the locations in the body where this can occur is in the arteries that carry oxygenated blood directly into heart muscle. These arteries are called coronary arteries. Build-up of plaque deposits in coronary arteries is called coronary heart disease or CHD. When one or more of the coronary arteries can no longer carry a sufficient amount of blood into the heart muscle a heart attack results. People are encouraged to monitor their cholesterol levels in their blood as high cholesterol levels are an indicator for possible coronary heart disease.

General vocabulary
voyage long journey by ship

Subject vocabulary
triglycerides fats or oils formed from three fatty acids and a glycerol molecule

phospholipid a type of lipid molecule that occurs in a bilayer to make up cell membranes

omega-3 fatty acid a fatty acid that has a double bond starting at the third carbon from the omega end of the molecule

omega-6 fatty acid a fatty acid that has a double bond starting at the sixth carbon from the omega end of the molecule

plaque build-up of cholesterol and other substances on the inner wall of arteries or biofilm on the surface of teeth

Figure 15.1 The two essential fatty acids shown in abbreviated form. Carbon number 1 is the carbon of the carboxyl group. Each angle change after that represents a carbon atom. Carbon atoms with double bonds are shown, and the first is numbered. Each carbon in the chain would have an appropriate number of hydrogens to make four bonds around each. The carbon on the far left of each structure is called the omega carbon. Counting from the omega carbon, you can easily see why these fatty acids are called omega-3 and omega-6, respectively. There is no reason to memorize these structures

As you may remember, there are 20 different amino acids within proteins. We need all 20, but we are capable of synthesizing only 11 of the 20. That means that 9 amino acids are essential in our diets. Obtaining these 9 essential amino acids is typically not a problem for someone who eats a variety of protein sources.

Understanding: Lack of essential amino acids affects the production of proteins.

Model sentence: Protein synthesis is affected if one or more essential amino acids is not included in the diet.

There are 20 types of amino acids. As you learned earlier, 9 of the 20 must be included in the diet. Anyone that regularly eats a variety of foods that contain protein will be getting all 20 different types. When their own cells are synthesizing proteins, there should be enough of each type of amino acid available.

In some areas of the world, people sometimes use a single crop as their primary protein source. One example is corn or maize. Maize is lacking in two essential amino acids, lysine and tryptophan. Researchers are working on new breeds of corn that have increased levels of lysine and tryptophan.

Understanding: Malnutrition may be caused by a deficiency, imbalance, or excess of nutrients in the diet.

Model sentence: Deficiencies, imbalances, or excesses of one or more nutrients in the diet can result in malnutrition.

Nutrition problems are collectively called malnutrition. There are three situations in which malnutrition can occur. Here are examples of all three:

1. Deficiency of one or more essential nutrient(s): it is obvious that as a person grows, their skeleton must grow as well. Most of the growth occurs at the ends of bones in areas called bone plates. When either vitamin D or the mineral calcium is not available, this growth does not occur in a normal way. Instead the ends of the bones become irregularly shaped and unusually thick. In children, this is a condition called rickets. The legs of children with rickets grow to become highly bowed inward or outward. They will never achieve their full potential height. Adults who do not consume enough vitamin D or calcium develop a condition called osteomalacia. Their bones become soft, and bowing and fracturing are more likely.

2. Imbalance of one or more essential nutrient(s): as mentioned above, some people live in areas of the world where food variety is a problem. Their source of protein may be primarily from a single type of crop. In this situation, one or more of the essential amino acids may be lacking.

3. Excesses of nutrient(s): obesity is a major health concern in many countries. There are many health conditions that are correlated with obesity. What is considered excess for one person may not be an excess for another. An example is shown in the following application.

Subject vocabulary

malnutrition an unhealthy condition due to insufficient, excessive, or unbalanced consumption of nutrients

rickets abnormal bone growth in children due to a deficiency of vitamin D or calcium or both

osteomalacia a condition leading to bone softening in adults due to a deficiency of vitamin D or calcium or both

Synonyms

deficiency ...... shortage/absence
bowed .... curved/bent

Subject vocabulary

phenylketonuria (PKU) a genetic disease leading to the inability to metabolize a single amino acid (phenylalanine)

appetite the desire to eat

hypothalamus a region of the brain that controls pituitary gland secretions and other autonomic functions

autonomic functions involuntary or unconscious functions

leptin hormone produced by body fat that lowers the appetite

anorexia an eating disorder where people eat very little in order to achieve what they perceive as an 'ideal' (too thin) body image

hypertension high blood pressure

type II diabetes a form of diabetes where one develops a resistance to the normal function of insulin

Application: Cause and treatment of phenylketonuria (PKU)

Some children are born with the inherited disease known as phenylketonuria or PKU. These children are unable to metabolize the amino acid phenylalanine because they lack the enzyme to do so. If left untreated phenylalanine will build up in their bloodstream and cells. This creates a toxic situation leading to mental deficiencies, behavioural problems, and seizures. In areas of the world where good medical care is available, it is common for all children to be tested for PKU right after birth. If the test is positive, the child is given protein sources that are low in phenylalanine. A diet that contains proteins known to be relatively low in phenylalanine is the only known treatment for PKU.

Understanding: Appetite is controlled by a centre in the hypothalamus.

Model sentence: An area of the brain called the hypothalamus contains a control centre for one's appetite.

The hypothalamus is in an area of your brain called your brainstem. Your brainstem, including the hypothalamus, controls activities that we call autonomic. These are activities that are controlled at the unconscious level.

After you eat a meal, there a variety of signals that provide your hypothalamus with information. For example:

- The swollen condition of your stomach full of food results in nervous system impulses being sent to the hypothalamus.
- The intestines and pancreas produce hormones that provide information to the hypothalamus.
- Adipose (fat) tissue produces a hormone called leptin that provides information to the hypothalamus.

The hypothalamus uses this information to reduce your appetite. All of this is occurring without your conscious knowledge and that is typical of brainstem actions.

Application: Breakdown of heart muscle due to anorexia

Anorexia is an eating disorder characterized by having an 'ideal' body image that is far too thin. The body image desired by someone with anorexia is too thin for proper health. Sometimes the greatly restricted diet is accompanied by a desire to exercise excessively. People who suffer from this eating disorder are not receiving the correct amount and type of essential nutrients. Many systems of the body are negatively affected. The heart is no exception. Without an adequate intake of protein for amino acids and other essential substances, the heart begins to get smaller and weaker over time. Successful treatment for the eating disorder can save a life in this instance.

Understanding: Overweight individuals are more likely to suffer hypertension and type II diabetes.

Model sentence: People who are overweight are more likely to develop hypertension and/or type II diabetes.

Hypertension is also called 'high blood pressure'. People with hypertension place a strain on both their heart and arteries as a result of the increased pressure. There are many factors that can contribute to hypertension and some of those are not controllable. Examples are age and genetic background. One factor that is controllable for most people is their body mass index or BMI. Your BMI is a calculation of body mass corrected for height. High BMI values have been positively correlated with hypertension.

Another health problem that has been positively correlated with high BMI is type II diabetes. People are not born with type II diabetes, they develop the disease at some point in their life. People with this disease do not **metabolize** glucose as they should within their cells. This is because their body cells have developed a **resistance** to the hormone insulin. Under normal circumstances, insulin is the hormone that adds plasma membrane channels that allow glucose to enter the cell. When channel proteins no longer respond to insulin properly, glucose is not able to enter cells and stays in the bloodstream.

Understanding: Starvation can lead to breakdown of body tissue.

Model sentence: Body tissues are digested when a person is starving.

Earlier you read about some health conditions that result when a specific nutrient is out of balance in the diet. But what happens when almost no nutrients are available? The answer is that the body begins to make use of its own stored nutrients.

You probably have seen photographs of people who are experiencing starvation conditions. They often appear as is they have very little to no muscle. This is because they have used their own **skeletal muscle** as a source of amino acids to make other proteins. The muscle is still there but has become so thin that it is hardly noticeable.

D.2 Digestion

Understanding: Nervous and hormonal mechanisms control the **secretion** of **digestive juices**.

Model sentence: Digestion of foods requires the secretion of digestive fluids controlled by the nervous and endocrine systems.

Digestion is a chemical process that requires various **glands** to secrete specific substances. These fluids are necessary in order to convert the relatively large molecular nutrients that we **ingest** into smaller molecular forms that can be absorbed into our blood stream. Many of the chemical reactions that occur are hydrolysis reactions that you studied in Chapter 2.

It would be wasteful and possibly harmful to have digestive secretions within the stomach and intestines all of the time. Therefore, there are **mechanisms** that the body uses in order to recognize when various secretions are needed.

Some of these mechanisms are under the control of your **nervous system**. Simply seeing, smelling, or thinking about food may trigger a nervous system response that begins some digestive secretions. Another system of your body that is involved is your **endocrine system.** The endocrine system includes all of your glands that secrete hormones into your bloodstream. You will learn about two of the hormones that help control stomach secretions in a later topic of this unit.

Subject vocabulary

metabolize to perform metabolism

resistance the inability of a tissue to respond normally to a chemical such as a hormone

skeletal muscle muscle that is used to move bones

secretion release of a substance from a cell, tissue, or gland

digestive juices fluid secretions that chemically aid the digestive process

digestion a chemical process whereby large molecules undergo reactions in order to become a molecular size that can be absorbed into the blood

ingest take food/substances into the body

nervous system system of the body that includes your brain, spinal cord and various nerves for communication with body tissues

endocrine system system of the body that includes all those glands that produce hormones secreted into the bloodstream

General vocabulary

gland an organ of the body which produces a substance

Synonyms

mechanism .... way/process

Subject vocabulary

exocrine gland a gland that secretes a substance into a duct for transport

lumen area within surrounding walls or membranes; usually used for the cavity of a tubular structure such as a blood vessel

duct a small tube

endocrine gland a gland that produces a hormone

gastric secretions fluid secreted into the stomach by cells of the stomach

autonomic nervous system that portion of your nervous system that controls unconscious activities

oesophagus tube of the alimentary canal that connects the mouth to the stomach

gastric pit small and numerous exocrine glands located in the inner wall of the stomach

pepsinogen an inactive form of a protein-digesting enzyme secreted into the lumen of the stomach

mucus a protective secretion produced by certain cells of the body including cells of the stomach

Synonyms

gut .... alimentary canal
cavity .... space (within)

General vocabulary

pit-like shaped like a small cave or pit

Understanding: Exocrine glands secrete to the surface of the body or the lumen of the gut.

Model sentence: Exocrine glands secrete substances either to the body surface or the interior of the gut.

Exocrine glands do not secrete into the blood. Instead, they secrete into a small tube called a duct. The duct takes the secretion to a specific location in the body for use. The ducts for some exocrine glands take the secretion to the surface of the body. Other exocrine glands take their secretions to the interior cavity of the gut. This interior cavity is called the lumen. Here are some examples of exocrine glands:

Exocrine gland	Secretion	Duct takes secretion to
lacrimal (tear) glands	tears	outer surface of each eye
sweat glands	sweat	surface of the skin
gastric glands	gastric fluid for digestion	lumen of the stomach
pancreas	pancreatic fluid for digestion	lumen of the small intestine

Note: the pancreas is also an endocrine gland as it produces hormones as well.

Hints for success: The two types of glands mentioned in this section have similar sounding names: exocrine and endocrine. Spend some time matching the names with the type of gland that the name applies to. Remember that exocrine glands secrete into a duct and endocrine glands secrete into the bloodstream.

Understanding: The volume and content of gastric secretions are controlled by nervous and hormonal mechanisms.

Model sentence: The nervous and endocrine systems control the volume and content of secretions into the stomach lumen.

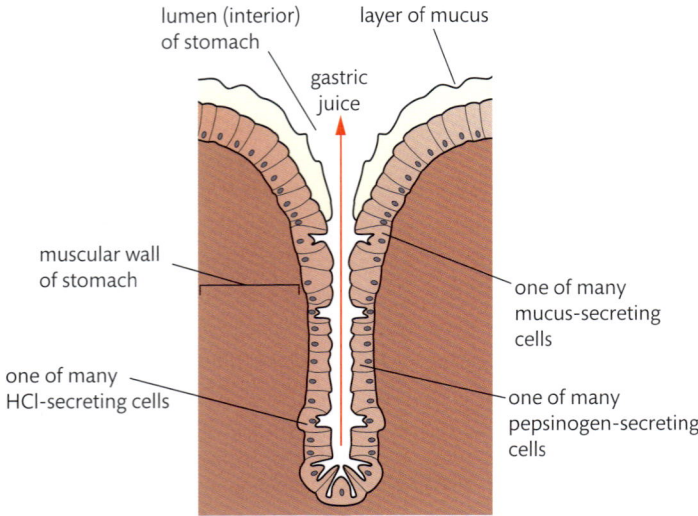

Figure 15.2 One of the many gastric pits located in the inner lining of the stomach. Each pit is shared by each of the glandular cell types creating and secreting one of the components of gastric juice (hydrochloric acid, pepsinogen, or mucus). Note the thin duct leading to the lumen of the stomach; the presence of this duct qualifies each of these pits as an exocrine gland

Even before you eat, your nervous system is preparing your gut for food. Even thinking about food may result in your autonomic nervous system sending signals to begin saliva and gastric juice secretions. After being swallowed, food goes through a tube called the oesophagus. The oesophagus takes the food to the stomach where it remains for a period of time.

Within the stomach are numerous very small exocrine glands called gastric pits. Each of these pit-like structures is lined with cells that secrete a substance into the lumen of the stomach. These secretions include hydrochloric acid, a protein digesting enzyme (pepsinogen) and mucus. Collectively, this fluid is called gastric fluid. The food that enters the stomach is mixed with this fluid. Muscle layers of the stomach create a churning motion in order to mix the food with the gastric fluid.

The nervous system impulses mentioned earlier that are being sent to the stomach also result in some stomach cells releasing a hormone. This hormone is called **gastrin**. Gastrin enters the bloodstream and makes its way to the cells in the gastric pits. This results in the production of even more gastric juice. Eating a full meal results in the stomach swelling. This results in a nervous system impulse being sent to the brainstem. The brainstem then sends impulses for even more gastric juice. Thus, the volume of gastric juice depends on the amount of food in the stomach.

Application: *Helicobacter pylori* infection as a cause of stomach ulcers

Stomach ulcers were once thought to be a result of stress. The thinking was that stress caused excess **hydrochloric acid** to be secreted. It was assumed that the excess acid both caused and irritated the ulcer. In the early 1980s, two researchers found a species of bacteria (*Helicobacter pylori*) in the stomach wall of ulcer patients. It surprised researchers, as up to that point everyone assumed no living thing could survive in this highly acidic environment. Ulcer patients who are successfully treated with antibiotics show that it was damage from the bacteria that was the cause of the ulcer.

Understanding: Acid conditions in the stomach favour some hydrolysis reactions and help to control **pathogens** in ingested food.

Model sentence: The hydrochloric acid secreted into the stomach helps prevent food poisoning and provides a favourable chemical environment for some hydrolysis reactions.

As mentioned in the previous section, hydrochloric acid is a component of gastric juice. This creates a very acidic environment within the lumen of the stomach. One benefit to this is that pathogens are often destroyed by stomach acid. We refrigerate many foods to keep bacteria and fungi from multiplying, but the majority of foods that we eat still contain many of these microorganisms.

A second benefit is the chemical environment provided by the acid. In the previous section, you learned that a protein hydrolysing enzyme called pepsinogen was a component of gastric juice. Pepsinogen is secreted as an inactive enzyme. Its structure is slightly modified when it enters an acidic environment and it becomes active. The active form of pepsinogen is called **pepsin**. Laboratory tests show that pepsin is most effective at digesting protein when at a low pH as provided by the stomach.

Application: The reduction of stomach acid secretion by proton pump inhibitor drugs

The highly acidic environment of the stomach can sometimes result in health problems. In a condition referred to as **acid reflux**, highly acidic gastric fluids irritate the inside wall of the oesophagus. An ulcer is a damaged area of the inside wall of the stomach or small intestine. The damage is made worse by the acid. Late in the 20th century, researchers developed a class of drugs called **proton pump inhibitors**. These drugs work by **inhibiting** the production of HCl by cells in the gastric pits. Healing of both acid reflux and ulcers is often possible, aided by the lowered production of acid.

Subject vocabulary

gastrin hormone produced by the stomach that leads to increased production of gastric juice

Helicobacter pylori species of bacteria that has been shown to be the cause of stomach ulcers

ulcer an open sore

pathogens disease-causing agents such as viruses and bacteria

food poisoning an illness that sometimes results when one eats food containing pathogenic organisms

pepsin the active form of a protein-hydrolysing enzyme in the stomach

acid reflux a painful condition caused by stomach acid irritating the lower portion of the oesophagus

proton pump inhibitors a class of drugs that result in gastric pit cells producing less hydrochloric acid

Synonyms

hydrochloric acid .... HCl

inhibiting .... preventing/ reducing

Subject vocabulary

epithelium cell layer that often forms a covering or outer cell layer of a structure (formed of epithelial cells)

absorption the passage of molecules through membranes

villus (plural: villi) a small finger-like projection that extends into the lumen of the small intestine

microvillus (plural: microvilli) cell membrane projections that greatly increase plasma membrane surface area

ATP a molecule used for a source of chemical energy

active transport cellular transport requiring energy (ATP) from the cell

General vocabulary

adapted efficient for a particular purpose

projection something that protrudes or projects outwards

Understanding: The structure of cells of the **epithelium** of the villi is **adapted** to the **absorption** of food.

Model sentence: The cells of small **projections** called villi, found in the small intestine, are adapted for the absorption of digested food.

When partially digested food leaves the stomach it enters the small intestine. Digestion will continue, but another important process begins. That process is absorption. Absorption occurs when the macromolecules within foods have become small enough to be taken through the cells of the intestine and enter the bloodstream.

The interior lumen of the small intestine is not smooth. It is lined with millions of very small finger-like projections called villi. The presence of villi greatly increases the surface area for absorption. Each **villus** (singular) has epithelial cells that are in contact with the fluid in the lumen. Digested molecules must pass through these epithelial cells before entering the interior of a villus. Inside of each villus is a capillary bed for absorption of the nutrients into the bloodstream.

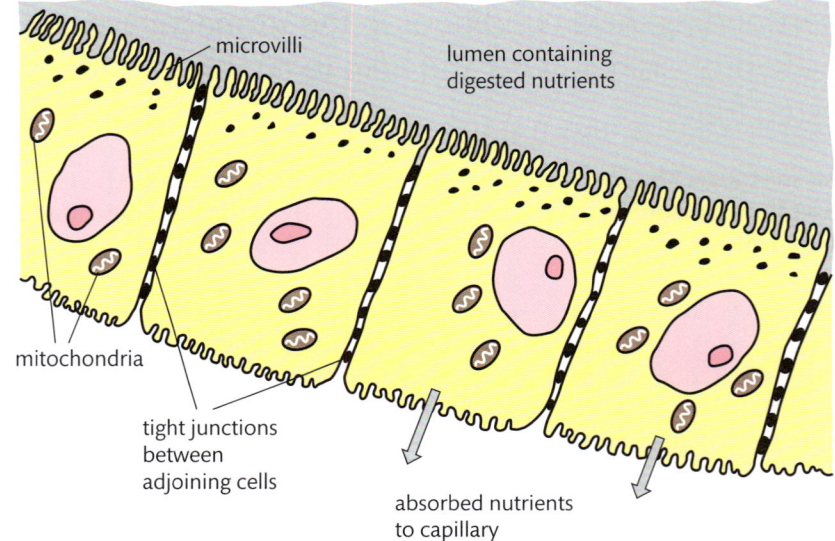

Figure 15.3 *Individual epithelial cells of a villus. Digested molecules must pass through these cells in order to reach a capillary bed*

Summary of villi epithelial cell adaptations for efficient food absorption:
- One side of the cell is in direct contact with digested molecules in the lumen of small intestine.
- Each villus cell has many cell membrane projections (**microvilli**) on that same side. This further increases the surface area for absorption.
- Epithelial cells are held tightly together by shared proteins. This is called a tight junction. This prevents undigested food from entering the villus without passing through a plasma membrane.
- Each villus has numerous mitochondria in order to provide **ATP**. Some molecules will be absorbed using an **active transport** mechanism.
- The inside of the cell is near to a capillary bed for absorption into the bloodstream.

Understanding: The rate of transit of materials through the large intestine is positively correlated with their fibre content.

Model sentence: Undigested foods move through the large intestine more efficiently when they contain a high fibre content.

Some natural foods that you eat have a relatively high fibre content. These foods typically come from a plant. This is because the highest components of fibre are cellulose and lignin. These two types of molecules are the largest components of plant cell walls. Therefore, whenever you eat any vegetable or fruit, you will be eating fibre.

The human digestive system does not produce any enzymes that digest cellulose or lignin. As a result, these two molecules pass through our gut relatively unchanged. Both are much too large to be absorbed through the villi of the small intestine. When each of these two molecules reaches the end of the small intestine they next enter the large intestine. The presence of a relatively high fibre content in the large intestine helps all of the solid waste to keep moving. This is considered to be healthy as solid waste (faeces) will not remain in the large intestine for as long a time period.

Application: Dehydration due to cholera toxin

Cholera is a disease caused by the bacterium *Vibrio cholera*. More specifically, cholera is a result of a toxin released by these bacteria. People typically become infected by drinking contaminated water. Often the water is contaminated with human or animal sewage. The toxin results in severe diarrhea. Prolonged diarrhea can lead to severe dehydration. The infection can be life threatening if not treated.

Understanding: Materials not absorbed are egested.

Model sentence: Solid wastes are egested as faeces.

The large intestine's primary function is to absorb water from the fluids that enter. The water content of the solid waste is much lower at the end of the large intestine as compared to the beginning. In addition, there are multitudes of bacteria that live within our large intestine. These bacteria are able to thrive given the water, warmth, and food material they are being provided. These bacteria provide a normal environment within the interior of our large intestine for us. They also produce vitamin K that we need for blood clotting purposes.

When the bacteria have finished acting on the waste and the water has been absorbed, the leftover material is called faeces. It is eliminated through our rectum in a process called egestion.

Synonyms

transit .... movement

Subject vocabulary

large intestine the final sections of the gut (much of the large intestine is often called the colon)

fibre food material that will not digest and cannot be absorbed

solid waste all of the undigested and unabsorbed substances in the gut

dehydration condition caused by losing more water than you are taking in

cholera a disease caused by a bacterium that results in severe diarrhea

diarrhea frequent loss of faeces in a very liquid form

egestion elimination of solid waste from our gut

vitamin K a vitamin produced by gut bacteria that is important for blood clotting

blood clotting a body response to minimize blood loss from small blood vessels

faeces solid waste from our gut

rectum the last portion of the large intestine

General vocabulary

contaminate to make something impure by the addition of a pollutant such as sewage

prolonged continuing for a long time

thrive grow/multiply well

D.3 Functions of the liver

Subject vocabulary

toxin a poisonous substance

detoxify to chemically modify a toxin to make it harmless

pesticide poison used to treat pest infestations

herbicide a chemical that kills selected plant life

hepatocytes the most numerous cells making up liver tissue

bone marrow soft tissue which fills the inner, hollow spaces of certain types of bones

haemoglobin a protein found in red blood cells used to carry oxygen in the blood

haem group the non-protein portions of haemoglobin molecules

bilirubin a main component of bile

Understanding: The liver removes **toxins** from the blood and **detoxifies** them.

Model sentence: When blood circulates through the liver, toxins are removed and are detoxified.

The human diet often contains many more toxins than most people are aware of. It is not uncommon for trace amounts of **pesticides** and **herbicides** to be included in and on some of the foods that we eat. Many people drink alcohol in beer, wine, and liquors. Each of these substances and many more are filtered out of our bloodstream by liver cells. These cells are called **hepatocytes.**

Hepatocytes also chemically alter toxins after filtering the substance from the blood. The chemical change results in the molecule becoming non-toxic. The resulting molecule is either used for a useful purpose or added back into the blood for eventual elimination by kidney filtration.

Understanding: Components of red blood cells are recycled by the liver.

Model sentence: Many of the molecules that make up red blood cells are recycled in the liver.

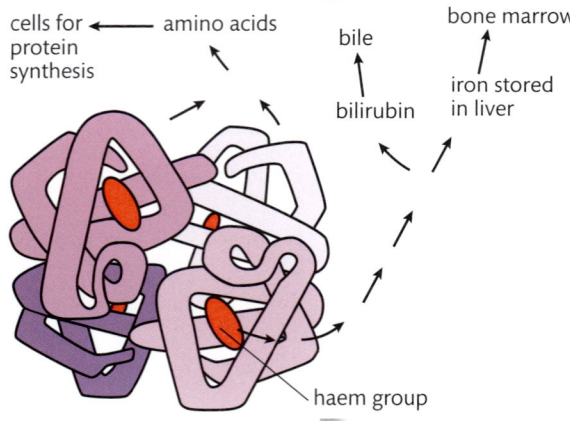

Figure 15.4 *The molecular components of haemoglobin are recycled when erythrocytes die after about 4 months*

Red blood cells are being continuously formed within our **bone marrow.** The reason for this is that red blood cells live for only about 120 days after being formed. Mature red blood cells have no nucleus. This limits their cellular life span. The body has developed chemical processes to ensure that components of these cells are recycled as much as possible. The liver is a key contributor to these processes.

Each red blood cell typically contains about 250 million **haemoglobin** molecules. This is a protein that binds to oxygen in the lungs and carries it to our tissues. When you consider that a human being has many trillions of red blood cells, you can see that recycling components of haemoglobin is very important.

In the figure shown above you can see a single haemoglobin molecule. This molecule is a large protein that is composed of four polypeptides. Each polypeptide contains a non-protein part near its centre called a **haem group.** Near the centre of each haem group is an iron atom. It is this iron atom that temporarily binds to an oxygen molecule in the lungs. The following events are all part of the recycling of haemoglobin within the liver:

- Each of the four polypeptides is hydrolysed into amino acids. The amino acids are returned to the blood for general body use.
- The iron is removed from each haem group and is sent to the bone marrow to be used for making new haemoglobin.
- The haem group is modified to become a molecule called **bilirubin.** Bilirubin is one of the main components of a substance called bile. Bile is produced by hepatocytes in the liver and sent to the small intestine to help in the digestion of lipids.

Understanding: The breakdown of erythrocytes starts with phagocytosis of red blood cells by Kupffer cells.

Model sentence: Kupffer cells within small liver blood vessels called sinusoids remove ageing red blood cells and haemoglobin by phagocytosis.

Very small blood vessels within the liver are lined by a type of white blood cell, called Kupffer cells. These cells specialize in removing red blood cells and haemoglobin from the blood by phagocytosis. Red blood cells are then lysed releasing haemoglobin within the Kupffer cell. Each haemoglobin is then chemically disassembled into its component parts. Some of the component parts are sent to the nearby hepatocytes for further modification and some are returned to the blood.

Understanding: Iron is carried to the bone marrow to produce haemoglobin in new red blood cells.

Model sentence: The iron that is removed from haemoglobin is sent to bone marrow so that new haemoglobin can be produced.

Iron is one of the most important components of haemoglobin to recycle. The iron that is removed from haemoglobin is sent by way of the blood stream to bone marrow. This is the location in the body where new red blood cells are formed. Our diet needs to include some iron each day. This is because the recycling of iron is not 100% efficient. In addition, any blood loss will not allow iron to be recycled and it will need to be replaced.

Figure 15.4 summarizes the recycling of haemoglobin that occurs in the liver. Haemoglobin is a large protein that is composed of four polypeptides. Each polypeptide contains a non-protein part near its centre called a haem group. Near the centre of each haem group is an iron atom. It is this iron atom that temporarily binds to an oxygen molecule in the lungs.

Understanding: Surplus cholesterol is converted to bile salts.

Model sentence: Bile salts are made from surplus cholesterol.

An important function of the liver is the production of a digestive secretion called bile. Bile is produced by hepatocytes in the liver. Bile can be stored in a sac called the gall bladder.

Ingested lipids are not water-soluble. Therefore, lipids tend to combine together to form lipid droplets within the lumen of the stomach and small intestine. The enzyme that digests lipids is called lipase. Lipase can only have access to the lipid molecules on the outside of a coalesced mass. This limits the rate of hydrolysis reactions catalysed by lipase. The function of bile is to emulsify lipids for faster digestion. Emulsification occurs when bile forces itself into a lipid mass and breaks it into smaller droplets. This increases the surface area to volume ratio and thus increases the rate of hydrolysis of lipids by lipase.

Bile has two primary components, bilirubin and bile salts. The formation of bilirubin was discussed in the previous section. The second component, bile salts, are formed in the liver from surplus cholesterol.

Subject vocabulary

Kupffer cell a type of white blood cell within sinusoids of the liver

sinusoids specialized capillaries found in the liver

phagocytosis active transport in which larger particles and substances are brought into the cell

lysed ruptured or broken open

hepatocytes the most numerous cells making up liver tissue

polypeptide polymer of many amino acids combined by peptide bonds

bile salts a component of bile made from cholesterol

gall bladder a storage sac for bile

lipase the enzyme that catalyses the hydrolysis of lipids into glycerol and fatty acids

emulsify to physically break a coalesced mass into smaller masses / droplets

General vocabulary

disassembled taken apart/ broken down

combine to add together to make a whole

droplets small drops

Subject vocabulary

plasma proteins protein molecules that circulate within blood plasma

albumin a plasma protein that helps regulate the osmotic balance of the blood

osmotic balance two fluids that have equal solute and water concentrations

fibrinogen the inactive form of the blood-clotting protein called fibrin

fibrin the active form of fibrinogen that forms the mesh of a blood clot

blood clot a protein mesh that traps cells and other substances to help seal a damaged blood vessel

organelles non-cellular structures within a cell which carry out organ-like processes

hepatic portal vein a major vein that brings blood from the small intestine to the liver

hepatic artery a blood vessel that brings oxygenated blood to the liver

Understanding: Endoplasmic reticulum and Golgi apparatus in hepatocytes produce **plasma proteins**.

Model sentence: Hepatocytes produce some plasma proteins with the help of endoplasmic reticulum and Golgi apparatus within hepatocytes.

The liquid part of blood is called plasma. Plasma proteins are those proteins that circulate within this liquid. There are many types of plasma proteins, but we are going to focus on just two:

1. **Albumin**: this is a plasma protein that is used to help regulate the **osmotic balance** of the blood. In addition, albumin is used as a carrier molecule for bile salts and some other fat-soluble molecules.

2. **Fibrinogen**: this plasma protein is needed for blood clotting. When a blood vessel is damaged, a series of chemical events occurs. These events ultimately lead to fibrinogen being converted into **fibrin**. Fibrin forms mesh-like protein fibres that trap cells and various other substances. This forms a **blood clot**.

Cells that secrete substances typically contain a great deal of endoplasmic reticulum and Golgi apparatus. Each of these **organelles** creates a membrane (a vesicle) around a group of molecules. The vesicle created by the endoplasmic reticulum is transported to the Golgi apparatus. Within the Golgi apparatus, the protein may be modified. The Golgi apparatus then creates another membrane vesicle around the modified plasma proteins. This vesicle is transported to the inner surface of the plasma membrane. A process called exocytosis or secretion then occurs. See Chapter 1 for a more complete description of exocytosis.

Understanding: The liver intercepts blood from the gut to regulate nutrient levels.

Model sentence: Blood from the villi of the small intestine is routed to the liver in order to help regulate nutrient levels.

In an earlier section you learned that inside of each villus of the small intestine there is a capillary bed. This capillary bed absorbs nutrients from digested foods. All of the capillary beds in all of the villi bring blood into a single vein. This vein is called the hepatic portal vein. The nutrient content of the blood in the **hepatic portal vein** varies greatly. This is because we eat different foods and at different times. Thus, nutrient absorption into the capillary beds within the villi varies greatly.

The hepatic portal vein brings this blood to the liver. The liver is then able to remove some of the nutrients from the blood. The blood that leaves the liver has a more stable nutrient level as compared to the blood that enters the liver through the hepatic portal vein.

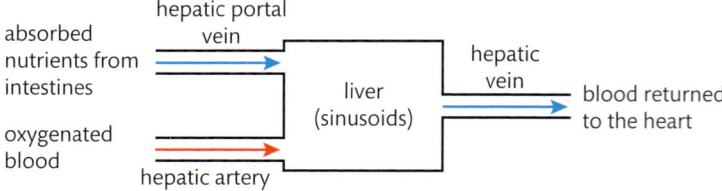

Figure 15.5 *A schematic showing the blood circulation pattern to and from the liver. Notice that the liver receives oxygenated blood from the* **hepatic artery** *in addition to the blood from the small intestine by way of the hepatic portal vein. This means that there are two major blood vessels sending blood to the liver but only one that takes blood away from the liver*

Understanding: Some nutrients in excess can be stored in the liver.

Model sentence: **The liver stores some surplus nutrients.**

One of the nutrients that is regulated by the liver is glucose. The liver is able to remove some of the excess glucose and store it. The liver stores it within hepatocytes. When the glucose enters a hepatocyte, the glucose is converted into a polysaccharide known as **glycogen**. It is common for hepatocytes to contain many vesicles filled with glycogen molecules.

If glucose levels are relatively low in the blood, the stored glycogen can be converted back to glucose. This glucose is then added back into the bloodstream.

D.4 The heart

Understanding: Structure of **cardiac muscle** cells allows **propagation** of stimuli through the heart wall.

Model sentence: **Heart muscle cells are highly adapted to allow efficient passage of electrical signals through the heart wall.**

The heart is a muscular pump composed of four chambers. The upper two have a thin muscular wall and are called atria. The lower two chambers have very thick muscular walls and are called ventricles. This section describes the muscle cells that make up the heart. This type of muscle is called cardiac muscle.

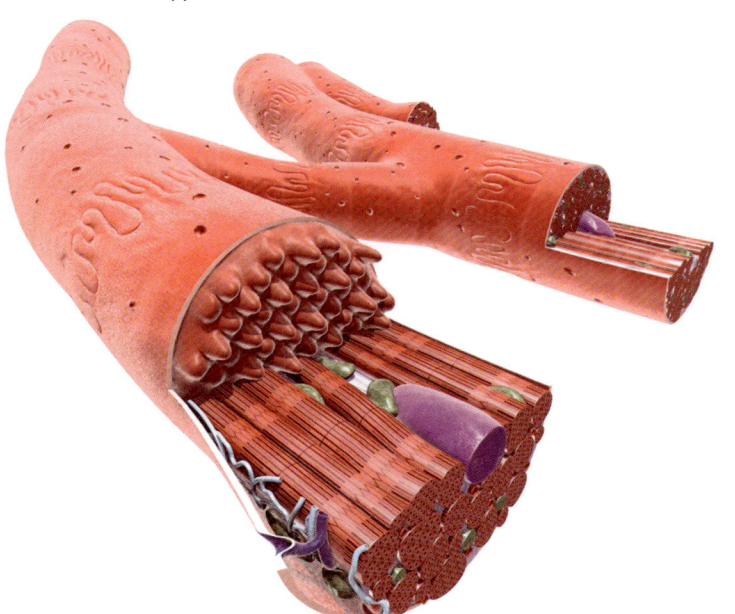

Subject vocabulary

glycogen a polysaccharide composed of many individual glucose units

cardiac muscle muscle type that makes up the heart

intercalated discs membrane projections that form interlocking units between adjoining cardiac muscle cells

General vocabulary

propagation the process of spreading to another area

Figure 15.6 *Illustration showing a small portion of cardiac muscle. Notice the branching between one area of muscle cells and another. There are several individual cardiac muscle cells shown, with two shown in section. The sections are shown with a portion of an intercalated disc cut in half. The sections also show sarcomeres and a large central nucleus (purple)*

The illustration above shows several cardiac muscle cells. Look carefully in one of the sectioned areas and you will see sarcomeres. Remember, sarcomeres are the contracting units of muscle. Individual cardiac muscle cells connect to each other by way of **intercalated discs**. The two muscle cells closest to you in the illustration show what the structure of an intercalated disc looks like. The cell that has been cut in a half-section would have had an opposite shape to the one shown. Thus, the two

Subject vocabulary

intercalate to insert into each other

sinoatrial node a specialized group of cells in the heart that send out spontaneous electrical signals leading to a resting heart rate

atrioventricular (AV) node a specialized group of cells in the heart that receives an impulse from the SA node and then sends an impulse to the ventricles

artificial pacemaker a battery-operated device that regulates heart rate when the SA node fails to do so

systole time period in which a heart chamber is undergoing a contraction

Synonyms

sinoatrial node .... SA node

originating (from) .... starting/coming (from)

General vocabulary

spontaneous something that happens without apparent external cause

---

would fit together and **intercalate**. Cytoplasm and electrical signals for contraction can be passed from cell to cell at these intercalated discs. Notice also that cells form branches. This means that cardiac muscle cells can chemically communicate with each other. This chemical communication is in the form of electrical signals that lead to contractions. All of the cardiac cells of both atria work together as a unit when they contract. Soon after, all of the cardiac cells of both ventricles contract together.

Cardiac muscle cells also contain nuclei and many mitochondria.

Understanding: Signals from the sinoatrial node that cause contraction cannot pass directly from atria to ventricles.

Model sentence: The sinoatrial node results in contraction of the atria only as its signal cannot be directly passed to the ventricles.

You learned in Chapter 6 that the **sinoatrial (SA) node** acts as the natural pacemaker of the heart. The SA node is a grouping of cells located in the right atrium. The impulse **originating** from the SA node only spreads through the atria. This spread is by way of the intercalated discs and numerous branches as described in the previous section. The intercalated discs and branching do not extend down into the muscle tissue of the ventricles.

The ventricles receive their electrical signals from a second node of cells called the **atrioventricular (AV) node**. The AV node is also located in the right atrium of the heart. The AV node does not send a **spontaneous** impulse like the SA node. In other words, the AV node does not act as a natural pacemaker. The AV node waits to receive an impulse from the SA node before sending its own electrical signal.

Application: Use of artificial pacemakers to regulate the heart rate

Some people have a heart condition where the SA node does not send out a signal at an optimum timing. This can lead to a heart rate that is too slow, too fast, or simply irregular. A common treatment is the insertion of a battery-operated device called an artificial pacemaker. The device is implanted under the skin, often in the chest area. The pacemaker will give off a small electrical signal that takes the place of the timing that normally occurs by way of the SA node. Artificial pacemakers have battery lives of about 7 years. At that time, the entire pacemaker is replaced.

Understanding: There is a delay between the arrival and passing on of a stimulus at the atrioventricular node.

Model sentence: The atrioventricular node receives an electrical signal from the sinoatrial node and then delays a short time before sending a signal to the ventricles.

All four chambers of the heart cannot contract at the same time. If this were to happen, the blood would not continue moving in a single useful direction. In order to prevent all four chambers from contracting at the same time, the AV node has a very short delay after receiving a signal from the SA node. This short delay allows both atria to undergo **systole**. Then when the AV node does send its signal, both ventricles will then undergo systole.

Application: Use of defibrillation to treat life-threatening cardiac conditions

During a heart attack, the heart is no longer beating or is beating in a pattern not consistent with a normal cardiac cycle. Defibrillation is a process carried out using a device that delivers an electric shock to the heart. This resets the electric signals and often the heart will begin normal electric activity. When successful, the heart will begin beating normally on its own once the shock has been delivered.

Small portable defibrillators have become common in places where people normally gather. These devices are called automated external defibrillators or AEDs. These devices can be used by anyone as they have built-in audible instructions and include components that are easy to use.

Subject vocabulary

atrioventricular valves valves located between each atrium and ventricle

semilunar valves valves located where blood exits each ventricle

cardiac cycle all of the events that comprise one heartbeat

trace a line drawn by a recording instrument

electrocardiogram a record of the electrical activity of the heart as measured by a device called an electrocardiograph

conducting fibres nerve fibres within and between the ventricles of the heart

Purkinje fibres branches of the main conducting fibres coming from the AV node in the ventricles of the heart

Understanding: This delay allows time for atrial systole before the atrioventricular valves close.

Model sentence: The delay between impulses of the two heart nodes gives enough time for both atria to contract and force blood into the ventricles before the atrioventricular valves close.

Notice the location of the right and left AV valves on the figure to the right. When these two valves are open, blood is able to move from the atria to the ventricles. Atrial systole is the event that completes blood moving into the ventricles for any single heart cycle. Atrial systole is initiated by the SA node and the actual contraction occurs during the short delay by the AV node.

Heart valves open and close based on pressure differences on either side of the valve. After the delay, the contraction of the ventricles raises the blood pressure inside of the ventricles. This increased pressure closes the AV valves to allow the ventricular pressure to increase even more. Eventually, the very high pressure in the ventricles opens the **semilunar valves** and the blood exits the ventricles.

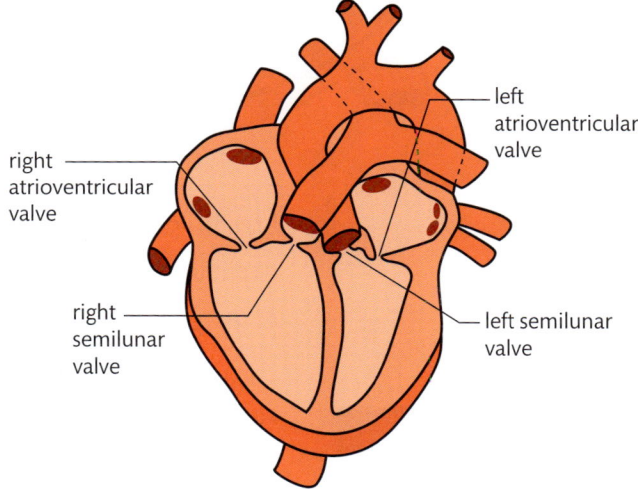

Figure 15.7 *The location of the four heart valves.*

Skill: Mapping of the cardiac cycle to a normal ECG trace

An ECG is the abbreviation for an **electrocardiogram**. An ECG is shown as a graph with electrical activity (voltage) shown on the *y*-axis and time on the *x*-axis. The electrical activity is from the SA and AV nodes.

How to read a normal ECG trace:
- P wave: shows the voltage given off by the SA node
- Point Q: shows the voltage given off by the AV node
- QRS complex: shows the voltage from the AV node spreading down the **conducting fibres** and **Purkinje fibres**
- T wave: the AV node is repolarizing (getting ready to send another impulse).

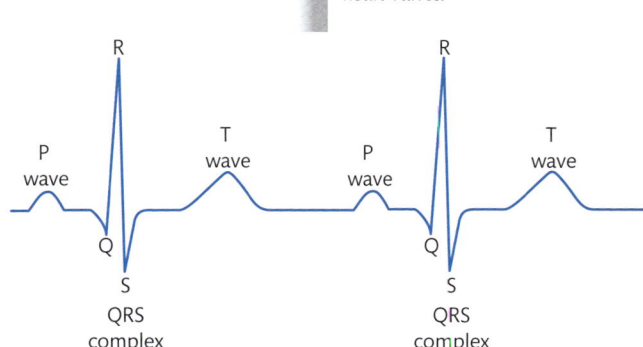

Figure 15.8 *ECG for a normal heart showing two heart cycles*

Understanding: Conducting fibres ensure coordinated contraction of the entire ventricle wall.

Model sentence: All of the muscle cells of the ventricles contract at the same time due to conducting fibres carrying the electrical signal from the atrioventricular node.

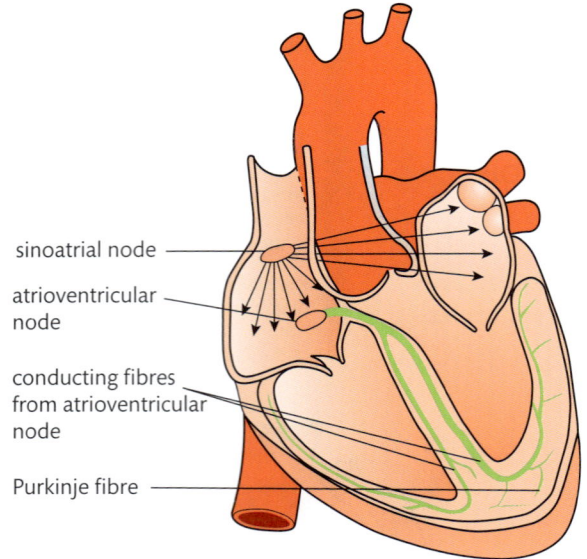

The muscular walls of the ventricles are very thick. This means that there are many more cardiac muscle cells making up the ventricles as compared to the atria. When the SA node sends an impulse the highly branched and intercalated cells spread the electrical signal quickly and both atria contract at the same time. There are too many cells making up the ventricles for cell-to-cell communication only to work in a timely manner. The ventricles also rely on conducting nerve fibres to quickly spread the electrical signal from the AV node.

Figure 15.9 This drawing of the human heart shows the location of the SA node, AV node and the conducting fibres spreading out through the ventricles from the AV node. The black arrows show an electrical signal coming from the SA node. After that there is a time delay before the AV node sends a signal through the conducting fibres to various branches called Purkinje fibres

Understanding: Normal heart sounds are caused by the atrioventricular valves and semilunar valves closing, causing changes in blood flow.

Model sentence: The normal sounds of the heart as heard through a **stethoscope** are caused by the closing of two sets of heart valves.

The sounds of the heart as heard through a stethoscope are often described as a 'lub' sound, followed by a 'dub' sound and then a silence. This same pattern is then repeated over and over. Each single set of sounds represents one heart cycle.

Heart sounds are created by valves closing. The first heart sound, 'lub', is created by the atrioventricular valves closing. There are two of these valves but they close at the same time. Therefore, there is only one sound. The second heart sound, 'dub', is created when both semilunar valves close. Once again, a single sound.

When valves close, the blood is routed in a direction opposite to the newly closed valve. This keeps the blood moving in a direction that is beneficial to body needs.

Hints for success: Use the heart diagrams in the previous sections to trace the flow of blood. Link blood flow to when heart chambers are contracting, valves are opening and closing, and the sounds of the heart.

Subject vocabulary

stethoscope a device used to listen to sounds made within the body

Skill: Interpretation of systolic and diastolic blood pressure measurements

A blood pressure in medical terms is actually two pressures. One is called the systolic pressure and the other the diastolic pressure. A typical example might be:

$$\frac{115 \text{ (systolic pressure)}}{68 \text{ (diastolic pressure)}}$$

These values are read as 115 over 68 (both pressure readings are in mm of Hg)
- Systolic pressure is a measurement of the pressure in arteries when the ventricles of the heart contract (undergo systole).
- Diastolic pressure is a measurement of the pressure when the ventricles are resting and refilling with blood.

Application: Causes and consequences of **hypertension** and thrombosis

Hypertension is a medical condition characterized by having blood pressure that is consistently higher than is considered to be healthy. Hypertension is a condition that typically develops slowly over many years. Loss of **elasticity** in blood vessels is one contributing factor. Another is the build-up of a substance called **plaque**. Plaque is long-term build-up of cholesterol and other substances on the inside wall of arteries. This can greatly decrease the volume of blood that the blood vessel can carry. Arteries blocked with plaque greatly increase the threat of a heart attack or **stroke**.

Thrombosis is a medical condition where a **thrombus** (clot) develops and breaks loose within a blood vessel. Often the origin of a thrombus is an area of plaque build-up. Sometimes a section of plaque breaks away and begins circulating. When this thrombus reaches a blood vessel diameter that it will no longer fit through, it becomes stuck. Two locations where this can become immediately life threatening are:
- in the coronary arteries feeding heart muscle
- in arteries within the lungs.

D.5 Hormones and metabolism

Understanding: **Endocrine glands** secrete **hormones** directly into the bloodstream.

Model sentence: Hormones from endocrine glands travel throughout the body because they are secreted directly into the blood.

The endocrine system is a diverse set of glands in the body. Two things unite this group of glands:

1. All endocrine glands secrete a molecule called a hormone.
2. All hormones are secreted into the bloodstream for delivery to cells of the body.

Cells that are capable of responding to a hormone are called **target cells** (of that hormone). For example in Chapter 11, you learned about **osmoregulation** in the kidneys. Osmoregulation is controlled by a hormone known as antidiuretic hormone (ADH). ADH is a hormone produced by the posterior lobe of the pituitary gland. The pituitary gland is located at the base of the brain. The target tissue of ADH is the collecting ducts of the kidneys. In order for ADH to have an effect on kidney cells it must travel to the kidney by way of the bloodstream. All hormones travel throughout the body by way of the bloodstream.

Subject vocabulary

hypertension high blood pressure

plaque build-up of cholesterol and other substances on the inner wall of arteries

stroke a sudden decrease in blood supply to a portion of the brain

thrombosis a clot that breaks loose and lodges in another smaller blood vessel in the body

thrombus a clot that develops in a blood vessel

endocrine gland a gland that produces a hormone

hormone chemical messenger produced in very small amounts by an endocrine gland

target cell cells that respond to a particular hormone

osmoregulation control mechanism used by an organism to regulate water balance

Synonyms

elasticity .... flexibility

Subject vocabulary

steroid lipid-soluble organic substance, e.g. cholesterol

solubility degree of how readily a substance will dissolve into another substance

transcription the process of creating RNA from DNA

regulatory area a section of DNA that determines whether a particular gene is currently active

Understanding: **Steroid** hormones bind to receptor proteins in the cytoplasm of the target cell to form a receptor–hormone complex.

Model sentence: Hormones classified as steroids enter the cytoplasm and bind to receptor proteins to become a receptor–hormone complex.

Steroid hormones are lipid molecules. Therefore, steroids have the **solubility** properties of lipids. This means that steroid hormones pass directly through the plasma membranes of a cell. You should remember from Chapter 1 that the plasma membrane is also a lipid structure. Once a steroid hormone enters a cell, it bonds to a receptor protein located in the cytoplasm of the cell. This forms a receptor–hormone complex.

Understanding: The receptor–hormone complex promotes the **transcription** of specific genes.

Model sentence: Transcription of specific genes is promoted within a target cell by the receptor–hormone complex.

In the simplest scenario, the receptor–hormone complex next passes through the nuclear membrane. Once inside the nucleus the complex binds to a **regulatory area** of a gene. The receptor–hormone complex acts to promote the activity of certain genes. When a particular gene is promoted by the receptor–hormone complex, the process of transcription is initiated for that gene. Thus, the steroid hormone is able to control the production of protein within a target cell. Examples of naturally occurring steroid hormones are oestrogen, progesterone, and testosterone.

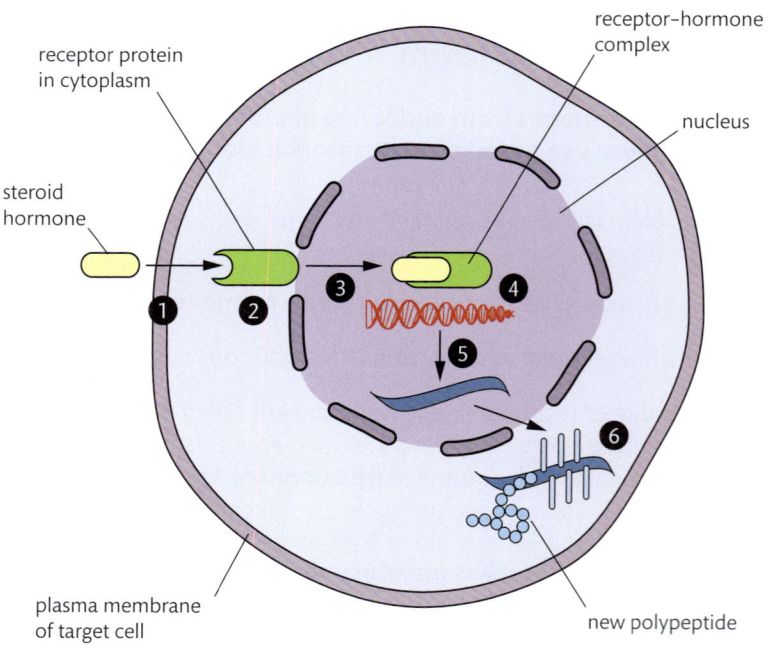

Figure 15.10 An illustrated version of the general mechanism of a steroid hormone. (1) A non-polar (lipid soluble) steroid hormone enters directly through the biphospholipid layer of the plasma membrane. (2) A steroid hormone binds to a receptor protein in the cytoplasm to make a receptor-hormone complex. (3) The receptor-hormone complex enters the nucleus through a nuclear pore. (4) The receptor-hormone complex binds to a specific gene of DNA and, in this example, promotes transcription for this gene. (5) Messenger (m)RNA molecules are synthesized as a result. (6) Ribosomes on the endoplasmic reticulum translate mRNA into a new polypeptide.

Understanding: **Peptide hormones** bind to receptors in the plasma membrane of the target cell.

Model sentence: **Hormones classified as peptide hormones affect target cells by binding to receptors in the plasma membrane.**

Peptide hormones are composed of amino acids. A peptide hormone recognizes a target cell by locating a part of a receptor molecule that extends out of the plasma membrane. The peptide hormone must form a 'fit' with this receptor molecule. This 'fit' is very similar to the way an enzyme and its substrate fit together. There must be a matching, but opposite, complementary shape and set of **charges** between the two molecules.

The receptor molecule extends all the way through the plasma membrane of the target cell. Therefore, a part of the receptor molecule also extends down into the cytoplasm of the cell. This will be important for the action **initiated** by the hormone that will be described in the next section.

Subject vocabulary

peptide hormone a hormone composed of amino acids

charges positive and negative area of molecules as a result of polar covalent bonding and other intramolecular forces

secondary messenger a molecule located on the inside of a plasma membrane that is activated when a peptide hormone binds to a receptor protein

transcription factor a molecule that affects when a gene is synthesizing RNA

Synonyms

initiated......... started/begun

General vocabulary

cascade a sequence of events, each one causing the next

Understanding: Binding of hormones to membrane receptors activates a **cascade** mediated by a second messenger inside the cell.

Model sentence: **When a peptide hormone binds to a membrane receptor it causes a secondary messenger to be activated inside the plasma membrane initiating a cascade of reactions within the cell.**

Assume a peptide hormone and a receptor protein fit each other. The peptide hormone will chemically induce the receptor protein to activate a molecule located on the inside of the plasma membrane. The molecule activated is called a **secondary messenger**. In this way peptide hormones can affect the internal chemistry of the cell without ever entering the cell.

Often the secondary messenger activates one or more other molecules in the cytoplasm. The final messenger molecule will typically do one of two things:

1 Activate an enzyme in the cytoplasm. This promotes one or more reactions that were not occurring before the peptide hormone began this sequence.

2 Activate a **transcription factor** that either promotes or inhibits production of a particular RNA molecule. Protein synthesis is directly affected.

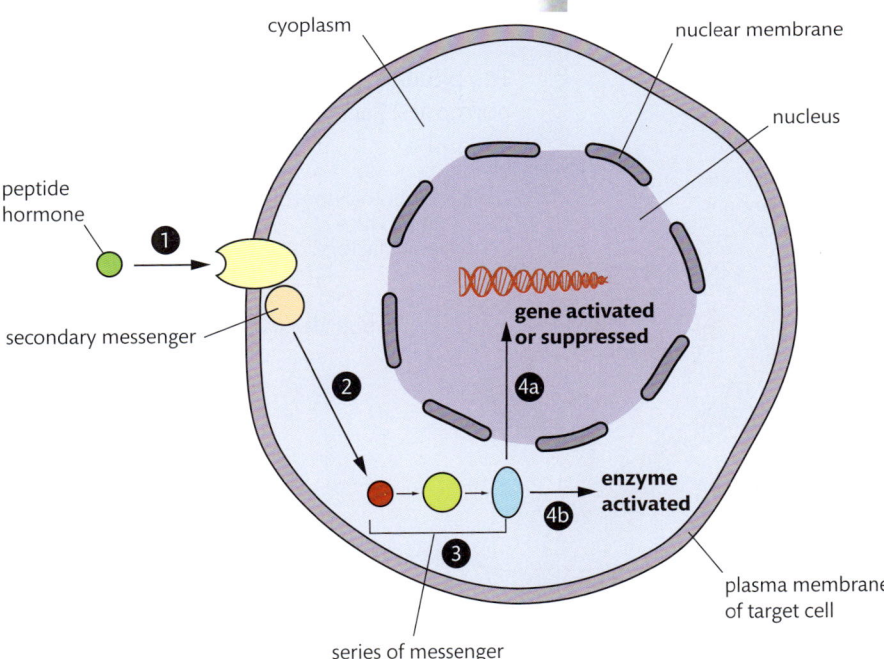

Figure 15.11 An illustrated version of the general mechanism of a peptide hormone. (1) A peptide hormone fits the complementary shape and charge of a receptor protein within the plasma membrane of a target cell. (2) A receptor protein signals the beginning of a cascade of reactions. (3) A series of second messenger molecules is activated. (4a) One possible consequence is a second messenger molecule that promotes or inhibits a gene, leading to more or less of a polypeptide being synthesized. (4b) A second possibility is that an enzyme is activated and a reaction or reaction sequence begins that is catalysed by that activated enzyme

15 Option D: Further human physiology | 343

Hints for success: When distinguishing between steroid and peptide hormones, take note that steroid hormones enter cells and peptide hormones do not enter cells.

Understanding: The **hypothalamus** controls hormone secretion by the anterior and posterior lobes of the pituitary gland.

Model sentence: Hormone secretion by the anterior and posterior lobes of the pituitary gland are controlled by the part of the brain called the hypothalamus.

Subject vocabulary

hypothalamus a region of the brain that controls pituitary gland secretions and other autonomic functions

axon long extension of a neurone that carries an impulse away from cell body

terminal buttons the small knob-like structures at the end of axons that release a neurotransmitter in neurones or a hormone for neurosecretory cells

releasing factors molecules produced and secreted from the hypothalamus that control secretion of hormones from the anterior pituitary gland

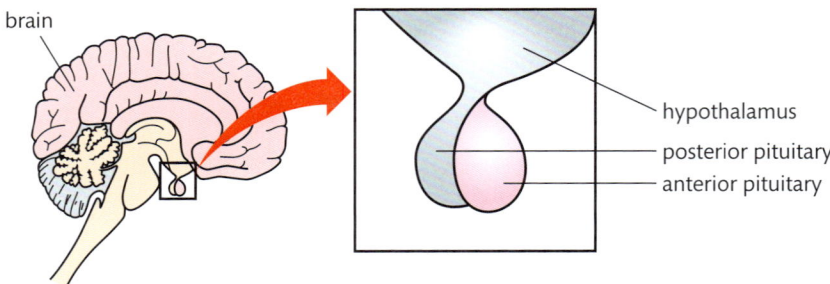

Figure 15.12 *The position of the hypothalamus and pituitary*

The pituitary gland is composed of two lobes. Each lobe secretes a different set of hormones. Each lobe is controlled by the hypothalamus, but in very different ways.

The posterior lobe of the pituitary secretes the two hormones, oxytocin and ADH. These two hormones are produced by cells in the hypothalamus. These cells are called neurosecretory cells. They have relatively long **axons** that extend down into the posterior pituitary. When physiological conditions call for secretion of either oxytocin or ADH, they are secreted from the **terminal buttons** into the blood stream at the ends of these long axons.

The anterior pituitary secretes many hormones. These include growth hormone (GH), prolactin, FSH, and LH among others. The hypothalamus controls the secretion of all anterior pituitary hormones by secretion of its own hormones. These hormones are called **releasing factors** or releasing hormones. The releasing factors from the hypothalamus are directly taken to the anterior pituitary by an interconnecting blood vessel. The hypothalamus controls anterior pituitary secretions by controlling which releasing factors are produced.

Hints for success: In an exam, take note whether a question is asking for location of production or location of secretion of a hormone. The hormones secreted from the posterior pituitary are produced in the hypothalamus.

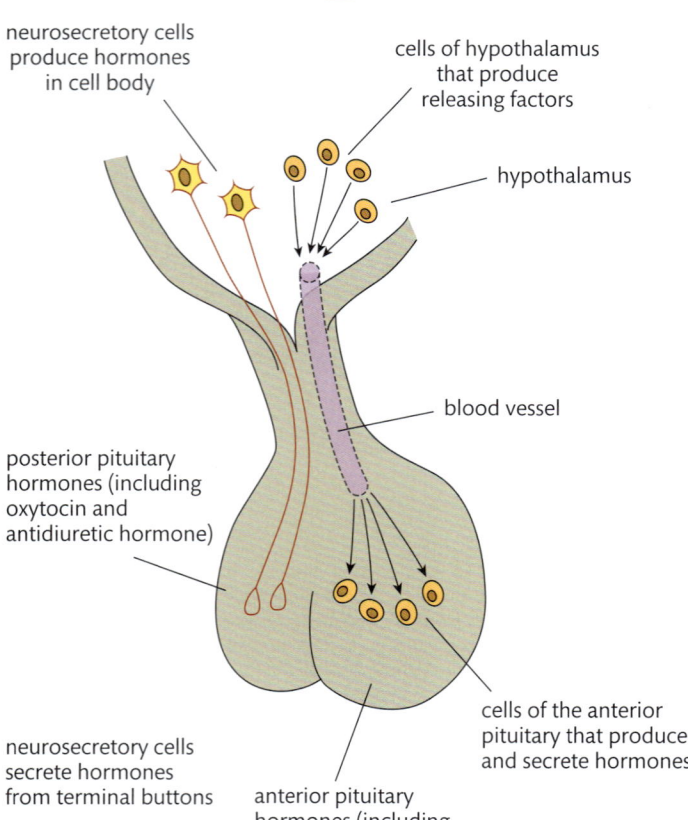

Figure 15.13 *The hypothalamus and pituitary*

344 | D.5 Hormones and metabolism

Understanding: Hormones secreted by the pituitary control growth, developmental changes, reproduction, and homeostasis.

Model sentence: **A variety of body processes are controlled by pituitary gland hormones, including: growth, developmental changes, reproduction, and homeostasis.**

Hormone	Category	Example
growth hormone (GH)	growth	stimulates growth in children and adolescents
FSH and LH	development	these two hormones are necessary for steroid production in both males and females
FSH and LH	reproduction	these two hormones are necessary for oocyte production in females and sperm production in males
ADH	homeostasis	needed for water balance (osmoregulation)

Application: **Some athletes take growth hormones to build muscles**

Even though there is very little research on the dangers involved, some athletes choose to take or inject growth hormones. Many professional sports organizations have banned the use of these substances. Time will tell whether there will be long-term physiological effects from this practice.

Application: **Control of milk secretion by oxytocin and prolactin**

Lactation is production and release of milk by a new mother. During pregnancy, the pituitary hormone, prolactin, stimulates development of milk producing cells in the breasts. The naturally high levels of oestrogen characteristic of a pregnancy inhibit the release of milk. At the time of birth, oxytocin, another hormone from the pituitary is secreted. The increase of oxytocin and the decrease of oestrogen (because of the birth) stimulate milk release. The production of both prolactin and oxytocin is further stimulated by stimulation of the breast nipple from the suckling activity of the newborn. This is an example of positive feedback control of a physiological process.

D.6 Transport of respiratory gases

Understanding: **Oxygen dissociation curves** show the **affinity** of haemoglobin for oxygen.

Model sentence: **Graphs called oxygen dissociation curves show haemoglobin's affinity for oxygen.**

Earlier in this chapter you learned that each **erythrocyte** contains about 250 million haemoglobin molecules. You also learned that a human being has many trillions of erythrocytes circulating in their blood at any given time. Each haemoglobin molecule is composed of four polypeptides, four haem groups with an iron atom at the centre of each **haem group.** An oxygen molecule can bond to each

General vocabulary

adolescent a person who has undergone puberty but has not reached maturity

Subject vocabulary

oxytocin a hormone secreted from the pituitary

prolactin anterior pituitary hormone that stimulates development of milk-producing cells

lactation production and release of breast milk

oxygen dissociation curve a graph that plots partial pressure of oxygen against percentage of haemoglobin saturation

affinity attraction for

haem group the non-protein portion of haemoglobin molecules

Synonyms

erythrocyte .... red blood cell

iron atom. Thus, each haemoglobin molecule is capable of transporting four **oxygen molecules**.

Synonyms

oxygen
molecule........ O_2

Subject vocabulary

saturated all four iron atoms within a single haemoglobin are bonded to an oxygen molecule

sigmoid having a shape like the letter 'S'

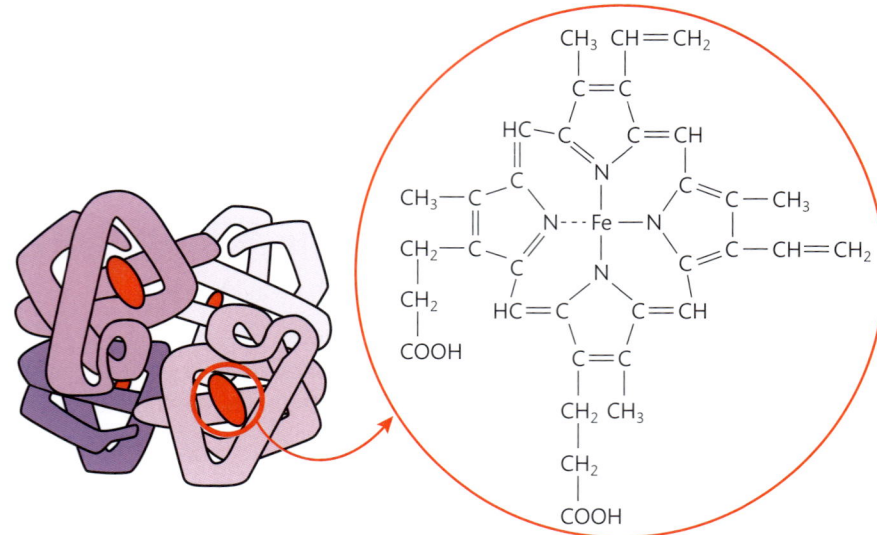

Figure 15.14 *Haemoglobin is a large protein consisting of four polypeptides with a haem group within each. The molecular structure of a haem group is shown on the right. Notice the iron atom at the centre of the molecule*

A graph called an oxygen dissociation curve shows haemoglobin's differing affinities for oxygen. Haemoglobin's affinity for oxygen is dependent on how many oxygen molecules are currently being 'carried'. When an oxygen molecule bonds to haemoglobin, it results in a molecular shape change to the haemoglobin. This change in molecular shape increases the affinity of haemoglobin for oxygen. In other words, haemoglobin that is already carrying three oxygen molecules has the greatest affinity for another oxygen molecule.

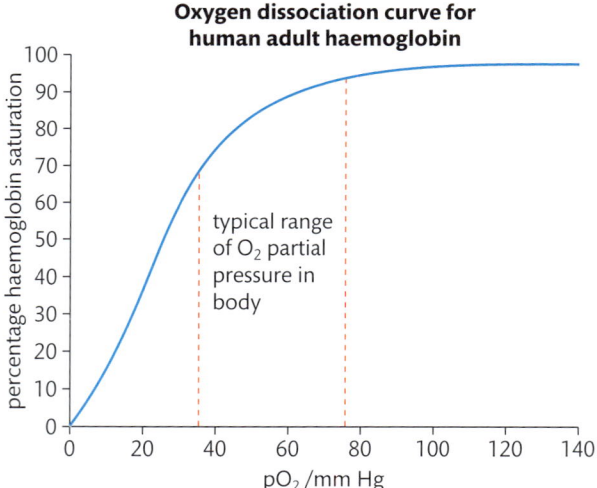

Figure 15.15 *This oxygen dissociation curve shows the range of oxygen partial pressure found in the body*

Notes to help you make sense of this graph:

- The *y*-axis shows percentage of haemoglobin that is **saturated**. This means saturated with oxygen molecules. Haemoglobin is only saturated with oxygen when it is carrying four oxygen molecules.
- The *x*-axis shows partial pressure of oxygen in mm Hg. The partial pressure of a gas (oxygen) is the pressure exerted by a single gas when it is in a mixture of gases. Oxygen is a single gas in the mixture of gases we call air.
- The reason the graph has a **sigmoid shape** ('S' shape) is because of haemoglobin's increase in affinity when already bonded to one or more oxygen molecules.
- The two dotted red lines will help you to better understand when haemoglobin loads oxygen and unloads oxygen. The term used for an oxygen molecule

breaking its bond to haemoglobin is dissociation. This is where these graphs derive their name. The red line on the right shows the partial pressure of oxygen in the lungs. Notice that over 90% of the haemoglobin molecules are saturated with oxygen. The red line on the left shows partial pressure of oxygen typical in body tissues. Notice that some, but not all haemoglobin molecules have given up at least one oxygen molecule to the cells. Saturation of haemoglobin has dropped to slightly less than 70%.

Understanding: Carbon dioxide is transformed in red blood cells into hydrogen carbonate ions.

Model sentence: Within the cytoplasm of red blood cells, carbon dioxide is transformed into hydrogen carbonate ions.

The cytoplasm of red blood cells contains an enzyme called **carbonic anhydrase**. This enzyme catalyses a reaction in which carbon dioxide and water combine to form carbonic acid (H_2CO_3). **Carbonic acid** then separates into a hydrogen carbonate ion and a hydrogen ion.

The hydrogen carbonate ions formed from this reaction exit the red blood cell through specialized protein channels. This is an example of **facilitated diffusion**.

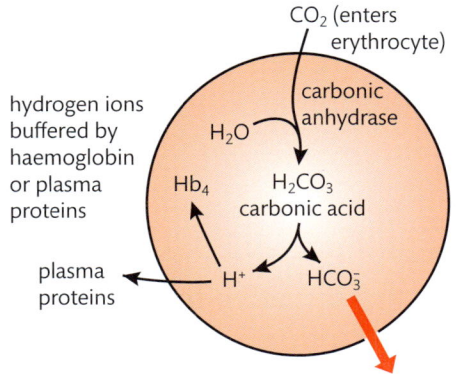

Figure 15.16 The events occurring when carbon dioxide enters a erythrocyte include the formation of carbonic acid and the resulting buffering by haemoglobin and plasma proteins

Subject vocabulary

hydrogen carbonate ions a negatively charged ion made of hydrogen, carbon, and three oxygen atoms

carbonic anhydrase the enzyme that catalyses hydrogen carbonate ion formation in red blood cells

facilitated diffusion diffusion of a substance through protein channels in a membrane

solution a solvent with one or more solutes (in the context used above the solution is referring to blood plasma)

Synonyms

carbonic acid .. H_2CO_3

Understanding: Carbon dioxide is carried in **solution** and bound to haemoglobin in the blood.

Model sentence: Carbon dioxide has various ways of being transported in blood, including being dissolved in blood plasma and bound to haemoglobin.

There are three ways that carbon dioxide is transported in the blood:
- The majority of carbon dioxide undergoes the reaction described in the previous section and becomes hydrogen carbonate ions (HCO_3^-). The majority of these ions diffuse out of erythrocytes into the blood plasma. When in the lung tissues, these ions will convert back to carbon dioxide molecules.
- A small percentage (about 5%) of carbon dioxide simply stays as carbon dioxide and dissolves into the solution of blood plasma.
- Some carbon dioxide (about 10%) enters red blood cells and temporarily binds to haemoglobin.

Subject vocabulary

Bohr shift an effect whereby an increase in carbon dioxide in the blood decreases the affinity of haemoglobin for oxygen

respiring actively engaged in cell respiration

chemoreceptors nervous system receptor cells that are sensitive to one or more chemicals

pH a measure of the acidity or alkalinity of a solution

Understanding: The **Bohr shift** explains the increased release of oxygen by haemoglobin in **respiring** tissues.

Model sentence: In an effect known as the Bohr shift, haemoglobin increases its release of oxygen in tissues that have increased their rate of cell respiration.

Haemoglobin's affinity for oxygen is reduced in an environment where carbon dioxide levels are high. Where in the body are carbon dioxide levels relatively high? Within body tissues that are most actively using cell respiration. The best example would be muscle tissue in a person who is exercising. Since haemoglobin loses some of its affinity for oxygen in active muscle tissue, the haemoglobin gives up more oxygen than it would have otherwise. This effect is called the Bohr shift.

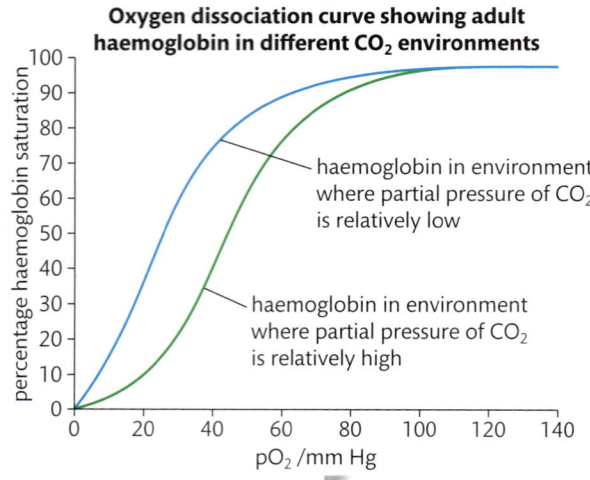

The Bohr shift can be seen on an oxygen dissociation curve by plotting haemoglobin in a non-exercise situation (blue line on left) and haemoglobin while exercising (green line on right). Notice that haemoglobin in body tissues that are exercising has a lower percentage of haemoglobin saturation. The reason for this is that the haemoglobin has given up more of its oxygen to the muscle tissues that need it.

Figure 15.17 The Bohr shift

Understanding: **Chemoreceptors** are sensitive to changes in blood **pH**.

Model sentence: Nervous system receptors called chemoreceptors monitor changes in blood pH.

Let's revisit the equation for production of hydrogen carbonate ions after carbon dioxide enters the blood.

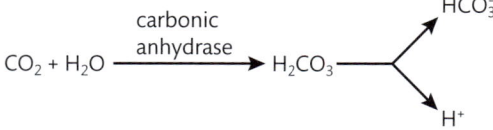

$$CO_2 + H_2O \xrightarrow{\text{carbonic anhydrase}} H_2CO_3 \longrightarrow HCO_3^- + H^+$$

You will notice that there are two products from the overall chemical reaction. One is hydrogen carbonate ions and the other is hydrogen ions. This reaction always produces these two products. When one exercises the rate of formation of these two products increases.

The increased production of hydrogen ions during exercise slightly lowers blood pH. We have very sensitive chemoreceptors that are able to detect even small decreases in blood pH.

Understanding: The **rate of ventilation** is controlled by the **respiratory control centre** in the **medulla oblongata**.

Model sentence: The number of times that we breathe in and out per minute is controlled by an area of the medulla oblongata called the respiratory control centre.

You have probably noticed that you do not have to think about breathing. It is just something that you do. Physiological activities like breathing and heart rate are under control of your autonomic nervous system. These activities do not need to be consciously controlled. Because of the way that the autonomic nervous system works, you do not have to think about the control mechanisms at the conscious level of thought.

The muscles that are involved in breathing (see section 6.4) do need to receive electrical signals from the brain in order to keep up their life maintaining activity. These electrical impulses are coming from an area of your brainstem called the medulla oblongata. Specifically an area called the respiratory control centre. Even when you are sleeping your respiratory control centre is sending out electrical signals. These impulses are going to your diaphragm and other muscles involved in ventilation so that you continue breathing.

Application: **Consequences of high altitude for gas exchange**

In today's world of rapid travel by airlines, it is not uncommon for someone to be living at or near sea level on one day and then find themselves at a high altitude location the next. For example, someone flying from sea level to Quito, Ecuador, would have an altitude increase of about 2800 m in a single day. Air at high altitude locations has a lower pressure than air at sea level. This means the individual molecules within the air are further apart in high altitude locations. When you breathe air in, you are breathing in fewer oxygen molecules at high altitude as compared to lower elevations.

When someone first arrives at a high altitude location, they often feel fatigued from just normal activities like walking or climbing stairs. This is because their body tissues are receiving less oxygen. Other symptoms can include vision problems, nausea, high pulse rate and difficulty in thinking clearly. These symptoms are often called altitude sickness or mountain sickness.

Over time the human body will compensate for the lowered amount of oxygen in a process called acclimatization. The following are involved in the acclimatization process:

- an increase in the number of erythrocytes and haemoglobin
- an increase in capillaries in both muscles and lungs
- an increase in lung volume
- an increase in myoglobin in muscle tissues.

Subject vocabulary

rate of ventilation number of times breathing in and out per unit of time

respiratory control centre the area of the medulla oblongata involved in control of rate of ventilation

medulla oblongata portion of the brainstem that controls many involuntary functions; also known as medulla of the brain

autonomic nervous system that portion of your nervous system that controls unconscious activities

altitude sickness symptoms due to oxygen deprivation at high altitude

myoglobin a protein found within muscles that bonds to an oxygen molecule

General vocabulary

elevation height above sea level

fatigue physical and/or mental tiredness

nausea a feeling of sickness with an urge to vomit

Understanding: During exercise the rate of ventilation changes in response to the amount of CO_2 in the blood.

Model sentence: Exercise results in an increase of carbon dioxide in the bloodstream resulting in an increase in the rate of ventilation.

The chemoreceptors that monitor blood pH are located in the aorta, carotid arteries, and in the medulla oblongata of our brain. Each of these receptors is able to send electrical signals to the respiratory control centre of the medulla oblongata. They do this when the pH of the blood begins to decrease as exercise begins.

When the respiratory control centre receives an electrical signal as a result of a lowered pH, the control centre sends out its own electrical impulses. These impulses go to the muscles that control ventilation. The mechanism of ventilation is not changed (see section 6.4), the rate of ventilation is just increased. The opposite occurs when body activity is lowered and the pH of the blood begins to increase slightly. The respiratory control centre responds by lowering the rate of ventilation.

Application: pH of blood is regulated to stay within the narrow range of 7.35 to 7.45

As you can see, humans have a very narrow range of blood pH. There are two primary homeostatic mechanisms that work to keep us within that range.

1. When our rate of activity increases we produce more hydrogen ions. If a large number of hydrogen ions are left in solution, a large drop in pH can result. Instead, we have molecules that act as buffers. The molecules acting as buffers temporarily bond to the hydrogen ions. This takes the ions out of solution and thus they do not affect the pH of the solution. Two of the most common molecules that act as buffers are haemoglobin and a variety of plasma proteins (see Figure 15.16).

2. Even with the effect of buffering, there will still be a small decrease in blood pH when we exercise. The chemoreceptors in our carotid arteries and medulla oblongata respond to this by increasing our rate of breathing and our heart rate. These two actions work to lower the amount of carbon dioxide in our blood stream. They do this by increasing the rate of carbon dioxide released in our lungs.

Application: Causes and treatments of emphysema

In section 6.4 you learned the mechanism of gas exchange between air in the alveoli of the lungs and respiratory gases travelling in the bloodstream. The tissue making up the alveoli and the small air ducts bringing air in and out is very delicate tissue. Emphysema is a disease where that delicate tissue has been damaged. Often the damage is from long-term cigarette smoking. Over a long exposure, cigarette smoke will result in the destruction of alveoli and their small air ducts. This leaves wide holes where healthy lung tissue once was found. Occasionally there are other causes for emphysema:

- marijuana smoking
- exposure to second-hand smoke
- exposure to some types of air pollution
- exposure to some manufacturing fumes
- exposure to coal or silica dust.

If emphysema is diagnosed early, some lung regeneration is possible due to natural healing. Often the disease is not diagnosed early for a variety of reasons. When

---

Subject vocabulary

aorta the largest artery in the body, taking oxygenated blood away from the left ventricle of the heart

carotid arteries large arteries in the neck that carry oxygenated blood to the brain, face, and neck

homeostatic system environment in which all conditions are steadily maintained

buffer a substance in solution that resists a change in pH

emphysema a lung disease where alveoli become damaged, typically due to smoking

Synonyms

ducts .... tubes

General vocabulary

second-hand smoke smoke inhaled by one person due to the smoke exhaled by another person smoking

the damage is severe, treatment typically centres around slowing further damage by stopping exposure to the causative agent. In addition, some medications can help with symptoms. Many people suffering from severe emphysema need to use additional oxygen from a container. This is given through small tubes into the nostrils.

Understanding: **Foetal haemoglobin** is different from adult haemoglobin allowing the transfer of oxygen in the **placenta** onto the foetal haemoglobin.

Subject vocabulary

foetal haemoglobin haemoglobin produced in a foetus before birth

placenta a structure found in the uterus that allows exchanges of gases, nutrients, and waste products between mother and foetus

placental capillaries blood vessels of the placenta that permit the exchanges of molecules between mother and foetus

Model sentence: Oxygen is transferred from the mother's haemoglobin to foetal haemoglobin because the structure of foetal haemoglobin allows a greater affinity for oxygen.

A foetus produces a different form of haemoglobin as compared to the haemoglobin it will produce after birth. The comparison is often referred to as foetal vs. adult haemoglobin, but the difference is actually pre-birth haemoglobin vs. post-birth haemoglobin. Post-birth haemoglobin will bond to oxygen molecules in the baby's lungs. Pre-birth haemoglobin will be receiving oxygen from the mother's haemoglobin within **placental capillaries**. Each is specialized for its function. Study the oxygen dissociation curve shown to the right that compares foetal haemoglobin to 'adult' haemoglobin.

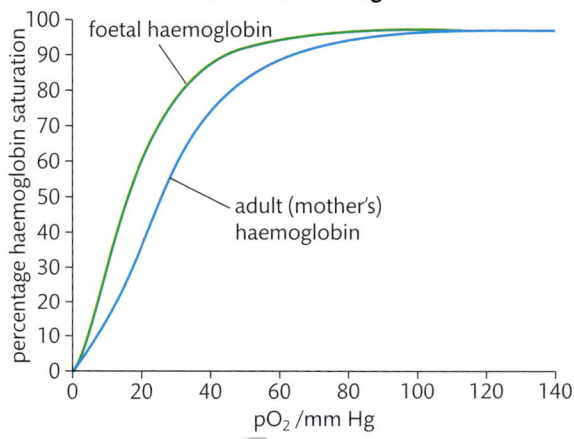

Figure 15.18 Foetal haemoglobin has a greater affinity for oxygen than adult haemoglobin in the range of partial pressures typical of human tissues

You will notice foetal haemoglobin has a higher affinity for oxygen molecules as compared to the mother's haemoglobin over all partial pressures except for very low and very high oxygen partial pressures. Notice that the curve for foetal haemoglobin is consistently to the left of the curve for the mother's haemoglobin. Any point selected on the x-axis shows that adult haemoglobin binds less oxygen at that partial pressure compared with foetal haemoglobin. This means that if an oxygen molecule is available in placental capillaries, foetal haemoglobin is more likely to bind to it than the mother's haemoglobin.

Skill: **Analysis of dissociation curves for haemoglobin and myoglobin**

Myoglobin is a molecule found within your muscle tissues. Unlike haemoglobin, myoglobin is formed of a single polypeptide, single haem group, and iron. Therefore, myoglobin can only bind with a single oxygen molecule. Myoglobin's function is to give up its bound oxygen molecule only when the muscle tissue is nearing an anaerobic condition. This typically only occurs during heavy exercise. You can think of myoglobin as providing a reserve of oxygen to delay the onset of anaerobic cell respiration. In humans, this would be lactic acid production (see Chapters 2 and 8).

You should be able to describe how this graph relates to myoglobin's ability to provide oxygen during heavy exercise.

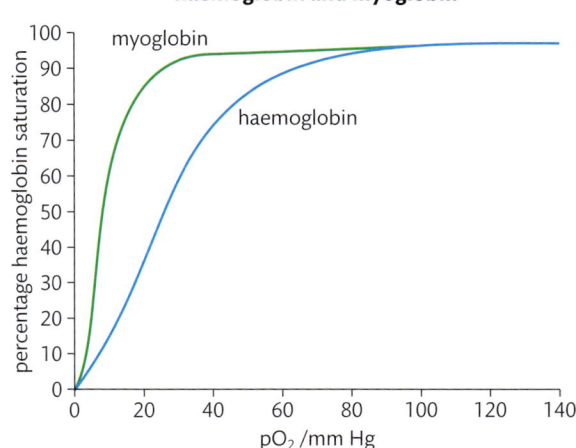

Figure 15.19 Oxygen dissociation curves of haemoglobin and myoglobin. Myoglobin dissociates oxygen only when the oxygen partial pressure gets very low, e.g. in actively respiring muscle tissues

15 Option D: Further human physiology

Internal assessment

Introduction

The internal assessment (IA) task for biology will consist of one investigation/scientific exploration. You will spend 10 hours doing this investigation. Your IA mark will provide 20% of your overall assessment for your IB biology score. The written assignment should be 6–12 pages in length. The individual investigation (II) can be:
- hands-on practical work
- using a spreadsheet for analysis and modelling
- extracting data from a database and analysing it graphically
- a combination of spreadsheet/database work and traditional hands-on investigation.

General information for internal assessment

- The internal assessment requires the application of your biology knowledge and skills.
- Work submitted for your IA must be your own personal work.
- Your instructor will help in making certain you have a thorough understanding of the internal assessment criteria.
- The IB animal experimentation policy must be followed.
- Your instructor will provide support and general guidance throughout the IA process.
- Your instructor may provide advice on the first draft of your IA product.
- Your instructor must be able to confirm that what you submit for your IA is your own work.

Internal assessment criteria

The following is a list of the five criteria used to assess the report of your individual investigation. Included are the total marks and the weighting for each criterion.

Criterion	Criterion total marks	Criterion weighting toward final mark
personal engagement	2	8%
exploration	6	25%
analysis	6	25%
evaluation	6	25%
communication	4	17%

Guidance on getting your individual investigation started

1 Find a topic and research question that interests you. Your instructor will usually provide suggestions on areas in biology from which to choose appropriate topics or research questions.

2 Be certain you have a purpose in mind when designing your independent investigation.

3 A research question may be as simple as, 'What is the influence of X on Y?', where X and Y are factors or variables that can be measured, controlled, or counted.

4 Be certain that anything mentioned in your research question can be measured using materials and techniques available to you in the school's lab.

5 Be precise in the writing of your research question.

6 Any organism or organisms used must be referred to by their scientific names.

7 Consider the time you have available in the planning of the independent investigation.

8 The independent or manipulated variable must be carefully considered before beginning the procedure for your independent investigation. Considerations for the independent variable are listed below.
- The independent variable is what you are testing the effects of in your experiment.
- The independent variable differs from one part of the experiment to another.
- Example: You would use a range of five different concentrations of a particular fertilizer to determine the fertilizer's effects on a particular plant's growth.

9 The dependent or measured variable is whatever you will be measuring as the result of your investigation.
- The dependent variable measures the changes in the experiment due to the variations of the independent variable.
- The design of the table into which the measured results of the experiment will be placed is extremely important.

10 The controlled variables are the things that are kept the same in all parts of the experiment.
- The controlled variables ensure a proper and meaningful experimental procedure.
- The controlled variables ensure that only the independent variable really is responsible for any changes recorded.
- A list of those controlled items which would have made a significant difference in the results should be presented.

11 Consider the number of samples you will use in your independent investigation. An adequate sample size is essential to be able to generate meaningful data. It is suggested you have at least five samples for each of the five variations of the investigation's independent variable.

12 It is expected that there will be some consideration of safety, ethics, and environmental impact. Consent forms will be expected where human volunteers are used in the protocol.

13 The procedure for your individual investigation may be based on a well-known procedure. However, it should be modified to represent a personal design and approach which will allow the collection of sufficient and reliable data.

14 Be as precise and as concise as possible in the writing of your procedure. Some things to consider are:

- The description of the steps of your procedure should be fully understandable to another person.
- Include the independent, dependent, and controlled variables in the writing of the procedure. All three of these variable types must be clearly stated in the procedure.
- Glassware, such as beakers and flasks, used should be described in the procedure to indicate volume and specific type. Standard sizes of test tubes used are usually sufficient. Test tubes used which possess unique characteristics should be fully described.
- Indicate safety measures within the procedure. Include how hot objects are to be handled. Explain any equipment used for cutting. Include the safe procedure for using any cutting or sharp instruments. Include safe procedures for handling harmful chemicals.
- Precise concentrations of any chemical solutions must be included within the procedure. Examples of concentrations may be % or moles per litre. Volumes used should be stated in ml or appropriate SI units.
- Be sure to include comments about anything in your investigation that could have an impact on the environment such as how you will properly dispose of any chemicals used.
- All measuring devices will need to be included in the procedure. This will include balances, electronic probes, any interface for electronic probes, thermometers, etc. Any unique use of any measuring device will need to be explained in the procedure.

Internal assessment criteria details

Each internal assessment criterion is presented in this section with the top-level descriptor for the maximum points. Guidance will be provided after each internal assessment criterion to help you in achieving the maximum marks possible.

Personal engagement

Marks	Top-level descriptors
2	• A personal approach is clearly evident within the investigation. • A clear explanation of the reason for choosing the topic and research question is presented. • There is clear personal interest, creativity in designing the experiment, and obvious initiative in the implementation of the investigation.

You will need to explain why you are willing to devote the suggested 10 hours of work into your specific topic and research question. This explanation may include background information involving the particular research question. Include a description as to why the investigation is significant to you. Be certain to include modifications in available procedures that indicate creativity on your part in your investigation of the research question.

Exploration

Marks	Top-level descriptors
6	• Topic and research question are clearly stated. The research question is appropriate for this higher level investigation. • Background information is provided so a clear understanding of the research question is possible. The background information also reinforces the significance of the investigation to the student. • The procedure for the investigation is directly related to the research question. All factors and variables are presented which could have a significant effect on the procedure's outcome. The procedure will lead to the gathering of data which will bring about a proper conclusion in relationship to the research question. • Safety and ethical considerations are apparent in the procedure. Any environmental issues involving the procedure are discussed.

The exploration criterion presents a major task. That task is to ensure the research question and the procedure for the investigation are at the proper level. This requires a thorough presentation of background information which has allowed the development of a focused research question. The procedure is an extremely important part of this criterion. You will need to modify any existing procedures you find in your research so that a unique approach is presented in the search to address the research question. The number of samples used to collect data must be adequate. It is essential that all factors which may have an effect on the investigation outcome are accounted for and discussed. Be certain to keep a proper record of all sources used in this phase and all other phases, as each will need to be presented in the report bibliography. All equipment used in the experimental phase must be properly named and described for a chance at a top mark in this criterion. Describe fully any unique ways in which equipment is used in your procedure.

Analysis

Marks	Top-level descriptors
6	- Both quantitative and qualitative data are presented which allow a relevant and valid conclusion to the research question. This includes raw and processed data. - The data presented are of sufficient amount and accuracy to allow a proper conclusion to the research question. Data are presented appropriately in visual forms including tables and graphs. - Any and all uncertainties are presented completely and appropriately. - Data processing indicates a proper relevance to the research question. The processed data allow a logical conclusion to the research question.

results
- qualitative
  - drawings, diagrams, annotated photos
  - descriptions of things that cannot be expressed in numbers
- quantitative
  - raw data with units and degrees of precision
  - processed data
    - calculations
    - graphs and trendlines
    - charts and tables
  - comments about limitations and weaknesses

This criterion asks to what extent your report provides evidence that you have selected, processed, analysed, and interpreted the data in the appropriate way to reach a valid conclusion to the research question. Raw data presented must include uncertainties. Both quantitative and qualitative data should be presented. Any tables presented should include a title and number. Rows and columns in the tables should be neat and orderly to allow easy interpretation. Headings of each column should include units and the degree of precision. All entries in each cell of the table should reflect the degree of precision at the heading of each column. All entries in each cell of the table should have the same number of decimal places. An appropriate method for analysing the data should be selected. Graphs presented must be proper, beginning with the independent variable being represented on the *x*-axis and the dependent variable being represented on the *y*-axis. Axes must be properly labelled with uncertainties included. Proper titles and numbers must be given for each graph. Statistical tests used must be appropriate so that a valid conclusion in relation to the research question may be deduced. Outliers should not be excluded from the processing without good reason and explanation.

Evaluation

Marks	Top-level descriptors
6	- The conclusion is detailed and is directly related to the research question. There is obvious use of data to justify the conclusion. A logical deduction from the data presented allows a valid conclusion to the research question.
- The conclusion is fully explained with adequate reference to data collected and presented.
- A detailed discussion of the strengths and weaknesses of the procedure is presented.
- Suggestions that may bring about a more valid conclusion are included. Methods used are analysed in relation to the accuracy and reliability of data obtained in the procedure. Modifications involving the procedures utilized for future research are presented along with their justification.

This criterion assesses your work by examining your ability to provide evidence that you have selected, processed, analysed, and interpreted the data to support your conclusion. You must show your conclusion is justified by the data you have collected. You should research similar investigations carried out by scientists and published in accepted journals. This will possibly increase the credibility and reliability of your data and conclusion. Be certain to include the sources researched in your bibliography. Comparing your data to accepted scientific theory might be necessary if you cannot find similar studies to your investigation in journals. It is important to discuss your conclusion in relationship to the hypothesis you presented early in the report. Use terms such as 'confirmed by data' or 'refuted by data' to relate your conclusion to the earlier presented hypothesis. Describe any unexpected results such as outliers in the data or any surprises in the outcome. Address how your data and conclusions relate to the theory you have learned in the biology classroom.

Communication

Marks	Top-level descriptors
4	• The report is clearly focused. The process and outcomes are clearly stated. • The information presented in the report is all relevant and coherent. • Information presented demonstrates conciseness. The information is clear, understandable, and to the point. Only information relevant and essential to the research question and conclusion is presented. • Proper terms are used to describe the science of the paper. Proper names of any organisms are provided. All equipment is named and described appropriately. • Labels, decimals places, headings, titles, etc., are all presented in a proper scientific manner. • The bibliography is presented in an accepted manner. All sources used in any manner in the report are presented in the bibliography. There is a minimum of sources mentioned which are not directly used in the report.

Write your report with these terms in mind:

- clear
- concise
- logical.

These terms will help you produce a report in which you effectively communicate with your reader. Be certain to read over the procedure before submitting the final product to ensure someone else could easily repeat your procedure. It is especially important that someone else would get similar results as you if they carried out your stated procedure. Make certain your data analysis is stated, so it is obvious why and how you processed your data. Any photographs included should be annotated. The photographs must include the source if they are not your own. Photographs which are yours may simply be labelled, 'author's photo'. The terminology used throughout the report should be consistent and scientifically acceptable.

Final internal assessment suggestions

Lab reports should be written using an impersonal style. This means that words such as 'I', 'we', 'my', and 'us' should be avoided. For example, instead of saying 'Next, I added soap to the Petri dish', you should write 'Next, soap was added to the Petri dish'. The phrase 'my hypothesis' should be rewritten as 'the hypothesis'. To avoid using 'I', say things like 'it was noticed that ...' instead of 'I noticed that ...'. Likewise, 'It is my personal opinion that ...' should be written as 'It is the investigator's personal opinion that ...'.

Proofread carefully before submitting the final report. Follow any general advice provided by your teacher after they read over your first draft. Be mindful that a 6–12 page report is expected. This page limit does not mean using a small font size or miniature graphs to fit the limit. It is also important to note this project is to involve roughly 10 hours of work on your part. Be certain your report reflects properly the suggested page length and time spent.

You should feel extremely proud as you turn in your final report!

Biology extended essay

Introduction

One of the requirements of the IB Diploma is to write an extended essay. An extended essay is an in-depth study of a limited topic within a particular subject area. It provides the opportunity to carry out independent research within a subject of your choice. Biology is a subject often selected by students for their extended essay. It is a popular subject because many of the topics studied in IB Biology stimulate further research ideas in students. Laboratory work carried out in the IB Biology course also provides a base for student ideas involving possible research questions. A good research question is essential for extended essay success.

General guidelines for all extended essays

Extended essays in all subjects have the following guidelines:

- an upper word limit of 4000 words which does not include the abstract, the bibliography, the contents page, appendices, or any labelling or captioning of graphs, diagrams, illustrations or tables
- should involve a recommended 40 hours of student work
- final product is externally assessed using published criteria
- each student is allocated a faculty member with extended essay training who will provide general guidance for the project
- schools set deadlines based on each school's particular circumstances
- it should represent a unique approach to addressing a specific research question
- it must be independent research
- select a topic with a research question which is of interest to you and be certain to show that interest in the writing of the paper.

General guidelines for biology extended essays

- Most successful biology extended essays involve some sort of independent, hands-on experimental work along with literature-based research.
- The extended essay should include a detailed procedure section representing the exact steps carried out in the experimental work. This section is known as the protocol.
- Some biology extended essays that are mostly literature based do well. These literature-based extended essays in biology should include a unique analysis of raw data generated by reputable protocols and procedures.
- Any research involving organisms must be ethical. Any animal research must follow the IB published guidelines concerning the use of animals in experimental procedures.
- Extended essays based on experimental or practical work at a laboratory outside the school must have a cover letter submitted with the essay detailing the student's role in the protocol design. This letter must also specifically describe any guidance received while in this type of situation. This is especially important when the research is done at a university or research institution.
- For safety and/or academic honesty reasons, some schools do not allow students to work outside the school, so check with your teacher.

Suggested steps toward a successful project

1. Initial research and planning
   a. Decide on your subject of interest. Pick something you are very enthusiastic about, because you will need to stay motivated for the entire process.
   b. Think of potential research questions.
   c. A biology extended essay must have a biological focus. It must directly relate to an organism in some specific way.
   d. IB states clearly that biology topics dealing with symptoms and treatment of particular human diseases are very rarely the subject of successful extended essays.
   e. Topics dealing with ethical issues, different general approaches to medical treatments, and surveys involving attitudes or opinions concerning science research are rarely successful biology extended essays.
   f. Meet with your faculty supervisor to discuss possible topics and research questions.
   g. One of the most important functions of the faculty supervisor is help in developing a proper research question for the extended essay
   h. Be sure to read the general criteria in the Extended Essay Guide as well as the criteria that are specific to biology. It is also a good idea to read past extended essays to see what they are like.

2. Continued research involving the chosen research question
   a. Research should involve a survey of the topic literature keeping a detailed account of the sources from which ideas and/or data are used.
   b. Plan your procedure for any experimental work.
   c. Discuss your research and procedure with your faculty supervisor.
   d. It may be necessary to refine the topic and research question as more information is gathered. The proper focus of the research question is essential. Always check with your supervisor before making any changes to the research question.

3. Experimental work
   a. Make certain the experimental procedure is safe and ethical in the opinion of your faculty supervisor before beginning the procedure.
   b. Arrange for all necessary equipment, chemicals, and specific needs before beginning the experimental work. This may involve sources outside of your school. Be certain all sources of materials outside your school are acceptable to your faculty supervisor.
   c. It is extremely important to consider the independent variables, the dependent variables, and the controlled variables in your procedure or procedures.
   d. An essential part of any experimental work involves an adequate sample size. Sample size is important and should be discussed with your faculty supervisor.
   e. Control groups and experimental groups must be carefully considered.
   f. A plan should be in place for the recording of raw data before the procedure ever begins. Qualitative data and quantitative data should both be considered in the data collection and recording stage.
   g. Processing and presentation of data are essential parts of the experimental work. Careful consideration should be given to tables, graphs, and statistical tests so that data will allow meaningful and proper conclusions.
   h. Your faculty supervisor may give general suggestions throughout this experimental work.

4   Writing the paper

   a   Your essay should have a structure which allows for an acceptable and appropriate presentation. An acceptable extended essay organisation is:
   - Title page
   - Abstract
   - Table of contents
   - Introduction with research question stated early and clearly
   - Hypothesis and explanation of hypothesis
   - Background information (keep this precise and **concise** rather than **exhaustive**)
   - Presentation of variables
   - Materials used
   - Protocol of experimental procedures
   - Data collection and presentation
   - Data analysis
   - Evaluation
   - Conclusion
   - Bibliography
   - Appendix (optional – may include details of protocols, raw data, or any calculations of the raw data. It is important to note that the paper should be sufficient without the presence of an appendix.)

   b   A first draft should be submitted to your faculty supervisor so that general directions may be provided in the writing of the final draft.
   c   The first draft should be checked against the IB marking criteria by you and your supervisor to make certain of a high mark.
   d   The style of the bibliography should be one used at your school. There is not a specific form of bibliography to use. It is important that some reference in the paper is made toward each bibliography source provided. Information to access online sources used must be appropriate and complete.

5   Final paper stage

   a   Make changes generally suggested in the first draft by your faculty supervisor.
   b   Proofreading is essential.
   c   Double-check your final paper against the 'formal presentation' criterion in the extended essay marking criteria.
   d   Arrange a meeting with your faculty supervisor to turn it into the final paper. You and your supervisor should go over the final paper together making certain the major sections have been included.

Synonyms

concise .... short

General Vocabulary

exhaustive very thorough and complete

The extended essay criteria and advice to achieve high marks for each criterion

Criterion	Advice
Research question – 2 marks	- A good research question is essential to a good extended essay. It should be stated early in the introduction and should be focused for a 4000 word essay. - Adequate time and thought must be put into writing the research question. - The research question should lend itself to discussion and even debate. This allows you to ultimately present a proper conclusion after the presentation of sound arguments and data concerning the research question.
Introduction – 2 marks	- This should provide an explanation of the research question. - The introduction should include discussion of the significance of the research question.

Investigation – 4 marks	- The procedure is the key.
	  - Is it unique?
	  - Does it allow for adequate data collection?
	  - Are controls used?
	  - Is the procedure truly biological in nature?
	  - Is the procedure relevant to the research question?
	- If the paper has a library-based component, this criterion involves a detailed look at how the data to be analysed were obtained.
	- Look at a variety of sources to arrive at a proper investigation approach.
	- Be certain the investigation will allow gathering of data which are relevant to the research question.

Knowledge and understanding of the topic studied – 4 marks	- The essay must show a thorough understanding of the topic. - Your essay should flow in a logical way toward the development of a proper conclusion concerning the research question. - Have you shown that you clearly understand all aspects of the essay? - Do your analyses represent an obvious understanding? - Any diagrams used should be explained to demonstrate their meaning to the research question and conclusion.
Reasoned argument – 4 marks	- In your search to confirm your hypothesis, are you logical and methodical in your approach and explanation? - Is a convincing argument presented? - All arguments or data presented must relate logically to the research question. - It is wise to present alternative views as you develop your argument.

Criterion	Advice
Application of analytical and evaluative skills – 4 marks	• Has there been careful analysis of all sources used in the essay? • Have all aspects of the experiment been evaluated for appropriateness? • Is the presentation of data logical? • Has there been adequate data analysis? • All sources used and cited should include validation. • All tables and graphs must be presented appropriately. • All tables and graphs must relate to the research question and to the conclusion.
Use of language appropriate to the subject – 4 marks	• Is the language appropriate to the topic and is it correctly used? • Is it clear and precise? • Does the terminology demonstrate your level of understanding? • Provide a definition for all terms which are essential to your procedure and to your development of a proper conclusion.
Conclusion – 2 marks	• Does the conclusion flow logically from the arguments in the essay? • Is the conclusion relevant to the research question and does it relate to the original hypothesis? • Does the conclusion include unresolved questions and potential future research? • Do not introduce any new arguments or content in your conclusion. • Limitations concerning the validity of your conclusion should be mentioned.
Formal presentation – 4 marks	• This includes elements such as title page, table of contents, page numbers, appropriate illustrations, proper citations and bibliography, and appropriate appendices, if used.

Abstract – 2 marks	• This is written last and includes three elements:
	  • research question
	  • investigative approach
	  • conclusion.
	• Is it within 300 words?

Holistic judgment – 4 marks	• This criterion is used to reward creative and unique approaches. • It also involves depth of understanding, insight, and apparent interest in the topic. • There should be a wide range of sources used in the essay as this indicates interest in the topic. • Make certain the conclusion is well supported with alternative possibilities discussed. • Sources should not just be from the internet. A range of reputable scientific journals and views should be included.

Final concerns for your extended essay

1. Be careful concerning plagiarism. Presenting someone else's ideas or work as your own is plagiarism. Be certain to give proper credit to all people whose ideas or work has been used in any way in your extended essay. A useful rule to follow: when in doubt, cite.

2. Your title page should include:
   - Title in the middle of the page. Many students use their research question as a title but this is not necessary and it often makes for a very long title to write on the cover sheet. Invent a shorter title and put your research question under it as a subtitle.
   - Your full name, candidate number, and date.
   - Word count – within the 4000 limit. To find the word count using Microsoft Word, select the text from the beginning of your introduction to the end of the conclusion and choose 'Statistics' from the 'Tools' menu. Un-tick the box that says to 'Include footnotes'. Headings and legends can be subtracted, too.

3. The abstract goes after the title page and should only be written once the essay is finished. It has specific requirements. Be certain it is not over the 300 word limit. Its word count is not included in the 4000 word count for the extended essay. The abstract is placed immediately after the title page in the final paper.

4. After the abstract is the table of contents, then the introduction. The introduction should state the research question early and clearly.

5. The introduction must present a strong reasoning for pursuing a conclusion to the presented research question. State clearly why the research question is significant for your extended essay.

6. Any experimental procedures should be clearly and appropriately presented in a way they can be easily repeated.

7. Show that ethical and safety factors have been thoroughly addressed.

8. Pages should be clearly numbered. The title page is not numbered. Sections of the paper should be clearly and appropriately labelled.

9. Citations, such as footnotes or in-line citations, must be proper and consistent. Sources not specifically used in the paper should be kept to a minimum and included in a 'Further reading' section after the bibliography.

10. All visual presentations must be clear, labelled appropriately, and must relate directly to the research question and conclusion.

11. The conclusion must be clearly related to the research question. Limitations to the conclusion should be discussed. It is suggested that a brief plan for possible further development of your research question is presented.

12. Any appendices used must be appropriate. Check with your supervisor for what should and should not go into an appendix.

Viva voce

The completion of your extended essay is signified by the *viva voce* (concluding interview). This is a 10 to 15 minute interview with your faculty supervisor. It provides an opportunity to reflect on successes and what has been learned.

Enjoy your research.

Index

A

A-B-O blood group 211
absorption of food 119-21, 332
absorption spectrum 52, 53
acetyl coenzyme A 163-4
acetylcholine 136
actin 220-1
action potential 135, 263
action spectrum 52, 53
activation energy 36, 158
active site 36
active transport 15-16, 134-5, 224
adaptations 103-4
adaptive radiation 99-100, 208
addiction 270
ADH 225-6
adipose tissue 138
aerobic cell respiration 49, 163-4
agricultural biotechnology 74-5, 282-8
air monitoring stations 91
albumin 336
algal blooms 320
alien species 310
alleles 55
  dominant/recessive 65, 67-70
  frequency 206-7, 210
allergy 213-14
Allium speciation 209
alpha helices 155
altitude sickness 349
alveoli 130-1
Amflora potato 284
amino acids
  cladistics 114
  essential 327
  polypeptide formation 32, 34, 35
  primary structure of protein 155
amniocentesis 64
amphetamines 268
anabolism 26, 157
anaerobic cell respiration 48-9
anaerobic microbes 86
anaesthetics 267
analogous traits 115, 116
ancestry 114
anorexia 328
antagonistic muscle action 133, 218-19
antibiotics 129
  resistance to 107, 129, 291
antibodies 128, 211-16
anticodon 46
antigens 128, 211, 215
anti-malarial drugs 161
antithrombin 295
aphid stylets 188
appetite 138, 328
Archaea 109
arteries 121-2, 123
artificial pacemakers 338
artificial selection 99
ascorbic acid 326

Aspergillus niger 280
ATP
  cell respiration 47-9
  chemiosmosis 167, 172-3
  glycolysis 163
  muscle contraction 221
  photosynthesis 170, 175, 176
ATP synthase 167, 172-3
atria 121
atrioventricular node 338
atrioventricular valves 339
autonomic nervous system 241-2
autoradiography 57
autosomes 60
autotrophs 78-9, 85, 86, 276
auxin efflux pumps 191
auxins 190, 191-2
axons 133-4, 236

B

B lymphocytes 212, 213
bacteriophages 292
balance 254
batch culture techniques 279, 280 281
behaviour
  ethology 271-5
  innate 255-9, 272-5
  learned 259-62, 272-5
benzene degradation 289
beta pleated sheets 155
bile 334, 335
binary fission 8
binomial nomenclature 107-8, 110
biodiversity
  classification 107-13
  conservation 312-15
biofilms 290-2
biofuels 88
biogas 278-9
bioinformatics 161, 284, 296-301
biomagnification 311
biomarkers 294, 295
biomass 85, 88, 307
biomes 308
biopharming 295
bioremediation 288-9
biotechnology
  environmental protection 288-92
  genetic modification 72-7, 282-8, 295
  in medicine 292-6
  microorganisms in industrial processes 276-82
biotic index 313
bipolar neurones 249, 252
birds
  blackcap migration 272-3
  blue tits feeding from milk bottles 272
  captive breeding of California condor 314
  courtship in birds of paradise 274-5
  Darwin's finches 100, 106

  inheritance and learning of birdsong 260
birth 233
blackcap migration 272-3
BLAST 298, 299
blastocysts 231
blood clotting 127
blood glucose control 137
blood pH 348, 350
blood pressure 122, 340-1
blood system 121-6
blood transfusion 211-12
blue tits 272
body mass index 31
body temperature control 138
Bohr shift 348
bones 217
bound ribosomes 154
Bowman's capsule 223
brain
  contralateral processing 245-6, 250-1
  functional specialization 239-47
  heart rate control 126, 240
  plasticity 237-8
brainstem 240
breathing 130-3, 349
Broca's area 244
bronchi 131
bronchioles 131
Bt corn 74-5
bulbs 184

C

Cairns, John 57
calcium carbonate 89
calcium ions 221
California condor 314
Calvin cycle 175-7
CAM plants 179
cancer 19, 23, 71, 132
capillaries 122-3
captive breeding 314
capture-mark-release-recapture method 316-17
carbohydrates
  in living things 25
  molecular biology 29-31
  photosynthesis 52
carbon bonds 24
carbon cycling 85-91
carbon dioxide
  carbon cycling 85-6, 87, 88
  climate change 92, 93, 95, 96
  photosynthesis 52, 53
  transport in blood 347
  ventilation 130
carbon fixation (Calvin) cycle 175-7
carbon fluxes 89-90
cardiac muscle 337-8
carrying capacity 318
catabolism 26, 157
catalysis 25-6, 36

cell body 133–4
cell cycle 22
cell theory 2
cells
　differentiation 4–5
　division 19–23
　drawings of 4, 8, 9, 10
　membrane structure 11–14
　membrane transport 15–17
　origin 17–19
　respiration 47–50, 84, 86, 161–9
　surface area to volume ratio 3
　ultrastructure 6–11
central nervous system (CNS) 236
central pattern generators 240
cerebellum 240
cerebral cortex 239, 242–3
cerebral hemispheres 239, 244–6
Chase, Martha 144
chemical energy 83
chemiosmosis 167, 172–3, 186
chemoreceptors 247–8, 348
Chernobyl accident 71
chi-squared test 80, 204–6
chiasma 198
chlorophyll 51, 52, 171
chloroplasts 169, 170, 177
cholera 333
cholesterol 13–14, 326
cholinergic synapses 136
chorionic villus sampling 64
chromatograph 51
chromosomes 5, 20, 54, 56–60, 143, 197
　abnormalities 63–4
circadian rhythms 138–9
circulation of blood 124
circumscription 110
cis isomers 30–1
citric acid production 280
clade 114
cladistics 114–18
cladograms 116–17, 300
classical conditioning 258–9
classification of species 107–13
climate change 92–7
climographs 308
clones 76–7
clotting factors 127
co-dominant alleles 67–70
coal 87–8
cocaine 268
cochlea 252, 253
cochlear implants 254
codons 17, 45, 46
coho salmon 273–4
collecting duct 225–6
colour blindness 70, 200, 250
colour vision 251–2
communities
　ecosystems and 81–2, 306–10
　species and 80–1, 302–5
competitive exclusion principle 305, 310

complementary base pairs 40, 41
concentrations of solute 16–17
condensation reaction 26
conditioning
　classical (reflex) 258–9
　operant 260–1
cone cells 248, 249, 251–2
conservation of biodiversity 312–15
consumers 79
continuous culture techniques 279, 280 281
continuous variation 203–4
contractile sarcomeres 220
contralateral processing 245–6, 250–1
coral reefs 89, 96, 304
coronary arteries 122
　blood clots 127
corpus callosum 239
cortical homunculus 245
Costus plants 110
courtship display 274–5
cross bridges 221
crossing over 62, 63, 197–8
crude oil 87–8
cuttlefish 256
cyclins 22
cystic fibrosis 55, 68–9
cytokinesis 19, 21

D

Darwin's finches 100, 106
databases 56, 58, 297, 300
Davson–Danielli model 13
DDT 311
decarboxylation 163, 164, 165
deer reproduction 142
defibrillation 339
degenerate code 115
degrees of freedom 205
dehydration 226
denature
　enzymes 37
　protein 156
dendrites 133–4
denitrifying bacteria 322–3
depolarization 135, 263
depressants 266
desert plants 179
determinate growth 188
detritivores 79
diabetes 137, 328–9
diaphragm 132, 133
diazepam 268
dichotomous key 113
dideoxyribonucleic acid 148
diffusion 15, 86
digestion 119–21, 329–33
dihybrid cross 200–1
diploid cells 58–9
dipolarity 27–8
directional selection 209
disaccharides 29
discrete variation 203–4
disruptive selection 209

DNA
　amplification using PCR 73
　double helix 40, 144
　gel electrophoresis 72
　genes 5, 34, 36, 54
　methylation patterns 149
　microarrays 292, 294
　mitosis 20
　mutations 18, 19, 55, 71, 103
　profiling (fingerprinting) 73–4, 148
　recombinant 286–8
　replication 41–2, 61–2, 143–8
　semi-conservative replication 41, 42, 144
　structure 39–40, 143–8
　transcription 41, 43, 148–50, 342
　translation 41, 44, 46, 151–6
　triplets 45
DNA polymerase 42, 145, 147
Dolly the sheep 77
domain 109
dominant alleles 65, 67–70
dopamine 262, 268, 269
double helix 40, 144
Down syndrome 60, 63–4
Drosophila melanogaster 59, 202, 203
drugs
　addiction to 270
　antibiotics 129
　psychoactive 266–9
　resistance to antibiotics 107, 129, 291

E

ear 252–4
ecosystems
　communities and 81–2, 306–10
　impact of humans 310–12
ecstasy 269
egestion 333
egg 228–9
elastic fibres 122
electrocardiogram (ECG) 339
electron carriers 161
electron micrographs 10
electron microscopes 6–7
electron tomography 169
electron transport chain 166
ELISA 292, 293
emergent property 290
emphysema 132, 350–1
encephalization quotient 243
encoding 261
end-product inhibition 160–1
endocrine glands 341
endocytosis 15, 16
endorphins 266–7
endoskeleton 217
endosymbiotic theory 18
energy flow 82–5
energy pyramid 85, 307
enhancers 150
environment and gene expression 150
environmental protection 288–92

environmental resistance 283
enzyme-linked immunosorbent assay (ELISA) 292, 293
enzymes
　activation energy 36, 158
　active site 36
　catalysis 25-6, 36
　denatured 37
　digestion 120
　DNA replication 145-6
　immobilized 38
　induced-fit model 158
　inhibitors 159-60
　metabolic pathway 157
　molecular biology 36-8
　reaction rates 37, 159
　substrates 36
epinephrine 126
Escherichia coli 161, 277
essential nutrients 325
EST data mining 301
ethology 271-5
eubacteria 109
eukaryotes
　cell structure 6, 8-11
　chromosomes 57-8
　classification 108, 109
　DNA 144
　endosymbiotic theory 18
　mRNA modification 149
Euphorbia pulchemrrima 194
eutrophication 324
evolution 98-102
ex situ conservation 314
exercise 350
exocrine glands 330
exocytosis 15, 16
exons 149
exoskeleton 217
expiration 132-3
exponential growth 317
extended essay 359-64
eye
　irrigation 16
　retina 137, 248-9

F

FAD 161, 165, 166
$FADH_2$ 165, 166
faeces 333
fatty acids 30-1, 326
feed conversion ratio 307
female reproductive system 140-1
fermentation 48-9, 88, 277-81
fertilization
　animals 230
　flowering plants 195
fibre 333
fibrin 127
fibrinogen 127, 336
figworts 117
finches, Darwin's 100, 106
fitness 105
flowering plants 5, 192-6

fluid mosaic model 13, 14
fluorescent proteins 295
foetal haemoglobin 351
food chains 83-4, 85, 306
food web 306
fossil fuels 87-8, 95, 96
fossil record 98
Franklin, Rosalind 144
frogs 312
fruit flies 59, 202, 203
functions of life 2-3

G

GABA 268
gametes 61, 64, 65-6
ganglion cells 249, 250
gas exchange 130-3, 349
gas transport 345-51
gastric secretions 330-1
gel electrophoresis 72
genes 54-6
　biotechnology 72-7, 282-8, 295
　cladistics 114
　DNA 5, 34, 36, 54
　expression 150
　inheritance 65-71, 200-6
　model organisms 298
　pools 206-10
　therapy 296
genetic code 45-6
genetic diseases 68-71
genetic engineering 74-5, 277
genetic markers 293
genetically modified organisms 74-5, 282-8, 295
genitalia
　female 140-1
　male 139-40
genome 5, 56
genus name 107-8
Gersmehl diagrams 309
giant leaf insect 105-6
glial cells 235, 236
glomerulus 223-4
glucagon 137
glucose 48, 162
glycerate 3-phosphate 175
glycolysis 48, 162-3
gradualism 101, 208
Gram staining 282
gravitropism 190
greenhouse effect 92-5
greenhouse gases 87, 92-5
growth hormones 345
guard cells 178

H

haemodialysis 224
haemoglobin 35, 156, 334, 335, 345-6, 348
　foetal 351
haemophilia 70, 200
hair cells 253, 254
halophytes 180

haploid cells 58-9
Hardy-Weinberg equation 210
Harvey, William 124, 142
HCG 230
hearing 252-4
heart 337-41
　beat 125
　blood flow through 124
　chambers 121
　muscle 337-8
　rate 126, 240
　sounds 340
　valves 123-4
heat energy 84
height 204
helicase 41, 146
Helicobacter pylori 331
hepatitis B antigen 284
Hershey, Alfred 144
heterotrophs 78-9, 276
hierarchical system 108
high altitude 349
highly repetitive sequences 147
histamines 213-14
histones 57, 143
HIV 128
homeostasis 137-9
homologous chromosomes 58, 197, 198
homologous structures 99-100, 116, 300
hormones 137-42, 189-90, 341-5
Human Genome Project 56
Huntington's disease 68, 69
hybridoma cells 216
hydrogen bonds 27, 155
hydrogen carbonate ions 86, 347
hydrolysis 26
hydrophilic substances 28
hydrophobic substances 28
hydrostatic pressure gradient 185, 186-8
hyperpolarization 263
hypertension 328-9, 341
hypertonic solution 17
hypothalamus 138, 239, 328, 344
hypotonic solution 17

I

immunity
　memory cells 214
　non-specific/specific 128
　vaccines 215
implantation 231
imprinting 260
impulses 133-4, 135
in situ conservation 313
indeterminate growth 188
indicator species 312-13
induced-fit model 158
industrial melanism 101
infectious disease defences 126-9
inheritance 65-71, 200-6
innate behaviour 255-9, 272-5

insecticides 136, 311
inspiration 132-3
insulin 46, 137
internal assessment (IA) 352-8
interphase 22
invasive species 310
iron 335
irrigating solutions 16
isotonic solutions 16
IVF 142

J
jet lag 139
joints 217-18

K
karyogram 59-60
keystones species 303
kidney 222-7
kinesis 255
kingdom 108
knockout technology 298
Krebs cycle 164-5
Kupffer cells 335

L
lactate 49
lactation 345
lactose-free milk 38
lagging strand 145
law of independent assortment 199
leaching 324
leading strand 145
learned behaviour 259-62, 272-5
learning 261, 265-6
leptin 138
leukocytes 128, 212
lichen 313
light-dependent reactions 169, 170, 171
light energy 82-3
light-independent reactions 170, 174-5
lignin 181
limestone 89
limiting factors 53, 302
limits of tolerance 302-3
link reaction 163-4
Linnaean system 107-8, 110
lion oestrus 275
lipids 25, 29-31
liver 334-7
local currents 135
logistic growth 318, 319
loop of Henle 224-5, 226
Lorenz, Konrad 260
luminescent probes 295
lungs
    cancer 132
    circulation 124
    gas exchange 130-3
lymphocytes 128, 212, 213
lysosomes 154

M
macromolecules 26, 120
macroplastics 312
malaria
    anti-malarial drugs 161
    control using DDT 311
male reproductive system 139-40
malnutrition 327-8
Malpighian tubules 222
marine resources 320
Marinobacter 289
marker genes 286
mast cells 213, 214
mature mRNA 149, 151
MDMA 269
mechanoreceptors 247, 253
medical biotechnology 292-6
medulla oblongata 126, 240, 349
meiosis 61-4, 66, 103, 197-9
melanism 101
melatonin 138-9
memory 261-2, 265-6
memory cells 213, 214
Mendel, Gregor 65
menstrual cycle 141-2
meristems 188, 189
mesocosm 82
messenger RNA (mRNA) 43, 44, 45, 46, 148, 149-50
metabolism 25-6, 138, 157-61, 341-5
metabolites 294
metastasis 23
methane 86-7, 92-3
methyl mercury 289
microorganisms
    biofilms 290-2
    bioremediation using 288-9
    in industrial processes 276-82
microplastics 312
micropropagation 190
mimicry 105-6
minerals 121, 325
mitochondria 166, 168-9
mitosis 19, 20-1, 189
mitotic index 23
model organisms 238, 298
molecular systematics 114
Mollusca 89
monoclonal antibodies 216
monomers 26, 120
monosaccharides 29
Morgan, Thomas Hunt 202
movement 217-21
mRNA 43, 44, 45, 46, 148, 149-50
mRNA-ribosmal complex 44
mucous membranes 126
muscle
    antagonistic action 133, 218-19
    arteries 122
    brain control 246
    cardiac 337-8
    contraction 220-1
    fibres 219-20
    lactate production 49
    skeletal 218-21

ventilation 132-3
mutagens 23, 71
mutations 18, 19, 55, 71, 103
mutualism 304
mutualistic relationship 182, 196, 321
myelination 134
myofibrils 220
myoglobin 35, 351
myosin 220-1

N
NAD 161, 163, 164, 166
NADH 163, 164, 165, 166
NADP 170, 173, 175
NADP reductase 173
NADPH 170, 173
natural classification system 110, 111-13
natural gas 86, 87-8
natural selection 98, 103-7, 271
neonicotinoid insecticides 136
nephrons 223, 224-5
nerve gases 159
nerve impulses 133-4, 135
neural development 234-8
neural pruning 237
neural tube 234-5, 239
neuromodulators 265
neurones 133-7, 234-8, 247
neuropharmacology 261-70
neurotransmitters 136, 262-6
niche 305
nitrogen cycle 321-3
nitrogenous waste 222, 227
nitrous oxides 92, 93
node of Ranvier 134
non-disjunction 63-4, 71
non-specific immunity 128
nuclear bombs 71
nucleic acids 25, 39
nucleosomes 57, 143, 149
nucleotides 39, 144
nucleus accumbens 244
null hypothesis 80
nutrient cycling 81
nutrition 78-9, 325-9

O
oestrogen 140-1, 233
oil degradation 289
olfactory receptors 247-8
omega fatty acids 326
oncogenes 23
oogenesis 228-9
open reading frame 285-6
operant conditioning 260-1
opioids 268
optic nerve 249, 250
osmoconformers 222
osmolarity 17
osmoregulation 222-7
osmosis 15
ovarian hormones 141-2
ovary 228, 229

overhydration 226
overweight 328-9
oxidation reaction 161, 163, 164-5, 166
oxidative phosphorylation 166, 167
oxygen
   from photolysis 51
   ventilation 130
   water of metabolism 167-8
oxygen dissociation curve 345-7
oxytocin 233, 345

P

pacemaker 125
   artificial 338
pancreas 10, 120, 137
parasympathetic system 241
parsimony 116
pathogens 212, 215, 292-3
pathway engineering 277
Pavlov, Ivan 259
PCR 73, 292, 293
peat 87
penicillin 129, 280
pentadactyl limb 99-100, 102
peppered moth 101
peptide hormones 343-4
perception 247-54
peripheral nervous system 236, 241
phagocytosis 16, 128
phenylketonuria 328
phloem 183-8
phloem sap 184, 185
phosphodiester bond 145
phospholipids 11-12
phosphorus cycle 323
phosphorylation 153, 162
photolysis 51, 171
photoperiodism 193-4
photophosphorylation 173
photoreceptors 137, 247, 248-9
photosynthesis 10, 50-3, 83, 169-77
photosystem I 170-1, 173-4
photosystem II 170-1, 172, 174
phototropism 190, 191
Phyllium giganteum 105-6
phylogenetics 300
phylograms 300
phylum 108
phytochrome 193-4
pigmentation 101
pineal gland 138
pituitary gland/hormones 141-2, 240, 344, 345
placenta 231, 232-3
plants
   cell structure 9
   clones 76
   cytokinesis 21
   DNA in flowering plants 5
   genetically-modified 74-5, 282-8, 295
   growth 10, 188-92
   hormones 189-90
   phloem 183-8

   reproduction 192-6
   xylem 178-83, 184-5
plaque 122, 326
plasma cells 213
plasma membrane 9, 211
plasma proteins 336
plasmids 57
plastic debris 312
plasticity of brain 237-8
plastocyanin 173
plastoquinone 172
platelets 127
pneumocytes (type I/II) 130-1
poinsettia 194
polar molecules 27, 28
pollination 192, 194-5
pollution 288-92, 311
polygenic traits 204
polymerase chain reaction (PCR) 73, 292, 293
polypeptides 32-5, 44, 151, 152-3
polysaccharides 29
polysomes 152
polyspermy 230
population ecology 316-20
postsynaptic neurone 136, 262, 263-4
potometer 179
pregnancy 230-3
   testing kits 216
pressure-flow hypothesis 187-8
presynaptic neurone 136
probes 281
progesterone 140-1, 230, 233
prokaryotes
   cell structure 6, 7-8
   chromosomes 57
   DNA 144
   plasmids 57
   translation 154
prolactin 345
promoter region 148
proteins
   cell membrane 12-13
   conjugated 156
   denatured 156
   gel electrophoresis 72
   gene expression 150
   in living things 25
   molecular biology 32-6
   primary structure 155
   quaternary structure 156
   secondary structure 155
   steps in synthesis 151
   tertiary structure 156
   tracking 295
proteome 36
proton (H^+) gradient 172-3
proton pump inhibitors 331
proton pumping 166
protoplasts 287
proximal convoluted tubule 224
Pseudomonas 289
psychoactive drugs 266-9
punctuated equilibrium 101, 208

Punnett grid 66, 67, 200-1, 203
pupil reflex 241-2
pyramid of energy 85, 307
pyruvate 48, 162, 163-4

Q

quadrat counting 316
quorum sensing 291-2

R

R-group 32, 155, 156
radiation exposure 71
random orientation 62, 199
rate of ventilation 349-50
receptor-hormone complex 342
recessive alleles 65, 67-70
recombinant DNA 286-8
recombinants 203
red blood cells 211, 334-5, 347
red-green colour blindness 70, 200, 250
reduction reaction 161
reflex arcs 257-8
reflex conditioning 258-9
reflexes 257
reinforcement 261
renal artery and vein 222, 223
repolarization 135
repressor proteins 150
reproduction
   flowering plants 192-6
   hormones 139-42
   in isolation 207-8
   sexual 103, 228-33
respiration 47-50, 84, 86, 161-9
respiratory control centre 349
respiratory gases
   exchange 130-3, 349
   transport 345-51
respirometers 50
resting potential 134-5
retina 137, 248-9
Rhizobium 321
ribosome-mRNA complex 151
ribosomes 9, 32, 44, 151, 154
ribulose biphosphate 174-7
RNA 39-40, 43, 44
RNA polymerase 43, 148
rod cells 248, 249, 251-2
root hairs 182
rubisco 175
RuBP 174-7
RuBP carboxylase 175
runaway greenhouse effect 95

S

saline-adapted plants 180
saltatory conduction 134
sampling techniques 316-17
saprotrophs 79, 276
sarcomeres 220
sarcoplasmic reticulum 219
Schwann cell 134
scientific names 107-8

secondary messenger 343
sedatives 266, 268
seed dispersal 195
seed germination 196
selective breeding 99
semicircular canals 254
semi-conservative replication 41, 42, 144
seminiferous tubule 228
sensory neurones 247
sequence alignment software 299
serotonin 269
severe combined immunodeficiency (SCID) 296
sewage treatment 290
sex chromosomes 60
sex-linked 70, 202
sexual reproduction 103, 228-33
shoot apex 189, 192
shore crab foraging 273
short tandem repeats 148
sickle cell disease 55, 69-70
sieve tube members 183-4
sieve tubes 184, 186-8
silencers 150
Simpson's reciprocal index of diversity 315
Singer-Nicolson model 13
sinoatrial node 125, 338
sister chromatids 20, 61-2, 197, 199
skeleton 217
skin 126
Skinner Box 260-1
small intestine 119, 120
small nuclear RNAs 149
smallpox 215
smell perception 247-8
snRNAs 149
sodium-potassium pump 15, 17
somatic cell nuclear transfer 77
somatic nervous system 241
somatic therapy 296
sound perception 252-4
soybeans, glyphosate-tolerant 283
spatial habitat 303
specialized tissue 4
speciation 100, 206-10
species
  classification 107-13
  communities and 80-1, 302-5
  diversity 314-15
  evolution 100
  indicator species 312-13
  keystone species 303
  nutrition 78-9
specific immunity 128
spermatogenesis 228-9
spina bifida 235
spinal cord 240
spliceosomes 149
splicing 149, 150
SRY gene 139
stabilizing selection 209
starvation 329
statistical significance 80-1

stem cells 6
stem-cuttings 76
steroid hormones 342, 344
stimulants 266, 267-9
stoma 178
stomach ulcers 331
strep throat 107
strokes 238
succession 310
sulphanilamide 159
summation 263
sunlight 82-3
supercoiling 20, 57, 143
surfactant 131
sympathetic system 241
synapses 136, 236, 237, 264
synaptic pruning 237
synovial joints 217-18

T

T lymphocytes 212
Taq DNA polymerase 42
target genes 284, 285
taxa 108
taxis 255
taxonomy 108
telomeres 147
test cross 67-8
testosterone 139
theory of evolution by natural selection 98
therapy
  biopharming 295
  gene therapy 296
thermoreceptors 247
threshold potential 135, 137
thrombin 127
thrombosis 341
thylakoids 169
thyroid gland 138
thyroxin 138
tissue 4
tobacco mosaic virus 284
trachea 131
trans isomers 30-1
transcription 41, 43, 148-50, 342
transcription activators 150
transect 305
transfer RNA (tRNA) 44, 46, 147, 151-2
  binding sites 152-3
transfusion 211-12
transgenic species 74-5, 282-8, 295
translation 41, 44, 46, 151-6
transpiration 178-80
transpirational pull 182
trichromatic vision 252
triglycerides 31
triose phosphate 162, 175-6
Triticum baeoticum 58
tRNA 44, 46, 147, 151-2
  binding sites 152-3
trophic levels 83-4, 306
tropism 190
tropomyosin 221
troponin 221

tumours *see* cancer
type I/II diabetes 137, 328-9
type I/II pneumocytes 130-1

U

ultrafiltration 223
unsaturated fatty acids 30-1
urea 26
urinary tests 224

V

vaccines 215
valves 123-4
vampire bats 273
vectors 288, 296
veins 123
ventilation 130-3, 349-50
ventricles 121
vesicles 16
vestibular system 254
villi 120-1, 332
viral vectors 296
viruses 129
visible light spectrum 50
visual cortex 244
visual perception 248-52
vitamins 121, 325-6
vive voce 364

W

water
  disinfection 292
  incompressibility 185
  of metabolism 167-8
  molecular biology 27-8
  photolysis 51, 171
  transport in xylem 178-83
water vapour 92, 93
wheat 58
white blood cells 128, 212
Wilkins, Maurice 144
withdrawal reflex 257-8

X

X chromosomes 60
X-ray diffraction 144
Xenopus 238
xerophytes 179
xylem 178-83, 184-5

Y

Y chromosome 60, 139
yeast fermentation 48-9

Z

Z-lines 220
zebras 105
zone of inhibition 282
zones of stress 302-3